Rick Steves'

D0006311

ENGLAND

2012

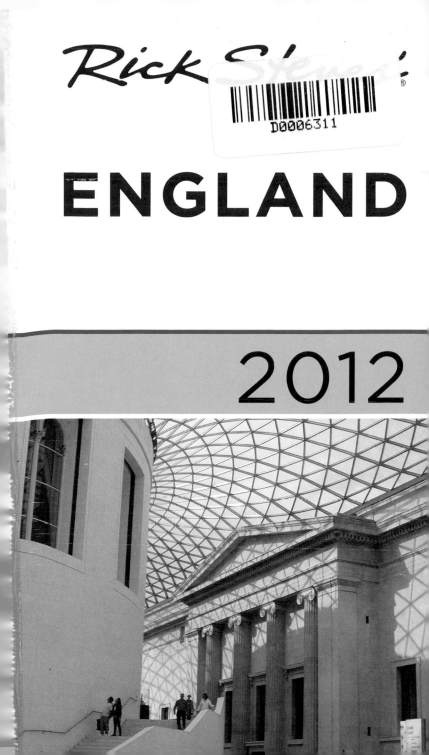

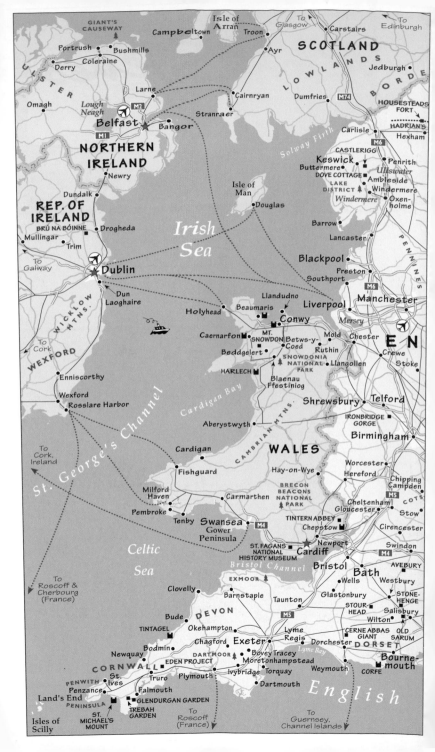

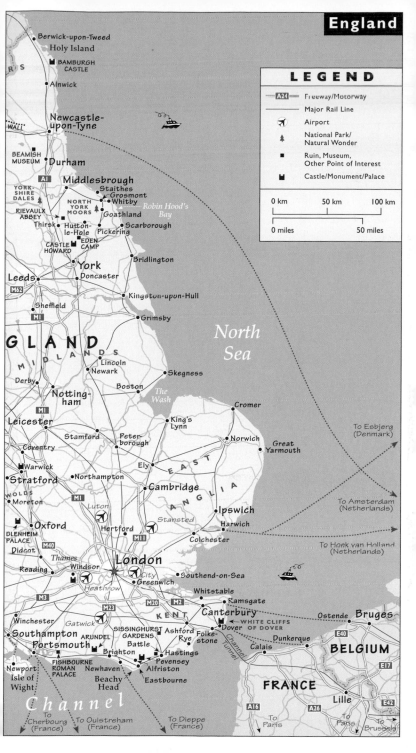

England

LEGEND

- **A24** — Freeway/Motorway
- —— Major Rail Line
- ✈ Airport
- ♠ National Park/Natural Wonder
- ■ Ruin, Museum, Other Point of Interest
- ▮ Castle/Monument/Palace

| 0 km | 50 km | 100 km |
| 0 miles | | 50 miles |

- Berwick-upon-Tweed
- Holy Island
- ■ BAMBURGH CASTLE
- Alnwick
- Newcastle-upon-Tyne
- WALL
- ■ BEAMISH MUSEUM
- Durham
- A1
- Middlesbrough
- YORKSHIRE DALES
- NORTH YORK MOORS
- Staithes
- Grosmont
- Whitby
- RIEVAULX ABBEY
- Thirsk
- Hutton-le-Hole
- Goathland
- Robin Hood's Bay
- Pickering
- Scarborough
- CASTLE HOWARD
- EDEN CAMP
- York
- Bridlington
- Leeds
- Doncaster
- M62
- Sheffield
- M1
- Kingston-upon-Hull
- Grimsby

North Sea

- **GLAND**
- MIDLANDS
- Derby
- Lincoln
- Newark
- Nottingham
- Boston
- Skegness
- *The Wash*
- M1
- Leicester
- Stamford
- Peterborough
- King's Lynn
- Cromer
- Coventry
- Warwick
- Northampton
- Ely
- Norwich
- Great Yarmouth
- Stratford
- WOLDS
- Moreton
- M1
- Luton
- Cambridge
- EAST ANGLIA
- Oxford
- BLENHEIM PALACE
- M40
- Didcot
- *Thames*
- Reading
- Windsor
- Hertford
- Stansted
- Ipswich
- M11
- Harwich
- Colchester
- London
- City
- Greenwich
- Heathrow
- Southend-on-Sea
- Whitstable
- M3
- Gatwick
- M23
- M20
- M2
- Ramsgate
- Canterbury
- KENT
- Winchester
- Southampton
- ARUNDEL
- SISSINGHURST GARDENS
- Ashford
- Folkestone
- WHITE CLIFFS OF DOVER
- Dover
- Ostende
- Bruges
- Portsmouth
- FISHBOURNE ROMAN PALACE
- Battle
- Rye
- *Channel*
- Dunkerque
- E40
- Newport
- Isle of Wight
- Brighton
- Newhaven
- Pevensey
- Hastings
- Calais
- BELGIUM
- Alfriston
- Beachy Head
- Eastbourne
- FRANCE
- E17
- A16
- A26
- Lille
- E42
- *Channel*
- To Cherbourg (France)
- To Oulstreham (France)
- To Dieppe (France)
- To Paris
- To Paris
- To Brussels
- To Esbjerg (Denmark)
- To Amsterdam (Netherlands)
- To Hoek van Holland (Netherlands)

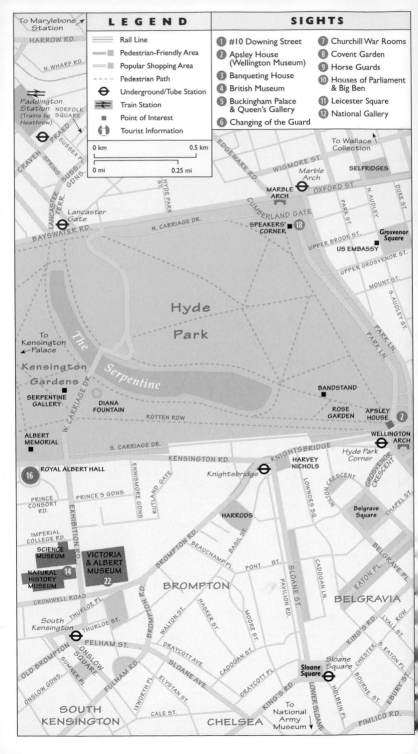

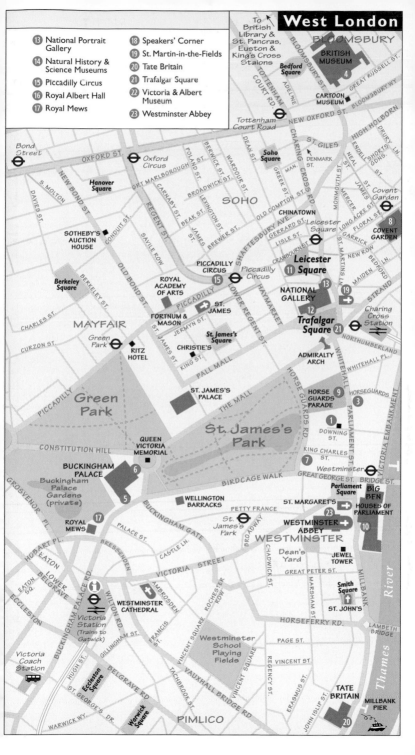

West London

- 13 National Portrait Gallery
- 14 Natural History & Science Museums
- 15 Piccadilly Circus
- 16 Royal Albert Hall
- 17 Royal Mews
- 18 Speakers' Corner
- 19 St. Martin-in-the-Fields
- 20 Tate Britain
- 21 Trafalgar Square
- 22 Victoria & Albert Museum
- 23 Westminster Abbey

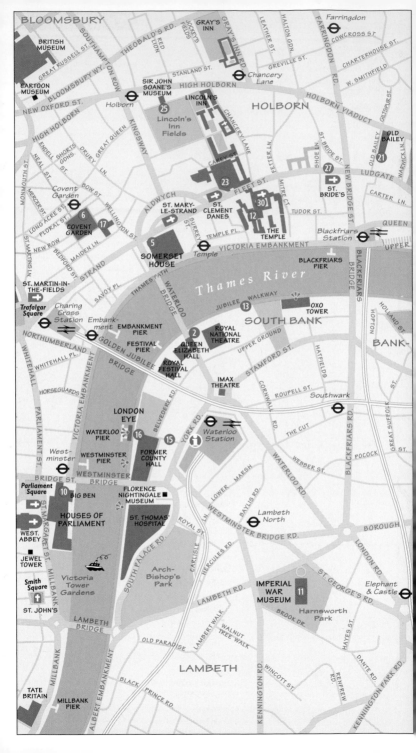

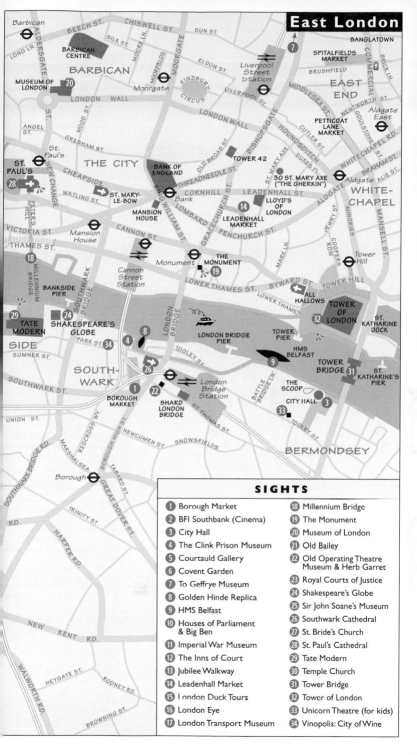

East London

SIGHTS

1. Borough Market
2. BFI Southbank (Cinema)
3. City Hall
4. The Clink Prison Museum
5. Courtauld Gallery
6. Covent Garden
7. To Geffrye Museum
8. Golden Hinde Replica
9. HMS Belfast
10. Houses of Parliament & Big Ben
11. Imperial War Museum
12. The Inns of Court
13. Jubilee Walkway
14. Leadenhall Market
15. London Duck Tours
16. London Eye
17. London Transport Museum
18. Millennium Bridge
19. The Monument
20. Museum of London
21. Old Bailey
22. Old Operating Theatre Museum & Herb Garret
23. Royal Courts of Justice
24. Shakespeare's Globe
25. Sir John Soane's Museum
26. Southwark Cathedral
27. St. Bride's Church
28. St. Paul's Cathedral
29. Tate Modern
30. Temple Church
31. Tower Bridge
32. Tower of London
33. Unicorn Theatre (for kids)
34. Vinopolis: City of Wine

Website
tfl.gov.uk

24 hour travel information
0843 222 1234*

*You pay no more than 5p per minute if calling from a BT landline. There may be a connection charge. Charges from mobiles or other landline providers may vary.

MAYOR OF LONDON

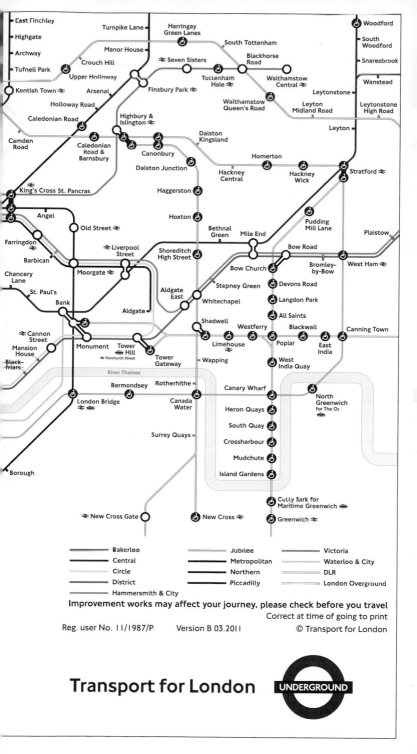

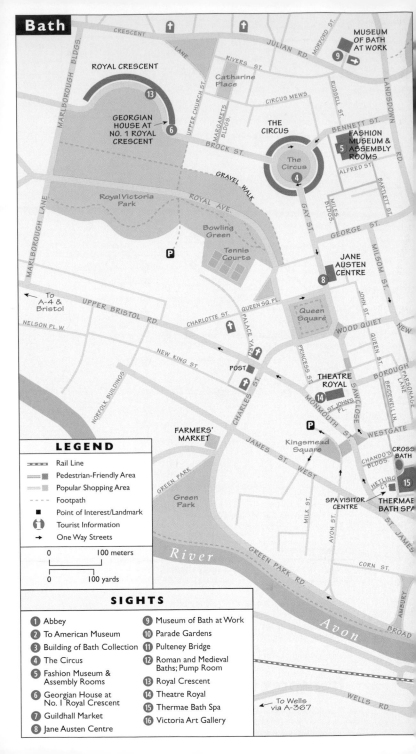

Bath

CRESCENT

MARLBOROUGH BLDGS.

ROYAL CRESCENT

LANE

JULIAN RD.

MORFORD ST.

MUSEUM
OF BATH
AT WORK
9

RIVERS ST.

Catharine
Place

CIRCUS MEWS

RUSSELL ST.

LANDSDOWN RD.

13

UPPER CHURCH ST.

MARGARETS BLDGS.

THE
CIRCUS

BENNETT ST.

FASHION
MUSEUM &
ASSEMBLY
ROOMS
5

GEORGIAN
HOUSE AT
NO. 1 ROYAL
CRESCENT
6

BROCK ST.

The
Circus
4

ALFRED ST.

BARTLETT ST.

GRAVEL WALK

GAY ST.

MILES BLDGS.

GEORGE ST.

MARLBOROUGH LANE

Royal Victoria
Park

ROYAL AVE.

Bowling
Green

P

Tennis
Courts

MILSOM ST.

JANE
AUSTEN
CENTRE
8

JOHN ST.

← To
A-4 &
Bristol

UPPER BRISTOL RD.

QUEEN SQ. PL.

Queen
Square

WOOD QUIET

QUEEN ST.

NEW

NELSON PL. W.

CHARLOTTE ST.

PALACE YARD

NEW KING ST.

POST

PRINCESS ST.

THEATRE
ROYAL
14

SAWCLOSE

ST. JOHN'S PL.

BOROUGH

PARSONAGE LANE

BRIDEWELL LN.

WESTGATE

NORFOLK BUILDINGS

CHARLES ST.

JAMES ST.

P

Kingsmead
Square

MONMOUTH ST.

CHANDO'S BLDGS.

CROSS
BATH

FARMERS'
MARKET

GREEN PARK

JAMES ST. WEST

HETLING CT.

15

Green
Park

MILK ST.

SPA VISITOR
CENTRE

THERMAE
BATH SPA

AVON ST.

ST. JAMES

River

GREEN PARK RD.

CORN ST.

Avon

ABBURY

BROAD

To Wells
via A-367 ←

WELLS RD.

LEGEND

- ▪▪▪▪ Rail Line
- ═══▪ Pedestrian-Friendly Area
- ═══▪ Popular Shopping Area
- - - - Footpath
- ▪ Point of Interest/Landmark
- ⬥ Tourist Information
- → One Way Streets

0	100 meters
0	100 yards

SIGHTS

1	Abbey	**9**	Museum of Bath at Work
2	To American Museum	**10**	Parade Gardens
3	Building of Bath Collection	**11**	Pulteney Bridge
4	The Circus	**12**	Roman and Medieval Baths; Pump Room
5	Fashion Museum & Assembly Rooms	**13**	Royal Crescent
6	Georgian House at No. 1 Royal Crescent	**14**	Theatre Royal
		15	Thermae Bath Spa
7	Guildhall Market	**16**	Victoria Art Gallery
8	Jane Austen Centre		

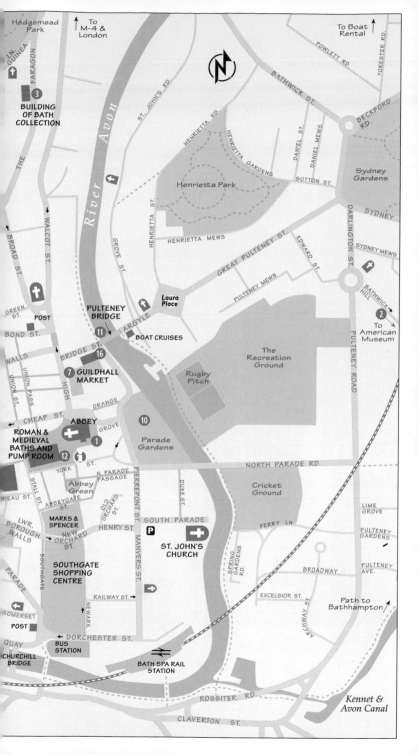

Rick Steves'

ENGLAND

2012

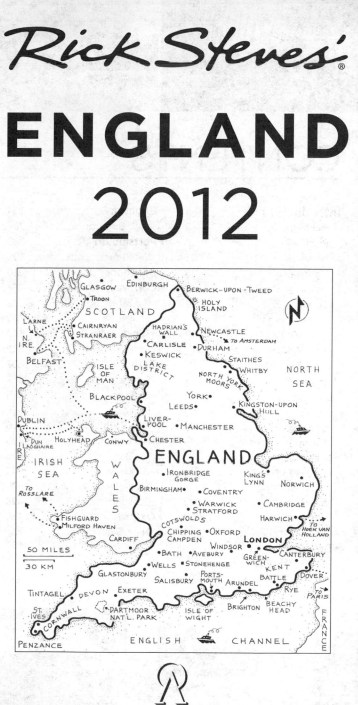

AVALON
TRAVEL

CONTENTS

Top Destinations in England

SCOTLAND

DURHAM & N.E. ENGLAND

LAKE DISTRICT

NORTH YORKSHIRE

BLACKPOOL LIVERPOOL

YORK

IRONBRIDGE GORGE

STRATFORD-UPON-AVON

THE COTSWOLDS

GREENWICH, WINDSOR & CAMBRIDGE

WALES

OXFORD

LONDON

BATH

CANTERBURY

NEAR BATH

BRIGHTON

DOVER & S.E. ENGLAND

DARTMOOR

PORTS-MOUTH

CORNWALL

DCH

INTRODUCTION

From the grandeur and bustle of London, to the pastoral country-side that inspired Shakespeare, to some of the quaintest towns you'll ever experience, England delights. Stand in a desolate field and ponder an ancient stone circle. Strike up a conversation just to hear the Queen's English. Bite into a scone smothered with clotted cream, sip a cup of tea, and wave your pinky as if it's a Union Jack.

This book breaks England into its top big-city, small-town, and rural destinations. It gives you all the information and opinions necessary to wring the maximum value out of your limited time and money in each of these locations.

Note that this book covers only England, which occupies the southern two thirds of the island of Great Britain. If you want to visit Wales and Scotland too, pick up a copy of *Rick Steves' Great Britain* instead.

Experiencing English culture, people, and natural wonders economically and hassle-free has been my goal for more than three decades of traveling, tour guiding, and travel writing. With this new edition, I pass on to you the lessons I've learned, updated for your trip in 2012.

While including the predictable biggies (such as Big Ben, Stratford-upon-Avon, and Stonehenge), the book also mixes in a healthy dose of Back Door intimacy (windswept Roman lookouts, angelic boys' choirs, and nearly edible Cotswold villages). This book is selective. For example, while Hadrian's Wall is more than 70 miles long, I recommend visiting just the best six-mile stretch.

The best is, of course, only my opinion. But after spending half my adult life researching Europe, I've developed a sixth sense for what travelers enjoy. The places featured in this book will knock your spots off.

INTRODUCTION

Map Legend

⅃⅄ Viewpoint		⊘ Airport		⌐ Tunnel	
↑ Entry Arrow		Ⓣ Taxi Stand		Pedestrian Zone	
✪ Tourist Info		⊤ Tram Stop		------ Railway	
WC Restroom		Ⓑ Bus Stop		.... Ferry/Boat Route	
⚑ Castle		Ⓟ Parking		⊢—⊣ Tram	
⌂ Church		⊖ Tube		⟜⟜⟜ Stairs	
■ Statue/Point of Interest		)(Mtn. Pass		- - - - Walk/Tour Route	
		▨ Park		------ Trail	

Use this legend to help you navigate the maps in this book.

About This Book

Rick Steves' England 2012 is a personal tour guide in your pocket. The book is organized by destination. Each destination is a mini-vacation on its own, filled with exciting sights, strollable neighborhoods, homey and affordable places to stay, and memorable places to eat. In the following chapters, you'll find these sections:

Planning Your Time suggests a schedule for how to best use your limited time.

Orientation includes specifics on public transportation, helpful hints, local tour options, easy-to-read maps, and tourist information.

Sights describes the top attractions and includes their cost and hours.

Self-Guided Walks take you through interesting neighborhoods, with a personal tour guide in hand.

Sleeping describes my favorite hotels, from good-value deals to cushy splurges.

Eating serves up a range of options, from inexpensive pubs to fancy restaurants.

Connections outlines your options for traveling to destinations by train, bus, and plane, plus route tips for drivers.

The **Great Britain: Past and Present** chapter is a quick overview of British history and culture.

The **appendix** is a traveler's tool kit, with telephone tips, useful phone numbers, transportation basics (on trains, buses, car rentals, driving, and flights), recommended books and films, a festival list, a climate chart, a handy packing checklist, a hotel reservation form, and a fun British-Yankee dictionary.

Browse through this book, choose your favorite destinations, and link them up. Then have a brilliant trip! Traveling like a temporary local, you'll get the absolute most out of every mile, minute,

Key to This Book

Updates
This book is updated every year, but things change. For the latest, visit www.ricksteves.com/update, and for a valuable list of reports and experiences—good and bad—from fellow travelers, check www.ricksteves.com/feedback.

Abbreviations and Times
I use the following symbols and abbreviations in this book:
Sights are rated:

▲▲▲   **Don't miss**
▲▲   **Try hard to see**
▲   **Worthwhile if you can make it**
No rating   **Worth knowing about**

Tourist information offices are abbreviated as **TI,** and bathrooms are **WCs.** To categorize accommodations, I use a **Sleep Code** (described on page 22).

Like Europe, this book uses the **24-hour clock** for schedules. It's the same through 12:00 noon, then keep going: 13:00, 14:00, and so on. For anything over 12, subtract 12 and add p.m. (14:00 is 2:00 p.m.).

When giving **opening times,** I include both peak season and off-season hours if they differ. So, if a museum is listed as "May-Oct daily 9:00-16:00," it should be open from 9 a.m. until 4 p.m. from the first day of May until the last day of October (but expect exceptions).

For **transit** or **tour departures,** I first list the frequency, then the duration. So, a train connection listed as "2/hour, 1.5 hours" departs twice each hour, and the journey lasts an hour and a half.

and dollar. I'm happy that you'll be visiting places I know and love, and meeting my favorite English people.

Planning

This section will help you get started on planning your trip—with advice on trip costs, when to go, and what you should know before you take off.

Travel Smart

Your trip to England is like a complex play—easier to follow and to really appreciate on a second viewing. While no one does the same trip twice to gain that advantage, reading this book in its entirety before your trip accomplishes much the same thing.

Design an itinerary that enables you to visit sights at the best possible times. Note festivals, holidays, specifics on sights, and

England at a Glance

▲▲▲**London** Thriving metropolis packed with world-class museums, monuments, churches, parks, palaces, theaters, pubs, Beefeaters, telephone boxes, double-decker buses, and all things British.

▲▲**Greenwich, Windsor, and Cambridge** Easy side-trips from London: famous observatory at the maritime center of Greenwich, the Queen's palace at Windsor, and England's best university town, Cambridge.

▲**Canterbury** Pleasant pilgrimage town with England's top church.

▲**Dover and Southeast England** The imposing Dover Castle, famous White Cliffs, lush Sissinghurst Gardens, hill town of Rye, and historic site of the Battle of Hastings.

▲**Brighton** Flamboyant beach resort on England's south coast, near the rolling hills of South Downs Way and the chalky cliffs at Beachy Head.

▲**Portsmouth** Newly rejuvenated shipbuilding city with top nautical sights at the Historic Dockyard, plus Roman ruins and stately Arundel Castle nearby.

▲**Dartmoor** Mysterious, desolate, moor-cloaked national park with wild ponies, hiking paths, and an ancient stone circle.

▲**Cornwall** Feisty peninsula littered with prehistoric ruins, plus the seaside resort towns of Penzance and St. Ives, King Arthur's supposed Tintagel Castle, the tip of England at Land's End, and other offbeat sights.

▲▲▲**Bath** Genteel Georgian showcase city, built around the remains of an ancient Roman bath.

▲▲**Near Bath** England's mysterious heart, including the prehistoric-meets-New Age hill at Glastonbury, spine-tingling stone circles at Stonehenge and Avebury, enjoyable cathedral towns of

Wells and Salisbury, and delightful Dorset countryside.

▲**Oxford** Stately university town with Blenheim Palace—one of England's best—on its doorstep.

▲▲**The Cotswolds** Remarkably quaint villages—including the cozy market town Chipping Campden, popular hamlet Stow-on-the-Wold, and handy transit hub Moreton-in-Marsh—scattered over a hilly countryside.

▲**Stratford-upon-Avon** Shakespeare's hometown and top venue for seeing his plays performed, plus the medieval Warwick Castle and Coventry's inspiring cathedral nearby.

▲**Ironbridge Gorge** Birthplace of the Industrial Revolution, with sights and museums that tell the earth-changing story.

▲**Liverpool** The Beatles' hometown, an increasingly rejuvenated port city.

Blackpool England's tackiest, most fun-loving beach resort.

▲▲**The Lake District** Idyllic lakes-and-hills landscape, with enjoyable hikes and joyrides, time-passed valleys, William Wordsworth and Beatrix Potter sights, and the charming home-base town of Keswick.

▲▲▲**York** Walled medieval town with grand Gothic cathedral, excellent museums (Viking, Victorian, Railway), and atmospheric old center.

▲**North Yorkshire** Smattering of ruined abbeys, desolate moors, seaside towns (including bustling Whitby and tiny Staithes), and other sights near York.

▲**Durham and Northeast England** Youthful working-class town with magnificent cathedral, plus (nearby) an open-air museum, the Roman remains of Hadrian's Wall, Holy Island, and Bamburgh Castle.

INTRODUCTION

days when sights are closed. If you're using public transportation, read up on the tips for trains and buses (see pages 787 and 791 of the appendix). If you're renting a car, study my driving tips and the examples of road signs (see page 796). A smart trip is a puzzle—a fun, doable, and worthwhile challenge.

Be sure to mix intense and relaxed periods in your itinerary. To maximize rootedness, minimize one-night stands. It's worth a long drive after dinner to be settled into a town for two nights. Hotels and B&Bs are more likely to give a better price to someone staying more than one night. Every trip (and every traveler) needs at least a few slack days (for picnics, laundry, people-watching, and so on). Pace yourself. Assume you will return.

Reread this book as you travel, and visit local TIs. Upon arrival in a new town, lay the groundwork for a smooth departure; write down (or print out from an online source) the schedule for the train or bus that you'll take when you depart. Drivers can study the best route to their next destination.

Get online at Internet cafés or at your hotel, and buy a phone card or carry a mobile phone: You can get tourist information, learn the latest on sights (special events, tour schedules, etc.), book tickets and tours, make reservations, reconfirm hotels, research transportation connections, check weather, and keep in touch with your loved ones.

Enjoy the friendliness of the British people. Connect with the culture. Set up your own quest for the best pub, cathedral, or chocolate bar. Slow down and be open to unexpected experiences. You speak the language—use it! Ask questions—most locals are eager to point you in their idea of the right direction. Keep a notepad in your pocket for confirming prices, noting directions, and organizing your thoughts. Wear your money belt, learn the currency, and figure out how to estimate prices in dollars. Those who expect to travel smart, do.

Trip Costs

Five components make up your trip costs: airfare, surface transportation, room and board, sightseeing and entertainment, and shopping and miscellany.

Airfare: A basic round-trip US-to-London flight can cost $800-1,300, depending on where you fly from and when (cheaper in winter). Smaller budget airlines may provide bargain service from several European capitals to many cities in England. If your trip extends beyond England, consider saving time and money by flying into one city and out of another—for instance, into London and out of Amsterdam.

Surface Transportation: For a three-week whirlwind trip of all my recommended English destinations, allow $550 per person for public transportation (train pass, key buses, and Tube fare in London). For a three-week car rental, tolls, gas, and insurance, allow $900 per person (based on two people sharing). Leasing is worth considering for trips of two and a half weeks or more. Car rental and leases are cheapest when arranged from the US. Train passes are normally available only outside of Europe (although you can buy a bus pass in England). You may save money by simply buying tickets as you go. For more on public transportation and car rental, see "Transportation" in the appendix.

Room and Board: You can thrive in England in 2012 on $115 per day per person for room and board (more in big cities). This allows $15 for lunch, $35 for dinner, and $65 for lodging (based on two people splitting the cost of a $130 double room that includes breakfast). Students and tightwads can enjoy England for as little as $60 ($30 for a bed, $30 for meals and snacks).

Sightseeing and Entertainment: Figure about $15-30 per major sight (Stonehenge-$12, Shakespeare's Birthplace in Stratford-$20, Westminster Abbey-$26, Tower of London-$32), $7 for minor ones (climbing church towers), and $20-40 for splurge experiences (e.g., walking tours and concerts). For information on various sightseeing passes, see page 20.

Fortunately, many of the best sights in London are free, including the British Museum, National Gallery, National Portrait Gallery, Tate Britain, Tate Modern, British Library, and the Victoria & Albert Museum (though most request donations). An overall average of $30 a day works in most cities (allow $50 for London). Don't skimp here. After all, this category is the driving force behind your trip—you came to sightsee, enjoy, and experience England.

Shopping and Miscellany: Figure roughly $2 per postcard, $3 for tea or an ice-cream cone, and $5 per pint of beer. Shopping can vary in cost from nearly nothing to a small fortune. Good budget travelers find that this category has little to do with assembling a trip full of lifelong and wonderful memories.

Sightseeing Priorities

Depending on the length of your trip, and taking geographic proximity into account, here are my recommended priorities:

3 days:	London
5 days, add:	Bath and nearby sights (take a minibus tour or choose some combination of Stonehenge, Avebury, Wells, Glastonbury, and Salisbury)
7 days, add:	Cotswolds
9 days, add:	York
11 days, add:	Lake District
14 days, add:	Durham, Stratford, Warwick

England's Best Three-Week Trip by Car

Day	Plan	Sleep in
1	Arrive at London's Heathrow Airport, bus to Bath	Bath
2	Bath	Bath
3	Pick up car, Avebury, Wells, Bath	Glastonbury
4	Early drive to Cornwall	Penzance
5	Cornwall	Penzance
6	Dartmoor	Salisbury
7	Salisbury, Portsmouth	Salisbury
8	Oxford, Blenheim	Chipping Campden
9	Explore the Cotswolds	Chipping Campden
10	Stratford, Warwick, Coventry	Ironbridge Gorge
11	Ironbridge Gorge	Liverpool
12	Liverpool, maybe side-trip to Blackpool	Liverpool
13	South Lake District	Keswick area
14	North Lake District	Keswick area
15	Hadrian's Wall and Durham, to York, turn in car	York
16	York	York
17	Early train to London	London
18	London	London
19	London	London
20	Canterbury, Dover	London
21	Greenwich, Windsor, Cambridge, Brighton (choose one)	London
22	Whew!	

While this three-week itinerary is designed to be done by car, it can be done by train and bus or, better yet, with a BritRail & Drive Pass (best car days: Cornwall/Dartmoor, Cotswolds, and Lake District); for more on the pass, see page 788. For three weeks without a car, I'd cut back on the recommended sights with the

17 days, add: Ironbridge Gorge, Liverpool
21 days, add: Cornwall, Dartmoor
24 days, add: Choose two of the following—Cambridge, Oxford, Blackpool, Coventry, Portsmouth, Brighton, Canterbury, or Dover

This list includes virtually everything on "England's Best Three-Week Trip by Car" itinerary and map (see next page).

Your itinerary will depend on your interests. Nature lovers will likely put the lovely Lake District and the more remote Dartmoor nearer the top of their list, while engineers are drawn

most frustrating public transportation (Cornwall, Dartmoor, and Ironbridge Gorge). Lacing together the cities by train is very slick, and buses get you where the trains don't go. With more time, everything is workable without a car.

like a magnet to Ironbridge Gorge. Beatlemaniacs make a pilgrimage to Liverpool. Coastal Blackpool offers amusement-park fun, refreshing for families and those who've had enough of museums. Literary fans like Cambridge, Oxford, Stratford, Bath, and the South Lake District.

When to Go

In England, July and August are peak season—my favorite time—with very long days, the best weather, and the busiest schedule of tourist fun.

Prices and crowds don't go up during peak times as dramatically in England as they do in much of Europe, except for holidays and festivals (see "Holidays and Festivals" in the appendix). Still, travel during "shoulder season" (May, early June, Sept, and early Oct) is easier and can be a bit less expensive. Shoulder-season travelers usually enjoy smaller crowds, decent weather, the full range of sights and tourist fun spots, and the ability to grab a room almost whenever and wherever they like—often at a flexible price. Winter travelers find absolutely no crowds and soft room prices, but shorter sightseeing hours and reliably bad weather. Some attractions are open only on weekends or are closed entirely in the winter (Nov-Feb). The weather can be cold and dreary, and nightfall draws the shades on sightseeing well before dinnertime. While rural charm falls with the leaves, city sightseeing is fine in the winter.

Plan for rain no matter when you go. Just keep traveling and take full advantage of bright spells. The weather can change several times in a day, but rarely is it extreme. As the locals say, "There is no bad weather, only inappropriate clothing." Bring a jacket and dress in layers. Temperatures below 32°F cause headlines, and days that break 80°F—while more frequent in recent years—are still rare in England. Weather-wise, July and August are not much better than shoulder months. May and June can be lovely anywhere in England. (For more information, see the climate chart in the appendix.) While sunshine may be rare, summer days are very long. The midsummer sun is up from 6:30 until 22:30. It's not uncommon to have a gray day, eat dinner, and enjoy hours of sunshine afterward.

Know Before You Go

Your trip is more likely to go smoothly if you plan ahead. Check this list of things to arrange while you're still at home.

You need a **passport**—but no visa or shots—to travel in Great Britain. You may be denied entry into certain European countries if your passport is due to expire within three to six months of your ticketed date of return. Get it renewed if you'll be cutting it close. It can take up to six weeks to get or renew a passport (for more on passports, see www.travel.state.gov). Pack a photocopy of your passport in your luggage in case the original is lost or stolen.

Book rooms well in advance if you'll be traveling during peak season and any major **holidays** (see page 809).

Most people fly into London and remain there for a few days. Instead, consider a gentler **small-town start** in Bath (the ideal jet-lag pillow), and let London be the finale of your trip. You'll be more rested and ready to tackle England's greatest city. Heathrow Airport has direct bus connections to Bath and other cities. (Bristol Airport is also near Bath.)

If you'll be in London or Stratford and want to **see a play,** check theater schedules ahead of time. For simplicity, I book plays while in England, but if there's something you just have to see, consider buying tickets before you go. For a current schedule of London plays and musicals, visit www.officiallondontheatre .co.uk. Tickets to performances at Stratford's Royal Shakespeare Theatre are likely to sell out (see www.rsc.org.uk), but if it's just Shakespeare you're after—with or without Stratford—you can see his plays in London, too.

At **Stonehenge,** anyone can see the stones from behind the rope line, but if you want to go inside the stone circle, you'll need advance reservations (see page 422).

Call your **debit- and credit-card companies** to let them know the countries you'll be visiting, to ask about fees, and more (see page 14).

Do your homework if you want to buy **travel insurance.** Compare the cost of the insurance to the likelihood of your using it and your potential loss if something goes wrong. Also, check whether your existing insurance (health, homeowners, or renters) covers you and your possessions overseas. For more tips, see www .ricksteves.com/insurance.

If you're bringing a mobile device, you can download free information from **Rick Steves Audio Europe,** featuring hours of travel interviews on Great Britain, audio tours of major sights in London, and more (via www.ricksteves.com, iTunes, or the Rick Steves Audio Europe smartphone app; for details, see page 802).

If you're planning on **renting a car** in Great Britain, you'll need your driver's license.

If traveling to continental Europe on the **Eurostar** train, consider ordering a ticket in advance (or buy it in Britain); for details, see page 206.

Think about buying a **railpass** after researching your options (see page 788 and www.ricksteves.com/rail for all the specifics).

Because **airline carry-on restrictions** are always changing, visit the Transportation Security Administration's website (www .tsa.gov/travelers) for an up-to-date list of what you can bring on the plane with you and what you must check. Some airlines may restrict you to only one carry-on (no extras like a purse or daypack); check with your airline or at Britain's transportation website for the latest (www.dft.gov.uk).

Practicalities

Emergency and Medical Help: In Great Britain, dial 999 for police help or a medical emergency. If you get sick, do as the Brits do and go to a pharmacist for advice. Or ask at your B&B or hotel for help—they'll know the nearest medical and emergency services.

Theft or Loss: To replace a passport, you'll need to go in person to an embassy or consulate (see page 782). If your credit and debit cards disappear, cancel and replace them (see "Damage Control for Lost Cards" on page 16). File a police report, either on the spot or within a day or two; it's required to submit an insurance claim for lost or stolen railpasses or travel gear, and can help with replacing your passport or credit and debit cards. For more information, see www.ricksteves.com/help. Precautionary measures can minimize the effects of loss: Back up photos and other files frequently, and use passwords to protect sensitive data on your electronic devices.

Time Zones: Britain, which is one hour earlier than most of continental Europe, is five/eight hours ahead of the East/West coasts of the US. The exceptions are the beginning and end of Daylight Saving Time: Europe "springs forward" the last Sunday in March (two weeks after most of North America), and "falls back" the last Sunday in October (one week before North America). For a handy online time converter, try www.timeand date.com/worldclock.

Business Hours: In England, most stores are open Monday through Saturday from roughly 10:00 to 17:00. In London, stores stay open later on Wednesday or Thursday (until 19:00 or 20:00), depending on the neighborhood. Sundays have the same pros and cons as they do for travelers in the US (special events, limited hours, banks and many shops closed, limited public transportation, no rush hours, street markets lively with shoppers). Saturdays are virtually weekdays with earlier closing hours and no rush hour (though transportation connections can be less frequent than on weekdays).

Watt's Up? Europe's electrical system is 220 volts, instead of North America's 110 volts. Most newer electronics (such as laptops, battery chargers, and hair dryers) convert automatically, so you won't need a converter plug, but you will need an adapter plug with three square prongs, sold inexpensively at travel stores in the US, and in British airports and drugstores. Avoid bringing older appliances that don't automatically convert voltage; instead, buy a cheap replacement in Europe. Low-cost hairdryers and other small appliances are sold at Superdrug, Boots, or Argos stores (ask your hotelier for the closest branch).

Discounts: Discounts (called "concessions" or "concs" in Britain) are not listed in this book. However, many sights offer discounts for youths (up to age 18), students (with proper identification cards, www.isic.org), families, seniors (loosely defined as retirees or those willing to call themselves a senior), and groups of 10 or more. Always ask. Some discounts are available only for EU citizens.

News: Americans keep in touch via the *International Herald Tribune* (published almost daily throughout Europe and online at www.iht.com). Another informative site is http://news.bbc.co.uk. Every Tuesday, the European editions of *Time* and *Newsweek* hit the stands with articles of particular interest to travelers in Europe. Sports addicts can get their daily fix online or from *USA Today.* Many hotels have BBC News (of course) and CNN television channels.

Money

This section offers advice on how to pay for purchases on your trip (including getting cash from ATMs and paying with plastic), dealing with lost or stolen cards, VAT (sales tax) refunds, and tipping.

What to Bring

Bring both a credit card and a debit card. You'll use the debit card at cash machines (ATMs) to withdraw pounds for most purchases, and the credit card to pay for larger items. Some travelers carry a third card, in case one gets demagnetized or eaten by a temperamental machine.

For an emergency reserve, bring several hundred dollars in hard cash in easy-to-exchange $20 bills. Avoid using currency exchange booths (lousy rates and/or outrageous fees); if you have foreign currency to exchange, take it to a bank. Don't use traveler's checks—they're not worth the fees or long waits at slow banks.

Cash

Cash is just as desirable in Britain as it is at home. Small businesses (hotels, restaurants, and shops) prefer that you pay your bills with cash. Some vendors will charge you extra for using a credit card, and some won't take credit cards at all. Cash is the best—and sometimes only—way to pay for bus fare, taxis, and local guides.

Throughout Europe, ATMs are the standard way for travelers to get cash. Most ATMs in Britain are located outside a bank. Try to use the ATM when the branch is open; if your card is munched by a machine, you can immediately go inside for help.

To withdraw money from an ATM (which locals call "cashpoints"), you'll need a debit card (ideally with a Visa or MasterCard logo for maximum usability), plus a PIN code. Know your PIN code in numbers; there are no letters on European keypads. For security, it's best to shield the keypad when entering your PIN at

Exchange Rate

I list prices in pounds (£) throughout this book.

1 British pound (£1) = about $1.60

While the euro (€) is now the currency of most of Europe, Britain is sticking with its pound sterling. The British pound (£), also called a "quid," is broken into 100 pence (p). Pence means "cents." You'll find coins ranging from 1p to £2, and bills from £5 to £50. Counterfeit pound coins are easy to spot (real coins have an inscription on their outside rims; the rims on the fakes look like tree bark).

London is so expensive that some travelers try to kid themselves that pounds are dollars. But when they get home, that £1,000 Visa bill isn't asking for $1,000...it wants $1,600. (To get the latest rate and print a cheat sheet, see www .oanda.com.)

an ATM. Although you can use a credit card for ATM transactions, it's generally more expensive because it's considered a cash advance rather than a withdrawal.

When using an ATM, try to withdraw large sums of money to reduce the number of per-transaction bank fees you'll pay. If the machine refuses your request, try again and select a smaller amount (some cash machines limit the amount you can withdraw—don't take it personally). If that doesn't work, try a different machine. (Be aware that some ATMs will tell you to take your cash within 30 seconds, and if you aren't fast enough, your cash may be sucked back into the machine—and you'll have a hassle trying to get it from the bank.) It's easier to pay for purchases with smaller bills; if the ATM gives you big bills, try to break them at major museums or larger stores.

Even in jolly olde England, you'll need to keep your cash safe. Use a money belt—a pouch with a strap that you buckle around your waist like a belt and wear under your clothes. Pickpockets target tourists. A money belt provides peace of mind, allowing you to carry lots of cash safely. Don't waste time every few days tracking down a cash machine—withdraw a week's worth of money, stuff it in your money belt, and travel!

Credit and Debit Cards

For purchases, Visa and MasterCard are more commonly accepted than American Express. Just like at home, credit and debit cards are accepted by larger hotels, restaurants, and shops. I typically use my debit card to withdraw cash to pay for most purchases. I use my credit card only in a few specific situations: to book hotel reservations by phone, to cover major expenses (such as car rentals, plane tickets, and long hotel stays), and to pay for things near the end of my trip (to avoid another visit to the ATM). While you could use a debit card to make most large purchases, a credit card offers a greater degree of fraud protection (because debit cards draw funds directly from your account).

Ask Your Credit- or Debit-Card Company: Before your trip, contact the company that issued your debit or credit cards.

• Confirm your card will work overseas, and alert them that you'll be using it in Europe; otherwise, they may deny transactions if they perceive unusual spending patterns.

• Ask for the specifics on transaction **fees.** When you use your credit or debit card—either for purchases or ATM withdrawals—you'll often be charged additional "international transaction" fees of up to 3 percent (1 percent is normal) plus $5 per transaction. If your fees are too high, consider getting a card just for your trip: Capital One (credit cards only, www.capitalone.com) and most credit unions have low-to-no international fees.

• If you plan to withdraw cash from ATMs, confirm your daily **withdrawal limit** (£300 is usually about the maximum). Some travelers prefer a high limit that allows them to take out more cash at each ATM stop, while others prefer to set a lower limit in case their card is stolen.

• Ask for your credit card's **PIN** in case you encounter Europe's chip-and-PIN system; since they're unlikely to tell you your PIN over the phone, allow time for the bank to mail it to you.

Chip and PIN: If your card is declined for a purchase in Europe, it may be because of chip and PIN, which requires cardholders to punch in a PIN instead of signing a receipt. Much of Europe, including Great Britain, Ireland, France, the Netherlands, and Scandinavia, is adopting this system. Some merchants rely on it exclusively. If, when you're using your card, you're prompted to enter your PIN but don't know it, ask if the cashier can swipe your card and print a receipt for you to sign instead; if not, just pay cash. You're most likely to encounter chip and PIN at automated payment machines—such as those at train stations, parking garages, luggage lockers, and self-serve pumps at gas stations. If a machine won't take your card, look for a cashier nearby who can make your card work, or see if one of the machines takes cash.

You can avoid potential hassles by getting your own chip-and-PIN card just for your trip, but so far your options are limited. Chase offers a Visa credit card with a chip called J.P. Morgan Select, but it comes with a hefty annual fee and requires a stellar credit rating. Travelex has a chip-and-PIN cash card called "Cash Passport" that's preloaded with euros or British pounds and sold at many airports; it comes with exorbitant exchange rates and only works at places that accept MasterCard. While handy, these cards are probably not worth it unless you're staying in Great Britain for several weeks and you're willing to pay for the convenience.

Dynamic Currency Conversion: If merchants offer to convert your purchase price into dollars (called dynamic currency conversion, or DCC), refuse this "service." You'll pay even more in fees for the expensive convenience of seeing your charge in dollars.

Damage Control for Lost Cards

If you lose your credit, debit, or ATM card, you can stop people from using it by reporting the loss immediately to the respective global customer-assistance centers. Call these 24-hour US numbers collect: Visa (410/581-9994), MasterCard (636/722-7111), and American Express (623/492-8427). Diner's Club has offices in Britain (0870-1900-011) and the US (702/797-5532, call collect).

At a minimum, you'll need to know the name of the financial institution that issued you the card, along with the type of card (classic, platinum, or whatever). Providing the following information will allow for a quicker cancellation of your missing card: full card number, whether you are the primary or secondary cardholder, the name exactly as printed on the card, billing address, home phone number, circumstances of the loss or theft, and identification verification (your birth date, your mother's maiden name, or your Social Security number—memorize this, don't carry a copy). If you are the secondary cardholder, you'll also need to provide the primary cardholder's identification-verification details. You can generally receive a temporary card within two or three business days in Europe (see www.ricksteves.com/help for more).

If you promptly report your card lost or stolen, you typically won't be responsible for any unauthorized transactions on your account, although many banks charge a liability fee of $50.

Tipping

Tipping in Britain isn't as automatic and generous as it is in the US, but for special service, tips are appreciated, if not expected. As in the US, the proper amount depends on your resources, tipping philosophy, and the circumstances, but some general guidelines apply.

Restaurants: At pubs where you order at the counter, you don't have to tip. (Regular customers ordering a round sometimes say, "Add one for yourself" as a tip for drinks ordered at the bar—but this isn't expected.) At a pub or restaurant with waitstaff, check the menu or your bill to see if the service is included; if not, tip about 10 percent. Many restaurants in London now add a 12.5 percent "optional" tip onto the bill—read your bill carefully, and tip only what you think the service warrants.

Taxis: To tip the cabbie, round up. For a typical ride, round up your fare a bit (for instance, if the fare is £4.50, give £5; for a £28 fare, give £30). If the cabbie hauls your bags and zips you to the airport to help you catch your flight, you might want to toss in a little more. But if you feel like you're being driven in circles or otherwise ripped off, skip the tip.

Special Services: Tour guides at public sights sometimes hold out their hands for tips after they give their spiel. If I've already paid for the tour, I don't tip extra unless they've really impressed me. At hotels, if you let porters carry your luggage, it's polite to give them 50p for each bag (another reason to pack light). If you like to tip maids, leave 50p per overnight at the end of your stay.

In general, if someone in the service industry does a super job for you, a small tip of a pound or two is appropriate, but not required.

When in doubt, ask. If you're not sure whether (or how much) to tip for a service, ask your hotelier or the TI; they'll fill you in on how it's done on their turf.

Getting a VAT Refund

Wrapped into the purchase price of your British souvenirs is a Value-Added Tax (VAT) of 20 percent. If you purchase more than £30 (about $48) worth of goods at a store that participates in the VAT-refund scheme, you're entitled to get most of that tax back. Typically, you must ring up the minimum at a single retailer—you can't add up your purchases from various shops to reach the required amount.

Getting your refund is usually straightforward and, if you buy a substantial amount of souvenirs, well worth the hassle. If you're lucky, the merchant will subtract the tax when you make your purchase. (This is more likely to occur if the store ships the goods to your home.) Otherwise, you'll need to:

Get the paperwork. Have the merchant completely fill out the necessary refund document, called a "Tax-Free Shopping Cheque." The newest ones look like a long receipt. You'll have to present your passport at the store. Be sure to retain your original sales receipt.

Get your stamp at the border or airport. Process your VAT document at your last stop in the EU (e.g., at the airport) with the customs agent who deals with VAT refunds. Before checking in for your flight, find the local customs office, and be prepared to stand in line. It's best to keep your purchases in your carry-on for viewing, but if they're too large or dangerous to carry on (such as knives), have your purchases easily accessible in the bag you're about to check, ready to show the customs agent. You're not supposed to use your purchased goods before you leave. If you show up at customs wearing your new Wellingtons, officials might look the other way—or deny you a refund.

Collect your refund. You'll need to return your stamped document to the retailer or its representative. Many merchants work with a service, such as Global Blue (www.global-blue.com) or Premier Tax Free (www.premiertaxfree.com), which have offices at major airports, ports, or border crossings (after check-in and security, probably strategically located near a duty-free shop). These services, which extract a 4 percent fee, can refund your money immediately in cash or credit your card (within two billing cycles). If the retailer handles VAT refunds directly, it's up to you to contact the merchant for your refund. You can mail the documents from home, or more quickly, from your point of departure (using a stamped, self-addressed envelope you've prepared or one that's been provided by the merchant). You'll then have to wait—it can take months.

Customs for American Shoppers
You are allowed to take home $800 worth of items per person duty-free, once every 30 days. You can also bring in duty-free a liter of alcohol. As for food, you can take home many processed and packaged foods: vacuum-packed cheeses, dried herbs, jams, chocolate, oil, vinegar, and honey. Fresh fruits and vegetables and most meats are not allowed. Any liquid-containing foods must be packed in checked luggage, a potential recipe for disaster. To check customs rules and duty rates, visit www.cbp.gov.

Sightseeing

Sightseeing can be hard work. Use these tips to make your visits to England's finest sights meaningful, fun, efficient, and painless.

Plan Ahead
Set up an itinerary that allows you to fit in all your must-see sights. For a one-stop look at opening hours in the bigger cities, see the "At a Glance" sidebars throughout this book. Most sights keep stable hours, but you can easily confirm the latest by checking with the TI or visiting museum's websites.

Don't put off visiting a must-see sight—you never know when a place will close unexpectedly for a holiday, strike, or restoration. On holidays (see list on page 809), expect reduced hours or closures. Many museums have shorter hours off-season.

When possible, visit major sights in the morning (when your energy is best) and save other activities for the afternoon. At sights, hit the highlights first, then go back to see the rest if you have the time and stamina.

Going at the right time helps avoid crowds. This book offers tips on specific sights. Try visiting very early, at lunch, or very late. Evening visits are usually peaceful, with fewer crowds. For specifics on London at night, see the sidebar on page 96.

Study up. To get the most out of the self-guided walks and sight descriptions in this book, read them before you visit.

At Sights

Here's what you can typically expect:

Some important sights may have metal detectors or conduct bag searches that will slow your entry, while others may require you to check daypacks and coats. They'll be kept safely. If you have something you can't bear to part with, stash it in a pocket or purse. To avoid checking a small backpack, carry it under your arm like a purse as you enter. From a guard's point of view, a backpack is generally a problem, while a purse is not.

At ticket desks, you'll constantly see references to "Gift Aid"—a complicated tax-deduction scheme that benefits both museums (which are often classified as charities) and their patrons who are British taxpayers. But unless you pay taxes in Britain, you can ignore this.

Flash photography is often banned, but taking photos without a flash is usually allowed. Look for signs or ask. Flashes damage oil paintings and distract others in the room. Even without a flash, a handheld camera will take a decent picture (or buy postcards or posters at the museum bookstore). If photos are permitted, video cameras are generally OK, too.

Museums may have special exhibits in addition to their permanent collection. Some exhibits are included in the entry price, while others come at an extra cost (which you may have to pay even if you don't want to see the exhibit).

Expect changes—artwork can be on tour, on loan, out sick, or shifted at the whim of the curator. To adapt, pick up any available free floor plans as you enter, and ask museum staff if you can't find a particular item.

Many sights rent audioguides, which generally offer excellent recorded descriptions (about £3.50; sometimes included with admission). If you bring along your own pair of headphones and a Y-jack, you can sometimes share one audioguide with your travel partner and save money. I've produced free downloadable audio tours of the major sights in London; see page 48.

Guided tours, which usually cost around £3-8 and vary widely in quality, are most likely to occur during peak season. If sights offer short films featuring their highlights and history, they're generally well worth your time.

Important sights and cathedrals often have an on-site café or cafeteria (usually a good place to rest and have a snack or light meal). The WCs are usually free and nearly always clean (it's smart to carry tissues in case a WC runs out of TP).

Many sights sell postcards that highlight their attractions. Before you leave a sight, scan the postcards and thumb through the biggest guidebook (or skim its index) to be sure you haven't overlooked something that you'd like to see.

Most sights stop admitting people 30-60 minutes before closing time, and some rooms close early (often about 45 minutes before the actual closing time). Guards usher people out, so don't save the best for last.

Every sight or museum offers more than what is covered in this book. Use the information in this book as an introduction—not the final word.

Sightseeing Passes and Memberships

Many sights in England are covered by the Great British Heritage Pass or these memberships: English Heritage or National Trust. If you're a whirlwind sightseer, seriously consider the Great British Heritage Pass, which covers the most sights.

Great British Heritage Pass: The best deal for busy travelers, this pass covers more than 600 British Heritage and National Trust properties, plus many others (including several major attractions in Scotland, Wales, and Northern Ireland). If you buy the pass online, you can save on the shipping charge by picking it up at various TIs throughout the country (£39/3 days, £69/7 days, £89/15 days, £119/30 days; child passes available but note that kids already get discounts at sights; tel. 0870-242-9988, www.british heritagepass.com).

Memberships: Many sights in England are managed by either the English Heritage or the National Trust (the sights don't overlap). Both organizations sell annual memberships that allow free or discounted entry to the sights they supervise; the English Heritage also sells passes. You can join the National Trust or English Heritage online or at just about any of their sights.

Membership in **English Heritage** includes free entry to more than 400 sights in England and half-price admission to about 100 more sights in Scotland and Wales. For most travelers, the **Overseas Visitor Pass** is a better choice than the pricier one-year membership (Visitor Pass: £21.50/7 days, £26/14 days, discounts for couples and families; Membership: £44 for one person, £77 for two, discounts for seniors and students, children under 19 free; toll tel. 0870-333-1182, www.english-heritage.org.uk).

Membership in the **National Trust** is best suited for garden-

and-estate enthusiasts, ideally those traveling by car. It covers more than 350 historic houses, manors, and gardens throughout Great Britain. From the US, it's easy to join online through the Royal Oak Foundation, the National Trust's American affiliate (one-year membership: $55 for one person, $80 for two, family and student memberships, www.royal-oak.org). Children under age five are always admitted free to National Trust properties (www.nationaltrust.org.uk).

Things to Consider: If you have children over the age of five and you're all avid sightseers, consider the Great British Heritage Pass or National Trust family membership—but remember that they get in free or cheaply at most sights. Similarly, people over 60 get "concessions" (discounted prices) at many English sights (and can get a senior discount on an English Heritage membership). If you're traveling by car and can get to the more remote sights, you're more likely to get your money's worth out of a pass or membership, especially during peak season (Easter-Oct). If you're traveling off-season (Nov-Easter) when many of the sights are closed, the deals are a lesser value.

The Bottom Line: These various deals can save a busy sight-seer money...but only if you choose carefully. Make a list of the sights you plan to see, check which ones are covered (visit the web-sites listed above), and then add up the total if you were to pay individual admissions to the covered sights. Compare the total to the cost of the pass or membership. Keep in mind that an advantage to any of these deals is that you'll feel free to dip into lesser sights that normally aren't worth the cost of their admission.

Sleeping

I favor accommodations that are handy to your sightseeing activities. In England, small bed-and-breakfast places (B&Bs) generally provide the best value, though I also include some bigger hotels. Rather than list lodgings scattered throughout a city, I describe two or three favorite neighborhoods and recommend the best accommodations values in each, from dorm beds to fancy doubles with all the comforts. Outside of pricey London, you can expect to find good doubles for £50-100 ($80-160), including cooked breakfasts and tax. (For specifics on London, see page 159.)

A major feature of this book is its extensive listing of good-value rooms.

Sleep Code

(£1 = about $1.60, country code: 44)

Price Rankings

To help you easily sort through my hotel listings, I've divided the accommodations into three categories based on the price for a double room with bath during high season:

> $$$ **Higher Priced**
> $$ **Moderately Priced**
> $ **Lower Priced**

I always rate hostels as $, whether or not they have double rooms, because they have the cheapest beds in town. Prices can change without notice; verify the hotel's current rates online or by email. For other updates, see www.rick steves.com/update.

Abbreviations

To pack maximum information into minimum space, I use the following code to describe accommodations in this book. Prices listed are per room, not per person. When a price range is given for a type of room (such as double rooms listing for £80-120), it means the price fluctuates with the season, size of room, or length of stay; expect to pay the upper end for peak-season stays.

S = Single room (or price for one person in a double).

D = Double or twin room. "Double beds" can be two twins sheeted together and are usually big enough for non-romantic couples.

T = Triple (generally a double bed with a single).

Q = Quad (usually two double beds; adding an extra child's bed to a T is usually cheaper).

b = Private bathroom with toilet and shower or tub.

s = Private shower or tub only. (The toilet is down the hall.)

According to this code, a couple staying at a "Db-£80" B&B would pay a total of £80 (about $130) for a double room with a private bathroom. Unless otherwise noted, breakfast is included and credit cards are accepted. For most places, the rates I list include the 20 percent VAT tax—but it's smart to ask when you book your room.

If I mention "Internet access" in a listing, there's a public terminal in the lobby for guests to use. If I say there's "Wi-Fi," you can generally access it in public areas and often (but not always) in your room, but only if you have your own laptop or other Wi-Fi device.

I like places that are clean, central, relatively quiet at night, reasonably priced, friendly, small enough to have a hands-on owner and stable staff, run with a respect for British traditions, and not listed in other guidebooks. (In Britain, for me, six of these eight criteria means it's a keeper.) I'm more impressed by a convenient location and a fun-loving philosophy than flat-screen TVs and shoeshine machines.

Book your accommodations well in advance if you'll be traveling during busy times. Mark these dates in red on your travel calendar: New Year's Day, Good Friday through Easter Monday, the Bank Holidays that occur on the first and last Mondays in May and on the last Monday in August, Christmas, and December 26 (Boxing Day). See page 809 for a list of major holidays and festivals in England; for tips on making reservations, see page 28.

England has a rating system for hotels and B&Bs. These diamonds and stars are supposed to imply quality, but I find that they mean only that the place sporting these symbols is paying dues to the tourist board. Rating systems often have little to do with value.

Travel Review Websites: TripAdvisor (www.tripadvisor.com) and similar review websites are popular tools for finding hotels, but have drawbacks. To write a review, people need only an email address—making it easy to hide their true identity. If a hotel is well reviewed in a guidebook or two, and also gets good ratings on TripAdvisor, it's probably a safe bet—but I wouldn't stay at a hotel based solely on a TripAdvisor recommendation.

Rates and Deals

I've described my recommended accommodations using a Sleep Code (see the sidebar). Prices listed are for one-night stays in peak season, usually include a hearty breakfast, and assume you're booking direct (not through a TI or online hotel-booking engine). Using an online booking service costs the hotel about 20 percent and logically closes the door on special deals. Book direct.

Given the economic downturn, hoteliers and B&B operators are willing and eager to make a deal. The government hiked the VAT tax in 2011, and B&B owners especially have been reluctant to raise their rates accordingly. I'd suggest emailing several hotels or B&Bs to ask for their best price. Comparison-shop and make your choice.

In general, prices can soften if you do any of the following: offer to pay cash, stay at least three nights, or mention this book. You can also try asking for a cheaper room or a discount, or offer to skip breakfast. When establishing prices, confirm if the charge is per person or per room (if a price is too good to be true, it's probably per person). Because many places in Britain charge per person,

INTRODUCTION

small groups often pay the same for a single and a double as they would for a triple. In this book, however, room prices are listed per room, not per person.

As you look over the listings, you'll notice that some accommodations promise special prices to my readers who book direct (without using room-finding services or hotel-booking websites, which take a commission). To get these rates, you must mention this book when you reserve, and then show the book upon arrival. Some readers with ebooks have reported difficulty getting a Rick Steves discount. If this happens to you, please show this to the hotelier: Rick Steves discounts apply to readers with ebooks as well as printed books.

Types of Accommodations

Hotels

Many of my recommended hotels have three floors of rooms and steep stairs; expect good exercise and be happy you packed light. You'll generally find an elevator (called a "lift" here) only at larger hotels. If you're concerned about stairs, call and ask about ground-floor rooms or pay for a hotel with a lift. Air-conditioning is rare (I've noted which of my listings have it), but most places have fans. On hot summer nights, you'll want your window open—though in big cities, you may have to put up with street noise.

"Twin" means two single beds, and "double" means one double bed (in my listings, I list all two-person rooms as "doubles"). If you will take either one, let the hotel know, or you might be needlessly turned away. Most hotels offer family deals, which means that parents with young children can easily get a room with an extra child's bed or a discount for larger rooms. Call to negotiate the price. Teenage kids are generally charged as adults. Kids under five almost always sleep free.

Be careful of the terminology: An "en suite" (pronounced "on sweet") room has a bathroom (toilet and shower/tub) actually inside the room; a room with a "private bathroom" can mean that the bathroom is all yours, but it's across the hall; and a "standard" room has access to a bathroom down the hall that's shared with other rooms. Figuring there's little difference between "en suite" and "private" rooms, some places charge the same for both. If you want your own bathroom inside the room, request "en suite." (Hotels sometimes distinguish between a "bathroom"—with an actual bathtub—and a "shower room." An "en suite" room can have either a tub or shower.)

If money's tight, ask for a standard room. You'll almost always have a sink in your room. And, as more rooms go "en suite," the hallway bathroom is shared with fewer standard rooms.

Confusingly, pricey hotels might call an en suite room

"standard" to differentiate it from a fancier "superior" or "deluxe" room—if you're not sure, ask for clarification.

Note that to be called a "hotel," a place technically must have certain amenities, including a 24-hour reception (though this rule is loosely applied). TVs are standard in rooms, but may come with only the traditional five British channels (no cable). Note that all of Britain's accommodations are now non-smoking.

If you're arriving early in the morning, your room probably won't be ready. You should be able to safely check your bag at the hotel and dive right into sightseeing.

Hoteliers (and B&B hosts) can be a great help and source of advice. Most know their city well and can assist you with everything from public transit and airport connections to finding a good restaurant, the nearest launderette, or an Internet café. But even at the best places, mechanical breakdowns occur: Air-conditioning malfunctions, sinks leak, hot water turns cold, and toilets gurgle and smell. Report your concerns clearly and calmly at the front desk. For more complicated problems, don't expect instant results.

If you suspect night noise will be a problem (if, for instance, your room is over a pub), ask for a quiet room in the back or on an upper floor. To guard against theft in your room, keep valuables out of sight. Some rooms come with a safe, and others have safes at the front desk. Use them if you're concerned.

Checkout can pose problems if surprise charges pop up on your bill. If you settle up your bill the day before you leave, you'll have time to discuss and address any points of contention (before 19:00, when the night shift usually arrives).

Above all, don't expect things to be the same as back home. Keep a positive attitude. Remember, you're on vacation. If your hotel is a disappointment, spend more time out enjoying the city you came to see.

Modern Hotel Chains: While most travelers prefer the classic British hotel or B&B experience, chain hotels—which are popping up in bigger cities all over Britain—can be a great value. They offer simple, clean, and modern rooms for up to four people (two adults/two children) for £60-100, depending on the location (more expensive in London). Some are located near the train station, on major highways, or outside the city center. What you lose in charm, you gain in savings.

These hotels are as cozy as a Motel 6, but they are especially worth considering for families, as kids sometimes stay for free. Most rooms have a double bed, single bed, five-foot trundle bed, private shower, WC, and TV. There's usually an attached restaurant, good security, an elevator, and a 24-hour staffed reception desk. Breakfast is always extra.

Book through the hotel's website, as it is often the easiest

Smoke-Free Great Britain

Great Britain's public places are now smoke-free. Hotels, B&Bs, and restaurants are required to be non-smoking (though hoteliers are permitted to designate specific rooms for smokers).

way to make reservations, and will generally net you a discount. Midweek prices are generally higher than weekend rates, and Sunday nights can be shockingly cheap. To find the going rate, punch in your dates on the hotel's online reservation form. Like airline tickets, pricing changes from day to day or week to week according to demand. The best deals typically require a prepaid, nonrefundable, three-week advance purchase.

The biggest chains are **Premier Inn** (www.premierinn.com, reservations tel. 0870-242-8000) and **Travelodge** (www.travelodge .co.uk, reservations tel. 0870-085-0950). Premier Inn has a "Premier Saver" option available on certain dates if booked at least three weeks in advance and prepaid in full (no changes or refunds). Travelodge has a similar prepaid "Saver" rate for 7- to 21-day advance bookings (nonrefundable, but changes possible for a small fee until up to a week ahead).

Other chains with properties in Britain include the Irish chain **Jurys Inn** (www.jurysinns.com) and the French-owned **Ibis** (www.ibishotel.com). Couples can consider **Holiday Inn Express,** which is spreading throughout England. Like a Holiday Inn lite, with cheaper prices and no restaurant, many of these hotels allow only two per room, although some take up to four (doubles about £60-100, make sure Express is part of the name or you'll pay more for a regular Holiday Inn, www.hiexpress.co.uk, reservations tel. 0871-423-4896).

Meanwhile, **easyHotel** is a different animal—an extremely basic, pay-as-you-go bargain chain with several branches in London (see page 175 for details).

For recommendations for online hotel deals in London, as well as using auction-type sites, see page 160.

Hotels Beyond This Book: If you're traveling beyond my recommended destinations, you'll find accommodations where you need them. Any town with tourists has a TI that books rooms or can give you a list and point you in the right direction. In the absence of a TI, ask people on the street or in pubs or restaurants for help. Online, visit www.smoothhound.co.uk, which offers a range of accommodations for towns throughout the UK (searchable by town, airport, hotel name, or price range).

Small Hotels and B&Bs

Places with "townhouse" or "house" (such as "London House") are like big B&Bs or small family-run hotels—with fewer amenities but more character than a hotel. B&Bs range from large guest houses with 15-20 rooms to small homes renting out a spare bedroom, but they typically have six rooms or fewer. The philosophy of the management determines the character of a place more than its size and facilities offered. I avoid places run as a business by absentee owners. My top listings are run by people who enjoy welcoming the world to their breakfast table.

Compared to hotels, B&Bs give you double the cultural intimacy for half the price. While you may lose some of the conveniences of a hotel—such as fancy lobbies, in-room phones, and frequent bed-sheet changes—I happily make the trade-off for the lower rates and personal touches. If you have a reasonable but limited budget, skip hotels and go the B&B way. Many B&Bs now take credit cards, but may add the card service fee to your bill (about three percent).

You'll generally pay £25-50 (about $40-80) per person for a double room in a B&B in Britain. Some big, impersonal chain hotels are offering rooms cheaper than the mom-and-pop places—but without breakfast (see "Modern Hotel Chains," earlier). When considering the price of a B&B or small hotel, remember you're getting two breakfasts (up to a £25 value) for each double room.

B&Bs are not hotels. Think of your host as a friendly acquaintance who's invited you to stay in her home, rather than someone you're paying to wait on you.

B&B proprietors are selective as to whom they invite in for the night. At some B&Bs, children are not welcome. If you'll be staying for more than one night, you are a "desirable." In popular weekend-getaway spots, you're unlikely to find a place to take you for Saturday night only. If my listings are full, ask for guidance. Mentioning this book can help. Owners usually work together and can call up an ally to land you a bed.

Small places usually serve a hearty fried breakfast of eggs and much more (for details on breakfast, see page 35). Because your B&B owner is also the cook, there's usually a quite-limited time span when breakfast is served (typically about an hour—make sure you know when it is before you turn in for the night). It's an unwritten rule that guests shouldn't show up at the very end of the breakfast period and expect a full cooked breakfast (try to arrive at least 15 minutes before the ending time). If you do arrive late (or need to leave before breakfast is served), most hosts are happy to let you help yourself to cereal, fruit or juice, and coffee; ask politely if it's possible.

Most B&Bs stock rooms with an electric kettle, along with

Making Reservations

Given the good value of the accommodations I've found for this book, I'd recommend that you reserve your rooms in advance, particularly if you'll be traveling during peak season. Book several weeks ahead, or as soon as you've pinned down your travel dates. Note that some national holidays jam things up and merit your making reservations far in advance (see "Holidays and Festivals" on page 809).

Phoning: To call England from the US or Canada, dial 011-44 and then the area code (without initial zero) and the local number. (The 011 is our international access code, and 44 is the country code for the entire United Kingdom.) If you're calling England from another European country, dial 00-44-area code (without initial zero) and the local number. (The 00 is Europe's international access code.) To make calls within England, dial the area code and local number. For more tips on calling, see page 776.

Requesting a Reservation: To make a reservation, contact hotels directly by email, phone, or fax. Email is the clearest and most economical way to make a reservation. Or you can go straight to the hotel website; many have secure online reservation forms and can instantly inform you of availability and any special deals. But be sure you use the hotel's official site and not a booking agency's site—otherwise you may pay higher rates than you should.

The hotelier wants to know these key pieces of information (also included in the sample request form in the appendix):
- number and type of rooms
- number of nights
- date of arrival
- date of departure
- any special needs (e.g., bathroom in the room or down the hall, twin beds vs. double bed, air-conditioning, quiet, view, ground floor, etc.)

When you request a room, use the European style for writing dates: day/month/year. For example, a two-night stay in July, I would request "1 double room for 2 nights, arrive 16/07/12, depart 18/07/12." Consider carefully how long you'll stay; don't just assume you can tack on extra days once you arrive. Make sure you mention any discounts—for Rick Steves readers or otherwise—when you make the reservation.

Confirming a Reservation: If the hotel's response includes its room availability and rates, it's not a confirmation. You must tell them that you want that room at the given rate. Most hoteliers will request your credit-card number for a one-night deposit to hold the room. While you can email your credit-card information (I do), it's safer to share that confidential info via phone call, fax, split between two emails, or via a secure online reservation form (if the hotel has one on its website).

Canceling a Reservation: If you must cancel your reservation, it's courteous to do so with as much advance notice as possible—at least three days. Simply make a quick phone call or send an email. Family-run hotels and B&Bs lose money if they turn away customers while holding a room for someone who doesn't show up. Understandably, many places bill no-shows for one night.

Cancellation policies can be strict: For example, you might lose a deposit if you cancel within two weeks of your reserved stay, or you might be billed for the entire visit if you leave early. Internet deals may require prepayment, with no refunds for cancellations. Ask about cancellation policies before you book.

If canceling via email, request confirmation that your cancellation was received to avoid being accidentally billed.

Reconfirming Your Reservation: Always call to reconfirm your room reservation a day or two in advance from the road. (Don't have a TI call for you; they may take a commission.) Smaller hotels and B&Bs appreciate knowing your estimated time of arrival. If you'll be arriving late (after 17:00), alert your hotelier. On the small chance that a hotel loses track of your reservation, bring along a hard copy of their emailed or faxed confirmation.

Reserving Rooms as You Travel: You can make reservations as you travel, calling hotels or B&Bs a few days to a week before your arrival. If everything's full, don't despair. Call a day or two in advance and fill in a cancellation. If you'd rather travel without any reservations at all, you'll have greater success snaring rooms if you arrive at your destination early in the day. When you anticipate crowds (weekends are worst), call hotels at about 9:00 or 10:00 on the day you plan to arrive, when the hotel clerk knows who'll be checking out and just which rooms will be available.

Most TIs in Britain can book you a room in their town, and also often in nearby towns. They generally charge a £4 fee, and you'll pay a 10 percent "deposit" at the TI and the rest at the B&B (meaning that you pay extra and the B&B loses money, as the TI keeps the "deposit"). While this can be useful in a pinch, it's a better deal for everyone (except the TIs) to book direct, using the listings in this book.

cups, tea bags, and coffee packets (if you prefer decaf, buy a jar at a grocery and dump the contents into a baggie for easy packing).

Americans sometimes assume they'll get new towels each day. The English don't, and neither should you. Hang towels up to dry and reuse.

Be aware of luggage etiquette. A large bag in a compact older building can easily turn even the most graceful of us into a bull in an English china shop. If you've got a backpack, don't wear it indoors. If your host offers to carry your bag upstairs, accept—they're adept at maneuvering luggage up tiny staircases without damaging their walls and banisters. Finally, use your room's luggage racks—putting bags on empty beds can dirty and scuff nice comforters. Treat these lovingly maintained homes as you would a friend's house.

Electrical outlets sometimes have switches that turn the current on or off; if your electrical appliance isn't working, flip the switch at the outlet. When you unplug your appliance, don't forget your adapter—most B&Bs have boxes of various adapters and converters that guests left behind (which is handy if you left yours at the last place).

You're likely to encounter unusual bathroom fixtures. The "pump toilet" has a flushing handle that doesn't kick in unless you push it just right: too hard or too soft, and it won't go. (Be decisive but not ruthless.) There's also the "dial-a-shower," an electronic box under the shower head where you'll turn a dial to select the heat of the water and (sometimes with a separate dial or button) turn on or shut off the flow of water. If you can't find the switch to turn on the shower, it may be just outside the bathroom.

Many B&Bs and small hotels are in older buildings, with thin walls and doors, and sometimes creaky floorboards. This can make for a noisy night, especially with people walking down the hall to use the bathroom. If you're a light sleeper, bring earplugs. And please be quiet in the halls and in your rooms (talk softly, and keep the TV volume low). Those of us getting up early will thank you for it.

Your B&B bedroom probably won't include a phone. In this mobile-phone age, street phone booths can be few and far between. Some B&B owners will allow you to use their phone, but many are disinclined to let you ring up charges. That's because most British people pay for each local call (whether from a fixed line or a mobile phone), and rates are expensive. Therefore, to be polite, ask to use their phone only in an emergency—and offer to use an international calling card or to pay for the call. If you plan to be staying in B&Bs and making frequent calls, consider buying a British mobile phone (see page 781).

With so many people traveling these days with a laptop or

other wireless device, nearly every B&B comes equipped with free Wi-Fi (as noted in my accommodations listings); however, the signal frequently won't reach up many stairs, so you may have to sit in the lounge to access it.

Many B&B owners are also pet owners. And, while pets are rarely allowed into guest rooms, and B&B proprietors are typically very tidy, visitors with pet allergies might be bothered. I've tried to list which B&Bs have pets, but if you're allergic, ask about pets when you reserve.

Remember that you may need to pay cash for your room. Plan ahead so you have enough cash to pay up when you check out.

Hostels

England has hundreds of hostels of all shapes and sizes. Choose your hostel selectively. Hostels can be historic castles or depressing tenements, serene and comfy or overrun by noisy school groups. You'll pay about £20-25 ($32-40) for a bed. Travelers of any age are welcome if they don't mind dorm-style accommodations and meeting other travelers. Most hostels offer kitchen facilities, Internet access, Wi-Fi, and a self-service laundry. Bring a sleeping sheet or rent one as you go. Family and private rooms may be available on request.

Independent hostels tend to be easygoing, colorful, and informal (no membership required); see www.hostelz.com, www.hostelseurope.com, www.hostels.com, and www.hostelworld.com. **Official hostels** are part of Hostelling International and adhere to various rules (such as a 17:00 check-in, lockout during the day, a curfew at night); they require that you either have a membership card or pay extra per night (www.hihostels.com). For more England hostel listings, consult www.yha.org.uk.

Eating

England's reputation for miserable food, while once well-deserved, is now dated. While some dreary pub food still exists, creative chefs are trying to push British cuisine forward with some new international influences. You'll find the cuisine scene here lively, trendy, and pleasantly surprising. (Unfortunately, it's also expensive.) Even the basic, traditional pub grub has gone upmarket—more and more "gastropubs" are serving locally sourced meats and fresh vegetables rather than microwaved pies, soggy fries, and mushy peas.

All English eateries are now smoke-free. Restaurants and pubs that sell food are non-smoking indoors; establishments keep their smokers contented by allowing them to light up in doorways and on outdoor patios.

Sounds Bad, Tastes Good

The English have a knack for making food sound funny. Here are a few examples:

Toad in the Hole: Sausage dipped in batter and fried

Bubble and Squeak: Leftovers, usually potatoes, veggies, and meat, all fried up together

Bap: Small roll

Treacle: Golden syrup, similar to light molasses

When restaurant-hunting, choose a spot filled with locals, not tourists. Venturing even a block or two off the main drag leads to higher-quality food for less than half the price of the tourist-oriented places. Locals eat better at lower-rent locales.

Budget Eating Tips

You have plenty of inexpensive choices: pub grub, daily lunch and early-bird specials, ethnic restaurants, cafeterias, fast food, picnics, fish-and-chips, greasy-spoon cafés, pizza, and more.

I've found that portions are huge and, with locals feeling the economic pinch, **sharing plates** is generally just fine. Ordering two drinks, a soup or side salad, and splitting a £10 meat pie can make a good, filling meal. If you are on a limited budget, share a main course in a more expensive place for a nicer eating experience.

Pub grub is the most atmospheric budget option. You'll usually get fresh, tasty buffets under ancient timbers, with hearty lunches and dinners priced reasonably at £6-10 (see "Pubs," later). Gastropubs, with better food, are more expensive.

Classier restaurants have some affordable deals. Lunch is usually cheaper than dinner; a top-end, £25-for-dinner-type restaurant often serves the same quality two-course lunch deals for £10-12. Look for early-bird dinner specials, allowing you to eat well and affordably (generally two courses-£17, three courses-£20), but early (usually last order by 18:30 or 19:00).

Ethnic restaurants from all over the world add spice to England's cuisine scene. Eating Indian, Bangladeshi, Chinese, or Thai is cheap (even cheaper if you do take-out). Middle Eastern stands sell gyro sandwiches, falafel, and *shwarmas* (lamb in pita bread). An Indian samosa (greasy, flaky meat-and-vegetable pie) costs £2, can be microwaved, and makes a very cheap, if small, meal. (For more, see "Indian Food," later.) You'll find all-you-can-eat Chinese and Thai places serving £6 meals and offering £3.50 take-away boxes. While you can't "split" a buffet, you can split a take-away box. Stuff the box full, and you and your partner can eat in a park for less than £2 each—making this England's cheapest hot meal.

Fish-and-chips are a heavy, greasy, but tasty English classic. Every town has at least one "chippy" selling a take-away box of fish-and-chips in a cardboard box or (more traditionally) wrapped in paper for about £3-7. You can dip your fries in ketchup, American-style, or "go English" and drizzle the whole thing with vinegar.

Most large **museums** (and some historic **churches**) have handy, moderately priced cafeterias.

Fast food places, both American and British, are everywhere.

Cheap chain restaurants, such as steak houses and pizza places, serve no-nonsense food in family-friendly settings (steakhouse meals about £10; all-you-can-stomach pizza about £5). For specific chains to keep an eye out for, see "Chain Restaurants," later.

Bakeries sell yogurt, cartons of "semi-skimmed" milk, pastries, meat pies, and pasties (PASS-teez). Pasties are heavy, savory meat pies that originated in the Cornish mining country; they had big crust handles so miners with filthy hands could eat them and toss the crust. The most traditional filling is beef stew, but you'll also find them with chicken, vegetable, lamb and mint, and even Indian flavors inside (see sidebar on page 348).

Picnicking saves time and money. You can easily get prepared food to go. Munch a relaxed "meal on wheels" picnic during your open-top bus tour or river cruise to save 30 precious minutes for sightseeing.

Good **sandwich shops** and corner **grocery stores** are a hit with local workers eating on the run. Try boxes of orange juice  (pure, by the liter), fresh bread, tasty English cheese, meat, a tube of Colman's English mustard, local eatin' apples, bananas, small tomatoes, a small tub of yogurt (drinkable), trail mix, nuts, plain or chocolate-covered digestive biscuits, and any local specialties. At **open-air markets** and **supermarkets,** you can get produce in small quantities (three tomatoes and two bananas cost about £1). Supermarkets often have good deli sections, even offering Indian dishes, and sometimes salad bars. Decent packaged sandwiches (£3-4) are sold everywhere (for a few options, see "Carry-Out Chains," later).

Chain Restaurants

I know—you're going to Britain to enjoy characteristic little hole-in-the-wall pubs, so mass-produced food is the furthest thing from your mind. But several good chains with branches across the UK can be a nice break from pub grub. I've recommended these restaurants throughout this book, but if you see a location that I haven't listed…go for it.

Sit-Down Chains

Wagamama Noodle Bar, serving up fresh and reliably delicious pan-Asian cuisine, is stylish, youthful, and mod. There's one in almost every midsize city in the UK, and after you've sampled their udon noodles, fried rice, or curry dishes, you'll know why. They're usually in a sprawling, loud, and modern hall filled with long shared tables and busy servers who scrawl your order on the placemat. Portions are huge enough for light eaters on a tight budget to share (typically £7-10 entrées, good vegetarian options).

At **Yo! Sushi,** freshly prepared sushi dishes trundle past on a conveyor belt. Color-coded plates tell you how much each dish costs (£1.75-5), and a picture-filled menu explains what you're eating. Just help yourself.

Gourmet Burger Company (GBK) offers £7-8 burgers that are, if not quite gourmet, very good. Choices range from a simple cheeseburger to more elaborate options, such as Jamaican. Choose a table and order at the counter—they'll bring the food to you.

Loch Fyne Fish Restaurant, a Scottish chain, serves up fish, oysters, and mussels in a lively, upscale-but-unpretentious setting (£10-15 main dishes, early-bird deals).

Ask and **Pizza Express** serve quality pasta and pizza in a pleasant, sit-down atmosphere that's family-friendly. **Jamie's Italian** (from celebrity chef Jamie Oliver) is hipper and pricier, and feels more upmarket.

Carry-Out Chains

While the following places might have some seating, they're an easy place to grab some prepackaged food on the go.

Major supermarket chains have smaller, offshoot branches that specialize in sandwiches, salads, and other prepared foods "to go." These can be a picnicker's dream come true. Some shops are stand-alone, while others are located inside a larger store. The most prevalent—and best—is **M&S Simply Food** (part of the Marks & Spencer department-store chain; no seating but plasticware is provided). **Sainsbury's Local** grocery stores also offer some decent prepared food; **Tesco Express** and **Tesco Metro** are a distant third.

Other "cheap and cheery" chains, such as **Pret à Manger** and **Eat,** provide office workers with good, healthful sandwiches, salads, and pastries to go.

West Cornwall Pasty Company sells a variety of these traditional savory pies for around £3— as do many smaller, independent
bakeries.

The Great English Breakfast

The traditional "fry," or "full English breakfast"—generally
included in the cost of your room—is famous as a hearty way to
start the day. Also known as a
"heart attack on a plate," the
breakfast is especially feast-
like if you've just come from
the land of the skimpy continental breakfast across the
Channel.

The standard fry gets off
to a healthy start with juice
and cereal or porridge. (Try
Weetabix, a soggy English
cousin of shredded wheat and perhaps the most absorbent material
known to humankind.) Next, with tea or coffee, you get a heated
plate with a fried egg, Canadian-style bacon or sausage, a grilled
tomato, sautéed mushrooms, baked beans, and sometimes hash
browns, kippers (herring), or fried bread (sizzled in a greasy skil-
let). Toast comes in a rack (to cool quickly and crisply) with butter
and marmalade. This protein-stuffed meal is great for stamina and
tides many travelers over until dinner.

You'll figure out quickly which parts of the fry you like and
don't like. Your host appreciates knowing this up front, rather than
serving you the whole shebang and having to throw out uneaten
food. There's nothing wrong with skipping some or all of the fry—
few Brits actually start their day with this heavy breakfast. Many
progressive B&B owners offer vegetarian, organic, or other creative variations on the traditional breakfast.

These days, the best coffee is served in a *cafetière* (also called a
"French press"). When your coffee has steeped as long as you like,
plunge down the filter and pour.

Afternoon Tea

People of leisure punctuate their day with an "afternoon tea" at
a tearoom. You'll get a pot of tea, small finger foods (like sandwiches with the crusts cut off), homemade scones, jam, and thick
clotted cream. A lighter "cream tea" gets you tea and a scone or
two. Tearooms, which often serve appealing light meals, are usually open for lunch and close at about 17:00, just before dinner. For
more on this most English of traditions, see page 194.

Pubs

Pubs are a basic part of the British social scene, and, whether you're a teetotaler or a beer-guzzler, they should be a part of your

travel here. "Pub" is short for "public house." It's an extended living room where, if you don't mind the stickiness, you can feel the pulse of England.

Smart travelers use the pubs to eat, drink, get out of the rain, watch sport-

ing events, and make new friends. Unfortunately, many city pubs have been afflicted with an excess of brass, ferns, and video slot machines. The most traditional, atmospheric pubs are in the countryside and in smaller towns.

Pub Grub

Pub grub gets better each year. In London, it offers the best indoor eating value. For £6-10, you'll get a basic budget hot lunch or dinner in friendly surroundings. The *Good Pub Guide* is excellent (www.thegoodpubguide.co.uk). Pubs that are attached to restaurants, advertise their food, and are crowded with locals are more likely to have fresh food and a chef—and less likely to be the kind of pub that sells only lousy microwaved snacks.

Pubs generally serve traditional dishes, such as fish-and-chips, vegetables, "bangers and mash" (sausages and mashed potatoes), roast beef with Yorkshire pudding (batter-baked in the oven), gammon (ham steak), and assorted meat pies, such as steak-and-kidney pie or shepherd's pie (stewed lamb topped with mashed potatoes). Side dishes include salads (sometimes even a nice self-serve salad bar), vegetables, and—invariably—"chips" (French fries). "Crisps" are potato chips. A "jacket potato" (baked potato stuffed with fillings of your choice) can almost be a meal in itself. A "ploughman's lunch" is a traditional English meal of bread, cheese, and sweet pickles that nearly every tourist tries...once. These days, you'll likely find more Italian pasta, curried dishes, and quiche on the menu than traditional fare.

Meals are usually served 12:00-14:00 and 18:00-20:00—generally not throughout the day. Since pubs make more money selling beer, many places stop serving meals early in the evening. There's often no table service. Order at the bar, then take a seat and they'll bring the food when it's ready (or sometimes you pick it up at the bar). Pay at the bar (sometimes when you order, sometimes after you eat). Don't tip unless it's a place with full table service.

Servings are hearty, service is quick, and you'll rarely spend more than £10 per person. (If you're on a tight budget, consider sharing a meal—note the size of portions around you before ordering.) A beer or cider adds another couple of pounds. (Free tap water is always available.)

If you want food that's a notch above, seek out a **gastropub**. Although similar to a regular pub, a gastropub pays more attention to the quality of its menu—with accordingly higher prices (£10-15 meals). You'll find a few gastropubs in the towns and cities, but some of the best are in countryside villages.

Beer and Other Beverages

The British take great pride in their beer. Many Brits think that drinking beer cold and carbonated, as Americans do, ruins the taste. Most pubs will have **lagers** (cold, refreshing, American-style beer), **ales** (amber-colored, cellar-temperature beer), **bitters** (hop-flavored ale, perhaps the most typical British beer), and **stouts** (dark and somewhat bitter, like Guinness). At pubs, long-handled pulls are used to pull the traditional, rich-flavored "real ales" up from the cellar. These are the connoisseur's favorites: fermented naturally, varying from sweet to bitter, often with a hoppy or nutty flavor. Notice the fun names. Short-hand pulls at the bar mean colder, fizzier, mass-produced, and less interesting keg beers. Mild beers are sweeter, with a creamy malt flavoring. Irish cream ale is a smooth, sweet experience. Try the draft cider (sweet or dry)...carefully.

Order your beer at the bar and pay as you go, with no need to tip. An average beer costs £3. Part of the experience is standing before a line of "hand pulls," or taps, and wondering which beer to choose.

As dictated by British law, draft beer and cider are served by the pint (20-ounce imperial size) or the half-pint (9.6 ounces). (It's almost feminine for a man to order just a half; I order mine with quiche.) The government recently sanctioned a new serving size—the two-thirds pint—hoping that more choice will woo more beer drinkers (a steady decline in beer consumption, which is taxed, has had a negative effect on tax revenues). Proper English ladies like a **shandy** (half beer and half 7-Up).

Besides beer, many pubs actually have a good selection of wines by the glass, a fully stocked bar for the gentleman's "G and T" (gin and tonic), and the increasingly popular bottles of alcohol-plus-sugar (such as Bacardi Breezers) for the younger, working-class set. **Pimm's** is a refreshing and fruity summer cocktail, traditionally popular during Wimbledon. It's an upper-class drink—a rough bloke might insult a pub by claiming it sells more Pimm's than beer.

> # How Was Your Trip?
>
> Were your travels fun, smooth, and meaningful? If you'd like to share your tips, concerns, and discoveries, please fill out the survey at www.ricksteves.com/feedback. I value your feedback. Thanks in advance—it helps a lot.

Teetotalers can order from a wide variety of soft drinks—both the predictable American sodas and other more interesting bottled drinks, such as ginger beer (similar to ginger ale but with more bite), root beers, or other flavors (Fentimans brews some unusual options that are stocked in many English pubs). Note that in Britain, "lemonade" is lemon-lime soda (like 7-Up). Children are served food and soft drinks in pubs, but you must be 18 to order a beer.

Pub hours vary. Pubs generally serve beer Monday-Saturday 11:00-23:00 and Sunday 12:00-22:30, though many are open later, particularly on Friday and Saturday. As it nears closing time, you'll hear shouts of "Last orders." Then comes the 10-minute warning bell. Finally, they'll call "Time!" to pick up your glass, finished or not, when the pub closes.

A cup of darts is free for the asking. People go to a public house to be social. They want to talk. Get vocal with a local. This is easiest at the bar, where people assume you're in the mood to talk (rather than at a table, where you're allowed a bit of privacy). The pub is the next best thing to having relatives in town. Cheers!

Indian Food

Eating Indian food is "going local" in cosmopolitan, multiethnic England. You'll find recommended Indian restaurants in most English cities, and even in small towns. Take the opportunity to sample food from Britain's former colony. Indian cuisine is as varied as the country itself. In general, they use more exotic spices than British or American cuisine—some hot, some sweet. (But if you like your food very hot, you'll find that Indian restaurants dull the spice for timid British palates—you'll have to be insistent if you want four-star heat.) Indian food is very vegetarian-friendly, offering many meatless dishes to choose from on any given menu.

For a simple meal that costs about £12-14, order one dish with rice and *naan* (Indian flatbread that can be served plain, with garlic, or other ways—usually one order is plenty for two people to share). You'll generally pay £2-3 extra for an order of rice (it's not included in the entrée price, as it often is at Indian restaurants in the US). Many restaurants have a fixed-price com-

British Chocolate

My chocoholic readers are enthusiastic about British choco-
lates. As with other dairy products, chocolate seems richer
and creamier here than it does in the US, so even the basics
like Kit Kat and Twix have a different taste. Some favorites include Cadbury Gold bars (filled with liquid caramel),
Cadbury Crunchie bars, Nestlé's Lion bars (layered wafers
covered in caramel and chocolate), Cadbury's Boost bars (a
shortcake biscuit with caramel in milk chocolate), Cadbury
Flake (crumbly folds of melt-in-your-mouth chocolate), Galaxy
chocolate bars (especially the ones with hazelnuts), and Aero
(a light-as-air chocolate bar filled with little bubbles). Thornton
shops (in larger train stations) sell a box of sweets called the
Continental Assortment, which comes with a tasting guide.
The highlight is the mocha white-chocolate truffle. British
M&Ms, called Smarties, are better than American ones. At ice-
cream vans, look for the beloved traditional "99p"—a vanilla
soft-serve cone with a small Flake bar stuck right into the
middle. For a break from chocolate, buy a roll of wine gums—
similar to Jujubes, but tangier and less sweet (Maynards is the
biggest brand).

bination meal that offers more variety, and is simpler and cheaper
than ordering à la carte. For about £20, you can make a mix-and-
match platter out of several sharable dishes, including *dal* (sim-
mered lentils) as a starter; one or two meat or vegetable dishes
with sauce (for example, chicken curry, chicken *tikka masala*
in a creamy tomato sauce, grilled fish tandoori, chickpea *chana
masala*, or a spicy *vindaloo* dish); *raita* (a cooling yogurt that's
added to spicy dishes); rice; *naan;* and an Indian beer (wine and
Indian food don't really mix) or chai (a cardamom- and cinna-
mon-spiced tea, usually served with milk). An easy way to taste a
variety of dishes (especially for a single diner) is to order a *thali*—
a sort of sampler plate, generally served on a metal tray, with
small servings of various specialties.

Desserts (Sweets or "Puddings")

To the British, the traditional word for dessert is "pudding,"
although it's also referred to as "sweets" these days. Sponge cake,
cream, fruitcake, and meringue are key players.

Trifle is the best-known British concoction, consisting of
sponge cake soaked in brandy or sherry (or orange juice for children), then covered with jam and/or fruit and custard cream.
Whipped cream can sometimes put the final touch on this "light"
treat.

Castle puddings are sponge puddings cooked in small molds

and topped with Golden Syrup (a popular brand and a cross between honey and maple syrup). Bread-and-butter pudding consists of slices of French bread baked with milk, cream, eggs, and raisins (similar to the American preparation), served warm with cold cream. Hasty pudding, supposedly the invention of people in a hurry to avoid the bailiff, is made from stale bread with dried fruit and milk. Queen of puddings is a breadcrumb pudding topped with warm jam, meringue, and cream. Treacle pudding is a popular steamed pudding whose "sponge" mixture combines flour, suet (animal fat), butter, sugar, and milk. Christmas pudding (also called plum pudding) is a dense mixture with dried and candied fruit served with brandy butter or hard sauce. Sticky toffee pudding is a moist cake made with dates, heated and drizzled with toffee sauce, and served with ice cream or cream. Banoffee pie is the delicious British answer to banana cream pie.

The English version of custard is a smooth, yellow liquid. Cream tops most everything custard does not. There's single cream for coffee. Double cream is really thick. Whipped cream is familiar, and clotted cream is the consistency of whipped butter.

Fool is a dessert with sweetened pureed fruit (such as rhubarb, gooseberries, or black currants) mixed with cream or custard and chilled. Elderflower is a popular flavoring for sorbet.

Scones are tops, and many inns and restaurants have their secret recipes. Whether made with fruit or topped with clotted cream, scones take the cake.

Traveling as a Temporary Local

We travel all the way to England to enjoy differences—to become temporary locals. You'll experience frustrations. Certain truths that we find "God-given" or "self-evident," such as cold beer, ice in drinks, bottomless cups of coffee, hot showers, and bigger being better, are suddenly not so true. One of the benefits of travel is the eye-opening realization that there are logical, civil, and even better alternatives. A willingness to go local ensures that you'll enjoy a full dose of English hospitality.

Europeans generally like Americans. But if there is a negative aspect to the English image of us, it's that we are loud, aggressive, impolite, rich, superficially friendly, and a bit naive.

The English (and Europeans in general) place a high value on speaking quietly in restaurants and on trains. Listen while on the bus or in a restaurant—the place can be packed, but the decibel level is low. Try to adjust your volume accordingly to show respect for their culture.

While the English look bemusedly at some of our Yankee excesses—and worriedly at others—they nearly always afford us individual travelers all the warmth we deserve.

Judging from all the happy feedback I receive from travelers who have used this book, it's safe to assume you'll enjoy a great, affordable vacation—with the finesse of an independent, experienced traveler.

Thanks, and have a brilliant holiday!

Back Door Travel Philosophy
From *Rick Steves' Europe Through the Back Door*

Travel is intensified living—maximum thrills per minute and one of the last great sources of legal adventure. Travel is freedom. It's recess, and we need it.

Experiencing the real Europe requires catching it by surprise, going casual..."Through the Back Door."

Affording travel is a matter of priorities. (Make do with the old car.) You can eat and sleep—simply, safely, and enjoyably—anywhere in Europe for $120 a day plus transportation costs (allow more for bigger cities). In many ways, spending more money only builds a thicker wall between you and what you traveled so far to see. Europe is a cultural carnival, and time after time, you'll find that its best acts are free and the best seats are the cheap ones.

A tight budget forces you to travel close to the ground, meeting and communicating with the people. Never sacrifice sleep, nutrition, safety, or cleanliness to save money. Simply enjoy the local-style alternatives to expensive hotels and restaurants.

Connecting with people carbonates your experience. Extroverts have more fun. If your trip is low on magic moments, kick yourself and make things happen. If you don't enjoy a place, maybe you don't know enough about it. Seek the truth. Recognize tourist traps. Give a culture the benefit of your open mind. See things as different, but not better or worse. Any culture has plenty to share.

Of course, travel, like the world, is a series of hills and valleys. Be fanatically positive and militantly optimistic. If something's not to your liking, change your liking.

Travel can make you a happier American, as well as a citizen of the world. Our Earth is home to nearly seven billion equally precious people. It's humbling to travel and find that other people don't have the "American Dream"—they have their own dreams. Europeans like us, but with all due respect, they wouldn't trade passports.

Thoughtful travel engages us with the world. In tough economic times, it reminds us what is truly important. By broadening perspectives, travel teaches new ways to measure quality of life.

Globetrotting destroys ethnocentricity, helping us understand and appreciate other cultures. Rather than fear the diversity on this planet, celebrate it. Among your most prized souvenirs will be the strands of different cultures you choose to knit into your own character. The world is a cultural yarn shop, and Back Door travelers are weaving the ultimate tapestry. Join in!

ENGLAND

ENGLAND

England (pop. 52 million) is a hilly country the size of Louisiana (50,346 square miles) and located in the lower two-thirds of the isle of Britain. Scotland is to the north and the English Channel to the south, with the North Sea to the east and Wales (and the Irish Sea) to the west. Fed by ocean air from the southwest, the climate is mild, with a chance of cloudy, rainy weather almost any day of the year.

England has an economy that can stand alongside many much larger nations. It boasts high-tech industries (software, chemicals, aviation), international banking, and textile manufacturing, and is a major exporter of beef. While farms and villages remain, England is now an urban, industrial, and post-industrial colossus.

England traditionally has been very class-conscious, with the wealthy landed aristocracy, the middle-class tradesmen, and the lower-class farmers and factory workers. While social stratification is fading with the new global economy, regional differences remain strong. Locals can often identify where someone is from by their dialect or local accent—Geordie, Cockney, or Queen's English.

One thing that sets England apart from its fellow UK countries (Scotland, Wales, and Northern Ireland) is its ethnic makeup. Traditionally, those countries had Celtic roots, while the English mixed in Saxon and Norman blood. In the 20th century, England welcomed many Scots, Welsh, and Irish as low-wage workers. More recently, it's become home to immigrants from former colonies of its worldwide empire—

particularly from India/Pakistan/Bangladesh, the Caribbean, and Africa—and to many workers from poorer Eastern European countries. These days it's not a given that every "English" person speaks English. Nearly one in three citizens does not profess the Christian faith. As the world becomes interconnected by communications technology, it's possible for many immigrants to physically inhabit the country while remaining closely linked to their home culture—rather than truly assimilating into England.

This is the current English paradox. England—the birthplace and center of the extended worldwide family of English-speakers—is losing its traditional Englishness. Where Scotland, Wales, and Northern Ireland have cultural movements to preserve their local languages and customs, England does not. Politically, there is no "English" party in the UK Parliament. While Scotland, Wales, and Northern Ireland have their own parliaments to decide local issues, England must depend on the decisions of the UK government at large. Except for the occasional display of an English flag at a soccer match (the red St. George's cross on a white background), many English people don't really think of themselves as "English"—more as "Brits," a part of the wider UK.

Today, England tries to preserve its rich past as it races forward as a leading global player. There are still hints of its legacy of farms, villages, Victorian lamplighters, and upper-crust dandies. But it's also a jostling world of unemployed factory workers, investment bankers, soccer matches, rowdy "stag parties," and faux-Tudor suburbs. Modern England is a culturally diverse land in transition. Catch it while you can.

LONDON

London is more than 600 square miles of urban jungle—a world in itself and a barrage on all the senses. On my first visit, I felt extremely small.

London is more than its museums and landmarks. It's the L.A., D.C., and N.Y.C. of Britain—a living, breathing, thriving organism...a coral reef of humanity. The city has changed dramatically in recent years, and many visitors are surprised to find how "un-English" it is. ESL (English as a second language) seems like the city's first language, as white people are now a minority in major parts of the city that once symbolized white imperialism. Arabs have nearly bought out the area north of Hyde Park. Chinese takeouts outnumber fish-and-chips shops. Eastern Europeans pull pints in British pubs. Many hotels are run by people with foreign accents (who hire English chambermaids), while outlying suburbs are home to huge communities of Indians and Pakistanis. London is a city of nearly eight million separate dreams, inhabiting a place that does its best to tolerate and encourage them. With the English Channel Tunnel and discount airlines making travel between Britain and the Continent easier than ever, London is learning—sometimes fitfully—to live as a microcosm of its formerly vast empire.

The city, which has long attracted tourists, seems perpetually at your service, with an impressive slate of sights, entertainment, and eateries, linked by a great transit system. In anticipation of the 2012 Olympic Games (July 27-August 12) and a greater onslaught of tourists than usual, London is busy spiffing up the place, especially the rapidly developing Olympic Park in East London.

With just a few days here, you'll get no more than a quick

splash in this teeming human tidal pool. But with a good orientation, you'll find London manageable and fun. You'll get a sampling of the city's top sights, history, and cultural entertainment, and a good look at its ever-changing human face.

Blow through the city on the open deck of a double-decker orientation tour bus, and take a pinch-me-I'm-in-London walk through the West End. Ogle the crown jewels at the Tower of London, hear the chimes of Big Ben, and see the Houses of Parliament in action. Cruise the Thames River, and take a spin on the London Eye. Hobnob with poets' tombstones in Westminster Abbey, and visit with Leonardo, Botticelli, and Rembrandt in the National Gallery. Enjoy Shakespeare in a replica of the Globe theater and marvel at a glitzy, fun musical at a modern-day theater. Whisper across the dome of St. Paul's Cathedral, then rummage through our civilization's attic at the British Museum. And sip your tea with pinky raised and clotted cream dribbling down your scone.

Planning Your Time

The sights of London alone could easily fill a trip to England. It's a great one-week getaway. But on a three-week tour of England,

I'd give London three busy days. You won't be able to see everything, so don't try—you'll keep coming back to London. After dozens of visits myself, I still enjoy a healthy list of excuses to return. If you're flying in to one of London's airports, consider starting your trip in Bath and making London your English finale. Especially if you hope to enjoy a play or concert, a night or two of jet lag is bad news.

In 2012, be aware that the **Olympic Games** will overtake London from July 27 to August 12. For more on the games and where they'll be played, see page 139.

Here's a suggested three-day schedule:

Day 1

9:00   Tower of London (crown jewels first, then Beefeater tour, then White Tower; note that on Sun-Mon, the Tower opens at 10:00).

13:00   Grab a picnic, catch a boat at Tower Pier, and relax with lunch on the Thames while cruising to Westminster Pier.

14:30   Tour Westminster Abbey, and consider their evensong service (at 15:00 Sat-Sun, at 17:00 Mon-Fri and Sat in summer).

Rick Steves' Free Audio Tours

I've produced free, self-guided audio versions of my tours of the major sights in London (download them via www.ricksteves.com/audioeurope, iTunes, or the free Rick Steves Audio Europe smartphone app). These user-friendly, easy-to-follow, fun, and informative audio tours are available for the British Museum, British Library, and St. Paul's Cathedral, as well as neighborhood walks in Westminster and The City of London. Compared to live tours, these audio tours are hard to beat: Nobody will stand you up, the quality is reliable, you can take the tour exactly when you like, and they're free.

17:00 (or after evensong) Follow my self-guided walk of Westminster. When you're finished, if it's a Monday or Tuesday, you could return to the Houses of Parliament and pop in to see the House of Commons in action (until 22:30).

Day 2

8:30   Take a double-decker hop-on, hop-off London sightseeing bus tour (from Green Park or Victoria) and hop off for the Changing of the Guard.

11:00   Buckingham Palace (guards change most days May-July at 11:30, alternate days Aug-April—confirm).

12:00   Walk through St. James's Park to enjoy London's delightful park scene.

13:00   Covent Garden for lunch, shopping, and people-watching.

14:30   Tour the British Museum.

Evening   Have a pub dinner before a play, concert, or evening walking tour.

Day 3 (or More)

Choose among these remaining London highlights: National Gallery, British Library, Churchill War Rooms, Imperial War Museum, the two Tates (Tate Modern on the South Bank for modern art, Tate Britain on the North Bank for British art), St. Paul's Cathedral, Victoria and Albert Museum, National Portrait Gallery, Natural History Museum, Courtauld Gallery, or the Museum of London; take a spin on the London Eye or a cruise to Kew Gardens or Greenwich; enjoy a play at Shakespeare's Globe; do some serious shopping at one of London's elegant department stores or open-air markets; or take another historic walking tour.

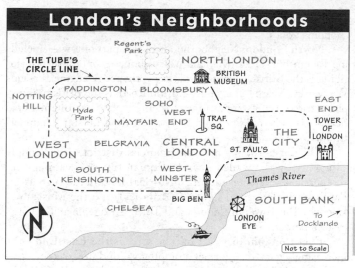

London's Neighborhoods

Regent's Park

THE TUBE'S CIRCLE LINE

NORTH LONDON

BRITISH MUSEUM

NOTTING HILL

PADDINGTON

BLOOMSBURY

EAST END

Hyde Park

SOHO

WEST END

MAYFAIR

TRAF. SQ.

TOWER OF LONDON

WEST LONDON

BELGRAVIA

CENTRAL LONDON

THE CITY

ST. PAUL'S

SOUTH KENSINGTON

WEST-MINSTER

Thames River

CHELSEA

BIG BEN

SOUTH BANK

LONDON EYE

To Docklands

Not to Scale

LONDON

Orientation to London

(area code: 020)

To grasp London more comfortably, see it as the old town in the city center without the modern, congested sprawl. (Even at that, it's still huge.)

The Thames River (pronounced "tems") runs roughly west to east through the city, with most of the visitor's sights on the North Bank. Mentally, maybe even physically, with scissors, trim down your map to include only the area between the Tower of London (to the east), Hyde Park (west), Regent's Park (north), and the South Bank (south). This is roughly the area bordered by the Tube's Circle Line. This four-mile stretch between the Tower and Hyde Park (about a 1.5-hour walk) looks like a milk bottle on its side (see map above), and holds 80 percent of the sights mentioned in this chapter.

Sprawling London becomes much more manageable if you think of it as a collection of neighborhoods:

Central London: This area contains Westminster and what Londoners call the West End. The **Westminster** district includes Big Ben, Parliament, Westminster Abbey, and Buckingham Palace—the grand government buildings from which Britain is ruled. **Trafalgar Square,** London's gathering place, has many major museums. The **West End** is the center of London's cultural life, with bustling squares: Piccadilly Circus and Leicester Square host cinemas, tourist traps, and nighttime glitz. Soho and Covent Garden are thriving people-zones with theaters, restaurants, pubs, and boutiques. And Regent and Oxford streets are the city's main shopping zones.

North London: Neighborhoods in this part of town—including Bloomsbury, Fitzrovia, and Marylebone—contain such major sights as the British Museum and the overhyped Madame Tussauds Waxworks. Nearby, along busy Euston Road, is the British Library plus a trio of train stations (one of them, St. Pancras International Station, is linked to Paris and Brussels by the Eurostar "Chunnel" train).

The City: Today's modern financial district, called simply "The City," was a walled town in Roman times. Gleaming skyscrapers are interspersed with historical landmarks such as St. Paul's Cathedral, legal sights (Old Bailey), and the Museum of London. The Tower of London and Tower Bridge lie at The City's eastern border.

East London: Just east of The City is the **East End**—the increasingly gentrified former stomping ground of Cockney ragamuffins and Jack the Ripper. Even farther to the east is London's version of Manhattan, the **Docklands,** filling the area around Canary Wharf. Energized by big businesses, the Docklands shows you London at its most modern. Historic **Greenwich** lies just south of the Docklands/Canary Wharf area, across the Thames. And the **2012 Olympic Park** is in the once-dreary Stratford district, a short train ride to the north.

The South Bank: The South Bank of the Thames River offers major sights (Tate Modern, Shakespeare's Globe, London Eye) linked by a riverside walkway. Within this area, **Southwark** (SUTH-uck) stretches from the Tate Modern to London Bridge. Pedestrian bridges connect the South Bank with The City and Trafalgar Square.

West London: This huge area contains neighborhoods such as Mayfair, Belgravia, Chelsea, South Kensington, and Notting Hill. It's home to London's wealthy and has many trendy shops and enticing restaurants. Here you'll find a range of museums (Victoria and Albert Museum, Tate Britain, and more), my top hotel recommendations, lively Victoria Station, and the vast green expanses of Hyde Park and Kensington Gardens.

With this neighborhood focus and a good orientation, you'll get a sampling of London's top sights, history, and cultural entertainment, and a good look at its ever-changing human face.

Tourist Information

The **Britain and London Visitors Centre,** a block off Piccadilly Circus, is the best tourist information service in town. However, it's scheduled to move after March 2012 when its lease expires; check its website for its new location (Mon-Fri 9:30-18:00, Sat-

Sun 10:00-16:00; 1 Lower Regent Street, tel. 0870-156-6366, www .visitbritain.com, www.visitlondon.com). Unfortunately, London's many "Tourist Information Centres" (which represent themselves as TIs at major train and bus stations, airports, and near major sights—including St. Paul's Cathedral) are now simply businesses, selling advertising space to companies with fliers to distribute.

The Britain and London Visitors Centre has many different departments. Along with getting tourist information, you can purchase advance tickets to big sights, buy sightseeing passes, arrange coach tours, get theater tickets (steep 20 percent booking fee), get online (£1/20 minutes, terminals upstairs), plan travel beyond London, and even book trains to the Continent. Bring your itinerary and a checklist of questions.

At the Tourist Information desk, pick up various free publications: the *London Planner* (a free monthly that lists all the sights, events, and hours), walking tours info, a theater guide, London bus map, and the *Guide to River Thames Boat Services*. The staff sells a good £1 map and all the various sightseeing passes (London Pass described later; country-wide passes described on page 20).

The Hotels and Travel desk sells long-distance bus tickets and passes, train tickets (convenient for reservations), and Fast Track tickets to some of London's attractions. These tickets, which allow you to skip the queue at the sights at no extra cost, are worthwhile for places that can have long ticket lines, such as the Tower of London, the London Eye, and Madame Tussauds Waxworks. If you're going to the Waxworks, buy tickets here, since—at £22.50—they're cheaper than at the sight itself. (Note that some souvenir shops sell discounted tickets for sights; you'll see signs in their windows.)

The Visitors Centre reserves hotel rooms, but you can avoid their £5 booking fee by contacting hotels on your own.

London Pass: This pass is pricey, and to save any money, you'd have to sightsee virtually nonstop (£43/1 day, £58/2 days, £71/3 days, £94/6 days; days are calendar days rather than 24-hour periods; comes with 160-page guidebook, also sold at major train stations and airports, tel. 0870-242-9988, www.londonpass.com). It lets you skip the lines and covers many sights, including the Tower of London, Westminster Abbey, and St. Paul's Cathedral, but not the London Eye or Madame Tussauds Waxworks. Think through your sightseeing plans, study their website to see what's covered, and do the math before you buy.

Arrival in London

For more information on travel by train, bus, and plane, see "London Connections," near the end of this chapter.

By Train: London has nine major train stations, all connected

Affording London's Sights

London is one of Europe's most expensive cities, with the dubious distinction of having some of the world's highest admission prices. Fortunately, many sights are free.

Free Museums: Many of the city's biggest and best museums won't cost you a dime. Free sights include the British Museum, British Library, National Gallery, National Portrait Gallery, Tate Britain, Tate Modern, Wallace Collection, Imperial War Museum, Victoria and Albert Museum, Natural History Museum, Science Museum, National Army Museum, Sir John Soane's Museum, the Museum of London, the Geffrye, and on the outskirts of town, the Royal Air Force Museum London.

About half of these museums request a donation of a few pounds, but whether you contribute or not is up to you. If I spend money for an audioguide, I feel fine about not otherwise donating. If that makes you uncomfortable, donate.

Free Churches: Smaller churches let worshippers (and tourists) in free, although they may ask for a donation. The big sightseeing churches—Westminster Abbey and St. Paul's—charge steep admission fees, but offer free evensong services daily (though you're not allowed to stick around afterward). Westminster Abbey also offers free organ recitals most Sundays at 17:45.

Other Freebies: London has plenty of free performances, such as lunch concerts at St. Martin-in-the-Fields (see page 95) and summertime movies at The Scoop amphitheater near City Hall (Tube: London Bridge, schedule at www.morelondon .com—click on "The Scoop"). For other freebies, check out www .freelondonlistings.co.uk. There's no charge to enjoy the pageantry of the Changing of the Guard, rants at Speaker's Corner in Hyde Park, displays at Harrods, the people-watching scene at Covent Garden, and the colorful streets of the East End. It's free to view the legal action at the Old Bailey and the legislature at work in the Houses of Parliament. And you can get into a bit of the Tower of London by attending Sunday services in the Tower's chapel (chapel access only).

Greenwich makes for a very cheap day out (see next chapter). Many of its sights are free, and the journey there is covered by a cheap Zones 1-2 Tube ticket.

Sightseeing Deals: If you buy a paper One-Day Travelcard or rail ticket at a National Rail station (such as Paddington or Victoria), you may be eligible for two-for-one discounts at many popular sights, such as the London Eye, Tower of London, Tate Modern, and Madame Tussauds Waxworks. This is a great deal if you can get it. To claim the discount, you must have a rail ticket that has been used and validated that day—for instance, if you are arriving by train into London (from elsewhere in England) or taking a short morning side-trip. Get details and print vouchers at www.daysoutguide.co.uk, or look for brochures with coupons at major train stations.

Good-Value Tours: The £5-8 city walking tours with professional guides are one of the best deals going. (Note that the guides for the "free" walking tours are unpaid and expect tips—I'd pay up front for a professionally guided tour instead.) Hop-on, hop-off big-bus tours, while expensive (£22-27), provide a great overview and include free boat tours as well as city walks. A one-hour Thames ride to Greenwich costs £10 one-way, but most boats come with entertaining commentary. A three-hour bicycle tour is about £20.

Pricey...but Worth It? Big-ticket sights worth their hefty admission fees are Kew Gardens (£14), Shakespeare's Globe (£11.50), and the Churchill War Rooms (£16).

The London Eye has become a London must-see—though if you're on a tight budget, it's difficult to justify its very high cost (£19). While Hampton Court Palace (£16) is expensive, it is well-presented and a reasonable value if you have an interest in royal history. The Queen charges royally to open her palace to the public: Buckingham Palace (£17.50, Aug-Sept only), and her art gallery and carriage museum (adjacent to the palace, £9 and £8, £15.50 for both) are expensive but interesting. Madame Tussauds Waxworks is pricey but still fun and popular (£29, £22.50 if purchased at TI, drops to £14 after 17:00 if booked online). The Vinopolis wine museum provides a way to get a buzz and call it museum-going (from £20, entry includes tastes of wine).

Many smaller museums charge low admission. My favorites include the Courtauld Gallery (£6, free on Mon until 14:00) and the Wellington Museum at Apsley House (£6.30, www.english-heritage.org.uk).

Totally Pants (Brit-speak for Not Worth It): The London Dungeon, at £23.50, is gimmicky, overpriced, and a terrible value...despite the long line at the door. It doesn't make sense to spend your pounds on Winston Churchill's Britain at War Experience (£13) when the Churchill War Rooms (£16) and the Imperial War Museum (free) cover the same themes much better.

Theater: Compared with Broadway's prices, London theater is a bargain. Seek out the freestanding "tkts" booth at Leicester Square to get discounts from 25 to 50 percent on good seats (though not necessarily for the hottest shows; see page 154). If you're willing to settle for the cheapest seats (possibly with obstructed views), ask the theater's box office for their best deal (even the most popular shows generally have some £10-25 tickets). A £5 "groundling" ticket for a play at Shakespeare's Globe is the best theater deal in town (see page 128). Tickets to the Open Air Theatre at north London's Regent's Park start at £12 (see page 156).

London doesn't come cheap. But with its many free museums and affordable plays, this cosmopolitan, cultured city offers days of sightseeing thrills without requiring you to pinch your pennies (or your pounds).

by the Tube (subway). All have ATMs, and many of the larger stations also have shops, fast food, exchange offices, and luggage storage. From any station, you can ride the Tube or taxi to your hotel. For more info on train travel, see www.nationalrail.co.uk.

By Bus: The main intercity bus station is Victoria Coach Station, one block southwest of Victoria train station (and the Victoria Tube station). For more on bus travel, see www.national express.com.

By Plane: London has five airports. Most tourists arrive at Heathrow or Gatwick airports, although flights from elsewhere in Europe may land at Stansted, Luton, or London City airports. For specifics on getting from London's airports to downtown, see "London Connections," near the end of this chapter; for hotels near Heathrow and Gatwick, see page 177.

Helpful Hints

Theft Alert: Wear your money belt. The Artful Dodger is alive and well in London. Be on guard, particularly on public transportation and in places crowded with tourists, who, considered naive and rich, are targeted. The Changing of the Guard scene is a favorite for thieves. And more than 7,500 purses are stolen annually at Covent Garden alone.

Pedestrian Safety: Cars drive on the left side of the road—which can be as confusing for foreign pedestrians as for foreign drivers. Before crossing a street, I always look right, look left, then look right again just to be sure. Most crosswalks are even painted with instructions, reminding foreign guests to "Look right" or "Look left."

Medical Problems: Local hospitals have good-quality 24-hour-a-day emergency care centers where any tourist who needs help can drop in and, after a wait, be seen by a doctor. Your hotel has details. St. Thomas' Hospital, immediately across the river from Big Ben, has a fine reputation.

Getting Your Bearings: London is well-signed for visitors. Through an initiative called Legible London, the city is erecting thoughtfully designed, pedestrian-focused maps around town. In this sprawling city—where predictable grid-planned streets are relatively rare—it's also smart to buy and use a good map. The *Benson's London Street Map* (£2.75), sold at many newsstands and bookstores, is my favorite for efficient sightseeing.

Festivals: In 2012, the big news in London is the **Olympics** (July 27-Aug 12). For one week in February and another in September, fashionistas descend on the city for **London Fashion Week** (www.londonfashionweek.co.uk). The famous

Chelsea Flower Show blossoms in late May (book ahead for this popular event at www.rhs.org.uk/chelsea). In 2012, the country will celebrate the Queen's **Diamond Jubilee** (her 60th year on the throne) with a long weekend and special exhibitions (June 2-5, www.direct.gov.uk/diamondjubilee). During the annual **Trooping the Colour** in June, there are military bands and pageantry, and the Queen's birthday parade (www.trooping-the-colour.co.uk). Tennis fans pack the stands at the **Wimbledon Tennis Championship** in late June to early July (www.wimbledon.org), and partygoers head for the **Notting Hill Carnival** in late August.

Traveling in Winter: London dazzles year-round, so consider visiting in winter, when airfares and hotel rates are generally cheaper and there are fewer tourists. For ideas on what to do, see the "Winter Activities in London" article at www.ricksteves.com/winteracts.

Internet Access: As nearly all hotels offer Internet access, and cafés all over town have free Wi-Fi, there are few actual Internet cafés. If you need to get online, you'll find Internet cafés near Trafalgar Square (456 Strand), on Oxford Street (at #358, opposite Bond Street Tube station), and near Victoria Station (at 164 Victoria Street).

Travel Bookstores: Located between Covent Garden and Leicester Square, the very good **Stanfords Travel Bookstore** stocks current editions of many of my books (Mon-Fri 9:00-19:30, Thu 9:00-20:00, Sat 10:00-20:00, Sun 12:00-18:00, 12-14 Long Acre, Tube: Leicester Square, tel. 020/7836-1321, www.stanfords.co.uk).

Two impressive **Waterstone's** bookstores have the biggest collection of travel guides in town: on Piccadilly (Mon-Sat 9:00-22:00, Sun 11:30-18:00, Costa Café, great views from top-floor bar—see sidebar on page 117, 203 Piccadilly, tel. 020/7851-2400) and on Trafalgar Square (Mon-Sat 9:00-21:00, Sun 11:30-18:00, Costa Café on second floor, tel. 020/7839-4411).

Baggage Storage: Train stations have replaced lockers with more secure baggage storage counters, known locally as "left luggage." Each bag must go through a scanner (just like at the airport), so lines can be slow. Expect long waits in the morning to check in (up to 45 minutes) and in the afternoon to pick up (each item-£8.50/24 hours, most stations daily 7:00-23:00). You can also store bags at the airports (similar rates and hours, www.excess-baggage.com). If leaving London and returning later, you may be able to store a box or bag at your hotel for free—assuming you'll be staying there again.

Getting Around London

To travel smart in a city this size, you must get comfortable with public transportation. London's excellent taxis, buses, and subway (Tube) system make a car unnecessary (see page 65 for details on driving in London—and why it's a bad idea).

Public-Transit Passes

London has the most expensive public transit in the world—save money on your Tube and bus rides by using a multi-ride pass. You have three options: Pay double by buying individual tickets as you go; buy a £5 Oyster card and top it up as needed to travel like a local for about £1-2 per ride; or get a Travelcard for unlimited travel on one or seven days.

The transit system has six zones. Since almost all of my recommended accommodations, restaurants, and sights are within Zones 1 and 2, those are the prices I've listed here—but you'll pay more to go farther afield. Specific fares and other details change constantly; for a complete and updated list of prices, check www .tfl.gov.uk.

Individual Transit Tickets

These days in London, individual paper tickets are a dinosaur; there's no point buying one unless you're literally taking just one ride your entire time in the city. Because individual fares (£4 per Tube ride, £2.20 per bus ride) are about double the cost of using a pay-as-you-go Oyster card (explained below), in just two or three rides you'll recoup the £5 added deposit for the Oyster. If you do buy a single ticket, avoid ticket-window lines in Tube stations by using the coin-op machines; practice on the punchboard to see how the system works (hit "Adult Single" and your destination). These tickets are valid only on the day of purchase.

Oyster Cards

A pay-as-you-go Oyster card (a plastic card embedded with a computer chip) is the standard, smart way to economically ride the Tube, buses, Docklands Light Railway (DLR), and Overground. On each type of transport, you simply lay the card flat against the yellow card reader at the turnstile or entrance, it flashes green, and the fare is automatically deducted. (You'll also touch your card again to  exit the Tube and DLR turnstiles, but not to exit buses.)

With an Oyster card, rides cost about half the price of individual paper tickets (£1.90 or £2.50 per Tube ride—depending on time of day, £1.30 per bus ride). You buy the card itself at any Tube station ticket window for a £5 deposit, then load it up with as much credit as you want. (For extra peace of mind, ask about registering your card against theft or loss.) When your balance gets low, simply add credit—or "top up"—at a ticket window or machine (note that American credit cards will work at the ticketing window, but not at the automated "top-up" stations). A price cap on the pay-as-you-go Oyster card guarantees you'll never pay more than the One-Day Travelcard price within a 24-hour period.

You can see how much credit remains on your card or review the trips you've taken so far by swiping it at any automatic ticket machine. Oyster card balances never expire (though they need reactivating at a ticket window every two years), so you can use the card whenever you're in London, or lend it to someone else. If you're done with the card (and don't mind a short wait), you can turn it in to reclaim your £5 deposit at any ticket window.

Travelcards

Like the Oyster card, Travelcards are valid on the Tube, buses, Docklands Light Railway (DLR), and Overground. The difference is that Travelcards let you ride as many times as you want within a one- or seven-day period for one fixed price.

Before you buy a card, estimate where you'll be going; there's a card for Zones 1 and 2, and another for Zones 1-6 (which includes Heathrow Airport). If Heathrow is the only ride you're taking outside Zones 1-2 (which is likely), you can pay a small supplement to make the Zones 1-2 Travelcard stretch to cover that one ride.

The **One-Day Travelcard** gives you unlimited travel for a day (Zones 1-2: £8, off-peak version £6.60; Zones 1-6: £15, off-peak version £8; off-peak cards are good for travel after 9:30 on weekdays and anytime on weekends). This Travelcard works like a traditional paper ticket: Buy it at any Tube station ticket window or machine, then feed it into a turnstile (and retrieve it) to enter and exit the Tube. On a bus, just show it to the driver when you get on.

The **Seven-Day Travelcard** is a great option if you're staying four or more days and plan to use the buses and Tube a lot. It's actually issued on a plastic Oyster card, but gives you unlimited travel anytime, anywhere in Zones 1 and 2 for a week (£27.60 plus the refundable £5 deposit for the Oyster card). As with an Oyster card, you'll touch it to the yellow pad when entering or exiting a Tube turnstile, or when boarding a bus.

Discounts

Groups: A gang of 10 or more adults can travel all day on the Tube for £4 each (but not on buses). Kids ages 11-17 pay £1.50 when part of a group of 10.

Families: A paying adult can take up to four kids (age 10 and under) for free on the Tube, Docklands Light Railway (DLR), and Overground all day, every day (kids 10 and under are always free on buses). At the Tube station, use the manual gate, rather than the turnstiles, to be waved in. Other child and student discounts are explained at www.tfl.gov.uk/tickets.

River Cruises: A Travelcard gives you a 33 percent discount on most Thames cruises (see "Cruises," later). If you pay for Thames Clippers (including the Tate-to-Tate museum boat) with your pay-as-you go Oyster card, you'll get a 10 percent discount.

Sightseeing Deal: Buy a paper One-Day Travelcard or rail ticket at a National Rail station, and you may qualify for two-for-one discounts at many popular sights (transport ticket must be used the same day as the sight discount; look for brochures with coupons at major train stations, or print vouchers at www.daysout guide.co.uk).

The Bottom Line

Struggling to choose which pass works best for your trip? First of all, skip the individual tickets. On a short visit (three days or fewer), if you think you'll be zipping around a lot, consider a One-Day Travelcard for each day you're here (or at least for your busiest days); if you'll be taking fewer, more focused rides, get an Oyster card and pay as you go. If you're in London four days or longer, the Seven-Day Travelcard will likely pay for itself.

By Tube

London's subway system (called the Tube or Underground—but never "subway," which refers to a pedestrian underpass) is one of this planet's great people-movers and often the fastest long-distance transport in town (runs Mon-Sat about 5:00-24:00, Sun about 7:00-23:00). While technically not part of the Tube, two other commuter rail lines are tied into the network and use the same tickets: The Docklands Light Railway (called DLR, runs to the Docklands, 2012 Olympics site, and Greenwich) and the Overground.

Get your bearings by studying a map of the system (free at any station).

Each line has a name (such as Circle, Northern, or Bakerloo) and two directions (indicated by the end-of-the-line stops). Find the line that will take you to your destination, and figure out roughly what direction (north, south, east, or west) you'll need to go to get there.

You can use an Oyster card, Travelcard, or individual tickets (all explained earlier) to pay for your journey. At the Tube station, touch your Oyster card flat against the turnstile's yellow card reader, both when you enter and exit the station. If you have a regular paper ticket or a One-Day Travelcard, feed it into the turnstile, reclaim it, and hang on to it—you'll need it later.

Find your train by following signs to your line and the (general) direction it's headed (such as Central Line: east). Since some

tracks are shared by several lines, double-check before boarding a train: First, make sure your destination is one of the stops listed on the sign at the platform. Also, check the electronic signboards that announce which train is next, and make sure the destination (the end-of-the-line stop) is the direction you want. Some trains, particularly on the Circle and District lines, split off for other directions, but each train has its final destination marked above its windshield.

Trains run roughly every 3-10 minutes. If one train is absolutely packed and you notice another to the same destination is coming in three minutes, wait to avoid the sardine routine. Rush hours (8:00-10:00 and 16:00-19:00) can be packed and sweaty. Bring something to do to make your waiting time productive. If you get confused, ask for advice from a local, a blue-vested staff person, or at the information window located before the turnstile entry.

You can't leave the system without touching your Oyster card to an electronic reader, or feeding your ticket or One-Day Travelcard into the turnstile. (If you have a single-trip paper ticket, the turnstile will eat your now-expired ticket; if it's a One-Day Travelcard, it will spit out your still-valid card.) Some stations, such as Hampton Court, do not have a turnstile, so you'll have to locate a reader to validate your Oyster card. If you skip this step, the highest fare will be deducted from your card. When leaving a station, save walking time by choosing the best street exit—check the maps on the walls or ask any station personnel.

The system can be fraught with construction delays and breakdowns (the Circle Line is notorious for problems). This will be especially noticeable as London gears up for the 2012 Olympics. Most construction is scheduled for weekends. Closures are known and publicized in advance (online at www.tfl.gov.uk and with posters in the Tube). Pay attention to signs and announcements explaining necessary detours. Closed Tube lines are often replaced by temporary bus service, but it can be faster to figure out alternate routes on the Tube; since the lines cross each other constantly,

Handy Bus Routes

Since London instituted a congestion charge for cars, the bus system has gotten faster, easier, and cheaper than ever. Tube-oriented travelers need to get over their tunnel vision, learn the bus system, and get around fast and easy. The best views are upstairs on a double-decker.

Here are some of the most useful routes:

Route #9: Knightsbridge (Harrods) to Hyde Park Corner to Piccadilly Circus to Trafalgar Square. This is one of two "Heritage Routes," using some old-style double-decker buses.

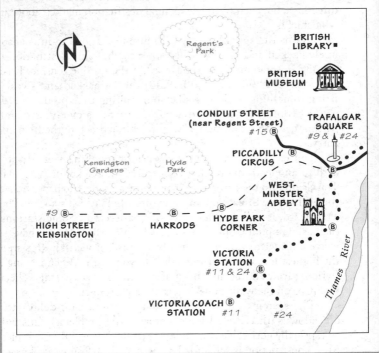

Routes #11 and #24: Victoria Station to Westminster Abbey to Trafalgar Square (#11 continues to St. Paul's and Liverpool Street Station).

Route #RV1 (a scenic South Bank joyride): Tower of London to Tower Bridge to Southwark Street (five-minute walk behind Tate Modern/Shakespeare's Globe) to London Eye/Waterloo Station/County Hall, then over Waterloo Bridge to Aldwych and Covent Garden.

Route #15: Regent Street to Piccadilly Circus to Trafalgar Square to Fleet Street to St. Paul's to Tower of London. This is the other "Heritage Route," using some old-style double-decker buses.

In addition, several buses (including #6, #13, #15, #23, #139, and #159) make the corridor run from Trafalgar, Piccadilly Circus, and Oxford Circus to Marble Arch. Check the bus stop closest to your hotel—it might be convenient to your sightseeing plans.

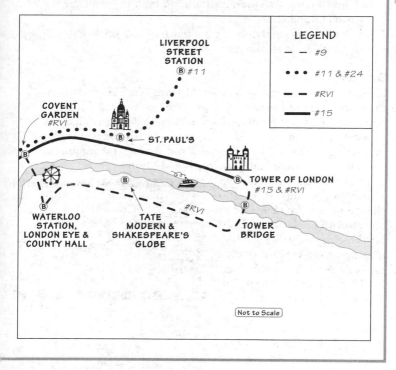

LEGEND

— — #9

• • • #11 & #24

– – #RV1

——— #15

LIVERPOOL STREET STATION
Ⓑ #11

COVENT GARDEN #RV1

Ⓑ ST. PAUL'S

Ⓑ

Ⓑ TOWER OF LONDON #15 & #RV1

Ⓑ

Ⓑ

Ⓑ #RV1

WATERLOO STATION, LONDON EYE & COUNTY HALL

TATE MODERN & SHAKESPEARE'S GLOBE

TOWER BRIDGE

Not to Scale

there are several ways to make any journey. For help, check out the "Journey Planner" at www.tfl.gov.uk.

Tube Etiquette

- When your train arrives, stand off to the side and let riders exit before you try to board.
- Avoid using the hinged seats near the doors of some trains when the car is jammed; they take up valuable standing space.
- If you're blocking the door when the train stops, step out of the car and off to the side, let others off, then get back on.
- Talk softly in the cars. Listen to how quietly Londoners communicate and follow their lead.
- On escalators, stand on the right and pass on the left. But note that in some passageways or stairways, you might be directed to walk on the left (the direction Brits go behind the wheel).
- When leaving a station, it's polite to hold the door for the person behind you.
- Discreet eating and drinking are fine (nothing smelly); drinking alcohol and smoking are not.

By Bus

If you figure out the bus system, you'll swing like Tarzan through the urban jungle of London. Pick up a free bus map at a TI, transport office (located at major Underground stations such as Victoria), or some major museums. This map lists the best bus routes for sightseeing (see the sidebar for a quick run-down of these routes).

Buses are covered by Travelcards and Oyster cards. Or you can buy individual tickets from a machine at bus stops (no change given). Any bus ride in downtown London costs £2.20 for those paying cash, or £1.30 if using an Oyster card (with a cap of £4 per day). If you're staying longer, consider the £17.80 Seven-Day bus pass.

The first step in mastering London's bus system is learning how to decipher the bus stop signs (see photo). In the first column, find your destination on the list—e.g., Paddington. In the next column, find a bus that goes there—the #23. The final column has a letter within

O		
Oakwood ⊖	N91	⊙ ⊗
Old Coulsdon	N68	Aldwych
Old Ford	N8	Oxford Circus
Old Kent Road Canal Bridge	53, N381	⊙
	453	⊙ ⊙
	N21	⊙
Old Street ⊖ ⇌	243	Aldwych
Orpington ⇌	N47	⊙
Oxford Circus ⊖	Any bus	⊙
	N18	⊙
P		
Paddington ⊖ ⇌	23, N15	⊙ ⊙ ⊙ ⊙
Palmers Green ⇌	N29	⊙
Park Langley	N3	⊙ ⊙
Peckham	12	⊙ ⊙
	N89, N343	⊙
	N136	⊙ ⊙
	N381	⊙
Penge Pawleyne Arms	176	⊙
	N3	⊙ ⊙
Petts Wood ⇌	N47	⊙
Pimlico Grosvenor Road	24	⊙ ⊙
Plaistow Greengate	N15	⊙ ⊙
Plumstead ⇌	53	⊙
Plumstead Common	53	⊙

a circle (e.g., "M") that tells you exactly which bus stop you need to stand at to catch your bus. (You'll find the same letter marked on a neighborhood map nearby.) Make your way to that stop—you'll know it's yours because it will have the same letter on its pole—and wait for the bus with your number on it to arrive. Hop on, and you're good to go.

As you board, touch your Oyster card to the electronic card reader, or, if you have a paper ticket or a One-Day Travelcard, show it to the driver. On "Heritage Routes" #9 and #15 (which use some older double-decker buses), you may still pay a conductor; take a seat, and he or she will come around to collect your fare or verify your pass. There's no need to tap your card or show your ticket when you hop off.

If you have an Oyster card or Travelcard, save your feet and get in the habit of hopping buses for quick little straight shots, even just to get to a Tube stop. During bump-and-grind rush hours (8:00-10:00 and 16:00-19:00), you'll usually go faster by Tube.

By Taxi

London is the best taxi town in Europe. Big, black, carefully regulated cabs are everywhere. (While historically known as "black

cabs," some of London's official taxis are now covered with wildly colored ads.) Some cabs are switching to biofuels—a good way to dispose of all that oil used to fry fish-and-chips.

I've never met a crabby cabbie in London. They love to talk, and they know every nook and cranny in town. I ride in a taxi each day just to get my London questions answered (drivers must pass a rigorous test on "The Knowledge" of London geography to earn their license).

If a cab's top light is on, just wave it down. Drivers flash lights when they see you wave. They have a tight turning radius (on new cabs, the back tires actually pivot), so you can hail cabs going in either direction. If waving doesn't work, ask someone where you can find a taxi stand. Telephoning a cab will get you one in a few minutes, but costs a little more (tel. 0871-871-8710; £2 surcharge, plus extra fee to book ahead by credit card).

Rides start at £2.20. The regular tariff #1 covers most of the day (Mon-Fri 6:00-20:00), tariff #2 is during "unsociable hours" (Mon-Fri 20:00-22:00 and Sat-Sun 6:00-22:00), and tariff #3 is for night (22:00-6:00) and on holidays. Rates go up about 15-20 percent with each higher tariff. All extra charges are explained in writing on the cab wall. Tip a cabbie by rounding up (maximum 10 percent).

Connecting downtown sights is quick and easy, and will cost you about £6-8 (for example, St. Paul's to the Tower of London). For a short ride, three adults in a cab generally travel at close to Tube prices—and groups of four or five adults should taxi everywhere. All cabs can carry five passengers, and some take six, for the same cost as a single traveler.

Don't worry about meter cheating. Licensed British cab meters come with a sealed computer chip and clock that ensures you'll get the correct tariff. The only way a cabbie can cheat you is by taking a needlessly long route. Another pitfall is taking a cab when traffic is bad to a destination efficiently served by the Tube. On one trip to London, I hopped in a taxi at South Kensington for Waterloo Station and hit bad traffic. Rather than spending 20 minutes and £2 on the Tube, I spent 40 minutes and £16 in a taxi.

If you overdrink and ride in a taxi, be warned: Taxis charge £40 for "soiling" (a.k.a., pub puke). If you forget this book in a taxi, call the Lost Property office and hope for the best (tel. 0845-330-9882).

By Bike

London is continuing its push to become more bike-friendly. The city continues to install bike lanes around town and in 2010, unveiled a citywide bike-rental program similar to ones in other major European cities.

Barclays Cycle Hire bikes, intended for quick point-to-point trips, are a snap to rent and a giddy joy to use, even for the most jaded London tourist. "Boris Bikes" (as they are affectionately called by locals, after cycle enthusiast and mayor Boris Johnson) are cruisers with big, cushy seats, a bag rack with elastic straps, and three gears.

Approximately 400 bike-rental stations are scattered throughout the city, each equipped with a computer kiosk. To rent a bike, you will need to pay an access fee (£1/day or £5/week). The first 30 minutes are free; if you hang on to the bike for longer, you'll be charged (£1 for 1 hour, £4 for 1.5 hours, £6 for 2 hours, and much steeper beyond that). When you are ready to ride, press "Hire a Cycle" and insert your credit card when prompted. You'll then get a ticket with a five-digit code (using a combination of 1s, 2s, and 3s). Take the ticket to any bike and punch in the number on the panel by the front tire. After the yellow light blinks, a green light will appear; at that point, firmly pull the bike out of the slot.

When your ride is over, find a station with an empty slot, then push your bike in until it locks and the green light flashes. You can hire bikes as often as you like (which will start your free 30-minute period over again), as long as you wait five minutes between each use. A map of the docking stations is essential—pick one up at any major Underground station. It's also available online at www.tfl .gov.uk (click on the "Road Users" tab, then look for the "Barclays Cycle Hire" link) and as a free smartphone app (http://cyclehire app.com).

Helmets are not provided, so ride carefully. Stay to the far-left side of the road and watch closely at intersections for *left*-turning cars. If riding on crowded streets feels intimidating, stick to parks and quiet back lanes.

By Car

If you have a car, stow it—you don't want to drive in London. If you need convincing, here's one more reason: A £10 **congestion charge** is levied on any private car entering the city center during peak hours (Mon-Fri 7:00-18:00, no charge Sat-Sun and holidays, fee payable at gas stations, convenience stores, and self-service machines at public parking lots, or online at www.cclondon.com). Traffic cameras photograph and identify every vehicle that enters the fee zone; if you get spotted and don't pay up by midnight that day (or pay £12 before midnight of the following day), you'll get socked with at least a £60 penalty. The system has been effective in cutting down traffic jam delays and bolstering London's public transit. The revenue that's raised subsidizes the buses, which are now cheaper, more frequent, and even more user-friendly than before. Today, the vast majority of vehicles in the city center are buses, taxis, and service trucks.

Tours in London

▲▲▲Hop-on, Hop-off Double-Decker Bus Tours

Two competitive companies (Original and Big Bus) offer essentially the same two tours of the city's sightseeing highlights, with nearly 30 stops on each route. Big Bus tours are a little more expensive (£27), while Original tours are cheaper (£22 with this book) and nearly as good.

These two-to-three hour, once-over-lightly bus tours drive by all the famous sights, providing a stress-free way to get your bearings and see the biggies. They stop at a core group of sights regardless of which overview tour you're on: Piccadilly Circus, Trafalgar Square, Big Ben, St. Paul's, the Tower of London, Marble Arch, Victoria Station, and elsewhere. With a good guide

Combining a London Bus Tour and the Changing of the Guard

For a grand and efficient intro to London, consider catching either of the bus companies' overview tours at 8:30, riding 90 percent of the loop (which takes just over two hours, depending on traffic), and hopping off at Buckingham Palace in time to catch the Changing of the Guard ceremony. Choose between the Big Bus Tour (catch it at the Green Park Tube station) or the Original Bus Tour (catch it at Grosvenor Gardens a block from Victoria Station). If you miss the 8:30 bus, there's generally another departure in 20 minutes that might get you to the ceremony a bit late (confirm with the driver).

and nice weather, I'd sit back and enjoy the entire tour. (If you don't like your guide, you can hop off and try your luck with the next departure.)

Each company offers at least one route with live (English-only) guides, and a second (sometimes slightly different route) comes with recorded, dial-a-language narration. In addition to the overview tours, both Original and Big Bus include the Thames River boat trip by City Cruises (similar to the River Red Rover ticket explained on page 75) and three 1.5-hour walking tours.

Pick up a map from any flier rack or from one of the countless salespeople, and study the complex system. Sunday morning—when the traffic is light and many museums are closed—is a fine time for a tour. Unless you're using the bus tour mainly for hop-on, hop-off transportation, consider saving time and money by taking a night tour (described on the next page).

Buses run about every 10-15 minutes in summer, every 20 minutes in winter, and operate daily. They start at about 8:30 and run until early evening in summer or late afternoon in winter. The last full loop usually leaves Victoria Station about 17:00 (confirm by checking the schedule or asking the driver).

You can buy tickets from drivers or from staff at street kiosks (credit cards accepted at kiosks at major stops such as Victoria, ticket good for 24 hours).

Original London Sightseeing Bus Tour—There are two versions of their basic highlights loop: **The Original Tour** (live guide, marked with a yellow triangle on the front of the bus) and the **City Sightseeing Tour** (essentially the same route but with recorded narration, a kids' soundtrack option, and a stop at Madame Tussauds; bus marked with a red triangle). Other routes include the blue-triangle **Museum Tour** (connecting far-flung museums and major shopping stops), and green, black, and purple triangle

routes (linking major train stations to the central route). All routes are covered by the same ticket. Keep it simple and just take one of the city highlights tours (£26, £22 with this book, limit four discounts per book, they'll rip off the corner of this page—raise bloody hell if the staff or driver won't honor this discount; also online deals, info center at 17 Cockspur Street, tel. 020/8877-1722, www.theoriginaltour.com).

Big Bus London Tours—For £27 (up to 30 percent discount online—requires printer), you get the same basic overview tours: Red buses come with a live guide, while the blue route has a recorded narration and a one-hour longer path that goes around Hyde Park. These pricier Big Bus tours tend to have better, more dynamic guides than the Original tours, and more departures as well—meaning shorter waits for those hopping on and off (daily 8:30-18:00, winter until 16:30, info center at 48 Buckingham Palace Road, tel. 020/7233-9533, www.bigbustours.com).

London by Night Sightseeing Tour—This tour offers a two-hour circuit, but after hours, with no extras (e.g., walks, river cruises), and at a lower price. While the narration can be pretty lame, the views at twilight are grand—though note that it stays light until late on summer nights, and London just doesn't do floodlighting as well as Paris (£16, £11 online, drivers accept cash only). From May through late September, open-top buses depart at 19:15, 20:00, 20:45, and 21:30 from Victoria Station (Jan-April and late Sept-late Dec departs at 19:30 only with closed-top bus, no tours between Christmas and New Year). Buses leave from the curb immediately in front of Victoria Station (closest to building at muster point C; or you can board at any stop, such as Paddington Station, Marble Arch, Trafalgar Square, London Eye, or Tower of London; tel. 020/8545-6109, www.london-by-night.net). For a memorable and economical evening, munch a scenic picnic dinner on the top deck. (There are plenty of take-away options within the train stations and near the various stops.)

▲▲Walking Tours

Several times each day, top-notch local guides lead (sometimes big) groups through specific slices of London's past. Look for brochures at TIs or ask at hotels, although the latter usually push higher-priced bus tours. *Time Out,* the weekly entertainment guide (£3 at newsstands), lists some, but not all, scheduled walks. Check with the various tour companies by phone or online to get their full picture.

Daily Reminder

Sunday: The Tower of London and British Museum are both especially crowded today. The Speakers' Corner in Hyde Park rants from early afternoon until early evening. These places are closed: Banqueting House, Sir John Soane's Museum, and legal sights (Houses of Parliament, City Hall, and Old Bailey; the neighborhood called The City is dead). Westminster Abbey and St. Paul's are open during the day for worship but closed to sightseers. With all these closures, this morning is a good time to take a bus tour. Most big stores open late (around 11:30) and close early (18:00). Street markets are flourishing at Camden Lock, Spitalfields, Petticoat Lane, Brick Lane, and Greenwich, but Portobello Road and Brixton markets are closed (though the Brixton farmer's market is open 10:00-14:00). Theaters are quiet, as most actors take today off. (There are a few exceptions, such as *The Lion King* and Shakespeare's Globe, which offer Sunday performances in summer.)

Monday: Virtually all sights are open except for Apsley House, Sir John Soane's Museum, Vinopolis, and a few others. The Courtauld Gallery is free until 14:00. The Houses of Parliament are usually open until 22:30.

Tuesday: Virtually all sights are open, except for Vinopolis and Apsley House. The British Library is open until 20:00. On the first Tuesday of the month, Sir John Soane's Museum is also open 18:00-21:00. The Houses of Parliament are usually open until 22:30.

Wednesday: Virtually all sights are open, except for Vinopolis.

Thursday: All sights are open, plus evening hours at the National Portrait Gallery (until 21:00) and Vinopolis (until 22:00).

To take a walking tour, simply show up at the announced location and pay the guide. Then enjoy two chatty hours of Dickens, Harry Potter, the Plague, Shakespeare, Legal London, the Beatles, Jack the Ripper, or whatever is on the agenda.

The Essential London Walk—Blue Badge Tourist Guides offer a basic two-hour walk 365 days a year at 10:00 (normally £9 but my readers pay £6; meet at the Eros statue on Piccadilly Circus—look for the guide with the Blue Badge umbrella, www.tourist guides.org.uk). Tours go rain or shine, and there's no need to pre-book—just show up. This is the best deal going, as you know you'll get a well-trained guide leading you through the historic core of London (from Piccadilly, you walk to Trafalgar Square, Whitehall, Westminster Abbey, the Houses of Parliament, and the Thames, and end at Buckingham Palace—just in time for the last part of the Changing of the Guard).

Friday: All sights are open, except the Houses of Parliament. Sights open late include the British Museum (selected galleries until 20:30), National Gallery (until 21:00), National Portrait Gallery (until 21:00), Vinopolis (until 22:00), Victoria and Albert Museum (selected galleries until 22:00), and Tate Modern (until 22:00). The Tate Britain is open until 22:00 on the first Friday of the month. Best street market today: Spitalfields.

Saturday: Most sights are open except legal ones (Old Bailey, City Hall, Houses of Parliament; skip The City). Vinopolis and the Tate Modern are open until 22:00. Today's the day to hit the Portobello Road street market; the Camden Lock and Greenwich markets are also good.

Notes: The St. Martin-in-the-Fields church offers concerts at lunchtime (Mon, Tue, and Fri at 13:00) and in the evening (several nights a week at 19:30, jazz Wed at 20:00).

Evensong occurs daily at St. Paul's (Mon-Sat at 17:00 and Sun at 15:15), Westminster Abbey (Mon-Fri at 17:00—may be spoken on Wed, Sat-Sun at 15:00 except Sat in summer, when it's at 17:00), and Southwark Cathedral (weekdays at 17:30, Sat at 16:00, Sun at 15:00, no service on Wed or alternate Mon). For more on evensong, see page 157.

London by Night Sightseeing Tour buses leave from Victoria Station each evening (every 45 minutes from 19:15 to 21:30, only at 19:30 in winter).

The London Eye spins nightly (last departure between 20:00 and 21:30, depending on the season).

In winter, Apsley House is only open on weekends (closed Mon-Fri).

London Walks—This leading company lists its extensive and creative daily schedule in a beefy, plain *London Walks* brochure. Pick it up at TIs, hotels, or St. Martin-in-the-Fields' Café in the Crypt on Trafalgar Square, or access it on their website. Just perusing their fascinating lineup of tours inspires me to stay longer in London. Their two-hour walks, led by professional guides and actors, cost £8 (cash only, walks offered year-round, private tours for groups-£120, tel. 020/7624-3978 for a live person, tel. 020/7624-9255 for a recording of today's or tomorrow's walks and the Tube station they depart from, www.walks.com).

London Walks also offers "Explorer Days" tours into the countryside, a good option for those with limited time and transportation (£14 plus £10-46 for transportation and any admission costs, cash only: Stonehenge/Salisbury, Oxford/Cotswolds, Cambridge, Bath, and so on). These are economical in part because everyone gets group discounts for transportation and admissions.

London

1 kilometer

1 mile

ZOO

ABBEY ROAD

Regent's Park

HARROW RD.

PARK RD.

ALBANY ST.

EDGEWARE ROAD

MARYLEBONE STATION

BAKER ST.

To Heathrow Airport & Bath

(M-4) WESTWAY

FLYOVER

WALLACE COLLECTION

OXFORD ST.

PADDINGTON STATION

Norfolk Square

MARBLE ARCH

PORTOBELLO ROAD MARKET

NOTTING HILL

BAYSWATER

BAYSWATER

SPEAKERS' CORNER

SO

To Heathrow Airport & Windsor

NOTTING HILL GATE

Hyde Park

MAYFAIR

Kensington Gardens

KENSINGTON PALACE

PICCADILLY

HOLLAND RD.

Holland Park

KNIGHTSBRIDGE

Green Park

KENSINGTON HIGH ST.

ROYAL ALBERT HALL

VICTORIA & ALBERT MUSEUM

BROMPTON RD.

HARRODS

BUCKINGHAM PALACE

To London Bridge (Arizona)

WARWICK RD.

EARL'S COURT RD.

CROMWELL RD.

SOUTH KENSINGTON

SLOANE

VICTORIA STATION

BUS STATION

TALGARTH RD.

EARL'S COURT

FULHAM RD.

KING'S RD.

CHELSEA

PIM

OLD BROMPTON

CHELSEA EMBANKMENT

To Kew Gardens & Hampton Court Palace

To Gatwick Airport

Sandemans New London "Free Royal London Tour"—This company employs English-speaking students (rather than licensed guides) who recite three-hour spiels covering the basic London sights. While the fast-moving, youthful tours are light and irreverent, and can be both entertaining and fun, it's misleading to call the tours "free," as tips are expected (the guides are unpaid). With the Essential London Walk (listed earlier) offered daily at a reasonable price by professional Blue Badge guides, taking this "free" tour makes no sense to me (daily at 11:00 and 13:00, meet at Wellington Arch, Tube: Hyde Park Corner, Exit 2). Sandemans also has other guided tours for a charge, including a Pub Crawl (£12, Tue-Sat at 19:30, meet at Belushi's at 9 Russell Street, Tube: Covent Garden, www.newlondon-tours.com).

Beatles Walks—Fans of the still-Fab Four can take one of three Beatles walks (London Walks has two that run 5 days/week; Big Bus includes a daily walk with their bus tour; both listed earlier). For more on Beatles sights, see page 112.

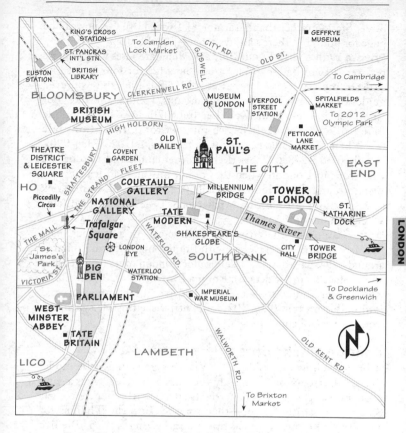

Jack the Ripper Walks—Each walking tour company seems to make most of its money with "haunted" and Jack the Ripper tours. Many guides are historians and would rather not lead these lightweight tours—but, in tourism as in journalism, "if it bleeds, it leads" (which is why the juvenile London Dungeon is one of the city's busiest sights).

Two reliably good two-hour tours start every night at the Tower Hill Tube station exit. **Ripping Yarns** is guided by off-duty Yeoman Warders—the Tower of London "Beefeaters" (£7, pay at end, nightly at 18:45, no tours between Christmas and New Year, mobile 07813-559-301, www.jack-the-ripper-tours.com). **London Walks'** guides leave from the same spot later each night (£7, pay at the start, nightly at 19:30, tel. 020/7624-3978, recorded info tel. 020/7624-9255, www.jacktheripperwalk.com). After taking both, I found the London Walks tour more entertaining, informative, and with a better route (along quieter, once-hooker-friendly lanes, with less traffic), starting at Tower Hill and ending at Liverpool

Street Station rather than returning to Tower Hill. Groups can be huge for both, but there's always room—just show up.

Private Walks with Local Guides—Standard rates for London's registered Blue Badge guides are about £127 for four hours and £200 or more for nine hours (tel. 020/7780-4060, www.tourist guides.org.uk or www.blue-badge.org.uk). I know and like four fine local guides: **Sean Kelleher** (tel. 020/8673-1624, mobile 07764-612-770, seankelleher@btinternet.com), **Britt Lonsdale** (£150/half-day, £250/day, great with families, tel. 020/7386-9907, mobile 07813-278-077, brittl@btinternet.com), and two others who work in London when they're not on the road leading my Britain tours, **Tom Hooper** (mobile 07986-048-047, tomh@rick steves.net) and **Gillian Chadwick** (mobile 07889-976-598, gillianc @ricksteves.net).

Driver-Guides—These two guides have cars or a minibus (particularly helpful for travelers with limited mobility) and charge around £290/half-day and £450/day for London tours (see websites and contact them for details): **Robina Brown** (tel. 020/7228-2238, www.driverguidetours.com, robina@driverguidetours.com) and **Janine Barton** (tel. 020/7402-4600, http://seeitinstyle.synthasite .com, jbsiis@aol.com).

London Duck Tours

A bright-yellow amphibious WWII-vintage vehicle (the model that landed troops on Normandy's beaches on D-Day) takes a gang of 30 tourists past some famous sights on land—Big Ben, Trafalgar Square, Piccadilly Circus—then splashes into the Thames for a cruise. All in all, it's good fun at a rather steep price. The live guide works hard, and it's kid-friendly to the point of goofiness (£20, April-Sept daily 10:30-18:00, shorter hours Oct-March, 1-4/ hour, 1.25 hours—45 minutes on land and 30 minutes in the river, £3 booking fee online, these book up in advance, departs from Chicheley Street—you'll see the big, ugly vehicle parked 100 yards behind the London Eye, Tube: Waterloo or Westminster, tel. 020/7928-3132, www.londonducktours.co.uk).

Bike Tours

London, like Paris, is committed to creating more bike paths, and many of its best sights can be laced together with a pleasant pedal through its parks. A bike tour is a fun way to see the sights and enjoy the city on two wheels.

London Bicycle Tour Company—Three tours covering London are offered daily from their base at Gabriel's Wharf on the South Bank of the Thames. Sunday is the best, as there is less car traffic (**Central Tour**—£17, daily at 10:30, 6 miles, 2.5 hours, includes Westminster, Covent Garden, and St. Paul's; **Royal West Tour**—

£20, April-Oct Sat-Sun at 12:00, Nov-March only on Sun, 9 miles, 3.5 hours, includes Westminster, Hyde Park, Buckingham Palace, and Covent Garden; **East Tour**—£20, April-Oct Sat-Sun at 14:00, Nov-March only on Sat at 12:00, 9 miles, 3.5 hours, includes south side of the river to Tower Bridge, then The City to the East End; book ahead for off-season tours). They also rent bikes (£3.50/hour, £20/day; office open daily 10:00-18:00, west of Blackfriars Bridge on the South Bank, 1a Gabriel's Wharf, tel. 020/7928-6838, www.londonbicycle.com).

Fat Tire Bike Tours—Daily bike tours cover the highlights of downtown London, on two different itineraries (£2 discount with this book): **Royal London** (£20, daily March-Nov at 11:00, June-Aug also at 15:30, 7 miles, 4 hours, meet at Queensway Tube station; includes Parliament, Buckingham Palace, Hyde Park, and Trafalgar Square) and **River Thames** (£30, mid-March-Nov Thu-Sat at 10:30, 5 hours, meet at Waterloo Tube station—exit 2; includes London Eye, St. Paul's, Tower of London, Trafalgar Square, Covent Garden, and boat trip on the Thames). The spiel is light and irreverent rather than scholarly, but the price is right. Reservations are easy online, and required for River Thames tours and kids' bikes (off-season tours can be arranged, mobile 078-8233-8779, www.fattirebiketourslondon.com). Confirm the schedule online or by phone.

Weekend Tour Packages for Students in London

Andy Steves (Rick's son) runs **Weekend Student Adventures,** offering experiential three-day weekend tours for €250 designed for American students studying abroad (see www.wsaeurope.com for details on tours of London and other great European cities).

▲▲Cruises

Boat tours with entertaining commentaries sail regularly from many points along the Thames. The options are plentiful, with several companies offering essentially the same trip. Your basic options are to use the boats either for a scenic joyride cruise within central London, or for transportation to an outlying sight (such as Greenwich or Kew Gardens).

Boats come and go from several docks in central London (see sidebar on the next page). The most popular places to embark are Westminster Pier (at the base of Westminster Bridge across the street from Big Ben) and Waterloo Pier (at the London Eye, across the river).

Buy boat tickets at the kiosks on the docks. While individual Tube and bus tickets don't work on the boats, a Travelcard can snare you a 33 percent discount on most cruises (just show the card

Thames Boat Piers

While Westminster Pier is the most popular, it's not the only dock in town. Consider all the options (listed from west to east, as the Thames flows):

Millbank Pier (north bank), at the Tate Britain Museum, is used primarily by the "Tate to Tate" service (express connection to Tate Modern at Bankside Pier).

Westminster Pier (north bank), near the base of Big Ben, offers round-trip sightseeing cruises and lots of departures in both directions (though the Thames Clippers boats don't stop here). Nearby sights include Parliament and Westminster Abbey.

Waterloo Pier (a.k.a. **London Eye Pier,** south bank), right at the base of the London Eye, is a good, less-crowded alternative to Westminster, with many of the same cruise options (Waterloo Station is nearby).

Embankment Pier (north bank) is near Covent Garden, Trafalgar Square, and Cleopatra's Needle (the obelisk on the Thames). This pier is used mostly for special boat trips (such as some RIB—rigid inflatable boat—trips, and lunch and dinner cruises).

Festival Pier (south bank) is next to the Royal Festival Hall, just downstream from the London Eye.

Blackfriars Pier (north bank) is in The City, not far from St. Paul's.

Bankside Pier (south bank) is directly in front of the Tate Modern and Shakespeare's Globe.

London Bridge Pier (a.k.a. **London Bridge City Pier,** south bank) is near the HMS *Belfast*.

Tower Pier (north bank) is at the Tower of London, at the east edge of The City and near the East End.

St. Katharine's Pier (north bank) is just downstream from the Tower of London.

Canary Wharf Pier (north bank) is at the Docklands, London's new "downtown."

In outer London, you might also use the piers at **Greenwich, Kew Gardens,** and **Hampton Court.**

when you pay for the cruise; no discount with the pay-as-you-go Oyster card except on Thames Clippers). Because different companies vary in the discounts they offer, always ask. Children and seniors generally get discounts. You can purchase drinks and scant, pricey snacks on board. Clever budget travelers pack a picnic and munch while they cruise.

Round-trip fares are only a bit more than one-way. Still, for pleasure and efficiency, consider combining a one-way cruise (to Kew, Greenwich, or wherever) with a Tube or train ride back.

Tourist-Oriented Cruises in Central London

London offers many made-for-tourist cruises, most on slow-moving, open-top boats accompanied by commentary about passing sights.

City Cruises runs boats from Westminster Pier across the river to Waterloo Pier, then downriver to Tower Pier and on to Greenwich (tel. 020/7740-0400, www.citycruises.com). If you want just a sample, hop on their 30-minute cruise only as far as Tower Pier (£8 one-way, £10.50 round-trip, daily April-Oct roughly 10:00-19:00, until 18:00 in winter, 2/hour). City Cruises also offers a £13.50 River Red Rover ticket good for all-day hop-on, hop-off travel (also included with the bus tours described on page 65)—though the line's limited stops in central London make this a lesser deal than it might seem.

Thames River Services runs a similar trip with even fewer stops: Westminster to St. Katharine's Pier to Greenwich (tel. 020/7930-4097, www.thamesriverservices.co.uk). They have classic boats and feel a little friendlier and more old-fashioned. For more details, see "Cruising Downstream, to Greenwich and the Docklands," later.

The **Circular Cruise** offered by Crown River Services is a handy hop-on, hop-off route with stops at the Westminster, Festival, Embankment, Bankside, London Bridge, and St. Katharine's piers (£3 to go one stop, £8.40 one-way for a longer trip, £11 for an all-day ticket, daily 11:00-18:30, every 30 minutes late May-early Sept, fewer stops and less frequent off-season, tel. 020/7936-2033, www.crownriver.com).

The **London Eye** operates its own river cruise, offering a 40-minute live-guided circular tour from Waterloo Pier. As it's much pricier than the alternatives for just a short loop, it's a poor value (£12, reservations recommended, 10 percent discount if you pre-book online, no Travelcard discounts, departures daily generally at :45 past the hour, April-Oct 10:45-18:45, Nov-March 11:45-16:45, closed mid-Jan-mid-Feb, tel. 0870-500-0600, www.londoneye.com).

Careening at Top Speed Along the Thames: Two competing companies invite you aboard a small, 12-person, high-speed rigid inflatable boat (RIB—similar to a Zodiac) for an adrenaline-fueled tour of the city (London RIB Voyages: stand-up comedian guides, £32.50/50 minutes, £45/1.25 hours, tel. 020/7928-8933, www.londonribvoyages.com; Thames RIB Experience: £32/50 minutes, £45/1.5 hours, tel. 0870-224-4200, www.thamesribexperience.com).

   Away from the Thames, on Regent's Canal: Consider exploring London's canals by taking a cruise on historic Regent's Canal in north London. The good ship *Jenny Wren* offers 1.5-hour guided canal boat cruises from Walker's Quay in Camden Town through scenic Regent's Park to Little Venice (£9.50; Aug daily at 10:30, 12:30, 14:30, and 16:30; April-July and Sept-Oct daily at 12:30 and 14:30, Sat-Sun also at 16:30; Walker's Quay, 250 Camden High Street, 3-minute walk from Tube: Camden Town; tel. 020/7485-4433, www.walkersquay.com). While in Camden Town, stop by the popular, punky Camden Lock Market to browse through trendy arts and crafts (daily 10:00-18:00, busiest on weekends, a block from Walker's Quay, www.camdenlockmarket.com).

Commuting by Clipper

Thames Clippers, which uses fast, sleek, 220-seat catamarans, is designed for commuters rather than sightseers. Think of the boats as express buses in the river—they zip no-nonsense through London every 20 minutes, stopping at most of the major docks en route: Embankment, Waterloo, Blackfriars or Bankside, London Bridge, Tower, Canary Wharf (Docklands), and Greenwich (roughly 20 minutes from Embankment to Tower, 10 more minutes to Docklands, 10 more minutes to Greenwich). However, the boats are less pleasant for joyriding than the cruises described earlier, with no commentary and no open deck up top (the only outside access is on a crowded deck at the exhaust-choked back of the boat, where you're jostling for photos). Any one-way ride costs £5.50, and a River Roamer all-day ticket costs £12.60 (33 percent discount with Travelcard, 10 percent off with a pay-as-you-go Oyster card, tel. 020/7001-2222, www.thamesclippers.com).

   Thames Clippers also offers two express trips. The **"Tate to Tate"** boat service, which directly connects the Tate Britain (Millbank Pier) and the Tate Modern (Bankside Pier), is made for art-lovers (£5.50 one-way, covered by £12.60 River Roamer day ticket; buy ticket at gallery desk, at kiosk by the dock, or on board; for frequency and times, see the Tate Britain and Tate Modern listings, later, or www.tate.org.uk/tatetotate). The **O2 Express** runs only on nights when there are events going on at the O2 (formerly the Millennium Dome; from Waterloo Pier, £6 one-way, £12 round-trip, 30 minutes).

Cruising Downstream, to Greenwich and the Docklands

Greenwich: Both of the big tour companies (City Cruises and Thames River Services, described earlier) head to Greenwich from Westminster Pier. The cruises are usually narrated by the captain, with most commentary given on the way to Greenwich. The companies' prices are the same (£10 one-way, £13 round-trip), though their itineraries are slightly different: **City Cruises** stops at Waterloo/London Eye Pier and Tower Pier on the way to Greenwich (if you buy their £13.50 River Red Rover ticket, you can hop on and off all day long; daily April-Oct generally 10:00-17:00, less off-season, 2/hour, 1.25 hours from Westminster to Greenwich; cheaper to go from Tower Pier to Greenwich—£8 one-way, £10.50 round-trip, only 30 minutes to Greenwich—but you miss all the scenery in central London). **Thames River Services** stops only at St. Katharine's Pier on the way to Greenwich, making the trip a little faster (April-Oct 10:00-16:00, July-Aug until 17:00, daily 2/hour; Nov-March shorter hours and runs every 40 minutes; 1 hour from Westminster to Greenwich).

The **Thames Clippers** boats, described earlier, are cheaper, faster, and make more stops downtown, but have no commentary and no seating up top (£5.50 one-way, £12.60 for an all-day pass, 3/hour, about 45 minutes from Westminster to Greenwich).

To maximize both efficiency and sightseeing, I'd take a boat to Greenwich one way, and go the other way on the DLR (Docklands Light Railway), with a stop in the Docklands (Canary Wharf station).

The **Docklands: Thames Clippers** connects the Docklands' Canary Wharf Pier to both central London and Greenwich (£5.50 one-way, £12.60 for an all-day pass, no commentary, 3/hour, roughly 10 minutes to Tower, 30 minutes to Waterloo, 10 minutes to Greenwich).

Cruising Upstream, to Kew Gardens and Hampton Court Palace

Boats operated by the Westminster Passenger Services Association leave for Kew Gardens from Westminster Pier (£12 one-way, £18 round-trip, cash only; 4/day, April-Oct daily at 10:30, 11:15, 12:00, and 14:00; 1.5 hours, about half the trip is narrated, tel. 020/7930-2062, www.wpsa.co.uk). Most boats continue on to Hampton Court Palace for an additional £3 (and another 1.5 hours). Because of the river current, you'll sometimes save 30 minutes cruising from Hampton Court back into town (depends on the tide—ask before you commit to the boat). Romantic as these rides sound, it can be a long trip...especially upstream.

Self-Guided Walk

Westminster Walk

Just about every visitor to London strolls along historic Whitehall from Big Ben to Trafalgar Square. This walk gives meaning to that

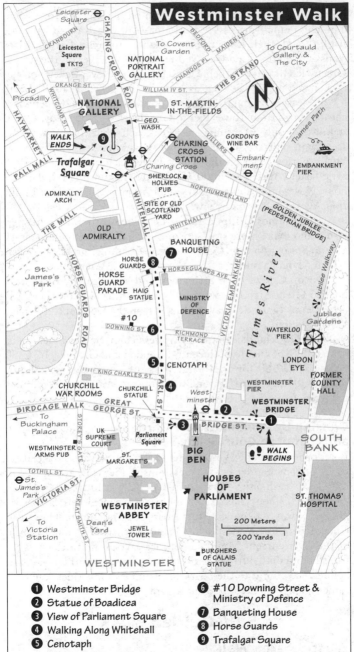

Westminster Walk

① Westminster Bridge
② Statue of Boadicea
③ View of Parliament Square
④ Walking Along Whitehall
⑤ Cenotaph
⑥ #10 Downing Street & Ministry of Defence
⑦ Banqueting House
⑧ Horse Guards
⑨ Trafalgar Square

touristy ramble (most of the sights you'll see are described in more detail later). Under London's modern traffic and big-city bustle lie 2,000 fascinating years of history. You'll get a whirlwind tour as well as a practical orientation to London. (You can download a free, extended **audio tour** version of this walk to your mobile device; see page 48.)

Start halfway across **Westminster Bridge** (❶) for that "Wow, I'm really in London!" feeling. Get a close-up view of the **Houses of Parliament** and **Big Ben** (floodlit at night). Downstream you'll see the **London Eye.** Down the stairs to Westminster Pier are boats to the Tower of London and Greenwich (downstream) or Kew Gardens (upstream).

En route to Parliament Square, you'll pass a **statue of Boadicea** (❷), the Celtic queen defeated by Roman invaders in A.D. 60.

For fun, call home from a pay phone near Big Ben at about three minutes before the hour to let your loved one hear the bell ring. You'll find four red phone booths lining the north side of **Parliament Square** (❸) along Great George Street—also great for a phone-box-and-Big-Ben photo op.

Wave hello to Winston Churchill and Nelson Mandela in Parliament Square. To Churchill's right is **Westminster Abbey,** with its two stubby, elegant towers. The white building (flying the Union Jack) at the far end of the square houses Britain's new **Supreme Court.**

Head north up Parliament Street, which turns into **Whitehall** (❹), and walk toward Trafalgar Square. You'll see the thought-provoking **Cenotaph** (❺) in the middle of the street, reminding passersby of the many Brits who died in the last century's world wars. To visit the **Churchill War Rooms,** take a left before the Cenotaph, on King Charles Street.

Continuing on Whitehall, stop at the barricaded and guarded **#10 Downing Street** (❻) to see the British "White House," home of the prime minister. Break the bobby's boredom and ask him a question. The huge building across Whitehall from Downing Street is the **Ministry of Defence** (MOD), the "British Pentagon."

Nearing Trafalgar Square, look for the 17th-century **Banqueting House** across the street (❼) and the **Horse Guards** (❽) behind the gated fence (Changing of the Horse Guards Mon-Sat at 11:00, Sun at 10:00, dismounting ceremony daily at 16:00).

The column topped by Lord Nelson marks **Trafalgar Square** (❾). The stately domed building on the far side of the square is the **National Gallery,** which has a classy café in the Sainsbury wing. To the right of the National Gallery is **St. Martin-in-the-Fields Church** and its Café in the Crypt.

To get to Piccadilly from Trafalgar Square, walk up Cockspur

Street to Haymarket, then take a short left on Coventry Street to colorful **Piccadilly Circus** (see map on page 98).

Near Piccadilly, you'll find a number of theaters. **Leicester Square** (with its half-price "tkts" booth for plays—see page 154) thrives just a few blocks away. Walk through seedy **Soho** (north of Shaftesbury Avenue) for its fun pubs. From Piccadilly or Oxford Circus, you can take a taxi, bus, or the Tube home.

Sights in Central London

Westminster

These sights are listed roughly in geographical order from Westminster Abbey to Trafalgar Square, and are linked in my self-guided Westminster Walk, earlier.

▲▲▲Westminster Abbey

Westminster Abbey is the greatest church in the English-speaking world, where the nation's kings and queens have been crowned and buried since 1066. The histories of Westminster Abbey and England are almost the same. A thousand years of English history—3,000 tombs, the remains of 29 monarchs, and hundreds of memorials to poets, politicians, and warriors—lie within its stained-glass splendor and under its stone slabs.

Cost and Hours: £16, £32 family ticket (covers 2 adults and 1 child), cash or credit cards accepted (line up in the correct queue to pay); ticket includes cloisters, audioguide, and Abbey Museum; abbey—Mon-Fri 9:30-16:30, Wed until 19:00 (main church only), Sat 9:30-14:30, last entry one hour before closing, closed Sun to sightseers but open for services; museum—daily 10:30-16:00; cloisters—daily 8:00-18:00, free access to cloisters through Dean Court (near west entrance); Tube: Westminster or St. James's Park.

When to Go: The place is most crowded on Saturdays, Mondays, and any midmornings. Visit early, during lunch, or late to avoid tourist hordes. Weekdays after 14:30 are less congested; come then and stay for the 17:00 evensong. The main entrance, on the Parliament Square side, often has a sizable line. Of the two queues at the admissions desk (cash or credit), the cash line is probably moving faster. There's talk of opening a "fast track" entry for London Pass holders; if you have the pass, it's worth asking to see if that's happened yet.

Music and Services: Mon-Fri at 7:30 (prayer), 8:00 (communion), 12:30 (communion), 17:00 evensong (on Wed the evensong may be spoken—no song); Sat at 8:00 (communion), 9:00 (prayer), 12:30 (communion), 15:00 (evensong; June-Sept it's at 17:00); Sun services generally come with more music: at 8:00 (communion), 10:00 (sung Matins), 11:15 (sung Eucharist), 15:00 (evensong), 18:30 (evening service). For more on evensong, see page 157. Services are free to anyone, though visitors who haven't paid church admission aren't allowed to linger afterward. Free organ recitals are often held Sun at 17:45 (30 minutes). For a schedule of services or recitals on a particular day, look for posted signs with schedules or check the Abbey's website; tel. 020/7654-4834, www.westminster-abbey.org.

➍ **Self-Guided Tour:** You'll have no choice but to follow the steady flow of tourists circling clockwise through the church. My tour covers the Abbey's top stops.

• *Walk straight in, through the north transept and into the center of the church.*

North Transept and View of Nave: The "high" (main) altar (which usually has a cross and candlesticks atop it) sits on the platform up the five stairs. This is the culminating point of the long, high-ceilinged nave. Nestled in the nave is the elaborately carved wooden seating of the choir (a.k.a. "quire" in British churchspeak), where monks once chanted their services and where, today, the Abbey boys' choir sings the evensong. The Abbey's 10-story nave is the tallest in England. The north transept is nicknamed "Statesmen's Corner" and specializes in the tombs of famous prime ministers.

• *Turn left and follow the crowd. Stop at the wooden staircase on your right.*

Tomb of Edward the Confessor: Step back and peek over the dark coffin of Edward I to see the tippy-top of the green-and-gold wedding-cake tomb of King Edward the Confessor—the man who built Westminster Abbey. God had told pious Edward to visit St. Peter's Basilica in Rome. But with the Normans thinking conquest, it was too dangerous for him to leave England. Instead, he built this grand church and dedicated it to St. Peter. It was finished just in time to bury Edward and to crown his foreign successor, William the Conqueror, in 1066. After Edward's death, people prayed at his tomb, and, after getting fine results, Pope Alexander III canonized him. This elevated, central tomb—which lost some of its luster when Henry VIII melted down the gold coffin-case— is surrounded by the tombs of eight kings and queens.

• *At the top of the stone staircase, veer left into the private burial chapel of Queen Elizabeth I.*

Tomb of Queen Elizabeth I and Mary I: Although there's only one effigy on the tomb (Elizabeth's), there are actually two queens buried beneath it, both daughters of Henry VIII (by different mothers). Bloody Mary—meek, pious, sickly, and Catholic—enforced Catholicism during her short reign (1553-1558) by burning "heretics" at the stake.

Elizabeth—strong, clever, and Protestant—steered England on an Anglican course. She holds a royal orb symbolizing that she's queen of the whole globe. When 26-year-old Elizabeth was crowned in the Abbey, her right to rule was questioned (especially by her Catholic subjects) because she was the bastard seed of Henry VIII's unsanctioned marriage to Anne Boleyn. But Elizabeth's long reign (1559-1603) was one of the greatest in English history, a time when England ruled the seas and Shakespeare explored human emotions. When she died, thousands turned out for her funeral in the Abbey. Elizabeth's face, modeled after her death mask, is considered a very accurate take on this hook-nosed, imperious "Virgin Queen."

• *Continue into the ornate, flag-draped room behind the main altar.*

Chapel of King Henry VII (a.k.a. the Lady Chapel): The light from the stained-glass windows; the colorful banners over-head; and the elaborate tracery in stone, wood, and glass give this room the festive air of a medieval tournament. The prestigious Knights of the Bath meet here, under the magnificent ceiling studded with gold pendants. The ceiling—of carved stone, not plaster (1519)—is the finest English Perpendicular Gothic and fan vaulting you'll see (unless you're going to King's College Chapel in Cambridge). The ceiling was sculpted on the floor in pieces, then jigsaw-puzzled into place. It capped the Gothic period and signaled the vitality of the coming Renaissance.

• *Go to the far end of the chapel and stand at the banister in front of the modern set of stained-glass windows.*

Royal Air Force Chapel: Saints in robes and halos mingle with pilots in parachutes and bomber jackets. This tribute to WWII flyers is for those who earned their angel wings in the Battle of Britain (July-Oct 1940). A bit of bomb damage has been preserved—look for the little glassed-over hole in the wall below the windows in the lower left-hand corner.

• *Exit the Chapel of Henry VII. Turn left into a side chapel with the tomb (the central one of three in the chapel).*

Tomb of Mary, Queen of Scots: The beautiful, French-educated queen was held under house arrest for 19 years by Queen Elizabeth I, who considered her a threat to her sovereignty. Elizabeth got wind of an assassination plot, suspected Mary was behind it, and had her first cousin (once removed) beheaded. When Elizabeth died heirless, Mary's son, James VI, King of Scots, also became King James I of England and Ireland. James buried his mum here (with her head sewn back on) in the Abbey's most sumptuous tomb.

• *Exit Mary's chapel. Ahead of you, at the foot of the stairs, is the...*

Coronation Chair: The gold-painted oak chair waits here—with its back to the high altar—for the next coronation. For every English coronation since 1308 (except two), it's been moved to its spot before the high altar to receive the royal buttocks. The chair's legs rest on lions, England's symbol.

• *Turn left into the south transept. You're in...*

Poets' Corner: England's greatest artistic contributions are in the written word. Here the masters of arguably the world's most complex and expressive language are remembered—Geoffrey Chaucer *(Canterbury Tales)*, Lord Byron, Dylan Thomas, W. H. Auden, Lewis Carroll *(Alice's Adventures in Wonderland)*, T. S. Eliot *(The Waste Land)*, Alfred, Lord Tennyson, Robert Browning, and Charles Dickens. Many writers are honored with plaques and monuments; relatively few are actually buried here. Shakespeare is commemorated by a fine statue that stands near the end of the transept, overlooking the others.

• *Return to the center of the church in front of the high altar.*

The Coronation Spot: This is where every English coronation since 1066 has taken place. Royalty are also given funerals here. Princess Diana's coffin was carried to this spot for her funeral service in 1997. The "Queen Mum" (mother of Elizabeth II) had her funeral here in 2002. This is also where most of the last century's royal weddings have taken place, including the unions of Queen Elizabeth II and Prince Philip (1947), Prince Andrew and Sarah Ferguson (1986), and Prince William and Kate Middleton (2011).

• *Exit the church (temporarily) at the south door, which leads to the...*

Cloisters and Abbey Museum: The buildings that adjoin the church housed the monks. Cloistered courtyards gave them a place to meditate on God's creations. The small Abbey Museum, formerly the monks' lounge, is worth a peek for its fascinating and well-described exhibits. Look into the impressively realistic eyes of Elizabeth I, Charles II, Admiral Nelson, and a dozen others, part of a compelling series of wax-and-wood statues that, for three centuries, graced coffins during funeral processions. The once-exquisite, now-fragmented Westminster Retable, which decorated the high altar in 1270, is the oldest surviving altarpiece in England.

• *Go back into the church and stand in the...*

Nave: On the floor near the west entrance of the Abbey is the flower-lined Tomb of the Unknown Warrior, one ordinary WWI soldier buried in soil from France with lettering made from

London at a Glance

▲▲▲**Westminster Abbey** Britain's finest church and the site of royal coronations and burials since 1066. **Hours:** Mon-Fri 9:30-16:30, Wed until 19:00, Sat 9:30-14:30, closed Sun to sightseers except for worship. See page 80.

▲▲▲**Churchill War Rooms** Underground WWII headquarters of Churchill's war effort. **Hours:** Daily 9:30-18:00. See page 87.

▲▲▲**National Gallery** Remarkable collection of European paintings (1250-1900), including Leonardo, Botticelli, Velázquez, Rembrandt, Turner, Van Gogh, and the Impressionists. **Hours:** Daily 10:00-18:00, Fri until 21:00. See page 91.

▲▲▲**British Museum** The world's greatest collection of artifacts of Western civilization, including the Rosetta Stone and the Parthenon's Elgin Marbles. **Hours:** Daily 10:00-17:30, Fri until 20:30 (selected galleries only). See page 104.

▲▲▲**British Library** Impressive collection of the most important literary treasures of the Western world. **Hours:** Mon-Fri 9:30-18:00, Tue until 20:00, Sat 9:30-17:00, Sun 11:00-17:00. See page 108.

▲▲▲**St. Paul's Cathedral** The main cathedral of the Anglican Church, designed by Christopher Wren, with a climbable dome and daily evensong services. **Hours:** Mon-Sat 8:30-16:30, closed Sun except for worship. See page 113.

▲▲▲**Tower of London** Historic castle, palace, and prison housing the crown jewels and a witty band of Beefeaters. **Hours:** March-Oct Tue-Sat 9:00-17:30, Sun-Mon 10:00-17:30; Nov-Feb Tue-Sat 9:00-16:30, Sun-Mon 10:00-16:30. See page 118.

▲▲▲**Victoria and Albert Museum** The best collection of decorative arts anywhere. **Hours:** Daily 10:00-17:45, Fri until 22:00 (selected galleries only). See page 134.

▲▲**Houses of Parliament** London's Neo-Gothic landmark, famous for Big Ben and occupied by the Houses of Lords and Commons. **Hours:** Generally Mon-Tue 14:30-22:30, Wed-Thu 11:30-17:50, closed Fri-Sun and most of Aug-Sept. See page 86.

▲▲**Trafalgar Square** The heart of London, where Westminster, The City, and the West End meet. **Hours:** Always open. See page 89.

▲▲**National Portrait Gallery** A *Who's Who* of British history, featuring portraits of this nation's most important historical figures. **Hours:** Daily 10:00-18:00, Thu-Fri until 21:00, first and second floors open Mon at 11:00. See page 94.

▲▲**Covent Garden** Vibrant people-watching zone with shops, cafés, street musicians, and an iron-and-glass arcade that once hosted a produce market. **Hours:** Always open. See page 97.

▲▲**Changing of the Guard at Buckingham Palace** Hour-long spectacle at Britain's royal residence. **Hours:** Generally May-July daily at 11:30, Aug-April every other day. See page 103.

▲▲**London Eye** Enormous observation wheel, dominating—and offering commanding views over—London's skyline. **Hours:** Daily July-Aug 10:00-21:30, April-June 10:00-21:00, Sept-March 10:00-20:00. See page 123.

▲▲**Imperial War Museum** Examines the military history of the bloody 20th century. **Hours:** Daily 10:00-18:00. See page 126.

▲▲**Tate Modern** Works by Monet, Matisse, Dalí, Picasso, and Warhol displayed in a converted powerhouse. **Hours:** Daily 10:00-18:00, Fri-Sat until 22:00. See page 127.

▲▲**Shakespeare's Globe** Timbered, thatched-roofed reconstruction of the Bard's original wooden "O." **Hours:** Theater complex, museum, and actor-led tours generally daily 9:00-17:00; in summer, morning theater tours only. Plays are also held here. See page 128.

▲▲**Tate Britain** Collection of British painting from the 16th century through modern times, including works by William Blake, the Pre-Raphaelites, and J. M. W. Turner. **Hours:** Daily 10:00-18:00, first Fri of the month until 22:00. See page 132.

▲▲**Natural History Museum** Packed with stuffed creatures, engaging exhibits, and enthralled kids. **Hours:** Daily 10:00-17:50. See page 135.

▲**Courtauld Gallery** Fine collection of paintings filling one wing of the Somerset House, a grand 18th-century palace. **Hours:** Daily 10:00-18:00. See page 100.

melted-down weapons from that war. Think about that million-man army from the empire and commonwealth, and all those who gave their lives. Their memory is so revered that, when Kate Middleton walked up the aisle on her wedding day, by tradition she had to step around the tomb (and her wedding bouquet was later placed atop this tomb, also in accordance with tradition).

▲▲Houses of Parliament (Palace of Westminster)

This Neo-Gothic icon of London, the royal residence from 1042 to 1547, is now the meeting place of the legislative branch of government. The Houses of Parliament are located in what was once the Palace of Westminster—long the palace of England's medieval kings—until it was largely destroyed by fire in 1834. The palace was rebuilt in the Victorian Gothic style (a move away from Neoclassicism back to England's Christian and medieval heritage, true to the Romantic Age) and completed in 1860.

Tourists are welcome to view debates in either the bickering House of Commons or the genteel House of Lords. You're only allowed inside when Parliament is in session, indicated by a flag flying atop the Victoria Tower at the south end of the building (generally Mondays through Thursdays). During the summer recess, when Parliament is not in session, visitors can take a guided tour. While the actual debates are generally quite dull, it is a thrill to be inside and see the British government inaction.

Cost and Hours: Free, both Houses usually open Mon-Tue 14:30-22:30, Wed-Thu 11:30-17:50, closed Fri-Sun and most of Aug-Sept, generally less action and no lines after 18:00, Tube: Westminster, tel. 020/7219-4272, see www.parliament.uk for schedule.

Touring the Houses of Parliament (HOP): Enter the venerable HOP midway along the west side of the building (across the street from Westminster Abbey) through the Visitor Entrance (with the tourist ramp, next to the St. Stephen's Entrance—if lost, ask a guard). As you enter, you'll be asked if you want to visit the House of Commons or the House of Lords. The House of Lords has more pageantry, shorter lines, but less interesting debates (tel. 020/7219-3107 for schedule, visit www.parliamentlive.tv for a preview). Inquire about the wait—an hour or two is not unusual. If there's a long line for the House of Commons and you just want a quick look inside the grand halls of this majestic building, start with the House of Lords. Once inside, you can switch if you like.

Just past security (where you'll be photographed and given a badge to wear around your neck), you enter the vast and historic **Westminster Hall,** which survived the 1834 fire. The cavernous hall was built in the 11th century, and its famous self-supporting hammer-beam roof was added in 1397. Racks of brochures here

explain how the British government works, and plaques describe the hall. The Jubilee Café, open to the public, has live video feeds showing exactly what's going on in each house. Just seeing the café video is a fun experience (and can help you decide which house—if either—you'd like to see). Walking through the hall and up the stairs, you'll enter the busy world of government with all its high-powered goings-on.

Houses of Parliament Tours: Though Parliament is in recess during much of August and September, you can get a behind-the-scenes peek at the royal chambers of both houses during these months with a tour (£15, 1.25 hours, generally Mon-Fri, times vary, so confirm in advance; book ahead through www.ticketmaster.co.uk). The same tours are offered Saturdays year-round.

Jewel Tower: Across the street from the Parliament building's St. Stephen's Gate, the Jewel Tower is a rare remnant of the old Palace of Westminster used by kings until Henry VIII. The crude stone structure (1365-1366) was a guard tower in the palace wall, overlooking a moat. It contains a fine little exhibit on Parliament and the tower (£3, daily March-Oct 10:00-17:00, Nov-Feb 10:00-16:00, tel. 020/7222-2219). Next to the tower (and free) is a quiet courtyard with picnic-friendly benches.

Big Ben: The 315-foot-high clock tower at the north end of the Palace of Westminster is named for its 13-ton bell, Ben. The light above the clock is lit when the House of Commons is sitting. The face of the clock is huge—you can actually see the minute hand moving. For a good view of it, walk halfway over Westminster Bridge.

Other Sights in Westminster

▲▲▲**Churchill War Rooms**—This is a fascinating walk through the underground headquarters of the British government's fight against the Nazis in the darkest days of the Battle of Britain. The attraction includes two parts: the war rooms themselves and a top-notch museum dedicated to the man who steered the war from here, Winston Churchill. For details on all the blood, sweat, toil, and tears, pick up the excellent, essential, and included audioguide at the entry, and dive in.

Cost and Hours: £16 (includes small donation), daily 9:30-18:00, last entry one hour before closing; on King Charles Street, 200 yards off Whitehall, follow the signs, Tube: Westminster, tel. 020/7930-6961, http://cwr.iwm.org.uk. The museum's gift shop is great for anyone nostalgic for the 1940s.

Cabinet War Rooms: The 27-room, heavily fortified nerve center of the British war effort was used from 1939 to 1945.

Churchill's room, the map room, and other rooms are just as they were in 1945. As you follow the one-way route, be sure to take advantage of the audioguide, which explains each room and offers first-person accounts of wartime happenings here (it takes about 45 minutes, not counting the Churchill Museum). Be patient—it's well worth it. While the rooms are spartan, you'll see how British gentility survived even as the city was bombarded—posted signs informed those working underground what the weather was like outside, and a cheery notice reminds you to turn off the light switch to conserve electricity.

Churchill Museum: Don't bypass this museum, which occupies a large hall about a half-dozen rooms into the war rooms. It dissects every aspect of the man behind the famous cigar, bowler hat, and V-for-victory sign. It's extremely well-presented and engaging, using artifacts, quotes, political cartoons, clear explanations, and high-tech interactive exhibits to bring the colorful statesman to life; this museum alone deserves an hour. You'll get a taste of Winston's wit, irascibility, work ethic, passion for painting, American ties, writing talents, and drinking habits. The exhibit shows Winston's warts as well: It questions whether his party-switching was just political opportunism, examines the basis for his opposition to Indian self-rule, and reveals him to be an intense taskmaster who worked 18-hour days and was brutal on his staffers (who deeply respected him nevertheless).

A long touch-the-screen timeline lets you zero in on events in his life from birth (November 30, 1874) to his first appointment as prime minister in 1940. Many of the items on display—such as a European map divvied up in permanent marker, which Churchill brought to England from the postwar Potsdam Conference—drive home the remarkable span of history this man lived through. Imagine: Churchill began his military career riding horses in the cavalry and ended it speaking out against the proliferation of nuclear armaments. It's all the more amazing considering that, in the 1930s, the man who would be my vote for greatest statesman of the 20th century was considered a washed-up loony ranting about the growing threat of fascism.

Eating: If you're hungry, get your rations at the Switch Room café (in the museum), or for a nearby pub lunch, try the Westminster Arms (food served downstairs, on Storey's Gate, a couple of blocks south of the museum).

Horse Guards—The Horse Guards change daily at 11:00 (10:00 on Sun), and a colorful dismounting ceremony takes place daily at 16:00. The rest of the day, they just stand there—terrible for video cameras (on Whitehall, between Trafalgar Square and #10 Downing Street, Tube: Westminster, www.changing-the-guard.com). Buckingham Palace pageantry is canceled when it rains, but the horse guards change regardless of the weather.

▲**Banqueting House**—England's first Renaissance building (1619-1622) was designed by Inigo Jones. Built by King James I and decorated by his son Charles I, the Banqueting House came to symbolize the Stuart kings' "divine right" management style—the belief that God himself had anointed them to rule. The house is one of the few London landmarks spared by the 1698 fire and the only surviving part of the original Palace of Whitehall. Today it opens its doors to visitors, who enjoy a restful 20-minute audiovisual history, a 30-minute audioguide, and a look at the exquisite banqueting hall itself. As a tourist attraction, it's basically one big room—but what a grand room it is, with sumptuous ceiling paintings by Peter Paul Rubens. At Charles I's request, these paintings drove home the doctrine of the legitimacy of the divine right of kings. Ironically, in 1649—divine right ignored—King Charles I was famously executed right here.

Cost and Hours: £4.80, includes audioguide, Mon-Sat 10:00-17:00, closed Sun, last entry at 16:30, subject to closure for government functions, aristocratic WC, immediately across Whitehall from the Horse Guards, Tube: Westminster, tel. 020/3166-6155, www.hrp.org.uk.

▲▲Trafalgar Square

London's central square—at the intersection of Westminster, The

City, and the West End—is the climax of most marches and demonstrations, and a thrilling place to simply hang out. A recent remodeling of the square has rerouted car traffic, helping reclaim the area for London's citizens. At the top of Trafalgar Square (north) sits the domed National Gallery with its grand

LONDON

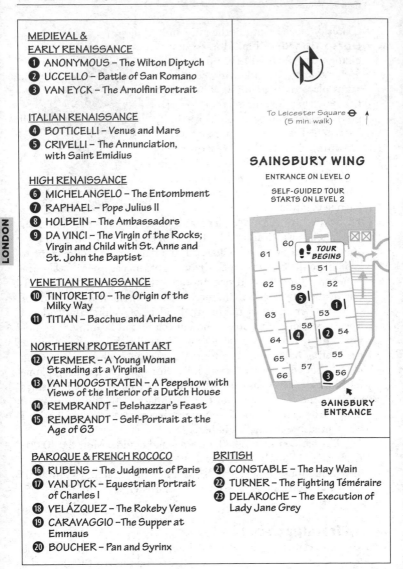

MEDIEVAL & EARLY RENAISSANCE
1. ANONYMOUS – The Wilton Diptych
2. UCCELLO – Battle of San Romano
3. VAN EYCK – The Arnolfini Portrait

ITALIAN RENAISSANCE
4. BOTTICELLI – Venus and Mars
5. CRIVELLI – The Annunciation, with Saint Emidius

HIGH RENAISSANCE
6. MICHELANGELO – The Entombment
7. RAPHAEL – Pope Julius II
8. HOLBEIN – The Ambassadors
9. DA VINCI – The Virgin of the Rocks; Virgin and Child with St. Anne and St. John the Baptist

VENETIAN RENAISSANCE
10. TINTORETTO – The Origin of the Milky Way
11. TITIAN – Bacchus and Ariadne

NORTHERN PROTESTANT ART
12. VERMEER – A Young Woman Standing at a Virginal
13. VAN HOOGSTRATEN – A Peepshow with Views of the Interior of a Dutch House
14. REMBRANDT – Belshazzar's Feast
15. REMBRANDT – Self-Portrait at the Age of 63

BAROQUE & FRENCH ROCOCO
16. RUBENS – The Judgment of Paris
17. VAN DYCK – Equestrian Portrait of Charles I
18. VELÁZQUEZ – The Rokeby Venus
19. CARAVAGGIO – The Supper at Emmaus
20. BOUCHER – Pan and Syrinx

BRITISH
21. CONSTABLE – The Hay Wain
22. TURNER – The Fighting Téméraire
23. DELAROCHE – The Execution of Lady Jane Grey

To Leicester Square (5 min. walk)

SAINSBURY WING

ENTRANCE ON LEVEL 0

SELF-GUIDED TOUR STARTS ON LEVEL 2

TOUR BEGINS

SAINSBURY ENTRANCE

staircase, and to the right, the steeple of St. Martin-in-the-Fields, built in 1722, inspiring the steeple-over-the-entrance style of many town churches in New England. In the center of the square, Lord Horatio Nelson stands atop his 185-foot-tall fluted granite column, gazing out toward Trafalgar, where he lost his life but defeated the French fleet. Part of this 1842 memorial is made from his victims' melted-down cannons. He's surrounded by spraying fountains, giant lions, hordes of people, and—until recently—even more

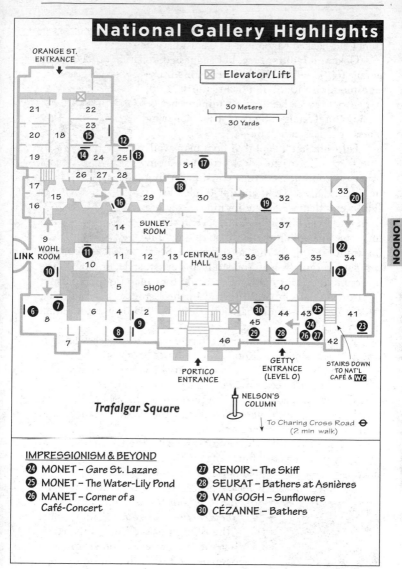

National Gallery Highlights

ORANGE ST. ENTRANCE

⊠ Elevator/Lift

30 Meters
30 Yards

21 · 22 · 23 · 20 · 18 · **15** · 19 · **14** · 24 · 25 · **12** · **13** · 26 · 27 · 28 · 31 · **17**

18 · 30 · 33 · **20**

17 · 15 · **16** · 29 · **19** · 32

16 · SUNLEY ROOM · 37

9 WOHL ROOM · 14 · **22**

LINK · **11** · 11 · 12 · 13 · CENTRAL HALL · 39 · 38 · 36 · 35 · 34 · **21**

10 · 10 · 5 · SHOP · 40

6 · **7** · 6 · 4 · 2 · **30** · 44 · 43 · **25** · 41

8 · **8** · **9** · 45 · **24** · **23**

7 · 46 · **29** · **28** · **26** · **27** · 42

PORTICO ENTRANCE

GETTY ENTRANCE (LEVEL 0)

STAIRS DOWN TO NAT'L CAFÉ & WC

NELSON'S COLUMN

Trafalgar Square

↓ To Charing Cross Road ⊖
(2 min walk)

IMPRESSIONISM & BEYOND
24 MONET – *Gare St. Lazare*
25 MONET – *The Water-Lily Pond*
26 MANET – *Corner of a Café-Concert*

27 RENOIR – *The Skiff*
28 SEURAT – *Bathers at Asnières*
29 VAN GOGH – *Sunflowers*
30 CÉZANNE – *Bathers*

pigeons. A former London mayor decided that London's "flying rats" were a public nuisance and evicted Trafalgar Square's venerable seed salesmen (Tube: Charing Cross).

▲▲▲National Gallery
Displaying Britain's top collection of European paintings from 1250 to 1900—including works by Leonardo, Botticelli, Velázquez, Rembrandt, Turner, Van Gogh, and the Impressionists—this is

one of Europe's great galleries. You'll peruse 700 years of art—from gold-backed Madonnas to Cubist bathers.

Cost and Hours: Free, but suggested donation of £2-3, temporary (optional) exhibits require an admission fee; daily 10:00-18:00, Fri until 21:00, last entry to special exhibits 45 minutes before closing; on Trafalgar Square, Tube: Charing Cross or Leicester Square.

Information: Helpful £1 floor plan available from information desk; free one-hour overview tours leave from Sainsbury Wing info desk daily at 11:30 and 14:30, plus Fri at 19:00; excellent £3.50 audioguides—choose from one-hour highlights tour, several theme tours, or tour option that lets you dial up info on any painting in the museum; ArtStart computer terminals help you study any artist, style, or topic in the museum, and print out a tailor-made tour map (located on first floor of the Sainsbury Wing and in the Espresso Bar); info tel. 020/7747-2885, switchboard tel. 020/7839-3321, www.national gallery.org.uk.

Eating: Consider splitting afternoon tea at the excellent-but-pricey National Dining Rooms, on the first floor of the Sainsbury Wing. The National Café, located near the Getty Entrance, also has afternoon tea (see page 194 for more info on both).

◑ Self-Guided Tour: Go in through the Sainsbury Entrance (in the smaller building to the left of the main entrance), and approach the collection chronologically.

Medieval and Early Renaissance: In the first rooms, you see shiny paintings of saints, angels, Madonnas, and crucifixions floating in an ethereal gold never-never land.

After leaving this gold-leaf peace, you'll stumble into Uccello's *Battle of San Romano* and Van Eyck's *The Arnolfini Portrait*, called by some "The Shotgun Wedding." This painting—a masterpiece of down-to-earth details—was once thought to depict a wedding ceremony forced by the lady's swelling belly. Today it's understood as a portrait of a solemn, well-dressed, well-heeled couple, the Arnolfinis of Bruges, Belgium (she likely was not pregnant—the fashion of the day was to gather up the folds of one's extremely full-skirted dress).

Renaissance: In painting, the Renaissance meant realism.

Artists rediscovered the beauty of nature and the human body, expressing the optimism and confidence of this new age. Look for Botticelli's *Venus and Mars*, Michelangelo's *The Entombment*, Raphael's *Pope Julius II*, and Leonardo's *The Virgin of the Rocks*.

Hans Holbein the Younger's *The Ambassadors* depicts two well-dressed, suave men flanking a shelf full of books, globes, navigational tools, and musical instruments—objects that symbolize the secular knowledge of the Renaissance. So what's with the gray, slanting blob at the bottom? If you view the blob from the right-hand edge of the painting (get real close, right up to the frame), the blob suddenly becomes...a skull, a reminder that—despite the fine clothes, proud poses, and worldly knowledge—we will all die.

In *The Origin of the Milky Way* by Venetian Renaissance painter Tintoretto, the god Jupiter places his illegitimate son, baby Hercules, at his wife's breast. Juno says, "Wait a minute. That's not

my baby!" Her milk spurts upward, becoming the Milky Way.

Northern Protestant: Greek gods and Virgin Marys are out, and hometown folks and hometown places are in. Highlights include Vermeer's *A Young Woman Standing at a Virginal* and Rembrandt's *Belshazzar's Feast.*

Rembrandt painted his *Self-Portrait at the Age of 63* in the year he would die. He was bankrupt, his mistress had just passed away, and he had also buried several of his children. We see a disillusioned, well-worn, but proud old genius.

Baroque: The museum's outstanding Baroque collection includes Van Dyck's *Equestrian Portrait of Charles I* and Caravaggio's *The Supper at Emmaus*. In Velázquez's *The Rokeby Venus,* Venus lounges diagonally across the canvas, admiring herself, with flaring red, white, and gray fabrics to highlight her rosy white skin and inflame our passion. This work by the king's personal court painter is a rare Spanish nude from that ultra-Catholic country.

British: The reserved British were more comfortable cavorting with nature than with the lofty gods, as seen in Constable's *The Hay Wain* and Turner's *The Fighting Téméraire*. Turner's messy, colorful style influenced the Impressionists and gives us our first glimpse into the modern art world.

Impressionism: At the end of the 19th century, a new breed of artists burst out of the stuffy confines of the studio. They donned scarves and berets and set up their canvases in farmers' fields or carried their notebooks into crowded cafés, dashing off quick sketches in order to catch a momentary...impression. Check out

Trafalgar Square

Impressionist and Post-Impressionist masterpieces such as Monet's *Gare St. Lazare* and *The Water-Lily Pond*, Renoir's *The Skiff*, Seurat's *Bathers at Asnières*, and Van Gogh's *Sunflowers*.

Cézanne's *Bathers* are arranged in strict triangles. Cézanne uses the Impressionist technique of building a figure with dabs of paint (though his "dabs" are often larger-sized "cube" shapes) to make solid, 3-D geometrical figures in the style of the Renaissance. In the process, his cube shapes helped inspire a radical new style—Cubism—bringing art into the 20th century.

Other Sights on Trafalgar Square

▲▲**National Portrait Gallery**—Put off by halls of 19th-century characters who meant nothing to me, I used to call this "as interesting as someone else's yearbook." But a selective walk through this 500-year-long *Who's Who* of British history is quick and free, and puts faces on the major characters in the story of England.

Some highlights: Henry VIII and wives; portraits of the "Virgin Queen" Elizabeth I, Sir Francis Drake, and Sir Walter Raleigh; the only real-life portrait of William Shakespeare; Oliver Cromwell and Charles I with his head on; portraits by Gainsborough and Reynolds; the Romantics (William Blake, Lord Byron, William Wordsworth, and company); Queen Victoria and her era; and the present royal family, including the late Princess Diana.

The collection is well-described, not huge, and in historical sequence, from the 16th century on the second floor to today's royal family on the ground floor. As 2012 marks the Queen's Diamond Jubilee (her 60th year on the throne), expect to see numerous portraits of her during the summer months.

Cost and Hours: Free, but suggested donation of £5, temporary (optional) exhibits require an admission fee, £3 audioguide, daily 10:00-18:00, Thu-Fri until 21:00—often with music and drinks offered in the evening, first and second floors open Mon at 11:00, last entry to special exhibits 45 minutes before closing, 100 yards off Trafalgar Square (around the corner from the National Gallery and opposite the Church of St. Martin-in-the-Fields), Tube: Charing Cross or Leicester Square, tel. 020/7306-0055, recorded info tel. 020/7312-2463, www.npg.org.uk.

▲**St. Martin-in-the-Fields**—The church, built in the 1720s with a Gothic spire atop a Greek-type temple, is an oasis of peace on wild and noisy Trafalgar Square. St. Martin cared for the poor. "In the fields" was where the first church stood on this spot (in the 13th century), between Westminster and The City. Stepping inside, you still feel a compassion for the needs of the people in this neighborhood—the church serves the homeless and houses a Chinese community center. The modern east window—with grillwork bent into the shape of a warped cross—was installed in 2008 to replace one damaged in World War II.

A freestanding glass pavilion to the left of the church serves as the entrance to the church's underground areas. There you'll find the concert ticket office, a gift shop, brass-rubbing center, and the recommended support-the-church Café in the Crypt.

Cost and Hours: Free, but donations welcome, £3.50 audioguide at shop downstairs; hours vary but generally Mon-Fri 8:30-13:00 & 14:00-18:00, Sat 9:30-13:00 & 14:00-18:00, Sun 15:30-17:00; Tube: Charing Cross, tel. 020/7766-1100, www.smitf.org.

Music: The church is famous for its concerts. Consider a free lunchtime concert (suggested £3.50 donation; Mon, Tue, and Fri at 13:00), an evening concert (£8-26, several nights a week at 19:30), or Wednesday night jazz in the church's café (£5-10, at 20:00). See the website for the concert schedule.

London for Early Birds and Night Owls

Most sightseeing in London is restricted to the hours between 10:00 and 18:00. Here are a few exceptions:

Sights Open Early

Every day, several sights open at 9:45 or earlier.

Westminster Cathedral: Daily at 7:00.

St. Paul's Cathedral: Mon-Sat at 8:30.

Shakespeare's Globe: Daily at 9:00.

Madame Tussauds Waxworks: Daily mid-July-Aug at 9:00, Sept-mid-July Mon-Fri at 9:30, Sat-Sun at 9:00.

Tower of London: Tue-Sat at 9:00.

Churchill War Rooms: Daily at 9:30.

Kew Gardens: Daily at 9:30.

Westminster Abbey: Mon-Sat at 9:30.

British Library: Mon-Sat at 9:30.

Buckingham Palace: Aug-Sept daily at 9:45.

Sights Open Late

Every night in London, at least one sight is open late (in addition to the London Eye and Madame Tussauds). Here's the scoop from Monday through Sunday:

London Eye: Last ascent July-Aug daily at 21:30, April-June at 21:00, Sept-March at 20:00.

Madame Tussauds: Mid-July-Aug daily until 21:00; Sept-mid-July Mon-Fri until 19:30, Sat-Sun until 20:00.

Clink Prison Museum: July-Sept daily until 21:00, Oct-June Sat-Sun until 19:30.

Houses of Parliament (when in session, roughly Oct-July): Mon-Tue until 22:30.

British Library: Tue until 20:00.

Sir John Soane's Museum: First Tue of month from 18:00 to 21:00.

British Museum (some galleries): Fri until 20:30.

National Portrait Gallery: Thu-Fri until 21:00.

Vinopolis: Thu-Sat until 22:00.

National Gallery: Fri until 21:00.

Victoria and Albert Museum: Fri until 22:00 (selected galleries).

Tate Modern: Fri-Sat until 22:00.

Tate Britain: First Fri of the month until 22:00.

The West End and Nearby

To explore this area during dinnertime, see my recommended restaurants on page 182.

▲**Piccadilly Circus**—Although this square is slathered with neon billboards and tacky attractions (think of it as the Times Square of London), the surrounding streets are packed with great shopping opportunities and swimming with youth on the rampage. For overstimulation in a grimy mall that smells like teen spirit, drop by the extremely trashy Trocadero Centre for its Funland arcade games, multiplex cinema, and 10-lane bowling alley (admission to Trocadero is free; individual attractions have separate admissions; located between Piccadilly and Leicester squares on Coventry Street).

Nearby Shaftesbury Avenue and Leicester Square teem with fun-seekers, theaters, Chinese restaurants, and street singers. To the northeast is London's Chinatown and, beyond that, the funky Soho neighborhood (described next). And curling to the northwest from Piccadilly Circus is genteel Regent Street, lined with the city's most exclusive shops.

▲**Soho**—North of Piccadilly, seedy Soho has become seriously trendy and is well worth a gawk. It's the epicenter of London's thriving and colorful youth, a fun and funky *Sesame Street* scene populated by people of every color of the racial rainbow...straight, gay, and everything in between.

Soho is also London's red light district (especially near Brewer and Berwick Streets), where "friendly models" wait in tiny rooms up dreary stairways, and voluptuous con artists sell strip shows. Though venturing up a stairway to check out a model is interesting, anyone who goes into any one of the shows will be ripped off. Every time. Even a £5 show in a "licensed bar" comes with a £100 cover or minimum (as it's printed on the drink menu) and a "security man." You may accidentally buy a £200 bottle of bubbly. And suddenly, the door has no handle. While this all sounds creepy, it's easy to avoid trouble if you're not looking for it. In fact, the sleazy joints share the block with respectable pubs and restaurants, and elderly couples out for a stroll pass neon signs that flash *Licensed Sex Shop in Basement*.

▲▲**Covent Garden**—This large square is swarming with people and street performers—jugglers, sword swallowers, and guitar

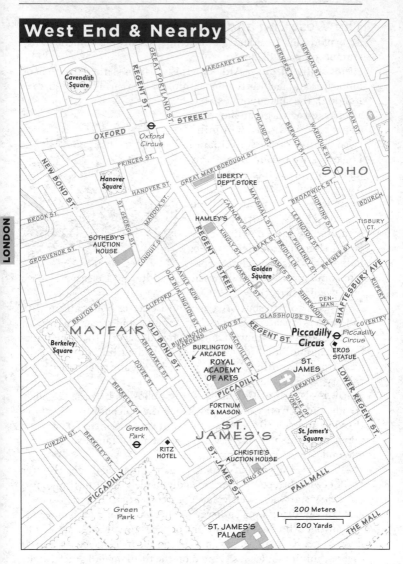

West End & Nearby

LONDON

players. London's buskers (including those in the Tube) are auditioned, licensed, and assigned times and places where they are allowed to perform.

The square's centerpiece is a covered marketplace. A market has been here since medieval times, when it was the "convent" garden owned by Westminster Abbey. In the 1600s, it became a housing development with this courtyard as its center, done in the Palladian style by Inigo Jones. Today's fine iron-and-glass structure was built in 1830 (when such buildings were all the Industrial Age

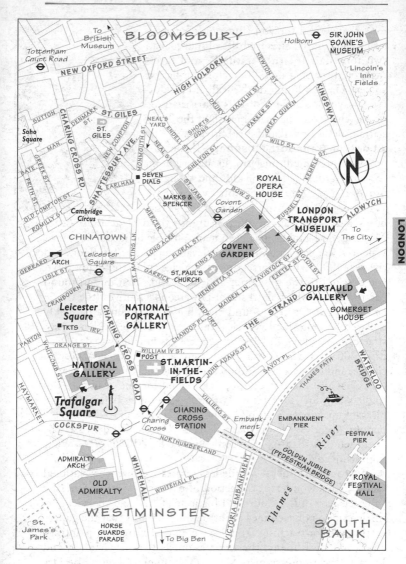

rage) to house the stalls of what became London's chief produce market. Covent Garden remained a produce market until 1973, when its venerable arcades were converted to boutiques, cafés, and antiques shops. A market still thrives here today (for details, see page 148).

The "Actors' Church" of St. Paul, the Royal Opera House, and the London Transport Museum (described next) all border the square, and venerable theaters are nearby. The area is a people-watcher's delight, with cigarette eaters, Punch-and-Judy acts, food that's good for you (but not your wallet), trendy crafts, sweet whiffs of marijuana, two-tone hair (neither natural), and faces that could set off a metal detector. For better Covent Garden lunch deals, walk a block or two away from the eye of this touristic hurricane (check out the places north of the Tube station, along Endell and Neal Streets).

▲**London Transport Museum**—This modern, well-presented museum, located right at Covent Garden, is fun for kids and thought-provoking for adults (if a bit overpriced). Whether you're cursing or marveling at the buses and Tube, the growth of Europe's third-biggest city (after Moscow and Istanbul) has been made possible by its public transit system. After you enter, take the elevator up to the top floor...and the year 1800, when horse-drawn vehicles ruled the road. Next, you descend to the first floor and the world's first underground Metro system, which used steam-powered locomotives (the Circle Line, c. 1865). On the ground floor, horses and trains are quickly replaced by motorized vehicles (cars, taxis, double-decker buses, streetcars), resulting in 20th-century congestion. How to deal with it? In 2003, car drivers in London were slapped with a congestion charge, and today, a half-billion people ride the Tube every year.

Cost and Hours: £13.50, ticket good for one year, Sat-Thu 10:00-18:00, Fri 11:00-18:00, last entry 45 minutes before closing, pleasant upstairs café with Covent Garden view, in southeast corner of Covent Garden courtyard, Tube: Covent Garden, switchboard tel. 020/7379-6344, recorded info tel. 020/7565-7299, www.ltmuseum.co.uk.

▲**Courtauld Gallery**—While less impressive than the National Gallery, this wonderful collection of paintings is still a joy. The gallery is part of the Courtauld Institute of Art, and the thoughtful description of each piece of art reminds visitors that the gallery is still used for teaching. You'll see medieval European paintings and works by Rubens, the Impressionists (Manet, Monet, and Degas), Post-Impressionists (such as Cézanne), and more. Besides the permanent collection, a quality selection of loaners and temporary exhibits are often included in the entry fee.

Cost and Hours: £6, free Mon until 14:00; open daily 10:00-18:00, last entry 30 minutes before closing, occasional late-night openings until 21:00—check website; at Somerset House along the Strand, Tube: Temple or Covent Garden, recorded info tel. 020/7848-2526, shop tel. 020/7848-2579, www.courtauld.ac.uk.

Somerset House: The Courtauld Gallery is located at Somerset House, a grand 18th-century civic palace that offers a marvelous public space (housing temporary exhibits) and a riverside terrace with several eateries (between the Strand and the Thames). The palace once held the national registry that recorded Britain's births, marriages, and deaths: "...where they hatch 'em, match 'em, and dispatch 'em." Step into the courtyard to enjoy the fountain. Go ahead...walk through it. The 55 jets get playful twice an hour. In the winter, this becomes a popular ice-skating rink with a toasty café for viewing (www.somerset-house.org.uk).

Buckingham Palace

Three palace sights require admission: the State Rooms (Aug-Sept

only), Queen's Gallery, and Royal Mews. You can pay for each separately, or buy a combo-ticket. The combo-ticket for £31 admits you to all three sights; a cheaper version for £15.50 covers the Queen's Gallery and Royal Mews. Many tourists are more interested in the Changing of the Guard, which costs nothing at all to view.

▲**State Rooms at Buckingham Palace**—This lavish home has been Britain's royal residence since 1837. When the Queen's at home, the royal standard flies (a red, yellow, and blue flag); otherwise, the Union Jack flaps in the wind. The Queen opens her palace to the public—but only in August and September, when she's out of town.

Cost and Hours: £17.50 for lavish State Rooms and throne room, includes audioguide; Aug-Sept only, daily 9:45-18:30, last admission 15:45; only 8,000 visitors a day by timed entry; come early to the palace's Visitor Entrance (opens 9:15), or book ahead in person or by phone or online (£1.25 extra); Tube: Victoria, tel. 020/7766-7300, www.royalcollection.org.uk.

▲**Queen's Gallery at Buckingham Palace**—Queen Elizabeth's personal collection of art is on display in a wing adjoining the palace. Her 7,000 paintings make up the finest private art collection in the world, rivaling Europe's biggest national art galleries. It's actually a collection of collections, built on by each successive monarch since the 16th century. She rotates her paintings, enjoying some privately in her many palatial residences while sharing others with her subjects in public galleries in Edinburgh and London. Small, thoughtfully presented, and always exquisite displays fill the five rooms open to the public. As you're in "the most important building in London," security is tight.

In addition to the permanent collection, you'll see temporary exhibits and a small room glittering with the Queen's personal

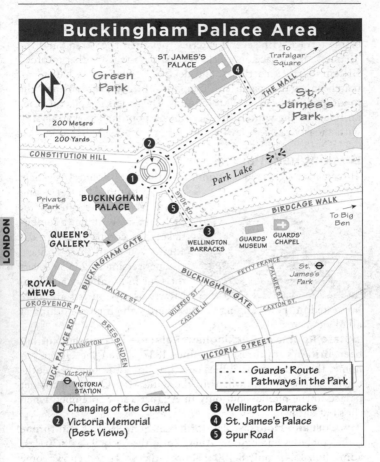

Buckingham Palace Area

- ❶ Changing of the Guard
- ❷ Victoria Memorial (Best Views)
- ❸ Wellington Barracks
- ❹ St. James's Palace
- ❺ Spur Road

· · · · · Guards' Route
- - - - - Pathways in the Park

jewelry. Compared to the crown jewels at the Tower, it may be Her Majesty's bottom drawer—but it's still a dazzling pile of diamonds. Temporary exhibits change about twice a year and are lovingly described by the included audioguide. While admission tickets come with an entry time, this is only enforced during rare days when crowds are a problem.

Cost and Hours: £9, daily 10:00-17:30, last entry one hour before closing, Tube: Victoria, tel. 020/7766-7301—but Her Majesty rarely answers. Men shouldn't miss the mahogany-trimmed urinals.

Royal Mews—Located to the left of Buckingham Palace, the Queen's working stables, or "mews," are open to visitors. The visit is likely to be disappointing unless you follow the included audioguide or the hourly guided tour, in which case it's thoroughly entertaining—especially if you're interested in horses and/or royalty. The 40-minute tours show off a few of the Queen's 30 horses, a fancy car, and a bunch of old carriages, finishing with the Gold State Coach (c. 1760, 4 tons, 4 mph). Queen Victoria said absolutely no cars. When she died, in 1901, the mews got its first Daimler. Today, along with the hay-eating transport, the stable is home to five Bentleys and Rolls-Royce Phantoms, with one on display.

Cost and Hours: £8, April-Oct daily 11:00-17:00, Nov-March Mon-Fri 10:00-16:00, closed Sat-Sun, last entry 45 minutes before closing, guided tours on the hour, Buckingham Palace Road, Tube: Victoria, tel. 020/7766-7302.

▲▲**Changing of the Guard at Buckingham Palace**—This is the spectacle every visitor to London has to see at least once: stone-

faced, red-coated, bearskin-hatted guards changing posts with much fanfare, in an hour-long ceremony accompanied by a brass band.

It's 11:00 at Buckingham Palace, and the on-duty guards are ready to finish their shift. Nearby at St. James's Palace (a half-mile northwest), a second set of guards is also ready for a break. Meanwhile, fresh replacement guards gather for a review and inspection at Wellington Barracks, 500 yards east of the palace (on Birdcage Walk).

At 11:15, the tired St. James's guards head out to the Mall, and then take a right turn for Buckingham Palace. At 11:30, the replacement troops, led by the band, also head for Buckingham Palace. Meanwhile, a fourth group—the Horse Guard—passes by along the Mall on their way back to Hyde Park Corner from their own changing-of-the-guard ceremony on Whitehall (which just took place at Horse Guards Parade at 11:00, or 10:00 on Sun).

At 11:45, the tired and fresh guards converge on Buckingham Palace in a perfect storm of Red Coat pageantry. Everyone parades around, the guard changes (passing the regimental flag, or "color") with much shouting, the band plays a happy little concert, and then they march out. At noon, two bands escort two detachments of guards away: the tired guards to Wellington Barracks and the fresh guards to St. James's Palace. As the fresh guards set up at St. James's Palace and the tired ones dress down at the barracks, the tourists disperse.

Cost and Hours: Free, daily May-July at 11:30, every other day Aug-April, no ceremony in very wet weather; exact schedule subject to change—call 020/7766-7300 for the day's plan, or check www.changing-the-guard.com or www.royalcollection.org.uk (click "Visit," then "Changing the Guard"); Buckingham Palace, Tube: Victoria, St. James's Park, or Green Park. Or hop into a big black taxi and say, "Buck House, please."

Sightseeing Strategies: Most tourists just show up and get lost in the crowds, but those who know the drill will enjoy the event more. The action takes place in stages over the course of an hour, at several different locations. The main event is in the forecourt right in front of Buckingham Palace (between Buckingham Palace and the fence) from 11:30 to 12:00. To see it close up, you'll need to get here no later than 10:30 to get a place right next to the fence.

But there's plenty of pageantry elsewhere. Get out your map and strategize. You could see the guards mobilizing at Wellington Barracks or St. James's Palace (11:00-11:15). Or watch them parade with bands down The Mall and Spur Road (11:15-11:30). After the ceremony at Buckingham Palace is over (and many tourists have gotten bored and gone home), the parades march back along those same streets (12:10).

Pick one event and find a good, unobstructed place from which to view it. The key is to get either right up front along the road or fence, or find some raised elevation to stand or sit on—a balustrade or a curb—so you can see over people's heads.

For the best overall view, stake out the high ground on the circular Victoria Memorial (come before 11:00 to get a place). From the memorial, you have good views of the palace as well as the arriving and departing parades along The Mall and Spur Road. The actual changing of the guard in front of the palace is a nonevent. It is interesting, however, to see nearly every tourist in London gathered in one place at the same time.

If you arrive too late to get a good spot, or you just don't feel like jostling for a view, stroll down to St. James's Palace and wait near the corner for a great photo-op. At about 12:15, the parade marches up The Mall to the palace and performs a smaller changing ceremony—with almost no crowds. Afterward, stroll through nearby St. James's Park.

Sights in North London

▲▲▲British Museum

Simply put, this is the greatest chronicle of civilization...anywhere. A visit here is like taking a long hike through *Encyclopedia Britannica* National Park. While the vast British Museum wraps around its Great Court (the huge entrance hall), the most popular sections of the museum fill the ground floor: Egyptian, Assyrian, and ancient

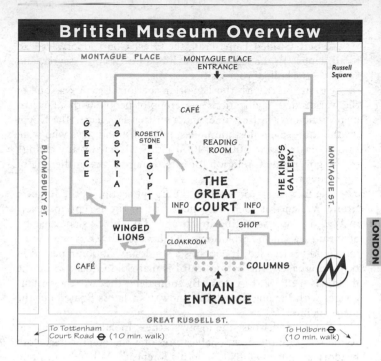

British Museum Overview

MONTAGUE PLACE

MONTAGUE PLACE ENTRANCE

Russell Square

CAFÉ

G R E E C E

A S S Y R I A

ROSETTA STONE

READING ROOM

E G Y P T

THE KING'S GALLERY

BLOOMSBURY ST.

MONTAGUE ST.

THE GREAT COURT

INFO

INFO

WINGED LIONS

CLOAKROOM

SHOP

CAFÉ

COLUMNS

MAIN ENTRANCE

GREAT RUSSELL ST.

To Tottenham Court Road ⊖ (10 min. walk)

To Holborn ⊖ (10 min. walk)

LONDON

Greek, with the famous Elgin Marbles from the Parthenon in Athens. The museum's stately Reading Room—famous as the place where Karl Marx hung out while formulating his ideas on communism and writing *Das Kapital*—sometimes hosts special exhibits.

Cost and Hours: Free but a £4, $5, or €5 donation requested; temporary exhibits usually extra; daily 10:00-17:30, Fri until 20:30 (selected galleries only), least crowded weekday late afternoons; Great Russell Street, Tube: Tottenham Court Road.

Information: Information desks offer a standard museum map (£1 suggested donation) and a £2 version that highlights important pieces. Free 30-minute **eyeOpener tours** are led by volunteers, who focus on select rooms (daily 11:00-15:45, generally every 15 minutes). The 1.5-hour **Highlights tours,** led by licensed guides, are expensive but meaty, giving an introduction to the museum's masterpieces (£9, daily at 10:30, 13:00, and 15:00). Free 45-minute **gallery talks** on specific subjects are offered Tue-Sat at 13:15. The £5 **multimedia guide** offers dial-up audio commentary and video on 200 objects, as well as several theme tours (must leave photo ID). There's also a fun children's audioguide (£3.50). And finally, you can download my free **audio tour** of this museum for your mobile device (see page 48). General info tel. 020/7323-8299, ticket desk tel. 020/7323-8181, collection questions tel.

020/7323-8838, www.britishmuseum.org.

○ Self-Guided Tour: From the Great Court, doorways lead to all wings. To the left are the exhibits on Egypt, Assyria, and Greece—the bulk of your visit.

Egypt: Start with the Egyptian section. Egypt was one of the world's first "civilizations"—a group of people with a government, religion, art, free time, and a written language. The Egypt we think of—pyramids, mummies, pharaohs, and guys who walk funny—lasted from 3000 to 1000 B.C. with hardly any change in the government, religion, or arts. Imagine two millennia of Eisenhower.

The first thing you'll see in the Egypt section is the **Rosetta Stone.** When this rock was unearthed in the Egyptian desert in 1799, it was a sensation in Europe. This black slab caused a quantum leap in the evolution of history. Finally, Egyptian writing could be decoded. It contains a single inscription repeated in three languages. The bottom third is plain old Greek, while the middle is medieval Egyptian. By comparing the two known languages with the one they didn't know, translators figured out the hieroglyphics.

Next, wander past the many **statues,** including a seven-ton Ramesses, with the traditional features of a pharaoh (goatee, cloth headdress, and cobra diadem on his forehead). When Moses told the king of Egypt, "Let my people go!" this was the stony-faced look he got. You'll also see the Egyptian gods as animals—these include Amun, king of the gods, as a ram, and Horus, the god of the living, as a falcon.

At the end of the hall, climb the stairs to **mummy** land. To mummify a body, disembowel it (but leave the heart inside), pack the cavities with pitch, and dry it with natron, a natural form of sodium carbonate (and, I believe, the active ingredient in Twinkies). Then carefully bandage it head to toe with hundreds of yards of linen strips. Let it sit 2,000 years, and...*voilà!* The mummy was placed in a wooden coffin, which was put in a stone coffin, which was placed in a tomb. The result is that we now have Egyptian bodies that are as well-preserved as Joan Rivers. Many of the mummies here are from the time of the Roman occupation, when they painted a fine portrait in wax on the wrapping. X-ray photos in the display cases tell us more about these people. Don't miss the animal mummies. Cats were popular pets. They were also considered incarnations of the goddess Bastet. Worshipped in life as the sun god's allies, preserved in death, and memorialized with statues, cats were given the adulation they've come to expect ever since.

Assyria: Long before Saddam Hussein, Iraq was home to other palace-building, iron-fisted rulers—the Assyrians, who conquered their southern neighbors and dominated the Middle East for 300 years (c. 900-600 B.C.). Their strength came from a superb army (chariots, mounted cavalry, and siege engines), a policy of terrorism against enemies ("I tied their heads to tree trunks all around the city," reads a royal inscription), ethnic cleansing and mass deportations of the vanquished, and efficient administration (roads and express postal service). They have been called "The Romans of the East."

Standing guard over the Assyrian exhibit halls are two human-headed **winged lions.** These lions guarded an Assyrian palace. Carved into the stone between the bearded lions' loins, you can see one of civilization's most impressive achievements—writing. This wedge-shaped (cuneiform) script is the world's first written language, invented 5,000 years ago by the Sumerians (of southern Iraq) and passed down to their less-civilized descendants, the Assyrians.

The **Nimrud Gallery** is a mini-version of the throne room of King Ashurnasirpal II's palace at Nimrud. It's filled with royal propaganda reliefs, 30-ton marble bulls, and panels depicting wounded lions (lion-hunting was Assyria's sport of kings).

Greece: During their Golden Age (500-430 B.C.), the ancient Greeks set the tone for all of Western civilization to follow. Democracy, theater, literature, mathematics, philosophy, science, gyros, art, and architecture, as we know them, were virtually all invented by a single generation of Greeks in a small town of maybe 80,000 citizens.

Your walk through Greek art history starts with **pottery,** usually painted red and black and a popular export product for the sea-trading Greeks. The earliest featured geometric patterns (eighth century B.C.), then a painted black silhouette on the natural orange clay, then a red figure on a black background. Later, painted vases show a culture that was really into partying.

The highlight is the **Elgin Marbles,** named for the shrewd British ambassador who had his men hammer, chisel, and saw them off the Parthenon at Athens' Acropolis in the early 1800s. Though the Greek government complains about losing its marbles—and recently built a state-of-the-art museum at the base of the Acropolis in an attempt to shame the British government into returning them—the Brits feel they rescued and preserved the sculptures. These much-wrangled-over bits of the Parthenon (from about 450 B.C.) are even more impressive than they look. The marble panels lining the walls of the large hall are part of the frieze that originally ran around the exterior of the Parthenon (under the eaves). The statues at either end of the hall once filled the Parthenon's triangular-shaped pediments and showed the birth of Athena. The relief panels known as metopes tell the story of the

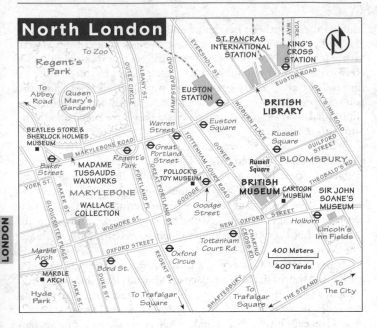

struggle between the forces of human civilization and animal-like barbarism.

The Rest of the Museum: Be sure to venture upstairs to see artifacts from **Roman Britain** that surpass anything you'll see at Hadrian's Wall or elsewhere in the country. Also look for the Sutton Hoo Ship Burial artifacts from a seventh-century royal burial on the east coast of England (Room 41). A rare Michelangelo cartoon (preliminary sketch) is in Room 90.

Other Sights in North London

▲▲▲**British Library**—The British Empire built its greatest monuments out of paper, and it's with literature that England made her lasting contribution to civilization and the arts. Here, in just two rooms—variously called "The Sir John Ritblat Gallery," "Treasures of the British Library," or just "The Treasures"—are the literary jewels of Western civilization, from early Bibles, to the Magna Carta, to Shakespeare's *Hamlet,* to Lewis Carroll's *Alice's Adventures in Wonderland.*

You'll see the Lindisfarne Gospels transcribed on an illuminated manuscript, as well as Beatles lyrics scrawled on the back of a greeting card. Pages from Leonardo da Vinci's notebook show his powerful curiosity, his genius for invention, and his famous backward and inside-out handwriting, which makes sense only if you know Italian and have a mirror. A *Beowulf* manuscript from A.D. 1000, *The Canterbury Tales,* and Shakespeare's First Folio also

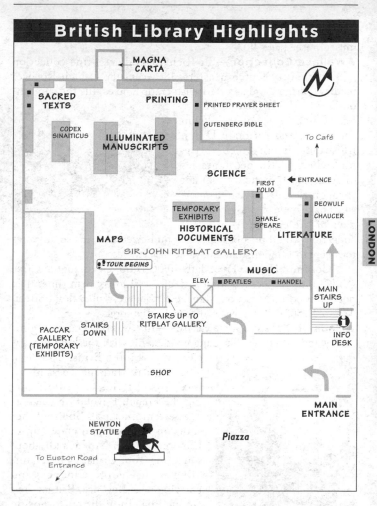

reside here. (If the First Folio is not out, the library should have other Shakespeare items on display.)

Note that exhibits generally change often, and many of the museum's old, fragile manuscripts need to "rest" periodically in order to stay well-preserved. If your heart's set on seeing that one particular rare Dickens book or letter penned by Gandhi, call ahead to make sure it's on display.

Cost and Hours: Free but £2 suggested donation, admission charged for some (optional) temporary exhibits, Mon-Fri 9:30-18:00, Tue until 20:00, Sat 9:30-17:00, Sun 11:00-17:00, 96 Euston Road, Tube: King's Cross St. Pancras or Euston, tel. 019/3754-6060 or 020/7412-7676, www.bl.uk.

Tours: While the British Library doesn't offer an audioguide or guided tours, you can download my free **audio tour** of this museum (see page 48).

▲**Wallace Collection**—Sir Richard Wallace's fine collection of 17th-century Dutch Masters, 18th-century French Rococo, medieval armor, and assorted aristocratic fancies fills the sumptuously furnished Hertford House on Manchester Square. From the rough and intimate Dutch lifescapes of Jan Steen to the pink-cheeked Rococo fantasies of François Boucher, a wander through this little-visited mansion makes you nostalgic for the days of the empire. While this collection would be a big deal in a mid-sized city, it's small potatoes here in London...but enjoyable nevertheless.

Cost and Hours: Free, daily 10:00-17:00, £4 audioguide, free guided tours or lectures almost daily—call to confirm times, just north of Oxford Street on Manchester Square, Tube: Bond Street. Tel. 020/7563-9500, www.wallacecollection.org.

▲**Madame Tussauds Waxworks**—This waxtravaganza is gimmicky and expensive, but dang good...a hit with the kind of travelers who skip the British Museum. The original Madame Tussaud did wax casts of heads lopped off during the French Revolution (such as Marie-Antoinette's). She took her show on the road and ended up in London in 1835. Now it's all about squeezing Tom Cruise's bum, gambling with George Clooney, and partying with Beyoncé, Britney, and Brangelina. In addition to posing with all the eerily realistic wax dummies—from Johnny Depp to Barack Obama to the Beatles—you'll have the chance to tour a hokey haunted-house exhibit; learn how they created this waxy army; hop on a people-mover and cruise through a kid-pleasing "Spirit of London" time trip; and visit with Spider-Man, the Hulk, and other Marvel superheroes. A nine-minute "4-D" show features a 3-D movie heightened by wind, "back ticklers," and other special effects.

Cost and Hours: £29, 10 percent discount and no waiting in line if you buy tickets on their website (also consider combo-deal with London Eye, sold cheaper online), £22.50 if purchased at TI, cheaper for kids. From 17:00 to closing, it's £14 if you buy in advance online. Children under 5 always free. Open Mid-July-

Aug and school holidays daily 9:00-21:00, Sept-mid-July Mon-Fri 9:30-19:30, Sat-Sun 9:00-20:00, last entry two hours before closing; Marylebone Road, Tube: Baker Street, tel. 0871-894-3000, www.madametussauds.com.

Crowd-Beating Tips: This popular attraction can be swamped with people. To avoid the hassle, buy your tickets and reserve an entry time in advance, either online (10 percent discount) or by phone (same price as box office). If you wait to buy tickets at the attraction, you'll discover that the ticket-buying line twists endlessly once inside the door (believe the posted signs warning you how long the wait will be—an hour or more is not unusual at busy times). If you buy your tickets at the door, try to arrive after 15:00.

▲**Sir John Soane's Museum**—Architects love this quirky place, as do fans of interior decor, eclectic knickknacks, and Back Door

sights. Tour this furnished home on a bird-chirping square and see 19th-century chairs, lamps, and carpets, wood-paneled nooks and crannies, and stained-glass skylights. (Note that some sections may be closed for restoration in 2012, but the main part of the house will be open.) The townhouse is cluttered with Soane's (and his wife's) collection of ancient relics, curios, and famous paintings, including Hogarth's series on *The Rake's Progress* (read the fun plot) and several excellent Canalettos. In 1833, just before his death, Soane established his house as a museum, stipulating that it be kept as nearly as possible in the state he left it. If he visited today, he'd be entirely satisfied. You'll leave wishing you'd known the man.

Cost and Hours: Free but donations much appreciated, Tue-Sat 10:00-17:00, open and candlelit the first Tue of the month 18:00-21:00, closed Sun-Mon, last entry 30 minutes before closing, long entry lines on Sat and first Tue, good £1 brochure, £5 guided tour Sat at 11:00, free, downloadable audio tours on their website, 13 Lincoln's Inn Fields, quarter-mile southeast of British Museum, Tube: Holborn, tel. 020/7405-2107, www.soane.org.

Cartoon Museum—This humble but interesting museum is located in the shadow of the British Museum. While its three rooms are filled with British cartoons unknown to most Americans, the satire of famous bigwigs and politicians—including Napoleon, Margaret Thatcher, the Queen, and Tony Blair—shows the power of parody to deliver social commentary. Upstairs, you'll see pages spanning from *Tarzan* to *Tank Girl,* and *Andy Capp* to the British *Dennis the Menace*—interesting only to comic-book diehards.

LONDON

Cost and Hours: £5.50, Tue-Sat 10:30-17:30, Sun 12:00-17:30, closed Mon, 35 Little Russell Street—go one block south of the British Museum on Museum Street and turn right, Tube: Tottenham Court Road, tel. 020/7580-8155, www.cartoon museum.org.

Pollock's Toy Museum—This rickety old house, with glass cases filled with toys and games lining its walls and halls, is a time-warp experience that brings back childhood memories to people who grew up without batteries or computer chips. Though the museum is small, you could spend a lot of time here, squinting at the fascinating toys and dolls that entertained the children of 19th- and early 20th-century England. The included information is great. The story of Theodore Roosevelt refusing to shoot a bear cub while on a hunting trip was celebrated in 1902 cartoons, resulting in a new, huggable toy: the Teddy Bear. It was popular for good reason: It could be manufactured during World War I without rationed products; it coincided with the new belief that soft toys were good for a child's development; it was an acceptable "doll for boys"; and it's *the* toy children keep long after they've grown up.

Cost and Hours: £5, kids-£2, generally Mon-Sat 10:00-17:00, closed Sun, last entry 30 minutes before closing, 1 Scala Street, Tube: Goodge Street, tel. 020/7636-3452, www.pollockstoy museum.com. A fun, retro toy shop is attached.

Beatles Sights—Central London is surprisingly devoid of sights associated with the famous '60s rock band. To see much of anything, consider taking a guided walk (see page 70).

For a photo op, go to **Abbey Road** and walk the famous crosswalk pictured on the *Abbey Road* album cover (Tube: St. John's Wood, get information and buy Beatles memorabilia at the small kiosk in the station). From the Tube station, it's a five-minute walk west down Grove End Road to the intersection with Abbey Road. The Abbey Road recording studio is the low-key, white

building to the right of Abbey House (it's still a working studio, so you can't go inside). Ponder the graffiti on the low wall outside, and...imagine. To re-create the famous cover photo, shoot the crosswalk from the roundabout as you face north up Abbey Road. Shoes are optional.

Nearby is **Paul McCartney's current home** (7 Cavendish Avenue): Continue down Grove End Road, turn left on Circus Road, and then right on Cavendish. Please be discreet.

The **Beatles Store** is at 231 Baker Street (Tube: Baker Street). It's small—some Beatles-logo T-shirts, mugs, pins, and old vinyl records like you might have in your closet—and has nothing of historic value (open eight days a week, 10:00-18:30, tel. 020/7935-4464, www.beatlesstorelondon.co.uk; another rock memorabilia store is across the street).

Sherlock Holmes Museum—A few doors down from the Beatles Store, this meticulous re-creation of the (fictional) apartment of the (fictional) detective sits at the (real) address of 221b Baker Street. Fans will like it. Others might enjoy the Victorian-era furniture, clothes, pipes, paintings, and chamber pots, which give a glimpse at daily life from the time.

Cost and Hours: £6, daily 9:30-18:00, last entry 30 minutes before closing, large gift shop for Holmes connoisseurs, Tube: Baker Street, tel. 020/7935-8866, www.sherlock -holmes.co.uk.

Sights in The City

When Londoners say "The City," they mean the one-square-mile business center in East London that 2,000 years ago was Roman Londinium. The outline of the Roman city walls can still be seen in the arc of roads from Blackfriars Bridge to Tower Bridge. Within The City are 23 churches designed by Sir Christopher Wren, mostly just ornamentation around St. Paul's Cathedral. Today, while home to only 7,000 residents, The City thrives with nearly 300,000 office workers coming and going daily. It's a fascinating district to wander on weekdays, but since almost nobody actually lives there, it's dull in the evenings and on Saturday and Sunday.

You can download my free **audio tour** of The City—which peels back the many layers of history in this oldest part of London—for your mobile device (see page 48).

▲▲▲St. Paul's Cathedral

Sir Christopher Wren's most famous church is the great St. Paul's, its elaborate interior capped by a 365-foot dome. There's been a church on this spot since 604. After the Great Fire of 1666 destroyed the old cathedral, Wren created this Baroque master-piece. And since World War II, St. Paul's has been Britain's symbol of resistance. Despite 57 nights of bombing, the Nazis failed to destroy the cathedral, thanks to the St. Paul's volunteer fire watch-men, who stayed on the dome.

Cost and Hours: £14.50, includes church entry, dome climb,

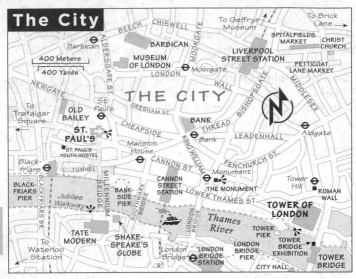

The City

To Geffrye Museum
To Brick Lane →

BEECH   CHISWELL

Barbican

BARBICAN

SPITALFIELDS MARKET
CHRIST CHURCH

400 Meters
400 Yards

MUSEUM OF LONDON
Moorgate

LIVERPOOL STREET STATION

PETTICOAT LANE MARKET

ALDERSGATE ST.
MOORGATE
NEWGATE
LONDON

THE CITY

LONDON WALL

BISHOPSGATE
MIDDLESEX

To Trafalgar Square

St. Paul's
OLD BAILEY

GRESHAM ST.

ST. PAUL'S

CHEAPSIDE

BANK

THREAD.

LEADENHALL

Aldgate

Mansion House

KINGWILLIAM ST.

Bank

Blackfriars

TUNNEL

FENCHURCH ST.

BLACKFRIARS PIER

BLACKFRIARS BR.

MILLENNIUM BRIDGE

CANNON ST.

Monument

Tower Hill

ROMAN WALL

Jubilee Walkway

BANK-SIDE PIER

CANNON STREET STATION

THE MONUMENT

LOWER THAMES ST.

SOUTHWARK BRIDGE

ST. PAUL'S YOUTH HOSTEL

TOWER OF LONDON

TATE MODERN

To Waterloo Station

SHAKE-SPEARE'S GLOBE

London Bridge

LONDON BRIDGE

Thames River

LONDON BRIDGE STATION

TOWER PIER

LONDON BRIDGE PIER

TOWER BRIDGE EXHIBITION

CITY HALL

TOWER BRIDGE

crypt, guided tour, and audioguide; free on Sun but officially open only to worshippers; Mon-Sat 8:30-16:30, last entry for sightseeing 16:00 (dome opens at 9:30, last entry at 16:15), closed Sun except for worship, sometimes closed for special events, Tube: St. Paul's.

Music and Services: Communion is Mon-Sat at 8:00 and 12:30. Sunday services are held at 8:00, 10:15 (Matins), 11:30 (sung Eucharist), 15:15 (evensong), and 18:00. Additional evensong services are held Mon-Sat at 17:00 (40 minutes, free to anyone—though visitors who haven't paid admission aren't allowed to linger after the service). For more on evensong, see page 157. If you're

here for evensong worship and sitting under the dome, at 16:45 you may be able to grab a big wooden stall in the choir, next to the singers.

Information: Admission includes an **audioguide** as well as a 1.5-hour **guided tour** (Mon-Sat at 10:45, 11:15, 13:30, and 14:00; confirm schedule at church or call 020/7246-8357). You can download my free **audio tour** of St. Paul's for your mobile device (see page 48). Recorded info tel. 020/7236-4128, reception tel. 020/7246-8350, www.stpauls.co.uk.

Touring the Cathedral: Even now, as skyscrapers encroach, the 365-foot-high dome of St. Paul's rises majestically above the

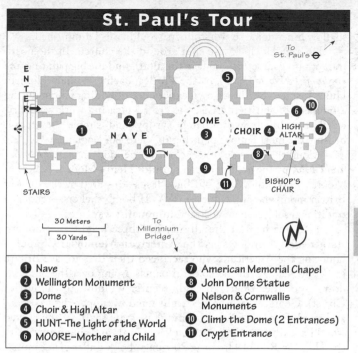

St. Paul's Tour

1 Nave

2 Wellington Monument

3 Dome

4 Choir & High Altar

5 HUNT—The Light of the World

6 MOORE—Mother and Child

7 American Memorial Chapel

8 John Donne Statue

9 Nelson & Cornwallis Monuments

10 Climb the Dome (2 Entrances)

11 Crypt Entrance

rooftops of the neighborhood. The tall dome is set on classical columns, capped with a lantern, topped by a six-foot ball, and iced with a cross. As the first Anglican cathedral built in London after the Reformation, it is Baroque: St. Peter's in Rome filtered through clear-eyed English reason. Often the site of historic funerals (Queen Victoria and Winston Churchill), St. Paul's most famous ceremony was a wedding—when Prince Charles married Lady Diana Spencer in 1981.

Inside, this big church *feels* big. At 515 feet long and 250 feet wide, it's Europe's fourth-largest, after Rome (St. Peter's), Sevilla, and Milan. The spaciousness is accentuated by the relative lack of decoration. The simple, cream-colored ceiling and the clear glass in the windows light everything evenly. Wren wanted this: a simple, open church with nothing to hide. Unfortunately, only this entrance area keeps his original vision—the rest was encrusted with 19th-century Victorian ornamentation.

The **dome** you see, painted with scenes from the life of St. Paul, is only the innermost of three. From the painted interior of the first dome, look up through the opening to see the light-filled lantern of the second dome. Finally, the whole thing is covered on the outside by the third and final dome, the shell of lead-covered wood that you see from the street. Wren's ingenious three-in-one design was psychological as well as functional—he wanted a low, shallow inner dome so worshippers wouldn't feel diminished.

Do a quick clockwise spin around the church. In the north transept (to your left as you face the altar), find the big painting *The Light of the World* (1904), by the Pre-Raphaelite William Holman Hunt. Inspired by Hunt's own experience of finding Christ during a moment of spiritual crisis, the crowd-pleasing work was criticized by art highbrows for being "syrupy" and "simple"—even as it became the most famous painting in Victorian England.

Along the left side of the choir is the modern statue *Mother and Child*, by the great modern sculptor Henry Moore. Typical of Moore's work, this Mary and Baby Jesus—inspired by the sight of British moms nursing babies in WWII bomb shelters—renders a traditional subject in an abstract, minimalist way.

The area behind the altar, with three bright and modern stained-glass windows, is the **American Memorial Chapel**— honoring the Americans who sacrificed their lives to save Britain in World War II. In the colorful panels arcing over the big windows, spot the American eagle (center window, to the left of Christ), George Washington (right window, upper-right corner), and symbols of all 50 states (find your state seal). In the carved wood beneath the windows, you'll see birds and foliage native to the US. The Roll of Honor (a 500-page book under glass, immediately behind the altar) lists the names of 28,000 US servicemen and women based in Britain who gave their lives during the war.

Around the other side of the choir is a shrouded statue honoring **John Donne** (1621-1631), a passionate preacher in old St. Paul's, as well as a great poet ("never wonder for whom the bell tolls—it tolls for thee").

In the south transept are monuments to military greats **Horatio Nelson,** who fought Napoleon, and **Charles Cornwallis,** who was finished off by George Washington at Yorktown.

Climbing the Dome: During your visit, you can climb 530 steps to reach the dome and great city views. Along the way, have some fun in the Whispering Gallery (257 steps up). Whisper sweet nothings into the wall, and your partner (and anyone else) standing far away can hear you. For best effects, try whispering (not talking) with your mouth close to the wall, while your partner stands a few dozen yards away with his or her ear to the wall.

Visiting the Crypt: The crypt is a world of historic bones and interesting cathedral models. Many legends are buried here—Horatio Nelson, who wore down Napoleon; the Duke of Wellington, who finished Napoleon off; and even Wren himself. Wren's actual tomb is marked by a simple black slab with no statue, since he considered the church itself to be his legacy. Back up in the nave, on the floor directly under the dome, is Christopher Wren's name

London's Best Views

Though London is a height-challenged city, you can get lofty perspectives on it from several high-flying places. For some viewpoints, you need to pay admission (cheapest at The Monument) and at the bars or restaurants, you'll likely get a drink; the only truly free spots are Primrose Hill and the viewpoint in front of Royal Observatory Greenwich.

London Eye: Ride the giant Ferris wheel for London's best, most expensive, and dizzying views. See page 123.

St. Paul's Dome: You'll earn a striking, unobstructed view by climbing hundreds of steps to the cramped balcony of the church's cupola. See page 113.

Tate Modern: Take in a classic vista across the Thames from the museum's seventh-floor restaurant and bar. See page 127.

The Monument: Though surrounded by modern buildings in the financial district, this 202-foot column memorializing the Great Fire of 1666 affords a nice view of The City. See page 118.

National Portrait Gallery: A mod top-floor restaurant peers over Trafalgar Square and the Westminster neighborhood. See page 94.

Waterstone's Bookstore: Its hip, low-key, top-floor café/bar has reasonable prices and sweeping views of the London Eye, Big Ben, and the Houses of Parliament (see page 55 for hours, 203 Piccadilly, Tube: Piccadilly Circus, tel. 020/7851-2433, www.5thview.co.uk).

OXO Tower: Perched high over the Thames River, the building's upscale restaurant/bar boasts views over London and St. Paul's, with al fresco dining in good weather (Barge House Street, Tube: Blackfriars, tel. 020/7803-3888, www.harveynichols.com/restaurants/oxo-tower-london).

London Hiltonhh Park Lane: You'll spot Buckingham Palace, Hyde Park, and the London Eye from Galvin at Windows, a 28th-floor restaurant/bar in an otherwise nondescript hotel (22 Park Lane, Tube: Hyde Park Corner, tel. 020/7208-4021, www.galvinatwindows.com).

Primrose Hill: For dramatic 360-degree city views, head to the huge grassy expanse at the summit of Primrose Hill, just north of Regent's Park (off Prince Albert Road, Tube: Chalk Farm or Camden Town, www.royalparks.gov.uk/The-Regents-Park).

The Thames River: Various companies offer boat trips on the Thames, offering a unique vantage point and unobstructed, ever-changing views of great landmarks (see page 73).

Royal Observatory Greenwich: Enjoy sweeping views of Greenwich's grand buildings in the foreground, the Docklands' skyscrapers in the middle ground, and The City and central London in the distance.

and epitaph (written in Latin): "Reader, if you seek his monument, look around you."

Near St. Paul's Cathedral

▲**Old Bailey**—To view the British legal system in action— lawyers in little blonde wigs speaking legalese with a British accent—spend a few minutes in the visitors' gallery at the Old Bailey, called the "Central Criminal Court." Don't enter under the dome; continue down the block about halfway to the modern part of the building—the entry is at Warwick Passage.

Cost and Hours: Free, generally Mon-Fri 9:45-13:00 & 14:00-16:30 depending on caseload, closed Sat-Sun, reduced hours in Aug; no kids under 14; no bags, mobile phones, cameras, iPods, or food, but small purses OK; Eddie, at Bailey's Café across the street at #27, stores bags for £2; 2 blocks northwest of St. Paul's on Old Bailey Street, follow signs to public entrance, Tube: St. Paul's, tel. 020/7248-3277.

▲**Museum of London**—This museum tells the fascinating story of London, taking you on a walk from its pre-Roman beginnings to the present. It features London's distinguished citizens through history—from Neanderthals, to Romans, to Elizabethans, to Victorians, to Mods, to today. The museum's displays are chrono- logical, spacious, and informative without being overwhelming. Scale models and costumes help you visualize everyday life in the city at different periods. In the last room, you'll see the museum's prized possession: the Lord Mayor's Coach, a golden carriage pulled by six white horses, looking as if it pranced right out of the pages of *Cinderella*. There are enough whiz-bang multimedia dis- plays (including ones on the Plague and the Great Fire) to spice up otherwise humdrum artifacts. This regular stop for the local school kids gives the best overview of London history in town.

Cost and Hours: Free, daily 10:00-18:00, galleries shut down 30 minutes before closing, see the day's events board for special talks and tours, on London Wall at Aldersgate Street, Tube: Barbican or St. Paul's plus a five-minute walk, tel. 020/7814-5660, www.museumoflondon.org.uk.

The Monument—Wren's 202-foot-tall tribute to London's Great Fire was recently restored. Climb the 331 steps inside the column for a view of The City that is still monumental.

Cost and Hours: £3, daily 9:30-17:30, last entry at 17:00, junc- tion of Monument Street and Fish Street Hill, Tube: Monument, tel. 020/7626-2717, www.themonument.info.

▲▲▲Tower of London

The Tower has served as a castle in wartime, a king's residence in peacetime, and, most notoriously, as the prison and execution site

of rebels. You can see the crown jewels, take a witty Beefeater tour, and ponder the executioner's block that dispensed with Anne Boleyn, Sir Thomas More, and troublesome heirs to the throne.

Cost and Hours: £18, family-£50, entry fee includes Beefeater tour (described later), skip the £4 audioguide; March-Oct Tue-Sat 9:00-17:30, Sun-Mon 10:00-17:30; Nov-Feb Tue-Sat 9:00-16:30, Sun-Mon 10:00-16:30; last entry 30 minutes before closing; Tube: Tower Hill, switchboard tel. 0844-482-7777, www.hrp.org.uk.

Advance Tickets: To avoid the long ticket-buying lines at the Tower, buy your ticket at the Trader's Gate gift shop, located down the steps from the Tower Hill Tube stop; at the Tower Welcome Centre to the left of the normal ticket lines (credit card only); or at any London TI at no extra cost. It's also easy to book online (www.hrp.org.uk, £1 discount, no fee) or by phone (tel. 0844-482-7799 within UK or tel. 011-44-20-3166-6000 from the US, £2 fee), then pick up your tickets at the Tower.

More Crowd-Beating Tips: It's most crowded in summer, on weekends (especially Sundays), and during school holidays. Any time of year, the line for the crown jewels—the best on earth—can be just as long as the line for tickets. For fewer crowds, arrive before 10:00 and go straight for the jewels, then tour the rest of the Tower. Crowds die down after 16:30.

Yeoman Warder (Beefeater) Tours: Today, while the Tower's military purpose is history, it's still home to the Beefeaters—the 35 Yeoman Warders and their families. (The original duty of the Yeoman Warders was to guard the Tower, its prisoners, and the jewels.) The free, worthwhile, one-hour Beefeater tours leave every 30 minutes from inside the gate (last one at 15:30, 14:30 in winter, they take a midday lunch break). The boisterous Beefeaters are great entertainers, and their talks include lots of bloody anecdotes about the Tower and its history.

Sunday Worship: For a refreshingly different Tower experience, come on Sunday mornings, when visitors are welcome on the grounds for free to worship in the Royal Chapel. You get in without the lines, but you can only see the chapel—no sightseeing (9:15 Communion or 11:00 service with fine choral music, meet at west gate 30 minutes early, dress for church, may be closed for ceremonies—call ahead).

Touring the Tower: William I, still getting used to his new title of "the Conqueror," built the stone **White Tower** (1077-1097)

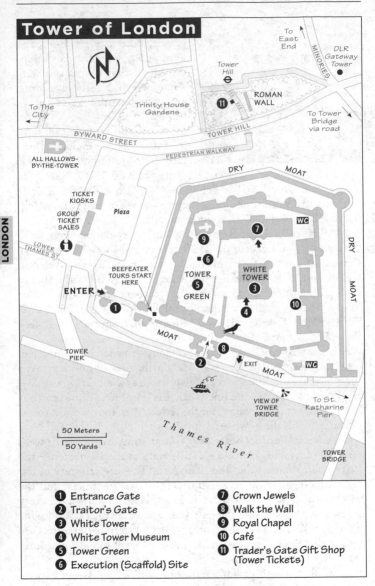

Tower of London

N

To East End

MINORIES

DLR Gateway Tower

Tower Hill

ROMAN WALL

To The City

Trinity House Gardens

11

To Tower Bridge via road

BYWARD STREET

TOWER HILL

PEDESTRIAN WALKWAY

ALL HALLOWS-BY-THE-TOWER

DRY   MOAT

TICKET KIOSKS

GROUP TICKET SALES

Plaza

9

WC

7

LOWER THAMES ST.

i

BEEFEATER TOURS START HERE

6

WHITE TOWER

DRY

ENTER

TOWER GREEN

5

3

10

MOAT

1

4

TOWER PIER

MOAT

8

2

EXIT   MOAT   WC

VIEW OF TOWER BRIDGE

To St. Katharine Pier

Thames River

50 Meters

50 Yards

TOWER BRIDGE

LONDON

1 Entrance Gate
2 Traitor's Gate
3 White Tower
4 White Tower Museum
5 Tower Green
6 Execution (Scaffold) Site

7 Crown Jewels
8 Walk the Wall
9 Royal Chapel
10 Café
11 Trader's Gate Gift Shop (Tower Tickets)

to keep the Londoners in line. Standing high above the rest of old London, the White Tower provided a gleaming reminder of the monarch's absolute power over his subjects. If you made the wrong move here, you could be feasting on roast boar in the Banqueting Hall one night and chained to the walls of the prison the next. It also served as an effective lookout for seeing invaders coming up the Thames.

The square, 90-foot-tall tower was the original structure that gave this castle complex of 20 towers its name. William's successors enlarged the complex to its present 18-acre size. Because of the security it provided, the Tower of London has served over the centuries as the Royal Mint, the Royal Jewel House, and as a prison and execution site.

Inside the White Tower is a **museum** with exhibits re-creating medieval life and the Tower's bloody history of torture and executions. In the Royal Armory, you'll see suits of armor of Henry VIII—slender in his youth (c. 1515), heavyset by 1540—with his bigger-is-better codpiece. On the top floor, see the Tower's actual execution ax and chopping block.

You'll find more bloody history per square inch in this original tower of power than anywhere else in Britain, though the actual **execution site** (in the middle of the Tower Green) looks just like a lawn. It was here that enemies of the crown would kneel before the king for the final time. With their hands tied behind their backs, they would say a final prayer, then lay their heads on a block, and—*shlit*—the blade would slice through their necks, their heads tumbling to the ground. Tower Green was the most prestigious execution site. Henry VIII axed a couple of his ex-wives here, including Anne Boleyn and his fifth wife, teenage Catherine Howard.

The Tower's hard stone and glittering **crown jewels** represent the ultimate power of the monarch. The Sovereign's Scepter is encrusted with the world's largest cut diamond—the 530-carat Star of Africa, beefy as a quarter-pounder. The Crown of the Queen Mother (Elizabeth II's famous mum, who died in 2002) has the 106-carat Koh-I-Noor diamond glittering on the front (considered unlucky for male rulers, it only adorns the crown of the king's wife). The Imperial State Crown is what the Queen wears for official functions, such as the annual opening of Parliament. Among its 3,733 jewels are Queen Elizabeth I's former earrings (the hanging pearls, top center), a stunning 13th-century ruby look-alike in the center, and Edward the Confessor's ring (the blue sapphire on top, in the center of the Maltese cross of diamonds).

The Tower was defended by state-of-the-art **walls** and fortifications in the 13th century. Walking along them offers a good look at the walls, along with a fine view of the famous Tower Bridge, with its twin towers and blue spans (described next).

After your visit, consider taking the boat to Greenwich from here (see cruise info on page 73).

Near the Tower of London

Tower Bridge—The iconic Tower Bridge (often mistakenly called London Bridge) has been recently painted and restored. The hydraulically powered drawbridge was built in 1894 to accommodate the growing East End. While fully modern, its design was a retro Neo-Gothic look.

You can tour the bridge at the **Tower Bridge Exhibition,** with a history display and a peek at the Victorian engine room that lifts the span. It's overpriced at £8, though the city views from the walkways are spectacular (daily 10:00-18:00 in summer, 9:30-17:30 in winter, last entry 30 minutes before closing, enter at the northwest tower, Tube: Tower Hill, tel. 020/7403-3761, www.tower bridge.org.uk).

The bridge is most interesting when the drawbridge lifts to let ships pass, as it does a thousand times a year, but it's best viewed from outside the museum. For the bridge-lifting schedule, check the website or call (see above for contact info).

Nearby: The best remaining bit of London's **Roman Wall** is just north of the Tower (at the Tower Hill Tube station). The chic **St. Katharine Dock,** just east of Tower Bridge, has private yachts, mod shops, the Medieval Banquet (see page 193), and the classic Dickens Inn, fun for a drink or pub lunch. Across the bridge is the South Bank, with the upscale Butlers Wharf area, City Hall, museums, and the Jubilee Walkway.

Sights in East London

▲**East End**—This formerly industrial area just beyond the Liverpool Street train and Tube stations has turned into one of London's trendy spots. It boasts a colorful mix of bustling markets, late-night dance clubs, the Bangladeshi ghetto (called "Banglatown"), and tenements of Jack the Ripper's London, all in the shadow of glittering new skyscrapers. Head up Brick Lane for a meal in "the curry capital of Europe," or check out the former Truman Brewery, which now houses a Sunday market, cool shops, and Café 1001 (good coffee). This neighborhood is best on Sunday afternoons, when the Spitalfields, Petticoat Lane, and Brick Lane markets thrive (for more on these markets, see page 147).

▲**Geffrye Museum**—This low-key but well-organized museum—housed in an 18th-century almshouse northeast of The City—is located north of Liverpool Street Station in the hip Shoreditch area. Walk past 11 English living rooms, furnished and decorated in styles from 1600 to 2000, then descend the circular stairs to see changing exhibits on home decor. In summer, explore the fragrant herb garden.

Cost and Hours: Free, Tue-Sat 10:00-17:00, Sun 12:00-17:00, closed Mon, garden open April-Oct, 136 Kingsland Road, tel. 020/7739-9893, www.geffrye-museum.org.uk.

Getting There: Take the Tube to Liverpool Street, then it's a 10-minute ride north on bus #149 or #242. Or take the East London line on the Overground to the Hoxton stop, which is right next to the museum (Tube tickets and Oyster cards also valid on Overground).

Sights on the South Bank

▲Jubilee Walkway—The South Bank is a thriving arts and cultural center tied together by this riverside path, a popular,  pub-crawling pedestrian promenade called the Jubilee Walkway. Stretching from Tower Bridge past Westminster Bridge, it offers grand views of the Houses of Parliament and St. Paul's. On a sunny day, this is the place to see London out strolling. The Walkway hugs the river except just east of London Bridge, where it cuts inland for a couple of blocks. Plans are under way to expand the path into a 60-mile "Greenway" that will circle the city, scheduled to open in 2012 for the Olympic Games and Elizabeth's 60th year as Queen (www.jubileewalkway.org.uk).

▲▲London Eye—This giant Ferris wheel, towering above London opposite Big Ben, is the world's highest observational  wheel and London's answer to the Eiffel Tower. While the experience is memorable, London doesn't have much of a skyline, and the price is borderline outrageous. But whether you ride or not, the wheel is a sight to behold.

The experience starts with a brief (four-minute), engaging show combining a 3-D movie with wind and water effects. Then it's time to spin around the Eye. Designed like a giant bicycle wheel, it's a pan-European undertaking: British steel and Dutch engineering, with Czech, German, French, and Italian mechanical parts. It's also very "green," running extremely efficiently and virtually silently. Twenty-five people ride in each of its 32 air-conditioned capsules for the 30-minute rotation (you go around only once). Each capsule has a bench, but most people stand. From

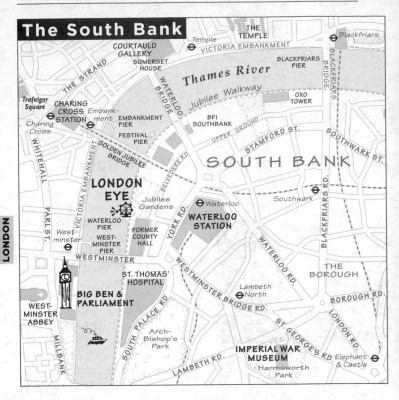

The South Bank

THE STRAND

COURTAULD GALLERY
SOMERSET HOUSE

Temple
⊖ VICTORIA EMBANKMENT
THE TEMPLE

Thames River

Jubilee Walkway

⊖ Blackfriars

BLACKFRIARS BRIDGE

Trafalgar Square

CHARING CROSS STATION ⊖
Charing Cross

Embank-
ment ⊖

EMBANKMENT PIER

WATERLOO BRIDGE

BFI SOUTHBANK

OXO TOWER

BLACKFRIARS PIER

WHITEHALL

FESTIVAL PIER

UPPER GROUND

STAMFORD ST.

SOUTHWARK ST.

GOLDEN JUBILEE BRIDGE

VICTORIA EMBANKMENT

BELVEDERE RD.

SOUTH BANK

LONDON EYE

Jubilee Gardens

⊖ Waterloo

Southwark ⊖

BLACKFRIARS RD.

PARL ST.

WATERLOO PIER

West-
minster ⊖

FORMER COUNTY HALL

WEST-
MINSTER PIER

YORK RD.

WATERLOO STATION

WATERLOO RD.

WESTMINSTER

THE BOROUGH

ST. THOMAS' HOSPITAL

WESTMINSTER BRIDGE RD.

Lambeth North ⊖

BOROUGH RD.

BIG BEN & PARLIAMENT

WEST-
MINSTER ABBEY

Arch-
Bishop's Park

SOUTH PALACE RD.

ST. GEORGE'S RD.

LONDON RD.

MILLBANK

LAMBETH RD.

IMPERIAL WAR MUSEUM

Harmsworth Park

⊖ Elephant & Castle

LONDON

the top of this 443-foot-high wheel—the highest public viewpoint in the city—even Big Ben looks small.

Cost: £19, or pay roughly twice as much for a combo-ticket with Madame Tussauds Waxworks (sold cheaper online), other packages available. Buy tickets at the box office (in the corner of the County Hall building nearest the Eye), in advance by calling 0870-500-0600, or save 10 percent by booking online at www.londoneye.com.

Hours: Daily July-Aug 10:00-21:30, April-June 10:00-21:00, Sept-March 10:00-20:00, these are last-ascent times, closed Dec 25 and a few days in Jan for annual maintenance, Tube: Waterloo or Westminster. Thames boats come and go from Waterloo Pier at the foot of the wheel.

Crowd-Beating Tips: The London Eye is busiest between 11:00 and 17:00, especially on weekends year-round and every day in July and August. When it's crowded, you might have to wait up to 30 minutes to buy your ticket, then another 30-45 minutes to board your capsule. If you plan to visit during a busy time, call ahead or go online to pre-book your ticket, then punch your confirmation code into the automated machine in the ticket office (no

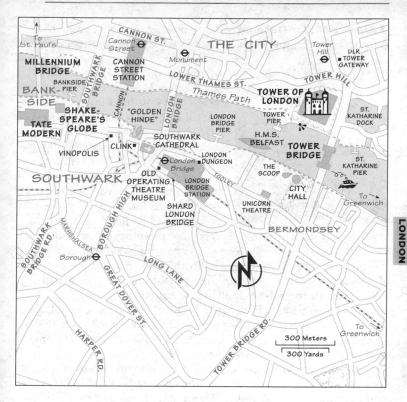

wait to get the ticket, but you'll still wait to board the wheel). You can pay an extra £10 for a Fast Track ticket that lets you jump the queue, but the time you save is probably not worth the expense.

By the Eye: The area next to the London Eye has developed a cotton-candy ambience of kitschy, kid-friendly attractions. There's an aquarium, game arcade, and "Movieum" dedicated to movies filmed in London, from *Harry Potter* to *Star Wars*.

Southwark

These sights are in Southwark (SUTH-uck), the core of the tourist's South Bank. Southwark was for centuries the place Londoners would go to escape the rules and decency of the city and let their hair down. Bearbaiting, brothels, rollicking pubs, and theater—you name the dream, and it could be fulfilled just across the Thames. A run-down warehouse district through the 20th century, it's been gentrified with classy restaurants, office parks, pedestrian promenades, major sights (such as the Tate Modern and Shakespeare's Globe), and a colorful collection of lesser sights. The area is easy on foot and a scenic—though circuitous—way to connect the Tower of London with St. Paul's.

▲▲Imperial War Museum—This impressive museum covers the wars of the last century—from World War I biplanes, to the rise of

fascism, to Montgomery's Africa campaign tank, to the Cold War, the Cuban Missile Crisis, the Troubles in Northern Ireland, the wars in Iraq, and terrorism. Rather than glorify war, the museum does its best to shine a light on the 100 million deaths of the 20th century. It shows everyday life for people back home and never neglects the powerful human side of one of humankind's most persistent

traits. Allow plenty of time, as this powerful museum—with lots of artifacts and video clips—can be engrossing. War wonks love the place, as do general history buffs who enjoy patiently reading displays. For the rest, there are enough multimedia exhibits and submarines for the kids to climb in to keep it interesting.

Cost and Hours: Free, daily 10:00-18:00, last entry 17:45, temporary exhibits extra, £4 audioguide, often guided tours on weekends—ask at info desk, Tube: Lambeth North, bus #12 or #159, tel. 020/7416-5000, www.iwm.org.uk.

Touring the Museum: The core of the **permanent collection,** located downstairs, takes you step-by-step through World Wars I and II. A special exhibit called "Monty: Master of the Battlefield" celebrates Field Marshal Bernard Montgomery. Then you move on to conflicts since 1945. Most of the displays are low-tech—glass cases hold dummies in uniforms, weapons, newspaper clippings, ordinary objects from daily life—but have excellent explanations and video clips. The Trench Experience lets you walk through a dark, chaotic, smelly WWI trench. The Blitz Experience film assaults the senses with the noise and intensity of a WWII air raid on London. Also, the cinema shows a rotating selection of films.

In the entry hall are the **large exhibits**—including Monty's

tank, several field guns, and, dangling overhead, vintage planes. Imagine the awesome power of the 50-foot V-2 rocket, the kind the Nazis rained down on London, which could arrive silently and destroy a city block. Its direct descendant is the Polaris missile, capable of traveling nearly 3,000 miles in 20 minutes and obliterating an entire city.

Two other sections are not to be missed: The **"Secret War"** peeks into the intrigues of espionage in World Wars I and II and in conflicts since. The section on the **Holocaust**, one of the best on the subject anywhere, tells the story with powerful videos, artifacts, and fine explanations.

The museum (which sits in an inviting park equipped with an equally inviting café) is housed in what was the Royal Bethlam Hospital. Also known as "the Bedlam asylum," the place was so wild that it gave the world a new word for chaos. Back in Victorian times, locals—without reality shows and YouTube—paid admission to visit the asylum on weekends for entertainment.

▲▲**Tate Modern**—Dedicated in the spring of 2000, the striking museum across the river from St. Paul's opened the new century

with art from the previous one. Its powerhouse collection of Monet, Matisse, Dalí, Picasso, Warhol, and much more is displayed in a converted powerhouse.

The permanent collection is on the third and fifth floors. Paintings are arranged according to theme, not chronologically or by artist. Paintings by Picasso, for example, are scattered all over the building. Don't just come to see the Old Masters of modernism. Push your mental envelope with more recent works by Pollock, Miró, Bacon, Picabia, Beuys, Twombly, and others.

Of equal interest are the many temporary exhibits featuring cutting-edge art. Each year, the main hall features a different monumental installation by a prominent artist—always one of the highlights of the art world. Note that the Tate is constructing an expansion wing to the south, which will double its exhibition space. Some parts may open in 2012.

Cost and Hours: Free, £3 donations appreciated, varying costs for temporary exhibits, £3.50 audioguide; daily 10:00-18:00, Fri-Sat until 22:00, last entry to temporary exhibitions 45 minutes before closing, museum especially crowded on weekend days (crowds thin out on Fri and Sat evenings); free 45-minute guided tours offered daily on Level 3 at 11:00 and 12:00, and on Level 5 at 14:00 and 15:00 (confirm at info desk); tel. 020/7887-8888, www.tate.org.uk.

Getting There: Cross the Millennium Bridge from St. Paul's; take Tube to Southwark, London Bridge, or Mansion House and walk 10-15 minutes; or connect by "Tate to Tate" boat from Tate Britain (£5.50 one-way or £12.60 for day ticket, 33 percent discount with Travelcard, buy ticket on board, departs every 40 minutes

Crossing the Thames on Foot

You can cross the Thames on any of the bridges that carry car traffic over the river, but London's two pedestrian bridges are more fun. The Millennium Bridge (see photo) connects the sedate St. Paul's Cathedral with the great Tate Modern. The Golden Jubilee Bridge, well-lit with a sleek, futuristic look, links bustling Trafalgar Square on the North Bank with the London Eye and Waterloo Station on the South Bank.

from 9:55 to 17:00, 18 minutes, check schedule at www.tate.org.uk /tatetotate).

▲**Millennium Bridge**—The pedestrian bridge links St. Paul's Cathedral and the Tate Modern across the Thames. This is London's first new bridge in a century. When it first opened, the $25 million bridge wiggled when people walked on it, so it promptly closed for an $8 million, 20-month stabilization; now it's stable and open again. Nicknamed the "blade of light" for its sleek minimalist design (370 yards long, four yards wide, stainless steel with teak planks), its clever aerodynamic handrails deflect wind over the heads of pedestrians.

▲▲**Shakespeare's Globe**—This replica of the original Globe Theatre was built, half-timbered and thatched, as it was in Shakespeare's time. (This is the first thatched roof constructed in London since they were outlawed after the Great Fire of 1666.) The Globe originally accommodated 2,200 seated patrons and another 1,000 standing. Today, slightly smaller and leaving space for reasonable aisles, the theater holds

800 seated and 600 groundlings. Its promoters brag that the theater melds "the three A's"—actors, audience, and architecture—with each contributing to the play. The working theater hosts authentic performances of Shakespeare's plays with actors in period costumes, modern interpretations of his works, and some works by other playwrights. For details on attending a play, see page 155.

The complex has three parts: the theater itself, the box office,

and a museum. The Globe Exhibition ticket includes both a tour of the theater and the museum.

Museum: First, you browse on your own through displays of Elizabethan-era costumes, music, script-printing, and special effects. There are early folios and objects that were dug up on site. A video and scale models help put Shakespearean theater within the context of the times. (The Globe opened one year after England mastered the seas by defeating the Spanish Armada. The debut play was Shakespeare's *Julius Caesar.*)

Theater: You must tour the theater at the time stamped on your ticket, but you can come back to the museum afterward; tick-

ets are good all day. The guide (usually an actor) leads you into the theater to see the stage and the various seating areas for the different classes of people. You take a seat and learn how the new Globe is similar to the old Globe (open-air performances, standing-room by the stage, no curtain) and how it's different (female actors today, lights for night performances, concrete floor). It's not a backstage tour—you don't see dressing rooms or costume shops or sit in on rehearsals, though you may see workers building sets for a new production. You mostly sit and listen. The guides are energetic, theatrical, and knowledgeable, bringing the Elizabethan period to life.

When matinee performances are going on, you can't tour the theater. But you can see the museum, then tour the nearby (and less interesting) Rose Theatre instead.

Cost and Hours: £11.50 includes museum and 40-minute tour, £9 when only the Rose Theatre is available for touring, tickets good all day; complex open daily 9:00-17:00; exhibition and tours: May-Sept—Globe tours offered mornings only with Rose Theatre tours in afternoon; Oct-April—Globe tours run all day, tours start every 15-30 minutes; on the South Bank directly across Thames over Southwark Bridge from St. Paul's, Tube: Mansion House or London Bridge plus a 10-minute walk; tel. 020/7902-1400 or 020/7902-1500, www.shakespeares-globe.org.

Eating: The Swan at the Globe café offers a sit-down res-taurant (for lunch and dinner, reservations recommended, tel. 020/7928-9444), a drinks-and-plates bar, and a sandwich-and-coffee cart (daily 9:00-closing, depending on performance times).

Vinopolis: City of Wine—While it seems illogical to have a huge wine museum in beer-loving London, Vinopolis makes a good case. Built over a Roman wine store and filling the massive

vaults of an old wine warehouse,
the museum offers an excellent audioguide with a light
yet earnest history of wine to
accompany your sips of various
mediocre reds and whites, ports,
and champagnes. Allow some
time, as the audioguide takes
an hour and a half—and the
sipping can slow things down

pleasantly. This place is popular. Booking ahead for Friday and
Saturday nights is a must.

Cost and Hours: Self-guided tour options range from £20
to £40—each includes about five wine tastes and an audioguide.
Other options are available for guided tours. Some packages also
include whiskey (the new wine), other spirits, or a meal. Open Thu-
Fri 14:00-22:00, Sat 12:00-22:00, Sun 12:00-18:00, closed Mon-
Wed, last entry 2.5 hours before closing, between Shakespeare's
Globe and Southwark Cathedral at 1 Bank End, Tube: London
Bridge, tel. 020/7940-3000, www.vinopolis.co.uk.

The Clink Prison Museum—Proudly the "original clink," this
was, until 1780, where law-abiding citizens threw Southwark trou-
blemakers. Today, it's a low-tech torture museum filling grotty old
rooms with papier-mâché gore. Unfortunately, there's little that
seriously deals with the fascinating problem of law and order in
Southwark, where 18th-century Londoners went for a good time.

Cost and Hours: Overpriced at £6; July-Sept daily 10:00-
21:00; Oct-June Mon-Fri 10:00-18:00, Sat-Sun until 19:30; 1 Clink
Street, Tube: London Bridge, tel. 020/7403-0900, www.clink
.co.uk.

***Golden Hinde* Replica**—This is a full-size replica of the 16th-
century warship in which Sir Francis Drake circumnavigated the
globe from 1577 to 1580. Commanding this ship, Drake earned his
reputation as history's most successful pirate. The original is long
gone, but this boat has logged more than 100,000 miles, including
a voyage around the world. While the ship is fun to see, its interior
is not worth touring.

Cost and Hours: £6, daily 10:00-17:30, sometimes closed for
private events, Tube: London Bridge, tel. 020/7403-0123, www
.goldenhinde.com.

Southwark Cathedral—While made a cathedral only in 1905,
it's been the neighborhood church since the 13th century, and
comes with some interesting history. The enthusiastic docents give
impromptu tours if you ask.

Cost and Hours: Free, but £4 suggested donation, daily 8:00-
18:00, last entry 30 minutes before closing, £2.50 guidebook, no

photos without permission, Tube: London Bridge. Tel. 020/7367-6700, http://cathedral.southwark.anglican.org.

Music: The cathedral hosts evensong services (Mon-Tue and Thu-Fri at 17:30, Sat at 16:00, Sun at 15:00, no service on Wed or alternate Mon).

▲**Old Operating Theatre Museum and Herb Garret**—Climb a tight and creaky wooden spiral staircase to a church attic where you'll find a garret used to dry medicinal herbs, a fascinating exhibit on Victorian surgery, cases of well-described 19th-century medical paraphernalia, and a special look at "anesthesia, the defeat of pain." Then you stumble upon Britain's oldest operating theater, where limbs were sawed off way back in 1821. The museum occasionally offers "demonstrations." While fun and interesting to some, they can be distressing to those who are squeamish or have a vivid imagination.

Cost and Hours: £6, cash only, daily 10:30-16:45, closed Dec 15-Jan 5, 9a St. Thomas Street, Tube: London Bridge, tel. 020/7188-2679, www.thegarret.org.uk.

HMS *Belfast*—"The last big-gun armored warship of World War II" clogs the Thames just upstream from the Tower Bridge. This huge vessel—now manned with wax sailors—thrills kids who always dreamed of sitting in a turret shooting off their imaginary guns. If you're into WWII warships, this is the ultimate. Otherwise, it's just lots of exercise with a nice view of the Tower Bridge.

Cost and Hours: £13.50, includes audioguide, daily March-Oct 10:00-18:00, Nov-Feb 10:00-17:00, last entry one hour before closing, Tube: London Bridge, tel. 020/7940-6300, http://hmsbelfast.iwm.org.uk.

City Hall—The glassy, egg-shaped building near the south end of Tower Bridge is London's City Hall, designed by Sir Norman Foster, the architect who worked on London's Millennium Bridge and Berlin's Reichstag. City Hall houses the office of London's

mayor—the blonde, flamboyant, conservative former journalist and author Boris Johnson. He consults here with the Assembly representatives of the city's 25 districts. An interior spiral ramp allows visitors to watch and hear the action below in the Assembly Chamber—ride the lift to the second floor (the highest visitors can go) and spiral down. On the lower ground floor is a large aerial photograph of London, an information desk, and a handy cafeteria. Next to City Hall is the outdoor amphitheater called The Scoop.

Cost and Hours: Free, open to visitors Mon-Thu 8:30-18:00, Fri 8:30-17:30, closed Sat-Sun; Tube: London Bridge station plus 10-minute walk, or Tower Hill station plus 15-minute walk; tel. 020/7983-4000, www.london.gov.uk.

Sights in West London

▲▲**Tate Britain**—One of Europe's great art houses, Tate Britain specializes in British painting from the 16th century through modern times. This is people's art,

with realistic paintings rooted in the culture, landscape, and stories of the British Isles. But the museum will be under renovation in 2012, and during this time, much of the permanent collection has been stored. Fortunately, a few paintings are on display in a single room, labeled "Key Works from the Historic Collection."

Look for Hogarth's sketches of gritty London life, Gainsborough's twinkle-toe ladies, Blake's glowing angels, Constable's clouds, the swooning realism of the Pre-Raphaelites, and room after room of J. M. W. Turner's proto-Impressionist tempests. In the modern art wing there are Francis Bacon's screaming nightmares, Henry Moore statues, and the camera-eye portraits of Hockney and Freud.

Even if these names are new to you, don't worry. You'll likely see a few "famous" works you didn't know were British and exit the Tate Britain with at least one new favorite artist.

Cost and Hours: Free, but £3 donation requested, admission fee for (optional) temporary exhibits, £1 map, £3.50 audioguide; daily 10:00-18:00, first Fri of the month until 22:00, last entry to special exhibitions at 17:15 (or 21:00 when open late); free tours on various topics offered throughout the day—ask at information desk or call ahead; switchboard tel. 020/7887-8888, recorded info tel. 020/7887-8008, www.tate.org.uk.

Getting There: It's on the Thames River, south of Big Ben and north of Vauxhall Bridge. Take the Tube to Pimlico, then walk seven minutes. Or hop on the "Tate to Tate" boat from the Tate Modern (£5.50 one-way, £12.60 day ticket, 33 percent discount with a Travelcard, buy ticket on board, departs every 40 minutes from 10:00 to 17:00, 18 minutes, www.tate.org.uk/tatetotate).

▲**Apsley House (Wellington Museum)**—Having beaten Napoleon at Waterloo, Arthur Wellesley, the First Duke of Wellington, was once the most famous man in Europe. He was

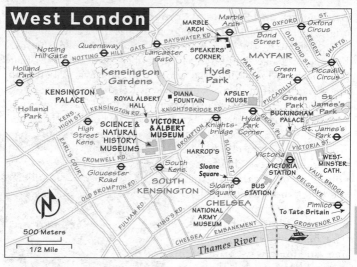

West London

MARBLE ARCH — Marble Arch — OXFORD — Oxford Circus — ST.
Notting Hill Gate — Queensway — BAYSWATER RD. — Bond Street — OLD BOND ST. — REGENT — SHAFTS.
NOTTING HILL GATE — Lancaster Gate — SPEAKERS' CORNER — PARK LN. — MAYFAIR — Green Park — Piccadilly Circus
Holland Park — Kensington Gardens — Hyde Park — Green Park — St. James's Park
KENSINGTON PALACE — ROYAL ALBERT HALL — DIANA FOUNTAIN — APSLEY HOUSE — PICCADILLY — BUCKINGHAM PALACE
Holland Park — KENSINGTON RD. — KNIGHTSBRIDGE RD. — Hyde Park Corner — St. James's Park
KENS. HIGH ST. — SCIENCE & NATURAL HISTORY MUSEUMS — VICTORIA & ALBERT MUSEUM — Knights-bridge — BROMPTON RD. — SLOANE ST. — Victoria — VICTORIA ST. — WEST-MINSTER CATH.
High Street Kens. — EARL'S COURT — HARROD'S — VICTORIA STATION — VAUX. BRIDGE
CROMWELL RD. — South Kens. — BUS STATION — BELGRAVE
Gloucester Road — SOUTH KENSINGTON — Sloane Square — Pimlico
OLD BROMPTON RD. — KING'S RD. — Sloane Square — To Tate Britain → — GROSVENOR RD.
FULHAM RD. — CHELSEA — NATIONAL ARMY MUSEUM
500 Meters — CHELSEA EMBANKMENT
1/2 Mile — Thames River

LONDON

given a huge fortune with which he purchased London's ultimate address, #1 London. His refurbished mansion offers a nice interior,

a handful of world-class paintings, and a glimpse at the life of the great soldier and two-time prime minister. The highlight is the large ballroom, the Waterloo Gallery, decorated with Anthony van Dyck's *Charles I on Horseback* (over the main fireplace), Diego Velázquez's earthy *The Water-Seller of Seville* (to the left of Van Dyck), Jan Steen's playful *The Dissolute Household* (to the right), and a large portrait of Wellington by Francisco Goya (farther right). Those who know something about Wellington ahead of time will appreciate the place much more than those who don't, as there's scarce biographical background. The place is well-described by the included audioguide, which has sound bites from the current Duke of Wellington (who still lives at Apsley).

Cost and Hours: £6.30, free on June 18—Waterloo Day, April-Oct Wed-Sun 11:00-17:00, closed Mon-Tue; Nov-March Sat-Sun 10:00-16:00, closed Mon-Fri; 20 yards from Hyde Park Corner Tube station, tel. 020/7499-5676, www.english-heritage .org.uk.

Nearby: Hyde Park's pleasant rose garden is picnic-friendly. **Wellington Arch,** which stands just across the street, is open to the public but not worth the £4 charge (elevator up, lousy views and boring exhibits).

▲**Hyde Park and Speakers' Corner**—London's "Central Park," originally Henry VIII's hunting grounds, has more than 600 acres of lush greenery, the huge man-made Serpentine Lake, the royal Kensington Palace and Orangery (described later), and the ornate Neo-Gothic Albert Memorial across from the Royal Albert Hall. The western half of the park is known as Kensington Gardens.

On Sundays, from just after noon until early evening, **Speakers' Corner** offers soapbox oratory at its best (northeast corner of the park, Tube: Marble Arch). Characters climb their stepladders, wave their flags, pound emphatically on their sandwich boards, and share what they are convinced is their wisdom. Regulars have resident hecklers who know their lines and are always ready with a verbal jab or barb. "The grass

roots of democracy" is actually a holdover from when the gallows stood here and the criminal was allowed to say just about anything he wanted to before he swung. I dare you to raise your voice and gather a crowd—it's easy to do.

The **Princess Diana Memorial Fountain** honors the "People's Princess," who once lived in nearby Kensington Palace. The low-key circular stream, great for cooling off your feet on a hot day, is in the south-central part of the park, near the Albert Memorial and Serpentine Gallery. (Don't be confused by signs to the Diana, Princess of Wales Memorial Playground, in the northwest corner of the park.)

▲▲▲**Victoria and Albert Museum**—The world's top collection of decorative arts (vases, stained glass, fine furniture, clothing, jewelry, carpets, and more) is a surprisingly interesting assortment of crafts from the West, as well as from Asian and Islamic cultures. The British Galleries are grand, but there's much more to see, including Raphael's tapestry cartoons and a cast of Trajan's Column that depicts the emperor's conquests.

You'll also see one of Leonardo da Vinci's notebooks, underwear through the ages, a Chihuly chandelier, a life-size *David* with detachable fig leaf, Henry VIII's quill pen, and Mick Jagger's sequined jumpsuit. From the worlds of Islam and India, there are stunning carpets, the ring of the man who built the Taj Mahal, and a mechanical tiger that eats Brits.

Best of all, the objects are all quite beautiful. You could spend days in the place. Pick up a museum map and wander at will.

Cost and Hours: Free, but £5 donation requested, sometimes pricey fees for (optional) special exhibits, £1 suggested donation for much-needed museum map; daily 10:00-17:45, some galleries open Fri until 22:00, free one-hour tours daily on the half-hour 10:30-15:30; on Cromwell Road in South Kensington, Tube: South Kensington, from the Tube station a long tunnel leads directly to museum; tel. 020/7942-2000, www.vam.ac.uk.

▲▲**Natural History Museum**—Across the street from Victoria and Albert, this mammoth museum is housed in a giant and

wonderful Victorian, Neo-Romanesque building. In the main hall, above a big dinosaur skeleton and under a massive slice of sequoia tree, Charles Darwin sits as if upon a throne overseeing it all. Built in the 1870s specifi-cally for the huge collection (50 million specimens), the building has two halves: the Life Galleries (creepy-crawlies, human biol-ogy, "our place in evolution," and awe-inspiring dinosaurs) and the Earth Galleries (meteors, volcanoes, earthquakes, and so on).

Exhibits are wonderfully explained, with lots of creative, inter-active displays. Pop in, if only for the wild collection of dinosaurs and to hear English children exclaim, "Oh my goodness!" Get ori-ented by talking with one of the many "visit planners" (helpful guides scattered throughout the museum), review the "What's on Today" board for special events and tours, and note which sections are closed (rather than "renovating," they say "we are evolving"). While the dinosaur hall often has a long line, everything else is wide open. Don't miss the vault in the mineralogy section (top floor of the green zone), with rare and precious stones, including a meteorite from Mars and the Aurora Pyramid of Hope, displaying 296 diamonds showing their full range of natural colors.

Cost and Hours: Free, fees for special exhibits, daily 10:00-17:50, last entry at 17:30, occasional tours, long tunnel leads directly from South Kensington Tube station to museum, tel. 020/7942-5000, exhibit info and reservations tel. 020/7942-5011, www.nhm.ac.uk.

▲**Science Museum**—Next door to the Natural History Museum, this sprawling wonderland for curious minds is kid-perfect, with themes such as measuring time, exploring space, climate change, and the evolution of modern medicine. It offers hands-on fun, from moonwalks to deep-sea exploration, with trendy technology exhibits and a state-of-the-art IMAX theater (£10, kids-£8)

Cost and Hours: Free, daily 10:00-18:00, Exhibition Road, Tube: South Kensington, tel. 0870-870-4868, www.science museum.org.uk.

Kensington Palace—In 2012, this historic palace will reopen after a major renovation. A new permanent exhibit, "Victoria Revealed," will showcase the life and times of Britain's longest-ruling monarch. The palace was once the residence of King William and Queen Mary, who moved from Whitehall in central London in 1689 to the more pristine and peaceful village of Kensington (now engulfed by London). Sir Christopher Wren converted an existing house into the palace, which became the center of English court life until 1760, when the royal family moved into Buckingham Palace. Since then, lesser royals have bedded down in Kensington Palace. Princess Diana lived here from her 1981 marriage to Prince Charles until her death in 1997. Today it's home to three of Charles' cousins. If you visit before the renovations are finished, skip the temporary and cheesy "Enchanted Palace" theatrical show.

Cost and Hours: £12.50, discounts for booking online, daily 10:00-18:00, until 17:00 in winter, last entry one hour before closing, a 10-minute hike through Kensington Gardens from either Queensway or High Street Kensington Tube station, tel. 0870-751-5170 or 0844-482-7777, www.hrp.org.uk.

Nearby: Garden enthusiasts enjoy popping into the secluded Sunken Garden, 50 yards from the exit. Consider afternoon tea at the nearby Orangery (see page 194), built as a greenhouse for Queen Anne in 1704.

Victoria Station—From underneath this station's iron-and-glass canopy, trains depart for the south of England and Gatwick Airport. While Victoria Station is famous and a major Tube stop, few tourists actually take trains from here—most just come to take in the exciting bustle. It's a fun place to just be a "rock in a river" teeming with commuters and services. The station is surrounded by big red buses and taxis, travel agencies, and lousy eateries. It's next to the main intercity bus station (Victoria Coach Station) and the best inexpensive lodgings in town.

Westminster Cathedral—This cathedral, the largest Catholic church in England and just a block from Victoria Station, is strikingly Neo-Byzantine, but not very historic or important to visit. Opened in 1903, the church has an unfinished interior, with a spooky, blackened ceiling waiting for the mosaics that are supposed to be placed there. While it's definitely not Westminster Abbey, half the tourists wandering around inside seem to think it is. Take the lift to the top of the 273-foot bell tower for a view of the glassy office blocks of Victoria Station.

Cost and Hours: Free entry, £5 for the lift, church—daily 7:00-19:00, tower—daily 9:30-17:00; 5-minute walk from Victoria Station, just off Victoria Street, Tube: Victoria, www.westminster cathedral.org.uk.

National Army Museum—This museum is not as awe-inspiring as the Imperial War Museum, but it's still fun, especially for kids who are into soldiers, armor, and guns. And while the Imperial War Museum is limited to wars of the 20th century, the National Army Museum tells the story of the British army from 1415 through the Bosnian conflict and Iraq, with lots of Redcoat lore and a good look at Waterloo. Kids enjoy trying on a Cromwellian helmet, seeing the skeleton of Napoleon's horse, and peering out from a World War I trench through a working periscope.

Cost and Hours: Free, daily 10:00-17:30, Royal Hospital Road, Chelsea, Tube: Sloane Square, tel. 020/7730-0717, www .national-army-museum.ac.uk.

Sights in Greater London

East of Central London
▲▲The Docklands
Once the primary harbor for the Port of London, the Docklands has been transformed into a vibrant business center, with ultra-tall skyscrapers, subterranean supermalls, trendy pubs, and peaceful parks with pedestrian bridges looping over canals. While not full of the touristy sights that many are seeking in London, the Docklands offers a refreshing look at the British version of a 21st-century city. It's best at the end of the workday, when it's lively with office workers. It's ideal on the way back from Greenwich, since both line up on the same train tracks. From the Docklands, it's also a relatively straightforward detour to see the Olympics 2012 sights (described next).

Getting to the Docklands from Central London: Take the Jubilee Line on the Tube to Canary Wharf station (15 minutes from Westminster, frequent departures). Or catch the Thames Clippers boat to Canary Wharf Pier (£5.50 one-way; boats leave every 20 minutes from the Waterloo, Embankment, Bankside, London Bridge, and Tower piers; 10-30-minute trip).

Combining the Docklands with Greenwich or Olympic Park: All three places lie along the north-south Docklands Light Rail train line, a few minutes apart. You could sightsee Greenwich in the morning and early afternoon, then make a brief stop at the Docklands (Canary Wharf station) on your way back to central London. To reach the Olympic Park viewing site (described later), catch a DLR train north toward Stratford and get off at the Pudding Mill Lane DLR stop.

▲**Museum of London Docklands**—Illuminating the gritty and fascinating history of this site, this museum traces the story of what was London's primary harbor. You'll see fascinating models of Old London Bridge, crammed with little houses and shops (not unlike how Florence's Ponte Vecchio still looks); a reconstruction of a "Legal Quay," where cargo was processed; and a re-creation of the fuel pipeline that was laid under the English Channel to supply the Allies on the Continent. You'll also walk through gritty "Sailortown," listening to the salty voices of those who lived and worked in quarters like these.

Cost and Hours: Free, daily 10:00-18:00, last entry 30 minutes before closing, West India Quay, Tube: West India Quay or Canary Wharf, tel. 020/7001-9844, www.museumindocklands .org.uk.

2012 London Olympic Park

From July 27 to August 12, 2012, all eyes will be on London as it hosts athletes from 205 nations in the 30th Olympiad. Though events will take place throughout the city, festivities will center around Olympic Park, filling the Lea Valley, about seven miles northeast of central London. Lea Valley used to be the site of derelict factories, mountains of discarded tires, and Europe's biggest refrigerator dump. But now, this area glistens with gardens, greenery, and state-of-the-art construction.

London is the first city to host the modern games three times—first in 1908, then in 1948 (the first post-World-War-II Olympics, known as the "Austerity Games"). The city won the 2012 bid for its grand and green vision, including a promise to permanently improve the least desirable part of the city. The site's connection to the broader world will be extraordinary: During the games, it will take less than three hours to go from Paris to Olympic Park (ride the Eurostar to St. Pancras International Station in downtown London, and connect via a seven-minute bullet train to Stratford International Station—covered by your Eurostar ticket).

These are the greenest games ever. There's no public parking at the site—event tickets include an all-day London Tube pass. About 90 percent of demolition material has been recycled. More

2012 Olympics Venues

Although most of the Olympic Games are being held in London's East End, there are sports and activities all over London and Britain. These are the main venues:

Olympic Park is the heart of the games. Here you'll find the 80,000-seat Olympic Stadium (for opening and closing ceremonies), the Olympic Village (where the athletes stay), and a giant climbable sculpture called the Orbit. A new 12,000-seat basketball arena will be completely dismantled when the games are over. The Aquatics Centre, with its swooping wave-like roofline, may become the architectural "face" of the games.

Central London is the site of—really?—beach volleyball. Tons of sand will be spread across the parking lot behind #10 Downing Street and Horse Guards, creating an urban beach ringed with bleachers. Triathletes compete in **Hyde Park,** swimming in Serpentine Lake, then biking and running around the park. **Greenwich Park** (near the *Cutty Sark;* see page 215) holds equestrian events, while the nearby **O2** arena (formerly the "Millennium Dome") hosts gymnastics and more basketball.

Farther afield, you'll find tennis at **Wimbledon** (of course), volleyball at **Earl's Court,** and football/soccer at **Wembley Stadium.** The Olympic torch will wend its way through various communities. And anywhere you go, you can't avoid the universally ridiculed Olympic mascots—those alien/Gumby/Cyclops-like creatures named Wenlock and Mandeville.

Tickets are being sold in phases through www.cosport.com (for residents of the US and Canada).

than half of the deliveries are by train or boat rather than by truck. Half a million trees have been planted, and 1.4 million tons of dirt have been cleansed of arsenic, lead, and other toxic chemicals—a reminder of this site's dirty industrial past. Locals whine about the cost—as locals have whined about big public building projects, I imagine, since the days great cities built great Gothic churches. But the $14 billion project is a stimulus plan, with 90 percent local investment and employment.

About 75 percent of the construction is "legacy building," giving these structures a practical life in a reinvigorated community after the games. Many of the buildings will be converted to housing, with half of these units designated for low-income people. Bridges leading to the site, built double-wide for huge crowds, will be scaled back. The commercial zone, Stratford City, will become the biggest shopping center in Europe. Between the bullet trains, Tube, regional rail services, and DLR, residents of post-Olympics Stratford will enjoy the best public transit in town, with multiple connections to central London. (Don't confuse it with Stratford-upon-Avon, the famous Warwickshire town where Shakespeare was born. That's two hours northwest of London.)

Suddenly, Stratford is a place with a future (and poor little grandmas who've called it home for years are now worth something to their relatives and developers...and now chocolate and flowers appear on Sundays). It seems fitting that this most multiethnic part of London will host these famously multiethnic games.

Viewing the Olympic Park Site

Olympic Park is huge—bigger than Hyde Park/Kensington Gardens. It's also quite beautiful, laced with canals and tributaries of the Lea River. During the games, it will be closed except to ticket-holders. Following the games, the area will become a public park. Until then, the site is viewable from a spot called the View Tube, which you can visit on your own or via a guided tour.

View Tube—You can see all the major landmarks—Olympic Stadium, the Orbit tower, and Aquatics Centre—from the View Tube, a covered shelter with a lookout tower, café, WC, and maps. It sits at the park's southern perimeter, perched on a 500-yard-long berm called the Greenway. While you're there, you may see some of the legion of Nepali Gurkhas who've been employed for security.

The View from the View Tube: Anchoring the complex is the big Olympic Stadium, which will host the opening and closing ceremonies. It's built with modular parts, so after the games, it may be partly dismantled and refitted to become a more intimate venue.

From the stadium, pan to the right to see the following:

On the far horizon, find the swooped wooden roofline of the bicycle track, or velodrome. To the right of that is the white ruffled exterior of the basketball arena. Immediately to the right of that are the Olympic Village apartments. After the 16,000 athletes move out at the end of the games, contractors will swoop in to install kitchens, turning these dorms into public housing.

In the near distance, the red, 350-foot viewing tower called the Orbit has been compared to a vertical roller coaster and a hubble bubble (a Middle-Eastern water pipe).

Pan to the right to see the Aquatics Centre, with its roofline meant to suggest a dolphin. Behind it are Stratford Station and the east entrance to the park.

From the View Tube, you can stroll along the Greenway's

500-yard-long sidewalk, providing other viewpoints. At the far end of the stadium is the media center where 20,000 journalists (more than one per athlete) will be stationed.

Cost and Hours: Free, daily 9:00-17:00, café mobile 07834-275-687, www.theviewtube.co.uk.

Getting There: From central London, it's about a 25-minute ride on the Tube and/or DLR to one of the stations that ring Olympic Park.

To the View Tube Viewpoint: The closest stop is the Pudding Mill Lane DLR Station, which will only be open before the games start, and will close during the games. It sits on the southern edge of the park, only 200 yards from the viewpoint. From central London, ride the Tube to any station that allows you to transfer to the DLR to Pudding Mill Lane. Good change points are Bow Road/Bow Church, Stratford, and Canary Wharf.

To Tube Stations a Pleasant Stroll South of Olympic Park: The West Ham Tube Station is three-quarters of a mile south of Olympic Park. Though it's not close to the park, it's on the Tube line, so you can get there directly from, say, Victoria Station, on the District Line. Once at West Ham Station, you can walk along a bike path to the park. The Bromley-by-Bow Tube Station is also south of the park and also nearly a mile away; from the station, stroll the paths along the River Lea to the park.

To the East Entrance of Olympic Park: There are two similarly named stations, located 400 yards apart. The Stratford Station is both a Tube and DLR stop. The Stratford International Station serves the DLR and the new high-speed train. During the games, the Javelin bullet train will dart to Stratford International direct from St. Pancras International Station in seven minutes.

Guided Tour—Blue Badge guides lead 1.5-hour guided walks of the area. It's a pleasant riverside stroll culminating at the View Tube. You'll learn about the Olympics, but you won't see any more of the park itself than you would on your own—plus, it takes longer.

Cost and Hours: £9, pay guide directly in cash, online reservations recommended but not required, daily at 11:00, meet at the Bromley-by-Bow Tube Station (District or Hammersmith Line), www.toursof2012sites.com.

West of Central London

▲▲**Kew Gardens**—For a fine riverside park and a palatial greenhouse jungle to swing through, take the Tube or the boat to every botanist's favorite escape, Kew Gardens. While to most visitors the Royal Botanic Gardens of Kew are simply a delightful opportunity to wander among 33,000 different types of plants, to the hardworking organization that runs the gardens, the Gardens are

Greater London

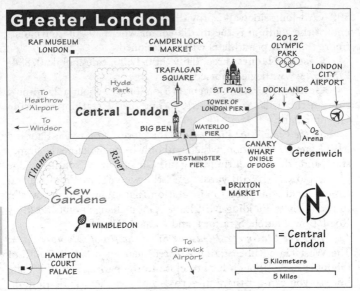

RAF MUSEUM LONDON

CAMDEN LOCK MARKET

2012 OLYMPIC PARK

LONDON CITY AIRPORT

To Heathrow Airport

Hyde Park

TRAFALGAR SQUARE

ST. PAUL'S

DOCKLANDS

Central London

TOWER OF LONDON PIER

To Windsor

BIG BEN

WATERLOO PIER

O_2 Arena

WESTMINSTER PIER

CANARY WHARF ON ISLE OF DOGS

Greenwich

Thames River

Kew Gardens

BRIXTON MARKET

N

= Central London

WIMBLEDON

To Gatwick Airport

HAMPTON COURT PALACE

5 Kilometers

5 Miles

LONDON

a way to promote understanding and preservation of the botanical diversity of our planet. The Kew Tube station drops you in an herbal little business community, a two-block walk from Victoria Gate (the main garden entrance). Pick up a map brochure and check at the gate for a monthly listing of best blooms.

Garden-lovers could spend days exploring Kew's 300 acres. For a quick visit, spend a fragrant hour wandering through three buildings: the Palm House,

a humid Victorian world of iron, glass, and tropical plants that was built in 1844; a Waterlily House that Monet would swim for; and the Princess of Wales Conservatory, a modern greenhouse with many different climate zones growing countless cacti, bug-munching carnivorous plants, and more. With extra time, check out the Xstrata Treetop Walkway, a 200-yard-long scenic steel walkway that puts you high in the canopy 60 feet above the ground. Young kids will love the Climbers and Creepers indoor/outdoor playground and little zip line, as well as a slow and easy ride on the hop-on, hop-off Kew Explorer tram (£4 for narrated 40-minute ride, departs on the hour from 11:00 from near Victoria Gate).

Cost: £14, discounted to £11.50 45 minutes before greenhouses close, kids under 17 free, £5 for Kew Palace only.

Hours: April-Aug Mon-Fri 9:30-18:30, Sat-Sun 9:30-19:30, closes earlier Sept-March, last entry to gardens 30 minutes before closing, galleries and conservatories close at 17:30 in high season—earlier off-season, free one-hour walking tours daily at 11:00 and 14:00, Tube: Kew Gardens, boats run April-Oct between Kew Gardens and Westminster Pier—see page 77, switchboard tel. 020/8332-5000, recorded info tel. 020/8332-5655, www.kew.org.

Eating: For a sun-dappled lunch or snack, walk 10 minutes from the Palm House to the Orangery Cafeteria (£8-12 lunches, daily 10:00-17:30, until 16:30 in winter, closes early for events, tel. 0844-482-7777 www.hrp.org.uk).

▲**Hampton Court Palace**—Fifteen miles up the Thames from downtown, the 500-year-old palace of Henry VIII is worth ▲▲

for palace aficionados. Actually, it was originally the palace of his minister, Cardinal Wolsey. When Wolsey, a clever man, realized Henry VIII was experiencing a little palace envy, he gave the mansion to his king. The Tudor palace was also home to Elizabeth I and Charles I. Sections were updated by Christopher Wren for William and Mary. The stately palace stands overlooking the Thames and includes some impressive Tudor rooms, including a Great Hall with a magnificent hammer-beam ceiling. The industrial-strength Tudor kitchen was capable of keeping 600 schmoozing courtiers thoroughly—if not well—fed. The sculpted garden features a rare Tudor tennis court and a popular maze.

The palace tries hard to please, but it doesn't quite sparkle. From the information center in the main courtyard, you can pick up audioguides for self-guided tours of various wings of the palace (free but slow, aimed mostly at school-aged children). For more in-depth information, strike up a conversation with the costumed characters or docents posted in each room. The Tudor portions of the castle, including the rooms dedicated to the young Henry, are most interesting; the Georgian rooms are pretty dull. The maze in the nearby garden is a curiosity some find fun (maze free with palace ticket, otherwise £3.85).

Cost and Hours: £16, or £43.50 for families, online discounts, daily April-Oct 10:00-18:00, Nov-March 10:00-16:30, last entry one hour before closing, café, tel. 0844-482-7777, www.hrp .org.uk.

Getting There: The train (2/hour, 35 minutes, Oyster cards OK) from London's Waterloo Station drops you across the river from the palace (just walk across the bridge). Consider arriving at or departing from the palace by boat (connections with London's Westminster Pier, see page 77); it's a relaxing and scenic three- to four-hour cruise past two locks and a fun new/old riverside mix.

Kew Gardens/Hampton Court Blitz: Because these two sights are in the same general direction (about £20 for a taxi between the two), you can visit both in one day. Here's a game plan: Start your morning at Hampton Court, tour the palace and garden, and have a Tudor-style lunch in the atmospheric dining hall. After lunch, take bus #R68 from Hampton Court Station to Richmond (40 minutes), then transfer to bus #65, which will drop you off at the Kew Gardens gate (5 minutes). After touring the gardens, have tea in the Orangery, then Tube or boat back to London.

North of Central London

Royal Air Force Museum London—A hit with aviation enthusiasts, this huge aerodrome and airfield contain planes from World War II's Battle of Britain up through the Gulf War. You can climb inside some of the planes, try your luck in a cockpit, and fly with the Red Arrows in a flight simulator.

Cost and Hours: Free, daily 10:00-18:00, last entry 30 minutes before closing, café, shop, parking-£2.50, Grahame Park Way, 30-minute ride from central London, Tube: Colindale—top of Northern Line Edgware branch, tel. 020/8205-2266, www.raf museum.org.uk.

Highgate Cemetery—Located in the tea-cozy-cute village of Highgate, north of the city, this Victorian cemetery represents a fascinating, offbeat piece of London history. Built as a private cemetery, this was the fashionable place to bury the wealthy dead in the late 1800s. It has themed mausoleums, professional mourners, and several high-profile residents in its East Cemetery, including Karl Marx, George Eliot, and Douglas Adams. The tomb of the "Godfather of Punk," Malcolm McLaren (former manager of the Sex Pistols), is often covered with rotten veggies.

Cost and Hours: East Cemetery—£3, Mon-Fri 10:00-17:00, Sat-Sun 11:00-17:00, closes one hour earlier in winter, last entry 30 minutes before closing; older, creepier West Cemetery—viewable by £7 guided tour only, Mon-Fri at 14:00, Sat-Sun hourly 11:00-16:00; Tube: Archway or bus #C2, tel. 020/8340-1834, www.high gate-cemetery.org.

Shopping in London

Most stores are open Monday through Saturday from roughly 10:00 to 18:00, and many close Sundays. Large department stores stay open later during the week (until 20:00 or 21:00) and are open shorter hours on Sundays. If you're looking for bargains, you can visit one of the city's many street markets.

Shopping Streets

London is famous for its shopping. The best and most convenient shopping streets are in the West End and West London (roughly between Soho and Hyde Park). You'll find mid-range shops along **Oxford Street** (running east from Tube: Marble Arch), and fancier shops along **Regent Street** (stretching south from Tube: Oxford Circus to Piccadilly Circus) and **Knightsbridge** (where you'll find Harrods and Harvey Nichols, described later; Tube: Knightsbridge). Other streets are more specialized, such as **Jermyn Street** for old-fashioned men's clothing (just south of Piccadilly Street) and **Charing Cross Road** for books.

Fancy Department Stores in West London

Harrods—Harrods is London's most famous and touristy department store. With more than four acres of retail space covering seven floors, it's a place where some shoppers could spend all day. (To me, it's still just a department store.) Big yet classy, Harrods has everything from elephants to toothbrushes (Mon-Sat 10:00-20:00, Sun 11:30-18:00, mandatory storage for big backpacks-£3, on Brompton Road, Tube: Knightsbridge, tel. 020/7730-1234, www.harrods.com).

While the store is famous partly for its Egyptian theme and its memorials to Princess Diana and her boyfriend, Dodi Fayed, those were the pet projects of Harrods' former owner, Mohamed Al Fayed (Dodi's Egyptian father). Al Fayed sold the store in 2010 to a Qatari investment group, so it's possible some of these features (especially the Di and Dodi stuff) could change.

Sightseers should pick up the free *Store Guide* at any info post. Here's what I enjoy: On the ground floor, find the Food Halls, with their Edwardian tiled walls, creative and exuberant displays, and staff in period costumes—not quite like your local supermarket back home.

Descend to the lower ground floor and follow signs to the Egyptian Escalator (in the center of the store), where you'll likely find a memorial to Dodi Fayed and Princess Diana. Photos and flowers honor the late Princess and her lover, who both died in a car crash in Paris in 1997. Inside a small, clear pyramid, you can see a wine glass still dirty from their last dinner and the engagement ring that Dodi purchased the day before they died. True Di-hards can go back up one level to the ground floor and follow signs to Door #3 in Menswear (near Men's Designer and Men's Tailoring, at the escalator). A huge (and more than a little creepy) bronze statue shows Di and Dodi releasing a symbolic albatross.

Back in the center of the store, ride the Egyptian Escalator—lined with pharaoh-headed sconces, papyrus-plant lamps, and hieroglyphic balconies—to the fourth floor. From the escalator, make a U-turn left and head to the far corner of the store (toys) to find child-size luxury pedal cars. If you have £10,000 to spare, these are the perfect gift for the child who has everything.

Also on the fourth floor is **The Georgian Restaurant,** where you can enjoy a fancy afternoon tea (see page 195). For non-tea drinkers, 27 other eateries are scattered throughout the store, including a sushi bar, kosher deli, pizzeria, classic pub, and—for the truly homesick—a Krispy Kreme.

Many of my readers report that Harrods is overpriced, snooty, and teeming with American and Japanese tourists. It's the only shopping mall I've seen with its own gift store. Still, it's the palace of department stores. The nearby Beauchamp Place is lined with classy and fascinating shops.

Harvey Nichols—Once Princess Diana's favorite, "Harvey Nick's" remains the department store *du jour* (Mon-Sat 10:00-20:00, Sun 11:30-18:00, near Harrods, 109-125 Knightsbridge, Tube: Knightsbridge, tel. 020/7235-5000, www.harveynichols.com). Want to pick up a little £20 scarf for the wife? You won't do it here, where they're more like £200. The store's fifth floor is a veritable food fest, with a gourmet grocery store, a fancy restaurant, a Yo! Sushi bar, and a lively café. Consider a take-away tray of sushi to eat on a bench in the Hyde Park rose garden two blocks away.

Fortnum & Mason—The official department store of the Queen, Fortnum & Mason embodies old-fashioned, British upper-class taste. While some may find it too stuffy, you won't find another store with the same storybook atmosphere (Mon-Sat 10:00-20:00, Sun 12:00-18:00, elegant tea served in St. James's Restaurant—see page 195, 181 Piccadilly, Tube: Green Park, tel. 020/7734-8040, www.fortnumandmason.com).

Liberty—Known for its gorgeous floral fabrics and well-stocked crafts department, Liberty is fun to stroll through just for a look at its hip, artful displays and castle-like interior (Mon-Sat 10:00-21:00, Sun 10:00-18:00, Great Marlborough St, Tube: Oxford Circus, tel. 020/7734-1234, www.liberty.co.uk).

Street Markets

Antique buffs, people-watchers, and folks who brake for garage sales love London's street markets. There's good early-morning market activity somewhere any day of the week. The best—which combine lively stalls and a colorful neighborhood with cute and characteristic shops of its own—are Portobello Road and Camden Lock Market. Any London TI has a complete, up-to-date list. If you like to haggle, there are no holds barred in London's street markets.

Warning: Markets attract two kinds of people—tourists and pickpockets.

In Notting Hill

Portobello Road Market—Arguably London's best street market, Portobello Road stretches for several blocks through the delightful, colorful, funky-yet-quaint Notting Hill neighborhood (immortalized by the Hugh Grant/Julia Roberts film of the same name). Already charming streets lined with pastel-painted houses and offbeat antiques shops are enlivened on Saturdays with 2,000 additional stalls (5:30-17:00), plus food, live music, and more. (It's also extremely crowded.) If you start at Notting Hill Gate and work your way north, you'll find these general sections: antiques, new goods, produce, more new goods, and a flea market. While Portobello Road is best on Saturdays, it's enjoyable to stroll this street on most other days as well, since the characteristic shops are fun to explore—but skip it on Sundays, when virtually everything is closed (Tube: Notting Hill Gate, near recommended accommodations, tel. 020/7229-8354, www.portobelloroad.co.uk).

In Camden Town

Camden Lock Market—This huge, trendy arts-and-crafts festival is divided into three areas, each with its own vibe. The main market, set alongside the picturesque canal, features a mix of shops and stalls selling boutique crafts and artisanal foods. The market to the opposite side of Chalk Farm Road is edgier, with cheap ethnic food and punk crafts. The Stables, a sprawling, incense-scented complex, is more lowbrow, with cheap clothes, junk jewelry, and loud music (daily 10:00-18:00, busiest on weekends, Tube: Chalk Farm, tel. 020/7485-7963, www.camdenlockmarket.com). Avoid the tacky, crowded area between the market and the Camden Town Tube station by getting off at the Chalk Farm stop; better yet, consider arriving via a scenic waterbus ride from Little Venice (tel. 020/7482-2660, www.londonwaterbus.com).

In the East End

All three of these East End markets are busiest and most interesting on Sundays.

Spitalfields Market—This huge, mod-feeling market hall (pronounced "spittle-fields") combines a shopping mall with old brick buildings and sleek modern ones, all covered by a giant glass roof. While the shops and a rainbow of restaurant options are open every day, the open space between them is filled with stalls during the week. It's best on Sundays (9:00-17:00), when all stalls and shops are open; you'll find a lively organic food market, many ethnic eateries, crafts, trendy clothes, bags, and an antiques-and-junk market. Thursdays are for antiques, Fridays specialize in cutting-edge fashion and art, and the first and third Wednesday of every month feature a record and book fair (all 10:00-16:00). It's quietest on Saturdays, Mondays, and Tuesdays, when only the shops are open—no stalls (shops open daily 11:00-19:00, Tube: Liverpool Street; from the Tube stop, take Bishopsgate East exit, turn left, walk to Brushfield Street, and turn right; tel. 020/7375-2963, www.visitspitalfields.com).

Petticoat Lane Market—Just a block from Spitalfields Market, this line of stalls sits on the otherwise dull, glass-skyscraper-filled Middlesex Street; adjoining Wentworth Street is grungier and more characteristic. Expect budget clothing, leather, shoes, watches, jewelry, and crowds (Sun 9:00-14:00, sometimes later; smaller market Mon-Fri 10:00-16:30 on Wentworth Street only; closed Sat; Middlesex Street and Wentworth Street, Tube: Liverpool Street). The Columbia Road flower market is nearby (Sun 8:00-15:00, http://columbiaroad.info).

Brick Lane Market—Housed in the former Truman Brewery, this market is in the heart of the "Banglatown" Bangladeshi community. Of the three East End markets, Brick Lane is the grittiest and most avant-garde, selling handmade clothes and home decor, as well as ethnic street food (Sun 10:00-17:00, 91 Brick Lane, Tube: Liverpool Street or Aldgate East, tel. 020/7770-6028, www.bricklanemarket.com).

In the West End

Covent Garden Market—Originally the convent garden for Westminster Abbey, the iron-and-glass market hall hosted a produce market until the 1970s (earning it the name "Apple Market"). Yesteryear's produce stalls are now open 10:00-18:00 daily with antiques (Mon); clothes, gifts, and foods (Tue-Fri); and handmade crafts (Sun; Tube: Covent Garden, tel. 020/7836-9136, www.coventgardenlondonuk.com). The **Jubilee Hall Market** to the south follows a similar schedule (antiques Mon 5:00-16:00, general market Tue-Fri 9:30-18:30, handcrafts Sat-Sun 9:30-17:30, tel. 020/7836-2139, www.jubileemarket.co.uk).

In South London

Brixton Market—This seedy neighborhood south of the Thames features yet another thriving market. Here the food, clothing, records, and hair-braiding throb with an Afro-Caribbean beat (stalls open Mon-Sat 8:00-18:00, Wed until 15:00, farmer's market Sun 10:00-14:00 but otherwise dead on Sundays; Tube: Brixton, www.brixtonmarket.net).

Borough Market—The Southwark neighborhood hosts a carnival of food under the Borough Bridge, with stalls selling produce, baked goods, cheeses, and other delicacies (Thu 11:00-17:00, Fri 12:00-18:00, Sat 8:00-17:00, closed Sun-Wed, Tube: London Bridge, tel. 020/7407-1002, www.boroughmarket.org.uk).

In Greenwich

With several sightseeing treats just a quick DLR ride from central London, Greenwich has its share of great markets. They're especially lively on weekends. For details, see page 213.

Famous Auctions

London's famous auctioneers welcome the curious public for viewing and bidding. You can preview estate catalogs or browse auction calendars online. To ask questions or set up an appointment, contact **Sotheby's** (Mon-Fri 9:00-16:30, closed Sat-Sun, café, 34-35 New Bond Street—see map on page 152, Tube: Oxford Circus, tel. 020/7293-5000, www.sothebys.com) or **Christie's** (Mon-Fri 9:00-17:00, Sat-Sun usually 12:00-17:00 but weekend hours vary—call ahead, 8 King Street, Tube: Green Park, tel. 020/7839-9060, www.christies.com).

Entertainment in London

For the best list of what's happening and a look at the latest London scene, pick up a current copy of *Time Out* (£3, www.timeout.com). The TI's free monthly *London Planner* covers sights, events, and plays at least as well as *Time Out*.

Theater (a.k.a. "Theatre")

London's theater rivals Broadway's in quality and usually beats it in price. Choose from around 200 offerings—Shakespeare, musicals, comedies, thrillers, sex farces, cutting-edge fringe, revivals starring movie celebs, and more. London does it all well. I prefer big, glitzy—even bombastic—musicals over serious chamber dramas, simply because London can deliver the lights, sound, dancers, and multimedia spectacle I rarely get back home. (If you're a regular visitor to Broadway or Las Vegas—where you have access to similar spectacles—you might prefer some of London's more low-key offerings.) For a rundown of what's hot right now, see the "What's On in the West End" sidebar.

There are also plenty of enticing plays to choose from, ranging

What's On in the West End

Here are some of the perennial favorites that you're likely to find among the West End's evening offerings. If spending the time and money for a London play, I like a full-fledged, high-energy musical (which all of these are). Generally you can book tickets for free at the box office or for a £2-3 fee by telephone or online. See the map on page 152 for locations.

Billy Elliot—This adaptation of the popular British film is part family drama, part story of a boy who just has to dance, set to a score by Elton John (£20-65, Mon-Sat 19:30, matinees Thu and Sat 14:30, Victoria Palace Theatre, Victoria Street, Tube: Victoria, tel. 0844-811-0055, www.billyelliotthemusical.com).

Chicago—A chorus-girl-gone-bad forms a nightclub act with another murderess to bring in the bucks (£26-63, Mon-Thu 20:00, Fri 17:30 and 20:30, Sat 15:00 and 20:00, Cambridge Theatre, Earlham Street, Tube: Covent Garden, booking tel. 0844-412-4652, www.chicagothemusical.com).

Jersey Boys—This fast-moving, easy-to-follow show tracks the rough start and rise to stardom of Frankie Valli and the Four Seasons. It's light, but the music is so catchy that everyone leaves whistling the group's classics (£20-65, Mon-Sat 19:30, matinees Tue and Sat 14:30, Prince Edward Theatre, Old Compton Street, Tube: Leicester Square, tel. 0844-482-5138, www.jerseyboys london.com).

Les Misérables—Claude-Michel Schönberg's musical adaptation of Victor Hugo's epic follows the life of Jean Valjean as he struggles with the social and political realities of 19th-century France. This inspiring mega-hit takes you back to the days of France's struggle for a just and modern society (£15-63, Mon-Sat 19:30, matinees Wed and Sat 14:30, Queen's Theatre, Shaftesbury Avenue, Tube: Piccadilly Circus, box office tel. 0844-482-5138, www.lesmis.com).

from revivals of classics to cutting-edge works by the hottest young playwrights. Many star huge-name celebrities (you'll see the latest offerings advertised all over the Tube and elsewhere). London is a magnet for movie stars who want to stretch their acting chops. For example, since 2003, Kevin Spacey has been the artistic director of the Old Vic theater. He has directed and appeared in several productions, and has enlisted many big-name film directors and actors for others (www.oldvictheatre.com).

Most theaters, marked on tourist maps, are found in the West End between Piccadilly and Covent Garden. Box offices, hotels, and TIs offer a handy free *Official London Theatre Guide* and *Entertainment Guide*. From home, you can look online at

The Lion King—In this Disney extravaganza, Simba the lion learns about the delicately balanced circle of life on the savanna (£21-64, Tue-Sat 19:30; matinees Wed, Sat, and Sun 14:30; Lyceum Theatre, Wellington Street, Tube: Charing Cross or Covent Garden, theater info tel. 020/7420-8100, booking tel. 0844-844-0005, www.thelionking.co.uk).

Mamma Mia!—This energetic, spandex-and-platform-boots musical weaves together a slew of ABBA hits to tell the story of a bride in search of her real dad as her promiscuous mom plans her Greek Isle wedding. The production has the audience dancing by the time it reaches its happy ending (£20-67, Mon-Thu and Sat 19:30, Fri 20:30, matinees Fri 17:00 and Sat 15:00, Prince of Wales Theatre, Coventry Street, Tube: Piccadilly Circus, box office tel. 0844-482-5115, www.mamma-mia.com).

Phantom of the Opera—A mysterious masked man falls in love with a singer in this haunting Andrew Lloyd Webber musical about life beneath the stage of the Paris Opera (£20-62.50, Mon-Sat 19:30, matinees Tue and Sat 14:30, Her Majesty's Theatre, Haymarket, Tube: Piccadilly Circus or Leicester Square, US toll-free tel. 800-334-8457, London booking tel. 0844-412-2707, www.thephantomoftheopera.com).

We Will Rock You—Whether or not you're a Queen fan, this musical tribute (more to the band than to Freddie Mercury) is an understandably popular celebration of their work (£30-62, Mon-Sat 19:30, matinee Sat 14:30, Dominion Theatre, Tottenham Court Road, Tube: Tottenham Court Road, Ticketmaster tel. 0844-847-1775, www.wewillrockyou.co.uk).

Wicked—This lively prequel to *The Wizard of Oz* examines how the Witch of the West met Glinda the Good Witch, and later became so, you know,...(£15-65, Mon-Sat 19:30, matinee Wed and Sat 14:30, Apollo Victoria Theatre, just east of Victoria Station, Tube: Victoria, Ticketmaster tel. 0844-826-8000, www.wicked themusical.co.uk).

www.officiallondontheatre.co.uk for the latest on what's currently playing in London.

Performances are nightly except Sunday, usually with one or two matinees a week (Shakespeare's Globe is the rare theater that does offer performances on Sun, late April-early Oct). Tickets range from about £15 to £60. Matinees are generally cheaper and rarely sell out.

Buying Theater Tickets

To book a seat, simply call the theater box office (which may ring through to a central ticketing office), ask about seats and available dates, and buy a ticket with your credit card. You can call

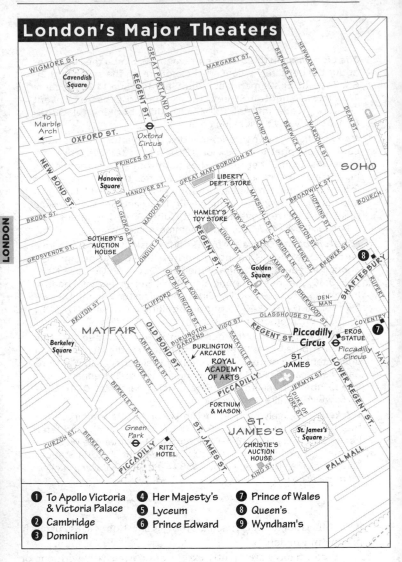

London's Major Theaters

LONDON

1 To Apollo Victoria & Victoria Palace
2 Cambridge
3 Dominion
4 Her Majesty's
5 Lyceum
6 Prince Edward
7 Prince of Wales
8 Queen's
9 Wyndham's

from the US as easily as from England. Arrive about 30 minutes before the show starts to pick up your ticket and avoid lines. (For money-saving tips, see "Cheap Theater Tricks" and "Half-Price 'tkts' Booth" on page 154.)

For a booking fee, you can reserve online on theater websites. Most link you to a preferred ticket vendor, usually www.ticket master.co.uk or www.seetickets.com. In the US, Keith Prowse Ticketing is also handy by phone or online (US tel. 212/398-4175, http://www.keithprowse.com/tickets/slink.buy).

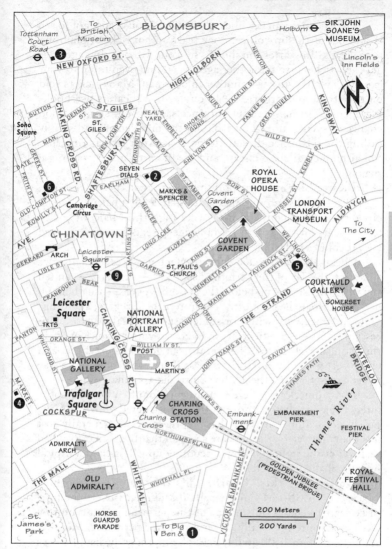

LONDON

Although booking through an agency is quick and easy, prices are inflated by a standard 25 percent fee. Ticket agencies (whether in the US, at London's TIs, or scattered throughout the city) are scalpers with an address. If you're buying from an agency, look at the ticket carefully (your price should be no more than 30 percent over the printed face value; the 20 percent VAT is already included in the face value), and understand where you're sitting according to the floor plan (if your view is restricted, it will state this on the ticket; for floor plans of the various theaters, see www.theatremonkey.com).

Agencies are worthwhile only if a show you've just got to see is sold out at the box office. They scarf up hot tickets, planning to make a killing after the show is sold out. US booking agencies get their tickets from another agency, adding even more to your expense by involving yet another middleman. Many tickets sold on the street are forgeries. Although some theaters use booking agencies to handle their advance sales, you'll stand a good chance of saving money by avoiding the middleman and simply calling the box office directly to purchase your tickets (international phone calls are cheap, and credit cards make booking a snap).

Theater Lingo: It's helpful to know these terms when booking tickets—stalls (ground floor), dress circle (first balcony), upper circle (second balcony), balcony (sky-high third balcony), slips (cheap seats on the fringes). Many cheap seats have a restricted view (behind a pillar).

Cheap Theater Tricks: Some theater box offices sell half-price tickets on the day of the performance ("tkts"—see below—can tell you which ones); line up before the box office opens—usually 10:00 or 10:30. Most theaters offer cheap returned tickets, standing-room, matinee, and senior or student standby deals. These "concessions" (discounted tickets) are indicated with a "conc" or "s" in the listings. Picking up a late return can get you a great seat at a cheap-seat price. Even if a show is "sold out," there's usually a way to get a seat. Call the theater box office and ask how.

If you don't care where you sit, you can often buy the absolutely cheapest seats—those with an obstructed view or in the nosebleed section—at the box office; these tickets generally cost less than £20. Many theaters are so small that there's hardly a bad seat. After the lights go down, scooting up is less than a capital offense. Shakespeare did it.

Half-Price "tkts" Booth: This famous ticket booth at Leicester (LESS-ter) Square sells discounted tickets for top-price seats to shows on the day of the performance and up to a week in advance (generally £3 service charge per ticket, Mon-Sat 10:00-19:00, Sun 11:00-16:00, lines often form early, list of shows available online at www.tkts.co.uk). Most tickets are half-price; other shows are discounted 25 percent, and some are full price (no service charge for full-price shows). Note that the real half-price booth (with its "tkts" name) is a freestanding kiosk at the edge of the garden in Leicester Square. Several dishonest outfits nearby advertise "official half-price tickets"—avoid these.

Here are sample prices: A top-notch seat to *Chicago* costs £59 if you buy directly from the theater; the same seat costs £32.50 at Leicester Square. The cheapest balcony seat is £25 through the theater. Half-price tickets can be a good deal, unless you want the cheapest seats or the hottest shows. But check the board; occasionally they sell cheap tickets to good shows.

Theater Options

West End Theaters: The commercial (nonsubsidized) theaters cluster around Soho (especially along Shaftesbury Avenue) and Covent Garden. With a centuries-old tradition of pleasing the masses, these present London theater at its glitziest (see the sidebar for a sampling of what's playing here).

Royal Shakespeare Company: If you'll ever enjoy Shakespeare, it'll be in Britain. The RSC performs at various theaters around London and in Stratford-upon-Avon year-round. To get a schedule, contact the RSC (Royal Shakespeare Theatre, Stratford-upon-Avon, tel. 0844-800-1110, www.rsc.org.uk).

Shakespeare's Globe: To see Shakespeare in a replica of the theater for which he wrote his plays, attend a play at the Globe. In this round, thatch-roofed, open-air theater, the plays are performed much as Shakespeare intended—under the sky and with no amplification.

The play's the thing from late April through early October (usually Mon 19:30, Tue-Sat 14:00 and 19:30, Sun either 13:00 and/or 18:30, tickets can be sold out months in advance). You'll pay £5 to stand and £15-35 to sit, usually on a backless bench. Because only a few rows and the pricier Gentlemen's Rooms have seats with backs, £1 cushions and £3 add-on back rests are considered a good investment by many. Dress for the weather.

The £5 "groundling" tickets—which are open to rain—are most fun. Scurry in early to stake out a spot on the stage's edge, where the most interaction with the actors occurs. You're a crude peasant. You can lean your elbows on the stage, munch a picnic dinner (yes, you can bring in food), or walk around. I've never enjoyed Shakespeare as much as here, performed as it was meant to be in the "wooden O." If you can't get a ticket, consider waiting around. Plays can be long, and many groundlings leave before the end. Hang around outside and beg or buy a ticket from someone leaving early (groundlings are allowed to come and go). A few non-Shakespeare plays are also presented each year. If you can't attend a show, you can take a guided tour of the theater and museum by day (see page 128).

To reserve tickets for plays, call or drop by the theater box office (Mon-Sat 10:00-18:00, Sun 10:00-17:00, open one hour later on performance days, New Globe Walk entrance, no extra charge to book by phone, tel. 020/7401-9919). You can also reserve online (www.shakespeares-globe.org, £2 booking fee). If the tickets are sold out, don't despair; a few often free up at the last minute. Try calling around noon the day of the performance to see if the box office expects any returned tickets. If so, they'll advise you to show up a little more than an hour before the show, when these tickets are sold (first-come, first-served).

The theater is on the South Bank, directly across the Thames over the Millennium Bridge from St. Paul's Cathedral (Tube: Mansion House or London Bridge). The Globe is inconvenient for public transport, but the courtesy phone in the lobby lets you get a minicab in minutes. (These minicabs have set fees—e.g., £8 to South Kensington—but generally cost less than a metered cab and provide fine and honest service.) During theater season, there's a regular supply of black cabs outside the main foyer on New Globe Walk.

Outdoor Theater in Summer: Enjoy Shakespearean drama and other plays under the stars at the Open Air Theatre, in leafy Regent's Park in north London. Food is allowed: You can bring your own picnic; order à la carte from the theater menu; or pre-order a £25 picnic supper from the theater at least 48 hours in advance (tickets £12-50; season runs late May-mid-Sept, box office open April-late May Mon-Sat 10:00-18:00, closed Sun; late May-mid-Sept Mon-Sat 10:00-20:00, Sun 10:00-until start of play on performance days only; order tickets online after mid-Jan or by phone Mon-Sun 9:00-21:00; £1 booking fee by phone, no fee if ordering online or in person; tel. 0844-826-4242, www.open airtheatre.org; grounds open 1.5 hours prior to evening perfor-mances, one hour prior to 2:30 matinee, and 30 minutes prior to earlier matinees; 10-minute walk north of Baker Street Tube, near Queen Mary's Gardens within Regent's Park; detailed directions and more info at www.openairtheatre.org).

Fringe Theater: London's rougher evening-entertainment scene is thriving, filling pages in *Time Out*. Choose from a wide range of fringe theater and comedy acts (generally £5).

Classical Music
Concerts at Churches
For easy, cheap, or free concerts in historic churches, ask the TI (or check *Time Out*) about **lunch concerts,** especially:
- St. Bride's Church, with free lunch concerts twice a week at 13:15 (generally Tue, Wed, or Fri—confirm by phone or online, church tel. 020/7427-0133, www.stbrides.com).
- St. James's at Piccadilly, with 50-minute concerts on Mon, Wed, and Fri at 13:10 (suggested £3.50 donation, info tel. 020/7381-0441, www.st-james-piccadilly.org).
- St. Martin-in-the-Fields, offering concerts on Mon, Tue, and Fri at 13:00 (suggested £3.50 donation, church tel. 020/7766-1100, www.smitf.org).

St. Martin-in-the-Fields also hosts fine **evening concerts** by

Evensong

One of my favorite experiences in Britain is to attend evensong at a great church. Evensong is an evening worship service that is typically sung rather than said (though some parts—including scripture readings, a few prayers, and a homily—are spoken). It follows the traditional Anglican service in the Book of Common Prayer, including prayers, scripture readings, canticles (sung responses), and hymns that are appropriate for the early evening—traditionally the end of the working day and before the evening meal. In major churches with resident choirs, this service is filled with quality, professional musical elements. A singing or chanting priest leads the service, and a choir—usually made up of both men's and boys' voices (to sing the lower and higher parts, respectively)—sings the responses. The singers are often a cappella, and sometimes accompanied by organ. While regular attendees follow the service from memory, visitors—who are welcome—are given an order of service or a prayer book to help them follow along. (If you're not familiar with the order of service, watch the congregation to know when to stand, sit, and kneel.)

The most impressive places for evensong include London (Westminster Abbey or St. Paul's), Cambridge (King's College Chapel), Canterbury Cathedral, Wells Cathedral, Oxford (Christ Church College), York Minster, and Durham Cathedral. While this list includes many of the grandest churches in England, be aware that evensong typically takes place in the small choir area—which is far more intimate than the main nave. (To see the full church in action, a concert is a better choice.) Evensong generally occurs daily between 17:00 and 18:00 (often two hours earlier on Sun)—check with individual churches for specifics. At smaller churches, evensong is sometimes spoken, not sung.

Note that evensong is not a performance—it's a somewhat somber worship service. If you enjoy worshipping in different churches, attending evensong can be a trip-capping highlight. But if regimented church services aren't your thing, consider getting a different music fix. Most major churches also offer organ or choral concerts—look for posted schedules or ask at the information desk or gift shop.

candlelight (£8-26, several nights a week at 19:30) and live jazz in its underground Café in the Crypt (£5-10 tickets, Wed at 20:00).

Evensong and Organ Recitals at Churches

Evensong services are held at several churches, including:
- St. Paul's Cathedral (Mon-Sat at 17:00, Sun at 15:15).
- Westminster Abbey (Mon-Tue and Thu-Fri at 17:00, Sat-Sun at 15:00 except Sat at 17:00 in summer; there's a service on

Wed, but it may be spoken, not sung).
- Southwark Cathedral (Mon-Tue and Thu-Fri at 17:30, Sat at 16:00, Sun at 15:00, no service on Wed or alternate Mon, tel. 020/7367-6700, www.southwark.anglican.org/cathedral).
- St. Bride's Church (Sun at 17:30, tel. 020/7427-0133, www .stbrides.com).

Free **organ recitals** are often held on Sunday at 17:45 in Westminster Abbey (30 minutes, tel. 020/7222-5152). Many other churches have free concerts; ask for the *London Organ Concerts Guide* at the TI.

Performances

Prom Concerts: For a fun classical event (mid-July–mid-Sept), attend a Prom Concert (shortened from "Promenade Concert") during the annual festival at the Royal Albert Hall. Nightly concerts are offered at give-a-peasant-some-culture prices to "Promenaders"—those willing to stand throughout the performance (£5 standing-room spots sold at the door, £7 restricted-view seats, most £20-54 but depends on performance, Tube: South Kensington, tel. 0845-401-5045, www.bbc.co.uk/proms).

Opera: Some of the world's best opera is belted out at the prestigious Royal Opera House, near Covent Garden (box office tel. 020/7304-4000, www.roh.org.uk), and at the London Coliseum (English National Opera, St. Martin's Lane, Tube: Leicester Square, box office tel. 0871-911-0200, www.eno.org). Or consider taking in an unusual opera at King's Head Pub in Islington, home of London's Little Opera House (11 Upper Street, Tube: Angel, tel. 020/7478-0160, www.kingsheadtheatre.com).

Dance: Sadler's Wells Theatre features both international and UK-based dance troupes (Rosebery Avenue, Islington, Tube: Angel, info tel. 020/7863-8198, box office tel. 0844-412-4300, www.sadlerswells.com).

Sightseeing

Evening Museum Visits: Many museums are open an evening or two during the week, offering fewer crowds. See the list on page 96.

Tours: Guided walks are offered several times a day. **London Walks** is the most established company. Daytime walks vary by theme: ancient London, museums, legal London, Dickens, Beatles, Jewish quarter, Christopher Wren, and so on. In the evening, expect a more limited choice: ghosts, Jack the Ripper, pubs, or literary-themed. Get the latest from their brochure or website, or call for a recorded listing of that day's walks. Show up at the listed time and place, pay the guide, and enjoy the two-hour tour (£8, cash only, tel. 020/7624-3978, recorded info tel. 020/7624-9255, www.walks.com).

To see the city illuminated at night, consider a bus tour. A two-hour **London by Night Sightseeing Tour** leaves every evening from Victoria Station and other points (see page 67).

Cruises: During the summer, boats sail as late as 19:00 between Westminster Pier (near Big Ben) and the Tower of London. (For details, see page 73.)

A handful of outfits run Thames River evening cruises with four-course meals and dancing. **London Showboat** offers the best value (£75, April-Oct Wed-Sun, March and Nov-Dec Thu-Sat, Jan-Feb Fri-Sat, 3.5 hours, departs at 19:30 from Westminster Pier and returns by 23:00, reservations necessary, tel. 020/7740-0400, www.citycruises.com). Dinner cruises are also offered by **Bateaux London** (£75-125, tel. 020/7695-1800, www.bateauxlondon.com). For more on cruising, get the *River Thames Boat Services* brochure from a London TI.

Summer Evenings Along the South Bank

If you're visiting London in summer, consider hitting the South Bank after hours.

Take a trip around the **London Eye** while the sun sets over the city (the wheel spins until late—last ascent at 21:30 July-Aug, 21:00 April-June, 20:00 Sept-March). Then cap your night with an evening walk along the pedestrian-only **Jubilee Walkway,** which runs east-west along the river. It's where Londoners go to escape the heat. This pleasant stretch of the walkway—lined with pubs and casual eateries—goes from the London Eye past Shakespeare's Globe to Tower Bridge (you can walk in either direction).

If you're in the mood for a movie, take in a flick at the **BFI Southbank,** located just across the river, alongside Waterloo Bridge. Run by the British Film Institute, the state-of-the-art theater shows mostly classic films, as well as art cinema (£9, £5 on Tue and weekday matinees, Tube: Waterloo or Embankment, box office tel. 020/7928-3232, check www.bfi.org.uk for schedules).

Farther east along the South Bank is **The Scoop**—an outdoor amphitheater next to City Hall. It's a good spot for movies, concerts, dance, and theater productions throughout the summer—with Tower Bridge as a scenic backdrop. These events are free, nearly nightly, and family-friendly. For the latest event schedule, see www.morelondon.com and click on "The Scoop" (next to City Hall, Riverside, The Queen's Walkway, Tube: London Bridge).

Sleeping in London

London is an expensive city for rooms. Cheaper rooms are relatively dumpy. Don't expect £130 cheeriness in an £80 room. For £70, you'll get a double with breakfast in a safe, cramped, and

Sleep Code

(£1 = about $1.60, country code: 44, area code: 020)
S = Single, **D** = Double/Twin, **T** = Triple, **Q** = Quad, **b** = bathroom, **s** = shower only. Unless otherwise noted, credit cards are accepted and prices include breakfast.

To help you sort through these listings easily, I've divided the accommodations into three categories, based on the price for a double room with bath:

$$$ Higher Priced—Most rooms £125 or more.
$$ Moderately Priced—Most rooms between £75-125.
$ Lower Priced—Most rooms £75 or less.

Prices can change without notice; verify the hotel's current rates online or by email. For other updates, see www.ricksteves.com/update.

dreary place with minimal service and the bathroom down the hall. For £90, you'll get a basic, clean, reasonably cheery double with a private bath in a usually cramped, cracked-plaster building, or a soulless but comfortable room without breakfast in a huge Motel 6-type place. My London splurges, at £160-290, are spacious, thoughtfully appointed places good for entertaining or romancing.

Looking for Hotel Deals Online: Given London's high hotel prices, using the Internet can help you score a deal. Various websites list rooms in high-rise, three- and four-star business hotels. You'll give up the charm and warmth of a family-run establishment, and breakfast probably won't be included, but you might find that the price is right.

Start by browsing the websites of several chains to get a sense of typical rates and online deals. For listings of no-frills, Motel 6-type places, see "Big, Good-Value, Modern Hotels," later. Pricier London hotel chains include Millennium/Copthorne (www.millenniumhotels.com), Thistle (www.thistle.com), Intercontinental/Holiday Inn (www.ichotelsgroup.com), Radisson (www.radisson.com), Hilton (www.hilton.com), and Red Carnation (www.redcarnationhotels.com).

Auction-type sites (such as www.priceline.com or www.hotwire.com) match flexible travelers with empty hotel rooms, often at prices well below the hotel's normal rates.

My readers report good experiences with these accommodation discount sites: www.londontown.com (an informative site with a discount booking service), http://athomeinlondon.co.uk and www.londonbb.com (both list central B&Bs), www.lastminute

London's Hotel Neighborhoods

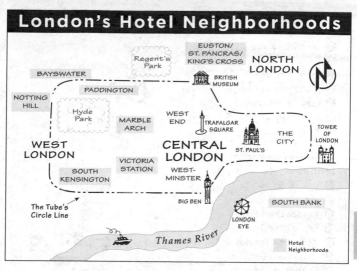

.com, www.visitlondon.com, http://roomsnet.com, and www.euro cheapo.com.

Victoria Station Neighborhood (Belgravia)

The streets behind Victoria Station teem with little, moderately priced-for-London B&Bs. It's a safe, surprisingly tidy, and decent

area without a hint of the trashy, touristy glitz of the streets in front of the station. I've divided these accommodations into two broad categories: west or east of the station. Decent eateries abound in both areas (see page 187). All the recommended hotels are within a five-minute walk of the Victoria Tube, bus, and train stations. On hot summer nights, request a quiet back room.

Near the hotels on the west side is the 400-space Semley Place NCP **parking garage** (£34/day, possible discounts with hotel voucher, just west of the Victoria Coach Station at Buckingham Palace Road and Semley Place, tel. 0845-050-7080, www.ncp .co.uk). The best laundry options are on the east side: The handy **Pimlico Launderette** is about five blocks southwest of Warwick Square (daily 8:00-19:00, self- or full-service, south of Sutherland Street at 3 Westmoreland Terrace, tel. 020/7821-8692), and **Launderette Centre** is a block northeast of Warwick Square (Mon-Fri 8:00-21:00, Sat 8:00-19:00, Sun 9:00-20:00, last wash 2 hours before closing, about £7 wash and dry, £9 full-service, 31 Churton Street, tel. 020/7828-6039).

Victoria Station Neighborhood

1. Lime Tree Hotel
2. Cartref House
3. Morgan House
4. Lynton Hotel B&B
5. Luna Simone Hotel
6. New England Hotel
7. Best Western Victoria Palace
8. Cherry Court Hotel
9. Jubilee Hotel
10. Bakers Hotel
11. easyHotel Victoria
12. Vandon House Hotel
13. Ebury Wine Bar
14. Jenny Lo's Tea House
15. La Bottega Deli
16. To The Duke of Wellington Pub
17. The Thomas Cubitt Pub
18. Grumbles Restaurant
19. Seafresh Fish Restaurant
20. The Jugged Hare Pub
21. St. George's Tavern
22. Grocery Stores (4)
23. Launderettes (2)
24. Bus Tours – Day (2)
25. Bus Tours – Night
26. Tube, Taxis, City Buses
27. Green Line Coach Terminal
28. Buses to Luton & Stansted Airports
29. Apollo Victoria Theatre
30. Victoria Palace Theatre

LONDON

West of Victoria Station

Here in Belgravia, the prices are a bit higher and your neighbors include Andrew Lloyd Webber and Margaret Thatcher (her policeman stands outside 73 Chester Square). All of these places line up along tranquil Ebury Street, two blocks over from Victoria Station.

$$$ Lime Tree Hotel, enthusiastically run by Charlotte and Matt, comes with 25 spacious, stylish, comfortable, thoughtfully

LONDON

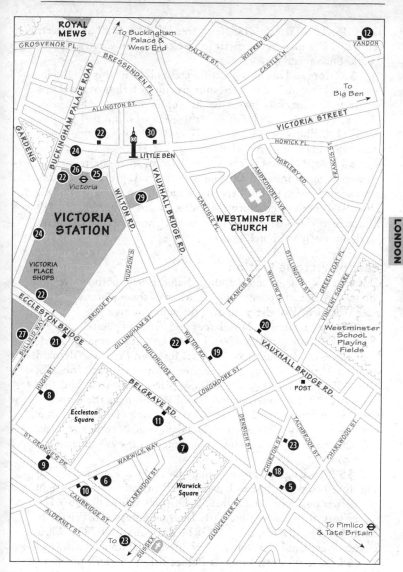

decorated rooms and a fun-loving breakfast room (Sb-£85-95, Db-£145, larger superior Db-£165, Tb-£190, family room-£205, free Internet access and Wi-Fi, small lounge opens onto quiet garden, 135 Ebury Street, tel. 020/7730-8191, www.limetree hotel.co.uk, info@limetreehotel.co.uk, trusty Alan covers the night shift).

$$ Cartref House B&B offers rare charm on Ebury Street, with 10 delightful rooms and a warm welcome (Sb-£82,

Db-£115, Tb-£151, Qb-£185, fans, free Wi-Fi, 129 Ebury Street, tel. 020/7730-6176, www.cartrefhouse.co.uk, info@cartrefhouse .co.uk, Sharon and Derek).

$$ Morgan House, a great budget choice in this neighborhood, has 11 rooms and is entertainingly run, with lots of travel tips and friendly chat from owner Rachel Joplin and her staff (S-£58, D-£78, Db-£98, T-£98, family suites-£138-148 for 3-4 people, Wi-Fi, 120 Ebury Street, tel. 020/7730-2384, www.morganhouse .co.uk, morganhouse@btclick.com).

$$ Lynton Hotel B&B is a well-worn, steep-stairs kind of place renting 13 inexpensive rooms with small prefab WCs. It's a decent value run by brothers Mark and Simon Connor (D-£85, Db-£105, these prices with this book in 2012, free Wi-Fi, 113 Ebury Street, tel. 020/7730-4032, www.lyntonhotel.co.uk, mark -and-simon@lyntonhotel.co.uk).

East of Victoria Station

This area is a bit less genteel-feeling than the neighborhood west of the station, but still plenty inviting. Most of these places are on or near Warwick Way, the main drag through this area.

$$ Luna Simone Hotel rents 36 fresh, spacious, nicely remodeled rooms with modern bathrooms. It's a smartly managed place, run for more than 40 years by twins Peter and Bernard and son Mark, and they still seem to enjoy their work (Sb-£75, Db-£105, Tb-£130, Qb-£160, these prices with cash and this book in 2012, free Internet access and Wi-Fi, near the corner of Charlwood Street and Belgrave Road at 47 Belgrave Road, handy bus #24 to Victoria Station and Trafalgar Square stops out front, tel. 020/7834-5897, www.lunasimonehotel.com, stay@lunasimone hotel.com).

$$ New England Hotel, run by Jay and the Patel family, has slightly worn public spaces but tidy, well-priced rooms in a tight old corner building (small Sb-£59, Db-£89, Tb-£119, Qb-£129, prices soft during slow times, pay Internet access and Wi-Fi, 20 Saint George's Drive, tel. 020/7834-8351, fax 020/7834-9000, www.newenglandhotel.com, mystay@newenglandhotel.com).

$$ Best Western Victoria Palace offers modern business-class comfort compared to the other creaky old hotels listed here. Choose between the 43 rooms in the main building (Db-£120, includes breakfast, elevator, 60-64 Warwick Way), or 22 rooms in the annex a half-block away (Db-£89, breakfast-£12.50, no elevator, 17 Belgrave Road, reception at main building). Both places have been recently renovated (air-con, free Wi-Fi, tel. 020/7821-7113, fax 020/7630-0806, www.bestwesternvictoriapalace.co.uk, info@bestwesternvictoriapalace.co.uk). Another 20-room annex may open by the time you visit.

$ Cherry Court Hotel, run by the friendly and industrious Patel family, rents 12 very small but bright and well-designed rooms in a central location (Sb-£50, Db-£58, Tb-£85, Qb-£100, Quint/b-£115, these prices with this book in 2012, 5 percent fee to pay with credit card, fruit-basket breakfast in room, air-con, free Internet access and Wi-Fi, laundry, peaceful garden patio, 23 Hugh Street, tel. 020/7828-2840, fax 020/7828-0393, www.cherry courthotel.co.uk, info@cherrycourthotel.co.uk).

$ Jubilee Hotel is a well-run slumbermill with 24 tiny, simple rooms and many tiny, neat beds (S-£39-45, Sb-£59-65, tiny D-£55-59, Db-£69-79, Tb-£79-95, Qb-£99-109, higher prices are for Fri-Sun, 5 percent Rick Steves discount if you book direct, Internet access and Wi-Fi, 31 Eccleston Square, tel. 020/7834-0845, www .jubileehotel.co.uk, stay@jubileehotel.co.uk, Bob Patel).

$ Bakers Hotel shoehorns 11 brightly painted rooms into a small building, but it's conveniently located and offers near-youth-hostel prices and a small breakfast (S-£40, D-£55, Db-£65, T-£65, Tb-£75, family room-£85, less for longer stays and on weeknights, pay Wi-Fi, 126 Warwick Way, tel. 020/7834-0729, www.bakers hotel.co.uk, reservations@bakershotel.co.uk, Amin Jamani).

$ easyHotel Victoria, at 36 Belgrave Road, is part of the budget chain described on page 175.

"South Kensington," She Said, Loosening His Cummerbund

To stay on a quiet street so classy it doesn't allow hotel signs, surrounded by trendy shops and colorful restaurants, call "South Ken" your London home. Shoppers like being a short walk from Harrods and the designer shops of King's Road and Chelsea. When I splurge, I splurge here. Sumner Place is just off Old Brompton Road, 200 yards from the handy South Kensington Tube station (on Circle Line, two stops from Victoria Station; and on Piccadilly Line, direct from Heathrow). A handy **launderette** is on the corner of Queensberry Place and Harrington Road (Mon-Fri 7:30-21:00, Sat 9:00-20:00, Sun 10:00-19:00, bring 50p and £1 coins).

$$$ Number Sixteen, for well-heeled travelers, packs over-the-top formality and class into its 41 rooms, plush lounges, and tranquil garden. It's in a labyrinthine building, with modern decor—perfect for an urban honeymoon (Db-from £215—but soft, ask for discounted "seasonal rates," especially on weekends and in Aug—subject to availability, does not include 20 percent VAT, breakfast buffet in the garden-£18, elevator, 16 Sumner Place, tel. 020/7589-5232, fax 020/7584-8615, US tel. 800-553-6674, www .firmdalehotels.com, sixteen@firmdale.com).

$$$ The Pelham Hotel, a 52-room business-class hotel with a pricey mix of pretense and style, is not quite sure which investment

LONDON

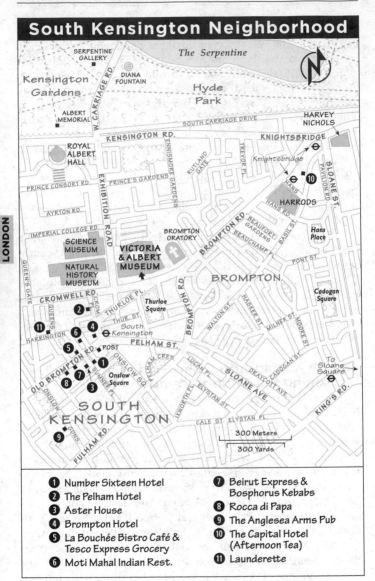

South Kensington Neighborhood

- **1** Number Sixteen Hotel
- **2** The Pelham Hotel
- **3** Aster House
- **4** Brompton Hotel
- **5** La Bouchée Bistro Café & Tesco Express Grocery
- **6** Moti Mahal Indian Rest.
- **7** Beirut Express & Bosphorus Kebabs
- **8** Rocca di Papa
- **9** The Anglesea Arms Pub
- **10** The Capital Hotel (Afternoon Tea)
- **11** Launderette

company owns it. It's genteel, with low lighting and a pleasant drawing room among the many perks (Db-£190-290, breakfast extra, does not include 20 percent VAT, lower prices on weekends and in Aug, Web specials can include free breakfast, air-con, elevator, free Internet access, pay Wi-Fi, gym, 15 Cromwell Place, tel. 020/7589-8288, fax 020/7584-8444, US tel. 1-888-757-5587, www.pelhamhotel.co.uk, reservations@pelhamhotel.co.uk).

$$$ Aster House, run by friendly and accommodating Simon and Leonie Tan, has a cheerful lobby, lounge, and breakfast room. Its rooms are comfy and quiet, with TV, phone, and air-conditioning. Enjoy breakfast or just lounging in the whisper-elegant Orangery, a glassy greenhouse. Simon and Leonie offer free loaner mobile phones to their guests (Sb-£125, Db-£190, bigger Db-£235, does not include 20 percent VAT, 20 percent discount with this book in 2012 if you book three or more nights, 25 percent discount for five or more nights, additional 5 percent off with cash, check website for specials, free Wi-Fi, 3 Sumner Place, tel. 020/7581-5888, fax 020/7584-4925, www.asterhouse .com, asterhouse@btinternet.com).

$$ Brompton Hotel is a humble, borderline-dreary place with 17 rooms above a jumble of cafés and clubs. There's a noisy bar and some street noise, so ask for a room in the back if you want quiet. It has old carpet and no public spaces, and they serve breakfast in your room. In spite of all this, it's cheap for London and very well-located (Sb-£95, Db-£100, Tb-£140, "deluxe" rooms are just like the others but with a tub, save a little by booking via their website, includes continental breakfast, Wi-Fi, across from the South Kensington Tube station at 30 Brompton Road, tel. 020/7584-4517, fax 020/7823-9936, www.bromhotel.com, book @bromhotel.com).

Notting Hill and Bayswater Neighborhoods

Residential Notting Hill has quick bus and Tube access to downtown, and, for London, is very "homely" (Brit-speak for cozy). It's also peppered with trendy bars and restaurants, and is home to the famous Portobello Road Market (see page 147).

Popular with young international travelers, the Bayswater street called Queensway is a multicultural festival of commerce and eateries. The neighborhood does its dirty clothes at **Galaxy Launderette** (£6 self-service, £8-10 full-service, daily 8:00-20:00, staff on hand with soap and coins, 65 Moscow Road, at corner of St. Petersburgh Place and Moscow Road, tel. 020/7229-7771). For **Internet access,** you'll find several stops along busy Queensway, and a self-serve bank of computer terminals on the food-circus level—third floor—of Whiteleys Shopping Centre (daily 8:30-24:00, corner of Queensway and Porchester Gardens).

Near Kensington Gardens Square

Several big, old hotels line quiet Kensington Gardens Square (not to be confused with the much bigger Kensington Gardens adjacent to Hyde Park), a block west of bustling Queensway, north of Bayswater Tube station. These hotels are quiet for central London, but the area feels a bit sterile, and the hotels here tend to

Notting Hill & Bayswater Neighborhoods

1 Vancouver Studios
2 Garden Court Hotel
3 Phoenix Hotel
4 Kensington Gardens Hotel
5 Princes Square Guest Accommodation
6 Westland Hotel
7 London Vicarage Hotel
8 The Gate Hotel
9 To Norwegian YWCA
10 Maggie Jones Restaurant

11 The Churchill Arms Pub & Thai Kitchen
12 The Prince Edward Pub
13 Café Diana
14 Royal China Restaurant
15 Whiteleys Shopping Centre (Food Court, Grocery, Internet)
16 Tesco Grocery
17 Spar Market
18 The Orangery (Afternoon Tea)
19 Launderette

be impersonal.

$$$ Vancouver Studios offers 45 modern rooms with fully equipped kitchenettes (utensils, stove, microwave, and fridge) rather than breakfast (Sb-£92, Db-£135, Tb-£175, extra bed-£20, can be more at busy times, 10 percent discount for seven or more nights, pay Internet access, free Wi-Fi, welcoming lounge and wonderful garden, near Kensington Gardens Square at 30 Prince's Square, tel. 020/7243-1270, fax 020/7221-8678, www.vancouver studios.co.uk, info@vancouverstudios.co.uk).

$$$ Garden Court Hotel is homey and understated, with 32 simple beige rooms and a peaceful garden in back. Edward takes pride in the hotel his family has run for more than 50 years (S-£50, Sb-£80, D-£80, Db-£130, Tb-£160, Qb-£180, these prices when booked direct with this book in 2012, elevator, free Wi-Fi, 30-31 Kensington Gardens Square, tel. 020/7229-2553, fax 020/7727-2749, www.gardencourthotel.co.uk, info@garden courthotel.co.uk).

$$ Phoenix Hotel, a Best Western modernization of a 125-room hotel, offers American business-class comforts; spacious, plush public spaces; and big, fresh, modern-feeling rooms. Its prices—which range from fine value to rip-off—are determined by a greedy computer program, with huge variations according to expected demand. Book online to save money (flexible prices, but usually Sb-£65, Db-£100, elevator, free Wi-Fi, 1-8 Kensington Gardens Square, tel. 020/7229-2494, fax 020/7727-1419, US tel. 800-528-1234, www.phoenixhotel.co.uk, info@phoenixhotel .co.uk).

$$ Kensington Gardens Hotel, which has the same owners as the Phoenix Hotel down the street (see above), laces 17 pleasant rooms together in a tall, skinny building with lots of stairs and no elevator (Ss-£57, Sb-£64, Db-£88, Tb-£110; book by phone or email for these special Rick Steves prices, rather than through the pricier website; continental breakfast served at Phoenix Hotel, free Wi-Fi, 9 Kensington Gardens Square, tel. 020/7243-7600, fax 020/7792-8612, www.kensingtongardenshotel.co.uk, info @kensingtongardenshotel.co.uk, Rowshanak).

$$ Princes Square Guest Accommodation is a big 50-room place that's well-located, practical, and a good value, especially with its online discounts (Sb-£65-70, Db-£80-90, Tb-£90-100, elevator, pay Wi-Fi, 23-25 Princes Square, tel. 020/7229-9876, www.princessquarehotel.co.uk, info@princessquarehotel.co.uk).

Near Kensington Gardens

$$$ Westland Hotel, conveniently located on a busy street a five-minute walk from the Notting Hill neighborhood, feels like a wood-paneled hunting lodge with a fine lounge. The 32 spacious rooms are comfortable, with old-fashioned charm. Their £130 doubles are the best value, but check their website for specials. It's been run by the Isseyegh family for three generations (Sb-£112, deluxe Sb-£127, Db-£133, deluxe Db-£155, cavernous premier Db-£176, sprawling Tb-£169-197, gargantuan Qb-£190-225, Quint/b-£239, elevator, pay Wi-Fi, garage-£12/day, between Notting Hill Gate and Queensway Tube stations at 154 Bayswater Road, tel. 020/7229-9191, fax 020/7727-1054, www.westlandhotel .co.uk, reservations@westlandhotel.co.uk, Shirley and Bertie).

$$$ London Vicarage Hotel is family-run, understandably popular, and elegantly British in a quiet, classy neighborhood. It has 17 rooms furnished with taste and quality, a TV lounge, a grand staircase, and facilities on each floor. Mandy and Monika maintain a homey atmosphere (S-£60, Sb-£102, D-£102, Db-£130, T-£130, Tb-£170, Q-£140, Qb-£185, 20 percent less in winter—check website, free Wi-Fi; 8-minute walk from Notting Hill Gate and High Street Kensington Tube stations, near Kensington Palace at 10 Vicarage Gate; tel. 020/7229-4030, fax 020/7792-5989, www .londonvicaragehotel.com, vicaragehotel@btconnect.com).

$$ The Gate Hotel has seven cramped but decent rooms on a delightful curved street near the start of the Portobello Road Market, in the heart of the characteristic Notting Hill neighborhood. While the lodgings are basic, the romantic setting might be worth it for some (Sb-£60, Db-£85, bigger "luxury" Db-£95, Tb-£115, each room £10 more Fri-Sat, 5 percent fee to pay with credit card, continental breakfast in room, no elevator, pay Wi-Fi, 6 Portobello Road, Tube: Notting Hill Gate, tel. 020/7221-0707, fax 020/7221-9128, www.gatehotel.co.uk, bookings@gatehotel .co.uk, Jasmine).

Near Holland Park

$ Norwegian YWCA (Norsk K.F.U.K.)—where English is definitely a second language—is open to any Norwegian woman, and to non-Norwegian women under 30. (Men must be under 30 with a Norwegian passport.) Located on a quiet, stately street, it offers a study, TV room, piano lounge, and an open-face Norwegian ambience (goat cheese on Sundays!). They have mostly quads, so those willing to share with strangers are most likely to get a bed (July-Aug: Ss-£41, shared double-£39/bed, shared triple-£34/bed, shared quad-£30.50/bed, includes breakfast year-round plus sack lunch and dinner Sept-June, £20 key deposit and £2 membership fee required, pay Wi-Fi, 52 Holland Park, Tube: Holland Park, tel. 020/7727-9346 or 020/7727-9897, www.kfukhjemmet.org.uk, kontor@kfukhjemmet.org.uk). With each visit, I wonder which is easier to get—a sex change or a Norwegian passport?

Paddington Station Neighborhood

The neighborhood near Paddington Station—while much less charming than the other areas I've recommended—is pleasant enough, and very convenient to the Heathrow Express airport train. The area is flanked by the Paddington and Lancaster Gate Tube stops. Most of my recommendations circle Norfolk Square, just two blocks in front of Paddington Station, yet still quiet and comfortable. Its main drag, London Street, is lined with handy eateries—pubs, Indian, Italian, Greek, Lebanese, and more—plus convenience stores and an Internet café. To reach this area, exit the station toward Praed Street (with your back to the tracks, it's to the left). Once outside, continue straight across Praed Street and down London Street; Norfolk Square is a block ahead on the left.

On Norfolk Square

These places (and many more on the same street) are similar; all offer small rooms at a reasonable price, in tall buildings with lots of stairs and no elevator. I've chosen the ones that offer the most reasonable prices and the warmest welcome.

$$ St. David's Hotels, run by the hospitable and energetic Neokleous family, has 60 fine rooms in several adjacent buildings (S-£60, Sb-£70, D-£70, Db-£90, Tb-£100, free Wi-Fi, 14-20 Norfolk Square, tel. 020/7723-3856, fax 020/7402-9061, www .stdavidshotels.com, info@stdavidshotels.com).

$$ Tudor Court Hotel has 38 colorful rooms run by the Gupta family (S-£40, Sb-£85, Db-£95, Tb-£115, family room-£135, 10-12 Norfolk Square, tel. 020/7723-5157, fax 020/7723-0727, www.tudorcourtpaddington.co.uk, reservations@tudorcourt paddington.co.uk).

$$ Ashley Hotel is a peeling-wallpaper kind of place with 54 rooms (S-£35-40, Sb-£50-60, Db-£70-80, pay Wi-Fi, 15-17 Norfolk Square, tel. 020/7723-3375, fax 020/7723-0173, www .ashleyhotellondon.com, info@ashleyhotellondon.com).

$ easyHotel, the budget chain described on page 175, has a branch at 10 Norfolk Place.

Elsewhere near Paddington Station

To reach these hotels, follow the directions above, but continue past Norfolk Square to the big intersection with Sussex Gardens; the Royal Park is a couple of blocks to the right, and the Springfield Hotel is immediately to the left.

$$$ The Royal Park is the neighborhood's classy splurge, with 48 plush rooms, polished service, a genteel lounge (free champagne for guests nightly 19:00-20:00), and all the little extras (standard Db-£139-149, bigger "executive" Db-£169-179, prices vary with demand, does not include 20 percent VAT or break-fast, free Internet access and Wi-Fi, 3 Westbourne Terrace, tel. 020/7479-6600, fax 020/7479-6601, www.theroyalpark.com, info @theroyalpark.com).

$$ Springfield Hotel is efficiently run and simple, with 17 updated rooms. It sits on the wide, busy street called Sussex Gardens (request a quieter back room), with several other similar hotels nearby if you're in a pinch (Sb-£60, Db-£80-90, Tb-£100, extra fee to pay with credit card, 154 Sussex Gardens, tel. 020/7723-9898, fax 020/7723-0874, www.springfieldhotellondon .co.uk, info@springfieldhotellondon.co.uk).

Other Neighborhoods

North of Marble Arch: **$$$ The 22 York Street B&B** offers a casual alternative in the city center, renting 10 traditional, hard-wood, comfortable rooms (Sb-£95, Db-£129, free Internet access and Wi-Fi, inviting lounge; from Baker Street Tube station, walk 2 blocks down Baker Street and take a right to 22 York Street—since there's no sign, just look for #22; tel. 020/7224-2990, www.22yorkstreet.co.uk, mc@22yorkstreet.co.uk, energetically run by Liz and Michael Callis).

$$$ The Sumner Hotel, renting 19 rooms in a 19th-century Georgian townhouse, is located a few blocks north of Hyde Park and Oxford Street, a busy shopping destination. Decorated with fancy modern Italian furniture, this swanky place packs in all the extras (Db-£170-220 depending on size, 20 percent discount with this book in 2012, extra bed-£50, air-con, elevator, free Wi-Fi, 54 Upper Berkeley Street just off Edgware Road, Tube: Marble Arch, tel. 020/7723-2244, fax 0870-705-8767, www.thesumner .com, hotel@thesumner.com).

Near Buckingham Palace: **$$ Vandon House Hotel,** run by Central College in Iowa, is packed with students most of the year, but rents its 32 rooms to travelers from late May through August at great prices. The rooms, while institutional, are comfy, and the location is excellent (S-£48, D-£75, Db-£95, Tb-£105, Qb-£125, apartment for up to 4 people-£125, only twin beds, a few rooms available year-round, elevator, pay Internet access and Wi-Fi; 3-minute walk west of St. James's Park Tube station or 7-minute walk from Victoria Station, near west end of Petty France Street on a tiny road, 1 Vandon Street; tel. 020/7799-6780, www.vandon house.com, info@vandonhouse.com).

Near Euston Station and the British Library: The **$$$ Methodist International Centre (MIC),** a modern, youthful Christian hotel and conference center, fills its lower floors with international students and its top floor with travelers. The 28

North London Accommodations

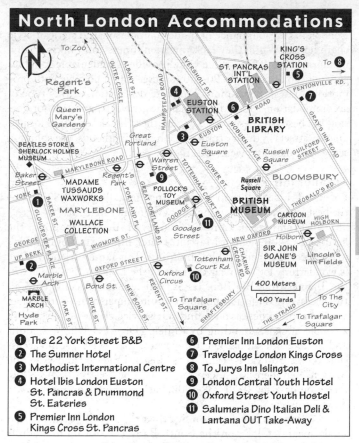

1. The 22 York Street B&B
2. The Sumner Hotel
3. Methodist International Centre
4. Hotel Ibis London Euston St. Pancras & Drummond St. Eateries
5. Premier Inn London Kings Cross St. Pancras
6. Premier Inn London Euston
7. Travelodge London Kings Cross
8. To Jurys Inn Islington
9. London Central Youth Hostel
10. Oxford Street Youth Hostel
11. Salumeria Dino Italian Deli & Lantana OUT Take-Away

rooms are modern and sleek yet comfortable, with fine bathrooms, phones, and desks. The atmosphere is friendly, safe, clean, and controlled; it also has a spacious lounge and game room (Sb-£119 Fri-Sun, £139 Mon-Thu; Db-£130 Fri-Sun, £149 Mon-Thu; pricier "deluxe" rooms also available, buying a £100 annual membership saves you £20-40 per night—do the math to see if it's worth paying for, check website for specials, elevator, pay Wi-Fi, on a quiet street a block west of Euston Station, 81-103 Euston Street—not Euston Road, Tube: Euston, tel. 020/7380-0001, www.micentre .com, reservations@micentre.com). In addition to the rooms in the main building, they have several "annex" rooms—three rooms in one house that share a single bathroom—which could work well for families (S-£85, D-£95). In June-August, when the students are gone, they also rent simpler twin rooms in the main building (S or D-£75, includes one breakfast, extra breakfast-£15).

Big, Good-Value, Modern Hotels

London has an abundance of modern, impersonal, American-style chain hotels. While they lack the friendliness and funkiness of a memorable B&B, the value they provide is undeniable; doubles generally go for around £90-100 (or less—often possible with promotional rates). For a more complete description of this type of accommodation—including amenities, caveats, and tips for getting the best rates—see page 23. As these hotels are often located on busy streets in dreary train-station neighborhoods, use common sense after dark and wear your money belt.

Premier Inn

For any of these, call their reservations line at 0870-242-8000 or—the best option—book online at www.premierinn.com.

$$ Premier Inn London County Hall, literally down the hall from a $400-a-night Marriott Hotel, fills one end of London's massive former County Hall building. This family-friendly place is wonderfully located near the base of the London Eye and across the Thames from Big Ben. Its 313 efficient rooms come with all the necessary comforts, though it's quite impersonal—rather than a real reception desk, you'll find self-service check-in kiosks with a couple of clerks standing by to help (Db-£109-170 for 2 adults and up to 2 kids under age 16, elevator, pay Wi-Fi, some accessible rooms, 500 yards from Westminster Tube stop and Waterloo Station, Belvedere Road, central reservations tel. 0870-242-8000, reception desk tel. 0870-238-3300, easiest to book online at www.premierinn.com).

$$ Premier Inn London Southwark, with 59 rooms, is near Shakespeare's Globe on the South Bank (Db for up to 2 adults and 2 kids-£99-169, elevator, pay Wi-Fi, Bankside, 34 Park Street, Tube: London Bridge, tel. 0871-527-8676, www.premierinn.com).

$$ Premier Inn London Kings Cross St. Pancras, with 276 rooms, is across the street from the east end of King's Cross Station and near the Eurostar terminus at St. Pancras Station (Db-£96-160, air-con, elevator, pay Wi-Fi, 26-30 York Way, Tube: King's Cross St. Pancras, tel. 0871-527-8672, www.premierinn.com).

Other **$$ Premier Inns** charging £90-170 per room include **London Euston** (big, blue Lego-type building packed with vacationing families, on handy but noisy street at corner of Euston Road and Dukes Road, Tube: Euston, tel. 0870-238-3301), **London Kensington Earl's Court** (11 Knaresborough Place, Tube: Earl's Court or Gloucester Road, tel. 0870-238-3304), **London Victoria** (82-83 Eccleston Square, Tube: Victoria, tel. 0870-423-6494), and **London Putney Bridge** (farther out, 3 Putney Bridge Approach, Tube: Putney Bridge, tel. 0870-238-3302). Avoid the

Tower Bridge location, which is an inconvenient 15-minute walk from the nearest Tube stop.

Other Chains

Travelodge: **$$ Travelodge London Kings Cross** is another typical chain hotel with 140 cookie-cutter rooms, just 200 yards south (in front) of King's Cross Station (Db-usually £85, family rooms, can be noisy, elevator, pay Wi-Fi, Grays Inn Road, Tube: King's Cross St. Pancras, tel. 0871-984-6256). Other convenient Travelodge London locations are nearby **Kings Cross Royal Scot, Euston, Marylebone, Covent Garden, Liverpool Street,** and **Farringdon.** For details on all Travelodge hotels, see www.travelodge.co.uk.

Ibis: **$$$ Hotel Ibis London Euston St. Pancras** rents 380 rooms on a quiet street a block west of Euston Station (Db-£89-149, usually £139, no family rooms, elevator, pay Internet access and Wi-Fi, 3 Cardington Street, Tube: Euston, tel. 020/7388-7777, fax 020/7388-0001, www.ibishotel.com, h0921@accor.com). There's also an **Ibis London City** (5 Commercial Street, Tube: Aldgate East, tel. 020/7422-8400), but the other Ibis locations are far from the center.

Jurys Inn: **$$ Jurys Inn Islington** rents 200-plus compact, comfy rooms near King's Cross Station (Db/Tb-£109-169, some discounted rooms available online, 2 adults and 2 kids under age 12 can share one room, 60 Pentonville Road, Tube: Angel, tel. 020/7282-5500, fax 020/7282-5511, www.jurysinns.com). You'll also find Jurys Inns at **Chelsea** (Imperial Road, Tube: Imperial Wharf, tel. 020/7411-2200) and near **Heathrow Airport** (see "Heathrow and Gatwick Airports," later).

easyHotel

With several hotels in good neighborhoods around London, easyHotel is a radical concept—offering what you need to sleep well and safe, and nothing more. Most of them are fitted into old buildings, so the rooms are all odd shapes, from tiny windowless closets to others that are quite spacious. All rooms are well-ventilated and come with an efficient "bathroom pod" that looks like it was popped out of a plastic mold—just big enough to take care of business. While they do have a 24-hour reception, everything else is spartan: you get two towels, liquid soap, and a clean bed—no breakfast, no fresh towels, and no daily cleaning. The base rate ranges from £21-65, depending on the room size and when you book—"The earlier you book, the less you pay." Prices are the same for one person or two, but then you're nickel-and-dimed with optional charges for the TV, Wi-Fi, luggage storage, and so on.

If you go with the basic package, it's like hosteling with privacy—a hard-to-beat value. But you get what you pay for; in my experience, easyHotels are cheap in every sense of the word (no elevator, thin walls, noisy halls filled with loud travelers seeking bargain beds, flimsy construction that often results in broken things in the room). And they're only a good deal if you book far enough ahead to get a good price, and skip the many extras...which can add up fast.

$ **easyHotel Victoria** is well-located in an old building near Victoria Station (77 rooms, 36 Belgrave Road—for location, see map on page 162, Tube: Victoria, tel. 020/7834-1379, enquiries@victoria.easyhotel.com). They also have branches at **South Kensington** (34 rooms, 14 Lexham Gardens, Tube: Earl's Court or Gloucester Road, tel. 020/7136-2870, enquiries@southken.easy hotel.com), **Earl's Court** (80 rooms, 44-48 West Cromwell Road, Tube: Earl's Court, tel. 020/7373-4546, enquiries@earlscourt .easyhotel.com), **Paddington** (47 rooms, 10 Norfolk Place, Tube: Paddington, tel. 020/7706-9911, enquiries@paddington.easy hotel.com), and **Heathrow** and **Luton** airports (Heathrow location described on next page). Regardless of the location, reserve through their website (www.easyhotel.com).

Hostels

For more London hostel listings, try www.hostellondon.com.

$ **London Central Youth Hostel** is the flagship of London's hostels, with 300 beds and all the latest in security and comfortable efficiency. Families and travelers of any age will feel welcome in this wonderful facility. You'll pay the same price for any bed in a 4- to 8-bed single-sex dorm—with or without private bathroom—so try to grab one with a bathroom (£20-30 per bunk bed—fluctuates with demand, £3/night extra for nonmembers, breakfast-£4; includes sheets, towel and locker; families welcome to book an entire room, pay Wi-Fi, members' kitchen, laundry, book long in advance, between Oxford Circus and Great Portland Street Tube stations at 104 Bolsover Street—see map on page 173, tel. 0870-770-6144 or 0845-371-9154, www.yha.org.uk, londoncentral@yha.org.uk).

$ **Oxford Street Youth Hostel,** newly opened, is right in the shopping and clubbing zone in Soho (£17-30 per bunk, 14 Noel Street, Tube: Oxford Street, tel. 0845-371-9133, www.yha.org.uk, oxfordst@yha.org.uk).

$ **St. Paul's Youth Hostel,** near St. Paul's, is clean, modern, friendly, and well-run. Most of the 190 beds are in shared, single-sex 3- to 11-bunk rooms (bed-around £20 depending on demand, twin D-£60, includes locker and sheets but not breakfast, non-members pay £3 extra, cheap meals, open 24 hours, 36 Carter

Lane, Tube: St. Paul's, tel. 020/7236-4965 or tel. 0845-371-9012, www.yha.org.uk, stpauls@yha.org.uk).

$ A cluster of three **St. Christopher's Inn** hostels, south of the Thames near London Bridge, have cheap dorm beds; one branch is for women only. All have loud and friendly bars attached (£22-32, must be over 18 years old, 161-165 Borough High Street, Tube: Borough or London Bridge, reservations tel. 020/8600-7500, www.st-christophers.co.uk).

Dorms

$$ The **University of Westminster** opens its dorm rooms to travelers during summer break, from mid-June through late September. Located in several high-rise buildings scattered around central London, the rooms—some with private bathrooms, others with shared bathrooms nearby—come with access to well-equipped kitchens and big lounges (S-£35, Sb-£60, D-£54, Db-£106, tel. 020/7911-5181, www.westminster.ac.uk/business/summer -accommodation, summeraccommodation@westminster.ac.uk).

$ **University College London** also has rooms for travelers, from mid-June until mid-September (S-£31-43, pay Internet access, tel. 020/7278-3895, www.ucl.ac.uk/residences).

$$ The **London School of Economics** has openings in its dorms from July through September (S-£33-43, Sb-£59-65, D-£52-60, Db-£76-94, tel. 020/7955-7575, www.lsevacations.co .uk, vacations@lse.ac.uk).

Heathrow and Gatwick Airports

At or near Heathrow Airport

It's so easy to get to Heathrow from central London, I see no reason to sleep there. But if you do, here are some options. The Yotel is actually inside the airport, while the rest are a short bus or taxi ride away. In addition to public buses, the cleverly named £4 "Hotel Hoppa" shuttle buses connect the airport to many nearby hotels (different routes serve the various hotels and terminals—may take a while to spot your particular bus at the airport).

$$ Yotel, at the airport inside Terminal 4, has small sleep dens that offer a popular place to catch a quick nap (four hours-£37-64), or to stay overnight (tiny "standard cabin"—£65/8 hours, "premium cabin"—£87/8 hours; cabins sleep 1-2 people; price is per cabin—not person, reserve online for free or by phone for small fee). Prices vary by day, week, and time of year, so check their website. All rooms are only slightly larger than a double bed, and have private bathrooms and free Internet access and Wi-Fi. These windowless rooms have oddly purplish lighting (tel. 020/7100-1100, www.yotel.com, customer@yotel.com).

$ easyHotel, your cheapest bet, is in a low-rent residential neighborhood a £5 taxi ride from the airport. Its 53 no-frills, pod-like rooms are on two floors. Before booking at this very basic place, read the explanation on page 175 (Db-£25-50, no breakfast, no elevator, pay Internet access and Wi-Fi, Brick Field Lane; take local bus #140 from airport's Central Bus Station or the "Hotel Hoppa" #H8 from Terminals 1 or 3, or the hotel can arrange a taxi to the airport; tel. 020/8897-9237, www.easyhotel.com, enquiries @heathrow.easyhotel.com).

$$ Hotel Ibis London Heathrow is a chain hotel offering predictable value (Db-£80 Mon-Thu, Db-£60 Fri-Sun, check website for specials as low as £35, breakfast-£7, pay Internet access and Wi-Fi; 112-114 Bath Road, take local bus #105, #111, #140, #285, #423, or #555 from airport's Central Bus Station or Terminal 4, or the "Hotel Hoppa" #H6 from Terminals 1 or 3, or #H56 from Terminals 4 or 5; tel. 020/8759-4888, fax 020/8564-7894, www .ibishotel.com, h0794@accor.com).

$$ Jurys Inn, another hotel chain, tempts tired travelers with 300-plus cookie-cutter rooms (Db-£89-105, check website for deals, breakfast extra; on Eastern Perimeter Road, Tube: Hatton Cross plus 5-minute walk; take the Tube one stop from Terminals 1, 2, or 3; or two stops from Terminals 4 or 5; or the "Hotel Hoppa" #H9 from Terminals 1 or 3, or #H53 from Terminals 4 or 5; or buses #285, #482, #490, or #555; tel. 020/8266-4664, fax 020/8266-4665, www.jurysinns.com).

At or near Gatwick Airport

$$ Yotel, with small rooms, has a branch right at the airport (Gatwick South Terminal; see prices and contact info in Heathrow listing, earlier).

$ Gatwick Airport Central Premier Inn rents cheap rooms 350 yards from the airport (Db-£40-75, breakfast-£8, £2 shuttle bus from airport—must reserve in advance, Longbridge Way, North Terminal, tel. 0871-527-8406, frustrating phone tree, www .premierinn.com). Four more Premier Inns are within a five-mile radius of the airport.

$$ Barn Cottage, a converted 16th-century barn flanked by a tennis court and swimming pool, sits in the peaceful countryside, with a good pub just two blocks away. Its two wood-beamed rooms, antique furniture, and large garden make you forget Gatwick is 10 minutes away (S-£60, D-£80, cash only, Church Road, Leigh, Reigate, Surrey, tel. 01306/611-347, warmly run by Pat and Mike Comer). Don't confuse this place with others of the same name. A taxi from Gatwick to here runs about £15; the Comers can take you back to the airport or train station for about £10.

$ Gatwick Airport Travelodge has budget rooms about two miles from the airport (Db-£39-57, breakfast extra, pay Wi-Fi, Church Road, Lowfield Heath, Crawley, £3 shuttle bus from airport, tel. 0871-984-6031, www.travelodge.co.uk).

Eating in London

In London, the sheer variety of foods—from every corner of its former empire and beyond—is astonishing. You'll be amazed at the number of hopping, happening new restaurants of all kinds.

If you want to dine (as opposed to eat), drop by a London newsstand to get a weekly entertainment guide or an annual restaurant guide (both have extensive restaurant listings). Visit www.london-eating.co.uk or www.squaremeal.co.uk for more options.

The thought of a £50 meal in Britain generally ruins my appetite, so my London dining is limited mostly to easygoing, fun, moderately priced alternatives. I've listed places by neighborhood—handy to your sightseeing or hotel. Considering how expensive London can be, if there's any good place to cut corners and stretch your budget, it's by eating cheaply. Pub grub (at one of London's 7,000 pubs) and ethnic restaurants (especially Indian and Chinese) are good low-cost options. Of course, picnicking is the fastest and cheapest way to go. Good grocery stores and sandwich shops, fine park benches, and polite pigeons abound in Britain's most expensive city.

Remember, London (and all of Britain) is smoke-free. Expect restaurants and pubs that sell food to be non-smoking indoors, with smokers occupying patios and doorways outside.

Central London
Near Trafalgar Square
These places are within about 100 yards of Trafalgar Square.

St. Martin-in-the-Fields Café in the Crypt is just right for a tasty meal on a monk's budget—maybe even on a monk's tomb. You'll dine sitting on somebody's gravestone in an ancient crypt. Their enticing buffet line is kept stocked all day, serving breakfast, lunch, and dinner (£6-10 cafeteria plates, hearty traditional desserts, free jugs of water). They also serve a restful cream tea (£6, daily 14:00-17:00). You'll find it directly under the St. Martin-in-the-Fields Church, facing Trafalgar Square (Mon-Tue 8:00-20:00, Wed 8:00-22:30, Thu-Sat 8:00-21:00, Sun 11:00-18:00, profits go to the church, Tube: Charing Cross, tel. 020/7766-1158 or 020/7766-1100). Wednesday evenings at 20:00 come with a live jazz band (£6-9 tickets). While here, check out the concert schedule for the busy church upstairs (or visit www.smitf.org).

LONDON

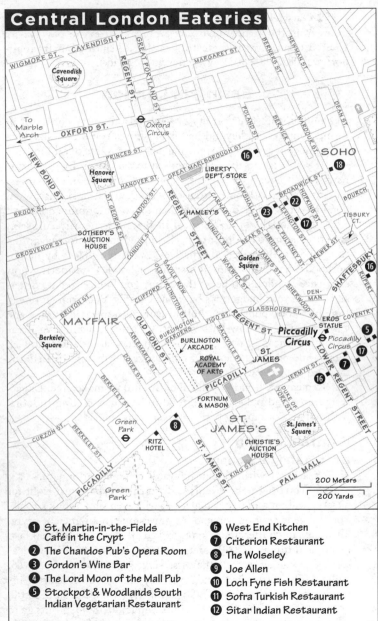

Central London Eateries

❶ St. Martin-in-the-Fields
Café in the Crypt

❷ The Chandos Pub's Opera Room

❸ Gordon's Wine Bar

❹ The Lord Moon of the Mall Pub

❺ Stockpot & Woodlands South
Indian Vegetarian Restaurant

❻ West End Kitchen

❼ Criterion Restaurant

❽ The Wolseley

❾ Joe Allen

❿ Loch Fyne Fish Restaurant

⓫ Sofra Turkish Restaurant

⓬ Sitar Indian Restaurant

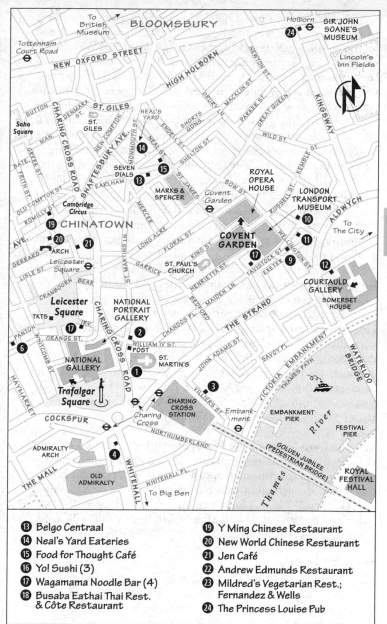

13 Belgo Centraal
14 Neal's Yard Eateries
15 Food for Thought Café
16 Yo! Sushi (3)
17 Wagamama Noodle Bar (4)
18 Busaba Eathai Thai Rest. & Côte Restaurant

19 Y Ming Chinese Restaurant
20 New World Chinese Restaurant
21 Jen Café
22 Andrew Edmunds Restaurant
23 Mildred's Vegetarian Rest.; Fernandez & Wells
24 The Princess Louise Pub

The Chandos Pub's Opera Room floats amazingly apart from the tacky crush of tourism around Trafalgar Square. Look for it opposite the National Portrait Gallery (corner of William IV Street and St. Martin's Lane) and climb the stairs (to the right of the pub entrance) to the Opera Room. This is a fine Trafalgar rendezvous point and wonderfully local pub. They serve traditional, plain-tasting £6-7 pub meals—meat pies and fish-and-chips are their specialty. The ground-floor pub is stuffed with regulars and offers snugs (private booths), the same menu, and more serious beer drinking. Chandos proudly serves the local Samuel Smith beer at £2 a pint (kitchen open daily 11:00-19:00, order and pay at the bar, 29 St. Martin's Lane, Tube: Leicester Square, tel. 020/7836-1401).

Gordon's Wine Bar, with a simple, steep staircase leading into a candlelit 15th-century wine cellar, is filled with dusty old bottles, faded British memorabilia, and nine-to-fivers. At the "English rustic" buffet, choose a hot meal or cold meat dish with a salad, or a hearty (and splittable) plate of cheeses, bread, and pickles (£7.75)—or share four plates for £12. Then step up to the wine bar and consider the many varieties of wine and port available by the glass (this place is passionate about port). The low carbon-crusted vaulting deeper in the back seems to intensify the Hogarth-painting atmosphere. Although it's crowded, you can normally corral two chairs and grab the corner of a table. On hot days, the crowd spills out onto a leafy back patio, where a barbecue cooks for a long line of tables (arrive before 17:00 to get a seat, Mon-Sat 11:00-23:00, Sun 12:00-22:00, 2 blocks from Trafalgar Square, bottom of Villiers Street at #47, Tube: Embankment, tel. 020/7930-1408, www.gordonswinebar.com, manager Gerard Menan).

The Lord Moon of the Mall pub, with real ales on tap and cheap pub grub such as fish-and-chips, is a good place to experience retro English cuisine from the days when it had a horrible reputation. The pub fills a great old former Barclays Bank building a block down Whitehall from Trafalgar Square (daily 9:00-22:00, kid-friendly menu but no kids after 20:00, 16-18 Whitehall, Tube: Charing Cross or Embankment, tel. 020/7839-7701).

Near Piccadilly

Hungry and broke in the theater district? Head for Panton Street (off Haymarket, two blocks southeast of Piccadilly Circus), where several hardworking little places compete, all seeming to offer a three-course meal for about £9. Peruse the entire block for your options (vegetarian, Pizza Express, Moroccan, Thai, Chinese, and two famous diners) before making your choice.

Stockpot is a meat, potatoes, gravy, and mushy-peas kind of place, famous and rightly popular for its edible, cheap English meals (Mon-Sat 7:00-23:00, Sun 7:00-22:00, 38-40 Panton Street, cash only). The **West End Kitchen** (across the street at #5, same hours and menu) is a direct competitor that's also well-known and just as good. Vegetarians may prefer the **Woodlands South Indian Vegetarian Restaurant,** which serves an impressive £18 *thali* (37 Panton Street).

The palatial **Criterion** offers grand-piano ambience beneath gilded tiles and chandeliers in a dreamy Byzantine church setting from 1880. It's right on Piccadilly Circus but a world away from the punk junk. It's a deal for the visual experience during lunch and before 19:00—but after 19:00, the menu becomes really expensive...and, at any hour, the service could care less. Anyone can drop in for coffee or a drink (£17-20 fixed-price meals, daily 12:00-14:30 & 17:30-19:00 & 22:00-23:30, 224 Piccadilly, tel. 020/7930-0488).

The **Wolseley** is the grand 1920s showroom of a long-defunct British car. The last Wolseley drove out with the Great Depression, but today this old-time bistro bustles with formal waiters serving traditional Austrian and French dishes in an elegant black-marble-and-chandeliers setting fit for its location next to the Ritz. Although the food can be unexceptional, prices are reasonable, and the presentation and setting are grand. Reservations are a must (£18 plates; cheaper soup, salad, and sandwich menu available; Mon-Fri 7:00-24:00, Sat 8:00-24:00, Sun 8:00-23:00, 160 Piccadilly—for exact location, see map on page 180, tel. 020/7499-6996). They're popular for their fancy cream or afternoon tea (for details, see page 194).

Near Covent Garden

Covent Garden bustles with people and touristy eateries. The area feels overrun, but if you must eat around here, there are some good options.

Joe Allen, tucked in a basement a block away, serves modern international and American cuisine with both style and hubbub. Downstairs off a quiet street with candles and white tablecloths, it's comfortably spacious and popular with the theater crowd (meals for about £30, £16 two-course specials and £18 three-course specials Mon-Wed and Sun, open daily 11:30-23:00, piano music after 21:00, 13 Exeter Street, tel. 020/7836-0651).

Loch Fyne Fish Restaurant is part of a Scottish chain that grows its own oysters and mussels. It offers an inviting atmosphere with a fine fishy energy and no pretense (£10-15 main dishes, £12.50 two-course special served 12:00-19:00, open daily, a couple of blocks behind Covent Garden at 2 Catherine Street, tel. 020/7240-4999).

Sofra Turkish Restaurant is good for quality Turkish with a touch of class. They have several menus: *meze* (Turkish tapas), vegetarian, and set (£8 before 19:00, £11 after 18:00, open long hours daily, 36 Tavistock Street, tel. 020/7240-3773).

Sitar Indian Restaurant is a well-respected Indian/Bangladeshi place serving dishes from many regions, fine fish, and a tasty £17 vegetarian *thali*. It's small and dressy, with snappy service (£15 main dishes, Mon-Fri 12:00-24:00, Sat-Sun 14:30-24:00, next to Somerset House at 149 Strand—see map on page 180, tel. 020/7836-3730).

Belgo Centraal serves hearty Belgian specialties in a vast 400-seat underground lair. It's a mussels, chips, and beer emporium dressed up as a mod-monastic refectory—with noisy acoustics and waiters garbed as Trappist monks. The classy restaurant section is more comfortable and less rowdy, but usually requires reservations. It's often more fun just to grab a spot in the boisterous beer hall, with its tight, communal benches (no reservations accepted). Both sides have the same menu and specials. Belgians claim they eat as well as the French and as heartily as the Germans. This place, which offers a stunning array of dark, blonde, and fruity Belgian beers, actually makes Belgian things trendy—a formidable feat (£10-14 meals, open daily 12:00-23:00; Mon-Fri £5-6.30 "beat the clock" meal specials 17:00-18:30—the time you order is the price you pay—including main dishes and fries; no meal-splitting after 18:30, and you must buy food with beer; daily £8 lunch special 12:00-17:00; 1 kid eats free for each parent ordering a regular entrée; 1 block north of Covent Garden Tube station at 50 Earlham Street, tel. 020/7813-2233).

Neal's Yard is *the* place for cheap, hip, and healthy eateries near Covent Garden. The neighborhood is a tabouli of fun, hippie-type cafés. One of the best is the venerable and ferociously vegetarian **Food for Thought,** packed with local health nuts (good £5 vegetarian meals, £8 dinner plates, Mon-Sat 12:00-20:30, Sun 12:00-17:30, 2 blocks north of Covent Garden Tube station at 31 Neal Street, near Neal's Yard, tel. 020/7836-0239).

Near Soho and Chinatown

London has a trendy scene that most Beefeater-seekers miss entirely. These restaurants are scattered throughout the hipster, gay, and strip-club district, teeming each evening with fun-seekers and theatergoers. Even if you plan to have dinner elsewhere, it's a treat just to wander around this lively area.

Beware of the extremely welcoming women standing outside the strip clubs (especially on Great Windmill Street). Enjoy the sales pitch—but only fools fall for the "£5 drink and show" lure. Seriously. If you go in, you'll leave with an empty wallet.

Yo! Sushi is a futuristic Japanese-food-extravaganza experience, complete with thumping rock music, Japanese cable TV, and a 195-foot-long conveyor belt. For £1.25, you get unlimited green tea or water. Snag a bar stool and grab dishes as they rattle by (priced by color of dish; check the chart: £1.75-5 per dish, daily 12:00-23:00, 2 blocks south of Oxford Street, where Lexington Street becomes Poland Street, 52 Poland Street, tel. 020/7287-0443). If you like Yo!, there are about 40 other locations around town, including a handy branch a block from the London Eye on Belvedere Road, as well as outlets within Selfridges, Harvey Nichols department stores, and Whiteleys Shopping Centre on Queensway.

Wagamama Noodle Bar is a noisy, pan-Asian, organic slurp-athon. As you enter, check out the kitchen and listen to the roar of the basement, where benches rock with happy eaters. Everybody sucks. Portions are huge and splitting is allowed (£7-10 meals, Mon-Sat 11:30-23:00, Sun 12:00-22:00, crowded after 19:00, 10A Lexington Street, tel. 020/7292-0990 but no reservations taken). If you like this place, handy branches are all over town, including one near the British Museum (4 Streatham Street), Kensington (26 High Street), in Harvey Nichols (109 Knightsbridge), Covent Garden (1 Tavistock Street), Leicester Square (14 Irving Street), Piccadilly Circus (8 Norris Street), Fleet Street (#109), and next to the Tower of London (Tower Place).

Busaba Eathai Thai Restaurant is a hit with locals for its snappy service, casual-yet-high-energy ambience, and good, inexpensive Thai cuisine. You'll sit communally around big, square 16-person hardwood tables or in two-person tables by the window—with everyone in the queue staring at your noodles. They don't take reservations, so arrive by 19:00 or line up (£7-10 meals, Mon-Thu 12:00-23:00, Fri-Sat 12:00-23:30, Sun 12:00-22:00, 106 Wardour Street, tel. 020/7255-8686). They have three other handy locations: on nearby Panton Street, just below Piccadilly Circus; at 22 Store Street, near the British Museum and Goodge Street Tube; and at 8-13 Bird Street, just off Oxford Street and across from the Bond Street Tube.

Côte Restaurant is a contemporary French bistro chain with no pretense, serving good-value French cuisine at the right prices (£9-13 mains, £12 three-course early dinner specials if you order by 19:00, open Mon-Wed 8:00-23:00, Thu-Fri 8:00-24:00, Sat 9:00-24:00, Sun 9:00-22:30, 124-126 Wardour Street, tel. 020/7287-9280).

Y Ming Chinese Restaurant—across Shaftesbury Avenue from the ornate gates, clatter, and dim sum of Chinatown—has dressy European decor, serious but helpful service, and authentic Northern Chinese cooking (good £11 meal deal offered 12:00-18:00, £7-11 plates, open Mon-Sat 12:00-23:45, closed Sun, 35-36 Greek Street, tel. 020/7734-2721).

New World Chinese Restaurant is a sprawling, old-fashioned Chinese diner that just feels real. It's a fixture in Chinatown, serving cheap Cantonese food, including dim sum and a similar dinner menu with an array of little £3 dishes (daily 11:00-24:00, dim sum daily 12:00-18:00, 1 Gerrard Place, tel. 020/7734-0677).

Jen Café, across the street, is a humble Chinese corner eatery much loved for its homemade dumplings. It's just stools and simple seating, with fast service, a fun, inexpensive menu, and a devoted following (£3-5 plates, long hours daily, 4 Newport Place, tel. 020/7287-9708).

On Lexington Street, in the Heart of Soho

Andrew Edmunds Restaurant is a tiny, candlelit place where you'll want to hide your camera and guidebook and not act like a tourist. This little place—with a jealous and loyal clientele—is the closest I've found to Parisian quality in a cozy restaurant in London. The modern European cooking and creative seasonal menu are worth the splurge (£6-8 starters, £10-20 main dishes, Mon-Sat 12:30-15:00 & 18:00-22:45, Sun 13:00-15:30 & 18:00-22:30, come early or call ahead, request ground floor rather than basement, 46 Lexington Street, tel. 020/7437-5708).

Mildred's Vegetarian Restaurant, across from Andrew Edmunds, has cheap prices, an enjoyable menu, and a pleasant interior filled with happy eaters (£7-9 meals, Mon-Sat 12:00-23:00, closed Sun, vegan options, 45 Lexington Street, tel. 020/7494-1634).

Fernandez & Wells is a delightfully simple little wine, cheese, and ham bar. Drop in and grab a stool as you belly up to the big wooden bar. Share a plate of top-quality cheeses and/or Spanish, Italian, or French hams with fine bread and oil, while sipping a nice glass of wine (Mon-Sat 11:00-22:00, Sun 12:00-19:00, quality sandwiches at lunch, wine/cheese/ham bar after 16:00, 43 Lexington Street, tel. 020/7734-1546).

Near the British Museum

Tiny Charlotte Place is lined with small eateries. It's a short walk from the Goodge Street Tube station and convenient to the British Museum and Pollock's Toy Museum (see map on page 173).

Salumeria Dino serves up hearty sandwiches, pasta, and Italian coffee. Dino, a native of Naples, has run his little shop for 30 years and has managed to create a classic Italian deli that's so authentic, you'll walk out singing "O Sole Mio" (£3-5 sandwiches, £1 take-away cappuccinos, Mon-Fri 9:00-17:00, closed Sat-Sun, #15, tel. 020/7580-3938).

Lantana OUT, next door to Salumeria Dino, sells modern soups, sandwiches, and salads at their take-away window. Their changing menu features a soup-salad-sweet combo deal for £5.50 (£3-7 meals, pricier sit-down café next door, Mon-Fri 7:30-15:00, café open Sat-Sun 9:00-15:00, #13, tel. 020/7637-3347).

West London
Near Victoria Station Accommodations

These restaurants are within a few blocks of Victoria Station—and all are places where I've enjoyed eating. As with the accommodations in this area, I've grouped them by location: east or west of the station (see the map on page 162).

Cheap Eats: For groceries, a handy **M&S Simply Food** is inside Victoria Station (Mon-Sat 7:00-24:00, Sun 8:00-22:00), along with a **Sainsbury's Market** (daily 6:00-23:00, at rear entrance, on Eccleston Street). A second Sainsbury's is just north of the station on Victoria Street, and a larger Sainsbury's is on Wilton Road near Warwick Way, a couple of blocks southeast of the station (Mon-Fri 7:00-23:00, Sat 7:00-22:00, Sun 11:00-17:00). A string of good ethnic restaurants lines Wilton Road (near the recommended Seafresh Fish Restaurant). For affordable if forgettable meals, try the row of cheap little eateries on Elizabeth Street.

West of Victoria Station

Ebury Wine Bar, filled with young professionals, provides a cut-above atmosphere, delicious £13-18 main dishes, and an £18 two-course and £23 three-course special anytime (three-course meal includes a glass of champagne that you're welcome to swap for wine). In the delightful back room, the fancy menu features modern European cuisine with a French accent; at the wine bar, find a cheaper bar menu that's better than your average pub grub. This is emphatically a "traditional wine bar," with no beers on tap (daily 11:00-23:00, reservations smart, at intersection of Ebury and Elizabeth Streets, 139 Ebury Street, tel. 020/7730-5447).

Jenny Lo's Tea House is a simple budget place serving up reliably tasty £7-9 eclectic Chinese-style meals to locals in the know. While the menu is small, everything is high quality. Jenny clearly learned from her father, Ken Lo, one of the most famous Cantonese chefs in Britain, whose fancy place is just around the corner (Mon-Fri 12:00-15:00 & 18:00-22:00, closed Sat-Sun, cash only, 14 Eccleston Street, tel. 020/7259-0399).

La Bottega is an Italian delicatessen that fits its upscale Belgravia neighborhood. It offers tasty, freshly cooked pastas (£6), lasagnas, and salads (lasagna and salad meal-£8), along with great sandwiches (£3) and a good coffee bar with pastries. While not cheap, it's fast (order at the counter), and the ingredients would please an Italian chef. Grab your meal to go, or enjoy the Belgravia good life with locals, either sitting inside or on the sidewalk

Pub Appreciation

The pub is the heart of the people's England, where all manner of folks have, for generations, found their respite from work and a home-away-from-home. England's classic pubs are national treasures, with great cultural value and rich history, not to mention good beer and grub.

The Golden Age for pub-building was in the late Victorian era (c. 1880-1905), when pubs were independently owned and land prices were high enough to make it worthwhile to invest in fixing up pubs. The politics were pro-pub as well: Conservatives, backed by Big Beer, were in, and temperance-minded Liberals were out.

Especially in class-conscious Victorian times, traditional pubs were divided into sections by elaborate screens (now mostly gone), allowing the wealthy to drink in a more refined setting, while commoners congregated on the pub's rougher side. These were really "public houses," featuring nooks (snugs) for groups and clubs to meet, friends and lovers to rendezvous, and families to get out of the house at night. Because many pub-goers were illiterate, pubs were simply named for the picture hung outside (e.g., The Crooked Stick, The Queen's Arms—meaning her coat of arms).

Historic pubs still dot the London cityscape. The only place to see the very oldest-style tavern in the "domestic tradition" is at **Ye Olde Cheshire Cheese,** which was rebuilt in 1667 (after the Great Fire) from a 16th-century tavern (£6-7 pub grub, £9-12 meals in the restaurant, open daily, 145 Fleet Street, Tube: Blackfriars, tel. 020/7353-6170). Imagine this place in the pre-Victorian era: With no bar, drinkers gathered around the fireplaces, while tap boys shuttled tankards up from the cellar. (This was long before barroom taps were connected to casks in the cellar. Oh, and don't say "keg"—that's a gassy modern thing.)

Late-Victorian pubs, such as the lovingly restored 1897 **Princess Louise** (Mon-Fri 11:00-23:00, Sat 12:00-23:00, closed Sun, 208 High Holborn, see map on page 181, Tube: Holborn, tel. 020/7405-8816), are more common. These places are fancy, often with heavily embossed wallpaper ceilings, decorative tile work, fine-etched glass, ornate carved stillions (the big central hutch for storing bottles and glasses), and even urinals equipped with a place to set your glass.

London's best Art Nouveau pub is **The Black Friar** (c. 1900-1915), with fine carved capitals, lamp holders, and quirky phrases worked into the decor (£7-12 meals, open daily, outdoor seating, 174 Queen Victoria Street, Tube: Blackfriars, tel. 020/7236-5474).

The "former-bank pubs" represent a more modern trend in

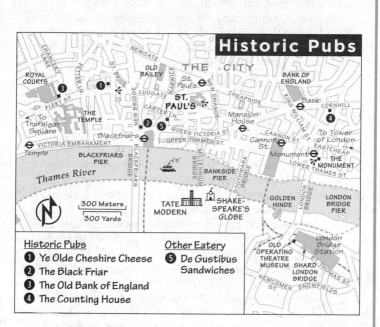

Historic Pubs

THE CITY

ROYAL COURTS

OLD BAILEY

St. Paul's

BANK OF ENGLAND

Bank

CORNHILL

LUDGATE

ST. PAUL'S

CHEAPSIDE

KING WILLIAM ST.

④

CARTER LN.

Mansion House

THE TEMPLE

②⑤

QUEEN VICTORIA ST.

UPPER THAMES ST.

CANNON ST.

Cannon St.

To Tower of London

EASTCHEAP

Blackfriars

VICTORIA EMBANKMENT

Monument ⊖

THE MONUMENT

Temple ⊖

BLACKFRIARS PIER

LOWER THAMES ST.

Thames River

BLACKFRIARS BRIDGE

MILLENNIUM BRIDGE

BANKSIDE PIER

SOUTHWARK BRIDGE

GOLDEN HINDE

LONDON BRIDGE

LONDON BRIDGE PIER

300 Meters
300 Yards

TATE MODERN

SHAKE-SPEARE'S GLOBE

London Bridge Station

To Trafalgar Square

Historic Pubs
① Ye Olde Cheshire Cheese
② The Black Friar
③ The Old Bank of England
④ The Counting House

Other Eatery
⑤ De Gustibus Sandwiches

OLD OPERATING THEATRE MUSEUM

SHARD LONDON BRIDGE

NEWCOMEN ST.

SNOWFIELDS

ST. THOMAS ST.

LONDON

pub-building. As banks increasingly go electronic, they're moving out of lavish, high-rent old buildings. Many of these former

banks are being refitted as pubs with elegant bars and freestanding stillions, providing a fine centerpiece. Three such pubs are **The Old Bank of England** (Mon-Fri 11:00-23:00, closed Sat-Sun, 194 Fleet Street, Tube: Temple, tel. 020/7430-2255), **The Jugged Hare** (open daily, 172 Vauxhall Bridge Road—see map on page 162, Tube: Victoria, tel. 020/7828-1543, also see listing on page 190), and **The Counting House** (Mon-Fri 11:00-23:00, closed Sat-Sun, 50 Cornhill, Tube: Bank, tel. 020/7283-7123, also see listing on page 193).

Go pubbing in the evening for a lively time, or drop by during the quiet late morning (from 11:00), when the pub is empty and filled with memories. For a guided tour, check out Bob Steel's London Heritage pub walks (about £50/group for a leisurely half-day private walk, www.aletrails.com, tel. 020/715-4815, info @aletrails.com).

(Mon-Fri 8:00-19:00, Sat 9:00-18:00, Sun 10:00-17:00, on corner of Ebury and Eccleston Streets, tel. 020/7730-2730).

The Duke of Wellington Pub is a classic neighborhood place with forgettable grub, woodsy sidewalk seating, and an inviting interior (dinner served Mon-Sat 18:00-21:00, 63 Eaton Terrace, tel. 020/7730-1782).

The Thomas Cubitt Pub, packed with young professionals, is a trendy neighborhood gastropub, great for a drink or pricey meal (44 Elizabeth Street, tel. 020/7730-6060).

East of Victoria Station

Grumbles brags it's been serving "good food and wine at nonscary prices since 1964." Offering a delicious mix of "modern eclectic French and traditional English," this unpretentious little place with cozy booths inside (on two levels, including a cellar) and four nice sidewalk tables is *the* spot to eat well in this otherwise workaday neighborhood. Their traditional dishes are their forte (£9-18 plates, £11 early-bird specials 18:00-19:00, open daily 12:00-14:30 & 18:00-23:00, reservations wise, half a block north of Belgrave Road at 35 Churton Street, tel. 020/7834-0149, Alex).

Seafresh Fish Restaurant is the neighborhood place for plaice—and classic and creative fish-and-chips cuisine. You can either take out on the cheap or eat in, enjoying a white fish ambience. Though Mario's father started this place in 1965, it feels like the chippie of the 21st century (meals-£6 to go, £10-15 to sit, Mon-Sat 12:00-15:00 & 17:00-22:30, closed Sun, 80-81 Wilton Road, tel. 020/7828-0747).

The Jugged Hare pub, a 10-minute walk from Victoria Station, sits in a lavish old bank building, with vaults replaced by tankards of beer and a fine kitchen. They have a fun, traditional menu with more fresh veggies than fries, and a plush, vivid pub scene good for a meal or just a drink (£6.25 sandwiches, £8-10 meals, food served daily 12:00-21:30, drinks served daily 11:00-23:00, 172 Vauxhall Bridge Road, tel. 020/7828-1543).

St. George's Tavern is *the* pub for a meal in this neighborhood. They serve dinner from the same fun menu in three zones: on the sidewalk to catch the sun and enjoy some people-watching, in the sloppy pub, and in a classier back dining room. They're proud of their sausages and "toad in the hole." The scene is inviting for just a beer, too (£7-10 meals, Mon-Sat 10:00-22:00, Sun until 21:30, corner of Hugh Street and Belgrave Road, tel. 020/7630-1116).

Near Notting Hill and Bayswater Accommodations

For locations, see the map on page 168.

Maggie Jones, a Charles Dickens-meets-Ella Fitzgerald splurge, is exuberantly rustic and very English, with a 1940s-jazz soundtrack. You'll get solid English cuisine, including huge plates of crunchy vegetables, served by a young and casual staff. It's pricey, but the portions are huge (especially the meat-and-fish pies, their specialty). You're welcome to save lots by splitting your main course. The candlelit upstairs is the most romantic, while the basement is kept lively with the kitchen, tight seating, and lots of action. If you eat well once in London, eat here—and do it quick, before it burns down (lunch—£5 starters, £7 main dishes; dinner—£6-9 starters, £10-23 main dishes; Mon-Sat 12:00-15:00 & 18:30-23:00, Sun 12:30-16:00 & 18:30-22:30, reservations recommended, 6 Old Court Place, just east of Kensington Church Street, near High Street Kensington Tube stop, tel. 020/7937-6462).

The Churchill Arms pub and **Thai Kitchen** (same location) are local hangouts, with good beer and a thriving old-English ambience in front, and hearty £8 Thai plates in an enclosed patio in the back. You can eat the Thai food in the tropical hideaway (table service) or in the atmospheric pub section (order at the counter and they'll bring it to you). They also serve basic English pub food at lunch (£3 sandwiches, £6 meals). The place is festooned with Churchill memorabilia and chamber pots (including one with Hitler's mug on it—hanging from the ceiling farthest from Thai Kitchen—sure to cure the constipation of any Brit during World War II). Arrive by 18:00 or after 21:00 to avoid a line. During busy times, diners are limited to an hour at the table (daily 12:00-22:00, 119 Kensington Church Street, tel. 020/7792-1246).

The Prince Edward serves good grub in a quintessential pub setting (£7-12 meals, Mon-Wed 10:00-23:00, Thu-Sat 10:00-23:30, Sun 10:00-22:30, plush-pubby indoor seating or sidewalk tables, family-friendly, pay Wi-Fi, 2 blocks north of Bayswater Road at the corner of Dawson Place and Hereford Road, 73 Prince's Square, tel. 020/7727-2221).

Café Diana is a healthy little eatery serving sandwiches, salads, and Middle Eastern food. It's decorated—almost shrine-like—with photos of Princess Diana, who used to drop by for pita sandwiches. You can dine in the simple interior, or order some food from the counter to go (£3-5 sandwiches, £6-8 meat dishes, daily 8:00-23:00, 5 Wellington Terrace, on Bayswater Road, opposite Kensington Palace Garden Gates, where Di once lived, tel. 020/7792-9606, Abdul).

On Queensway: The road called Queensway is a multiethnic food circus, lined with lively and inexpensive eateries—browse the options along here and choose your favorite. For a cut above, head for **Royal China Restaurant**—filled with London's Chinese population, who consider this one of the city's best eateries. It's dressed up in black, white, and gold, with candles and brisk waiters. While it's pricier than most neighborhood Chinese restaurants, the food is noticeably better (£9-13 dishes, Mon-Thu 12:00-23:00, Fri-Sat 12:00-23:30, Sun 11:00-22:00, dim sum until 17:00, 13 Queensway, tel. 020/7221-2535). For a lowbrow alternative, **Whiteleys Shopping Centre Food Court**—at the top end of Queensway—offers a fun selection of ethnic and fast-food chain eateries among Corinthian columns, and a multiscreen theater in a delightful mall (daily 9:00-23:00; options include Yo! Sushi, good salads at Café Rouge, pizza, Starbucks, and a coin-op Internet place; third floor, corner of Porchester Gardens and Queensway).

Supermarkets: **Tesco** is a half-block from the Notting Hill Gate Tube stop (Mon-Sat 7:00-23:00, Sun 12:00-18:00, near intersection with Pembridge Road, 114-120 Notting Hill Gate). The smaller **Spar Market** is at 18 Queensway (Mon-Sat 7:00-24:00, Sun 9:00-24:00), and **Marks & Spencer** can be found in Whiteleys Shopping Centre (Mon-Sat 9:00-20:00, Sun 12:00-18:00).

South Kensington

Popular eateries line Old Brompton Road and Thurloe Street (Tube: South Kensington), and a good selection of cheap eateries are clumped around the Tube station. For locations, see the map on page 166.

La Bouchée Bistro Café is a classy hole-in-the-wall touch of France. This candlelit and woody bistro, with very tight seating, serves a two-course, £11.50 special on weekdays during lunch and from 17:30-18:30, and £17 *plats du jour* all *jour.* Reservations are smart in the evening (daily 12:00-15:00 & 17:30-23:30, 56 Old Brompton Road, tel. 020/7589-1929).

Moti Mahal Indian Restaurant, with minimalist-yet-classy mod ambience and attentive service, serves mostly Bangladeshi cuisine that's delicious. Consider chicken *jalfrezi* if you like spicy food, and buttery chicken if you don't (£10 dinners, daily 12:00-14:30 & 17:30-23:00, 3 Glendower Place, tel. 020/7584-8428).

Beirut Express has fresh, well-prepared Lebanese cuisine. In the front, you'll find take-away service as well as barstools for quick service (£4 sandwiches). In the back is a sit-down restaurant with £14 plates (daily 12:00-23:00, 65 Old Brompton Road, tel. 020/7591-0123).

Bosphorus Kebabs is the student favorite for a quick, fast, and hearty Turkish dinner. While mostly for take-away, they have a few tight tables indoors and on the sidewalk (£5 meals, Turkish kebabs, daily until 24:00, 59 Old Brompton Road, tel. 020/7584-4048).

Rocca di Papa is a bright and dressy Italian place with a heated terrace (£8 pizza, pasta, and salads; open daily, 73 Old Brompton Road, tel. 020/7225-3413).

The Anglesea Arms, with a great terrace surrounded by classy

South Kensington buildings, is a destination pub that feels like the classic neighborhood favorite. It's a thriving and happy place, with a woody ambience and a mellow back dining room a world away from any tourism. Chef Julian Legge freshens up traditional English cuisine and prints up a daily menu listing his creative meals. While it'd be a shame to miss his cooking, this is also a fine place to just have a beer (£6 starters, £13 main dishes, meals served daily 12:00-15:00 & 18:00-22:00; from Old Brompton Road, turn right at Onslow Gardens and go down a few blocks to 15 Selwood Terrace; tel. 020/7373-7960).

Supermarket: **Tesco Express** is handy for picnics (daily 7:00-24:00, 50-52 Old Brompton Road).

Elsewhere in London

Medieval Banquet, near the Tower of London: In an underground, brick-arched room, costumed wenches bring you a tasty four-course medieval-themed meal (includes ale and red wine) as minstrels, knights, jesters, and contortionists perform. Couples, families, tour groups, and stag and hen parties sit at tables in alcoves; entertainers take turns performing in front of each alcove (in 15-minute segments, with breaks in between). To show you like an act, pound on the table. The nearly nightly show starts at 20:00 (Sun at 18:00) and ends about 22:15 (20:15 on Sun). Reserve in advance online or by phone (£49.95, family deal-£110 Sun-Thu, 15 percent discount for Rick Steves readers, veggie option possible, medieval garb rentable, The Medieval Banquet Ivory House, St. Katharine Docks, enter docks off East Smithfield Street, Tube: Tower Hill, tel. 020/7480 5353, www.medievalbanquet.com).

Between St. Paul's and the Tower: **The Counting House,** formerly an elegant old bank, offers great £8-10 meals, nice homemade meat pies, fish, and fresh vegetables. The fun "nibbles menu" is available starting in the early evening until 22:00 (or until 21:00 on Mon-Tue; open Mon-Fri 11:00-23:00, gets really busy with the buttoned-down 9-to-5 crowd after 12:15 especially Thu-Fri, closed Sat-Sun, near Mansion House in The City, 50 Cornhill—see map on page 189, tel. 020/7283-7123).

Near St. Paul's: **De Gustibus Sandwiches** is where a top-notch artisan bakery meets the public, offering fresh, you-design-it sandwiches, salads, and soups. Just one block below St. Paul's, it has simple seating or take-out picnic sacks for lugging to one of the great nearby parks (Mon-Fri 7:00-17:00, closed Sat-Sun, from church steps follow signs to youth hostel a block downhill—see map on page 189, 53-55 Carter Lane, tel. 020/7236-0056; another outlet is inside the Borough Market in Southwark).

Near the British Library: Drummond Street (running just west of Euston Station—see map on page 173) is famous in London for cheap and good Indian vegetarian food (£5-10 dishes, £7 lunch buffet). Consider **Chutneys** (124 Drummond, tel. 020/7388-0604) and **Ravi Shankar** (133-135 Drummond, tel. 020/7388-6458) for a good *thali* (both open long hours daily).

Taking Tea in London

Once the sole province of genteel ladies in fancy hats, afternoon tea has become more democratic in the 21st century. While some tearooms—such as the wallet-draining £40-a-head tea service at the Ritz and the finicky Fortnum & Mason—still require a jacket and tie (and a bigger bank account), most happily welcome tourists in jeans and sneakers.

Tea Terms

The cheapest "tea" on the menu is generally a "cream tea"; the most expensive is the "champagne tea." **Cream tea** is simply a pot of tea and a homemade scone or two with jam and thick clotted cream. (For maximum pinkie-waving taste per calorie, slice your scone thin like a miniature loaf of bread.) **Afternoon tea**—what Americans usually call "high tea"—generally is a cream tea plus a tier of three plates holding small finger foods (such as cucumber sandwiches) and an assortment of small pastries. **Champagne tea** includes all of the goodies, plus a glass of champagne. **High tea** to the English generally means a more substantial late-afternoon or early-evening meal, often served with meat or eggs.

Tearooms, which often also serve appealing light meals, are usually open for lunch and close about 17:00, just before dinner. At all the places listed below, it's perfectly acceptable for two people to order one afternoon tea and one cream tea (at about £5) and share the afternoon tea's goodies.

Places to Sip Tea

The Wolseley serves a good afternoon tea in between their meal service. Split one with your companion and enjoy two light meals at a great price in classic elegance (£10 cream tea, £21 afternoon tea, served Sun-Fri 15:30-18:30, Sat 15:30-17:30, see full listing on page 183).

The Orangery at Kensington Palace serves four different varieties of tea meals, from the £15 "Orangery tea" to the £35 "Tregothnan tea" in its bright white hall near Princess Di's former residence. You can also order treats à la carte. The portions aren't huge, but who can argue with eating at a princess' orangery or on the terrace? (Tea served 12:00-18:00, no reservations taken; a 10-minute walk through Kensington Gardens from either Queensway or High Street Kensington Tube stations to the orange brick building, about 100 yards from Kensington Palace—see map on page 168; tel. 020/3166-6113, www.hrp.org.uk.)

The National Dining Rooms, a restaurant and café within the National Gallery on Trafalgar Square, are convenient and have a nondescript modern ambience. Although the restaurant can book up in advance, you can generally waltz in for afternoon tea at the café. To play it safe, arrive in the early afternoon to reserve a tea time, then tour the National Gallery before or after your appointed time (£4 cakes and tarts, £5.75 cream tea, £17 afternoon tea, tea served 15:00-17:00, located in Sainsbury Wing of National Gallery, Tube: Charing Cross or Leicester Square, tel. 020/7747-2525, www.peytonandbyrne.co.uk). **The National Café,** at the other end of the building (across the street from St. Martin-in-the-Fields), also serves tea in a more appealing, old-fashioned atmosphere—and their afternoon tea is a bit cheaper (£6 cream tea, £15 afternoon tea, tea served 15:00-17:30).

The Café at Sotheby's, located on the ground floor of the auction giant's headquarters, is manna for shoppers taking a break from fashionable New Bond Street. There are no windows—just a long leather bench, plenty of mirrors, and a dark-wood room where waiters serve sweet treats and the £6.50 mix-and-match Neal's Yard cheese plate to locals in the know (£3 cakes and creams, £7 "small tea," £12 afternoon tea, £18.75 champagne tea, café open Mon-Fri only 9:30-11:30 & 12:00-16:45, afternoon tea served 15:00-16:45, reservations recommended, 34-35 New Bond Street—see map on page 180, Tube: Bond Street or Oxford Circus, tel. 020/7293-5077, www.sothebys.com/cafe).

The Capital Hotel, a luxury hotel a half-block from Harrods, caters to weary shoppers with its intimate five-table, linen-table-cloth tearoom. It's where the ladies-who-lunch meet to decide whether to buy that Versace gown they've had their eye on. Even so, casual clothes, kids, and sharing plates are all OK (£20.50 afternoon tea, daily 14:30-17:30, call to book ahead—especially on weekends, see map on page 166, 22 Basil Street, Tube: Knightsbridge, tel. 020/7589-5171, www.capitalhotel.co.uk).

Fortnum & Mason's St. James's Restaurant, on the fourth floor, offers plush seats under the elegant tearoom's chandeliers. You'll get the standard three-tiered silver tea tray: finger sandwiches on the bottom, fresh scones with jam and clotted cream on the first floor, and decadent pastries and "tartlets" on the top floor, with unlimited tea. At this price, consider it dinner (about £34-38, Mon-Sat 12:00-18:30, Sun 12:00-16:30, dress up a bit for this—no shorts, "children must be behaved," see map on page 180, 181 Piccadilly, reserve in advance online or at tel. 0845-602-5694, www.fortnumandmason.com).

Harrods' Georgian Restaurant is where you (along with 200 of your closest friends) can enjoy a fancy tea under a skylight as a pianist tickles the keys of a Bösendorfer, the world's most expensive piano (£26 afternoon tea, includes finger sandwiches and pastries with free refills, tea served Mon-Fri from 15:00, Sat-Sun from 15:45, last order at 17:15, on Brompton Road, Tube: Knightsbridge, reservations tel. 020/7225-6800, www.harrods.com).

Cheaper Options: Taking tea is not just for tourists and the wealthy—it's a true English tradition. If you want the teatime experience but are put off by the price, most department stores on Oxford Street (including those between Oxford Circus and Bond Street Tube stations) offer an afternoon tea (some more affordable than others). For example, **John Lewis** has a mod third-floor brasserie that serves a nice £10 afternoon tea platter from 15:00 (on Oxford Street one block west of the Bond Street Tube station, tel. 020/3073-0626, www.johnlewis.com). Many museums and bookstores have cafés serving afternoon tea goodies à la carte, where you can put together a spread for less than £10—**Waterstone's** fifth-floor café and the **Victoria and Albert Museum** café are two of the best. **Teapod,** a modern option near the Tower Bridge, advertises the "best-value afternoon tea in London," serving cream tea for £5.50 and afternoon tea for £14, along with sandwiches, soups, salads, and pastries (Mon-Fri 8:00-18:00, Sat 9:00-19:00, Sun 10:00-19:00, 31 Shad Thames, 200 yards from the Tower Bridge on the South Bank, tel. 020/7407-0000; another branch at 22 Wellington Street in Covent Garden; www.teapodtea.co.uk).

In Bath: The **Pump Room** is reason enough to put off tea in London—assuming you're visiting the city of Bath. This historic, elegant Georgian hall with live music lets anyone enjoy the ritual of tea in grand style (see page 370).

London Connections

By Plane

Phone numbers and websites for London's airports and major airlines are listed in the appendix. For accommodations at or near the major airports, see page 177. Note that a number of discount airlines fly into and out of London's smaller airports, making this a nice, cheap option for traveling to other destinations. For more information, see "Cheap Flights" on page 800.

Heathrow Airport

Heathrow Airport is one of the world's busiest airports. Think about it: 68 million passengers a

London's Airports

50 Kilometers
50 Miles

Cambridge

LUTON

STANSTED

ENGLAND

North Sea

LONDON · LONDON CITY

Bath · Reading

HEATHROW

GATWICK

CHANNEL TUNNEL

English Channel

To Paris & Brussels

year on 470,000 flights from 180 destinations riding 90 airlines, like some kind of global maypole dance. Read signs and ask questions. For Heathrow's airport, flight, and transfer information, call the switchboard at tel. 0844-335-1801, or visit the helpful website at www.heathrowairport.com.

Heathrow has five terminals: T-1 (mostly domestic and Irish flights, with some service to Europe and the US); T-2 (closed for renovation, should reopen in 2013); T-3 (North and South American, Asian, and some European flights); T-4 (European and US flights); and T-5 (British Airways flights only). You can walk between T-1 and T-3. To travel between the other terminals, you can take the Heathrow Express trains (free), buses (free), or the Tube (requires a ticket). Unlike most American airports, there is no train that links all the terminals together on one line, so you may have to transfer if you're going to T-4 or T-5.

If you're flying out of Heathrow, it's critical to confirm which terminal your flight will use (check the Web or call your airline in advance)—because if it's T-4 or T-5, you'll need to allow extra time. Taxi drivers generally know which terminal you'll need, but bus drivers may not.

Services: Each terminal has an airport information desk (generally daily 6:00-22:00), car-rental agencies, exchange bureaus, ATMs, a pharmacy, a VAT refund desk (tel. 020/8910-3682; you must present the VAT claim form from the retailer here to get your tax rebate on items purchased in Britain—see page 17 for details), and baggage storage (£8.50/item for 24 hours, hours vary by terminal but generally daily 5:30-23:00, www.left-baggage.co.uk). Get online 24 hours a day at Heathrow's Internet access points (at each terminal—T-4's is up on the mezzanine level) or with your laptop (pay Wi-Fi provided by Boingo, www.boingo.com). A post office is on the first floor of T-3. Each terminal has cheap eateries.

Heathrow's small **"TI"** (tourist info shop), even though it's a for-profit business, is worth a visit to pick up free information: a simple map, the *London Planner*, and brochures (daily 6:30-22:00, 5-minute walk from T-3 in Tube station, follow signs to Underground; bypass queue for transit info to reach window for London questions).

Getting to London from Heathrow Airport

You have five basic options for traveling the 14 miles between Heathrow Airport and downtown London: Tube (£5/person), bus (£5/person), direct shuttle bus (£21.50/person), express train with connecting Tube or taxi (about £20/person), or taxi (about £55 per group).

By Tube (Subway): For £5, the Tube takes you from any Heathrow terminal to downtown London in 50-60 minutes on the Piccadilly Line (6/hour; depending on your destination, may require a transfer, buy ticket at the Tube station ticket window). If you plan to use the Tube for transport in London, it may make sense to buy a Travelcard or pay-as-you-go Oyster card at the Tube station ticket window at the airport. (For information  on these passes, see page 56.) If your Travelcard covers only Zones 1-2, it does not include Heathrow (Zone 6); however, you can pay a small supplement for the initial trip from Heathrow to downtown.

If you're taking the Tube from downtown London *to* the airport, note that the Piccadilly Line trains don't stop at every terminal. Trains either stop at T-4, then T-1/T-3 (also called Heathrow Central), in that order; or T-1/T-3 and T-5. When leaving central London on the Tube, allow extra time if going to T-4 or T-5; since you have to be sure you get on a train going to your terminal, carefully check the destination information before you board.

By Bus: Most buses depart from the outdoor common area in the heart of the Heathrow complex called the Central Bus Station. It serves T-1 and T-3, and is a 5-minute walk from these terminals. To get to T-4 or T-5 from the Central Bus Station, go inside, downstairs, and follow signs to take Heathrow Express trains to your terminal (free, but only runs every 15-20 minutes to those terminals); or catch one of the free buses that circulate between terminals.

National Express has regular service from Heathrow's Central Bus Station to Victoria Coach Station in downtown London, near several of my recommended hotels. While slow, the bus is affordable and convenient for those staying near Victoria Station (£5, 1-2/hour, less frequent from Victoria Station to Heathrow, 45-60 minutes depending on time of day, tel. 0871-781-8181, www.nationalexpress.com).

By Shuttle: SkyShuttle operates buses about every half-hour between all Heathrow terminals and hotels in central London (£21.50/person one-way, £34.40/person round-trip; reservations tel. 0845-481-0960, call between 6:00-22:00; www.skyshuttle.co.uk).

By Train: Two different trains (slow for £8.50, fast for £16.50) run between Heathrow Airport and London's Paddington Station. At Paddington Station, you're in the thick of the Tube system, with easy access to any of my recommended neighborhoods—my Paddington hotels are just outside the front door, and Notting Hill Gate is just two Tube stops away. The **Heathrow Connect** train is the slightly slower, much cheaper option, serving T-1 and T-3 at one station called Heathrow Central; use free transfers if you're coming from either T-4 or T-5 (£8.50 one-way, 2/hour, 30 minutes, tel. 0845-678-6975, www.heathrowconnect.com). The **Heathrow Express** train is fast (15 minutes to downtown from T-1 and T-3; 21 minutes from T-5; transfer required from T-4) and runs more frequently (4/hour), but it's pricey (£16.50 "express class" one-way, £32 round-trip, ask about discount promos at ticket desk, buy ticket before you board or pay a £3 surcharge to buy it on the train, covered by BritRail pass, daily 5:10-23:25, tel. 0845-600-1515, www.heathrowexpress.co.uk). At the airport, you can use Heathrow Express as a free transfer between terminals.

By Taxi: Taxis from the airport cost about £45-70 to west and central London (one hour). For four people traveling together, this can be a deal. Hotels can often line up a cab back to the airport for about £30-40. For the cheapest taxi to the airport, don't order one from your hotel. Simply flag down a few and ask them for their best "off-meter" rate. Locals refer to hired cars that do the trip off-meter as "mini-cabs." These are reliable and generally cost about what you'd pay for a taxi in good traffic, but—with a fixed price—they can save you money when taxis are snarled in congestion with the meter running.

Getting to Bath from Heathrow Airport

By Bus: Direct buses run daily from Heathrow to Bath (£19-42, 10/day direct, 2-4 hours, more frequent but slower with transfer in London, tel. 0871-781-8181, www.nationalexpress.com). BritRail passholders may prefer the 2.5-hour Heathrow-Bath bus/train connection via Reading (BritRail passholders just pay £15 for bus; otherwise £50-65 depending on time of day, about £10 cheaper when bought in advance; tel. 0118-957-9425, buy bus ticket from www.railair.com, train ticket from www.firstgreatwestern.co.uk). First catch the RailAir Link shuttle bus (2/hour, 45 minutes) to Reading (RED-ding), then hop on the express train (2/hour, 1 hour) to Bath. Factoring in the connection in Reading—which can add at least an hour to the trip—the train is a less convenient option than the direct bus to Bath.

Gatwick Airport

More and more flights land at Gatwick Airport, halfway between London and the South Coast (tel. 0844-335-1802, www.gatwick airport.com). Gatwick has two terminals, North and South, which are easily connected by a free monorail (two-minute trip, runs 24 hours daily). Note that boarding passes say "Gatwick N" or "Gatwick S" to indicate your terminal. British Airways flights generally use Gatwick North. The Gatwick Express trains (described next) stop only at Gatwick South. Schedules in each terminal show only arrivals and departures from that terminal.

Getting to London: Gatwick Express trains are clearly the best way into London from this airport. They shuttle conveniently between Gatwick South and London's Victoria Station, with many of my recommended hotels close by (£18, £31 round-trip, 10 percent discount online, 4/hour, 30 minutes, runs 5:00-24:00 daily, purchase tickets on train at no extra charge, tel. 0845-850-1530, www.gatwickexpress.com). If you buy your tickets at the station before boarding, ask about their deal where three adults travel for the price of two, or four for the price of three. (If you see others in the ticket line, suggest buying your tickets together—you'll save more than £5 each.)

You can save a few pounds by taking Southern Railway's slower and less frequent **shuttle train** between Gatwick South and Victoria Station (£11, up to 4/hour, 45 minutes, tel. 0845-127-2920, www.southernrailway.com).

A train also runs from Gatwick South to **St. Pancras International Station** (£9, 8/hour, 1 hour, www.firstcapital connect.co.uk)—useful for travelers taking the Eurostar train (to Paris or Brussels) or staying in the St. Pancras/King's Cross neighborhood.

Even slower, but cheap and handy to the Victoria Station neighborhood, you can take the **bus** from Gatwick to Victoria (£7.50, hourly, 1.5 hours, tel. 0871-781-8181, www.nationalexpress .com).

Getting to Bath: To get to Bath from Gatwick, you can catch a bus to Heathrow and take the bus to Bath from there (10/ day, 4-5 hours total, £25 one-way, transfer at Heathrow Airport, www.nationalexpress.com—see "Getting to Bath from Heathrow Airport," previous page). By train, the best Gatwick-Bath connection involves a transfer in Reading (£48-58 one-way depending on time of day, cheaper in advance, hourly, 2.5 hours, www.first greatwestern.co.uk; avoid transfer in London, where you'll have to change stations).

London's Other Airports

Stansted Airport: If you're using Stansted (tel. 0870-0000-303, www.stanstedairport.com), you have several options for getting into or out of London. Two different **buses** connect the airport and downtown London's Victoria Station neighborhood: National Express (£10, £17 round-trip, every 20 minutes, 1.75 hours, runs 24 hours a day, picks up and stops throughout London, ends at Victoria Coach Station, tel. 0871-781-8181, www.nationalexpress .com) and Terravision (£9, 2-3/hour, 1.25 hours, ends at Green Line Coach Station just south of Victoria Station). Or you can take the faster, pricier Stansted Express **train** (£18-20 one-way, £25-27 round-trip, connects to London's Tube system at Tottenham Hale and Liverpool Street, 4/hour, 45 minutes, 5:00-23:00, tel. 0845-850-0150, www.stanstedexpress.com). Stansted is expensive by **cab**; figure £120 one-way from central London.

Luton Airport: For Luton (airport tel. 01582/405-100, www .london-luton.co.uk), there are two choices into or out of London. The fastest way to go is by **rail** to London's St. Pancras International Station (£12 one-way, 1-5/hour, 25-45 minutes—check schedule to avoid the slower trains, tel. 0845-712-5678, www.eastmidlands trains.co.uk); catch the 10-minute shuttle bus (£1) from outside the terminal to the Luton Airport Parkway Station. The Green Line express **bus** #757 runs to Buckingham Palace Road, just south of London's Victoria Station (£13 one-way, £16 round-trip, small discount for easyJet passengers who buy online, 2-4/hour, 1.25-1.5 hours, 24 hours a day, tel. 0844-801-7261, www.greenline.co.uk). If you're sleeping at Luton, consider easyHotel (see listing on page 176).

London City Airport: There's a slim chance you might use London City Airport (tel. 020/7646-0088, www.londoncity airport.com). To get into London, take the Docklands Light Railway (DLR) to the Bank Tube station, which is one stop east of St. Paul's on the Central Line (£4 one-way, covered by Travelcard, £2.50-2.90 on Oyster card, 22 minutes, tel. 020/7222-1234, www .tfl.gov.uk/dlr).

Connecting London's Airports by Bus

More and more travelers are taking advantage of cheap flights out of London's smaller airports. A handy **National Express bus** runs between Heathrow, Gatwick, Stansted, and Luton airports—easier than having to cut through the center of London—although

London's Major Train Stations

traffic can be bad and increase travel times (tel. 0871-781-8181, www.nationalexpress.com).

From Heathrow Airport to: Gatwick Airport (1-4/ hour, 1-1.5 hours, £21.50 one-way, £40 round-trip, allow at least three hours between flights), **Stansted Airport** (1-2/hour, 1.5-1.75 hours, £24 one-way, £31 round-trip), **Luton Airport** (hourly, 1-1.5 hours, £21 one-way, £31 round-trip).

By Train

Britain is covered by a myriad of rail systems (owned by different companies), which together are called National Rail. London, the country's major transportation hub, has a different train station for each region. There are nine main stations (see the map above):

Euston—Serves northwest England, North Wales, and Scotland.

King's Cross—Serves northeast England and Scotland, including York and Edinburgh.

Liverpool Street—Serves east England, including Essex and Harwich.

London Bridge—Serves south England, including Brighton.

Public Transportation near London

Marylebone—Serves southwest and central England, including Stratford-upon-Avon.

Paddington—Serves south and southwest England, including Heathrow Airport, Windsor, Bath, South Wales, and the Cotswolds.

St. Pancras International—Serves north and south England, plus the Eurostar to Paris or Brussels (see "Crossing the Channel," later).

Victoria—Serves Gatwick Airport, Canterbury, Dover, and Brighton.

Waterloo—Serves southeast England, including Salisbury.

In addition, there are other, smaller train stations in London that you are not likely to use, such as **Charing Cross** or **Blackfriars.**

Any train station has schedule information, can make reservations, and can sell tickets for any destination. Most stations offer a baggage-storage service (£8/bag for 24 hours, look for *left luggage* signs); because of long security lines, it can take a while to check or pick up your bag (www.excess-baggage.com). For more details on the services available at each station, see www.nationalrail.co.uk /stations.

Buying Tickets: For general information, call 0845-748-4950 (or visit www.nationalrail.co.uk or www.eurostar.com; £5 booking fee for telephone reservations). If you book far enough ahead, you might find discounted train tickets on certain routes at www .megatrain.com (tel. 0871-266-3333; as they also sell bus tickets, be careful to specify that you want to take the train).

Railpasses: For train travel outside London, consider getting a BritRail pass. Options include passes that cover England as well as Scotland and Wales, England-only passes, England/ Ireland passes, "London Plus" passes (good for travel in most of southeast England but not in London itself), and BritRail & Drive passes (which include a car rental). For specifics, contact your travel agent, or see www.ricksteves.com/rail.

Train Connections from London
To Points West
From Paddington Station to: Bath (2/hour, 1.5 hours; also consider a guided Evan Evans tour by bus—see page 205), **Oxford** (2/hour direct, 1 hour, more possible with transfer in Reading), **Penzance** (every 1-2 hours, 5-5.5 hours, possible change in Plymouth or Newton Abbot), and **Cardiff** (2/hour, 2 hours).

To Points North
From King's Cross Station: Trains run at least hourly, stopping in **York** (2 hours), **Durham** (3 hours), and **Edinburgh** (4.5 hours). Trains to **Cambridge** also leave from here (3/hour, 45-60 minutes).

From Euston Station to: Conwy (nearly hourly, 3.25 hours, transfer in Chester), **Liverpool** (hourly, 2 hours, more with transfer), **Blackpool** (1-2/hour, 2.75-3.25 hours, 1-2 transfers), **Keswick** (hourly, 4.5 hours, transfer to bus at Penrith), and **Glasgow** (1-2/ hour, 4.5-5 hours).

From London's Other Stations
Trains run between London and **Canterbury,** leaving from St. Pancras International Station and arriving in Canterbury West (1-2/hour, 1 hour), as well as from London's Victoria Station and arriving in Canterbury East (2/hour, 1.5 hours).

Direct trains leave for **Stratford-upon-Avon** from Marylebone Station, located near the southwest corner of Regents Park (5/day direct, more with transfers, 2.25 hours).

To Other Destinations: Dover (hourly, 1.25 hours, direct from St. Pancras International Station; also hourly, 2 hours, direct from Victoria Station or Charing Cross Station), **Brighton** (4-5/ hour, 1 hour, from Victoria Station and London Bridge Station), **Portsmouth** (3/hour, 1.5-2 hours, most from Waterloo Station, a few from Victoria Station), and **Salisbury** (1-2/hour, 1.5 hours, from Waterloo Station). For trains to **Windsor, Cambridge, Greenwich,** or **Bath,** check those chapters.

By Bus

Buses are slower but considerably cheaper than trains for reaching destinations around Britain, and beyond. Most depart from **Victoria Coach Station,** which is one long block south of Victoria Station (near many recommended accommodations and Tube: Victoria). Inside the station, you'll find basic eateries, kiosks, and a helpful information desk stocked with schedules and ready to point you to your bus or answer any questions.

Most domestic buses are operated by **National Express** (tel. 0871-781-8181, www.nationalexpress.com); their international departures are called **Eurolines** (tel. 0871-781-8177, www.eurolines.co.uk). A newer, smaller company called **Megabus** undersells National Express with deeply discounted promotional fares—the further ahead you buy, the less you pay (some trips for just £1.50, tend to be slower than National Express, toll tel. 0900-160-0900, www.megabus.com). They also sell discounted train tickets on selected routes.

Try to avoid bus travel on Friday and Sunday evenings, when weekend travelers are more likely to make buses sell out.

To ensure getting a ticket—and to save money with special promotions—you can book your ticket in advance online (see websites listed earlier). The cheapest pre-purchased tickets can be changed (for a £5 fee), but they're nonrefundable. If you have a British mobile phone, you can buy an "M-Ticket," which sends your paperless confirmation number right to your phone.

If you're planning to buy your ticket at the station, try to arrive an hour before the bus departs—or drop by the day before. (For buses to Stansted Airport and Oxford, you can buy the ticket on board; otherwise you'll buy it at a ticket window.) Watch your bags carefully—luggage thieves thrive at the station.

To Bath: The National Express bus leaves from Victoria Coach Station (nearly hourly, 2.5-3.75 hours, avoid those with layover in Bristol, sample fares: one-way-£22, round-trip-£29).

To get to Bath via Stonehenge, consider taking a guided bus tour from London to Stonehenge, Salisbury, and Bath, and abandoning the tour in Bath (be sure to confirm that Bath is the last stop on that particular tour). **Evan Evans'** tour is £74 and includes admissions. The tour leaves from Victoria Coach Station every morning at 8:45 (you can stow your bag in a compartment under the bus), stops in Salisbury (for a look at its magnificent cathedral) and Stonehenge, and then stops in Bath before returning to London (offered year-round; they also offer another tour to Stonehenge and Bath via Windsor Castle). You can book the tour at the Victoria Coach Station or the Evan Evans office (258 Vauxhall Bridge Road, near Victoria Coach Station, tel. 020/7950-1777, US tel. 209/830-1521, www.evanevans.co.uk). **Golden Tours** also runs a Stonehenge-Bath tour (£59, check website for seasonal tour days; departs from Fountain Square, located across from Victoria Coach Station, US tel. 800-548-7083, tel. 0844-880-5050, www.goldentours.com).

To Other Destinations: Oxford (2-4/hour, about 1.5 hours), **Cambridge** (hourly, 2-2.5 hours), **Canterbury** (about hourly, 2-2.5 hours), **Dover** (about hourly, 2.5-3.25 hours), **Penzance** (5/day, 8.5-10 hours, overnight available), **Cardiff** (hourly, 3.25 hours), **Liverpool** (8/day direct, 5.25-6 hours, overnight available), **Blackpool** (4/day direct, 6.25-7 hours, overnight available), **York** (4/day direct, 5.25 hours), **Durham** (4/day direct, 6.5-7.5 hours), **Glasgow** (3/day direct, 8-9 hours, train is a much better option), **Edinburgh** (2/day direct, 8.75-9.75 hours, go by train instead).

To Dublin, Ireland: This bus/boat journey, operated by National Express, takes 10-12 hours (£26-48, 1/day, departs Victoria Coach Station at 18:00, check in with passport one hour before). Consider a cheap 1.25-hour Ryanair flight instead (www.ryanair.com).

To the Continent: Especially in summer, buses run to destinations all over Europe, including Paris, Amsterdam, Brussels, and Germany (sometimes crossing the Channel by ferry, other times through the Chunnel). For any international connection, you need to check in with your passport one hour before departure. For details, call 0871-781-8177 or visit www.eurolines.co.uk. For information on crossing the Channel by bus, see the end of this chapter.

Crossing the Channel
By Eurostar Train

The fastest and most convenient way to get from Big Ben to the Eiffel Tower is by rail. Eurostar, a joint service of the Belgian, British, and French railways,

is the speedy passenger train that zips you (and up to 800 others in 18 sleek cars) from downtown London to downtown Paris or Brussels (15+/day, 2.25-2.5 hours) faster and more easily than flying. The actual tunnel crossing is a 20-minute, silent, 100-mile-per-hour nonevent. Your ears won't even pop. Get ready for more high-speed connections: Eurostar's monopoly expired at the beginning of 2010, and Germany's national railroad wants to run its bullet trains to London by 2013.

Eurostar Fares

Channel fares are reasonable but complicated. Prices vary depending on how far ahead you reserve, whether you can live with restrictions, and whether you're eligible for any discounts (children, youths, seniors, round-trip travelers, and railpass holders all qualify).

Fares can change without notice, but typically a **one-way, full-fare ticket** (with no restrictions on refundability) runs about $425 first-class and $300 second-class. **Cheaper seats** come with more restrictions and can sell out quickly (figure $100-160 for second-class, one-way). Those traveling with a railpass that covers France or Britain should look first at the **passholder** fare ($85-130 for second-class, one-way Eurostar trips). For more details, visit my *Guide to Eurail Passes* (www.ricksteves.com/eurostar), Rail Europe (www.raileurope.com), or go directly to Eurostar (www.eurostar.com).

A tour company called BritainShrinkers sells one- or two-day tours to Paris, Brussels, or Bruges, enabling you to side-trip to these cities from London for less than most train tickets alone. For example, you'll pay about $175 for a one-day Paris "tour" (unescorted Mon-Sat day trip with Métro pass; tel. 020/7713-1311 or www.britainshrinkers.com). This can be a particularly good option if you need to get to Paris from London on short notice, when only the costliest fares are available.

Buying Eurostar Tickets

Because only the most expensive (full-fare) ticket is fully refundable, don't reserve until you're sure of your plans. But if you wait too long, the cheapest tickets will get bought up.

Once you're confident about the time and date of your crossing, you can check and book fares by phone or online. Ordering online through Eurostar or major agents offers a print-at-home e-ticket option. You can also order by phone through Rail Europe at US tel. 800-EUROSTAR for home delivery before you go, or

Eurostar Routes

ENGLAND

London

Ebbsfleet

Ashford

English Channel

Calais Fréthun

Lille-Europe

Amsterdam

NETH.

Brussels

BELG.

FRANCE

Paris

50 Kilometers

50 Miles

----- Eurostar

········· Channel Tunnel

········· Other Rail

through Eurostar (tel. 0870-518-6186, priced in euros) and pick up your ticket at the train station. In continental Europe, you can buy your Eurostar ticket at any major train station in any country or at any travel agency that handles train tickets (expect a booking fee). In Britain, tickets can be issued only at the Eurostar office in St. Pancras International Station. You can purchase passholder discount tickets at Eurostar departure stations, through US agents, or by phone with Eurostar, but they may be harder to get at other train stations and travel agencies, and are a discount category that can sell out.

Remember that Britain's time zone is one hour earlier than France or Belgium. Times listed on tickets are local times (departure from London is British time, arrival in Paris is French time).

Taking the Eurostar

Eurostar trains depart from and arrive at London's St. Pancras International Station. Check in at least 30 minutes in advance for your Eurostar trip. It's very similar to an airport check-in: You pass through airport-like security, show your passport to customs officials, and find a TV monitor to locate your departure gate. There are a few airport-like shops, newsstands, horrible snack bars, and cafés (bring food for the trip from elsewhere), pay-Internet terminals, and a currency-exchange booth with rates about the same as you'll find on the other end.

Crossing the Channel Without Eurostar

The old-fashioned ways of crossing the Channel are cheaper than Eurostar (taking the bus is cheapest). They're also twice as romantic, complicated, and time-consuming.

By Train and Boat

To Paris: You'll take a train from London to the port of Dover, then catch a ferry to Calais, France, before boarding another train for Paris. Trains go from London's St. Pancras International to **Dover's** Priory Station (hourly, 1.25 hours; bus or taxi from train station to ferry dock). P&O Ferries sail from Dover to Calais; TGV trains run from Calais to Paris. You'll need to book your own train tickets to Dover and from Calais to Paris. The prices listed here are for the ferry only (from £35 one-way or £60 round-trip online, more at dock or by phone, book early for best fares; 22/day, 1.5 hours, tel. 08716-642-020, www.poferries.com).

To Amsterdam: Stena Line's Dutchflyer service combines train and ferry tickets between London and Amsterdam via the ports of **Harwich** and Hoek van Holland. Trains go from London's Liverpool Street Station to Harwich (hourly, 1.75 hours, most transfer in Manningtree). Stena Line ferries sail from Harwich to Hoek van Holland (7.75 hours), where you can transfer to a train to Amsterdam or other Dutch cities (ferry—from £34, from £63 with cabin, book at least 2 weeks in advance for best price, 13 hours total travel time, Dutchflyer tel. 0844-576-2762, www.stenaline.co.uk, Dutch train info at www.ns.nl).

For additional European ferry info, visit www.aferry.to. For UK train and bus info, go to www.traveline.org.uk.

By Bus
You can take the bus from London direct to **Paris** (4/day, 8.25-9.75 hours), **Brussels** (3-4/day, 12 hours), or **Amsterdam** (4/day, 12 hours) from Victoria Coach Station (via ferry or Chunnel, day or overnight). You'll pay the same to Paris, Brussels, or Amsterdam. The price depends on when you book (for example: £28 one-way, £38 round-trip if purchased at least a week ahead; £40 one-way, £55 round-trip if purchased the day before; £44 one-way, £61 round-trip if purchased same day; no discounts and £5 more for any ticket during peak times such as holiday weekends; tel. 0871-781-8177; visit www.eurolines.co.uk and look for "funfares").

By Plane
Check with budget airlines for cheap round-trip fares to Paris or Brussels (see "Cheap Flights" on page 800).

GREENWICH, WINDSOR, AND CAMBRIDGE

Three of the best day-trip possibilities near London are Greenwich, Windsor, and Cambridge. Greenwich, technically within London's city limits, is England's maritime capital; Windsor, west of the city, has a very famous castle; and Cambridge, an hour to the north, is England's best university town.

Getting Around

By Train: The British rail system uses London as a hub and normally offers same-day round-trip fares that cost virtually the same as one-way fares. For day trips, these "off-peak day return" tickets, available if you depart London outside rush hour (usually after 9:30 on weekdays and anytime Sat-Sun), are best. Note that a "day return" (round-trip within a single day) is different—and cheaper—than a "return," so be sure to buy the right ticket. You can also save a little money if you purchase tickets before 18:00 the day before your trip.

By Train Tour: London Walks offers a variety of "Explorer Days" tours year-round by train, including a Cambridge itinerary (£14 plus transportation and admissions costs, pick up their brochure at the TI or hotels, tel. 020/7624-3978, www.walks .com).

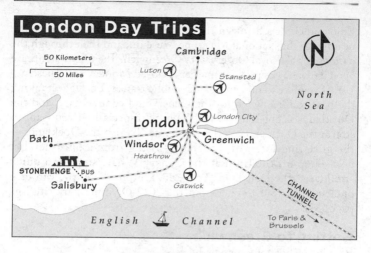

Greenwich

Tudor kings favored the palace at Greenwich (GREN-ich). Henry VIII was born here. Later kings commissioned architects Inigo Jones and Christopher Wren to beautify the town and palace, and William and Mary built a grand hospital to care for retired seamen (which later became a college for training naval officers).

Greenwich is England's maritime capital, and visitors come here for all things salty. (The *Cutty Sark* clipper ship, the area's premier attraction, is slated to reopen in the spring of 2012 after a long restoration.) The town is synonymous with timekeeping and astronomy, and at the Royal Observatory Greenwich, you can learn how those pursuits relate to seafaring. Greenwich also has stunning Baroque architecture, appealing markets, a fleet of nautical shops, plenty of parks, kid-friendly museums, and hordes of tourists. Since many of the major sights here are free to enter, and you can travel between central London and Greenwich on a cheap Tube ticket, it's a wonderfully inexpensive day out. And where else can you set your watch with such accuracy?

Planning Your Time

Upon arrival, stroll past the *Cutty Sark* dry dock to the Discover Greenwich exhibit and TI, then drop into the grand buildings of the Old Royal Naval College and walk the shoreline promenade.

Enjoy lunch or a drink in the venerable Trafalgar Tavern before heading to the National Maritime Museum, and then through the park up to the Royal Observatory Greenwich. The town's sights are open daily, but its popular market is closed Monday and Tuesday.

If you like to mix and match public transit, I'd suggest taking the boat to Greenwich for the scenery and commentary, and the Docklands Light Railway (DLR) back, especially if you want to stop at the Docklands on the way home. To visit the Docklands—the glittering forest of skyscrapers rising from a once-derelict port—hop off the train at the Canary Wharf stop for a quick stroll (see "The Docklands," page 137). From there, you can tack on a small detour to check out the 2012 Olympic Park site (see page 138).

Getting to Greenwich

It's a joy by boat or a snap by DLR.

By Boat: From central London, you can cruise scenically down the Thames to Greenwich. Various tour boats—with commentary and open-deck seating up top—leave from the piers at Westminster, Waterloo, and the Tower of London (2/hour, about 1 hour); note that most boats have commentary only on the way to Greenwich, not on the way back.

Thames Clippers offers faster trips, with no commentary and only a small deck at the stern (departs every 20 minutes from several piers in central London, 45 minutes). Thames Clippers also connects Greenwich to the Docklands' Canary Wharf Pier (3/hour, 10 minutes).

For cruising details, see page 73.

By DLR: From Bank station (also accessible from the Monument Tube station) in central London, take the DLR to Cutty Sark station in central Greenwich; it's one stop before the main—but less central—Greenwich station (departs at least every 10 minutes, 20 minutes, all in Zone 2, covered by any Tube pass). Many DLR trains terminate at Canary Wharf, so make sure you get on one that continues to Lewisham or Greenwich. Some DLR trains terminate at Island Gardens—you can generally catch another train to Greenwich's Cutty Sark station within a few minutes, though it may be more memorable to walk under the river through the long Thames pedestrian tunnel.

By Train: Mainline trains also go from London (Cannon Street and London Bridge stations) several times an hour to Greenwich station (10-minute walk from the sights). Although the train is fast and cheap, the DLR is preferable because it drops you right in the heart of town.

By Bus: Catch bus #188 from Russell Square near the British Museum (about 45 minutes to Greenwich).

Orientation to Greenwich

(area code: 020)

Still well within the city limits of London, Greenwich feels like a small town all its own. Covered markets and outdoor stalls make

for lively weekends. Save time to browse the town. Wander beyond the touristy Church Street and Greenwich High Road to where flower stands spill onto the side streets and antique shops sell brass nautical knickknacks. King William Walk, College Approach, Nelson Road, and Turnpin Lane (all in the vicinity of Greenwich Market) are all worth a look. If you need pub

grub, Greenwich has almost 100 pubs, with some boasting that they're mere milliseconds from the prime meridian.

Markets: Thanks to its markets, Greenwich throbs with day-trippers on weekends. The **Greenwich Market** is an entertaining mini-Covent Garden, located in the middle of the block between the Cutty Sark DLR station and the Old Royal Naval College—right on your way to the sights (Wed-Sun 10:00-17:30, closed Mon-Tue; farmers' market on Wed, food court on Thu-Sun, antiques on Thu-Fri, arts and crafts on Fri-Sun; tel. 020/7515-7153, www.greenwichmarket.net). The **Clocktower Market** sells old odds and ends at high prices on Greenwich High Road, near the post office (Sat-Sun and bank holidays only 10:00-17:00, www.clocktowermarket.co.uk).

Tourist Information

The TI is inside the Discover Greenwich visitors center (described later, under "Sights in Greenwich"). From the DLR station, exit straight ahead to the monumental gateway for the Old Royal Naval College complex; Discover Greenwich is just inside the gate on the left (daily 10:00-17:00, Pepys House, 2 Cutty Sark Gardens, tel. 0870-608-2000, www.visitgreenwich.org.uk).

Guided walks, which depart from the TI, offer an overview of the town and go past most of the big sights (£6, daily at 12:15 and 14:15, 1.5 hours; the only sights you enter are the Painted Hall and Chapel of St. Peter and St. Paul, and only on the 14:15 tour).

Sights in Greenwich

I've organized these listings as a handy sightseeing walk through town, starting right next to the Cutty Sark DLR station.

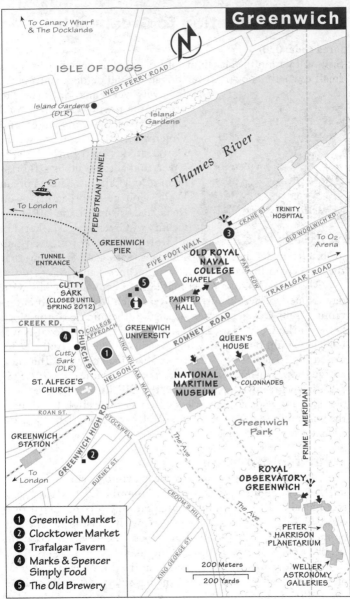

Greenwich

To Canary Wharf
& The Docklands

ISLE OF DOGS

WEST FERRY ROAD

Island Gardens
(DLR)

Island
Gardens

Thames River

To London

PEDESTRIAN TUNNEL

GREENWICH
PIER

FIVE FOOT WALK

CRANE ST.

TRINITY
HOSPITAL

OLD WOOLWICH RD

To O₂
Arena

❸

TUNNEL
ENTRANCE

CUTTY
SARK
(CLOSED UNTIL
SPRING 2012)

❺

ⓘ

OLD ROYAL
NAVAL
COLLEGE

CHAPEL

PAINTED
HALL

PARK ROW

TRAFALGAR ROAD

CREEK RD.

COLLEGE APPROACH

CHURCH ST.

GREENWICH
UNIVERSITY

ROMNEY ROAD

QUEEN'S
HOUSE

❹

Cutty
Sark
(DLR)

KING WILLIAM WALK

NELSON WALK

ST. ALFEGE'S
CHURCH

NATIONAL
MARITIME
MUSEUM

COLONNADES

ROAN ST.

GREENWICH HIGH RD.

STOCKWELL

Greenwich
Park

PRIME MERIDIAN

GREENWICH
STATION

❷

To
London

BURNEY ST.

The Ave

CROOM'S HILL

ROYAL
OBSERVATORY
GREENWICH

KING GEORGE ST.

The Ave

PETER
HARRISON
PLANETARIUM

200 Meters

200 Yards

WELLER
ASTRONOMY
GALLERIES

❶ Greenwich Market
❷ Clocktower Market
❸ Trafalgar Tavern
❹ Marks & Spencer
   Simply Food
❺ The Old Brewery

GREENWICH

▲▲*Cutty Sark*—The Scottish-built *Cutty Sark* was the last of the great China tea clippers, and was the queen of the seas when first launched in 1869. With 32,000 square feet of sail, she could blow with the wind 300 miles in a day. After a five-year-long restoration, the ship is scheduled to open again to the public in the spring of 2012. The new display space allows visitors to walk above and below the suspended ship.

Cost and Hours: Call or look online for the latest information, tel. 020/8858-2698, www.cuttysark.org.uk.

Discover Greenwich—This visitors center (which also houses the TI) is located at the corner of the Old Royal Naval College closest to the *Cutty Sark*. While it's hardly a museum, it offers a decent introduction to Greenwich and some fun exhibits for kids. In the center, a model of the town lights up to tell its history. Surrounding the model are displays and artifacts from various people who have left their mark on the town, along with exhibits about the architecture and construction of Greenwich's fine buildings. Adjoining Discover Greenwich are the TI and a recommended pub, The Old Brewery.

Cost and Hours: Free, daily 10:00-17:00, tel. 020/8269-4747, www.oldroyalnavalcollege.org.

▲**Old Royal Naval College**—The college was originally a hospital founded by Queen Mary II and King William III in 1692 as a charity to care for retired or injured naval officers (called pensioners). William and Mary spared no expense, hiring the great Christopher Wren to design the complex (though other architects completed it). Its days as a hospital ended in 1869, and it served as a college for training naval officers from 1873 to 1998. Now that the Royal Navy has moved out, the public is invited to view the college's elaborate Painted Hall and Chapel of St. Peter and St. Paul, which are in symmetrical buildings that face each other overlooking a broad riverfront park.

Cost and Hours: Free, daily 10:00-17:00, sometimes closed for private events, service Sun at 11:00 in chapel—all are welcome. Guides give 1.5-hour tours covering the hall and chapel, along with other areas not open to the general public (£6, daily at 14:00, departs from TI, call ahead to check availability). Tel. 020/8269-4799, www.oldroyalnavalcollege.org.

❷ Self-Guided Tour: Good descriptions are free to borrow in each building, or you can buy the fun *Nasty Naval College* brochure, with offbeat facts about the place (£1). Guides called Yeoman Warders are often standing by to answer questions.

Here's an overview of what you'll see:

Painted Hall: Originally intended as a dining hall for pensioners, this sumptuously painted room was deemed too glorious (and, in the winter, too cold) for that purpose. So almost as soon

as it was completed, it became simply a place to impress visitors.

Enter the hall, climb the stairs, and gape up at one of the largest painted ceilings in Europe—112 feet long. It's a big propaganda scene, glorifying the building's founders, Queen Mary II and King William III (who, as a Protestant monarch, had recently trounced the Catholic French King Louis XIV in a pivotal battle). Crane your neck—or use the clever wheeled mirrors—to examine the scene. In the center are William and Mary. Under his foot, William is crushing a dark figure with a broken sword...Louis XIV. He is handing a red cap (representing liberty) to the woman on the right, who holds the reins of a white horse (symbolizing Europe). On the left, a white-robed woman hands him an olive branch, a sign of peace. The message: William has granted Europe liberty by saving it from the tyranny of Louis XIV. Below the royal couple, the Spirit of Architecture shows them the plans for this very building (commemorating the sad fact that Mary died before its completion). Ringing the central image are the four seasons (represented by Zodiac signs), the four virtues, and—at the top and bottom—a captured Spanish galleon and a British man-of-war battleship.

Up the steps at the end of the room, along the wall of the **upper hall,** is a portrait of the family of King George I. On the right is the artist who spent 19 years of his life painting this hall, James Thornhill (he finally finished it in 1727). He's holding out his hand—reportedly, he didn't feel he was paid enough for this Sistine-sized undertaking.

• *Exit the hall, and cross the field to enter the...*

Chapel of St. Peter and St. Paul: Not surprisingly, you'll sense a nautical air in this fine chapel. Notice the rope motif in the floor tiles down the aisle.

The painting above the altar, by American Benjamin West, depicts the shipwreck of St. Paul on the island of Malta. According to the Bible, Paul disturbed a poisonous viper but managed to throw it in a fire, miraculously without being harmed. Soon after the chapel was completed, it was gutted by a fire and had to be redecorated all over again. The plans were too ambitious, so the designers cut corners. Some of the columns and capitals are fake,

GREENWICH

and the "sculptures" lining the nave high above are actually *trompe l'oeil*—3-D paintings meant to look real. But some items, such as the marble frame around the main door, are finely crafted from expensive materials.

• *Leave the chapel, and walk straight down to the water—enjoying the sweeping views across to the Docklands. When you hit the river, turn right for the...*

Thames to Trafalgar Tavern Stroll—Wander east along the Thames on Five Foot Walk (named for the width of the path). Notice that the Old Royal Naval College is split into two parts; reportedly, Queen Mary didn't want the view from the Queen's House blocked. Looking up from the river, you'll see the college's twin-domed towers (one giving the time, the other the direction of the wind) framing the Queen's House, and the Royal Observatory Greenwich crowning the hill beyond.

Continuing downstream, just past the college, you'll find the **Trafalgar Tavern.** Dickens knew the pub well, and he used it as the setting for the wedding breakfast in *Our Mutual Friend.* Built in 1837 in the Regency style to attract Londoners downriver, the tavern is popular with locals (and tourists) for its fine lunches. The upstairs Nelson Room is still used for weddings. Its formal moldings and elegant windows with balconies over the Thames

are a step back in time. In addition to the casual pub, the tavern also has an elegant ground-floor dining room (£6-11 pub grub; £6-8 starters and £11-17 main courses in restaurant; food served Mon-Sat 12:00-22:00, Sun 12:00-17:00, Park Row, tel. 020/8858-2909).

A mile downstream from the pub, the **O2** (a.k.a. "the Dome") languished for nearly a decade after its controversial construction

and brief life as the Millennium Dome. Intended to be a world's fair-type site and the center of London's year 2000 celebration, it ended up being the topic of heated debates about cost overruns and its controversial looks. While post-2000 plans for a casino and hotel project fell through, it's come in handy as an emergency homeless shelter. The site was finally bought by a developer a few years ago and rechristened "The O₂" in honor of the telecommunications company that paid for the naming rights.

Currently, it hosts sporting events and concerts (at the time of his death, Michael Jackson was planning a massive concert series here), and will see action during the 2012 Summer Olympics.

• *From the Trafalgar Tavern, walk two long blocks up Park Row, and turn right (through the gate near the corner) into the park. The palatial buildings in the middle of the park are the Queen's House and the National Maritime Museum; the Royal Observatory Greenwich is on the hilltop beyond.*

Queen's House—This building, the first Palladian-style villa in Britain, was designed in 1616 by Inigo Jones for James I's wife, Anne of Denmark. All traces of the queen are long gone, and the Great Hall and Royal Apartments now serve as an art gallery for the National Maritime Museum. Predictably, most of the art is nautical-themed, with plenty of paintings of ships and sea battles, and portraits of admirals and captains. The Orangery is home to various Christ-like paintings depicting the death of Admiral Horatio Nelson—the maritime hero who is so adored here in England's naval capital. Among these is the great J. M. W. Turner painting *Battle of Trafalgar* (1824), the artist's only royal commission. The painting is often out on loan, so ask at the entry before you look for it.

Cost and Hours: Free, free audioguide, daily 10:00-17:00, last entry 30 minutes before closing, tel. 020/8858-4422, www.nmm.ac.uk.

▲**National Maritime Museum**—Great for anyone interested in the sea, this museum holds everything from a giant working pad-

dlewheel to the uniform Admiral Nelson wore when he was killed at Trafalgar (look for the bullet hole, in the left shoulder). A big glass roof tops three levels of slick, modern, kid-friendly exhibits about all things seafaring.

The Explorers exhibit covers early expeditions and an ill-fated Arctic trip, complete with a soundtrack of creaking wooden ships and crashing waves. One room displays stained-glass windows honoring members of London's Baltic Exchange (an important shipping consortium) killed in World War I. Kids like the All Hands and Bridge galleries, where they can send secret messages by Morse code and operate a miniature dockside crane. Along with displays of lighthouse technology and a whaling cannon, you'll see model ships, nautical paintings, and various salty odds and ends. Note that some parts of the museum are closed for renovation until 2012, though there's still plenty to see.

Cost and Hours: Free, daily 10:00-17:00, last entry 30 minutes before closing; look for family-oriented events posted at entrance—singing, treasure hunts, storytelling—particularly on weekends; tel. 020/8312-6608, www.nmm.ac.uk.

• *The final sight in town—the Royal Observatory Greenwich—is at the top of the hill just behind the National Maritime Museum. To reach it, cross through the colonnade connecting the museum and the Queen's House, then follow the crowds as they huff up the steep hill (allow 10-15 minutes).*

▲▲**Royal Observatory Greenwich**—Located on the prime meridian (0° longitude), the observatory is famous as the point from which all time is measured. The observatory's early work, however, had nothing to do with coordinating the world's clocks to Greenwich Mean Time (GMT). The observatory was founded in 1675 by Charles II for the purpose of improving navigation by more accurately charting the night sky. Today, the Greenwich time signal is linked with the BBC (which broadcasts the famous "pips" worldwide at the top of the hour). A visit here gives you a taste of the sciences of astronomy, timekeeping, and seafaring—and how they all meld together—along with great views over Greenwich and the distant London skyline.

Cost and Hours: £10, includes astronomy galleries, ticket good for re-entry for one year; daily 10:00-17:00, later in summer—can be as late as 19:00, courtyard sometimes open later than buildings, last entry 30 minutes before closing; tel. 020/8858-4422, www.nmm.ac.uk.

Planetarium: Shows cost £6.50, last 30 minutes, and generally run every hour (usually Mon-Fri 13:00-16:00, Sat-Sun 11:00-16:00, fewer shows in winter, schedule can change from day to day). Confirm times by calling ahead, checking online, or picking up a flier (which you'll see around the observatory). As these shows can sell out, consider calling ahead to order tickets (see phone number above).

❍ **Self-Guided Tour:** As you hike up the hill to the observatory, look along the roof for the orange **Time Ball**—also visible from the Thames—which drops daily at 13:00. Nearby, under the analog clock just outside the courtyard, see how your foot measures up to the foot where the public standards of length are cast in bronze.

Entering the observatory, you're directed to choose between two routes: the meridian route, to the right, and the astronomy route, to the left. Since the meridian route is more interesting, do that first.

Meridian Route: Following signs, you'll have the chance to rent an audioguide (£3.50, 1 hour), then enter the courtyard. Running through the middle of this space is The Line—the

The Longitude Problem

Around 1700, as the ships of seafaring nations began to venture farther from their home bases, the alarming increase in the number of shipwrecks made it clear that navigational tools had to be improved. Determining latitude—the relative position between the equator and the North or South Pole—was straightforward; sailors needed only to measure the angle of the sun at noon. But figuring out longitude, or their east-west position, was not as easy without a fixed point (such as the equator) from which to measure.

In 1714, the British government offered the £20,000 Longitude Prize. Two successful solutions emerged, and both are tied to Greenwich.

The first approach was to map the stars in the night sky over Greenwich. Then, sailors at sea could compare the stars overhead to the Greenwich map and calculate their east-west position. Visitors to the Royal Observatory can still see the giant telescopes—under retractable roofs—that were used to carefully chart the movement of the stars night after night.

The second approach was to create a clock that would remain completely accurate on voyages—no easy feat back then, when turbulence and changes in weather and humidity made timepieces notoriously unreliable at sea. John Harrison spent 45 years working on this problem, finally succeeding in 1760 with his fourth effort, the H4 (which won him the Longitude Prize). All four of his attempts are on display at the Royal Observatory.

So, how can a clock determine longitude? Every 15° of longitude equals an hour when comparing the difference in sunrise or sunset times between two places. For example, the time gap between Greenwich and New York City is five hours, which translates into a longitudinal difference of 75°. Equipped with an accurate timepiece set to Greenwich Mean Time, sailors could figure out their longitude by comparing sunset time at their current position with sunset time back in Greenwich.

Notice that both approaches use Greenwich as a baseline—either on an astral map or on a clock. That's why, to this day, the prime meridian and official world time are both centered in this unassuming London suburb.

prime meridian. Visitors wait patiently to have their photographs taken as they straddle the line in front of the monument, with one foot in each hemisphere. While watching all this fuss over a little line, consider that—unlike the equator—the placement of the prime meridian is totally arbitrary. It could well have been at my house, in Timbuktu, or just a few feet over—as, for a time, it was (the trough along the building's roofline shows where one astronomer had placed it). While waiting for your turn, set your wristwatch to the digital clock showing GMT to a tenth of a second.

Three different attractions are scattered around this courtyard. First, hiding in a corner is a **camera obscura.** This thrillingly low-tech device projects a live image from Greenwich onto a flat disc in a darkened room simply by manipulating light, without electricity or machinery. Bizarre as this seems today, imagine how astonishing it was in the days before television.

The smaller building is the **Flamsteed House,** named for John Flamsteed, the first king-appointed Astronomer Royal (in 1675). It contains the apartments that he lived in and the Wren-designed Octagon Room, where he carried out some of his work. Downstairs is a fascinating exhibit on the "Longitude Problem" and how it was solved (see sidebar, earlier). Also on display are all four of John Harrison's sea clocks. Compared to his other contraptions, the fourth and final attempt looks like an oversized pocket watch. But, in terms of its impact, this little timepiece is right up there with the printing press, the cotton gin, the telegraph, and the money belt on the scale of human achievement.

Finally, the **Telescopes Exhibition,** in the larger house, has a wide assortment of historical telescopes, including a couple of room-sized ones.

• *Now head out back for the...*

Astronomy Route: Walk past the giant rusted-copper cone top of the planetarium. The building beyond houses the **Weller Astronomy Galleries,** where interactive, kid-pleasing displays allow you to guide a space mission and touch a 4.5-billion-year-old meteorite. You can also buy tickets for and enter the state-of-the-art, 120-seat **Peter Harrison Planetarium** from here (for details, see "Planetarium," earlier).

Before you leave the observatory grounds, enjoy the **view** from

the overlook—the symmetrical royal buildings, the Thames, the Docklands and its busy cranes (including the prominent Canary Wharf Tower, with its pyramid cap), the huge O2 dome, and the square-mile City of London, with its skyscrapers and the dome of St. Paul's Cathedral. At night

GREENWICH

(17:00-24:00), look for the green laser beam the observatory projects into the sky (best viewed in winter), extending along the prime meridian for 15 miles.

Eating in Greenwich

If you're in town on a weekend, be sure to drop by the **Greenwich Market,** which hosts a sprawling food court (Thu-Sun 10:00-17:30, directly in front of Cutty Sark DLR station). Another handy place to pick up ready-made food is **Marks & Spencer Simply Food,** between the DLR station and the *Cutty Sark* dry dock (Mon-Sat 8:30-21:00, Sun 10:00-21:00, 55 Greenwich Church Street, tel. 020/8853-1840).

The **Trafalgar Tavern,** described on page 217, is good (Mon-Sat 12:00-22:00, Sun 12:00-17:00, Park Row, tel. 020/8858-2909).

The **Old Brewery,** in the Discover Greenwich center on the Old Royal Naval College grounds, is an upscale gastropub decorated with all things beer. A brewery on this site once provided the daily ration of four pints of beer for pensioners at the hospital. Today it's a microbrewery offering 50 different beers, while a beer sommelier suggests the right pairings with food on the menu (£6-15 pub grub; part of the pub becomes a fancier restaurant in the evenings with £5-6 starters and £11-17 main courses; daily 10:00-23:00, lunch 12:00-17:00, dinner from 18:00, tel. 020/3327-1280).

Windsor

Windsor, a compact and easy walking town of about 30,000 people, originally grew up around the royal residence. In 1070, William the Conqueror continued his habit of kicking Saxons out of their various settlements, taking over what the locals called "Windlesora" (meaning "riverbank with a hoisting winch")—which eventually became "Windsor." William built the first fortified castle on a chalk hill above the Thames; later, kings added on to his early designs, rebuilding and expanding the castle and surrounding gardens.

By setting up primary residence here, modern monarchs increased Windsor's popularity and prosperity—most notably, Queen Victoria, whose stern statue glares at you as you approach the castle. After her death, Victoria rejoined her beloved husband, Albert, in the Royal Mausoleum at Frogmore House, a mile south of the castle in a private section of the Home Park (house and mausoleum rarely open). The current Queen considers Windsor her primary residence, and the one where she feels most at home. You can tell if Her Majesty is in residence by checking to see which flag is flying above the round tower: If it's the royal standard (a red, yellow, and blue flag) instead of the Union Jack, the Queen is at home.

While 99 percent of visitors just come to tour the castle and go, some enjoy spending the night. Windsor's charm is most evident when the tourists are gone. Consider overnighting here—parking and access to Heathrow Airport are easy, and an evening at the horse races (on Mondays) is hoof-pounding, heart-thumping fun.

Getting to Windsor

By Train: Windsor has two train stations—Windsor & Eton Central (5-minute walk to palace; TI in adjacent shopping center) and Windsor & Eton Riverside (5-minute walk to palace and TI). First Great Western trains run between London's Paddington Station and Windsor & Eton Central (3/hour, 35 minutes, change at Slough; £8 one-way standard class, £8.50-11 same-day return, www.firstgreatwestern.co.uk). South West Trains run between London's Waterloo Station and Windsor & Eton Riverside (2/hour, 1 hour; £8.60 one-way standard class, £9-15 same-day return, info tel. 0845-748-4950, www.nationalrail.co.uk).

If you're day-tripping into London from Windsor, ask at the train station about combining a same-day return train ticket with a One-Day Travelcard—you'll end up with one ticket that covers rail transportation to and from London and doubles as an all-day Tube and bus pass in town (£12-21, lower price for travel after 9:30, rail ticket may also qualify you for half-price London sightseeing discounts—ask or look for brochure at station, or go to www.daysoutguide.co.uk).

By Bus: Green Line buses #701 and #702 run from London's Victoria Colonnades (between the Victoria train and coach stations) to the Parish Church stop on Windsor's High Street, before continuing on to Legoland (£1-9 one-way, £9.50-13.50 round-trip, prices vary depending on time of day, 1-2/hour, 1.25 hours to Windsor, tel. 01344/782-222, www.rainbowfares.com).

By Car: Windsor is about 20 miles from London and just off Heathrow Airport's landing path. The town (and then the castle and Legoland) is well-signposted from the M4 motorway. It's a convenient first stop if you're arriving at and renting a car from Heathrow, and saving London until the end of your trip.

From Heathrow Airport: Buses #71 and #77 run between Terminal 5 and Windsor, dropping you in the center of town on Peascod Street (about £7, 1-2/hour, 45 minutes, tel. 0871-200-2233, www.firstgroup.com). London black cabs can charge whatever they like from Heathrow to Windsor (and do); avoid them by calling a local cab company, such as Windsor Radio Cars (£25, tel. 01753/677-677, www.windsorcars.com).

Orientation to Windsor

(area code: 01753)
Windsor's pleasant pedestrian shopping zone litters the approach to its famous palace with fun temptations. You'll find most shops and restaurants around the castle on High and Thames Streets, and down the pedestrian Peascod Street (PESS-cot), which runs perpendicular to High Street.

Tourist Information
The TI is immediately adjacent to Windsor & Eton Central Station, in the Windsor Royal Shopping Centre's Old Booking Hall (May-Sept Mon-Fri 9:30-17:30, Sat 9:30-17:00, Sun 10:00-16:00; Oct-April Mon-Sat 10:00-17:00, Sun 10:00-16:00; tel. 01753/743-900, www.windsor.gov.uk). The TI sells discount tickets to Legoland (see "More Sights in Windsor," later).

Arrival in Windsor
By Train: The train to Windsor & Eton Central Station from Paddington (via Slough) will spit you out into the Windsor Royal shopping pavilion (which houses the TI), only a few minutes' walk from the castle. If you arrive instead at Windsor & Eton Riverside Station (from Waterloo Station), you'll see the castle as you exit—just follow the wall to the castle entrance.

By Car: Follow signs from the M4 motorway for pay-and-display parking in the center. River Street Car Park is closest to the castle, but pricey and often full. The cheaper, bigger Alexandra Car Park (near the riverside Alexandra Gardens) is farther west. To walk to the town center from the Alexandra Car Park, head east through the tour-bus parking lot toward the castle. At the souvenir shop, walk up the stairs (or take the elevator) and cross the overpass to the Windsor & Eton Central Station. Just beyond the station, you'll find the TI in the Windsor Royal Shopping Centre.

Helpful Hints
Internet Access: Get online at the **library,** located on Bachelors' Acre, between Peascod and Victoria Streets (£1.50 for 30 minutes, Mon and Thu 9:30-17:00, Tue 9:30-20:00, Wed 14:00-17:00, Fri 9:30-19:00, Sat 9:30-15:00, closed Sun, tel. 01753/743-940, www.rbwm.gov.uk).

Supermarkets: Pick up picnic supplies at **Marks & Spencer** (Mon-Sat 9:00-18:00, Sun 11:00-17:00, 130 Peascod Street,

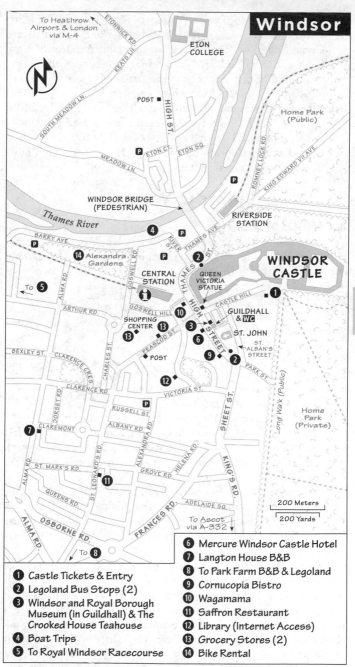

Windsor

To Heathrow Airport & London via M-4

ETONWICK RD.

ETON COLLEGE

KEATS LN.

HIGH ST.

SOUTH MEADOW LN.

POST ■

Home Park (Public)

ROMNEY LOCK RD.

KING EDWARD VII AVE.

MEADOW LN.

ETON CT. ETON SQ.

P

P

WINDSOR BRIDGE (PEDESTRIAN)

Thames River

RIVERSIDE STATION

BARRY AVE.

P

4

RIVER ST.

THAMES AVE.

P

WINDSOR CASTLE

14 Alexandra Gardens

GOSWELL RD.

2

THAMES ST.

Queen Victoria Statue

1

To 5

ALMA RD.

CENTRAL STATION

i

ARTHUR RD.

GOSWELL HILL

10

HIGH STREET

CASTLE HILL

GUILDHALL & WC

3

ST. JOHN

BEXLEY ST.

CLARENCE CRES.

SHOPPING CENTER

13

13

6

ST. ALBAN'S STREET

2

CHARLES ST.

PEASCOD ST.

9

PARK ST.

CLARENCE RD.

POST ♦

SHEET ST.

12

Home Park (Private)

DORSET RD.

VICTORIA ST.

Long Walk (Public)

RUSSELL ST.

P

CLAREMONT

7

ALBANY RD.

ALEXANDRA RD.

KING'S RD.

ST. LEONARD'S RD.

ST. MARK'S RD.

GROVE RD.

HELENA RD.

11

QUEENS RD.

ADELAIDE SQ.

FRANCES RD.

ALMA RD.

OSBORNE RD.

To Ascot via A-332

200 Meters

200 Yards

To 8

1 Castle Tickets & Entry
2 Legoland Bus Stops (2)
3 Windsor and Royal Borough Museum (in Guildhall) & The Crooked House Teahouse
4 Boat Trips
5 To Royal Windsor Racecourse
6 Mercure Windsor Castle Hotel
7 Langton House B&B
8 To Park Farm B&B & Legoland
9 Cornucopia Bistro
10 Wagamama
11 Saffron Restaurant
12 Library (Internet Access)
13 Grocery Stores (2)
14 Bike Rental

WINDSOR

tel. 01753/852-266) or at **Waitrose** (Mon-Tue and Sat 8:30-19:00, Wed-Fri 8:30-20:00, Sun 11:00-17:00, King Edward Court Shopping Centre, just south of the Windsor & Eton Central Station, tel. 01753/860-565). Just outside the castle, you'll find long benches near the statue of Queen Victoria—great for people-watching while you munch.

Bike Rental: Extreme Motion, near the river in Alexandra Gardens, rents 21-speed mountain bikes as well as helmets (£12/4 hours, £17/day, helmets £1-1.50, £100 credit-card deposit required, bring passport as ID, summer daily 10:00-22:00, closed off-season, tel. 01753/830-220).

Sights in Windsor

▲▲Windsor Castle

Windsor Castle, the official home of England's royal family for 900 years, claims to be the largest and oldest occupied castle in the world. Thankfully, touring it is simple. You'll see immense grounds, lavish staterooms, a crowd-pleasing dollhouse, an art gallery, and the chapel.

Cost: £16.50, family pass £43.50, ticket good for re-entry for one year if stamped at exit; to skip the lines, purchase tickets in advance online or at the Buckingham Palace ticket office, then go in through a fast entry door.

Hours: Daily March-Oct 9:45-17:15, Nov-Feb 9:45-16:15, last entry 1.25 hours before closing, often closed for special events such as the Garter Service in mid-June—call or check website to make sure it's open when you want to go.

Information: As you enter, ask about the warden's free 30-minute guided walks around the grounds (2/hour). They cover the grounds but not the castle, which is well described by the included audioguide (skip the official guidebook); tel. 020/7766-7304, www.royalcollection.org.uk.

Other Activities: The **Changing of the Guard** takes place Monday through Saturday at 11:00 (April-July) and on alternating days the rest of the year (check website to confirm schedule; ceremonies begin a little earlier—get there by 10:45). There is no Changing of the Guard on Sundays or in very wet weather. An **evensong** takes place in the chapel nightly at 17:15—free for worshippers.

Touring the Castle: Immediately upon entering, you pass through a simple modern building housing a **historical overview**

of the castle. This excellent intro is worth a close look—you're basically on your own after this. Inside, you'll find the motte (artificial mound) and bailey (fortified stockade around it) of William the Conqueror's castle. Dating from 1080, this was his first castle in England.

Follow the signs to the staterooms/gallery/dollhouse. **Queen Mary's Dollhouse**—a palace in miniature (1:12 scale, from 1924) and "the most famous dollhouse in the world"—often has the longest wait. If dollhouses aren't your cup of tea, you can skip that line and go immediately into the lavish **staterooms.** Strewn with history and the art of a long line of kings and queens, they're the best I've seen in Britain—and well restored after a devastating 1992 fire. Take advantage of the talkative docents in each room, who are happy to answer your questions.

The adjacent gallery is a changing exhibit featuring the **royal art collection** (and some big names, such as Michelangelo and Leonardo). Signs direct you (downhill) to **St. George's Chapel.** Housing numerous royal tombs, it's a fine example of Perpendicular Gothic, with classic fan-vaulting spreading out from each pillar (dating from about 1500). The simple chapel containing the tombs of the current Queen's parents, King George VI and "Queen Mother" Elizabeth, and younger sister, Princess Margaret, is along the church's north aisle.

Next door is the sumptuous 13th-century **Albert Memorial Chapel,** redecorated after the death of Prince Albert in 1861 and dedicated to his memory.

More Sights in Windsor

Legoland Windsor—Paradise for Legomaniacs under 12, this huge, kid-pleasing park has dozens of tame but fun rides (often

with very long lines) scattered throughout its 150 acres. The impressive Miniland has 40 million Lego pieces glued together to create 800 tiny buildings and a minitour of Europe; the Creation Centre boasts an 80 percent scale-model Boeing 747 cockpit, made of two million bricks. Several of the more exciting rides involve getting wet, so dress accordingly or buy a cheap disposable poncho in the gift shop. While you may be tempted to hop on the Hill Train at the entrance, it's faster and more convenient to walk down into the park. Food is available in the park, but you can save money by bringing a picnic.

Cost: Adults-£41.40, £37.20 in advance online, £36 from

Windsor TI; children-£31.20, £27.60 online, £26 from TI, 2-for-1 deals sometimes available; free for ages 3 and under; optional Q-Bot or Q-Bot Express ride-reservation gadget allows you to bypass lines (£10-40 depending on when you go and how much time you want to save); coin lockers-£1.

Hours: Convoluted schedule, but generally mid-March-July Mon-Fri 10:00-17:00, Sat-Sun 10:00-18:00, sometimes closed Tue-Wed in spring; Aug daily 9:30-20:00; Sept-Oct Thu-Mon 10:00-17:00, until 18:00 Sat-Sun, closed Tue-Wed; closed Nov-mid-March. Call or check website for exact schedule, tel. 0871-222-2001, www.legoland.co.uk.

Getting There: A £4.50 round-trip shuttle bus runs from opposite Windsor's Theatre Royal on Thames Street, and from the Parish Church stop on High Street (2/hour). If day-tripping from London, ask about rail/shuttle/park admission deals from Paddington or Waterloo train stations. For drivers, the park is on B3022 Windsor/Ascot road, two miles southwest of Windsor and 25 miles west of London. Legoland is clearly signposted from the M3, M4, and M25 motorways. Parking is easy and free.

Eton College—Across the bridge from Windsor Castle you'll find many post-castle tourists filing toward the most famous "public" (the equivalent of our "private") high school in Britain. Eton was founded in 1440 by King Henry VI; today it educates about 1,300 boys (ages 13-18), who live on campus. Eton has molded the characters of 19 prime ministers as well as members of the royal family, most recently princes William and Harry. The college is sparse on sights, but the public is allowed into the schoolyard, chapel, cloisters, and the Museum of Eton Life

Cost and Hours: £6.50, access only by one-hour guided tour at 14:00 and 15:15; tours available late March-Sept, usually Wed and Fri-Sun but daily during spring and summer holiday; closed Oct-late March and about once a month for special events, so call ahead; no photos in chapel, no food or drink allowed; tel. 01753/671-177, www.etoncollege.com.

Windsor and Royal Borough Museum—Tucked into a small space beneath the Guildhall, this little museum does its best to give some insight into the history of Windsor and the surrounding area. Ask at the desk if visits are being allowed to the Guildhall itself (where Prince Charles remarried); if not, it's probably not worth the price of admission.

Cost and Hours: £3, £1 audioguide, Tue-Sat 10:00-16:00, Sun 12:00-16:00, closed Mon, located in the Guildhall on High Street, tel. 01628/796-846, www.rbwm.gov.uk.

Boat Trips—Cruise up and down the Thames River for classic views of the castle, the village of Eton, Eton College, and the Royal Windsor Racecourse. Choose from a 40-minute or two-hour tour, then relax onboard and nibble a picnic. Boats leave from the riverside promenade adjacent to Barry Avenue.

Cost and Hours: 40-minute tour—£5.40, family pass from £13.50, mid-Feb-Oct 1-2/hour daily 10:00-17:00, Nov Sat-Sun hourly 10:00-16:00; 2-hour tour—£8.60, April-Oct only, 1-2/day; closed Dec-mid-Feb; tel. 01753/851-900, www.frenchbrothers .co.uk.

Horse Racing—The horses race near Windsor every Monday at the Royal Windsor Racecourse (£10-23 entry, online discounts, those under 18 free with an adult, April-Oct, no races in Sept, off A308 between Windsor and Maidenhead, tel. 01753/498-400, www.windsor-racecourse.co.uk). The romantic way to get there from Windsor is by a 10-minute shuttle boat (£6 round-trip, www .frenchbrothers.co.uk). The famous Ascot Racccourse (described below) is also nearby.

Near Windsor

Ascot Racecourse—Located seven miles southwest of Windsor and just north of the town of Ascot, this royally owned track is one of the most famous horse-racing venues in the world. The horses first ran here in 1711, and the course is best known for June's five-day Royal Ascot race meeting, attended by the Queen and 299,999 of her loyal subjects. For many, the outlandish hats worn on Ladies Day (Thursday) are more interesting than the horses. Royal Ascot is usually the third week in June (likely June 19-23 in 2012); the pricey tickets go on sale the preceding November but are often available close to the date (see website for details). In addition to Royal Ascot, the racecourse runs the ponies year-round—funny hats strictly optional.

Cost: Regular tickets generally £10-29, Royal Ascot £17-69, online discounts, those 17 and under free; parking £5-7, more for special races; dress code enforced in some areas and on certain days, tel. 0870-727-1234, www.ascot.co.uk.

Sleeping in Windsor

(area code: 01753)

Most visitors stay in London and do Windsor as a day trip. But here are a few suggestions for those staying the night.

$$$ Mercure Windsor Castle Hotel, with 108 business-class rooms, is as central as can be, just down the street from Her Majesty's weekend retreat (Db-£120-165, nonrefundable online deals, breakfast-£16, air-con, free Wi-Fi, 18 High Street, tel. 01753/851-577, www.mercure.com, h6618@accor.com).

$$ Langton House B&B is a stately Victorian home with four well-appointed rooms lovingly maintained by Paul and Sonja Fogg

Sleep Code

(£1 = about $1.60, country code: 44)
S = Single, D = Double/Twin, T = Triple, Q = Quad, b = bathroom, s = shower only. Unless otherwise noted, credit cards are accepted.

To help you sort through these listings easily, I've divided the rooms into three categories based on the price for a standard double room with bath:

$$$ **Higher Priced**—Most rooms £100 or more.
$$ **Moderately Priced**—Most rooms between £60-100.
$ **Lower Priced**—Most rooms £60 or less.

Prices can change without notice; verify the hotel's current rates online or by email. For other updates, see www.ricksteves.com/update.

WINDSOR

(Sb-£70, Db-£99, Tb-£119, Qb-£145, 5 percent extra if paying by credit card, lower prices off-season, family-friendly, guest kitchen, free Internet access and Wi-Fi, 46 Alma Road, tel. 01753/858-299, www.langtonhouse.co.uk, paul@langtonhouse.co.uk).

$$ **Park Farm B&B,** bright and cheery, is convenient for drivers visiting Legoland (Sb-£65, Db-£89, Tb-£105, Qb-£120, ask about family room with bunk beds, cash only—credit card solely for reservations, free Wi-Fi, access to shared fridge and microwave, free off-street parking, 1 mile from Legoland on St. Leonards Road near Imperial Road, 5-minute bus ride or 1-mile walk to castle, £4 taxi ride from station, tel. 01753/866-823, www.parkfarm.com, stay@parkfarm.com, Caroline and Drew Youds).

Eating in Windsor

Elegant Spots with River Views: Several places flank Windsor Bridge, offering romantic dining after dark. The riverside promenade, with cheap take-away stands scattered about, is a delightful place for a picnic lunch or dinner with the swans.

Touristy Places Around the Palace: Strolling the streets and lanes around the palace entrance, you'll find countless trendy and inviting eateries. **Cornucopia Bistro** serves tasty international dishes (£11 two-course lunches, £10-14 main courses at dinner, daily 12:00-14:30 & 18:00-21:30, Fri-Sat until 22:00, closed Sun night, 6 High Street). **The Crooked House** is a touristy 17th-century timber-framed teahouse, serving fresh, hearty £8-10 lunches and cream teas in a tipsy interior or outdoors on its cobbled lane (daily 10:30-18:00, 51 High Street). **Wagamama** offers modern Asian food, mostly in the form of noodle soups, in an informal and communal setting (£7-10 dishes, daily 12:00-23:00, on the left as you face the Windsor Royal Shopping Centre).

Ethnic Food Along St. Leonards Road: Residents enjoy the vast selection of unpretentious little eateries (including a fire-station-turned-pub) just past the end of pedestrian Peascod Street. You'll also find a handful of ethnic eateries. **Saffron Restaurant** is the local choice for South Indian cuisine, with a modern interior and attentive waiters who struggle with English but are fluent at bringing out tasty dishes. Their vegetarian *thali* is a treat (open daily for lunch from noon, dinner 17:30-23:00, 99 St. Leonards Road, tel. 01753/855-467).

Cambridge

Cambridge, 60 miles north of London, is world famous for its prestigious university. Wordsworth, Isaac Newton, Tennyson, Darwin, and Prince Charles are a few of its illustrious alumni. The university dominates—and owns—most of Cambridge, a historic town of 100,000 people. Cambridge is the epitome of a university town, with busy bikers, stately residence halls, plenty of bookshops, and proud locals who can point out where DNA was originally modeled, the atom first split, and electrons discovered.

In medieval Europe, higher education was the domain of the Church and was limited to ecclesiastical schools. Scholars lived in "halls" on campus. This academic community of residential halls, chapels, and lecture halls connected by peaceful garden courtyards survives today in the colleges that make up the universities of Cambridge and Oxford. By 1350 (Oxford is roughly 100 years older), Cambridge had eight colleges, each with a monastic-type courtyard, chapel, library, and lodgings. Today, Cambridge has 31 colleges, each with its own facilities. In the town center, these grand old halls date back centuries, with ornately decorated facades that try to one-up each other. While students' lives revolve around their independent colleges, the university organizes lectures, presents degrees, and promotes research.

The university schedule has three terms: Lent term from mid-January to mid-March, Easter term from mid-April to mid-June, and Michaelmas term from early October to early December. During exam time (roughly the month of May), the colleges are closed to visitors, which can impede access to all the picturesque little corners of the town. But the main sights—King's College Chapel and Trinity Library—stay open, and Cambridge is never sleepy.

Planning Your Time

Cambridge is worth most of a day. Start by taking the TI's walking tour, which includes a visit to the town's only must-see sight, the King's College Chapel (first tour at 11:00, later on Sun, call ahead to confirm and reserve—see "Tours in Cambridge," later). Spend the afternoon touring the Fitzwilliam Museum (closed Mon), or simply enjoying the ambience of this stately old college town.

Getting to Cambridge

By Train: It's an easy trip from London and less than an hour away. Catch the train from London's King's Cross Station (3/hour, fast trains leave at :15 and :45 past the hour and run in each direction, 45 minutes, £20 one-way standard class, £21 same-day return after 9:30, make sure to ask for "day return" and not the more expensive "return" ticket, operated by First Capital Connect, tel. 0845-748-4950, www.firstcapitalconnect.co.uk or www.nationalrail.co.uk). Trains also run from London's Liverpool Street Station—though more frequent, they take longer (4/hour, 1.25 hours).

By Bus: National Express coaches run from London's Victoria Coach Station to the Parkside stop in Cambridge (hourly, 2-2.5 hours, £11.50, tel. 08717-818-181, www.nationalexpress.co.uk).

Orientation to Cambridge

(area code: 01223)
Cambridge is congested but small. Everything is within a pleasant walk. There are two main streets, separated from the Cam River by the most interesting colleges. The town center, brimming with tearooms, has a TI and a colorful open-air market square. The train station is about a mile to the southeast.

Tourist Information

Cambridge's TI is well run and well signposted, just off Market Square in the town center. They book rooms for £5, offer walking tours (see "Tours in Cambridge," later), and sell bus tickets, a £0.60 town map, and a bigger £1 map/guide (Mon-Sat 10:00-17:00, Easter-Sept also Sun 11:00-15:00—otherwise closed Sun, phones answered from 9:00, Peas Hill, tel. 0871-226-8006, room-booking tel. 01223/457-581, www.visitcambridge.org).

Arrival in Cambridge

By Train: Cambridge's train station doesn't have baggage storage, but you can pay to leave your bags at the nearby bike-rental shop (see "Helpful Hints," below). The station does not have a TI, but it does have automated machines that dispense city maps for a £1 coin.

To get from the station to downtown Cambridge, you have several options. You can **walk** for about 25 minutes (exit straight ahead on Station Road, bear right at the war memorial onto Hills Road, and follow it into town); take public **bus** #1, #3, or #7 (note that buses are referred to as "Citi 1," "Citi 3," and so on in print and online, but only the number is marked on the bus; £1.30, pay driver, runs every 5-10 minutes, get off at Emmanuel Street stop—look for Grand Arcade shopping mall on the left); pay about £5 for a **taxi;** or ride a City Sightseeing **bus tour** (described later, buy ticket at kiosk next to bus stop).

By Car: Drivers can follow signs from the M11 motorway to any of the handy and central short-stay parking lots. Or you can leave the car at one of five park-and-ride lots outside the city, then take the shuttle into town (free parking, shuttle costs £2.30 round-trip if you buy ticket from machine, or £2.60 from driver).

Helpful Hints

Festival: The **Cambridge Folk Festival** gets things humming and strumming (July 26-29 in 2012, www.cambridgefolkfestival .co.uk).

Bike Rental: Station Cycles, located about a block to your right as you exit the station, rents bikes (£7/4 hours, £10/day, helmets 50p, £60 deposit, cash or credit card) and stores luggage (£3-4/bag depending on size; Mon-Fri 8:00-18:00, Wed until 19:00, Sat 9:00-17:00, Sun 10:00-16:00, tel. 01223/307-125, www.stationcycles.co.uk). They have a second location near the center of town (inside the Grand Arcade shopping mall, Mon-Fri 8:00-19:00, Wed until 20:00, Sat 9:00-18:00, Sun 10:00-18:00, tel. 01223/307-655).

Tours in Cambridge

▲▲**Walking Tour of the Colleges**—A walking tour is the best way to understand Cambridge's mix of "town and gown." The walks can be more educational (read: dry) than entertaining. But they do provide a good rundown of the historic and scenic highlights of the university, some fun local gossip, and plenty of university trivia. For example, why are entering students called "undergraduates"? Because long ago, new students at Cambridge were assigned to a mentor who already had a degree...so they were

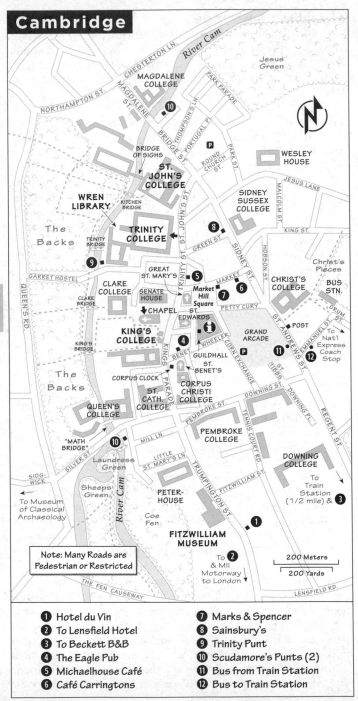

Cambridge

Note: Many Roads are Pedestrian or Restricted

200 Meters
200 Yards

1. Hotel du Vin
2. To Lensfield Hotel
3. To Beckett B&B
4. The Eagle Pub
5. Michaelhouse Café
6. Café Carringtons
7. Marks & Spencer
8. Sainsbury's
9. Trinity Punt
10. Scudamore's Punts (2)
11. Bus from Train Station
12. Bus to Train Station

"under" the supervision of a "graduate."

The TI offers **daily walking tours** that include the King's College Chapel, as well as another college—usually Queen's College (£14.50, 2 hours, includes admission fees; July-Aug daily at 11:00, 12:00, 13:00, and 14:00, no 11:00 tour on Sun; Sept-June Mon-Sat at 11:00, 13:00, and another time—likely at 12:00, Sun only at 13:00 and possibly at 12:00; tel. 01223/457-574, www .visitcambridge.org). It's smart to call ahead to reserve a spot (they'll take your credit-card number), or you can drop by in person (try to arrive 30 minutes before the tour). Notice that the 12:00 tour overlaps with the limited opening times of the Wren Library—so you'll miss out on the library if you take the noon tour.

Private guides are available through the TI (basic 1-hour tour-£4/person, £60 minimum; 1.5-hour tour-£4.50/person, £67.50 minimum; 2-hour tour-£5/person, £75 minimum; does not include individual college entrance fees, tel. 01223/457-574, tours @cambridge.gov.uk).

Walking and Punting Ghost Tour—If you're in Cambridge on the weekend, consider a £6 ghost walk to where spooky sightings have been reported, Friday evenings at 18:00, or a creepy £17.50 trip on the River Cam followed by a walk, most Saturdays at dusk (20:00 in summer; book ahead for either tour, organized by the TI, tel. 01223/457-574).

Bus Tours—City Sightseeing hop-on, hop-off bus tours are informative and cover the outskirts, including the American WWII Cemetery. But keep in mind that buses can't go where walking tours can—right into the center (£13, 80 minutes for full 21-stop circuit, cash only, departs every 20 minutes in summer, every 40 minutes in winter, first bus leaves train station at 10:06, last bus at 17:46, recorded commentary, tel. 01223/423-578, www.city-sight seeing.com). If arriving by train, you can buy your ticket from the kiosk directly in front of the station, then ride the bus into town.

Sights in Cambridge

Cambridge has many impressive old college buildings to explore, with fancy facades and tranquil grassy courtyards. I've featured the two most interesting (King's and Trinity), but feel free to wander beyond these. You might notice several bricked-up windows on the old buildings around town. This dates from a time when taxes were calculated per window...so filling them in saved money.

▲**King's Parade and Nearby**—The lively street in front of King's College, called King's Parade, seems to be where everyone in Cambridge gathers. Looming across the street from the college is **Great St. Mary's Church,** with a climbable bell tower (£3, Mon-Sat 9:30-17:00, Sun 12:30-16:00, 123 stairs). On the street

out front, students hawk punting tours on the Cam River (see
"Punting on the Cam," later).

Behind the church is the
thriving **Market Square.** The
big market is on Sunday (9:30-
16:30) and features produce,
arts, and crafts. On other days,
you'll find mostly clothes and
food (Mon-Sat 9:30-16:00).

The imposing Neoclassical building at the top (north) end
of King's Parade is the **Senate House,** the meeting place of the
university's governing body. In June, you might notice green boxes
lining the front of this house. Traditionally at the end of the term,
students would come to these boxes to see whether or not they'd
earned their degree; if a name was not on the list, the student had
flunked. Amazingly, until 2010 this was the only notification students received about their status. (Now they also get an email.)

In the opposite direction (south), at Benet Street, look for the
strikingly modern **Corpus Clock.** Designed and commissioned by
alum John Taylor, the clock was ceremonially unveiled by Stephen
Hawking in 2008. It uses concentric golden dials with blue LED
lights to tell the time, but it's precise only every five minutes; its
otherwise-irregular timekeeping mimics the unpredictability of
life. Perched on top is Chronophage, the "eater of time"—a gro-
tesque giant grasshopper that keeps the clock moving and periodically winks at passersby. Creepy and disturbing? Exactly, says
Taylor...so is the passage of time.

Just down Benet Street on the left is the recommended **Eagle
Pub**—Cambridge's oldest pub and a sight in itself; it's worth poking into the courtyard to learn about its dynamic history, even if
you don't eat or drink here. Across the street from the pub stands
the oldest surviving building in Cambridgeshire, **St. Benet's
Church.** The Saxons who built the church included circular holes
in its bell tower, to encourage owls to roost there and keep the
mouse population under control.

▲▲King's College Chapel—Built from 1446 to 1515 by Henrys
VI through VIII, England's best example of Perpendicular Gothic
architecture is the single most impressive building in town.

Cost and Hours: £6.50, erratic hours depending on school
schedule and events; during academic term usually Mon-Fri 9:30-
15:30, Sat 9:30-15:15, Sun 13:15-14:30; during breaks (see page 231)
usually Mon-Sat 9:30-16:00, Sun 10:00-17:00; tel. 01223/331-212,
recorded info tel. 01223/331-155, www.kings.cam.ac.uk/chapel.

Evensong: When school's in session, you're welcome to enjoy
an evensong service in this glorious space, with a famous choir

made up of men and boys (free, Mon-Sat at 17:30, Sun at 15:30; for more on evensong, see page 157).

Getting There: You'll see the regal front facade of King's College along King's Parade. To enter the chapel, curl around the back: Facing the college on King's Parade, head right and take the first left possible (just after the Senate House, on Senate House passage); at the dead end, bear left on Trinity Lane to reach the gate where you can pay to enter the chapel.

❷ Self-Guided Tour: Stand inside, look up, and marvel, as Christopher Wren did, at what was the largest single span of **vaulted roof** anywhere—2,000 tons of incredible fan vaulting, held in place by the force of gravity (a careful balancing act resting delicately on the buttresses visible outside the building).

While Henry VI—who began work on the chapel—wanted it to be austere, his descendants decided it should glorify the House of Tudor (of which his son, Henry VII, was the first king). Lining the walls are giant **Tudor coats-of-arms.** The shield includes a fleur-de-lis because an earlier ancestor, Edward III, woke up one day and—citing his convoluted lineage—somewhat arbitrarily declared himself king of France. The symbols on the left (a rose and the red dragon of Wales, holding the shield) represent the family of Henry VII's father, the Tudors. On the right, the greyhound holding the shield and the portcullis (the iron grate) symbolize the family of Henry VII's mother, Lady Margaret Beaufort, who prodded her son for years to complete this chapel.

The 26 **stained-glass windows** date from the 16th century. It's the most Renaissance stained glass anywhere in one spot. (Most

of the stained glass in English churches dates from Victorian times, but this glass is much older.) The lower panes show scenes from the New Testament, while the upper panes feature corresponding stories from the Old Testament. Considering England's turbulent history, it's miraculous that these windows have survived for nearly half a millennium in such a pristine state. After Henry VIII separated from the Catholic Church in 1534, many such windows and other Catholic features around England were destroyed. (Think of all those ruined abbeys dotting the English countryside.) However, since Henry had just paid for these windows, he couldn't bear to get rid of them. A century later, in the days of Oliver Cromwell, another wave of iconoclasm destroyed more windows around England. Though these windows were slated for removal, they stayed put. (Historians speculate that Cromwell's troops, who were garrisoned in this building, didn't want the windows removed in the chilly wintertime.) Finally, during World War II, the windows were taken out and hidden away to keep them safe and then painstakingly replaced.

The **choir screen** that bisects the church was commissioned by King Henry VIII to commemorate his marriage to Anne Boleyn. By the time it was finished, so was she (beheaded). But it was too late to remove her initials, which were carved into the screen (look for *R.A.*, for *Regina Anna*—"Queen Anne").

Behind the screen is the **choir** area, where the King's College Choir performs a daily evensong (see details earlier). On Christmas Eve, a special service is held here and broadcast around the world on the BBC—a tradition near and dear to the hearts of Brits.

Finally, walk to the altar and admire Rubens' masterful *Adoration of the Magi* (1634). It's actually a family portrait: The admirer in the front (wearing red) is a self-portrait of Rubens, Mary looks an awful lot like his much-younger wife, and the Baby Jesus resembles their own newborn at the time.

▲▲**Trinity College and Wren Library**—More than a third of Cambridge's 83 Nobel Prize winners have come from this richest and biggest of the town's colleges, founded in 1546 by Henry VIII.

Cost and Hours: Grounds—£3, daily 9:30-17:00, last entry 45 minutes before closing; library—free, Mon-Fri 12:00-14:00, Nov-mid-June also Sat 10:30-12:30, closed Sun; only 19 people allowed in at a time; to see Wren Library without paying for the grounds, enter from the riverside entrance, located by the Garret Hostel Bridge; tel. 01223/338-400, www.trin.cam.ac.uk.

◐ **Self-Guided Tour:** The college has three sights to see: the entrance gate, the grounds, and the magnificent Wren Library.

Trinity Gate: You'll notice gates like these adorning facades of colleges around town. Above the door is a statue of **King Henry VIII,** who founded Trinity because he feared that Cambridge's existing colleges were too cozy with the Church. Notice Henry's right hand: it holds a chair leg instead of the traditional crown jewels scepter. This is courtesy of Cambridge's Night Climbers, who first replaced the scepter a century ago, and continue to periodically switch it out for other items.

According to campus legend, decades ago some of the world's most talented mountaineers enrolled at Cambridge...in one of the flattest parts of England. (Cambridge was actually a seaport until Dutch engineers drained the surrounding swamps.) Lacking opportunities to practice their skill, they began scaling the frilly facades of Cambridge's college buildings under cover of darkness (if caught, they'd be expelled). In the 1960s, climbers actually managed to haul an entire automobile onto the roof of the Senate House. The university had to bring in the army to cut it into pieces and remove it. Only 50 years later, at a class reunion, did the guilty parties finally 'fess up.

In the little park to the right, notice the lone **apple tree.** Supposedly, this tree is a descendant of the very one that once stood in the garden of Sir Isaac Newton (who spent 30 years at Trinity). According to legend, Newton was inspired to investigate gravity when an apple fell from the tree onto his head. This tree stopped bearing fruit long ago; if you do see apples, they've been tied on by mischievous students.

• *If you like, head through the gate into the...*

Trinity Grounds: The grounds are enjoyable to explore, if not quite worth the cost of admission. Inside the **Great Court,**

the clock (on the tower on the right) double-rings at the top of each hour. It's a college tradition to take off running from the clock when the high noon bells begin (it takes 43 seconds to clang 24 times), race around the courtyard, touching each of the four corners without setting foot on the cobbles, and return to the same spot by the time the ringing ends. Supposedly only one student (a young lord) ever managed the feat—a scene featured in *Chariots of Fire* (but filmed elsewhere).

The **chapel** (entrance under clock)—which pales in comparison to the stunning King's College Chapel—feels like a shrine to thinking, with statues honoring great Trinity minds both familiar (Isaac Newton, Alfred Lord Tennyson, Francis Bacon) and unfamiliar. Who's missing? The poet Lord Byron, who was such a hellraiser during his time at Trinity that a statue of him was deemed unfit for Church property; his statue stands in the library instead.

Wren Library: Don't miss the 1695 Christopher Wren-designed library, with its wonderful carving and fascinating original manuscripts. Just outside the library entrance, Sir Isaac Newton clapped his hands and timed the echo to measure the speed of sound as it raced down the side of the cloister and back. In the library's 12 display cases (covered with cloth that you flip back), you'll see handwritten works by Sir Isaac Newton and John Milton, alongside A. A. Milne's original *Winnie the Pooh* (the real Christopher Robin attended Trinity College).

▲▲**Fitzwilliam Museum**—Britain's best museum of antiquities and art outside of London is the Fitzwilliam, housed in a grand Neoclassical building a 10-minute walk south of Market Square. The Fitzwilliam's broad collection is like a mini-British Museum/National Gallery rolled into one. The ground floor features an extensive range of antiquities and applied arts—everything from Greek vases, Mesopotamian artifacts, and Egyptian sarcophagi to Roman statues, fine porcelain, and suits of armor.

Upstairs is the painting gallery, with works that span art history: Italian Venetian masters (such as Titian and Canaletto), a worthy English section (featuring Gainsborough, Reynolds, Hogarth, and others), and a nice array of French Impressionist art (including Manet, Renoir, Pissarro, and Sisley). Rounding out the collection are old manuscripts, including some musical compositions from Handel. Watch your step—in 2006, a visitor tripped and accidentally smashed three 17th-century Chinese vases. Amazingly, the vases were restored (with donations from the community) and are now on display in Gallery 17...in a protective case.

Cost and Hours: Free, but suggested £3 donation, audio/videoguide-£3, Tue-Sat 10:00-17:00, Sun 12:00-17:00, closed Mon except bank holidays, no photos, Trumpington Street, tel. 01223/332-900, www.fitzmuseum.cam.ac.uk.

Museum of Classical Archaeology—Although this museum contains no originals, it offers a unique chance to study accurate copies (19th-century casts) of virtually every famous ancient Greek and Roman statue. More than 450 statues are on display. If you've seen the real things in Greece, Istanbul, Rome, and elsewhere, touring this collection is like a high school reunion..."Hey, I know you!" But since it takes some time to get here, this museum is best left to devotees of classical sculpture.

Cost and Hours: Free, Mon-Fri 10:00-17:00, Sat 10:00-13:00 during term, closed Sun, Sidgwick Avenue, tel. 01223/335-153, www.classics.cam.ac.uk/museum.

Getting There: The museum is a five-minute walk west of Silver Street Bridge; after crossing the bridge, continue straight until you reach a sign reading *Sidgwick Site*. The museum is in the long building on the corner to your right; the entrance is on the opposite side, and the museum is upstairs.

▲**Punting on the Cam**—For a little levity and probably more exercise than you really want, try hiring one of the traditional flat-bottom punts at the river and pole yourself up and down (or around and around, more likely) the lazy Cam. Once you get the hang of it, it's a fine way to enjoy the scenic side of Cambridge. It's less crowded in late afternoon (and less embarrassing).

Several companies rent punts and offer tours. Hawkers try to snare passengers in the thriving people zone in front of King's College. Prices are soft in slow times—try talking them down a bit before committing.

Trinity Punt, just north of Garret Hostel Bridge, is run by Trinity College students (£14/hour, £40 deposit, 45-minute tours-£30/boat, can share ride and cost with up to 2 others, cash only, ask for quick and free lesson, Easter-mid-Oct Mon-Fri 11:00-17:30, Sat-Sun 10:00-17:30, return punts by 18:30, no rentals mid-Oct-Easter, tel. 01223/338-483). **Scudamore's** has two locations: Mill Lane, just south of the central Silver Street Bridge, and the less convenient Quayside at Magdalene Bridge, at the north end of town (£16-18/hour, £80 deposit required—can use credit card; 45-minute tours-£15/person, £12.50 if you book at the TI; open daily June-Aug 9:00-22:00 or later, Sept-May at least 10:00-16:00, weather permitting, tel. 01223/359-750, www.scudamores.com).

Near Cambridge

Imperial War Museum Duxford—This former airfield, nine miles south of Cambridge, is nirvana for aviation fans and WWII buffs. Wander through seven exhibition halls housing 200 vintage aircraft (including Spitfires, B-17 Flying Fortresses, a Concorde, and a Blackbird) as well as military land vehicles and special displays on Normandy and the Battle of Britain. On many weekends, the museum holds special events, such as air shows (extra fee)—check the website for details.

Cost and Hours: £16.50 (includes small donation), show local bus ticket for discount, daily mid-March-late Oct 10:00-18:00, late Oct-mid-March 10:00-16:00, last entry one hour before closing; Concorde interior open until 17:00, 15:00 off-season; tel. 01223/835-000, http://duxford.iwm.org.uk.

Getting There: The museum is located off A505 in Duxford. From Cambridge, take bus #7 from the train station (45 minutes) or from Emmanuel Street's Stop A (55 minutes, bus runs 2/hour Mon-Sat, www.stagecoachbus.com/cambridge). On Sundays and bank holidays, catch the #132 bus, run by private bus operator Myalls, from the train station or the Drummer Street bus station (40 minutes, first bus around 10:00, then every 2 hours until 18:00, tel. 01763/243-225).

Sleeping in Cambridge

(£1 = about $1.60, country code: 44, area code: 01223)
While Cambridge is an easy side-trip from London, its subtle
charms might convince you to spend the night. Cambridge has
very few accommodations in the city center, and none in the tight
maze of colleges and shops where you'll spend most of your time.
These recommendations are about a 10- to 15-minute walk south of
the town center, toward the train station.

$$$ **Hotel du Vin** blends France, England, and wine. This
worthwhile splurge has 41 comfortable, spacious rooms above a
characteristic bistro that offers good deals for guests and nonguests
alike. This mod place manages to be classy yet unpretentious (Db-
£120-150, fancier suites available, check online for special offers,
breakfast-£10 if booked ahead, air-con, elevator, pay Wi-Fi, just
down the street from the Fitzwilliam Museum at Trumpington
Street 15-17, tel. 01223/227-330, fax 01223/227-331, www.hoteldu
vin.com, reception.cambridge@hotelduvin.com).

$$$ **Lensfield Hotel,** popular with visiting professors, has
30 old-fashioned rooms (Sb-£69, Db-£105, pricier rooms also
available, pay Wi-Fi, 53 Lensfield Road, tel. 01223/355-017, fax
01223/312-022, www.lensfieldhotel.co.uk, enquiries@lensfield
hotel.co.uk).

$ **Debbie and Michael Beckett** rent one room in their mod-
ern home, next door to a big church halfway between downtown
and the train station. The room, with a private bathroom on the
hall, makes you feel like a houseguest (S-£40, D-£55, includes
breakfast, 15 St. Paul's Road, tel. 01223/315-832, debbie.beckett2
@googlemail.com).

Eating in Cambridge

While picnicking is scenic and saves money, the weather may not
always cooperate. Here are a few ideas for fortifying yourself with
a lunch in central Cambridge.

The Eagle Pub, near the TI, is the oldest pub in town, and a
Cambridge institution with a history so rich that a visit here practically qualifies as sightseeing.
Find your way into the delightful courtyard, with outdoor seating and a good look at the place's
past. The second-floor windows
were once guest rooms, back
when this was a coachmen's inn
as well as a pub. Notice that the
window on the right end is open;

any local will love to tell you why. Follow the signs into the mis-named "RAF Bar," where US Air Force pilots signed the ceiling while stationed here during World War II. Science fans can celebrate the discovery of DNA—Francis Crick and James Watson first announced their findings here in 1953 (£6-8 lunches, £6-11 dinners, food served daily 10:00-22:00, drinks until 23:00, 8 Benet Street, tel. 01223/505-020).

The **Michaelhouse Café** is a heavenly respite from the crowds, tucked into the repurposed St. Michael's Church, just north of Great St. Mary's Church. At lunch, choose from salads, soups, and sandwiches, as well as a few hot dishes and a variety of tasty baked goods (£5-10 light meals, Mon-Sat 8:00-17:00, breakfast served 8:00-11:00, lunch served 11:30-15:30, hot drinks and baked goods always available, closed Sun, Trinity Street, tel. 01223/309-147). Near the end of the day—after 14:30—you can pay £4 to fill your plate with whatever they have left.

Café Carringtons is a cozy cafeteria that serves traditional British food at reasonable prices, including a Sunday roast lunch (£6-8 meals, £5 sandwiches, Mon-Sat 8:00-17:00, Sun 10:00-16:00, down the stairs at 23 Market Street, tel. 01223/361-792).

Supermarkets: There's a **Marks & Spencer Simply Food** at the train station and a larger Marks & Spencer department store on Market Square (Mon-Thu 9:00-18:00, Wed until 19:00, Fri 9:00-19:00, Sat 9:00-18:30, Sun 11:00-17:00, tel. 01223/355-219). **Sainsbury's** supermarket has longer hours (Mon-Sat 8:00-23:30, Sun 11:00-17:00, 44 Sidney Street, at the corner of Green Street).

A good picnic spot is Laundress Green, a grassy park on the river, at the end of Mill Lane near the Silver Street Bridge punts. There are no benches, so bring something to sit on. Remember, the college lawns are private property, so walking or picnicking on the grass is generally not allowed. When in doubt, ask at the college's entrance.

Cambridge Connections

From Cambridge by Train to: York (1-2/hour, 2.5 hours, transfer in Peterborough), **Oxford** (2/hour, 2.5 hours, change in London involves Tube transfer between train stations), **London** (King's Cross Station: 3/hour, 45-60 minutes; Liverpool Street Station: 4/hour, 1.25 hours). Train info: Tel. 0845-748-4950, www.nationalrail.co.uk.

By Bus to: London (hourly, 2-2.5 hours), **Heathrow Airport** (1-2/hour, 2-3 hours). Bus info: Tel. 08717-818-181, www.nationalexpress.com.

CANTERBURY

Canterbury is one of England's most important religious destinations. For centuries, it has welcomed hordes of pilgrims to its grand cathedral. While these days you'll probably see more iPods than Bibles in this college town, Canterbury's cathedral and medieval core still beckon with rich history and architectural splendor.

Pleasant, walkable Canterbury, like many cities in southern England, was originally founded by the pagan Romans. Then along came St. Augustine, sent by the pope to convert England's King Ethelbert of Kent to Christianity. Ethelbert (who had a Christian wife) joined the Church and allowed St. Augustine to set up a monastery on the edge of town. As Christianity became more established in England, Canterbury became its center, and the Archbishop of Canterbury emerged as one of the country's most powerful men.

The famous pilgrimages to Canterbury began in the 12th century, after the assassination of Archbishop Thomas Becket by followers of King Henry II (with whom Becket had been in a long fight). Becket was canonized as a martyr, rumors of miracles at the cathedral spread, and flocks of pilgrims showed up at its doorstep. Along the way, they'd stop off at inns and entertain each other with tales—sometimes bawdy and just for fun, sometimes devout and meaningful.

Today, much of the medieval city—heavily bombed during World War II—exists only in fragments. Miraculously, the cathedral and surrounding streets are fairly well-preserved. Thanks to its huge student population and thriving pedestrian-and-shopper-friendly zone in the center, Canterbury is an exceptionally livable and fun-to-visit town.

Planning Your Time

Because of its impressive cathedral, compact tourist zone, and relaxing break-from-a-big-city ambience, Canterbury is an ideal day trip from London. With more time, it merits an overnight. (You could even come straight from the airport to Canterbury and sleep here for two nights, with a day of sightseeing.) If visiting for just a few hours, head straight for the cathedral, then spend the rest of your time strolling the town's pleasant pedestrian core, and maybe drop into some of Canterbury's other sights. Consider sticking around for evensong in the cathedral (Mon-Fri at 17:30, Sat-Sun generally at 15:15).

Ambitious sightseers can fit both Canterbury and Dover (see next chapter) into a hectic one-day trip from London: Take an early train to Dover, taxi to Dover Castle, munch a picnic lunch on the train to Canterbury, tour Canterbury Cathedral, then enjoy the evensong and dinner in Canterbury before returning by train to London.

Orientation to Canterbury

(area code: 01227)

With about 45,000 people, Canterbury is big enough to be lively but small enough to be manageable. The center of town is enclosed by the old city walls, a ring road, and the Stour River to the west. High Street (also known as St. Peter's Street at one end and St. George's Street at the other) bisects the town center. During the day, the action is on High Street and in the knot of medieval lanes surrounding the cathedral. (At night, the city is quiet all around.) The center is walkable—it's only about 20 minutes on foot from one end to the other.

Tourist Information

The TI, in front of Christ Church Gate, assists modern-day pilgrims. Pick up the free Visitors Guide with a map (Mon-Sat 9:00-17:30, Sun 10:00-17:00; 12-13 Sun Street, tel. 01227/378-100, www.canterbury.co.uk).

Combo-Ticket: The TI sells a "Canterbury Attractions

Canterbury

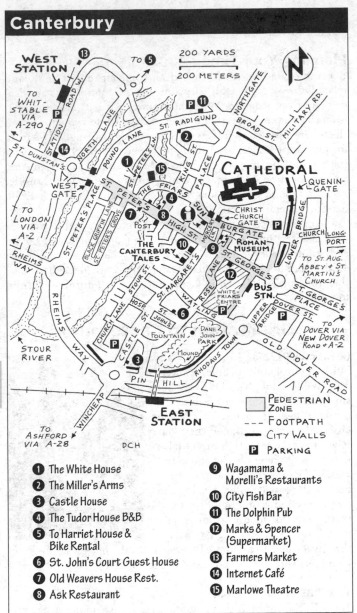

WEST STATION

TO WHITSTABLE VIA A-290

TO LONDON VIA A-2

RHEIMS WAY

STOUR RIVER

TO ASHFORD VIA A-28

DCH

WEST GATE

ST. DUNSTAN'S

ROAD W.

STATION RD.

NORTH LANE

POUND LANE

ST. PETER'S ST.

ST. PETER'S PLACE

BLACK GRIFFIN LANE

ST. PETER'S GROVE

ST. PETER'S

THE FRIARS

HIGH ST.

Post

STOUR ST.

ST. MARGARET'S

CHURCH LANE

CASTLE ST.

ST. JOHN'S

HOSP.

WATLING

Fountain

PIN HILL

WINCHEAP

RHEIMS WAY

CASTLE ST.

ST. RADIGUND

KING ST.

PALACE ST.

SUN ST.

MERCERY LANE

BURGATE

CHRIST CHURCH GATE

CATHEDRAL

QUENIN-GATE

BROAD ST.

MILITARY RD.

NORTHGATE

ROMAN MUSEUM

ST. GEORGE'S

ROSE LANE

UPPER BRIDGE ST.

BUS STN.

WHITE-FRIARS CENTRE

DANE JOHN PARK

Mound

RHODAUS TOWN

LOWER BRIDGE

CHURCH ST.

LONG-PORT

TO ST. AUG. ABBEY & ST. MARTIN'S CHURCH

ST. GEORGE'S PLACE

DOVER ST.

TO DOVER VIA NEW DOVER ROAD & A-2

OLD DOVER ROAD

EAST STATION

THE CANTERBURY TALES

200 YARDS

200 METERS

TO ⑤

PEDESTRIAN ZONE

--- **FOOTPATH**

— **CITY WALLS**

P **PARKING**

Legend:

- ① The White House
- ② The Miller's Arms
- ③ Castle House
- ④ The Tudor House B&B
- ⑤ To Harriet House & Bike Rental
- ⑥ St. John's Court Guest House
- ⑦ Old Weavers House Rest.
- ⑧ Ask Restaurant
- ⑨ Wagamama & Morelli's Restaurants
- ⑩ City Fish Bar
- ⑪ The Dolphin Pub
- ⑫ Marks & Spencer (Supermarket)
- ⑬ Farmers Market
- ⑭ Internet Café
- ⑮ Marlowe Theatre

CANTERBURY

Passport" that covers the cathedral, St. Augustine's Abbey, the Canterbury Tales audio-visual show, and either the Roman Museum or another lesser sight. It's a good deal only if you plan to see everything (£20, saves about £6, sold only at TI).

Arrival in Canterbury

Canterbury's two train stations (East and West) flank the town center. Trains from London's Victoria Station arrive at Canterbury's East Station; trains from London's St. Pancras and Charing Cross stations arrive at Canterbury's West Station. Each train station is about a 10-minute walk from downtown. The bus station is at the end of the High Street pedestrian area, inside the city walls just past the big Whitefriars shopping center.

Helpful Hints

Guided Walk: Canterbury Tourist Guides offer a 1.5-hour walk departing from the TI (£6, daily at 11:00, July-Sept also at 14:00, www.canterbury-walks.co.uk, tel. 01227/459-779).

Internet Access: Dot Café, just outside of the city gate, has several Internet terminals and does computer repair (£3/hour, Mon-Sat 9:00-21:00, Sun 10:30-17:30, upstairs at 19-21 St. Dunstan's Street, tel. 01227/478-778, www.ukdotcafe.com). The recommended **Dolphin Pub** has free Wi-Fi for paying customers.

Shopping: A **Marks & Spencer** department store, with a supermarket at the back on the ground floor, is located near the east end of High Street (Mon-Sat 9:00-19:00, Sun 11:00-17:00, tel. 01227/462-281). Sprawling behind it is a vast shopping complex called **Whitefriars Centre** (most shops open Mon-Sat 9:00-18:00, Sun 10:00-16:00). A modest **farmers' market** is held every day except Monday at The Goods Shed (Tue-Sat 9:00-19:00, Sun 10:00-16:00), just to the north of the West Station, adjacent to the parking lot.

Bike Rental: Downland Cycles rents and repairs bikes (£15/day, helmets-£3, multiple-day discounts, Mon-Sat 9:00-17:30, closed Sun; up the street from the West Station on Malthouse Road, just off St. Stephen's Road; tel. 01227/479-643, www.downlandcycles.co.uk). For a pleasant daylong ride in the countryside, ask for a map of the Crab and Winkle Way, a popular biking trail from Canterbury to the charming fishing village of Whitstable.

Theater: The **Marlowe Theatre,** named for Christopher Marlowe (Shakespeare's famous competitor and native of Canterbury) opens for its first full season in 2012, offering an array of ballet, Broadway productions, speakers, and musicians (book tickets online or at TI, The Friars, tel. 01227/787-787, www.marlowetheatre.com).

Sights in Canterbury

▲▲▲Canterbury Cathedral

This grand landmark of piety, one of the most important churches in England, is the headquarters of the Anglican Church—in terms of church administration, it's something like

the English Vatican. It's been a Christian site ever since St. Augustine, the cathedral's first archbishop, broke ground in 597. In the 12th century, the cathedral became world-famous because of an infamous act: the murder of its then-archbishop, Thomas Becket. Canterbury became a prime destination for religious pilgrims, trumped in importance only by Rome and Santiago de Compostela, Spain. The dramatic real-life history of Canterbury Cathedral is the tale of two King Henrys (Henry II and Henry VIII), and of the martyred Becket.

Cost and Hours: £8, Easter-Oct Mon-Sat 9:00-17:30, Sun 12:30-14:00, slightly shorter hours Nov-Easter, last entry 30 minutes before closing, tel. 01227/762-862, www.canterbury-cathedral.org.

Tours: Guides wearing golden sashes are posted throughout the cathedral to answer your questions. Guided £5 tours are offered Mon-Fri at 10:30, 12:00, and 14:30 (14:00 in winter); and Sat at 10:30, 12:00, and 13:30 (no tours Sun). At the shop inside the cathedral, you can rent a dry but informative £3.50 audioguide.

Evensong: The choral evensong is easy even for atheists. As you enter, they'll hand you a laminated placard telling you what to say for group responses, when to sit and stand, and when the music begins (free, Mon-Fri at 17:30, Sat-Sun generally at 15:15). Weekend schedules are subject to change, so it's smart to stop by or call to confirm (tel. 01227/762-862). For more on evensong, see page 157.

◐ Self-Guided Tour: Although guided tours and audioguides are available, it's simple just to wander through on your own.

• *Begin your tour in the pedestrian shopping zone just outside the cathedral grounds, by the TI. Before going through the passageway, take a moment to appreciate the...*

Christ Church Gate: This highly decorated gate is the cathedral yard's main entrance. Find the royal seals and symbols on the gate, including the Tudor rose. This rose was the symbol of Henry VIII, who—shortly after the Christ Church Gate was built—divorced both his wife and the Vatican, establishing the Anglican Church.

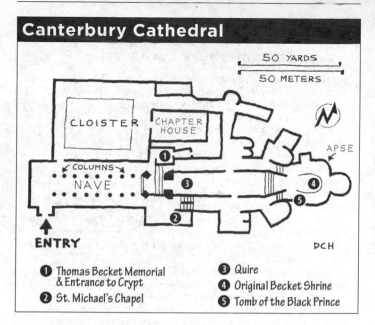

Canterbury Cathedral

50 YARDS
50 METERS

CLOISTER

CHAPTER HOUSE

APSE

COLUMNS

NAVE

❶

❸

❹

❺

❷

ENTRY

DCH

❶ Thomas Becket Memorial & Entrance to Crypt
❷ St. Michael's Chapel
❸ Quire
❹ Original Becket Shrine
❺ Tomb of the Black Prince

• *Go through the gate (where you'll buy your ticket) and walk into the courtyard that surrounds this massive, impressive church. Examine the...*

Cathedral Exterior: Notice the cathedral's length, and how each section is distinctive. The church was already considered large in pre-pilgrim days, but in the 15th century, builders began another 100 years of construction (resulting in a patchwork effect that you'll notice in the interior).

• *Enter the church through the side door—the front doors of English cathedrals tend to be used only for special occasions—and pick up a map at the desk before you take a seat in the...*

Nave: The interior of the nave shows the inner workings of this sprawling, eclectic structure. Look around, and you'll see a church that's had many incarnations. Archaeological excavations in the early 1990s showed that the building's core is Roman. Through the ages, new sections were added on, with the biggest growth during the 1400s, when the cathedral had to be expanded to hold all of its pilgrims.

While tourists still flock here, this is also a working church, the headquarters of the Anglican Church, and the seat of the Archbishop of Canterbury. The current archbishop, Rowan Williams, has made headlines with his liberal and accepting views on homosexuality and the ordination of women, as well as his concern about Britain's involvement in the Iraq War. He's been quoted as saying that creationism should not be taught in schools.

Thomas Becket and Canterbury Cathedral

In the 12th century, Canterbury Cathedral had already been a Christian church for more than 500 years. The king at the time was Henry II (who rebuilt and expanded nearby Dover Castle, described in the next chapter). Henry was looking for a new archbishop, someone who would act as a yes-man and allow him to gain control of the Church (and its followers). He found a candidate in his drinking buddy and royal chancellor: Thomas Becket (also called

Thomas à Becket). In 1162, the king's friend was consecrated as archbishop.

But Becket surprised the king, and maybe even himself. Inspired by his new position—and wanting to be a true religious leader to his mighty flock—he cleaned up his act, became dedicated to the religious tenets of the Church (dressing as a monk), and refused to bow to the king's wishes. As tensions grew, Henry wondered aloud, "Will no one rid me of this turbulent priest?" Four knights took his words seriously, and assassinated Becket during vespers in the cathedral. The act shocked the medieval world. King Henry later submitted to walking barefoot through town while being flogged by priests as an act of pious penitence.

Not long after Becket's death in 1170, word spread that miracles were occurring in the cathedral, prompting the pope to canonize Becket. Soon the pilgrims came, hoping some of Becket's steadfast goodness would rub off (perhaps they also wanted to see the world—just like travelers today).

• *From here, we'll follow the route laid out by the map you picked up when you entered. Head up the right aisle. When you get to the quire (marked by a beautifully carved stone portal in the center of the nave), go left through the small tunnel underneath. Immediately to your right as you exit the tunnel is the...*

Thomas Becket Memorial: This is where Thomas Becket was martyred. You'll see a humble plaque and a wall sculpture of lightning-rod arrows pointing to the place where he died.

• *Continue down the stairs next to the memorial and enter the...*

Crypt: Notice the heavy stone arches. This lower section was started by the Normans, who probably built on top of St. Augustine's original church. Cross over to the other (right) side of the crypt. The small chapel marked *Église Protestante Française* celebrates a Mass in French every Sunday at 15:00. This chapel has been used for hundreds of years by French (Huguenot) and Belgian (Walloon) Protestant communities, who fled persecution in their home countries for the more welcoming atmosphere in Protestant England.

• *Facing this chapel, turn right, walk to the end of the crypt, and climb up the stairs. At the landing, turn left to find...*

St. Michael's Chapel: Also known as the Warrior's Chapel, this was built by Lady Margaret Holland (d. 1439) to house family tombs. The chapel is also associated with the Royal East Kent Regiment ("The Buffs"). Notice the bell on the wall to the left, which once rang from the HMS *Canterbury,* a ship that waged war against those disobedient colonists during the American Revolution. Each day at 11:00, the bell is rung and a prayer is said here to honor those who have lost their lives in battle.

• *Head up the stairs across from the tomb, and go through the ornate stone portal we passed earlier. This will bring you into the **quire,** where the choir sings evensong. Walk toward the high altar, then turn left through the gate and walk with the quire on your right to the far end of the church (the apse). Behind the quire, you'll see a candle in the center of the floor. This was the site of the...*

Original Becket Shrine: Beginning in the 12th century, hundreds of thousands of pilgrims came to this site to leave offerings. Imagine this site in the Dark Ages. You're surrounded by humble, devout pilgrims who've trudged miles upon miles to reach this spot. (Try to ignore the B.O.) Now that they've finally arrived, they're hoping to soak up just a bit of the miraculous power that's supposed to reside here.

Then came King Henry VIII, who broke away from the pope so he could marry on his own terms. In 1538, he destroyed the original altar (and lots more, including the original abbey on the edge of town). Dictatorial Henry VIII—no fan of a priest who would stand up to a king—had Thomas Becket's body removed from the cathedral. Legend says that Henry had Becket's body burned and the ashes scattered as part of his plan to drive religious pilgrims away from the site.

• *Adjacent to the shrine, in the apse, is the...*

Tomb of the Black Prince: This is the final resting place of the Black Prince, Edward of Woodstock (d. 1376). The Prince of Wales and the eldest son of Edward III, the Black Prince was famous for his cunning in battle and his chivalry—the original

The Canterbury Tales

"Whan that Aprill, with his shoures soote
The droghte of March hath perced to the roote..."

So begins *The Canterbury Tales*, one of the earliest and most influential works of English literature. In the late 14th century, author and diplomat Geoffrey Chaucer (c. 1343-1400) was so inspired by the cross-section of humanity undertaking the pilgrimage to Canterbury that he penned a collection of 24 tales told by fictional travelers. *The Canterbury Tales* is arguably the oldest surviving travelogue, and the greatest work written in the Middle English vernacular—a bold move at a time when Latin and French were the literary languages of choice. (Because Middle English is essentially a different language—see the first two lines, above—the work is most often read today in present-day English translation.)

Chaucer demonstrates an impressive range of themes and genres within these tales, ranging from tragedy to romance to humor. *The Canterbury Tales* is a microcosm of human experience, featuring yarns spun by people from diverse walks of life: knight, miller, cook, lawyer, wife, merchant, squire, physician, monk, nun. Despite their obvious differences, all of these travelers were drawn together by a shared faith and the desire to experience the power of the shrine of Thomas Becket...and by a mutual appreciation for a good story.

"knight in shining armor."

Our tour is finished. As you leave the cathedral, consider this: Even with all their power, wealth, and influence, two English kings were unable to successfully eradicate Thomas Becket's influence (if they had, the line to get into the cathedral would be shorter). A man of conscience—who once stood up to the most powerful ruler in England—continues to inspire visitors, nearly a thousand years after his death.

More Sights in the Old Town

▲The Canterbury Tales—If your visit to Canterbury gives you English Lit flashbacks, this corny audio-visual show offers a good review—or, if you're unfamiliar with Chaucer, it provides a decent introduction. Making use of creepy mannequins, primitive lighting effects, and medieval smells, it dramatizes five of the tales. More hokey than literary, the exhibit is useful as a CliffsNotes to Chaucer's masterpiece.

Cost and Hours: £8, includes audioguide, daily 10:00-17:00, July-Aug from 9:30, Nov-Feb until 16:30, St. Margaret's Street, tel. 01227/454-888, recorded info tel. 01227/479-227, www.canterburytales.org.uk.

Roman Museum—The colorful displays in this slight museum illustrate Canterbury's Roman origins and end with a view of sections of still-intact foundations and mosaics. Included are several shamelessly self-congratulatory exhibits celebrating the museum archaeologist...nice touch.

Cost and Hours: £6, free for kids, Mon-Sat 10:00-17:00, in summer also open Sun 11:00-16:00, last entry one hour before closing, Butchery Lane, across from City Arms Inn, tel. 01227/785-575, www.canterbury-museums.co.uk.

East of the Old Town

While historically significant, these two sights—about a 10-minute walk east of the Old Town walls—aren't worth the trek for most visitors.

St. Augustine's Abbey—These ruins of the original abbey—founded by the man himself, St. Augustine—sit right on the edge of town. At its height, the abbey was a hive of activity, with a large church, cloister, and a cluster of service buildings for the monks. In the 16th century, King Henry VIII grew jealous of the wealth and influence held by England's monks, so he closed down the monasteries, retired the monks, and sold off the land and buildings. The abbey's buildings were converted to houses, while the large church was slowly dismantled and used as a building-material quarry for projects in the area.

Today, the site is dull even compared to other ruined abbeys. A modest museum sets up your visit. Outside, the foundations and some fragments of the original structures are still visible in a grassy field, and the uninspired audioguide struggles to bring the site to life. Pace the square of the cloister and imagine yourself as a monk in the early days of Christianity in England.

Cost and Hours: £4.50, includes audioguide; April-June Wed-Sun 10:00-17:00, closed Mon-Tue; July-Aug daily 10:00-18:00; Sept-March Sat-Sun 10:00-16:00, until 17:00 Sept-Oct, closed Mon-Fri; sometimes closes at 15:00 for concerts, last entry 30 minutes before closing, tel. 01227/767-345, www.english-heritage.org.uk.

St. Martin's Church—Set in the center of an old, slanted graveyard, humble little St. Martin's has the honor of being the oldest parish church in England. In continual use since 650, it sits on the foundations of a Roman temple, and features an elegant Norman-era baptismal font to the right of the entrance.

Cost and Hours: Free; generally open Tue, Thu, and Sat 11:00-15:00; tel. 01227/768-072. Because the church is run by volunteers, it has very sporadic hours, so call to confirm. To find the church, continue on the busy road 100 yards past the abbey, and turn down the first real road to the left (North Holmes Road);

you'll see the churchyard's wooden entry gate from the main road.

Sleeping in Canterbury

Canterbury is a pleasant college town with lots of shops, restaurants, and pubs, making it a fine home base. There are relatively few options within the old walls, but I've listed my favorites. The roads heading out of town, particularly New Dover Road, have clusters of B&Bs that are slim on charm but suitable for tired drivers.

$$$ **The White House** is a classy and elegant B&B. Its seven renovated rooms, on a quiet residential lane just two blocks from the bustle of High Street, offer more modern flair than other Canterbury options in this price range (Sb-£65-80, Db-£95-175 depending on size, 6 St. Peter's Lane, tel. 01227/761-836, www .whitehousecanterbury.co.uk, info@whitehousecanterbury.co.uk, Adrian and Sharon).

$$$ **Castle House,** a 10-minute walk from the cathedral, has 13 spacious, inn-like rooms. It overlooks a major roundabout, but the double-glazed windows keep noise to a minimum (Sb-£60-90, Db-£65-100, family apartment-£85-140, free Wi-Fi, free parking, 28 Castle Street, tel. 01227/761-897, www.castlehousehotel.co.uk, enquiries@castlehousehotel.co.uk).

$$$ **The Miller's Arms** offers 11 comfy rooms adjacent to a cozy pub and restaurant, on a quiet street across from the Stour River (Sb-£65, Db-£75-95, Wi-Fi, parking-£5/day, 1 Mill Lane, tel. 01227/456-057, www.millerscanterbury.co.uk, millersarms @shepherdneame.co.uk).

Sleep Code

(£1 = about $1.60, country code: 44, area code: 01227)
S = Single, **D** = Double/Twin, **T** = Triple, **Q** = Quad, **b** = bathroom, **s** = shower only. You can assume credit cards are accepted and breakfast is included unless otherwise noted.

To help you sort easily through these listings, I've divided the accommodations into three categories based on the price for a standard double room with bath:

$$$ **Higher Priced**—Most rooms £80 or more.
$$ **Moderately Priced**—Most rooms between £45-80.
$ **Lower Priced**—Most rooms £45 or less.

Prices can change without notice; verify the hotel's current rates online or by email. For other updates, see www .ricksteves.com/update.

$$ The Tudor House B&B has seven slanted-floor, older-feeling, Victorian-wallpaper rooms in a 1600s home. Located in Canterbury's center, just two blocks from the cathedral, it has a garden with a river view (S-£35, Sb-£50, D-£59, Db-£69, T-£75, 6 Best Lane, tel. 01227/765-650, www.tudorhousecanterbury.co.uk, info@tudorhousecanterbury.co.uk, Mazi Gerogan and Mamad Arabnia).

$$ Harriet House offers seven tidy, small rooms with sophisticated decor. Since it's a 15-minute walk down a busy street from the town center, it works best for drivers (Sb-£45-55, Db-£65-75, family rooms available, pay Wi-Fi, some road noise, parking, 3 Broad Oak Road, tel. 01227/457-363, www.harriethouse.co.uk, enquiries@harriethouse.co.uk, Terry and Chris).

$ St. John's Court Guest House is a good value on a quiet street within the walls. No-nonsense Liz Rowe rents eight basic but bright rooms (all with shared bathrooms down the hall) in a quaint brick building (S-£25-30, D-£45, T-£65, cash only, no young children, parking, St. John's Lane, tel. 01227/456-425, www.stjohnscourtguesthouse.co.uk, nigelnrw@aol.com).

Eating in Canterbury

As a student town, Canterbury is packed with eateries—especially along the pedestrianized shopping zone. However, many places serve only lunch, leaving options pretty thin for dinner. Of these listings, only Morelli's is closed for dinner.

Old Weavers House serves solid English food in a pleasant, historic building along the river. Sit inside beneath sunny walls

and creaky beams, or outside on their riverside garden patio. This is the most atmospheric of my listings (£6-7 lunch specials, £10-18 dinner plates, daily 11:00-23:00, 1 St. Peter's Street, tel. 01227/464-660).

Ask, over a small bridge from Old Weavers House, is in a renovated home. This chain restaurant offers decent Italian food at moderate prices. The garden in back, while pleasant, lacks the Old Weavers House's river view (£8-12 meals, daily 12:00-23:00, big and splittable salads and pasta bowls, 24 High Street, tel. 01227/767-617).

Wagamama, part of the wildly popular British chain known for slinging delicious pan-Asian fare, has a convenient location just off the main shopping street (£7-13 main dishes, daily 12:00-22:00, 7-11 Longmarket Street, tel. 01227/454-307).

Morelli's Restaurant serves typical soups, sandwiches, and "jacket potatoes" with take-away options. You'll find it above the recommended Wagamama on Longmarket Street, with glassy indoor seating or fine outdoor tables (£4-7 light lunches, daily 8:00-17:00, tel. 01227/784-700).

City Fish Bar is your quintessential British "chippie," serving several kinds of fried fish. Get yours for take-away or grab a sidewalk table on this charming pedestrian street (£5-8 fish-and-chips, Mon-Sat 10:00-19:00, Sun 11:00-19:00, 30 St. Margaret's Street, tel. 01227/760-873).

Pub: **The Dolphin,** a local favorite, is a homey spot with carefully chosen ales. The food is a cut above typical pub grub, with quality local ingredients, and daily specials. Sit in the main bar, in the sunroom, or—in nice weather—at a picnic table in the grassy garden (large £8-15 plates, daily 12:00-24:00, free Wi-Fi, 17 St. Radigunds St, tel. 01227/455-963).

Canterbury Connections

Remember that Canterbury has two train stations, East and West.

From Canterbury by Train to: London (2-4/hour, 1-2 hours, some with transfers, trains run from Canterbury West Station to London's St. Pancras or Charing Cross stations, also from Canterbury East Station to London's Victoria Station), **Dover** (2/hour, 20-30 minutes, from Canterbury East to Dover Priory), **Rye** (hourly, 1 hour, from Canterbury West, transfer at Ashford International), **Hastings** (hourly, 1.25 hours, from Canterbury West, transfer at Ashford International), **Brighton** (1-2/hour, 2.25-2.5 hours, 1-3 transfers, can be complicated—best connections through London's St. Pancras or Ashford International, from Canterbury West). Train info: tel. 0845-748-4950, www.national rail.co.uk.

By Bus to: London's Victoria Coach Station (roughly hourly, 2-2.5 hours), **Dover** (roughly hourly, 45 minutes). Bus info: tel. 0870-781-8181, www.nationalexpress.com.

DOVER AND SOUTHEAST ENGLAND

Dover—like much of southern England— sits on a foundation of chalk. Miles of cliffs stand at attention above the beaches; the most famous are the White Cliffs of Dover. Sitting above those cliffs is the impressive Dover Castle, England's primary defensive strong- hold from Roman through modern times. From the nearby port, ferries, hydrofoils, and hovercrafts shuttle people and goods back and forth across the English Channel. France is only 23 miles away—on a sunny day, you can see it off in the distance.

Because of its easy access from the Continent, many travelers have a sentimental attachment to Dover as the first place they saw in England. But in recent years—especially since the opening of the English Channel Tunnel in 1994—this workaday town has lost whatever luster it once had. The run-down town center isn't worth a second look. Focus instead on a fun in-and-out visit to Dover's looming castle, standing guard as it has for almost a thousand years. Geologists and romantics may want to take a cruise to get the best view of the famous White Cliffs. (Or, for a more rural and idyllic white cliff experience, visit Beachy Head near Brighton— described on page 286.)

In the southeast English countryside near Dover, you can explore a castle and charming cottage garden at Sissinghurst; stroll the cobbles of the huggable hill town of Rye; and visit the Battle of Hastings site—in the appropriately named town of Battle—where England's future course was charted in 1066.

Planning Your Time

Dover works best as a day trip from Canterbury or London, and is worth a quick visit if you're passing through anyway. Ambitious sightseers can tackle both Dover and Canterbury as a one-day side-trip from London (see page 245).

Orientation to Dover

(area code: 01304)

Gritty, urban-feeling Dover seems bigger than its population of 30,000. The town lies between two cliffs, with Dover Castle on one side and the Western Heights on the other. While the streets stretch longingly toward the water, the core of the town is cut off from the harbor by the rumbling A20 highway (connecting Dover with cities to the west) and a long, eyesore apartment building. Unless you're taking a boat somewhere, or are interested in the goings-on of a busy industrial harbor, there's not much reason to visit the waterfront. Biggin Street is the town's nondescript, mostly pedestrianized shopping area, running between Market Square and Town Hall.

Tourist Information

You'll find the TI in the center of town, attached to the old jail. The TI sells ferry and bus tickets, and books rooms for a £3 fee (June-Aug daily 9:00-17:30; April-May and Sept Mon-Fri 9:00-17:30, Sat-Sun 10:00-16:00; Oct-March Mon-Fri 9:00-17:30, Sat 10:00-16:00, closed Sun; Old Town Gaol, Biggin Street, tel. 01304/205-108, www.whitecliffscountry.org.uk).

Arrival in Dover

Trains arrive on the west side of town, a five-minute walk from the main pedestrian area and the TI. **Drivers** find that parking is plentiful close to the water—just follow *P* signs. If you arrive by **boat** at the Eastern Docks, walk about 20 minutes along the base of the cliffs into town (with the sea on your left), or catch a shuttle bus to the train station (3/hour, daily 7:00-21:00).

Sights in Dover

▲▲Dover Castle

This powerful castle perches grandly atop the White Cliffs of Dover. English troops were garrisoned within the castle's medieval walls for almost 900 years, protecting the coast from European invaders (a record of military service rivaled only by Windsor Castle and the Tower of London). With a medieval Great Tower as its centerpiece and battlements that survey 360 degrees of wind-

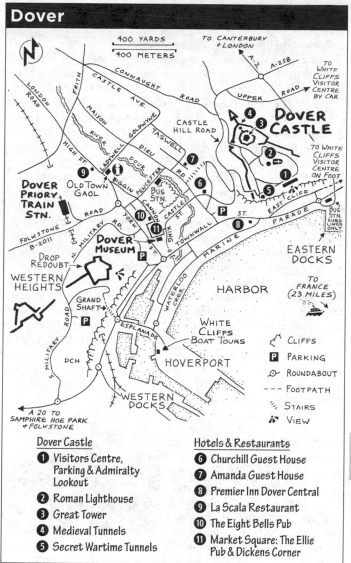

Dover

Dover Castle
1 Visitors Centre, Parking & Admiralty Lookout
2 Roman Lighthouse
3 Great Tower
4 Medieval Tunnels
5 Secret Wartime Tunnels

Hotels & Restaurants
6 Churchill Guest House
7 Amanda Guest House
8 Premier Inn Dover Central
9 La Scala Restaurant
10 The Eight Bells Pub
11 Market Square: The Ellie Pub & Dickens Corner

swept coast, Dover Castle has undeniable majesty. Today, the biggest invading menaces are the throngs of school kids on field trips, so it's best to arrive early. While the historic parts of the castle are unexceptional, the exhibits in the WWII-era Secret Wartime Tunnels are unique and engaging.

Cost and Hours: £16, £42 family ticket; April-Sept daily 10:00-18:00, from 9:30 in Aug; Oct daily 10:00-17:00; Nov-March

Sat-Sun 10:00-16:00, closed Mon-Fri; last entry one hour before closing, parts of the castle may close in high winds, tel. 01304/211-067, www.english-heritage.org.uk/dovercastle.

Avoiding Lines: Arrive early for the fewest crowds (busiest on summer bank holidays and weekends). Consider seeing the Secret Wartime Tunnels first—when you buy your ticket, ask about wait times for the tunnels and the included Underground Hospital tour (with a 30-person maximum, these can fill up quickly in high season).

Getting There: Drivers follow signs from A20 or the town center. For those without a car, getting up to the castle is tricky. Bus #15 departs hourly from the bus station (on Pencester Road) and heads up to the castle. Otherwise, you can take a taxi from downtown (about £5 one-way) or hoof it up the steep hill (30-45 minutes straight up; 1.5 miles from train station). By the time you get to the top, you'll know why no invading army ever successfully took the castle. The hike back down is easier, of course—ask for walking directions (using shortcut staircases) at the castle's visitors center before you leave.

Getting Around the Castle: The sporadic and free "land train" does a constant loop around the castle's grounds, shuttling visitors between the Secret Wartime Tunnels, the entrance to the Great Tower, and the Medieval Tunnels (at the lower end of the castle). Though handy for avoiding the ups and downs, the train doesn't run every day. Nothing at the castle is more than a 10-minute walk from anything else—so you'll likely spend more time waiting for the train than you would walking.

Background: A linchpin for English defense starting in the Middle Ages, Dover Castle was heavily used in the time of Henry VIII and Elizabeth I. After a period of decline, the castle was reinvigorated during the Napoleonic Wars, and became a central command in  World War II (when naval headquarters were buried deep in the cliffside). Dover Castle was retired from active duty in 1984.

➲ Self-Guided Tour: Start your tour of strategically located Dover Castle—considered "the key to England" by potential invaders—at the visitors center. Here you can pick up a free map describing the sights, including the Battlements Walk—a great addition if time allows. Adjust the order of this tour based on wait times for the Secret Wartime Tunnels—if it's looking crowded, do the tunnels first and then follow this tour afterward. (Be aware that the last tour of the tunnels' Underground Hospital exhibit leaves one hour before the castle closes.)

• *Leave the visitors center to the right, and walk around the officers' barracks to find a grassy slope overlooking...*

Admiralty Lookout: The White Cliffs of Dover are directly beneath you. Take in the superb view across the Channel. Can you see France from here? The statue is of British Admiral Sir Bertram Ramsay, who heroically orchestrated the "Miracle of Dunkirk" by rescuing hundreds of thousands of surrounded Allied troops from the French coast during World War II. You'll learn more about him in the Secret Wartime Tunnels.

• *Backtrack past the visitors Center, and hike up the path through the guard tower. Emerging on the other side of the guard tower, look up the hill to your right. The round tower behind the flagpole is the oldest structure at the castle, the...*

Roman Lighthouse: The lighthouse *(pharos)* was built during the first century A.D., when Julius Caesar's Roman fleet for the colony of Britannia was based in the harbor below. To guide the boats, they burned wet wood by day (for maximum smoke), and dry wood by night (for maximum light). When the Romans finally left England 400 years later, the *pharos* is said to have burst into flames as the last ship departed. Adjacent to the lighthouse is the unimpressive St. Mary-in-the-Castle Church, built to guard against invading Saxons in the sixth century.

• *Pass through the archway and into the courtyard of...*

Henry II's Great Tower: The heart of this frontier fortress first beat in 1066, when a castle was built here after the Battle of Hastings (see page 270). In the 12th century, King Henry II (the bad guy in the Thomas Becket story—see page 250 in the Canterbury chapter) added heavy castle fortifications. For centuries, Dover Castle was the most secure fortress in all of England, and an important symbol of royal might on the coast.

Examine the central building, which was the original tower (also called a "keep"). The walls are up to 20 feet thick. King

Henry II slept on the top floor, surrounded by his best protection against an invading army. Imagine the attempt: As the thundering enemy cavalry makes its advance, the king's defenders throw caltrops (four-starred metal spikes meant to cut through the horses' hooves). His knights unsheathe their swords, and trained crossbow archers ring the tower, sending arrows into foreign armor. Later kings added buildings near the tower (along the inner bailey, which lines the keep yard) to garrison troops during wartime and provide extra rooms for royal courtiers during peacetime.

Inside the Great Tower, you'll find a kid-oriented exhibit (with colorful furnishings and sound effects) that gives a sense of what the castle was like in King Henry VIII's time. On summer weekends, and for most of August, costumed actors add to the fun. Find the well, which helped make the tower even more siege-resistant. Fans of Thomas Becket can look for his chapel, a tiny sacristy called the "upper chapel." If you're feeling energetic, climb all the way to the top of the tower's spiral staircase for a sweeping view of the town and sea beyond. The basement holds the medieval kitchen and royal armory.

• *After leaving the Great Tower, walk a few paces across the courtyard to the...*

Garrison: This structure surrounding the tower once housed knights and men-at-arms. It's now home to the vaguely interesting Princess of Wales's Royal Regiment and Queen's Regiment Museum, a collection of military memorabilia (sorry, no Princess Diana items).

• *Exit the keep yard at the far end through the King's Gate. Cross a stone bridge and then descend a wooden staircase. Under these stairs is the entrance to the...*

Medieval Tunnels: This system of tunnels was originally built in case of a siege. While enjoyable for a kid-in-a-castle experience, there's actually little to see in these tunnels. From here, you can catch the tourist train (if it's running) or do the Battlements Walk. Much of Dover's success as a defendable castle came from these unique concentric walls—the battlements—which protected the inner keep.

• *There's one more thing to see, and it's the castle's undisputed highlight: the Secret Wartime Tunnels. If the "land train" is running today, you can wait for it; otherwise walk (about 10 minutes total) along the inside of the castle's outer wall (with the wall on your right) and through the gate. Continue along the wall until you reach the entrance to the...*

Secret Wartime Tunnels: In the 1790s, with the threat of Napoleon looming, the castle's fortifications were beefed up again. So many troops were stationed here that they needed to tunnel

into the chalk to provide sleeping areas for up to 2,000 men. These tunnels were vastly expanded during World War II, when operations for the war effort moved into a bomb-proofed, underground air-raid shelter safe from Hitler's feared Luftwaffe planes. Winston Churchill watched air battles from here, while Allied commanders looked out over a battle zone nicknamed "Hellfire Corner."

Your visit to the tunnels includes three new exhibits. The first, **Operation Dynamo,** is named for the May 1940 rescue mission wherein the British managed, in just 10 days, to evacuate some 338,000 Allied soldiers from the beaches of Dunkirk, in Nazi-occupied France. The effort was coordinated from these tunnels by Admiral Ramsay, and you can see his elaborate communications center, telephone exchange, and command center. The original furnishings and equipment have been restored and are placed where they stood during World War II. Newsreel footage, sounds, and even scents help recreate the wartime atmosphere.

The next exhibit, **Wartime Tunnels Uncovered,** uses diaries, uniforms, archival films, and other artifacts to chart the development of the tunnels from the Napoleonic era to the Cold War.

Seeing the third exhibit, the **Underground Hospital,** requires lining up for a 30-minute guided tour (no reservations possible, tours depart every 10 minutes, last tour departs one hour before closing). Follow the story of an injured pilot, told through audiovisual effects, while touring a recreated 1941 operating room and a narrow hospital ward.

Other Sights in Dover

Dover Museum—This refurbished museum, right off the tiny main square, houses a large, impressive, and well-preserved

Bronze Age boat unearthed near Dover's shoreline. The boat is displayed on the top floor along with other finds from the site and an exhibit on boat construction techniques (£3; Mon-Sat 10:00-17:00, also Sun 10:00-15:00 April-Aug; tel. 01304/201-066, www.dover museum.co.uk).

The Cliffs of Dover—The cliff called **Western Heights**—opposite Dover Castle, just outside of town—provides a sweeping view of Dover (and occasionally of France). The trail along the cliff weaves around former gun posts that were originally installed during Napoleonic times, but were used most extensively during World War II. It was here that the British military amassed huge decoy forces in an effort to fool the Germans into thinking that a Dover-based attack was imminent. This fake-out maneuver was meant to disguise the plan for the Normandy D-Day invasion. Today, the bunkers are abandoned, but in decent condition. This is the place where you always wished you could play war as a kid... and with a little imagination, you still can. Peaceniks find it an excellent picnic spot. To drive there, take A20 west past the harbor to the Western Heights roundabout, take the Aycliff exit onto Military Road, wind uphill for about half a mile, then turn right at the small brown sign onto Drop Redoubt Road. For more information, see www.doverwesternheights.org.

For a different (and many say better) view from the cliffs, as well as a fascinating look at one of the world's busiest ports, head east of town to the **White Cliffs of Dover Visitor Centre** (free, parking-£3, daily March-Oct 10:00-17:00, Nov-Feb 11:00-16:00, Upper Road, Langdon Cliffs, tel. 01304/202-756, www.nationaltrust.org.uk). You'll find exhibits about the cliffs and local flora and fauna, plus a handy café and ample space for

picnicking. You can walk to the visitor center from Dover (about 2.5 miles from the train station—just walk along the base of the cliffs with the sea on your right, following footpath signs from the town center), or you can drive: Head up the Castle Hill Road, pass the castle entrance, then take a sharp right turn onto Upper Road. After crossing over the A2 highway, look for the visitors center entrance at the next hairpin turn. If the first parking area is full, keep going—there are several.

If you have the energy, you can walk two miles along the cliff top from the visitor center to the **South Foreland Lighthouse,** built in 1843, and enjoy the glorious view (£4.20, admission only with 30-minute guided tour, Fri-Mon 11:00-17:30, closed Tue-Thu except Aug and school holidays, last tour 30 minutes before closing, tel. 01304/852-463, www.nationaltrust.org.uk).

Samphire Hoe—This man-made park, less than two miles south of Dover, makes a good stop for those who wish to see more of the white cliffs—without the industrial crush of the busy Dover

docks. Samphire Hoe, a chalk meadowland beneath the cliffs, was created using more than six million cubic yards of chalk left over from the construction of the Channel Tunnel in the early 1990s. What could have been a dumping ground is now a grassy expanse hosting a rich variety of plants and wildlife. The park has walking paths and a tea kiosk, as well as a mile-long seawall that attracts anglers, wave watchers, and swimmers aiming for France.

Cost and Hours: Free, park open daily 7:00-dusk; tea kiosk daily Easter-Sept, weekends only in winter; tel. 01304/225-649, www.samphirehoe.co.uk.

Getting There: From Dover, drivers take A20 heading to Folkestone and watch for the Samphire Hoe exit. After waiting for the green light at the 007-style tunnel, you'll emerge at a pay-and-display parking lot. Walkers can follow the North Downs Way footpath, while cyclists can use the National Cycle Network Route 2; both are signposted from Dover—ask the TI for specifics.

Boat Tours—The famous White Cliffs of Dover are almost impossible to appreciate from town. A 40-minute Dover White Cliffs Boat Tour around the bay will give you all the photo ops you need.

Cost and Hours: £8, £20 family ticket, more expensive bus-and-boat combos available, May-Aug daily at 12:00, 14:00, and 16:00; Sept-April by appointment only—book at least 24 hours ahead, tel. 01303/271-388, mobile 07971/301-379, www.dover whiteclifftours.com.

Ferries to France—In the mood for a glass of wine and some escargot? A day trip to Calais, France, is only a short boat ride away (walk-on passengers generally £13-15 round-trip, car prices vary with demand—usually £30-75 but can double on Sat, 1.25-1.75 hours). Several companies make the journey: P&O Ferries (tel. 0871-664-2121, www.poferries.com), SeaFrance (cars only—tel. 0871-423-7119, www.seafrance.com), and DFDS Seaways (cars only—to Dunkirk, 2 hours, tel. 0871-574-7235, www.dfdsseaways .co.uk).

Sleeping in Dover

(£1 = about $1.60, country code: 44, area code: 01304)
I'd rather sleep in Canterbury, but in a pinch, Dover has a variety of B&Bs spread throughout town (if arriving late at night, take a cab). The guest houses below can recommend another B&B if they're booked up.

$$ Churchill Guest House, neatly run by Alastair and Betty Dimech, is a comfortable, traditional type of place. It's perfectly located, just at the base of the castle hill, with eight rooms plus a family-friendly flat (Sb-£40-50, Db-£60-80, 5-person basement apartment-£80-135, 6 Castle Hill Road, tel. 01304/204-622, http://churchillhouse.homestead.com, toastofdover@gmail.com).

The homier **$$ Amanda Guest House,** on one of the quietest streets in town, works best for drivers (Db-£60-70, cash only but reserve with credit card, easy parking, 20-minute walk from train

station to 4 Harold Street, tel. 01304/201-711, www.amandaguest
house.com, amandaguesthouse@hotmail.com, Mike and Anne).

Sleeping near the Waterfront: **$$ Premier Inn Dover Central**
is handy to the ferry and cruise terminal, with dozens of identical,
prefab rooms (Db-£62-82 depending on demand—up to £130 on
summer weekends, sleeps up to 2 adults and 2 kids, check website
for specials, breakfast-£5-8, restaurant, pay Wi-Fi, free parking,
Marine Court, Marine Parade, tel. 0871-527-8306, fax 0871-527-
8307, www.premierinn.com).

Eating in Dover

Your dining options in downtown Dover are few, and not worth
writing home about. Consider having lunch at one of the castle's
cafés or cafeterias.

La Scala is tiny, but in a romantic way, and serves a good vari-
ety of Italian dishes (£8-16 meals, Mon-Sat 12:00-14:30 & 18:00-
22:30, closed Sun, 19 High Street, tel. 01304/208-044).

The Eight Bells, smoky and wood-paneled, is a huge pub that
feels like a Vegas lounge. It has good beer and an excellent local
reputation. Along with La Scala, it's one of two dinner options
downtown (£6-9 meals, daily 8:00-24:00, kids OK before 20:00,
19 Cannon Street, tel. 01304/205-030).

Lunch Eateries on Market Square: Dover's main shopping
square is surrounded by places for a quick lunch. **The Ellie,** a
generic, modern pub at a convenient location (right next door to the
Dover Museum), spills out onto Market Square (£4 sandwiches,
£6 main dishes, open daily 10:00-24:00, food served 11:00-15:00
only, inviting outdoor seating on the square, tel. 01304/215-685).
Across the square is the more genteel **Dickens Corner,** a comfy
diner with a tearoom upstairs (£3-5 "jacket potatoes" and soups,
Mon-Sat 8:30-16:30, closed Sun, 7 Market Square, tel. 01304/206-
692).

Dover Connections

While the train will get you to most big destinations on the South
Coast, the bus has better connections to smaller towns. Stagecoach
offers good one-day "Explorer" (£5.80) or one-week "Megarider
Gold" (£19) tickets covering anywhere they go in southeast
England (tel. 0871-200-2233, www.stagecoachbus.com).

The Dover train station is called Dover Priory. Most buses
stop at the "bus station" (it's more of a lot) on Pencester Road in
the town center. Eurolines buses stop at the Eastern Docks, near
the ferries to and from France.

From Dover by Train to: London (hourly, 1.25 hours, direct to St. Pancras; also hourly, 2 hours, direct to Victoria Station or Charing Cross Station), **Canterbury** (2/hour, 20-30 minutes, arrives at Canterbury East Station), **Rye** (hourly, 1.25 hours, transfer at Ashford International), **Hastings** (hourly, 1.5 hours, transfer at Ashford International), **Brighton** (2/hour, 2.75-3 hours, transfer at Ashford International or London Bridge Station). Train info: tel. 0845-748-4950, www.nationalrail.co.uk.

By Bus: National Express (tel. 0871-781-8181, www.national express.com) goes to **London** (roughly hourly, 2.5-3.25 hours) and **Canterbury** (roughly hourly, 45 minutes). Stagecoach (tel. 0871-200-2233, www.stagecoachbus.com) goes to **Rye** (hourly, 2 hours) and **Hastings** (hourly, 3 hours).

Near Dover

Sissinghurst Castle Garden

For a taste of traditional English gardening, this elegant home and well-maintained garden is worth seeking out. Vita Sackville-West,

socialite and lover of Virginia Woolf, purchased this castle and land in the early 20th century with her husband, diplomat-author Harold Nicolson. The two of them transformed the grounds into a beautiful English cottage garden. The gardens are laid out in sections, each with a theme, such as the Herb Garden and the Lime Walk. Every section feels like a small outdoor room. There is always something blooming here, but the best show is in June, when the famous White Garden bursts with fragrant roses. The castle, formerly a vast and grand affair, has disappeared for the most part, but an Elizabethan tower still stands. Inside are a few small exhibits, and—on the second floor—a series of illustrations that show the development, disintegration, and rebirth of the estate. At the top of the tower, you can survey the garden and orchard from up high. Inside the library wing, a portrait of Vita Sackville-West hangs over the fireplace, along with paintings of other family members, some of whom still live on the property.

Cost and Hours: £10, parking-£2; garden open mid-March-Oct Fri-Tue 10:30-17:00 or until dusk, last entry 30 minutes before closing, closed Wed-Thu; shorter hours for castle and library, café, tel. 01580/710-701, www.nationaltrust.org.uk/sissinghurst.

Getting There: Sissinghurst is about 55 miles west of Dover,

DOVER & SE ENGLAND

Southeast England

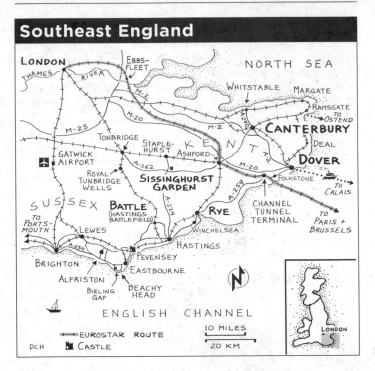

off A262, near Cranbrook. **Trains** from London connect to Staplehurst, about five miles away (2/hour, 1 hour from Charing Cross Station, tel. 0845-748-4950, www.nationalrail.co.uk). From Staplehurst, you can take a **taxi** directly to the garden (£10-12, tel. 01580/890-003), or a **bus** to the village of Sissinghurst, where you can **walk** along an idyllic footpath about a mile to the garden (for bus specifics, call 0871-200-2233, or use the journey planner at www.travelinesoutheast.org.uk).

Rye

If you dream of half-timbered pubs and wisteria-covered stone churches, Rye is the photo op you've been looking for. A busy sea-port village for hundreds of years, Rye was frozen in time as silt built up and the sea retreated in the 16th and 17th centuries, leaving only a skinny waterway to remind it of better days. While ship-building and smuggling were the mainstays of the economy back then, antique shops and expensive B&Bs drive business these days.

Rye is England's version of a hill town, packed with tourists trying to soak up some charm.

Arrival in Rye: As you approach town, notice the canal filled with boats. Follow it along to the old quays. The water line used to come up to this area, and the parking lot on Strand Quay would have been the wharf. Drivers should ignore the confusing *P* signs, which direct you to parking lots away from the town center—instead, try to squeeze into the small lot next to the Rye Heritage Centre (by the antique shops) or the larger one across the street.

Tourist Information: The TI is located at the top of the hill, just below the Church of St. Mary the Virgin (daily April-Oct 10:00-17:00, Nov-March 10:00-16:00, 4-5 Lion Street, tel. 01797/229-049, www.visitrye.co.uk).

Sights in Rye: Rye's sights try to make too much of this little town, but a stroll along the cobbles is enjoyable. Start at the **Rye Heritage Centre,** which has an impressive scale model of the town, presented in a 20-minute sound-and-light show (£3.50, every 30 minutes, if it's not running you can peek in at the model for free; daily April-Oct 10:00-17:00, Nov-March 10:00-16:00; town audioguide-£4, Strand Quay/A259, tel. 01797/226-696, www.rye heritage.co.uk).

From near the Rye Heritage Centre, Mermaid Street leads up into the medieval heart of Rye. Along this street (on the left), look for the **Mermaid Inn,** rebuilt in 1420 after the original burned down. Step inside and have a peek into Rye's heyday, or splurge for an expensive lunch (£21-25 fixed-price lunches, daily 12:00-14:30 & 19:00-21:30, tel. 01797/223-065). Today, it's a pricey upscale hotel—look for photos of recent celebrity customers just inside the door.

Continuing up Mermaid Street, jog right up West Street to Church Square. The old **Church of St. Mary the Virgin** has a pleasant interior and an 84-step tower you can climb for a country-side view (church—free, daily 9:15-17:15, shorter hours in winter; tower—£2.50, same hours as church but may close in bad weather; tel. 01797/224-935).

Beyond the square is a miniature castle called the Ypres Tower, housing the **Rye Castle Museum,** with a lookout tower and a modest collection of items from the town's past. Striking up a conversation with the museum's custodian, a lifelong resident, may be the museum's most interesting attraction (£3; April-Oct daily 10:30-17:00; Nov-March daily

10:30-15:30; last entry 30 minutes before closing, tel. 01797/226-728, www.ryemuseum.co.uk). On summer weekends you can visit the museum's second location, which features a 1745 fire engine and more about Rye's shipbuilding past (£2.50, £5 combo-ticket with castle museum, April-Oct Sat-Sun 10:30-17:00, closed Mon-Fri and Nov-March, 3 East Street).

Getting There: Rye is about 35 miles southwest of Dover on A259 (the route to Brighton). **Trains** connect to Rye from London (hourly, 1.25 hours from St. Pancras Station, 2 hours from Charing Cross Station, transfer at Ashford International) and Dover (hourly, 1.25 hours, transfer at Ashford International). Stagecoach **bus** #100 provides a direct connection to Dover (hourly, 2 hours, tel. 0871-200-2233, www.stagecoachbus.com).

Near Rye: Compared to sugary-sweet Rye, modest **Winchelsea** feels like an antacid. Small, inviting, and just far enough away from the maddening crowd, the town makes a good stop for a picnic lunch. The grocery shop on the square sells all you need for a quiet meal on the little village green. Winchelsea is about three miles southwest of Rye on A259, toward Hastings.

▲Battle of Hastings Abbey and Battlefield

Located about an hour southwest of Dover by car, the town of Battle commemorates a fight no Brit can forget—the Battle of Hastings. In 1066, a Norman (French) king was victorious in the Battle of Hastings and seized control of England, leading to a string of Norman kings and forever changing the course of English history and the English language. The battlefield and adjoining ruined abbey (built soon after the battle to atone for all the spilled blood) are worth ▲▲▲ to British-history buffs, but anyone can appreciate the dramatic story behind the grassy field. Ignore the tourists and take a journey back in time...these fields would have looked almost the same 1,000 years ago. Gaze across the unassuming little valley and imagine thousands of invading troops. Your visit can last from three minutes to three hours, depending on your imagination.

Cost and Hours: £7.50, includes audioguide, £19 family ticket; April-Sept daily 10:00-18:00; Oct-March Sat-Sun 10:00-16:00, closed Mon-Fri except in Oct; last entry 30 minutes before closing, children's play area, tel. 01424/775-705, www.english-heritage.org.uk/battleabbey.

Getting There: The town of Battle isn't on a major road, but **drivers** find that it's well-signposted from busy A259, whether you're coming from the east (Dover) or from the west (Brighton). There's a pricey £3 coin-op parking lot next to the abbey. Battle can be reached by **train** from London's Charing Cross or Cannon

Street stations (2/hour, 1.5 hours, some require transfer), Hastings (2/hour, 15 minutes), or Dover (2-3/hour, 2-2.5 hours, 1-2 transfers). The entrance to Battle Abbey is at the south end of High Street; follow signs from the train station.

Background: The most epic of all of Europe's medieval *Lord of the Rings*-style battles took place on the most memorable date of the Middle Ages: October 14, 1066. The pivotal Battle of Hastings came about because the celibate King Edward the Confessor of England had died without an heir, and two nobles claimed the throne.

An Anglo-Saxon noble named Harold, Earl of Wessex, claimed that Edward gave him the throne on his deathbed. He was also chosen king by the traditional council, but support for Harold was weak. Meanwhile, across the English Channel, French-born William, Duke of Normandy, claimed that Edward had personally selected *him* as his successor. As the descendant of Vikings who'd once settled England, William claimed he had royal blood. His enemies called him William the Bastard because his mother was the former Duke of Normandy's mistress.

With the pope's blessing, William patiently gathered and trained a large army and sailed across the Channel. Harold raced south to meet him, his own army exhausted from battling enemies in the north. Near the town of Hastings in southern England, Harold assembled his troops into a wall atop the highest hill and waited for William.

Early in the morning on October 14th, the Norman soldiers trudged up the hill, and the battle was on. First, Norman archers

rained arrows on the English. Next, foot soldiers on both sides fought hand-to-hand. William's army began to retreat (a tactical maneuver, say the French). Seeing them flee, the English charged ahead, pursuing them down the hill. Suddenly, the Normans turned and attacked. Riding on horseback, the Norman soldiers were armed with a secret weapon: stirrups, which gave them a foothold to put force behind their lances.

The two sides fought a fierce 14-hour battle, with heavy casualties. Ultimately the Normans decimated the English force. In the battle's climactic finale, Harold was killed (supposedly by an arrow through the eye). William—now "the Conqueror"—marched on to London, where he was crowned King of England in Westminster Abbey on Christmas Day, 1066. William commemorated the dead by building an abbey on the spot of the decisive battle.

The Norman Conquest of England propelled the isolated isle of Britain into the European mainstream. William centralized the government and imported the Romanesque style of architecture—seen at places such as the White Tower at the Tower of London, and Durham Cathedral. The English call this style "Norman." Historians speculate that, were it not for the stirrup, England would have remained on the fringe of Europe (like Scandinavia), French culture and language would have prevailed in the New World...and you'd be reading this book today in French. *Sacré bleu!* William's conquest also muddied the political waters, setting in motion 400 years of conflict between England and France that would not be resolved until the end of the Hundred Years' War, in 1453.

Visiting the Abbey and Battlefield: A small museum, battleground overlook, and remaining Battle Abbey buildings illuminate the historical significance of the Battle of Hastings. After buying your ticket and picking up the essential, included audioguide, head to the nearby **visitors center** to watch an excellent 15-minute film that recounts the story of the battle, with animated scenes from the famous Bayeux Tapestry (pic-

tured on previous page) and impressive live-action reenactments. Also in the center are replicas of weapons used by the fighters—lift them to appreciate how the Brits invented heavy metal long before Led Zeppelin.

Then head outside, where you have two choices with your audioguide: Follow the short tour along a terrace overlooking the **battlefield** (about 15 minutes), or take the longer version out through the woods and across the fateful field (about 40 minutes).

With sound effects and a witty but not corny commentary, the audioguide really injects some life into the site. Finally, you'll wind up at the remains of the **abbey,** where the audioguide relates details of monastic lifestyles. It's interesting and a bit more intact than many other ruined abbeys, but it pales in comparison to the drama of the battle. Walking back to the entrance, notice that the abbey's former Great Hall now houses another famous English institution—a private school.

Eating in Battle: The **Pilgrims Restaurant,** across the street from the abbey, is an atmospherically crooked half-timbered house serving decent but pricey food with outdoor terrace seating (£7-10 soups, sandwiches, and salads, open daily 9:15-17:30, 1 High Street, tel. 01424/772-314).

BRIGHTON

Brighton—brash and flamboyant, with a carnival flair—is refreshing if you're suffering from an excess of doilies and museums. The city boasts a garish 19th-century Royal Pavilion, a loud and flashy carnival pier, England's most thriving gay community, and a long stretch of cobbled beach. It's no wonder that youthful bohemians and blue-collar Londoners alike make this town their holiday destination of choice.

In the 1790s, with Napoleon's armies running rampant on the Continent, aristocrats could no longer travel abroad on a traditional "Grand Tour" of Europe. King George IV chose the village of Brighthelmstone to build a vacation palace for himself, and royal followers began a frenzy of construction on the seashore. Soon this once-sleepy seaside village was transformed into an elegant resort town. With the rise of train travel, connections to London became quick and cheap, making Brighton an inviting getaway for working-class Londoners.

The countryside near Brighton is packed with tempting sights and worthwhile stopovers for drivers. Go for a walk on the South Downs Way, lick an ice-cream cone in the postcard-pretty village of Alfriston, visit the best white cliffs in England at Beachy Head, and explore the evocative ruins of a Roman fort at Pevensey.

Planning Your Time

Brighton's sights—its Royal Pavilion, Museum and Art Gallery, and pleasure pier—can be seen in just a few hours, making this a doable day trip from London. If you've got a full day and a car, spend the rest of your day at Alfriston and Beachy Head.

Debating between Brighton and Portsmouth? Travelers

Brighton

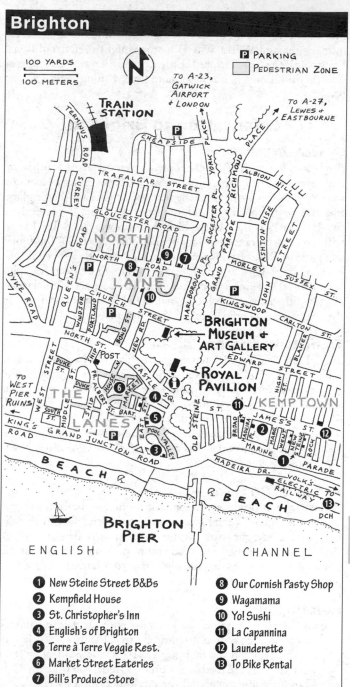

P PARKING
PEDESTRIAN ZONE

100 YARDS
100 METERS

N

TRAIN STATION

TO A-23, GATWICK AIRPORT & LONDON

TO A-27, LEWES & EASTBOURNE

TERMINUS ROAD

CHEAPSIDE

TRAFALGAR STREET

YORK PLACE

RICHMOND PLACE

ALBION HILL

SURREY ROAD

GLOUCESTER ROAD

GLOUCESTER PL.

GRAND PARADE

ASHTON RISE

STREET

NORTH LAINE

NORTH ROAD

MARLBOROUGH PL.

MORLEY

JOHN

SUSSEX ST.

DYKE ROAD

QUEEN'S ROAD

WINDSOR

PORTLAND

CHURCH STREET

BOND ST.

NEW RD.

KINGSWOOD

CARLTON STREET

NORTH ST.

BRIGHTON MUSEUM & ART GALLERY

EDWARD STREET

BLAKER

HIGH ST.

TO WEST PIER RUINS

WEST STREET

DUKE ST.

SHIP ST.

DUKE

PRINCE ALBERT ST.

SHIP ST.

SOUTH ST.

MIDDLE ST.

Post

THE LANES

MARKET

ST. JAMES'S ST.

CASTLE SQ.

Royal Pavilion

OLD STEINE

KEMPTOWN

BROAD ST.

MADEIRA PL.

MANCHESTER ST.

NEW STEINE

ROCK Y

ST.

EAST ST.

POOL VALLEY

KING'S ROAD

GRAND JUNCTION ROAD

MARINE PARADE

MADEIRA DR.

VOLK'S ELECTRIC TO RAILWAY

BEACH

BEACH

DCH

BRIGHTON

BRIGHTON PIER

ENGLISH   CHANNEL

1 New Steine Street B&Bs
2 Kempfield House
3 St. Christopher's Inn
4 English's of Brighton
5 Terre à Terre Veggie Rest.
6 Market Street Eateries
7 Bill's Produce Store

8 Our Cornish Pasty Shop
9 Wagamama
10 Yo! Sushi
11 La Capannina
12 Launderette
13 To Bike Rental

interested in the arts, shopping, and the restaurant scene are more likely to be turned on by lively Brighton, while those interested in maritime and World War II history might prefer traditional Portsmouth (see next chapter). Either destination works as an easy day trip from London, but with more time, visiting both is a great plan.

Orientation to Brighton

(area code: 01273)
Brighton is big, with 160,000 people. It feels surprisingly urban for a seaside resort—like the Nice of England. Most tourists focus on the area near the waterfront. The heart of Brighton is the Brighton Pier and, several blocks inland, the Royal Pavilion. Between these two landmarks is the twisty old center of town called The Lanes, with good restaurants and lots of shopping. North of The Lanes and past the Royal Pavilion is the popular, recently revived neighborhood of North Laine, with more shopping and eateries, plus occasional street-music performances. The best accommodations cluster to the east of The Lanes, within a block of the seafront, in the colorful neighborhood called Kemptown.

Tourist Information

The TI is in the Royal Pavilion's gift shop and has a good, free color map of Brighton. They also book rooms (£1.50/person) and sell tickets to various sights and theater productions, as well as bus and train tickets (daily 10:00-17:00, possibly later in summer, tel. 01273/290-337, www.visitbrighton.com).

A walking-tour audioguide of Brighton is available for download to your iPod or other MP3 player (£6, covers 3 miles, www.coolcitywalks.com).

Arrival in Brighton

Trains arrive at Brighton Station, a 15-minute walk from the center. Drivers on A23 enter town on the tree-lined Grand Parade, which goes straight to the water (ending near Brighton Pier). Parking is tricky: Signs will lead you to parking garages near the center, but if you're staying the night, ask your hotelier for the best place to leave your car.

Helpful Hints

Crowd Control: Brighton can overflow with visitors in summer and on weekends. The Brighton Festival (May, www.brightonfestival.org) and the Summer LGBT Pride Festival (second week of Aug) are the busiest times. Off-season (roughly Oct-March), visitors may find the city quiet, prices slashed, and attractions shuttered.

Laundry: St. James's Laundry is in Kemptown, near my recommended accommodations (self-service open Mon-Sat 8:30-16:00, or drop off Mon-Fri 9:00-12:00 for same-day full-service, closed Sun, 53 St. James's Street, tel. 01273/672-395).

Bike Rental: Ask at the TI or try **Brighton Sports Company,** down by the water next to the bike path (£6/hour, £12/3 hours, helmet-£1, picture ID and £100 credit-card deposit required, daily Easter-Oct 10:00-18:00, closed Nov-Easter, 10-minute walk east of recommended New Steine B&Bs, halfway between Brighton Pier and Brighton Marina, Madeira Drive, mobile 07917-753-794, www.brightonsports.co.uk, Mark).

Getting Around Brighton

Brighton's well-run bus system is handy, especially if you're staying in one of my recommended guest houses on Kemptown's New Steine Street (£1.60/ride, £3.70 CitySaver day pass; buy from driver, at TI, or online for slight discount; tel. 01273/886-200, www.buses.co.uk).

Sights in Brighton

▲▲**Brighton Royal Pavilion**—Famous for his scandalous secret marriage to Catholic widow Mrs. Fitzherbert, King George IV was

lively, decadent, and trendsetting. He loved to vacation by the sea and host glamorous dinner parties. George was enamored with Asian cultures, styling his vacation home with exotic decorations from the East. The result is colorful and exuberant...some would say gaudy. Like Brighton itself, the place smacks of faded elegance—but it's fun to tour. It's free to enter the restored Regency gardens surrounding the Pavilion, and the nearby Brighton Museum and Art Gallery (described later).

Cost and Hours: £10, includes audioguide, daily April-Sept 9:30-17:45, Oct-March 10:00-17:15, last entry 45 minutes before closing, head up East Street from The Lanes, bus stop on Old Steine Road, tel. 03000-290-900, www.royalpavilion.org.uk. If there's a line to buy tickets, dip into the TI (at the gift shop next door) and purchase them for the same price.

❍ **Self-Guided Tour:** Pick up the free and informative audioguide as you enter. It'll tell you more about these highlights (and other points of interest) along the one-way route.

While George planned the palace as a royal holiday residence, it was used mainly as a party pad to entertain guests. They'd be suitably impressed by the grand **Long Gallery.** Here and throughout the Pavilion, examine the fine detail work—such as the "bamboo" stairway decoration that's actually carved from wood.

If guests were impressed by the Long Gallery, they were blown away by the **Banqueting Room.** Imagine England's elite nibbling crumpets under the one-ton chandelier...with its dragons exhaling light through lotus-shaped shades. Notice that the ornate table is permanently set for the dessert course.

The elaborate **Kitchen** was one of the most innovative of its time. Smoke from the fireplace rotated a huge rotisserie that could cook enough meat to feed a hundred hungry diners. The king was so particular about his food that he insisted his kitchen be attached to the dining room (unheard-of at the time). He also had a warming table built to keep food at the optimum temperature.

Head through the gallery and salon into a room dedicated to George's true passion: music. In the massive **Music Room,** the royal band serenaded guests. Take a moment to appreciate the Chinese-inspired decor here and throughout the palace. Known as *chinoiserie,* it was the height of fashion in those days.

The **Private Apartments** were on the ground floor, to more easily accommodate the ailing king (who spent less and less time here near the end of his life). Note that this space is more intimate and cozy than the showpiece halls we've seen elsewhere. (If you're intrigued by all this, dip into the dry but informative 18-minute film about the Pavilion's history.)

Continuing upstairs, you'll stroll through the restored **Yellow Bow Rooms,** then **Queen Victoria's Apartments,** where you'll learn the epilogue to the story of George's party palace. George was a big spender, piling up huge debts. No expense was spared. Prudish Queen Victoria, who took the throne seven years after George's death, wanted more privacy than the Pavilion provided and scorned the excesses in George's court—so she quickly offloaded the decadent Pavilion to the local town council (which still owns it today). Only recently did Queen Elizabeth II bring the original furniture out of storage and loan it to the Pavilion.

Brighton Museum and Art Gallery—This gallery, similar to the Victoria and Albert Museum in London, displays decorative arts with a heavy focus on 20th-century art and design. The modern pseudo-kitsch includes the Dalí-inspired *Mae West Lips Sofa* and Frank Gehry's *Wiggle Chair.* The café above the gallery has a pleasant view of the action.

Cost and Hours: Free, Tue-Sun 10:00-17:00, closed Mon except holidays, just north of the Royal Pavilion, tel. 03000-290-900, www.virtualmuseum.info.

Brighton Pier—Glittering and shiny with amusement rides and carnival games, Brighton Pier is *the* place to go for a fix of

"candy floss" (cotton candy), fortune-tellers, and tacky souvenirs. The pier, opened in 1899 and long known as Palace Pier, has gone in and out of fashion; in recent years, it's come back to life, thanks to a restoration. The main pavilion is a 19th-century gem. If you ignore the fancy video games, you might be able to imagine yourself as a Victorian Londoner out on holiday, seeing brilliant electric lights for the first time.

Cost and Hours: Free entry to pier, rides run Sun-Fri 11:00-20:00, Sat 11:00-22:00, arcade usually open until 22:00, closing time depends on crowds, tel. 01273/609-361, www.brightonpier.co.uk.

Nearby: Check out the ruins of the pier to the west. Due to disrepair, the shorter but once equally festive **West Pier** disintegrated into the water in the 1970s. Watch for the long-planned construction of a new observation tower here. Designed by the architects of the London Eye, the **i360** tower's doughnut-like elevator will someday lift tourists to a bird's-eye view over the town. Unfortunately, due to construction delays, it's unlikely to be open in 2012.

Beach—OK, so it isn't Hawaii, but you can walk along the large, flattened cobbles, called "shingles," and get your feet wet.

Sleeping in Brighton

Brighton's bohemian character is fun during the day, but the town can be a little shady at night. The recommended accommodations are in the gay-friendly Kemptown neighborhood, about a block from the beach and within a 10-minute walk of the Brighton Pier and Royal Pavilion.

The best Brighton accommodations are variations on the same theme: a guest house with about a dozen rooms. A guest house offers more professionalism and anonymity than a B&B, and more character(s) than a hotel. As rooms vary in size, one hotel can have four or five different prices for their doubles. ("Sea views" here are unimpressive, and not worth paying extra for.) To complicate matters, in summer, prices skyrocket by £15-30 on weekends, making otherwise good-value places suddenly way overpriced. Summer weekends are also plagued with noisy partygoers roaming the streets until dawn. Avoid sleeping in Brighton on a summer

BRIGHTON

Sleep Code

(£1 = about $1.60, country code: 44, area code: 01273)
S = Single, **D** = Double/Twin, **T** = Triple, **Q** = Quad, **b** = bathroom,
s = shower only. You can assume credit cards are accepted
and breakfast is included unless otherwise noted.

To help you sort easily through these listings, I've divided
the accommodations into three categories based on the price
for a standard double room with bath:

$$$ Higher Priced—Most rooms £100 or more.
$$ Moderately Priced—Most rooms between £60-100.
$ Lower Priced—Most rooms £60 or less.

Prices can change without notice; verify the hotel's
current rates online or by email. For other updates, see www
.ricksteves.com/update.

weekend if you can help it—but if you must sleep here, ask for a
quieter room away from the road. I've listed the summer ranges;
you can assume the lower rates are for weeknights and smaller
rooms, while the higher rates are for weekends and fancier and/or
view rooms. You'll often get a better deal off-season (especially on
weeknights).

On New Steine Street

Kemptown's New Steine Street (pronounced "steen")—essentially
a long square with a park in the middle—is lined with about a
dozen different guest houses.
After visiting all of them, these
are my favorites. Marine View
is more traditional; Sea Spray,
New Steine, Gulliver's, and
Hamptons are mod, stylish, and
gay-friendly; and Strawberry
Fields is somewhere in between.

Handy bus #7 runs every
10 minutes from just outside the
train station to the top of New Steine Street (10-minute ride). To
return to the center, walk to the bottom of the road and cross the
oceanfront street to the bus stand (you'll find schedules there).

$$$ Sea Spray is an innovative concept hotel: Each of the 15
rooms has a different theme, from the Renaissance to New York
to Elvis. It's a memorable place to spend the night, with art-filled
public spaces (Db-£60-145, sea views, some with balconies, pricier
suites, free Wi-Fi, sauna and massage, at #26, tel. 01273/680-332,

BRIGHTON

www.seaspraybrighton.co.uk, seaspray@brighton.co.uk, Neil).

$$$ New Steine B&B, with 22 coffee-and-cream-colored rooms, combines Old World charm with contemporary chic (S-£49-55, Db-£85-135, Tb-£132-159, Qb-£181-186, check website for discounts, dinner option, free Wi-Fi, bistro, at #10-11, tel. 01273/681-546, www.newsteinehotel.com, reservation@newsteine hotel.com).

$$$ Gulliver's, their sister hotel two doors down, has similar decor and slightly cheaper prices (Sb-£44-50, Db-£80-130, Tb-£127-154, at #12a, tel. 01273/695-415, www.gullivershotel.com, reservation@gullivershotel.com).

$$$ Hamptons Brighton has crisp and stylish nautical decor right out of New England—but with Union Jack accents (S-£40-45, Sb-£45-55, D-£85, Db-£85-130 depending on size, at #3, tel. 01273/675-436, www.hamptonsbrighton.com, hamptonsbrighton @hotmail.co.uk).

$$ Strawberry Fields Hotel has 27 rooms with a fun strawberry theme. Sharon and her friendly and competent assistant, Anna, look after you (Ss-£30-49, D-£60-75, Db-£70-99, T-£90-105, free Wi-Fi on lower floors, at #6-7, tel. 01273/681-576, www.strawberry-fields-hotel.com, strawberryfields@pavilion.co.uk).

$$ Marine View has 11 comfortable rooms (S-£35-50, Db-£65-85, family room-£85-150, some with sea and pier views, free Wi-Fi, at #24, tel. 01273/603-870, www.mvbrighton.co.uk, info@mvbrighton.co.uk).

Elsewhere in Brighton

Madeira Place, a few blocks closer to the town center than New Steine Street, has its own stretch of guest houses. The best of these is **$$ Kempfield House,** tastefully run in a Georgian townhouse. The 13 rooms are elegantly simple and nicely appointed (Sb-£50-75, Db-£70-110, huge Db-£85-125, check website for discounts, 2-night minimum on weekends, free Wi-Fi, 18 Madeira Place, tel. 01273/567-521, www.kempfieldhouse.co.uk, info@kempfieldhouse.co.uk).

$ St. Christopher's Inn is your budget hostel option. Smackdab in the middle of the action, on the main seafront road across from the Brighton Pier, this self-described "party hostel" offers cheap doubles and dorm beds for young people wanting to live it up in Brighton. The ground-floor bar and basement disco can be noisy—light sleepers can try requesting a higher floor (£13-28 for a bunk in 4- to 8-bed dorms, Db-£54-110, prices change dramatically by day and season—check online for best deals, elevator, 10-12 Grand Junction Road, booking tel. 020/7407-1856, reception tel. 01273/202-035, www.st-christophers.co.uk).

Eating in Brighton

If you haven't filled yourself up with greasy boardwalk fare, you'll find plenty of good, affordable restaurants around town.

In The Lanes

The area known as The Lanes has the best concentration of both trendy and traditional restaurants. My first two listings are pricey, while the Market Street eateries are easier on a tight budget.

English's of Brighton, hiding on the side of the little square on East Street, is a venerable local institution that's been serving seafood specialties for more than 150 years to luminaries such as Charlie Chaplin and Laurence Olivier. The white-tablecloth-classy interior sprawls through several rooms on two floors, and there's seating out on the square (£13-15 fixed-price lunches, £15-20 fixed-price dinners, £17-25 main dishes, Mon-Sat 12:00-22:00, Sun 12:00-21:30, reservations smart, 29-31 East Street, tel. 01273/327-980).

Terre à Terre keeps vegetarians and healthy eaters happy with imaginative dishes and friendly service (£15 main dishes, Mon-Fri 12:00-22:30, Sat 12:00-23:00, Sun 12:00-22:00, 71 East Street, tel. 01273/729-051).

On Market Street: This bustling area—more a long, wide square than a "street"—is packed with affordable eateries. Take a spin around to choose your favorite, but check out the following: **Fat Leo** gets high marks from locals for big portions of pasta and the best bang-for-your-pound in a bright, modern interior with seating on two levels. It's not haute cuisine, but it's cheap (£3-10 main dishes, daily 12:00-22:00, at #16-17, tel. 01273/325-135). For a seafront picnic, pick up some pastries and pasties at **Forfars Fresh,** baking in Brighton since 1818 (eat at their upstairs café for a few pence more, Mon-Sat 8:00-18:00, Sun 10:00-18:00, café closes one hour before store, at #44, tel. 01273/327-458). **Giggling Squid** serves up tasty Thai dishes in a simple, two-story interior (£4-8 light "Thai tapas" lunch dishes, bigger £6-10 dinners, Mon-Fri 12:00-16:00 & 17:30-23:00, Sat-Sun 12:00-22:00, at #11, tel. 01273/737-373). **The Burger Bar** is a cute little quasi-diner slinging burgers and all-day breakfast fare. As there's no interior seating, you'll have to grab a table on the square (£3-5, cash only, open daily 9:00-18:00, at #11a, tel. 01273/205-979).

In North Laine

Just north of The Lanes and the Royal Pavilion, this former warehouse district is now the cool place to explore, with new restaurants and fun quirky shops popping up all the time.

Bill's Produce Store is a unique café (and, yes, produce store) that's immensely popular with locals for its fresh, inventive dishes and smoothies. Get here before the lunch rush to nab a seat and ogle the surroundings—and the fresh-flower-bedecked cakes behind the counter (£4-8 breakfasts, £5-12 lunches and dinners, take-away sandwiches, Mon-Sat 8:00-22:00, Sun 9:00-22:00, 100 North Road, tel. 01273/692-894).

Our Cornish Pasty Shop offers excellent versions of its namesake, including vegetarian varieties, and delicious homemade desserts (Mon-Sat 9:00-18:00, Sun 11:00-17:00, 24 Gardner Street, tel. 01273/688-063, Ian and Nese).

Two reliable Asian chains have branches here (a block apart from each other, off North Road). At **Wagamama,** diners slurp pan-fried, pan-Asian noodles at long, shared tables in a single hall as the harried wait staff scurries around (£7-12 main dishes, Mon-Sat 12:00-23:00, Sun 12:00-22:00, 30 Kensington Street, tel. 01273/688-892). **Yo! Sushi** features a conveyor belt of tasty and creative raw fish (£2-5/plate, Mon-Sat 12:00-23:00, Sun 12:00-22:30, last orders 30 minutes before closing, 6-7 Jubilee Street, tel. 01273/258-711).

In Kemptown

To dine closer to home, simply wander the lively streets of Kemptown. St. James's Street, running parallel to the seafront a block inland, is lined with all types of cuisine: cheap burgers and fish-and-chips, Thai, Mediterranean, pub grub, and more. For Italian, try **La Capannina,** a cozy one-room restaurant with a run-by-an-Italian-family feel (£6-10 pizzas and pastas, Mon-Fri 12:00-15:30 & 18:00-23:00, Sat-Sun 18:00-23:00, just off St. James's Street at 15 Madeira Place, tel. 01273/680-839).

Brighton Connections

Brighton is well-connected to London and most coastal towns.

From Brighton by Train to: London's **Gatwick Airport** (at least hourly, 25-40 minutes), **London's** Victoria Station (1-2/hour direct, 1 hour; also to London Bridge Station, 1-2/hour direct, 1 hour), **Portsmouth** (hourly direct, 1.25 hours, more with transfer), **Hastings** (2/hour direct, 1-1.25 hours), **Dover** (2/hour, 2.5-3 hours, 1-3 transfers), **Canterbury** (2-3/hour, 2-3 hours, 1-3 transfers). Train info: tel. 0845-748-4950, www.nationalrail.co.uk.

By Bus: National Express (tel. 0871-781-8181, www.national express.com) runs buses to London's **Gatwick Airport** (at least hourly, 1 hour), **Heathrow Airport** (at least hourly, 2.5 hours, transfer possible), **London's** Victoria Coach Station (hourly, 2.5 hours), and **Portsmouth** (1/day direct, 2 hours). Stagecoach buses (tel. 0871-200-2233 or 0845-121-0190, www.stagecoachbus.com)

go to **Portsmouth** (3-4/hour, 4.25 hours) and **Arundel** (2/hour, fewer on Sun, 2 hours, some require transfer).

Near Brighton

Stretching east of Brighton is a coastline fringed with broad, rolling green downs, or hills—an area known as the South Downs Way. These hills are an excellent place to practice a favorite sport of the English: walking. Paths, well-tended by local walking clubs, weave through much of the English countryside, attracting weekend and holiday strollers, and anyone looking for fresh air and exercise. On a quick visit, the highlights here are the adorable hamlet of Alfriston and the dramatic chalk cliff of Beachy Head. Just beyond is the ruined Roman fort at Pevensey. I've listed these attractions as you'll reach them, traveling eastward from Brighton.

Planning Your Time

These sights can be combined to make a good half-day side trip from Brighton (better in the afternoon; allow more time if you want to squeeze in a South Downs Way walk en route). Drive east on A27, dip down through Alfriston to stroll the cute village center and poke into the clergy house, then continue on to Beachy Head—arriving when the cliffs are gorgeously lit by the late-afternoon sun. Pevensey is skippable but makes for an easy quick visit, as it's just off the main A27/A259 road connecting Brighton to points eastward (Dover or Canterbury).

▲Alfriston

The South Downs Way winds itself inland at Alfriston, set in a peaceful green valley. This tidy, picturesque little one-street vil-

lage—half red-brick, half half-timbered, all quaint—is packed with tourists and walkers.

Arrival in Alfriston: Drivers follow *Alfriston* signs south from A27. Park in the giant lot at the north end of town, then stroll up the main drag. Alfriston, while cute, isn't worth the trouble if you don't have a car, but you could take bus #12 or #12A from Brighton south to Seaford, then catch bus #126 to Alfriston (tel. 0871-200-2233, www.traveline.org.uk).

Sights: A block behind the main street is the landmark **St. Andrew's Church,** overlooking an inviting green (the church

Near Brighton

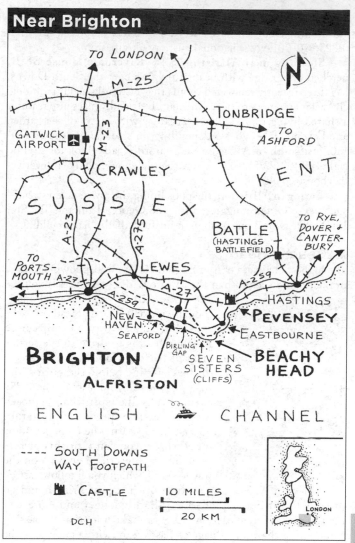

sometimes hosts concerts—look for the schedule in the entry-way). Tucked behind the church (on the right side) is the humble, thatched **Alfriston Clergy House.** This 14th-century house was the first property ever acquired by the National Trust—for just £10—in 1896. Its small garden is filled with delphiniums and roses, and the interior of the building is well-preserved. This place gives you a look at the lifestyles of the medieval and pious. Docents are sometimes waiting inside to tell you more (£4.50, skimpy £3.50 guidebook; Sat-Wed mid-March-Oct 10:30-17:00, shorter hours

BRIGHTON

off-season; closed Thu and Fri year-round except open Fri in Aug; closed mid-Dec-Feb; last entry 30 minutes before closing, tel. 01323/870-001, www.nationaltrust.org.uk/alfriston).

Sleeping near Alfriston: $$$ Riverdale House B&B, perched on a ridge with beautiful views over the South Downs, has three recently renovated rooms that tastefully meld traditional character and modern hues. This family-friendly place also features a shared living room and conservatory with views of the garden and beyond (Db-£90-115 depending on size, family suite-£140-160, just south of Alfriston on Seaford Road—look for sign on right, tel. 01323/871-038, www.riverdalehouse.co.uk, info@river dalehouse.co.uk).

Eating in Alfriston: The pubs lining the town's main street— such as Ye Olde Smugglers Inn, The George Inn, and The Star Inn—offer typical pub grub in beautiful half-timbered buildings.

▲▲Beachy Head

The highest chalk sea cliff in England is less well-known but more dramatic and scenic than the White Cliffs of Dover. If you see

one white cliff in England (and one is enough), make it Beachy Head.

The easiest way to appreciate Beachy Head is to drive to the settlement of **Birling Gap,** with easy access to the coastline below the cliff. From Brighton, make your way to the A259 coastal road. (The most scenic approach is to head east on speedy A27, then turn off and head south when you see signs for *Alfriston;* you can visit this picturesque town—described above—on the way to A259, which you'll follow east.)

Once on A259, you can turn off just past Friston and go directly to Birling Gap or—for a slightly longer and more scenic route—continue east on A259 to make a loop of it, passing through the charming village of East Dean (with a good pub, the Tiger Inn, on the village green). Shortly after leaving East Dean on A259, you'll see a turnoff on the right for Beachy Head. Follow this road as it rises over the hills, with views over grassy fields on one side and the English Channel on the other. Soon you'll spot the Countryside Centre on your right, with information for walkers and other visitors (Easter-Oct daily 10:00-16:00, Nov-Dec likely Sat-Sun only 10:00-15:30 but call to confirm, closed Jan-Easter, tel. 01323/737-273). Then continue on Beachy Head Road, which eventually drops you down into Birling Gap.

Once you arrive in Birling Gap, park at the big pay-and-

South Downs Way

The South Downs Way (often abbreviated SDW) runs for 100 miles along the chalk hills of England's south coast, from Winchester (25 miles inland in Hampshire) to Eastbourne (on the coast of East Sussex). This long, scenic ridge has attracted walkers for thousands of years, and in April of 2011, the area surrounding the trail became England's 10th national park. Locals consider these trails a birthright.

The SDW is a bridleway, which means you can walk, bike, or ride a horse. To keep on course, look for the blue arrow signs with a white acorn in the middle or dots of blue paint on posts or trees. It's always a good idea to have a map; the UK Ordnance Survey Explorer maps are excellent and widely available (#123 covers the area around Beachy Head).

Walkers have priority over horses and bicycles, but it's polite to step aside and let them pass. While motorized vehicles are not allowed on the SDW itself, much of the path runs along farm tracks, so you may encounter tractors. Keep a safe distance or you may be plowed under.

While you can walk along almost the entire southern coast, the best part for a day hike is the three-mile stretch

out to Beachy Head from Eastbourne (find the path at the west end of King Edward's Parade, also called B2103; the small car park is often full, so you may need to park on a nearby street).

Many people walk the entire 100 miles, staying in B&Bs or hostels in towns along the way, or camping in designated areas. The SDW winds its way through or near many towns and villages, including Exton, Buriton, Arundel, Lewes, and Alfriston. Two good websites are www.southdowns.gov.uk and www.nationaltrail.co.uk. You can buy a guidebook at most UK bookshops or online through www.amazon.co.uk. Titles include *South Downs Way* by Jim Manthorpe, *South Downs Way National Trail Guide* by Paul Millmore, and *Walks in the South Downs National Park* by Kev Reynolds.

display lot next to the Birling Gap Hotel, and use the staircase to reach the beach. As you stroll under the grand chalky monster, marvel at the otherworldly whiteness of the cliff and the stones underfoot. Pick up a chunk of chalk to feel how soft and crumbly it is—the constant sloughing off is why these cliffs are so steep, dramatic, and pearly-white (signs warn you to stay away from the immediate base of the cliffs). Stretching to your right (as you face the sea) are the Seven Sisters cliffs, offering chalky splendor as far as the eye can see.

If you have time for a **walk,** there are two good routes to consider. For a clifftop walk with great sea views, but not the best vistas of the cliff face itself, hike from the lighthouse called Belletout (you'll see it as you approach the cliffs from the west) to the Countryside Centre. Or, for head-on views of the cliff as you walk, start out in Seaford and hike up the ridge to Hope Gap. Both of these trails are fairly steep, and it's important to watch your step: Long windblown grass fields come to an abrupt end at the cliff edge, with no barrier between you and the sea crashing hundreds of feet below.

If you don't have a car, take buses #12A or #13X, which offer good daily service between Brighton and Birling Gap, Seaford, and Beachy Head (2/hour, 45-90 minutes, tel. 01273/886-200 or 0871-200-2233, www.traveline.org.uk).

Pevensey

This nondescript village, 25 miles east of Brighton (where the A259 coastal route and faster A27 inland route intersect), is a one-street town leading up to a large, brooding Roman fortress. Originally built as a coastal fortification in the fourth century, **Pevensey Castle** was also used by the Normans, who landed in 1066 with William the Conqueror at Norman's Bay, just within

sight. The moat around the inner castle was probably flushed by the incoming tidewater, although the present coastline has moved farther to the south. The ruins of the castle were also put into action during World War II. While you can pay to go into the castle itself, the best activity—wandering the scenic and grassy field around it—is free.

Cost and Hours: Castle entry-£4.80, includes audioguide; April-Sept daily 10:00-18:00; Oct daily 10:00-16:00; Nov-March Sat-Sun only 10:00-16:00, closed Mon-Fri; tel. 01323/762-604, www.english-heritage.org.uk/pevensey.

Getting There: Non-drivers can take the train from Brighton to Pevensey (2/hour, 1 hour, possible change in Lewes, tel. 0845-748-4950, www.nationalrail.co.uk).

PORTSMOUTH

Portsmouth, the age-old home of the Royal Navy and Britain's second-busiest ferry port after Dover, is best known for its Historic Dockyard and many nautical sights. For centuries, Britain, a maritime superpower, relied on the fleets in Portsmouth to expand and maintain its vast empire and guard against invaders. When sea power was needed, British leaders—from Henry VIII to Winston Churchill to Tony Blair—called upon Portsmouth to ready the ships.

As a major military target, the city of Portsmouth was flattened by WWII bombs (ironically, the Historic Dockyard was relatively unscathed). Postwar reconstruction was hasty and poorly planned, and the city became infamous for its bad architecture. But an impressive gentrification is underway here. Efforts to rejuvenate tourism have included refurbishing Old Portsmouth, building a sprawling new waterfront shopping complex, and adding an odd, pointy monolith to the skyline. While Brighton rests on its holiday-making laurels—and revels in its shabby-chic—Portsmouth feels increasingly gentrified.

The old nautical sights are as impressive as ever. Visiting landlubbers can tour the HMS *Victory*, which played a key role in Britain's battles with Napoleon's navy, and see artifacts from the *Mary Rose*, a 16th-century warship. But the new spirit of Portsmouth is equally enticing. Portsmouth seems to

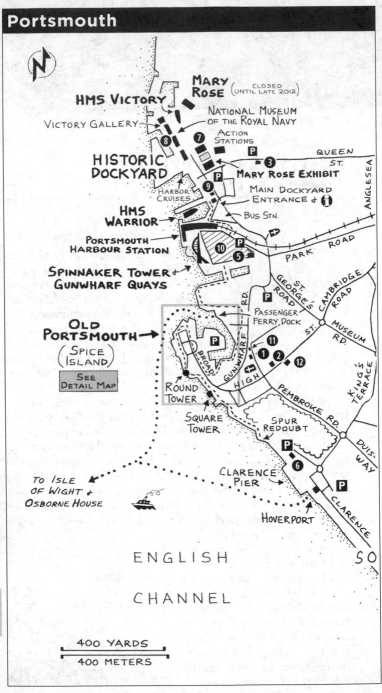

Portsmouth

N

MARY ROSE (CLOSED UNTIL LATE 2012)

HMS VICTORY

VICTORY GALLERY

NATIONAL MUSEUM OF THE ROYAL NAVY

8

7   ACTION STATIONS

P

3   QUEEN ST.

ANGLESEA

HISTORIC DOCKYARD

P   MARY ROSE EXHIBIT

HARBOR CRUISES

9   MAIN DOCKYARD ENTRANCE & 🛈

BUS STN.

HMS WARRIOR

PORTSMOUTH HARBOUR STATION

PARK ROAD

ST. GEORGE'S ROAD

10   P   5   CAMBRIDGE ROAD

SPINNAKER TOWER & GUNWHARF QUAYS

P

PASSENGER FERRY DOCK

ST. JAMES RD.

MUSEUM RD.

OLD PORTSMOUTH → (SPICE ISLAND)

SEE DETAIL MAP

P   BROAD ST.

11   1   2   12

GUNWHARF   HIGH

KING'S TERRACE

ROUND TOWER

SQUARE TOWER

PEMBROKE RD.

SPUR REDOUBT

DUIS-WAY

TO ISLE OF WIGHT & OSBORNE HOUSE

CLARENCE PIER

P   6

P

HOVERPORT

CLARENCE

SO

ENGLISH

CHANNEL

400 YARDS
400 METERS

TO LONDON VIA M-3, SALISBURY, CHICHESTER, ARUNDEL & BRIGHTON

1 Lombard House
2 The Duke of Buckingham Pub & Rooms
3 The Royal Maritime Club
4 Portsmouth & Southsea Backpackers Lodge
5 Express by Holiday Inn
6 Premier Inn Southsea
7 Boathouse No. 7 Cafeteria
8 Georgian Tearooms
9 Costa Coffee & Historic Dockyard Tickets
10 Gunwharf Quays Eateries
11 A Bar Bistro
12 Good Fortune Chinese Rest.

MARKETWAY
ALFRED
COMMERCIAL ROAD
EDIN. RD.
ARUNDEL
ROAD

PORTSMOUTH & SOUTHSEA STATION

CHURCHILL AVE.

MIDDLE ST.

KING'S RD.
ELM GROVE

GROVE RD. S.

KENT ROAD

--- MILLENNIUM PROMENADE
P PARKING
VIEW

BURG
OSBORNE
CLARENCE PARADE
CLARENDON ROAD

AVE. DE CAEN

FLORENCE ROAD

UTHSEA

ESPLANADE

D-DAY MUSEUM & OVERLORD EMBROIDERY

CASTLE

DCH

PORTSMOUTH

expertly balance its dual status as both a city of the past, and one of the future.

Near Portsmouth, on the road to Brighton, are two very different palaces: the ancient remains of Fishbourne Roman Palace, with its striking mosaics; and thriving Arundel Castle, still the proud home of England's top duke.

Planning Your Time

Portsmouth works well as a day trip from London, Bath, or Salisbury. The city's top sights—at the Historic Dockyard—can be seen in a few hours. But thanks to the bustling Gunwharf Quays and Spinnaker Tower, the D-Day Museum, and a seaside-holiday atmosphere, you'll have no trouble filling a whole day. Consider spending the night.

Orientation to Portsmouth

(area code: 023)

Portsmouth, situated on a large peninsula, feels smaller than its population of 200,000. Almost all of its visit-worthy sights line up along a two-mile stretch of waterfront, from the Historic Dockyard in the north to the Southsea neighborhood in the south—with its D-Day Museum, beaches, and hovercraft to the Isle of Wight.

Tourist Information

The main TI is located on The Hard, just left of the **Historic Dockyard** gate. On most Sundays, the TI offers guided walks, usually at 14:30 for £3—ask for details (open daily 9:30-17:15, tel. 023/9282-6722, www.visitportsmouth.co.uk, vis@portsmouthcc.gov.uk). A second TI is two miles away, near the D-Day Museum in **Southsea** (March-Oct daily 9:30-17:15, likely shorter hours off-season, Clarence Esplanade, tel. 023/9282-6722).

At either TI, pick up the free, virtually useless black-and-white map, or shell out a couple of pounds for a good color one. If you're planning to visit the Spinnaker Tower, get your ticket at the main TI for a small discount.

To tempt you to cross the town and see more of Portsmouth, the main TI sells 10-percent-off tickets for the D-Day Museum (located near the Southsea TI), and the Southsea TI sells 10-percent-off tickets for the Historic Dockyard (located near the main TI). Cheapskates can save a couple of pounds by taking advantage of both tickets: On your way into town, swing by the main TI to buy the discounted D-Day Museum ticket. Cross town to tour that museum, and before leaving, visit the Southsea TI to pick up the discounted Historic Dockyard ticket—then head back to that sight, near the main TI.

Bus Tours: With vintage double-decker buses and live guides, **Local Haunts** does a 1.5-hour tour through Portsmouth (£9, buy tickets from guide or at TI, late April-Sept Wed-Thu and Sun at 14:00, leaves from Stand A at The Hard Interchange bus station near Historic Dockyard, toll-free tel. 0800-389-6897, www.local haunts.com, info@localhaunts.com).

Arrival in Portsmouth

Portsmouth has two **train** stations. Stay on the train until the final stop at the Portsmouth Harbour Station, conveniently located one long block from the main TI and the entrance to the Historic Dockyard. The Hard Interchange bus station is just across from the train station (buses #5 and #700 run from here to Southsea). High-speed, passenger-only catamarans to Ryde on the Isle of Wight depart from the waterfront in front of the train station (explained later, under "Portsmouth Connections").

Drivers approach Portsmouth on the M27 motorway. First take the *Portsmouth (W)* exit, then follow signs for *Historic Waterfront*. As you get closer, individual parking lots are well-signposted (the one called "Historic Dockyard" is a garage just two blocks from the main TI).

Getting Around Portsmouth

The walkable core contains the top sights: the Historic Dockyard, Spinnaker Tower (views), Gunwharf Quays (shopping complex), Millennium Promenade Walk, and Old Portsmouth. To get to the D-Day Museum two miles away in Southsea, catch bus #5 or #700 from the Hard Interchange bus station, between the main TI and the train station (£1/ride, £4 day pass, 2/hour Mon-Sat, hourly Sun, 10 minutes).

Sights in Portsmouth

I've listed Portsmouth's sights by neighborhood, from north to south.

▲▲Historic Dockyard

When Britannia ruled the waves, it did so from Portsmouth's Historic Dockyard. Britain's great warships, known as the "Wooden Walls of England," were all that lay between the island nation and invaders from the Continent. Today, this harbor is still the base of the Royal Navy. (If you sneak a peek beyond the guard stations, you can see the British military at work.) The shipyard offers visitors a glimpse of maritime attractions new and old. Marvel at the modern-day warships anchored on the docks, then explore the fantastic collection of historic memorabilia and

Nelson's Victory over Napoleon

Admiral Lord Horatio Nelson (1758-1805), a small man who suffered seasickness throughout his career, was a brilliant military strategist. He developed a new plan for taking on Napoleon's fleet: Instead of pulling parallel to the ships and firing broadside, he would drive a line of ships head-on, perpendicular to his opponent's fleet. When the English attacked, they decimated the French, who were unable to return adequate fire. Victory was won, but Nelson, who courageously wore his bright uniform to inspire his men, was lost to a sniper's bullet. While sailors are usually buried at sea, Nelson's body was returned to London, where he was given a grand funeral and then entombed in St. Paul's Cathedral. The victory at Trafalgar solidified British dominance of the seas. Although Napoleon would menace Europe for another 10 years, he would never again challenge the British Royal Navy.

preserved ships.

The museum complex has several parts: HMS *Victory*, National Museum of the Royal Navy, *Mary Rose* exhibit, HMS *Warrior*, Action Stations, and a harbor cruise. The highlight is the HMS *Victory*, arguably the most important ship in British history. From its deck, Admiral Nelson defeated Napoleon's French fleet at Trafalgar, saving Britain from invasion and escargot.

Cost: You can stroll around the Dockyard to see the exteriors of the HMS *Victory* and HMS *Warrior* for free (except during special events), but going inside the attractions requires a £21.50 ticket that covers everything. The Southsea TI, across town, sells 10-percent-off tickets for this sight (see "Tourist Information," earlier). Day-trippers who arrive by train can save more by purchasing a combined ticket (see "Day-Trip Deal," below).

Hours: The Dockyard is open daily April-Oct 10:00-18:00, Nov-March 10:00-17:30 (last tickets sold 1.5 hours before closing, most attractions close 30 minutes before the Dockyard closes, tel. 023/9283-9766, recorded info tel. 023/9286-1512, www.historic dockyard.co.uk). Friendly and knowledgeable docents throughout the complex happily answer questions and capably tell tales of the sea.

Day-Trip Deal: If visiting the Historic Dockyard as a day trip via train from London, knock about £4 off the admission price by buying a combined rail-and-dockyard ticket (most trains depart from London's Waterloo Station, smart to buy at least one day ahead, tel. 0845-600-0650, www.southwesttrains.co.uk).

Crowd-Beating Tips: To skip the line, buy tickets in advance, either at the Southsea TI (which gives a 10 percent discount) or online (www.historicdockyard.co.uk/tickets). Otherwise, you might have to wait up to 45 minutes to buy tickets, especially in July and August, when school is out. Ticket lines are worst at midday, so try to arrive either right when the Dockyard opens or after lunchtime. In summer, there's usually a second, cash-only ticket desk (ask the greeter as you enter the Dockyard). You can tour the *Victory* on your own in summer, but in winter (Oct-March), you can enter the ship only with a 50-minute tour (you'll get an appointment time for the tour, but as they can fill up by early afternoon, it's best to arrive early in winter).

Because most visitors slowly plod their way back to the *Victory*, the best plan is to do the reverse: Head there first, then work your way back through the other exhibits. This also gets you to the best sights before you get "shipped out." I've listed the attractions in that order.

▲▲▲**HMS *Victory***—This grand historic warship changed the course of world history. At the turn of the 19th century, Napoleon's forces were terrorizing the Continent. In 1805, Napoleon amassed a fleet of French and Spanish ships for the purpose of invading England. The Royal Navy managed to blockade the fleets, but some French ships broke through. Admiral Nelson, commander of the British fleet, pursued the ships aboard the HMS *Victory*, cornering them at Cape Trafalgar, off the coast of Spain (see sidebar). Today, the dry-docked HMS *Victory* is so well-preserved that it feels ready to haul anchor and pull out of the harbor at any moment. In fact, it's still a commissioned warship, the world's oldest. For the British, this ship is more a cathedral than a museum.

۞ Self-Guided Tour: Visitors follow a one-way route that spirals up and down through the ship's six decks. Though restoration work is underway throughout 2012, the ship remains open. Here are the highlights.

In the **great cabin,** you'll see Admiral Nelson's quarters. Imagine Nelson and his officers dining at the elegant table—or hunched over maps here to plan an attack. While it looks like an officer's stately quarters, this space is also designed for action: All of the wood furniture was foldable and could be stored away during battle. The black-and-white checkerboard "tile" flooring—inspired by Nelson's love of southern Italy (and its women)—is actually painted canvas, which could, like the carpets, be rolled up at a moment's notice. It took the crew less than 10 minutes to clear away all the upper-class trappings and turn this space into a fully functional cannon deck. Leaving the Great Cabin, you'll pass Nelson's hanging bunk—even the master of this ship slept on a glorified hammock rather than a bed. (We'll see humbler hammocks soon.)

The **upper gun deck** is filled with original cannons. To prevent the ship from tipping, the lightest were placed higher on the ship, with the heavy ones below. It took a well-trained British sailor two minutes to ready a cannon for firing, compared to the eight minutes French gunners needed to fire their cannons.

Heading up to the **upper deck,** you'll see Captain Hardy's cabin—not quite as posh as his boss Nelson's, but still not bad. Before descending the stairs, notice the small golden plaque on the deck marking the spot where "Nelson fell" during that fateful Battle of Trafalgar—shot by a sniper. From here, the crew rushed him below deck to care for him during his dying hours.

Down in the **middle gundeck,** you can see how the sailors on the ship lived where they worked. When not in battle, they strung hammocks between the guns and ate at tables wedged under their strung-up beds. Sailors ate from square plates to save space. When a man died, his hammock was his burial cloth—his body was sewn up in the hammock, with a last stitch through the nose to ensure the man was really dead. (Since military service was obligatory, faking death was common.)

As you progress deeper into the bowels of the ship, the space becomes smaller and darker (watch your head). It's down here, in the **orlop deck,** that Nelson died, gasping his final words: "Thank God, I have done my duty." The painting next to the spot of his death shows the admiral glowing like a saint as sailors look on in grief. (Whether or not this is an eyewitness account is suspect; check the size of the ship—either people were much smaller back then or the painter had never been aboard the *Victory*.) After his death, Nelson was put in a cask filled with brandy to preserve his body. Legend has it that the cask was not quite as full by the time the sailors arrived in London.

National Museum of the Royal Navy—This museum, situated in three buildings, is packed with model ships, paintings, uniforms, and lots more Nelson hero-worship. While interesting, it gets old quickly for all but serious naval history fans. If you dip into only one part, choose the one nearest the *Victory*, called the Victory Gallery. The corny but informative 15-minute "Trafalgar Experience" multimedia show—with movies, mannequins, sound effects, and smoke—offers a blow-by-blow account of the Battle of Trafalgar. It culminates with a viewing of a panoramic painting of the battle.

▲Mary Rose—If you're here in late 2012, you'll get to see the new, £35 million home of the *Mary Rose*. Until then, the eerie, melancholy carcass of the ship is closed to the public, but its artifacts are on display in a separate museum.

This 16th-century warship was Henry VIII's favorite, named after his sister (Mary) and his family emblem (the rose). In July 1545, when a French fleet approached the English coastline, the

Mary Rose was sent out to engage the enemy. Suddenly, just two miles offshore, a stiff breeze caught the ship and it tipped over. Since all of the gun bays were open, ready for battle, the water overwhelmed the ship and it began to sink. Netting over the hold was intended to keep boarding parties at bay, but instead it trapped 400 sailors as they frantically scrambled to escape. Eventually, the ship and its doomed crew settled, stuck in the mud, in relatively shallow water.

In 1982, about 15 years after the wreck was located, the half of the ship that was encased in mud—and thus preserved—was raised. Today, the *Mary Rose* is still undergoing conservation. Since allowing the ship to dry out too quickly would cause the structure to disintegrate, for years its remains were constantly sprayed with a sealing wax solution. In 2011, officials finally started to let the hull dry out—a process that will take several years.

Inside the wreck were found all sorts of Tudor-era items, such as clothes, dishes, weapons, and even a backgammon board and an oboe-like instrument. Until the new museum opens, a selection of these items is shown off in an exhibit that's back near the entrance of the Dockyard. A 15-minute film runs every half-hour, telling the story of how they raised the *Mary Rose*. While the exhibit is a little too kid-oriented and lacks the decorum a shipwreck site deserves, it's still a fascinating look at everyday shipboard life from almost 500 years ago.

HMS *Warrior*—This ship, while impressive, never saw a day of battle...which explains why it's in such good condition. The

Warrior was the first ironclad warship, a huge technological advance. Compare this ship, built in 1860, with the *Victory*, which was similar to the common warships at the time. The *Warrior* was unbeatable, and the enemy knew it. Its very existence was sufficient to keep the peace. The late 19th century didn't see many sea battles, however, and by the time warships were needed again, the *Warrior* was obsolete.

Action Stations—Thinly veiled propaganda for the military, this collection of interactive, high-tech exhibits and simulators is aimed mostly at the young and/or prospective Royal Navy recruits. It's like an Army commercial combined with a noisy video arcade—persuasively fun for kids but irritating to weary adults.

Harbor Cruise—You can scoot around the harbor and back to the Historic Dockyard in about 45 minutes by boat. As the boat also stops at Gunwharf Quays, taking this cruise at the very end of your Dockyard visit can be a smart way to eliminate the 10- to

15-minute walk to the Spinnaker Tower and surrounding mall.

Cost and Hours: £5, included in £21.50 Historic Dockyard ticket, departs about hourly during the summer starting at 11:00, last cruise usually leaves at 16:00 from just inside Dockyard entrance, weather-dependent, tel. 01983/564-602.

Gunwharf Quays and the Spinnaker Tower

If walking to this area from the Historic Dockyard, walk south on the main road past Portsmouth Harbour train station, keeping the water on your right. Then turn right through the archway marked *Gunwharf Quays*, walking under the old brick rail bridge.

Gunwharf Quays—Part of the major (and successful) makeover of Portsmouth, the bustling Gunwharf Quays (pronounced "keys") is an American-style outdoor-shopping-center-on-steroids, with restaurants, shops, and entertainment. You'll find all the top shops here, as well as a casino, a bowling alley, a 14-screen cinema, trendy eateries with good views of the water, and an Express by Holiday Inn.

Hours: Mall open Mon-Fri 10:00-19:00, Sat 9:00-19:00, Sun 10:00-17:00, tel. 023/9283-6700, www.gunwharf-quays.com.

Spinnaker Tower—Out at the far end of the shopping zone is this can't-miss-it edifice. Like Seattle's vaguely futuristic Space Needle, the Spinnaker Tower has quickly become an icon of its city. The 557-foot-tall tower is evocative of the billowing ships' sails that have played such a key role in the history of this city and country. You can ride to the 330-foot-high view deck for a panorama of the port and sea beyond, or court acrophobia with a stroll across "Europe's biggest glass floor."

Cost and Hours: £8, £7.20 if bought at main TI; daily 10:00-18:00, last entry 30 minutes before closing; since it can be crowded at midday July-Aug, it's smart to book ahead—and doing so online gets you a 10 percent discount; info tel. 023/9285-7520, booking tel. 023/9285-7521, www.spinnaker tower.co.uk.

Old Portsmouth

Portsmouth's historic district—once known as "Spice Island" after the ships' precious cargo—is surprisingly quiet. For a long time, the old sea village was dilapidated and virtually empty. But successful revitalization efforts have brought a few inviting pubs and B&Bs. It's a pleasant place to stroll around and imagine how different this district was in the old days, when it was filled with salty fishermen and sailors who told tall tales and sang sea shanties in rough-and-tumble pubs.

Getting There: To walk to Old Portsmouth from the Historic Dockyard, first follow the above directions to the Spinnaker Tower. From the tower, head south along the plaza with the water on your right. Cross over the small canal, follow the public pathway to the right around the condo complex, then head inland with the ferry port on your right. When you emerge at busy Gunwharf Road, turn right and follow the decorative chain links in the sidewalk to skirt the ferry port and reach the old town (some of the sidewalk markers may be partially obscured by construction). Eventually you emerge onto Broad Street, with the water in front of you. Head to the right, and in a few blocks, you'll reach the small peninsula of Old Portsmouth.

Old Portsmouth Millennium Promenade Walk—Stylized chain links in the sidewalk mark the Millennium Promenade (also called the Renaissance Trail on some historical markers). The chain symbol recalls the great steel chain that once spanned the mouth of the harbor and was raised to block invading warships. For a pleasant hour-long after-dinner stroll, walk the portion of the trail south of Old Portsmouth along the oceanfront. Interpretive panels along the way give you insights into Portsmouth's fascinating history.

• *From the tip of Old Portsmouth, follow the trail around on the ocean side to small* **Capstan Square,** *where the harbor-spanning chain was raised to keep out enemy ships. Pass through a narrow gate and climb up the stairs to the top of the 15th-century* **Round Tower.** *A plaque shows where the wreck of the* Mary Rose *was found. After taking in the view, follow the top of the old stone fortifications down to the Square Tower.*

The 15th-century **Square Tower,** originally the residence of the governor of Portsmouth, was later used to store gunpowder. South of the Square Tower on the left is the small, roofless Royal Garrison Church. Founded in 1212 as a hospice, it was used as a shelter for overseas pilgrims traveling to Canterbury, Chichester, and Winchester. The church was later used by garrisoned troops before the nave lost its roof in a WWII bombing raid.

• *After walking south about a quarter-mile, you'll see a small moat on the left.*

You've reached the **Spur Redoubt,** part of the outer fortifications (see interpretive sign down by moat)—and the end of our walk. To avoid the huge crowds that had gathered in town to see him, Admiral Nelson supposedly passed through this area on September 14, 1805, on his way to the Battle of Trafalgar. From the beach, he was rowed out to the *Victory,* waiting off the Isle of Wight. He didn't return to England alive.

• *Cross the metal bridge over the moat, pass through a tunnel under*

the earthen fortifications, and immediately turn right and climb up the
short path to the top. Walk back along the top of the grassy fortifications.
Benches invite you to stop and watch the many passing ferries and other
ships or to simply enjoy the sunset. If the weather's clear, you can see the
Isle of Wight from here.

Southsea

On a sunny day, this appealing seafront neighborhood—with its
long, broad, grassy park stretching for miles in front of fine old
townhouses—bustles with locals enjoying their city. While it's
studded with some humdrum sights, the main reason to venture to
Southsea is for its interesting D-Day Museum.

▲**D-Day Museum and Overlord Embroidery**—This small
museum, worth ▲▲ to history buffs, was built to commemorate

the 40th anniversary of the
D-Day invasions. Though it
feels a bit dated and faded, it
still does an excellent job of
re-creating both the atmosphere of WWII England
and the planning and exe-
cution of the Normandy
landing.

The centerpiece of the exhibit is the 272-foot long **Overlord
Embroidery** (named for the invasion's code name). The 34 appli-
quéd panels—stitched together over five years by a team of seam-
stresses, and originally displayed in a brewery's boardroom—were
inspired by the Bayeux Tapestry that recorded William the
Conqueror's battles during the Norman invasion of England a
thousand years earlier. The panels chronologically trace the years
from 1940 to 1944, from the first British men receiving their call-
up papers in the mail to the successful implementation of D-Day.
It celebrates everyone from famous WWII figures to unsung
heroes of the home front. A worthwhile audioguide narrates the
whole thing, panel by panel (rent when you buy your ticket).

In the center of the embroidery hall, a movie theater shows
a good 15-minute film—a montage of archival wartime footage
set to period music (included in entry ticket). Then you'll wander
through an exhibit that thoughtfully explains the Battle of Britain
and D-Day, including some vehicles that were actually used for
the landing. Allow at least 1.5 hours for your visit.

Cost and Hours: £6.50, audioguide-£2, discounted tickets sold at main TI—see page 292, daily April-Oct 10:00-17:30,
Nov-March 10:00-17:00, last entry 30 minutes before closing. A
café is on site (open April-Sept). The museum is on the waterfront
about two miles south of the Spinnaker Tower, next to a car park

(Clarence Esplanade, Southsea, tel. 023/9282-7261, www.dday museum.co.uk).

Getting There: To get from Portsmouth's Hard Interchange bus station to the museum, take bus #5 or #700 (see "Getting Around Portsmouth," earlier; ask at info booth about last return-bus times). Drivers can park in the pay-and-display parking lot.

Sleeping in Portsmouth

If you just can't get enough of ships and sea air, Old Portsmouth, just a 15-minute walk from the Historic Dockyard (cutting through the outdoor Gunwharf Quays mall), is charming, fairly quiet, and has several accommodation options.

In Old Portsmouth

$$$ Fortitude Cottage, quaint and cozy, rents six modern-feeling rooms and one apartment in two adjoining row houses just a block from the water. Everything is done with care, making these some of the best rooms in Portsmouth. The main building has views, and the top-floor room has its own roof terrace. The new annex rooms are more spacious, with large modern bathrooms (Db-£90-120, Sb pays the Db rate except during slow times, free Wi-Fi, 51 Broad Street, tel. 023/9282-3748, www.fortitudecottage.co.uk, info@fortitudecottage.co.uk, Maggie and Mike).

$$$ Oyster Cottage is for those who want their B&B to themselves. Witty Carol, who might remind you of Carol Channing, has just one large, light-filled, updated room with a bay-window sitting area, ideal for watching passing boats right

---

Sleep Code

(£1 = about $1.60, country code: 44, area code: 023)
S = Single, **D** = Double/Twin, **T** = Triple, **Q** = Quad, **b** = bathroom, **s** = shower only. You can assume credit cards are accepted and breakfast is included unless otherwise noted.

To help you sort easily through these listings, I've divided the accommodations into three categories based on the price for a standard double room with bath:

   $$$ **Higher Priced**—Most rooms £75 or more.
   $$ **Moderately Priced**—Most rooms between £40-75.
   $ **Lower Priced**—Most rooms £40 or less.

Prices can change without notice; verify the hotel's current rates online or by email. For other updates, see www.ricksteves.com/update.

up close (Db-£70-90, free parking, 9 Bath Square, tel. 023/9282-3683, www.theoystercottage.co.uk, info@theoystercottage.co.uk).

$$ Sailmaker's Loft B&B, next door, is a straightforward, unpretentious B&B. Originally built as a warehouse, it has one en-suite room and two others that share a bathroom. The two rooms on the ocean side offer front-row seats of the bustling harbor. Owner Bob is an ex-seaman who loves his home port (S-£30, twin D-£60, Db-£70, free parking, 5 Bath Square, tel. 023/9282-3045, mobile 0796-619-4030, www.sailmakersloft.org.uk, sailmakers loft@aol.com).

Between Old Portsmouth and Gunwharf Quays

$$ Lombard House rents two rooms on a quiet residential street next to the cathedral, a 10-minute walk from the Historic Dockyard. The public areas are tastefully decorated in red and fea-ture original artwork. In 2005, as part of the bicentennial of the Battle of Trafalgar, actor-owners Alex and Finni traveled around Europe as Admiral Nelson and his mistress, Lady Emma Hamil-ton. Alex's museum-quality admiral's uniform is on display in their atmospheric breakfast cellar, which also boasts old oak ship beams (Sb-£40-49, Db-£70, cash only, free Wi-Fi, 9 Lombard Street, tel. 023/9286-2294, mobile 0776-200-1528, finni@victoryfilms.co.uk).

$$ The Duke of Buckingham Pub, a few blocks inland from Old Portsmouth, is likely to have rooms when others are full. While the accommodations take a backseat to the popular pub, the 19 basic rooms—some above the bar, some out back in separate cottages—are clean and cozy (D-£59, Db-£65, no breakfast, free Wi-Fi in the pub, 119 High Street, tel. 023/9282-7067, www.duke ofbuckingham.co.uk, buckingham119@aol.com).

Elsewhere in Portsmouth

$$$ The Royal Maritime Club offers a home away from home to sailors in town who don't want to bunk on the boat. Just two blocks up the road from the Historic Dockyard entrance, it also welcomes tourists, who share its grand public spaces, generous facilities (including a swimming pool, fitness center, game room, self-service laundry, even barbershop) and 100 comfortable, sur-prisingly newish rooms. The catch: They rent out their ballroom for parties, which can sometimes be noisy into the wee hours—if you're a light sleeper, try requesting a quieter room. It's located two blocks from the Historic Dockyard and four blocks from the train station, opposite the oval-shaped Admiralty Tower (Sb-£48, Db-£90, family suites, elevator, free Wi-Fi, Queen Street, tel. 023/9282-4231 or 023/9283-7681, fax 023/9229-3496, www.royal maritimeclub.co.uk, info@royalmaritimeclub.co.uk).

Old Portsmouth Accommodations & Eateries

TO ISLE OF WIGHT

TO SPINNAKER TOWER

1. Fortitude Cottage
2. Oyster Cottage
3. Sailmaker's Loft B&B
4. The Spice Island Inn
5. The Still & West Country House Pub
6. Sallyport Tea Rooms

BATH SQ.

WEST TOWER ST.

EAST ST.

SEAGER'S CT.

P

CAPSTAN SQUARE

ROUND TOWER

FORTIFICATIONS

BROAD ST. (A-3)

WHITE HART ROAD

HIGH ST.

SQUARE TOWER

TO SPUR REDOUBT

DCH

100 YARDS
100 METERS

OLD PORTSMOUTH MILLENNIUM PROMENADE WALK

P PARKING

VIEW

$ Portsmouth & Southsea Backpackers Lodge is your budget option, with dorm beds and some cheap doubles in a faded old house. This strictly run place is in Southsea, a five-minute walk from the D-Day Museum and about two miles from the central sights (£17 bunks in 4- to 8-bed dorms, D-£34, Db-£38, reception open 7:30-23:00, free Wi-Fi, laundry, 4 Florence Road, tel. 023/9283-2495, www.portsmouthbackpackers.co.uk, reservations @magnusproperties.co.uk).

Big Chain Hotels

The following hotels (with elevators and 24-hour reception) may have rooms when the other accommodations are full.

$$$ Express by Holiday Inn, located in the shadow of the Spinnaker Tower and within the Gunwharf Quays shopping complex, rents 130 cookie-cutter rooms not far from the Portsmouth Harbour train station and Historic Dockyard (£110-145 per room, check website for specials, includes continental breakfast and discounts at some Gunwharf Quays restaurants; free parking for first 24 hours, then £2/day; US reservations tel. 888-465-4329, British reservations toll-free tel. 0800-405-060, reception tel. 023/9289-4240, fax 023/9289-4241, www.hiexpress.co.uk, portsmouth@kew green.co.uk).

PORTSMOUTH

$$ Premier Inn Southsea, a half-mile south of Old Portsmouth along the waterfront, offers 48 somewhat tired rooms next to the kitschy, cotton-candy-carnival ambience of Clarence Pier (the noisy pier attractions close down at about 22:30). It's popular with business travelers on weeknights and families on weekends—as the hordes of screaming kids in the family restaurant downstairs can attest (Db for up to two adults and two kids-£68, may be up to £119 during special events, check website for specials, continental breakfast-£5.25, full English breakfast-£8, pay Wi-Fi, limited free parking, Long Curtain Road, just off Pier Road, Southsea, tel. 023/9273-4622 or tel. 0871-527-9014, www.premierinn.com).

Eating in Portsmouth

At the Historic Dockyard

The Historic Dockyard has an acceptable **cafeteria,** called **Boathouse No. 7,** with a play area that kids enjoy (£4-8 meals, daily 10:00-15:00). The **Georgian Tearooms** are across the pedestrian street in Storehouse #9, with good sandwich and cake offerings (daily 10:00-17:00). The **Costa Coffee** inside the entrance building offers surprisingly good grilled sandwiches, and coffee drinks to go (daily 10:00-17:00).

At Gunwharf Quays

Eating options abound at this bustling mega-mall. Most restaurants line up along the waterfront by the Spinnaker Tower. You'll pay too much in this high-rent district—and many of the places are chains selling mall food—but it's the most convenient one-stop neighborhood for dining. Familiar restaurant names include Wagamama, Yo! Sushi, Loch Fyne, Jamie's Italian, and Pizza Express (see descriptions on page 34).

In and near Old Portsmouth

Dinnertime is the best time to head over to Old Portsmouth, eat at a pub, and then stroll along the Millennium Promenade (described earlier, under "Sights in Portsmouth"). The first two pubs listed here sling overpriced pub grub with gorgeous views, within a French fry's toss of the water—the busy maritime traffic makes for a fascinating backdrop. The next two listings are clustered between Old Portsmouth and Gunwharf Quays, along quiet, mostly residential streets. The last listing is a charming tearoom that closes before dinnertime.

The Spice Island Inn, at the tip of the Old Portsmouth peninsula, has terrific outdoor seating, a family-friendly dining room upstairs, and many vegetarian offerings (£5-9 lunches, £7-12 dinners, food served daily 11:00-21:30, bar open longer, 1 Bath Square, tel. 023/9287-0543).

The Still & West Country House Pub has dining in two appealing zones. Eat from the simpler and cheaper menu on the main floor, or outside on the picnic benches with fantastic views of the harbor (£7 baguette sandwiches and £8 fish-and-chips). Or head upstairs to the dining room, with higher prices (£9-17 main dishes) but a gorgeous glassed-in conservatory that offers sea views—especially enticing in cold weather (dining room open Mon-Sat 12:00-15:00 & 18:00-21:00, Sun 12:00-19:00, longer hours in the bar, 2 Bath Square, tel. 023/9282-1567).

The **A Bar Bistro** is a relaxed, seafood-and-wine kind of place, and is handy for those staying near the cathedral or Old Portsmouth (£9-18 main dishes, Mon-Sat 11:00-24:00, Sun 12:00-22:00, 58 White Hart Road, tel. 023/9281-1585).

The **Good Fortune,** across the street from the Duke of Buckingham Pub, is a Chinese restaurant favored by locals (£5-9 main dishes, £13-20 multi-course meals, Wed-Mon 18:00-23:00, closed Tue, 21 High Street, tel. 023/9286-3293).

Tearoom: If you're in Old Portsmouth before dinner and could do with a proper afternoon tea, visit the **Sallyport Tea Rooms,** named for a gateway in a fortification—specifically, the one in Portsmouth's ramparts that Nelson passed through on his final departure (£4-5 sandwiches, £7 afternoon tea—order in advance, daily 10:00-17:00, 35 Broad Street, tel. 023/9281-6265).

Portsmouth Connections

From Portsmouth by Train to: London (3/hour, 1.5-2 hours, most to Waterloo Station, a few to Victoria Station), **Gatwick Airport** (2/hour, 1.5-2 hours, some require transfer), **Bath** (hourly, 2.25 hours), **Salisbury** (hourly, 1.25 hours), **Brighton** (direct trains hourly, 1.25 hours, more with transfer), **Exeter** (hourly, 3-3.5 hours, change in Salisbury). Train info: tel. 0845-748-4950, www.national rail.co.uk.

By Bus: For most connections, the train is faster—take the bus only if you're on a tight budget. Stagecoach runs the #700 Coastliner bus to **Brighton** (2/hour Mon-Sat, hourly Sun, 4 hours; tel. 0871-200-2233, www.stagecoachbus.com). National Express buses also go to **Brighton** (1 direct bus/day, 1.75 hours), **Salisbury** (1 direct bus/day, 1.5 hours), and **Bath** (1 direct bus/day, 3 hours; tel. 0871-781-8181, www.nationalexpress.com).

By Ferry to the Isle of Wight: Wightlink Ferries has service to **Fishbourne** (2/hour, 40 minutes, cars and passengers) and a catamaran to **Ryde** (2/hour, 22 minutes, passengers only, tel. 0871-376-1000, www.wightlink.co.uk). Hovertravel operates a passenger-only hovercraft from Southsea (2 miles south of Portsmouth) to **Ryde** (£15 same-day round-trip, at least 2/hour, 10 minutes, tel. 023/9281-1000, www.hovertravel.co.uk).

Serious royal-family fans can consider a day trip from Portsmouth to the Isle of Wight to see **Osborne House,** Queen Victoria's beloved getaway—ask about a combo-ticket that combines the round-trip boat ride, bus #4 to and from the estate, and admission (£28.50, buy online at www.hovertravel.co.uk or at Hovertravel's Southsea terminal on the day of travel; Osborne House open April-Sept daily 10:00-17:00; Oct daily 10:00-16:00; Nov-March open erratically—call first or check online; Osborne House tel. 01983/200-022, www.english-heritage.org.uk).

By International Ferry: Brittany Ferries (tel. 0871-244-0744, www.brittanyferries.com) sails to France: **Caen** (2-4/day, 4.5 hours on high-speed boat, 6-7 hours on slower boat), **Cherbourg** (1-2/day, 4 hours), **St. Malo** (night crossing, 1/day, 12 hours); and to northern Spain: **Santander** (1/week, 25 hours). LD Lines (toll-free tel. 0800-917-1201 or toll tel. 0844-576-8836, www.ldlines.co.uk) sails to **Le Havre,** France (1-2/day, 4.5-9 hours).

Near Portsmouth

These sights are very near the main A27 road that connects Portsmouth with Brighton. They're worth considering for a stopover if you have time as you pass through.

Fishbourne Roman Palace

In the 1930s, a farmer just outside of Chichester found the remains of a Roman palace on his land. Wary of archaeologists, he didn't disclose his find until 1960. The ensuing dig revealed a huge Roman-era villa, probably owned by a local tribal chief who was loyal to the Roman Empire. In the main museum building, you'll find the collection's impressive centerpiece: well-preserved floor mosaics, which are on display in  their original locations (visitors walk above them on an elevated walkway). Also in the main building is a museum telling the story of the palace and Fishbourne's Roman era. The garden outside was reconstructed to resemble the original Roman plan. Across the parking lot, the Discovery Centre lets you peek into the offices and warehouses of the archaeologists at work—like a zoo for people in

Near Portsmouth

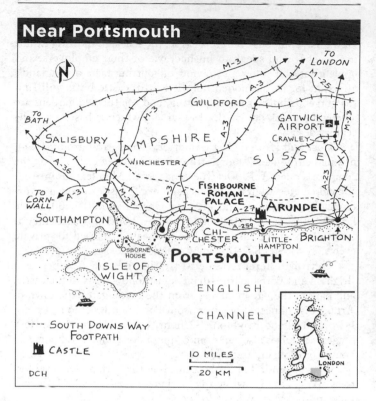

Map labels: TO LONDON, M-3, A-3, M-25, GUILDFORD, GATWICK AIRPORT, M-23, TO BATH, CRAWLEY, SALISBURY, HAMPSHIRE, SUSSEX, A-36, WINCHESTER, A-3, A-23, TO CORNWALL, A-31, M-27, FISHBOURNE ROMAN PALACE, ARUNDEL, SOUTHAMPTON, A-27, CHI-CHESTER, A-259, LITTLE-HAMPTON, BRIGHTON, OSBORNE HOUSE, PORTSMOUTH, ISLE OF WIGHT, ENGLISH CHANNEL, ---- SOUTH DOWNS WAY FOOTPATH, CASTLE, DCH, 10 MILES, 20 KM, LONDON

lab coats. You'll learn how the artifacts are handled on their long journey from the ground to the display case. The palace is fairly interesting to most, but likely to fascinate true fans of Roman history.

Cost and Hours: £8, £2 guidebook outlines a very detailed tour, £2.50 illustrated book is good for kids, daily March-Oct 10:00-17:00, Nov-mid-Dec and Feb 10:00-16:00, closed mid-Dec-Jan, café, tel. 01243/789-829, www.sussexpast.co.uk/fishbourne.

Getting There: It's on the southwestern outskirts of the large town of Chichester, well-signed from the main A27 motorway connecting Brighton and Portsmouth. First head for the town of Fishbourne, then follow *Roman Palace* signs through a very residential-feeling neighborhood to the museum. From the Fishbourne train station, the palace is a five-minute walk.

▲Arundel Castle

This impressive castle of Arundel (AIR-uhn-dull) graces the valley below with straight-out-of-a-storybook appeal. The Duke of Norfolk—the top dog among all English dukes—still lives here, in what amounts to a museum of his own family (the Fitzalan-Howards). Pompous even for a castle, the self-aggrandizing exhibits, docents who speak in hushed awe of their employers, and opulent interiors offer a somehow off-putting taste of England's affection for its outmoded nobility. Still, castle buffs will find the gorgeous interior worth visiting, and the themed gardens are a delight—check out the Earl's Garden, which is based on 17th-century designs.

Cost and Hours: Castle interior, chapel, and grounds-£14, private bedrooms-£2 more; grounds and chapel only-£7.50. The complex is open April-Oct Tue-Sun, closed Mon (except in Aug) and closed Nov-March. Various parts of the castle are open at different times: grounds and Fitzalan Chapel—10:00-17:00; castle keep—11:00-16:30; main castle rooms—12:00-17:00; last entry at 16:00. Parts of the castle can be unexpectedly closed for private events. Tel. 01903/882-173, www.arundelcastle.org.

Getting There: Arundel Castle is right on A27 between Brighton and Portsmouth—**drivers** just follow signs to the castle, and park at the pay lot across from the castle gate. The town of Arundel is connected by **train** from Portsmouth (2/hour, 1 hour, 1-2 transfers) and Brighton (1-2/hour, 1.25-1.5 hours, 1 transfer); Stagecoach **buses** also run from Brighton to Arundel (2/hour, 2.25 hours, some require transfer).

Background: The castle seems like the perfect medieval fortress. Well, almost...while the castle dates back to the 11th century, most of what you see today is actually a Victorian restoration. The owners of the castle, the Catholic Dukes of Norfolk, weren't very popular in this Protestant country, and neither was their castle, which endured multiple sieges. The dukes persevered, however, rebuilding their castle in the 18th and 19th

centuries along with a large Catholic church. As you explore the castle, posted explanations fill in the story (such as an English Civil War exhibit with a Catholic spin). For a primer before you begin, consider stopping by the little information room in the gate as you enter the castle grounds (across from the ticket booth).

❸ Self-Guided Tour: The castle is all about its intimidating bulk and opulent interior—so little explanation is necessary. But here are a few tidbits to bring meaning to your visit. Notice that various parts of the castle have different opening times (listed earlier); if you're here in the morning, visit them according to when they open.

Castle Keep: This ancient centerpiece of the castle is a classic motte-and-bailey design, with a stout windowless fortress atop a man-made hill—double defense against attackers. Later, as the castle grew around it, the keep became the last resort in case of an attack. Walking across the bridge to the keep, ponder how easy it would be to keep the keep—it's connected to the outside only by one bridge, and is well defended by strategically placed arrow slits. Inside the keep yard, stairs lead down to a cellar used as both a dungeon and a storehouse for resources in case the keep had to be used for a final stand. If the flag is flying up top, it means the Duke of Norfolk or his heir (the Earl of Arundel) is around.

Main Castle Rooms: This was—and remains—the gorgeously appointed residence of the Duke of Norfolk. As you ogle the decor, docents explain what you're looking at, and they are always eager to tell you about the lineage, heraldry, and personalities of their beloved dukes. You'll pass through a spectacular private **chapel** (19th-century "Catholic Revival") before entering the **Baron's Hall,** with a pair of giant fireplaces and some fine furniture (including a gorgeous inlaid-wood chest). This room is still used for functions...and, occasionally, for filming the British version of *Antiques Roadshow.* Then you'll pass through a **picture gallery** displaying a *Who's Who* of the Dukes of Norfolk (no, really... who *are* these people?) and enjoy strolling through the formal state dining room, bedrooms, and drawing rooms. Finally, you'll reach the highlight: a wonderful old **library** with rich mahogany woodwork and 10,000 leather-bound books on two levels.

Fitzalan Chapel: This family church—across a tree-filled garden from the main castle—is the final resting place of many of the Dukes of Norfolk. In the nave of the church, notice the grisly double-decker tomb of a 15th-century earl. Called a *memento mori,* or "reminder of death," this was carved during the earl's lifetime—with his virile, healthy self on the top level, and a rotting corpse on the bottom level—to remind him of his own mortality. Flanking the aisle, find the plaques dedicated to the most recent D.'s of N.: Bernard (who died in 1975) and his cousin Miles Francis (died in 2002). Today's Duke—Edward Fitzalan-Howard—is the 18th to hold the title...and you just walked through his house.

Arundel Town: If you have time to kill, check out the adjacent village of Arundel, where you'll find many fine pubs and shops. The **TI**—if it survives budget cuts to remain open in 2012—is also happy to suggest nearby boat trips and activities in town (daily in summer 10:00-16:00, 1-3 Crown Yard Mews, River Road, tel. 01903/882-268, www.sussexbythesea.com).

DARTMOOR

Windswept and desolate, Dartmoor—one of England's best national parks—is one of the few truly wild places you'll find in this densely populated country. Dartmoor's vast medieval commons are still places where all can pass, anyone can graze their sheep, and ponies run wild. Old stone-slab clapper bridges remind hikers that for thousands of years, humans have trod these same paths. In other parts of England, stone circles, stone rows, and standing stones are cause for a tourist frenzy. In Dartmoor, where the terrain is littered with the highest concentration of prehistoric monuments in the UK, they're barely worth a detour.

Locals brag that Dartmoor is England as it was 50 years ago. Maybe that's why it's increasingly a retreat of the rich and famous. You'll find yourself sharing the narrow roads with luxury SUVs, as many retired CEOs and washed-up celebrities have resettled here, in an idyllic and remote countryside far from prying eyes. The area around Chagford has become known as the "Golden Triangle."

All that wealth aside, Dartmoor remains first and foremost the terrain of hikers. Dartmoor gives you a chance to be alone with England's history, jittery sheep, stately wild ponies, and seemingly endless moors. It's also a moody place: At sunset on a clear evening, the gold-tinged heather and rolling hills can be romantic; but on a gray and misty day, it's foreboding—and if you listen hard enough, you might just hear the howl of the hound of the Baskervilles.

Planning Your Time

Dartmoor works well as a stopover between Cornwall (see next chapter) and the rest of England. While you could get a taste of Dartmoor with one overnight (after breakfast, do my self-guided driving tour and/or Scorhill Stone Circle before moving on in the afternoon), it really deserves at least one full day and two overnights to fully appreciate its majesty and mystery. This is one of those places where time slows down...and puts a crimp in an ambitious itinerary.

Getting Around Dartmoor

By Car: Drivers have Dartmoor by the tail—but a good map is essential...as is a fair amount of courage. Dartmoor's narrow lanes are the most challenging in England: barely as wide as a single car, and often flanked by tall stone hedges covered in greenery (with an occasional jutting rock near the base that's made to order for slashing tires). As most roads are too narrow for two cars to easily pass, you'll often have to pull up or reverse to the nearest wide spot in the road when encountering another car. Just follow the other driver's lead, pull in your mirrors as needed, and don't be shy to wave a thank you. For driving in Dartmoor, rent the smallest car you can tolerate, and you'll breathe easier.

By Bus: Dartmoor is tricky for visitors without a car, but there are some bus connections (tel. 0871-200-2233, www.dartmoor -npa.gov.uk or www.traveline.org.uk). Okehampton and Ivybridge are both on minor rail lines, but the closest major city is Exeter.

During high season, the **Haytor Hoppa/#271** bus runs Saturdays only to cover the eastern side of Dartmoor (£5 hop-on/ hop-off ticket, late April-Oct 4/day), looping from Bovey Tracey up to Haytor and on to Widecombe-in-the-Moor, before returning to Bovey Tracey. The **Transmoor Link #82** bus runs five times a day Sundays only June through mid-September. It leaves from Exeter and stops in Moretonhampstead, Postbridge, and Princetown (£2). Two other bus routes from Exeter also connect to Dartmoor towns (Mon-Sat year-round, no buses Sun): **Bus #173** to Chagford and Moretonhampstead (5/day), and **bus #359** to Moretonhampstead (6/day).

The **Sunday Rover** day pass lets you travel on summer Sundays and Bank Holidays on most buses and trains in Dartmoor (£7.50, buy ticket on bus or train, late May-mid-Sept, tel. 0871-200-2233, www.carfreedaysout.com/dartrover.html).

Orientation to Dartmoor

Dartmoor National Park is vast (368 square miles), but I've focused on the most accessible chunk, at the northeastern end of the park between the A30 and A38 highways.

Throughout Dartmoor, there are more than 10,000 ancient monuments, all accessible to walkers. Princetown, in the center of the moors, has the park's primary information office, with

DARTMOOR

Dartmoor National Park

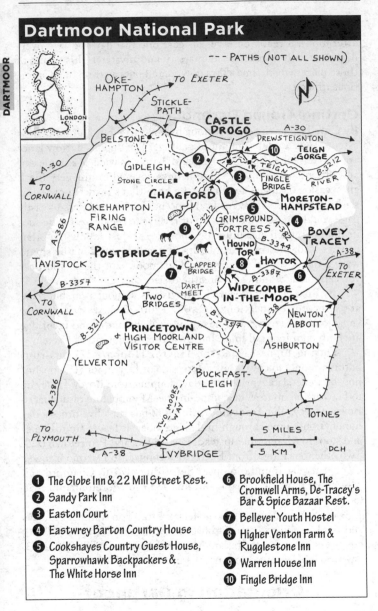

OKE-HAMPTON
TO EXETER
- - - PATHS (NOT ALL SHOWN)
STICKLE-PATH
CASTLE DROGO
A-30
DREWSTEIGNTON
BELSTONE
②
⑩
TEIGN GORGE
A-30
B-3212
TEIGN RIVER
GIDLEIGH
TO CORNWALL
③
FINGLE BRIDGE
STONE CIRCLE
CHAGFORD
①
MORETON-HAMPSTEAD
OKEHAMPTON FIRING RANGE
⑤
GRIMSPOUND FORTRESS
④
BOVEY TRACEY
A-386
⑨
B-3212
A-382
B-3344
HOUND TOR
POSTBRIDGE
⑧
HAYTOR
A-38
TAVISTOCK
⑦
CLAPPER BRIDGE
⑥
TO EXETER
B-3357
DART-MEET
B-3387
WIDECOMBE-IN-THE-MOOR
TWO BRIDGES
A-38
TO CORNWALL
B-3212
B-3357
NEWTON ABBOT
PRINCETOWN
+ HIGH MOORLAND VISITOR CENTRE
ASHBURTON
YELVERTON
A-386
BUCKFAST-LEIGH
TOTNES
TO PLYMOUTH
TWO MOORS WAY
A-38
IVYBRIDGE
5 MILES
5 KM
DCH

① The Globe Inn & 22 Mill Street Rest.
② Sandy Park Inn
③ Easton Court
④ Eastwrey Barton Country House
⑤ Cookshayes Country Guest House, Sparrowhawk Backpackers & The White Horse Inn

⑥ Brookfield House, The Cromwell Arms, De-Tracey's Bar & Spice Bazaar Rest.
⑦ Bellever Youth Hostel
⑧ Higher Venton Farm & Rugglestone Inn
⑨ Warren House Inn
⑩ Fingle Bridge Inn

DARTMOOR

other branches at Postbridge and Haytor (all described later, under "Tourist Information"). The small villages that encroach on the park are charming, and a few (such as Chagford, Moretonhampstead, and Bovey Tracey) are good as home bases for exploring the moors.

Two pieces of gear are essential: good shoes (resistant to mud and "Dartmoor landmines"—wild-horse patties) and an Ordnance Survey map (essential for drivers). You'll need this highly detailed map, not just because the land can be boggy, but also because roads and walking paths are twisty and confusing. (Only two major roads cross the moor, but there are dozens of lesser roads twisting through the countryside—it seems there are five different ways to get between any two points.) The Ordnance Survey produces two good maps of the region. The 1:25,000 Dartmoor map (Explorer #OL28) is ideal for serious hikers, since it shows every ridge, feature, and landmark, but its detail can be overwhelming for drivers. The 1:50,000 map (called "Okehampton & North Dartmoor," Landranger Map #191) is more useful for drivers, and still includes enough detail to use for basic hikes.

Dangers: Parts of the moors are used by the military for target practice. These areas are clearly shown on maps, and marked by red flags when in use—but before going for a hike, always check with a park information office to ensure your route is OK. Other dangers include ticks and adders (a poisonous snake with a black-and-white zigzag stripe). Weather can change quickly here, so wear layers and be prepared for "four seasons in one day" (as locals say). Because Dartmoor is so vast and empty, getting lost is a real threat—a good map and a compass are essential if you're going more than a short distance from your car.

Tourist Information

Most of the bigger villages surrounding Dartmoor have TIs, but the main information center for the park is the **High Moorland Visitor Centre** in Princetown. In addition to hiking info, this office has an interactive exhibit on the history, wildlife, and "countryside code" for walking the moors (free, exhibit-£1.50, daily April-Sept 10:00-17:00, March and Oct 10:00-16:00, Nov-Feb 10:30-15:30, Tavistock Road, tel. 01822/890-414, www.dartmoor-npa.gov.uk). There are also good branches in **Postbridge** (at the big parking lot near the Clapper Bridge, relaxing video upstairs about Dartmoor ponies, daily April-Sept 10:00-17:00, Oct 10:00-16:00, closed Nov-March, tel. 01822/880-272) and by **Haytor** (April-Sept daily 10:00-17:00; Oct daily 10:00-16:00; March Thu-Sun 10:00-16:00, closed Mon-Wed; Nov-Feb Thu-Sun 10:30-15:30, closed Mon-Wed; tel. 01364/661-520).

At any of these offices, you can buy your Ordnance Survey

DARTMOOR

map and pick up their free information-packed *Enjoy Dartmoor 2011-2012* guide and the *Explore Dartmoor* brochure listing guided walks and events (both brochures also downloadable online). These offices are the best source of advice on hikes or driving routes, and each one sells an illustrated £1.50 booklet with suggestions for self-guided walks. If you have an iPod or other wireless device, you can download free, six-mile audio walks starting at the three park information centers (www.dartmoor-npa.gov.uk; click on "Visiting").

Guided Walks: Consider taking a guided walk offered by the **national park** (£3.50-9/person depending on length, get schedule at www.dartmoor-npa.gov.uk or in *Explore Dartmoor* brochure). You can also go with your own guide for a hike of your choosing at a similar price—try **Tom Soby,** who offers a range of walks, including a popular one exploring the places featured in *The Hound of the Baskervilles* (£7-10/person to join a scheduled walk, 3- to 4-hour private tours-£50, mobile 07516-042-316, tomstors@hot mail.com).

Phil Page, a former Dartmoor park manager, offers walks all year on topics from butterflies to literary novels set in Dartmoor (£10/hour for up to 6 people, tel. 07858/421-148, mobile 07849-840-126, www.dartmoornaturetours.co.uk, enquiries@dartmoor naturetours.co.uk). His wife, Hanneke, runs a two-room B&B (see page 325).

Self-Guided Driving Tour

▲▲▲Pony, Lamb, and Moor Joyride

This all-day driving route is a convenient framework for your

Dartmoor exploration. Linger at the desolate viewpoints you find most appealing, and don't be afraid to venture off this plan for a walk to a secluded stone row or circle. If you have enough time, chase down leads suggested by locals—there are many hidden gems embedded in Dartmoor. This circular route begins and ends in Chagford, but you can join or leave it wherever you like.

• *Begin in the village of...*

Chagford

Perched on the edge of the moor, this tiny town is not only charming but actually feels like a real, normal slice of English life (www .chagford-parish.co.uk). The small-town ambience here may make you feel like you've stepped into a time warp (or maybe a quaint BBC sitcom). Villages like this one, which was probably established in Saxon times, were built around Dartmoor as bases for the tin-mining industry. In 1305, Chagford became one of four Dartmoor stannary towns, a main center for "weighing and paying" the miners. The eight-sided Market House in the village square (known as the "pepper pot") is located on the site of the old stannary court/assayer's office.

St. Michael's Parish Church, at the upper end of town, mostly dates from the 15th century and is built out of the typical stone of the area, gray granite. The hard rock is tough to work, so most buildings here are fairly simple. An incident occurred here that is said to have inspired R. D. Blackmore's *Lorna Doone:* A bride named Mary Whiddon was shot dead by a former suitor as she left the church during her wedding in 1641 (pamphlet available inside). Look among the pews at the needlepoint cushions, a few of which bear a tinner's symbol: three rabbits in a circle that each have two ears, but appear to share only three ears among them. (This motif also shows up in the stained-glass window over the door of the wine store on the town square.)

The little **village square** has all the essentials: bank, post office, small grocery store, pharmacy, butcher, delicatessen, and

a few hardware shops that sell any hiking gear that you might have forgotten (including Ordnance Survey maps). Moorland Dairy, next to the Three Crowns Hotel, sells ice-cream cones, interesting cheeses from the area, and clotted cream by the pound (tel. 01647/432-479). Go gawk inside Bowden's hardware store to see how everything you could possibly ever need can be neatly crammed into one place—don't miss the glassed-in antique-hardware room way in the back, and the loft full of dozens of Wellington boots (tel. 01647/433-271).

• *Hop in your car and follow* Postbridge *signs directing you to the road south of Chagford, which will take you to busy B3212. Soon after you turn right onto B3212, you'll cross some...*

Cattle Grates

Welcome to wild-pony country. The rumble of your tires over cattle grates—which you'll cross several times on our drive—tells you that you've entered an area without fences, where livestock of all kinds can roam freely. It's also a reminder to slow down and watch the road closely, especially around blind corners—the animals find cars more interesting than scary, and you may well find some sunning themselves in the middle of the road. I've had to lean on my horn several times to convince a dozing sheep to let me pass. As throughout England, you'll see sheep grazing and fluffy little lambs bounding through the heather. But Dartmoor adds its own unique touch: famously "wild," but remarkably tame, horses. (In fact, the horses are all owned by

local farmers, who keep an eye on them as they graze the moors—notice that some horses are branded.) The horses have free rein of Dartmoor, so you may not see them immediately, but eventually you may find a few (or possibly an entire herd). Horses have wandered here for centuries, and the brown ones are probably the most closely related to the ancestral Dartmoor breed. The park discourages people from feeding or even approaching the horses—they get used to mooching, so they often readily come up to people, but may bite or kick without warning.

• *After crossing the cattle grates, you're really into the heart of...*

The Moors

England's green, bucolic landscape is occasionally interrupted by brown, scrubby moorlands like these. It's tricky to define a "moor"—but once you've spent time on one, you'll know them when you see them. A moor is characterized by its relative lack of vegetation, save for high grasses and heather—a dull-brown shrub that thrives here (and briefly turns a brilliant purple when it flowers in late summer). The long, undulating expanses of open land, almost unbroken by trees but scattered with long-forgotten prehistoric stone monuments, makes Dartmoor feel even more evocative and mysterious than other English moors.

• *On the left, you may notice the remains of a hilltop settlement. If you're up for a hike to get a closer look, consider this optional detour: Turn left at the* Widecombe *sign, and follow the road for a few minutes—keeping an eye on those hilltop ruins above you on the left. Just before the big curve to the right, look for a pullout on the right, and four stone steps on the left. You can park and use these steps to climb up to...*

Grimspound

Dating from 2000 B.C., this late-Bronze Age fortress was a settlement for 800 years. The outer stone wall was a defense wall, and the inner circles would have been stone huts. Well-populated in ancient times, the moors are thought to have become unlivable in about 1200 B.C. because of climate change, and settlements like these were abandoned.

• *Backtrack to the main road you were on, and continue south. Very soon on the left, just before the little parking lot, look for the worn and weathered stub of a...*

Celtic Cross

All along the road, look for tall stone crosses like this one. These marked the way for villagers to cross the moor, often for funeral processions.

• *Soon after the cross, on the right, you'll see the...*

Warren House Inn

Named for a warrener (rabbit-raiser) who fed bunnies to hungry miners, this pub comes with a fun history. This site has reputedly been occupied by a travelers' rest stop for more than 900 years. In 1845, a pub across the road was falling down from disrepair, so this "new" structure was built. Supposedly embers from the old fire were used to light the fire in the new building—which has burned ever since. While the story is questionable, the food here is good—specializing in (of course) rabbit pie, as well as steak-and-ale pie. The glorious moorside seating, at picnic benches out front and across the road, make it an enticing stop for a meal or drink (£6-12 main dishes, open Easter-mid-Nov daily for lunch and dinner, mid-Nov-Easter closed Mon-Tue evenings, tel. 01822/880-208, www.warrenhouseinn.co.uk).

• *There's a lot moor to see (sorry), so let's keep moving. Carry on along the same road into the town of...*

Postbridge

This functional village comes with one of Dartmoor's classic views. As you cross the bridge in the heart of town, on the left you'll

see an ancient bridge parallel to the road. Bridges like this one—essentially a post and a wide flat stone lintel—dot the moor. Called clapper bridges, they date from the Middle Ages, if not earlier. For a closer look, pull over at the big parking lot on the right soon after the bridge, near the handy and very helpful national park office. If you have time, consider a hike—Postbridge is a good base for moor walks (pick up their £1.50 booklet for walks from here).

• *Continue down to the village of Two Bridges, where you hit B3357. Our route turns left (east) on this road, but consider detouring to the right (west) to the town of **Princetown** (pronounced "Princeton"), with its High Moorland Visitor Centre (see "Tourist Information," earlier).*

Princetown is also home to a high-security prison that held French pris-
oners during the Napoleonic Wars, and American POWs during the
War of 1812. (But if you've already gotten your fill of park info from the
Postbridge office, Princetown is skippable.)

   Heading east on B3357, you'll soon have to use some narrower back
roads to reach our next stop. You'll feel lost, but use your map and track
signs closely: First follow signs down into Dartmeet, then uphill toward
Ashburton. After coming back down from the moor, watch for the turn-
off on the left to Ponsworthy, then our next stop...

Widecombe-in-the-Moor

Set in the center of the rolling hills, this adorable but often
shopper-choked village is a scenic stop—and feels crowded after a

drive on the empty moor. There's a
farmers' market usually the fourth
Saturday of every month (10:00-
16:00), and generally a Thursday
craft market during the summer
at the 1537 Church House (late
May-early Oct 10:00-16:00, www
.widecombe-in-the-moor.com). If
you're ready for a meal, carry on
(turning right at the sign by the
Church House) down the country road to the **Rugglestone Inn**—
which is more likely to have local farmers drinking a pint than
tourists. The prices are surprisingly low, and the quality is good...
but watch out for the high-powered local cider (£8-10 main dishes,
food served daily 11:30-15:00 & 18:00-23:30 with mid-day break
on weekends, tel. 01364/621-327, www.ruggelstoneinn.co.uk).
• *Leave Widecombe, following signs for* Bovey Tracey *and enjoying the*
sky-high views. (On a clear day, you can see all the way to the English
Channel.) Now we'll take a look at two of the better-known "tors" of
Dartmoor. If you're tight on time, choose one: Haytor is famous and
offers better views, but is more difficult to hike to, while Hound Tor is
the more impressive formation.

   On the Bovey Tracey road, you'll spot a turnoff on the left toward
Moretonhampstead, *which we'll take later (or now, if you want to*
skip Haytor). To see Haytor, continue 1.5 miles farther on—you'll spot it
on the hilltop above you on the left. Use the giant parking lot on the right
(after a smaller one on the left) and hike up to the grand...

Haytor

Dartmoor sits up on a granite plateau, and occasionally bare granite
"peaks" poke up through the heather. Like lonesome watchtowers
looming above the barren landscape, these "tors" are Dartmoor's
most distinctive landmarks—and Haytor is the most famous and

popular, thanks to its excellent vantage point for panoramic views. Tors basically look like piles of boulders that you can imagine might have been dragged and dropped on hilltops by prehistoric developers, but they're all natural, caused by weathering. This area is divided into two parts: Haytor itself, and the adjacent Haytor Rocks.

• *If you'd like to detour into the town of **Bovey Tracey** (described under "Sights in Dartmoor," later), now's the time—it's 10 minutes away on B.3387, down in the valley beyond the Haytor park information center.*

Or, to continue our loop, backtrack to the Moretonhampstead turn-off (M'hampstead for short), which you'll now follow north through the moors. Soon you'll see another tor ahead and on the right. When you get to the little fork, follow the P signs to the right and park to walk up to...

Hound Tor

Perhaps the most striking tor in Dartmoor, and the inspiration for the Sherlock Holmes story *The Hound of the Baskervilles,*

this mighty clump of rocks impresses. According to legend, this stand of stones was once a pack of hunting dogs that had disrupted a witches' coven. As a punishment, the pooches were petrified. (The hunter that owned the dogs

was turned into the nearby tor called Bowerman's Nose, about a mile north of here.) Hike up and scramble over the many levels. In the valley beyond this ridge are the faint remains of some old Devon longhouses. These were situated at a gentle angle, with animals in the lower part and people in the upper part—liquids and other waste would run downhill, while the heat generated by the livestock would warm its owners above.

• *Our tour is nearly finished. From the Hound Tor parking lot, backtrack a few yards to the little fork and turn right, following signs to* M'hampstead. *You'll drive through the countryside before reaching the larger but still charming town of **Moretonhampstead**—a nice place for a stroll, dining at the recommended White Horse Inn (see "Eating in Dartmoor," later), or to browse the selection of local guidebooks at the TI (daily 9:30–17:00, off-season Fri-Sun only 10:00–16:30, Internet access, New Street, tel. 01647/440-043, www.moretonhampstead.com).*

If you still have daylight left, consider heading north out of

Letterboxing

The local pastime of letterboxing began as a way to collect tourist postcards. What has evolved is a secret system of log-books hidden all over Dartmoor—inside metal boxes, squir-reled away under rocks, or stuffed in the brush. Your goal: Find the logbook and stamp, and add your name and stamp to as many books as possible (bring your own inkpad just in case). Since this practice is a bit of a secret, you'll need to enlist a local to help you get started. Ask at a local TI or at Bellever Hostel (near Postbridge), or check out www.dartmoorletter boxing.org and www.letterboxingondartmoor.co.uk.

Moretonhampstead on A382 until the turnoff (to the right) for Drewsteignton and the **Fingle Bridge;** *or head back through Chagford and venture to the* **Scorhill Stone Circle** *(both described under "Sights in Dartmoor," next).*

Sights in Dartmoor

▲**Walks on the Moors**—Pick up your Ordnance Survey map at any local shop or TI and start walking. The Princetown TI also has a map with suggestions for routes through the moors. Postbridge, in the heart of the moorlands, is a fine launch pad for good walks, and has a park information center that can suggest well-outlined routes. Other good walking bases include Belstone in the north (for rugged scenery) and Ivybridge in the south (more forested). You can go almost anywhere—except the firing ranges. These are technically open for walking when not in use (you'll see red flags if they're closed), but it's probably best to avoid them entirely. For more pointers, read "Orientation to Dartmoor," earlier.

▲▲**Scorhill Stone Circle**—Thousands of Neolithic ruins dot the landscape of Dartmoor, but the Scorhill (SCO-rill) Stone Circle near Gidleigh may be the best. Stonehenge, *the* iconic stone circle, is much bigger—but it's also packed with crowds and right off a busy road (described in the Near Bath chapter). Tranquil, forgotten Scorhill is yours alone—the way a stone circle should be. As it comes with a scenic stroll across a moor, it's a great sampling of what Dartmoor is all about—as  much about the journey as about the destination.

Getting There: The trailhead is about a 15-minute drive west of Chagford. The trailhead is tricky to find—be patient, use your Ordnance Survey map, and solicit help from a local. (I wouldn't attempt it in a heavy fog—but if you do, take along a compass.) From Chagford, follow signs to *Gidleigh*—you'll drive west out of town, bear right (uphill) at the fork, then turn right at the next intersection; from there, cross over the very narrow bridge and go through Murchington, then stay straight, going up and down the hills through Gidleigh. Keep following the same off-the-beaten-path road through the hamlet of Berrydown, until you dead-end at a little parking lot (if in doubt, follow signs for *Scorhill*). Park, then walk through the gate and hike about 15 minutes straight ahead up and over the moor (with a long stone fence on either side of you). After cresting the hill, head down into the gentle valley and look for the circle below (slightly to the left—assuming you've walked straight from the gate). Once there, you'll be alone with the heather, broom, ancient history...and, often, sheep and wild ponies.

▲**Teign Gorge and Fingle Bridge**—Near the town of Drewsteignton, a narrow road leads down into the Teign River Valley. At the end of the road is the **Fingle Bridge Inn,** a pub set along a river and a pictur-

esque old bridge. The food is good and reasonably priced, with daily specials and a hearty ploughman's lunch of open-face sandwiches (£4-8 lunches and cream tea served 12:00-16:30, £7-10 dinners served 18:00-21:00, no dinner Sun; open June-Sept Mon-Sat 11:00-22:00, Sun 11:00-18:00; Oct-May daily 11:00-16:00, until 22:00 Fri-Sat; tel. 01647/281-287, www.fingle bridgeinn.com). A popular spot for weddings and fly-fishing, the trail across the road makes for an excellent post-meal amble along the river (from B3219, head to Drewsteignton, then look for signs to *Fingle Bridge*).

Up the road, you'll come across **Castle Drogo,** an elaborate country house—complete with a circular croquet lawn and formal gardens—that has the honor of being the last castle built in England, finished in 1930 (£8.20, grounds only-£5.10, mid-March-Oct daily

11:00-17:00, grounds and visitor center open at 9:00, closes earlier or open weekends only off-season, closed late Dec-mid-Feb, last entry 30 minutes before closing, on-site café, tel. 01647/433-306, www.nationaltrust.org.uk/castledrogo). Some trails on the estate lead down to Fingle Bridge.

Bovey Tracey—This town on the southeastern side of Dartmoor National Park is a good base and offers a few indoor options to explore when the rains chase you off the moors (just 10 minutes' drive west of Haytor on B3387). With about 7,000 people, it's a metropolis by Dartmoor standards. The **TI** is located on the main street at the main pay-and-display lot on the right as you drive into town (March-Oct daily 10:00-16:00, Nov-Feb sporadic hours, tel. 01626/834-217, www.boveytracey.gov.uk). You can get online at the library (up to 30 minutes free, Mon-Tue and Thu-Fri 10:00-12:30 & 14:00-17:30, Sat 10:00-12:30 only, closed Wed and Sun, Abbey Road, tel. 01626/832-026, www.devon.gov.uk/library). Accommodations and eateries in Bovey Tracey are suggested later in this chapter.

Bovey Tracey, a pottery town until the 1950s, is becoming known as a center for fine crafts. Clay was quarried nearby, and Josiah Wedgwood even nosed around here when deciding where to locate his china factory (he later chose Staffordshire). The **Devon Guild of Craftsmen** has a gallery/museum and shop in a restored riverside mill downtown (free, daily 10:00-17:30, café, just after crossing the river on Station Road, tel. 01626/832-223, www.crafts.org.uk), and hosts a contemporary arts fair the second weekend in June (www.craftsatboveytracey.co.uk).

The **House of Marbles** sounds goofy enough that you might want to visit. It's basically a giant gift shop inside a historic pottery with some interesting glassmaking displays. Check out the marble museum displaying antique marbles, ones made of odd materials, and fun, kinetic wire marble mazes in action that always draw a crowd. The place is now the home of Teign Valley Glass Studios, and you can watch artisans at work creating contemporary glassware using traditional and modern techniques (free, artists in action generally Tue-Sat 9:00-16:30, Sun 10:00-15:00, lunch and tea breaks posted). Outside in the courtyard are old, circa-1900 "muffle" kilns (signs describe their history). In the gift shop, kids of all ages will love digging through the giant bins of multicolored marbles—they're actually made in Mexico, but big piles of them look really cool (free, Mon-Sat 9:00-17:00, Sun 10:00-17:00, café, about 1.5 miles south of town toward Newton Abbot just off A382, at The Old Pottery on Pottery Road, tel. 01626/835-358, www.houseofmarbles.com).

Sleeping in Dartmoor

Befitting such a mysterious destination, accommodations in Dartmoor tend to be quirkier than the English norm, with more character(s) than the staid, hotelesque accommodations in more mainline destinations. Sleeping here really feels like "going local."

Near Chagford
(area code: 01647)

For a description of the handy home-base town of Chagford, see page 314. Most of these accommodations aren't in Chagford itself, but in other villages (or the countryside) nearby. I've provided general directions, but given the confusing spaghetti of back roads here, it's always smart to call ahead for precise arrival instructions.

$$$ Along Chagford's main street, several pubs rent rooms upstairs. The best bet is **The Globe Inn,** with seven decent rooms (Sb-£65, Db-£80-95, family room, Wi-Fi, 9 High Street, pay parking lot nearby, tel. 01647/433-485, www.theglobeinnchagford.co.uk, graham@theglobeinnchagford.co.uk, Graham and Mary). They're also open for meals (£7-16, daily 12:00-14:30 & 18:00-21:00).

$$ Easton Court offers five bright, flowery rooms that overlook the gardens where *Brideshead Revisited* was written (decorated with a faux stone circle to ponder). A bit less "colorful" than the other accommodations here (in a good way), it feels like the ideal thatched-roof English guest house (classic Db-£75, superior Db-£85, Sb-£15 less, all rooms £5 cheaper off-season or if staying at least 2 nights, free Internet access and Wi-Fi, parking, tel.

Sleep Code

(£1 = about $1.60, country code: 44)
S = Single, **D** = Double/Twin, **T** = Triple, **Q** = Quad, **b** = bathroom, **s** = shower only. You can assume credit cards are accepted and breakfast is included unless otherwise noted.

To help you sort easily through these listings, I've divided the accommodations into three categories based on the price for a standard double room with bath:

$$$ Higher Priced—Most rooms £80 or more.
$$ Moderately Priced—Most rooms between £50-80.
$ Lower Priced—Most rooms £50 or less.

Prices can change without notice; verify the hotel's current rates online or by email. For other updates, see www.ricksteves.com/update.

01647/433-469, www.easton.co.uk, stay@easton.co.uk, Debra and
Paul). It's at the crossroads called Easton, just east of Chagford,
right on A382.

$$ Sandy Park Inn rents five well-appointed but overpriced
rooms above a busy upmarket pub. Although it's in a creaky old
16th-century shell, it comes with modern touches (Sb-£45, smaller
Ds-£69, Db-£79, some have private bathrooms across the hall,
cheaper for longer stays, Wi-Fi, tel. 01647/433-267, www.sandy
parkinn.co.uk, info@sandyparkinn.co.uk, Matt). It's on A382 east
of Chagford, at the turnoff for the Teign Gorge. For more on the
pub, see "Eating in Dartmoor," later.

In or near Moretonhampstead
(area code: 01647)

Moretonhampstead—larger and less quaint than Chagford or
Widecombe-in-the-Moor—is a handy home base with its own
share of half-timbered appeal.

$$$ Eastwrey Barton Country House is set on a ter-
raced lawn halfway up the side of the Wray Valley between
Moretonhampstead and Bovey Tracey. It has five warm and spacious rooms in a restored Georgian country house (standard Sb-£70,
superior Sb-£80, standard Db-£100, superior Db-£120, £29 three-
course dinners for guests, no children under 10, free Wi-Fi, several nice lounges, on A382 near Lustleigh, tel. 01647/277-338,
www.eastwreybarton.co.uk, reservations@eastwreybarton.co.uk,
friendly Sharon and Patrick).

$$ Cookshayes Country Guest House, on the main B3212
road in the heart of Moretonhampstead, has seven traditional,
homey rooms in a big house. They also serve good dinners for
guests with advance notice (Sb-£40-45, Db-£50-60, 33 Court
Street, tel. 01647/440-374, fax 01647/440-453, www.cookshayes
.co.uk, cookshayes@aol.com, gregarious Tracy and chef Barry).

$ Sparrowhawk Backpackers rents cheap beds in the
Moretonhampstead town center, in the light-filled loft of a restored
stone stable (£17 bunks in coed dorm with curtains, D-£38, family
room, bedding provided, kitchen, 45 Ford Street, tel. 01647/440-
318, mobile 07870-513-570, www.sparrowhawkbackpackers.co.uk,
ali@sparrowhawkbackpackers.co.uk).

In or near Bovey Tracey
(area code: 01626)

Sleep here if you want to be close to a real town on the edge of the
national park, rather than the rustic villages inside Dartmoor. For
more on Bovey Tracey, see page 322.

$$ Brookfield House offers three lovely bedrooms in a spacious 1906 Edwardian house set on two acres of lawns and gardens

(Sb-£53-57, Db-£76-84, no children under 12, closed Dec-Jan, Challabrook Lane, tel. 01626/836-181, www.brookfield-house .com, enquiries@brookfield-house.com, Frances and Laurence).

$$ The Cromwell Arms is a 16th-century coaching inn right in the middle of the action with 12 simple, comfortable rooms (Sb-£55, Db-£72.50, family Tb or Qb-£100, minimum 2-night stay on weekends, Fore Street, tel. 01626/833-473, www.thecromwellarms .co.uk, info@thecromwellarms.co.uk, Gary and Julie). For more on the downstairs pub, see "Eating in Dartmoor," later.

At **$$ Yarrow Lodge,** Hanneke and local guide Phil rent two rooms (with a shared bath) in their home in the midst of Yarner Wood, a nature reserve within the national park between Bovey Tracey and Haytor (S-£35, D-£70, March-Oct only, tel. 01626/836-589, mobile 07849-840-126, www.yarrowlodge.co.uk, enquiries@yarrowlodge.co.uk).

Near Postbridge

$ Bellever Youth Hostel offers 34 beds in seven rooms on the moors. It's simple and institutional, but it comes with an impressive wildlife area out front to learn about the local terrain (£18-20/bunk in 4- to 8-bed rooms, Q-£66, £1/night discount if arriving by bus, bicycle, or on foot; £3 more for non-members, £6-8 dinners, £2 self-service laundry, members' kitchen, open all year, reception open 7:30-10:00 & 17:00-22:30, tel. 0845-371-9622, www.yha.org .uk, bellever@yha.org.uk). It's about a mile south of Postbridge, well-signed from the main road.

Near Widecombe-in-the-Moor

$$ Higher Venton Farm is a simple, middle-of-nowhere 1560 farmhouse renting three basic rooms with eclectic, outmoded decor (S-£32, twin D-£60, Db-£70, tel. 01364/621-235, www .ventonfarm.com, info@ventonfarm.com). It's about a half-mile outside the village of Widecombe-in-the-Moor (follow signs from main intersection to *Rugglestone Inn,* then continue on the same road beyond the inn to the farm).

Eating in Dartmoor

In or near Chagford

Several pubs in Chagford serve microwaved pub grub, but locals recommend venturing into the countryside for a better meal. Many accommodations serve affordable meals to their guests—but always ask in advance so they have time to shop and prepare.

22 Mill Street, pricey but well-regarded, is a cut above the other eateries lining Chagford's main street, both in terms of class and quality (£16-25 fixed-price lunches, £36-59 fixed-price dinners, open Tue-Sat 12:00-15:00 & 19:00-22:00, closed Sun-Mon, reservations smart, tel. 01647/432-244). They also rent two good rooms upstairs with a breakfast and five-course dinner package (Db-£250, www.22millst.com).

Sandy Park Inn, which also rents rooms, has a characteristic 16th-century pub and a cozy dining room that serves pricey but good food with great Old World atmosphere (£5-6 sandwiches at lunch, £5-14 main dishes, open daily 11:00-23:00, tel. 01647/433-267). It's a few minutes from Chagford—for location details, see "Sleeping in Dartmoor," earlier.

In Moretonhampstead

The White Horse Inn has tasty Mediterranean-inspired dishes, as well as more traditional pub fare and pizzas. You can sit in the pub or a few steps down in the quieter, more modern dining room (£7.50-11 pizzas, £12-21 main dishes, dining room open April-Oct daily 12:30-2:30 & 18:30-21:00, no lunch service off-season, reservations recommended on weekends, 7 George Street, tel. 01647/440-242).

In Bovey Tracey

De-Tracey's Bar offers traditional pub fare in the upper part of the town (£6-10 meals, food served daily 11:00-23:00 except Sun from 12:00, 56 Fore Street, tel. 01626/833-465).

Spice Bazaar offers good Indian food (£7-15 main dishes, daily 12:00-14:00 & 18:00-23:30, 38 Fore Street, tel. 01626/833-111).

The Cromwell Arms serves good meals in a traditional atmosphere (food served daily 12:00-14:00 & 18:00-21:30, Fore Street, tel. 01626/833-473).

Elsewhere in Dartmoor

Earlier in this chapter, I've described three restaurants that make for good lunch or dinner stops as you explore the moors: **Warren House Inn,** perched atop a moor south of Chagford (see page 317); **Rugglestone Inn,** just outside the village of Widecombe-on-the-Moor (see page 318); and the **Fingle Bridge Inn,** in the Teign Gorge (see page 321).

CORNWALL

*Penzance • St. Ives • The Penwith Peninsula •
East Cornwall*

Set on a rocky peninsula in the southwest of England, Cornwall has a Celtic vibe. Its rugged scenery and wild, uncultivated appeal make you feel as if you're approaching the end of the world (and many natives would say it's exactly that). Harboring the remnants of an endangered Celtic culture (Cornish), an extinct tin-mining industry, and a gaggle of visit-worthy sights, this is one of England's most popular holiday regions—especially among the English.

Cornwall—part of the "Celtic fringe" of Britain—grew up as a very different place from England, with its own language, called Cornish, which thrived for centuries. Fishing, shipping, and smuggling were the main businesses here for hundreds of years, but in the 18th century, tin-mining became the major industry. The 20th century dealt a double blow to Cornwall: The local pilchard fish became depleted, and cheap Asian and South American tin put an end to mining. Today's predominant trade is tourism, as evidenced by the many tacky tourist traps littering the landscape.

But visitors flock here for good reason. Not only is the area packed with ancient sites, precious villages, and historic monuments, but the climate is also unusually mild. The Gulf Stream often brings warm, almost tropical weather to Cornwall—making it perfect for gardening, walking, basking on the beach, and generally enjoying life.

To see Cornwall, set yourself up in a home base (Penzance or St. Ives) and spend most of your time venturing out on day trips. Romantic St. Ives has an artsy beach-bum ambience and is crowded with holiday-makers in summer. Penzance, on the other hand, is all business—a working-class shipping port with plenty of high-quality accommodations and welcoming eateries. Since Cornwall is best suited for day-tripping, Penzance's relative lack of tourist charm is actually an asset—it's much easier to drive in and out of, and has better public-transportation connections, making it my preferred home base. Sleep in St. Ives only if you're serious about gallery-hopping.

Venture to quaint seaside villages, a dramatic theater, a telegraph museum, a dead tin mine, and a thought-provoking stone circle. Cry "Land Ho!" at Land's End, and consider a chopper or ferry ride to the castaway Isles of Scilly. Farther northeast, the castle of a king named Arthur tickles travelers' imaginations, while unusual gardens thrill those with green thumbs.

Planning Your Time

Brits spend weeks here on holiday. But for a speedy traveler, two nights based in Penzance or St. Ives, with one solid day rambling around the peninsula, offer a suitable first taste.

Given that it takes so long to get to this edge of the world from the heart of England (figure about a day each way by car or train), it makes sense not to rush your visit. Spending three nights and two days here allows you to slow down, see all the sights, and get a better feel for Cornish culture. Most of the noteworthy sights and villages wrap around the Penwith Peninsula, so you can line them up and see them on a handy circular drive.

The attractions farther east—Tintagel Castle and the gardens—are ideal for breaking up the long journey to or from Cornwall (en route to Bath or Dartmoor).

Getting to Cornwall

By Train: Train travelers arrive in Cornwall at Penzance, the most central and largest city on the coast (see "Penzance Connections" on page 339).

By Plane: Cornwall's main airport is Newquay-Cornwall International (www.newquay-airport.co.uk), 5 miles from Newquay and 35 miles northeast of Penzance. Airlines that serve Newquay include Air Southwest (from Glasgow, Bath/Bristol, Dublin, and more; www.airsouthwest.com), Flybe (from Edinburgh or London-Gatwick, www.flybe.com), bmibaby (from Manchester and East Midlands, www.bmibaby.com), and Lufthansa (from Dusseldorf, www.lufthansa.com). Avis (www.avis.com), Europcar (www.europcar.co.uk), and Hertz (www.hertz.com) rent cars at or

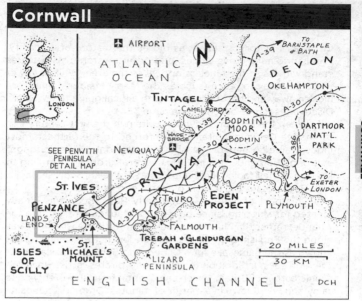

near the airport. Public-transportation connections into Penzance can be tricky—contact the Newquay TI for suggestions (tel. 01637/854-020, www.visitnewquay.org), or try BioTravel's airport transfer service (tel. 01637/880-006, www.biotravel.co.uk).

Getting Around Cornwall

This region is most satisfying by car, which allows you to pack a lot into each day. It's challenging but doable by public transportation, in which case you'll have to be more selective. Note that all public-transit routes run less frequently off-season (Oct-April). A tour with Western Discoveries (see page 334) is a handy way to get into the countryside.

By Car: The coastal road—which passes through Penzance and above St. Ives—links together almost all of the best sights. Driving in Cornwall is generally easy, but parking is not, especially in summer—small villages often have tiny parking lots near the water and larger ones outside of town, so it's a good idea to arrive early in the day. Roads can get very congested on Bank Holiday weekends and in August, so allow extra time, especially on main routes such as A30 and A38. Narrow, twisty Cornish lanes criss-cross the spine of the peninsula, and can save time if the main routes are crowded—but you'll need a good map (try the 1:100,000 Ordnance Survey) and, even more importantly, a good navigator. For current traffic conditions, listen to the radio—many rental-car stereos have a setting for automatic traffic updates (often marked

Cornish History

Cornwall's history is almost as old as the history of humanity. Prehistoric huts, stone circles, and other mysterious structures stand witness to the timeless appeal of the area. While a few of these are easy to reach (such as the Merry Maidens), most are hidden away and best uncovered with a local guide (try Western Discoveries tours—described on page 334).

When the Romans arrived in Britain in the first century B.C., the native Celtic inhabitants were forced to the farthest, most inhospitable corners of the island. To this day, a "Celtic fringe" still rings England. This includes several groups struggling to keep alive their fading languages, such as Welsh, Scottish Gaelic, Irish Gaelic, Manx (on the Isle of Man)...and Cornish.

This part of Britain—specifically Penzance—was ideally located for shipping, since boats could launch straight into the Atlantic, rather than having to tack from farther east all the way along the English Channel. It's no wonder that Penzance is best known as the namesake for a Gilbert and Sullivan musical about the high seas. In addition to sailors and pirates, artists love this scenic corner of Britain, which can change from sun-drenched to rainy and windblown in a matter of minutes. Dramatic clouds hit Cornwall like a hammer, and the sea here changes color with the sky.

Rich deposits of metals—especially tin—have linked this rugged spit of land to the rest of the world, making Cornwall unexpectedly cosmopolitan. Cornish tin has been found in ancient plumbing as far away as Turkey and Pompeii (Italy). Cornwall wasn't conquered by the Romans—partly because of its remoteness—but also because the Cornish were already Roman trading partners. (You'll find no Roman forts in Cornwall, but you will find Roman goods.) Cornish trading came with an influx of exotic products—Cornish cooking is unique in England for its use of saffron, likely bartered with the Near East for metals.

In the 18th century, Cornwall's tin-mining industry enjoyed a boom (see sidebar on page 348). But when the industry went bust in the late 19th century, many miners had to find work elsewhere. Though tin-mining was a back-breaking, menial job, it

by the letters TA or TP; see page 795).

By Bus: It's slow but possible to reach most Cornwall sights by bus, some of which go topless May through September. Most buses are run by First (tel. 0845-600-1420 or Traveline tel. 0871-200-2233, www.firstgroup.com), though Western Greyhound handles the #504 route (tel. 01637/871-871, www.westerngreyhound .com). First has a useful one-day pass called "FirstDay Cornwall" for the region that includes Penzance, St. Ives, Land's End, and the surrounding area (£7, pay driver).

You'll find the following bus routes useful:

also required highly skilled miners. Mine owners from around the world began to recruit and relocate unemployed Cornish miners. Throughout the 1860s, 20 percent of Cornish people emigrated, and this "Cornish diaspora" spread the culture from this corner of England across the face of the earth. For example, hundreds of Cornish miners went to California to get in on the Gold Rush. Locals brag, "Anywhere you find a hole in the ground, you'll find a Cornishman at the bottom of it." Similarly, Cornish graveyards read like a geography textbook, as headstones often list the places where the person lived.

The great migration of the late 19th century also left behind many ghost towns, which still dot the Cornish countryside. Today, many of these long-abandoned homes are being bought up by Londoners and converted into holiday villas—driving up prices and forcing out the few remaining locals.

The Cornish language—related to Welsh, and more distantly related to Scottish Gaelic and Irish Gaelic—was widely spoken here through the late 18th century. As the Industrial Revolution shrunk England and church leaders refused to offer services in Cornish, the language became obsolete. Cornish survived only among a handful of speakers through the 19th and early 20th centuries. But, remarkably, Cornish held on, and—after a recent EU designation as an official minority language—it's now allowed to be taught in schools again. More people speak Cornish today than two centuries ago, and raising kids to be bilingual is in vogue.

Today, feisty Cornwall, with a half-million residents, is officially and for all practical purposes part of England (unlike Wales or Scotland). But native-born Cornishmen and Cornishwomen still cling to what makes them unique—they're Cornish first, British second. The fledgling Cornish independence movement has never really gotten anywhere, but that doesn't stop locals from displaying the flag of Cornwall: a black field (representing the earth) with a white cross (the tin flowing through the earth). Also look for bumper stickers boasting the Cornish word for "Cornwall": *Kernow*.

Buses **#1** and **#1A** connect Penzance with Newlyn and Land's End (Mon-Sat 2/hour, Sun 5/day, 10 minutes to Newlyn, 50 minutes to Land's End); #1A also stops at Porthcurno, near the Telegraph Museum and a steep uphill climb to the Minack Theatre (Mon-Sat 4/day, Sun 2/day, 40 minutes).

Buses **#2** and **#2A** run between Penzance and Falmouth, stopping at Marazion near St. Michael's Mount (Mon-Sat 2/hour, Sun every 2 hours, 10 minutes to Marazion, 1.75 hours to Falmouth).

Buses **#6** and **#6A** connect Penzance with Newlyn and Mousehole (2-3/hour, 10 minutes to Newlyn, 20 minutes to

Mousehole). Buses **#5** and **#5A** also go to Newlyn.

Buses **#17**, **#17A**, and **#17B** connect Penzance and St. Ives (1-2/hour, 35-50 minutes). Bus **#17B** also stops at Marazion (St. Michael's Mount).

Bus **#300** is a topless tourist bus that does a big, 3.5-hour loop around the Penwith Peninsula (daily late April-Sept only, 4/day), connecting Penzance, St. Ives (40 minutes), and Land's End (2.5 hours). Along the way, it stops at Marazion (St. Michael's Mount), Geevor Tin Mine, Sennen Cove, and Newlyn. From late May to late August, it also stops in Porthcurno.

Bus **#504** connects Penzance to some otherwise difficult-to-reach destinations along the southern edge of Penwith (Mon-Sat 2-4/day, none on Sun): Newlyn (10 minutes), Mousehole (15 minutes), Merry Maidens (30 minutes), Porthcurno (50 minutes), Minack Theatre (50 minutes), Land's End (1.25 hours), and Sennen Cove (1.5 hours).

By Train: A scenic (read: slow) rail line connects Penzance and St. Ives, mostly running along the coast (2/day direct, 20 minutes; roughly hourly with transfer in St. Erth, 30-60 minutes; tel. 0845-748-4950, www.nationalrail.co.uk).

Penzance

Sure enough, Penzance had its share of pirates. Strategically situated near the very tip of Britain, the town was an ideal spot for pirates to hijack and plunder ships returning from the New World with untold treasures. But today's Penzance is less of a rough-and-tumble pirate smuggler's cove and more of a blue-collar transportation hub. Penzance can't compete with the artsy vibe of St. Ives or the precious jewel-box quality of nearby Mousehole, but it's cornered the market on functionality: Well-located B&Bs, good restaurants, train and bus stations, and easy parking make Penzance the most practical home base for exploring the Cornish coast.

Orientation to Penzance

(area code: 01736)
Penzance, with about 20,000 people, is situated on a small peninsula. The eastern part of the peninsula has the TI, harbor, and train and bus stations. The southern part has a broad and inviting promenade, with most of the town's B&Bs nearby. Climbing uphill from the water are various streets, including the bustling Market Jew Street (derived from the Cornish *Marghas Yow*, mean-

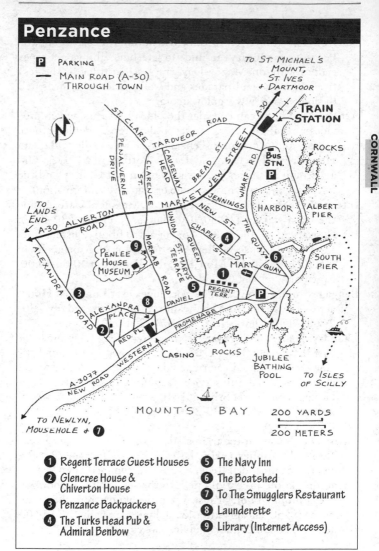

Penzance

P PARKING
— MAIN ROAD (A-30) THROUGH TOWN

TO ST. MICHAEL'S MOUNT, ST. IVES & DARTMOOR

TRAIN STATION

ROCKS

Bus STN.

ST. CLARE ST.

TARDVEOR ROAD

PENALVERNE DRIVE

CAUSEWAY HEAD

CLARENCE ST.

BREAD ST.

MARKET JEW STREET

WHARF RD.

TO LAND'S END
A-30 ALVERTON ROAD

JENNINGS

NEW ST.

THE QUAY

HARBOR

ALBERT PIER

UNION ST.

CHAPEL ST.

ST. MARY'S TERRACE

QUEEN ST.

ST. MARY

ST. MARY QUAY

SOUTH PIER

ALEXANDRA ROAD

MORRAB ROAD

PENLEE HOUSE MUSEUM

REGENT TERR.

ALEXANDRA PLACE

RED. PL.

DANIEL

PROMENADE

WESTERN

CASINO

A-3077 NEW ROAD

ROCKS

JUBILEE BATHING POOL

TO ISLES OF SCILLY

TO NEWLYN, MOUSEHOLE & **7**

MOUNT'S BAY

200 YARDS
200 METERS

1 Regent Terrace Guest Houses
2 Glencree House & Chiverton House
3 Penzance Backpackers
4 The Turks Head Pub & Admiral Benbow
5 The Navy Inn
6 The Boatshed
7 To The Smugglers Restaurant
8 Launderette
9 Library (Internet Access)

CORNWALL

ing "Thursday Market") and the more atmospheric, restaurant-lined Chapel Street. The hill is capped by the spire of the Church of St. Mary, and the grandly domed Market House, now a bank.

Tourist Information

Budget cuts closed the Penzance TI in May of 2011, and plans to reopen it are uncertain. Ask your hotelier whether anything has taken its place, or check www.visitcornwall.com.

Helpful Hints

Festival: The annual **Golowan (Midsummer) Festival** engulfs Penzance for 10 days in mid- to late-June. Things get especially rowdy on Mazey Day, the last Saturday of the festival, with colorful parades and well-lubricated crowds (tel. 01736/369-686, www.golowan.org).

Art Pass: Art buffs can consider the £14.50 Art Pass, which provides unlimited access for seven days to the Penlee House Gallery and Museum in Penzance; the Tate Gallery, Barbara Hepworth Museum, and Leach Pottery in St. Ives; and a discount at the shops in the Newlyn Art Gallery and the Exchange in Newlyn (www.tate.org.uk/stives/information).

Internet Access: You can get online at **Steamers Café**, inside the train station (£0.50/10 minutes, Mon-Sat 7:30-17:30, closed Sun, tel. 01736/360-369) or at the **library,** just up from the Penlee House Gallery and Museum on Morrab Road (£0.90/15 minutes, Mon-Fri 9:00-17:00, Sat 10:00-16:00, closed Sun, tel. 0300-1234-111).

Baggage Storage: You can stow your luggage at **Longboat Hotel,** across the street from the train station (£2/bag, daily 7:30-24:00, Market Jew Street, tel. 01736/364-137).

Laundry: Penzance's big waterfront **casino,** along the promenade past the Regent Terrace B&Bs, is attached to a handy little launderette (around the right side of the casino; self-service-about £8-10/load, full service-about £14.50, same-day full service possible if you bring it soon after the attendant arrives at 9:00, open daily 7:30-20:00, start last load by 18:30, tel. 01736/333-978).

Taxis: Cabs line up at the train station taxi stand. Or you can call the reliable **Stones Taxi** (tel. 01736/363-400) for the £3-4 fare to my recommended Regent Terrace accommodations.

Swimming Pool: Take a dip next to the sea in the outdoor, Art Deco **Jubilee Pool,** or just watch the action from the promenade (£4.50, cheaper after 15:30, June-Sept daily 10.30-18:00, tel. 01736/369-224, www.jubileepool.co.uk).

Tours in Penzance

▲Western Discoveries Tours—If you want to explore Cornwall's hidden nooks and crannies with a local, a minivan tour is a must. Russ Peake is an enthusiastic, energetic young guide with a broad knowledge of Cornwall's history, geology, and culture. He packs up to eight people into his van and takes them on Cornwall's twistiest back lanes to track down forgotten Neolithic monuments and Iron Age settlements. You won't see any of the big attractions listed in this book—Russ takes you way off the beaten path. The

route and specific sights covered change based on the weather and the interests of the group. This is a great way to experience the real Cornwall...away from the tourist congestion on the coast (£30/person for 4 hours, departs Penzance train station at 9:30; can also pick up near St. Ives train station at 9:10 for £5 extra; 5 or more go cheaper with £130 private tour, may also be able to pick up at your Penzance hotel, essential to book ahead by phone or email, tel. 01736/362-763, www.westerndiscoveries.co.uk, info@western discoveries.co.uk).

Boat Tours—The beautiful Cornish coast is best seen from the water, and the catamaran trips run by **Marine Discovery** are a fun way to sample it with an ecological emphasis. A variety of tours are offered, with a chance to see seals, dolphins, porpoises, seabirds, and even basking sharks (£18-35 depending on length of tour, less for kids—though some tours have age restrictions, cash only, April-Oct, may be cancelled in bad weather, depart from either Albert Pier or South Pier depending on tides, best to reserve at least 2 days ahead, tel. 01736/874-907, mobile 07749-277-110, www.marinediscovery.co.uk, info@marinediscovery .co.uk).

Sights in Penzance

Penlee House Gallery and Museum—Filling a Victorian house in Penlee Park, the gallery hosts a fine collection from painters of the local Newlyn School. These Post-Impressionists, attracted to Cornwall in the late 1800s by the quality of light and the low cost of living, painted seascapes, portraits, and scenes of daily life. The ground floor shows off rotating exhibits from the museum's permanent collection. The upstairs has more paintings and a modest museum about Penzance's prehistoric and more recent history (learn how Penzance, Newlyn, and Mousehole were burned by Spanish raiders in 1595). It's smart to call ahead, as the museum closes some or all of its galleries for a week several times a year to rearrange its collection.

    Cost and Hours: £4.50, free on Sat, open Easter-Sept Mon-Sat 10:00-17:00, Oct-Easter Mon-Sat 10:30-16:30, closed Sun year-round, last entry 30 minutes before closing, café, Morrab Road, tel. 01736/363-625, www.penleehouse.org.uk.

Waterfront Stroll to Newlyn and Mousehole—A broad pedestrian promenade follows the coast around Mount's Bay, from

Penzance to Newlyn—perfect for an early-morning or after-dinner stroll (about 30 minutes one-way). From Newlyn, a coastal footpath extends farther to Mousehole (another 30-minute walk; for more on Mousehole, see page 345). Locals say that any fishing that happens these days goes out of Newlyn.

Sleeping in Penzance

Guest Houses on Regent Terrace

Set just a block off the seashore, the upmarket guest houses on this street are central and convenient. Rooms in front usually have views of the sea, while those in back overlook a churchyard. Most breakfast rooms are downstairs on the garden level. Though they're all run by friendly proprietors, these places feel more like small hotels than B&Bs. All offer free parking, along with free Wi-Fi and Internet access to guests. Drivers should get precise directions from their hotelier in order to find the narrow and easy-to-miss Regent Terrace.

$$$ **Camilla House** is relaxed and modern, with contemporary class, neutral colors, a sophisticated black-and-white lounge, and lots of luxurious touches throughout. Friendly, helpful Simon and Susan rent eight comfy, sunny rooms, and are a great source for travel tips (Sb-£37.50, Db-£75-90 depending on size and view, 3-night minimum April-Oct if booking in advance, at #12, tel. & fax 01736/363-771, www.camillahouse.co.uk, info@camillahouse.co.uk).

$$$ **Lombard House Hotel** offers a chandeliered Georgian townhouse atmosphere. The nine rooms come with slightly older furniture and fixtures than my other listings, but the two top-floor attic rooms are cozy and have fine views (Sb-£46, Db-£92, Tb-£138, large family Qb-£138-145, at #16, tel. & fax 01736/364-897, www.lombardhousehotel.com, rita.kruge@lombardhousehotel.com, Rita and Tom).

$$$ **Warwick House** has seven fine rooms with a casually posh feel (Sb-£45, Db-£80-88, at #17, tel. & fax 01736/363-881, www.warwickhousepenzance.co.uk, enquiry@warwickhousepenzance.co.uk, Chris and Julie). They also rent a two-bedroom seafront cottage in the off-season (www.tremorvahcottage.co.uk).

$$$ **Chy-an-Mor Guest House** has nine rooms, some decorated in a vintage, French-traditional style. Tea and cakes are ready for you upon arrival (Sb-£37-42, Db-£70-90, no children under 14, closed Dec-mid-March, at #15, tel. 01736/363-441, www.chyanmor.co.uk, reception@chyanmor.co.uk, Louise and Richard).

$$$ **Blue Seas Hotel** has eight sleek, modern rooms (Sb-£40-45, Db-£80-90, check website for special discounts, closed mid-

Sleep Code

(£1 = about $1.60, country code: 44, area code: 01736)
S = Single, **D** = Double/Twin, **T** = Triple, **Q** = Quad, **b** = bathroom,
s = shower only. You can assume credit cards are accepted
and breakfast is included unless otherwise noted.

To help you sort easily through these listings, I've divided
the accommodations into three categories based on the price
for a standard double room with bath:

$$$ Higher Priced—Most rooms £75 or more.
$$ Moderately Priced—Most rooms between £50-75.
$ Lower Priced—Most rooms less than £50.

Prices can change without notice; verify the hotel's
current rates online or by email. For other updates, see www
.ricksteves.com/update.

Dec-Jan, at #13, tel. 01736/364-744, www.blueseashotel-penzance
.co.uk, info@blueseashotel-penzance.co.uk, Arnaud and Fiona).

Cheaper Options on or near Alexandra Road

Alexandra Road, about a five-minute walk down the promenade
from Regent Terrace (and therefore a bit farther from the town
center and restaurants), is lined with midrange accommodations
and a hostel. All of the below offer free Wi-Fi; additional Internet
access is available nearby at the library for a small fee.

$$ Glencree House, with eight rooms in a beautiful gran-
ite Victorian townhouse, offers charming antique furniture,
thoughtful little touches, and comparable quality to the Regent
Terrace guest houses at a slightly lower price (S-£27-37, Sb-£33-41,
Db-£58-86, Tb-£80-119, Qb-£99-135, price depends on length of
stay and season, just off Alexandra Road on quiet Mennaye Road
at #2, tel. 01736/362-026, www.glencreehouse.co.uk, stay@glen
creehouse.co.uk, Andrew and Lynsey).

$$ Chiverton House is a stone Victorian home with six small-
ish rooms packed with wood furnishings (Sb-£30-40, Db-£50-
70, cash only, just off Alexandra Road at 9 Mennaye Road, tel.
01736/332-733, www.chivertonhousebedandbreakfast.co.uk, alan
.waller@sky.com, Alan and Sally).

$ Penzance Backpackers, with 30 beds in seven rooms, is
situated in a townhouse on a B&B-studded stretch of Alexandra
Road. This is your best bet for budget dorm beds (£16 beds in
6-person dorms, D-£36, reception open 9:00-12:00 & 17:00-22:00,
no lockout, tel. 01736/363-836, www.pzbackpack.com, info@pz
backpack.com).

CORNWALL

Eating in Penzance

Wherever you eat, check the daily specials lists—most pubs serve fresh local fish and crab, along with the usual options.

On Chapel Street

This historic street, running up into town from the waterfront near Regent Terrace, has several tempting options. Eat before 19:00 to take advantage of early-bird dinner specials.

The Turks Head Pub, the oldest pub in Penzance, is a dark, low-beamed gem. It's an all-around pub, serving tasty food and local ales. This is a popular spot—so be sure to arrive early. There are dining rooms in the back and downstairs, but the pub in front is ideal for rubbing elbows with locals (£6-8 lunches, £9-18 dinners, food served Mon-Sat 11:00-22:00, Sun 12:00-21:00, on Chapel Street near intersection with Abbey Street, no street number, tel. 01736/363-093).

Admiral Benbow is a memorable tourist trap overloaded with over-the-top nautical decor—it's worth poking inside for a lesson on how a theme can be taken to the extreme (£5-8 lunches, £10-13 dinners, food served daily 12:00-14:30 & 17:30-21:30, 46 Chapel Street, tel. 01736/363-448).

Along the Promenade

The Navy Inn is a friendly, low-key pub that's equal parts traditional/nautical and modern (£4-10 meals, daily 12:00-21:30, just up Queen Street from The Promenade, tel. 01736/333-232).

The Boatshed is a modern wine bar and restaurant tucked across the road from the South Pier and just around the corner from recommended Regent Terrace accommodations (£5-7 sandwiches, £8 pizzas, £8-15 dinners, food served daily 11:00-15:00 & 18:30-21:30, The Quay, tel. 01736/368-845).

Out of Town, in Newlyn

The Smugglers Restaurant is the best option for white-tablecloth dining (dinners only). This is where locals go to celebrate special occasions. Located 1.5 miles southwest of my recommended B&Bs, it faces the harbor along the main road in Newlyn (£12-20 main dishes; summer daily 19:00-21:30; winter Wed-Sat 19:00-21:30, closed Sun-Tue; 12 Fore Street, tel. 01736/331-501). They also rent out three rooms (Db-£75-90, www.smugglersnewlyn.co.uk, smugglersnewlyn@btconnect.com, Stephen).

Penzance Connections

For connections within Cornwall, see page 329.

From Penzance by Train to: London's Paddington Station (about hourly, 5-6 hours, possible transfer in Plymouth or Newton Abbot), **Salisbury** (about hourly, 5-6 hours, 1-2 transfers), **Edinburgh** (every 1-2 hours, 10-17 hours, 1 direct, most transfer in London), **York** (every 1-2 hours, 8-11 hours, 1 direct, most transfer in London), **Exeter** (roughly hourly, 3 hours). Train info: tel. 0845-748-4950, www.nationalrail.co.uk.

By Bus to: Exeter (1-3/day, 5.5-6 hours, possible transfer in Plymouth), **Brighton** (3/day, 11.5-12 hours, transfers in Plymouth, Heathrow, or London), **Portsmouth** (2-3/day, 11-12.5 hours, transfer in Plymouth), **London** (5/day direct, 8.5-10 hours, overnight available). Bus info: tel. 0871-781-8181, www.nationalexpress.com.

St. Ives

Picturesque St. Ives enjoys three claims to fame: It's a major artists' colony, a top fun-in-the-Cornish-sun holiday destination, and

England's surfing mecca. Tourists hit the town like a tidal wave in summer (July-Sept)—when, as a local told me, "You can smell the sweat and suntan oil for miles around." An annual music and arts festival keeps things humming in September (www.stivesseptember festival.co.uk). But even in the feeding frenzy of peak season, St. Ives remains mellow. British bohemians and British surfers—two kinds of people you probably didn't expect to meet in England—both abound in St. Ives.

The town's artsy aura is nothing new. With golden light reflecting off the aquamarine waves and twisty lanes, St. Ives began to attract artists in the early 20th century. The potter Bernard Leach practiced his craft here, as did sculptor Barbara Hepworth, and both have galleries in town—along with dozens of other, lesser-known artists. (The TI assured me there are an "untold number" of galleries—and handed me two different brochures suggesting gallery-hopping routes through town.) Museum junkies will seek out St. Ives' branch of the Tate Gallery.

Orientation to St. Ives

(area code: 01736)
About half the size of Penzance, with 11,000 people, St. Ives occupies a few steep bits of land between sandy beaches. The town clusters around its sandy harbor, with a bulbous spit of land just beyond called The Island. From the quaint, waterfront old town, newer development sprawls uphill toward the main road. Thanks to its warren of convoluted lanes, small St. Ives can be difficult to navigate.

Tourist Information
The TI, tucked inside the Guildhall, narrowly avoided the budget axe in 2011 and will likely have limited hours and services in 2012 (may be open June-Sept Mon-Fri 9:00-17:00, Sat 10:00-16:00, Sun 10:00-14:00; Oct-May Mon-Fri 9:00-17:00, Sat 10:00-13:00, closed Sun; Street an Pol, tel. 01736/796-297, www.visit-west cornwall.com).

Arrival in St. Ives
By Car: St. Ives is a nightmare for drivers—parking is scarce, and the streets are congested with slow-moving pedestrians. If you dare—and if it's not too crowded—you can drive right through the heart of St. Ives. Dip down into town, pass along the harbor, then head back up the hill at the far end to reach a pay lot by The Island (near my recommended accommodations).

However, most drivers avoid the tight, pedestrian-clogged lanes by parking at the huge Trenwith parking lot above town, near the Leisure Centre (£5.50 all day until 20:00; £6.50/24 hours), and take the handy £1 shuttle into town. (To find the parking lot, just before you descend into town, follow the signs to the right with the blue *P* icon.) The shuttle lets you off in town near the movie theater (take note: this is also where you'll catch the shuttle for the return trip).

By Train or Bus: The train and bus stations are near the waterfront; just exit and walk with the sea on your right into the heart of town. To get here, you can take the cute, historic St. Ives Bay Line that runs above the coast from St. Erth to St. Ives. Catch the train in Penzance, in St. Erth, or at the park-and-ride lot at Lelant Saltings on the way to St. Ives (Traveline tel. 0871-200-2233 or tel. 0845-748-4950, www.nationalrail.co.uk). If you use the train park-and-ride, you get £1 off your Tate Gallery entry fee.

Helpful Hints
Internet Access: You can get online at the library, which is at the corner of Gabriel and Tregenna, just up from the Guildhall

(£3.60/hour, Mon and Thu-Fri 9:30-17:00, Tue 9:30-18:30, Sat 10:00-13:00, closed Wed and Sun, tel. 0300-1234-111).

Surf's Up: Find your inner dude by taking surfing lessons from **St. Ives Surf School** on Porthmeor Beach (£30/person, daily 9:30-18:00, tel. 01736/793-938, www.stivessurfschool.co.uk).

Sights in St. Ives

Art-lovers can save money by buying the Art Pass, which includes the first three sights mentioned here, plus others in Cornwall (see page 334).

Tate Gallery—St. Ives very proudly hosts a branch of the prestigious London art museum. The modern building impresses, but the collection—focusing mostly on modern works by relatively obscure local artists—can be a letdown to non-art-lovers.

Cost and Hours: £6.25, £9.75 combo-ticket includes Barbara Hepworth Museum and Sculpture Garden; March-Oct daily 10:00-17:20; Nov-Feb Tue-Sun 10:00-16:20, closed Mon; last entry 20 minutes before closing, closes periodically to change exhibits, tel. 01736/796-226, www.tate.org.uk/stives.

▲Barbara Hepworth Museum and Sculpture Garden—Many visitors find this collection more accessible than the Tate's. Barbara Hepworth was one of the first sculptors to create non-representational art (that is, totally abstract works that didn't attempt to imitate the real world), and she lived most of her life in St. Ives. This modest museum, with a sculpture garden and replica of her studio, shows off Hepworth's curvaceous, undulating forms —inspired by, if not quite resembling, the sea, wind, sand, and light of St. Ives.

Cost and Hours: £5.25, £9.75 combo-ticket includes the Tate, same hours and tel. as the Tate, at the corner of Ayr Lane and Barnoon Hill, www.tate.org.uk/stives/hepworth.

Leach Pottery Museum—This museum celebrates Bernard Leach, considered one of the founders of the mid-20th-century British studio-pottery movement. New pieces are produced on-site, and a gallery showcases work by leading contemporary potters.

Cost and Hours: £5.50; March-Oct Mon-Sat 10:00-17:00, Sun 11:00-16:00; Nov-Feb Mon-Sat 10:00-17:00, closed Sun; last entry 30 minutes before closing, Higher Stennack/B3306, tel. 01736/799-703, www.leachpottery.com.

Getting There: The studio is well-marked from the upper outskirts of St. Ives, on the road into town. From Royal Square in the center of town, it's a 15-minute walk. Or park at the Trenwith car park (described earlier under "Arrival in St. Ives"); the studio is a six-minute walk from there (disabled parking only at the studio). In summer, a frequent shuttle (£1) usually runs between the studio and the town center.

Stroll the Town—Besides gallery-hopping, the best way to enjoy St. Ives is by taking an ice-cream cone on a waterfront stroll. The slate-tile-clad High Street and pleasant waterfront have plenty of shops and ice-cream stands to entertain even the pickiest kids. Boats departing from the harbor can take you on trips around the cliffs and to the coves, a good way to appreciate why the Cornish coast was so popular with bootleggers and pirates.

Hit the Beach—St. Ives is popular with Brits on a "bucket-and-spade" holiday because it's surrounded by sandy beaches. In addition to the sandy, central harbor—home to boats as well as swimmers—you'll find family-friendly Porthminster Beach (west) and surfer-friendly Porthmeor Beach (east). Tiny, secluded Porthgwidden Beach—hiding between the rocks under the high peninsula called The Island—is worth the hike.

Sleeping in St. Ives

(£1 = about $1.60, country code: 44, area code: 01736)
The town's charm wears thin with the hordes of tourists in high season, but the evenings are quiet enough to consider staying over. Both of these options are in tight, twisty old buildings—climbing to your room can feel like spiraling up through a ship's hull.

$$$ Cornerways rents six rooms with lots of grays, blacks, and exposed beams. It's got a smooth nautical-meets-contemporary vibe, with easygoing Tim at the helm (Sb-£40-60, Db-£80-95, cheaper off-season, free Wi-Fi, 1 Bethesda Place, tel. 01736/796-706, mobile 07815-796-706, www.cornerwaysstives.com, cornerwaysstives@aol.com).

$$$ The Anchorage has four cozy rooms and claustrophobic ceilings (S-£40-80, Db-£75-100, 5 Bunkers Hill, tel. 01736/797-135, mobile 07977-928-540, www.anchoragestives.co.uk, info @anchoragestives.co.uk, Christopher).

Eating in St. Ives

Opening times for most St. Ives eateries can change from one day to the next, depending on weather and crowds.

Along the Harborfront: The main drag along the harbor has plenty of dining options. Peruse the menus and views, and choose your favorite. I ate well at **Café Coast,** with tasty and well-priced fusion cuisine (English, Thai, and Italian) and a nicely sleek, contemporary, sea-view ambience (£8-12 pizzas, pastas, and main dishes; daily 9:00-16:00 & 17:30-22:00, right on the harborfront Wharf Street, tel. 01736/794-925).

Above Porthmeor Beach: Across the street from the Tate Gallery, the **Porthmeor Beach Café** is suspended above this popular surfing beach (£6-9 sandwiches, tapas, salads, and pizzas; £10-15 dinners, daily 9:00-21:00, tel. 01736/793-366).

On Fore Street: Running parallel to the harbor one block inland, Fore Street is lined with tourist shops and some good budget eateries. Near the corner of Salubrious Place, follow the heavenly scent to the **Cornish Bakehouse** for traditional Cornish pasties (daily 9:00-19:00, tel. 01736/793-632). Just around the corner, **The Dolphin** has good fish-and-chips to take away. Or, for about £1 more, you can eat upstairs, with a sea view—the server will hoist your food up the dumbwaiter for you (tel. 01736/795-701).

On Fish Street: Just up the hill from the harbor and the landmark Sloop Inn, **Saltwater** is a small but upscale place, serving Mediterranean-inspired seafood dishes (£13-16 main dishes, Tue-Sat 18:30-21:30, closed Sun-Mon, smart to reserve, 14 Fish Street, tel. 01736/794-928).

And for Dessert: You'll see places hawking "Cornish Ice Cream"—the frozen version of clotted cream, which means it's much creamier than the norm. For something deliciously different, try the lavender-and-honey flavor.

St. Ives Connections

The **bus** is more practical than the train for most connections. The most useful lines are #17 and #17A to Penzance; #17B to Penzance via Marazion (St. Michael's Mount); and #300 to Land's End and Penzance (via Geevor Tin Mine, Sennen Cove, and Marazion, plus Porthcurno late-May-late Aug only). For details, see page 330.

All **train** connections from St. Ives to points eastward go through St. Erth, where you'll switch from the cute little St. Ives Bay Line to the main line to Penzance (see "Penzance Connections" on page 339).

The Penwith Peninsula

The western tip of Cornwall, called the Penwith Peninsula, is a virtual pincushion of worthwhile stops. Literally meaning "headland," Penwith features rugged, rocky, windblown scenery and the best-preserved bits of traditional Cornish culture. With Penzance or St. Ives as a home base, all of the following destinations are within easy striking distance for a day trip. I've listed them roughly clockwise from Penzance (the first sight, St. Michael's Mount, is east of—and visible from—Penzance). Drivers: Note that B3315

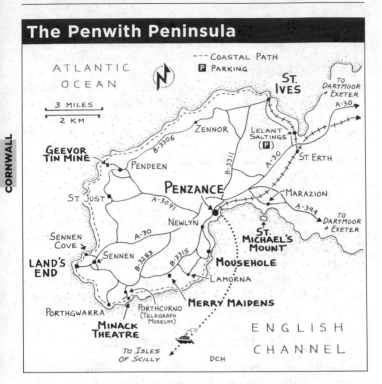

The Penwith Peninsula

- - - COASTAL PATH
P PARKING

ATLANTIC OCEAN

ST. IVES

TO DARTMOOR + EXETER

A-30

3 MILES
2 KM

ZENNOR

LELANT SALTINGS (P)

B-3306

GEEVOR TIN MINE

PENDEEN

ST. ERTH

PENZANCE

MARAZION

ST. JUST

A-3071

A-394

TO DARTMOOR + EXETER

NEWLYN

ST. MICHAEL'S MOUNT

SENNEN COVE

A-30

B-3283

B-3315

MOUSEHOLE

LAND'S END

SENNEN

LAMORNA

PORTHGWARRA

PORTHCURNO (TELEGRAPH MUSEUM)

MERRY MAIDENS

ENGLISH

MINACK THEATRE

CHANNEL

TO ISLES OF SCILLY

DCH

travels west from Penzance, passing the Merry Maidens stone circle and Porthcurno en route to Land's End.

St. Michael's Mount

Similar to France's Mont St. Michel, but on a smaller scale, this dramatic rock island has been inhabited for 1,500 years. Originally a Benedictine monastery, the castle was built up by the St. Aubyn family, who still own it today in partnership with the National Trust. If the tide is out, a pedestrian causeway connects the island to the town of Marazion. Otherwise, a short ride in a motorboat (£1.50 each way) will bring you up to the lower gates. A steep and rocky path curves its way up to the castle entrance.

Once inside, the castle is surprisingly petite. The most interesting rooms are the chapel (probably part of the original monastery) and the Chevy Chase room (which will disappoint *Saturday Night Live* fans). Family portraits, some as recent as 1993, adorn the walls. Contrary to popular belief, most of England's castles are now owned by the state or by charities. The Great Depression bankrupted many noble English families, who were forced to sell off family estates and heirlooms. This is one of the few open to the public that has remained associated with the same family since the Middle Ages.

Out on the terrace, views of the Penwith Peninsula are grand, and they get even better when you climb the tower. The windswept gardens below the castle are worth a look for die-hard gardeners.

Locals claim that Jesus Christ visited Cornwall during his teen years. Supposedly he landed here at St. Michael's Mount, then traveled up to Glastonbury (near Bath). While this might seem patently bogus, natives persuasively insist that it could have happened: Joseph of Arimathea, who was a wealthy disciple of Jesus, was also a metal trader. He might have brought Jesus to this metal-rich peninsula on a business trip. All that we know of Jesus' life between his adolescence and age 30 is that he traveled in the "wilderness"...which Britain (and most of Europe) certainly was at that time.

Cost and Hours: Castle and garden-£8.75, castle only-£7, garden only-£3.50; castle open late March-Oct Sun-Fri 10:30-17:00, closed Sat, last entry 45 minutes before closing; Nov-late March castle tours run from the mount's café "when tides and weather are favourable," usually Tue and Fri at 11:00 and 14:00—call to confirm; garden open May-June Mon-Fri 10:30-17:00, July-Sept Thu-Fri only 10:30-17:00, closed off-season; tel. 01736/710-507, ferry and tide info tel. 01736/710-265, www.stmichaelsmount.co.uk.

Getting There: Buses #2, #2A, #17B, and #300 run from Penzance to Marazion, from which you can walk or catch the boat to St. Michael's Mount (£1.50, Mon-Sat 2/hour, Sun every 1-2 hours, 10 minutes). Drivers can park in either of two waterfront parking lots (£3, fee charged 9:00-20:00).

Eating at St. Michael's Mount: For a convenient and good lunch option, try the mount's café or restaurant.

Mousehole

Tiny and salty as a barnacle on a sloop, Mousehole (MOW-zle) is adorable. Mousehole is typical of the many charming and now touristy fishing villages that sugar this coastline. It's famous for smuggling, for fishing, and for being the last place where the pre-Roman language of Cornish was spoken. Today, Mousehole harvests more tourists than fish. The little harbor maintains a small fleet, but was busier in the past. The tiny passage out of the harbor is said to be what gave the town its curious name. The best time to enjoy the simple charm of Mousehole is early in the day, when it's enhanced by fresh sea air and noisy seagulls. The beachside path from Newlyn makes an excellent 30-minute stroll (described on page 335). Drivers might want to skip Mousehole's maddeningly narrow and twisty lanes.

Getting There: Buses #6 and #6A go from Penzance to Newlyn, then on to Mousehole (1-2/hour, 10 minutes to Newlyn, 20 minutes to Mousehole). Buses #5 and #5A from Penzance also serve Newlyn. Bus #504 provides similar but less frequent service to Newlyn (Mon-Fri 4/day, Sat 3/day, none on Sun, 10 minutes) and Mousehole (Mon-Sat 3-4/day, none on Sun, 15 minutes).

Merry Maidens Stone Circle

In ancient times, stone circles had some sort of significant purpose—probably as a site for religious ceremonies, as a community meeting place, or, most famously, as a calendar. This particular stone circle, far simpler than the famous ones at Stonehenge and Avebury, is a reminder that the Penwith Peninsula was inhabited in the Neolithic Age (roughly 2000 B.C. or earlier). The story behind the name, most likely concocted in

the Middle Ages, goes like this: A group of village women decided to go into the fields on the Sabbath for some merriment and dancing. This displeased God, who turned the women to stone to serve as a warning to others.

Getting There: The Merry Maidens are in a grassy field just off B3315 (on the way from Penzance to Land's End). They're easy to miss if you're driving. Coming from Penzance, after passing through Boleigh, look for a pullout on the left near three gates; you'll also see a bus stop and a low-profile stone marker, and, on the right, a green arrow pointing across the road with a faded *Merry Maidens* sign. If you don't have a car, bus #504 takes you from Penzance to the Merry Maidens (Mon-Sat 2/day, none on Sun, 30 minutes).

Porthcurno

This humdrum hamlet, just off B3315 between Penzance and Land's End, has two worthwhile sights.

▲**Minack Theatre**—For good Cornish theater, try the Minack. This local open-air theater has just about the most spectacular setting of any place—theater or otherwise—in England. This gorgeously landscaped facility can seat up to 750 theatergoers. With seats actually carved into a rocky cliff and a terrace stage perched hundreds of feet over the sea, the Minack is quite a sight. Imagine watching *The Tempest* with only the sunset and crashing waves for scenery. If you aren't a theater buff or don't happen to be here dur-

ing the theater season, the site is still worth a visit for the unbeatable views of the rocky cliffs. The small exhibit on the history of the Minack includes a short video on Rowena Cade, the visionary theater-lover who persevered to build it. There's also a cliff-hanging coffee house.

Cost and Hours: You can visit the theater just to see it (£4; May-Sept daily 9:30-17:30—except Wed and Fri mid-May-Sept, when it closes at 11:30 for a matinee; call ahead or check website for other sporadic closures; Oct-April daily 10:00-16:00; last entry 30 minutes before closing), or you can attend a **performance** during peak season (£8-9.50, £1 booking fee if you use a credit/debit card, performances generally mid-May-mid-Sept, usually Mon-Fri at 20:00, also Wed and Fri at 14:00, rarely cancelled but dress for the weather, tel. 01736/810-181, www.minack.com).

Getting There: The theater is up an extremely narrow and twisty road above Porthcurno, well-signed from town, with free parking. From Penzance, bus #504 goes to the theater (2/day Mon-Sat only, none on Sun, 50 minutes). If you're willing to hike, you can also take buses #1A or #300 from Penzance to the stop in Porthcurno, with a steep, quarter-mile uphill climb to the theater (#1A runs Mon-Sat 4/day, Sun 2/day, 40 minutes; #300 goes daily 4/day late May-late Aug only, 40 minutes). During the summer, the last bus #1A leaves Porthcurno for Penzance after the show, at 23:00 (Mon-Sat only).

Telegraph Museum—In 1870, a telegraph cable was laid from Porthcurno to India. By the time World War II broke out, 14 cables tethered this village to the rest of the world. In 1940, defensive tunnels were built to protect the telegraph station and cables from the Nazis—who were then just 80 miles away in France.

Today, those tunnels house a surprisingly interesting museum, tracing the history of the "Victorian Internet." You'll learn how underwater cables were made possible thanks to a new insulating material (a resin from a Malaysian tree called gutta-percha), how the cables were even more heavily armored in shallower water (where they could be damaged by the anchors of passing ships), and how ruptured cables were repaired in the briny deep. About once an hour, a docent gives a history lesson on underwater telegraphy...which, like the museum, is better than it sounds.

Cost and Hours: £6; mid-April-Oct daily 10:00-17:00, Wed until 19:30 in summer; Nov-mid-April Sun-Mon only 10:00-17:00, closed Tue-Sat; last entry one hour before closing, next to main

CORNWALL

Cornwall's Tin-Mining Legacy

Cornwall's history is tied to its tin-mining industry. While Cornwall has always been known for its metal deposits, a major tin boom began here in the mid-1700s, as new steam-engine-powered pumps allowed tin to be mined below the water table. The industry peaked 200 years ago, when tin was the cutting edge of technology, and Cornwall was the Silicon Valley of Britain.

Miners would climb down into the narrow shafts, and use a hammer and a long bit to slowly drive deep, skinny holes into a vein of tin. Then they'd insert sticks of dynamite. Before safety fuses were invented, quills from bird feathers were used as fuses, so miners setting off gunpowder never knew how much time they had to reach safety before the explosion.

Deadly cave-ins were frequent. These were supposedly caused by mischievous Tommyknockers, Cornish pixies similar to leprechauns. But these mysterious creatures might simply have been a creation of the oxygen-starved imaginations of exhausted miners.

Mines employed the notorious "company store" system, where workers were paid in tokens that could only be redeemed at the store run by the mine (an obvious conflict of interest—which always worked to the company's advantage). To save money, miners made their own "hardhats." They'd take a felt hat and harden it by dipping it alternately in hot tree resin and soil. Then they'd stick a candle on the brim for light while they worked. Since miners had to buy their own candles (from the company store, of course), they'd extinguish them during their lunch break to make them last longer.

After working all morning underground, Cornish tin miners looked forward to their traditional lunch of a **pasty** (PASS-tee).

parking lot in Porthcurno on the road up to Minack Theater—look for big white building marked *Museum*, tel. 01736/810-966, www .porthcurno.org.uk.

Getting There: Buses #1A and #504 from Penzance stop in Porthcurno near the museum (Mon-Sat 4-6/day, Sun 2/day, 40 minutes), as does #300 (daily late May-late Aug only, 4/day, 40 minutes).

Land's End

The westernmost point in all of England should seem like a desolate, rugged place. In reality, it's a tacky tourist trap where greedy businesses have chewed up whatever small bit of charm or authenticity this place might once have had. As you approach, you'll see endless signs bragging "the last" (or, in a too-cute spin, "the first and last")...everything: inn, hotel, refreshment stand, postal box, and so on. Come here only if you want to be able to say you've been

Basically a beef stew wrapped in a pastry crust, pasties had a thick, crimped edge that miners could grab with dirty hands without contaminating their food. Because real flour was expensive, early miners skimped by using barley wheat—making for a very tough package. Leftover chunks of dough were often dropped into the mineshaft to appease the Tommyknockers.

Originally a pasty would be filled half with stew, and the rest with dessert, such as jam or apples. Nowadays there's a nice variety of flavors, like lamb and mint, but the full meal deal is rare. The British government is currently seeking trademark protection from the European Union for the Cornish pasty. That means the name could only be applied to those pasties made in Cornwall using traditional techniques and recipes (www.cornishpasty association.co.uk). Look for pasties all over Cornwall, even in posh St. Ives. One of the best places is McFadden and Sons Butchers in St. Just, near Geevor Tin Mine (see page 350).

Other than savory pasties, the crumbling smokestacks that dot the landscape today are the only remnants of Cornwall's now-dead tin mining industry, which couldn't compete with cheap tin from Asia and South America. The ground underfoot is still honeycombed with forgotten tin mines. Older Cornish natives can still remember being in their houses and hearing the miners working underground.

CORNWALL

to Land's End. (Consider lying.)

If you do visit, pay the £4 parking fee (enforced 24 hours/day; coins required 17:00-9:00) and walk straight from the parking lot through the low-budget theme park (stop at your own risk) out to the viewpoint. This was once considered the end of the civilized world, the last (or first) thing to be seen by departing (or arriv-

ing) ships. After gazing at the sea and guessing how far away from home you are, find out how close you were by checking your hometown at the picture stand on the right. For £11-14, they'll take your photo with a personalized signpost and mail it to you (tel. 01736/741-222, theme park tel. 0871-720-0044, www.landsend-landmark.co.uk).

"Back Door" Approach to Land's End: To appreciate the majesty of this location while avoiding the tourist logjam, consider hiking in from nearby **Sennen Cove.** From the road just north of Land's End, turn off to drive down the steep and narrow road into the village of Sennen, then park at the harbor (where the road dead-ends at the end of town). It's a steep, uphill, but rewarding one-mile hike over the windswept headlands to Land's End, following the South West Coast Path, Britain's longest national trail (for a description, see www.southwestcoastpath.com).

Getting There: Buses #1, #1A, #300, and #504 connect Penzance with Land's End (Mon-Sat every 1-2 hours, Sun every 2 hours, 40 minutes-2.5 hours), while #300 and #504 also stop at Sennen Cove (#300—daily, 4/day, 50 minutes; #504—2/day, none on Sun, 1.5 hours).

▲Geevor Tin Mine

Once 2,100 feet deep and extending almost a mile under the ocean, the Geevor Mine closed in 1990. Today, it's been converted into a museum, but it retains most of its original buildings and machinery. Exploring the remnants of this recently defunct industry—which for centuries was an integral part of Cornish life—you'll gain an appreciation for the simple, noble life of miners. Even if you're not into heavy metal, this unique look at tin mining is fascinating—and worth ▲▲▲ to those interested in engineering.

Cost and Hours: £9.75, Easter-Oct Sun-Fri 9:00-17:00, Nov-Easter Sun-Fri 9:00-16:00, last entry one hour before closing, closed Sat year-round; self-guided "free flow" visits in summer, but guided tours at 11:00, 13:00, and 15:00 in winter; wear good shoes, pick up the free map at entry to follow the route, café, tel. 01736/788-662, www.geevor.com.

Getting There: It's just off the B3306 road along the north coast of Penwith. Or, if you're driving in from the A30 Penzance bypass, take A3071 to St. Just and follow the brown *Historic Mining Area* signs. Take the right fork on B3318 to Pendeen, turn left at the crossroads to drive through Pendeen, and turn right at the Geevor entrance. You can also get here on buses #10A and #300 from Penzance, or #300 from St. Ives and Land's End (buy combo-ticket for bus plus mine entry from driver).

Touring the Mine: Put on your hard hat and wander through the **museum.** A short film explains the tin-mining process, and a giant model, once used to help engineers keep track of the network of shafts, makes it clear how extensive the mining industry was here.

Then head **outside,** where you'll walk from shed to shed to see the various parts of the day-to-day workings of the mine. The two-story Hard Rock museum features exhibits for all ages about mining and the rocks that harbor valuable ores. The most interesting area is "The Dry," where the miners showered, changed, and dried their uniforms between shifts. Though it closed almost two decades ago, it feels as though the miners could show up at any time to clock in. Enjoy the old time-punch clock, the fun stickers on the miners' lockers, and graffiti showing their sense of humor (such as the *Ear Protection Must Be Worn* sign posted next to the toilets). In "The Mill," you'll see how a vast warehouse of "shaking tables"—like giant machines panning for gold—separated the miners' haul into its useable parts.

The finale is a half-hour **underground tour** of an 18th-century mine (which predates the more recent mine that the current buildings supported, and was discovered by modern miners). A docent, often a former mine employee, gives you a coverall and leads you in. The mines—narrow and low (you'll be hunched for most of the tour, and claustrophobes will be miserable)—give you a sense of the difficult life of miners and the perilous conditions under which they worked.

Eating near the Mine: You can get hot, authentic, delicious Cornish pasties on the main square of the humble town of St. Just, at **McFadden and Sons Butchers** (Mon-Sat 8:00-17:00, until 16:00 in winter, closed Sun, 11 Market Square, tel. 01736/788-136). For more on pasties, see the sidebar.

Isles of Scilly

Just off the coast of Cornwall, this group of islands (pronounced "silly") sits right in the path of the Gulf Stream. The warm (or at least warmer) climate is perfect for growing a wide variety of exotic plants, so the islands boast plenty of gardens to visit. But half the fun is getting there: A fleet of old, creaky, Penzance-based **helicopters** is ready to whisk you to precarious heights (£99-179 round-trip depending on time, season, and ticket type, 20-minute flight, Mon-Sat year-round, no flights Sun or winter holidays, £3 shuttle from Penzance train station to heliport 45 minutes before each flight, tel. 01736/363-871, www.islesofscillyhelicopter.com). Alternatively, you can take a very slow **boat** called the *Scillonian III* from Penzance (£30-35 same-day return, £47.50 one-way, £95 round-trip, 2.75 hours each way, sporadic schedule but generally departs Mon-Sat at 9:15 in summer from the Penzance Quay/ Lighthouse Pier, no boats Nov-mid-March, tel. 0845-710-5555, www.ios-travel.co.uk). The boat company also runs **planes** out to the islands from the Land's End airport (£70-90 same-day return, £70 one-way, £125-140 round-trip, 15-minute flight).

East Cornwall

These destinations are a bit farther from Penzance, and closer to Dartmoor National Park (see previous chapter). I've listed them from farthest to nearest to Penzance. Consider visiting them in this order as you approach the tip of Cornwall.

▲▲Tintagel Castle

Wild, rocky, remote, and romantic, Tintagel (tin-TAD-jell) is as dramatic as a castle can be. The real King Arthur—if he actually

existed—was supposedly born here and ruled his lands from this rocky point. While the popular tales of Camelot are flights of fantasy, they may be based on a real person. Even though there's no physical record of King Arthur (other than a pottery shard discovered in the 1990s),

the verbal tradition is strong enough that experts think a fifth- or sixth-century ruler by that name probably lived in this area, possibly basing himself in modern Camelford (which might be where "Camelot" comes from). Regardless of whether Arthur is fact or fiction, windblown Tintagel Castle is striking. If you can handle lots of steep hiking up and down, this is one of England's most rewarding ruined-castle experiences. And as a bonus, you get to enjoy a spectacularly scenic stretch of Cornish coastline. Bring a picnic to have lunch with a view, or eat at the on-site café.

Cost and Hours: £5.50; daily April-Sept 10:00-18:00, Oct 10:00-17:00; Nov-March Sat-Sun 10:00-16:00, closed Mon-Fri; tel. 01840/770-328, www.english-heritage.org.uk.

Information: For the full story, invest in the TI's £4 illustrated guidebook. It's keyed to numbered plaques around the site (which I've also made use of in my self-guided tour, below).

Getting There: The castle clings to the coast below the tacky town of Tintagel. If you're arriving by car, look for *Tintagel* signs from A39 as it passes through Camelford. Once you enter town, take your pick of parking lots, then hike down the steep road to the main entrance at the rocky bay. Or, if you prefer, take the Land Rover shuttle (£2 each way, runs continuously April-Oct). By public transportation from Penzance, it's a three- to four-hour journey, involving a train and two buses: Take a train from Penzance to Bodmin Parkway, then bus #555 to Wadebridge, where you catch bus #594 to Tintagel (for specifics, call 0871-200-2233, or use the journey planner at www.travelinesw.com). For bus info, contact Western Greyhound (tel. 01637/871-871, www.westerngreyhound.com).

❸ **Self-Guided Tour:** The main part of the castle is on what's called The Island (actually a rocky peninsula attached by a narrow spit; take care on the 100-plus steps); nearby, on the mainland, is a separate section called the Mainland Courtyard. Here are the highlights:

After buying your ticket at the main entrance, watch the good seven-minute **film** called *Searching for King Arthur,* which considers the historical and legendary underpinnings of this evocative site.

Next, head up to the viewpoint overlooking the cove. As you

approach the bridge, look for the hole in the cliff below the ruins—supposedly **Merlin's cave.** (If the tide is out, you can climb down to explore the famous wizard's former home...and ponder how he managed to keep the carpet dry and prevent seals from climbing on the furniture.)

Now look up to the top of the giant chunk of rock above Merlin's cave. Appreciate the naturally fortified, easily defensible position of this rock-top castle. Note the narrow and difficult approach to this hunk of land, and you can understand why Tintagel—meaning "fortress with narrow entrance"—is aptly named.

Head up the steps and cross the footbridge, then tackle the very steep climb up to the top of the cliffs, or **The Island.** We'll do a roughly counterclockwise spin around these grounds.

As you enter through the back door, you reach the **Island Courtyard**—castle remnants dating from the Middle Ages (with a *3* plaque). Rather than belonging to Arthur (who would have lived centuries earlier), these structures were built for the brother of a 13th-century king. Notice that the walls are made of stacked sheets of slate, which was mined on this site for many years.

Continue through the ruins and up to the viewpoint platform (marked with a *4* plaque). All around you—including directly below—you'll see the foundations of ruined **Dark Age houses,** which actually date from the time when Arthur most likely lived (the fifth century A.D.). Here archaeologists have found remains of items from as far away as North Africa and the Eastern

Mediterranean—evidence of the wealth and status of this castle's owner.

Climb on up to the top of The Island. As you explore, you'll come across several interesting sites. In the walled area called the **garden** (marked *5*), medieval residents could relax and entertain visitors in the summer. The **well** (marked *8*) was the source of water in the Middle Ages, and remains today's last resort in case of fire. The 11th-century **chapel** (marked *10*) is recognizable for the altar at its far end. If you have time, linger up here. The craggy peaks across the tops of the cliffs make a perfect, windblown picnic spot.

After the chapel, you'll head back down the steep steps to the footbridge. From here, for extra credit, consider hiking up the steps across the bridge to the **Mainland Courtyard,** with more medieval remains. If you decide to climb up, you can take a much less steep path behind this courtyard back down to rejoin the main path up the valley.

▲The Eden Project

Set in an abandoned china-clay mine, the Eden Project is an ambitious and futuristic work-in-progress—a theme park of global gardening with an environmental conscience. Exotic plants from all over the world are showcased in two giant biomes, reputedly the largest greenhouses in the world. The displays focus on sustainable farming and eco-conscious planting, but the most interesting thing here is the sheer audacity of the idea. If you're looking for a quaint English cottage garden, this isn't it. Rather than a flowery look at  England's past, this "global garden" gives you a sense of how the shrinking of the world will affect us in the future.

Cost and Hours: £20, discounts for booking online or arriving by public transport, daily mid-March-Oct 9:00-18:00, Nov-mid-March 10:00-16:30, last entry 1.5 hours before closing, domes can close as early as 15:00 for private events and off-season—check online or call first to confirm closing time, cafés, tel. 01726/811-911, www.edenproject.com.

Crowd Alert: The Eden Project is popular and can be crowded, especially on rainy days and weekdays June-Aug (they told me "wet Wednesdays" are the worst). During peak-of-peak times, you may have to wait up to an hour to get in. To avoid this, consider arriving after 13:00.

Getting There: Drivers will find the Eden Project well-signposted from both A30 and A39—you'll be directed to A391, and follow signs from there. Park at one of the many outlying lots, note your parking lot's fruity symbol, then walk down into the Project (or take the free park-and-ride shuttle bus). By public transit, first take the train to St. Austell, where you'll meet hourly bus #101 (daily, tel. 0871-200-2233 or 0845-600-1420, www.firstgroup .com) or #527 (Mon-Sat hourly, Sun 5/day, tel. 01637/871-871, www .westerngreyhound.com). Buses meet most arriving trains for the 20-minute run to the complex (ask driver about combo-ticket for bus and entry fee).

Touring the Eden Project: After buying your ticket, zigzag down into the pit and work your way through the various exhibits, including the enormous, hot, and hazy Rainforest Biome (where my camera completely fogged up; you can seek relief in an air-conditioned hut about halfway through); the smaller and more arid Mediterranean Biome; an eatery-filled walkway connecting them called The Link; The Core, with educational exhibits; and lots of gardens. A land train and an elevator from The Core make it easier to get back up to the visitors center when you're done. Kid-oriented programs, rock and pop concerts, and other special events run throughout the year.

It's an impressive concept, and the biomes are striking. But the educational exhibits are a bit too conceptual to be effective—leaving the whole, expensive experience feeling somehow unmoored.

Gardens near Falmouth

Cornwall has many wonderful gardens, some with subtropical varieties of plants that thrive in this mild climate (www.great gardensofcornwall.co.uk). These two gardens are a few miles apart on the same backcountry road, just south of Falmouth.

Getting There: If you're driving, take A39 or A394 into Falmouth until you see brown-and-white *Garden* signs—track these closely for four miles through the countryside to the gardens (Glendurgan is the better-signed of the two). If you're without a car, take buses #500 or #535 from Falmouth toward Helston (15-30 minutes, tel. 01637/871-871, www.westerngreyhound.com or Traveline tel. 0871-200-2233, www.travelinesw.com).

Sleeping near the Gardens: To maximize your time exploring the gardens, consider spending the night in salty Falmouth, a tidy harbor town nestled near the Tudor fortress of Pendennis Castle. **$$$ Greenbank Hotel** is right on the water with a seagull-eye's view of the many boats moored in the Fal Estuary. Look near the hotel lobby for displays about Kenneth Grahame, who wrote parts of *The Wind in the Willows* while staying here (Db-£119-195, check for online deals, Internet access, free Wi-Fi, Harbourside, tel. 01326/312-440, fax 01326/211-362, www.greenbank-hotel .co.uk, reception@greenbank-hotel.co.uk).

▲Trebah Garden—The "Garden of Dreams" at Trebah (TREE-bah) is a lush and tropical spectacle. Set on 26 acres that bunny-hop down a ravine to the beach below, this tropical garden is an unexpected treat. While most of England suffers from chilly arctic air, the Cornish peninsula is bathed in warmer air from the Gulf Stream—making average temperatures here much milder (the sea here never drops below 50 degrees Fahrenheit). Palms, succulents, bamboo, large azaleas, giant rhubarbs, and the prehistoric-looking gunnera might make you think (or wish) that you're in the tropics rather than in Cornwall. The garden's exoticism

impresses even non-gardeners. While garden-lovers wander in ecstasy, history buffs can ponder the fact that the beach below was used by some US troops in World War II to launch the D-Day attack on Omaha Beach.

Cost and Hours: £8 March-Oct, £4 Nov-Feb, show bus ticket for discount, open daily 10:00-17:00, until dusk in winter, last entry 30 minutes before closing, colorful year-round but flowers are best late March and April, café, tel. 01326/252-200, www.trebahgarden.co.uk.

Glendurgan Garden—Just up the road from Trebah, Glendurgan has a smaller collection of tropical plants mingled with more traditional English garden fare. Similarly set in a broad basin angled to the sea, Glendurgan is bigger but less striking than its neighbor. However, it comes with an extensive, kid-friendly hedge maze (about waist-high—but still entertaining—for an adult), built by the former owner to amuse his 12 children. Gardeners may appreciate its good orchids and its small "Holy Bank" of biblical-themed plants. And down at the seashore, the fishing hamlet of Durgan makes it feel less like just an overblown backyard for aristocrats.

Cost and Hours: £6.50, worthwhile £3.50 map/guide, mid-Feb-Oct Tue-Sat 10:30-17:30, closed Sun-Mon except Aug when it's open Mon, closed Nov-mid-Feb, last entry 30 minutes before closing, best in spring, café, tel. 01326/250-906 or 01326/252-020, www.nationaltrust.org.uk.

BATH

The best city to visit within easy striking distance of London is Bath—just a 1.5-hour train ride away. Two hundred years ago, this city of 85,000 was the trendsetting Hollywood of Britain. If ever a city enjoyed looking in the mirror, Bath's the one. It has more "government-listed" or protected historic buildings per capita than any other town in England. The entire city, built of the creamy warm-tone limestone called "Bath stone," beams in its cover-girl complexion. An architectural chorus line, it's a triumph of the Neoclassical style of the Georgian era—named for the four Georges who sat as England's king from 1714 to 1830. Proud locals remind visitors that the town is routinely banned from the "Britain in Bloom" contest to give other towns a chance to win. Bath's narcissism is justified. Even with its mobs of tourists (2 million per year) and greedy prices, Bath is a joy to visit.

Bath's fame began with the allure of its (supposedly) healing hot springs. Long before the Romans arrived in the first century, Bath was known for its warm waters. Romans named the popular spa town Aquae Sulis, after a local Celtic goddess. The town's importance carried through Saxon times, when it had a huge church on the site of the present-day abbey and was considered the religious capital of Britain. Its influence peaked in 973 with King Edgar's sumptuous coronation in the abbey. Later, Bath prospered as a wool town.

Bath then declined until the mid-1600s, wasting away to just a huddle of huts around the abbey, with hot, smelly mud and 3,000 residents, oblivious to the Roman ruins 18 feet below their dirt floors. In fact, with its own walls built upon ancient ones, Bath was no bigger than that Roman town. Then, in 1687, Queen Mary, fighting infertility, bathed here. Within 10 months she gave birth to a son...and a new age of popularity for Bath.

The revitalized town boomed as a spa resort. Ninety percent of the buildings you'll see today are from the 18th century. The classical revivalism of Italian architect Andrea Palladio inspired a local father-and-son team—both named John Wood (the Elder and the Younger)—to build a "new Rome." The town bloomed in the Neoclassical style, and streets were lined not with scrawny sidewalks but with wide "parades," upon which women in their stylishly wide dresses could spread their fashionable tails.

Beau Nash (1673-1762) was Bath's "master of ceremonies." He organized the daily social regimen of aristocratic visitors, and he made the city more appealing by lighting the streets, improving security, banning swords, and opening the Pump Room. Under his fashionable baton, Bath became a city of balls, gaming, and concerts—the place to see and be seen in England. This most civilized place became even more so with the great Neoclassical building spree that followed.

These days, modern tourism has stoked the local economy, as has the fast morning train to London. (A growing number of Bath professionals catch the 7:13 train to Paddington Station every morning.) With renewed access to Bath's soothing hot springs at the Thermae Bath Spa, the venerable waters are in the spotlight again, attracting a new generation of visitors in need of a cure or a soak.

Planning Your Time

Bath deserves two nights even on a quick trip. On a three-week Britain getaway, spend three nights in Bath, with one day for the city and one day for side-trips (see next chapter). Ideally, use Bath as your jet-lag recovery pillow, and do London at the end of your trip.

Consider starting a three-week British vacation this way:

Day 1: Land at Heathrow. Connect to Bath by National Express bus—the better option—or the less convenient bus/train combination (for details, see page 199). While you don't need or want a car in Bath, and some rental companies have an office there, those who land early and pick up their cars at the airport can visit Windsor Castle (near Heathrow) and/or Stonehenge on their way to Bath. (You can also consider flying into Bristol.) If you have the evening free in Bath, take a walking tour.

Day 2: 9:00-Tour the Roman Baths; 10:30-Catch the free city walking tour; 12:30-Picnic on the open deck of a Bath tour bus; 14:00-Free time in the shopping center of old Bath; 15:30-Tour the Fashion Museum or Museum of Bath at Work. Take the evening walking tour (unless you did last night), enjoy the Bizarre Bath comedy walk, consider seeing a play, or go for a nighttime soak in the Thermae Bath Spa.

Day 3 (and possibly 4): By car, explore nearby sights. Without a car, consider a one-day Avebury/Stonehenge/cute towns minibus tour from Bath (Mad Max tours are best; see "Tours in Bath," later).

Orientation to Bath

(area code: 01225)

Bath's town square, three blocks in front of the bus and train station, is a cluster of tourist landmarks, including the abbey, Roman and Medieval Baths, and the Pump Room. Bath is hilly. In general, you'll gain elevation as you head north from the town center.

Tourist Information

The TI is in the abbey churchyard (Mon-Sat 9:30-18:00, Sun 10:00-16:00, closes one hour earlier Mon-Sat Oct-May, pricey toll tel. 0906-711-2000—50p/minute, www.visitbath.co.uk). The TI sells various visitor guides and maps—survey your options before buying one (£1-1.50). Only the most basic visitor guide, with a very rudimentary map, is free. The TI books rooms and theater tickets for no extra fee (booking tel. 0844-847-5256). If you're a Jane Austen fan, ask about the walking tours that leave from the abbey square on weekends. Entertainment listings from the local paper are posted on the bulletin board. You can also buy the Great British Heritage Pass here (see page 20).

Arrival in Bath

The Bath Spa **train station** has a national and international ticket desk and a privately run travel agency masquerading as a TI. Directly in front of the train station is Bath's brand-new SouthGate Bath shopping center. To get from the train station to the TI, exit straight ahead, walk two blocks up Manvers Street, and turn left at the triangular "square" overlooking the riverfront park, following the small TI arrow on a signpost.

The **bus station** is west of the train station, along Dorchester Street.

My recommended B&Bs are all within a 10- to 15-minute walk or a £4-5 taxi ride from the train and bus stations.

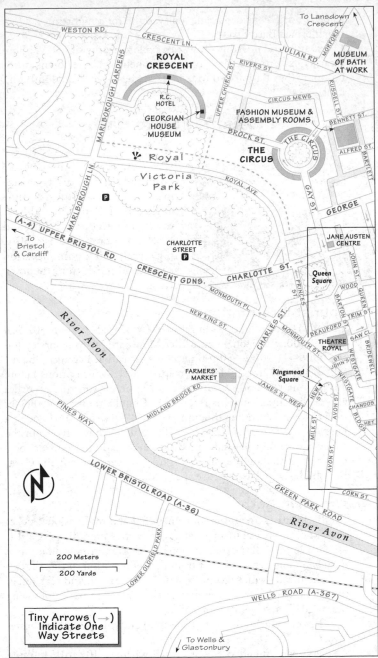

BATH

WESTON RD.

CRESCENT LN.

To Lansdown
Crescent

MORFORD

JULIAN RD.

MUSEUM
OF BATH
AT WORK

ROYAL
CRESCENT

RIVERS ST.

RUSSELL ST.

UPPER CHURCH ST.

CIRCUS MEWS

BENNETT ST.

R.C.
HOTEL

FASHION MUSEUM &
ASSEMBLY ROOMS

GEORGIAN
HOUSE
MUSEUM

BROCK ST.

THE
CIRCUS

ALFRED ST.

BARTLETT

MARLBOROUGH GARDENS

♥ Royal

THE
CIRCUS

Victoria
Park

ROYAL AVE.

GAY ST.

GEORGE

MARLBOROUGH LN.

P

JANE AUSTEN
CENTRE

(A-4) UPPER BRISTOL RD.

CHARLOTTE
STREET

Queen
Square

JOHN ST.

To
Bristol
& Cardiff

P

CHARLOTTE ST.

WOOD

QUEEN ST.

CRESCENT GDNS.

PRINCES ST.

BARTON ST.

TRIM ST.

River Avon

MONMOUTH PL.

BEAUFORD SQ.

SAW CL.

NEW KING ST.

CHARLES ST.

MONMOUTH ST.

THEATRE
ROYAL

BRIDEWELL

ST. JOHN'S PL.

WESTGATE

WESTGATE
BLDGS.

Kingsmead
Square

FARMERS'
MARKET

JAMES ST. WEST

NEW ST.

AVON ST.

CHANDOS

HET.

PINES WAY

MIDLAND BRIDGE RD.

MILK ST.

AVON ST.

N

LOWER BRISTOL ROAD (A-36)

GREEN PARK ROAD

CORN ST.

River Avon

LOWER OLDFIELD PARK

200 Meters

200 Yards

WELLS ROAD (A-367)

Tiny Arrows (→)
Indicate One
Way Streets

To Wells &
Glastonbury

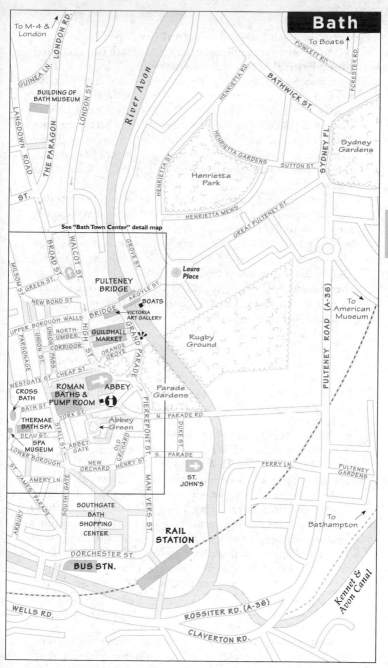

Bath

To M-4 & London

POWLETT RD.

To Boats

GUINEA LN.

LONDON RD.

FORESTER RD.

BATHWICK ST.

LANSDOWN ROAD

THE PARAGON

LONDON ST.

BUILDING OF BATH MUSEUM

River Avon

HENRIETTA RD.

SYDNEY PL.

Sydney Gardens

ST.

HENRIETTA ST.

HENRIETTA GARDENS

SUTTON ST.

Henrietta Park

HENRIETTA MEWS

GREAT PULTENEY ST.

See "Bath Town Center" detail map

BATH

MILSOM ST.

BROAD ST.

WALCOT ST.

GROVE ST.

GREEN ST.

PULTENEY BRIDGE

ARGYLE ST.

Laura Place

NEW BOND ST.

BRIDGE

BOATS

PULTENEY ROAD (A-36)

To American Museum

UPPER BOROUGH WALLS

UNION ST.

HIGH ST.

VICTORIA ART GALLERY

PARSONAGE

NORTH-UMBER.

GUILDHALL MARKET

GRAND PARADE

CORRIDOR

ORANGE GROVE

Rugby Ground

WESTGATE ST.

CHEAP ST.

CROSS BATH

ROMAN BATHS & PUMP ROOM

ABBEY

Parade Gardens

BATH ST.

PIERREPONT ST.

THERMAE BATH SPA

YORK ST.

Abbey Green

N. PARADE RD.

BEAU ST.

BALL'S

SPA MUSEUM

ABBEY-GATE

OLD ORCHARD

DUKE ST.

LOWER BOROUGH

NEW ORCHARD

HENRY ST.

S. PARADE

FERRY LN.

PULTENEY GARDENS

ST. JAMES PARADE

AMERY LN.

MAN VERS ST.

ST. JOHN'S

SOUTH GATE

SOUTHGATE BATH SHOPPING CENTER

To Bathampton

ARBURY

DORCHESTER ST.

RAIL STATION

WELLS RD.

BUS STN.

Kennet & Avon Canal

ROSSITER RD. (A-36)

CLAVERTON RD.

Helpful Hints

Festivals: The **Bath Literature Festival** is an open book March 2-11 in 2012 (www.bathlitfest.org.uk). The **Bath International Music Festival** bursts into song every spring (classical, folk, jazz, contemporary; May 30-June 10 in 2012, www.bath musicfest.org.uk), overlapped by the eclectic **Bath Fringe Festival** (theater, walks, talks, bus trips; generally similar dates to the Music Festival, www.bathfringe.co.uk). The **Jane Austen Festival** unfolds genteelly in late September (www .janeausten.co.uk/festival). And for three weeks in December, the squares around the abbey are filled with a **Christmas market.**

Bath's festival **box office** sells tickets for most events (but not for those at the Theatre Royal), and can tell you exactly what's on tonight (a block down from the TI at 2 Church Street, tel. 01225/463-362, www.bathfestivals.org.uk). The city's weekly paper, the *Bath Chronicle,* publishes a "What's On" events listing (www.thisisbath.com).

Internet Access: Ask your hotel or the TI for the closest Internet café. You can also get online at the Bath **library** (£1.20/20 minutes, slightly cheaper with free library membership, Mon 9:30-18:00, Tue-Thu 9:30-19:00, Fri-Sat 9:30-17:00, Sun 13:00-16:00, in the Podium Shopping Centre on Northgate Street near Pulteney Bridge, tel. 01225/394-041, www.bath nes.gov.uk).

Bookstore: Topping & Company, an inviting bookshop, has posters in the windows advertising frequent author readings, free coffee and tea for browsers, and tables filled with tidy stacks of carefully selected volumes (daily 9:00-20:00, near the bottom of the street called "The Paragon"—where it meets George Street, tel. 01225/428-111, www.toppingbooks.co.uk).

Laundry: The **Spruce Goose Launderette** is between the Circus and the Royal Crescent, on the pedestrian lane called Margaret's Buildings. Bring lots of £1 coins for washing and £0.20 coins for drying, as there are no change machines (self-service: about £4-5/load, daily 8:00-20:00, last load at 19:30; full-service: £12/load, Mon, Wed, Fri-Sat 8:00-12:00; tel. 01225/483-309). **Speedy Wash** can pick up your laundry anywhere in town on weekdays before 11:00 for same-day service (£12/small bag, Mon-Fri 7:30-17:30, Sat 8:30-13:00 but no pickup, closed Sun, no self-service, most hotels work with them, 4 Mile End, London Road, tel. 01225/427-616).

Car Rental: Enterprise provides a pickup service for customers to and from their hotels (extra fee for one-way rentals, at Lower Bristol Road outside Bath, tel. 01225/443-311, www.enterprise.com). Others include **Thrifty** (pickup service and one-way rentals available, in the Burnett Business Park in Keynsham—between Bath and Bristol, tel. 01179/867-997, www.thrifty.co.uk), **Hertz** (one-way rentals possible, at Windsor Bridge, tel. 0843/309-3004, www.hertz.co.uk), and **National/Europcar** (one-way rentals available, £7 by taxi from the train station, at Brassmill Lane—go west on Upper Bristol Road, tel. 01225/481-982 or 01761/479-205). Skip **Avis**—it's a mile from the Bristol train station; you'd need to rent a car to get there. Most offices close Saturday afternoon and all day Sunday, which complicates weekend pickups. Ideally, take the train or bus from downtown London to Bath, and rent a car as you leave Bath.

Parking: Parking in the city center is difficult. Short-term street parking is available but pricey (about £2.50/hour, 2-hour maximum, buy pay-and-display tickets from machine). You'll pay less per hour in long-stay lots (figure £9/24 hours; the Charlotte Street car park is handy). For more info on parking, visit www.bathnes.gov.uk/bathnes.

Tours in Bath

▲▲▲**Walking Tours**—Free two-hour tours are led by **The Mayor's Corps of Honorary Guides,** volunteers who want to share their love of Bath with its many visitors (as the city's mayor first did when he took a group on a guided walk back in the 1930s). These chatty, historical, and gossip-filled walks are essential for your understanding of this town's amazing Georgian social scene. How else would you learn that the old "chair ho" call for your sedan chair evolved into today's "cheerio" farewell? Tours leave from outside the Pump Room in the abbey churchyard (free, no tips, year-round Sun-Fri at 10:30 and 14:00, Sat at 10:30 only; additional evening walks May-Sept Tue and Fri at 19:00; tel. 01225/477-411, www.bathguides.org.uk). Tip for theatergoers: When your guide stops to talk outside the Theatre Royal, skip out for a moment, pop into the box office, and see about snaring a great deal on a play for tonight.

For a **private tour,** call the local guides' bureau, Bath Parade Guides (£60/2 hours, tel. 01225/337-111, www.bathparadeguides .co.uk, bathparadeguides@yahoo.com). For **Ghost Walks** and **Bizarre Bath** tours, see "Nightlife in Bath," later.

▲▲**City Bus Tours**—City Sightseeing's hop-on, hop-off bus tours zip through Bath. Jump on a bus anytime at one of 17 signposted pickup points, pay the driver, climb upstairs, and hear recorded commentary about Bath. City Sightseeing has two

Bath at a Glance

▲▲▲**Walking Tours** Free top-notch tours, helping you make the most of your visit, led by The Mayor's Corps of Honorary Guides. **Hours:** Sun-Fri at 10:30 and 14:00, Sat at 10:30 only; additional evening walks offered May-Sept Tue and Fri at 19:00. See page 363.

▲▲▲**Roman and Medieval Baths** Ancient baths that gave the city its name, tourable with good audioguide. **Hours:** Daily July-Aug 9:00-22:00, March-June and Sept-Oct 9:00-18:00, Nov-Feb 9:30-17:30. See page 367.

▲▲**The Circus and the Royal Crescent** Stately Georgian (Neoclassical) buildings from Bath's late-18th-century glory days. **Hours:** Always viewable. See page 374.

▲▲**Fashion Museum** 400 years of clothing under one roof, plus the opulent Assembly Rooms. **Hours:** Daily March-Oct 10:30-18:00, Nov-Feb 10:30-17:00. See page 375.

▲▲**Museum of Bath at Work** Gadget-ridden circa-1900 engineer's shop, foundry, factory, and office, best enjoyed with a live tour. **Hours:** April-Oct daily 10:30-17:00, Nov and Jan-March weekends only, closed in Dec. See page 376.

▲**Pump Room** Swanky Georgian hall, ideal for a spot of tea or a taste of unforgettably "healthy" spa water. **Hours:** Daily 9:30-12:00 for coffee and breakfast, 12:00-14:30 for lunch, 14:30-16:30 for afternoon tea (open for dinner during Bath International Music Festival, July-Aug, and Christmas holidays only). See page 370.

BATH

45-minute routes: a city tour (unintelligible audio recording on half the buses, live guides on the other half—choose the latter), and a "Skyline" route outside town (all live guides, stops near the American Museum—15-minute walk). On a sunny day, this is a multitasking tourist's dream come true: You can munch a sandwich, work on a tan, snap great photos, and learn a lot, all at the same time. Save money by doing the bus tour first—ticket stubs get you minor discounts at many sights (£11.50, ticket valid for 2 days and both tour routes, generally 4/hour daily in summer 9:30-18:30, in winter 10:00-15:00, tel. 01225/444-102, www.city-sightseeing.com).

Taxi Tours—Local taxis, driven by good talkers, go where big buses can't. A group of up to four can rent a cab for an hour (about £20) and enjoy a fine, informative, and—with the right cabbie—entertaining private joyride. It's probably cheaper to let

▲**Thermae Bath Spa** Relaxation center that put the bath back in Bath. **Hours:** Daily 9:00-22:00. See page 371.

▲**Bath Abbey** 500-year-old Perpendicular Gothic church, graced with beautiful fan vaulting and stained glass. **Hours:** April-Oct Mon-Sat 9:00-18:00, Sun 13:00-14:30 & 16:30-17:30; Nov-March Mon-Sat 9:00-16:30, Sun 13:00-14:30 & 16:30-17:30. See page 372.

▲**Pulteney Bridge and Parade Gardens** Shop-strewn bridge and relaxing riverside gardens. **Hours:** Bridge—always open; gardens—Easter-Sept daily 11:00-17:00, shorter hours off-season. See page 373.

▲**Georgian House at No. 1 Royal Crescent** Best opportunity to explore the interior of one of Bath's high-rent Georgian beauties. **Hours:** Mid-Feb-Oct Tue-Sun 10:30-17:00, Nov Tue-Sun 10:30-16:00, closed Mon and Dec-mid-Feb. See page 375.

▲**American Museum** An insightful look primarily at colonial/early-American lifestyles, with 18 furnished rooms and eager-to-talk guides. **Hours:** Mid-March-Oct Tue-Sun 12:00-17:00, closed Mon and Nov-mid-March. See page 378.

Jane Austen Centre Exhibit on 19th-century Bath-based novelist, best for her fans. **Hours:** Mid-March-mid-Nov daily 9:45-17:30, July-Aug Thu-Sat until 19:00; mid-Nov-mid-March Sun-Fri 11:00-16:30, Sat 9:45-17:30. See page 377.

the meter run than to pay for an hourly rate, but ask the cabbie for advice.

To Stonehenge, Avebury, and the Cotswolds

Bath is a good launch pad for visiting Wells, Avebury, Stonehenge, and more.

Mad Max Minibus Tours—Operating daily from Bath, Maddy and Paul offer thoughtfully organized, informative tours that run with entertaining guides. Book ahead—as far ahead as possible in summer—for these popular tours. Their **Stone Circles** full-day tour covers 110 miles and visits Stonehenge, the Avebury Stone Circles, and two cute villages: Lacock and Castle Combe. Photogenic Lacock (LAY-cock) is featured in parts of the BBC's *Pride and Prejudice* and the Harry Potter movies, and Castle Combe, the southernmost Cotswold village, is as sweet as they come (£32.50 plus £7.50 Stonehenge entry, tours run daily 8:45-16:30, arrive 15 minutes early, leaves early to beat the Stonehenge hordes). Their shorter tour of **Stonehenge and Lacock** leaves daily at 13:15 and returns at 17:15; occasionally, it also leaves at 8:45 and returns at 12:45 (£17.50 plus £7.50 Stonehenge entry). Most of their tours are limited to 16 people, though on busy days, the half-day tour might have up to 24.

Mad Max also offers a **Cotswold Discovery** full-day tour, a picturesque romp through the countryside with stops and a cream-tea opportunity in the quainter Cotswolds villages, including Stow-on-the-Wold, Bibury, Tetbury, the Coln Valley, The Slaughters (optional walk between the two villages), and others (£35; runs Sun, Tue, and Thu 8:45-17:15; arrive 15 minutes early). If you ask in advance, you can bring your luggage along and use the tour as transportation to Stow or, for £5 extra, Moreton-in-Marsh, with easy train connections to Oxford.

All tours depart from Bath at the Glass House shop on the corner of Orange Grove, a one-minute walk from the abbey. Arrive 15 minutes before your departure time and bring cash (it's possible to pay with credit card only if you book online at least 48 hours in advance—£1 discount). Online or email reservations are preferable to calling (phone answered daily 8:00-18:00, tel. 07990/505-970, www.madmaxtours.co.uk, maddy@madmaxtours.co.uk). Please honor or cancel your seat reservation.

More Bus Tours—If Mad Max is booked up, don't fret. Plenty of companies in Bath offer tours of varying lengths, prices, and destinations. Note that the cost of admission to sights is usually not included with any tour.

Scarper Tours runs a minibus tour to Stonehenge (£14, 10 percent Rick Steves discount if you book direct, doesn't include £7.50 Stonehenge entry fee, departs from behind the abbey; daily mid-June-Aug at 9:30, 13:00, and 16:30; mid-March-mid-June and Sept-mid-Oct at 10:00 and 14:00; mid-Oct-mid-March at 13:00; tel. 07739/644-155, www.scarpertours.com). The three-hour tour (two hours there and back, an hour at the site) includes driver narration en route.

Celtic Horizons, run by retired teacher Alan Price, offers tours from Bath to a variety of destinations, such as Stonehenge, Avebury, and Wells. Alan can provide a convenient transfer service (to or from London, Heathrow, Bristol Airport, the Cotswolds, and so on), with or without a tour itinerary en route. Allow about £25/hour for a group (his comfortable minivans seat 4, 6, or 8 people) and £150 for Heathrow-Bath transfers (1-4 persons). It's best to make arrangements and get pricing information by email at alan@celtichorizons.com (cash only, tel. 01373/461-784, http://celtichorizons.com).

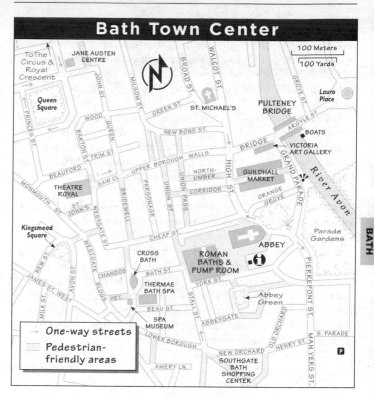

Bath Town Center

One-way streets
Pedestrian-friendly areas

Sights in Bath

In the Town Center

▲▲▲**Roman and Medieval Baths**—In ancient Roman times, high society enjoyed the mineral springs at Bath. From Londinium—and throughout the empire—Romans traveled so

often to Aquae Sulis, as the city was called, to "take a bath" that finally it became known simply as Bath. Today, a fine museum surrounds the ancient bath. With the help of a great audioguide, you'll wander past well-documented displays, Roman artifacts, a temple pediment with an evocative bearded face, a bronze head of the goddess Sulis Minerva, excavated ancient foundations, and the actual mouth of the spring. At the end you'll have a chance to walk around the big pool itself, where Romans once lounged, splished, splashed, and thanked the gods for the gift of naturally hot water.

Cost and Hours: £12.50, £0.75 more in July-Aug, includes audioguide, £15.50 combo-ticket includes Fashion Museum—a £3.50 savings, family ticket available, daily July-Aug 9:00-22:00, March-June and Sept-Oct 9:00-18:00, Nov-Feb 9:30-17:30, last entry one hour before closing, tel. 01225/477-785, www.roman baths.co.uk.

Crowd-Beating Tips: As this is the top sight in this touristy town, it can be very busy on Saturdays and any day in summer (though you'll never wait longer than about 30 minutes to get in). On any day, the least crowded time to visit is before 11:00. If you're here in July or August, the best time is after 19:00, when the baths are romantic, gas-lit, and all yours.

Tours: Take advantage of the included, essential **audioguide,** which will make your visit easy and informative. In addition to the basic commentary, look for posted numbers to key into your audioguide for specialty topics—including a kid-friendly tour and insightful musings from American expat writer Bill Bryson. For those with a big appetite for Roman history, in-depth **guided tours** leave from the end of the museum at the edge of the actual bath (included with ticket, on the hour, a poolside clock is set for the next departure time, 20-40 minutes depending on the guide). You can revisit the museum after the tour.

● Self-Guided Tour: Follow the one-way route through the bath and museum complex. This self-guided tour offers a basic overview; for more in-depth commentary, make ample use of the included audioguide.

Begin by walking around the upper **terrace,** overlooking the Great Bath. This terrace—lined with sculptures of VIRs (Very Important Romans)—evokes ancient times but was built in the 1890s. The ruins of the bath complex sat undisturbed for centuries before finally being excavated and turned into a museum in the late 19th century.

Head inside to the **museum,** where exhibits explain the dual purpose of the buildings that stood here in Roman times: a bath complex, for relaxation and for healing; and a temple dedicated to the goddess Sulis Minerva, who was believed to be responsible for the mysterious and much-appreciated thermal springs. Cut-away diagrams and models resurrect both parts of this complex and help you establish your bearings among the remaining fragments and foundations.

Peer down into the **spring,** where little air bubbles remind you that 240,000 gallons of water a day emerge from the earth—

magically, it must have seemed to Romans—at a constant 115°F.

Go downstairs to get to know the Romans who built and enjoyed these baths. The fragments of the **temple pediment**— carved by indigenous Celtic craftsmen but with Roman themes—

represent a remarkable cultural synthesis. Sit and watch for a while, as a slide projection fills in historians' best guesses as to what once occupied the missing bits. The identity of the circular face in the middle puzzles researchers. (God? Santa Claus?) It could be the head of the Gorgon monster after it was slain by Perseus—are those snakes peeking through its hair and beard? And yet, the Gorgon was traditionally depicted as female. Perhaps instead it's Neptune, the god of water—appropriate for this aquatic site.

The next exhibits examine the importance of Aquae Sulis (the settlement here) in antiquity. Much like the pilgrimage sites of the Middle Ages, this spot exerted a powerful pull on people from all over the realm, who were eager to partake in its healing waters and to worship at the religious site. You'll see some of the small but extremely heavy carved-stone tables that pilgrims hauled here as an offering to the gods.

As you walk through the temple's original foundations, keep an eye out for the sacrificial altar. The gilded-bronze head of the goddess **Sulis Minerva** (in the dis-

play case) once overlooked a flaming cauldron inside the temple, where only priests were allowed to enter. Similar to the Greek goddess Athena, Sulis Minerva was considered to be a life-giving mother goddess. The next room displays some of the requests (inscribed on sheets of pewter or iron) that visitors made of the goddess. Take time to read some of these—many are comically spiteful and petty, offering a warts-and-all glimpse into day-to-day Roman culture.

Engineers enjoy a close-up look at the spring overflow and the original **drain system**—built two millennia ago—that still carries excess water to the River Avon. Marvel at the cleverness and durability of Roman engineering, created in (what we usually imagine to be) a "primitive" time. A nearby exhibit on pulleys and fasteners lets you play with these inventions.

Head outside to the **Great Bath** itself (where you can join one of the included guided tours—look for the clock with the next start time). Take a slow lap (by foot) around the perimeter, imagining the frolicking Romans who once immersed themselves up to their necks in this five-foot-deep pool. (On busy days, when costumed characters hang out by the bath, you may not have to imagine.) The water is greenish because of algae—don't drink it. The best views are from the west end, looking back toward the abbey. Nearby is a giant chunk of roof span, from a time when this was a cavernous covered swimming hall. At the corner, you'll step over a small canal where hot water still trickles into the main pool. Nearby, find a length of original lead pipe, remarkably well preserved since antiquity.

Symmetrical bath complexes branch off at opposite ends of the Great Bath (perhaps dating from a conservative period when the Romans maintained separate facilities for men and women). The **East Baths** show off changing rooms and various bathing rooms, each one designed for a special therapy or recreational purpose (immersion therapy tub, sauna-like heated floor, and so on), as described in detail by the audioguide.

When you're ready to leave, head for the **West Baths** (including a sweat bath and a *frigidarium*, or "cold plunge" pool) and take another look at the spring and more foundations. After returning your audioguide, exit through the gift shop and dip into the attached **Pump Room** to drink a spot of tea or to gag on the spa water (get a free sample with your bath ticket).

▲**Pump Room**—For centuries, Bath was forgotten as a spa. Then, in 1687, the previously barren Queen Mary bathed here, became

pregnant, and bore a male heir to the throne. A few years later, Queen Anne found the water eased her painful gout. Word of its wonder waters spread, and Bath earned its way back on the aristocratic map. High society soon turned the place into one big pleasure palace. The Pump Room, an elegant Georgian hall just above the Roman Baths, offers visitors their best chance to raise a pinky in Chippendale grandeur. Above the newspaper table and sedan chairs, a statue of Beau Nash himself sniffles down at you. Come for a light meal, or for just the price of a coffee (£3), drop in anytime—except during lunch—to enjoy live music and the atmosphere.

Cost and Hours: Daily 9:30-12:00 for coffee and £6-15 breakfast, 12:00-14:30 for £6-16 lunches, 14:30-16:30 for £17.50 traditional afternoon tea, tea/coffee and pastries also available in the afternoons; open for dinner July-Aug, during Bath International Music Festival, and Christmas holidays only; live music daily—string trio or piano, times vary; tel. 01225/444-477.

The Spa Water: This is your chance to eat a famous (but forgettable) "Bath bun" and split a drink of the awful curative water (£0.50 or free with your Roman and Medieval Baths ticket—just head to the little alcove on the right and show them your ticket). The water comes from the King's Spring and is brought to you by an appropriately attired server, who explains that the water is 10,000 years old, pumped up from nearly 100 yards deep, and marinated in 43 wonderful minerals. Convenient public WCs (which use plain old tap water) are in the entry hallway that connects the Pump Room with the baths.

▲**Thermae Bath Spa**—After simmering unused for a quarter-century, Bath's natural thermal springs once again offer R&R for

the masses. The state-of-the-art spa is housed in a complex of three buildings that combines historic structures with controversial (and expensive) new glass-and-steel architecture.

Is the Thermae Bath Spa worth the time and money? The experience is pretty pricey and humble compared to similar German and Hungarian spas. The tall, modern building in the city center lacks a certain old-time elegance. Jets in the pools are very limited, and the only water toys are big foam noodles. There's no cold plunge—the only way to cool off between steam rooms is to step onto a small, unglamorous balcony. The Royal Bath's two pools are essentially the same, and the water isn't particularly hot in either—in fact, the main attraction is the rooftop view from the top one (best with a partner or as a social experience).

That said, this is the only natural thermal spa in the UK and your chance to bathe in Bath. Bring your swimsuit and come for a couple of hours (Fri night and all day Sat-Sun are most crowded). Consider an evening visit, when—on a chilly day—Bath's twilight glows through the steam from the rooftop pool.

Cost: The cheapest spa pass is £25 for two hours, which gains you access to the Royal Bath's large, ground-floor "Minerva Bath"; four steam rooms and a waterfall shower; and the view-filled, open-air, rooftop thermal pool. Longer stays are £35/4 hours and £55/day (towel, robe, and slippers are an extra £9). If you arrived in Bath by train, your used rail ticket will score you a four-hour session for the price of two (£25, Mon-Fri). The much-hyped £42 Twilight Package includes three hours and a meal (one plate, drink, robe, towel, and slippers). The appeal of this package is not the mediocre meal, but being on top of the building at a magical hour (which you can do for less money at the regular rate).

Thermae has all the "pamper thyself" extras: massages, mud wraps, and various healing-type treatments, including "watsu"—water shiatsu (£40-70 extra). Book treatments at www.thermae bathspa.com.

Hours: Daily 9:00-22:00, last entry at 19:30. No kids under 16 are allowed. It's 100 yards from the Roman and Medieval Baths, on Beau Street, tel. 01225/331-234. There's a salad-and-smoothies café for guests.

The Cross Bath: This renovated, circular Georgian structure across the street from the main spa provides a simpler and less-expensive bathing option. It has a hot-water fountain that taps directly into the spring, making its water hotter than the spa's (£15/1.5 hours, daily 10:00-20:00, last entry at 18:30, check in at the bath's main office across the street and you'll be escorted to the Cross Bath, changing rooms, no access to Royal Bath, no kids under 12).

Spa Visitor Centre: Also across the street, in the Hetling Pump Room, this free, one-room exhibit explains the story of the spa (Mon-Sat 10:00-17:00, Sun 10:00-16:00, £2 audioguide).

▲**Bath Abbey**—The town of Bath wasn't much in the Middle Ages, but an important church has stood on this spot since Anglo-Saxon times. King Edgar I was crowned here in 973, when the

church was much bigger (before the bishop packed up and moved to Wells). Dominating the town center, today's abbey—the last great medieval church of England—is 500 years old and a fine example of the Late Perpendicular Gothic style, with breezy fan vaulting and enough stained glass to earn it the nickname "Lantern of the West."

The **facade** (c. 1500, but mostly restored) is interesting for some of its carvings. Look for the angels going down the ladder. The statue of Peter (to the left of the door) lost its head to mean iconoclasts; it was recarved out of Peter's once supersized beard. Take a moment to appreciate the abbey's architecture from the Abbey Green square.

Going **inside** is worth the small suggested contribution. The glass, red-iron gas-powered lamps, and the heating grates on the floor are all remnants of the 19th century. The window behind the altar shows 52 scenes from the life of Christ. A window to the left of the altar shows Edgar's coronation.

Cost and Hours: £2.50 suggested donation; April-Oct Mon-Sat 9:00-18:00, Sun 13:00-14:30 & 16:30-17:30; Nov-March Mon-Sat 9:00-16:30, Sun 13:00-14:30 & 16:30-17:30; handy flier narrates a self-guided 19-stop tour, schedule of events—including concerts, services, and evensong—posted on the door and online, tel. 01225/422-462, www.bathabbey.org.

Climbing the Tower: You can reach the top of the tower but only with an official 50-minute guided tour. You'll hike up 212 steps for views across the rooftops of Bath and down into the Roman and Medieval Baths (£5, sporadic schedule but generally at the top of each hour Mon-Sat April-Oct 10:00-16:00, Nov-March 11:00-14:00, more often during busy times, no tours Sun, buy tickets in abbey gift shop).

▲**Pulteney Bridge, Parade Gardens, and Cruises**—Bath is inclined to compare its shop-lined Pulteney Bridge to Florence's Ponte Vecchio. That's pushing

it. But to best enjoy a sunny day, pay £1 to enter the Parade Gardens below the bridge (Easter-Sept daily 11:00-17:00, shorter hours off-season, includes deck chairs, ask about concerts held some Sun at 15:00 in summer, entrance a block south of bridge, www .bathnes.gov.uk). Relaxing peacefully by the riverside provides a wonderful break (and memory).

Across the bridge at Pulteney Weir, tour boat companies run **cruises** (£8 round-trip, £4 one-way, up to 7/day if the weather's good, one hour to Bathampton and back, WCs on board, tel. 01225/312-900). Just take whatever boat is running—all stop in Bathampton—allowing you to hop off and walk back (about 45-60 minutes; for details on the walk, see "Activities in Bath," later). Boats come with picnic-friendly sundecks.

Guildhall Market—The little, old-school shopping mall located across from Pulteney Bridge is a frumpy time warp in this affluent town. It's fun for browsing and picnic shopping, and its recommended Market Café is a cheap place for a bite.

Victoria Art Gallery—This gallery, next to Pulteney Bridge, has two parts: The ground floor houses temporary exhibits, while the upstairs is filled with paintings from the late 17th century to the present, along with a small collection of decorative arts.

Cost and Hours: Free, Tue-Sat 10:00-17:00, Sun 13:30-17:00, closed Mon, WC, tel. 01225/477-233, www.victoriagal.org.uk.

Northwest of the Town Center

Several worthwhile public spaces and museums can be found a slightly uphill 10-minute walk away.

▲▲**The Circus and the Royal Crescent**—If Bath is an architectural cancan, these are its knickers. These first Georgian "condos"—built in the mid-18th century by the John Woods (the Circus by the Elder, the Royal Crescent by the Younger)—are well explained by the city walking tours. "Georgian" is British for "Neoclassical." These two building complexes, conveniently located a block apart from each other, are quintessential Bath.

Circus: True to its name, this is a circular housing complex. Picture it as a coliseum turned inside out. Its Doric, Ionic, and Corinthian capital decorations pay homage to its Greco-Roman origin, and are a reminder that Bath (with its seven hills) aspired to be "the Rome of England." The frieze above the first row of columns has hundreds of different panels representing the arts, sciences, and crafts. The ground-floor entrances were made large enough that aristocrats could be carried right through the door in their sedan chairs, and women could enter without disturbing their sky-high hairdos. The tiny round windows on the top floors were the servants' quarters. While the building fronts are uniform, the backs are higgledy-piggledy, infamous for their "hanging loos" (bathrooms added years later). Stand in the middle of the Circus among the grand plane trees, on the capped old well. Imagine the days when there was no indoor plumbing, and the servant girls gathered here to fetch water—this was gossip central. If you stand on the well, your clap echoes three times around the circle (try it).

Royal Crescent: A long, graceful arc of buildings—impossible to see in one glance unless you step way back to the edge of the big park in front—evokes the wealth and gentility of Bath's glory days. As you cruise the Crescent, pretend you're rich. Then pretend you're poor. Notice the "ha ha fence," a drop-off in the front yard that acted as a barrier, invisible from the windows, for keeping out sheep and peasants.

The refined and stylish **Royal Crescent Hotel** sits unmarked in the center of the Crescent (with the giant rhododendron growing over the door). You're welcome to (politely) drop in to explore its fine ground-floor public spaces and back garden. A gracious and traditional tea is served in the garden out back (£14 cream tea, £23.50 afternoon tea, daily 15:00-17:00, sharing is OK, reserve a day in advance in summer, tel. 01225/823-333).

▲**Georgian House at No. 1 Royal Crescent**—This museum (corner of Brock Street and Royal Crescent) offers your best look into a period house. Your visit is limited to four roped-off rooms, but it's worth the admission to get behind one of those classy Georgian facades, especially if you take the time to talk with the docents stationed in each room. The docents know all the fascinating details of Georgian life...like how high-class women shaved their eyebrows and pasted on carefully trimmed strips of furry mouse skin in their place. On the bedroom dresser sits a bowl of black beauty marks and a head-scratcher from those pre-shampoo days. Fido spent his days in the kitchen treadmill powering the rotisserie.

Cost and Hours: £6.50, mid-Feb-Oct Tue-Sun 10:30-17:00, Nov Tue-Sun 10:30-16:00, closed Mon and Dec-mid-Feb, last entry 30 minutes before closing, £2 guidebook available, no photos, "no stiletto heels, please," tel. 01225/428-126, www.bath-preservation-trust.org.uk. Its WC is accessible from the street (under the entry steps, across from the exit and shop).

▲▲**Fashion Museum**—Housed underneath Bath's Assembly Rooms, this museum displays four centuries of fashion on one floor.

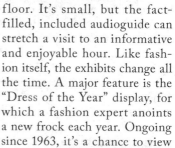

It's small, but the fact-filled, included audioguide can stretch a visit to an informative and enjoyable hour. Like fashion itself, the exhibits change all the time. A major feature is the "Dress of the Year" display, for which a fashion expert anoints a new frock each year. Ongoing since 1963, it's a chance to view nearly a half-century of fashion trends in one sweep of the head. (The menswear version—awarded sporadically—shows a bit less variation, but has flashes of creativity.) Many of the exhibits are organized by theme (bags, shoes, underwear, wedding dresses). You'll see how fashion evolved—just like architecture and other arts—from one historical period to the next: Georgian, Regency, Victorian, the Swinging '60s, and so on. If you're intrigued by all those historic garments, go ahead and lace up your own trainer corset (which looks more like a lifejacket) and try on a hoop underdress.

Cost and Hours: £7.25, £15.50 combo-ticket also covers Roman Baths, family ticket available, daily March-Oct 10:30-18:00, Nov-Feb 10:30-17:00, last entry one hour before closing, self-service café, Bennett Street, tel. 01225/477-789, www.fashionmuseum.co.uk.

Assembly Rooms: Whether or not you're touring the Fashion

Museum, poke into the building that houses it, where you can wander the big, grand, empty Assembly Rooms. Card games, concerts, tea, and dances were held here in the 18th century, before the advent of fancy hotels with grand public spaces made them obsolete. Note the extreme symmetry (pleasing to the aristocratic eye) and the high windows (assuring privacy). After the Allies bombed the historic and well-preserved German city of Lübeck, the Germans picked up a Baedeker guide and chose a similarly lovely city to bomb: Bath. The Assembly Rooms—gutted by WWII bombs in this wartime tit-for-tat—have since been restored to their original splendor. (Only the chandeliers are original.)

Nearby: Below the Fashion Museum (to the left as you leave, 20 yards away, at the door marked *14* and *Alfred House*) is one of the few surviving sets of **iron house hardware.** "Link boys" carried torches through the dark streets, lighting the way for big shots in their sedan chairs as they traveled from one affair to the next. The link boys extinguished their torches in the black conical "snuffers." The lamp above was once gas-lit. The crank on the left was used to hoist bulky things to various windows (see the hooks). Few of these sets survived the dark days of the WWII Blitz, when most were collected and melted down, purportedly to make weapons to feed the British war machine. (Not long ago, these well-meaning Brits finally found out that all of their patriotic extra commitment to the national struggle had been for naught, since the metal ended up in junk heaps.)

Shoppers head down **Bartlett Street,** just below the Fashion Museum, to browse the antique shops.

▲▲Museum of Bath at Work—This modest but lovable place explains the industrial history of Bath. The museum is a vivid

reminder that there's always been a grimy, workaday side to this spa town.

The core of the museum is the well-preserved, circa-1900 fizzy-drink business of one Mr. Bowler. It includes a Dickensian office, engineer's shop, brass foundry, and factory floor. It's just a pile of meaningless old gadgets—until the included audioguide resurrects Mr. Bowler's creative genius. Each item has its own story to tell.

Upstairs are display cases featuring other Bath creations through the years, including a 1914 Horstmann car, wheeled sedan chairs (this *is* Bath, after all), and versatile plasticine (colorful proto-Play-Doh—still the preferred medium of Aardman Studios, creators of the stop-motion animated *Wallace and Gromit* movies). At the snack bar, you can buy your own historic fizzy drink (a descendant of the ones once made here). On your way out, don't miss the intriguing collection of small exhibits on the ground floor, featuring cabinetmaking, the traditional methods for cutting the local "Bath Stone," a locally produced six-stroke engine, and more.

Cost and Hours: £5, people over 60 pay £3.50, April-Oct daily 10:30-17:00, Nov and Jan-March weekends only, closed Dec, last entry at 16:00, Julian Road, 2 steep blocks up Russell Street from Assembly Rooms, tel. 01225/318-348, www.bath-at-work .org.uk.

Sightseeing Tip: Notice the proximity of this museum to the very different Fashion Museum (described earlier). Museum attendants told me that—while open-minded spouses appreciate both places—it's standard for husbands to visit the Museum of Bath at Work while their wives are touring the Fashion Museum. Maybe it's time to divide and conquer?

Jane Austen Centre—This exhibition focuses on Jane Austen's tumultuous, sometimes troubled five years in Bath (circa 1800, during which time her father died) and the influence the city had on her writing. There's little of historic substance here. You'll walk through a Georgian townhouse that she didn't live in (one of her real addresses in Bath was a few houses up the road, at 25 Gay Street), and you'll see mostly enlarged reproductions of things associated with her writing, but none of that seems to bother the steady stream of happy Austen fans touring through the house.

The museum does describe various places from two novels set in Bath (*Persuasion* and *Northanger Abbey*). Guides give an intro talk (15 minutes, 2/hour, starts at :15 and :45 past the hour) about the romantic but down-to-earth Austen, who skewered the silly, shallow, and arrogant aristocrats' world, where "the doing of nothing all day prevents one from doing anything." They also show a 15-minute video; after that, you're free to wander through the rest of the exhibit. The well-stocked gift shop—with "I love Mr. Darcy" tote bags and Colin Firth's visage emblazoned on teacups, postcards, and more—is a shopping spree in the making for Austen fans.

Cost and Hours: £7.50; mid-March-mid-Nov daily 9:45-17:30, July-Aug Thu-Sat until 19:00; mid-Nov-mid-March Sun-Fri 11:00-16:30, Sat 9:45-17:30; between Queen's Square and the Circus at 40 Gay Street, tel. 01225/443-000, www.janeausten .co.uk.

Tea: Upstairs, the award-winning **Regency Tea Rooms** (free entrance) hits the spot for Austenites, with costumed waitstaff and themed teas (£6-10), including the all-out "Tea with Mr. Darcy" for £12 (also £6 sandwiches, same hours as the Centre, last orders 45 minutes before closing).

Sightseeing Tip: Jane Austen-themed **walking tours** of the city begin at the KC Change shop in the abbey square and end at the Centre (£5, buy tickets at KC Change shop, 1.5 hours, Sat-Sun at 11:00, July-Aug also Fri-Sat at 16:00, no reservation necessary).

Building of Bath Collection—This unique collection offers an intriguing behind-the-scenes look at how the Georgian city was actually built (£4, mid-Feb-Nov Sat-Mon 10:30-17:00, last entry 30 minutes before closing, closed Tue-Fri and Dec-mid-Feb, a short walk north of the city center on a street called "The Paragon," tel. 01225/333-895, www.bath-preservation-trust.org.uk).

Outer Bath

▲**American Museum**—I know, you need this in Bath like you need a Big Mac. The UK's sole museum dedicated to American history, this may be the only place that combines Geronimo and Groucho Marx. It has thoughtful exhibits on the history of Native Americans and the Civil War, but the museum's heart is with the decorative arts and cultural artifacts that reveal how Americans lived from colonial times to the mid-19th century. Each of the 18 completely furnished rooms (from a plain 1600s Massachusetts dining/living room to a Rococo Revival explosion in a New Orleans bedroom) is hosted by eager guides waiting to fill you in on the everyday items that make domestic Yankee history surprisingly interesting. (In the Lee Room, look for the original mouse holes, strategically backlit, in the floor boards.) One room is a quilter's nirvana. You could easily spend an afternoon here, enjoying the surrounding gardens, arboretum, and trails.

Cost and Hours: £9, mid-March-Oct Tue-Sun 12:00-17:00, closed Mon and Nov-mid-March, last entry one hour before closing, at Claverton Manor, tel. 01225/460-503, www.american museum.org.

Getting There: The museum is outside of town and a headache to reach if you don't have a car, involving a 10-15-minute walk from bus #18 or the hop-on, hop-off bus stop.

Activities in Bath

Walking—The Bath Skyline Walk is a six-mile wander around the hills surrounding Bath (leaflet at TI). Plenty of other scenic paths are described in the TI's literature. For additional options, get *Country Walks around Bath,* by Tim Mowl (£4.50 at TI or bookstores).

Hiking the Canal to Bathampton—An idyllic towpath leads two miles from the Bath Spa train station, along the Kennet and Avon Canal, to the sleepy village of Bathampton. Immediately behind the station in Bath, cross the footbridge, turn left, and find where the canal hits the River Avon. Head northeast along the small canal, noticing the series of Industrial Age locks and giving thanks that you're not a horse pulling a barge. After the path criss-crosses the canal a few times, you'll mostly walk with the water on your right. You'll be in Bathampton in less than an hour, where The George, a classic pub, awaits with a nice meal and cellar-temp beer (reservations smart, tel. 01225/425-079).

Boating—The Bath Boating Station, in an old Victorian boat-house, rents rowboats, canoes, and punts (£7/person for first hour, then £3/additional hour, Easter-Sept daily 10:00-18:00, closed off-season, intersection of Forester and Rockcliffe roads, one mile northeast of center, tel. 01225/312-900, www.bathboating.co.uk).

Swimming and Kids' Activities—The Bath Sports and Leisure Centre has a fine pool for laps as well as lots of waterslides. Kids have entertaining options in the mini-gym "Active Club" area, which includes a rock wall and a "Zany Zone" indoor playground (swimming: £3.80 for adults, £2.40 for kids; kids and their parents pay £4 each to use "Active Club" plus pool; Mon-Fri 6:30-22:00, Sat 6:30-19:00, Sun 8:00-20:00, kids' hours limited, call for open-swim times, just across the bridge on North Parade Road, tel. 01225/486-905, www.aquaterra.org).

Shopping—There's great browsing between the abbey and the Assembly Rooms (Fashion Museum). Shops close at about 17:30, and many are open on Sunday (11:00-16:00). Explore the antique shops lining Bartlett Street, below the Fashion Museum.

Nightlife in Bath

For an up-to-date list of events, pick up the local weekly newspaper, the *Bath Chronicle,* which includes a "What's On" schedule (www.thisisbath.com). Younger travelers may enjoy the party-ready bar, club, and nightlife recommendations at www.itchybath .co.uk.

▲▲**Bizarre Bath Street Theater**—For an entertaining walking-tour comedy act "with absolutely no history or culture," follow Dom, J. J., or Noel Britten on their creative and lively Bizarre Bath walk. This 1.5-hour "tour," which combines stand-up comedy with cleverly executed magic tricks, plays off unsuspecting passersby as well as tour members. It's a belly laugh a minute (£8, or £7 if you show your Rick Steves book, April-Oct nightly at 20:00, smaller groups Mon-Thu, promises to insult all nationalities and sensitivities, just racy enough but still good family fun, leaves from The Huntsman pub near the abbey, confirm at TI or call 01225/335-124, www.bizarrebath.co.uk).

▲**Theatre Royal Performance**—The 18th-century, 800-seat Theatre Royal, recently restored and one of England's loveliest, offers a busy schedule of London West End-type plays, including many "pre-London" dress-rehearsal runs (£15-39, shows generally start at 19:30 or 20:00, matinees at 14:30, box office open Mon-Sat 10:00-20:00, Sun 12:00-20:00 if there's a show, £3 extra to book online or by phone with a credit card, on Saw Close, tel. 01225/448-844, www.theatreroyal.org.uk).

Forty nosebleed spots on a bench (misnamed "standbys") go on sale at noon Monday through Saturday for that day's evening performance (£6, 2 tickets maximum, can book ahead but subject to £3 fee; no fee if bought at box office but cash only). If the show is sold out, same-day "standing places" go on sale at 18:00 (12:00 for matinees) for £4 (2 tickets maximum, cash only). Also at the box office, you can snatch up any "last minute" seats for £10-15 a half-hour before "curtain up" (cash only).

Sightseeing Tip: During the free Bath walking tour, your guide stops here. Pop into the box office, ask what's playing, and see if there are many seats left for that night. If the play sounds good and plenty of seats remain unsold, you're fairly safe to come back 30 minutes before curtain time to buy a ticket at the cheaper price. Oh...and if you smell jasmine, it's the ghost of Lady Grey, a mistress of Beau Nash.

Evening Walks—Take your choice: comedy (Bizarre Bath, described earlier), history, or ghost tour. The free **city history walks** (a daily standard described on page 363) are offered on some summer evenings (2 hours, May-Sept Tue and Fri at 19:00, leave from Pump Room). **Ghost Walks** are a popular way to pass the after-dark hours (£7, cash only, 1.5 hours, year-round Thu-Sat at 20:00, leave from The Garrick's Head pub—to the left and behind Theatre Royal as you face it, tel. 01225/350-512, www.ghostwalks ofbath.co.uk). The cities of York and Edinburgh—which have houses thought to be actually haunted—are better for these walks.

Pubs—Most pubs in the center are very noisy, catering to a rowdy twentysomething crowd. But at the top end of town, you can still find some classic old places with inviting ambience and live music. These are listed in order from closest to farthest away:

The Old Green Tree, the most convenient of all these pubs, is a rare traditional pub right in the town center (locally brewed real ales, no children, 12 Green Street; also recommended for lunch—see "Eating in Bath," later).

The Star Inn is much appreciated by local beer-lovers for its fine ale and "no machines or music to distract from the chat." It's a spit 'n' sawdust place, and its long bench, nicknamed "death row," still comes with a complimentary pinch of snuff from tins on the ledge. Try the Bellringer Ale, made just up the road (Mon-Fri 12:00-14:30 & 17:30-24:00, Sat-Sun 12:00-24:00, no food served, 23 The Vineyards, top of The Paragon/A4 Roman Road, tel.

01225/425-072, generous and friendly welcome from Paul, who runs the place).

The Bell has a jazzy, pierced-and-tattooed, bohemian feel, but with a mellow older crowd. Some kind of activity is brewing nearly every night, usually live music (£2.50 sandwiches, pizza Fri-Sat only, Mon-Sat 11:30-23:00, Sun 12:00-22:30, 103 Walcot Street, tel. 01225/460-426, www.walcotstreet.com).

Summer Nights at the Baths—In July and August, you can stretch your sightseeing day at the Roman Baths, open nightly until 22:00 (last entry 21:00), when the gas lamps flame and the baths are far less crowded and more atmospheric. To take a dip yourself, consider popping over to the Thermae Bath Spa (last entry at 19:30).

Sleeping in Bath

Bath is a busy tourist town. Accommodations are expensive, and low-cost alternatives are rare. By far the best budget option is the

YMCA—it's central, safe, simple, very well-run, and has plenty of twin rooms available. To get a good B&B, make a telephone reservation in advance. Competition is stiff, and it's worth asking any of these places for a weekday, three-nights-in-a-row, or off-season deal. Friday and Saturday nights are tightest (with many rates going

Sleep Code

(£1 = about $1.60, country code: 44, area code: 01225)
S = Single, **D** = Double/Twin, **T** = Triple, **Q** = Quad, **b** = bathroom, **s** = shower only. Unless otherwise noted, credit cards are accepted.

To help you sort easily through these listings, I've divided the rooms into three categories based on the price for a standard double room with bath:

  $$$ Higher Priced—Most rooms £100 or more.
   $$ Moderately Priced—Most rooms between £60-100.
    $ Lower Priced—Most rooms £60 or less.

Prices can change without notice; verify the hotel's current rates online or by email. For other updates, see www.ricksteves.com/update.

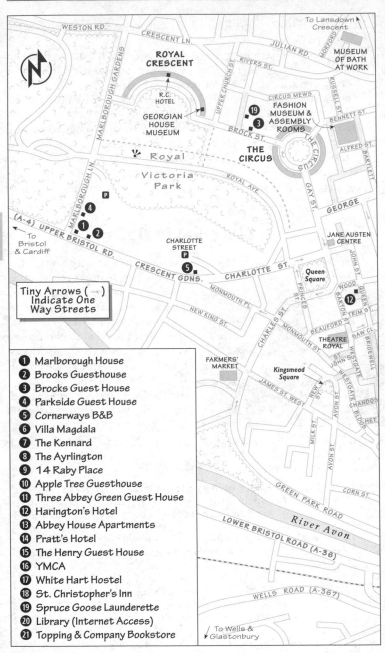

WESTON RD.
CRESCENT LN.
JULIAN RD.
To Lansdown Crescent
MORFORD
MUSEUM OF BATH AT WORK
ROYAL CRESCENT
RIVERS ST.
RUSSELL ST.
MARLBOROUGH GARDENS
UPPER CHURCH ST.
CIRCUS MEWS
R.C. HOTEL
BENNETT ST.
GEORGIAN HOUSE MUSEUM
FASHION MUSEUM & ASSEMBLY ROOMS
⑲
③
BROCK ST.
ALFRED ST.
BARTLETT
MARLBOROUGH LN.
Royal
THE CIRCUS
THE CIRCUS
Victoria Park
ROYAL AVE.
GAY ST.
GEORGE
P
④
① ②
(A-4) UPPER BRISTOL RD.
To Bristol & Cardiff
JANE AUSTEN CENTRE
JOHN ST.
CHARLOTTE STREET
WOOD
Queen Square
P
⑤
CRESCENT GDNS.
CHARLOTTE ST.
QUEEN SQ.
BARTON ST.
TRIM ST.
MONMOUTH PL.
PRINCES ST.
⑫
SAW CL.
BRIDEWELL
Tiny Arrows (→) Indicate One Way Streets
NEW KING ST.
CHARLES ST.
MONMOUTH ST.
BEAUFORD SQ.
THEATRE ROYAL
ST. JOHN'S
WESTGATE
BLDGS.
FARMERS' MARKET
Kingsmead Square
ST. JOHN'S PL.
WESTGATE
CHANDOS
HET.
JAMES ST. WEST
NEW ST.
AVON ST.
MILK ST.
GREEN PARK ROAD
CORN ST.
River Avon
LOWER BRISTOL ROAD (A-36)
WELLS ROAD (A-367)
To Wells & Glastonbury

① Marlborough House
② Brooks Guesthouse
③ Brocks Guest House
④ Parkside Guest House
⑤ Cornerways B&B
⑥ Villa Magdala
⑦ The Kennard
⑧ The Ayrlington
⑨ 14 Raby Place
⑩ Apple Tree Guesthouse
⑪ Three Abbey Green Guest House
⑫ Harington's Hotel
⑬ Abbey House Apartments
⑭ Pratt's Hotel
⑮ The Henry Guest House
⑯ YMCA
⑰ White Hart Hostel
⑱ St. Christopher's Inn
⑲ Spruce Goose Launderette
⑳ Library (Internet Access)
㉑ Topping & Company Bookstore

BATH

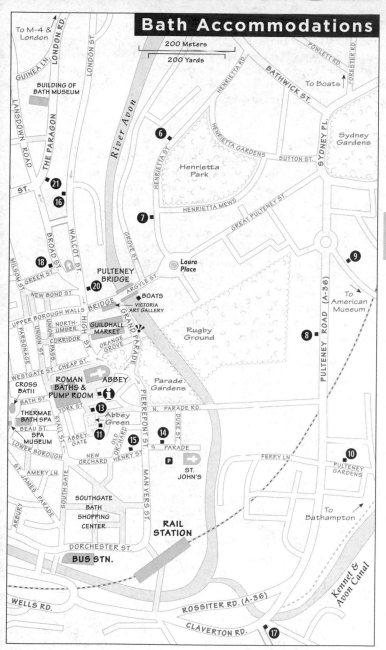

Bath Accommodations

200 Meters
200 Yards

To M-4 &
London

GUINEA LN.

LONDON RD.

LONDON ST.

POWLETT RD.

FORESTER RD.

BATHWICK ST.

To Boats

BUILDING OF
BATH MUSEUM

THE PARAGON

LANSDOWN ROAD

ST.

River Avon

HENRIETTA RD.

HENRIETTA ST.

HENRIETTA GARDENS

SUTTON ST.

SYDNEY PL.

Sydney
Gardens

Henrietta
Park

6

21

16

GROVE ST.

HENRIETTA MEWS

GREAT PULTENEY ST.

7

BROAD ST.

WALCOT ST.

MILSOM ST.

GREEN ST.

NEW BOND ST.

Laura
Place

18

9

PULTENEY
BRIDGE

ARGYLE ST.

20

BRIDGE

Boats

HIGH ST.

VICTORIA
ART GALLERY

GUILDHALL
MARKET

GRAND PARADE

Rugby
Ground

To
American
Museum

PULTENEY ROAD (A-36)

UPPER BOROUGH WALLS

PARSONAGE

UNION PASS.

NORTH-
UMBER.

CORRIDOR

ORANGE
GROVE

8

WESTGATE ST.

CHEAP ST.

CROSS
BATH

BATH ST.

ROMAN
BATHS &
PUMP ROOM

ABBEY

Parade
Gardens

THERMAE
BATH SPA

YORK ST.

13

Abbey
Green

PIERREPONT ST.

N. PARADE RD.

BEAU ST.
SPA
MUSEUM

ABBEY-
GATE

11

OLD
ORCHARD

15

14

DUKE ST.

S. PARADE

FERRY LN.

To
Bathampton

10

PULTENEY
GARDENS

LOWER BOROUGH

NEW
ORCHARD

HENRY ST.

MANVERS ST.

P

ST.
JOHN'S

ST. JAMES PARADE

AMERY LN.

ARBURY

SOUTH GATE

SOUTHGATE
BATH
SHOPPING
CENTER

RAIL
STATION

DORCHESTER ST.

BUS STN.

WELLS RD.

ROSSITER RD. (A-36)

CLAVERTON RD.

17

Kennet &
Avon Canal

up by about 25 percent)—especially if you're staying only one night, since B&Bs favor those lingering longer. If staying only Saturday night, you're very bad news to a B&B hostess. If you're driving to Bath, stowing your car near the center will cost you (though some less-central B&Bs have parking)—see "Parking" on page 363, or ask your hotelier. Almost every place provides Wi-Fi at no charge to its guests.

Near the Royal Crescent

These listings are all a 15-minute uphill walk or an easy £4-5 taxi ride from the train station. Or take any hop-on, hop-off bus tour from the station, get off at the stop nearest your accommodation (likely Royal Avenue—confirm with driver), check in, then finish the tour later in the day. The Marlborough Lane places have easier parking but are less centrally located.

$$$ **Marlborough House**, exuberantly run by Peter, mixes modern style with antique furnishings and features a welcoming breakfast room with an open kitchen. Each of the six rooms comes with a sip of sherry (Sb-£70-95, Db-£85-125, Tb-£95-135, organic vegetarian breakfasts and toiletries, free Wi-Fi, free parking, some street noise, 1 Marlborough Lane, tel. 01225/318-175, fax 01225/466-127, www.marlborough-house.net, mars@manque .dircon.co.uk).

$$$ **Brooks Guesthouse** is the biggest of the bunch, with 21 modern rooms and classy Victorian public spaces (Sb-£59-89, Db-£80-120, Tb-£109-150, great breakfasts with non-traditional and vegetarian options, free Wi-Fi, 1 Crescent Gardens, Upper Bristol Road, tel. 01225/425-543, www.brooksguesthouse.com, info@brooksguesthouse.com, Andrew and Carla).

$$ **Brocks Guest House** has six rooms in a Georgian townhouse built by John Wood in 1765. Located between the prestigious Royal Crescent and the courtly Circus, it has been redone in a way that would make the great architect proud (standard Db-£79-85, superior Db-£87-95, family room-£115-125, higher rates are for Fri-Sat, free Wi-Fi, little top-floor library, 32 Brock Street, tel. 01225/338-374, fax 01225/334-245, www.brocksguesthouse.co.uk, brocks@brocksguesthouse.co.uk, Richard).

$$ **Parkside Guest House** has five large, thoughtfully appointed Edwardian rooms. It's tidy, clean, homey, and well priced—and has a spacious back garden (Sb-£60, Db-£80, these prices are for Rick Steves readers, free Wi-Fi, limited free parking, 11 Marlborough Lane, tel. & fax 01225/429-444, www.parkside bandb.co.uk, post@parksidebandb.co.uk, kind Inge Lynall).

$$ **Cornerways B&B**, located on a noisy street, is simple and well worn, with three rooms and old-fashioned homey touches (Sb-£45-55, Db-£65-75, 15 percent discount with this book and

3-night stay in 2012, free Wi-Fi, DVD library, free parking, 47 Crescent Gardens, tel. 01225/422-382, www.cornerwaysbath.co.uk, info@cornerwaysbath.co.uk, Sue Black).

East of the River

These listings are a 10-minute walk from the city center. While generally a better value, they are not quite as conveniently located.

$$$ **Villa Magdala** rents 18 stately, hotelesque rooms in a freestanding Victorian townhouse opposite a park. In a city that's so insistently Georgian, it's fun to stay in a mansion that's Victorian (Db-£120-140 depending on size and demand, family rooms, inviting lounge, free Wi-Fi, free parking, in quiet residential area on Henrietta Street, tel. 01225/466-329, fax 01225/483-207, www.villamagdala.co.uk, enquiries@villamagdala.co.uk).

$$$ **The Kennard,** with 12 rooms immaculately maintained by proud owners Giovanni and Mary Baiano, is a short walk through a genteel neighborhood from the Pulteney Bridge. Each of the rooms is different, but all are colorfully and elaborately decorated (prices are for Sun-Thu/Fri-Sat: S-£65/£70, Sb-£89/£120, Db-£110/£130, Tb-£150/£180, free Wi-Fi, free street parking permits, thoughtfully planned Georgian garden out back, 11 Henrietta Street, tel. 01225/310-472, fax 01225/460-054, www.kennard.co.uk, reception@kennard.co.uk).

$$$ **The Ayrlington,** next door to a lawn-bowling green, has 16 attractive rooms with Asian decor and hints of a more genteel time. Though this well-maintained hotel fronts a busy street, it's reasonably quiet and tranquil. Rooms in the back have pleasant views of sports greens and Bath beyond. For the best value, request a standard top-floor double with a view of Bath (twin Db-£80-100, standard Db-£100-125, superior Db-£120-150, big deluxe Db-£130-170, higher price is for Fri-Sun, free Wi-Fi, fine garden, free and easy parking, 24-25 Pulteney Road, tel. 01225/425-495, fax 01225/469-029, www.ayrlington.com, mail@ayrlington.com, Ling Roper).

$$ **14 Raby Place** is a good value, mixing Georgian glamour with homey warmth and modern, artistic taste within its five rooms. Muriel Guy keeps things simple and endearingly friendly. She's a fun-loving live wire who serves organic food for breakfast (S with private bathroom on the hall-£35, Db-£75, Tb-£80, cash only; 14 Raby Place—go over bridge on North Parade Road, left on Pulteney Road, cross to church, Raby Place is first row of houses on hill; tel. 01225/465-120, murieljeanguy@gmail.com).

$$ **Apple Tree Guesthouse** offers six comfortable rooms near a shady canal (Sb-£55-66, Db-£85-110, Tb-£120-132, 2-night minimum Fri-Sat nights, free Wi-Fi, free parking, 7 Pulteney

Gardens, tel. 01225/337-642, www.appletreeguesthouse.com, enquiries@appletreeguesthouse.co.uk, Les and Lynsay Redwood).

In the Town Center

You'll pay a premium to sleep right in the center. And, since Bath is so pleasant and manageable by foot, a downtown location isn't essential. Still, these are particularly well located.

$$$ Three Abbey Green Guest House, with seven rooms, is bright, cheery, and located in a quiet, traffic-free courtyard only 50 yards from the abbey and the Roman Baths. Its spacious rooms are a fine value (Db-£95-145, four-poster Db-£145-180, family rooms-£140-200, price depends on season and size of room, 2-night minimum on weekends, free Internet access and Wi-Fi, tel. 01225/428-558, www.threeabbeygreen.com, stay@threeabbey green.com; Sue, Derek, and daughter Nicola). They also rent self-catering apartments (Db-£140-160, Qb-£170-200, 2-night minimum).

$$$ Harington's Hotel rents 13 fresh, modern rooms on a quiet street in the town center. This stylish place feels like a boutique hotel, but with a friendlier, laid-back vibe (Sb-£79-155, standard Db-£88-145, superior Db-£98-155, large superior Db-£108-165, Tb-£138-195, prices vary substantially depending on demand, free Wi-Fi, 10 Queen Street, tel. 01225/461-728, fax 01225/444-804, www.haringtonshotel.co.uk, post@haringtons hotel.co.uk). Melissa and Peter offer a 5 percent discount with this book for two-night stays except on Fridays, Saturdays, and holidays. They also rent two self-catering apartments down the street—one can sleep up to three (Db-£125, Tb-£145), and the other can sleep up to eight (prices on request; for apartments: 2-night minimum on weekdays, 3-night minimum on weekends).

$$$ Abbey House Apartments consist of five flats on Abbey Green and several others scattered around town—all tastefully restored by Laura (who, once upon a time, was a San Francisco rock musician). The apartments called Abbey View and Abbey Green (which comes with a washer and dryer) have views of the abbey from their nicely equipped kitchens. These are especially practical and economical if you plan on cooking. Laura provides everything you need for simple breakfasts, and it's fun and cheap to stock the fridge or get take-away for a meal in your flat. When Laura meets you to give you the keys, you become a local (Sb-£90, Db-£100-175, price depends on size, 2-night minimum, rooms can sleep four with Murphy and sofa beds, apartments clearly described on website, free Wi-Fi, Abbey Green, tel. 01225/464-238, www .laurastownhouseapartments.co.uk, bookings@laurastownhouse apartments.co.uk).

$$$ **Pratt's Hotel** is as proper and olde English as you'll find in Bath. Its creaks and frays are aristocratic, and even its public places make you want to sip a brandy. The 46 rooms show their age a bit, but are comfy and spacious. Since it's near a busy street, occasionally it can get noisy—request a quiet room, away from the street (Sb-£60-100, Db-£90-140, price depends on demand, breakfast-£10, check website for current rates and specials, dogs £7.50—but children under 15 free with 2 adults, elevator, pay Wi-Fi, attached restaurant-bar, 4-6 South Parade, tel. 01225/460-441, fax 01225/448-807, www.forestdale.com, pratts@forestdale.com).

$$$ **The Henry Guest House** is a simple, vertical place, renting eight clean rooms. It's friendly, well run, and just two blocks from the train station. Ask Liz about personalized tours of the area (Sb-£60-65, Db-£100-110, higher prices are for bigger "premier" rooms, extra bed-£15, family room-£155, 2-night minimum on weekends, free Wi-Fi, 6 Henry Street, tel. 01225/424-052, www.thehenry.com, stay@thehenry.com). Liz also rents two self-catering apartments nearby that sleep up to eight with roll-away beds and a sleeper couch (email them for rates).

Bargain Accommodations

Bath's Best Budget Beds: $ The **YMCA,** centrally located on a leafy square, has 210 beds in industrial-strength rooms—all with sinks and minimal furnishings. Although it smells a little like a gym, this place is a godsend for budget travelers—safe, secure, quiet, and efficiently run. With lots of twin rooms and no double beds, this is the only easily accessible budget option in downtown Bath (rates for Sun-Thu/Fri-Sat: S-£31/£35, twin D-£53/£59, T-£65/£74, Q-£76/£88, dorm beds-£18/£20, WCs and showers down the hall, includes continental breakfast, cooked breakfast-£2.50, cheap lunches, free linens, rental towels, lockers, pay Internet access, free Wi-Fi, laundry facilities, down a tiny alley off Broad Street on Broad Street Place, tel. 01225/325-900, fax 01225/462-065, www.bathymca.co.uk, stay@bathymca.co.uk).

Sloppy Backpacker Dorms: $ **White Hart Hostel** is a friendly and colorful nine-room place offering adults and families good, cheap beds in two- to six-bed dorms (£15/bed, S-£25, D-£40, Db-£50-70, kitchen, fine garden out back, 5-minute walk behind the train station at Widcombe—where Widcombe Hill hits Claverton Street, tel. 01225/313-985, www.whitehartbath.co.uk). The White Hart also has a pub with a reputation for good, although not cheap, food. $ **St. Christopher's Inn,** in a prime central location, is part of a chain of low-priced, high-energy hubs for backpackers looking for beds and brews. Their beds are so cheap because they know you'll spend money on their beer. The inn sits above the lively, youthful Belushi's pub, which is where you'll find the reception (54 beds in 6- to 12-bed rooms–£15-25, D–£52-60, higher prices are for weekends and walk-ins—it's always cheaper to book online, check website for specials, no guests under 18, pay Internet access, free Wi-Fi, laundry facilities, lounge, 9 Green Street, tel. 01225/481-444, www.st-christophers.co.uk).

Eating in Bath

Bath is bursting with eateries. There's something for every appetite and budget—just stroll around the center of town. A picnic dinner of deli food or take-out fish-and-chips in the Royal Crescent Park or down by the river is ideal for aristocratic hoboes. The restaurants I recommend are small and popular—reserve a table on Friday and Saturday evenings. Most pricey little bistros offer big savings with their two- and three-course lunches and "pre-theatre" specials. In general, you can get two courses for £10 at lunch or £12 in the early evening (compared to £15 for a main course after 18:30 or 19:00). Restaurants advertise their early-bird specials, and as long as you order within the time window, you're in for a cheap meal.

Romantic, Upscale French and English

Tilleys Bistro serves healthy French, English, and vegetarian meals with candlelit ambience. Owners Dawn and Dave make you feel as if you are guests at a dinner party in their elegant living room. Their fun menu lets you build your own meal, beginning with an interesting array of £6-9 starters. Cap things off with the cheese plate and a glass of the house port, a passion of Dave's. While it's pricey and the portions are modest, this is a memorable splurge (£10-19 main courses; lunch specials: £12.50/2 courses, £15/3 courses; Mon-Sat 12:00-14:30 & 18:00-22:30, Sun 18:00-21:00 only, reservations smart, 3 North Parade Passage, tel. 01225/484-200).

The Garrick's Head is an elegantly simple gastropub right around the corner from the Theatre Royal, with a pricey restaurant on one side and a bar serving affordable snacks on the other. You're welcome to eat from the bar menu, even if you're in the fancy dining room or outside enjoying some great people-watching. The word on the street: The fish-and-chips here are the best in town (£6-10 pub grub, £11-16 main courses on the fancier menu, Mon-Sat 11:00-22:00, Sun 12:00-22:00, drinks until later, 8 St. John's Place, tel. 01225/318-368).

The Circus Café and Restaurant is a relaxing little eatery serving well-executed English cuisine with European flair. Choose between the minimalist modern interior—with seating on the main floor or in the cellar—and the four tables on the peaceful street connecting the Circus and the Royal Crescent (£8 lunches, £7 starters and £13 main courses at dinner, open Mon-Sat 10:00-24:00, closed Sun, reservations smart, 34 Brock Street, tel. 01225/466-020).

Casanis French Bistro-Restaurant is a local hit. Chef Laurent, who hails from Nice, cooks "authentic Provençal cuisine" from the south of France, while his wife, Jill, serves. The decor matches the cuisine—informal, relaxed, simple, and top quality. The intimate Georgian dining room upstairs is a bit nicer and more spacious than the ground floor (lunch specials: £13.50/2 courses, £17/3 courses; dinner special available 18:00-19:00: £17/2 courses, £21/3 courses; open Tue-Sat 12:00-14:00 & 18:00-22:00, closed Sun-Mon, immediately behind the Assembly Rooms at 4 Saville Row, tel. 01225/780-055).

Casual Alternatives

Whether ethnic food or vegetarian, there are plenty of ways to get some fun culinary variation in this town.

Demuths Vegetarian Restaurant is highly rated and ideal for the well-heeled vegetarian. Its tight, stark, understated interior comes with a vegan vibe (£6-11 lunches, £7 starters and £13-15 main courses at dinner, daily 12:00-15:30 & 17:00-21:30, 2 North Parade Passage, tel. 01225/446-059).

Yen Sushi is your basic little sushi bar—plain and sterile, with stools facing a conveyor belt that constantly tempts you with a variety of freshly made delights on color-coded plates. When you're done, the waitstaff will tally your plates and give you the bill (£1.50-4 plates, you can fill up for £12 or so, daily 12:00-15:00 & 17:30-22:30, 11 Bartlett Street, tel. 01225/333-313).

Martini Restaurant, a hopping, purely Italian place, has class and jovial waiters (£9-12 pastas and pizzas, £14-19 meat and fish dishes, daily 12:00-14:30 & 18:00-22:30, open all day long on Sat, plenty of veggie options, daily fish specials, extensive wine list, reservations smart on weekends, 9 George Street, tel. 01225/460-818; Nunzio, Franco, and chef Luigi).

Rajpoot Tandoori serves—by all assessments—the best Indian food in Bath. You'll hike down deep into a sprawling cellar, where the plush Indian atmosphere and award-winning cooking make paying the extra pounds palatable. The seating is tight and the ceilings low, but it's air-conditioned (£8.25 three-course lunch special, £9-11 main courses; figure £20 per person with rice, naan, and drink; daily 12:00-14:30 & 18:00-23:00, 4 Argyle Street, tel. 01225/466-833, Ali).

Thai Balcony Restaurant's open, spacious interior is so plush, it'll have you wondering, "Where's the Thai wedding?" While locals debate which of Bath's handful of Thai restaurants serves

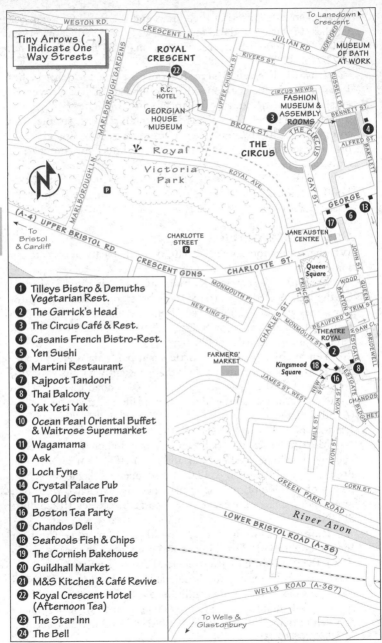

Tiny Arrows (→)
Indicate One
Way Streets

1 Tilleys Bistro & Demuths
   Vegetarian Rest.
2 The Garrick's Head
3 The Circus Café & Rest.
4 Casanis French Bistro-Rest.
5 Yen Sushi
6 Martini Restaurant
7 Rajpoot Tandoori
8 Thai Balcony
9 Yak Yeti Yak
10 Ocean Pearl Oriental Buffet
    & Waitrose Supermarket
11 Wagamama
12 Ask
13 Loch Fyne
14 Crystal Palace Pub
15 The Old Green Tree
16 Boston Tea Party
17 Chandos Deli
18 Seafoods Fish & Chips
19 The Cornish Bakehouse
20 Guildhall Market
21 M&S Kitchen & Café Revive
22 Royal Crescent Hotel
    (Afternoon Tea)
23 The Star Inn
24 The Bell

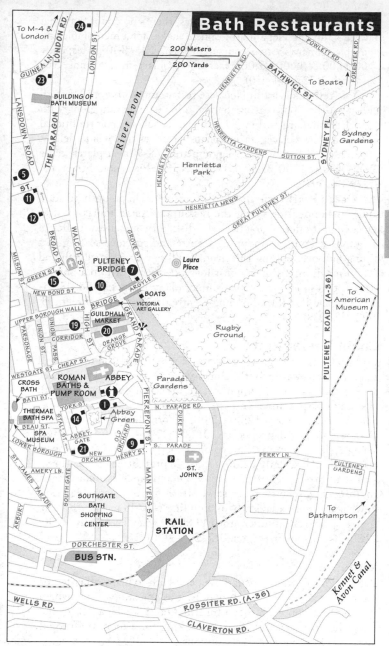

Bath Restaurants

the best food or offers the lowest prices, there's no doubt that Thai Balcony's fun and elegant atmosphere makes for a memorable and enjoyable dinner (£9 two-course lunch special, £8-10 plates, daily 12:00-14:00 & 18:00-22:00, reservations smart on weekends, Saw Close, tel. 01225/444-450).

Yak Yeti Yak is a fun Nepalese restaurant, with both Western and sit-on-the-floor seating. Sera and his wife, Sarah, along with their cheerful, hardworking Nepali team, cook up great traditional food (and plenty of vegetarian plates) at prices that would delight a sherpa (£7-9 lunches, £5 veggie plates, £8-9 meat plates, daily 12:00-14:30 & 17:00-22:30, downstairs at 12 Pierrepont Street, tel. 01225/442-299).

Ocean Pearl Oriental Buffet, inside a shopping mall food court, is famous for being the restaurant Asian tourists eat at repeatedly. It offers a practical, 40-dish, all-you-can-eat buffet in the modern Podium Shopping Centre and spacious seating in a dining hall overlooking the river. You'll pay £6.50 for lunch and £11.50 for dinner. But it's best for take-away—fill up a box for just £3.50 at lunch or £4.50 at dinner (daily 12:00-15:00 & 18:00-22:30, in the Podium Shopping Centre on Northgate Street, tel. 01225/331-238).

Chain Restaurants

With so many homegrown favorites, I see little reason to frequent a chain restaurant in Bath. But if you're a fan, you'll find three decent choices (all of which can be found throughout Britain): **Wagamama** specializes in pan-Asian cuisine (£7-9 meals, Mon-Sat 12:00-23:00, Sun 12:00-22:00, 1 York Buildings, corner of George and Broad streets, tel. 01225/337-314, www.wagamama .com); **Ask** dishes up Italian comfort food (£8-10 pizzas and pastas, good salads, daily 12:00-23:00, George Street but entrance on Broad Street, tel. 01225/789-997); and **Loch Fyne,** a bright, youthful, high-energy place serves fresh fish at reasonable prices in what was once a lavish bank building (£10-18 meals, £10 two-course special from lunch until 19:00 on weekdays, daily 12:00-22:30, 24 Milsom Street, tel. 01225/750-120).

Pubs

Bath is not a good pub-grub town, and with so many other tempting options, eating at a pub here isn't as appealing as elsewhere. For the best pub grub, head for **The Garrick's Head** gastropub (described earlier). But if you're looking for a more traditional, lowbrow place, consider these options.

Crystal Palace Pub is an inviting place just a block away from the abbey, facing the delightful little Abbey Green. With a focus on food rather than drink, they serve "pub grub with a Continental flair" in three different spaces, including a picnic-table back patio (£9-12 meals, food served Mon-Fri 11:00-21:00, Sat 11:00-20:00, Sun 12:00-20:00, last orders for drinks at 23:00, no kids after 16:30, Abbey Green, tel. 01225/482-666).

The Old Green Tree, in the old town center, serves satisfying lunches to locals in a characteristic pub setting (real ales on tap, £6-7 sandwiches, £9 meals, lunch served Mon-Sat 12:00-15:00 only, open daily for drinks, no children, can be crowded on weekend nights, 12 Green Street, tel. 01225/448-259).

For a pub to drink and hang out in, rather than eat at, check out **The Star Inn** or **The Bell** (described on pages 380 and 381).

Simple Options

For a fast, handy, and tasty meal on the go, try one of these easy places. If you get take-away (possible at most of these), you can munch your picnic while watching street musicians from a bench on the abbey square.

The **Boston Tea Party** chain is what Starbucks aspires to be—the neighborhood coffeehouse and hangout. Its extensive breakfasts, light lunches, and salads are fresh and healthy. The outdoor seating overlooks a busy square. They also host musical events, and their walls are decorated with works by local artists (£3-7 breakfasts, £5-7 lunches, Mon-Sat 7:30-19:00, Sun 9:00-19:00, free Wi-Fi, 19 Kingsmead Square, tel. 01225/313-901).

Chandos Deli has good coffee and tasty £3-5 sandwiches made on artisan breads. This upscale but casual five-table place serves breakfast pastries and lunch to dedicated foodies who don't want to pay too much (Mon-Sat 9:00-17:30, Sun 11:00-17:00, 12 George Street, tel. 01225/314-418).

Seafoods Fish & Chips is respected by lovers of greasy fried fish in Bath. There's diner-style and outdoor seating, or you can get your food to go for a bit cheaper (£4-5 take-away meals, Mon-Sat 11:30-22:00, closed Sun, 38 Kingsmead Square, tel. 01225/465-190).

The Cornish Bakehouse, tucked down a shopping gallery across from the Guildhall Market, has freshly baked £3 take-away pasties (Mon-Sat 8:30-17:30, Sun 10:00-17:00, off High Street at 11A The Corridor, tel. 01225/426-635).

Produce Market and Café: **Guildhall Market,** across from Pulteney Bridge, has produce stalls with food for picnickers. At its inexpensive **Market Café,** you can slurp a curry or sip a tea while surrounded by stacks of used books, bananas on the push list, and honest-to-goodness old-time locals (£3-5 traditional English meals including fried breakfasts all day, Mon-Sat 8:00-17:00, closed Sun, tel. 01225/461-593 a block north of the abbey, on High Street).

Supermarkets: **Waitrose,** at the Podium Shopping Centre, is great for picnics and has a good salad bar (Mon-Fri 8:30-20:00, Sat 8:30-19:00, Sun 11:00-17:00, just west of Pulteney Bridge and across from post office on High Street). **Marks & Spencer,** near the train station, has a grocery at the back of its department store and two eateries: **M&S Kitchen** on the ground floor and the pleasant, inexpensive **Café Revive** on the top floor (Mon-Fri 8:30-19:00, Sat 8:30-18:00, Sun 11:00-17:00, 16-18 Stall Street).

Bath Connections

Bath's train station is called Bath Spa (tel. 0845-748-4950). The National Express bus station is just west of the train station (bus info tel. 0871-781-8181, www.nationalexpress.com). For all public bus services in southwestern England, see www.travelinesw.com.

From Bath to London: You can catch a **train** to London's Paddington Station (2/hour, 1.5 hours, best deals for travel after 9:30 and when purchased in advance, www.firstgreatwestern .co.uk), or save money—but not time—by taking the National Express **bus** to Victoria Coach Station (direct buses nearly hourly, 2.5-3.75 hours, sample fares: one-way-£22, round-trip-£29).

From Bath to London's Airports: You can reach **Heathrow** directly and easily by National Express bus (10/day, 2-4 hours, £19-42 one-way, tel. 0871-781-8181, www.nationalexpress.com) or by a train-and-bus combination (take twice-hourly train to Reading, catch twice-hourly airport shuttle bus from there, allow 2.5 hours total, £50-65 depending on time of day, about £10 cheaper when bought in advance, BritRail passholders just pay £15 for bus). Or take the Celtic Horizons minibus to Heathrow (see page 366).

You can get to **Gatwick** by train (about hourly, 2.5 hours, £48-58 one-way depending on time of day, cheaper in advance, transfer in Reading) or by bus (10/day, 4-5 hours, £25 one-way, transfer at Heathrow Airport).

Between Bristol Airport and Bath: Located about 20 miles west of Bath, this airport is closer than Heathrow, but they haven't worked out good connections to Bath yet. From Bristol Airport, your most convenient options are to take a taxi (£35) or call Alan Price (see "Celtic Horizons" on page 366). Otherwise, at the airport you can hop aboard the Bristol Airport Flyer (bus #A1), which takes you to the Temple Meads train station in Bristol (£7, 2-6/hour, 30 minutes, buy bus ticket at airport info counter or from driver, tell driver you want the Temple Meads train station). At the Temple Meads Station, check the departure boards for trains going to the Bath Spa train station (4/hour, 15 minutes, £6). To get from Bath to Bristol Airport, take the train to Temple Meads, then catch the Bristol Airport Flyer bus.

From Bath by Train to: Salisbury (1-2/hour, 1 hour), **Portsmouth** (hourly, 2.25 hours), **Exeter** (1-2/hour, 1.5-2 hours, transfer in Bristol or Westbury), **Penzance** (1-2/hour, 4.5-5 hours, one direct, most 1-2 transfers), **Moreton-in-Marsh** (hourly, 2.5-3 hours, 2-3 transfers), **York** (hourly with transfer in Bristol, 4.25-4.5 hours, more possible with additional transfers), **Oxford** (hourly, 1.25 hours, transfer in Didcot), **Cardiff** (hourly, 1-1.5 hours), **Birmingham** (2/hour, 2 hours, transfer in Bristol), and **points north** (from Birmingham, a major transportation hub, trains depart for Blackpool, Scotland, and North Wales; use a train/bus combination to reach Ironbridge Gorge and the Lake District).

From Bath by Bus to: Salisbury (hourly, 2.75 hours, transfer in Warminster; or 1/day direct at 17:05, 1.5 hours on National Express #300), **Portsmouth** (1/day direct, 3 hours), **Exeter** (4/day, 3.5-4 hours, transfer in Bristol), **Penzance** (2/day, 7-8 hours, transfer in Bristol), **Cheltenham** or **Gloucester** (4/day, 2.5 hours, transfer in Bristol), **Stratford-upon-Avon** (1/day, 4 hours, transfer in Bristol), and **Oxford** (1/day direct, 2 hours, more with transfer). Buses to **Wells** depart nearly hourly, but the last direct bus back leaves before the evensong service is finished (1.25 hours, last return 17:43—except Sun, when there are also buses at 18:46 and 20:16; or take 18:15 bus to Bristol, then train to Bath—see page 415). For bus connections to **Avebury** and **Glastonbury,** see the next chapter.

NEAR BATH

Glastonbury • Wells • Avebury • Stonehenge • Salisbury

Ooooh, mystery, history. Glastonbury is the ancient home of Avalon, King Arthur, and the Holy Grail. Nearby, medieval Wells gathers around its grand cathedral, where you can enjoy an evensong service. Then get Neolithic at every Druid's favorite stone circles, Avebury and Stonehenge. Salisbury is known for its colorful markets and soaring cathedral.

Planning Your Time

Avebury, Glastonbury, and Wells make a wonderful day out from Bath. With a car, you can do all three in a day if you're selective with your sightseeing in each town (no lingering). Splicing in Stonehenge is possible, but really stretching it. If you want to squeeze a little less into each day, choose either the sights to the west (Wells and Glastonbury), or those to the east (Avebury, Stonehenge, and Salisbury). Ideally, try to see Stonehenge on your way from London, saving your Bath side-tripping day for the other sights.

Everybody needs to see Stonehenge, but I'll tell you now, it looks just like it looks. You'll know what I mean when you pay to get in and rub up against the rope fence that keeps tourists at a distance. Avebury is the connoisseur's stone circle: more subtle and welcoming.

Wells is simply a cute town, much smaller and more medieval than Bath, with a uniquely beautiful cathedral that's best experienced at the 17:15 evensong service (Sun at 15:00). Glastonbury can be covered well in three to four hours: See the abbey, climb the Tor, and ponder your hippie past (and where you are now). Just an hour from Bath, Salisbury makes a pleasant stop, particularly on a

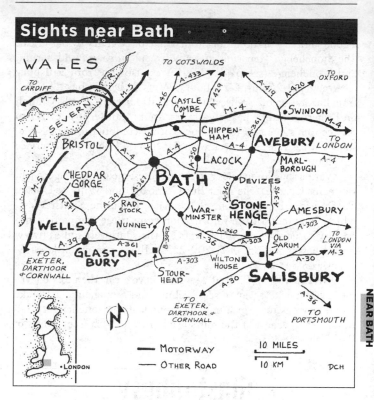

Sights near Bath

market day (Tue, Sat, and every other Wed), though its cathedral is striking anytime.

Getting Around the Region

By Car: Drivers can do a 133-mile loop, from Bath to Avebury (25 miles) to Stonehenge (30 miles) to Glastonbury (50 miles) to Wells (6 miles) and back to Bath (22 miles).

By Bus and Train: Wells and Glastonbury are both easily accessible by bus from Bath. Bus #173 goes direct from Bath to **Wells** (nearly hourly, less frequent on Sun, 1.25 hours), where you can catch bus #375, #376, #377, or #29 to continue on to **Glastonbury** (4/hour, 20 minutes). Note that there are no direct buses between Bath and Glastonbury. Wells and Glastonbury are also connected to each other by a 9.5-mile foot and bike path (though, alas, neither town has bike rental).

Many different buses run between Bath and **Avebury,** all requiring one or two transfers (hourly, 2 hours, transfer at Trowbridge or Devizes). There is no bus between Avebury and Stonehenge.

A one-hour train trip connects Bath to **Salisbury** (1-2/hour).

With the best public transportation of all these towns, Salisbury is a good jumping-off point for Stonehenge or Avebury by bus or car. The Stonehenge Tour runs buses between Salisbury, Old Sarum, and Stonehenge (see page 428). Buses also run from Salisbury to Avebury (1-2/hour, 2-2.5 hours; Wilts & Dorset bus #2 leaves from bus station on Endless Street and also from St. Paul's Church on Fisherton Street, near the train station; transfer in Devizes to Stagecoach's bus #49 to Avebury; other combinations possible, some with 2 transfers; check with Salisbury TI on possible service reductions).

Various bus companies run these routes, including Stagecoach, Bodmans Coaches, the First Bus Company, and Wilts & Dorset. To find fare information, check with Traveline South West, which combines all the information from these companies into an easy-to-use website that covers all the southwest routes (www.travelinesw.com, tel. 0871-200-2233). Buses run much less frequently on Sundays.

By Tour: From Bath, if you don't have a car, the most convenient and quickest way to see Avebury and Stonehenge is to take an all-day bus tour, or a half-day tour just to Stonehenge. Mad Max is the liveliest of the tours leaving from Bath (see "Tours in Bath" on page 363).

Glastonbury

Marked by its hill, or "tor," and located on England's most powerful line of prehistoric sites (called a "ley line"), the town of Glastonbury gurgles with history and mystery.

In A.D. 37, Joseph of Arimathea—Jesus' wealthy uncle—brought vessels containing the blood of Jesus to Glastonbury, and, with them, Christianity came to England. (Joseph's visit is plausible—long before Christ, locals traded lead to merchants from the Levant.) While this story is "proven" by fourth-century writings and accepted by the Church, the King-Arthur-and-the-Holy-Grail legends it inspired are not.

Those medieval tales came when England needed a morale-boosting folk hero for inspiration during a war with France. They pointed to the ancient Celtic sanctuary at Glastonbury as proof enough of the greatness of the fifth-century warlord Arthur. In 1191, his supposed remains (along with those of Queen Guinevere) were dug up from the abbey garden, and Glastonbury became woven into the Arthurian legends. Reburied in the abbey choir, their gravesite is a shrine today. Many think the Grail trail ends at the bottom of the Chalice Well, a natural spring at the base of the Glastonbury Tor.

The Glastonbury Abbey was England's most powerful by the 10th century, and was part of a nationwide network of monasteries that by 1500 owned one-sixth of all English land and had four times the income of the Crown. Then Henry VIII dissolved the abbeys in 1536. He was particularly harsh on Glastonbury—he not only destroyed the abbey but also hung and quartered the abbot, sending the parts of his body on four different national tours...at the same time.

But Glastonbury rebounded. In an 18th-century tourism campaign, thousands signed affidavits stating that they'd been healed  by water from the Chalice Well, and once again Glastonbury was on the tourist map. Today, Glastonbury and its Tor are a center for searchers, too creepy for the mainstream church but just right for those looking for a place to recharge their crystals.

Part of the fun of a visit to Glastonbury is just being in a town where every other shop and eatery is a New Age place. If you need spiritual guidance or just a rune reading, wander through the Glastonbury Experience, a New Age mall at the bottom of High Street. Locals who are not into this complain that on High Street you can buy any kind of magic crystal or incense, but not a roll of TP. But, as this counterculture is their town's bread and butter, they do their best to sit in their pubs and go "Ommmmm."

Orientation to Glastonbury

(area code: 01458)

Tourist Information

The TI is on High Street—as are many of the dreadlocked folks who walk it. It occupies a fine 15th-century townhouse called The Tribunal (Mon-Sat 10:00-16:00, closed Sun, pay Internet access, 9 High Street, tel. 01458/832-954, www.glastonburytic.co.uk). The TI sells several booklets about cycling and walking in the area, including the *Glastonbury and Street Guide,* with local listings and a map (£1.75); and the *Glastonbury Millennium Trail* pamphlet, which sends visitors on a historical scavenger hunt, following 20

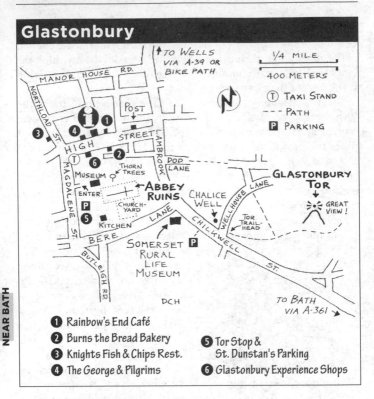

Glastonbury

1 Rainbow's End Café
2 Burns the Bread Bakery
3 Knights Fish & Chips Rest.
4 The George & Pilgrims
5 Tor Stop & St. Dunstan's Parking
6 Glastonbury Experience Shops

numbered marble plaques embedded in the pavement throughout the town (£1). The TI also offers walking tours (£5, call ahead for schedule).

Above the TI is the marginally interesting **Lake Village Museum,** with two humble rooms featuring tools made of stones, bones, and antlers. Preserved in and excavated from the local peat bogs, these tools offer a look at the lives of marshland people in pre-Roman times (£2.50, extensive descriptions, same hours as TI).

Helpful Hints

Market Day: Tuesday is market day for crafts, knickknacks, and produce on the main street. There's also a country market Tuesday mornings in the Town Hall.

Glastonbury Festival: Almost every summer, the gigantic Glastonbury Festival—billing itself as the "largest music and performing arts festival in the world"—brings all manner of postmodern flower children to its notoriously muddy "Healing Fields." Music fans and London's beautiful people make the trek to see the hottest new English and American bands. There won't be a festival in 2012 because of the London Olympics, but if you're near Glastonbury during the 2013 festival, anticipate increased traffic and crowds (especially on public transportation; the more than 135,000 tickets generally sell out), even though the actual music venue is six miles east of town (www.glastonburyfestivals.co.uk).

Sights in Glastonbury

I've listed these sights in the order you'll reach them, moving from the town center to the Tor.

▲▲Glastonbury Abbey

The evocative ruins of the first Christian sanctuary in the British Isles stand mysteriously alive in a lush 36-acre park. Because it

comes with a fine museum, a dramatic history, and enthusiastic guides dressed in period costume, this is one of the most engaging to visit of England's many ruined abbeys.

Cost and Hours: £6, daily June-Aug 9:00-18:00, Sept-May 9:30 or 10:00 to dusk, closing times vary in the winter, last entry 30 minutes before closing, nearby pay parking, tel. 01458/832-267, www.glastonburyabbey .com. Enter the abbey from Magdalene Street (around the corner from High Street, near the St. Dunstan's parking lot).

Tours and Demonstrations: Costumed guides offer tours and presentations throughout the day (all included with your ticket). These include a fun medieval kitchen demo (described later) and earnest, costumed "Living History" re-enactments (generally daily March-Oct at 10:30, 12:00, 14:00, and 16:00). As you enter, confirm these times, and ask about other tour and show times. Or, if you're coming on a slow day (off-season weekdays), call ahead to get the schedule.

Eating: Picnicking is encouraged—bring something from one of the shops in town (see "Eating in Glastonbury," later), or buy food at the small café on site.

Background: The space that these ruins occupy has been sacred ground for centuries. The druids used it as a pagan holy site, and during Joseph of Arimathea's supposed visit, he built a simple place of worship here. In the 12th century—because of that legendary connection with Joseph of Arimathea—Glastonbury was the leading Christian pilgrimage site in all of Britain. The popular abbey grew very wealthy and employed a thousand people to serve

NEAR BATH

the needs of the pilgrims. Then, in 1171, Thomas Becket was martyred at Canterbury, and immediately canonized by the pope (who thanked God for the opportunity to rile up the Christian public in England against King Henry II). This was a classic church-state power struggle. The king was excommunicated, and had to crawl through the streets of London on his knees and submit to a whipping from each bishop in England. Religious pilgrims abandoned Glastonbury for Canterbury, leaving Glastonbury suddenly a backwater.

In 1184, there was a devastating fire in the monastery, and in 1191, the abbot here "discovered"—with the help of a divine dream—the tomb and bodies of King Arthur and Queen Guinevere. Of course, this discovery rekindled the pilgrim trade in Glastonbury.

Then, in 1539, King Henry VIII ordered the abbey's destruction. When Glastonbury Abbot Richard Whiting questioned the king's decision, he was branded a traitor, hung at the top of Glastonbury Tor (after carrying up the plank that would support his noose), and his body cut into four pieces. His head was stuck over the gateway to the former abbey precinct. After this harsh example, the other abbots accepted the king's dissolution of England's abbeys. Many returned to monastic centers in France.

Today, the abbey attracts people who find God within. Tie-dyed, starry-eyed pilgrims seem to float through the grounds, naturally high. Others lie on the grave of King Arthur, whose burial site is marked off in the center of the abbey ruins.

● **Self-Guided Tour:** After buying your ticket, tour the informative **museum** at the entrance building. A model shows the abbey in its pre-Henry VIII splendor, and exhibits tell the story of a place "grandly constructed to entice the dullest minds to prayer." You'll often see costumed guides here who are eager to share the site's story, and might even offer an impromptu tour.

Then head out to explore the green park, dotted with bits of the **ruined abbey.** You come face-to-face with the abbey's west (entrance) end. The abbey was long and skinny, but vast. At 580 feet long, it was the longest in Britain.

Before poking around the ruins, circle to the left behind the entrance building to find the two **thorn trees.** According to legend, when Joseph of Arimathea came here, he climbed nearby Wearyall Hill and stuck his staff into the soil. A thorn tree sprouted, and its descendant still stands there today; these are its offspring. In 2010, vandals hacked off the branches of the original tree on Wearyall Hill, but miraculously, the stump put out small green shoots the following spring. The trees inside the abbey grounds bloom twice a year, at Easter and at Christmas. If the story seems far-fetched to you, don't tell the Queen—a blossom from the abbey's trees sits proudly on her breakfast table every Christmas morning.

Now hike along the ruins to the far end of the abbey. You can stand and, from what was the altar, look down at what was the nave. In this area, you'll find the tombstone (formerly in the floor of the church's choir) where the supposed relics of Arthur and Guinevere were interred.

Continue around the far side of the abbey ruins, feeling free to poke around the park. Head back toward the front of the church, noticing all of the foundation rubble in the field adjoining the abbey; among these were the former churchyard, where Arthur and Guinevere's bones were originally found.

Head for the only surviving intact building on the grounds—the abbot's conical **kitchen.** Here, you'll often find Matilda the pilgrim (or another costumed docent) demonstrating life in the abbey kitchen in a kind of medieval cooking show.

Near Glastonbury Tor

These sights are about a 15-minute walk from the town center, toward the Tor (see "Getting There," on page 404).

Somerset Rural Life Museum—Exhibits in this free and extremely kid-friendly museum include peat digging, cider-making, and cheesemaking. The Abbey Farmhouse is now a collection of domestic and work mementos that illustrate the life of Victorian farm laborer John Hodges "from the cradle to the grave." The fine 14th-century tithe barn (one of 30 such structures that funneled tithes to the local abbey), with its beautifully preserved wooden ceiling, is filled with Victorian farm tools and enthusiastic schoolchildren.

Cost and Hours: Free, Tue-Sat 10:00-17:00, closed Sun-Mon, last entry 30 minutes before closing, free parking, at intersection of Bere Lane and Chilkwell Street, tel. 01823/278-805, www.somerset.gov.uk/museums.

Chalice Well—According to tradition, Joseph of Arimathea brought the chalice from the Last Supper to Glastonbury in A.D. 37. Supposedly it ended up in the bottom of a well, which is now the centerpiece of a peaceful and inviting garden.

Even if the chalice is not in the bottom of the well and the water is red from iron ore and not Jesus' blood, the tranquil setting is one where nature's harmony is a joy to ponder. To find the well itself, follow the gurgling stream uphill, passing several places to drink from or wade in the healing water, as well as areas designated for silent reflection. The stones of the well shaft date from the 12th century, and are believed to have come from the church in Glastonbury Abbey (which was destroyed by fire). During the 18th century, pilgrims flocked to Glastonbury for the well's healing powers. Have a drink or take some of the precious water home—they sell empty bottles to fill.

Cost and Hours: £3.60, daily April-Oct 10:00-18:00, Nov-March 10:00-16:30, last entry 30 minutes before closing, on Chilkwell Street/A361, drivers park at Rural Life Museum and walk 5 minutes—see instructions below, tel. 01458/831-154, www.chalicewell.org.uk.

▲Glastonbury Tor

Seen by many as a Mother Goddess symbol, the Tor—a natural plug of sandstone on clay—has an undeniable geological charisma.

Climbing the Tor is the essential activity on a visit to Glastonbury. A fine Somerset view rewards those who hike to its 520-foot summit. From its top you can survey a former bogland that is still below sea level at high tide. The ribbon-like man-made drainage canals that glisten as they slice through the farmland are the work of Dutch engineers, imported centuries ago to turn the marshy wasteland into something usable.

Looking out, find Glastonbury (at the base of the hill) and Wells (marked by its cathedral) to the right. Above Wells, a TV tower marks the 996-foot high point of the Mendip Hills. It was lead from these hills that attracted the Romans (and, perhaps, Jesus' uncle Joe) so long ago. Stretching to the left, the hills define what was the coastline before those Dutch engineers arrived.

The Tor-top tower is the remnant of a chapel dedicated to St. Michael. Early Christians often employed St. Michael, the warrior angel, to combat pagan gods. When a church was built upon a pagan holy ground like this, it was frequently dedicated to Michael. But apparently those pagan gods fought back: St. Michael's Church was destroyed by an earthquake in 1275.

Getting There: The Tor is a steep hill at the southeastern edge of the town (it's visible from just about everywhere). The base of the Tor is a 20-minute **walk** from the TI and town center. From the base, a trail leads up to the top (figure another 15-20 uphill minutes, if you keep a brisk pace). While you can hike up the Tor from either end, the less-steep approach (which most people take) starts next to the Chalice Well.

If you have a **car,** drive to the Somerset Rural Life Museum, where you can park for free, then walk five minutes to the trailhead (walk up the lane between the parking lot and the museum, turn right onto Chilkwell Street, and watch on the left for the Chalice Well, then the trailhead).

If you're without a car and don't want to walk to the Tor trailhead, you have two options: The **Tor Bus** shuttles visitors from the town center to the base of the Tor. If you ask, the bus will also stop at the Somerset Rural Life Museum and the Chalice Well (£3 round-trip, 2/hour, on the half-hour, Easter-Sept daily 9:30-12:30 & 14:00-19:00, doesn't run Oct-Easter, catch bus at St. Dunstan's parking lot in the town center—to the right as you face the abbey entrance, pick up schedule at TI). A **taxi** to the Tor trailhead costs about £5 one-way—an easier and more economical choice for couples or groups. Remember, these take you only to the bottom of the Tor; to reach the top, you have to hike.

Eating in Glastonbury

Rainbow's End is one of several fine, healthy, vegetarian lunch cafés for hot meals (different every day), salads, herbal teas, yummy homemade sweets, and New Age people-watching (£7-8 meals, cheaper salads sold by the portion, vegan and gluten-free options, counter service, daily 10:00-16:00, a few doors up from the TI, 17 High Street, tel. 01458/833-896). If you're looking for a midwife or a male-bonding tribal meeting, check their notice board.

Burns the Bread makes hearty pasties (savory meat pies) as well as fresh pies, sandwiches, delicious cookies, and pastries. Ask about the Torsy Moorsy Cake (a type of fruitcake made with cheddar), or try a gingerbread man made with real ginger. Grab a pasty and picnic with the ghosts of Arthur and Guinevere in the abbey ruins (£1.50 pasties and pastries, Mon-Sat 6:00-17:00, Sun 11:00-17:00, 14 High Street, tel. 01458/831-532).

Knights Fish and Chips Restaurant, which has been in the same family since 1909, is the town's top chippy—and another fine option for a picnic at the abbey (£6 to go, about £1 more for table service, Mon 17:00-21:30, Tue-Sat 12:00-14:15 & 17:00-21:30, closed Sun, 5 Northload Street, tel. 01458/831-882).

The George & Pilgrims Hotel's wonderfully Old World pub might be exactly what the doctor ordered for visitors suffering a New Age overdose. The French owners mix a few French dishes into the traditional pub-grub menu (£5 sandwiches, £8-11 meals, Mon-Sat 11:00-23:00, Sun 12:00-22:30, food served 12:00-15:00 & 18:00-21:00, 1 High Street, tel. 01458/831-146). They also rent rooms (Db-£75).

Glastonbury Connections

The nearest train station is in Bath. Local buses are run by First Bus Company (tel. 0845-606-4446, www.firstgroup.com).

From Glastonbury by Bus to: Wells (4/hour, 20 minutes, bus #375/#376/#377 runs frequently, bus #29 about 10/day), **Bath** (hourly, allow 2 hours, take bus #375/#376/#377 or #29 to Wells, transfer to bus #173 to Bath, 1.25 hours between Wells and Bath). Buses are sparse on Sundays (generally one bus every other hour). If you're heading to points west, you'll likely connect through **Taunton** (which is a transfer point for westbound buses from Bristol).

Wells

Because this well-preserved little town has a cathedral, it can be called a city. While it's the biggest town in Somerset, it's England's smallest cathedral city (pop. 9,400), with one of its most interesting cathedrals and a wonderful evensong service. Wells has more medieval buildings still doing what they were originally built to do than any town you'll visit. Market day fills the town square on Wednesday (farmers' market) and Saturday (general goods).

Orientation to Wells

(area code: 01749)

Tourist Information

The TI is in the lobby of the Wells Museum across the green from the cathedral. It has useful information about the town's sights and nearby cheese factories (April-Oct Mon-Sat 10:00-17:00, Nov-March Mon-Sat 11:00-16:00, closed Sun, 8 Cathedral Green, tel. 01749/671-770, www.visitsomerset.co.uk). They give out a free schematic map of town and sell a better one for £0.10. Consider the *Wells City Trail* booklet for £0.60. On Wednesdays and Saturdays at 11:00, they offer a one-hour walking tour of town for £4.

Arrival in Wells

If you're coming by **bus,** you'll arrive at the big, well-organized but unstaffed bus parking lot, about a five-minute walk from the town center. (The big church tower you see is *not* the cathedral.) Find the Wells map at the head of the stalls to get oriented; the signpost at the main exit directs you downtown. **Drivers** will find pay parking right on the main square, but because of confusing one-way streets, it's hard to reach; instead, it's simpler to park at the Princes Road lot near the bus station (enter on Priory Road) and walk five minutes to the cathedral.

Helpful Hints

Local Guide: Edie Westmoreland offers town walks in the summer by appointment (£15/group of 2-5 people, £4/person for 8 or more, 1.5-hour tours usually start at Penniless Porch on town square, book three days in advance, tel. 01934/832-350, mobile 07899-836-706, ebwestmoreland@btinternet.com).

Best Views: It's hard to beat the grand views of the cathedral from the green in front of it...but the reflecting pool tucked inside the Bishop's Palace grounds tries hard. For a fine cathedral-and-town view from your own leafy hilltop bench, hike 10 minutes up Tor Hill.

Sights in Wells

▲▲Wells Cathedral

England's first completely Gothic cathedral (dating from about 1200) is the highlight of the city. Locals claim this church has the largest collection of medieval statuary north of the Alps. It certainly has one of the widest and most elaborate facades I've seen, and unique figure-eight supports in the nave to boot.

Cost and Hours: Requested £6 donation—not intended to keep you out, daily Easter-Sept 7:00-19:00, Oct-Easter 7:00-18:00; to take pictures, pay £3 photography fee at info desk or at coin-op machine inside cathedral, no flash in choir; one-hour tours April-Oct Mon-Sat at 10:00, 12:00, 13:00, 14:00, and 15:00; Nov-March Mon-Sat usually at 12:00 and 14:00—unless other events are going on in the cathedral; good shop, handy Chapter Two restaurant, tel. 01749/674-483, www.wellscathedral.org.uk.

Ͽ Self-Guided Tour: Begin on the vast, inviting **green** in front of the cathedral. In the Middle Ages, the cathedral was enclosed within "The Liberty," an area free from civil jurisdiction until the 1800s. The Liberty included the green on the west side of the cathedral, which, from the 13th to the 17th centuries, was a burial place for common folk, including 17th-century plague victims. During the Edwardian period, a local character known as Boney Foster used to dig up the human bones and sell them to tourists. The green later became a cricket pitch, then a field for grazing animals. Today, it's the perfect setting for an impressive cathedral.

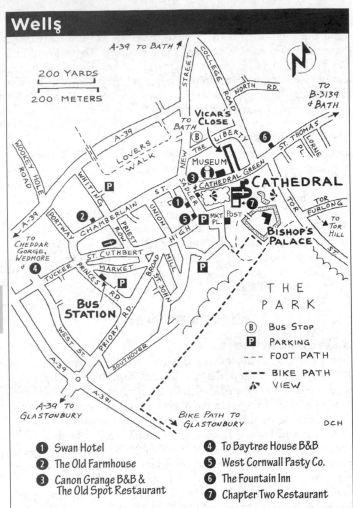

Wells

A-39 TO BATH

200 YARDS
200 METERS

COLLEGE ROAD
STREET
NORTH RD.
TO B-3139 & BATH
ST. THOMAS PL.
LORNE
VICAR'S CLOSE
THE LIBERTY
TO BATH
A-39
LOVERS WALK
WOOKEY HOLE ROAD
WHITING
NEW ST.
SADLER ST.
ST. CUTHBERT
MUSEUM
CATHEDRAL GREEN
CATHEDRAL
ST. THOMAS ST.
TOR
TOR FURLONG
TO TOR HILL
CHAMBERLAIN
PRIEST ROW
UNION ST.
HIGH ST.
MKT PL.
POST
BISHOP'S PALACE
PORTWAY
TO CHEDDAR GORGE, WEDMORE
TUCKER
PRINCES RD.
MARKET
BROAD ST.
ST. JOHN
MILL
THE PARK
BUS STATION
WEST ST.
PRIORY RD.
SOUTHOVER
A-39
A-371
A-39 TO GLASTONBURY
BIKE PATH TO GLASTONBURY
DCH

ⓑ BUS STOP
ⓟ PARKING
- - - FOOT PATH
– – – BIKE PATH
↖ VIEW

① Swan Hotel
② The Old Farmhouse
③ Canon Grange B&B & The Old Spot Restaurant
④ To Baytree House B&B
⑤ West Cornwall Pasty Co.
⑥ The Fountain Inn
⑦ Chapter Two Restaurant

Peer up at the impressive **facade.** The recently restored west front displays almost 300 original 13th-century carvings of kings and the Last Judgment. The bottom row of niches is empty, too easily reached by Cromwell's men, who were hell-bent on destroying "graven images." Stand back and imagine it as a grand Palm Sunday welcome with a cast of hundreds—all gaily painted back then, choristers singing boldly from holes above the doors and trumpets tooting through the holes up by the 12 apostles.

Now head **inside.** Most of the time, visitors enter by going to the right, through the door under the small spire into the lobby and welcome center. (At certain times—generally 7:00-9:00 and

17:00-19:00—you can enter through the cathedral's main door.)

At the **welcome center,** you'll be warmly greeted and reminded how expensive it is to maintain the cathedral. Pay the donation, buy a £3 photo-permission sticker (if you choose), and pick up a map of the cathedral's highlights. Then head through the cloister and into the cathedral.

At your first glance down the nave, you're immediately struck by the general lightness and the unique "scissors" or hourglass-shaped **double arch** (added in 1338 to transfer weight from the west—where the foundations were sinking under the tower's weight—to the east, where they were firm). The warm tones of the stone interior give the place a modern feel. Until Henry VIII and the Reformation, the interior was painted a gloomy red and green. Later it was whitewashed. Then, in the 1840s, the church experienced the Victorian "great scrape," as locals peeled moldy whitewash off and revealed the bare stone we see today. The floral ceiling painting is based on the original medieval design. A single pattern was discovered under the 17th-century whitewash and repeated throughout.

Small, ornate 15th-century pavilion-like chapels flank the altar, carved in lacy Gothic for wealthy townsmen. The **pulpit** features a post-Reformation, circa-1540 English script—rather than the standard Latin. Since this was not a monastery church, the Reformation didn't destroy it as it did the Glastonbury Abbey church.

We'll do a quick clockwise spin around the cathedral's interior. First walk down the left aisle until you reach the north transept. The medieval **clock** does a silly but much-loved joust on the quarter-hour. If you get to watch the show, notice how—like clockwork—every other rider gets clobbered. The clock's face, which depicts the earth at the center of the universe, dates from 1390. The outer ring shows hours, the second ring shows minutes, and the inner ring shows the dates of the month and phases of the moon. Beneath the clock, the fine **crucifix** was carved out of a yew tree by a German prisoner of war during World War II. After the war ended, many of England's German prisoners figured there was little in Germany to go home to, so they stayed, assimilating into English culture.

Also in the north transept is the door with well-worn steps leading up to the grand, fan-vaulted **Chapter House**—an intimate place for the theological equivalent of a huddle among church officials.

Now continue down the left aisle. On the right is the entrance to the **choir** (or "quire," the central zone where the daily services are sung). Go in and take a close look at the embroidery work on the cushions, which celebrate the hometowns of important local church leaders. Up above the east end of the choir is "Jesse's Window," depicting Jesus' family tree. It's also called the "Golden Window," because it's bathed in sunlight each morning.

Head back out to the aisle the way you came in, and continue to the end of the church. In the apse you'll find the **Lady Chapel.** Examine the medieval stained-glass windows. Do they look jumbled? In the 17th century, Puritan troops trashed the precious original glass. Much was repaired, but many of the broken panes were like a puzzle that was never figured out. That's why today many of the windows are simply kaleidoscopes of colored glass.

Now circle around and head up the other aisle. As you walk, notice that many of the black **tombstones** set in the floor have decorative recesses that aren't filled with brass (as they once were). After the Reformation in the 1530s, the church was short on cash, so they sold the brass to raise money for roof repairs.

Once you reach the south transept, you'll find several items of interest. The **old font** survives from the previous church (A.D. 705) and has been the site of Wells baptisms for almost a thousand years. In the far end of this transept, a little of the muddy green and red that wasn't whitewashed survives.

Nearby, notice the **carvings** at the tops of the pillars, which depict medieval life. On the first pillar, notice the man with a toothache, and another man with a thorn in his foot. The second pil-

NEAR BATH

lar tells a story of medieval justice:
On the left, we see thieves stealing
grapes; on the right, the woodcutter
(with an axe) is warning the farmer
(with the pitchfork) what's happening.
Circle around to the back of the pillar
for the rest of the story: On the left,
the farmer chases one of the thieves,
grabbing him by the ear. On the right,
he clobbers the thief over the head
with his pitchfork—so hard the farmer's hat falls off.

Also in the south transept, you'll find the entrance to the
cathedral **Reading Room.** Housing a few old manuscripts, it
offers a peek into a real 15th-century library (£1, April-Oct Fri-Sat
14:30-16:30 only; might also be possible to step in for a quick look
on weekday mornings and afternoons).

And finally, the south transept is also where you'll exit the
cathedral: Head out into the cloister, then cross the courtyard back
to the welcome center, shop, Chapter Two restaurant, and exit. Go
in peace.

More Cathedral Sights

▲▲Cathedral Evensong Service—The cathedral choir takes
full advantage of heavenly acoustics with a nightly 45-minute
evensong service. You will sit right in the old "quire" as you listen
to a great pipe organ and boys', girls', and men's voices.

Cost and Hours: Free, Mon-Sat at 17:15, Sun at 15:00, generally no service when school is out July-Aug unless a visiting choir
performs, to check call 01749/674-483 or visit www.wellscathedral
.org.uk. At 17:05 (Sun at 14:50) the verger ushers visitors to their
seats. There's usually plenty of room.

Returning to Bath after the Evensong: On weekdays and
Saturdays, if you need to catch the 17:43 bus to Bath, request a
seat on the north side of the presbytery, so you can slip out the
side door without disturbing the service (10-minute walk to station
from cathedral, bus also departs from The Liberty—a 4-minute
walk away—at 17:47; or go at 18:15 via Bristol—explained under
"Wells Connections," later).

Other Cathedral Concerts: The cathedral also hosts several
evening concerts each month (£10-26, most about £18, generally
Thu-Sat at 19:00 or 19:30, box office in cathedral gift shop, open
Mon-Sat 14:00-16:30, closed Sun, tel. 01749/832-201). Concert
tickets are also available at the TI.

Vicar's Close—Lined with perfectly pickled 14th-century houses,
this is the oldest continuously occupied complete street in Europe

(since 1348; just a block north of the cathedral—go under the big arch and look left). It was built to house the vicar's choir, and it still houses church officials (and some of the houses can be rented for a weeklong holiday; contact the cathedral office for details).

▲**Bishop's Palace**—Next to the cathedral stands the moated Bishop's Palace, built in the 13th century and still in use today as the residence of the Bishop of Bath

and Wells. While the interior of the palace itself is dull, the grounds and gardens surrounding it are spectacular—the most tranquil and scenic spot in Wells, with wonderful views of the cathedral. It's just the place for a relaxing walk in the park.

Cost and Hours: £6, April-Oct daily 10:30-18:00, closed Nov-March, often closed on Sat for special events—call to confirm, last entry one hour before closing, tel. 01749/988-111, www.bishopspalace.org.uk.

Touring the Palace and Gardens: The palace's spring-fed moat was built in the 14th century to protect the bishop during squabbles with the borough. Now it serves primarily as a pool for mute swans, who have been trained to ring a bell to ask for food. The bridge was last drawn in 1831. Crossing that bridge, you'll buy your ticket and enter the grounds (past the old-timers playing a proper game of croquet—daily after 13:30). Pass through the evocative ruins of the Great Hall (which was deserted and left to gradually deteriorate), and stroll through the chirpy south lawn. If you're feeling energetic, hike up to the top of the ramparts that encircle the property.

Circling around the far side of the mansion, cross the little bridge and follow the path to the wells (springs) that gave the city its name. Surrounding a reflecting pool with the cathedral towering overhead, these flower-bedecked pathways are idyllic. Nearby are an arboretum, picnic area, and sweet little pea-patch gardens.

After touring the gardens, the mansion's interior is a letdown—despite the borrowable descriptions that struggle to make

NEAR BATH

the dusty old place meaningful. Have a spot of tea in the café (with outdoor garden seating), or climb the creaky wooden staircase to wander long halls lined with portraits of bishops past.

Near Wells

The following stops are best for drivers.

Cheddar Cheese—If you're in the mood for a picnic, drop by any local aromatic cheese shop for a great selection of tasty Somerset cheeses. Real farmhouse cheddar puts American cheddar to Velveeta shame. The **Cheddar Gorge Cheese Company,** eight miles west of Wells, is a dairy farm with a guide and a viewing area, giving guests a chance to see the cheesemaking process and enjoy a sample (£2, daily 10:00-16:00; take A39, then A371 to Cheddar Gorge; tel. 01934/742-810, www.cheddargorgecheeseco .co.uk).

Scrumpy Farms—Scrumpy is the wonderfully dangerous hard cider brewed in this part of England. You don't find it served in many pubs because of the unruly crowd it attracts. Scrumpy, at 8 percent alcohol, will rot your socks. "Scrumpy Jack," carbonated mass-produced cider, is not real scrumpy. The real stuff is "rough farmhouse cider." This is potent stuff. It's said some farmers throw a side of beef into the vat, and when fermentation is done only the teeth remain.

TIs list local cider farms open to the public, such as **Mr. Wilkins' Land's End Cider Farm,** a great Back Door travel experience (free, Mon-Sat 10:00-20:00, Sun 10:00-13:00; west of Wells in Mudgley, take B3139 from Wells to Wedmore, then B3151 south for 2 miles, farm is a quarter-mile off B3151—tough to find, get close and ask locals; tel. 01934/712-385, www.wilkinscider.com).

Apples are pressed from August through December. Hard cider, while not quite scrumpy, is also typical of the West Country, but more fashionable, "decent," and accessible. You can get a pint of hard cider at nearly any pub, drawn straight from the barrel— dry, medium, or sweet.

Castle of Nunney—The centerpiece of the charming village of Nunney (between Bath and Glastonbury, off A361) is a striking 14th-century castle surrounded by a fairy-tale moat. Its rare, French-style design brings to mind the Paris Bastille. The year 1644 was a tumultuous one for Nunney. Its noble family was royalist (and likely closet Catholics). They defied Parliament, so Parliament ordered their castle "slighted" (deliberately destroyed) to ensure that it would threaten the order of the land no more. Looking at this castle, so daunting in the age of bows and arrows, you can see how it was no match for the modern cannon. The pretty Mendip village of Nunney, with its little brook, is also worth a wander.

Sleeping in Wells

(area code: 01749)
Wells is a pleasant overnight stop, with a handful of agreeable B&Bs. The first three places listed below are within a short walk of the cathedral.

$$ Swan Hotel, a Best Western facing the cathedral, is a big, comfortable 48-room hotel. Prices for their Tudor-style rooms vary based on whether you want extras like a four-poster bed or a view of the cathedral. They also rent five apartments in the village (Sb-£108, Db-£140, superior Db-£164, deluxe Db-£188, apartments-£114-149, ask about weekend deals, free Wi-Fi, Sadler Street, tel. 01749/836-300, fax 01749/836-301, www.swanhotel wells.co.uk, info@swanhotelwells.co.uk).

$$ The Old Farmhouse, a five-minute walk from the town center, welcomes you with a secluded front garden and two tastefully decorated rooms (Db-£80-85, 2-night minimum, secure parking, next to the gas station at 62 Chamberlain Street, tel. 01749/675-058, www.wellsholiday.com, theoldfarmhousewells@hotmail.com, charming owners Felicity and Christopher Wilkes).

$ Canon Grange B&B is a 15th-century watch-your-head beamed house directly in front of the cathedral. It has seven homey rooms and a cozy charm (S-£55, Db-£72, Db with spectacular cathedral view-£74, family room, free Wi-Fi, on the cathedral green, tel. 01749/671-800, www.canongrange.co.uk, canongrange@email.com, Annette and Ken).

$ Baytree House B&B is a modern and practical home at the edge of town (on a big road, a 10-minute walk to the bus station) renting five fresh, bright, and comfy rooms. Amanda and

Paulo Bellini run the place with Italian enthusiasm (Db-£64-70, Tb-£75-90, two rooms have private bathrooms on the hall, free Wi-Fi, plush lounge, free parking, near where Strawberry Way hits the A39 road to Cheddar at 85 Portway, tel. 01749/677-933, mobile 07745-287-194, www.baytree-house.co.uk, stay@baytree -house.co.uk).

Eating in Wells

Downtown Wells is tiny. A fine variety of eating options is within a block or two of its market square, including classic pubs, little delis and bakeries serving light meals, and a branch of **West Cornwall Pasty Company,** selling good savory pasties to go (Mon-Sat 8:00-18:00, Sun 10:00-17:00, 1a Sadler Street, tel. 01749/671-616).

The Fountain Inn, on a quiet street 50 yards behind the cathedral, serves good pub grub (£9-10 lunches, £10-13 dinners, open daily, St. Thomas Street, tel. 01749/672-317).

Chapter Two, the modern restaurant in the cathedral welcome center, offers a handy if not heavenly lunch (£6-7 lunches, Mon-Sat 10:00-17:00, Sun 11:00-17:00, may close earlier in winter, tel. 01749/676-543).

The Old Spot is a dressy, modern place with a cathedral view. The food is elegant and well-prepared, although pricey (£13-16 fixed-price lunch, Wed-Sat 12:30-14:30 & 19:00-22:30, Sun 12:30-14:30, Tue 19:00-22:30, closed Mon, 12 Sadler Street, tel. 01749/689-099).

Wells Connections

The nearest train station is in Bath. The bus station in Wells is at a well-organized bus parking lot at the intersection of Priory and Princes roads. Local buses are run by First Bus Company (for Wells, tel. 0845-606-4446, www.firstgroup.com), while buses to and from London are run by National Express (tel. 0871-781-8181, www.nationalexpress.com).

From Wells by Bus to: Bath (nearly hourly, 1.25 hours, last bus #173 leaves at 17:43—except Sun, when there are also buses at 18:46 and 20:16; if you miss the Mon-Sat 17:43 bus to Bath, catch the 18:15 bus to Bristol, then a 15-minute train ride to Bath, arriving 19:35), **Glastonbury** (4/hour, 20 minutes, bus #375/#376/#377 runs frequently, bus #29 about 10/day), **London**'s Victoria Coach Station (£28-30, 1/day direct, departs Wells at 6:55, arrives London at 11:20; otherwise hourly with a change in Bristol, 4 hours).

Avebury

Avebury is a prehistoric open-air museum, with a complex of fascinating Neolithic sites all gathered around the great stone henge (circle). Because the area sports only a thin skin of topsoil over chalk, it is naturally treeless (similar to the area around Stonehenge). Perhaps this unique landscape—where the land connects with the big sky—made it the choice of prehistoric societies for their religious monuments. Whatever the case, Avebury dates to 2800 B.C.—six centuries older than Stonehenge. This complex, the St. Peter's Basilica of Neolithic civilization, makes for a fascinating visit. Many enjoy it more than Stonehenge.

Orientation to Avebury

(area code: 01672)
Avebury, just a little village with a big stone circle, is easy to reach by car, but may not be worth the hassle by public transportation (see "Getting Around the Region," page 397).

Tourist Information

The TI is located within the town chapel. Notice the stone work: It's a mix of bricks and broken stones from the ancient circle (April-Oct Tue-Sat 9:30-17:00, Sun 9:30-14:30, closed Mon; Nov-March likely open Wed-Sat 9:30-16:00, Sun 9:30-14:30, closed Mon-Tue; Green Street, tel. 01672/539-179, www.visitwiltshire.co.uk). For good information on the Avebury sights, see the websites of the English Heritage (www.english-heritage.org.uk) and the National Trust (www.nationaltrust.org.uk).

Arrival by Car

If driving, you must pay to park in Avebury, and your only real option is the flat-fee National Trust parking lot, which is a three-minute walk from the village (£5, £3 after 15:00, summer 9:00-18:00, off-season 9:00-16:00). No other public parking is available in the village.

Stone Circles: The Riddle of the Rocks

Britain is home to roughly 800 evocative stone circles, most of them rudimentary, jaggedly sparse boulder rings that lack

the iconic upright-and-lintel form of Stonehenge. But their misty, mossy settings provide curious travelers with an intimate and accessible glimpse of the mysterious people who lived in prehistoric Britain.

Bronze Age Britain (2000-600 B.C.) was populated by farming folk who had mastered the craft of smelting heated tin and copper together to produce bronze, which was used to produce more durable tools and weapons. Late in the Bronze Age, many of these primitive, clannish communities also chose to put considerable time and effort into gathering huge rocks and arranging them into ceremonial circles for use in rituals with long-forgotten meanings. Scholars believe that these circles may have been used as solar observatories, to calculate solstices and equinoxes as they planned life-sustaining seasonal crop-planting cycles. Archaeologists have discovered a few ancient remains in the center of some circles, but their primary use seems to have been ceremonial rather than as burial sites. And without any written records, we can only make educated guesses as to their exact purpose.

The superstitious people of the Middle Ages, who hadn't quite perfected their carbon-dating techniques, came up with colorful explanations for the circles. Stonehenge, for example, was believed to have been arranged by giants (makes sense to me). Later, several circles were thought to be petrified partiers who had dared to dance on the Sabbath; nearby standing stones were supposedly the frozen figures of the pipers who had been playing the dance tunes.

England's stone circles generally lie at the fringes of the country, clustering mostly in the southwest (particularly on the Cornwall peninsula) and in the hills north of Manchester. Dedicated travelers seeking stone circles will find them marked in the Ordnance Survey atlas and signposted along rural roads. Ask a local farmer for directions—and savor the experience (wear shoes impervious to grass dew and sheep doo). I've highlighted my favorites in this book: **Stonehenge** and **Avebury** (both described in this chapter), **Castlerigg** (in the Lake District, near Keswick—see page 630), Cornwall's **Merry Maidens** (see page 346), and **Scorhill Stone Circle,** probably the best of the many circles in Dartmoor National Park (see page 320).

Sights in Avebury

All of Avebury's prehistoric sights are free to visit and always open.

▲▲**Avebury Stone Circle**—The stone circle at Avebury is bigger (16 times the size), less touristy, and, for many, more interesting than Stonehenge. You're free to wander among 100 stones, ditches, mounds, and curious patterns from the past, as well as the village of Avebury, which grew up in the middle of this fascinating 1,400-foot-wide Neolithic circle.

In the 14th century, in a kind of frenzy of religious paranoia, Avebury villagers buried many of these mysterious pagan stones. Their 18th-century descendants hosted social events in which they broke up the remaining pagan stones (topple, heat up, douse with cold water, and scavenge broken stones as building blocks). In modern times, the buried stones were dug up and re-erected. Concrete markers show where the missing broken-up stones once stood.

To make the roughly half-mile walk around the circle, you'll hike along an impressive earthwork henge—a 30-foot-high outer bank surrounding a ditch 30 feet deep, making a 60-foot-high rampart. This earthen rampart once had stones standing around the perimeter, placed about every 30 feet, and four grand causeway entries. Originally, two smaller circles made of about 200 stones stood within the henge.

▲**Ritual Procession Way**—Also known as West Kennet Avenue, this double line of stones provided a ritual procession way leading from Avebury to a long-gone wooden circle dubbed "The Sanctuary." This "wood henge," thought to have been 1,000 years older than everything else in the area, is considered the genesis of Avebury and its big stone circle. Most of the stones standing along the procession way today were reconstructed in modern times.

▲**Silbury Hill**—This pyramid-shaped hill is a 130-foot-high, yet-to-be-explained mound of chalk just outside of Avebury. More than 4,000 years old, this mound is considered the largest man-made object in prehistoric Europe (with the surface area of London's Trafalgar Square and the height of the Nelson Column). It's a reminder that we've only just scratched the surface of England's mysterious and ancient religious landscape.

Inspired by a legend that the hill hid a gold statue in its center, locals tunneled through Silbury Hill in 1830, undermining the structure. Work is currently underway to restore the hill, which

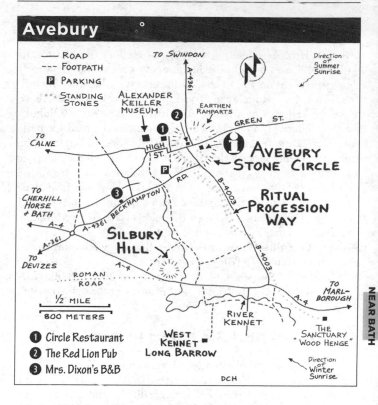

Avebury

— ROAD
--- FOOTPATH
P PARKING
° ° STANDING STONES

TO SWINDON

N
Direction of Summer Sunrise

ALEXANDER KEILLER MUSEUM

EARTHEN RAMPARTS

GREEN ST.

TO CALNE

HIGH ST.

AVEBURY STONE CIRCLE

TO CHERHILL HORSE & BATH

BECKHAMPTON RD.

RITUAL PROCESSION WAY

B-4003

A-4
A-4361

SILBURY HILL

TO DEVIZES

A-361

ROMAN ROAD

A-4

TO MARL-BOROUGH

A-4

½ MILE
800 METERS

❶ Circle Restaurant
❷ The Red Lion Pub
❸ Mrs. Dixon's B&B

WEST KENNET LONG BARROW

RIVER KENNET

THE SANCTUARY "WOOD HENGE"

Direction of Winter Sunrise

DCH

NEAR BATH

remains closed to the public. Archaeologists (who date things like this by carbon-dating snails and other little critters killed in its construction) figure Silbury Hill took only 60 years to build, in about 2200 B.C. This makes Silbury Hill the last element built at Avebury and contemporaneous with Stonehenge. Some think it may have been an observation point for all the other bits of the Avebury site. You can still see evidence of a spiral path leading up the hill, and a moat at its base.

The Roman road detoured around Silbury Hill. (Roman engineers often used features of the landscape as visual reference points when building roads. Their roads would commonly kink at the crest of hills or other landmarks, where they realigned with a new visual point.) Later, the hill sported a wooden Saxon fort, which likely acted as a lookout for marauding Vikings. And in World War II, the Royal Observer Corps stationed men up here to count and report Nazi bombers on raids.

West Kennet Long Barrow—A pullout on the road just past Silbury Hill marks the West Kennet Long Barrow (a 15-minute walk from Silbury Hill). This burial chamber, the best-preserved Stone Age chamber tomb in the UK, stands intact on the ridge. It lines up with the rising sun on the summer solstice. You can walk inside the barrow.

Cherhill Horse—Heading west from Avebury on A4 (toward Bath), you'll see an obelisk (a monument to some important earl) above you on the downs, or chalk hills, near the village of Cherhill. You'll also see a white horse carved into the chalk hillside. Above it are the remains of an Iron Age hill fort known as Oldbury Castle—described on an information board at the roadside pull-out. There is one genuinely prehistoric white horse in England (the Uffington White Horse); the Cherhill Horse, like all the others, is just an 18th-century creation. Prehistoric discoveries were all the rage in the 1700s, and it was a fad to make your own fake ones. Throughout southern England, you can cut into the thin layer of topsoil and find chalk. Now, so they don't have to weed, horses like this are cemented and painted white.

Alexander Keiller Museum—This archaeology museum has an interactive exhibit in a 17th-century barn.

Cost and Hours: £4.90, daily April-Oct 10:00-18:00, Nov-March 10:00-16:30, last entry 30 minutes before closing, tel. 01672/539-250.

Eating and Sleeping in Avebury

(£1 = about $1.60, country code: 44, area code: 01672)

The pleasant **Circle Restaurant** serves healthy, hearty à la carte lunches, including vegan and gluten-free dishes, and cream teas on most days (daily April-Oct 10:00-18:00, Nov-March 10:00-16:00, next to National Trust store and the Alexander Keiller museum, tel. 01672/539-514).

The Red Lion has inexpensive, greasy pub grub; a creaky, well-worn, dart-throwing ambience; and a medieval well in its dining room (£6-12 meals, daily 12:00-22:00, tel. 01672/539-266).

Sleeping in Avebury makes lots of sense, since the stones are lonely and wide-open all night. **$ Mrs. Dixon's B&B,** up the road from the public parking lot, rents three cramped and homey rooms. Look for the green-and-white *Bed & Breakfast* sign from the main road (S-£40, D-£60, these prices promised with this book in 2012, cash only, parking available in back, 6 Beckhampton Road, tel. 01672/539-588, run by earthy Mrs. Dixon and crew).

Stonehenge

As old as the pyramids, and older than the Acropolis and the Colosseum, this iconic stone circle amazed medieval Europeans, who figured it was built by a race of giants. And it still impresses visitors today. As one of Europe's most famous sights, Stonehenge does a valiant job of retaining an air of mystery and majesty (partly because cordons, which keep hordes of tourists from trampling all over it, foster the illusion that it stands alone in a field). Although some people are underwhelmed by Stonehenge, most of its almost one million annual visitors find that it's worth the trip. And the ancient site continues to reveal its mysteries: In 2010, within sight of Stonehenge, archaeologists discovered another 5,000-year-old henge, or ditch, which they believe once encircled a wooden "twin" of the famous circle.

Getting to Stonehenge

By Public Transportation: Catch a train to Salisbury, then go by bus or taxi to Stonehenge (for details, see page 428). Note that there is no public transportation between Avebury and Stonehenge.

By Car: Stonehenge is well-signed just off A303. It's about 15 minutes north of Salisbury, an hour east of Glastonbury, and an hour south of Avebury. From Salisbury, head north on A345 (Castle Road) through Amesbury, go west on A303 for 1.5 miles, veer right onto A344, and it's just ahead on the left, with the parking lot on the right. In 2012, construction may begin on a new visitors center, which will change the parking location; check online or ask local TIs for details.

By Bus Tour: For tours of Stonehenge from Bath, see page 365 (Mad Max is best); for tours from Salisbury, see page 428.

Orientation to Stonehenge

Cost: £7.50, covered by English Heritage Pass and Great British Heritage Pass (see page 20).

Hours: Daily June-Aug 9:00-19:00, mid-March-May and Sept-mid-Oct 9:30-18:00, mid-Oct-mid-March 9:30-16:00, last entry 30 minutes before closing.

When to Go: Shorter hours and possible closures June 20-22 due to huge, raucous solstice crowds; £3 parking fee likely in summer—refundable with paid admission.

Information: Entry includes a worthwhile hour-long audioguide, tel. 01980/623-108 or 0870-333-1181, www.english-heritage.org.uk/stonehenge.

Reaching the Inner Stones: Special one-hour access to the stones' inner circle—before or after regular visiting hours—costs an extra £15.30 and must be reserved well in advance. Details are on the English Heritage website (go to "Explore Stonehenge," then click on the Stone Circle Access link), or call 01722/343-834.

Planned Changes: Stonehenge officials want to build a new visitors center and museum that will blend in with the landscape and make the stone circle feel more pristine. Visitors will park farther away and ride a shuttle bus to the site. Construction is scheduled to begin in April of 2012.

Self-Guided Tour

The entrance fee includes a good audioguide, but this commentary will help make your visit even more meaningful.

Walk in from the parking lot, buy your ticket, pick up your included audioguide, and head through the ugly underpass beneath the road. On the way up the ramp, notice the artist's rendering of what Stonehenge once looked like. As you approach the massive structure, walk right up to the knee-high cordon and let your fellow 21st-century tourists melt away. It's just you and the druids...

England has hundreds of stone circles, but Stonehenge—which literally means "hanging stones"—is unique. It's the only one that has horizontal cross-pieces (called lintels) spanning the vertical monoliths, and the only one with stones that have been made smooth and uniform. What you see here is a bit more than half the original structure—the rest was quarried centuries ago for

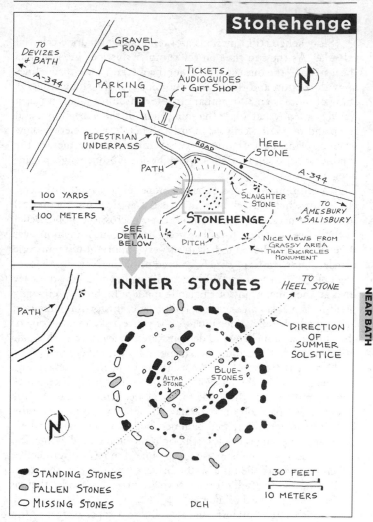

Stonehenge

TO
DEVIZES
& BATH

A-344

GRAVEL
ROAD

PARKING
LOT

TICKETS,
AUDIOGUIDES
& GIFT SHOP

N

PEDESTRIAN
UNDERPASS

ROAD

HEEL
STONE

PATH

A-344

100 YARDS

100 METERS

SEE
DETAIL
BELOW

SLAUGHTER
STONE

STONEHENGE

TO
AMESBURY
& SALISBURY

DITCH

NICE VIEWS FROM
GRASSY AREA
THAT ENCIRCLES
MONUMENT

INNER STONES

TO
HEEL STONE

PATH

DIRECTION
OF
SUMMER
SOLSTICE

ALTAR
STONE

BLUE-
STONES

N

● STANDING STONES
◐ FALLEN STONES
○ MISSING STONES

30 FEET

10 METERS

DCH

NEAR BATH

other buildings.

Now do a slow counterclockwise spin around the monument, and ponder the following points. As you walk, mentally flesh out the missing pieces and re-erect the rubble. Knowledgeable guides posted around the site are happy to answer your questions.

This was a hugely significant location to prehistoric peoples. There are some 500 burial mounds within a three-mile radius of Stonehenge—most likely belonging to kings and chieftains. Built in phases between 3000 and 1500 B.C., Stonehenge originally was used as a cremation cemetery (so goes one recently popular theory). But that's not the end of the story, as the monument was expanded over the millennia.

Stonehenge still functions as a remarkably accurate celestial calendar. As the sun rises on the summer solstice (June 21), the "heel stone"—the one set apart from the rest, near the road—lines up with the sun and the altar at the center of the stone circle. A study of more than 300 similar circles in Britain found that each was designed to calculate the movement of the sun, moon, and stars, and to predict eclipses in order to help early societies know when to plant, harvest, and party. Even in modern times, as the summer solstice sun sets in just the right slot at Stonehenge, pagans boogie.

In addition to being a calendar, Stonehenge is built at the precise point where six ley lines intersect. Ley lines are theoretical lines of magnetic or spiritual power that crisscross the globe. Belief in the power of these lines has gone in and out of fashion over time. They are believed to have been very important to prehistoric peoples, but then were largely ignored until the New Age movement of the 20th century. Without realizing it, you follow these ley lines all the time: Many of England's modern highways, following prehistoric paths, and churches, built over prehistoric monuments, are located where ley lines intersect. If you're a skeptic, ask one of the guides at Stonehenge to demonstrate the ley lines with a pair of L-shaped divining rods...it's creepy and convincing.

Notice that two of the stones (facing the entry passageway) are blemished. At the base of one monolith, it looks like someone has pulled back the stone to reveal a concrete skeleton. This is a clumsy repair job to fix damage done long ago by souvenir-seekers, who actually rented hammers and chisels to take home a piece of Stonehenge. Look to the right of the repaired stone: The back of another stone is missing the same thin layer of protective lichen that covers the others. The lichen—and some of the stone itself—was sandblasted off to remove graffiti. (No wonder they've got Stonehenge roped off now.)

Stonehenge's builders used two different types of stone. The tall, stout monoliths and lintels are sandstone blocks called sarsen stones. Most of the monoliths weigh about 25 tons (the largest is 45 tons), and the lintels are about 7 tons apiece. These sarsen stones were brought from "only" 20 miles away. The shorter stones in the middle, called bluestones, came from the south coast of Wales—240 miles away (close if you're taking a train, but far if you're packing a megalith). Imagine the logistical puzzle of floating six-ton stones up the River Avon, then rolling them on logs about 20 miles to this position...an impressive feat, even in our era of skyscrapers.

Why didn't the builders of Stonehenge use what seem like perfectly adequate stones nearby? This, like many other questions about Stonehenge, remains shrouded in mystery. Think again about the ley lines. Ponder the fact that many experts accept none of the explanations of how these giant stones were transported. Then imagine congregations gathering here 5,000 years ago, raising thought levels, creating a powerful life force transmitted along the ley lines. Maybe a particular kind of stone was essential for maximum energy transmission. Maybe the stones were levitated here. Maybe psychics really do create powerful vibes. Maybe not. It's as unbelievable as electricity used to be.

Salisbury

Salisbury, set in the middle of the expansive Salisbury Plain, is a favorite stop for its striking cathedral and intriguing history.

Salisbury was originally settled during the Bronze Age, possibly as early as 600 B.C., and later became a Roman town called Sarum. The modern city of Salisbury developed when the old settlement outgrew its boundaries, prompting the townspeople to move the city from a hill to the river valley below. Most of today's visitors come to marvel at the famous Salisbury Cathedral, featuring England's tallest spire and largest cathedral green. Collectors, bargain-hunters, and foodies will savor Salisbury's colorful market days. And archaeologists will dig the region around Salisbury, with England's highest concentration of ancient sites. The town itself is pleasant and walkable, and is a convenient base camp for visiting the ancient sites of Stonehenge and Avebury, or for exploring the countryside.

Orientation to Salisbury

(area code: 01722)
Salisbury (pop. 45,000) stretches along the River Avon in the shadow of its huge landmark cathedral. The heart of the city clusters around Market Square, which is also a handy parking lot on non-market days. High Street, a block to the west, leads to the medieval North Gate of the Cathedral Close. Shoppers explore the streets south of the square. The area north of Market Square is generally residential, with a few shops and pubs.

Tourist Information

The TI, just off Market Square, hands out free city maps, books local rooms for no fee, and sells train tickets with a £1.50 surcharge (April-Sept Mon-Sat 10:00-17:00, Oct-March Mon-Sat 10:00-16:00, closed Sun, Fish Row, tel. 01722/334-956, www.visit wiltshire.co.uk).

Ask the TI about 1.5-hour **walking tours** (£4, April-Oct daily at 11:00, Nov-March Sat-Sun only, depart from TI; other itineraries available, including £4 Ghost Walk May-Sept Fri at 20:00; tel. 01722/320-349, www.salisburycityguides.co.uk).

Arrival in Salisbury

By Train: From the train station, it's a 10-minute walk into the town center. Leave the station to the left, walk about 50 yards down South Western Road, and take the first right (at The Railway Tavern) onto Mill Road, following it around the bend and through the traffic roundabouts. Soon you'll see the Queen Elizabeth Gardens and the cathedral spire on your right. The road becomes Crane Bridge Road, then Crane Street, and finally New Street before intersecting with Catherine/St. John Street. Market Square and the TI are one long block north (left) on Catherine Street, and it's another two short blocks beyond that to the bus station. The Salisbury Cathedral and recommended Exeter Street B&Bs are to the south (right), down St. John Street (which becomes Exeter Street).

By Bus: The bus station is located in the town center, just off Market Square on Endless Street.

By Car: Drivers will find several pay parking lots in Salisbury—simply follow the blue *P* signs. The "Central" lot, behind the giant red-brick Sainsbury's store, is within a 10-minute walk of the TI or cathedral and is best for overnight stays (enter from Churchill Way West or Castle Street, lot open 24 hours). The "Old George Mall" parking garage is closer to the cathedral and has comparable daytime rates (£1/hour, 1 block north of cathedral, enter from New Street; garage open Mon-Sat 7:00-20:00, Sun 10:00-17:00).

Helpful Hints

Market Days: For centuries, Salisbury has been known for its lively markets. On Tuesdays and Saturdays, Market Square hosts the charter market, with general goods. Every other Wednesday is the farmers' market. There are also special markets, such as one with French products. Ask the TI for a current schedule.

Festivals: The **Salisbury International Arts Festival** runs for just over two weeks at the end of May and beginning of June

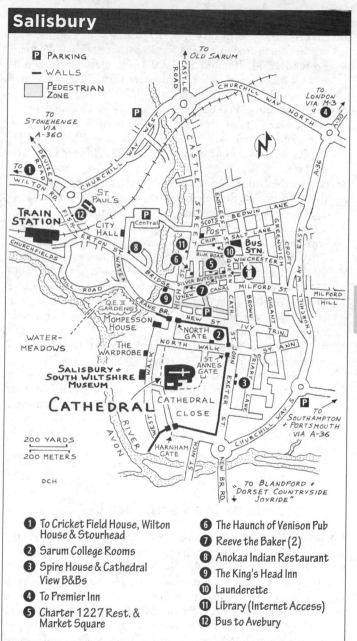

Salisbury

P PARKING
— WALLS
☐ PEDESTRIAN ZONE

TO OLD SARUM

TO STONEHENGE VIA A-360

TO LONDON VIA M-3

TRAIN STATION

ST. PAUL'S

CITY HALL

WATER-MEADOWS

MOMPESSON HOUSE

THE WARDROBE

SALISBURY & SOUTH WILTSHIRE MUSEUM

CATHEDRAL

CATHEDRAL CLOSE

HARNHAM GATE

RIVER AVON

200 YARDS
200 METERS

DCH

TO SOUTHAMPTON & PORTSMOUTH VIA A-36

TO BLANDFORD & DORSET COUNTRYSIDE JOYRIDE

NEAR BATH

❶ To Cricket Field House, Wilton House & Stourhead
❷ Sarum College Rooms
❸ Spire House & Cathedral View B&Bs
❹ To Premier Inn
❺ Charter 1227 Rest. & Market Square

❻ The Haunch of Venison Pub
❼ Reeve the Baker (2)
❽ Anokaa Indian Restaurant
❾ The King's Head Inn
❿ Launderette
⓫ Library (Internet Access)
⓬ Bus to Avebury

(www.salisburyfestival.co.uk).

Internet Access: The **library** has 12 terminals for visitors, who can use them free of charge for 30 minutes (Mon-Wed and Fri 9:00-19:00, Thu and Sat 9:00-17:00, closed Sun, sign in at desk for access number, computers turned off 10 minutes before closing, Market Place, tel. 01722/324-145).

Laundry: Washing Well has full-service (£7.50-13/load depending on size, 2-hour service, Mon-Sat 8:30-17:30) as well as self-service (Mon-Sat 15:30-20:00, Sun 7:00-20:30, last self-service wash one hour before closing; 28 Chipper Lane, tel. 01722/421-874).

Getting to the Stone Circles: You can get to Stonehenge from Salisbury on **The Stonehenge Tour** bus. Their distinctive red-and-black double-decker buses leave from the Salisbury train station and make a circuit to Stonehenge and Old Sarum, with lovely scenery and light commentary along the way (£11, £18 with Stonehenge and Old Sarum admission, tickets good all day, buy ticket from driver, June-Aug daily 9:30-17:00, 1-2/hour, may not run June 21 due to solstice crowds, shorter hours off-season, 30 minutes from station to Stonehenge, also stops at bus station, tel. 01983/827-005, check www.thestone hengetour.info for timetable).

A **taxi** from Salisbury to Stonehenge can be a good deal for groups (£40-50, call or email for exact price, includes round-trip from Salisbury to Stonehenge plus an hour at the site, entry fee not included, 5-6 people maximum, best to reserve ahead, tel. 01722/339-781, briantwort@ntlworld .com, Brian). Brian also offers a three-hour Stonehenge visit for £80, which includes Old Sarum, Woodhenge, Durrington Walls, and Woodford's thatched cottages.

For buses to Avebury's stone circle, see "Salisbury Connections," later.

Sights in Salisbury

▲▲**Salisbury Cathedral**—This magnificent cathedral, visible for miles around because of its huge spire (the tallest in England at 404 feet), is a wonder to behold. The surrounding enormous grassy field (called a "close") makes the Gothic masterpiece look even larger. What's more impressive is that all this was built in a mere 38 years—astonishingly fast for the Middle Ages. When the old hill town of Sarum was moved down to the valley, its cathedral had to be replaced in a hurry. So, in 1220, the townspeople began building, and in 1258 their sparkling-new cathedral was ready for ribbon-cutting. Since the structure was built in just a few decades, its style is uniform, rather than the patchwork of styles common in

Salisbury Cathedral

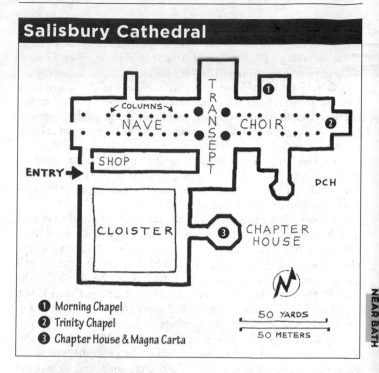

COLUMNS

NAVE

TRANSEPT

CHOIR

ENTRY →

SHOP

CLOISTER

CHAPTER HOUSE

DCH

N

❶ Morning Chapel
❷ Trinity Chapel
❸ Chapter House & Magna Carta

50 YARDS
50 METERS

cathedrals of the time (which often took centuries to construct).

Cost and Hours: £5.50 suggested donation; mid-June-Aug Mon-Sat 7:15-19:15, Sun 7:15-18:15; Sept-mid-June daily 7:15-18:15; Chapter House usually opens Mon-Sat at 9:30, Sun at 12:45, closes 30-45 minutes before the rest of the cathedral, and closes entirely for special events; choral evensong Mon-Sat at 17:30, Sun at 15:00; excellent cafeteria, tel. 01722/555-120, recorded info tel. 01722/555-113, www.salisburycathedral.org.uk. This working cathedral opens early for services—be respectful if you arrive when one is in session.

Tower Tours: Imagine building a cathedral on this scale before the invention of cranes, bulldozers, or modern scaffolding. An excellent tower tour (1.5-2 hours) helps visitors understand how it was done. You'll climb in between the stone arches and the roof to inspect the vaulting and trussing; see a medieval winch that was used in the construction; and finish with the 330-step climb up the narrow tower for a sweeping view of the Wiltshire countryside

(£8.50; early April–Sept Mon–Sat at 11:15, 12:15, 13:15, 14:15, and 15:15, Sun at 13:00 and 14:30; fewer off-season but usually one at 13:15, no tours in Dec except Christmas week; maximum 12 people, can reserve by calling 01722/555-156).

⊙ Self-Guided Tour: Entering the church, you'll instantly feel the architectural harmony. Volunteer guides posted at the entry are ready to answer your questions. (Free guided tours of the cathedral nave are offered—about twice hourly—when enough people assemble.)

As you look down the nave, notice how the stone columns march identically down the aisle, like a thick gray forest of tree trunks. The arches overhead soar to grand heights, helping church-goers appreciate the vast and amazing heavens.

From the entrance, head to the far wall (the back-left corner). You'll find a model showing how this cathedral was built so quickly in the 13th century. Next to that is the "oldest working clock in existence," dating from the 14th century (the hourly bell has been removed, so as not to interrupt worship services). On the wall by the clock is a bell from the decommissioned ship HMS *Salisbury*. Look closely inside the bell to see the engraved names of crew members' children who were baptized on the ship.

Wander down the aisle past monuments and knights' tombs. When you get to the transept, examine the columns where the arms of the church cross. These posts were supposed to support a more modest bell tower, but when a heavy tower was added 100 years later, the columns bent under the enormous weight, causing the tower to lean sideways. Although the posts were later reinforced, the tower still tilts about two and a half feet.

Continue down the left side of the choir and dip into the Morning Chapel. At the back of this chapel, find the spectacular glass prism engraved with images of Salisbury—donated to the church in memory of a soldier who died at the D-Day landing at Normandy.

The oldest part of the church is at the apse (far end), where construction began in 1220: the Trinity Chapel. The giant, modern stained-glass window ponders the theme "prisoners of conscience."

After you leave the nave, pace the cloister and follow signs to the medieval **Chapter House.** All English cathedrals have a chapter house, so called because it's where the daily Bible verse, or chapter, is read. These spaces often served as gathering places for conducting church or town business. Here you can see a modest display of cathedral items plus one must-see display: one of the four original copies of the Magna Carta, a document as important to the English as the Constitution is to Americans. This "Great Charter," dating from 1215, settled a dispute between the slimy King John and some powerful barons. Revolutionary for limiting the monarch's power, the Magna Carta constitutionally guaranteed that the monarch was not above the law. This was one of the first major victories in the long battle between monarchs and nobles.

▲**Cathedral Close**—The enormous green surrounding the cathedral is the largest in England, and one of the loveliest. It's cradled

in the elbow of the River Avon and ringed by row houses, cottages, and grand mansions. The church owns the houses on the green and rents them to lucky people with holy connections. A former prime minister, Edward Heath, lived on the green, not because of his political influence, but because he was once the church organist.

The benches scattered around the green are an excellent place for having a romantic moonlit picnic or for gazing thoughtfully at the leaning spire. Although you may be tempted to linger until it's late, don't—this is still private church property...and the heavy medieval gates of the close shut at about 23:00.

A few houses are open to the public, such as the overpriced Mompesson House and the medieval Wardrobe. The most interesting attraction is the...

▲**Salisbury and South Wiltshire Museum**—Occupying the building just opposite the cathedral entry, this eclectic and sprawling collection was heralded by American expat travel writer Bill Bryson as one of England's best. While that's a stretch, the museum does offer a little something for everyone, including exhibits on local archaeology and history, a costume gallery, the true-to-its-name "Salisbury Giant" puppet once used by the tailors' guilds during parades, some J. M. W. Turner paintings of the cathedral interior, and a collection of exquisite Wedgwood china and other ceramics. The highlight is the Stonehenge Gallery, with informative and interactive exhibits explaining the ancient structure. Since there's not yet a good visitors center at the site itself, this makes for a good pre- or post-Stonehenge activity.

Cost and Hours: £6, Mon-Sat 10:00-17:00, July-Aug Sun 12:00-17:00, Sept-June closed Sun, check with desk about occasional tours, 65 The Close, tel. 01722/332-151, www.salisbury museum.org.uk.

Sleeping in Salisbury

(£1 = about $1.60, country code: 44, area code: 01722)
Salisbury's town center has very few affordable accommodations, and I've listed them below—plus a couple of good choices a little

farther out. The town gets particularly crowded during the arts festival (late May through early June).

$$ Cricket Field House, outside of town on A36 toward Wilton, overlooks a cricket pitch and golf course. It has 17 clean, comfortable rooms, a gorgeous garden, and plenty of parking (Sb-£60-68, Db-£85-105, price depends on season, Wilton Road, tel. & fax 01722/322-595, www.cricketfieldhouse.co.uk, cricketfield cottage@btinternet.com, Brian and Margaret James). While this place works best for drivers, it's just a 20-minute walk from the train station or a five-minute bus ride from the city center.

$$ Sarum College is a theological college that rents 40 rooms in its building right on the peaceful Cathedral Close. Much of the year, it houses visitors to the college, but it usually has rooms for tourists as well—except the week after Christmas, when it closes. The slightly institutional but clean rooms share hallways with libraries, bookstores, and offices, and the five attic rooms come with grand cathedral views (Sb-£60, Db-£95-105 depending on size, meals available at additional cost, elevator, 19 The Close, tel. 01722/424-800, fax 01722/338-508, www.sarum.ac.uk, hospitality @sarum.ac.uk).

$$ Spire House B&B, just off the Cathedral Close, is classy and cozy. The four bright, surprisingly quiet rooms come with busy wallpaper, and two have canopied beds (Db-£80-90, Tb-£90-100, cash only, no kids under age 8, free Wi-Fi, 84 Exeter Street, tel. 01722/339-213, www.salisbury-bedandbreakfast.com, spire .enquiries@btinternet.com, friendly Lois).

$ Cathedral View B&B, with four rooms next door at #83, is similar and offers a good value in an outstanding location (Db-£75, Tb-£90-105, cash only, 2-night minimum on weekends, no kids under age 10, free Wi-Fi, 83 Exeter Street, tel. 01722/502-254, www.cathedral-viewbandb.co.uk, info@cathedral-viewbandb .co.uk, Wenda and Steve).

$ Premier Inn, two miles from the city center, offers dozens of prefab and predictable rooms ideal for drivers and families (Db-£66-100, more during special events, 2 kids ages 15 and under sleep free, breakfast-£5-8, pay Wi-Fi, possible noise from nearby trains, off roundabout at A30 and Pearce Way, tel. 0871-527-8956, fax 0871-527-8957, www.premierinn.com).

Eating in Salisbury

There are plenty of atmospheric pubs all over town. For the best variety of restaurants, head to the Market Square area. Many places offer great "early bird" specials before 20:00.

Charter 1227, an upstairs eatery overlooking Market Square, is a handy place for a nice meal (£12.50 two-course lunch, open

Tue-Sat 12:00-14:30 & 18:00-21:30, closed Sun-Mon, dinner reservations smart, 6 Ox Row, tel. 01722/333-118).

The Haunch of Venison, possibly dating back to 1320, is a Salisbury institution with creaky, sticky, crooked floors and the mummified hand of a cheating card player on display (actually a replica; to the left of the fireplace in the House of Lords room). Downstairs, the "occasionally haunted" half-timbered pub serves nouvelle pub grub (£5-8 meals). The restaurant upstairs, while a little pretentious, has a good reputation for its traditional fare (£8-18 main dishes; pub open Mon-Sat 11:00-23:00, Sun 12:00-22:00, food served 12:00-14:30 & 18:00-21:00, reservations smart for dinner, 1 Minster Street, tel. 01722/411-313).

Reeve the Baker, with a branch just up the street from the TI, crafts an array of high-calorie delights and handy pick-me-ups for a fast and affordable lunch. The long cases of pastries and savory treats will make you drool (Mon-Fri 8:00-17:30, Sat 8:00-17:00, Sun 10:00-16:00, cash only; one location is next to the TI at 2 Butcher Row, another much smaller one is at the corner of Market and Bridge streets at 61 Silver Street, tel. 01722/320-367).

Anokaa is a splurge that's highly acclaimed for its updated Indian cuisine. You won't find the same old chicken *tikka* here, but clever newfangled variations on Indian themes, dished up in a dressy contemporary setting (£9-15 main dishes, £9 lunch buffet, daily 12:00-14:00 & 17:30-22:30, 60 Fisherton Street, tel. 01722/414-142).

The King's Head Inn is a youthful chain pub with a big, open, modern interior and fine outdoor seating overlooking the pretty little River Avon. Its extensive menu has something for everyone (£3-5 sandwiches, £4-9 main dishes, Mon-Fri 7:00-24:00, Sat-Sun 8:00-24:00, food served until 22:00, kids welcome during the day but they must order meals by 20:30, free Wi-Fi, 1 Bridge Street, tel. 01722/342-050).

Salisbury Connections

From Salisbury by Train to: London's Waterloo Station (1-2/hour, 1.5 hours), **Bath** (1-2/hour, 1 hour), **Oxford** (hourly, 2 hours, transfer in Reading and Basingstoke), **Portsmouth** (hourly, 1.25 hours), **Exeter** (1-2/hour, 2 hours, some require transfers), **Penzance** (about hourly, 5.5-6 hours, 1-2 transfers). Train info: tel. 0845-748-4950, www.nationalrail.co.uk.

By Bus to: Bath (hourly, 2.75 hours, transfer in Warminster, www.travelinesw.com; or one direct bus/day at 10:35, 1.5 hours on National Express #300, tel. 0871-781-8181, www.national express.com), **Avebury** (1-2/hour, 2-2.5 hours, transfer in Devizes, www.travelinesw.com). Many of Salisbury's long-distance buses

NEAR BATH

are run by Wilts & Dorset (tel. 01722/336-855 or 01983/827-005, www.wdbus.co.uk). National Express buses go once a day to **Bath** (morning only at 10:35, 1.5 hours) and **Portsmouth** (evenings only at 18:25, 1.5 hours, tel. 0871-781-8181, www.nationalexpress.com).

Near Salisbury

Old Sarum

Right here, on a hill overlooking the plain below, is where the original town of Salisbury was founded many centuries ago. While little remains of the old town, the view of the valley is amazing...and a little imagination can transport you back to *very* olde England.

Human settlement in this area stretches back to the Bronze Age, and the Romans, Saxons, and Normans all called this hilltop home. From about 500 B.C. through A.D. 1220, Old Sarum flourished, giving rise to a motte-and-bailey castle, a cathedral, and scores of wooden homes along the town's outer ring. The town grew so quickly that by the Middle Ages, it had outgrown its spot on the hill. In 1220, the local bishop successfully petitioned to move the entire city to the valley below, where space and water was plentiful. So, stone by stone, Old Sarum was packed up and shipped to New Sarum, where builders used nearly all the rubble from the old city to create a brand-new town with a magnificent cathedral.

Old Sarum was eventually abandoned altogether, leaving only a few stone foundations. The grand views of Salisbury from here have "in-spired" painters for ages and provided countless picnickers with a scenic backdrop: Grab a sandwich or snacks from one of the grocery stores in Salisbury or at the excellent Waitrose supermarket at the north end of town—just west of where A36 meets A345.

Cost and Hours: £3.70, daily July-Aug 9:00-18:00, April-June and Sept 10:00-17:00, Oct and March 10:00-16:00, Nov-Jan 11:00-15:00, Feb 11:00-16:00, last entry 30 minutes before closing, tel. 01722/335-398, www.english-heritage.org.uk.

Getting There: It's two miles north of Salisbury off A345, accessible by Wilts & Dorset bus #X5 or via The Stonehenge Tour bus (see page 428).

Wilton House

This sprawling estate, with a grand mansion and lush gardens, has been owned by the Earls of Pembroke since King Henry VIII's time. Inside the mansion, you'll find a collection of paintings by Rubens, Rembrandt, Van Dyck, and Brueghel, along with quirky odds-and-ends, such as a lock of Queen Elizabeth I's hair. The perfectly proportioned Double Cube Room has served as every-

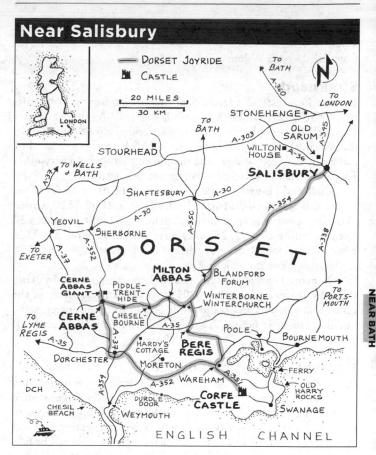

thing from a 17th-century state dining room to a secret D-Day planning room during World War II...if only the portraits could talk. The Old Riding School houses a skippable 20-minute film that dramatizes the history of the family. Outside, classic English gardens feature a river lazily winding its way through grasses and under Greek-inspired temples. Jane Austen fans particularly enjoy this stately home, where parts of 2005's Oscar-nominated *Pride and Prejudice* were filmed. But, alas, Mr. Darcy has checked out.

Cost and Hours: House and gardens-£14, gardens only-£5.50; house open Easter weekend and May-Aug Sun-Thu 11:30-16:30, last entry 45 minutes before closing, closed Fri-Sat except holiday weekends; gardens April-Aug daily 11:00-17:00, Sept Sat-Sun 11:00-17:00, last entry 30 minutes before closing; house and gardens closed Oct-April, except house open Easter weekend and gardens open mid-April; recorded info tel. 01722/746-729, tel. 01722/746-714, www.wiltonhouse.com.

Getting There: It's five miles west of Salisbury via A36 to Wilton's Minster Street; or buses #2, #13, #25, #26, #27, or #R3 from Salisbury to Wilton.

Stourhead

For a serious taste of a traditional English landscape, don't miss this 2,650-acre delight. Stourhead, designed by owner Henry Hoare II in the mid-18th century, is a wonderland of rolling hills, meandering paths, placid lakes, and colorful trees, punctuated by classically inspired bridges and monuments. It's what every other English estate aspires to be—like nature, but better.

Cost and Hours: House and garden-£12.10, or £7.30 to see just one; house open mid-March-Oct Fri-Tue 11:00-17:00, closed Wed-Thu; garden open year-round daily 9:00-18:00, last entry 30 minutes before closing, 28 miles west of Salisbury off B3092 in town of Stourton, 3 miles northwest of Mere, tel. 01747/841-152, www.nationaltrust.org.uk.

Nearby: Drivers or ambitious walkers can visit nearby **King Alfred's Tower** and climb its 205 steps for glorious views of the estate and surrounding countryside (£2.90 to climb tower, same opening times as house, 2.5 miles northwest of Stourhead, off Tower Road).

Dorset Countryside Joyride

The region of Dorset, just southwest of Salisbury, is full of rolling fields, winding country lanes, quaint cottages, and villages stuffed with tea shops. Anywhere you go in the area will take you someplace charming, so consider this tour only a suggestion and feel free to get pleasantly lost in the English countryside. You'll be taking some less-traveled roads, so bring along a good map.

Starting in Salisbury, take A354 through Blandford Forum to Winterborne Whitechurch. From here, follow signs and small back roads to the village of Bere Regis, where you'll find some lovely 15th-century buildings, including one with angels carved on the roof. Follow A35 and B3075 to Wareham, where T. E. Lawrence (a.k.a. Lawrence of Arabia) lived; he's buried in nearby Moreton. Continue south on A351 to the dramatic and romantic **Corfe Castle.** This was a favorite residence for medieval kings until it was destroyed by a massive gunpowder blast during a 17th-century siege (£6.20, daily April-Sept 10:00-18:00, March and Oct 10:00-17:00, Nov-Feb 10:00-16:00, last entry 30 minutes before closing, tel. 01929/481-294, www.nationaltrust.org.uk). Retrace A351 to Wareham, and then take A352 to Dorchester.

Just northeast of Dorchester on A35, near the village of Stinsford, novelist Thomas Hardy was born in 1840; you'll find **Hardy's family's cottage** nearby in Higher Bockhampton (£4,

May-Oct Thu-Mon 11:00-17:00, closed Tue-Wed and Nov-April, last entry 30 minutes before closing, tel. 01305/262-366, www .nationaltrust.org.uk). While Hardy's heart is buried in Stinsford with his first wife, Emma, the rest of him is in Westminster Abbey's Poets' Corner. Take A35 back to Dorchester. Just west of Dorchester, stay on A35 until it connects to A37; then follow A352 north toward Sherborne.

About eight miles north of Dorchester, on the way to Sherborne, you'll find the little town of **Cerne Abbas** (surn AB-iss), named for an abbey in the center of town. There are only two streets to wander down, so take this opportunity to recharge with a cup of tea and a scone. Abbots Tea Room has a nice cream tea (pot of tea, scone, jam, and clotted cream, 7 Long Street, tel. 01300/341-349). Up the street, you can visit the abbey and its well, reputed to have healing powers.

Just outside of town, a large chalk figure, the **Cerne Abbas Giant,** is carved into the green hillside. Chalk figures such as this one can be found in many parts of the region. Because the soil is only a few inches deep, the overlying grass and dirt can easily be removed to expose the bright white chalk bedrock beneath, creating the outlines. While nobody is sure exactly how old the figures are, or what their original purpose was, they are faithfully maintained by the locals, who mow and clear the fields at least once a year. This particular figure, possibly a fertility god, looks friendly...maybe a little too friendly. Locals claim that if a woman who's having trouble getting pregnant sleeps on the giant for one night, she will soon be able to conceive a child. (A few years back, controversy surrounded this giant, as a 180-foot-tall, donut-hoisting Homer Simpson was painted onto the adjacent hillside. No kidding.)

Leaving Cerne Abbas on country roads toward Piddletrenthide (on the aptly named River Piddle), continue through Cheselbourne to **Milton Abbas.** (This area, by the way, has some of the best town names in the country, such as Droop, Plush, Pleck, and Folly.) The village of Milton Abbas looks overly perfect. In the 18th century, a wealthy man bought up the town's large abbey and estate. His new place was great...except for the neighbors, a bunch of vulgar villagers with houses that cluttered his view from the garden. So, he had the town demolished and rebuilt a mile away. What you see now is probably the first planned community, with identical houses, a pub, and a church. The estate is now a "public school," which is what the English call an expensive private school. From Milton Abbas, signs lead you back to Winterborne Whitechurch, and A354 to Salisbury.

OXFORD

For centuries, the University of Oxford's stellar graduates have influenced Western civilization—ever since the first homework was assigned here in 1167. But that doesn't mean that Oxford is stodgy. Although you may see professors in their traditional black robes, this is a fun, young college town, filled with lots of shopping, cheap eats around every corner, and rowdy, rollicking pubs.

While a typical American-style university has one campus, Oxford (like Cambridge) has colleges scattered throughout town. But the sightseers' Oxford is walkable and compact. Many of the streets in the center are pedestrian-only during the day. Stick to the center, and you'll get a feel for workaday Oxford, where knowledge is the town business—and procrastinating over a pint is the students' main hobby. (Local shops sell T-shirts that say, "Don't ask me about my thesis.")

Sample the spirit of Oxford. Step off the busy, urban-feeling High Street into the hushed sanctuary of a grassy college quad. See the dining hall that inspired the one where Harry Potter eats his meals, or the pub where J. R. R. Tolkien first spoke about the Hobbits.

If you haven't yet tried pub grub—or sampled a local British ale—make a point to do so in Oxford, just as its famous local writers did. In Oxford, a town known for traditions, the pubs are where the action is.

Perhaps better than anything in Oxford itself is the excellent Blenheim Palace. It's England's best countryside estate, just outside Oxford and described at the end of this chapter. Don't miss it.

Oxford or Cambridge?

England is home to two world-renowned universities: Oxford and Cambridge. Seeing one is enough. While I prefer the town of Cambridge (see page 231), Oxford's historic university makes it a heavyweight sight. If you're choosing between them, consider this: Cambridge feels like a lazy, easygoing small town; Oxford has a slightly more urban vibe, and even more stately buildings than its rival. Cambridge is not really on the way to anything, making it better as a side-trip from London than as a stopover. For convenience, you can't beat Oxford, which sits near the Cotswolds, Stratford-upon-Avon, Blenheim Palace, and other major sights.

Planning Your Time

Oxford is a convenient stop for people visiting the Cotswolds, Blenheim Palace (a 30-minute drive away), Stratford-upon-Avon, and Bath. Because of Oxford's proximity to other worthwhile destinations and its relative scarcity of good-value accommodations, a stop-off here on the way to somewhere else is ideal.

Oxford's colleges are generally open to visitors, but each has its own visiting hours (which can be unpredictable). There are three terms: Michaelmas (Oct-Dec), Hilary (Jan-March), and Trinity (April-June). Public spaces in the colleges are more likely to be closed during exams in early to mid-June.

Orientation to Oxford

(area code: 01865)

Oxford was first built where oxen crossed, or forded, the Cherwell and Isis rivers. (The Isis is another name for the Thames; back then you could row to London from Oxford...in just five days.) Property in the town center is divided about evenly among three different groups: the university; the colleges (which are independent entities); and private shops and homes.

Despite its relatively compact town center, Oxford can be confusing to navigate. All those colleges start to look alike, and streets tend to change names from block to block. Use the biggest buildings as navigational landmarks, and don't be shy about asking students for directions.

The main arteries are the north-south Cornmarket/St. Aldate's, and the east-west Queen Street/High Street. At the intersection of these streets stands the stubby, 14th-century Carfax Tower (named for the French *carrefour*, or "crossroads"). From here, pedestrianized Cornmarket—essentially an outdoor mall lined

OXFORD

Oxford

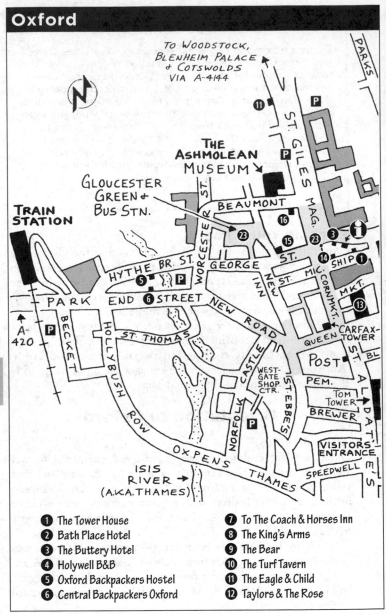

TO WOODSTOCK,
BLENHEIM PALACE
& COTSWOLDS
VIA A-4144

THE
ASHMOLEAN
MUSEUM

GLOUCESTER
GREEN &
BUS STN.

TRAIN
STATION

ST. GILES MAG.

PARKS

BEAUMONT

ST. GEORGE

HYTHE BR. ST.

WORCESTER ST.

PARK END STREET

NEW INN

ST. MIC.

SHIP

MKT.

CORNMKT.

NEW ROAD

BECKET

HOLLYBUSH ROW

ST. THOMAS

A-420

NORFOLK

CASTLE

WEST-GATE SHOP. CTR.

ST. EBBE'S

QUEEN

CARFAX TOWER

POST

PEM.

TOM TOWER

BREWER

VISITORS' ENTRANCE

SPEEDWELL

OXPENS

THAMES

ISIS
RIVER
(A.K.A. THAMES)

OXFORD

1. The Tower House
2. Bath Place Hotel
3. The Buttery Hotel
4. Holywell B&B
5. Oxford Backpackers Hostel
6. Central Backpackers Oxford
7. To The Coach & Horses Inn
8. The King's Arms
9. The Bear
10. The Turf Tavern
11. The Eagle & Child
12. Taylors & The Rose

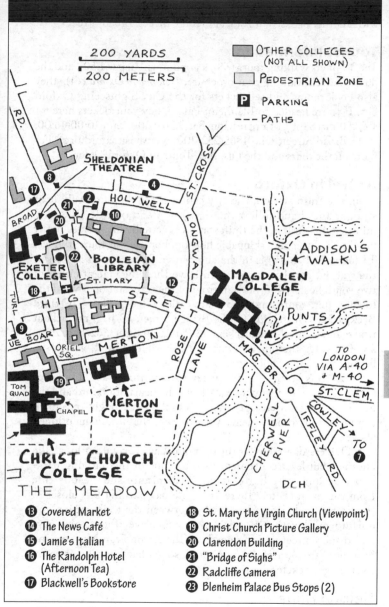

200 YARDS
200 METERS

OTHER COLLEGES (NOT ALL SHOWN)
PEDESTRIAN ZONE
P PARKING
- - - PATHS

RD.

SHELDONIAN THEATRE

⑧

⑰

ST. CROSS

④

HOLYWELL

BROAD

②

㉑

⑩

⑳

LONGWALL

ADDISON'S WALK

⑫

MAGDALEN COLLEGE

㉒

EXETER COLLEGE

BODLEIAN LIBRARY

ST. MARY

⑱

PUNTS

HIGH

STREET

TURL

⑨

UE BOAR

ORIEL SQ.

MERTON

ROSE LANE

MAG BR.

TO LONDON VIA A-40 & M-40

CHERWELL RIVER

ST. CLEM.

COWLEY

IFFLEY RD.

TO ⑦

⑲

TOM QUAD

CHAPEL

MERTON COLLEGE

CHRIST CHURCH COLLEGE

THE MEADOW

DCH

OXFORD

⑬ Covered Market
⑭ The News Café
⑮ Jamie's Italian
⑯ The Randolph Hotel (Afternoon Tea)
⑰ Blackwell's Bookstore

⑱ St. Mary the Virgin Church (Viewpoint)
⑲ Christ Church Picture Gallery
⑳ Clarendon Building
㉑ "Bridge of Sighs"
㉒ Radcliffe Camera
㉓ Blenheim Palace Bus Stops (2)

with shops and chain restaurants—heads north, where it intersects with another pedestrian zone at George Street/Broad Street.

Tourist Information

The TI offers walking tours (£8), a good town map (£1.50), and the do-it-yourself walking-tour brochure, *Welcome to Oxford* (£1). They also book rooms and sell tickets for the City Sightseeing Oxford bus. If you're headed to Blenheim Palace, buy your tickets here for a £2.50 discount (TI open Mon-Sat 9:30-17:00, Sun 10:00-16:00, 15-16 Broad Street, tel. 01865/252-200, www.visitoxford.org). For more on the tours and the bus, see "Tours in Oxford," later.

Arrival in Oxford

From the **train** station, the city center is a 10-minute walk (exit straight ahead and follow the signs) or a £5 taxi ride. The "city information" desk in the train station is actually just a sales outlet for City Sightseeing's skippable hop-on, hop-off bus tours; the real TI (described above) is in the city center. There are no lockers at the station, but day-trippers can leave their luggage at either of two youth hostels 400 yards in front of the train station toward the town center; confusingly, both are called "Backpackers" (Oxford Backpackers Hostel, 9A Hythe Bridge Street, £3/bag, no lockout times; and Central Backpackers, 13 Park End Street, £2/bag, 7:00-23:00). Note: The official Oxford YHA youth hostel, which sits behind the station, does not store bags.

The **bus** station, a bit closer to downtown at Gloucester Green, is just a five-minute walk from the heart of Oxford and the TI: Turn left onto George Street and follow it straight into town (no lockers at station—leave your bags at the hostels mentioned above).

Drivers day-tripping into Oxford have several options. The cheapest but least convenient is to use one of the outlying park-and-ride lots, which are about a 10-minute shuttle-bus ride from the town center. There are some pay parking lots closer to the center (including a handy one between the train station and downtown), but they're much more expensive. There's also pay-and-display street parking north of The Ashmolean Museum, on St. Giles Street (carefully monitored, so get back in time or you're likely to get ticketed).

Helpful Hints

Bookstore: One of the world's largest bookstores, **Blackwell's** boasts miles of shelves in its main location (additional satellite shops around town). The vast Norrington Room in the basement holds stacks of books (Mon-Sat 9:00-18:30, Sun 11:00-17:00, coffee shop upstairs, WC on top floor, 48-51 Broad

Street, tel. 01865/792-792, www.blackwells.co.uk). Ask here about literary walking tours (see "Tours in Oxford," later).

Best Views: At the University Church of St. Mary the Virgin, climb the 127 narrow, twisting stairs of the 13th-century bell tower for views of Oxford's many spires and colleges (church free, tower-£3, daily 9:00-17:00, July-Aug until 18:00, tower opens Sun at 11:45, last entry to tower 30 minutes before closing, coffee shop in vault, High Street, tel. 01865/279-111, www.university-church.ox.ac.uk). For an easier climb, skip up the 99 steps of Carfax Tower (£2.20, daily April-Oct 10:00-17:30, Nov-March 10:00-15:00).

Harry Potter Sights: In the movies, the look of Hogwarts School was partially based on a few real-life Oxford sights. For details, see page 806, and consider taking a Harry Potter tour (see below).

Tours in Oxford

▲**Walking Tours**—The TI's **"City and University"** walking tours, led by Blue Badge guides, explain the local history and traditions and take you inside one or two of the colleges. More informative than entertaining, these dry talks give you a solid historical background (£8, 2 hours, daily at 10:45 and 14:00, Sat also at 11:00 and 13:00, additional tours on busy days—ask at TI for schedule; 10:45 tours generally include Divinity School and cost £0.50 extra; book any tour inside TI, tours depart from sidewalk out front). They also have a wide variety of themed tours, including **Harry Potter tours** (£12) and **literary tours** about C. S. Lewis, J. R. R. Tolkien, and others (£8); pick up the latest schedule at the TI, or check online to see what's offered during your visit (www.visit oxford.org). All of these tours are popular and can sell out (especially on Sat); it's smart to reserve at least an hour ahead (drop by, call, or go online).

Blackwell's Walking Tours, led by proper British gentlemen, focus on literary and historic Oxford. Their Inklings tour visits J. R. R. Tolkien's and C. S. Lewis' former haunts. Check Blackwell's bookstore for current tours and times (£7, mid-April-Oct Tue-Fri, 1.5 hours, 48-51 Broad Street, tour info tel. 01865/333-606).

Other tours include the more casual **Oxford Walking Tours,** which depart hourly from the Trinity College gates (£8.50, daily 11:00-16:00, also evening ghost tours, mobile 07790-734-387, Stuart). But take a pass on the "free" tours led by Footprints Walking Tours. Although led by young, enthusiastic guides, they aren't really free since they expect a tip at the end.

Bike Cart Tours—Rickshaws called **Oxon Carts** pedal you on a tour around the major sights of central Oxford (one-hour tour-£25,

30-minute spin—£15, cart holds 2 people, weather permitting, reserve in advance, mobile 07747-024-600, www.oxoncarts.com, info@oxoncarts.com).

Hop-on, Hop-off Bus Tours—**City Sightseeing Oxford** runs bright-red double-decker buses around town, shuttling tourists from one sight to the next (20 stops in all). Because Oxford is fairly compact, with colleges that have to be seen on foot, consider this tour only if you've missed a walking tour or have tired feet. If you do go, take a seat up top to see over the college walls (£12.50, pay driver or buy tickets at TI, 4/hour, daily 9:30-18:30, last bus at 18:00, in winter goes 2/hour and stops running earlier, commentary is live on some buses and recorded on others, tel. 01865/790-522, www.citysightseeingoxford.com).

Minivan Tours—Run by Philip Baum, **Cotswold Roaming** offers a different minivan tour each day with scenic itineraries that include the Cotswolds, Blenheim Palace, Stratford/Warwick Castle, Bath/Castle Combe, and Salisbury/Stonehenge/Avebury (includes admissions for everywhere but Bath and Shakespeare sights). They can also arrange custom tours for small groups on request (£27.50 for half-day tours to the Cotswolds, £42.50-55 for full-day tours, tours may not run if there aren't enough people, tel. 01865/308-300, www.cotswold-roaming.co.uk).

Sights in Oxford

The Colleges

You could spend a lot of time going from college to college here—but since they all have similar features, frankly, if you've seen one, you've seen them all. If you just take the TI's walking tour, you'll get a sufficient taste of one or two—for most visitors, it's overkill to visit more. Save your time for the excellent Ashmolean Museum, Bodleian Library, or punting.

The entrance to each college is easy to spot—just look for a doorway with crests and a flagpole on the top. Each entry has an office with a porter (live-in caretaker). Inquire there to find out which buildings are open to visitors, and if any plays, music, or lectures are scheduled.

▲**Christ Church College**—This is the alma mater of William Penn (founder of Pennsylvania), John Wesley (influential Methodist leader), Charles Dodgson (a.k.a. Lewis Carroll), and 13 prime ministers. Its grounds include a grand old dining hall, a giant quad, and an impressive chapel that doubles as a cathedral.

Of Oxford's colleges, Christ Church is the largest and most prestigious (and, some think, most pretentious). It's also the most popular (and most expensive) for tourists to visit—partly thanks to its historic fame, but mostly because scenes in the Harry Potter movies were filmed here. While Christ Church is fun to see, it's no better or more representative than any other of Oxford's colleges; if your time is short and you can live without seeing the dining hall that inspired Harry's, a visit here isn't obligatory.

Cost and Hours: £7.50, family ticket-£15, Mon-Sat 9:00-17:30, Sun 14:00-17:30, church closes at 16:30, dining hall closes at 16:30, tel. 01865/276-492, www.chch.ox.ac.uk.

Dining Hall Closure: Note that the dining hall—the prime attraction for Harry Potter fans—is closed to outsiders when students are actually lunching here (usually Mon-Sat 11:30-14:30 during term). Plan your visit accordingly.

Evensong: Every day in Christ Church Cathedral, an excellent choir of students (and fidgety little boys) sings along to the church's pipe organ. This delightful service is open to anyone; linger after the service ends to hear the organist jam (free, daily at 18:00, enter at Tom Tower). For more on evensong, see page 157.

● Self-Guided Tour: The college is located on St. Aldate's; follow *Visitors' Entrance* signs (past the big tower and all the way to the end of the biggest building, toward the river).

As you enter the grounds through the visitors' entrance, you'll pass through a bit of countryside spreading out to the river. This is actually part of the college. Called **Christ Church Meadow,** it was the setting Lewis Carroll used for the croquet scenes in *Alice's Adventures in Wonderland* (free, open in summer 7:00-dusk). Consider taking a stroll here, either now or after your college visit (though you'll exit at the opposite end of the college complex).

Buy your ticket and pick up the essential self-guided tour booklet with map. Follow the one-way route to be sure you don't miss anything. Gentlemen wearing derby hats, called Custodians, are posted around the college to answer questions.

First you'll head into the small **cloister** (where some Harry Potter scenes were filmed), then you'll reach the base of the grand staircase leading up to the **dining hall** (closed 11:30-14:30 during term). Appreciate its grand scale and the splendid, Gothic, hammer-beam roof. While Harry Potter scenes were filmed along the staircase, they never actually filmed in the dining hall itself; set designers merely based their dining hall on this grand space. (Custodians report that astute kids who visit immediately know it's not the "real" Hogwarts—since there are three long rows of tables, not four.)

You'll then enter the impressive **Tom Quad,** a grassy field surrounded by college buildings. In the middle is a small fish pond

OXFORD

The Colleges of Oxford

While we think of it as one big university, Oxford consists of 38 autonomous, self-funded colleges. The role of the university is to provide lectures, administer exams, and award degrees, but the colleges are where students spend most of their time. Students directly apply to—and study at—one of these colleges, rather than the university (although they can submit an open application and have the university choose the college for them). Most colleges offer all of the traditional majors, but specialized majors have fewer choices. For example, 31 colleges offer history as a major, but only seven offer archaeology. Rivalry among the colleges is fierce, both academically and in sports (rowing is a favorite).

Many of the colleges, dating back hundreds of years, have historic old buildings that are open to the public. While some of these are free to enter, the more famous and interesting ones charge admission. Most are open only in the afternoons, but they can be unexpectedly closed due to exam schedules and special events.

History: The first school is thought to have been founded here in the 11th century, but Oxford really took off in 1167, when, during a period of political tension between England and France, Henry II banned English students from attending the University of Paris. The students—mostly poor peasant kids who'd been fortunate enough to be educated in Latin at monastic schools (the language of higher learning of the day)—gathered in Oxford to pursue their studies. The teachers took students under their wing, rented out boarding houses, and lived with and taught their charges in an almost monastic environment. Students often clashed with residents in this market town, just as university students tussle with "townies" the world over. But in medieval Oxford, these "town-and-gown fights" were often violent and claimed many casualties.

Anatomy of a College: Gradually, little campuses evolved that consisted of four parts: a library, dormitories, a dining hall, and a chapel. In its purest form, a college would have these four buildings surrounding a central courtyard, where students could exercise and which could be locked at night for security—the origin of today's quadrangle (though planting those spaces with golf course-quality grass was a much later

innovation). Today, visitors touring a college will still find these same four components.

Notice that many of the chapels are shaped like a capital "T," rather than like a typical cross-shaped church floor plan. One of the earliest chapels (at New College) was planned on a cross shape, but wasn't able to acquire the land they needed. Their modified, truncated plan (missing the top, or apse) caught on with the other colleges. Many chapels host evensong services at 18:00, which are usually open to the public.

In the Harry Potter-esque dining halls, long rows of tables (for students) lead toward the elevated high table, where the faculty dines. Hanging above the high table is usually a portrait of the college's founder, while portraits of other rectors and important alums also decorate the space. Students still really do eat in these halls at these long tables—which is why during term periods, you can't enter them at lunchtime (generally from about 11:00 to 14:30, depending on the college).

Oxford Today: About a quarter of applicants are accepted, and about a third of the student body hails from other countries—giving the city an international feel. You'll hear more American accents here than just about anywhere in England. Tuition, room, board, and books run about £10,000 a year for UK and EU residents; non-EU students pay double.

Students enter the college in October and spend their first year (through the following June) preparing for preliminary exams, which they must pass to remain enrolled. Once that hurdle is cleared, they study for two more years preparing for their final exams.

If you visit in June, you might see students wearing traditional academic robes on their way to their finals. (Well, not entirely traditional—while students can be penalized if they're not properly clad, the faculty years ago refused to legislate the length of female students' skirts. Many of today's young women express their individuality amid all that stuffiness by raising their gowns' hemlines...sometimes dramatically.) Students taking their finals wear carnations on their lapels: white on the first day, pink on the second day, and red on the final day. When students emerge from their final exam wearing a red carnation, they're greeted by friends and family who douse them with flour, glitter, and champagne or beer (a tradition called "trashing"). There's usually a happy ending: Among those who remain at Oxford all three years, the graduation rate is nearly 100 percent.

with a statue of Mercury. Notice the outlines of archways ringing the quad; the architect wanted to create a giant cloister here, but funding ran out.

The tall tower, designed by Christopher Wren, holds a seven-ton bell called **Great Tom.** According to tradition, this clangs out 101 times every night at 21:05. Why not on the hour? When the tradition began, time zones had yet to be standardized—and since Oxford was five minutes of longitude west of Greenwich, clocks here were set five minutes earlier. That means 21:05 Greenwich Mean Time was 21:00 on the dot Oxford time.

Continue a few steps along the quad, and enter the 800-year-old **chapel** (on the right). This is the only university chapel in the

world that also serves as a cathedral (bishop's seat). The interior feels dark and mysterious. Pick up the free sheet identifying the highlights, including the shrine to the obscure local saint, St. Frideswide, and a 1320 stained-glass window honoring Thomas Becket (whose face was blacked out to help him survive the Reformation). For information on the musical service that takes place here nightly, see "Evensong," earlier.

Exiting the chapel, you'll be steered back around the cloister, where you can view a 15-minute video about Christ Church. Then circle back around past the base of the dining hall stairs, pass through the Tom Quad again, and head straight to exit out the far end.

As you pass by the library, look for the tall **chestnut tree** behind the wall. Lewis Carroll would watch a cat belonging to a little girl named Alice (the dean's daughter) sitting in the tree. When he later wrote his story about Alice's visit to Wonderland, it inspired him to include the Cheshire Cat character.

Continue past more buildings. On the right just before the exit is Christ Church's final sight, the picture gallery described next.

Christ Church Picture Gallery—This sleepy gallery has a good collection that houses a rotating exhibition of drawings and sketches by Albrecht Dürer, Michelangelo, Leonardo da Vinci, Raphael, and other Old Masters. Because the drawings are fragile, they need to "rest" periodically—so don't be disappointed if your favorite is missing. There's also a permanent collection of oil paintings by the likes of Tintoretto, Veronese, Van Dyck, and Frans Hals.

Cost and Hours: £3, £1.50 if you paid to enter the college; May-Sept Mon-Sat 10:30-17:00, Sun 14:00-17:00; Oct-April Mon-Sat 10:30-13:00 & 14:00-16:30, Sun 14:00-16:30; tel. 01865/276-172.

Getting There: If you're visiting Christ Church College, the one-way tour route will eventually lead you here—look for signs to the *Picture Gallery.* To visit only the gallery—or if the main campus is closed to visitors—you can enter the gallery directly from the street (at Canterbury Gate, off Oriel Square).

Magdalen College—Sitting on the upper edge of town, this college (pronounced "maudlin") has the largest grounds of any of the Oxford colleges (big enough to include its own deer park). The best-known path through the college, Addison's Walk across the river, was frequented by C. S. Lewis. Visitors can tour the chapel, the dining hall, and the expansive grounds.

Cost and Hours: £4.50, daily July-Sept 12:00-19:00, Oct-June 13:00-18:00 or dusk, last entry 30 minutes before closing; evensong with the renowned boys' choir Oct-June Mon and Wed-Sat at 18:00, none July-Sept; High Street next to Magdalen Bridge, tel. 01865/276-000, www.magd.ox.ac.uk.

Merton College—The third-oldest college (at not quite 750 years old), Merton boasts the oldest quad (Mob Quad, from the 14th century). *The Lord of the Rings* author J. R. R. Tolkien taught here. Visitors have access to the quad and the chapel, but to get inside the superb medieval "chained" library—the oldest in Oxford—you'll have to take a tour.

Cost and Hours: College entry without tour-£2, Mon-Fri 14:00-17:00, Sat-Sun 10:00-17:00, last entry 30 minutes before closing, Merton Street, tel. 01865/276-310, www.merton.ox.ac.uk.

Tours: Guided tours, which are available in the summer for around £3, include the college, chapel, and library; usually held July-Sept at 14:00, 15:00, and 16:00; confirm times at the Porters' Lodge, 45 minutes.

Exeter College—A smaller college, Exeter is worth a peek. The highlight is Sir George Gilbert Scott's jewel-like Neo-Gothic

chapel. This replica of Paris' Sainte-Chapelle was recently cleaned, so the stone is gleaming. It features William Morris' *The Adoration of the Magi* tapestry.

Cost and Hours: Free, usually open daily 14:00-17:00, Turl Street, tel. 01865/279-600.

University Buildings

While each individual college has its own admirable complex of historic buildings, Oxford University's facilities aren't too shabby, either. As if trying to one-up all the colleges, the biggest and best university buildings cluster near the intersection of Broad Street/Holywell Street and Parks Road/Catte Street. These are the classic, iconic Oxford buildings you often see in movies.

Landmark University Buildings—Across the little square from the Sheldonian Theatre, the big Neoclassical building with the columns out front is the **Clarendon Building,** originally built to house the Oxford University Press. Among the books printed here was the Lincoln Bible—used to inaugurate Presidents Lincoln and Obama.

Across the street, you'll see the **"Bridge of Sighs,"** modeled after the one in Venice. It was built to connect the two parts of Hetford College.

The next two buildings sit in a quaint cobblestoned square, just down Catte Street from the others.

The most distinctive university building of all is the round, columned **Radcliffe Camera.** Built as a medical library, today it's used as a reading room for a gigantic library complex that runs through tunnels underneath the square. (It's named for the alum who funded it, not for the Harry Potter film star.)

The tall steeple belongs to the **Church of St. Mary the Virgin,** which is the university church and has a climbable tower (see page 443) and a café in the crypt.

The following two are the only university facilities that welcome visitors: Bodleian Library and Sheldonian Theatre.

▲Bodleian Library—With some 11 million books and more than 100 miles of shelving in its underground stacks, "the Bod" is one of the world's largest and most famous libraries. Founded by Thomas Bodley in 1602, this is one of six "legal deposit" libraries in the UK—so it must receive a copy of every book printed in the nation. The palatial building—with a big courtyard and frilly spires along the roofline—

has two areas that are open to the public: the Divinity School on the ground floor (which you can visit with a £1 ticket, or on a tour), and the medieval Duke Humfrey's Library (only with a tour).

The **Divinity School,** an impressive fan-vaulted hall, has a ceiling carved with intricately detailed religious symbolism.

Above the entry, notice that the crucifix (directly over the door) and St. Peter were defaced by Reformation forces. The colorful stained-glass windows that once lined the hall were another casualty. Above the door at the far end of the hall is a statue of Mary... holding a book. Students gather here to put on their gowns before walking to their graduation ceremony at the theater next door. Before leaving, imagine hospital beds lining this hall...yes, it's the infirmary from the Harry Potter films.

Upstairs in **Duke Humfrey's Library** are the musty, creaky old shelves of ancient-looking books, stacked neatly under a beautifully painted wooden ceiling. The required tour shows you only a small section of the library—basically one hall, and a view down another—but even at that, it gives you a good feel for the place. You'll learn about the library's history, and about the huge stockpile of books that sits beneath this part of Oxford. Because this is purely a reference library (none of the books can be checked out), they need plenty of space. They have a rare-books collection—with everything from a Shakespearean First Folio to a couple of Magna Cartas—that they're hoping to eventually display to the public after a planned renovation (in 2015 at the soonest).

Cost and Hours: You'll pay £1 to enter the Divinity School on your own (Mon-Fri 9:00-17:00, Sat 9:00-16:30, Sun 11:00-17:00), but to see the library you must take a dry but informative **tour** (£4.50/30-minute tour of Divinity School and library, £6.50/one-hour version). Tours run several times daily—check the schedule and buy your ticket at the kiosk in the passage across the courtyard from the library entrance, or call 01865/277-224.

Sheldonian Theatre—Graduations, matriculations, and other important campus events take place in this grand theater. Before it was built, these ceremonies took place in churches—but the music and celebratory tone were deemed inappropriate

Literary Oxford

Oxford's list of alums is almost laughably impressive. A virtual factory for famous politicians—among them a couple dozen prime ministers (including current PM David Cameron), Indira Gandhi, and Bill Clinton (who took classes here as a Rhodes scholar)—it's also the home of some of the most important scientists of the 20th century. Stephen Hawking (*A Brief History of Time*) went to Oxford, Richard Dawkins (*The Selfish Gene*) teaches at Oxford, and Tim Berners-Lee—inventor of the World Wide Web—got in trouble for hacking into Oxford's computers. But Oxford may be most famous for its literary past.

J. R. R. Tolkien (1892-1973) graduated from the university and was a professor at Oxford, teaching the glories of Anglo-Saxon language and English literature through one of his favorite works, the epic poem *Beowulf*. He spent years in Oxford writing the books he's most famous for: *The Hobbit* and the three volumes of *The Lord of the Rings*, beloved by millions of readers.

C. S. Lewis (1898-1963), Tolkien's good friend, was a fellow at Oxford for almost 30 years. Lewis sent generations of children through the back of a wardrobe in his series *The Chronicles of Narnia*. During his time in Oxford, Lewis was also the ringleader of a famous writing society called the Inklings, who met regularly at The Eagle and Child pub (which they called the "Bird and Baby"—see page 458). Picture these literary geniuses sitting in the pub's familiar confines. Lewis orders another round, while Tolkien tells Frodo's tale—with a pipe in hand—for the first time.

The Oxford-educated poet **W. H. Auden** (1907-1973) was a lifelong friend and correspondent of Tolkien's. (He was one of the first critics to publicly praise *The Lord of the Rings*.) Auden may be most familiar to Americans for the line of his poem "Funeral Blues" that was quoted in the film *Four Weddings and a Funeral:* "He was my North, my South, my East and West, / My working week and my Sunday rest, / My noon, my midnight, my talk, my song; / I thought that love would last for ever: I was wrong."

Lewis Carroll (1832-1898), the pen name of Charles Lutwidge Dodgson, was a mathematician who taught at Oxford, where he met young Alice Liddell, the dean's daughter and the real-life inspiration for his most famous book, *Alice's Adventures in Wonderland*. The author lived at Christ Church College, and Carroll and Liddell would regularly play croquet—without the

OXFORD

for a sacred space, so this theater was purpose-built. (Despite its misleading name, no theatrical presentations take place here, though music concerts sometimes do.) This was the first major building project designed by Sir Christopher Wren, then a physics professor and budding architect who went on to rebuild much of London after the great fire (including the landmark St. Paul's Cathedral). While the interior isn't too exciting, you'll see the

Queen of Hearts—in The Meadow.

Aldous Huxley (1894-1963), a prolific novelist and Oxford student, wrote the early science-fiction classic *Brave New World*, about a disturbing, mindless future. His later book, *The Doors of Perception,* was written under the influence of mescaline. (Jim Morrison, another fan of mind-altering experiences, named his band The Doors after the book.)

Literary great **Virginia Woolf** (1882-1941) was banned from using Oxford's library because she was a woman (Oxford didn't begin admitting women until 1920, though they could attend some classes before that). She later wrote her most important essay, "A Room of One's Own," where she parodied the university she nicknamed "Oxbridge," a combination of Oxford and Cambridge.

Oscar Wilde (1854-1900) did well at Oxford (graduating with the highest grade possible) and went on to become famous for his novels *(The Picture of Dorian Gray)*, plays *(The Importance of Being Earnest),* homosexuality (his famous trial sent him to jail), and memorably witty quotes, such as "Men marry because they are tired; women, because they are curious: both are disappointed." Another of his quotes: "I can resist everything except temptation." And another: "We are all in the gutter, but some of us are looking at the stars."

Oxford's other notable literary stars include the poet **Percy Bysshe Shelley, Jonathan Swift** *(Gulliver's Travels),* **T. S. Eliot** *(The Waste Land),* **John le Carré** *(The Spy Who Came in from the Cold),* **Philip Pullman** *(The Golden Compass,* part of his children's book series *His Dark Materials),* **Martin Amis** *(Time's Arrow),* **Helen Fielding** *(Bridget Jones's Diary),* and—maybe most important of all to generations of children's book readers—Theodor Seuss Geisel (a.k.a. **Dr. Seuss**).

In addition to the **Harry Potter** connection, visiting Brits are enthralled by locations relating to the Oxford-set **Inspector Morse** television series, which was an enormous hit in the UK from 1987 to 2000 (the sequel, **Inspector Lewis,** is now being filmed here). Sort of the British Columbo or a modern-day Sherlock Holmes, this fictional police detective was quirky, cultured, and extremely effective.

round main hall, with its painted ceiling, gold trim, stone columns, pipe organ, and chandeliers. Your ticket also includes admission to the building's cupola, with 360-degree views over the many spires of Oxford.

Cost and Hours: £2.50, Mon-Sat 10:00-12:30 & 14:00-16:30, until 15:30 in winter, sometimes closed for special events, closed Sun except July-Aug, Broad Street, tel. 01865/277-299.

Other Sights

▲▲**The Ashmolean Museum of Art and Archaeology**—This eclectic museum was founded in 1683 by a royal gardener, John Tradescant, who loved to collect interesting items while traveling in search of plants. All these years later, the collection is huge, and the building recently underwent a thorough £63 million renovation.

Cost and Hours: Free, £3 audioguide, Tue-Sun 10:00-18:00, closed Mon, rooftop café, Beaumont Street, tel. 01865/278-000, www.ashmolean.org.

Touring the Museum: While the collection doesn't rank with the big-league museums of London, it's very impressive for a small city. The vast collection features everything from antiquities to fine porcelain to paintings by some of the Old Masters. Rather than featuring any particularly famous items, it has a broad range of offbeat bits and pieces (such as Lawrence of Arabia's ceremonial dress, prehistoric Cycladic figurines from Greece, gorgeous Turkish and Middle Eastern tiles, a Stradivarius violin, and so on). What distinguishes this place is that it's all exceptionally well-presented, with engaging descriptions that pull you in to topics you didn't realize were of interest to you.

The museum is loosely organized chronologically, starting in the basement and working up through five floors of history; it's also arranged geographically, with excellent collections of Chinese, Middle Eastern, Indian, Mediterranean, and other regional art and artifacts. As you move up the building, the exhibit shows how these very different civilizations came together as the world shrunk. For an engaging introduction, head for the basement and peruse the "Exploring the Past" themed exhibits, which bring together various eras of history and corners of the globe while examining a particular topic (such as money, the human image, and reading and writing). Then browse the collection to your heart's content, and find your own favorites (I enjoyed the paintings of royal elephants from India).

There's also a fine painting gallery, showcasing lesser-known pieces by Degas, Pissarro, Van Gogh, and others. It's fun to see artist J. W. M. Turner's view down High Street in Oxford...then walk a block to see today's version. If nothing else, The Ashmolean provides visitors to this university town a way to see a respectable range of English glass, Chinese porcelain, ancient sculpture, and tapestries without having to ride the train.

Punting—Long, flat boats can be rented for punting (pushing with a long pole) along the River Cherwell. Chauffeurs are avail-

OXFORD

able, but the do-it-yourself crowd is having more fun...even if they are a little wet.

Cost and Hours: £16/hour—or £20/hour on weekends, £30 deposit, chauffeured punts-£23/30 minutes, rowboats and paddle boats available for the less adventurous, cash only, daily March-Nov 9:30-dusk, closed off-season and in bad weather, Magdalen Bridge Boathouse, tel. 01865/202-643, www.oxfordpunting.co.uk).

Sleeping in Oxford

(area code: 01865)

Sleeping cheaply in Oxford is not easy. The colleges and university own much of the town, so boarding space is at a premium. There are a few high-end hotels in the center, and B&Bs crowd the main roads out of town. Noise is an issue in this college town—mostly from students conversing or singing loudly in the streets on the way home from the pub. Try requesting a quiet room, but expect some noise regardless. Given the easy connections by train to the Cotswolds (Moreton-in-Marsh) and London, I'd make Oxford a day trip, and sleep elsewhere. But if you're spending the night, here are some centrally located, reasonable options.

$$$ The Tower House, with tight spaces and low ceilings, has small, worn-but-sweet rooms, and couldn't be more central. Three of the seven rooms share a bathroom with a spacious shower (S-£70, Sb-£90, D-£80, Db-£110, includes continental breakfast, free Wi-Fi, no parking, request a quieter back room, 15 Ship Street, tel. 01865/246-828, fax 01865/247-508, www.oxfordhotelsandinns .com, thetowerhouse@btconncct.com).

OXFORD

Sleep Code

(£1 = about $1.60, country code: 44)

S = Single, **D** = Double/Twin, **T** = Triple, **Q** = Quad, **b** = bathroom, **s** = shower only. Unless otherwise noted, breakfast is included and credit cards are accepted.

To help you sort easily through these listings, I've divided the accommodations into three categories based on the price for a double room with bath:

$$$ Higher Priced—Most rooms £100 or more.
$$ Moderately Priced—Most rooms between £50-100.
$ Lower Priced—Most rooms £50 or less.

Prices can change without notice; verify the hotel's current rates online or by email. For other updates, see www .ricksteves.com/update.

$$$ Bath Place Hotel is a creaky place with 16 cute, flowery, slightly scruffy rooms connected by a maze of impossibly steep and narrow stairways. It's tucked down a tiny lane—just follow the trail of students going to the very popular pub below. The pub closes and things calm down after 23:30 on weeknights, or 24:00 on weekends—if you're a light sleeper and want to turn in early, request a quieter room (Sb-£85-95—or £110 on Fri-Sat, Db-£118-145, Tb-£150-220, Qb-£170-238, price depends on room size, includes buffet breakfast, free Wi-Fi, limited parking-£10/day, free parking farther away, 4 Bath Place, tel. 01865/791-812, fax 01865/791-834, www.bathplace.co.uk, info@bathplace.co.uk, Yolanda).

$$$ The Buttery Hotel, up steep steps above a café/bakery (hence the name) and two doors down from the TI, rents 16 comfortable, good-value rooms. The "deluxe" rooms are larger and have big windows overlooking bustling Broad Street—nice for views but not for noise; the cheaper "standard" rooms are quieter (tiny Sb-£60, bigger Sb-£80-85, standard Db-£100-110, deluxe Db-£125-135, Tb-£155-165, higher rates are for Fri-Sat, free Wi-Fi, no parking, 11-12 Broad Street, tel. 01865/811-950, fax 01865/811-951, www.thebutteryhotel.co.uk, enquiries@thebutteryhotel.co.uk, Felicity).

$$ Holywell Bed & Breakfast, run by local tour guide Stuart and his American wife Carrie, is hidden away in an ancient row house on quiet Holywell Street, across from New College. Its four twin rooms share two bathrooms (S-£60-80, D-£80-100, higher prices are for Fri-Sat, book well in advance, no children under age 12, steep stairs, free Wi-Fi, free parking in adjacent lot, guests also receive free walking tour with Stuart, 14 Holywell Street, tel. 01865/721-880, www.holywellbedandbreakfast.com, info@holywellbedandbreakfast.com).

Hostels

This youthful town has two different hostels that are called "Backpackers," at opposite sides of the same block (a 3-minute walk from the train station on the way to the town center). Both of them are willing to store non-guests' bags for a fee (£3/bag at Oxford Backpackers, £2/bag at Central Backpackers).

$ Oxford Backpackers Hostel rents 92 beds in single-sex and mixed dorms. While the ambience is somewhere between grotty and funky, hard-core hostelers appreciate the cheap beds (£16-18/bed in large dorm, £19/bed in 4-person dorm, includes continental breakfast, reception open 8:00-23:00, free Wi-Fi, laundry service, 9A Hythe Bridge Street, tel. 01865/721-761, fax 01865/203-293, www.hostels.co.uk, oxford@hostels.co.uk).

$ Central Backpackers Oxford, loosely run by gregarious Aussie Mick, rents 50 beds in 4- to 12-bed dorms around an inviting covered patio. It feels a bit more tame than Oxford Backpackers (£19-22/bed depending on room size, includes basic continental breakfast, free Internet access and Wi-Fi, laundry service, 13 Park End Street, tel. 01865/242-288, www.centralbackpackers.co.uk).

Near Oxford

$$ The Coach & Horses Inn, a charming 16th-century inn and pub, is located seven miles southeast of Oxford in Chislehampton, across the street from a bus stop that connects the two towns (Sb-£62, Db-£75, free Wi-Fi, tel. 01865/890-255, fax 01865/891-995, www.coachhorsesinn.co.uk, enquiries@coachhorsesinn.co.uk).

Eating in Oxford

Pubs

These pubs perfectly conform to what Americans imagine a British pub to be: a rambling series of cozy, well-worn rooms on sloping wooden floors filled with tight clusters of friends enjoying food and ale around ancient-feeling tables. The hours listed below are for when food is served—most stay open later to serve drinks.

The King's Arms, across from Blackwell's Bookstore and the Sheldonian Theatre, has an approachable, open, convivial atmosphere. They offer good traditional English fare (£5 sandwiches, £8-10 pub grub, food served daily 11:00-21:30, 40 Holywell Street at corner of Parks Road, across from the Sheldonian, tel. 01865/242-369).

The Bear, hidden down a side street and close to the Christ Church Picture Gallery, is one of Oxford's oldest and most charm-

ing pubs. This teensy place proudly sports no right angles (go ahead—check) since 1242. Peruse the framed collections of amputated clothing on the walls and hold on to your tie if you're wearing one. If you're coming for lunch, arrive before 13:00, when they're typically swamped and tables are in short supply (£7-10 meals, food served daily 12:00-21:00, 6 Alfred Street at corner of Blue Boar Street, tel. 01865/728-164). There are a few picnic tables out back—leave through

the pub's side door to find them, or walk to the left as you're facing the front.

The Turf Tavern—big, boisterous, and tucked into a short alley—is popular for its good food, outdoor beer garden, and warren of claustrophobic rooms nestled against the old city wall

(£6-9 pub grub, food served daily 11:00-21:00, 4 Bath Place, tel. 01865/243-235). To find it from Holywell Street, listen for the chatter of students enjoying a beer (down Bath Lane); otherwise, head for the gap marked *St. Helen's Passage* under the Bridge of Sighs on New College/Queen's Lane.

The **Eagle and Child,** a long and thin series of rooms, is subdued, smaller, and more intimate than the other pubs listed. A five-minute walk from the city center, it's more famous for its history and ambience than its very traditional food. This was the gathering place of the writers known as the Inklings (see sidebar on page 452), and a literary vibe still haunts the place. If you're a fan of Middle-earth and Narnia, stop in for a drink under photos of J. R. R. Tolkien and C. S. Lewis (£6-10 pub grub, read the history on the menu, food served Mon-Fri 11:00-22:00, Sat-Sun 10:00-22:00, 49 St. Giles Street, tel. 01865/302-925).

Eating Cheaply

Taylors is a student favorite for affordable £3-5 hot or cold sandwiches with a wide range of fillings. There are a few tables, but most people get food to go and find a scenic spot for a picnic (daily 8:00-20:00, closes at 17:00 July-Aug and other times students are away, 58 High Street, tel. 01865/723-152). You'll see several Taylors locations around Oxford.

The **Covered Market**—a farmers'-market maze of shops, fruit stands, deli counters, and cafés—has a fine selection for breakfast, lunch, or a picnic (daily 9:00-17:30, between Market Street and High Street, near Carfax Tower).

Other Eateries

The **News Café,** with a cheerful and bright interior, buzzes with locals. They serve light food for lunch and early dinner, and hearty meals, big salads, and cheaper cream teas than at the large hotels. It's a nice break from the chain eateries on nearby Cornmarket (£7-10 meals, Sun-Thu 9:00-19:00, Fri-Sat 9:00-22:00, 1 Ship Street, tel. 01865/242-317).

Chain Restaurants on Cornmarket and Nearby: On Cornmarket, you'll find a slew of chain eateries, including **Pret à Manger** and **West Cornwall Pasty Company.** Nearby is **Jamie's Italian,** part of a chain owned by British TV's celebrity chef Jamie Oliver and serving up classic Italian cuisine in a sprawling, industrial-mod interior (£6-8 pastas, £11-16 main dishes, Mon-Sat 12:00-23:00, Sun 12:00-22:30, 24-26 George Street, tel. 01865/838-383).

There's a **Marks & Spencer** on Queen Street, across from Carfax Tower.

Afternoon Tea: **The Randolph Hotel** is a swanky place where proud parents take their graduating students for a fancy afternoon tea (reserve ahead, especially near the end of the term). You'll enjoy impeccable service and classic English afternoon tea under high ceilings and chandeliers (£19 afternoon tea, £12.25 traditional cream tea, daily 12:00-22:00, tea served until 18:00, Beaumont Street, directly opposite Ashmolean Museum, tel. 01865/256-400). **The Rose** is a local favorite for a spot of tea and warm scones in a more modern atmosphere (£11 afternoon tea, £6.50 cream tea, Tue-Sat 9:00-18:00, Sun 10:00-18:00, 51 High Street, tel. 01865/244-429).

Oxford Connections

From Oxford by Train to: London's Paddington Station (2/ hour direct, 1 hour, more possible with transfer in Reading; cheap £21.40 "day return" ticket good Mon-Fri after 9:01 from Oxford or 9:21 from London, or all day Sat-Sun), **Bath** (hourly, 1.25 hours, transfer in Didcot), **Moreton-in-Marsh** (about hourly, 40 minutes), **Stratford-upon-Avon** (every 2 hours, 1.5 hours, transfer in Leamington Spa or Banbury), **Salisbury** (hourly, 2 hours, transfer in Reading and Basingstoke), **Portsmouth** (2-4/hour, 2.5-2.75 hours, 1-2 transfers), **York** (hourly, 4 hours). Train info: tel. 0845-748-4950, www.nationalrail.co.uk.

By Bus: The Oxford Tube bus runs every 12-20 minutes to London's Marble Arch and Victoria Coach Station (£14 one-way, £20 round-trip, tel. 01865/772-250, www.oxfordtube.com). The competing Oxford Espress runs every 15 minutes during peak times to the same London stops (otherwise about 2-3/hour; £13 one-way, £20 round-trip, tel. 01865/785-400, www.oxfordbus.co.uk) Both companies take about 1.75 hours to make the trip, and all buses depart from the Gloucester Green bus station—just show up and ask which leaves first.

An independent bus service called The Airline shuttles students and visitors directly between Oxford and **Heathrow Airport** 24 hours a day (2/hour, 1.5 hours, £22 one-way, £26 round-trip) and to **Gatwick Airport** (hourly, 2-2.5 hours, £27 one-way, £36 round-trip, tel. 01865/785-400, www.oxfordbus.co.uk).

National Express (tel. 0871-781-8181, www.nationalexpress.com) runs buses to **Stratford-upon-Avon** (1/day direct, 1 hour). For details on taking a public bus to **Blenheim Palace,** see the next section.

Near Oxford: Blenheim Palace

Just 30 minutes' drive from Oxford (and convenient to combine with a drive through the Cotswolds), Blenheim Palace is one of England's best—worth ▲▲▲. Too
many palaces can send you into a
furniture-wax coma, but everyone
should see Blenheim. The Duke of
Marlborough's home—the largest
in England—is still lived in, which
is wonderfully obvious as you
prowl through it. The 2,000-acre
yard, well-designed by Lancelot

"Capability" Brown, is as majestic to some as the palace itself. The view just past the outer gate as you enter is a classic. Even if you're in a hurry, you'll need two hours to see the basic sights—but if you have more time, you could spend all day here. Note: Americans who pronounce the place "blen-HEIM" are the butt of jokes. It's "BLEN-em."

Cost and Hours: £20, discount tickets that save £2.50 are available at TIs in surrounding towns—including Oxford and Moreton-in-Marsh; family ticket for two adults and two kids—£50, £5 guidebook; open mid-Feb-Oct daily 10:30-17:30, last tour departs at 16:45; Nov-mid-Dec Wed-Sun 10:30-17:30; park open but palace closed Nov-mid-Dec Mon-Tue and mid-Dec-mid-Feb; tel. 01993/810-530, recorded info tel. 0800-849-6500, www .blenheimpalace.com.

Getting There: Blenheim Palace sits at the edge of the cute cobbled town of Woodstock. The train station nearest the palace (Hanborough, 1.5 miles away) has no taxi or bus service.

From **Oxford**, take bus #S3 (Mon-Sat 2/hour, less frequent on Sun, 30 minutes; bus tel. 01865/772-250, www.stagecoachbus .com). It departs from downtown Oxford at George Street (near the corner with Cornmarket), then stops at Oxford's bus station at Gloucester Green and sometimes also at Oxford's train station (check the schedule). It stops twice near Blenheim Palace: the "Blenheim Palace Gates" stop is along the main road about a half-mile walk to the palace itself; the "Woodstock/Marlborough Arms" stop puts you right in the heart of the village of Woodstock (handy if you want to poke around town before heading to the palace; this adds just a few more minutes' walking than the other bus stop). The Woodstock gate also offers the most spectacular view of the palace and lake.

If you're coming from the **Cotswolds,** your easiest train connection is from Moreton-in-Marsh to Oxford, where you can catch the bus to Blenheim (note that bus #S3 doesn't always stop at the

Oxford train station—you may have to walk five minutes to the bus station).

Drivers head for Woodstock (from the Cotswolds, follow signs for *Oxford* on A-44); the palace is well-signposted once in town, just off the main road. Buy your ticket at the gate, then drive up the long driveway to park near the palace.

Background: John Churchill, first duke of Marlborough, defeated Louis XIV's French forces at the Battle of Blenheim in 1704. This pivotal event marked a turning point in the centuries-long struggle between the English and the French, and some historians claim that if not for his victory, we'd all be speaking French today. (They're probably exaggerating, but *qui sait?*) A thankful Queen Anne rewarded Churchill by building him this nice home, perhaps the finest Baroque building in England (designed by playwright-turned-architect John Vanbrugh). Ten dukes of Marlborough later, it's as impressive as ever. (The current, 11th duke considers the would-be 12th more of an error than an heir, and what to do about him is quite an issue.) In 1874, a later John Churchill's daughter-in-law, Jennie Jerome, gave birth at Blenheim to another historic baby in that line...and named him Winston. The history continues.

◒ Self-Guided Tour: From the parking lot, stop off at the "Falstaff" info booth to pick up a free map and head through the small courtyard. You'll emerge into a grand courtyard in front of the palace's columned yellow facade. Most of the attractions are reached by going through the palace's main entry.

You'll enter into the truly great **Great Hall.** Before taking the well-organized tour, spend some time on your own in the fine **Winston Churchill Exhibition,** which displays letters, paintings, and other artifacts of the great statesman who was born here. The highlight is the bed in which Sir Winston was born in 1874 (prematurely...his mother went into labor suddenly while attending a party here).

When you've had your fill of Churchill, catch the 45-minute guided tour of the **state rooms**—the fancy halls the dukes use to impress visiting dignitaries (tours leave every 10 minutes, included with ticket, last one at 16:45). This fascinating tour lets visitors ogle some of the most sumptuous rooms in the palace, ornamented with fine porcelain, gilded ceilings, portraits of past dukes, photos of the present duke's family, and "chaperone" sofas designed to give courting couples just enough privacy...but not *too* much. When the palace is really busy (most likely on Sun), they dispense with guided tours and go "free flow," allowing those with an appetite for learning to strike up conversations with docents in each room.

Enjoy the series of 10 Brussels tapestries that commemorate military victories of the First Duke of Marlborough, including the

Battle of Blenheim. After winning that pivotal conflict, he scrawled a quick note on the back of a tavern bill notifying the Queen of his victory (you'll see a replica). The tour offers insights into the quirky ways of England's fading nobility—for example, in exchange for this fine palace, the duke still pays "rent" to the Queen in the form of one ornamental flag per year (called "quit-rent standard").

The palace items come with tales of past dukes of Marlborough and their families. You'll learn about Consuelo Vanderbilt—of the New York Vanderbilts—who was forced against her will to marry into this aristocratic family. She was miserable, but dutifully produced two sons (whom she dubbed "the heir and the spare") before the marriage fell apart after 10 years.

Finish with the remarkable "long library"—with its tiers of books and stuccoed ceilings—before exiting through the chapel, near the entrance to the gardens (described later). But before taking off to explore the gardens, consider two more attractions inside the main palace.

The Untold Story (to the left as you enter the Great Hall) is a modern, 45-minute, multimedia "visitors' experience" (runs every 10 minutes, included in your ticket). You'll travel from room to room—as doors open and close behind you—guided through 300 years of history by a maid named Grace Ridley. (If you have limited time to spend at the palace, this is skippable.)

For a more extensive visit, follow up the general tour with a 30-minute guided walk through the **private apartments** of the duke. Tours leave at the top and bottom of each hour; however, since you'll see where the duke's family actually resides today, tours are cancelled if His Grace is in his jammies (£4.50, irregular schedule but generally daily 12:00-16:30, most likely to be open in spring, tickets are limited, buy from table in library or at Flagstaff info booth outside main gates, enter in corner of courtyard to left of grand palace entry).

The palace's expansive **gardens** stretch nearly as far as the eye can see in every direction. Access them from the courtyard, by going through the little door near the "Churchill Shop" (as you face the main palace entrance, it's to the right). You'll emerge into the Water Terraces; from there, you can loop around to the left, behind the palace, to see (but not enter) the Italian Garden. Or, head down to the lake to walk along the waterfront trail; going left takes you to the rose gardens and arboretum, while turning right brings you to the Grand Bridge. You can explore on your own (using the map and good signposting), or rent a £3 audioguide

that outlines three different walks around the property (40-90 minutes depending on tour; rent it in the "Churchill Shop" next to the door to the gardens). A café sits at the garden exit for basic lunch and teatime treats.

Finally, in the "stables block" (under the gateway to the right, as you face the main palace entrance) is the **"Churchill's Destiny" exhibit,** which traces the military leadership of two great men who shared that name: John, who defeated Louis XIV at the Battle of Blenheim in the 18th century, and in whose honor this palace was built; and Winston, who was born in this palace, and who won the Battle of Britain and helped defeat Hitler in the 20th century. The exhibit offers a painstaking, blow-by-blow account of each of the battles. It's remarkable that arguably two of the most important military victories in the nation's history were overseen by distant cousins—England is a small island indeed. (Winston Churchill fans can visit his tomb, just over a mile away in the Bladon town churchyard—the church is faintly visible from inside the palace.)

The final attraction is actually on the way out of the palace complex: the kid-friendly **pleasure garden,** where a lush and humid greenhouse flutters with butterflies. A kid zone includes a few second-rate games and the "world's largest symbolic hedge maze." The maze is worth a look if you haven't seen one and could use some exercise. If you have a car, you'll pass these gardens as you drive down the road toward the exit; otherwise, you can take the tiny train from the palace parking lot to the garden (2/hour).

Sleeping near Blenheim Palace, in Woodstock

(£1 = about $1.60, country code: 44, area code: 01993)
$$ Blenheim Guest House, charming and 200 years old, has six rooms in the town center. A bit musty, it's located above a tea-room literally next door to the gateway into the palace grounds (Sb-£55, Db-£68-80 depending on size, free Wi-Fi, 17 Park Street, tel. 01993/813-814, fax 01993/813-810, www.theblenheim.co.uk, theblenheim@aol.com).

$$ The Blenheim Buttery has six modern, comfortable rooms fitted into a half-timbered, slanted-floor building (Sb-£85, Db-£110, free Wi-Fi, 7 Market Place, tel. 01865/811-950, www.the blenheimbuttery.co.uk, info@theblenheimbuttery.co.uk, Felicity).

THE COTSWOLDS

Chipping Campden • Stow-on-the-Wold •
Moreton-in-Marsh

The Cotswold Hills, a 25-by-90-mile chunk of Gloucestershire, are dotted with enchanting villages. As with many fairy-tale regions of Europe, the present-day beauty of the Cotswolds was the result of an economic disaster. Wool was a huge industry in medieval England, and Cotswold sheep grew the best wool. A 12th-century saying bragged, "In Europe the best wool is English. In England the best wool is Cotswold." The region prospered. Wool money built fine towns and houses. Local "wool" churches are called "cathedrals" for their scale and wealth. Stained-glass slogans say things like "I thank my God and ever shall, it is the sheep hath paid for all."

With the rise of cotton and the Industrial Revolution, the woolen industry collapsed. Ba-a-a-ad news. The wealthy Cotswold towns fell into a depressed time warp; the homes of impoverished nobility became gracefully dilapidated. Today, visitors enjoy a harmonious blend of man and nature—the most pristine of English countrysides decorated with time-passed villages, rich wool churches, tell-me-a-story stone fences, and "kissing gates" you wouldn't want to experience alone. Appreciated by throngs of 21st-century Romantics, the Cotswolds are enjoying new prosperity.

The north Cotswolds are best. Two of the region's coziest towns, Chipping Campden and Stow-on-the-Wold, are eight and four miles, respectively, from Moreton-in-Marsh, which has the best public transportation connections. Any of

these three towns makes a fine home base for your exploration of the thatch-happiest of Cotswold villages and walks.

Planning Your Time

The Cotswolds are an absolute delight by car and, with patience, enjoyable even without a car. On a three-week British trip, I'd spend at least two nights and a day in the Cotswolds. The Cotswolds' charm has a softening effect on many uptight itineraries. You could enjoy days of walking from a home base here.

Home Bases: Chipping Campden and **Stow-on-the-Wold** are quaint without being overrun, and both have good accommodations. Stow has a bit more character for an overnight stay, and offers the widest range of choices. The plain town of **Moreton-in-Marsh** is the only one of the three with a train station, and is only worth visiting as a transit hub. While Moreton has the most convenient connections, non-drivers can also make it work to home-base in Chipping Campden or Stow—especially if you don't mind sorting through bus schedules or springing for the occasional taxi to connect towns. (But note that this becomes even more challenging on Sundays, when there is essentially no bus service.) With a car, consider really getting away from it all by staying in one of the smaller villages.

Nearby Sights: If you want to take in some Shakespeare, note that Stow, Chipping Campden, and Moreton are only a 30-minute drive from **Stratford,** which offers a great evening of world-class entertainment (see next chapter). And England's greatest countryside palace, **Blenheim,** is located at the eastern edge of the Cotswolds, between Moreton and Oxford (see previous chapter).

One-Day Driver's 100-Mile Cotswold Blitz: Use a good map and reshuffle this plan to fit your home base:

9:00	Browse through Chipping Campden, following my self-guided walk.
10:30	Joyride through Snowshill, Stanway, and Stanton.
12:30	Have lunch in Stow-on-the-Wold, then follow my self-guided walk there.
15:00	Drive to the Slaughters, Bourton-on-the-Water, and Bibury; or, if you're up for a hike instead of a drive, walk from Stow to the Slaughters to Bourton, then catch the bus back to Stow.
18:00	Have dinner at a countryside gastropub (reserve in advance by phone), then head home; or drive 30 minutes to Stratford-upon-Avon for a Shakespeare play.

Don't miss Blenheim Palace, which deserves a half-day. Thanks to its location at the Cotswolds' eastern edge, Blenheim fits well on the way into or out of the region.

Cotswold Appreciation 101

Much history can be read into the names of the area. *Cotswold* could come from the Saxon phrase meaning "hills of sheep's cotes" (shelters for sheep). Or it could mean shelter ("cot" like cottage) on the open upland ("wold").

In the Cotswolds, a town's main street (called High Street) needed to be wide to accommodate the sheep and cattle being marched to market (and today, to park tour buses). Some of the most picturesque cottages were once humble row houses of weavers' cottages, usually located along a stream for their waterwheels (good examples in Bibury and Lower Slaughter). The towns run on slow clocks and yellowed calendars. An entire village might not have a phone booth.

Fields of yellow (rapeseed) and pale blue (linseed) separate pastures dotted with black and white sheep. In just about any B&B, when you open your window in the morning you'll hear sheep baa-ing. The decorative "toadstool" stones dotting front yards throughout the region are medieval staddle stones, which buildings were set upon to keep the rodents out.

Cotswold walls and roofs are made of the local limestone. The limestone roof tiles hang by pegs. To make the weight more bearable, smaller and lighter tiles are higher up. An extremely strict building code keeps towns looking what many locals call "overly quaint."

Two-Day Plan by Public Transportation: This plan is best for any day except Sunday—when virtually no buses run—and assumes you're home-basing in Moreton-in-Marsh.

Day 1: Take the morning bus (likely around 9:30) to Chipping Campden to explore that town. If you want to stretch your legs, hike 30 minutes (each way) into Broad Campden. Then take the bus from Chipping Campden to Moreton and transfer to a Stow-bound bus. After poking around Stow, hike from Stow through the Slaughters to Bourton-on-the-Water (about 3 hours at a relaxed pace), then return by bus to Moreton for dinner. (For less walking and more time for an early dinner in Stow, do just part of the hike, or take the bus from Stow to Bourton and back.) Note that the last bus back to Moreton departs Stow at about 18:50 (departs Bourton at 18:40, this bus runs Mon-Sat only—none on Sun except May-Aug, confirm times locally).

Day 2: Take a day trip to Blenheim Palace via Oxford (train to Oxford, bus to palace—explained on page 460); or rent a bike and

While you'll still see lots of sheep, the commercial wool industry is essentially dead. It costs more to shear a sheep than the 50 pence the wool will fetch. In the old days, sheep lived long lives, producing lots of wool. When they were finally slaughtered, the meat was tough and eaten as "mutton." Today, you don't find mutton much because the sheep are raised primarily for their meat, and slaughtered younger. When it comes to Cotswold sheep these days, it's lamb (not mutton) for dinner (not sweaters).

Towns are small, and everyone seems to know everyone. The area is provincial yet ever-so-polite, and people commonly rescue themselves from a gossipy tangent by saying, "It's all very...mmm...yaaa."

In contrast to the village ambience are the giant manors and mansions whose private, gated driveways you'll drive past. Many of these now belong to A-list celebrities, who have country homes here. If you live in the Cotswolds, you can call Madonna, Elizabeth Hurley, Kate Moss, and Kate Winslet your neighbors.

This is walking country. The English love their walks and vigorously defend their age-old right to free passage. Once a year the Ramblers, Britain's largest walking club, organizes a "Mass Trespass," when each of the country's 50,000 miles of public footpaths is walked. By assuring that each path is used at least once a year, they stop landlords from putting up fences. Any paths found blocked are unceremoniously unblocked.

Questions to ask locals: Do you think foxhunting should have been banned? Who are the Morris men? What's a kissing gate?

ride to Chastleton House; or take a daylong countryside walk (best to bus to Stow or Chipping Campden and walk from there).

Tourist Information

Local TIs stock a wide array of helpful resources. Ask for the *Cotswold Lion* weekly newspaper, which includes suggestions for walks and hikes (summers only); the monthly *Cotswold Events* guide; the *Explore the Cotswolds by Public Transport* bus timetable brochure, as well as individual bus schedules for the routes you'll be using; and the *Attractions and Events Guide 2012* (with updated prices and hours for Cotswolds sights). Each village also has its own assortment of brochures about the place itself, and the surrounding countryside, often for a small fee (£0.50-1). While paying for these items seems chintzy, realize that Cotswolds TIs have lost much of their funding and are struggling to make ends meet (some even have volunteer staff).

The Cotswolds

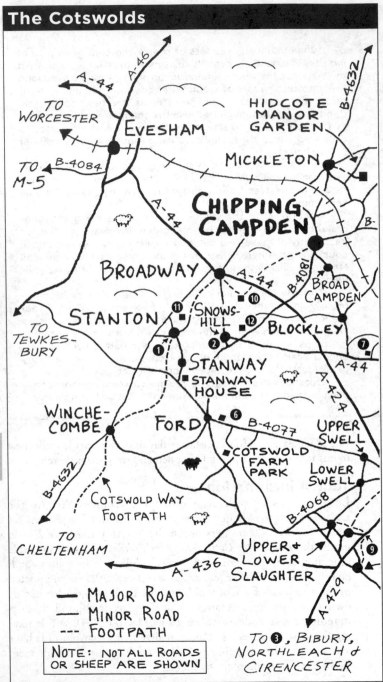

THE COTSWOLDS

TO WORCESTER

A-44

A-46

TO M-5

B-4084

EVESHAM

HIDCOTE MANOR GARDEN

MICKLETON

B-4632

CHIPPING CAMPDEN

BROADWAY

A-44

BROAD CAMPDEN

B-4081

B-

STANTON

11

SNOWS-HILL

10

12

BLOCKLEY

TO TEWKES-BURY

1

2

7

A-44

STANWAY

STANWAY HOUSE

A-424

WINCHE-COMBE

FORD

6

B-4077

UPPER SWELL

B-4632

COTSWOLD FARM PARK

LOWER SWELL

COTSWOLD WAY FOOTPATH

B-4068

TO CHELTENHAM

A-436

UPPER + LOWER SLAUGHTER

9

A-429

— MAJOR ROAD
— MINOR ROAD
--- FOOTPATH

NOTE: NOT ALL ROADS OR SHEEP ARE SHOWN

TO 3, BIBURY, NORTHLEACH & CIRENCESTER

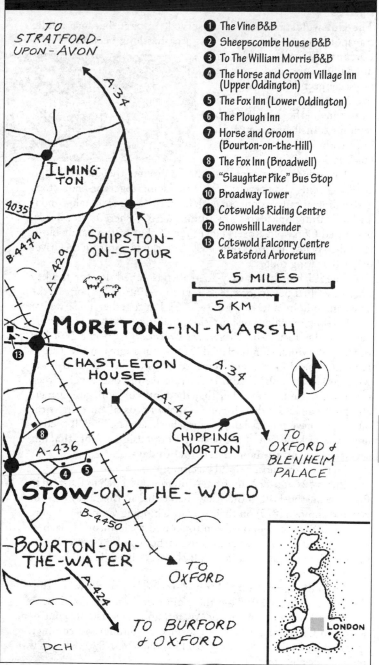

Getting Around the Cotswolds
By Bus

The Cotswolds are so well-preserved, in part, because public transportation to and within this area has long been miserable.

Fortunately, larger towns are linked by trains, and a few key buses connect the more interesting villages. Centrally located Moreton-in-the-Marsh is the region's transit hub—with the only train station and several bus lines.

To explore the towns, use the bus routes that hop through the Cotswolds about every 1.5 hours, lacing together main stops and ending at rail stations. In each case, the entire trip takes about an hour. Individual fares are around £2-3. (There is an all-day, unlimited Cotswold Rover Ticket for £6, but of the handy buses described below, it covers only #855. You can buy it from the driver on participating routes.)

The TI hands out easy-to-read bus schedules for the key lines described below (or check www.traveline.org.uk, or call the Traveline info line, tel. 0871-200-2233). Put together a one-way or return trip by public transportation, making for a fine Cotswolds day. Ask the TI for the *Explore the Cotswolds by Public Transport* timetables, which summarize all of the bus routes in the area in separate central, north, and south sections (or download them at www.cotswoldsaonb.org.uk). If you're traveling one-way between two train stations, remember that the Cotswold villages—generally pretty clueless when it comes to the needs of travelers without a car—have no official baggage-check services. You'll need to improvise; ask sweetly at the nearest TI or business. **Note that bus service is essentially nonexistent on Sundays.**

Here are the most helpful bus lines:

Buses **#21** and **#22** run from Moreton-in-Marsh to Batsford to Bourton-on-the-Hill to Blockley, then either to Broadway (#21) or Broad Campden (#22) on their way to Chipping Campden, before ending at Stratford-upon-Avon (operated by Johnsons Coaches, tel. 01564/797-000, www.johnsonscoaches.co.uk). Note that this route is the only one that goes all the way through to Chipping Campden.

Bus **#801** goes from Moreton-in-Marsh to Stow-on-the-Wold to "Slaughter Pike" (on the main road just south of the two Slaughters) to Bourton-on-the-Water, and then usually continues on to Cheltenham (limited service on Sundays in summer, operated by Pulham & Sons Coaches, tel. 01451/820-369, www.pulhamscoaches.com).

Bus **#855** (called the Fosse Link) goes from Moreton-in-Marsh to Stow-on-the-Wold to Bourton-on-the-Water to Northleach to Cirencester, and then (in the morning and evening) on to the Kemble train station (operated by Pulham & Sons Coaches, tel. 01451/820-369, www.pulhamscoaches.com).

Note that no single bus connects the three major towns described in this chapter (Chipping Campden, Stow, and Moreton); to get between Chipping Campden and Stow, you'll have to change buses in Moreton.

By Bike

Despite narrow roads, high hedgerows (blocking some views), and even higher hills, bikers enjoy the Cotswolds free from the constraints of bus schedules. For each area, TIs have fine route planners that indicate which peaceful, paved lanes are particularly scenic for biking. In summer, it's smart to book your rental bike a couple of days ahead.

In **Moreton-in-Marsh,** the nice folks at the **Toy Shop** rent mountain bikes. You can stop in the shop to rent a bike, or call ahead to pick up or drop off at other times—they're flexible (£15/day with route maps, bike locks, and helmets; shop open Mon and Wed-Fri 9:00-13:00 & 14:00-17:00, Sat 9:00-17:00, closed Sun and Tue, High Street, tel. 01608/650-756).

In **Chipping Campden,** you have two options: **Cycle Cotswolds,** right in town at the Volunteer Inn pub, is the most convenient (£10/day, £15/24 hours, daily 7:00-21:00, Lower High Street, tel. 01789/720-193, www.cyclecotswolds.co.uk). Otherwise, try **Cotswold Country Cycles** (£15/day, tandem-£30/day, includes helmets and route maps, delivery for a fee, daily 9:30-dusk, 2 miles north of town at Longlands Farm Cottage, tel. 01386/438-706, mobile 07746-107-728, www.cotswoldcountrycycles.com); they also offer self-led bike tours of the Cotswolds and surrounding areas (2-7 days, see website for details).

Stow-on-the-Wold does not have any bike-rental shops.

By Foot

Walking guidebooks and leaflets abound, giving you a world of choices for each of my recommended stops (choose a book with clear maps). If you're doing any hiking whatsoever, get the excellent Ordnance Survey Explorer OL #45 map, which shows every road, trail, and ridgeline (£8 at local TIs). Nearly every hotel and B&B has a box or shelf of local walking guides and maps, including Ordnance Survey #45. Don't hesitate to ask for a loaner. For a quick circular hike from a particular village, peruse the books and brochures offered by that village's TI. Villages are generally no more than three miles apart, and most have pubs that would love

THE COTSWOLDS

to feed and water you. For a list of guided walks, ask at any TI for the free *Cotswold Lion* newspaper. The walks range from 2 to 12 miles, and often involve a stop at a pub or tearoom (April-Sept; *Lion* newspaper also online at www.cotswoldsaonb.org.uk—click on "Publications").

There are many options for hikers, ranging from the "Cotswold Way" path that leads 100 miles from Chipping Campden all the way to Bath, to easy loop trips to the next village. Serious hikers enjoy doing a several-day loop, walking for several hours each day and sleeping in a different village each night. One popular route is the **"Cotswold Ring"**: Day 1—Moreton-in-Marsh to Stow-on-the-Wold to the Slaughters to Bourton-on-the-Water (12 miles); Day 2—Bourton-on-the-Water to Winchcombe (13 miles); Day 3—Winchcombe to Stanway to Stanton (7 miles), or all the way to Broadway (10.5 miles total); Day 4—On to Chipping Campden (just 5.5 miles, but steeply uphill); Day 5—Chipping Campden to Broad Campden, Blockley, Bourton-on-the-Hill or Batsford, and back to Moreton (7 miles).

Realistically, on a short visit, you won't have time for that much hiking. But if you have a few hours to spare, consider venturing across the pretty hills and meadows of the Cotswolds. Each of the home-base villages I recommend has several options. Stow-on-the-Wold, immersed in pretty but not-too-hilly terrain, is within easy walking distance of several interesting spots, and is probably the best starting point. Chipping Campden sits along a ridge, which means that hikes from there are extremely scenic, but also more strenuous. Moreton—true to its name—sits on a marsh, offering flatter and less picturesque hikes.

Here are a few hikes to consider, in order of difficulty (easiest first). I've selected these for their convenience to the home-base towns, and because the start and/or end points are on bus lines, allowing you to hitch a ride back to where you started (or on to the next town) rather than backtracking by foot.

Stow, the Slaughters, and Bourton-on-the-Water: Walk from Stow to Upper and Lower Slaughter, then on to Bourton-on-the-Water (which has bus service back to Stow on #801 or #855). One big advantage of this walk is that it's mostly downhill (4 miles, about 2-3 hours one-way). For details, see page 497.

Chipping Campden, Broad Campden, Blockley, and Bourton-on-the-Hill: From Chipping Campden, it's an easy mile walk into charming Broad Campden, and from there, a more strenuous hike to Blockley and Bourton-on-the-Hill (which are both connected by buses #21 and #22 to Chipping Campden and Moreton). For more details, see page 477.

Winchcombe, Stanway, Stanton, and Broadway: You can reach the charming villages of Stanway and Stanton by foot, but it's tough going—lots of up and down. The start and end points (Winchcombe and Broadway) have decent bus connections, and in a pinch some buses do serve Stanton (but carefully check schedules before you set out).

Broadway to Chipping Campden: The hardiest hike of those I list here, this takes you along the Cotswold Ridge. Attempt it only if you're a serious hiker (5.5 miles).

Bibury and the Coln Valley are pretty, but lack of bus access makes hiking there less appealing.

By Car

Joyriding here truly is a joy. Winding country roads seem designed to spring bucolic village-and-countryside scenes on the driver at every turn. Distances here are wonderfully short—but only if you invest in the Ordnance Survey map of the Cotswolds, sold locally at TIs and newsstands (the £8 Explorer OL #45 map is excellent but almost too detailed for drivers; the £5 Tour Map #8 covers a wider area in less detail). Here are driving distances from Moreton: **Stow-on-the-Wold** (4 miles), **Chipping Campden** (8 miles), **Broadway** (10 miles), **Stratford-upon-Avon** (17 miles), **Warwick** (23 miles), **Blenheim Palace** (20 miles).

Car hiking is great. In this chapter, I cover the postcard-perfect (but discovered) villages. With a car and the local Ordnance Survey map, you can easily ramble about and find your own gems. The problem with having a car is that you are less likely to walk. Consider taking a taxi or bus somewhere, so that you can walk back to your car and enjoy the scenery (see suggestions earlier).

Car Rental: Two places near Moreton-in-Marsh rent cars by the day. **Value Self Drive,** based in Shipston-on-Stour (about six miles north of Moreton) and run by accommodating Julian, has affordable rates (£23-33/day including insurance and taxes, automatic for no extra charge, Mon-Sat 8:30-19:00, might also be open Sun, call ahead to arrange, mobile 07974-805-485, valueselfdrive @btinternet.com). Conveniently, Julian will deliver a car to you in Moreton for £5 extra, provided you drive him back to Shipston (or pay £20 for a taxi). **Robinson Goss Self Drive,** also six miles north of Moreton-in-Marsh, is a bit more expensive, and won't bring the car to you in Moreton (£31-52/day including everything but gas, Mon-Fri 8:30-17:00, Sat 8:30-12:00, closed Sun, tel. 01608/663-322, www.robgos.co.uk).

By Taxi

Two or three town-to-town taxi trips can make more sense than renting a car. While taking a cab cross-country seems extravagant (about £2.50/mile), the distances are short (Stow to Moreton is 4 miles, Stow to Chipping Campden is 10), and one-way walks are

The Cotswolds at a Glance

Chipping Campden and Nearby

▲▲**Chipping Campden** Picturesque market town with the finest High Street in England, accented by a 17th-century Market Hall, wool-tycoon manors, and a characteristic Gothic church. See page 476.

▲▲**Stanway House** Grand, aristocratic home of the Earl of Wemyss, complete with the tallest fountain in Britain and a 14th-century tithe barn. **Hours:** June-Aug Tue and Thu only 14:00-17:00, closed Sept-May. See page 486.

▲**Stanton** Classic Cotswold village with flower-filled exteriors and 15th-century church. See page 488.

▲**Snowshill Manor** Eerie mansion packed to the rafters with eclectic curiosities collected over a lifetime. **Hours:** July-Aug Wed-Mon 11:30-16:30, closed Tue; April-June and Sept-Oct Wed-Sun 12:00-17:00, closed Mon-Tue; closed Nov-March. See page 489.

▲**Hidcote Manor Garden** Fragrant garden organized into color-themed "outdoor rooms" that set a trend in 20th-century garden design. **Hours:** July-Aug daily 10:00-18:00; mid-March-June and Sept Sat-Wed 10:00-18:00, closed Thu-Fri; Oct Sat-Wed 10:00-17:00, closed Thu-Fri; closed Nov-mid-March except Nov-Christmas Sat-Sun 12:00-15:00. See page 491.

▲**Broad Campden, Blockley, and Bourton-on-the-Hill** Trio of villages with sweeping views and quaint homes, far from the madding crowds. See page 492.

Stow-on-the-Wold and Nearby

▲▲**Stow-on-the-Wold** Convenient Cotswolds home base with charming shops and pubs clustered around town square, plus popular day-hikes. See page 493.

THE COTSWOLDS

lovely. If you call a cab, confirm that the meter will start only when you are actually picked up. Consider hiring a cab at the hourly "touring rate" (generally around £30), rather than the meter rate (e.g., £20-25 Stow to Chipping Campden). For a few more bucks, you can have a joyride peppered with commentary.

Note that the drivers listed are not typical city taxi services (with many drivers on call), but are mostly individuals—it's smart to book ahead if you're arriving in high season, since they can book up in advance on weekends.

▲**Lower and Upper Slaughter** Inaptly named historic villages—home to a working waterwheel, peaceful churches, and a folksy museum. See page 504.

▲**Bourton-on-the-Water** The "Venice of the Cotswolds," touristy yet undeniably striking, with petite canals and impressive Motor Museum. See page 504.

▲**Cotswold Farm Park** Kid-friendly park with endangered breeds of local animals, farm demonstrations, and tractor rides. **Hours:** Mid-March–early-Sept daily 10:30-17:00; closed off-season. See page 506.

▲**Keith Harding's World of Mechanical Music** Tiny museum brimming with self-playing musical instruments, demonstrations, and Victorian music boxes. **Hours:** Daily 10:00-17:00. See page 507.

▲**Bibury** Village of antique weavers' cottages, ideal for outdoor activities like fishing and picnicking. See page 507.

▲**Cirencester** Ancient 2,000-year-old city noteworthy for its crafts center and museum, showcasing artifacts from Roman and Saxon times. See page 508.

Moreton-in-Marsh and Nearby
▲**Moreton-in-Marsh** Relatively flat and functional home base with best transportation links in Cotswolds and a bustling Tuesday market.

▲**Chastleton House** Lofty Jacobean-era home with a rich family history. **Hours:** April-Sept Wed-Sat 13:00-17:00, closed Sun-Tue; Oct Wed-Sat 13:00-16:00, closed Sun-Tue; closed Nov-March.

To scare up a driver in Moreton, call **Moreton Taxis** (toll-free tel. 0800-955-8584), Richard at **Four Shires** (mobile 07747-802-555), or **Iain Swallow Taxis** (mobile 07789-897-966); in Stow, call Iain (above) or **Tony Knight** (mobile 07887-714-047); and in Chipping Campden, call Iain (above) or Paul at **Cotswold Private Hire** (mobile 07980-857-833). Tim Harrison at **Tour the Cotswolds** specializes in tours of the Cotswolds and its gardens (mobile 07779-030-820, www.tourthecotswolds.co.uk; Tim co-runs a recommended B&B in Snowshill—see page 491).

By Tour

Departing from Bath, **Mad Max Minibus Tours** offers a "Cotswold Discovery" full-day tour, and can drop you off in Stow with your luggage if you arrange it in advance (see page 366 of the Bath chapter).

While none of the Cotswold towns offers regularly scheduled walks, many have voluntary warden groups who love to meet visitors and give walks for just a small donation (about £3/person; specific contact information appears below for Chipping Campden).

Chipping Campden

Just touristy enough to be convenient, the north Cotswolds town of Chipping Campden (CAMden) is a ▲▲ sight. This market town, once the home of the richest Cotswold wool merchants, has some incredibly beautiful thatched roofs. Both the great British historian G. M. Trevelyan and I call Chipping Campden's High Street the finest in England.

Orientation to Chipping Campden

(area code: 01386)
To get your bearings, walk the full length of High Street; its width is characteristic of market towns. Go around the block on both ends. On one end, you'll find impressively thatched homes (out Sheep Street, past the public WC, and right on Westington Street). Walking north on High Street, you'll pass the Market Hall, the wavy roof of the first great wool mansion, a fine and free memorial garden, and, finally, the town's famous 15th-century Perpendicular Gothic "wool" church. (This route is the same as my self-guided town walk.)

Tourist Information

Chipping Campden's TI is tucked away in the old police station on High Street. Get the £1 town guide, which includes a map (April-Oct daily 9:30-17:00; Nov-March Mon-Thu 9:30-13:00, Fri-Sun 9:30-16:00; tel. 01386/841-206, www.chippingcampdenonline .org).

Helpful Hints

Festivals: Chipping Campden's biggest festival is the **Cotswold Olimpicks,** a series of tongue-in-cheek countryside games (such as competitive shin-kicking) atop Dover's Hill, just above town (first Fri-Sat after Late May Bank Holiday, www .olimpickgames.co.uk). They also have an **open gardens festival** the third weekend in June and a **music festival** in mid-May.

Internet Access: Try the occasionally open **library** (closed Tue, Thu, and Sun; High Street, tel. 01386/840-692) or **Butty's at the Old Bakehouse**, a casual eatery and Internet café (£1.50/15 minutes, £2.50/30 minutes, £4/hour, free Wi-Fi, Mon-Sat 8:30-14:00, closed Sun, Lower High Street, tel. 01386/840-401).

Bike Rental: Call **Cycle Cotswolds** or **Cotswold Country Cycles** (see page 471).

Taxi: Try **Cotswold Private Hire** or **Tour the Cotswolds** (see page 475).

Parking: Find a spot anywhere along High Street and park for free with no time limit. There's also a pay-and-display lot (1.5-hour maximum) on High Street (across from TI).

Tours: The local members of the **Cotswold Voluntary Wardens** would be happy to show you around town for a small donation to their conservation society (£3/person, 1-hour walk, walks June-Sept Tue at 14:30, meet at Market Hall). Tour guide and coordinator Ann Colcomb can help arrange for a walk on other days as well (tel. 01386/832-131, www.cotswolds aonb.com).

Walks and Hikes from Chipping Campden: Since this is a particularly hilly area, long-distance hikes are challenging. The easiest and most rewarding stroll is to the thatch-happy Hobbit village of **Broad Campden** (about a mile, mostly level). From there, you can walk or take the bus (#22) back to Chipping Campden.

Or, if you have more energy, continue from Broad Campden up over the ridge and into picturesque **Blockley**—and, if your stamina holds out, all the way to **Bourton-on-the-Hill** (Blockley and Bourton-on-the-Hill are also connected by buses #21 and #22 to Chipping Campden and Moreton).

Alternatively, you can hike up to **Dover's Hill,** just north of the village. Ask locally about this easy circular one-hour walk that takes you on the first mile of the 100-mile-long Cotswold Way (which goes from here to Bath).

For more about hiking, see "Getting Around the Cotswolds—By Foot" on page 471.

Self-Guided Walk

Welcome to Chipping Campden

This stroll through "Campden" (as locals call their town) takes you from the Market Hall west to the old silk mill, and then back east the length of High Street to the church. It takes about an hour.

Market Hall: Begin at Campden's most famous monument—the Market Hall. It stands in front of the TI, marking the town

center. The Market Hall was built in 1627 by the 17th-century Lord of the Manor, Sir Baptist Hicks. (Look for the Hicks family coat of arms in the building's facade.) Back then, it was an elegant—even over-the-top—shopping hall for the townsfolk who'd come here to buy their produce. In the 1940s, it was almost sold to an American, but the townspeople heroically raised money to buy it first, then gave it to the National Trust for its preservation.

The timbers inside are true to the original. Study the classic Cotswold stone roof, still held together with wooden pegs nailed in from underneath. (Tiles were cut and sold with peg holes, and stacked like waterproof scales.) Buildings all over the region still use these stone shingles. Today, the hall, which is rarely used, stands as a testimony to the importance of trade to medieval Campden.

Adjacent to the Market Hall is the sober WWI monument—a reminder of the huge price paid by every little town. Walk around it, noticing how 1918 brought the greatest losses.

The TI is just across the street, in the old police courthouse. If it's open, you're welcome to climb the stairs and peek into the **Magistrate's Court** (free, same hours as TI, ask at TI to go up). Under the open-beamed courtroom, you'll find a humble little exhibit on the town's history.

• *Walk west a few steps, to the Red Lion Pub. Across High Street (and*

a bit to the right) from the pub, look for the house with a sundial, called...

"Green Dragons": The house's decorative black cast-iron fixtures once held hay and functioned much like salad bowls for horses. Fine-cut stones define the door, but "rubble stones" make up

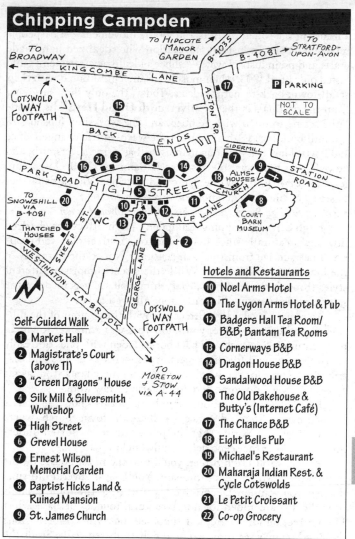

Chipping Campden

TO BROADWAY

TO HIDCOTE MANOR GARDEN

TO STRATFORD-UPON-AVON

B-4035 · B-4081

KINGCOMBE LANE

COTSWOLD WAY FOOTPATH

P PARKING

NOT TO SCALE

BACK ENDS

ASTON RD

CIDERMILL

PARK ROAD · HIGH STREET

STATION ROAD

ALMS-HOUSES

CHURCH

TO SNOWSHILL VIA B-4081

THATCHED HOUSES

SHEEP ST.

WC

CALF LANE

COURT BARN MUSEUM

WESTINGTON · CATBROOK

GEORGE LANE

COTSWOLD WAY FOOTPATH

TO MORETON & STOW VIA A-44

Self-Guided Walk
1 Market Hall
2 Magistrate's Court (above TI)
3 "Green Dragons" House
4 Silk Mill & Silversmith Workshop
5 High Street
6 Grevel House
7 Ernest Wilson Memorial Garden
8 Baptist Hicks Land & Ruined Mansion
9 St. James Church

Hotels and Restaurants
10 Noel Arms Hotel
11 The Lygon Arms Hotel & Pub
12 Badgers Hall Tea Room/ B&B; Bantam Tea Rooms
13 Cornerways B&B
14 Dragon House B&B
15 Sandalwood House B&B
16 The Old Bakehouse & Butty's (Internet Café)
17 The Chance B&B
18 Eight Bells Pub
19 Michael's Restaurant
20 Maharaja Indian Rest. & Cycle Cotswolds
21 Le Petit Croissant
22 Co-op Grocery

THE COTSWOLDS

the rest of the wall. The pink stones are the same limestone but have been heated, and likely were scavenged from a house that burned down.

• At the Red Lion Pub, leave High Street and walk a block down Sheep Street. Just past the public loo, on the right-hand side, is the old...

Silk Mill: The tiny Cam River powered a mill here since about 1790. Today it houses the handicraft workers guild and some interesting history. In 1902, Charles Robert Ashbee (1863-1942) revitalized this sleepy hamlet of 2,500 by bringing a troupe of London artisans and their families (160 people in all) to town. Ashbee was a leader in the romantic Arts and Crafts movement—craftspeople repulsed by the Industrial Revolution who idealized handmade crafts and preindustrial ways. Ashbee's idealistic craftsmen's guild lasted only until 1908, when most of his men grew bored with their small-town, back-to-nature ideals. Today, the only shop surviving from the originals is that of **silversmith David Hart.** His grandfather came to town with Ashbee, and the workshop (upstairs in the mill building) is an amazing time warp—little changed since 1902. Mr. Hart is a gracious man as well as a fine silversmith, and he welcomes browsers six days a week (Sat until 12:00, closed Sun, tel. 01386/841-100). (While you could continue 200 yards farther to see some fine thatched houses, this walk doesn't.)

• *Return to High Street, turn right, and walk through town.*

High Street: Chipping Campden's High Street has changed little architecturally since 1840. (The town's street plan and property lines survive from the 12th century.) Notice the harmony of the long rows of buildings. While the street comprises different styles through the centuries, everything you see was made of the same Cotswold stone—the only stone allowed today.

To remain level, High Street arcs with the contour of the hillside. Because it's so wide, you know this was a market town. In past centuries, livestock and packhorses laden with piles of freshly shorn fleece would fill the streets. Campden was a sales and distribution center for the wool industry, and merchants from as far away as Italy would come here for the prized raw wool.

High Street has no house numbers: Locals know the houses by their names. In the distance, you'll see the town church (where this walk ends). Notice that the power lines are buried underground, making the scene delightfully uncluttered.

As you stroll High Street, you'll find the finest houses on the uphill side—which gets more sun. You'll pass several old sundials as you wander. Decorative features (like the Ionic capitals near the TI) are added for non-structural touches of class. Most High Street buildings are half-timbered, but with cosmetic stone facades. You may see some exposed half-timbered walls. Study the crudely beautiful framing, made of hand-hewn oak (you can see the adze marks) and held together by wooden pegs.

Peeking down alleys, you'll notice how the lots are narrow but very deep. Called "burgage plots," this platting goes back to 1170. In medieval times, rooms were lined up like train cars, long and skinny: Each building had a small storefront, followed by a workshop, living quarters, staff quarters, stables, and a pea patch-type garden at the very back. Now the private alleys that still define many of these old lots lead to comfy gardens. While some of today's buildings are wider, virtually all the widths are exact multiples of that basic first unit (for example, a modern building may be three times wider than its medieval counterpart).

• *Hike up High Street toward the church, to just before the first intersection, to find the....*

Grevel House: In 1367, William Grevel built what's considered Campden's first stone house (on the left). Sheep tycoons had big homes. Imagine back then, when this fine building was surrounded by humble wattle-and-daub huts. It had newfangled chimneys, rather than a crude hole in the roof. (No more rain inside!) Originally a "hall house" with just one big, tall room, it got its upper floor in the 16th century. The finely carved central bay window is a good early example of the Perpendicular Gothic style. The gargoyles scared away bad spirits—and served as rain spouts. The boot scrapers outside each door were fixtures in that muddy age—especially in market towns, where the streets were filled with animal dung.

• *Continue up High Street for about 100 yards. Go past Church Street (which we'll walk up later). On the right, you'll find a small Gothic arch leading into a garden.*

Ernest Wilson Memorial Garden: Once the church's vegetable patch, this small and secluded garden is a botanist's delight today. It's filled with well-labeled plants that the Victorian botanist Ernest Wilson brought back to England from his extensive travels in Asia. There's a complete history of the garden on the board to the left of the entry (free, open daily until dusk).

• *Backtrack to Church Street. Turn left, walk past the recommended Eight Bells Inn, and hook left with the street. Along your right-hand side stretches...*

Baptist Hicks Land: Sprawling adjacent to the town church, the area known as Baptist Hicks Land held Hicks' huge estate

and manor house. This influential Lord of the Manor was from "a family of substance," who were merchants of silk and fine clothing as well as moneylenders. Beyond the ornate gate (which you'll see ahead, near the church), only a few outbuildings and the charred corner of his **mansion** survive. The mansion was burned by Royalists in 1645 during the Civil War—notice how Cotswold stone turns red when burned. Hicks housed the poor, making a show of his generosity, adding a long row of almshouses (with his family coat of arms) for neighbors to see as they walked to church. These almshouses (lining Church Street on the left) house pensioners today, as they have since the 17th century.

On the right, filling the old **Court Barn**, is a museum about crafts and designs from the Arts and Crafts movement, with works by Ashbee and his craftsmen (£4, Tue-Sun 10:30-17:00, closed Mon, tel. 01386/841-951, www.courtbarn.org.uk).

• *Next to the Court Barn, a scenic, tree-lined lane leads to the front door of the church. On the way, notice the 12 lime trees, one for each of the apostles, that were planted in about 1760 (sorry, no limes).*

St. James Church: One of the finest churches in the Cotswolds, St. James Church graces one of its leading towns. Both the town and the church were built by wool wealth. Go inside. The church is Perpendicular Gothic, with lots of light and strong verticality. Notice the fine vestments and altar hangings (intricate c. 1460 embroidery) behind protective blue curtains (near the back of the church). Tombstones pave the floor in the chancel (often under protective red carpeting)—memorializing great wool merchants through the ages.

At the altar is a brass relief of William Grevel, the first owner of the Grevel House (described earlier), and his wife. But it is Sir Baptist Hicks who dominates the church. His huge, canopied

tomb is the ornate final resting place for Hicks and his wife, Elizabeth. Study their faces, framed by fancy lace ruffs (trendy in the 1620s). Adjacent—as if in a closet—is a statue of their daughter, Lady Juliana, and her husband, Lutheran Yokels. Juliana commissioned the statue in 1642, when her husband died, but had it closed off until *she* died in 1680. Then, the doors were opened, revealing these two people holding hands and living happily ever after—at least in marble. The hinges were likely used only once.

As you leave the church, look immediately around the corner to the left of the door. A small tombstone reads "Thank you Lord for Simon, a dearly loved cat who greeted everyone who entered this church. RIP 1980."

Sleeping in Chipping Campden

(area code: 01386)

In Chipping Campden—as in any town in the Cotswolds—B&Bs offer a better value than hotels. Rooms are generally tight on Saturdays (when many charge a bit more and are reluctant to rent to one-nighters) and in September, which is considered a peak month. Parking is never a problem. Always ask for a discount if staying longer than one or two nights.

Sleep Code

(£1 = about $1.60, country code: 44)

S = Single, **D** = Double/Twin, **T** = Triple, **Q** = Quad, **b** = bathroom, **s** = shower only. Unless noted otherwise, you can assume credit cards are accepted and breakfast is included.

To help you sort easily through these listings, I've divided the accommodations into three categories based on the price for a standard double room with bath:

$$$ Higher Priced—Most rooms £90 or more.

$$ Moderately Priced—Most rooms between £65-90.

$ Lower Priced—Most rooms £65 or less.

Prices can change without notice; verify the hotel's current rates online or by email. For other updates, see www .ricksteves.com/update.

$$$ Noel Arms Hotel, the characteristic old hotel on the main square, has welcomed guests for 600 years. Its lobby was recently remodeled in a medieval-meets-modern style, and its 27 rooms are well-furnished with antiques (Sb-£140, standard Db-£150, bigger Db-£180, fancier four-poster Db-£200, midweek deals, some ground-floor doubles, free Wi-Fi in lobby, attached restaurant/bar and café, free parking, High Street, tel. 01386/840-317, fax 01386/841-136, www.noelarmshotel.com, reception@noel armshotel.com).

$$$ The Lygon Arms Hotel (pronounced "lig-un"), attached to the popular pub of the same name, has small public areas and 10 cheery, open-beamed rooms (one small older Db-£80-85, huge "superior" Db-£115-120, lovely courtyard Db-£145-165, lower prices are for midweek or multi-night stays, family deals, free Wi-Fi, free parking, High Street, go through archway and look for hotel reception on the left, tel. 01386/840-318, www.lygonarms .co.uk, sandra@lygonarms.co.uk, Sandra Davenport).

$$$ Badgers Hall Tea Room, also listed later under "Eating in Chipping Campden," rents three pricey rooms (Db-£98, or £110 on weekends, 2-night minimum, includes breakfast and tea, no kids under age 10, free Wi-Fi, High Street, tel. 01386/840-839, www.badgershall.com, Karen).

$$ Cornerways B&B is a fresh, bright, and comfy modern home (not "oldie worldie") a block off High Street. It's run by the delightful Carole Proctor, who can "look out the window and see the church where we were married." The two huge, light, airy loft rooms are great for families (Db-£70, Tb-£90, Qb-£110, 2-night minimum, £5 off for 3 or more nights, children's discount, cash only, free Wi-Fi, off-street parking, George Lane, just walk through the arch beside Noel Arms Hotel, tel. 01386/841-307, www.cornerways.info, carole@cornerways.info).

$$ Dragon House B&B rents two tidy rooms—with medieval beams and a shared lounge—right on the center of High Street. They have laundry machines and a sumptuous, stay-awhile garden (Db-£68, £5 off for 3 or more nights, cash only, free Wi-Fi, free off-street parking available, near Market Hall, tel. & fax 01386/840-734, www.dragonhouse-chipping-campden.com, info@dragonhouse-chipping-campden.co.uk, Valerie and Graeme the retired potter). They also have a cottage that sleeps up to six (Sat-Sat only, £250-750/week depending on month).

$$ Sandalwood House B&B is a big, comfy, heavily potpourri-scented home with a pink flowery lounge and a sprawling back garden. Just a five-minute walk from the center of town, it's in a quiet, woodsy setting. Its two cheery, pastel rooms are bright and spacious (D/Db-£74, T-£91, 2-night minimum, cheaper if you order a light breakfast instead of full, self-catering apartment sleeps four-£450/week, cash only, no kids under age 10, free Wi-Fi, free off-street parking, tel. & fax 01386/840-091, sandalwoodhouse @hotmail.com, Diana Bendall). To get to Sandalwood House, go west on High Street, and at the church and the Volunteer Inn, turn right and then right again; look for a sign in the hedge on the left, and head up the long driveway.

$$ The Old Bakehouse, run by energetic young mom Zoe, rents two small but pleasant twin-bedded rooms in a 600-year-old home with a plush fireplace lounge (Sb-£55, Db-£70, cash only, free Wi-Fi, Lower High Street, tel. & fax 01386/840-979, www .theoldbakehouse.org.uk, zoegabb@yahoo.co.uk).

$$ The Chance B&B rents three tastefully decorated rooms in a modern home with Cotswolds charm about a 10-minute walk from the town center (Sb-£65, Db-£70, discounts for long stays, cash only, free Wi-Fi, free parking, 1 Aston Road, tel. 01386/849-079, www.the-chance.co.uk, enquiries@the-chance.co.uk, Sally and Paul).

Eating in Chipping Campden

This town—so filled with wealthy residents and tourists—comes with many choices. I've listed some local favorites below. If you have a car, consider driving to one of the excellent countryside pubs mentioned in the sidebar on page 502.

Eight Bells Pub is a charming 14th-century inn on Leysbourne with a classy and woody restaurant and a more colorful pub. For over a decade now, Neil and Julie have enjoyed keeping their seasonal menu as locally sourced as possible. They serve a daily special, are proud of their fish dishes, and always have a good vegetarian dish. As this is rightly considered the best deal going in town for top-end pub dining, reservations are smart (£13-16 dinners, £13 two-course fixed-price meal weekdays, daily 12:00-14:00 & 18:30-21:00, later Fri-Sat, tel. 01386/840-371).

The Lygon Arms Pub is cozy and inviting, with a good, basic bar menu. You can order from the same menu in the colorful pub or the more elegant dining room across the passage (£7 sandwiches, £8-15 meals, daily 11:30-14:30 & 18:00-22:00).

Michael's, a fun Mediterranean restaurant on High Street, serves hearty portions and breaks plates at closing every Saturday night. Michael, who runs his place with a contagious passion and love of life, is from Cyprus: The forte here is Greek, with plenty of *mezes*—small dishes for £5-10 (also £14-17 larger dishes, £7 *meze* lunch platter, Tue-Sun 11:00-14:30 & 19:00-22:00, closed Sun nights and Mon, tel. 01386/840-826).

Maharaja Indian Restaurant in the Volunteer Inn, while forgettable, is the only Indian place in town (£8-12 meals, daily 17:30-22:30, grassy courtyard out back, Lower High Street, tel. 01386/849-281).

Light Meals

If you want a quick, take-away sandwich, consider these options. Munch your lunch on the benches on the little green near the Market Hall.

Le Petit Croissant, a cheery little French deli with a tearoom in the back, serves pastries, quiche, cheese, and wine (£4 sandwiches, more to eat in, Mon-Fri 9:00-17:00, Sat 8:30-17:00, Sun 10:00-16:00, Lower High Street, tel. 01386/841-861).

Butty's at the Old Bakehouse offers tasty £2-4 sandwiches and wraps made to order (Mon-Sat 8:30-14:00, closed Sun, Lower High Street, tel. 01386/840-401). They also have Internet access (see "Helpful Hints," earlier).

Picnic: The **Co-op** grocery store is the town's small "supermarket" (Mon-Sat 7:00-22:00, Sun 8:00-22:00, next to TI on High Street).

Tearooms

To visit a cute tearoom, try one of these places, located in the town center.

Badgers Hall Tea Room is great for a wide selection of savory dishes and desserts. A tempting table of homemade cakes, crumbles, and scones just inside the door lures passersby into its delightful half-timbered dining room. Along with light lunches, they serve a generous afternoon tea—a tall and ritualistic tray of dainty sandwiches, pastries, and scones with tea—for half the London price (£25 for 2 people, daily 10:00-17:00, High Street).

Bantam Tea Rooms, near the Market Hall, is also a good value (£7 teas, £6 sandwiches, Mon-Sat 10:00-17:00, Sun 10:30-17:00, High Street, tel. 01386/840-386).

Near Chipping Campden

Because the countryside around Chipping Campden is particularly hilly, it's also especially scenic. This is a very rewarding area to poke around in and discover little thatched villages.

West of Chipping Campden

Due west of Chipping Campden lies the famous and touristy town of Broadway. Just south of that, you'll find my nominations for the cutest Cotswold villages. Like marshmallows in hot chocolate, Stanway, Stanton, and Snowshill nestle side by side, awaiting your arrival. (Note the Stanway House's limited hours when planning your visit.)

Broadway

This postcard-pretty town, a couple of miles west of Chipping Campden, is filled with inviting shops and fancy teahouses. With a "broad way" indeed running through its middle, it's one of the bigger towns in the area. This means you'll likely pass through at some point if you're driving—but, since all the big bus tours seem to stop here, I usually give Broadway a miss. However, with a new road that allows traffic to skirt the town, Broadway has gotten cuter than ever. Broadway has good bus connections with Chipping Campden (on bus #21).

Just outside Broadway, on the road to Chipping Campden, you might spot signs for the **Broadway Tower,** which looks like a turreted castle fortification stranded in the countryside without a castle in sight. This 55-foot-tall observation tower is a "folly"—a uniquely English term for a quirky, outlandish novelty erected as a giant lawn ornament by some aristocrat with more money than taste. If you're also weighted down with too many pounds, you can relieve yourself of £4.50 to climb to its top for a view over the pastures (daily 10:30-17:00).

Stanway

More of a humble crossroads community than a true village, sleepy Stanway is worth a visit mostly for its manor house, which offers an intriguing insight into the English aristocracy today. If you're in the area when it's open, it's well worth visiting.

▲▲**Stanway House**—The Earl of Wemyss (pronounced "Weemz"), whose family tree charts relatives back to 1202, opens his melan-

choly home and grounds to visitors just two days a week in the summer. Walking through his house offers a unique glimpse into the lifestyles of England's eccentric and fading nobility.

Cost and Hours: £7, June-Aug Tue and Thu only 14:00-17:00, closed Sept-May, tel. 01386/584-469, www.stanwayfountain.co.uk. His lordship himself narrated the audioguide to his home (£2).

Getting There: By car, leave B4077 at a statue of (the Christian) George slaying the dragon (of pagan superstition); you'll round the corner and see the manor's fine 17th-century Jacobean gatehouse. There's no public transportation to Stanway.

Touring the Manor: Start with the grounds, then head into the house itself.

The Earl recently restored "the tallest **fountain** in Britain" on the grounds—300 feet tall, gravity-powered, and quite impressive (fountain spurts for 30 minutes at 14:45 and 16:00 on open days).

The bitchin' **Tithe Barn** (near where you enter the grounds) dates to the 14th century, and predates the manor. It was originally where monks—in the days before money—would accept one-tenth of whatever the peasants produced. Peek inside: This is a great hall for village hoedowns. While the Tithe Barn is no longer used to greet motley peasants and collect their feudal "rents," the lord still gets rent from his vast landholdings, and hosts community fêtes in his barn.

Stepping into the obviously very lived-in **manor,** you're free to wander around pretty much as you like, but keep in mind that a family does live here. His lordship is often roaming about as well. The place feels like a time warp. Ask a staff member to demonstrate the spinning rent-collection table. In the great hall, marvel at the one-piece oak shuffleboard table and the 1780 Chippendale exercise chair (half an hour of bouncing on this was considered good for the liver).

The manor dogs have their own cutely painted "family tree," but the Earl admits that his last dog, C. J., was "all character and no breeding." Poke into the office. You can psychoanalyze the lord by the books that fill his library, the DVDs stacked in front of his bed (with the mink bedspread), and whatever's next to his toilet.

The place has a story to tell. And so do the docents stationed in each room—modern-day peasants who, even without family trees, probably have relatives going back just as far in this village. Really. Talk to these people. Probe. Learn what you can about this side of England.

From Stanway to Stanton: These towns are separated by a row of oak trees and grazing land, with parallel waves echoing the furrows plowed by medieval farm-

ers. Centuries ago, farmers were allotted long strips of land called "furlongs." The idea was to dole out good and bad land equitably. (One square furlong equals an acre.) Over centuries of plowing these, furrows were formed. Let some-one else drive, so you can hang out the window under a canopy of oaks, passing stone walls and sheep. Leaving Stanway on the road to Stanton, the first building you'll see (on the left, just outside Stanway) is a thatched cricket pavilion overlooking the village cricket green. Dating only from 1930, it's raised up (as medieval buildings were) on rodent-resistant staddle stones. Stanton is just ahead; follow the signs.

▲Stanton

Pristine Cotswold charm cheers you as you head up the main street

of the village of Stanton. Go on a photo safari for flower-bedecked doorways and windows. (A scant few buses serve Stanton, but they're unpredictable—inquire locally.)

Stanton's **Church of St. Michael** (with the pointy spire) betrays a pagan past. It's safe to assume any church dedicated to St. Michael (the archangel who fought the devil) sits upon a sacred pagan site. Stanton is actu-ally at the intersection of two ley lines (geographic lines along which many prehistoric sights are found). You'll see St. Michael's well-worn figure (and, above that, a sundial) over the door as you enter. Inside, above the capitals in the nave, find the pagan symbols for the sun and the moon. While the church probably dates back to the ninth cen-tury, today's building is mostly from the

15th century, with 13th-century transepts. On the north transept (far side from entry), medieval frescoes show faintly through the 17th-century whitewash. (Once upon a time, these frescoes were considered too "papist.") Imagine the church interior colorfully decorated throughout. Original medieval glass is behind the altar. The list of rectors (at the very back of the church, under the organ loft) goes back to 1269. Finger the grooves in the back pews, worn away by sheepdog leashes. (A man's sheepdog accompanied him everywhere.)

Horse Riding: Anyone can enjoy the Cotswolds from the saddle. Jill Carenza's **Cotswolds Riding Centre,** set just outside

Stanton village, is in the most scenic corner of the region. The facility has 50 horses, and takes rank beginners on a scenic "hack" through the village and into the high country (per-hour prices: £29/person for a group hack, £39/person for a semi-private hack, £49 for a private one-person hack; lessons, longer rides, rides for experts, and pub tours available; tel. 01386/584-250, www .cotswoldsriding.co.uk). From Stanton, head toward Broadway and watch for the riding center on your right after about a third of a mile.

Sleeping in Stanton: **$$$ The Vine B&B** has five rooms in a characteristic old Cotswolds house near the center of town. Owned by Jill from the riding center (described earlier), it takes a backseat to the horses: It's basically self-service, so there's no greeting or check-in, and guests wander around wondering which room is theirs. Still, it's the best option in Stanton, and convenient if you want to ride all day (Ss-£55-75, Ds-£75, Db-£95, cottage with kitchen and 2 bedrooms-£150, most rooms with 4-poster beds, some stairs, tel. 01386/584-250, info@cotswoldsriding.co.uk).

Snowshill

Another nearly edible little bundle of cuteness, the village of Snowshill (SNOWS-hill) has a photogenic triangular square with a characteristic pub at its base.

▲**Snowshill Manor**—Dark and mysterious, this old palace is filled with the lifetime collection of Charles Paget Wade. It's one big, musty celebration of craftsmanship, from finely carved spinning wheels to frightening samurai armor to tiny elaborate figurines carved by prisoners from the bones of meat served at dinner. Taking seriously his family motto, "Let Nothing Perish," Wade dedicated his life and fortune to preserving things finely crafted. The house (whose management made me promise not to promote

it as an eccentric collector's pile of curiosities) really shows off Mr. Wade's ability to recognize and acquire fine examples of craftsmanship. It's all very...mmm...yaaa.

Cost and Hours: £9.50; manor house open July-Aug Wed-Mon 11:30-16:30, closed Tue; April-June and Sept-Oct Wed-Sun 12:00-17:00, closed Mon-Tue; closed Nov-March; gardens and ticket window open at 11:00, last entry 50 minutes before closing, restaurant, tel. 01386/852-410, www.nationaltrust.org.uk/snowshillmanor.

Getting There: The manor overlooks the town square, but there's no direct access from the square; instead, the entrance and parking lot are about a half-mile up the road toward Broadway. Park there and follow the long walkway through the garden to get to the house. A golf-cart-type shuttle to the house is available for those who need assistance.

Getting In: This popular sight strictly limits the number of entering visitors by doling out entry times. No reservations are possible; to get a slot, you must report to the ticket desk. It can be up to an hour's wait—even more on busy days, especially weekends (when they can sell out for the day as early as 14:00). Tickets go on sale and the gardens open at 11:00. Therefore, a good strategy is to arrive close to the opening time, and if there's a wait, enjoy the gardens (it's a 10-minute walk to the manor). If you have more time to kill, head into the village of Snowshill itself (a half-mile away) to wander and explore—or get a time slot for later in the day, and return in the afternoon.

Snowshill Lavender—In 2000, farmer Charlie Byrd realized that tourists love lavender. He planted his farm with 250,000

plants, and now visitors come to wander among his 53 acres, which burst with gorgeous lavender blossoms from mid-June through late August. His fragrant fantasy peaks late each July. Lavender—so famous in France's Provence—is not indigenous to this region, but it fits the climate and soil just fine. A free flier in the shop explains the variations of flowers blooming. Farmer Byrd produces lavender oil (an herbal product valued since ancient times for its healing, calming, and fragrant qualities) and sells it in a delightful shop,

THE COTSWOLDS

along with many other lavender-themed items. In the café, enjoy a pot of lavender-flavored tea with a lavender scone.

Cost and Hours: £2.50 to walk through the fields and the distillery, free to enter shop and café; June-Aug daily 10:00-17:00; April-May and Sept-Oct Wed-Sun 10:00-17:00, closed Mon-Tue; closed Nov-March; tel. 01386/854-821, www.snowshill-lavender .co.uk, info@snowshill-lavender.co.uk.

Getting There: It's a half-mile out of Snowshill on the road toward Chipping Campden (easy parking). Entering Snowshill from the road to the manor (described above), take the left fork, then turn left again at the end of the village.

Sleeping near Snowshill: The pretty, one-pub village of Snowshill holds a gem of a B&B. **$$$ Sheepscombe House B&B** is a clean and pristine home on a working sheep farm. It's immersed in the best of Cotswold scenery, with plenty of sheep in the nearby fields. Jacki and Tim Harrison rent three modern, spacious, and thoughtfully appointed rooms (Db-£90-100, Tb-£130-150, folding cots available, free Wi-Fi, just a third of a mile south of Snowshill—look for signs, tel. 01386/853-769, www.broadway -cotswolds.co.uk/sheepscombe.html, reservations@snowshill -broadway.co.uk). Tim, who's happy to give you a local's perspective on this area, also runs the Tour the Cotswolds car service (see page 475).

East of Chipping Campden

These lie roughly between Chipping Campden and Stow (or Moreton)—handy if you're connecting those towns.

▲Hidcote Manor Garden

Located northeast of Chipping Campden, this is less "on the way" between towns than the other sights in this section—but the grounds around this manor house are well worth a detour if you like gardens. Hidcote is where garden designers pioneered the notion of creating a series of outdoor "rooms," each with a unique theme (e.g., maple room, red room, and so on) and separated by a yew-tree hedge. The garden's design, inspired by the Arts and Crafts movement, is most formal near to the house and becomes more pastoral as it approaches the countryside. Follow your nose through a clever series of small gardens that lead delightfully from one to the next. Among the best in England, Hidcote Gardens are at their fragrant peak from May through August. But don't expect much indoors—the manor

THE COTSWOLDS

house has only a few rooms open to the public.

Cost and Hours: £10.50; July-Aug daily 10:00-18:00; mid-March-June and Sept Sat-Wed 10:00-18:00, closed Thu-Fri; Oct Sat-Wed 10:00-17:00, closed Thu-Fri; last entry one hour before closing; closed Nov-mid-March except Nov-Christmas Sat-Sun 12:00-15:00; tearoom, restaurant, tel. 01386/438-333, www.nationaltrust.org.uk/hidcote.

Getting There: If you're driving, it's four miles northeast of Chipping Campden—roughly toward Ilmington. Both gardens are accessible by bus and a 45-minute country walk. Buses #21 and #22 take you to Mickleton (one stop past Chipping Campden), where a footpath begins next to the churchyard. Continuing more or less straight, the path leads uphill through sheep pastures and ends at Hidcote's driveway.

Nearby: Gardening enthusiasts will want to also stop at **Kiftsgate Court Garden,** just across the road from Hidcote. While not as impressive, these private gardens are a fun contrast since they were designed at the same time and influenced by Hidcote (£7; May-Aug Sat-Wed 12:00-18:00, except Aug opens at 14:00, closed Thu-Fri; April and Sept Sun-Mon and Wed only 14:00-18:00; closed Oct-March; tel. 01386/438-777, www.kiftsgate.co.uk).

▲Broad Campden, Blockley, and Bourton-on-the-Hill

This trio of pleasant villages lines up along an off-the-beaten-path road between Chipping Campden and Moreton or Stow. **Broad Campden,** just on the outskirts of Chipping Campden, has some of the cutest thatched-roof houses I've seen. **Blockley,** nestled higher in the picturesque hills, is a popular setting for films. The same road continues on to **Bourton-on-the-Hill** (pictured), with fine views looking down into a valley and an excellent gastropub (Horse and Groom, described on page 502). All three of these towns are connected to Chipping Campden by bus #22 (#21 goes only to Bourton and Blockley), or you can walk (easy to Broad Campden, more challenging to the other two—see page 472).

Stow-on-the-Wold

Located 10 miles south of Chipping Campden, Stow-on-the-Wold—with a name that means "meeting place on the uplands"—is

the highest point of the Cotswolds. Despite its crowds, it retains its charm, and it merits ▲▲. Most of the tourists are day-trippers, so nights—even in the peak of summer—are peaceful. Stow has no real sights other than the town itself, some good pubs, antiques stores, and cute shops draped seductively around a big town square. Visit the church, with its evocative old door guarded by ancient yew trees and the tombs of wool tycoons. A visit to Stow is not complete until you've locked your partner in the stocks on the village green.

Orientation to Stow-on-the-Wold

(area code: 01451)

Tourist Information

Stow's TI, an independent business called Go Stow, is on a little alley right between the main street and Market Square. Get the handy little £0.50 walking-tour brochure called *Town Trail* and the free monthly *Cotswold Events* guide (Mon-Sat 10:00-17:00, Sun 11:00-16:00—except Oct-April until 16:30, 12 Talbot Court, tel. 01451/870-150, www.go-stow.co.uk).

At the TI, you can rent an **audioguide** town tour (£8, £12/2 people). You'll borrow an iPod Shuffle with the tour, and follow it to a dozen or so points around town for 80 minutes. While well-produced and easy to follow, there's not a lot of substance beyond my self-guided walk.

Helpful Hints

Internet Access: Try the erratically open **library** in St. Edwards Hall on the main square (closed Sun-Mon and Thu, tel. 01451/830-352), or the **youth hostel** (open long hours daily).

Taxi: See "Getting Around the Cotswolds—By Taxi" (page 473).

Parking: Park anywhere on Market Square free for two hours, or overnight between 16:00 and 11:00 (free 18:00-9:00 plus any 2 hours—they note your license, so you can't just move to another spot; £50 tickets for offenders). There's a pay-and-display lot for longer stays at the bottom of town (toward the

THE COTSWOLDS

Oddingtons), and a free long-stay lot 400 yards north of the town square at the Tesco supermarket (follow the signs).

Self-Guided Walk

Welcome to Stow-on-the-Wold

This little four-stop walk covers about 500 yards and takes about 45 minutes.

Start at the **Stocks on the Market Square.** Imagine this village during the time when people were publicly ridiculed here as a punishment. Stow was born in pre-Roman times; it's where

three trade routes crossed at a high point in the region (altitude: 800 feet). This square was the site of an Iron Age fort, and then a Roman garrison town. It hosted an international fair starting in 1107, and people came from as far away as Italy for the wool fleeces. This grand square was a vast, grassy expanse. Picture it in the Middle Ages (before the buildings in the center were added): a public commons and grazing ground, paths worn through the grass, and no well. Until the late 1800s, Stow had no running water; women fetched water from the "Roman Well" a quarter-mile away.

With as many as 20,000 sheep sold in a single day, this square was a thriving scene. And Stow was filled with inns and pubs to keep everyone housed, fed, and watered. A thin skin of topsoil covers the Cotswold limestone, from which these buildings were made. The **Stow Lodge** (next to the church) lies a little lower than the church; the lodge sits on the spot where locals quarried stones for the church. That building, originally the rectory, is now a hotel.

The church (where we'll end this little walk) is made of Cotswold stone, and marks the summit of the hill upon which the town was built. The stocks are a great photo op (lock dad up for a great family Christmas card).

• *Walk past the youth hostel and The White Hart inn to the market, and cross to the other part of the square. Notice how locals seem to be a part of a tight-knit little community.*

For 500 years, the **Market Cross** stood in the market reminding all Christian merchants to "trade fairly under the sight of God." Notice the stubs of the iron fence in the concrete base—

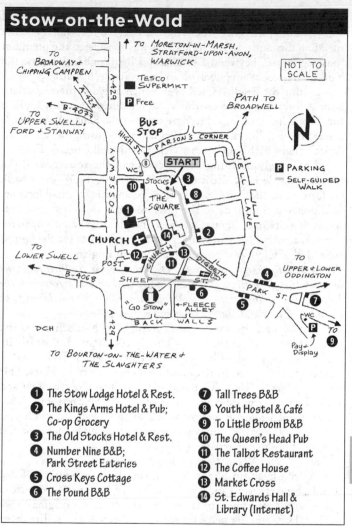

Stow-on-the-Wold

1 The Stow Lodge Hotel & Rest.
2 The Kings Arms Hotel & Pub; Co-op Grocery
3 The Old Stocks Hotel & Rest.
4 Number Nine B&B; Park Street Eateries
5 Cross Keys Cottage
6 The Pound B&B

7 Tall Trees B&B
8 Youth Hostel & Café
9 To Little Broom B&B
10 The Queen's Head Pub
11 The Talbot Restaurant
12 The Coffee House
13 Market Cross
14 St. Edwards Hall & Library (Internet)

a reminder of how countless wrought-iron fences were cut down and given to the government to be melted down during World War II. (Recently, it's been disclosed that all that iron ended up in junk heaps—frantic patriotism just wasted.) The plaque on the cross honors the Lord of the Manor, who donated money back to his tenants, allowing the town to finally finance running water in 1878.

Scan the square for a tipsy shop that locals call the "wonky house" (next to The Kings Arms). Because it lists (tilts) so severely, it's a listed building—the facade is protected (but the interior is modern and level). The Kings Arms, with its great gables and scary chimney, was once where travelers parked their horses before spending the night. In the 1600s, this was considered the premium "posting house" between London and Birmingham. Today, the Kings Arms cooks up pub grub and rents rooms upstairs.

During the English Civil War, which pitted Parliamentarians against Royalists, Stow-on-the-Wold remained staunchly loyal to the king. (Charles I is said to have eaten at the Kings Arms before a great battle.) Because of its allegiance, the town has an abundance of pubs with royal names (King's This and Queen's That).

The stately building in the center of the square with the wooden steeple is **St. Edwards Hall.** Back in the 1870s, a bank couldn't locate the owner of an account containing a small fortune, so it donated the funds to the town to build this civic center. It serves as a city hall, library, and meeting place. When it's open for some local event, you can wander around upstairs to see the largest collection of Civil War portrait paintings in England.

• *Walk past The Kings Arms down Digbeth Street to the little triangular park located in front of the Methodist Church and across from the Royalist Hotel. This hotel—along with about 20 others—claims to be the oldest in England, dating from 947.*

Just beyond the small grassy triangle with benches was the place where locals gathered for bloody cockfights and bearbaiting (watching packs of hungry dogs tear at bears). Today this is where—twice a year, in May and October—the Stow Horse Fair attracts nomadic Roma (Gypsies) and Irish Travellers from far and wide. They congregate down the street on the Maugersbury Road. Locals paint a colorful picture of the Roma, Travellers, and horses inundating the town. The young women dress up because the fair also functions as a marriage market.

• *Hook right and hike up the wide street.*

As you head up **Sheep Street,** you'll pass a boutique-filled former brewery yard (on the left). Notice its fancy street-front office, with a striking flint facade. Sheep Street was originally not a street, but a staging place for medieval sheep markets. The sheep would be gathered here, then paraded into the Market Square down narrow alleys—just wide enough for a single file of sheep to walk down, making it easier to count them. You'll see several of these so-called "fleece alleys" as you walk up the street.

• *Just past a fine antique bookstore (Wychwood Books), turn right onto Church Street, which leads past the best coffee shop in town (The Coffee House), and find the church.*

Before entering the **church,** circle it. On the back side, a door is flanked by two ancient yew trees. While many view it as the Christian "Behold, I stand at the door and knock" door, J. R. R. Tolkien fans see something quite different. Tolkien hiked the Cotswolds, and had a passion for sketching evocative trees such as this. *Lord of the Rings* enthusiasts are convinced this must be the inspiration for the door into Moria.

While the church (open daily—apart from services—9:00-18:00) dates from Saxon times, today's structure is from the 15th century. Its history is played up in leaflets and plaques just inside the door. The floor is paved with the tombs of big shots who made their money from wool and are still boastful in death. (Find the tombs crowned with the bales of wool.) Most of the windows are traditional Victorian designs (19th-century), but the two sets high up in the clerestory are from the dreamier Pre-Raphaelite school.

On the right wall as you approach the altar, a monument remembers the many boys from this small town who were lost in World War I (50 out of a population of 2,000). There were far fewer in World War II. The biscuit-shaped plaque (to the left) remembers an admiral from Stow who lost four sons defending the realm. It's sliced from an ancient fluted column (which locals believe is from Ephesus, Turkey).

During the English Civil War (1615), the church was ransacked, and more than 1,000 soldiers were imprisoned here. The tombstone in front of the altar remembers the Royalist Captain Keyt. His long hair, lace, and sash indicate he was a "cavalier," and true-blue to the king (Cromwellians were called "round heads"—named for their short hair). Study the crude provincial art—childlike skulls and (in the upper corners) symbols of his service to the king (armor, weapons).

Finally, don't miss the kneelers tucked in the pews. These are made by a committed band of women known as "the Kneeler Group." They meet most Tuesday mornings (except sometimes in summer) at 10:30 in the Church Room to needlepoint, sip coffee, and enjoy a good chat. (The vicar assured me that any tourist wanting to join them would be more than welcome. The help would be appreciated and the company would be excellent.)

Hiking from Stow

Stow/Lower Slaughter/Bourton Day Hike

Stow is made-to-order for day hikes. The most popular is the downhill, four-mile stroll to Lower Slaughter, then on to Bourton-on-the-Water. It's a two-hour walk if you don't stop. Allow about

three hours if you dawdle. From
Bourton-on-the-Water, a bus can
bring you back to Stow. Any B&B
or hotel can loan you a map for this
hike. Note that these three towns
are described in more detail starting on page 504.

Leaving Stow, walk through
the cemetery and down the big
A429 road for about 200 yards, then cross the road and catch the
well-marked trail. Follow it for a delightful hour across farms, over
romantic gates, and past Gainsborough-painting vistas. You'll
enjoy an intimate backyard look at local farm life. Although it
seems like you might lose the trail, tiny signs keep you on target.
Finally, passing a cricket pitch, you reach **Lower Slaughter,** with
its fine church and a mill creek leading up to its mill.

Hiking from Lower Slaughter up to **Upper Slaughter** is a
worthwhile one-mile, 15-minute detour each way, if you have the
time and energy.

From Lower Slaughter, it's a less-scenic 15-minute walk to the
bigger town of **Bourton-on-the Water.** Leave Lower Slaughter
along its mill creek, then follow a bridle path back to A429 and
into Bourton. Walking into Bourton, you'll pass the bus stop for
the ride back to Stow (buses #801 or #855 depart roughly hourly
Mon-Sat, none on Sun except May-Aug 2/day for #801 only,
10-minute ride, £1.30).

Sleeping in Stow

(£1 = about $1.60, country code: 44, area code: 01451)

$$$ The Stow Lodge Hotel fills the historic church rectory with
lots of old English charm. Facing the town square, with its own
sprawling and peaceful garden, this lavish old place offers 21 large,
thoughtfully appointed rooms with soft beds, stately public spaces,
and a cushy-chair lounge (slippery rates but generally Db-£120,
£10 extra on Sat, cheaper Oct-April, closed Jan, pay Internet access
and free Wi-Fi, free off-street parking, The Square, tel. 01451/830-
485, fax 01451/831-671, www.stowlodge.co.uk, enquiries@stow
lodge.com, helpful Hartley family).

$$$ The Kings Arms, with 10 rooms above a pub, manages to
keep its historic Cotswolds character while still feeling fresh and
modern in all the right ways (Sb-£60, Db-£100, steep stairs, three
"cottages" out back, free Wi-Fi, free off-street parking, Market
Square, tel. 01451/830-364, www.kingsarmsstow.co.uk, info@kings
armsstow.co.uk, Lucinda and Richard).

$$$ The Old Stocks Hotel, facing the town square, is a good value, even though the building itself is classier than its 18 big, simply furnished rooms. It's friendly and family-run, yet professional as can be. With man-killer beams and all beds equipped with footboards, it's a challenge for anyone over six feet tall (Sb-£48, standard Db-£95, refurbished "superior" Db-£115, Tb-£125, each room £10 extra on Sat, family deals, ground-floor room, free Wi-Fi in some rooms, attached bar and restaurant, garden patio, free off-street parking, The Square, tel. 01451/830-666, fax 01451/870-014, www.oldstockshotel.co.uk, info@oldstockshotel .co.uk, Allen family).

$$ Number Nine has three large, bright, recently refurbished, and tastefully decorated rooms. This 200-year-old home comes with watch-your-head beamed ceilings and old wooden doors (Sb-£45-55, Db-£60-75, free Internet access and Wi-Fi, 9 Park Street, tel. 01451/870-333, mobile 07779-006-539, www.number-nine .info, enquiries@number-nine.info, James and Carol Brown).

$$ Cross Keys Cottage offers four smallish but smartly updated rooms with bright floral decor and modern bathrooms. Kindly Margaret and Roger Welton take care of their guests in this 350-year-old beamed cottage (Sb-£55-65, Db-£70-75, free Wi-Fi, Park Street, tel. & fax 01451/831-128, rogxmag@hotmail .com).

$ The Pound is the quaint, 500-year-old, slanty, cozy, and low-beamed home of Patricia Whitehead. She offers two bright, inviting, twin-bedded rooms and a classic old fireplace lounge (D £50-60, T-£85, cash only, downtown on Sheep Street,  tel. & fax 01451/830-229, patwhitehead1@live.co.uk).

$ Tall Trees B&B, on Oddington Road at the bottom end of Stow, comes with horses and chickens on four acres of land. Run by no-nonsense Jennifer, the four contemporary rooms are in an old-style building (Sb-£40-50, Db-£60-70, price depends on size, family room-£100; she also rents out the whole place for up to 8 people—£450/3 days, £800/week; cash only, two ground-floor rooms, free Wi-Fi, free off-street parking, tel. 01451/831-296, fax 01451/870-049, talltreestow@aol.com).

$ Hostel: The **Stow-on-the-Wold Youth Hostel,** on Stow's main square, is the only hostel in the Cotswolds, with 48 beds in nine rooms. It has a friendly atmosphere and a members' kitchen (dorm bed-£18, non-members-£3 extra, includes sheets, some family rooms with private bathrooms, evening meals, pay Internet access and Wi-Fi, lockers, reserve long in advance, tel. 01451/830-497, fax 01451/870-102, www.yha.org.uk, stow@yha.org.uk, manager Don).

Near Stow
$$ Little Broom B&B hides out in the neighboring hamlet of Maugersbury, which enjoys the peace Stow once had. It rents three cozy rooms that share a fine garden and a pool (S-£30, Sb-£45–65, D-£55, Db-£60–75, apartment Db-£75 for two people plus £15 for each extra person, cash only, pay Wi-Fi, tel. & fax 01451/830-510, www.cotswolds.info/webpage/little-broom.htm, brendarussell @hotmail.co.uk). Brenda has racehorses, and her greenhouse keeps the pool warm throughout the summer (guests welcome). It's an easy eight-minute walk from Stow: Head east on Park Street and stay right toward Maugersbury. Turn right into Chapel Street and take the first right uphill to the B&B.

Eating in and near Stow

While Stow has several good dining options, consider venturing out of town for a meal. You can walk to the pub in nearby Broadwell, or—better yet—drive to one of the many enticing gastropubs in the surrounding villages (see sidebar on page 502).

In Stow
These places are all within a five-minute walk of each other, either on the main square or downhill on Queen and Park streets. For dessert, consider munching a treat or fruit (there's plenty for sale at the late-hours grocery on the square) under the trees on the square's benches and watching the sky darken, the lamps come on, and visitors having their photo fun in the stocks.

Restaurants and Pubs
The Stow Lodge is the choice of the town's proper ladies. There are two parts: The formal but friendly bar serves fine pub grub (hearty £8-11 lunches and dinners, daily 12:00-14:00 & 19:00-20:30). The restaurant serves a popular £25 three-course dinner (nightly, veggie options, good wines, just off main square, tel. 01451/830-485, Val). On a sunny day, the pub serves lunch in the well-manicured garden, where you'll feel quite aristocratic.

The Old Stocks Hotel Restaurant, which might at first glance seem like a tired and big hotel dining room, is actually a classy place to dine. With attentive service and an interesting menu, they provide tasty and well-presented food. It's good, basic pub grub at pub prices served in a fancy dining room with views of the square. In good weather, the garden out back is a hit (£8-9 lunches, £10-13 dinners, cheaper "snack" menu before 17:00, dinner served nightly 18:30-20:30, reservations recommended on weekends, tel. 01451/830-666).

The Queen's Head faces the Market Square, next to the Stow Lodge. With a classic pub vibe, it's a great place to bring your dog and watch the eccentrics while you eat pub grub and drink the local Cotswold brew, Donnington Ale (£6-7 sandwiches, £8-10 lunches, £9-13 dinners, beer garden out back, daily 12:00-14:30 & 18:30-21:00, tel. 01451/830-563, John).

The Talbot has a more stylish and contemporary feel, with creative, modern dishes (£6-8 lunches, £10-12 dinners). They serve drinks until midnight or later (meals served 12:00-14:30 & 18:30-21:00). With couches to cuddle up on and free Wi-Fi, it works hard to be a popular hangout. On Friday and Saturday evenings after 22:00, they crank up the music, making it the liveliest place in town (The Square, tel. 01451/870-934).

The Old Butchers feels like a breath of fresh air in staid old Stow. Trendy, with good food and slow, snooty service, it dishes up classic English cuisine with a French foodie flair and a passion for meat (£14-18 main dishes, daily 11:00-15:30 & 18:00-21:30, open all day long Sat-Sun, 7 Park Street, reservations likely necessary, tel. 01451/831-700).

Cheaper Options and Ethnic Food

Head to the grassy triangle where Digbeth hits Sheep Street; there you'll find take-out fish-and-chips, Chinese, and Indian food. You can picnic at the triangle, or on the benches by the stocks on Market Street.

Greedy's Fish and Chips, on Park Street, is a favorite with locals for take-out. There's no seating, but they do have benches in front (£4.50 fish-and-chips, Mon-Sat 12:00-14:00 & 16:30-21:00, closed Sun, tel. 01451/870-821).

Jade Garden Chinese Take-Away is appreciated by locals who don't want to cook (Wed-Sun 17:00-23:00, closed Tue, Park Street, tel. 01451/870-288).

The Prince of India offers good Indian food to take out or eat in (£7-8 main dishes, nightly 18:00-23:30, 5 Park Street, tel. 01451/830-099).

The Coffee House provides a nice break from the horses-and-hounds traditional cuisine found elsewhere. You can get your food to go, or eat here—there's pleasant garden seating out back (£9-10 soups, salads, and sandwiches; good coffee, Mon-Sat 9:30-17:00, Sun 10:00-16:00, Church Street, tel. 01451/870-802).

The **Youth Hostel Café** (facing the Market Square) serves drinks and meals all day and is family-friendly, with great prices

Great Country Gastropubs

These places—known for their high-quality meals and fine settings—are very popular. Arrive early or phone in a reservation. (If you show up at 20:00, it's unlikely that they'll be able to seat you for dinner if you haven't called first.) These pubs allow "well-behaved children," and are practical only for those with a car. If you have wheels, make a point to dine at one (or more) of these—no matter where you're sleeping.

Near Stow

The first two (in Oddington, about three miles from Stow) are more trendy and fresh, yet still in a traditional pub setting. The Plough (in Ford, a few miles farther away) is your jolly olde dark pub.

The Horse and Groom Village Inn in Upper Oddington is a smart place in a 16th-century inn, serving modern English and Continental food with a good wine list (32 wines by the glass) and serious beer (lunch: £7-10 sandwiches, £10-15 main dishes; dinner: £14-17 main dishes; daily 12:00-14:00 & 18:30-21:00, tel. 01451/830-584).

The Fox Inn, a different Fox Inn than the one in Broadwell (see "Pub Dinner Hike from Stow"), is old but fresh and famous among locals for its quality cooking (£12-17 main dishes, daily 12:00-14:00 & 18:30-22:00, garden and winter garden, in Lower Oddington, tel. 01451/870-555). They also rent three rooms (Db-£75-95, www.fox inn.net)

and tables in the backyard garden (£5 breakfast, £6-7 dinner, tel. 01451/830-497).

Even Cheaper: Small grocery stores face the main square (**Co-op,** open daily 7:00-22:00, is next to the Kings Arms), and a big **Tesco** supermarket is 400 yards north of town.

Pub Dinner Hike from Stow

From Stow, consider taking a half-hour countryside walk to the village of Broadwell, where you'll find a traditional old pub serving good, basic grub in a convivial atmosphere. **The Fox Inn** serves pub dinners and draws traditional ales—including the local Donnington ales (£8-10 meals, food served Mon-Sat 11:30-14:00 & 18:30-21:00, Sun 12:00-14:00 only, outdoor tables in garden out back, on the village green, tel. 01451/870-909, Mike and Carol).

Getting There: If you walk briskly, it's just 20 minutes downhill from Stow. While the walk is not particularly scenic (it's one-

The Plough Inn, in the hamlet of Ford, fills a fascinating old building, once an old coaching inn and later a courthouse. Ask

the bar staff for some fun history—like what "you're barred" means. Eat from the same traditional English menu in the restaurant, bar, or garden. They are serious about both their beer and—judging by the extensive list of homemade temptations— their desserts (£11-16 meals, food served daily 12:00-14:00 & 18:00-21:00, all day long Fri-Sun and June-Aug, 4 miles from Stow on Tewkesbury Road, reservations smart, tel. 01386/584-215).

Near Moreton-in-Marsh, in Bourton-on-the-Hill

The hill-capping Bourton—about a five-minute drive (or two-mile uphill walk) above Moreton—offers sweeping views over the Cotswold countryside. Perched at the top of this steep, picturesque burg is an enticing destination pub.

Horse and Groom is a new-feeling gastropub serving delicious modern English fare in a light and spacious modern-meets-traditional interior. The service is friendly, and the place is lively (£12-19 meals, food served daily 12:00-14:00 & 19:00-21:00, until 21:30 on Fri-Sat, tel. 01386/700-413). They also rent rooms (Db-£110-160 depending on size, www.horseandgroom.info). Don't confuse this with The Horse and Groom Village Inn in Upper Oddington, near Stow (described earlier).

third paved lane, and the rest on an arrow-straight bridle path), it is peaceful, and the exercise is a nice way to start and finish your meal. The trail is poorly marked, but it's hard to get lost: Leave Stow at Parson's Corner, continue downhill, pass the town well, follow the bridle path straight until you hit the next road, then turn right at the road and walk downhill into the village of Broadwell. You can often hitch a ride with someone from the pub back to Stow after you eat.

Near Stow-on-the-Wold

These sights are all south of Stow: Some are within walking distance (the Slaughters and Bourton-on-the-Water), and one is 20 miles away (Cirencester). The Slaughters and Bourton are tied together by the countryside walk described on page 497.

▲Lower and Upper Slaughter

"Slaughter" has nothing to do with lamb chops. It comes from the sloe tree (the one used to make sloe gin). You can reach these towns on bus #801 at the "Slaughter Pike" stop (along the main road, near the villages).

Lower Slaughter is a classic village, with ducks, a charming little church, a working water mill, and usually an artist busy at her easel somewhere. The Old Mill Museum is a folksy ensemble with a tiny museum, shop, and tea house complete with a delightful terrace overlooking the mill pond, enthusiastically run by Gerald and his daughter Laura (who just can't resist giving generous tastes of their homemade ice cream). Just behind the Old Mill, two kissing gates lead to the path that goes to nearby Upper Slaughter (a 15-minute walk or 2-minute drive away). And if you follow the mill creek downstream, a bridle path leads to Bourton-on-the-Water (described next).

In **Upper Slaughter,** walk through the yew trees (sacred in pagan days) down a lane through the raised graveyard (a buildup of centuries of graves) to the peaceful church. In the back of the fine graveyard, the statue of a wistful woman looks over the tomb of an 18th-century rector (sculpted by his son).

If driving, the small roads from Upper Slaughter to **Ford** and **Kineton** (and the Cotswold Farm Park, described later) are some of England's most scenic. Roll your window down and joy-ride slowly.

▲Bourton-on-the-Water

I can't figure out whether they call this "the Venice of the Cotswolds" because of its quaint canals or its miserable crowds. Either way, it's very pretty. This town—four miles south of Stow and a mile from Lower Slaughter—gets overrun by midday and weekend hordes. Surrounding Bourton's green are sidewalks

jammed with disoriented tourists wearing nametags. If you can avoid them, it's worth a drive-through and maybe a short stop. While it can be mobbed with tour groups during the day, it's pleasantly empty in the early evening and after dark. It's conveniently connected to Stow and Moreton

THE COTSWOLDS

by buses #801 and #855.

Parking: Finding a spot here is predictably tough. Even during the busy business day, rather than park in the pay-and-display parking lot a five-minute walk from the center, drive right into town and wait for a spot on High Street just past the village green (where the road swings left, turn right to go down High Street; there's a long row of free two-hour spots in front of the Edinburgh Woolen Mills Shop, on the right).

Tourist Information: The TI is tucked across the stream a short block off the main drag, just off Victoria Street (April-Oct Mon-Fri 9:30-17:00, Sat 9:30-17:30, closed Sun, closes one hour earlier Nov-March, tel. 01451/820-211, www.bourtoninfo.com).

Sights: Bourton's attractions are tacky tourist traps, but the three listed below might be worth considering. All are on High Street in the town center. In addition to these, families also enjoy Bourton's kid-perfect **leisure center** (big pool and sauna, 5-minute walk from town center off Station Road, open daily, call for public hours, tel. 01451/824-024).

▲**Motor Museum**—Lovingly presented, this good, jumbled museum shows off a lifetime's accumulation of vintage cars, old

lacquered signs, threadbare toys, and prewar memorabilia. If you appreciate old cars, this is nirvana. Wander the car-and-driver displays, from the automobile's early days to the stylish James Bond era. Don't miss the back door (marked *village life exhibition*), which leads to old carriage houses filled with even more cars. Talk to an elderly Brit who's touring the place for some personal memories (£4.35, mid-Feb-early Dec daily 10:00-18:00, closed off-season, in the mill facing the town center, tel. 01451/821-255, www.cotswold-motor-museum.com).

Model Railway Exhibition—This exhibit of three model railway layouts is impressive only to train buffs (£2.50, June-Aug daily 11:00-17:00, Sept-May Sat-Sun only, limited Jan hours, located in the back of a hobby shop, tel. 01451/820-686, www.bourton modelrailway.co.uk).

Model Village—This light but fun display recreates the town on a 1:9 scale in a tiny outdoor park, and has an attached room full of tiny models showing off various bits of British domestic life (£3.50 for the park, £1 more for the model room, daily 10:00-17:45, until 15:45 in winter, tel. 01451/820-467).

Walk to the Slaughters—From Bourton-on-the-Water, it's about a 30-minute walk (or a two-minute drive) to Upper and

Lower Slaughter (described previously); taken together, they make for an easy two-hour round-trip walk from Bourton. (You could also walk from Stow through the Slaughters to Bourton—hike described on page 497.)

▲Cotswold Farm Park

Here's a delight for young and old alike. This park is the private venture of the Henson family, who are passionate about preserving

rare and endangered breeds of local animals. While it feels like a kids' zone (with all the family-friendly facilities you can imagine), it's actually a fascinating chance for anyone to get up close and (very) personal with piles of mostly cute animals, including the sheep that made this

region famous—the big and woolly Cotswold Lion. A busy schedule of demonstrations gives you a look at local farm life—check the events board as you enter for times for the milking, "farm safari," shearing, and well-done "sheep show." Join the included, 20-minute tractor ride, with recorded narration by the founder's son, Adam Henson, filled with the family passion for the farm's mission. Buy a bag of seed (£0.50) upon arrival, or have your map eaten by munchy goats as I did. Tykes love the little tractor rides, maze, and zip line, but the "touch barn" is where it's at for little kids.

Cost and Hours: £7.70, kids-£6.25, family ticket for 2 adults and 2 kids-£25, mid-March-early Sept daily 10:30-17:00, last entry 30 minutes before closing, closed off-season, good £2 guidebook, decent cafeteria, tel. 01451/850-307, www.cotswoldfarmpark .co.uk.

Getting There: It's well-signposted about halfway between Stow and Stanway (15 minutes from either) just off Tewkesbury Road (B4077, toward Ford from Stow). A visit here makes sense if you're traveling from Stow to Chipping Campden.

Northleach

One of the "untouched and untouristed" Cotswold villages, Northleach is worth a short stop. The town's impressive main square and church attest to its position as a major wool center in the Middle Ages. Park in the square called The

THE COTSWOLDS

Green or the adjoining Market Place. The town has no TI, but you can pick up a free town map and visitor guide at Keith Haring's World of Mechanical Music (described next) or at the post office on the Market Place (Mon-Fri 9:00-13:00 & 14:00-17:30, Sat 9:00-12:30, closed Sun) and at other nearby shops. Information: www.northleach.gov.uk.

Getting There: Northleach is nine miles south of Stow, down A429. Bus #855 connects it to Stow and Moreton (tel. 01451/820-369, www.pulhamscoaches.com).

▲**Keith Harding's World of Mechanical Music**—In 1962, Keith Harding, tired of giving ad-lib "living room tours," opened this delightful little one-room place. It offers a unique opportunity to listen to 300 years of amazing self-playing musical instruments. It's run by people who are passionate about the restoration work they do on these musical marvels. The curators delight in demonstrating about 20 of the museum's machines with each hour-long tour. You'll hear Victorian music boxes and the earliest polyphones (record players) playing cylinders and then discs—all from an age when music was made mechanically, without the help of electricity. The admission fee includes an essential hour-long tour.

Cost and Hours: £8, daily 10:00-17:00, last entry at 16:00, tours go constantly—join one in progress, High Street, Northleach, tel. 01451/860-181, www.mechanicalmusic.co.uk.

Church of Saints Peter and Paul—This fine Perpendicular Gothic church has been called the "cathedral of the Cotswolds." It's one of the Cotswolds' finest two "wool" churches (along with Chipping Campden's), paid for by 15th-century wool tycoons. Find the oldest tombstone. The brass plaques on the floor memorialize big shots, showing sheep and sacks of wool at their long-dead feet, and inscriptions mixing Latin and the old English.

THE COTSWOLDS

▲Bibury

Six miles northeast of Cirencester, this village is a favorite with British picnickers fond of strolling and fishing. Bibury (BYE-bree) offers some relaxing sights, including a row of very old weavers' cottages, a trout farm, a stream teeming with fat fish and proud ducks, and a church surrounded by rosebushes, each tended by a volunteer of the parish. A protected wetlands area on the far side of the stream hosts newts and water voles. Walk up the main street, then turn right along the old weavers' Arlington Row and back

on the far side of the marsh, peeking into the rushes for wildlife.

For a closer look at the fish, cross the little bridge to the 15-acre **Trout Farm,** where you can feed them—or catch your own (£4 entrance fee to walk the grounds, fish food-£0.50, rod rental-£3.75, daily April-Sept 8:00-18:00, March and Oct 8:00-17:00, Nov-Feb daily 8:00-16:00, catch-your-own only available weekends daily July-Aug and March-June and Sept-Oct, tel. 01285/740-215, www.biburytroutfarm.co.uk).

Don't miss the scenic **Coln Valley drive** from A429 to Bibury through the enigmatic villages of Coln St. Dennis, Coln Rogers, Coln Powell, and Winson. Unfortunately, no buses reach Bibury.

Sleeping in Bibury: If you'd like to spend the night in tiny Bibury, consider **$$ The William Morris B&B,** named for the 19th-century designer and writer (small Db-£75, big Db-£85, £10 more Fri-Sun, cash only, 2 rooms, 200 yards from the bridge toward the church at 11 The Street, tel. 01285/740-555, www.thewilliammorris.com, info@thewilliammorris.com).

▲Cirencester

Almost 2,000 years ago, Cirencester (SIGH-ren-ses-ter) was the ancient Roman city of Corinium. It's 20 miles from Stow down A429, which was called Fosse Way in Roman times. Bus #855 connects Cirencester to Stow and Moreton. Drivers follow *town centre* signs and try to find parking right on the market square; if it's parked up, retreat to the

Waterloo pay-and-display lot (a five-minute walk away).

In Cirencester, stop by the impressive **Corinium Museum** to find out why they say, "If you scratch Gloucestershire, you'll find Rome." The museum chronologically displays well-explained artifacts from the town's rich history, with a focus on Roman times—when Corinium was the second-biggest city in the British Isles (after Londinium). You'll see column capitals and fine mosaics, before moving on to the Anglo-Saxon and Middle Ages exhibits (£4.80; April-Oct Mon-Sat 10:00-17:00, Sun 14:00-17:00; Nov-March Mon-Sat 10:00-16:00, Sun 14:00-16:00; Park Street, tel. 01285/655-611, www.cirencester.co.uk/coriniummuseum).

The **TI**, in the Corinium Museum shop, answers questions and sells a £0.50 town map and a £1 town walking-tour brochure (same hours as museum, tel. 01285/654-180).

Cirencester's church is the largest of the Cotswolds "wool" churches. The cutesy New Brewery Arts crafts center entertains visitors with traditional weaving and potting, workshops, an interesting gallery, and a good coffee shop. Monday and Friday are general-market days, Friday features an antiques market, and a crafts market is held on most Saturdays.

Moreton-in-Marsh

This workaday town—worth ▲—is like Stow or Chipping Campden without the touristy sugar. Rather than gift and antiques shops, you'll find streets lined with real shops: ironmongers selling cottage nameplates and carpet shops strewn with the remarkable patterns that decorate B&B floors. A shin-kickin' traditional market of 100-plus stalls fills High Street each Tuesday, as it has for the last 400 years (8:00-16:00, handicrafts, farm produce, clothing, great people-watching,  best if you go early). The Cotswolds has an economy aside from tourism, and you'll feel it here.

Orientation to Moreton-in-Marsh

(area code: 01608)
Moreton has a tiny, sleepy train station two blocks from High Street, lots of bus connections, and the best **TI** in the region. The TI offers a room-booking service, pay Internet access, and discounted tickets for major sights (such as Blenheim Palace). Peruse the racks of fliers, confirm rail and bus schedules, and consider the £0.50 *Town Trail* self-guided walking tour leaflet (Mon 8:45-16:00, Tue-Thu 8:45-17:15, Fri 8:45-16:45, Sat 10:00-13:00—or until 12:30 in winter, closed Sun, good public WC, tel. 01608/650-881).

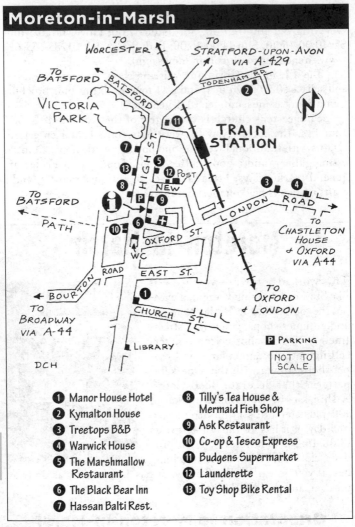

Moreton-in-Marsh

1 Manor House Hotel
2 Kymalton House
3 Treetops B&B
4 Warwick House
5 The Marshmallow Restaurant
6 The Black Bear Inn
7 Hassan Balti Rest.
8 Tilly's Tea House & Mermaid Fish Shop
9 Ask Restaurant
10 Co-op & Tesco Express
11 Budgens Supermarket
12 Launderette
13 Toy Shop Bike Rental

Helpful Hints

Internet Access: It's available for a price at the **TI** and free at the erratically open **library** (down High Street where it becomes Stow Road, tel. 01608/650-780).

Baggage Storage: While there is no formal baggage storage in town, the **Black Bear Inn** (next to the TI) might let you leave bags there—especially if you buy a drink. Or you can pay £2 to leave a bag at the **launderette** (see below).

Laundry: The handy launderette is a block in front of the train station on New Road (daily 7:00-19:00, last wash at 18:00, £3.40

self-service wash, £2-3 self-service dry, or drop off Mon-Fri 8:00-11:00 for £2.50 extra and same-day service—pick up by 17:00, tel. 01608/650-888).

Bike Rental, Taxis, and Car Rental: See "Getting Around the Cotswolds" (page 470).

Parking: It's easy—anywhere on High Street is fine any time, as long as you want, for free (though there's a 2-hour limit for parking in the small lot in the middle of the street). On Tuesdays, when the market makes parking tricky, you can park at the **Budgens** supermarket for £3—refundable if you spend at least £5 in the store.

Hikes and Walks from Moreton-in-Marsh: As its name implies, Moreton-in-Marsh sits on a flat, boggy landscape, making it a bit less appealing for hikes; I'd bus to Chipping Campden or to Stow, both described earlier, for a better hike (this is easy, since Moreton is a transit hub). If you do have just a bit of time to kill in Moreton, consider taking a fun and easy walk a mile out to the arboretum and falconry center in **Batsford** (described later).

Sleeping in Moreton-in-Marsh

(£1 = about $1.60, country code: 44, area code: 01608)

$$$ Manor House Hotel is Moreton's big old hotel, dating from 1545 but sporting such modern amenities as toilets and electricity. Its 35 classy-for-the-Cotswolds rooms and its garden invite relaxation (Sb-£120, Db-£155, family suite-£220, £40 more for Sat night, rates are soft—often a bit less, includes breakfast, elevator, pay Wi-Fi, log fire in winter, attached restaurants, free parking, on far end of High Street away from train station, tel. 01608/650-501, fax 01608/651-481, www.cotswold-inns-hotels.co.uk, info@manorhousehotel.info).

$$ Kymalton House (KYE-mal-ton) has two bright, tastefully decorated rooms in a gracious modern house. With a pleasant garden, it's set back off of a busy street just outside the town center (Db-£75, cheaper for 3 or more nights, double beds only, cash only, closed Dec-Jan, tel. 01608/650-487, kymalton@uwclub.net, Sylvia and Doug Gould). It's a seven-minute walk from town (walk past Budgens supermarket, turn right on Todenham Road, look for house on the right). They'll happily pick up and drop off train travelers at the station.

$ Treetops B&B is plush, with seven spacious, attractive rooms, a sun lounge, and a three-quarter-acre backyard. Liz and Ben (the family dog) will make you feel right at home—if you meet their two-night minimum on weekends (large Db-£65, gigantic Db-£70, two wheelchair-accessible ground-floor rooms have

THE COTSWOLDS

patios, free Wi-Fi, set far back from the busy road, London Road, tel. & fax 01608/651-036, www.treetopscotswolds.co.uk, info@tree topscotswolds.co.uk, Liz and Brian Dean). It's an eight-minute walk from town and the railway station (exit station, keep left, go left on bridge over train tracks, look for sign, then long driveway).

$ Warwick House, just down the road from Treetops, is where enterprising "half-American" Charlie Grant rents three rooms in a contemporary, casual, slightly rough-around-the-edges house. It's on a busy road, but the windows keep out most noise. Charlie will do your laundry if you stay three or more nights (Sb-£38, Db-£62, Tb-£75, 3 percent extra with credit card, no kids under age 12, healthy breakfast option, free Wi-Fi and loaner laptop, free parking, will pick up from train station, London Road, tel. 01608/650-773, www.snoozeandsizzle.com, charlie@warwick housebnb.demon.co.uk).

Eating in Moreton-in-Marsh

A stroll up and down High Street lets you survey your small-town options.

The Marshmallow is relatively upscale but affordable, with a menu that includes traditional English dishes as well as lasagna and salads (£9-11 main dishes, £12.50 high tea, £14 fancy teas, Sun-Mon 10:00-19:00, Tue 10:00-16:00, Wed-Sat 10:00-20:00, reservations smart, shady back garden for summer dining, tel. 01608/651-536).

The Black Bear Inn offers traditional English food. As you enter, choose between the dining room on the left or the pub on the right (£5-10 meals and daily specials, restaurant open daily 12:00-14:00 & 18:30-21:00, pub open daily 11:00-1:00 in the morning, tel. 01608/652-992).

Hassan Balti, with tasty Bangladeshi food, is a fine value for sit-down or take-out (£7-12 meals, daily 12:00-14:00 & 17:30-23:30, High Street, tel. 01608/650-798).

Tilly's Tea House serves fresh soups, salads, sandwiches, and pastries for lunch in a cheerful spot on High Street across from the TI (£5-7 light meals, good cream tea-£5, Mon-Sat 9:00-16:30, closed Sun, tel. 01608/650-000).

Ask, a chain restaurant across the street, has decent pastas, pizzas, and salads, and a breezy, family-friendly atmosphere (£8-11 pizzas, daily 12:00-23:00, take-out available, tel. 01608/651-119).

Mermaid fish shop is popular for its take-out fish and tasty selection of traditional savory pies (£5 fish-and-chips, £2 pies, Mon-Sat 12:00-14:00 & 17:00-22:30, closed Sun).

Picnic: There's a small **Co-op** grocery on High Street in the town center (Mon-Sat 7:00-20:00, Sun 8:00-20:00), and a **Tesco**

Express one door down (Mon-Fri 6:00-23:00, Sat-Sun 7:00-23:00). The big **Budgens** supermarket is indeed super (Mon-Sat 8:00-22:00, Sun 10:00-16:00, far end of High Street). There are picnic tables across the busy street, in pleasant Victoria Park.

Nearby: The excellent **Horse and Groom** gastropub in Bourton-on-the-Hill is a quick drive or uphill two-mile walk away (see page 502).

Moreton-in-Marsh Connections

Moreton, the only Cotswolds town with a train station, is also the best base for exploring the region by bus (see "Getting Around the Cotswolds," page 470).

From Moreton by Train to: London's Paddington Station (one-way-£29-31, round-trip after 8:15-£29, every 1-2 hours, 2.25-2.5 hours), **Bath** (hourly, 2.5-3 hours, 2-3 transfers), **Oxford** (about hourly, 40 minutes), **Ironbridge Gorge** (hourly, 2.75-3.5 hours, 2-3 transfers; arrive Telford, then catch bus or cab 7 miles to Ironbridge Gorge—see page 557), **Stratford-Upon-Avon** (almost hourly, 3 hours, 2-3 transfers, slow and expensive, better by bus). Train info: tel. 0845-748-4950, www.nationalrail.co.uk.

From Moreton by Bus to: Stratford-Upon-Avon (#21 and #22 end there, Mon-Sat about hourly, none on Sun, 1-1.25 hours, Johnsons Coaches, tel. 01564/797-000, www.johnsonscoaches.co.uk).

Near Moreton-in-Marsh

▲Chastleton House

This stately home, located about five miles southeast of Moreton-in-Marsh, was actually lived in by the same family from 1607

until 1991. It offers a rare peek into a Jacobean gentry house. (Jacobean, which comes from the Latin for "James," indicates the style from the time of King James I—the early 1600s.) Built, like most Cotswold palaces, with wool money, it gradually declined with the fortunes of its aristocratic family until, according to the last lady of the house, it was "held together by cobwebs." It came to the National Trust on condition that they would maintain its musty Jacobean ambience. Wander on creaky floorboards, many of them original, and chat with volunteer guides stationed in each room. It's an uppity place that doesn't encourage spontaneity. The docents are proud to play

on one of the best croquet teams in the region (the rules of croquet were formalized in this house in 1868). Page through the early
20th-century family photo albums in the room just off the entry.

Cost and Hours: £9.10; April-Sept Wed-Sat 13:00-17:00,
closed Sun-Tue; Oct Wed-Sat 13:00-16:00, closed Sun-Tue; ticket
office opens 12:30, last entry one hour before closing; closed Nov-
March; 10-minute drive southeast of Moreton, well-signposted,
5-minute hike to house from free parking lot, recorded info tel.
01494/755-560, www.nationaltrust.org.uk/chastleton.

Getting In: Only 180 visitors a day are allowed into the home
(25 people every 30 minutes), and reservations are not possible—
it's first-come, first served. At the busiest times, you might have
to wait a bit to enter the house. Wednesday and Thursday are the
quietest days, with the shortest wait times.

Batsford

This village, just a mile west of Moreton, has two side-by-side
attractions that might appeal if you have a special interest or time
to kill. These are also connected to Moreton by buses #21 and #22,
or an easy 45-minute country walk.

Cotswold Falconry Centre—Along with the Cotswolds' hunting heritage comes falconry—and this place, with dozens of specimens of eagles, falcons, owls, and other birds, gives a sample of
what these deadly birds of prey can do. You can peruse the cages to
see all the different birds, but the demonstration, with vultures or
falcons swooping inches over your head, is what makes it fun.

Cost and Hours: £7, discount at Batsford Arboretum with
ticket, mid-Feb-mid-Nov daily 10:30-17:30, last entry at 17:00; flying displays at 11:30, 13:30, and 15:00, plus in summer at 16:30;
Batsford Park, tel. 01386/701-043, www.cotswold-falconry.co.uk.

Batsford Arboretum—This sleepy grove, with 2,800 trees from
around the world, pales in comparison to some of the Cotswolds'
genteel manor gardens. But it's next door to the Falconry Centre,
and handy to visit if you'd enjoy strolling through a diverse wood.
The arboretum's café serves lunch and tea on a terrace with sweeping views of the Gloucestershire countryside.

Cost and Hours: £6.60, ticket good for discount at Falconry
Centre, daily 10:00-18:00, last entry at 16:45, closed Wed in Dec-
Jan, tel. 01386/701-441, www.batsarb.co.uk.

THE COTSWOLDS

STRATFORD-UPON-AVON

Stratford-upon-Avon • Warwick • Coventry

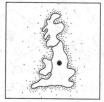

Stratford is Shakespeare's hometown. To see or not to see? Stratford is a must for every big bus tour in England, and one of the most popular side-trips from London. English majors and actors are in seventh heaven here. Sure, it's touristy, and non-literary types might find it's much ado about nothing. But nobody back home would understand if you skipped Shakespeare's house.

Shakespeare connection aside, the town's riverside and half-timbered charm, coupled with its hardworking tourist industry, makes Stratford a fun stop. But the play's the thing to bring the Bard to life—and you've arrived just in time to see the Royal Shakespeare Company (the world's best Shakespeare ensemble) making the most of their new theater complex. If you'll ever enjoy a Shakespeare performance, it'll be here...even if you flunked English Lit.

While you're in the area, explore Warwick, England's finest medieval castle, and stop by Coventry, a blue-collar town with a spirit that the Nazis' bombs couldn't destroy.

Planning Your Time

Stratford, Warwick, and Coventry are a made-to-order day for drivers connecting the Cotswolds with points north (such as Ironbridge Gorge or North Wales). While connections from the Cotswolds to Ironbridge Gorge are tough, Stratford, Warwick, and Coventry are well-served by public transportation.

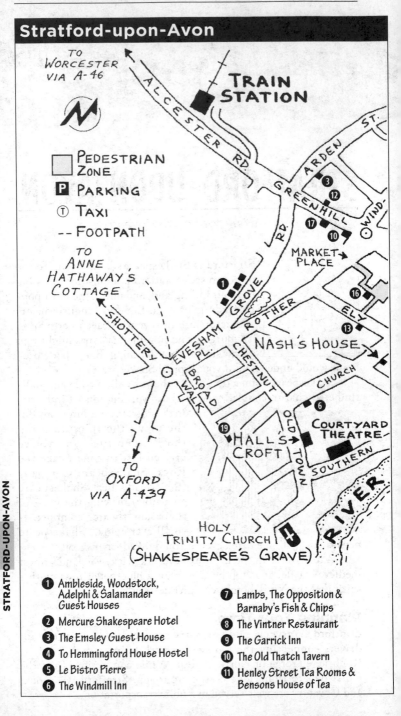

Stratford-upon-Avon

TO WORCESTER VIA A-46

TRAIN STATION

ALCESTER RD.

ARDEN ST.

GREENHILL

WIND ST.

☐ PEDESTRIAN ZONE

Ⓟ PARKING

Ⓣ TAXI

-- FOOTPATH

TO ANNE HATHAWAY'S COTTAGE

GROVE RD.

MARKET PLACE

ROTHER

ELY

SHOTTERY

EVESHAM PL.

CHESTNUT

NASH'S HOUSE

CHURCH

BROAD WALK

HALL'S CROFT

OLD TOWN

COURTYARD THEATRE

SOUTHERN

TO OXFORD VIA A-439

HOLY TRINITY CHURCH (SHAKESPEARE'S GRAVE)

RIVER

STRATFORD-UPON-AVON

❶ Ambleside, Woodstock, Adelphi & Salamander Guest Houses

❷ Mercure Shakespeare Hotel

❸ The Emsley Guest House

❹ To Hemmingford House Hostel

❺ Le Bistro Pierre

❻ The Windmill Inn

❼ Lambs, The Opposition & Barnaby's Fish & Chips

❽ The Vintner Restaurant

❾ The Garrick Inn

❿ The Old Thatch Tavern

⓫ Henley Street Tea Rooms & Bensons House of Tea

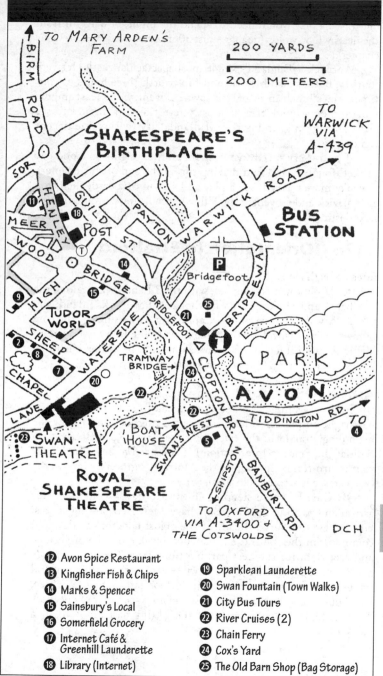

TO MARY ARDEN'S FARM

BIRM. ROAD

200 YARDS
200 METERS

TO WARWICK VIA A-439

SHAKESPEARE'S BIRTHPLACE

SOR

HENLEY

MEER

WOOD

GUILD

PAYTON ST.

Post

T

WARWICK ROAD

BUS STATION

P Bridgefoot

HIGH

BRIDGE

14

15

9

TUDOR WORLD

BRIDGEFOOT

25

21

i

BRIDGEWAY

PARK

2

SHEEP

8

7

WATERSIDE

TRAMWAY BRIDGE →

20

22

24

CLOPTON BR.

A V O N

CHAPEL

LANE

22

SWAN'S NEST

BOAT HOUSE

5

TIDDINGTON RD.

TO 4

23

SWAN THEATRE

SHIPSTON RD.

BANBURY RD.

ROYAL SHAKESPEARE THEATRE

TO OXFORD VIA A-3400 & THE COTSWOLDS

DCH

12 Avon Spice Restaurant
13 Kingfisher Fish & Chips
14 Marks & Spencer
15 Sainsbury's Local
16 Somerfield Grocery
17 Internet Café & Greenhill Launderette
18 Library (Internet)

19 Sparklean Launderette
20 Swan Fountain (Town Walks)
21 City Bus Tours
22 River Cruises (2)
23 Chain Ferry
24 Cox's Yard
25 The Old Barn Shop (Bag Storage)

If you're just passing through Stratford, it's worth a half-day, but to see a play, you'll need to spend the night, or drive in from the nearby Cotswolds (doable—just 30 minutes away; see previous chapter).

Warwick is England's single most spectacular castle. It's very touristy, but it's also historic and fun (worth three hours of your time). Have lunch in Warwick town. Coventry, the least important stop on a quick trip, is most interesting as a chance to see a real, struggling, industrial Midlands city (with some decent sightseeing).

If you're very speedy, you can hit all three sights on a one-day drive-through (you'll find driving tips at the end of this chapter). If you're more relaxed, see a play and stay in Stratford, then stop at Warwick and Coventry the following morning en route to your next destination.

Orientation to Stratford

(area code: 01789)
Stratford's old town is compact, with the TI and theater along the riverbank, and Shakespeare's Birthplace a few blocks inland; you can easily walk to everything except Mary Arden's place. The core of town is lined with half-timbered houses. The River Avon has an idyllic yet playful feel, with a park along both banks, paddleboats, hungry swans, and a fun old crank-powered ferry.

Arrival in Stratford

By Train: It's simple: Exit straight ahead from the train station, bear right up the hill (alongside the parking lot), and follow the main drag straight to the river. (For the Grove Road B&Bs, turn right at the first big intersection.) If you need to buy a picnic for your return train trip, stop at the Morrison's grocery store nearby (you can see it across the tracks).

By Car: If you're sleeping in Stratford, ask your B&B for arrival and parking details (many have a few free parking spaces, but it's best to reserve ahead). If you're just here for the day, and coming from the south (i.e., the Cotswolds), cross the big bridge and veer right for the best parking (following *Through Traffic, P,* and *Wark* signs, go around the block—turning right and right and right—and enter the multistory Bridgefoot garage; first hour free, £6/6 hours, £20/10-24 hours, you'll find no place easier or cheaper). The City Sightseeing bus stop and the TI (if it hasn't moved) are a block away.

Tourist Information

The TI has moved around in recent years; in 2012 you'll probably find it in a small brick building on Bridgefoot where the main street hits the river, or across from Shakespeare's birthplace on Henley Street. If not, ask around, or get information from your B&B (TI likely open daily 9:00-16:00, tel. 01789/264-293, www .discover-stratford.com).

Helpful Hints

Name That Stratford: If you're coming by train or bus, be sure to request a ticket for "Stratford-upon-Avon," not just "Stratford." Another Stratford—also known as Stratford Langthorne, just outside London—is the location for several events in the 2012 Olympics, and is nowhere near where you're trying to go.

Festival: Every year on the weekend following Shakespeare's birthday (traditionally considered to be April 23—also the day he died), Stratford celebrates. The town hosts free events, including activities for children. In coordination with the 2012 Olympic Games, Stratford's taking part in the 2012 Cultural Olympics, hosting theater troupes from around the world in June and July.

Internet Access: Get online at **Cyber Junction** (£3.50/hour, Mon-Fri 9:15-17:30, Sat 9:30-17:00, closed Sun, 28 Greenhill Street, tel. 01789/263-400, www.thecyberjunction.co.uk) or the **library** (£5/hour, Mon-Fri 9:00-17:30, Sat 9:30-17:00, Sun 12:00-16:00; if all computers are in use, reserve a time at the desk; tel. 01789/292-209).

Baggage Storage: Located directly behind the TI, **The Old Barn** shop stores bags—but be back to pick them up before the store closes, or you're out of luck for the night (£2/bag, Mon-Sat 10:00-17:00, Sun 10:00-16:00, tel. 01789/269-567).

Laundry: Sparklean is a 10-minute walk from the city center, or about five minutes from the Grove Road B&Bs (self-serve wash and dry-£8.50, daily 8:00-21:00, last wash at 20:00, 74 Bull Street, tel. 01789/269-075). On weekdays, Sparklean's kindly Jane will do the wash for you for £10-12 in a few hours if you drop it off by 12:00 (if you're in a pinch, she may even be able to pick up or drop off at your B&B). **Greenhill Launderette** is more central, but not as friendly (self-service wash-£3.50, dryer-£1/15 minutes, daily 8:00-22:00, last wash at 20:45, Greenhill Street).

Taxis: Try **007 Taxis** (tel. 01789/414-007) or the taxi stand on Woodbridge, near the intersection with High Street. To arrange for a private car and driver, contact **Platinum Cars** (£25/hour, tel. 01789/264-626, www.platinum-cars.co.uk).

Tours in Stratford

Stratford Town Walks—These entertaining, award-winning 1.5-hour walks introduce you to the town and its famous playwright. Tours run daily year-round, rain or shine. Just show up at the Swan fountain (on the waterfront, opposite Sheep Street) in front of the Royal Shakespeare Theatre and pay the guide (£5, kids-£2, ticket stub offers good discounts to some sights, Mon-Wed at 11:00, Thu-Sun at 14:00, tel. 01789/292-478 or 07855/760-377, www.stratford townwalk.co.uk). They also run an evening ghost walk led by a professional magician (£6, kids-£3; Mon, Thu, and Fri-Sat at 19:30; must book in advance).

City Sightseeing Bus Tours—Open-top buses constantly make the rounds, allowing visitors to hop on and hop off at all the Shakespeare sights. Given the far-flung nature of two of the Shakespeare sights, and the value of the fun commentary provided, this tour makes the town more manageable. The full 12-stop circuit takes about an hour, and comes with a steady and informative commentary (£11.75, discount with town walk ticket stub, buy tickets on bus or as you board, ticket good for 24 hours, buses leave from the river every 20 minutes in high season from 9:30-17:00, every 30 minutes off-season; buses alternate between tape-recorded commentary and live guides—for the best tour, wait for a live guide; tel. 01789/412-680, www.citysightseeing-stratford .com).

Shakespearean Sights

Stratford's five biggest Shakespeare sights are run by the same organization, the Shakespeare Birthplace Trust (www.shakespeare .org.uk). While these sights are promoted as if they were tacky tourist attractions—and are designed to be crowd-pleasers rather than to tickle academics—they're well-run and genuinely interesting. Shakespeare's Birthplace, Nash's House, and Hall's Croft are in town; Mary Arden's Farm and Anne Hathaway's Cottage are just outside Stratford. Each has a tranquil garden and helpful, eager docents who love to tell a story; and yet, each is quite different, so visiting all five gives you a well-rounded look at the Bard.

If you're here for Shakespeare sightseeing—and have time to venture to the countryside sights—you might as well buy the "Five House" combo-ticket and drop into them all. If your time is more limited, visit only Shakespeare's Birthplace, which is the most convenient to reach (right in the town center) and offers the best historical introduction to the playwright.

Combo-Tickets: Admission to the three Shakespeare Birthplace Trust sights in town requires one of two combo-tickets; no individual tickets are sold. Individual tickets are sold for the outlying Anne Hathaway's Cottage (£8) and Mary Arden's Farm (£10), but make sense only if you visit just these two sights. To visit only Shakespeare's Birthplace, Hall's Croft, and Nash's House, get the £12.50 **Shakespeare Birthplace combo-ticket.** To add Anne Hathaway's Cottage and Mary Arden's Farm, get the £19 **Shakespeare Five House combo-ticket.** If you've taken a walking tour with Stratford Town Walks (described under "Tours in Stratford," earlier), show your ticket stub to get the Shakespeare Five House combo-ticket for just £12.50. Tickets are sold at participating sights, and are good for one year. Shakespeare's grave isn't covered by either combo-ticket.

Closing Times: What the Shakespeare sights list as their "closing time" is actually their last-entry time. If you show up at the closing time I've noted below, you'll still be able to get in, but will have limited time to enjoy the sight (since they start closing things down soon after).

In Stratford

▲▲Shakespeare's Birthplace

Touring this sight, you'll experience a modern multimedia exhibit before seeing Shakespeare's actual place of birth. While the birthplace itself is a bit underwhelming, the exhibit, helpful docents, and sense that Shakespeare's ghost still haunts these halls make it a good introduction to the Bard.

Cost and Hours: Covered by either combo-ticket, daily April-Oct 9:00-17:00, July-Aug until 18:00, Nov-March 10:00-16:00, in town center on Henley Street, tel. 01789/204-016.

◆ Self-Guided Tour: The **"Shakespeare: Life, Love, and Legacy"** exhibit provides an entertaining and easily digestible introduction (or, for some, review) about what made the Bard so great. You'll walk through a series of four rooms, and in each one watch a four-minute video clip about Shakespeare's life and career: movie clips of his works; his upbringing in Stratford and his family life; his career in London; and the impact he's had on many facets of our culture. You'll also see fancy displays (such as a mannequin Shakespeare hunched over his desk), as well as actual historic artifacts that are illuminated when they're described in the video presentation, including an original 1623 First Folio of Shakespeare's work. It would be nice to linger over the First Folio, but the presentation hustles you into the next room after just a short glance.

William Shakespeare
(1564-1616)

To many, William Shakespeare is the greatest author, in any language, period. In one fell swoop, he expanded and helped define modern English—the unrefined tongue of everyday people—and granted it a beauty and legitimacy that put it on par with Latin. In the process, he gave us phrases like "one fell swoop," which we quote without knowing that no one ever said it before Shakespeare wrote it.

Shakespeare was born in Stratford-upon-Avon in 1564 to John Shakespeare and Mary Arden. Though his parents were probably illiterate, Shakespeare is thought to have attended Stratford's grammar school, finishing his education at age 14. When he was 18, he married a 26-year-old local girl, Anne Hathaway (she was three months pregnant with their daughter Susanna).

The very beginnings of Shakespeare's writing career are shrouded in mystery: Historians have been unable to unearth any record of what he was up to in his early 20s. We only know that seven years after his marriage, Shakespeare was living in London as a budding poet, playwright, and actor. He soon hit the big time, writing and performing for royalty, founding (along with his troupe) the Globe Theatre (a functioning replica of which now stands along the Thames' South Bank—see page 128), and raking in enough dough to buy New Place, a swanky mansion back in his hometown. Around 1611, the rich-and-famous playwright retired from the theater, moving back to Stratford, where he died at the age of 52.

With plots that entertained both the highest and the lowest minds, Shakespeare taught the play-going public about human nature. His tool was an unrivaled linguistic mastery of English. Using borrowed plots, outrageous puns, and poetic language, Shakespeare wrote comedies (c. 1590—*Taming of the Shrew, As*

Leaving the exhibit, walk through the garden and to the **birthplace,** a half-timbered Elizabethan building where young William grew up. I find the old house a bit disappointing, as if millions of visitors have rubbed it clean of anything authentic. It was restored in the 1800s, and, while the furnishings seem tacky and modern, they're supposed to be true to 1575, when William was 11. To liven up the otherwise dead-feeling house, chat up the well-versed attendants posted here and there, eager to answer your questions. You'll be greeted by a costumed guide who offers an introductory

You Like It), tragedies (c. 1600—*Hamlet, Othello, Macbeth, King Lear*), and fanciful combinations (c. 1610—*The Tempest*), exploring the full range of human emotions and reinventing the English language.

Perhaps as important was his insight into humanity. His father was a glove maker and wool merchant, and his mother was the daughter of a landowner from a Catholic family. Some scholars speculate that Shakespeare's parents were closet Catholics, practicing their faith during the rise of Protestantism. It is this tug-of-war between two worlds, some think, that helped enlighten Shakespeare's humanism. Think of his stock of great characters and great lines: Hamlet ("To be or not to be, that is the question"), Othello and his jealousy ("It is the green-eyed monster"), ambitious Mark Antony ("Friends, Romans, countrymen, lend me your ears"), rowdy Falstaff ("The better part of valor is discretion"), and the star-crossed lovers Romeo and Juliet ("But soft, what light through yonder window breaks"). Shakespeare probed the psychology of human beings 300 years before Freud. Even today, his characters strike a familiar chord.

The scope of his brilliant work, his humble beginnings, and the fact that no original Shakespeare manuscripts survive raise a few scholarly eyebrows. Some have wondered if Shakespeare had help on several of his plays. After all, they reasoned, how could a journeyman actor with little education have written so many masterpieces? And he was surrounded by other great writers, such as his friend and fellow poet, Ben Jonson. Most modern scholars, though, agree that Shakespeare did indeed write the plays and sonnets attributed to him.

His contemporaries had no doubts about Shakespeare—or his legacy. As Jonson wrote in the preface to the First Folio, "He was not of an age, but for all time!"

talk, then set free to explore on your own. Shakespeare's father, John—who came from humble beginnings, but bettered himself by pursuing a career in glove-making (you'll see the window where he sold them to customers on the street)—provided his family with a comfortable, upper-middle-class existence. The guest bed in the parlor was a major status symbol: They must have been rich to afford such a nice bed that wasn't even used every day. This is also the house where Shakespeare and his bride, Anne Hathaway, began their married life together. Upstairs are the rooms where young Will, his siblings, and his parents slept. After Shakespeare's father died and William inherited the building, the thrifty playwright converted it into a pub to make a little money.

Exit into the fine **garden.** The ugly modern building in the middle of the complex sometimes hosts temporary exhibits. If you hear a commotion, it's likely Shakespearean **actors,** who perform brief scenes in the garden. Pull up a bench and listen, imagining the playwright as a young boy stretching his imagination in this very place.

Nash's House—Nash was the first husband of Shakespeare's granddaughter...not exactly a close connection. However, this

house is next to the garden that was once the site of New Place, the house where Shakespeare retired. Archaeologists have been excavating the remains of New Place, and if they're still at it when you're here, you can enjoy an engaging, kid-friendly temporary exhibit (called "Dig for Shakespeare") in the otherwise dull parlor of Nash's House. Even better, you might be able to walk around the garden, watch the archaeologists at work, and (sometimes) lend a hand with the excavation and cleaning of the artifacts. Because Shakespeare is, in many ways, still a historical enigma, this work might yield important clues about his life. This opportunity will only last as long as the excavation does, so the house might be back to its boring old self by the time you visit.

Cost and Hours: Covered by either combo-ticket; daily April-Oct 10:00-17:00, July-Aug until 18:00; Nov-March 11:00-16:00; Chapel Street, tel. 01789/292-325.

Hall's Croft—This former home of Shakespeare's eldest daughter, Susanna, is in the Stratford town center. A fine old Jacobean house, it's the fanciest of the group. Since she married a doctor, the exhibits here are focused on 17th-century medicine. If you have time to spare and one of the combo-tickets, it's worth a quick pop-in. To make the exhibits interesting,

Stratford Thanks America

Residents of Stratford are thankful for the many contributions Americans have made to their city and its heritage. Along with pumping up the economy day in and day out with tourist visits, Americans paid for half the rebuilding of the Royal Shakespeare Theatre after it burned down in 1926. The Swan Theatre renovation was funded entirely by American aid. Harvard University inherited—you guessed it—the Harvard House, and it maintains the house today. London's much-loved theater, Shakespeare's Globe, was the dream (and gift) of an American. And there's even an odd but prominent "American Fountain" overlooking Stratford's market square on Rother Street, which was given in 1887 to celebrate the Golden Jubilee of the rule of Queen Victoria.

ask the docent for the 15- to 20-minute introduction, which helps bring the plague—and some of the bizarre remedies of the time—to life.

Cost and Hours: Covered by either combo-ticket, same hours as Nash's House, on-site tearoom, between Church Street and the river on Old Town Street, tel. 01789/292-107.

Shakespeare's Grave—To see his final resting place, head to the riverside Holy Trinity Church. Shakespeare was a rector for this

church when he died. While the church is surrounded by an evocative graveyard, the Bard is entombed in a place of honor, right in front of the altar inside. The church marks the ninth-century birthplace of the town, which was once a religious settlement.

Cost and Hours: £2 donation, not covered by either combo-ticket, free to view for churchgoers; April-Sept Mon-Sat 8:30-17:30, Sun 12:30-17:00; Oct-March until 17:00 or 16:00; 10-minute walk past the theater—see its graceful spire as you gaze down the river, tel. 01789/266-316, www.stratford-upon-avon.org.

Just Outside Stratford

To reach either of these sights, it's best to drive or take the hop-on, hop-off bus tour (see "Tours in Stratford," earlier)—unless you're staying at one of the Grove Road B&Bs, which are an easy 20-minute walk from Anne Hathaway's Cottage. Both sights are well-signposted (with brown signs) from the major streets and ring roads around Stratford. If driving between the sights, ask for directions at the sight you're leaving.

▲▲**Mary Arden's Farm**—Along with Shakespeare's Birthplace, this is my favorite of the Shakespearean sights. Famous as the girl-hood home of William's mom, this homestead is in Wilmcote (about three miles from Stratford). Built around two historic farm-houses, it's an open-air folk museum depicting 16th-century farm life...which happens to have ties to Shakespeare. The Bard is basically an afterthought here.

The museum hosts many special **events,** including the fal-conry show described below. The day's events are listed on a chalk-board by the entry, or you can call ahead to find out what's on. There are always plenty of activities to engage kids: It's an active, hands-on place.

Follow the Tudor roses from building to building, through farmhouses with good displays about farm life. Throughout the complex, you'll see period interpreters in Tudor costumes. They'll likely be going through the day's chores as people back then would have done—activities such as milking the sheep and cutting wood to do repairs on the house. They're there to answer questions and provide fun, gossipy insight into what life was like at the time.

The first building, **Palmer's farm** (mistaken for Mary Arden's home for hundreds of years, and correctly identified in 2000), is furnished as it would have been in Shakespeare's day.

Mary Arden actually lived in the neighboring **farmhouse,** covered in brick facade and seemingly less impressive. Dorothy Holmes, who lived here until 1979, left it as a 1920s time warp, and that's just what you'll see today.

Of the many events here, the most enjoyable is the **falconry demonstration,** with lots of mean-footed birds (only on weekends and local school holidays—

including July-Aug; usually at 11:00, 13:00, and 15:00). Chat with the falconers about their methods for earning the birds' trust. The birds' hunger sets them to flight (a round-trip earns the bird a bit of food; the birds fly when hungry—but don't have the energy if they're *too* hungry). Like Katherine, the wife described as "my falcon" in *The Taming of the Shrew,* these birds are tamed and trained with food as a reward. If things are slow, ask if you can feed one.

Cost and Hours: £10, covered by £19 combo-ticket, daily April-Oct 10:00-17:00, visitors must leave by 17:30, likely closed Nov-March, tel. 01789/293-455.

Getting There: The most convenient way to get here is by car (free parking) or the hop-on, hop-off bus tour, but it's also possible to reach by train. The Wilmcote train station is directly across the street from Mary Arden's House (£2 round-trip fare, one stop from Stratford-upon-Avon on Birmingham-bound train, 5-minute trip, train runs about every hour, call London Midland to confirm departure time—tel. 0844-811-0133, www.londonmidland.com).

▲**Anne Hathaway's Cottage**—Located 1.5 miles out of Stratford (in Shottery), this home is a 12-room farmhouse where the Bard's

wife grew up. William courted Anne here—she was 26, he was only 18—and his tactics proved successful. (Maybe a little too much, as she was several months pregnant at their wedding.) Their 34-year marriage produced two more children, and lasted until his death in 1616 at age 52. The Hathaway family lived here for 400 years, until 1911, and much of the family's 92-acre farm remains part of the sight.

After buying your ticket, turn left and head down through the garden to the thatch-roofed **cottage,** which looks cute enough to eat. The house offers an intimate peek at life in Shakespeare's day. In some ways, it feels even more authentic than his birthplace, and it's fun to imagine the writer of some of the world's greatest romances wooing his favorite girl right here during his formative years. Docents are posted in the first and last rooms to provide meaning and answer questions; while most tourists just stampede through, you'll have a more informative visit if you pause to listen to their commentary. (If the place shakes, a tourist has thunked his or her head on the low beams.)

Maybe even more interesting than the cottage are the **gardens,** which have several parts (including a prizewinning "traditional cottage garden"). If you head uphill (to the right from the entry), you'll find a "Woodland Walk," along with a fun sculpture garden littered with modern interpretations of Shakespearean characters (such as Falstaff's mead gut, and a great photo-op statue of the British Isles sliced out of steel). From April through June, the gardens are at their best, with bulbs in bloom and a large sweet-pea display. You might also find rotating exhibits, generally on a gardening theme.

Cost and Hours: £8, covered by £19 combo-ticket, daily April-Oct 9:00-17:00, Nov-March 10:00-16:00, tel. 01789/292-100.

Getting There: It's a 30-minute walk, a stop on the hop-on, hop-off tour bus, or a quick taxi ride from Stratford; well-signposted for drivers entering Stratford from any direction, easy £1 parking.

▲▲▲Plays Performed by the Royal Shakespeare Company

The Royal Shakespeare Company (RSC), undoubtedly the best Shakespeare company on earth, performs year-round in Stratford and in London. Seeing a play here in the Bard's birthplace is a must for Shakespeare fans, and a memorable experience for anybody. Between its excellent acting and remarkable staging, the RSC makes Shakespeare as accessible and enjoyable as it gets.

The RSC is enjoying new popularity after the 2011 opening of its cutting-edge Royal Shakespeare Theatre. The smaller, attached Swan Theatre hosts plays on a more intimate scale, with only about 400 seats. (Nearby, the Courtyard Theatre—built to house the company during the main theater's renovation—is seeing its final year in 2012.)

The Royal Shakespeare Company makes it easy to take in some theater, thanks to their very user-friendly website (www.rsc.org.uk), painless ticket-booking system, and chock-a-block schedule that fills the summer with mostly big-name Shakespeare plays (with a few more obscure titles to please the die-hard aficionados, as well). Outside January and February, there's almost always something playing.

Performances: Performances take place most days (Mon-Sat generally around 19:00 or 19:30, matinees around 13:00, sporadic Sun shows). Shows generally last three hours or more, with one intermission; for an evening show, don't count on getting back to your room much before 23:00. There's no strict dress code—and people dress casually (nice jeans and short-sleeve shirts are fine)—but shorts are discouraged. You can buy a program for £3.50. If you're feeling bold, buy a £5 standing ticket and then slip into an open seat as the lights dim—if nothing is available during the play's first half, something might open up after intermission.

Getting Tickets: Tickets range from £5 (standing) to £58, with most around £35. Saturday evening shows—the most popular—are most expensive. You can book tickets as you like it: online (www.rsc.org.uk), by phone (tel. 0844-800-1110), or in person at the box office (Mon-Sat 9:30-20:00, Sun 10:00-18:00). Pay by credit card, get a confirmation number, then pick up your tickets at the theater 30 minutes before "curtain up." Because it's so easy to get tickets online or by phone, it makes absolutely no sense to pay extra to book tickets through any other source.

Tickets go on sale months in advance. Saturdays and very famous plays (such as *Romeo and Juliet* or *Hamlet*) sell out the fastest; the earlier in the week the performance is, the longer it takes to sell out (e.g., Thursdays sell out faster than Mondays). Before your trip, check the schedule on their website, and consider buying tickets if something strikes your fancy. But demand is difficult to predict, and some tickets do go unsold. On my last visit, on a sunny Friday in June, the riverbank was crawling with tourists. I stepped into the RSC on a lark to see if they had any tickets. An hour later, I was watching King Lear lose his marbles.

Even if there aren't any seats available, you may be able to buy a returned ticket on the same day of an otherwise sold-out show. To increase your chances, be at the box office when it opens in the morning, and be prepared to wait.

Touring the Theaters: Theatrical and well-informed RSC volunteers lead entertaining, one-hour building tours that cover the main theater, the Swan, and some behind-the-scenes spaces, such as the space-age control room (£6.50; 4/day—usually at 9:15, 11:15, 13:15, and 17:15; book online or at the box office). For a God's-eye view of all of Shakespeare's houses, take a tour of the RSC's new **tower** (£2.50, tours depart every 20 minutes, daily 9:15-17:15, elevator).

The Food's the Thing: The main theater has a casual café with a terrace overlooking the river (£3 sandwiches, open daily from 9:00 until the show's over), as well as a fancier restaurant on the top floor that can count the Queen as a patron (£11.50 lunch menu, daily 11:30 until late, tel. 01789/403-449).

Theaters
The Royal Shakespeare Theatre—The newly remodeled flagship theater of the RSC has an interesting past. The original theater

was built in 1879 to honor the Bard, but burned down in 1926. The big building you see today (facing the riverside park) was erected in 1932 and outfitted with a stodgy Edwardian "picture frame"-style stage, even though the more dynamic "thrust"-style stage—better for engaging the audience—was the actors' choice. (It's also closer in design to Shakespeare's Globe stage, which juts into the crowd.)

A recent, multiyear renovation addressed this ill-conceived

design—post-remodel, the theater has an updated, thrust-style stage. They've left the shell of the 1930s theater, but outfitted it in an unconventional deconstructed-industrial style, with the seats stacked at an extremely vertical pitch. Though smaller, the redesigned theater can seat the same size audience as before, but now there's not a bad seat in the house—no matter what, you're no more than 15 yards from the stage (the cheapest "gallery" seats look down right onto Othello's bald spot). The redesign took great care to respect the ghosts of the former theater; for example, floorboards from the 1932 stage were re-laid in the theater's entry foyer, so as you wait for your play, you're walking on theater history.

The Swan Theatre—Adjacent to the RSC Theatre is the smaller, Elizabethan-style Swan Theatre, a galleried playhouse that opened in 1986. This smaller theater is used for new (non-Shakespearean) works and smaller productions. Occasionally the lowest level of seats is removed to accommodate "groundling" (standing-only) tickets, much like at the Globe Theatre in London.

The Courtyard Theatre—A two-minute walk down Southern Lane from the original Royal Shakespeare Theatre, this 1,000-seat theater (affectionately called the "rusty shed" by the locals) was built as a replacement venue while the Royal Shakespeare Theatre was being renovated. It was used as a prototype for the main theater—a testing ground for the lights, seats, and structure of its big brother. Everything in the building, with the exception of the roof, can be recycled—and might be, as the whole thing must be removed (possibly to be dismantled and sold) by December of 2012.

Non-Shakespearean Sights

Tudor World at the Falstaff Experience—This attraction is tacky, gimmicky, and more about entertainment than education. (And, while it's named for a Shakespeare character, the exhibit isn't about the Bard.) Filling Shrieve's House Barn with fun exhibits (mannequins and descriptions, but few real artifacts), it sweeps through Tudor history from the plague to Henry VIII's privy chamber to a replica 16th-century tavern. If you're into ghost-spotting, their nightly ghost tours may be your best shot.

Cost and Hours: Museum-£5, daily 10:30-17:30, last entry 30 minutes before closing; ghost tours-£7.50, daily at 18:00; Sheep Street, tel. 01789/298-070, www.falstaffexperience.co.uk.

The Look of Stratford

There's much more to Stratford than Shakespeare sights. Take time to appreciate the look of the town itself. While the main street goes back to Roman times, the key date for the city was 1196, when the king gave the town "market privileges." Stratford was shaped by its marketplace years. The market's many "departments" were located on logically named streets, whose names still remain: Sheep Street, Corn Street, and so on. Today's street plan—and even the 57' 9" width of the lots—survives from the 12th century. (Some of the modern storefronts in the town center are still that exact width.)

Starting in about 1600, three great fires gutted the town, leaving very few buildings older than that era. After those fires, tinderbox thatch roofs were prohibited—the Old Thatch Tavern on Greenhill Street is the only remaining thatch roof in town, predating the law and grandfathered in.

The town's main drag, Bridge Street, is the oldest street in town, but looks the youngest. It was built in the Regency style—a result of a rough little middle row of wattle-and-daub houses being torn down in the 1820s to double the street's width. Today's Bridge Street buildings retain that early 19th-century style: Regency.

Throughout Stratford, you'll see striking black-and-white, half-timbered buildings, as well as half-timbered structures that were partially plastered over and covered up in the 19th century. During Victorian times, the half-timbered style was considered low-class, but in the 20th century—just as tourists came, preferring ye olde style—timbers came back into vogue, and the plaster was removed on many old buildings. But any black and white you see is likely to be modern paint. The original coloring was "biscuit yellow" and brown.

Avon Riverfront—The River Avon is a playground of swans and canal boats. The swans have been the mascots of Stratford since 1623, when, seven years after the Bard's death, a poem in his First Folio nicknamed him "the sweet swan of Avon." Join in the bird-scene fun and buy **swan food** (£0.50) to feed swans and ducks; ask at the ice-cream stand for details. Don't feed the Canada geese, which locals disdain (they say the geese are vicious and have been messing up the eco-balance since they were imported by a king in 1665).

The **canal boats** saw their workhorse days during the short window of time between the start of the Industrial Revolution and the establishment of the railways. Today, they're mostly pleasure boats. The boats are long and narrow, so two can pass in the slim canals. There are 2,000 miles of canals in England's Midlands, built to connect centers of industry with seaports and provide vital transportation during the early days of the Industrial Revolution. Stratford was as far inland as you could sail on natural rivers from Bristol; it was the terminus of the man-made Birmingham Canal, built in 1816. Even today, you can motor your canal boat all the way to London from here.

For a little bit of mellow river action, rent a **rowboat** (£4/hour per person) or, for more of a challenge, pole yourself around on

a Cambridge-style **punt** (canal is poleable—only 4 or 5 feet deep; same price as the rowboat and more memorable/embarrassing if you do the punting—don't pay £8/hour per person for a waterman to do the punting for you). Take a short stop on your lazy tour of the English countryside, and moor your canal boat at Stratford's Canal Basin. You can try a sleepy half-hour **river cruise** (£4.50, no commentary, Avon Boating, board boat in Bancroft Gardens near the RSC theater or at Swan's Nest Boathouse across the Tramway Footbridge, tel. 01789/267-073, www.avon-boating .co.uk), or jump on the oldest surviving **chain ferry** (c. 1937) in Britain (£0.50), which shuttles people across the river just beyond the theater.

Cox's Yard, a riverside timber yard until the 1990s, is a rare

physical remnant of the days when Stratford was an industrial port. Today, Cox's is a touristy entertainment center with pubs that have live music most nights (£5-15, schedule at tel. 01789/404-600 or www .coxsyard.co.uk).

Sleeping in Stratford

(area code: 01789)
If you want to spend the night after you catch a show, options abound. Ye olde timbered hotels are scattered through the city center. Most B&Bs are a short walk away on the fringes of town, right on the busy ring roads that route traffic away from the center. (The

Sleep Code

(£1 = about $1.60, country code: 44)
S = Single, **D** = Double/Twin, **T** = Triple, **Q** = Quad, **b** = bathroom, **s** = shower only. Unless noted otherwise, you can assume credit cards are accepted and breakfast is included.

To help you sort easily through these listings, I've divided the accommodations into three categories based on the price for a standard double room with bath:

$$$ Higher Priced—Most rooms £90 or more.
$$ Moderately Priced—Most rooms between £60-90.
$ Lower Priced—Most rooms £60 or less.

Prices can change without notice; verify the hotel's current rates online or by email. For other updates, see www .ricksteves.com/update.

recommended places below generally have double-paned windows for rooms in the front, but still get some traffic noise.)

Local hoteliers expect the London Olympics and the newly reopened theater to hike up demand in 2012; book as far ahead

as possible. In general, the weekend after Shakespeare's birthday (April 28-29 in 2012) is particularly tight, but Fridays and Saturdays are busy throughout the season. This town is so reliant upon the theater for its business that some B&Bs have secondary insurance covering their loss if the Royal Shakespeare Company ever stops performing in Stratford.

On Grove Road

These accommodations are at the edge of town on busy Grove Road, across from a grassy park. From here, it's about a 10-minute walk either to the town center or to the train station (opposite directions).

$$ Ambleside Guest House is run with quiet efficiency and attentiveness by owners Peter and Ruth. Each of the seven rooms has been completely renovated, including the small but tidy bathrooms. The place has a homey, airy feel, with none of the typical B&B clutter (S-£30-38, Db-£60-80, Tb-£85-115, Qb-£100-140, ground-floor rooms, free parking, free Wi-Fi, 41 Grove Road, tel. 01789/297-239, fax 01789/295-670, www.amblesideguest house.com, ruth@amblesideguesthouse.com—include your phone number in your request, since they like to call you back to confirm with a personal touch).

$$ Woodstock Guest House is a friendly, frilly, family-run, and flowery place with five comfortable rooms (Sb-£35-48, Db-£60-85, family room-£75-125 depending on number of people, cash only, deals for 2 or more nights, ground-floor room, free Wi-Fi, free parking, 30 Grove Road, tel. 01789/299-881, www .woodstock-house.co.uk, enquiries@woodstock-house.co.uk, owners Denis and bubbly Jackie).

$$ Adelphi Guest House has six rooms, two with four-poster beds. Martin and Ellen have filled the house with antiques and run the place with Scottish charm. For breakfast, they offer a wide variety beyond the standard "English fry" (S-£40, Db-£75-100, Tb-£120, 5 percent surcharge on credit cards, 10 percent discount off these prices if you stay at least 2 nights in 2012—mention this book when you reserve, free Wi-Fi, free parking if booked in advance, 39 Grove Road, tel. 01789/204-469, www.adelphi-guest house.com, info@adelphi-guesthouse.com).

$ Salamander Guest House, run by gregarious Frenchman Pascal and his wife, Anna, rents seven clean, simple, good-value rooms (S-£30-40, Db-£50-65, Tb-£60-75, Qb-£80-90, free Wi-Fi, free on-site parking, 40 Grove Road, tel. & fax 01789/205-728, www.salamanderguesthouse.co.uk, p.delin@btinternet.com).

Elsewhere in Stratford

$$$ Mercure Shakespeare Hotel, centrally located in a black-and-white building just up the street from Nash's House, has 73 business-class rooms, each one named for a Shakespearean play or character. Some of the rooms are old-style Elizabethan higgledy-piggledy (with modern finishes), while others are contemporary style—note your preference when you reserve (Sb-£80, standard Db-£110, deluxe Db-£130-150, breakfast-£15/person, prices soft depending on demand, parking-£10/day, free Wi-Fi in lobby, pay Wi-Fi in rooms, Chapel Street, tel. 01789/294-997, fax 01789/415-411, www.mercure.com, h6630-re@accor.com).

$$ The Emsley Guest House holds five bright, modern rooms named after different counties in England. It's conscientiously run by Melanie and Ray Coulson, who give it a homey and inviting atmosphere (Db-£64-80, Tb-£90-120, Q-£120-160, 5-person family room with extra bathroom, families welcome, free Wi-Fi, free off-street parking, 5 minutes from station at 4 Arden Street, tel. 01789/299-557, www.theemsley.co.uk, mel@theemsley .co.uk).

$ *Hostel*: Hemmingford House, with 130 beds in 2- to 10-bed rooms, is a 10-minute bus ride from town (from £26 for non-members, includes breakfast; take bus #15, #18, or #18A two miles to Alveston; tel. 01789/297-093 or 0845-371-9661, stratford @yha.org.uk).

Eating in Stratford

Stratford's numerous restaurants vie for your pre-theater business, with special hours and meal deals. (Most offer light two- and three-course menus 17:30-19:00.) You'll find many hardworking places on Sheep Street and Waterside. Unfortunately, post-theater dinners are more challenging, as most places close early.

Le Bistro Pierre, across the river near the boating station, is a relatively new French eatery that's been impressing Stratford residents. They have indoor or outdoor seating and slow service (£9 two-course lunches; £14 two-courses meals before 19:00, otherwise £10-13 main courses; Mon-Fri 12:00-15:00 & 17:00-22:30, Sat 12:00-16:00 & 17:00-23:00, Sun 12:30-16:00 & 18:00-22:00, Swan's Nest, Bridgefoot, tel. 01789/264-804). They also have a pub with a different menu.

The Windmill Inn serves decent, modestly priced fare in a 17th-century inn. It combines old and new style, and—since it's a few steps beyond the heart of the tourist zone—actually attracts some locals as well. Order drinks and food at the bar, settle into a comfy chair, and wait for your meal (£7-10 pub grub, daily 12:00-22:00, Church Street, tel. 01789/297-687).

Sheep Street Eateries: The next three places, part of the same chain, line up along Sheep Street, offering trendy ambience and "modern English" cuisine, with relatively high prices and small portions (you'll pay separately for side dishes): **Lambs** is intimate, and serves meat, fish, and veggie dishes with panache. The upstairs feels dressy, under low half-timbered beams (specials before 19:00: £12 two-course meals, £15 three-course meals; otherwise £12-16 main courses, Mon 17:00-21:00, Tue-Sat 12:00-14:00 & 17:00-21:00, may be open Sun 12:00-14:00 & 18:00-21:00, 12 Sheep Street, tel. 01789/292-554). **The Opposition,** next door, has a less formal "bistro" ambience (£12 two-course meals before 19:00; otherwise £8-10 light meals, £13-15 main courses; Mon-Thu 12:00-14:00 & 17:00-21:00, Fri-Sat 12:00-14:00 & 17:00-22:30, Sun 12:00-14:00 & 18:00-21:00, tel. 01789/269-980). **The Vintner,** just up the street, has the best reputation and feels even trendier than its siblings, but still with old style. They're known for their £10 burgers (£7-10 light meals, £11-15 main courses, Mon-Thu 9:30-21:30, Fri-Sat until 22:00, Sun until 21:00, 4-5 Sheep Street, tel. 01789/297-259).

The Garrick Inn bills itself as the oldest pub in town, and comes with a cozy, dimly lit restaurant vibe. Choose between the pub or table-service section; either way, you'll dine on bland, pricey pub grub (£8-11 dishes, daily 12:00-23:00, 25 High Street, tel. 01789/292-186).

Drinking: **The Old Thatch Tavern** is, according to natives, the best place in town for beer, including local brews from the Purity Brewery. The food is a cut above what you'll get in the other pubs; enjoy it either in the tight, candle-lit restaurant or out on the quiet patio (£7-15 main courses, daily 11:00-23:00, on Greenhill Street overlooking the market square, tel. 01789/295-216).

Tea Room: **Henley Street Tea Rooms,** across the street from Shakespeare's Birthplace, has indoor seating plus outdoor tables right on the main pedestrian mall, and friendly service (£4 cream tea, £10 afternoon tea, teas available all day, daily 9:00-17:30, 40 Henley Street, tel. 01789/415-572). The same people run Bensons House of Tea & Gift Shop, just down the street (at #33).

Indian: **Avon Spice** has a good reputation and good prices (£7-11 main courses, daily 17:00-23:30, 7 Greenhill Street, tel. 01789/267-067).

Fish-and-Chips: **Barnaby's** is a greasy fast-food fish-and-chips joint near the waterfront—but it's convenient if you want to get takeout for the riverside park just across the street (£4-6 fish-and-chips, daily 11:00-20:00, at Sheep Street and Waterside). For better food, queue up with the locals at **Kingfisher,** then ask for the freshly battered haddock (£6-7 fish-and-chips, Mon-Sat 11:30-13:45 & 17:00-22:00, closed Sun, a long block up at 13 Ely Street, tel. 01789/292-513).

Picnics: For groceries, find **Marks & Spencer** on Bridge Street (Mon-Sat 9:00-18:00, Sun 10:30-16:30, small coffee-and-sandwiches café upstairs, tel. 01789/292-430). Across the street, the **Sainsbury's Local** stays open later than other supermarkets in town (daily 7:00-22:00). Nearby, **Somerfield** is in the Town Centre mall (Mon-Sat 8:00-19:00, Sun 10:00-16:00, tel. 01789/292-604). To picnic, head to the canal and riverfront park between the Royal Shakespeare Theatre and the TI. Choose a bench with views of the river or of vacation houseboats, and munch your fish-and-chips while tossing a few fries into the river to attract swans. It's a fine way to spend a midsummer night's eve.

Stratford Connections

Remember: When buying tickets or checking schedules, ask for "Stratford-upon-Avon," not just "Stratford" (which is a different town). Notice that a single train (running about every 2 hours) connects most of these destinations: Warwick, Leamington Spa (change for Coventry or Oxford), then London.

From Stratford-upon-Avon by Train to: London (6/day direct, more with transfers, 2.25 hours, to Marylebone Station),

Warwick (10/day, 30 minutes), Coventry (at least hourly, 1.75 hours, change in Leamington Spa or Birmingham), Oxford (every 2 hours, 1.5 hours, change in Leamington Spa or Banbury). Train info: tel. 0845-748-4950, www.nationalrail.co.uk.

By Bus to: Cotswolds towns (bus #21 or #22, Mon-Sat about hourly, none on Sun, 35 minutes to Chipping Campden, 1-1.25 hours to Moreton-in-Marsh; also stops at Broadway, Blockley, and Bourton-on-the-Hill; Johnsons Coaches, tel. 01564/797-000, www.johnsonscoaches.co.uk), Warwick (hourly by bus, 20 minutes, tel. 01788/535-555, www.stagecoachbus.com), Coventry (hourly, 1.25 hours, tel. 01788/535-555, www.stagecoachbus.com). A direct bus runs to Oxford once a day; otherwise, change in Chipping Norton (train is better). Most intercity buses stop on Stratford's Bridge Street (a block up from the TI). For bus info that covers all the region's companies, call Traveline at tel. 0871-200-2233 (www.travelinemidlands.co.uk).

By Car: Driving is easy and distances are brief: Stow-on-the-Wold (22 miles), Warwick (8 miles), Coventry (19 miles).

Route Tips for Drivers

Stratford to Points North via Warwick and Coventry: Leaving the Bridgefoot garage in downtown Stratford (see map on page 516), circle to the right around the same block, but stay on "the Wark" (Warwick Road, A439). Warwick is eight miles away. The castle is just south of town on the right. (For parking advice, see page 541.) When you're trying to decide whether to stop in Coventry or not, factor in Birmingham's rush hour—try to avoid driving through that city between 14:00-20:00, if you can.

If You're Including Coventry: After touring Warwick Castle, carry on through the center of Warwick town and follow signs to Coventry (still A439, then A46). If you're stopping in Coventry, follow signs painted on the road to the *City Centre*, and then to *Cathedral Parking*. Grab a place in the high-rise parking lot. Leaving Coventry, follow signs to *Nuneaton* and *M6 North* through lots of sprawl, and you're on your way. (See below.)

If You're Skirting Coventry: Take M69 (direction: Leicester) and follow M6 as it threads through giant Birmingham.

Once You're on M6: The highway divides into a free M6 and an "M6 Toll" road (designed to help drivers cut through the Birmingham traffic chaos). Take the toll road—£5 is a small price to pay to avoid all the nasty traffic (www.m6toll.co.uk).

When battling through sprawling Birmingham, keep your sights on M6. If you're heading for any points north—Ironbridge Gorge (Telford), North Wales, Liverpool, Blackpool, or the Lakes (Kendal for the South Lake District, Keswick for the North Lake District)—just stay relentlessly on M6 (direction: North West).

Each destination is clearly signed directly from M6. For specifics on getting to Ironbridge Gorge, see page 567.

Near Stratford-upon-Avon

Warwick

The pleasant town of Warwick ("WAR-ick") is home to England's finest medieval castle, which dominates the banks of the River Avon just upstream from Strat-

ford. The castle is impressive in itself, but its line-up of theme-park-type experiences makes it particularly entertaining, especially for kids. The castle-related attractions, while pricey, offer something for everyone, and on a sunny day the grounds are a treat to explore.

Meanwhile, Warwick town—with a fine market square and some good eateries—goes about its business almost oblivious to the busloads of tourists passing through. While handy for an overnight, Warwick offers relatively little to see beyond its castle.

Orientation to Warwick

(area code: 01926)

With about 24,000 people, Warwick is small and manageable. The castle and old town center sit side-by side, with the train station about a mile to the north. From the castle's main gate, a lane leads into the old town center a block away, where you'll find the TI, plenty of eateries (see "Eating in Warwick," later), and a few minor sights.

Arrival in Warwick

By Train: Warwick has two train stations; you want the one called simply "Warwick" (Warwick Parkway Station is farther from the castle). Day-trippers can leave bags at the train station's Castle Cars office for an extortionate £10 a day. It's much cheaper to carry your bags into town and use the £1 lockers near the castle (at the entrance to the Stables Car Park; if lockers are all taken—unlikely but possible—try asking very nicely at the castle information desk).

Near Stratford

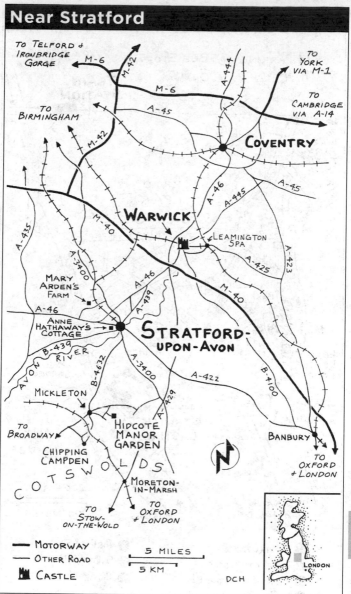

TO TELFORD &
IRONBRIDGE
GORGE

M-6

M-42

TO
YORK
VIA M-1

A-444

TO
CAMBRIDGE
VIA A-14

M-6

A-45

TO
BIRMINGHAM

M-42

COVENTRY

A-45

A-46

A-445

A-435

WARWICK

M-40

LEAMINGTON
SPA

A-425

A-423

MARY
ARDEN'S
FARM

A-3400

A-46

A-439

M-40

A-46

ANNE
HATHAWAY'S
COTTAGE

STRATFORD-
UPON-AVON

B-439

RIVER

B-4632

A-3400

A-422

B-4100

AVON

A-429

MICKLETON

TO
BROADWAY

HIDCOTE
MANOR
GARDEN

BANBURY

TO
OXFORD
& LONDON

CHIPPING
CAMPDEN

N

COTSWOLDS

MORETON-
IN-MARSH

TO
STOW-
ON-THE-WOLD

TO
OXFORD
& LONDON

—— MOTORWAY
—— OTHER ROAD
🏰 CASTLE

5 MILES

5 KM

DCH

LONDON

STRATFORD-UPON-AVON

Warwick

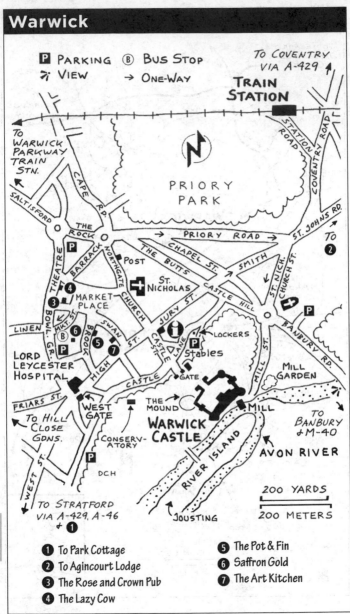

P PARKING Ⓑ BUS STOP
⫸ VIEW → ONE-WAY

TO COVENTRY
VIA A-429

TRAIN STATION

TO WARWICK PARKWAY TRAIN STN.

SALTISFORD

CAPE RD.

THE ROCK

PRIORY PARK

STATION ROAD

COVENTRY ROAD

ST. JOHNS RD.

PRIORY ROAD

CHAPEL ST.

SMITH

TO ②

BARRACK

NORTHGATE

CHURCH ST.

POST

THE BUTTS

ST. NICHOLAS

CASTLE HILL

ST. NICH. CHURCH ST.

BANBURY RD.

THEATRE

BOWL. GR.

LINEN

MKT. ST.

MARKET PLACE

BROOK

SWAN ST.

JURY ST.

ℹ

CASTLE LANE

LOCKERS

Ⓑ

LORD LEYCESTER HOSPITAL

HIGH

CASTLE

P STABLES

GATE

MILL ST.

MILL GARDEN

FRIARS ST.

TO HILL CLOSE GDNS.

WEST GATE

CONSERV-ATORY

THE MOUND

WARWICK CASTLE

MILL

AVON RIVER

TO BANBURY & M-40

WEST ST.

P

DCH

RIVER ISLAND

200 YARDS

200 METERS

TO STRATFORD VIA A-429, A-46
& ①

JOUSTING

① To Park Cottage
② To Agincourt Lodge
③ The Rose and Crown Pub
④ The Lazy Cow

⑤ The Pot & Fin
⑥ Saffron Gold
⑦ The Art Kitchen

STRATFORD-UPON-AVON

A **taxi** from the station to the castle or town center costs £5. The station is about a 15-minute **walk** from the castle or town center: Exit straight ahead down the street, then bear right onto Coventry Road, where you'll start to see signs for the castle. From here, at the traffic light, turn right onto St. John's Road. At the three-way fork, take Smith Street (the middle fork), which leads you through the old gateway straight up Warwick's High Street. After a long block, the TI appears on your left, with the main castle gate just beyond (up Castle Street). To reach the market square and restaurants from the TI, go one more block and turn right.

By Car: The main Stratford-Coventry road cuts right through Warwick. Coming from Stratford (8 miles to the south), you'll hit the castle parking lots first (£5, buy token from machine to exit lot; if these are full, lurk until a few cars leave and they'll let you in). The four castle lots are expensive, and three of them are a 10- to 15-minute walk from the actual castle; the closest one, just off Castle Lane, is the Stables Car Park, which costs more (£8). Street parking in the town center is cheaper (less than £2), but there's a two- to three-hour maximum—not enough time to fully experience the castle.

Tourist Information

Warwick's TI sells same-day tickets to Warwick Castle—there's no discount, but it can save you time in line at the castle (Mon-Fri 9:30-17:00, Sat 10:00-17:00, Sun 10:00-16:30, closes 30 minutes earlier Oct-May, tel. 01926/492-212, www.visitwarwick.co.uk). The TI has Internet access (£0.50 to get online for a few minutes) and a room-booking service (pay 10 percent here and the rest at your B&B).

Sundays at 11:00, a 1.5-hour walking tour of the town of Warwick departs from the TI (£3).

Sights in Warwick

▲▲Warwick Castle

Almost too groomed and organized, this theme park of a castle

gives its crowds of visitors a decent value for the stiff entry fee. The cash-poor but enterprising Earl of Warwick hired the folks at Merlin Entertainments (which owns many other big-name British attractions) to wring maximum tourist dollars out of his castle. They've made the place entertaining indeed, and packed it with lively exhibits...but

also watered down the history a bit, and added several layers of gift shops, overpriced concessions, and nickel-and-dime add-ons. The greedy feel of the place can be a little annoying, considering the already-steep admission. But—especially for kids—there just isn't a better medieval castle experience in England. With a lush, green, grassy moat and fairy-tale fortifications, Warwick Castle will entertain you from dungeon to lookout.

The castle is a 14th- and 15th-century fortified shell, holding an 18th- and 19th-century royal residence, surrounded by another one of dandy "Capability" Brown's landscape jobs (like at Blenheim Palace). You can tour the sumptuous staterooms, climb the towers and ramparts for the views, stroll through themed exhibits populated by aristocratic wax figures, explore the sprawling grounds and gardens, and—best of all—interact with costumed docents who explain the place and perform fantastic demonstrations of medieval weapons and other skills.

Cost and Hours: Steep £21 entry fee (£15 for kids under age 12, £16.20 for seniors) includes gardens and most castle attractions except for the gory Castle Dungeon (£7.80) and the *Merlin: The Dragon Tower* show (£4.80). Combo-tickets are available. Open daily April-Oct 10:00-18:00, Nov-March 10:00-17:00.

Advance Tickets: Booking in advance at www.warwick-castle.com (or at the Stratford TI) saves substantial money and time waiting in the ticket line (advance tickets bought at the Warwick TI let you avoid the line, but they don't save you money).

Information: The dry, nine-stop audioguide leads you through the staterooms (£2.50, or £4/2 people), but the posted information is more concise and interesting. The £5 guidebook gives you nearly the same script in souvenir-booklet form. There's also a children's audioguide called "A Knight's Tale" (£1.50). Both the audioguide and the guidebook are available at the gift shop near the entrance (not the ticket booth). If you tour the castle without help, pick the brains of the earnest and talkative docents. Recorded info tel. 0871-265-2000, www.warwick-castle.com.

Demonstrations and Events: It's the well-presented demos and other events that make this castle particularly worthwhile. These can include jousting competitions, archers showing off their longbow skills, sword fights, jester acts, falconry shows, demonstrations of the trebuchet (like a catapult) and ballista (a type of giant slingshot). They're offered year-round, but most frequently in summer and on weekends and school holidays. When you buy your castle ticket, be sure to pick up the daily events flier and plan your day around these events.

Eating at the Castle: Consider bringing your own picnic to enjoy at the gorgeous grounds. Otherwise you'll be left with overpriced concessions stands serving variations on the same mass-produced food. The stands are scattered around the castle grounds (and marked on the map you get with your ticket). **The Coach House** has cafeteria fare and grungy seating (located just before the turnstiles). **The Undercroft** has a sandwich buffet line (located inside, in basement of palace); you can sit under medieval vaults or escape with your food and picnic outside. The **riverside pavilion** sells sandwiches and fish-and-chips, and has fine outdoor seating (in park just before the bridge, behind castle). Fortunately, just 100 yards from the castle turnstiles—through a tiny gate in the wall—is Warwick town's workaday commercial district, with several better (and better-value) lunch options. It's worth the walk (see "Eating in Warwick," later).

○ Self-Guided Tour: Buy your ticket and head through the turnstile into the moat area, where you'll get your first view of the dramatic castle. In good weather, this lawn-like zone is filled with tents populated by costumed docents demonstrating everyday medieval lifestyles.

From the moat, two different entrance gateways lead to the

castle's **inner courtyard.** Within these mighty walls, there's something for every taste (described below); look for signs for where to enter each one.

The bulge of land at the far end of the courtyard, called **The Mound**, is where the original Norman castle of 1068 stood. Under this "motte," the wooden stockade (the "bailey") defined the courtyard in the way the castle walls do today. You can climb up to the top for a view down into the castle courtyard (do this at the end, since you can exit down the other side, toward the riverbank).

The main attractions are in the largest buildings along the side of the courtyard: the Great Hall, five lavish staterooms, and the chapel. Progressing through these rooms, you'll see how the castle complex evolved over the centuries, from the militarized Middle Ages to civilized Victorian times, from a formidable defensive fortress to a genteel manor home.

Enter through the cavernous **Great Hall,** decorated with suits of equestrian armor. Adjoining the Great Hall is the state

dining room, with portraits of English kings and princes. Then follow the one-way route through the **staterooms,** keeping ever more esteemed company as you go—the rooms closest to the center of the complex were the most exclusive, reserved only for those especially close to the Earl of Warwick. You'll pass through a series of three drawing rooms (abbreviated from "withdrawing," from a time when these provided a retreat into a more intimate area after a to-do in the larger, more public rooms): first, one decorated in a deep burgundy; then

the cedar drawing room, with intricately carved wood paneling, a Waterford crystal chandelier, and a Carrara marble fireplace; and finally the green drawing room, with a beautiful painted coffered ceiling and wax figures of Henry VIII and his six wives. The sumptuous Queen Anne Room was decorated in preparation for a planned 1704 visit by the monarch (unfortunately, Queen Anne never came—she got wind that one of her ladies-in-waiting, with whom she was fiercely competitive, was also coming, so she cancelled at the last minute). Finally comes the blue boudoir, an oversized closet decorated in blue silk wallpaper. The portrait of King Henry VIII over the fireplace faces a clock once owned by Marie-Antoinette.

On your way out, you'll pass the earl's private **chapel.** The earl's family worshipped in the pews in front of the stone screen, while the servants would stand behind it. Notice the ornate wood-carved relief depicting a scene of the Greeks fighting the Amazons, based on a painting by Peter Paul Rubens. The organ in the back of the chapel was powered by a hand-pumped bellows.

Back out in the courtyard, to the left of the staterooms, are the entrances to two other, less impressive exhibits. The **Kingmaker** exhibit (set in 1471) uses mannequins, sound effects, and smells to show how medieval townsfolk prepared for battle—from the black-smiths and armory, to the wardrobe, to the final rallying cry, with costumed docents standing by. The **Secrets and Scandals of the Royal Weekend Party** exhibit lets you explore staterooms staged as they appeared in 1898, but with an added narrative element: The philandering Daisy Maynard, Countess of Warwick—considered the most beautiful woman in Victorian England—is throwing a party, and big-name aristocrats are in attendance, including a young Winston Churchill. Among the guests is the Prince of Wales (the future King Edward VII), with whom Daisy reportedly also had a long-time affair. Gossipy "servants" clue you in on who's flirting with whom. The rooms are populated by eerily convincing

Madame Tussauds-style wax figures, and posted information and soundtracks loosely narrate the scandal. Unfortunately, it's more dry than titillating, and a bit hard to follow unless you're versed in the ins and outs of late-19th-century aristocratic intrigue.

You can climb up onto the **ramparts and tower**—a one-way, no-return route that leads you up and down (on very tight spiral stairs) the tallest tower, leaving you at a fun perch from which to fire your imaginary longbow. The halls and stairs can be very crowded with young kids, and—as the signs warn—it takes 530 steep steps (both up and down) to follow the whole route; claustrophobes should consider it carefully.

The **Princess Tower** offers children (ages 3-8) the chance to dress up as princesses and princes for a photo op. While it's included in the castle ticket, those interested must first sign up for a 15-minute time slot at the information tent in the middle of the courtyard, near the staterooms.

Two other pricey and skippable add-on attractions can also be entered from the courtyard (if you didn't buy a combo-ticket at the entrance, you can buy individual tickets at the information tent near the staterooms). **The Castle Dungeon,** a gory, tacky knock-off of the London Dungeon, features a series of costumed hosts who entertain and spook visitors on a 45-minute tour. *Merlin: The Dragon Tower,* a 20-minute live-action stage show with special effects, is based on a popular BBC television series.

Outside of the inner courtyard area are additional diversions. Surrounding everything is a lush, peacock-patrolled, picnic-perfect park, complete with a Victorian rose garden. The castle grounds are often enlivened by a knight in shining armor on a horse that rotates with a merry band of musical jesters. The grassy moat area is typically filled with costumed characters and demonstrations, including archery and falconry. Near the entrance to the complex is the **Pageant Playground,** with medieval-themed slides and climbing areas for kids. Down by the river is a bridge across to River Island, and—tucked around the back of the castle—a restored **mill and engine house**, with an exhibit that explains how the castle was electrified in 1894.

More Sights in Warwick

While Warwick has a few attractions beyond the castle, most are not that exciting.

The most photogenic building in town (aside from the castle) is the **Lord Leycester Hospital,** a gaggle of adjoining 14th-century half-timbered houses next to the southern gate of High Street. Converted into a "hospital" (rest home for the elderly or ill) in 1571, it has a chapel, great hall, maze of old rooms, and pretty garden (overpriced at £4.90, borrow self-

guided tour brochure at entry, Tue–Sun 10:00-17:00, until 16:00 in winter, closed Mon year-round, High Street, tel. 01926/491-422, www.lordleycester.com).

Garden fans will find three good ones in Warwick. Most appealing is the **Mill Garden,** down the quaint and half-timbered

Mill Street from the castle gate; this small garden, which adjoins the castle property, has fantastic views of the River Avon and castle (£2, April-Oct daily 9:00-18:00, closed Nov-March, 55 Mill Street, tel. 01926/492-877). **Hill Close Gardens,** at the other end of town near the racecourse, has 16 small Victorian garden plots but limited hours (£3, Fri and Sun 14:00-17:00, Sat 11:00-17:00, closed Mon-Thu, Bread and Meat Close, tel. 01926/493-339, www.hillclosegardens.com). The garden at the **Lord Leycester Hospital** (described above) rounds out your options.

Sleeping in Warwick

(£1 = about $1.60, country code: 44, area code: 01926)
$$ Park Cottage fills a creaky 1521 half-timbered house (once the dairy for the castle) with seven rooms and teddy-on-the-beddy

STRATFORD-UPON-AVON

touches. It's on the main road at the opposite end of town from the train station (near the racecourse), but Stuart and Janet will pick you up if their schedule allows (Sb-£59, Db-£74-79, family room-£10 extra per child, free Wi-Fi, free parking, 113 West Street/A429, tel. 01926/410-319, www.parkcottagewarwick.co.uk, janet @parkcottagewarwick.co.uk).

Several B&Bs line Emscote Road (A445) at the train-station end of town. The closest to town—and best—is **$$ Agincourt Lodge,** renting six comfortable rooms in an 1843 Victorian house (Sb-£40-55 depending on size, D with private b on the hall-£60, Db-£68, larger Db with four-poster bed-£78, Tb-£85, Qb-£95, free Wi-Fi, free parking, 36 Coten End, tel. 01926/499-399, www .agincourtlodge.co.uk, enquiries@agincourtlodge.co.uk, Mike and Marisa).

Eating in Warwick

All of these are on or within a short stroll of Market Place.

The Rose and Crown is a popular gastropub serving English food with a modern twist. Enjoy the cozy but not claustrophobic interior (order food at the bar, or dine in the table-service area), or sit outside (lunch—£5-7 light meals, £11-13 larger dishes; dinner—£11-18 main courses, £3 sides; food served daily 8:00-15:00 & 18:00-22:00, open longer for drinks, 30 Market Place, tel. 01926/411-117).

The Lazy Cow, a newer competitor a few doors down, is a bit more trendy and pricey, with a focus on steaks (in the open kitchen, see the aging cabinet and the indoor barbecue). Vegetarians may be put off by both the meat-heavy menu and the cow-themed decor (£5-8 starters, £10-20 main courses, open daily 7:00-24:00, food served in bar until 19:00 Fri-Sat, in sit-down restaurant until closing, 10 Theatre Street, tel. 08451-200-666)

The Pot & Fin serves up excellent fish-and-chips in a charming, rustic cottage setting a block off of Market Place (toward the castle). Everything is made fresh in-house. If you order takeaway (£4-7), you can grab one of the tables; or head upstairs for the pricier table-service menu, with £8 main courses (Sun-Mon 12:00-15:00, Tue-Fri 11:30-14:00 & 17:00-21:00, Sat 11:30-21:00, 48 Brook Street, tel. 01926/492-426).

Saffron Gold is a well-regarded Indian restaurant serving tasty £7-13 meals in an upscale setting with good service (Sun-Thu 17:30-23:30, Fri-Sat 17:30-24:00, just a block off Market Square but tricky to find—in drab Westgate House building near the Marks & Spencer, on Market Street, tel. 01926/402-061).

The Art Kitchen, right on the main pedestrian shopping street, is a mod Thai bistro surrounding a bar (£8-14 meals,

Sun-Thu 11:00-23:00, Fri-Sat 10:00-23:00, 7 Swan Street, tel. 01926/494-303).

Warwick Connections

Warwick is on the train line between Birmingham's Moor Street Station and London's Marylebone Station; most other connections require a change in the adjacent town of Leamington Spa.

From Warwick by Train to: Leamington Spa (about 2/hour, 3-10 minutes), **Stratford** (10/day, 30 minutes—buses are better, see below), **Coventry** (nearly hourly, 25-40 minutes, transfer in Leamington Spa), **Oxford** (nearly hourly, 50-70 minutes, transfer in Leamington Spa), **London**'s Marylebone Station (3/hour direct, 1.75 hours). Train info: tel. 0845-748-4950, www.national rail.co.uk.

By Bus to: Stratford (hourly, 20 minutes, bus #X17, also slower #15/ #18), **Coventry** (10/day, 1 hour, bus #X17, www.stage coachbus.com).

Coventry

Coventry was bombed to smithereens in 1940 by the Nazi Luftwaffe (air force). From that point on, the German phrase for "to really blast the heck out of a place" was (roughly) "to coven-trate" it. But Coventry rose from its ashes, and its message to our world is one of forgiveness, reconciliation, and the importance of peace.

Before it was infamous as a victim of World War II, Coventry had an illustrious history. According to legend, Coventry's most famous hometown girl, Lady Godiva, rode bareback and bare-naked through the town in the 11th century to convince her stubborn husband to lower taxes. You'll see her bronze statue on the market square a block from the cathedral, and a fun exhibit about her in the Herbert Museum.

The cloth trade made Coventry one of England's leading cities in the Middle Ages. Its fortunes rose and fell over time, and by the 20th century it had become a major industrial center—first as Britain's main bicycle manufacturer, later as its top car-making city, and eventually as a major center of armaments and aircraft assembly (making it a key target for the Nazis' Luftwaffe bombers). The city was utterly devastated by the Blitz; aside from the human toll, its greatest loss was its proud and famous St. Michael's Cathedral, which burned to the ground—the only English cathedral destroyed by the Nazis. Tellingly, Coventry's sister cities include two other places synonymous with horrific WWII destruction: Dresden, Germany, and Volgograd (formerly Stalingrad), Russia.

Today's Coventry isn't pretty. While many other WWII-damaged English towns were rebuilt quaint and cobbled, Coventry is all characterless modern concrete. But its cathedral—combining the still bombed-out shell of the old building, and a highly symbolic, starkly modern new one—is poignant and inspiring, and its other museums are quite good (and free). While I wouldn't go out of my way to visit Coventry, if you're passing by, consider stopping off to browse through a bit of normal, everyday, urban England.

Orientation to Coventry

(area code: 02476)

Coventry is a big city—with about 310,000 people—but everything of interest to visitors is in the small central core, which is bound by a busy ring road. You can walk from one end of the ring to the other in about 15 minutes. The train station is just south of the ring; the cathedral, TI, St. Anne's Guildhall, and Herbert Museum are in the northeastern part of the ring; and the Transport Museum is about a 10-minute walk west of the cathedral.

Arrival in Coventry

If you're passing through Coventry by public transportation, baggage storage is a problem—there's none at the train station. The cathedral and Transport Museum will store your bags while you visit each sight, but otherwise you're stuck. If your train route takes you through Birmingham's New Street Station (a transit hub for the area), consider using the left luggage desk there.

By Train: From the train station (which sits just outside the ring road), it's about a 15-minute walk to the cathedral. Exit straight ahead and find the blue line in the pavement, which leads you through the confusing maze of ring road overpasses to the edge of downtown; from there, simply follow signs for the cathedral (or the Transport Museum) through the modern shopping district. The cathedral is the taller of the two pointy spires.

By Car: Use the pay parking lot on Cox Street (just off of Fairfax Street), near the cathedral. From the ring road, take junction (exit) 2. The parking lot is basically under the ring road, across from the Coventry Sports and Leisure Centre.

Tourist Information

The **TI,** at the base of the cathedral tower, hands out free maps and brochures (Mon-Fri 9:30-17:00, Sat 10:00-16:30, Sun 10:00-12:00

& 13:00-16:30, closes 30 minutes earlier off-season, tel. 02476/225-616, www.visitcoventryandwarwickshire.co.uk, tic@cvone.co.uk).

Sights in Coventry

▲▲St. Michael's Cathedral

The symbol of Coventry is the bombed-out hulk of its old cathedral, with the huge new one adjoining it. This inspiring complex welcomes visitors.

Cost and Hours: The ruins of the old cathedral are free to enter (gates open daily roughly 8:30-17:00), though you'll pay to climb the tower (see below). Entering the new cathedral costs a hefty £7 (consider it a donation to a worthwhile cause). It's open Mon-Sat 9:00-16:30; on Sun, the church interior is free to enter and open 12:00-16:00, but the museum and café are closed. The front desk will hold your bags while you visit. Tel. 02476/521-1200, www.coventrycathedral.org.uk.

Tower Climb: You can walk 180 steps up to the top of the tower for views over the cathedral complex and city. Buy your ticket and enter at the TI, at the base of the tower (£2.50, open same hours as TI).

◑ Self-Guided Tour: A visit to the cathedral complex has two parts: First explore the ruins of the original building, then head into the new cathedral. You can pick up the free *Guide to the Ruined Cathedral* pamphlet at the TI; the new cathedral also hands out a floor plan that includes both the old and new churches.

Old Cathedral Ruins: Coventry's grand Perpendicular Gothic cathedral was the second to stand on this spot (built 1373-1460).

Its towering, 303-foot-tall steeple—the third-highest in England—was a symbol for the city. On the night of November 14, 1940, Nazi Luftwaffe bombers filled the skies above Coventry. They dropped incendiary devices (firebombs) to light up the ground so they could see their targets. One of these hit the roof of the cathedral, which was quickly consumed in flames. (The tower survived.) Today the footprint and surviving walls stand as a testament to the travesty of war.

At the apse of the ruined structure (far end from tower) is a replica of the **charred cross;** the original is inside the new cathedral. While surveying the wreckage after the bombing, workers found these beams lying on the ground in the shape of a cross—so they lashed them together and erected it here. The message "Father

Forgive" (spoken by Christ on the cross) makes it clear that this is a symbol not of anger, but of reconciliation. Every Friday at 12:00, the Coventry Litany of Reconciliation is said in these ruins—asking forgiveness for the seven deadly sins.

Various **monuments** are scattered around the ruins. Directly to the left of the charred cross is the bronze memorial to an early 20th-century bishop. In a chilling bit of irony, there's a swastika on his headband—dating from a time when this was just a good-luck symbol, before it had been appropriated by Hitler and painted on the planes that destroyed this place. Closer to the tower, you'll see the modern *Ecce Homo* sculpture (depicting Christ before Pilate) and a reconciliation monument, showing two people embracing across a gulf.

Before going inside the new cathedral building, head out to the plaza just beyond the complex and look back at it: old and new cathedrals, set perpendicular to each other, creating a continuous ensemble of worship. The large sculpture on the side of the new cathedral depicts St. Michael triumphing over the devil, as foretold by the Book of Revelation.

The cathedral's visitors center is to the right; in this undercroft is a museum about the history of all three cathedrals that have stood on this site, with artifacts from each one. (Also notice, to your left, the glassy entrance to the Herbert Art Gallery and Museum—a good post-cathedral stop, it's described later.)

• *Now head into the new cathedral interior. If the main door (up the stairs) is open, head inside and buy a ticket; otherwise, enter through the visitors center.*

New Cathedral: By the morning after the cathedral burned, the people of Coventry had already decided to rebuild it. The architect Basil Spence won the contest to design this re-imagining of the important church: The ruined old cathedral represents death and sacrifice, while the new structure—part of the same continuum—represents resurrection. While at first the cold gray walls inside the building make it feel gloomy and uninspired—almost (perhaps appropriately) like a giant bomb shelter—its highly symbolic design reveals itself to those who take the time to explore it.

Stand at the top of the main nave, on the giant letters that create a **gathering area** for the congregation. In the center of the nave near these letters, look for the maple leaf embedded in the floor—a thank-you to Canadians whose donations helped fund this building. Looking down the nave, notice that the cathedral follows the same basic traditional

layout of much older churches (long nave, choir area, high altar and apse at the far end) but features decidedly modern designs and decorations.

Turn right to take in the gigantic and gorgeous stained-glass window of the **baptistery**—a starburst with intensely warm colors

at the center, cool colors at the perimeter. Beneath this is the baptismal font, which is carved into a chunk of rock from the hills near Bethlehem. Looking down the nave, notice that otherwise, the cathedral has relatively little stained glass...from here, at least.

Across the nave from the baptistery, walk up the stairs into the **Chapel of Unity.** With its circular shape and floor mosaics depicting the five continents, this chapel preaches understanding among all Christian faiths—an ecumenism that echoes the cathedral's mission of reconciliation.

Back out in the main nave, walk down the central aisle. Notice the well-worn **copper coins** embedded in the floor. Dating from 1962 (when the cathedral was consecrated), these help choir members keep a straight line as they process into the church.

Pause in front of the **choir,** with its modern, dramatically prickly canopy, designed to evoke Jesus' crown of thorns—or possibly birds in flight. The Christmas-tree-shaped tower marks the seat of the bishop.

The green artwork that fills the far wall is not a fresco but a 74-foot-by-38-foot **tapestry** that depicts Jesus in a Byzantine Pantocrator ("creator of all") pose, surrounded by symbols of the four evangelists. Notice the faint outline of a small human being standing protected between Jesus' feet.

Turn around and look back down the **nave.** Remember how stained glass seemed in short supply from the far end of the church? From this direction, you can clearly see how the sawtooth-shaped design allows for row after row of colorful glass to be seen by worshippers as they return to their seats after taking communion. At the far end, notice that instead of a wall sealing off the church, there's a giant glass window—to emphasize the connection between this new cathedral and the old one just outside. Both buildings also use the same local red sandstone. This is intended to be one big, unified space.

Now circle around the left side of the choir, to the back-left corner of the church, where stairs lead down to WCs, the church museum, and a café. Hanging at the top of the stairwell is the **original charred cross** that was found in the ruins of the cathedral after the bombing.

Now cross toward the other side of the church. Right in the middle, you'll pass a misshapen cross above the main altar; in its center is a smaller cross consisting of three nails from the medieval church, which were also found in the wreckage. This **"cross of nails"** has become a symbol worldwide for postwar reconciliation. Several such crosses have been made, many of them given to other cities that were devastated by the war; one stands above the high altar of the recently rebuilt Frauenkirche in Dresden, Germany.

(You can buy a small replica of the cross of nails in the cathedral shop, across from the main door.)

Continue to the far side of the church. You'll pass the **Chapel of Gethsemane,** with a crown of thorns-shaped screen around the window. Beyond that, walk down the hallway and into the **Chapel of Christ the Servant.** The clear (rather than stained-glass) windows remind worshippers to extend their faith and stewardship outside the walls of this building. Also displayed here are fragments of the old cathedral's original stained-glass windows.

Near the Cathedral

▲**Herbert Art Gallery and Museum**—Recently expanded, this impressive museum complex and cultural center combines town history exhibits and art collections. Since it's free and directly behind the cathedral, it's well worth dropping in if you have some time to spare. As there are several different exhibits—both permanent and temporary—be sure to explore the entire building (ask for a floor plan).

Near the entrance is the History Gallery, with enjoyable

interactive exhibits that trace the city's story from its beginnings to the Blitz to today. You'll see actual artifacts from the Blitz and hear locals describe living through it. Beyond the informa-

tion desk are small exhibits on peace and reconciliation (Coventry has understandably become a very pacifist city), and the small but entertaining "Discover Godiva" exhibit, which examines the legend (and possible fact) of Lady Godiva. Her husband, Earl Leofric, increased taxes dramatically on his subjects. She pleaded with him for a tax cut, and he agreed—provided that she ride naked through town on horseback. A fun animated video shows how the legend evolved, with each generation of storytellers adding their own flourishes. One popular version says that the townspeople respectfully averted their eyes, except for one "Peeping Tom"—who was struck blind for his voyeurism. You'll also see various paintings of the Lady, clips of various movies about her, and various companies that have appropriated her as a mascot. Upstairs is the museum's modest but enjoyable gallery of sculpture, Old Masters, modern and contemporary artwork, and temporary exhibits.

Cost and Hours: Free, Mon-Sat 10:00-16:00, Sun 12:00-16:00, Jordan Well, tel. 02476/832-386, www.theherbert.org.

▲**St. Mary's Guildhall**—The origins of this fine half-timbered building, sitting next to the cathedral, are rooted in the fascinating

history of England's often-overlooked King Henry VI (r. 1422-1461). Afflicted with what today would be diagnosed as catatonic schizophrenia, Henry seemed to his medieval subjects to exist between our world and another—he'd drift into a trance and be unreachable for

days or weeks at a time, and emerge reporting the vibrant visions he'd had. During the Wars of the Roses, Henry briefly moved the capital of England to Coventry, creating a special bond with the city. After his death, Henry's corpse reportedly bled in front of observers, leading them to conclude that he was miraculous. A cult of followers sprang up around Henry, centered here in Coventry. People began to pray for divine intervention from the man they came to call "Saint Henry." One young girl, who had been crushed under a wagon wheel, was miraculously healed when her mother prayed to Henry. (The pope sent delegates to verify some 300 reported miracles, and Henry would likely have been formally canonized—if his son, Henry VII, hadn't refused to pay the hefty sum for sainthood. By the time his grandson, Henry VIII, broke away from the Vatican, all bets were off.) The local businessmen's guilds of Coventry built this fine hall to venerate their favorite king and unofficial saint.

While it's fun and a bit spooky to explore the maze of tight old rooms, the highlight here is the great hall. The semicircular stained-glass window traces Henry VI's royal lineage—that's him in the center, flanked by his supposed ancestors, William the Conqueror, King Arthur, and the Roman emperor Constantine (notice that Constantine's cross is bigger than the others'—his mother, St. Helen, supposedly discovered Jesus' "true cross"). Below the window is a remarkable, if faded, 14th-century tapestry that also honors Henry (ask the attendants to briefly turn on the light to see it better). More than 500 years old, this tapestry is still in situ—in the location for which it was intended. The hall is staffed by knowledgeable attendants who love to explain its history. If you dare, also ask them about the constant ghost sightings in this building—so frequent they've become routine.

Cost and Hours: Free, £0.50 pamphlet, £1 detailed descriptions, Easter-Sept Sun-Thu 10:00-16:00, closed Fri-Sat, during events, and off-season, tel. 02476/833-328, www.coventry.gov.uk/stmarys.

▲Coventry Transport Museum

A 10-minute walk from the cathedral, this good museum pays homage to Coventry's car-making heritage. For much of the 20th

century, Coventry was the main auto production center of Britain, and in the 1950s and 60s, more than a third of the city's population built cars. On two floors of a sprawling modern building, you can see the first, fastest, and most famous cars that came from this "British Detroit." The museum also shows off a collection of tractors, bicycles, motorcycles, and tanks...if it had wheels, they made it here. For car-lovers, it's worth ▲▲.

The exhibit focuses on local production (Daimler, Standard, Mandslay, and others), but a few famous non-Coventry cars are also included, such as Monty's staff car, Princess Di's modest Austin Metro car (a gift from Prince Charles before they married), a Delorean, a 1949 Land Rover, and Ewan McGregor's motorcycle from the BBC series *Long Way Round*. Aside from the cars, you'll find the "Landmarques Show" (recreated streets of old-time Coventry, circa 1868-1948), the "Coventry Blitz Experience" (a low-tech, walk-through simulation of war-torn Coventry with sound and light effects), and—upstairs—the thought-provoking "Ghost Town?" exhibit (tracing the decline of the Coventry auto industry from 1980 to 2010).

Cost and Hours: Free, good £5 souvenir guidebook, £1 lockers for use only while on the premises, daily 10:00-17:00, tel. 02476/234-270, www.transport-museum.com.

Coventry Connections

From Coventry by Train to: Warwick (hourly, 30 minutes, change in Leamington Spa), **Stratford-upon-Avon** (at least hourly, 1.75 hours, change in Leamington Spa or Birmingham), **Oxford** (hourly, 50 minutes), **London**'s Euston Station (3/hour, 1 hour), **Telford Central** (near Ironbridge Gorge; 2/hour, 1.5 hours, change in Birmingham). Train info: tel. 0845-748-4950, www.nationalrail.co.uk.

IRONBRIDGE GORGE

The Industrial Revolution was born in the Severn River Valley. In its glory days, this valley (blessed with abundant deposits of iron ore and coal, and a river for transport) gave the world its first iron wheels, steam-powered locomotive, and cast-iron bridge (begun in 1779). The museums in Ironbridge Gorge, which capture the flavor of the Victorian Age, take you back into the days when Britain was racing into the modern era, and pulling the rest of the West with her.

Near the end of the 20th century, the valley went through a second transformation: Photos taken just 30 years ago show an industrial wasteland. Today the Severn River Valley is lush and lined with walks and parkland. Even its bricks, while still smoke-stained, seem warmer and more inviting.

Planning Your Time

Without a car, Ironbridge Gorge isn't worth the headache. Drivers can slip it in between the Cotswolds/Stratford/Warwick and points north (such as the Lake District or North Wales). Speed demons zip in for a midday tour of the Blists Hill Victorian Town, look at the famous Iron Bridge and quaint Industrial Age town that sprawls around it, and head out. For an overnight visit, arrive in the early evening to browse the town, see the bridge, and walk along the river. Spend the morning touring the Blists Hill Victorian Town, have lunch there, and head to your next destination.

With more time—say, a full month in Britain—I'd spend two nights and a leisurely day: 9:30-Iron Bridge and the town; 10:30-Museum of the Gorge; 11:30-Coalbrookdale Museum of

Iron; 14:30-Blists Hill Victorian Town; then dinner at the recommended Golden Ball Inn.

Orientation to Ironbridge Gorge

(area code: 01952)
The town is just a few blocks gathered around the Iron Bridge,
which spans the peaceful, tree-lined Severn River. While the
smoke-belching bustle is long gone, knowing that this wooded,
sleepy river valley was the "Silicon Valley" of the 19th century
makes wandering its brick streets almost a pilgrimage. The actual
museum sites are scattered over three miles. The modern cooling
towers (for coal, not nuclear energy) that loom ominously over
these red-brick remnants seem strangely appropriate.

Tourist Information
The Museum of the Gorge, just west of the town center, has a
TI with lots of booklets for sale, including pamphlets describing nearby walks (Mon-Fri 9:00-17:00, Sat-Sun 10:00-17:00, tel.
01952/433-424, www.ironbridge.org.uk).

Getting Around Ironbridge Gorge
On weekends from Easter through October, **Gorge Connect**
buses link the museum locations (£0.50/ride, £3 day ticket, free
with Passport Ticket—described on the next page, 2/hour, Sat-
Sun 9:30-17:30 only, no buses Mon-Fri; schedule at www.iron
bridge.org.uk—click on "Plan Your Visit," then "Travel Advice,"
then "Using Public Transport"; tel. 01952/200-005). For connections from the Telford train or bus stations to the sights, see the
end of the chapter.
    If you need a **taxi** while in Ironbridge Gorge, call Central
Taxis at tel. 01952/501-050.

Sights in Ironbridge Gorge

▲▲Iron Bridge
While England was at war with her American colonies, this first
cast-iron bridge was built in 1779 to show off a wonderful new
building material. Lacking experience with cast iron, the builders
erred on the side of sturdiness and constructed it as if it were made
out of wood. Notice that the original construction used traditional
timber-jointing techniques rather than rivets. (Any rivets are from
later repairs.) The valley's centerpiece is free, open all the time,
and thought-provoking. Walk across the bridge to the tollhouse.
Read the fee schedule and notice the subtle slam against royalty.
(England was not immune to the revolutionary sentiment brewing

in the colonies at this time.) Pedestrians paid half a penny to cross; poor people crossed cheaper by coracle—a crude tub-like wood-and-canvas shuttle ferry. Cross back to the town and enjoy a pleasant walk downstream along the towpath. Where horses once dragged boats laden with Industrial Age cargo, locals now walk their dogs.

▲▲Ironbridge Gorge Museums

Ten museums located within a few miles of each other focus on the Iron Bridge and all that it represents. Not all the sights are worth your time. The Blists Hill Victorian Town is by far the best. The Museum of the Gorge attempts to give a historic overview, but the displays are humble—its most interesting feature is the 12-minute video. The Coalbrookdale Museum of Iron tells the story of iron—interesting to metalheads. Enginuity is just for kids. And the original Abraham Darby Furnace is a free shrine to 18th-century technology. The best sights are described in greater detail below.

Cost: This group of widely scattered sights has varied admission charges (most sights £3-9; Blists Hill is £15); the £22.50 **Passport Ticket** (families-£61.50) covers admission to all of them. If you're visiting the area's top three sights—Blists Hill Victorian Town, the Museum of the Gorge, and the Coalbrookdale Museum of Iron—you'll save about £3.50 with the Passport Ticket.

Hours: Unless otherwise noted, the sights share the same opening hours and contact info: daily 10:00-17:00, tel. 01952/433-424, www.ironbridge.org.uk, tic@ironbridge.org.uk.

Sightseeing Strategies: It helps to see the introductory movie at the Museum of the Gorge first, to help put everything else into context. To see the most significant sights by car, you'll park three times: once in town (either in the pay lot just over the bridge or in the lot at the Museum of the Gorge—the Iron Bridge and Gorge Museum are connected by an easy, flat walk); once at the Blists Hill parking lot; and once outside of the Coalbrookdale Museum of Iron (Enginuity is across the lot, and the Darby Houses are a three-minute uphill hike away). While you'll pay separately to park at the Museum of the Gorge, a single ticket is good for both pay-and-display lots at the Coalbrookdale Museum and Blists Hill.

If you're visiting on a weekend, you can leave your car in a town lot and take the Gorge Connect bus instead (runs Easter-Oct).

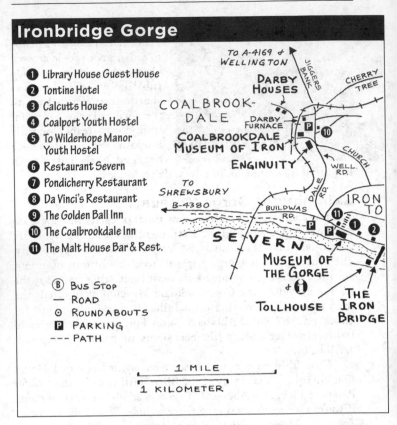

Ironbridge Gorge

1 Library House Guest House
2 Tontine Hotel
3 Calcutts House
4 Coalport Youth Hostel
5 To Wilderhope Manor Youth Hostel
6 Restaurant Severn
7 Pondicherry Restaurant
8 Da Vinci's Restaurant
9 The Golden Ball Inn
10 The Coalbrookdale Inn
11 The Malt House Bar & Rest.

Ⓑ BUS STOP
— ROAD
◉ ROUNDABOUTS
🅿 PARKING
--- PATH

1 MILE
1 KILOMETER

TO A-4169 & WELLINGTON
JIGGERS BANK
CHERRY TREE
DARBY HOUSES
COALBROOK-DALE
DARBY FURNACE
COALBROOKDALE MUSEUM OF IRON
ENGINUITY
CHURCH
WELL RD.
TO SHREWSBURY B-4380
DALE RD.
BUILDWAS RD.
IRON TO
SEVERN
MUSEUM OF THE GORGE & ⓘ
TOLLHOUSE
THE IRON BRIDGE

Museum of the Gorge

Orient yourself to the valley here in the Old Severn Warehouse. The 12-minute introductory movie (on a continuous loop) lays the groundwork for what you'll see in the other museums. Check out the exhibit and the model of the gorge in its heyday. Farther upstream from the museum parking lot is the fine riverside Dale End Park, with picnic areas and a playground.

Cost: £3.75, 500 yards upstream from the bridge, parking-£1.10.

Blists Hill Victorian Town

Save most of your time and energy for this wonderful town—an immersive, open-air folk museum. You'll wander through 50 acres of Victorian industry, factories, and a re-created community from the 1890s. Pick up the Blists Hill guidebook for a good step-by-step rundown.

The map you're given when entering is very important—it shows which stops in the big park are staffed with lively docents in

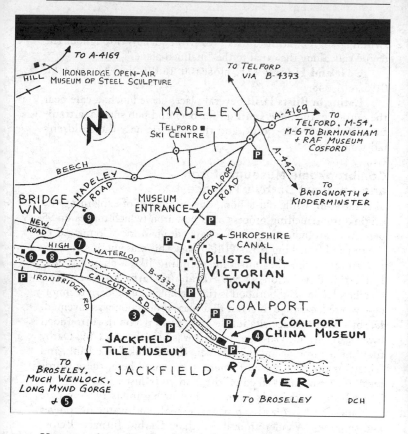

Victorian dress. Pop in to say hello to the banker, the lady in the post office, the blacksmith, and the girl in the candy shop. Maybe the boys are singing in the pub. It's fine to take photos. Asking questions and chatting with the villagers is encouraged. What's a shilling? How was the pay? What about health care in the 1800s?

Stop by the pharmacy and check out the squirm-inducing setup of the dentist's chair—it'll make you appreciate the marvel of modern dental care. Down the street, kids like watching the candlemaker at work. Check the events in the barn across the path,

where hands-on candlemaking and other activities take place.

Just as it would've had in Victorian days, the village has a working pub, a greengrocer's shop, a fascinating squatter's cottage, and a snorty, slippery pigsty. Don't miss the explanation of the "winding engine" at the Blists Hill Mine (demos throughout the day). Walk along the canal to the "inclined plane."

Cost and Hours: £15, closes at 16:00 Nov-March, tel. 01952/601-048.

Eating in Blists Hill: Several places serve lunch: a café near the entrance, the New Inn Pub for beer and pub snacks, a traditional fish-and-chips joint, and the cafeteria near the children's old-time rides.

Coalbrookdale Museum of Iron and Abraham Darby's Furnace

The **museum,** while old-school, does a fine job of explaining the original iron-smelting process, and how iron (which makes up 95 percent of all industrial metal) changed our world. Compared to the fun and frolicking Blists Hill village, this museum is sleepy.

Across from the museum, standing like a shrine to the Industrial Revolution, is the **Abraham Darby Furnace.** The Coalbrookdale neighborhood is the birthplace of modern technology, where locals like to claim that mass production was invented. Darby's blast furnace sits inside a big glass pyramid, surrounded by evocative Industrial Age ruins. It was here that, in 1709, Darby first smelted iron, using coke as fuel. To me, "coke" is a drink, and "smelt" is the past tense of smell...but around here, these words recall the event that kicked off the modern Industrial Age.

All the ingredients of the recipe for big industry were here in abundance—iron ore, top-grade coal, and water for power and shipping. Wander around Abraham Darby's furnace. Before this furnace was built, iron ore was laboriously melted by charcoal. With huge waterwheel-powered bellows, Darby burned topgrade coal at super-hot temperatures (burning off the impurities to make "coke"). Local iron ore was dumped into the furnace and melted. Impurities floated to the top, while the pure iron sank to the bottom of a clay tub in the bottom of the furnace. Twice a day, the plugs were knocked off, allowing the "slag" to drain away on the top and the molten iron to drain out on the bottom. The lowgrade slag was used locally on walls and paths. The high-grade iron trickled into molds formed in the sand below the furnace. It cooled into pig iron (named because the molds look like piglets suckling their mother). The pig-iron "planks" were broken off by sledgehammers and shipped away. The Severn River became one of Europe's busiest, shipping pig iron to distant foundries, where it was melted again and made into cast iron (for projects such as the Iron Bridge), or to forges, where it was worked like toffee into wrought iron.

Cost: Museum-£8.75, includes entry to the Darby Houses

(listed later); £1 less in winter—when Darby Houses are closed for lack of light; furnace-free. A café is on site.

Enginuity

Enginuity is a hands-on funfest for kids. Riffing on Ironbridge's engineering roots, this converted 1709 foundry is full of entertaining-to-kids water contraptions, pumps, magnets, and laser games. Build a dam, try your hand at earthquake-proof construction, navigate a water maze, operate a remote-controlled robot, or power a turbine with your own steam.

Cost: £8, across the parking lot from the Coalbrookdale Museum of Iron.

Darby Houses

The Darby family, Quakers who were the area's richest residents by far, lived in these two homes located just above the Coalbrookdale Museum.

The 18th-century Darby mansion, **Rosehill House,** features a collection of fine china, furniture, and trinkets from various family members. It's decorated in the way the family home would have been in 1850. If the gilt-framed mirrors and fancy china seem a little ostentatious for the normally wealth-shunning Quakers, keep in mind that these folks were rich beyond reason, and—as docents will assure you—considering their vast wealth, this was relatively modest.

Skip the adjacent **Dale House.** Dating from the 1780s, it's older than Rosehill, but almost completely devoid of interior furniture, and its exhibits are rarely open.

Cost and Hours: Included in Coalbrookdale Museum of Iron ticket, otherwise £4.75; closed Nov-March.

Coalport China Museum, Jackfield Tile Museum, and Broseley Pipeworks

Housed in their original factories, these showcase the region's porcelain, decorated tiles, and clay tobacco pipes. These industries were developed to pick up the slack when the iron industry shifted away from the Severn Valley in the 1850s. Each museum features finely decorated pieces, and the china and tile museums offer low-energy workshops.

Cost and Hours: £5-8 each; Broseley Pipeworks open only in summer afternoons (mid-May-mid-Sept 13:00-17:00, closed mid-Sept-mid-May).

Near Ironbridge Gorge

Ironbridge Open-Air Museum of Steel Sculpture—This park is a striking tribute to the region's industrial heritage. Stroll the 10-acre grounds and spot works by Roy Kitchin and other sculptors stashed in the forest and perched in rolling grasslands.

Cost and Hours: £3, March-Nov Tue-Sun 10:00-17:00, closed Mon except bank holidays, closed Dec-Feb, free parking, 2 miles from Iron Bridge, Moss House, Cherry Tree Hill, Coalbrookdale, Telford, tel. 01952/433-152, http://steelsculpture.go2.co.uk.

Skiing and Swimming—There's a small, brush-covered **ski and snowboarding slope** with two Poma lifts at Telford Snowboard and Ski Centre in Madeley, two miles from Ironbridge Gorge; you'll see signs for it as you drive into Ironbridge Gorge (£11/hour including gear, less for kids, open practice times vary by day—schedule posted online, tel. 01952/382-688, www.telford.gov.uk /skicentre). A public **swimming pool** is up the road on Court Street (5-minute drive from town, Madeley Court Sports Centre, tel. 01952/382-770).

Royal Air Force (RAF) Museum Cosford—This Red Baron magnet displays more than 80 aircraft, from warplanes to rockets. Get the background on ejection seats and a primer on the principles of propulsion.

Cost and Hours: Free, parking-£2, daily March-Oct 10:00-18:00, Nov-Feb 10:00-17:00, last entry one hour before closing, Shifnal, Shropshire, on A41 near junction with M54, tel. 01902/376-200, www.rafmuseum.org.uk/cosford.

More Sights—If you're looking for reasons to linger in Ironbridge Gorge, these sights are all within a short drive: the medieval town of Shrewsbury, the abbey village of Much Wenlock, the scenic Long Mynd gorge at Church Stretton, the castle at Ludlow, and the steam railway at the river town of Bridgnorth. Shoppers like Chester (en route to points north).

Sleeping in Ironbridge Gorge

$$$ **Library House Guest House** is *Better Homes and Gardens*-elegant. Located in the town center, a half-block downhill from the bridge, it's a classy, friendly gem that actually used to be the village library. Each of its four rooms is a delight. The Chaucer Room, which includes a small garden, is the smallest and least expensive. Lizzie Steel offers a complimentary drink upon arrival (small Db-£80, larger Db-£90, twin Db-£100, £15 less for Sb, DVD library, Wi-Fi, free parking just up the road, 11 Severn Bank, Ironbridge Gorge, tel. 01952/432-299, www.libraryhouse .com, info@libraryhouse.com). Lizzie may be able to pick you up

---

Sleep Code

(£1 = about $1.60, country code: 44, area code: 01952)
S = Single, **D** = Double/Twin, **T** = Triple, **Q** = Quad, **b** = bathroom,
s = shower only. You can assume credit cards are accepted
and breakfast is included unless noted otherwise.

To help you sort easily through these listings, I've divided
the accommodations into three categories based on the price
for a standard double room with bath during high season:

$$$ Higher Priced—Most rooms £65 or more.
$$ Moderately Priced—Most rooms between £45-65.
$ Lower Priced—Most rooms £45 or less.

Prices can change without notice; verify the hotel's
current rates online or by email. For other updates, see www
.ricksteves.com/update.

---

from the Telford train station if you request it in advance.

$$ Tontine Hotel is the town's big, 12-room, musty,
Industrial Age hotel. Check out the historic photos in the bar
(S-£25, Sb-£40, D-£40, Db-£56, breakfast-£5, family rooms, if
booking in advance ask about discount with this book, restaurant,
The Square, tel. 01952/432-127, fax 01952/432-094, www.tontine
-hotel.com, tontinehotel@tiscali.co.uk).

Outside of Town

$$$ Calcutts House rents seven rooms in their 18th-century iron-
master's home and adjacent coach house. Rooms in the main house
are elegant, while the coach-house rooms are bright, modern, and
less expensive. Their inviting living room and garden are a plus.
Ask the owners, Colin and Sarah Williams, how the rooms were
named (Db-£55-90, price depends on room size, Wi-Fi, located
on Calcutts Road, tel. 01952/882-631, www.calcuttshouse.co.uk,
info@calcuttshouse.co.uk). From Calcutts House, it's a delightful
15-minute stroll down a former train track into town.

$ Coalport Youth Hostel, plush for a hostel, fills an old fac-
tory at the China Museum in Coalport (£15-20 bunks in mostly
4-bed dorms, bunk-bed Db-£32-48, £3 more for non-members,
includes sheets, reception open 7:30-23:00, no lockout, kitchen,
self-service laundry, High Street, tel. 01952/588-755, www.yha.org
.uk, ironbridge@yha.org.uk). Don't confuse this hostel with another
area hostel, Coalbrookdale, which is only available for groups.

$ Wilderhope Manor Youth Hostel, a beautifully remote
Elizabethan manor house from 1586, is one of Europe's best hostels.

On Wednesday and Sunday afternoons, tourists actually pay to see what hostelers get to sleep in (£19-23 bunks, under 18-£13.50, £3 more for non-members, single-sex dorms, family rooms available, reservations recommended, reception closed 12:00-15:00, restaurant open 17:30-20:00, laundry, tel. 01694/771-363, www.yha.org.uk, wilderhope@yha.org.uk). It's in Longville-in-the-Dale, six miles from Much Wenlock down B4371 toward Church Stretton.

Eating in Ironbridge Gorge

Restaurant Severn is the local favorite for a place with style that serves contemporary dishes. Choose from a £25 two-course fixed-price meal or a £28 three-course offering (evenings Wed-Sun, closed Mon-Tue, across from the Iron Bridge in the town center, reservations smart—especially on weekends, 33 High Street, tel. 01952/432-233).

Pondicherry, in a renovated former police station, serves delicious Indian curries and a few British dishes to keep the less adventurous happy. The mixed vegetarian sampler is popular even with meat-eaters. The basement holding cells are now little plush lounges—a great option if you'd like your pre-dinner drink "in prison" (£12-16 plates, daily 17:00-23:00, starts to get hopping after 19:00, 57 Waterloo Street, tel. 01952/433-055).

Da Vinci's serves good, though pricey, Italian food and has a dressy ambience (£15-20 main courses, Tue-Sat 19:00-22:00, closed Sun-Mon, 26 High Street, tel. 01952/432-250).

The Golden Ball Inn, a brewery back in the 18th century, is a popular pub known for its quality food and great atmosphere. Check out chef/owner Kevin Price's creative dishes listed on the big blackboard. You can dine with the friendly local crowd in the "bar," eat in back with the brewing gear in the more quiet—and formal—dining room, or munch on the lush garden patio. Kevin is serious about his beer, listing featured ales daily (£10-15 meals, food served Mon-Fri 12:00-14:30 & 18:00-21:00, Sat-Sun 12:00-20:30, reservations smart on weekends, 5-minute hike up Madeley Road from the town roundabout, 1 Newbridge Road, tel. 01952/432-179).

The Coalbrookdale Inn is filled with locals enjoying excellent ales and good food. This former "best pub in Britain" has a tradition of offering free samples from a lineup of featured beers. Ask which real ales are available (Mon-Thu 17:00-23:30, Fri-Sun 12:00-23:30, food served 12:00-14:00 & 18:00-21:00, no food Sun evening, reservations unnecessary for the bar but a good idea for the fancier restaurant, lively ladies' loo, across street from Coalbrookdale Museum of Iron, 1 mile from Ironbridge Gorge,

12 Wellington Road, tel. 01952/433-953, www.coalbrookdaleinn .co.uk).

The Malt House, located in an 18th-century beer house, is a very popular scene with the local twentysomething gang (£9-15 main courses, bar menu at their Jazz Bar, daily 12:00-22:00, near Museum of the Gorge, 5-minute walk from center, The Wharfage, tel. 01952/433-712). For nighttime action, The Malt House is *the* vibrant spot in town, with live rock music and a fun crowd (generally Thu-Sat).

Ironbridge Gorge Connections

Ironbridge Gorge is five miles southwest of Telford, which has the nearest train station.

Getting between Telford and Ironbridge Gorge: From Telford's train station, you can take Arriva bus #44 (2/hour) to Madeley High Street, where you can catch the Gorge Connect bus to get to the sights (for more on the Gorge Connect, see page 558). Or, if the timing is better, you may want to zip over to the Telford bus station on bus #55 (4/hour) or #44 (2/hour; either bus covered by £5 "Day Saver" fare), or pay £3 for a cab. Then, from the Telford bus station, take bus #77, #88, or #99 (covered by £5 "Day Saver" fare, 1-2/hour, 20-45 minutes, none on Sun) to get to the Ironbridge Gorge sights (and the Gorge Connect bus). The Telford bus station is part of a large modern mall, an easy place to wait for the buses to Ironbridge Gorge. Buses are run by Arriva (www .arrivabus.co.uk), but you can also call Traveline for departure times and other information (tel. 0871-200-2233, www.traveline .org.uk).

A **taxi** from Telford to Ironbridge Gorge costs about £10.

By Train from Telford to: Birmingham (2/hour, 1.25 hours, change in Wolverhampton), **Conwy** in North Wales (9/day, 2.25 hours, some change in Chester or Shrewsbury), **Blackpool** (hourly, 2.75 hours, 2 changes), **Keswick/Lake District** (every 1-2 hours, 4.5-5.5 hours; 3-3.75 hours to Penrith with 1-2 changes, then catch a bus to Keswick, hourly except Sun 8/day, 40 minutes, www .stagecoachbus.com), **Edinburgh** (every 1-2 hours, 4.5-5.5 hours, 1-2 changes). Train info: tel. 0845-748-4950, www.nationalrail .co.uk.

By Car from the South: Driving in from the **Cotswolds** and **Stratford,** take M40 to Birmingham, then M6 (direction northwest) through Birmingham. The traffic northbound through Birmingham is miserable from 14:00 to 20:00, especially on Fridays. Take one of two M6 options: free with traffic through the city center; or M6 Toll, which, for around £5, skirts you north of the center with nearly no traffic—a very good bet during rush hour. After Birmingham, follow signs to *Telford* via M54 (if on toll road, it'll be via A5). Leave M54 at the Telford/Ironbridge exit (Junction 4). Follow the brown *Ironbridge* signs through several roundabouts to Ironbridge Gorge. (Note: On maps, Ironbridge Gorge is often referred to as "Iron Bridge" or "Iron-Bridge.")

LIVERPOOL

Wedged between serene North Wales and the even-more-serene Lake District, Liverpool provides an opportunity to sample the "real" England, and is the best look at urban England outside of London.

Beatles fans flock to Liverpool to learn about the Fab Four's early days, but the city has much more to offer: most notably an excellent maritime-history museum and two good art museums, as well as a pair of striking cathedrals, a dramatic skyline mingling old red-brick nautical buildings and glassy new skyscrapers, and—most of all—the charm of the Liverpudlians.

Sitting at the mouth of the River Mersey, Liverpool has long been a major shipping center. Its port played a key role in several centuries of world history—as a point in the "triangular trade" of African slaves, a gateway for millions of New World-bound European emigrants, and a staging ground for the British Navy's Battle of the Atlantic against the Nazi's U-boat fleet. But Liverpool was devastated physically by WWII bombs, then economically by the advent of container shipping in the 1960s. Liverpudlians looked on helplessly as postwar recovery resources were steered elsewhere, the city's substantial wartime contributions seemingly ignored.

Despite the pride and attention garnered in the 1960s by a certain quartet of favorite sons, Liverpool continued to decline through the 1970s and 80s. The Toxteth Riots of 1981, sparked by the city's dizzyingly high unemployment, brought worldwide attention to Liverpool's troubles.

In recent years, however, things are finally looking up. The city's status as the 2008 European Capital of Culture spurred

On the Scouse

Nicknamed "Scousers" (after a traditional local stew, originally brought here by Norwegian immigrants), the people of Liverpool have a reputation for being relaxed, easygoing, and welcoming to visitors. The Scouse dialect comes with a distinctive lilt and quick wit (the latter likely a means of coping with long-term hardship)—think of the Beatles' familiar accents, and all their famously sarcastic off-the-cuff remarks, and you

get the picture. Many Liverpudlians attribute these qualities to the Celtic influence here: Liverpool is a melting pot of not only English culture, but also loads of Irish and Welsh, as well as arrivals from all over Europe and beyond (Liverpool's diverse population includes many of African descent). Liverpudlians are also famous for their passion for football (i.e., soccer), and the Liverpool FC team—as locals will be quick to tell you—is one of England's best.

major gentrification, EU funding, and a cultural renaissance. And, with some 50,000 students attending three universities in town, Liverpool is also a youthful city, with a pub or nightclub on every corner. Anyone who still thinks of Liverpool as a depressed industrial center is about a decade behind the times.

Planning Your Time

Liverpool deserves at least a few hours, but those willing to give it a full day or more won't be disappointed.

For the quickest visit, focus your time at the Albert Dock, home to The Beatles Story, Merseyside Maritime Museum, Tate Gallery (for contemporary art-lovers). If time allows, consider a Beatles bus tour (which also depart from the Albert Dock).

A full day buys you time either to delve into the rest of the city (explore the rejuvenated urban core, tour the city's cathedrals, and—for art-lovers—visit the Walker Art Gallery near the train station), to binge on more Beatles sights (visiting the boyhood homes of John and Paul), or a bit of both.

If you're here just for the Beatles, you can easily fill a day with Fab Four sights: Do the tour of John and Paul's homes in the morning, then return to the Albert Dock to visit The Beatles Story. Take an afternoon bus tour from the Albert Dock to the other Beatles sights in town, winding up at the "Cavern Quarter" to enjoy a Beatles cover band in the reconstructed Cavern Club. (Beatles bus tours zip past the John and Paul houses from the outside, but visiting the interiors takes more time and should be reserved well in advance.)

International Beatles Week, celebrated the last week of August, is a very busy time in Liverpool, with lots of live musical performances.

Orientation to Liverpool

(area code: 0151)
With about a half-million people, Liverpool is Britain's fifth-biggest city. Fortunately, most points of interest for visitors are concentrated in the generally pedestrian-friendly downtown area. You can walk from one end of this zone to the other in about 25 minutes. Since interesting sights and colorful neighborhoods are scattered throughout this area, it's enjoyable to connect your sight-seeing on foot. (Beatles sights, however, are spread far and wide—it's much easier to connect them with a tour.)

Tourist Information

Liverpool's TI is at the **Albert Dock** (daily 10:00-17:30, Nov-March until 17:00, just inland from The Beatles Story, tel. 0151/707-0729 or 0151/233-2008, www.visitliverpool.com). Pick up the free, good city map and the comprehensive *Liverpool Visitor Guide*, crammed with updated lists of museums, hotels, restaurants, shops, and more. Note: The Queens Square Centre pavilion marked with an "i" symbol provides local transit info only—it's not a TI.

Arrival in Liverpool

By Train: Most trains use the main **Lime Street train station.** The station has eateries, shops, and baggage storage (per item: 3

hours-£3, 6 hours-£5, 24 hours-£7, Mon-Thu 7:00-21:00, Fri-Sun 7:00-23:00; most bus tours and private minivan/car tours are able to accommodate people with luggage).

From this station to the Albert Dock, it's about a 20-minute walk (you can trim some time by riding a bus partway) or a £4-5 **taxi** trip.

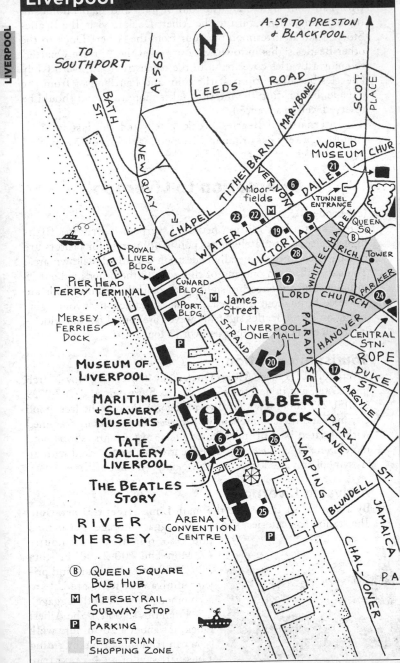

Liverpool

LIVERPOOL

TO SOUTHPORT

A-59 TO PRESTON & BLACKPOOL

BATH ST.

A-565

NEW QUAY

LEEDS ROAD

TITHE-BARN

MARYBONE

SCOT. PLACE

WORLD MUSEUM

CHUR.

21

CHAPEL

WATER

Moor-fields

VERNON

DALE

6

TUNNEL ENTRANCE

QUEEN SQ.

B

Royal Liver Bldg.

23

22

M

19

5

RICH.

Tower

VICTORIA

28

WHITECHAPEL

Pier Head Ferry Terminal

Cunard Bldg.

2

PARKER

Mersey Ferries Dock

M

James Street

Port. Bldg.

STRAND

LORD

CHURCH

HANOVER

24

Liverpool One Mall

PARADISE

Central Stn.

ROPE

Museum of Liverpool

P

20

17

DUKE ST.

Maritime & Slavery Museums

ALBERT DOCK

ARGYLE

PARK LANE

Tate Gallery Liverpool

i

6

26

WAPPING

The Beatles Story

7

27

25

BLUNDELL ST.

JAMAICA

RIVER MERSEY

Arena & Convention Centre

P

CHAL-ONER

PA

B QUEEN SQUARE BUS HUB

M MERSEYRAIL SUBWAY STOP

P PARKING

PEDESTRIAN SHOPPING ZONE

400 YARDS

400 METERS

CHILL

WALKER ART GALLERY

ST. GEORGE'S HALL

LONDON RD.

TO M-62

NELSON

LIME

LIME STREET STATION

METROPOLITAN CATHEDRAL (CATHOLIC)

SKEL.

BROWNLOW HILL

ELL.

LIME

RANE.

MOUNT

RENSHAW

PLEASANT

OX.

❸

❹

WALKS

SEEL

LEECE

HARD-MAN

❽

HOPE ST.

❶❶

MUL.

❶❻

BOMBED-OUT CHURCH

❶❺

❶

❶❹

MYRTLE

CHINA-TOWN

GREAT

❶❸

❶❷

❶❶

❶❽

MOUNT

UPPER DUKE

CANNING

LIVERPOOL CATHEDRAL (ANGLICAN)

JAMES

GEORGE

HOPE ST.

CATH.

ST.

ST.

RLIAMENT

A-562 TO WIDNES

TO SPEKE HALL, PENNY LANE & AIRPORT

Liverpool PENNY LANE L18

DCH

1 Hope Street Hotel
2 Hard Day's Night Hotel
3 Aachen Guest Accom.
4 Best Western Feathers Hotel
5 Sir Thomas Hotel
6 Premier Inns (2)
7 Holiday Inn Express
8 Internat'l Inn Hostel & Cocoon Pod Hotel
9 The Quarter Rest.
10 HOST
11 The Side Door
12 60 Hope Street
13 Yuet Ben
14 The Philharmonic Dining Rooms Pub
15 The Fly in the Loaf Pub
16 Alma de Cuba
17 Liverpool One Bridewell
18 Duke Street Eateries
19 Delifonseca
20 Liverpool One Eateries
21 The Ship and Mitre Pub
22 Thomas Rigby's Pub
23 Ye Hole in Ye Wall Pub
24 The Globe Pub
25 National Trust Beatles Tour Pick-Up Point (Mornings Only)
26 Magical Mystery Big Bus Tour Pick-Up Point
27 Yellow Duckmarine Tickets
28 Cavern Quarter (Mathew Street & Site of Original Cavern Club)

LIVERPOOL

Taxis wait outside either of the side doors of the station.

To **walk** (or take the **bus**), exit straight out the front door. On your right, you'll see the giant, Neoclassical St. George's Hall; the Walker Art Gallery is just beyond it. But to reach Albert Dock, go straight ahead across the street, then head down the hill between St. George's Hall (on your right) and the big blob-shaped mall (on your left). This brings you to Queens Square Centre, a hub for buses. (The round pavilion with the "i" symbol is a transit info center—see "Getting Around Liverpool," later.) To ride the bus the rest of the way to the Albert Dock, go to stall 2 (near the bottom of the row of buses) and take bus #C1 (2/hour, £1.60 one-way, £3.30 all-day ticket). But the bus isn't necessary, as the walk from here is pleasant and passes through Liverpool's spiffed-up central core: Walk around the right side of the transit-info pavilion, then turn left onto Whitechapel Street, which soon becomes a slick pedestrian zone lined with shopping malls. Follow this all the way down to the waterfront, where you'll see the big red-brick warehouses of the Albert Dock.

Regional trains also arrive at the much smaller, confusingly named **Central Station,** which is essentially a subway stop, located just a few blocks south.

By Plane: From Liverpool John Lennon Airport, take bus #500 to the city center; it stops both at the Queens Square Centre bus hub and at Lime Street train station (2/hour, £3). In front of the airport, look for the yellow submarine.

By Car: Drivers approaching Liverpool first follow signs to *City Centre* and *Waterfront,* then brown signs to *Albert Dock,* where you'll find a huge pay parking lot at the dock. If coming from Wales, take the toll tunnel under the River Mersey (£1.50) and follow signs for *Albert Dock.*

Getting Around Liverpool

The city is walkable (and fun to explore), so you likely won't need to take advantage of the local bus network. But if you do, and you'd like public-transit information, visit the Merseytravel pavilion at the main bus hub on Queens Square Centre, between Lime Street Station and the Albert Dock (Mon-Sat 8:30-18:00, Sun 10:00-17:00, Queens Square, tel. 0871-200-2233, www.merseytravel.gov.uk).

Tours in Liverpool

Beatles Bus Tours

If you want to see as many Beatles-related sights as possible in a short time, these tours are the way to go. Each drives by the houses where the Fab Four grew up (exteriors only), places they

LIVERPOOL

performed, and spots made famous by the lyrics of their hits ("Penny Lane," "Strawberry Fields," the Eleanor Rigby graveyard, and so on). Even lukewarm fans will enjoy the commentary and seeing the shelter on the roundabout, the barber who shaves another customer, and the banker who never wears a mack in the pouring rain. (Very strange.)

Several cheaper private-taxi tours have popped up around Liverpool. While I've heard some good reports about them, the quality is less reliable, and some of the guides aren't as well-versed in Beatles and Liverpool lore. I'd stick with the better-established companies listed below.

Magical Mystery Big Bus Tour—Beatles fans enjoy loading onto this old, psychedelically painted bus for a spin past Liverpool's main Beatles landmarks, with a few photo ops off the bus. With an enthusiastic, live commentary and Beatles tunes cued to famous landmarks, it leaves people happy (£16, 1.75 hours; daily year-round at 14:30; April-Oct and on off-season weekends and school holidays also at 12:00; often at other times as well—ask TI, call, or check online for schedule; buses depart from the Albert Dock near The Beatles Story and TI, tel. 0151/236-9091, www.beatlestour .org). As these tours often fill up, you'd be wise to book at least a day ahead by phone (through the Liverpool TI at tel. 0151/233-2459), or in person at the TI.

Phil Hughes Mini-Bus Beatles and Liverpool Tours—For something more extensive, fun, and intimate, consider a four-hour minibus Beatles tour from Phil Hughes. It's longer because it includes information on historic Liverpool, along with the Beatles stuff (and, for the *Titanic* centennial in 2012, Phil's added some sights related to that famous Liverpool-registered vessel). Phil organizes his tour to fit your schedule and will do his best to accommodate you (£17/person, £88/private group tour, can coordinate times with National Trust tour of Lennon and McCartney homes, 8-seat minibus, mobile 07961-511-223, tel. 0151/228-4565, www.tourliverpool.co.uk, tourliverpool@hotmail.com).

Jackie Spencer Private Tours—To tailor a visit to your schedule and interests, Jackie Spencer is at your service...just say when and where you want to go (up to 5 people in her minivan—£150, 2.5 hours, longer tours available, will pick you up at hotel or train station, mobile 0799-076-1478, www.beatleguides.com, jackie @beatleguides.com).

Other Tours

City Bus Tour—Two different hop-on, hop-off bus tours cruise around town, offering a quick way to get an overview that links all the major sights. The options are **City Sightseeing** (£8, buy ticket from driver, valid for 24 hours, recorded commentary, 15 stops, daily April-Oct 10:00-17:00, 3-4/hour, less frequent Nov-March, tel. 0151/203-3920, www.city-sightseeing.com) and **City Explorer** (£7, pay driver, ticket valid 24 hours, live guides, 12 stops; March-Oct 2/hour 10:00-16:00; Nov-Feb until 15:00—1/hour Mon-Fri, 2/hour Sat-Sun; tel. 0151/933-2324, www.cityexplorerliverpool .co.uk).

Ferry Cruise—Mersey Ferries offers narrated cruises that depart from the Pier Head ferry terminal, an easy five-minute walk north of the Albert Dock. The 50-minute cruise makes two brief stops on the other side of the river; you can hop off and catch the next boat back (£6.70, runs year-round, Mon-Fri 10:00-15:00, Sat-Sun 10:00-18:00, leaves Pier Head at top of hour, café, WCs onboard, tel. 0151/330-1000, www.merseyferries.co.uk).

"Yellow Duckmarine" Harbor and City Tour—This company runs wacky one-hour tours of Liverpool's waterfront, city, and docks by land and by sea in its amphibious WWII-era tourist assault vehicles. You'll spend a half-hour on land, and a half-hour in the water (in the docks, not actually out on the River Mersey). Be prepared to quack (£10, increases to £13 in summer and on school holidays, £29 family ticket for 2 adults and 2 kids jumps to £38 in summer and on holidays, buy tickets at office on the Albert Dock near The Beatles Story, departs from the Albert Dock every 30 minutes daily 10:30-17:00, more frequently and until 18:00 on busy days, tel. 0151/708-7799, www.theyellowduckmarine.co.uk).

Sights in Liverpool

▲Lennon and McCartney Homes

John and Paul's boyhood homes are now owned by the National Trust and have both been restored to how they looked during their 1950s childhoods. While some Beatles bus tours stop here for photo ops, only the National Trust minibus tour gets you inside the homes. This isn't Graceland—you won't find an over-the-top rock-and-roll extravaganza here. If you don't know the difference between John and Paul, you'll likely be bored. But for die-hard Beatles fans who want to get a glimpse into the time and place that created these musical masterminds, the National Trust tour is worth ▲▲▲.

Because the houses are in residential neighborhoods—and still share walls with neighbors—the National Trust runs only four tours per day in summer (Wed-Sun only), limited to 15

Beatlemaniacs each. Just 7,000 people pass through these doors each year.

Cost and Reservations: £20; because only 15 people are allowed on each tour, it's smart to make a reservation ahead of time, especially for morning tours and on weekends. If you're here in July, Aug, or any summer weekend or holiday, it's smart to reserve up to two weeks ahead; at other times, a day or two in advance is usually enough. You can reserve online (www.national trust.org.uk/beatles), or by calling 0151/427-7231. If you haven't reserved ahead, you can try to book a same-day tour (for the morning tours, call 0151/707-0729). Afternoon tours are less likely to be full, but that's because it takes 30 minutes (by car or taxi) to reach the tour's starting point from central Liverpool—see below.

Tour Options: A National Trust minibus will take you first to John's home, then Paul's, with about 45 minutes inside each. From mid-March to Oct, tours run four times per day Wed-Sun (no tours Mon-Tue). Morning tours (at 10:00 and 10:50) follow a more scenic route that includes a quick pass by Penny Lane; these are more convenient, as they depart from the Jurys Inn at the Albert Dock (south across the bridge from The Beatles Story, near the Ferris wheel).

Afternoon tours (at 14:30 and 15:20) leave from Speke Hall, an out-of-the-way National Trust property located eight miles southeast of Liverpool. Drivers should allow 30 minutes from the city center to Speke Hall—follow the brown *Speke Hall* signs through dozens of roundabouts, heading in the general direction of the airport. If you don't have a car, you'll need to hop in a taxi.

From either starting point, the entire visit takes about two hours round-trip.

Off-Season: From late Feb to mid-March and in Nov, tours leave Wed-Sun at 10:00, 12:30, and 15:00, and all depart from the handy Jurys Inn at the Albert Dock. No tours run in winter (Dec-late Feb).

Guides: Each home has a live-in caretaker who acts as your guide. These folks give an entertaining, insightful-to-fans 20- to 30-minute talk, and then leave you time (10-15 minutes) to wander through the house on your own. Ask lots of questions if their spiel peters out early—these docents are a wealth of information.

Mendips (John Lennon's Home)—Even though he sang about being a working-class hero, John grew up in the suburbs of Liverpool, surrounded by doctors, lawyers, and—beyond the back fence—Strawberry Field.

This was the home of John's Aunt Mimi, who raised him in this house from the time he was five years old and once told him, "A guitar's all right, John, but you'll never earn a living by it." (John later bought Mimi a country cottage with those fateful

The Beatles in Liverpool

The most iconic rock-and-roll band of all time was made up of four Liverpudlians who spent their formative years amidst the bombed-out shell of WWII-era Liverpool. The city has become a pilgrimage site for Beatlemaniacs, but even those with just a passing interest in the Fab Four are likely to find themselves humming their favorite tunes around town. Most Beatles sights in Liverpool relate to their early days, before the psychedelia, transcendental meditation, Yoko, and solo careers. Because these sights are so spread out, the easiest way to connect all of them in one go is by tour (see "Tours in Liverpool").

All four of the Beatles were born in Liverpool, and any tour of town glides by the **home** most identified with each one's childhood: John Lennon at "Mendips," Paul McCartney at 20 Forthlin Road, George Harrison at 12 Arnold Grove, and Ringo Starr (a.k.a. Richard Starkey) at 10 Admiral Grove.

Behind John's house at Mendips is a wooded area called **Strawberry Field** (he added the "s" for the song). This surrounds a Victorian mansion that was, at various times, a Salvation Army home and an orphanage. John enjoyed sneaking into the trees around the mansion to play. Today visitors pose in front of Strawberry Field's red gate (a replica of the original).

During the Beatles' formative years in the mid-1950s, skiffle music (American-inspired rockabilly/folk) swept through Liverpool. As a teenager, John formed a skiffle band called the Quarrymen. Paul met John for the first time when he saw the Quarrymen on July 6, 1957, at **St. Peter's Church** in Woolton. After the show, in the social hall across the street, Paul noted that John played only banjo chords (his mother had taught him to play on a banjo rather than a guitar—he didn't even know how to tune a guitar), and improvised many lyrics. John, two years older, realized he was a better improviser than a musician, so he was impressed when Paul borrowed a guitar, tuned it effortlessly, and played a note-perfect rendition of Eddie Cochran's "Twenty Flight Rock." Before long, Paul had joined the band.

In the St. Peter's Church graveyard is a headstone for a woman named **Eleanor Rigby.** But to this day, Paul swears that he never saw it, and made up the name for that famous song. Either he's lying, the name crept into his subconscious, or it's a truly remarkable coincidence.

The boys went to school on **Mount Street** in the center of Liverpool (near Hope Street, between the two cathedrals). John and his friend Stuart Sutcliffe attended the Liverpool College of Art, and Paul and his pal George Harrison went to Liverpool Institute High School for Boys. (When Paul introduced George to John as a possible new member for the band, John dismissed him as being too young...until he heard George play. He immediately became the lead guitarist.) Paul later bought his old school building and turned it into the Liverpool Institute for Performing Arts (LIPA)—nicknamed the "Fame Academy" for the similar school on the American TV series.

As young men, the boys rode the bus together to school—waiting at a bus stop in the **Penny Lane** neighborhood. Later they wrote a nostalgic song about the things they would observe while waiting there: The shelter by the roundabout, the barbershop, and so on. (While they also sing about the fireman with the clean machine, the firehouse itself is not actually on Penny Lane, but around the corner.)

After a series of lineup shuffles, by 1960 the group had officially become The Beatles: John Lennon, Paul McCartney,

George Harrison, and...Pete Best and Stu Sutcliffe. The quintet gradually built a name for themselves in Liverpool's "Merseybeat" scene, performing at local clubs. While the famous **Cavern Club** is gone (the one you see advertised is a reconstruction, but does offer similar ambience and good cover bands), the original **Casbah Coffee Club**—which the group felt more attached to—still exists and is open for tours (3.5 miles northwest of downtown in Pete Best's former basement, www.casbahcoffeeclub.com).

The group went to Hamburg, Germany, to cut their teeth in the thriving music scene there. They wound up performing as the backing band for Tony Sheridan's single "My Bonny." When this caught on back in Liverpool, record-store owner and promoter Brian Epstein took note, and signed the act. His shrewd management would eventually propel the Beatles to superstardom.

Many different people could be considered the "Fifth Beatle." John's friend Stu, who performed with the group in Hamburg, left to pursue his own artistic interests. Pete Best was the band's original drummer, but he was a loner and producers questioned his musical chops, so he was replaced with Ringo Starr. (John later said, "Pete Best was a great drummer, but Ringo was a Beatle.") Brian Epstein, the manager who marketed the Beatles brilliantly before his untimely death, is another candidate. But—in terms of long-term musical influence—it's hard to ignore the case for George Martin, who produced all of the Beatles' albums except *Let It Be,* and was instrumental in both forging and developing the Beatles sound.

By 1963, the Beatles were already world-famous—but, as evidenced by their songs about Penny Lane and Strawberry Fields, they never forgot their Merseyside home.

words etched over the fireplace.) John moved out at age 23, but his first wife, Cynthia, bunked here for a while when John made his famous first trip to America. Yoko Ono bought the house in 2002, and gave it as a gift to the National Trust (generating controversy among the neighbors). The stewards, Colin and Sylvia, make this place come to life.

On the surface, it's just a 1930s house carefully restored to how it would have been in the past. But delve deeper. It's been lovingly cared for—restored to be the tidy, well-kept place Mimi would have recognized (down to her apron hanging in the kitchen). It's a lucky quirk of fate that the house's interior remained mostly unchanged after the Lennons left: The bachelor who owned it decades after them didn't upgrade much, so even the light switches are true to the time.

If you're a John Lennon fan, it's fun to picture him as a young boy drawing and imagining at his dining room table. It also makes for an interesting comparison to Paul's humbler home, which is the second part of the tour.

20 Forthlin Road (Paul McCartney's Home)—In comparison to Aunt Mimi's house, the home where Paul grew up is simpler, much less "posh," and even a little ratty around the edges. Michael, Paul's brother, wanted it that way—their mother, Mary (famously mentioned in "Let It Be"), died when the boys were young, and it never had the tidiness of a woman's touch. It's been intentionally scuffed up around the edges to preserve the historical accuracy. Notice the differences—Paul has said that John's house was vastly different and more clearly middle class; at Mendips, there were books on the bookshelves.

More than a hundred Beatles songs were written in this house (including "I Saw Her Standing There") during days Paul and John spent skipping school. The photos from Michael, taken in this house, help make the scene of what's mostly a barren interior much more interesting.

On the Waterfront

In its day, Liverpool was England's greatest seaport, but trade declined after 1890, as the port wasn't deep enough for the big new ships. The advent of mega container ships in the 1960s put the final nail in the port's coffin, and by 1972 it was closed entirely.

But over the last decade, this formerly derelict and dangerous area has been the focus of the city's rejuvenation efforts. Liverpool's waterfront is now a venue for some of the city's top attractions. Three zones interest tourists (from south to north): The Wapping Dock area, with Liverpool's futuristic new arena, conference center, and adjacent Ferris wheel; the red-brick Albert Dock complex, with some of the city's top museums and lively restaurants and nightlife; and Pier Head, with the new Museum of Liverpool, ferries across the River Mersey, and buildings both old/stately and new/glassy. Below are descriptions of the main sights at the Albert Dock and Pier Head.

At the Albert Dock

Opened in 1852 by Prince Albert, and enclosing seven acres of water, the Albert Dock is surrounded by five-story brick warehouses. A half-dozen trendy eateries are lined up here, protected from the rain by arcades and padded by lots of shopping mall-type distractions. There's plenty of pay parking.

▲**The Beatles Story**—It's sad to think the Beatles are stuck in a museum. Still, this exhibit—while overpriced and a bit small—

is well-done, the story's a fascinating one, and even an avid fan will pick up some new information. The Beatles Story has two parts: the original, main exhibit at the south end of the Albert Dock; and a much smaller branch in the Pier Head ferry terminal, near the Museum of Liverpool just to the north.

Cost and Hours: £13 covers both parts, includes audioguide, daily May-Sept 9:00-19:00, Oct-April 10:00-18:00, last entry 2 hours before closing, tel. 0151/709-1963, www.beatlesstory.com.

Main Exhibit: Listen to the audioguide as you take a chronological stroll through the evolution of the Beatles, focusing on their Liverpool years: meeting as schoolboys, performing at (and helping decorate) the Casbah Coffee Club, making a name for themselves in Hamburg, meeting their manager Brian Epstein, and

LIVERPOOL

the advent of worldwide Beatlemania (with some help from Ed Sullivan). There are many actual artifacts (from George Harrison's first boyhood guitar to John Lennon's orange-tinted "Imagine" glasses), as well as large dioramas celebrating landmarks in Beatles lore (a reconstruction of the Cavern Club, a life-size recreation of the *Sgt. Pepper* album cover, and a walk-through yellow submarine). The last few rooms trace the members' solo careers, and the last few steps are reserved for reverence about John's peace work, including a re-creation of the white room he used while writing "Imagine." Rounding out the exhibits are a "Discovery Zone" for kids, and (of course) the "Fab Store," with an impressive pile of Beatles buyables.

The great audioguide, narrated by Julia Baird (John Lennon's little sister), captures the Beatles' charm and cheekiness in a way the stiff wax mannequins can't. You'll hear clips of interviews from the actual participants in the Beatles' story—their families, friends, and collaborators. Cynthia Lennon, John's first wife, still marvels at the manic power of Beatlemania.

While this is a fairly sanitized look at the Fab Four (LSD and Yoko-related conflicts are glossed over), the exhibits remind listeners of all that made the group earth-shattering—and even a little edgy—at the time. For example, performing before the Queen Mother, John Lennon famously quips: "Will the people in the cheaper seats clap your hands? And the rest of you, if you'll just rattle your jewelry."

Pier Head Exhibit: The second part of The Beatles Story is less interesting, but since it's included with the ticket, it's worth dropping into if you have the time. You'll find it upstairs in the Pier Head ferry terminal, about a 10-minute walk north (at the opposite end of the Albert Dock, then another 5-minute walk across the bridge and past the Museum of Liverpool). The main feature here is a corny "Fab 4D Experience," an animated movie that strings together Beatles tunes into something resembling a plot while mainly offering an excuse to play around with 3-D effects and other surprises (such as the smell of strawberries when you hear "Strawberry Fields Forever"). The Hidden Gallery displays recently rediscovered early photos of the moptops by then-teenaged photographer Paul Berriff. Through 2013, the museum also features the temporary exhibit "Elvis and Us," about the relationship between the Beatles and their fellow 1960s music icon.

▲**Merseyside Maritime Museum and International Slavery Museum**—These museums tell the story of Liverpool, once the second city of the British Empire. The third floor covers slavery, while the first, second, and basement handle other maritime topics.

Cost and Hours: Free, daily 10:00-17:00, café, tel. 0151/478-

4499, www.liverpoolmuseums.org.uk.

Background: Liverpool's port prospered in the 18th century as one corner of a commerce triangle with Africa and America. British shippers profited greatly through exploitation: About 1.5 million enslaved African people passed through Liverpool's docks (that's 10 percent of all African slaves). From Liverpool, the British exported manufactured goods to Africa in exchange for enslaved Africans; the slaves were then shipped to the Americas, where they were traded for raw material (cotton, sugar, and tobacco); and the goods were then brought back to Britain. While the merchants on all three sides made money, the big profit came home to England (which enjoyed substantial income from customs, duties, and a thriving smugglers' market). As Britain's economy boomed, so did Liverpool's.

After participation in the slave trade was outlawed in Britain in the early 1800s, Liverpool kept its port busy as a transfer point for emigrants. If your ancestors came from Scandinavia, Ukraine, or Ireland, they likely left Europe from this port. Between 1830 and 1930, nine million emigrants sailed from Liverpool to find their dreams in the New World.

Touring the Museums: Begin by riding the elevator up to Floor 3—we'll work our way back down.

On the Floor 3, three galleries make up the **International Slavery Museum.** First is a description of life in West Africa, which re-creates traditional domestic architecture and displays actual artifacts. Then comes a harrowing exhibit about enslavement and the "Middle Passage." The tools of the enslavers—chains, muzzles, and a branding iron—and the intense film about the Middle Passage sea voyage to America, drive home the horrifying experience of being abducted from your home and taken in wretched, life-threatening conditions thousands of miles away to toil for a wealthy stranger. Finally the museum examines the legacy of slavery—both the persistence of racism in contemporary society, and the substantial positive impact that people of African descent have had on European and American cultures. Walls of photos celebrate important people of African descent, and the music desk lets you sample songs from a variety of African-influenced genres.

Continue down the stairs to the **Maritime Museum,** on Floor 2. This celebrates Liverpool's shipbuilding heritage and displays actual ship components, model boats, and a gallery of nautical paintings.

Floor 1 shows footage and artifacts of three big Liverpool-related **shipwrecks:** the *Lusitania*, the *Empress of Ireland*, and the *Titanic* (all of which were destroyed—by a German U-Boat, accidental crash with a coal freighter, and iceberg, respectively—in a tragically short span of time between 1912 and 1915). Also on this floor, an extensive exhibit traces the **Battle of the Atlantic** (during World War II, Nazi U-Boats attacked merchant ships bringing supplies to Britain, in an attempt to cripple this island nation). You'll see how crew members lived aboard merchant ships. The **Hello Sailor!** exhibit explains how gay culture flourished at sea at a time where it was taboo in almost every other walk of British life.

Make your way to the basement, where exhibits describe the tremendous wave of **emigration** through Liverpool's port (between 1830 and 1930, some 9 million Europeans charted their course to the New World through the docks of Liverpool). And the **Seized!** exhibit looks at the legal and illegal movement of goods through that same port, including thought-provoking displays on customs, taxation, and smuggling.

Tate Gallery Liverpool—This prestigious gallery of modern art is near the Maritime Museum. It won't entertain you as well as its London sister, the Tate Modern, but if you're into modern art, any Tate's great. Its two airy floors, dedicated to the rotating collection of statues and paintings from the 20th century, are free; the top and ground floors are devoted to special exhibits.

Cost and Hours: Free, £3 suggested donation, £7-13 for special exhibits; daily 10:00-18:00 except closes at 17:00 mid-Oct-March, tel. 0151/702-7400, www.tate.org.uk/liverpool. The Tate has a nice, inexpensive café.

At Pier Head, North of the Albert Dock

A five-minute walk across the bridge north of the Albert Dock takes you to the Pier Head area, with the following sights.

▲Museum of Liverpool—This brand-new museum, in the blocky white building just across the bridge north of the Albert Dock, promises to "capture Liverpool's vibrant character and demonstrate the city's unique contribution to the world."

Displays are divided into four main themes: **The Great Port** details the story of Liverpool's defining industry, and how it developed through the Industrial Revolution. On display are an 1838 steam locomotive and a car from the turn-of-the-century Liverpool Overhead Railway (with 1897 movie footage shot from the elevated train line). **Global City** considers how Liverpool's status as a major British shipping center made it the gateway to a global empire upon which the sun never set. This area also features "The Liverpool Story" film about the history of the city. **People's Republic** examines what it is to be a

Liverpudlian (a.k.a. "Scouser"). As industrialized Liverpool has long been a hotbed of the labor movement, exhibits here also detail the political side of the city. And **Wondrous Place** celebrates the Liverpudlians who have made an impact on the rest of the world, including an exhibit on the city's famous passion for its local soccer teams (the "Kicking and Screaming" film immerses the viewer in the enthusiasm), and the original stage from St. Peter's Church, where John Lennon was performing the first time Paul McCartney laid eyes on him.

Also look for two dramatic depictions of Liverpool: The Liverpool Map is a 3-D glass sculpture of the city and its landmarks, while Ben Johnson's painting *The Liverpool Cityscape, 2008* is a remarkable and fun-to-examine melding of old and new art styles. At first glance, it's a typical skyline painting, but Johnson used computer models to create perfect depictions of each building before he put brush to canvas. This method allows for a photorealistic, highly detailed, but completely sanitized portrait of a city. Notice there are no cars or people.

Cost and Hours: Free, daily 10:00-17:00, Mann Island, Pier Head, www.liverpoolmuseums.org.uk/mol.

The Three Graces—Three towering buildings near the Museum of Liverpool, remnants of a time of great seafaring prosperity, are

known collectively as Liverpool's Three Graces: The double-clock-towered Royal Liver Building, with spires topped by the city's mythical mascot, the "Liver birds"; the relatively dull and boxy Cunard Building; and the domed Port of Liverpool Building, which strains to evoke memories of St. Paul's Cathedral in London. A 2002 plan to create a Fourth Grace—a metallic, glassy, and yellow blob called The Cloud—never panned out (it's being built in Toronto instead), and that site is now home to the

Museum of Liverpool (described earlier). While you can see the Three Graces from along the embankment—which is also lined with monuments to important Liverpudlians—the best views are from across the River Mersey (see page 598 for details on riding the ferry; note that the Pier Head ferry terminal also hosts some exhibits from The Beatles Story).

Downtown

Beatles Sights in the "Cavern Quarter"

The narrow, bar-lined Mathew Street, right in the heart of downtown, is ground zero for Beatles fans. The Beatles frequently performed in their early days together at the original Cavern Club, deep in a cellar along this street. While that's long gone, a mockup of the historic nightspot (built with many of the original bricks) lives on a few doors down. Still billed as "the **Cavern Club**," this is worth a visit to see the reconstructed cellar that's often filled by Beatles cover bands. While touristy, dropping by in the afternoon for a live Beatles tribute act in the Cavern Club somehow just feels right. You'll have Beatles songs stuck in your head all day anyway, so you might as well see a wannabe John

and Paul strumming and harmonizing a close approximation of the original (live music daily from 15:30, no cover charge except Thu-Sun after 20:00; open daily 11:00-24:00, later Thu-Sat, tel. 0151/236-9091, www.cavernclub.org).

Across the street and run by the same owners, the **Cavern Pub** lacks its sibling's troglodyte aura, but makes up for it with walls lined with old photos and memorabilia from the Beatles and other bands who've performed here. Like the Cavern Club, the pub features frequent performances by Beatles cover bands and

other acts (no cover, similar hours to the Club).

Out front is the Cavern's **Wall of Fame,** with a too-cool-for-school bronze John Lennon leaning up against a wall with bricks engraved with the names of musical acts that have graced the Cavern stage.

At the corner is the recommended **Hard Day's Night Hotel,** decorated inside and out to honor the Fab Four. Notice the statues of John, Paul, George, and Ringo on the second-story corners,

and the Beatles gift shop (one of many in town) on the ground floor.

Museums near the Train Station

Both of these museums are just a five-minute walk from the train station.

▲**Walker Art Gallery**—Though it has few recognizable works, Liverpool's main art galley offers an enjoyable walk through an easy-to-digest collection of European (mostly British) paintings, sculpture, and decorative arts. There's no audioguide, but many of the works are well-explained by posted descriptions.

LIVERPOOL

Cost and Hours: Free, £2 suggested donation, daily 10:00-17:00, William Brown Street, tel. 0151/478-4199, www.liverpool museums.org.uk.

○ **Self-Guided Tour:** The ground floor has an information

desk, café, children's area, small decorative arts collection, and sculpture gallery focusing on British Neoclassical works from the 19th century. The sculpture gallery has many works by John Gibson, a Welshman who grew up in Liverpool, and later studied under the Italian master Antonio Canova. Gibson's *Tinted Venus* was considered scandalous to Victorian mores because of the nude sculpture's lifelike pinkish tint.

Upstairs is a concise 15-room painting gallery, plus special exhibits. For a chronological spin, from the top of the stairs

head straight back to find Room 1, with a famous Nicholas Hilliard portrait of Queen Elizabeth I (nicknamed "The Pelican," for her brooch). In the adjacent Room 3 is another well-known royal portrait, of Henry VIII by Hans Holbein, as well as bombastic Baroque works by Rubens and Murillo. Room 4 features a Rembrandt self-portrait, while Room 5 focuses on 18th-century English painting, including canvases by Gainsborough, Hogarth (find the painting of the great actor David Garrick in the role of Richard III), and lots of George Stubbs. Rooms 6-8 feature a delightful array of Pre-Raphaelite works, among them Millias' evocative portrait of Isabella (Room 6). You'll find some Turners (a mushy landscape and a more sharp-focus Linlithgow Castle) in Room 7. For a counterpoint to the lyrical, mystical Pre-Raphaelite works, step into Room 9, with very literal Victorian narrative paintings depicting slices of English life, such as Sadler's *Friday* (showing Dominican monks feasting on fish) and Yeams' *And When Did You Last See Your Father?* On this chilling canvas, showing a scene from the English Civil War, authorities are slyly interrogating a naive, cherub-like boy while his family watches from behind, terrified that the child will reveal where his father is hiding.

Room 10 makes the transition to the 20th century and Impressionism, while modern British art dominates the rest of the gallery. In Room 11, Bernard Fleetwood-Walker's *Amity* shows a pair of chaste but (apparently) sexually charged teenagers relaxing in the grass.

World Museum—This catch-all family museum features five floors of kid-oriented exhibits. You'll see dinosaurs, an aquarium, artifacts from ancient Greece and Egypt, a planetarium and theater (get free tickets at the info desk in the lobby for these), and more.

   Cost and Hours: Free but £2 suggested donation, daily 10:00-17:00, William Brown Street, tel. 0151/478-4393, www.liverpool museums.org.uk.

Cathedrals

Liverpool has not one but two notable cathedrals—one Anglican, the other Catholic. (As the Spinners song puts it, "If you want a cathedral, we've got one to spare.") Both are huge, architecturally significant, and well worth visiting. Near the eastern edge of downtown, they're connected by a 10-minute, half-mile walk on pleasant Hope Street, which is lined with theaters and good restaurants (see "Eating in Liverpool," later).

   Liverpudlians enjoy pointing out that they have not only the world's only Catholic cathedral designed by a Protestant architect, but also the only Protestant one designed by a Catholic. With its large Irish-immigrant population, for much of its history Liverpool suffered from tension between its Catholic and Protestant communities. But during the city's darkest stretch of the depressed 1970s, the bishops of each church—Anglican Bishop David Sheppard and Catholic Archbishop Derek Worlock—came together and worked hard to reconcile the two communities for the betterment of Liverpool. (Liverpudlians nicknamed this dynamic duo "fish and chips" because they were "always together, and always in the newspaper.") It worked: Liverpool is a bold new cultural center, and relations between the two faiths remain healthy here. Join in this ecumenical spirit by visiting both of their main churches.

   ▲▲Metropolitan Cathedral of Christ the King (Catholic)—This daringly modern building, a cone topped with a crowned cylinder, seems almost out of place in its workaday Liverpool neighborhood. But the cathedral you see today bears no resemblance to Sir Edwin Lutyens' original 1930s plans for a stately Neo-Byzantine cathedral bigger than St. Peter's Basilica in Vatican City. (Lutyens was desperate to one-up the grandiose plans of Sir Giles Gilbert Scott, who was building the

Anglican Cathedral down the street—described next.) The crypt for the ambitious church was excavated in the 1930s, but World War II stalled progress for decades. In the 1960s, the plans were scaled back, and this smaller (but still impressive) house of worship was completed in 1967.

Cost and Hours: Cathedral—free entry but donations accepted, daily 8:00-18:00 (until 17:00 on Sun in winter)—but after 17:15 only people attending Mass are allowed inside; crypt—£3, Mon-Sat 10:00-16:00, last entry at 15:15, closed Sun, enter from inside church near organ; visitors center/café/gift shop—Mon-Sat 10:00-17:00, Sun 11:00-16:00; Mount Pleasant, tel. 0151/709-9222, www.liverpoolmetrocathedral.org.uk.

Touring the Cathedral: On the stepped plaza in front of the church, you'll see the entrance to the cathedral's visitors center and café (on your right). You're standing on a big concrete slab that provides a roof to the humongous Lutyens Crypt, underfoot. The existing cathedral occupies only a small part of the would-be cathedral's footprint. Imagine what might have been—"the greatest building never built." Because of the cathedral's tentlike appearance and ties to the local Irish community, some Liverpudlians dubbed it "Paddy's Wigwam."

Climb up the stairs to the main doors, step inside, and let your eyes adjust to this magnificent, dimly lit space. Unlike a typical nave-plus-transept cross-shaped church, this cathedral has a round foot-print, with seating for a congregation of 3,000 fully surrounding the white marble altar. Like a "theater in the round," it was designed to involve worshippers in the service. Suspended above the altar is a stylized crown of thorns.

Spinning off from the round central sanctuary are 13 smaller chapels, many of them representing different stages of Jesus' life. Each chapel is different. Explore, tuning into the symbolic details in each one. Also keep an eye out for the exquisite bronze Stations of the Cross by local artist Sean Rice.

The massive **Lutyens Crypt** (named for the ambitious original architect)—the only part of the originally planned cathedral to be completed—doesn't quite match the church. But it's interesting to explore its huge vaults and vast halls, visit the treasury, and see an exhibit about the cathedral's construction.

▲▲**Liverpool Cathedral (Anglican)**—The largest cathedral in Great Britain, this gigantic house of worship hovers at the south end of downtown. Tour its cavernous interior and consider scaling its tower.

Cost and Hours: Free but £3 suggested donation, daily 8:00-18:00; £5 ticket includes tower climb, audioguide, and 10-minute "Great Space" film—last showing at 16:00 Mon-Sat and 13:30 on Sun, last tower ascent at 16:30 Mon-Sat and 15:30 on Sun; St. James Mount, tel. 0151/709-6271, www.liverpoolcathedral.org.uk.

❍ **Self-Guided Tour:** Over the main door is a modern *Risen Christ* statue by Elisabeth Frink. Liverpudlians, not thrilled with the featureless statue and always quick with a joke, have dubbed it **"Frinkenstein."**

Stepping inside, pick up a floor plan at the information desk, go into the main hall, and take in the size of the place. When Liverpool was officially designated a "city" (seat of a bishop), they wanted to build a huge house of worship as a symbol of Liverpudlian pride. Built in bold Neo-Gothic style (like London's Parliament), it seems to trumpet with modern bombast the importance of this city on the Mersey. Begun in 1904, the cathedral's construction was interrupted by the tumultuous 20th century, and not completed until 1973.

Go to the big, circular tile in the very center of the cathedral, under the highest tower. This is a plaque for the building's architect, **Sir Giles Gilbert Scott** (1880-1960). While the church you're surrounded by may seem like his biggest legacy, he also designed an icon that's synonymous with Britain: the classic red telephone box. Flanking this aisle, notice the highly detailed sandstone carvings.

Take a counterclockwise spin around the church interior, heading up the right aisle. Find the **model** of the original plan for the cathedral (press the button to light it up). Scott was a very young architect, and received the commission with the agreement that he work closely under the wing of his more established mentor, George Bodley. These two architects' visions clashed, and Bodley usually won...until he died early in the planning stages, leaving Scott to pursue his own muse. If Bodley had survived, the cathedral would probably look more like this model. As it was, only one corner of the complex (the Lady Chapel, which we're about to see)

was completed before Giles changed plans to create the version you see today.

Nearby, the **"whispering arch"** spanning over the sarcophagus has remarkable acoustics, carrying voices from one end to the other. Try it.

Continuing down the church, notice the very colorful, modern painting of *The Good Samaritan* (by Adrian Wiszniewski, 1995) high above on the right. The naked

crime victim (who has been stabbed in his side, like the Crucifixion wound of Jesus) has been ignored by the well-dressed yuppies in the foreground, but the female Samaritan is finally taking notice. The canvas is packed with symbolism (for example, the Swiss Army knife, in a pool of blood in the left foreground, is open in the 3 o'clock position—the time that Jesus was crucified). This contemporary work of art demonstrates that this is a new, living church. But the congregation has its limits. This painting used to hang closer to the front of the church, but now they've moved it here, out of sight.

Proceeding to the corner, you'll reach the entrance to the oldest part of the church (1910): the **Lady Chapel,** with stained-glass

windows celebrating important women. (Sadly, the original windows were destroyed in World War II; these are replicas.)

Back up in the main part of the church, continue behind the main altar, to the **Education Centre,** with a fun, sped-up video showing all of the daily work it takes to make this cathedral run.

Circling around the far corner of the church, you'll pass the children's chapel and chapterhouse, and then pass under another modern Wiszniewski painting *(The House Built on Rock).* Across from that painting, go into the choir to get a good look at the Last Supper altarpiece above the **main altar.**

Continuing back up the aisle, you'll come to the **war chapel.** At its entrance is a book listing Liverpudlians lost in war. Battle flags fly high on the wall above.

You'll wind up at the gift shop, where you can buy a ticket to climb up to the top of the tower. The cathedral's café is up the stairs, above the gift shop.

Hope Street—The street connecting the cathedrals is the main artery of Liverpool's "uptown," a lively and fun-to-explore district loaded with dining and entertainment options. In addition to well-respected theaters, this street is home to the Philharmonic and its namesake pub (see "Eating in Liverpool," later). At the intersection with Mount Street is a monument consisting of concrete suitcases; just down this street are the high schools that Paul, George, and John attended (for details, see "The Beatles in Liverpool" sidebar, earlier).

Nightlife in Liverpool

Liverpool hops after hours, especially on weekends. The most happening zone is the area called **Ropewalks,** just east of the downtown shopping district and Albert Dock. Part of the protected historic area of Liverpool's docklands, the Ropewalks area has been redeveloped over the last few years and is now filled mostly with trendy pubs, nightclubs, and lounges—some of them rough around the edges, others posh and sleek. While this area is aimed primarily at the college-aged crowd, it's still worth a stroll, and has a few eateries worth considering.

Pubs

The "Eating in Liverpool" section, later, lists several pubs good for either a drink or a meal. Liverpool also has a wide range of watering holes best for serious drinkers and beer aficionados. The food at these palaces, all in the city center, is an afterthought, but they're a great spot for a pint: **The Ship and Mitre,** overlooking an off-ramp at the edge of downtown, has perhaps Liverpool's best selection of beers—with 40 types on tap—as well as frequent beer festivals; it can get very crowded (133 Dale Street, tel. 0151/236-0859, see festival schedule at www.theshipandmitre.com). **Thomas Rigby's** has hard-used wooden floors that spill out into a rollicking garden courtyard (21 Dale Street). Around the corner and much more sedate, **Ye Hole in Ye Wall** brags it's Liverpool's oldest pub, from 1726. Notice the men's room on the ground floor—the women's room (required by law to be added in the 1970s) is upstairs (just off Dale Street on Hackins Hey). A few blocks over, right in the heart of downtown and surrounded by modern mega-malls, is **The Globe**—a tight, cozy, local-feeling pub with five real ales and sloping floors (17 Cases Street).

Sleeping in Liverpool

Your best budget options in this thriving city are the boring, predictable, and central chain hotels—though I've listed a couple of more colorful options also worth considering. Many hotels, including the ones listed below, charge more on weekends (particularly Sat), especially when the Liverpool FC soccer team plays a home game. Rates shoot up even higher two weekends a year: during the Grand National horse race (April 12-14 in 2012) and during Beatles Week at the end of August—avoid these times if you can. Prices plummet on Sunday nights.

$$$ Hope Street Hotel is a class act that sets the bar for Liverpool's hotels. Located across from the Philharmonic on Hope Street (midway between the cathedrals, in an enticing dining neighborhood), it has 89 luxurious rooms with lots of hardwood, exposed brick, and elegant little extras (standard Db-officially £180, but often £140-160 Fri-Sat and £107 Mon-Thu, even less on Sun; fancier and pricier deluxe rooms and suites available; breakfast-£10, elevator, free Wi-Fi; parking-£10 in limited on-site spots or £5 nearby; 40 Hope Street, tel. 0151/709-3000, www.hope streethotel.co.uk, sleep@hopestreethotel.co.uk).

$$$ Hard Day's Night Hotel is the ideal splurge for Beatles pilgrims. Located in a carefully restored old building smack in the heart of the Cavern Quarter, its decor is purely Beatles, from its public spaces (lobby, lounge, bar, restaurant) to its 110 rooms. But what could have been a tacky travesty is instead tasteful, with a largely black-and-white color scheme and subtle nods to the Fab

---

Sleep Code

(£1 = about $1.60, country code: 44, area code: 0151)
S = Single, **D** = Double/Twin, **T** = Triple, **Q** = Quad, **b** = bathroom, **s** = shower only. You can assume credit cards are accepted unless otherwise noted.

To help you sort easily through these listings, I've divided the accommodations into three categories based on the price for a standard double room with bath:

  $$$ Higher Priced—Most rooms £90 or more.
   $$ Moderately Priced—Most rooms between £45-90.
    $ Lower Priced—Most rooms £45 or less.

Prices can change without notice; verify the hotel's current rates online or by email. For other updates, see www.rick steves.com/update.

Four (standard Db-£105, deluxe Db-£125, prices can spike dramatically during peak times, especially busy for Sat weddings in their own wedding chapel/reception hall, breakfast-£10 if you pre-book, air-con, elevator, free Wi-Fi, Central Building, North John Street, tel. 0151/236-1964, www.harddaysnighthotel.com, enquiries@harddaysnighthotel.com).

$$ Aachen Guest Accommodations has 17 modern, straightforward rooms in an old Georgian townhouse on a pleasant street just uphill from the heart of downtown (Sb-£45-55, Db-£49-75, Tb-£95-115, rates depend on demand—higher price is usually for weekends, includes breakfast, free Wi-Fi, 89-91 Mount Pleasant, tel. 0151/709-3477, www.aachenhotel.co.uk, enquiries@aachenhotel.co.uk).

$$ Best Western Feathers Hotel, nearly next door in a stately old Georgian building, has tight hallways and 81 small rooms with mod decor and amenities (Db-£64-74 on weekdays, £89-99 Fri, £109 Sat, includes breakfast, no elevator and six floors, free Internet access and Wi-Fi, parking-£7.50, 115-125 Mount Pleasant, tel. 0151/709-9655, www.feathers.uk.com, feathershotel@feathers.uk.com).

$$ Sir Thomas Hotel is a centrally located hotel that was once a bank. The lobby has been redone in trendy style, and the 39 rooms are comfortable. As windows are thin and it's a busy neighborhood, ask for a quieter room (Db-£65 midweek, £89-99 on non-event weekends, little difference between "standard" and "superior" rooms, one stately "luxury" room with heavy decor-£129, includes breakfast, elevator, free Wi-Fi, 10-minute walk from station, 24 Sir Thomas Street at the corner of Victoria Street, tel. 0151/236-1366, fax 0151/227-1541, www.sirthomashotel.co.uk, reservations@sirthomashotel.co.uk).

$$ Premier Inn, which has 186 pleasant, American-style rooms and a friendly staff, is inside the giant converted warehouses on the Albert Dock; many rooms have exposed brick from the original structure (Db-£68-121, averages £70-75 on weekdays, check website for specific rates, breakfast-£8, elevator, expensive Wi-Fi, discounted parking in nearby garage-£7.50, next to The Beatles Story, tel. 0871-527-8622, www.premierinn.com). There's also a second, downtown **$$ Premier Inn** with 165 rooms. While it's farther from the Albert Dock sights, it's just a 10-minute walk from the Lime Street train station and handy to downtown (Db-£53-121, check online for rates, Vernon Street, just off Dale Street, tel. 0151/242-7650). Both locations can fill up quickly on weekends.

$$ Holiday Inn Express has a branch at the Albert Dock, next door and nearly identical to the Premier Inn described above. Its 135 rooms are a smidge more basic—and cheaper—than the Premier Inn's; you might as well check both hotels' websites to see which has the better deal going (Db-generally around £70 on weekdays, £125 Sat, £58 Sun, includes breakfast, pay Wi-Fi, nearby parking-£7.50, beyond The Beatles Story at the Albert Dock, tel. 0844-875-7575, www.exliverpool.com, enquiries@exliverpool.com).

$ International Inn Hostel, run by the daughter of the Beatles' first manager, rents 100 budget beds in a former Victorian warehouse. Most nights, the hostel puts on fun, free food-themed events for guests—like serving scouse, the traditional Liverpudlian stew (Db-£36-45, bed in 2- to 10-bed room-£15-20, includes sheets and towels, all rooms have bathrooms, guest kitchen with free toast and tea/coffee available 24 hours, free Wi-Fi, laundry room, game room/TV lounge, video library, 24-hour reception, café with pay Internet access, 4 South Hunter Street, tel. & fax 0151/709-8135, www.internationalinn.co.uk, info@internationalinn.co.uk). In the hostel's basement is the **$$ Cocoon Pod Hotel,** offering 32 small, no-nonsense, modern rooms for people who have outgrown hosteling. As all the rooms are underground, there are no windows, which can make rooms a bit stuffy, though very quiet (except on weekends, when the hotel attracts some rowdy stag and hen parties). Choose either two twins or a king (Sb or Db-£43 Sun-Thu, £53 Fri-Sat; 1- to 3-bedroom apartments from £65; same location, amenities, and contact info as hostel; www.cocoonliverpool.co.uk). From the Lime Street Station, the hostel/Cocoon Pod are an easy 15-minute walk; if taking a taxi, tell them it's on South Hunter Street near Hardman Street.

Eating in Liverpool

Liverpool has an exciting and quickly evolving culinary scene; as a rollicking, youthful city, it's a magnet for creative chefs as well as upscale chain restaurants. I've arranged my listings by neighborhood. Consider my suggestions, but also browse the surrounding streets. This is a city where restaurant-finding is a joy rather than a chore.

On and near Hope Street

Hope Street, which connects the two cathedrals, is also home to several excellent restaurants. The Quarter, Host, and 60 Hope Street— which cluster near the corner of Hope and Falkner streets—are owned by brothers.

The Quarter serves up Mediterranean food at rustic tables that sprawl through several connected houses. It's trendy but cozy. They also serve breakfast and have carryout coffee and cakes (£4-6 starters, £7-10 pizzas and pastas, chalkboard specials, daily 8:30-24:00, 7 Falkner Street, tel. 0151/707-1965).

HOST (short for "Hope Street") features Asian fusion dishes in a casual, colorful, modern atmosphere (£4-6 small plates, £8-11 big plates, daily 11:00-23:00, 31 Hope Street, tel. 0151/708-5831).

The Side Door is a tight, upscale, and inviting little one-room bistro with a constantly changing menu of highly regarded modern English food. While this place is pricey, their "pre-theatre menu" is a good value (£19 two-course meals, £21 three-course meals, available before 19:00 Tue-Fri or 18:30 Sat; open Mon-Sat 12:00-14:30 & 17:30-22:30, closed Sun, 29a Hope Street, tel. 0151/707-7888).

60 Hope Street has modern English cuisine made with "as locally sourced as possible" ingredients in an upscale atmosphere. While the prices are high (£8-9 starters, £19-30 main dishes), their early-bird specials are a good deal (£15 two-course meals, £20 three-course meals including wine); they're available in the main restaurant only at lunchtime and until 18:30, but you can get them anytime (except Sun) in the more casual basement bistro (Mon-Fri 12:00-14:30 & 17:00-22:30, Sat 17:00-22:30 only, Sun 12:00-

20:00, reservations smart on weekends, 60 Hope Street, tel. 0151/707-6060).

Chinatown: A few blocks southwest of Hope Street is Liverpool's thriving Chinatown neighborhood, with the world's biggest Chinese arch. Lots of enticing options dishing up Chinese grub line up along Berry Street in front of the arch, and Cornwallis Street behind it. Among these, **Yuet Ben** (facing the arch from across Berry Street at 1 Upper Duke Street, closed Mon) is one of the most established.

Pubs near Hope Street

The Philharmonic Dining Rooms, kitty-corner from the actual Philharmonic, is actually a pub—but what a pub. This place wins the "atmosphere award" for its old-time elegance. The bar is a work of art, the marble urinals are downright genteel, and the three sitting areas on the ground floor (including the giant hall) are an enticing place to nurse a pint. This is a better place to drink than to eat—£4-10 pub grub is served only in the less-atmospheric upstairs (daily 12:00-21:30). John Lennon once said that his biggest regret about fame was "not being able to go to the Phil for a drink" (open for drinks daily 11:00-24:00, corner of Hope and Hardman streets, tel. 0151/707-2837).

The Fly in the Loaf has a classic pub exterior and interior, with efficient service, eight hand-pulls for real ales, and good food (£3-4 sandwiches, £6-7 meals; served until 19:00 Tue-Sat, until 17:00 Sun; open daily 12:00-24:00, 13 Hardman Street, tel. 0151/708-0817).

Ropewalks

While primarily a nightlife zone (see "Nightlife in Liverpool," earlier), this gentrified area also has a smattering of unique restaurants—including one in a former church, and another in a former police station.

Alma de Cuba fills the former Polish Catholic Church of St. Peter's with a trendy bar (downstairs, in the nave and altar area) and restaurant (upstairs, looking down into the nave). While the food (an eclectic international mix) is an afterthought, the "hedonists' church" atmosphere is nothing short of remarkable, at least to those who don't find it all a bit sacrilegious (£3-7 starters, £10-18 main dishes, daily 10:30-17:00 & 19:00-23:00, live music Thu from 22:30, live DJ with flower-petal shower and samba dancers Fri-Sat from 23:00, gospel brunch with small gospel choir Sun 13:30-17:30, Seel Street, tel. 0151/702-7394).

Liverpool One Bridewell pub fills a circa-1850 police station with a lively pub atmosphere. Downstairs, past the bar, several jail cells have been converted into cozy seating areas, while another bar and dining area sprawl upstairs (£7-9 pub grub, open daily for drinks 12:00-23:00; food served Mon until 16:00, Tue-Thu until 19:45, Sat-Sun until 20:45, Sun until 18:00; 1 Campbell Square, Argyle Street, tel. 0151/709-7000).

On Duke Street: A range of big, modern, popular, chain-feeling restaurants—Japanese, Mexican, Italian, and more—line up along Duke Street in the heart of the Ropewalks area (concentrated on the block between Kent Street and the Chinatown arch). While not high cuisine, these crowd-pleasers are close to the nightlife action.

Downtown

Delifonseca is a trendy delicatessen with two parts. In the cellar is the picnic-perfect deli counter, with prepared salads sold by weight, a wide range of meats and cheeses, and made-to-order £3 sandwiches. Upstairs is a casual bistro serving British, Mediterranean, and international cuisine (£7-10 sandwiches and salads, £10-13 chalkboard main dishes). While not cheap, the food here is high quality (both open Mon-Sat 8:00-21:00, last orders in the bistro around 21:30 on weekends, closed Sun, 12 Stanley Street, tel. 0151/255-0808).

Liverpool One: This shopping center, right in the heart of town, is nirvana for British chain restaurants. The upper Leisure Terrace has a row of some popular chains—including Café Rouge (French), Wagamama Noodle Bar, Gourmet Burger Company, Pizza Express, and more—all with outdoor seating. If you want to dine on predictable mass-produced food, you'll have a wide selection here.

At the Albert Dock

The eateries at the Albert Dock aren't high cuisine, but they're handy to your sightseeing. A slew of trendy restaurants come alive with club energy at night, but are sedate and pleasant in the afternoon and early evening. For lunch near the sights, consider the café in the **Tate Gallery** (£3-4 sandwiches and soups, £7-9 main dishes, daily 10:00-18:00 except closes at 17:00 mid-Oct-March).

Liverpool Connections

By Train

Note that many connections from Liverpool transfer at the Wigan North Western Station, which is on a major north-south train line.

From Liverpool by Train to: Blackpool (hourly, 1.5 hours), **Keswick/Lake District** (train to Penrith—roughly hourly with change in Wigan and possibly elsewhere, 1.75-2.25 hours; then bus to Keswick—hourly except Sun 9/day, 1 hour), **York** (hourly, 2.25 hours), **Edinburgh** (hourly, 3.5-3.75 hours, change in Wigan and possibly also Lancaster or Preston), **Glasgow** (1-2/hour, 3.25-3.75 hours, change in Wigan and possibly elsewhere), **London**'s Euston Station (hourly direct, 2 hours, more with changes), **Crewe** (2/hour, 45 minutes), **Chester** (2/hour, 45 minutes). Train info: tel. 0845-748-4950, www.nationalrail.co.uk.

By Ferry

By Ferry to Dublin, Republic of Ireland: P&O Irish Sea Ferries runs a car ferry only—no foot passengers (2-3/day, 8-hour trip, prices vary widely—roughly £150 for car and 2 passengers, over-night ferry includes berth and meals, 20-minute drive north of the city center at Liverpool Freeport—Gladstone dock, check in 1-2 hours before departure, tel. 0871-664-4777, www.poirishsea.com). Those without cars can take a ferry to Dublin via the Isle of Man (www.steam-packet.com), or ride the train to North Wales, and catch the Dublin ferry from Holyhead (www.stenaline.co.uk).

By Ferry to Belfast, Northern Ireland: Ferries sail from nearby Birkenhead roughly twice a day (8 hours, fares vary widely, tel. 0871-230-0330, www.stenaline.co.uk). Birkenhead's dock is a 15-minute walk from Hamilton Square Station on Merseyrail's Wirral Line.

Route Tips for Drivers

From Liverpool to Blackpool: Leaving Liverpool, drive north along the waterfront, following signs to *M58* (Preston). Once on M58 (and not before), follow signs to *M6*, and then *M55* into Blackpool.

BLACKPOOL

Blackpool is Britain's tacky, laid-back underbelly. It's one of England's most-visited attractions, the private domain of its working class, a faded and sticky mix of Coney Island, Las Vegas, and Denny's. It can be fun or depressing, thought-provoking or mind-numbing. Some people love it...others hate it. But it is, without a doubt, a spectacle.

Blackpool grew up with the Industrial Revolution. In the mid-1800s, entire mill towns would close down and take a two-week break here. They came to drink in the fresh air (much needed after a hard year in the mills) and—literally—the seawater. (Back then they figured it was healthy.) Supposedly, because Blackpool lies in a "rain shadow," it gets fewer rainy days than some other parts of England.

Blackpool's heyday is long past now, as more and more working people can afford cheap flights to sunny Spain. The resort has become popular for "stag" and "hen" (bachelor and bachelorette) parties—basically a cheap drunk weekend for the twentysomething crowd. Consequently, there are two Blackpools: the daytime Blackpool of kids riding roller coasters and grannies tucking into early-bird specials; and the drunken, debauched, late-night Blackpool of glass-dance-floor clubs and bars.

Blackpool is working to reinvent itself and draw more visitors. An overhaul of The Promenade wrapped up in 2011, and Merlin Entertainments (the deep-pocketed owner of Madame Tussauds, the London Eye, and Warwick Castle) has recently invested heavily here—buying and completely rehabbing Blackpool Tower, and opening a new Madame Tussauds just down the street. And yet

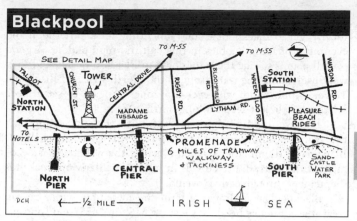

Blackpool

SEE DETAIL MAP

TO M-55

TO M-55

TALBOT RD.

CHURCH ST.

TOWER

CENTRAL DRIVE

MADAME TUSSAUDS

NORTH STATION

RUGBY RD.

BLOOMFIELD RD.

WATER-LOO RD.

LYTHAM RD.

SOUTH STATION

WATSON RD.

PLEASURE BEACH RIDES

TO HOTELS

PROMENADE
6 MILES OF TRAMWAY WALKWAY, & TACKINESS

NORTH PIER

CENTRAL PIER

SOUTH PIER

SAND-CASTLE WATER PARK

DCH ← ½ MILE →

IRISH SEA

BLACKPOOL

the town remains an accessible and affordable fun zone for the Flo and Andy Capps of northern England. People come year after year. They stay for a week, and they love it.

Be warned: Some of you will get to Blackpool and wonder, "Why did Rick send me *here*?" Most Americans don't even consider a stop in Blackpool. Many won't like it. It's an ears-pierced-while-you-wait, tipsy-toupee kind of place. Tacky, yes. Lowbrow, OK. More than a little run-down in parts, sure. If you're before or beyond kids, and not into kitsch and greasy spoons, skip it. But if you have kids, they'll enjoy Blackpool

WOW THERE'S EVEN MORE TO SEE DOWN HERE!

(hey, it's cheaper than Disneyland). And for those who are into nightlife, this town delivers. If you believe (as I do) that an itinerary should feature as many different facets of a culture as possible, consider a stop here. Blackpool is as English as the Queen—and considerably more fun.

A million greedy doors try every trick to get you inside. Huge arcade halls advertise free toilets and broadcast bingo numbers into the streets; the wind machine under a wax Marilyn Monroe blows at a steady gale; and the smell of fries, tobacco, and sugar is everywhere. Spend the day "muckin' about" the beach promenade of fortune-tellers, fish-and-chips joints, amusement piers, warped mirrors, and Englanders wearing hats with built-in ponytails. Scream down roller coasters and eat "candy floss" until you're deliriously queasy.

Planning Your Time

Ideally, get to Blackpool around lunchtime for an afternoon and evening of making bubbles in this cultural mud puddle. A good overall plan is to ride the tram down to Pleasure Beach, and then walk back along the waterfront to the North Pier and Blackpool Tower, dipping into whatever fun zones appeal. To see a more pristine beach, just keep walking north.

The evening light here is great, with the sun setting over the sea. Walk out along the peaceful North Pier at twilight. Blackpool's Illuminations, when much of the waterfront is decorated with lights, draws crowds in fall, particularly on weekends (September through early November).

Blackpool is easy by car or train. Speed demons with a car can treat it as a midday break (it's just off M6, on M55) and continue north. If the weather's great and you love nature, the lakes are just two hours north. A visit to Blackpool sharpens the wonders of Windermere.

Orientation to Blackpool

(area code: 01253)

Everything clusters along The Promenade, a tacky, glittering six-mile-long beachfront good-time strip mall punctuated by three fun-filled piers reaching out into the sea. The Pleasure Beach rides are near the South Pier. Jutting up near the North Pier is Blackpool's stubby Eiffel-type tower. The most interesting shops, eateries, and theaters are inland from the North Pier. For a break from glitz, walk north along The Promenade or the sandy beach—a residential neighborhood stretches for miles. When you've had enough, just hop on the tram or a bus for a quick ride back.

Tourist Information

The TI is in the wedding chapel on The Promenade, across from Blackpool Tower (Mon-Sat 9:00-17:00, closed Sun; tel. 01253/478-222—answered during the day, recorded entertainment info after hours; www.visitblackpool.com). There you'll find a city map, brochures on the amusement centers, and a helpful staff. The free *Events Programme* lists local happenings; the TI can book shows for you for a £2.50 fee. The TI books rooms for no fee (but collects a 10 percent deposit, which hotels don't recoup; room-finding service closes at 16:30).

If you're going to Blackpool Tower, Sandcastle Waterpark, or many other local attractions, buy your tickets here to save a few pounds. The **Resort Pass** gives you access to virtually all the big-name sights (the Blackpool Tower, Madame Tussauds, Pleasure Beach, and more) for one high price.

Arrival in Blackpool

By Train: The main (north) train station is three blocks from the town center (no maps given but one is posted). Exiting the station, turn right and look for the pedestrian underpass. Go left up the ramp, then right at the sign for *town centre*, and walk straight into town (on Talbot Road, ending at the North Pier and The Promenade).

The only **luggage storage** in Blackpool is about a 15-minute walk southwest of the train station, at the National Express bus office, in the big parking lot at the corner of New Bonny Street and Central Drive, behind the row of pay toilets (£1.50/day per item, Mon-Fri 7:00-17:00, Sat 7:30-16:30, closed Sun).

By Car: The motorway funnels you down Yeadon Way into a giant parking zone. If you're just here for the day, head for one of the huge pay garages. If you're spending the night, drive to the waterfront and head north. My top accommodations are north of the center, on The Promenade (easy parking). Leaving Blackpool to go anywhere, follow signs to *M55*, which starts at Blackpool and zips you to M6 (for points north or south).

Helpful Hints

Markets: At the indoor **Abingdon Street Market,** vendors sell baked goods, fruit, bras, jewelry, eggs, and more (daily 9:00-17:00). Eight miles north, the **Fleetwood Market** is huge, with two buildings full of produce, clothes, and crafts spilling out onto the street (Tue and Thu-Sat 8:00-17:00, closed Wed and Sun-Mon, www.fleetwoodmarket.co.uk; catch tram marked *Fleetwood*, 30 minutes, £2.70 one-way).

Tipping: The pubs of Blackpool have a unique tradition of "and (name an amount) your own, luv." Say that here, and your barmaid will add that amount to your bill and drop it into her tip jar. (Say it anywhere else...and they won't know what you mean.)

Internet Access: The public library, in the big domed building on Queen Street, lets visitors stand and use its computers for 15 minutes (free, Mon and Fri 9:00-17:00, Tue and Thu 9:00-19:00, Wed and Sat 10:00-17:00, Sun 11:00-14:00, tel. 01253/478-111).

Post Office: The main P.O. is in the basement of the WH Smith store, at 12-16 Bank Hey Street (Mon-Sat 9:00-17:30, closed Sun).

Car Rental: If you decide to tour the Lake District by car, you'll find plenty of rental agencies in Blackpool (closed Sat afternoon and Sun), including **Avis** (at the airport—just south of the South Pier, tel. 0844-544-6029) and **Budget** (434 Waterloo Road—just north of the South Pier, tel. 01253/691-632).

Getting Around Blackpool

Trams trundle 13 miles up and down the waterfront, connecting all the sights. They come in all shapes and colors (some vintage, some modern, some dressed up like boats), but are all on the same system and take the same tickets. This electric tramway—the first in Europe—dates from 1885 (about £2/ride depending on length of trip, pay conductor, trams come every 10-15 minutes or so year-round 6:00-23:15). Many **buses** also run along The Promenade—make sure you're not standing at a tram stop if you're waiting for a bus (similar prices, pay conductor, tel. 01253/473-001, www.black pooltransport.com). For £6, you can purchase a day pass that covers both trams and buses; buy it on board, at their office on Market Street, or at the TI.

Taxis are easy to snare in Blackpool, and three to five people travel cheaper by cab than by tram. Hotels can get you a taxi by phone within three minutes (no extra charge).

Sights in Blackpool

▲▲▲**People-Watching**—Blackpool's top sight is its people. You'll see England here as nowhere else. Grab someone's hand and a big baton of "rock" (candy), and stroll. Grown men walk around with huge teddy bears looking for places to play "bowlingo," a short-lane version of bowling. "Gypsy" psychics with celebrity photos in their windows promise to reveal your future. Ponder the thought of actually retiring here and spending your last years, day after day, wearing plaid pants and a bad toupee, surrounded by Blackpool. This place puts people in a talkative mood. Start up conversations. Ask a young couple on the street, "What's there to do here?" Find someone to explain the difference between tea and supper. Back at your hotel, join in the chat sessions in the lounge.

▲▲**The Piers**—Blackpool's famous piers were originally built for Victorian landlubbers who wanted to go to sea but were afraid

of getting seasick. Each of the three amusement piers has its own personality and is a joy to wander (all are free and open with demand early March-early Nov). The rides you'll see operate on a token system (buy tokens from kiosks along the pier).

The sedate **North Pier** is most traditional and refreshingly uncluttered. Dance down its empty planks at twilight to the early English rock playing on its speakers. Its Carousel Bar at the end is great for families—with a free kids' DJ

nightly in summer from 19:00 to 23:00 (parents drink good beer while the kids bunny-hop and boogie). At its tip is a big theater offering corny shows.

The something-for-everyone **Central Pier** is lots of fun. Ride its great Ferris wheel for the best view in Blackpool (rich photography at twilight, get the operator to spin you as you bottom out). The family bar at the end of the pier is a hit with kids.

The rollicking **South Pier** has classic carnival rides, such as bumper cars and carousels. The two very pricey adventure rides—Skycoaster and Skyscreamer—treat riders like rocks in a giant slingshot. This pier is also home to the Laughing Donkey Family Bar.

From the far end of any pier, look out at the horizon to see the natural-gas drilling platforms in the Irish Sea. In the distance, off the North Shore, castaway wind turbines capture energy.

▲**Blackpool Tower**—This mini-Eiffel Tower is a 100-year-old vertical fun center. Recently refurbished head-to-toe, it has preserved some of its oldie-but-goodie attractions, and added some glitzy new ones. Work your way up from the bottom through layer after layer of noisy entertainment: a circus (2-3 acts a day, runs Easter-first weekend in Nov); Jungle Jim's kiddie area; a gory "Blackpool Dungeon" attraction; and a wonderful old ballroom with barely live music and golden oldies dancing to golden oldies all day. Enjoy a break at the dance-floor-level pub or on a balcony perch. Kids love this place. With a little marijuana, adults would, too. Ride the elevator to the "Blackpool Tower Eye" viewpoint at the tip of this 518-foot-tall symbol of Blackpool, where you can stroll across the "Air Walk" glass floor and enjoy a smashing view, especially at sunset. Also up top is a "4D" cinema (3-D plus other startling effects).

Cost and Hours: Pricing is à la carte, depending on which attractions you choose: Admission to the Eye alone is £12; a ticket for the Eye, Circus, and Jungle Jim's costs £21—see website for complete pricing options (kid and family tickets available). Open daily from 10:00, closing times vary per attraction and with the season, some attractions may close for events, top of tower closes when excessively windy, tel. 01253/622-242, www.theblackpool tower.co.uk.

▲Madame Tussauds Blackpool—Just south of the Blackpool Tower along The Promenade, this kid-sister to the famous waxworks in London features eerily realistic wax copies of famous people with whom you can pose for a hundred goofy photos. However, while the London Tussauds focuses on international stars, the one in Blackpool (understanding its target audience) focuses on British celebs. Reality-TV stars, comedians, and other media personalities from the UK are featured, as well as such icons as a replica of the Rovers Return pub from the beloved-by-Brits soap opera *Coronation Street*. The average American likely won't recognize the vast majority of the waxy faces in here (with a few exceptions—notably Simon Cowell and Susan Boyle—plus international guest-stars such as Michael Jackson, Lady Gaga, Britney Spears, and Tiger Woods), and the price tag is hefty. But fans of British pop culture will enjoy seeing Graham Norton, Gok Wan, and Alan Carr, and superstar competitive dart-thrower Phil Taylor. And anyone will be impressed by the remarkably lifelike features of the figures.

Cost and Hours: Adults-£17.40, kids-£13.20, cheaper if you buy in advance online, Mon-Fri 10:00-16:30, Sat-Sun 10:00-18:00, hours can vary—check website, near the Central Pier on The Promenade, tel. 0871-282-9200, www.madametussauds.com.

▲Pleasure Beach—Rated ▲▲▲ for roller-coaster enthusiasts, these 42 acres across The Promenade from the beach attract nearly six million visitors annually, and are littered with rides galore, an ice show, circus and illusion shows, and varied amusements. The Nickelodeonland area features rides and characters tied into the American children's TV network (also popular in the UK). Many rides are tame enough for the under-10 set, but the top few offer some of the best thrills in Europe: the Pepsi Max Big One (with a peak of 235 feet and 85 mph, it's one of the world's fastest, highest, and steepest roller coasters), the Infusion (a twisty, loopy speed rush that you ride with your feet dangling),  and the IceBlast (which rockets you straight up before letting you bungee down). The Bling ride spins gondola riders in three different directions 100 feet above the ground at speeds of more than 60 mph. Also memorable is the Steeplechase—carousel horses stampeding down a roller coaster track (a dream come true for *Mary Poppins* fans). The Irn Bru Revolution speeds you over a steep drop and upside-down in a loop, then does it again backwards, while the Valhalla ride zips you on a Viking boat in watery darkness past scary Nordic things like lutefisk. With two 80-foot drops and lots of hype, first you're scared, then you're soaked, and—finally—you're just glad you survived. The park also offers several old wooden-framed rides full of historic charm—but brittle travelers will want to consider their necks and backs. The tame-looking Wild Mouse, built in 1958, is the jerkiest, and has no doubt kept generations of Blackpool chiropractors in the money.

Cost: £5 admission includes a few attractions, then you can pay individually for rides with £1 tickets (2-8 tickets per ride), or get unlimited rides with an armband (adults-£32, kids-£27, family ticket available, cheaper if purchased in advance on their website). If you haven't pre-purchased your pass, pay the £5 entry fee and have a look around (figure out how long lines are for the top rides)—once you've paid admission to the park, you can upgrade to the armband by paying the difference.

Hours: Daily Easter-early Nov, also open some weekends in Nov and Feb-Easter; opens at about 10:30 and closes as early as 17:00 or as late as 20:00, depending on season, weather, and demand—check website; closed entirely Dec-Jan, tel. 0871-222-1234, www.blackpoolpleasurebeach.com.

Avoiding Lines: The park can be jam-packed in summer (July-Aug) and on school holidays, causing long ticket lines from about 10:30 to 13:00; during these times, try to arrive early (ticket office opens at 9:30).

Getting There: Pleasure Beach is about two miles (a 45-minute walk) south of the North Pier, so consider taking the tram or bus.

Sandcastle Waterpark—This popular indoor attraction, across the street from Pleasure Beach, has a big pool, long slides, a wave machine, and water, water, everywhere, at a constant temperature of 84 degrees. Featuring the longest tube waterslide in the world (called "Masterblaster")—and some brand-new rides (Montazooma and Aztec Falls)—this is a place where most kids could easily spend a day.

Cost and Hours: Basic adult admission-£12, kids-£10; pay £3.75 extra for access to the "Hyperzone" area with the best rides; family passes and 10 percent discount tickets available online and at TI; daily April-Oct but hours change constantly, opening between 9:30 and 10:30 and closing between 16:30 (off-season) and 18:00 (late July-Aug), weekends only Nov-March; last admission one hour before closing, tel. 01253/343-602, www.sandcastle-waterpark.co.uk.

▲**Illuminations**—Blackpool was the first town in England to "go electric" in 1879. Now, every fall, from early September through early November, Blackpool stretches its tourist season by illuminating its six miles of waterfront with countless lights, all blinking and twinkling. People here speak with wonder about these lights.

The American in me kept saying, "I've seen bigger, and I've seen better," but I stuffed his mouth with cotton candy and just had some simple fun like everyone else on my specially decorated tram. Look for the animated tableaux up along the North Shore (www .blackpool-illuminations.net).

St. Annes-on-Sea—Had enough greasy food and flashing lights? The seaside village of St. Annes is an easy 20-minute bus ride away to the south, and offers a welcome break (buses #7 and #11 run from the Blackpool Tower every 10 minutes, covered by the all-day tram/bus pass). Get off at St. Annes Square, which is the first stop after the bus turns left following the long, dune-side straightaway. The town's promenade and the end of the simple Victorian pier (once you pass the noisy game arcade) feel like a breath of sanity. The broad sand beach is perfect for flying a kite, building a sandcastle, or watching happy dogs play in the surf. Consider strolling the beach northward all the way to the southern edge of The Promenade (about three miles—you can see the Pleasure Beach roller coasters from here); if you max out on sand and sea before that, simply cross the dunes back to the seaside road and find the nearest bus stop.

Nightlife in Blackpool

▲**Showtime**—Blackpool always has a few razzle-dazzle music, dancing-girl, racy-humor, magic, and tumbling shows. Box offices around town can give you a rundown on what's available (£7-30 tickets). Your hotel has the latest. Blackpool is also a staging ground for some London West End plays—giving you a chance to enjoy a show for a fraction of the London cost. You might try the Opera House for musicals (booking tel. 0844-856-1111, info tel. 01253/625-252) and the Grand Theatre for drama and ballet (£15-25, tel. 01253/290-190, www.blackpoolgrand.co.uk). Both are on Church Street, a couple of blocks behind the tower. For the latest in evening entertainment, see the window displays at the TI on The Promenade (www.blackpoollive.com).

▲▲**Funny Girls**—Blackpool's hot bar is in a dazzling venue a couple of blocks from the tower. Most nights from 20:00 to 23:30, Funny Girls puts on a "glam bam thank you ma'am" burlesque-in-drag show that delights footballers and grannies alike. A troop of a dozen or so gorgeous guys go through an entire wardrobe, putting on skits and dances that range

from the Charleston to Beyoncé to a very vampy *Sound of Music.* Between songs, the high-heeled MC entertains.

Get your drinks at the bar...unless the transvestites are dancing on it. The show, while racy, is not raunchy. The music is very loud. The crowd is young, old, straight, gay, very down-to-earth, and fun-loving. A weeknight is both a less-expensive and less-crushed experience, as Fridays and Saturdays are jammed. While the area up front can be a mosh pit, there are more sedate tables in back, where service comes with a vampish smile. If you want to experience the show without being immersed in a bar crowd, pay extra to sit.

Cost: Admission is charged according to whether you're sitting or standing (Sun £4 to stand, £14.50 to sit; Tue-Thu £3.50 to stand, £11.50 to sit; Fri £6 to stand, £18.50 to sit; Sat £8.50 to stand, £20.50 to sit; no shows Mon). Getting dinner here before the show runs about £16 (dinner reservations required, must be 18 to enter, 5 Dickson Road, TI sells tickets; to reserve in advance, call 01253/624-901, or visit box office at 44 Queen Street, next door to the Flying Handbag—open Mon-Sat 9:30-17:15, closed Sun, www.funnygirlsshowbar.co.uk).

Birley Street Light Show—This recently pedestrianized street, right in the heart of town, has silver arches bunny-hopping up and down its length. Nightly in peak season (July-early Nov), and on weekends off-season, a sound-and-light display called "Brilliance" enlivens the street after dark with flashing lights and music.

Other Nightspots—More than 100 years old, the **Mitre Pub** serves beer (but no real ales) in a cozy, truly rare, old-time Blackpool ambience. Drop in anytime to survey the fun photos of old Blackpool and for the great people scene (daily 11:00-23:00, food served 11:00-17:00 only—£4-7 meals, 3 West Street, tel. 01253/623-718). Other pubs in the center that are more traditional than rowdy (though admittedly touristy) are **The Pump and Truncheon** on Bonny Street behind Madame Tussauds (basic £5 pub grub with exposed brick and a billiards table), and **Scruffy Murphy's** on Corporation Street (food only at lunchtime, live music most weekends).

Blackpool's clubs and discos are cheap, with live bands and an interesting crowd (nightly 22:00-2:00 in the morning). With all the stag and hen parties, the late-night streets can be clotted with rude rowdies.

Sleeping in Blackpool

Blackpool's 140,000 people provide 120,000 beds in 3,500 mostly dumpy, cheap, nondescript hotels and B&Bs. Remember, this town's in the business of accommodating the people who can't afford to go to Spain. Most places have the same design—minimal character, maximum number of springy beds—and charge £20-25 per person. Empty beds abound except summer weekends and from September through early November (during Illuminations, when everyone bumps up prices). With the huge number of hotels in town, prices get really soft off-season. I've listed regular high-season prices. There's likely a launderette within a five-minute walk of your hotel; ask your host.

North of the Tower

These listings are on or near the waterfront in the quiet area they call "the posh end," a mile or two north of Blackpool Tower, with easy parking and easy access to the center by tram or bus. The first two listings have classy extras you wouldn't expect in Blackpool, and aren't far from the North Pier. The last two are B&Bs with welcoming owners and lots of stairs, a short tram ride or approximately 35-minute walk from the North Pier.

$$$ Barceló Imperial Hotel would like to brag that it's where the Queen would stay in Blackpool. (They boast that every prime minister since they opened has visited their #10 Bar.) With 180 rooms, it's the kind of grand, monumental hotel that they don't make anymore. But its dark-paneled Old World elegance has faded over time, especially in the rooms themselves (standard

---

Sleep Code

(£1 = about $1.60, country code: 44, area code: 01253)
S = Single, **D** = Double/Twin, **T** = Triple, **Q** = Quad, **b** = bathroom, **s** = shower only. You can assume credit cards are accepted unless otherwise noted.

To help you sort easily through these listings, I've divided the accommodations into three categories based on the price for a standard double room with bath:

  $$$ Higher Priced—Most rooms £90 or more.
    $$ Moderately Priced—Most rooms between £45-90.
      $ Lower Priced—Most rooms £45 or less.

Prices can change without notice; verify the hotel's current rates online or by email. For other updates, see www.ricksteves.com/update.

Central Blackpool

NOT TO SCALE
NORTH PIER TO CENTRAL PIER IS ABOUT ½ MILE (800 METERS)

+–+– TROLLEY LINE
P PARKING
☐ PEDESTRIAN ZONE

1. To Hotels North of the Tower
2. To The Lonsdale & Valdene Hotels
3. St. John's Square Eateries
4. Abingdon Barbeque
5. Marks & Spencer
6. AJ's Bistro
7. Yorkshire Fisheries
8. Kwizeen
9. Sapori
10. Michael Wan's Mandarin Restaurant
11. To Red Bank Road Eateries
12. The Mitre Pub
13. Scruffy Murphy's Pub
14. Funny Girls (Bar & Show)
15. Funny Girls (Box Office)
16. Nat'l Express Bus Office; Bag Storage & WCs

Db-£95-168 depending on size of room, season, and day of week, average is about Db-£109, check website for deals but call front desk for best standard room available, sea-view rooms-£60 extra, children 15 and under stay free, elevator, free Wi-Fi in lobby, pay Wi-Fi in rooms, parking-£2.50/day, tram stop: Imperial Hotel, North Promenade, tel. 01253/623-971, fax 01253/751-784, www.barcelo-hotels.co.uk, imperialblackpool@barcelo-hotels.co.uk).

$$$ The **Hilton Hotel** is good if you need a splurge. Yes, I know, staying at the Hilton in Blackpool is like wearing a tux to eat a corndog. But this is a grand 274-room place with lots of views, a pool, sauna, gym, and comfortable rooms (Db-£110-170, "club deal" Db with lots of extras-£25 more, ask about "special rates," best deals online, some rates include breakfast—otherwise £9.50 extra, call front desk to request view room for no extra charge, expensive

Wi-Fi in some rooms, tram stop: Warley Road, North Promenade, tel. 01253/623-434, fax 01253/294-371, www1.hilton.com).

$$ Beechcliffe Private Hotel has seven clean rooms run by a friendly couple, Ken and Carol Selman. The rooms are tight and simple, but this place has a homey touch (Sb-£25, Db-£50, extra person-£25 but kids half-price, tram stop: Cabin; turn left from tram stop, then right at Shaftesbury Avenue, and walk a block away from beach; 16 Shaftesbury Avenue, North Shore, tel. 01253/353-075, www.beechcliffe.co.uk, info@beechcliffe.co.uk). Ken offers guests rides to or from the train station for no charge.

$$ Robin Hood Hotel is a cheery place with a big, welcoming living room and nine spacious rooms with big beds and some sea views. If you don't mind the stairs, ask for the top room, #9, which features great views over the beach and sea (Sb-£25, Db-£50, extra person-£25 but kids half-price, under 6 free, tram stop: St. Stephen's Avenue and walk a block north, 1.5 miles north of tower across from a peaceful stretch of beach, 100 Queens Promenade, North Shore, tel. 01253/351-599, www.robinhoodhotel.co.uk, info@robinhoodhotel.co.uk, Paul and Kathy).

Near the Train Station

Both of these hotels are located on quiet Cocker Street, which provides an oasis of sanity and affordable comfort in a handy, if rough, neighborhood just a few short blocks from the train station and the Blackpool Tower and North Pier. These hotels are family-run, have strict security and noise standards, and cater to couples and families rather than to revelers.

$$ The Lonsdale Hotel offers five rooms in an oasis of peace behind a lush front porch garden. The plush lounge, with Edwardian paintings and furnishings, takes you to another era. Steve has managed the place for 25 years (Sb-£45, Db-£60, free Wi-Fi, free parking, at the corner of Lord Street and Cocker Street at 25 Cocker Street, tel. 01253/621-628, www.blackpool accommodation.net, lonsdalehotel@hotmail.co.uk).

$$ The Valdene Hotel, with a small garden facing the street, rents 10 rooms above its generous and inviting lounge. Old-time Blackpool photos on the walls create a peaceful and nostalgic atmosphere (Db-£50, 16 Cocker Street, tel. 01253/291-080, www .valdene-hotel.co.uk, valdenehotel@aol.com, Bob, Linda, and Simon Ablett).

Eating in Blackpool

Considering what's in demand here, I wouldn't hope for great food in Blackpool. Generally, food in the tower and along The Promenade is terrible. But if you explore the streets in the real town center, a few blocks up from The Promenade, you'll find some decent options. Because there's no real "destination" restaurant in town, I've organized them by streets that are worth browsing—just select whichever place appeals to you.

St. John's Square and Nearby

This recently pedestrianized square is fronted by several popular eateries. Trendy cafés—including Lounge, Number Five, Relish, and Sugar[3]—line the top of the square (all open only until about 17:00, no dinner). To fill the tank, head to **Quilligans,** a local favorite, across the square from the church. This kitschy, retro Blackpool diner suits the city's lowbrow aesthetic perfectly, with huge portions of comfort food (£3-5 light meals, £6-7 bigger meals). At the bottom of the square, West Coast Rock Café is popular with teens for its gigantic portions.

Carryout Options near St. John's Square: These two places are good options for picking up some take-away food; you can sit on a bench on St. John's Square, or—better yet—head for the beach. **Abingdon Barbeque,** with its expansive deli counter, is mobbed with hungry locals at lunch, munching on cheap roasted chicken and meat pies (daily 7:00-17:00, take-away only, 44 Abingdon Street, tel. 01253/621-817). **Marks & Spencer** has a big supermarket in its basement (Mon-Wed and Fri 9:00-18:00, Thu 9:00-19:00, Sat 9:00-18:00, Sun 10:30-16:30, just south of St. John's Square on Church Street).

Topping Street and Nearby

This somewhat dingy, urban-feeling street sits about halfway between the train station and The Promenade. But its lack of glitz helps keep some of the tourists away, making this a relatively local-feeling strip. Your options here include a pair of Thai restaurants, two pubs with great old-fashioned ambience and passable food (Washington and Churchill), an Italian joint, and the two places listed below.

AJ's Bistro, named for owners Andrew and Julie, features quality modern English cuisine (with an emphasis on seafood and steaks, and mostly gluten-free) in a casual atmosphere. Their £9.50 "evening menu"—like an early-bird deal but available anytime (except Sat)—includes two courses and a drink. Two people can have three courses each, plus a bottle of wine, for £50, or order from the pricey à la carte menu (£5-7 starters, £13-19 main dishes, Tue-Fri 17:30-23:00, Sat 12:00-23:00, Sun 15:00-23:00, closed Mon, 65 Topping Street, tel. 01253/626-111).

Fish-and-Chips: **Yorkshire Fisheries** is the locals' choice for best chippy, and promises better-quality fish-and-chips than the greasy joints that line The Promenade. Order at the counter, then either take it away or eat there (£3-6 meals, Mon-Sat 11:30-19:00, closed Sun, 16 Topping Street, tel. 01253/627-739).

Near Topping Street: **Kwizeen,** on a dingy street a block up from Topping Street, is an elegant bistro that serves Mediterranean and modern English dishes with a focus on locally sourced and creatively prepared food (£6-7 starters, £13-16 main dishes, £16 two-course and £19 three-course early-bird specials 18:00-19:00; open Mon-Fri 12:00-13:30 & 18:00-21:00, Sat 18:00-21:00, closed Sun; 47-49 King Street, tel. 01253/290-045).

Clifton Street

Stretching up from the Promenade and the TI, this street has a few ethnic offerings, including Italian, Indian, and Chinese. These two have the best reputation.

Sapori offers good Italian food in a sophisticated atmosphere that makes you forget that the tackiness of Blackpool is just outside the front door (£7-8 pizzas and pastas, £12-19 main dishes, daily 17:00-23:00, 36 Clifton Street, tel. 01253/627-440).

Michael Wan's Mandarin Restaurant is a local fixture; they've been providing Blackpool with authentic Chinese cuisine since 1961 (£6-10 meals, daily 12:00-14:00 & 17:30-23:00, 27 Clifton Street, tel. 01253/622-687).

In the North End: Red Bank Road

If you're staying at the hotels at the north end of The Promenade, and don't want to venture into the rowdy downtown for dinner, locals recommend riding the tram north to Bishpam. From here, Red Bank Road has several acceptable eateries including Indian, Italian, fish-and-chips, and steakhouse choices. The basic, diner-style **Bishpam Kitchen** has stick-to-your-ribs English comfort food, including good fish-and-chips (£5-7 meals, Sun-Thu 8:00-20:30, Fri-Sat 8:00-21:00, at #14-16). None of these places is high cuisine—the pickings are slim—but it's relatively convenient to accommodations in the north end.

Blackpool Connections

If you're heading to (or from) Blackpool by train, you'll usually need to transfer at **Preston** (4/hour, 22-27 minutes). The following trains leave from Blackpool's main (north) station. The information desk can print you a schedule for your requested journey.

From Blackpool to: Liverpool (hourly, 1.5 hours), **Keswick/ Lake District** (roughly hourly, allow at least 3.5 hours total for journey: transfer in Preston—30 minutes away, then 1 hour to Penrith, then catch a bus to Keswick, hourly except Sun 8/day, 40 minutes; alternatively, you could take the hourly 2-hour train to Windermere—with a change in Preston and sometimes also Oxenholme—and ride the bus from there to Keswick), **Conwy** in North Wales (roughly hourly, 3 hours, 3 transfers), **Edinburgh** (roughly hourly, 3.5 hours, transfer in Preston), **Glasgow** (1-2/hour, 3.25-3.5 hours, transfer in Preston), **York** (direct trains hourly, 3 hours, more with change in Manchester), **Moreton-in-Marsh** in the Cotswolds (hourly, 4.25-5 hours, 3 transfers), **Bath** (hourly, 4.5-4.75 hours, 2-3 transfers), **London**'s Euston Station (1-2/hour, 2.75-3.25 hours, 1-2 transfers), Telford near **Ironbridge Gorge** (hourly, 2.25 hours, 2 transfers), **Oban** (2/day, 7.25-7.75 hours, 3 transfers). Train info: tel. 0845-748-4950, www.nationalrail.co.uk.

BLACKPOOL

THE LAKE DISTRICT

In the pristine Lake District, William Wordsworth's poems still shiver in trees and ripple on ponds. Nature rules this land, and humanity keeps a wide-eyed but low profile. Relax, recharge, take a cruise or a hike, and maybe even write a poem. Renew your poetic license at Wordsworth's famous Dove Cottage.

The Lake District, about 30 miles long and 30 miles wide, is nature's lush, green playground. Explore it by foot, bike, bus, or car. While not impressive in sheer height (Scafell Pike, the tallest peak in England, is only 3,206 feet), there's a walking-stick charm about the way nature and the culture mix here. Locals are fond of declaring that their mountains are older than the Himalayas and were once as tall, but have been worn down by the ages. Walking along a windblown ridge or climbing over a rock fence to look into the eyes of a ragamuffin sheep, even tenderfeet get a chance to feel very outdoorsy. The tradition of staying close to the land remains true—albeit in an updated form—in the 21st century; you'll see restaurants serving organic foods as well as stickers advocating for environmental causes in the windows of homes.

Dress in layers, and expect rain mixed with brilliant "bright spells" (pubs offer atmospheric shelter at every turn). Drizzly days can be followed by delightful evenings.

Plan to spend the majority of your time in the unspoiled North Lake District. In this chapter, I focus on the town of Keswick, the lake called Derwentwater, and the vast, time-passed Newlands Valley. The North Lake District works great by car or by bus (with easy train access via Penrith), delights nature-lovers, and has good accommodations to boot.

The South Lake District—slightly closer to London—is famous primarily for its Wordsworth and Beatrix Potter sights, and gets the promotion, the tour crowds, and the tackiness that comes with them. I strongly recommend that you focus on the north. Ideally, enter the region from the north, via Penrith. Make your home base in or near Keswick, and side-trip from here into the South Lake District only if you're interested in the Wordsworth and Beatrix Potter sights.

Planning Your Time

On a three-week trip to Britain, I'd spend two days and two nights in this area. Penrith is the nearest train station, just 40 minutes by bus or car from Keswick. Those without a car will use Keswick as a springboard: Cruise the lake and take one of the many hikes in the Catbells area. Non-hikers can hop on a minibus tour. If great scenery is commonplace in your life, the Lake District can be more soothing (and rainy) than exciting. If you're rushed, you could make this area a one-night stand—or even a quick drive-through.

Two-Day Driving Plan: Here's the most exciting way for drivers coming from the south—who'd like to visit South Lake District sights en route to the North Lake District—to max out their time here:

Day 1: Get an early start, aiming to leave the motorway at Kendal by 10:30; drive along Windermere and through Ambleside.

11:30 Tour Dove Cottage and the Wordsworth Museum.

13:00 Backtrack to Ambleside, where a small road leads up and over the dramatic Kirkstone Pass (far more scenic northbound than southbound—get out and bite the wind) and down to Glenridding on Lake Ullswater.

15:00 Catch the Ullswater boat and ride to Howtown. Hike six miles (3-4 hours, roughly 15:30-19:00) from Howtown back to Glenridding. Or, for a shorter, one-hour Ullswater experience, hike up to the Aira Force waterfall (described later).

19:00 Drive to your Keswick hotel or farmhouse B&B near Keswick, with a stop as the sun sets at Castlerigg Stone Circle.

Day 2: Spend the morning (3-4 hours) splicing the Catbells high-ridge hike into a circular boat trip around Derwentwater. In the afternoon, make the circular drive from Keswick through the Newlands Valley, Buttermere, Honister Pass, and Borrowdale. You could tour the Honister Slate Mine en route (last tour at 15:30) and/or pitch-and-putt nine holes in Keswick before a late dinner.

Getting Around the Lake District
With a Car

Nothing is very far from Keswick and Derwentwater. Pick up a good map (any hotel can loan you one), get off the big roads, and leave the car, at least occasionally, for some walking. In summer, the Keswick-Ambleside-Windermere-Bowness corridor (A591) suffers from congestion.

Keswick Motor Company rents cars in Keswick (from £32/ day with insurance, Mon-Sat 8:30-17:15, closed Sun, ages 21-70 only, must have passport and International Driving Permit— see page 792, Lake Road, a block from Moot Hall in town center, tel. 017687/72064, http://keswickmotorcompany.co.uk).

Parking is tight throughout the region. It's easiest to just park in the pay-and-display lots (gather small coins, as most machines don't make change). If you're parking free on the roadside, don't block the vital turnouts. Never park on double yellow lines.

Without a Car

Those based in Keswick without a car manage fine. Because of the region's efforts to "green up" travel and cut down on car traffic, the bus service is quite efficient for your hiking and sightseeing. (You could even make a case for leaving your car in town and using the bus for many sightseeing and hiking agendas.)

By Bus: Keswick has no real bus station; buses stop at a turn-out in front of the Booths Supermarket. Local buses take you quickly and easily (if not always frequently) to all nearby points of interest. Check the schedule carefully to make sure you can catch the last bus home. The exhaustive *Cumbria & Lakes Rider* bus brochure (free, at TI or on any bus) explains the schedules. On board, you can purchase one-day Explorers passes (£9.75), or get one-day passes for certain routes. A four-day pass is available at the Keswick TI/National Park Visitors Centre. For bus and rail info, visit www.traveline.org.uk.

Bus **#X50** connects Penrith train station to Keswick (hourly Mon-Sat, 8/day Sun, 40 minutes, £5.50); note that the same bus changes names to #X4 and #X5 when going to points beyond Keswick.

Bus **#77/#77A,** the Honister Rambler, makes the gorgeous circle from Keswick around Derwentwater, over Honister Pass, through Buttermere, and down the Whinlatter Valley (4/day clockwise, 4/day "anticlockwise," daily Easter-Oct, weekends only in Nov, 1.5-hour loop, £6.50 Honister Dayrider all-day pass).

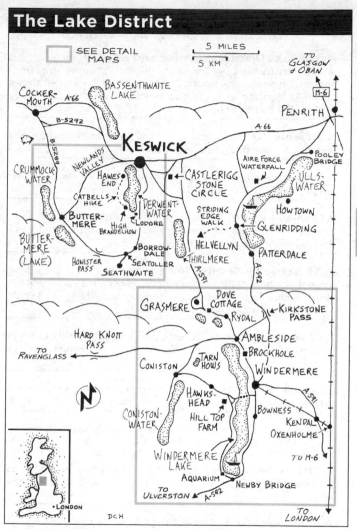

The Lake District

Bus **#78,** the Borrowdale Rambler, goes topless in the summer, affording a wonderful sightseeing experience in and of itself, heading from Keswick to Lodore Hotel, Grange, Rosthwaite, and Seatoller at the base of Honister Pass (roughly hourly, 2/hour mid-July-Aug, 8/day on Sun, 25 minutes each way, £6.50 Borrowdale Dayrider all-day pass).

Bus **#108,** the Patterdale Bus, runs between Penrith and Glenridding, stopping in Pooley Bridge (Mon-Sat 4-6/day, Sun 2/day, no Sun service Sept-Easter, 45 minutes, £14 Ullswater Bus & Boat day pass covers this bus route as well as steamers

The Lake District at a Glance

North Lake District: Keswick and Nearby

▲▲**Theatre by the Lake** Top-notch theater a pleasant stroll from Keswick's main square. **Hours:** Shows at 20:00 in summer, shows generally start earlier fall through spring; box office open daily 9:30-20:00. See page 637.

▲**Derwentwater** Lake immediately south of Keswick, with good boat service and trails. See page 628.

▲**Pencil Museum** Paean to graphite-filled wooden sticks. **Hours:** Daily 9:30-17:00. See page 629.

▲**Pitch-and-Putt Golf** Cheap, easygoing nine-hole course in Keswick's Hope Park. **Hours:** Daily from 9:30, last start at 19:45 or dusk, may close Nov-Easter. See page 629.

▲▲▲ **Scenic Circle Drive South of Keswick** Hour-long drive through the best of the Lake District's scenery, with plenty of fun stops (including the fascinating Honister Slate Mine) and short side-trip options. See page 635.

▲▲**Castlerigg Stone Circle** Evocative and extremely old (even by British standards) ring of Neolithic stones. **Hours:** Always viewable. See page 630.

▲▲**Catbells High Ridge Hike** Two-hour hike along dramatic ridge southwest of Keswick. See page 630.

▲▲**Buttermere Hike** Four-mile, low-impact lakeside loop in a gorgeous setting. See page 634.

▲▲**More Hikes from Keswick** Scenic hikes with varying degrees of difficulty: Latrigg Peak, Latrigg Trail, Walla Crag. See page 634.

▲▲**Ullswater Hike and Boat Ride** Long lake best enjoyed via steamer boat and seven-mile walk. **Hours:** Boats run daily 9:45-16:40, less off-season. See page 647.

on Ullswater).

Bus **#505,** the Coniston Rambler, connects Windermere with Hawkshead (daily Easter-Oct, about hourly, 35 minutes).

Bus **#517,** the Kirkstone Rambler, runs between Windermere and Glenridding (3/day mid-July-Aug, Sat-Sun only Easter-mid-July, 1 hour).

Buses **#555** and **#556** connect Keswick with the south (hourly,

▲**Honister Slate Mine Tour** A 1.5-hour hike through a 19th-century mine at the top of Honister Pass. **Hours**: Daily at 10:30, 12:30, 14:00, and 15:30; Dec–Jan 12:30 tour only.

▲**Aira Force Waterfall** Easy uphill hike to thundering waterfall. **Hours**: Always open.

South Lake District
▲▲**Dove Cottage and Wordsworth Museum** The poet's humble home, with a museum that tells the story of his remarkable life. **Hours:** Daily March-Oct 9:30–17:30, Nov-Dec and Feb until 16:30, closed Jan. See page 651.

▲**Rydal Mount** Wordsworth's later, more upscale home. **Hours:** March–Oct daily 9:30–17:00; Nov–Dec and Feb Wed–Sun 11:00–16:00, closed Mon–Tue; closed Jan. See page 652.

▲**Hill Top Farm** Beatrix Potter's painstakingly preserved cottage. **Hours:** June-Aug Sat–Thu 10:00–17:00, April–May and Sept-Oct Sat–Thu 10:30–16:30, shorter hours off-season, closed Fri and Nov–mid-Feb, often a long wait to visit—call ahead. See page 653.

▲**Beatrix Potter Gallery** Collection of artwork by and background on the creator of Peter Rabbit. **Hours:** June-Aug Sat–Thu 10:30–17:00, April–May and Sept-Oct Sat–Thu 11:00–17:00, shorter hours off-season, closed Fri and Nov–mid-Feb. See page 654.

The World of Beatrix Potter Touristy exhibition about the author. **Hours:** Daily April–Sept 10:00–18:00, Oct–March until 17:00. See page 655.

Brockhole National Park Visitors Centre Best place to gather info on Lake Windermere and the surrounding area, grandly situated in a lakeside mansion. **Hours:** Daily April–Oct 10:00–17:00, Nov–March until 16:00. See page 655.

1 hour to Windermere).

Bus **#599**, the open-top Lakes Rider, runs along the main Windermere corridor, connecting the big tourist attractions in the south (3/hour daily Easter-Aug, 50 minutes each way, £6.50 Central Lakes Dayrider all-day pass, route: Grasmere and Dove Cottage-Rydal Mount-Ambleside-Brockhole-Windermere-Bowness Pier).

By Bike: Several shops in Keswick rent road bikes and mountain bikes. Bikes come with helmets, touring maps, and advice for good trips. Keswick works well as a springboard for several fine days out on a bike; consider a three-hour trip up Newlands Valley and the Latrigg loop up a former train track (now a biking path), and back via Castlerigg Stone Circle.

Good places to rent bikes in Keswick include **Whinlatter Bikes** (£12/half-day, £15/day, daily 10:00-17:00, 82 Main Street, tel. 017687/73940, www.whinlatterbikes.com) and **Keswick Mountain Bikes** (£12/half-day, £15/day, Mon-Sat 9:00-17:30, Sun 10:00-17:30; right off the town square, at the recommended Lakeland Pedlar Restaurant; tel. 017687/75202, www.keswick bikes.co.uk). The **Keswick Motor Company** also rents bikes (£10/half-day, £15/day, £20 deposit; see listing under "Getting Around the Lake District," earlier).

By Boat: A circular boat service glides you around Derwentwater, with several hiker-aiding stops along the way (for a cruise/hike option, see "Derwentwater Lakeside Walk" on page 630).

By Foot: Hiking information is available everywhere. Don't hike without a good, detailed map (wide selection at Keswick TI and at the many outdoor gear stores, or borrow one from your B&B). Helpful fliers at TIs and B&Bs describe the most popular routes. For an up-to-date weather report, ask at a TI or call 0844-846-2444. Wear suitable clothing and footwear (you can rent boots in town; B&Bs can often loan you a good coat or an umbrella if weather looks threatening). Plan for rain. Watch your footing. Injuries are common. And every year, several people die while hiking in the area (some from overexertion; others are blown off ridges).

By Tour: For organized bus tours that run the roads of the Lake District, see "Tours in Keswick," later.

Keswick and the North Lake District

As far as touristy Lake District towns go, Keswick (KEZ-ick, population 5,000) is far more enjoyable than Windermere, Bowness, or Ambleside. Many of the place names around Keswick have Norse origins, inherited from the region's 10th-century settlers. An important mining center for slate, copper, and lead through the Middle Ages, Keswick became a resort in the 19th century. Its fine Victorian buildings recall those Romantic days when city slickers first learned about "communing with nature." Today, the compact town is lined with tearooms, pubs, gift shops, and hiking-gear shops. The lake called Derwentwater is a pleasant 10-minute walk from the town center.

THE LAKE DISTRICT

Orientation to Keswick

(area code: 017687)
Keswick is an ideal home base, with plenty of good B&Bs, an easy bus connection to the nearest train station at Penrith, and a prime location near the best lake in the area, Derwentwater. In Keswick, everything is within a 10-minute walk of everything else: the pedestrian town square, the TI, recommended B&Bs, grocery stores, the wonderful municipal pitch-and-putt golf course, the main bus stop, a lakeside boat dock, the post office (with Internet access upstairs), and a central parking lot. Thursdays and Saturdays are market days in the town square, but the square is lively every day throughout the summer.

Keswick town is a delight for wandering. Its centerpiece, Moot Hall (meaning "meeting hall"), was a 16th-century copper warehouse upstairs with an arcade below (closed after World War II). "Keswick" means "cheese farm"—a legacy from the time when the town square was the spot to sell cheese. When the town square went pedestrian-only a few years back, locals were all abuzz about people tripping over the curbs. (The English, seemingly thrilled by ever-present danger, are endlessly warning visitors to "watch your head," "duck or grouse," "watch the step," and "mind the gap.")

Keswick and the Lake District are popular with English

Keswick

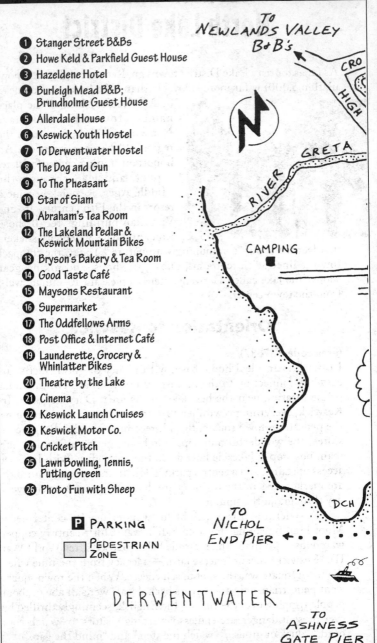

1 Stanger Street B&Bs
2 Howe Keld & Parkfield Guest House
3 Hazeldene Hotel
4 Burleigh Mead B&B;
Brundholme Guest House
5 Allerdale House
6 Keswick Youth Hostel
7 To Derwentwater Hostel
8 The Dog and Gun
9 To The Pheasant
10 Star of Siam
11 Abraham's Tea Room
12 The Lakeland Pedlar &
Keswick Mountain Bikes
13 Bryson's Bakery & Tea Room
14 Good Taste Café
15 Maysons Restaurant
16 Supermarket
17 The Oddfellows Arms
18 Post Office & Internet Café
19 Launderette, Grocery &
Whinlatter Bikes
20 Theatre by the Lake
21 Cinema
22 Keswick Launch Cruises
23 Keswick Motor Co.
24 Cricket Pitch
25 Lawn Bowling, Tennis,
Putting Green
26 Photo Fun with Sheep

P PARKING

PEDESTRIAN
ZONE

TO NEWLANDS VALLEY B&B's

CRO
HIGH

RIVER GRETA

CAMPING

DCH

TO NICHOL END PIER

DERWENTWATER

TO ASHNESS GATE PIER

THE LAKE DISTRICT

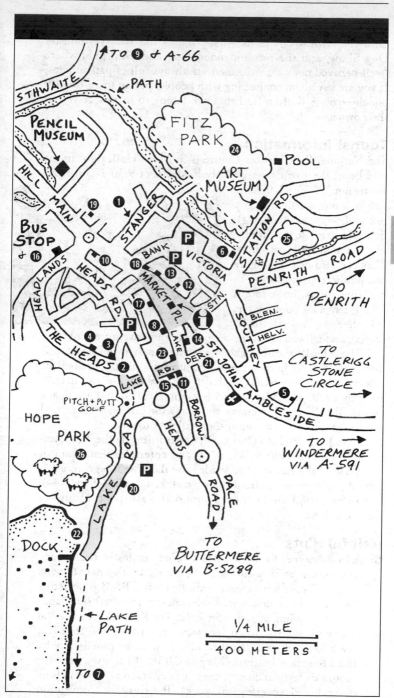

TO **9** & A-66

STHWAITE

PATH

PENCIL MUSEUM

FITZ PARK

POOL

ART MUSEUM

HILL

MAIN

19

1

STANGER

BUS STOP

16

HEADLANDS

HEADS RD.

10

18

BANK

VICTORIA

P

P

13

12

STN.

6

STATION RD.

25

PENRITH ROAD

TO PENRITH

SOUTHEY

BLEN.

HELV.

MARKET PL.

17

8

4

3

2

23

LAKE

14

DER.

21

ST. JOHNS

AMBLESIDE

5

TO CASTLERIGG STONE CIRCLE

TO WINDERMERE VIA A-591

THE HEADS

P

LAKE RD.

15

11

BORROW-

HEADS

DALE ROAD

PITCH + PUTT GOLF

HOPE PARK

26

LAKE ROAD

P

20

DOCK

22

LAKE PATH

TO **7**

TO BUTTERMERE VIA B-5289

¼ MILE

400 METERS

THE LAKE DISTRICT

holiday-makers who prefer to bring their dogs with them on vacation. The town square in Keswick can look like the Westminster Dog Show, and the recommended Dog and Gun pub, where "well-behaved dogs are welcomed," is always full of patient pups. If you are shy about connecting with people, pal up to an English pooch—you will often find they are happy to introduce you to their owners.

Tourist Information

The National Park Visitors Centre is in Moot Hall, right in the middle of the town square (daily Easter-Oct 9:30-17:30, Nov-

Easter until 16:30, tel. 017687/ 72645, www.lakedistrict.gov .uk and www.keswick.org). Staffers are pros at advising you about hiking routes. They can also help you figure out public transportation to outlying sights, book rooms (you'll pay a £4 booking fee; it's cheaper to call B&Bs direct), and tell you about the region's various adventure activities.

The TI sells theater tickets, Keswick Launch tickets (at a £1 discount), fishing licenses, and brochures and maps that outline nearby hikes (£0.60-1.80, including a very simple and driver-friendly £1.80 *Lap Map* featuring sights, walks, and a mileage chart). The TI also has books and maps for hikers, cyclists, and drivers (more books are sold at shops all over town).

Check the "What's On Locally" boards (inside the TI's foyer) for information about walks, talks, and entertainment. You can also pick up the *Events 2012* guide. The daily weather forecast is posted just outside the front door (weather tel. 0844-846-2444). For information about the TI's guided walks, see "Tours in Keswick," later.

Helpful Hints

Book in Advance: Keswick hosts a variety of festivals and conventions, especially during the summer, so it's smart to book ahead. Please honor your bookings—the B&B proprietors here lose out on much-needed business if you don't show up.

A sampling of events for 2012: The Keswick Jazz Festival mellows out the town in early May (May 3-6 in 2012, www.keswickjazzfestival.co.uk), followed immediately by the Mountain Festival (May 16-20 in 2012, www.keswick mountainfestival.co.uk), then a beer festival in early June (www.keswickbeerfestival.co.uk). The Keswick Convention packs the town with 4,000 evangelical Christians for three weeks each summer (mid-July-early Aug, www.keswick ministries.org).

Several Bank Holiday Mondays in spring and summer (May 7, June 4, and Aug 27 in 2012) draw vacationers from all over the island for three-day weekends.

If you have trouble finding a room (or a B&B that accepts small children), try www.keswick.org to search for available rooms.

Internet Access: U-Compute, located above the store that contains the post office, provides Internet access in a pleasant and airy perch (£2/30 minutes, £3/hour, unused time valid for 2 weeks, daily May-mid-Sept 8:30-21:00, mid-Sept-April 9:00-17:30, 16 terminals and Wi-Fi—same price, corner of Main and Bank streets, tel. 017687/75127). The **launderette** listed next also has Wi-Fi (£2/hour).

Laundry: For now, it's around the corner from the bus station on Main Street, next to the Co-op grocery, but sometime in 2012 it will move to a new location behind the Pencil Museum (self-service Mon-Fri 8:00-19:00, Sat-Sun 9:00-18:00, £6/load wash and dry, change machine and coin-op soap dispenser; full-service for a reasonable £1.20 service charge extra; tea and Wi-Fi for £2, tel. 017687/75448).

Midges: Tiny biting insects called midges—similar to no-see-ums—might bug you in this region from late May through September, particularly at dawn and dusk. The severity depends on the weather since wind and sunshine can deter them, and insect repellant fends them off: Ask the locals what works if you'll be hiking.

Tours in Keswick

Guided Walks—Walks of varying levels of difficulty depart from the TI several times a week at 10:00. They're led by local guides, leave regardless of the weather, and sometimes incorporate a bus ride into the outing (£7.50/half-day, £15/day, Easter-Oct, no tours during religious convention in July, wear suitable clothing and footwear, bring lunch and water, full-day tours return by 17:00, tel. 017687/72645, www.keswickrambles.org.uk). TIs throughout the region also offer free walks led by "Voluntary Rangers" (generally from Keswick on Sun and Wed in summer, ask for the *Events 2012* guide).

Bus Tours—These are great for people with bucks who'd like to wring maximum experience out of their limited time and see the area without lots of hiking or messing with public transport. For a cheaper alternative, take public buses.

Mountain Goat Tours is the region's dominant tour company. Unfortunately, they run their minibus tours out of Windermere, with pick-ups in Bowness and Ambleside, and sometimes in Kendal and Grasmere. They only pick up in Keswick on Fridays for their High Adventure tour—subject to demand. For those based in Keswick, add about an extra hour of driving, round-trip, if you join their tours in Windermere (tours run daily, £26/half-day, £36/day, year-round if there are sufficient sign-ups, minimum 4 people to a maximum of 16 per hearty bus, book in advance by calling 015394/45161, www.mountain-goat.com).

Show Me Cumbria Private Tours runs personalized tours all around the Lake District, and can pick you up in Keswick and other locations. They charge per hour, not per person, so their tours are a fine value for small groups (£30/hour, small groups of 1-6 people, tel. 01768/866-880, mobile 0780-902-6357, based in Penrith, www.showmecumbria.co.uk, andy@showmecumbria.co.uk).

Sights in Keswick

▲**Derwentwater**—One of Cumbria's most photographed and popular lakes, Derwentwater has four islands, good circular boat service, and plenty of trails. The pleasant town of Keswick is a short stroll from the shore, near the lake's north end. The roadside views aren't much, and while you can walk around the lake (fine trail, floods in heavy rains, 9 miles, 4 hours), much of the walk is boring. You're better off mixing a hike and boat ride (see "Hikes and Drives in the North Lake District," later), or simply enjoy the circular boat tour of the lake (described next).

Boating on Derwentwater: Keswick Launch runs two **cruises** an hour, alternating clockwise and "anticlockwise" (departing on the half-hour, daily 10:00-16:30, July-Aug until 17:30, in winter 5-6/day generally weekends and holidays only, at end of Lake Road, tel. 017687/72263, www.keswick-launch.co.uk). Boats make seven stops on each 50-minute round-trip (may skip some stops or not run at all if the water level is very high—such as after a heavy rain). The boat trip costs £9 per circle (£1 less if you book through TI) with free stopovers, or about £2 per segment. Stand at the end of the pier Gilligan-style, or the boat may not stop. Keswick Launch also rents **rowboats** for up to three people (£8/30 minutes, £12/hour, open Easter-Oct, larger rowboats and motor boats available).

Keswick Launch's **evening cruise** is a delightful little trip that comes with a glass of wine and a mid-lake stop for a short commentary (£9.20, £22 family ticket, 1 hour, mid-July-Aug at 18:30 and 19:30 every evening—weather permitting and if enough people show up; 6 is the minimum). You're welcome to bring a picnic dinner and munch scenically as you cruise.

▲**Pencil Museum**—Graphite was first discovered centuries ago in Keswick. A hunk of the stuff proved great for marking sheep in the 15th century. In 1832, the first crude Keswick pencil factory opened, and the rest is history (which is what you'll learn about here). While you can't actually tour the 150-year-old factory where the famous Derwent pencils were made, you can enjoy the smell of thousands of pencils getting sharpened for the first time. The adjacent charming and kid-friendly museum is a good way to pass a rainy hour; you may even catch an artist's demonstration. Take a look at the "war pencils" made for WWII bomber crews (filled with tiny maps and compasses) and relax for 10 minutes watching *The Humble Pencil* video in the theater, followed by a sleepy animated-snowman short.

Cost and Hours: £3.75, daily 9:30-17:00, last entry one hour before closing, humble café on-site, 3-minute walk from the town center, signposted off Main Street, tel. 017687/73626, www.pencil museum.co.uk).

Fitz Park—An inviting, grassy park stretches alongside Keswick's tree-lined, duck-filled River Greta. There's plenty of room for kids to burn off energy. Consider an after-dinner stroll on the footpath. You may catch men in white (or frisky schoolboys in uniform) playing a game of cricket. There's the serious bowling green (where you're welcome to watch the experts play, and enjoy the cheapest cuppa—i.e., tea—in town), and the public one where tourists are welcome to give lawn bowling a go (£3). You can try tennis on a grass court (£7/hour for 2 people, includes rackets) or enjoy the putting green (£2). Find the rental pavilion across the road from the art gallery (open daily 9:30-19:45 or until dusk).

▲**Golf**—A lush nine-hole pitch-and-putt golf course near the gardens in Hope Park separates the town from the lake and offers a classy, cheap, and convenient chance to golf near the birthplace of the sport. This is a great, fun, and inexpensive experience—just right after a day of touring and before dinner (£3.95 for, £2.60 for putting, £2.80 for 18 tame holes of "obstacle golf," daily from 9:30, last round starts at 19:45 or dusk, may close Nov-Easter, tel. 017687/73445).

Swimming—While the leisure center doesn't have a serious adult pool, it does have an indoor pool kids love, with a huge waterslide and wave machine (swim times vary by day and by season—call or check website, no towels or suits for rent, lockers-£1 deposit, 10-minute walk from town center, follow Station Road past Fitz Park and veer left, tel. 017687/72760, www.carlisleleisure.com).

Near Keswick

▲▲**Castlerigg Stone Circle**—For some reason, 70 percent of England's stone circles are here in Cumbria. Castlerigg is one of the best and oldest in Britain, and an easy stop for drivers. The circle—90 feet across and 5,000 years old—has 38 stones mysteriously laid out on a line between the two tallest peaks on the horizon. They served as a celestial calendar for ritual celebrations. Imagine the ambience here, as ancient people filled this clearing in spring to celebrate fertility, in late summer to commemorate the harvest, and in the winter to celebrate the winter solstice and the coming renewal of light. Festival dates were dictated by how the sun rose and set in relation to the stones. The more that modern academics study this circle, the more meaning they find in the placement of the stones. The two front stones face due north, toward a cut in the mountains. The rare-for-stone-circles "sanctuary" lines up with its center stone to mark where the sun rises on May Day. (Party!) For maximum "goose pimples" (as they say here), show up at sunset (free, open all the time, 3 miles east of Keswick—follow brown signs, 3 minutes off A66, easy parking).

Hikes and Drives in the North Lake District

From Keswick

Derwentwater Lakeside Walk—There's a trail all along Derwentwater, but much of it (especially the Keswick-to-Hawes End stretch) is not that interesting. The best hour-long section is the 1.5-mile path between the docks at High Brandelhow and Hawes End in Keswick, where you'll stroll a level trail through peaceful trees. This walk works best in conjunction with the lake boat (see "Boating on Derwentwater," earlier).

▲▲**Catbells High Ridge Hike**—For a great "king of the mountain" feeling, 360-degree views, and a close-up look at the weather blowing over the ridge, hike above Derwentwater about two hours from Hawes End up along the ridge to Catbells (1,480 feet) and down to High Brandelhow. Because the mountaintop is basically treeless, you're treated to dramatic panoramas the entire way up.

From High Brandelhow, you can catch the boat back to Keswick, or take the easy path along the shore of Derwentwater to your Hawes End starting point. (Extending the hike farther around the lake to Lodore takes you to a waterfall, rock climbers, a fine café, and another boat dock for a convenient return to Keswick—see "Car Hiking: A Scenic Circle Drive South of Keswick," later.) Note: When the water level is very high (for example, after a heavy rain), boats can't stop at Hawes End—ask at the TI or boat dock before setting out.

Catbells is probably the most dramatic family walk in the area (but wear sturdy shoes, bring a raincoat, and watch your footing). From Keswick, the lake, or your farmhouse B&B, you can see silhouetted figures hiking along this ridge.

Getting There: To reach the trailhead from Keswick, catch the "anticlockwise" boat (see "Boating on Derwentwater," earlier) and ride for 10 minutes to the second stop, Hawes End. (You can also ride to High Brandelhow and take this walk in the other direction, but I don't recommend it—two rocky scrambles along the way are easier, and safer, to navigate going uphill from Hawes End.) Note the schedule for your return boat ride, as boats generally run only hourly. Drivers can park free at Hawes End, but parking is limited and the road can be hard to find—get very clear directions in town before heading out. The Keswick TI sells a *Catbells* brochure about the hike (£0.95).

The Route: The path is not signposted, but it's easy to follow, and you'll see plenty of other walkers. From Hawes End, walk away from the lake, through a kissing gate to the turn just before the car park. Then turn left and go up, up, up. After about 20 minutes, you'll hit the first of two short scrambles (where the trail vanishes into a cluster of steep rocks), which leads to a bluff.

From the first little summit (great for a picnic break), and then along the ridge, you'll enjoy sweeping views of the lake on one side, and of Newlands Valley on the other. The bald peak in the distance is Catbells. Broken stones crunch under each step, wind buffets your ears, clouds prowl overhead, and the sheep baa comically. To anyone looking up from the distant farmhouse B&Bs, you are but a stick figure on the ridge.

Derwentwater & Newlands Valley

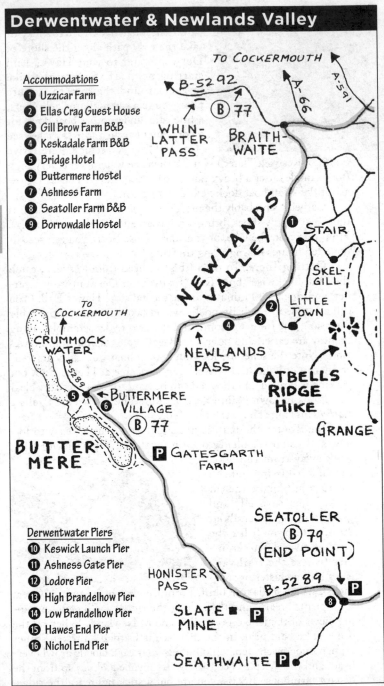

Accommodations
1. Uzzicar Farm
2. Ellas Crag Guest House
3. Gill Brow Farm B&B
4. Keskadale Farm B&B
5. Bridge Hotel
6. Buttermere Hostel
7. Ashness Farm
8. Seatoller Farm B&B
9. Borrowdale Hostel

Derwentwater Piers
10. Keswick Launch Pier
11. Ashness Gate Pier
12. Lodore Pier
13. High Brandelhow Pier
14. Low Brandelhow Pier
15. Hawes End Pier
16. Nichol End Pier

THE LAKE DISTRICT

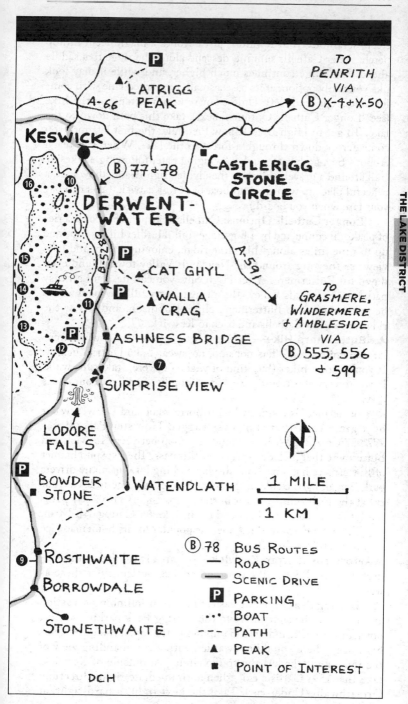

THE LAKE DISTRICT

Just below the summit, the trail disintegrates into another short, steep, scramble. Your reward is just beyond: a magnificent hilltop perch. After Catbells summit, descend along the ridge to a saddle ahead. The ridge continues much higher, and while it may look like your only option, at its base a small, unmarked lane with comfortable steps leads left. Unless you're up for extending the hike (see "Longer Catbells Options," next), take this path down to the lake. To get to High Brandelhow Pier, take the first left fork you come across down through a forest to the lake. When you reach Abbot's Bay, go left through a swinging gate, following a lakeside trail around a gravelly bluff, to the idyllic High Brandelhow Pier, a peaceful place to wait for your boat back to Keswick. (You can pay your fare when you board.)

Longer Catbells Options: Catbells is just the first of a series of peaks all connected by a fine ridge trail. Hardier hikers continue up to nine miles along this same ridge, enjoying valley and lake views as they arc around the Newlands Valley toward (and even down to) Buttermere. After High Spy, you can descend an easy path into Newlands Valley. The ultimate, very full day-plan would be to take a bus to Buttermere, climb Robinson, and follow the ridge around to Catbells and back to Keswick.

▲▲**Buttermere Hike**—The ideal little lake with a lovely, circular four-mile stroll offers nonstop, no-sweat Lake District beauty. If you're not a hiker (but kind of wish you were), take this walk. If you're very short on time, at least stop here and get your shoes dirty.

Buttermere is connected with Borrowdale and Derwentwater by a great road that runs over rugged Honister Pass. Buses #77/#77A make a 1.5-hour round-trip loop between Keswick and Buttermere that includes a trip over this pass. The two-pub hamlet of Buttermere has a pay-and-display parking lot, but many drivers park free along the side of the road. You're welcome to leave your car at the Fish Inn if you eat in their pub. There's also a pay parking lot at the Honister Pass end of the lake (at Gatesgarth Farm, £3). The Syke Farm in Buttermere is popular for its homemade ice cream (tel. 01768/77022).

▲▲**More Hikes from Keswick**—The area is riddled with wonderful hikes. B&Bs all have good advice, but consider these as well:

Latrigg Peak: For the easiest mountain-climbing sensation around, take the short drive to the Latrigg Peak parking lot just north of Keswick, and hike 15 minutes to the top of the 1,200-foot-high hill, where you'll be rewarded with a commanding view of the town and lake. At the traffic circle just outside of Keswick, take the A591 Carlisle exit, then an immediate right (direction: Ormathwaite/Underscar). Take the next right, a hard right, at the *Skiddaw* sign, where a long, steep, one-lane road leads to the Latrigg car park at the end of the lane. With more time, you can walk all the way from your Keswick B&B to Latrigg and back (it's a popular evening walk for locals). Or extend it even farther with the full Latrigg Trail, described next.

Latrigg Trail: Right from downtown Keswick, you can walk the seven-mile Latrigg trail, which includes a stretch along an old train track and the Castlerigg Stone Circle described earlier (pick up £0.60 map/guide from TI).

Walla Crag: From your Keswick B&B, a fine two-hour walk to Walla Crag offers great fell (mountain) walking and a ridge-walk experience without the necessity of a bus or car. Start by strolling along the lake to the Great Wood parking lot (or drive to this lot), and head up Cat Ghyl (where "fell runners"—trail-running enthusiasts—practice) to Walla Crag. You'll be treated to great panoramic views over Derwentwater and surrounding peaks. You can do a shorter version of this walk from the parking lot at Ashness Bridge.

▲▲▲Car Hiking: A Scenic Circle Drive South of Keswick— This hour-long drive, which includes Newlands Valley, Buttermere, Honister Pass, and Borrowdale, gives you the best scenery you'll find in the North Lake District. (To do a similar route without a car from Keswick, take loop bus #77/#77A.) Distances are short, roads are narrow and have turnouts, and views are rewarding. Get a good map and ask your B&B host for advice.

From Keswick, leave town on Crosthwaite Road, then, at the roundabout, head west on Cockermouth Road (A66, following signs toward *Cockermouth* and *Workington*). Don't take the first Newlands Valley exit, but do take the second one (through Braithwaite), and follow signs up the majestic Newlands Valley (also signed for *Buttermere*).

If the **Newlands Valley** had a lake, it would be packed with tourists. But it doesn't—and it isn't. The valley is dotted with

500-year-old family-owned farms. Shearing day is reason to rush home from school. Sons get school out of the way ASAP, and follow their dads into the family business. Neighbor girls marry those sons and move in. Grandparents retire to the cottage next door. With the price of wool depressed, most of the wives supplement the family income by running B&Bs (virtually every farm in the valley rents rooms). The road has one lane, with turnouts for passing. From the Newlands Pass summit, notice the glacial-shaped wilds, once forested, now not.

From the parking lot at **Newlands Pass,** at the top of Newlands Valley (unmarked, but you'll see a waterfall on the left), there's an easy 300-yard hike to the little waterfall. On the other side of the road, there's also an easy one-mile hike up to **Knottrigg,** which probably offers more TPCB (thrills per calorie burned) than any walk in the region. If you don't have time for even a short hike, at least get out of the car and get a feel for the setting.

After Newlands Pass, descend to **Buttermere** (scenic lake, tiny hamlet with a pub and ice-cream store—see "Buttermere Hike," earlier), turn left, drive the length of the lake, and climb over rugged **Honister Pass**—strewn with glacial debris, remnants from the old slate mines, and curious, shaggy Swaledale sheep (looking more like goats with their curly horns). The U-shaped valleys you'll see are textbook examples of those carved out by glaciers. Look high on the hillsides for "hanging valleys"—small glacial-shaped scoops cut off by the huge flow of the biggest glacier, which swept down the main valley.

The **Honister Slate Mine,** England's last still-functioning slate mine (and worth ▲), stands at the summit of Honister Pass.

The youth hostel next to it was originally built to house miners in the 1920s. The mine offers worthwhile tours (perfect for when it's pouring outside): You'll put on a hardhat, load onto a bus for a short climb, then hike into a shaft to learn about the region's slate industry. It's a long, stooped hike into the mountain, made interesting by the guide, and punctuated by the sound of your helmet scraping against low bits of the shaft. Standing deep in the mountain, surrounded by slate scrap and the beams of thirty headlamps fluttering around like fireflies, you'll learn of the hardships of miners' lives and how "green gold" is trendy once again, making the mine viable. Even if you don't have time to take the tour, stop here for its slate-filled shop (café and nice WCs, £10, 1.5-hour tour; departs daily at 10:30, 12:30, 14:00, and 15:30; Dec-Jan 12:30 tour only, call ahead to confirm times and to book a spot, helmets and lamps provided, tel. 017687/77230, www.honister-slate-mine.co.uk).

After stark and lonely Honister Pass, drop into sweet and homey **Borrowdale,** with a few lonely hamlets and fine hikes from Seathwaite. Circling back to Keswick past Borrowdale, B5289 takes you past a number of popular attractions: You can climb stairs to the top of the house-size **Bowder Stone** (signposted, a few minutes walk off the main road). Farther along, **Lodore Falls** is a short walk from the road (behind Lodore Hotel). **Shepherds Crag,** a cliff overlooking Lodore, was made famous by pioneer rock climbers. (Their descendants hang from little ridges on its face today.) This is serious climbing, with several fatalities a year.

For a great lunch, or tea and cakes, drop into the much-loved **High Lodore Farm Café,** where sheep farmer Martin is busy feeding hikers and day-trippers (Easter-Oct daily 9:00-17:00, closed Nov-Easter, short drive uphill from the main road and over a tiny bridge, tel. 017687/77221).

A very hard right off B5289 (signposted *Ashness Bridge, Watendlath*) and a steep half-mile climb on a narrow lane takes you to the postcard-pretty **Ashness Packhorse Bridge** (a quintessential Lake District scene, parking lot just above on right). A half-mile farther up (parking lot on left, no sign), and you're startled by the "surprise view" of Derwentwater—great for a lakes photo op. Continuing from here, the road gets extremely narrow en route to the hamlet of **Watendlath,** which has a tiny lake and lazy farm animals.

Return to B5289, the Borrowdale Valley Road, and back to Keswick. If you have yet to see it, cap your drive with a short detour from Keswick to the Castlerigg Stone Circle (described earlier).

Nightlife in Keswick

▲▲Theatre by the Lake—Keswickians brag that they enjoy "London theater quality at Keswick prices." Their theater offers events year-round and a wonderful rotation of six plays through the summer (plays vary throughout the week, with music concerts on some Sun). There are two stages: The main one seats 400, and the smaller "studio" theater seats 100 (and features edgier plays with rough language and nudity). Attending a play here is a fine opportunity to enjoy a classy night out.

Cost and Hours: £10-26, box office open daily 9:30-20:00, discounts for old and young, 20:00 shows in summer, shows generally start earlier fall through spring, café, smart to book ahead, parking at the adjacent lot is free after 18:30, tel. 017687/74411; book by phone, at TI, or at www.theatrebythelake.com.

▲▲Evening Activities—For a small and remote town, Keswick has lots going on in the evening. Remember, at this latitude it's light until 22:00 in midsummer. Along with the Theatre by the Lake (described above), you can **golf** (fine course, pitch-and-putt, goofy golf, or just enjoy the putting green, last start at 19:45) or **walk** among the grazing sheep in Hope Park as the sun gets ready to set (between the lake and the golf course, access from just above the beach, great photo ops on balmy evenings).

To socialize with locals, head to a pub for one of their special evenings: There's **quiz night** at The Dog and Gun (21:30 on most Thu; £1, proceeds go to Keswick's Mountain Rescue team, which rescues hikers and the occasional sheep). At a quiz night, tourists are more than welcome. Drop in, say you want to join a team, and you're in. If you like trivia, it's a great way to get to know people here.

Also in the town center, The Oddfellows Arms has free **live music** most summer nights (usually classic rock, from 21:30).

You can join Bob, the **Town Crier,** when he does his routine many summer Tuesday evenings (£2.50, 1.5 hours, usually starts at 19:30, weekly late May-early July, details at TI). Catch a **movie** at the Lonsdale Alhambra Cinema (St. Johns Street, tel. 017687/72195, www.keswick-alhambra.co.uk), a restored old-fashioned movie theater a few minutes' walk from the town center. An **evening lake cruise** is perfect for an extremely scenic, bring-your-own-picnic dinner (£10, 1 hour, with narration, mid-July-Aug at 18:30 and 19:30, weather permitting, see page 629).

Sleeping in Keswick

The Lake District abounds with attractive B&Bs, guest houses, and hostels. It needs them all when the summer hordes threaten the serenity of this Romantic mecca.

Reserve your room in advance in high season. From November through March, you should have no trouble finding a room. But to get a particular place (especially on Saturdays), call ahead. If you're using public transportation, you should sleep in Keswick. If you're driving, staying outside Keswick is your best chance for a remote farmhouse experience. Lakeland hostels offer £20 beds and come with an interesting crowd of all ages.

For Keswick, I've featured B&Bs and small hotels mainly on two streets, each within three blocks of the bus station and town square. Stanger Street, a bit humbler but quiet and handy, has smaller homes and more moderately priced rooms. "The Heads" is a classier area lined with proud Victorian houses, close to the lake and theater, overlooking a golf course. In addition to these two streets, Keswick abounds with many other options that are equally good; for example, the southeast area of the town center (around Eskin, Blencathra, and Helvellyn streets) is a few minutes' walk farther out, but has several B&Bs with easier parking.

Many of my Keswick listings charge extra for a one-night stay.

Sleep Code

(£1 = about $1.60, country code: 44, area code: 017687)
S = Single, **D** = Double/Twin, **T** = Triple, **Q** = Quad, **b** = bathroom, **s** = shower only. You can assume credit cards are accepted unless otherwise noted, and all B&B stays include breakfast.

To help you sort easily through these listings, I've divided the accommodations into three categories based on the price for a double room with bath:

$$$ Higher Priced—Most rooms £75 or more.
$$ Moderately Priced—Most rooms between £30-75.
$ Lower Priced—Most rooms £30 or less.

Prices can change without notice; verify the hotel's current rates online or by email. For other updates, see www.ricksteves.com/update.

Most won't book one-night stays on weekends (but if you show up and they have a bed free, it's yours) and don't welcome children under 12 (unless extremely well-behaved). Owners are enthusiastic about offering plenty of advice to get you on the right walking trail. Most accommodations have inviting lounges with libraries of books on the region and loaner maps. Take advantage of these lounges to transform your humble B&B room into a suite.

This is still the countryside—expect huge breakfasts (often with a wide selection, including vegetarian options), no phones in the rooms, and shower systems that might need to be switched on to get hot water. Parking is pretty easy (each place has a line on parking).

On Stanger Street

This street, quiet but just a block from Keswick's town center, is lined with B&Bs situated in Victorian slate townhouses. Each of these places is small, family-run, and accepts cash only. They are all good, offering comfortably sized rooms and a friendly welcome.

$$$ Badgers Wood B&B, at the top of the street, has six modern, bright, un-frilly view rooms, each named after a different tree (Sb-£39, Db-£74-78, 2-night minimum, no children under age 10, special diets accommodated, free Wi-Fi, 30 Stanger Street, tel. 017687/72621, www.badgers-wood.co.uk, enquiries@badgers-wood.co.uk, Andrew and Anne).

$$ Dunsford Guest House rents four rooms decorated with a Victorian feel, at a good price. Stained glass and wooden pews give the blue-and-cream breakfast room a country-chapel vibe (Db-£66, this price promised with this book in 2012, no children under

THE LAKE DISTRICT

age 16, free Wi-Fi, parking, 16 Stanger Street, tel. 017687/75059, www.dunsford.net, enquiries@dunsford.net, Deb and Keith).

$$ Heckberry House's two light, airy rooms are both on the first floor (Db-£66, 2-night minimum, no children, will pick up from bus station, 12 Stanger Street, tel. 017687/71277, www.heckberry.co.uk, enquiries@heckberry.co.uk, friendly Judith and David).

$$ Abacourt House, with a daisy-fresh breakfast room, has five pleasant doubles (Db-£70-74, no children, free Wi-Fi, £5 sack lunches available, 26 Stanger Street, tel. 017687/72967, www.abacourt.co.uk, abacourt.keswick@btinternet.com, John and Heather).

On The Heads

These B&Bs are in an area known as The Heads. This area is classier, with bigger and grander Victorian architecture and great

views overlooking the pitch-and-putt range and out into the hilly distance. The golf-course side of The Heads has free parking, if you can snare a spot (easy at night). A single yellow line on the curb means you're allowed to park there for free, but only overnight (16:00-10:00).

$$$ Howe Keld has the polished feel of a boutique hotel, but offers all the friendliness of a B&B. Its 14 contemporary-posh rooms, two on the ground floor, are spacious and tastefully decked out in native woods and slate. It's warm, welcoming, and family-run, with one of the best breakfasts I've had anywhere in England (Sb-£55-60, standard Db-£95-100, superior Db-£100-120, cash and 2-night minimum preferred, discount with 2 or more nights, family deals, free Wi-Fi, tel. 017687/72417 or toll-free 0800-783-0212, www.howekeld.co.uk, david@howekeld.co.uk, run with care by David and Valerie Fisher).

$$$ Parkfield Guest House, thoughtfully run and decorated by John and Susan Berry, is a big Victorian house. Its seven bright and pastel rooms have fine views (Sb-£60, Db-£80, Db suite-£95-100, these prices promised with this book through 2012, 2-night minimum, no children under age 16, Wi-Fi, off-street parking available, tel. 017687/72328, www.parkfield-keswick.co.uk, parkfieldkeswick@hotmail.co.uk).

$$$ Burleigh Mead B&B is a slate mansion from 1892 with wild carpeting. Gill (pronounced "Jill," short for Gillian) rents seven lovely rooms for a great value, and offers a friendly welcome, as well as a lounge and peaceful front-yard sitting area that's perfect for enjoying the view (Sb-£48, Db-£76, Db suite-£96, cash only, tel. 017687/75935, www.burleighmead.co.uk, info@burleigh mead.co.uk).

$$$ Hazeldene Hotel, on the corner of The Heads, rents 10 spacious rooms, many with commanding views. It's run with care by delightful Helen and her family (Db-£75-100 depending on view, Tb-£113, family room, free Wi-Fi, free parking, tel. 017687/72106, www.hazeldene-hotel.co.uk, info@hazeldene-hotel .co.uk).

$$ Brundholme Guest House has three bright and comfy rooms, all with grand views—especially from the front side—and a friendly and welcoming atmosphere (Sb-£38, Db-£68, free Wi-Fi, tel. 017687/73305, mobile 0773-943-5401, www.brundholme.co.uk, bazaly@hotmail.co.uk, Barry and Allison Thompson).

On Eskin Street

The area just southeast of the town center has several streets lined with good B&Bs, and is still within easy walking distance of downtown and the lake.

$$$ Allerdale House, a classy, nicely decorated stone mansion, holds six rooms and is well-run by Barbara and Paul (Sb-£38, Db-£76, larger Db-£90, these prices promised for 2012, free Internet access and Wi-Fi, free parking, 1 Eskin Street, tel. 017687/73891, www.allerdale-house.co.uk, reception@allerdale -house.co.uk).

Hostels in and near Keswick

The Lake District's inexpensive hostels, mostly located in great old buildings, are handy sources of information and social fun. These two hostels—both part of the Youth Hostels Association (www .yha.org.uk)—are former hotels, offering Internet access, laundry machines, and three cheap meals daily; at these, non-members pay about £3 extra a night, or buy a £16 membership.

$ Keswick Youth Hostel, with 85 beds in a converted old mill that overlooks the river, has a great riverside balcony and plenty of handy facilities, including a big lounge and library. Travelers of all ages feel at home here, but book ahead—beds here can be hard to come by from July through September (£21 beds in mostly 3- to 6-bed rooms, breakfast-£5, family rooms, includes sheets, Internet access and Wi-Fi, café, bar, laundry, office open 7:00-23:00, center of town just off Station Road before river, tel. 017687/72484, keswick@yha.org.uk).

$ Derwentwater Hostel, in a 220-year-old mansion on the shore of Derwentwater, is two miles south of Keswick and has 88 beds. The hostel was sold in 2011 so check to make sure it's still operating when you visit (£20 beds in 4- to 22-bed rooms, family rooms, Internet access and Wi-Fi, laundry, 23:00 curfew, follow B5289 from Keswick, look for sign 100 yards after Ashness exit, tel. 017687/77246, derwentwater@yha.org.uk).

West of Keswick, in the Newlands Valley

If you have a car, drive 10 minutes past Keswick down the majestic Newlands Valley (described earlier, under "Car Hiking: Scenic Circle Drive South of Keswick"). This valley is studded with 500-year-old farms that have been in the same family for centuries, and now rent rooms to supplement the family income. Each place offers easy parking, grand views, and perfect tranquility. The rooms are plainer and generally more dated than the B&Bs in town, and come with steep and gravelly roads, plenty of dogs, and an earthy charm. Traditionally, farmhouses lacked central heating, and while they are now heated, you can still request a hot-water bottle to warm up your bed.

Getting to the Newlands Valley: Leave Keswick via the roundabout at the end of Crosthwaite Road, and then head west on Cockermouth Road (A66). Take the second Newlands Valley exit through Braithwaite, and follow signs through Newlands Valley (drive toward Buttermere). All of my recommended B&Bs are on this road: Uzzicar Farm (under the shale field, which local kids love hiking up to glissade down), Ellas Crag Guest House, then Gill Brow Farm, and finally—the last house before the stark summit—Keskadale Farm (about four miles before Buttermere). The one-lane road has turnouts for passing. These are listed in geographical order, the first being a 10-minute drive from Keswick and the last being at the top of the valley (about a 15-minute drive from Keswick).

$$$ Uzzicar Farm is a big, rustic place with three comfy guest rooms in a low-ceilinged, 16th-century farmhouse—watch out for ducks. It's a particularly intimate and homey setting, where you'll feel like part of the family (S-£40, Db-£75-80, discount for 2 or more nights, family rooms, cash only, tel. 017687/78026, www.uzzicarfarm.co.uk, stay@uzzicarfarm.co.uk, Helen, David, and three daughters).

$$ Ellas Crag Guest House, with three rooms—each with a great view—is more of a comfortable stone house than a farm. This homey B&B offers a good mix of modern and traditional decor, including beautifully tiled bathrooms (Ss-£50, Sb-60, Ds-£64, Db-£68, singles available Mon-Thu only, these prices guaranteed with this book through 2012, cash only, 2-night minimum, local free-range meats and eggs for breakfast, sack lunches available, huge DVD library, laundry-£10/load, tel. 017687/78217, www.ellascrag.co.uk, info@ellascrag.co.uk, Jane and Ed Ma and their children).

$$ Gill Brow Farm is a rough-hewn, working farmhouse more than 300 years old where Anne Wilson rents two simple but fine rooms (D or Db-£56-60, tel. 017687/78270, www.gillbrow-keswick.co.uk, info@gillbrow-keswick.co.uk).

$$ Keskadale Farm is another good farmhouse experience, with Ponderosa hospitality. One of the valley's oldest, the house—with two guest rooms and a cozy lounge—is made from 500-year-old ship beams. This working farm is an authentic slice of Lake District life and is your chance to get to know lots of curly-horned sheep and the dogs that herd them. Now that her boys are old enough to help Dad in the fields, Margaret Harryman runs the B&B (Sb-£40-50, Db-£60-80, £2 extra for one-night stays, cash only, closed Dec-Feb, sack lunches available, tel. 017687/78544, www.keskadalefarm.co.uk, info@keskadalefarm.co.uk). They also rent a two-bedroom apartment (£400/week).

Southwest of Keswick, in Buttermere

$$$ Bridge Hotel, just beyond Newlands Valley at Buttermere, offers 21 beautiful rooms—most of them quite spacious—and a classic Old World countryside-hotel experience. On Fridays and Saturdays, a £29 dinner is required (standard Db-£130, fancier rooms for more, apartments available, check website for specials, minimum 2-night stay on weekends, free Wi-Fi in lobby, tel. 017687/70252, www.bridge-hotel.com, enquiries@bridge-hotel.com). There are no shops within 10 miles—only peace and quiet a stone's throw from one of the region's most beautiful lakes. The hotel has a dark-wood pub/restaurant on the ground floor.

$ Buttermere Hostel, a quarter-mile south of Buttermere village on Honister Pass Road, has good food, 70 beds, family rooms, and a peacefully rural setting (£20 beds in mostly 4- to 6-bed rooms, £2 cheaper mid-week, non-members-£3 more, includes breakfast, inexpensive lunches and dinners, laundry, office open 8:30-10:00 & 17:00-22:30, 23:00 curfew, tel. 0845-371-9508, www.yha.org.uk, buttermere@yha.org.uk).

South of Keswick, near Borrowdale

$$$ Ashness Farm sits alone, ruling its valley high above Derwentwater. If you want to be immersed in farm sounds and lakeland beauty, this is the place. On this 750-acre working farm, now owned by the National Trust, people have raised sheep and cattle for centuries. Today Anne and her son Henry are "tenant farmers" keeping this farm operating, and renting five rooms to boot (Sb-£49, Db-£78-90, less for 2 nights, cozy lounge, eggs and sausage literally fresh off the farm for breakfast, sack lunches available, just above Ashness Bridge, tel. 017687/77361, www.ashnessfarm.co.uk, inquiries@ashnessfarm.co.uk).

$$ Seatoller Farm B&B is a rustic 16th-century house on another working farm owned by the National Trust. Christine Simpson rents three rooms in her B&B, one of five buildings in this hamlet. The old windows are small, but the abundant flower boxes keep things bright (Db-£70-74, less for 2 or more nights, cottage available, closed mid-Dec-mid-Jan, tel. 017687/77232, www.seatollerfarm.co.uk, info@seatollerfarm.co.uk).

$ Borrowdale Hostel, in secluded Borrowdale Valley just south of Rosthwaite, is a well-run place surrounded by many ways to immerse yourself in nature. The hostel serves cheap dinners, offers sack lunches, and keeps the pantry well-stocked (86 beds, £18-22 beds in 2- to 8-bed dorms, D-£44, non-members-£3 more, family rooms, pay Internet access and Wi-Fi, laundry machines, 3 cheap meals daily, office open 7:30-22:30, 23:00 curfew, tel. 0845-371-9624, www.yha.org.uk, borrowdale@yha.org.uk). To reach this hostel from Keswick by bus, take #78, the "Borrowdale Rambler" (£6.50 Borrowdale Dayrider all-day pass, roughly hourly, 2/hour mid-July-Aug, 8/day on Sun, 25 minutes; last bus from Keswick at 17:40 most of year, at 18:00 mid-July-Aug).

Eating in Keswick

Keswick has a huge variety of eateries catering to its many visitors, but I've found nothing particularly enticing at the top end; the places listed here are just good, basic values. Most stop serving by 21:00.

The Dog and Gun serves good pub food (I love their rump of lamb) with great pub ambience. Upon arrival, muscle up to the bar to order your beer and/or meal. Then snag a table as soon as one opens up. Mind your head, and tread carefully: Low ceilings and wooden beams loom overhead, while paws poke out from under tables below, as Keswick's canines wait patiently for their masters to finish their beer (£6–10 meals, daily 12:00–21:00, goulash, no chips and proud of it, dog treats, 2 Lake Road, tel. 017687/73463).

The Pheasant is a walk outside town, but locals trek here regularly for the food. The menu offers Lake District pub standards (fish pie, Cumbrian sausage, guinea fowl), as well as more inventive choices. Check the walls for caricatures of pub regulars, sketched at these tables by a Keswick artist. While they have a small restaurant section, I much prefer eating in the bar (£9-13 meals, daily 12:00-14:00 & 19:00-20:30, Crosthwaite Road, tel. 017687/72219). From the town square, walk past the Pencil Museum, hang a right onto Crosthwaite Road, and walk 10 minutes. For a more scenic route, cross the river into Fitz Park, go left along the riverside path until it ends at the gate to Crosthwaite Road, turn right, and walk five minutes.

Star of Siam serves authentic Thai dishes in a tasteful dining room (£8-10 plates, daily 12:00-14:30 & 17:30-22:30, 89 Main Street, tel. 017687/71444).

Abraham's Tea Room, popular with townspeople, is a fine value for lunch. It's tucked away on the first floor of the giant George Fisher outdoor store (£4-6 soups and sandwiches, Mon-Fri 10:00-17:00, Sat 9:30-17:00, Sun 10:30-16:30, on the corner where Lake Road turns right).

The Lakeland Pedlar, a wholesome, pleasant café (with a bike shop upstairs), serves freshly baked vegan and vegetarian fare, including soups, organic bread, and daily specials. Their interior is cute. Outside tables face a big parking lot (£8 meals, daily 9:00-17:00, Thu-Sat until 21:00 in summer, Hendersons Yard, find the narrow walkway off Market Street between pink Johnson's sweet shop and The Golden Lion, tel. 017687/74492).

Bryson's Bakery and Tea Room has an enticing ground-floor bakery, with sandwiches and light lunches. The upstairs is a popular tearoom. Order lunch to go from the bakery, or for a few pence more, eat there, either sitting on stools or at a couple of sidewalk tables. Consider their £16 two-person Cumberland Cream Tea, which is like afternoon tea in London, but cheaper, and made with local products. Sandwiches, scones, and little cakes are served on a three-tiered platter with tea (£4-8 meals, Mon-Sat 9:00-17:30, Sun 9:30-17:00, 42 Main Street, tel. 017687/72257).

Good Taste has a small café space but a huge following, and is known for its fresh ingredients and its chef's expertise. Stop by for a light snack of homemade muffins and an espresso, or try a wild-boar burger (Mon-Sat 8:30-16:30, closed Sun, 19 Lake Road, tel. 017687/75973).

Maysons Restaurant, with Californian ambience, is fast and easy, with a buffet line of curry, Cajun, and vegetarian options. The food is cooked fresh on the premises, but it's nothing fancy: You point, they dish up and microwave (£6-8 plates, cash only; April-Oct daily 10:30-20:30; Nov-March Mon-Thu 11:45-17:00, Fri-Sun 11:45-20:30; family-friendly, also take-out—great for evening cruise picnic, 33 Lake Road, tel. 017687/74104).

Picnic: The fine **Booths supermarket** is right where all the buses arrive (Mon-Sat 8:00-21:00, Sun 9:30-16:00, The Headlands). The recommended **Bryson's Bakery** does good sandwiches to go (described earlier). **The Old Keswickian,** on the town square, serves up old-fashioned fish-and-chips to go (daily 9:00-21:30, upstairs restaurant closes earlier). Just around the corner, **The Cornish Pasty** offers an enticing variety of fresh meat pies to go (£2-3 pies, daily 9:30-17:30 or until the pasties are all gone, across from The Dog and Gun on Borrowdale Road, tel. 017687/72205).

In the Newlands Valley

The farmhouse B&Bs of Newlands Valley don't serve dinner, so their guests have two good options: Go into Keswick, or take the lovely 10-minute drive to Buttermere for an evening meal at the **Fish Inn Pub,** which has fine indoor and outdoor seating, but takes no reservations (£8-10 meals, daily 12:00-14:00 & 18:00-21:00, family-friendly, good fish and daily specials with fresh vegetables, tel. 017687/70253). The neighboring **Bridge Hotel Pub** is a bit cozier and serves "modern-day nibbles and good classic pub grub" (£10-12 meals, daily 12:00-21:30, tel. 017687/70252).

Keswick Connections

The nearest train station to Keswick is in Penrith (ticket window open Mon-Sat 5:30-21:00, Sun 11:30-21:00, no lockers). For train and bus info, check at a TI, visit www.traveline.org.uk, or call 0845-748-4950 (for train), or 0871-200-2233 (£0.10/minute). Most routes run less frequently on Sundays.

From Keswick by Bus: For connections, see page 618.

From Penrith by Bus to: Keswick (Mon-Sat roughly hourly 7:20-22:45, 8/day on Sun, 40 minutes, £5.50, pay driver, Stagecoach bus #X50), **Ullswater** and **Glenridding** (6/day, 45 minutes, bus #108). The Penrith bus stop is just outside the train station (bus schedules posted inside and outside station).

From Penrith by Train to: Blackpool (roughly 2/hour, 1.75 hours, change in Preston), **Liverpool** (roughly hourly, 1.75-2.25 hours, change in Wigan or Preston), **Birmingham**'s New Street Station (roughly hourly, 2.5-3 hours, some with change in Preston), **Durham** (hourly, 3 hours, change in Carlisle and Newcastle), **York** (roughly 2/hour, 3.5-4 hours, 1-2 transfers), **London**'s Euston Station (9/day, 3-3.5 hours), **Edinburgh** (nearly hourly, 1.75 hours), **Glasgow** (10/day, 1.5-2 hours), **Oban** (2/day, morning train 5.75 hours, evening train 6.75 hours, both require changing stations in Glasgow, evening train requires additional change in Carlisle).

Route Tips for Drivers

From Points South (such as Blackpool, Liverpool, or North Wales) to the Lake District: The direct, easy way to Keswick is to leave M6 at Penrith, and take the A66 highway for 16 miles to Keswick. For the scenic sightseeing drive through the south lakes to Keswick, exit M6 on A590/A591 through the towns of Kendal and Windermere to reach Brockhole National Park Visitors Centre. From Brockhole, the A road to Keswick is fastest, but the high road—the tiny road over Kirkstone Pass to Glenridding and lovely Ullswater—is much more dramatic.

Coming from (or Going to) the West: Only 1,300 feet above sea level, Hard Knott Pass is still a thriller, with a narrow, winding, steeply graded road. Just over the pass are the scant but evocative remains of the Hard Knott Roman fortress. The great views can come with miserable rainstorms, and it can be very slow and frustrating when the one-lane road with turnouts is clogged by traffic. Avoid it on summer weekends.

Near Keswick: Ullswater

▲▲Ullswater Hike and Boat Ride

Long, narrow Ullswater, which some consider the loveliest lake in the area, offers eight miles of diverse and grand Lake District scenery. While you can drive it or cruise it, I'd ride the boat from the south tip halfway up (to Howtown—which is nothing more than a dock) and hike back. Or walk first, then enjoy an easy ride

back. Old-fashioned "steamer" boats (actually diesel-powered) leave **Glenridding** regularly for Howtown (departs daily 9:45-16:40, mid-April-early Sept 9/day, early Sept-Oct 6/day, fewer off-season, 40 minutes; £5.80 one-way, £9.30 round-trip, covered by £14 Ullswater Bus & Boat day pass, family rates; drivers can use safe pay-and-display parking lot—£2/2 hours, £4/12 hours; take bus #108 from Penrith or bus #517 from Windermere; café at dock, brochure shows walking route, tel. 017684/82229, www.ullswater-steamers.co.uk).

From Howtown, spend three to four hours hiking and dawdling along the well-marked path by the lake south to Patterdale, and then along the road back to Glenridding. This is a serious seven-mile walk with good views, varied terrain, and a few bridges and farms along the way. For a shorter hike from Howtown Pier, consider a three-mile loop around Hallin Fell. A rainy-day plan is to ride the covered boat up and down the lake to Howtown and back, or to Pooley Bridge at the northern tip of the lake (mid-April-early Sept 7/day, fewer off-season, 2.25 hours, £12.70 round-trip). Boats don't run in really bad weather—call ahead if it looks iffy.

▲Aira Force Waterfall

At Ullswater, there's a delightful little park with parking, a ranger trailer, and easy trails leading half a mile uphill to a powerful 60-foot-tall waterfall. You'll read about how Wordsworth was inspired to write three poems here...and after taking this little walk, you'll know why. The car park (£3, open daily) is just where the Troutbeck road from A66 hits the lake, on A592 between Pooley Bridge and Glenridding.

Helvellyn

Considered by many the best high-mountain hike in the Lake District, this breathtaking round-trip route from Glenridding includes the spectacular Striding Edge—about a half-mile along the ridge. Be careful; do this six-hour hike only in good weather, since the wind can be fierce. While it's not the shortest route, the Glenridding ascent is best. Get advice from the Keswick TI, which has a helpful *Helvellyn from Glenridding* leaflet on the hike (£0.60).

South Lake District

The South Lake District has a cheesiness that's similar to other popular English resort destinations. Here, piles of low-end vacationers suffer through terrible traffic, slurp ice cream, and get candy floss caught in their hair. The area around Windermere is worth a drive-through if you're a fan of Wordsworth or Beatrix Potter, but you'll still want to spend the majority of your Lake District time (and book your accommodations) up north.

Getting Around

By Car: Driving is your best option to see the small towns and sights clustered in the South Lake District; consider combining your drive with the bus trip mentioned below. If you're coming to or leaving the South Lake District from the west, you could take the Hard Knott Pass for a scenic introduction to the area.

By Bus: Buses are a fine and stress-less way to lace together this gauntlet of sights in the congested Lake Windermere neighborhood. The open-top Lakes Rider bus #599 stops at Bowness Pier (lake cruises), Windermere (train station), Brockhole (National Park Visitors Centre), Ambleside, Rydal Mount, and Grasmere (Dove Cottage). Consider leaving your car at Grasmere and enjoying the breezy and extremely scenic ride, hopping off and on as you like (3/hour daily Easter-Aug, 50 minutes each way, £6.50 Central Lakes Dayrider all-day pass—buy from driver). Buses #555 and #556 run between Windermere and Keswick.

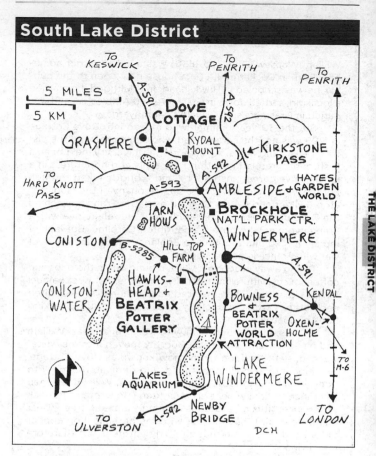

South Lake District

Sights in the South Lake District

Wordsworth Sights

William Wordsworth was one of the first writers to reject fast-paced city life. During England's Industrial Age, hearts were muzzled and brains ruled. Science was in, machines were taming nature, and factory hours were taming humans. In reaction to these brainy ideals, a rare few—dubbed Romantics—began to embrace untamed nature and undomesticated emotions.

Back then, nobody climbed a mountain just because it was there—but Wordsworth did. He'd "wander lonely as a cloud" through the countryside, finding inspiration in "plain living and high thinking." He soon attracted a circle of like-minded creative friends.

The emotional highs the Romantics felt weren't all natural. Wordsworth and his poet friends Samuel Taylor Coleridge and

Wordsworth at Dove Cottage

William Wordsworth (1770-1850) was a Lake District home-boy. Born in Cockermouth (in a house now open to the public), he was schooled in Hawkshead. In adulthood, he married a local girl, settled down in Grasmere and Ambleside, and was buried in Grasmere's St. Oswald's churchyard.

But the 30-year-old man who moved into Dove Cottage in 1799 was not the carefree lad who'd once roamed the district's lakes and fields. At Cambridge University, he'd been a C student, graduating with no job skills and no interest in a nine-to-five career. Instead, he and a buddy hiked through Europe, where Wordsworth had an epiphany of the "sublime" atop Switzerland's Alps. He lived a year in France, watching the Revolution rage. It stirred his soul. He fell in love with a Frenchwoman who bore his daughter, Caroline. But lack of money forced him to return to England, and the outbreak of war with France kept them apart.

Pining away in London, William hung out in the pubs and coffeehouses with fellow radicals, where he met poet Samuel Taylor Coleridge. They inspired each other to write, edited each other's work, and jointly published a groundbreaking book of poetry.

In 1799, his head buzzing with words and ideas, William and his sister (and soul mate) Dorothy moved into the white-washed, slate-tiled former inn now known as Dove Cottage. He came into a small inheritance, and dedicated himself to poetry full time. In 1802, with the war over, William returned to France to finally meet his daughter. (He wrote of the rich experience: "It is a beauteous evening, calm and free.../Dear child! Dear Girl! that walkest with me here,/If thou appear untouched by solemn thought,/Thy nature is not therefore less divine.")

Having achieved closure, Wordsworth returned home to marry a former kindergarten classmate, Mary. She moved into Dove Cottage, along with an initially jealous Dorothy. Three of their five children were born here, and the cottage was also home to Mary's sister, the family dog Pepper (a gift from Sir Walter Scott; see Pepper's portrait), and frequent houseguests who bedded down in the pantry: Scott, Coleridge, and Thomas de Quincey, the Timothy Leary of opium.

After almost nine years here, Wordsworth's family and social status had outgrown the humble cottage. They moved first to a house in Grasmere before settling down in Rydal Hall. Wordsworth was changing. After the Dove years, he would write less, settle into a regular government job, quarrel with Coleridge, drift to the right politically, and endure criticism from old friends who branded him a sellout. Still, his poetry—most of it written at Dove—became increasingly famous, and he died honored as England's Poet Laureate.

Thomas de Quincey got stoned on opium and wrote poetry, combining their generation's standard painkiller drug with their tree-hugging passions. Today, opium is out of vogue, but the Romantic movement thrives as visitors continue to inundate the region.

▲▲**Dove Cottage and Wordsworth Museum**—For poets, this two-part visit is the top sight of the Lake District. Take a short

tour of William Wordsworth's humble cottage and be inspired in its excellent museum, which displays original writings, sketches, personal items, and fine paintings.

The poet whose appreciation of nature and a back-to-basics lifestyle put this area on the map spent his most productive years (1799-1808) in this well-preserved stone cottage on the edge of Grasmere. After functioning as the Dove and Olive Bow pub for almost 200 years, it was bought by his family. This is where Wordsworth got married, had kids, and wrote much of his best poetry. Still owned by the Wordsworth family, the furniture was his, and the place comes with some amazing artifacts, including the poet's passport and suitcase (he packed light). Even during his lifetime, Wordsworth was famous, and Dove Cottage was turned into a museum in 1891—predating even the National Trust, which protects the house today.

Even if you're not a fan, Wordsworth's appreciation of nature, his Romanticism, and the ways his friends unleashed their creative talents with such abandon are appealing. The 30-minute cottage **tour** (departures on the hour and half-hour) and adjoining **museum**—with lots of actual manuscripts handwritten by Wordsworth and his illustrious friends—are both excellent. In dry weather, the garden where the poet was much inspired is worth a wander. (Visit this after leaving the cottage tour, and pick up the description at the back door. The garden is closed when wet.) Allow 1.5 hours for this visit.

Cost and Hours: £7.50, daily March-Oct 9:30-17:30, Nov-Dec and Feb until 16:30, closed Jan, last entry 30 minutes before closing, last tour at 16:50, café, bus #555 or #556 from Keswick, bus #555 or #599 from Windermere, tel. 015394/35544, www.wordsworth.org.uk. Parking costs £5 in the Dove Cottage lot facing the main road (A591), 50 yards from the site (coins only; grants you £4 rebate on Dove Cottage ticket).

Poetry Readings: On some Tuesday evenings in summer, the Wordsworth Trust puts on poetry readings, where national poets read their own works. They're hoping to continue the poetry tradition of the Lake District. Readings are held in Grasmere Village

Wordsworth's Poetry at Dove

At Dove Cottage, Wordsworth was immersed in the beauty of nature and the simple joy of his young, growing family. It was here that he reflected on both his idyllic childhood and his troubled twenties. The following are select lines from two well-known poems from this fertile time.

Ode: Intimations of Immortality

There was a time when meadow, grove, and stream,
The earth, and every common sight, to me did seem
Apparelled in celestial light, the glory and the freshness
    of a dream.
It is not now as it hath been of yore; turn wheresoe'er I
    may, by night or day,
The things which I have seen I now can see no more.
Now while the birds thus sing a joyous song...
To me alone there came a thought of grief...
Whither is fled the visionary gleam?
Where is it now, the glory and the dream?
Our birth is but a sleep and a forgetting:
The Soul...cometh from afar...
Trailing clouds of glory do we come
From God, who is our home.

I Wandered Lonely as a Cloud

I wandered lonely as a cloud
That floats on high o'er vales and hills,
When all at once I saw a crowd,
A host, of golden daffodils;
Beside the lake, beneath the trees,
Fluttering and dancing in the breeze...
For oft, when on my couch I lie
In vacant or in pensive mood,
They flash upon that inward eye
Which is the bliss of solitude;
And then my heart with pleasure fills,
And dances with the daffodils.

either at St. Oswald's Church or at the Wordsworth Hotel (every other Tue at 18:45, generally May-Sept only, two 45-minute sessions, £8 at the door or £7 pre-booked, tel. 015394/35544).

▲**Rydal Mount**—Located just down the road from Dove Cottage, this sight is worthwhile for Wordsworth fans. The poet's final, higher-class home, with a lovely garden and view, lacks the humble charm of Dove Cottage, but still evokes the time and creative spirit of the literary giant who lived here for 37 years. His family repurchased it in 1969 (after a 100-year gap), and his great-great-great-granddaughter still calls it home on occasion, as shown by

recent family photos sprinkled throughout the house.

After a short intro by the attendant, you'll be given an explanatory flier and are welcome to roam. Wander through the garden William himself designed, which has changed little since then. Surrounded by his nature, you can imagine the poet enjoying them with you. "O happy gardens! Whose seclusion deep, so friendly to industrious hours; and to soft slumbers, that did gently steep our spirits carry with them dreams of flowers, and wild notes warbled among leafy bowers."

Cost and Hours: £6.50; March-Oct daily 9:30-17:00; Nov Dec and Feb Wed-Sun 11:00-16:00, closed Mon-Tue; closed Jan, tea room, 1.5 miles north of Ambleside, well-signed, free and easy parking, bus #555 or #556 from Keswick, tel. 015394/33002, www .rydalmount.co.uk.

Beatrix Potter Sights

Of the many Beatrix Potter commercial ventures in the Lake District, there are two serious Beatrix Potter sights: her farm (Hill Top Farm); and her husband's former office, which is now the Beatrix Potter Gallery, filled with her sketches and paintings. The sights are two miles apart, in or near Hawkshead, a 20-minute drive south of Ambleside. If you're coming over from Windermere, catch the cute little 15-car ferry (runs constantly except when it's extremely windy, 10-minute trip, £4 car fare includes all passengers). Note that both of the major sights are closed on Friday.

On busy summer days, the wait to get into Hill Top Farm can last several hours (only 8 people are allowed in every 5 minutes, and the timed-entry tickets must be bought in person). If you like cutesy tourist towns (Hawkshead), this can be a blessing. Otherwise, you'll wish you were in the woods somewhere with Wordsworth.

▲**Hill Top Farm**—A hit with Beatrix Potter fans (and skippable for others), this dark and intimate cottage, swallowed up in the inspirational and rough nature around it, provides an enjoyable if quick experience. The six-room farm was left just as it was when she died in 1943. At her request, the house is set as if she had just stepped out—flowers on the tables, fire on, low lights. While there's no printed information here, guides in each room are eager to explain things. Call the farm for the current tour-wait times (if no one answers, leave a message for the administrator; someone will call you back).

THE LAKE DISTRICT

Beatrix Potter
(1866-1943)

As a girl growing up in London, Beatrix Potter vacationed in the Lake District, where she became inspired to write her popular children's books. Unable to get a publisher, she self-published the first two editions of *The Tale of Peter Rabbit* in 1901 and 1902. When she finally landed a publisher, sales of her books were phenomenal. With the money she made, she bought Hill Top Farm, a 17th-century cottage, and fixed it up, living there from 1905 until she married in 1913. Potter was more than a children's book writer; she was a fine artist, an avid gardener, and a successful farmer. She married a lawyer and put her knack for business to use, amassing a 4,000-acre estate. An early conservationist, she used the garden-cradled cottage as a place to study nature. She willed it—along with the rest of her vast estate—to the National Trust, which she enthusiastically supported. The events of Potter's life were dramatized in the 2007 movie *Miss Potter*, starring Renée Zellweger as Beatrix.

Cost and Hours: farmhouse-£7, tickets often sell out by 14:00; gardens-free; June-Aug Sat-Thu 10:00-17:00, April-May and Sept-Oct Sat-Thu 10:30-16:30, shorter hours off-season, closed Fri and Nov-mid-Feb; last entry 30 minutes before closing, in Near Sawrey village, 2 miles south of Hawkshead, bus #505 or #525 from Hawkshead, Mountain Goat Tours' hourly shuttle bus from ferry dock, tel. 015394/36269, www.nationaltrust.org.uk/beatrix potter. Drivers can park and buy tickets 150 yards down the road, and walk back to tour the place.

▲**Beatrix Potter Gallery**—Located in the cute but extremely touristy town of Hawkshead, this gallery fills Beatrix's husband's former law office with the wonderful and intimate drawings and watercolors that she did to illustrate her books. The best of the Potter sights, the gallery has plenty of explanation about her life and work. Even non-Potter fans find her art surprisingly interesting. Of about 700 works in the gallery's possession, a rotation of about 50 are shown at any one time. As you enter, pick up a page identifying each work of art—then you'll know (for example) that it's Mrs. Tittle Mouse meeting Bappity Bumble.

Cost and Hours: £4.60, tiny discount with Hill Top Farm,

June-Aug Sat-Thu 10:30-17:00, April-May and Sept-Oct Sat-Thu 11:00-17:00, shorter hours off-season, closed Fri and Nov-mid-Feb, last entry 30 minutes before closing, bus #505 from Windermere, Main Street, drivers use the nearby pay-and-display lot and walk 200 yards to the town center, tel. 015394/36355, www.national trust.org.uk/beatrixpotter.

Hawkshead Grammar School Museum—The town of Hawkshead is engulfed in Potter tourism, and the extreme quaintness of it all is off-putting. Just across from the pay-and-display parking lot is the interesting Hawkshead Grammar School Museum, founded in 1585, where William Wordsworth studied from 1779 to 1787. It shows off old school benches and desks whittled with penknife graffiti.

Cost and Hours: £2 includes guided tour; April-Sept Mon-Sat 10:00-13:00 & 14:00-17:00, Sun 13:00-17:00; Oct until 15:30, closed Nov-March, bus #505 from Windermere, tel. 015394/36735, www.hawksheadgrammar.org.uk.

The World of Beatrix Potter—This tour, a hit with children, is a gimmicky exhibit with all the historical value of a Disney ride. The 45-minute experience features a five-minute video trip into the world of Mrs. Tiggywinkle and company, a series of Lake District tableaux starring the same imaginary gang, and an all-about-Beatrix section, with an eight-minute video biography.

Cost and Hours: £6.75, kids-£3.50, daily April-Sept 10:00-18:00, Oct-March until 17:00, last entry 30 minutes before closing, tea room, in Bowness near Windermere town, tel. 08445-041-233, www.hop-skip-jump.com.

More Sights at Lake Windermere

Brockhole National Park Visitors Centre—Look for a stately old lakeside mansion between Ambleside and Windermere on A591. Set in a nicely groomed lakeside park, the center offers a free 30-minute video on life in the Lake District (played upon request), an information desk, organized walks (see the park's free *Visitor Guide*), exhibits, a bookshop (excellent selection of maps and guidebooks), a cafeteria, gardens, nature walks, and a large parking lot.

Cost and Hours: Free entry but steep £3 parking fee—coins only, or buy ticket at the Visitors Centre 100 yards away from parking lot; daily April-Oct 10:00-17:00, Nov-March until 16:00, bus #555 from Keswick, buses #505 and #599 from Windermere, tel. 015394/46601, www.lakedistrict.gov.uk.

Cruise: For a joyride around famous Lake Windermere, you can catch the Brockhole "Green" cruise here (£7, runs hourly April-Oct, 2/hour mid-July-Aug, 45-minute circle, scant narration, tel. 015394/43360, www.windermere-lakecruises.co.uk).

Lakes Aquarium—This aquarium gives a glimpse of the natural history of Cumbria. Exhibits describe the local wildlife living in lake and coastal environments, including otters, eels, pike, sharks, and the "much maligned brown rat." Experts give various talks throughout the day.

Cost and Hours: £9.15, kids under 16-£6.10, cheaper online, family deals, daily 9:00-18:00, until 17:00 in winter, last entry one hour before closing, in Lakeside, by Newby Bridge, at south end of Lake Windermere, tel. 015395/30153, www.lakesaquarium.co.uk.

Hayes Garden World—This extensive gardening center, a popular weekend excursion for locals, offers garden supplies, a bookstore, a playground, and gorgeous grounds. Gardeners could wander this place all afternoon. Upstairs is a fine cafeteria-style restaurant (Mon-Sat 9:00-17:30, Sun 11:00-17:00, at south end of Ambleside on main drag, see *Garden Centre* signs, located at north end of Lake Windermere, tel. 015394/33434, www.hayesgarden world.co.uk).

THE LAKE DISTRICT

YORK

Historic York is loaded with world-class sights. Marvel at the York Minster, England's finest Gothic church. Ramble The Shambles, York's wonderfully preserved medieval quarter. Enjoy a walking tour led by an old Yorker. Hop a train at Europe's greatest railway museum, travel to the 1800s in the York Castle Museum, and head back a thousand years to Viking York at the Jorvik Viking Centre.

York has a rich history. In A.D. 71, it was Eboracum, a Roman provincial capital—the northernmost city in the empire. Constantine was proclaimed emperor here in A.D. 306. In the fifth century, as Rome was toppling, a Roman emperor sent a letter telling England it was on its own, and York became Eoforwic, the capital of the Anglo-Saxon kingdom of Northumbria.

A church was built here in 627, and the town became an early Christian center of learning. The Vikings later took the town, and from the 9th through the 11th centuries, it was a Danish trading center called Jorvik. The invading and conquering Normans destroyed then rebuilt the city, fortifying it with a castle and the walls you see today.

Medieval York, with 9,000 inhabitants, grew rich on the wool trade and became England's second city. Henry VIII used the city's fine Minster as the northern capital of his Anglican Church. (In today's Anglican Church, the Archbishop of York is second only to the Archbishop of Canterbury.)

In the Industrial Age, York was the railway hub of northern England. When it was built, York's train station was the world's largest. During World War II, Hitler chose to bomb York by picking the city out of a travel guidebook.

Today, York's leading industry is tourism. It seems like everything that's great about Britain finds its best expression in this manageable town. While the city has no single claim to fame, York is more than the sum of its parts. With its strollable cobbles and half-timbered buildings, grand cathedral and excellent museums, thriving restaurant scene and welcoming locals, York delights.

Planning Your Time

After London, York is the best sightseeing city in England. On even a 10-day trip through England, it deserves two nights and a day. For the best 36 hours, follow this plan: Catch the 18:45 free city walking tour on the evening of your arrival (evening tours offered June-Aug only). Splurge on dinner at one of the city's creative bistros. The next morning, be at the York Castle Museum when it opens (at 9:30)—it's worth about two hours. Then browse and sightsee the rest of town. Train buffs love the National Railway Museum, and the Yorkshire Museum displays artifacts from the region's long history. Tour the Minster at 16:00 before catching the 17:15 evensong service (Sun at 16:00, usually none on Mon). Finish your day with an early-evening stroll along the wall (wall gates close at 20:00) and through the abbey gardens, and consider the Haunted Walk for a spooky take on York (Easter-Oct nightly at 20:00).

This schedule assumes you're here in the summer (when the evening orientation walk is going) and that there's an evensong on. Confirm your plans with the TI.

Orientation to York

(area code: 01904)

York has roughly 195,000 people; about one in ten is a student. But despite the city's size, the sightseer's York is small. Virtually everything is within a few minutes' walk: sights, train station, TI, and B&Bs. The longest walk a visitor might take (from a B&B across the old town to the York Castle Museum) is about 25 minutes.

Bootham Bar, a gate in the medieval town wall, is the hub of your York visit. (In York, a "bar" is a gate and a "gate" is a street. You can blame the Vikings.) At Bootham Bar and on Exhibition Square, you'll find the starting points for most walking tours and bus tours, handy access to the medieval town wall, a public WC, and Bootham Street (which leads to my recommended B&Bs). To find your way around York, use the Minster's towers as a navigational landmark, or follow the strategically placed signposts, which point out all places of interest to tourists.

Tourist Information

York's TI, which is a block in front of the Minster, sells a £1 *York Map and Guide*. Ask for the free monthly *What's On* guide and the *York MiniGuide*, which includes a map and some discounts (April-Oct Mon-Sat 9:00-18:00, Sun 10:00-17:00; Nov-March Mon-Sat 9:00-17:00, Sun 10:00-16:00; 1 Museum Street, tel. 01904/550-099, www.visityork.org). The TI books rooms for a £4 fee and has an Internet terminal (£3/hour). A screen lists "Today's Events in Town."

Yorkshire Pass: The TI sells an expensive pass that covers most York sights and a lot of other major sights in the region, and gives you discounts on the City Sightseeing hop-on, hop-off bus tours. But you'd have to be a very busy sightseer to make this pass worth it (£30/1 day, £42/2 days, £50/3 days, £72/6 days, www.yorkshirepass.com).

Arrival in York

By Train: The train station is a 10-minute walk from town. Day-trippers can store baggage at the window next to the Europcar office on platform 1 (£5/24 hours, baggage window open Mon-Sat 8:00-20:30, Sun 9:00-20:30).

Recommended B&Bs are a 10-minute walk or a £5 taxi ride from the station—for specific walking directions to the B&Bs, see page 685.

To walk downtown from the station, turn left down Station Road, veer through the gap in the wall and then left across the river, and follow the crowd toward the Gothic towers of the Minster. After the bridge, a block before the Minster, you'll come upon the TI on your right.

By Car: As you near York (and your B&B), you'll hit the A1237 ring road. Follow this to the A19/Thirsk roundabout (next to river on northeast side of town). From the roundabout, follow signs for *York City*, traveling through Clifton into Bootham. All recommended B&Bs are four or five blocks before you hit the medieval city gate (see neighborhood map on page 686). If you're approaching York from the south, take M1 until it becomes A1M, exit at junction 45 onto A64, and follow it for 10 miles until you reach York's ring road (A1237), which allows you to avoid driving through the city center. If you have more time, A19 from Selby is a slower and more scenic route into York.

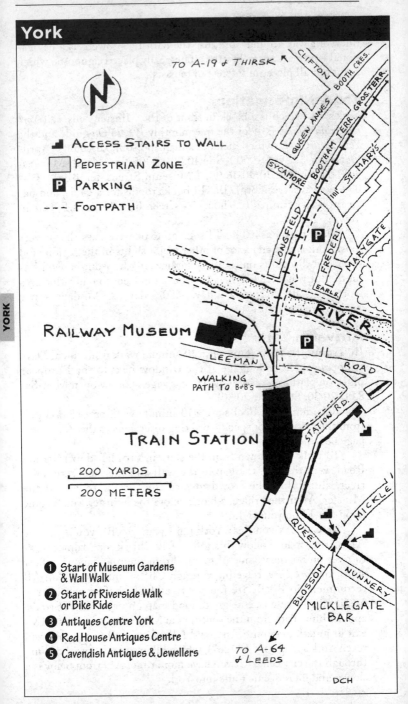

York

ACCESS STAIRS TO WALL

PEDESTRIAN ZONE

P PARKING

--- FOOTPATH

TO A-19 & THIRSK

CLIFTON
BOOTH CRES.
GROS. TERR.
QUEEN ANNE'S
BOOTHAM TERR.
ST. MARY'S
SYCAMORE
LONGFIELD
FREDERIC
MARYGATE
EARLS.

P

RIVER

RAILWAY MUSEUM

P

LEEMAN

ROAD

WALKING PATH TO B&B's

TRAIN STATION

STATION RD.

200 YARDS

200 METERS

MICKLE'

QUEEN

BLOSSOM

NUNNERY

MICKLEGATE BAR

TO A-64 & LEEDS

1 Start of Museum Gardens & Wall Walk

2 Start of Riverside Walk or Bike Ride

3 Antiques Centre York

4 Red House Antiques Centre

5 Cavendish Antiques & Jewellers

DCH

YORK

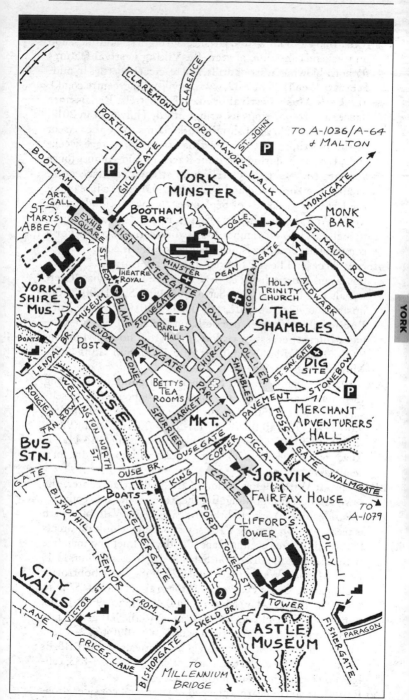

Helpful Hints

Festivals: Book a room well in advance during festival times, and on weekends any time of year. The **Viking Festival** features *lur* horn-blowing, warrior drills, and re-created battles in mid-February (Feb 11-19 in 2012, www.jorvik-viking-centre.co.uk). The **Early Music Festival** (medieval minstrels, Renaissance dance, and so on) zings its strings in July (July 6-14 in 2012, www.ncem.co.uk/yemf.shtml). York claims to be the "Ascot of the North," and the town fills up on horse-race weekends, especially during the **Ebor Races** in mid-August (once a month May-Oct, check schedules at www.yorkracecourse.co.uk). The **York Food and Drink Festival** takes a bite out of the last two weekends of September (www.yorkfoodfestival.com). And the St. Nicholas Fayre Christmas market jingles its bells in late November (www.yorkfestivals.com). For a complete list of festivals, see www.yorkfestivals.com.

Internet Access: The **TI** has one Internet terminal (£3/hour, hours and address listed earlier). **Evil Eye Lounge** has 10 terminals in a hip bar (Mon-Sat 10:00-24:00, Sun 11:00-23:00, upstairs at 42 Stonegate, tel. 01904/640-002). The **York Public Library**'s reference desk, on the first floor up, provides Internet access to visitors (£1/up to 2 hours, Mon-Thu 9:00-20:00, Fri 9:00-18:00, Sat 9:00-17:00, Sun 11:00-16:00, Museum Street, tel. 01904/552-828).

Laundry: The nearest place is **Haxby Road Launderette,** a long 15-minute walk north of the town center (about £8/load self-service, about £1.50 more for drop-off service, Mon-Wed 9:00-17:45, Thu 10:00-18:00, Fri-Sat 9:00-17:15, Sun 9:00-16:00, start last loads 1.5 hours before closing, 124 Haxby Road, tel. 01904/623-379). Some B&Bs will do laundry for a small charge.

Bike Rental: With the exception of the pedestrian center, the town's not great for biking. But there are several fine countryside rides from York, and the riverside New Walk bike path is pleasant. **Bob Trotter Cycles,** just outside Monk Bar, rents bikes and has free cycling maps (£15/day, helmet and map free with this book in 2012, Mon-Sat 9:00-17:30, closed Sun, 13-15 Lord Mayor's Walk, tel. 01904/622-868, www.bobtrottercycles.com). **Cycle Heaven** is at the train station (£5/hour, £10/half-day, £15/day, Mon-Fri 7:00-18:00, Sat 9:00-18:00, Sun 10:00-17:00, closed Sun off-season, to the left as you face the main station entrance from outside, tel. 01904/622-701).

Taxi: From the train station, taxis zip new arrivals to their B&Bs for £5. Queue up at the taxi stand, or call 01904/638-833; cabbies don't start the meter until you get in.

Car Rental: If you're nearing the end of your trip, consider dropping your car upon arrival in York. The money saved by turning it in early just about pays for the train ticket that whisks you effortlessly to London. In York, you'll find these agencies: **Avis** (Mon-Fri 8:00-18:00, Sat 8:00-13:00, closed Sun, 3 Layerthorpe, tel. 0844-544-6117); **Hertz** (Mon-Fri 8:00-17:00, Sat 9:00-13:00, closed Sun, at train station, tel. 01904/612-586); **Budget** (Mon-Fri 8:00-18:00, Sat 8:00-13:00, closed Sun, near the National Railway Museum at 75 Leeman Road, tel. 01904/644-919); and **Europcar** (Mon-Fri 8:00-18:00, Sat 8:00-16:00, closed Sun, train station platform 1, tel. 0844-846-4003).

Beware: Car-rental agencies close early on Saturday afternoons and all day Sunday—when dropping off is OK, but picking up is only possible by prior arrangement (and for a fee).

Tours in York

▲▲▲Walking Tours

Free Walks with Volunteer Guides—Charming locals give energetic, entertaining, and free two-hour walks through York (daily at 10:15 all year, plus 14:15 April-Oct, plus 18:45 June-Aug, depart from Exhibition Square in front of the art gallery). These tours often go long because the guides love to teach and tell stories. You're welcome to cut out early—but say so or they'll worry, thinking they've lost you.

Yorkwalk Tours—These are more serious 1.5- to 2-hour walks with a history focus. They do four different walks—Essential York, Roman York, Secret York, and The Snickelways of York—as well as a variety of "special walks" on more specific topics (£5.50 each, Feb-Nov daily at 10:30 and 14:15 plus Wed at 18:00, Dec-Jan weekends only, depart from Museum Gardens Gate, just show up, tel. 01904/622-303, www.yorkwalk.co.uk—check website, TI, or call for schedule). Tours go rain or shine, with as few as two participants.

Ghost Walks—Supposedly certified by the Guinness Book of World Records as "the world's most haunted city," York features a wide variety of evening ghost tours. You'll see fliers all over town. Most of these crowd-pleasing walks tend to be more about entertainment than genuine scares (goofy characters, jokes and stunts, spooky surprises, audience participation, and magic tricks rather than creepy-crawly goose pimples).

But my favorite is the scariest of them all: **Haunted Walk,** which has been led for nearly 30 years by brothers-in-law Tony and Leigh. These brilliant storytellers know how to terrify their groups with a plain old well-told ghost story...the quieter, the

York at a Glance

▲▲▲**York Minster** York's pride and joy, and one of England's finest churches, with stunning stained-glass windows, textbook Decorated Gothic design, and glorious evensong services. **Hours:** Open for worship daily from 7:00 and for sightseeing Mon-Sat from 9:00 (9:30 Nov-March), Sun from 12:30; flexible closing time (usually 18:30); shorter hours for tower and undercroft; evensong services Tue-Sat at 17:15, Sun at 16:00, occasionally on Mon, sometimes no services mid-July-Aug. See page 665.

▲▲▲**York Castle Museum** Far-ranging collection displaying everyday objects from Victorian times to the present. **Hours:** Daily 9:30-17:00. See page 680.

▲▲**National Railway Museum** Train buff's nirvana, tracing the history of all manner of rail-bound transport. **Hours:** Daily 10:00-18:00. See page 682.

▲▲**Yorkshire Museum** Sophisticated archaeology and natural history museum with York's best Viking exhibit, plus Roman, Saxon, Norman, and Gothic artifacts. **Hours:** Daily 10:00-17:00. See page 675.

▲▲**Jorvik Viking Centre** Entertaining and informative Disney-style exhibit/ride exploring Viking lifestyles and artifacts. **Hours:** Daily April-Oct 10:00-17:00, Nov-March until 16:00. See page 678.

▲**The Shambles** Atmospheric old butchers' quarter, with colorful, tipsy medieval buildings. **Hours:** Always open. See page 676.

▲**Fairfax House** Glimpse into an 18th-century Georgian family house, with enjoyably chatty docents. **Hours:** Tue-Sat 10:00-16:30, Sun 12:30-16:00, Mon by tour only at 11:00 and 14:00. See page 679.

scarier. The tales they spin (such as the legion of Roman soldiers who marched solemnly through a 20th-century basement, or the orphanage where dead children were stuffed under the floorboards) will have you seeing things in the shadows as you try to get to sleep in your creaky old B&B (£4, Easter-Oct nightly at 20:00, weekends only Nov-Easter, 1.5 hours, just show up, depart from Exhibition Square in front of the art gallery, end in The Shambles, tel. 01904/621-003).

▲City Bus Tours

Two companies run hop-on, hop-off bus tours circling York. While you can hop on and off all day, York is so compact that these have no real transportation value. If taking a bus tour, I'd catch either one at Exhibition Square (near Bootham Bar) and ride it for an orientation all the way around. Consider getting off at the National Railway Museum, skipping the last five minutes.

City Sightseeing—This outfit's half-enclosed, bright-red, double-decker buses take tourists past secondary York sights that the city walking tours skip—the mundane perimeter of town. About half the buses (twice hourly) run a "Heritage Tour" route with a live guide (£10, £13.50 combo-ticket with Yorkboat cruise—described later, pay driver, cash only, ticket valid 48 hours, Easter-Sept departs every 12 minutes, daily 9:15-17:00, less frequent off-season, about 1 hour, tel. 01904/633-990, www.yorkbus.co.uk).

York Pullman Bus Tours—These classic old-time buses are slightly less expensive, with fewer stops. They always have live guides (£7.50/24 hours, £8.50/48 hours; buy ticket from driver, office on Exhibition Square, or TI; mid-June-Oct departs 6/hour from Exhibition Square daily 9:20-17:15, off-season 2-3/hour until about 16:00, 45 minutes, enclosed bus used when wet, tel. 01904/622-992, www.yorkpullmanbus.co.uk).

Boat Cruise

YorkBoat does a lazy, narrated 45-minute lap along the River Ouse (£7.50, £13.50 combo-ticket with City Sightseeing bus tours—see above, April-Oct runs every 30 minutes, daily 10:30-15:00, off-season 4/day; 1.25-hour evening cruise at 21:15 for £9.50; leaves from Lendal Bridge and King's Staith landings, near Skeldergate Bridge, tel. 01904/628-324, www.yorkboat.co.uk).

Sights in York

▲▲▲York Minster

The pride of York, this largest Gothic church north of the Alps (540 feet long, 200 feet tall) brilliantly shows that the High Middle Ages were far from dark. The word "minster" comes from the Old English for "monastery," but is now simply used to imply that it's an important church. As it's the seat of a bishop, York Minster is also a cathedral. While Henry VIII destroyed England's great abbeys,

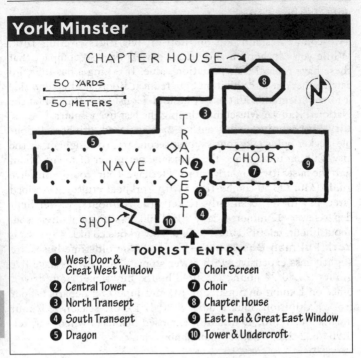

York Minster

- ① West Door & Great West Window
- ② Central Tower
- ③ North Transept
- ④ South Transept
- ⑤ Dragon
- ⑥ Choir Screen
- ⑦ Choir
- ⑧ Chapter House
- ⑨ East End & Great East Window
- ⑩ Tower & Undercroft

this was not part of a monastery and was therefore left standing. It seats 2,000 comfortably; on Christmas and Easter, at least 4,000 worshippers pack the place. Today, more than 250 employees and 500 volunteers work to preserve its heritage and welcome the 1.3 million visitors each year.

Cost and Hours: The **cathedral** opens for worship daily at 7:00. It's open for sightseeing Mon-Sat from 9:00 (9:30 Nov-March) and Sun from 12:30, when they begin charging £9 admission (includes guided tour and entry to the undercroft, treasury, and crypt). The closing time flexes with activities (usually at 18:30—check the day's closing time posted outside the church, or call for details, tel. 01904/557-217 or 0844-393-0011, www.york minster.org). The Minster may also close for special events (check calendar on their website).

Two sights within the Minster have shorter hours: the **undercroft** (included in cathedral ticket, opens at 9:00 or 9:30, last entry at 17:00, no photos) and the **tower** (£5.50, opens at 10:45, last ascent at 16:15 in summer but as early as 15:15 in winter, no children under 8, not good for acrophobes, closes in bad weather).

Tours: After buying your ticket, go directly to the welcome desk, pick up the worthwhile *Welcome to the York Minster* flier, and ask when the next free guided tour departs (roughly 2/hour, Mon-

Sat 10:30-14:00, one hour, they go even with just one or two people; you can join a tour in progress, or if none is scheduled, request a departure). The helpful Minster guides, some wearing blue armbands, are happy to answer your questions.

Stained-glass enthusiasts can take a special behind-the-scenes tour to learn about the restoration of the Minster's glass-terpiece, the Great East Window (£7.50; Mon, Wed, and Fri at 14:00; one hour, 10-person maximum).

Evensong: To experience the cathedral in musical and spiritual action, attend an evensong (Tue-Sat at 17:15, Sun at 16:00, visiting choirs occasionally perform on Mon, 45 minutes). When the choir is off on school break (mid-July-Aug), visiting choirs usually fill in (confirm at church or TI). Arrive 15 minutes early and wait just outside the choir in the center of the church. You'll be ushered in and can sit in one of the big wooden stalls. For more on evensong, see page 157.

Church Bells: If you're a fan of church bells, you'll experience ding-dong ecstasy daily except Mon (Sun morning about 10:00, Tue practice 19:30-21:30, and Tue-Sat at 16:45 to announce evensong). These performances are especially impressive, as the church holds a full carillon of 35 bells (it's the only English cathedral to have such a range). Stand in front of the church's west portal and imagine the gang pulling on a dozen ropes (halfway up the right tower—you can actually see the ropes through a little window) while one talented carillonneur plays 22 more bells with a baton-keyboard and foot pedals. On special occasions, you might even catch them playing a Beatles tune.

➲ **Self-Guided Tour:** Upon entering, head left, to the back (west end) of the church. Stand in front of the grand **west door** (used only on Sun) on the *Deo Gratias 627-1927* plaque—a place of worship for 1,300 years, thanks to God. Flanking the door, the list of bishops (and other church officials) goes unbroken back to the 600s. The statue of Peter with the key and Bible is a reminder that the church is dedicated to St. Peter, and the key to heaven is found through the word of God. While the Minster sits on the remains of a Romanesque church (c. 1100), today's church was begun in 1220 and took 250 years to complete. Up above, look for the female, headless "semaphore saints," using semaphore flag code to spell out a message with golden discs: "Christ is here."

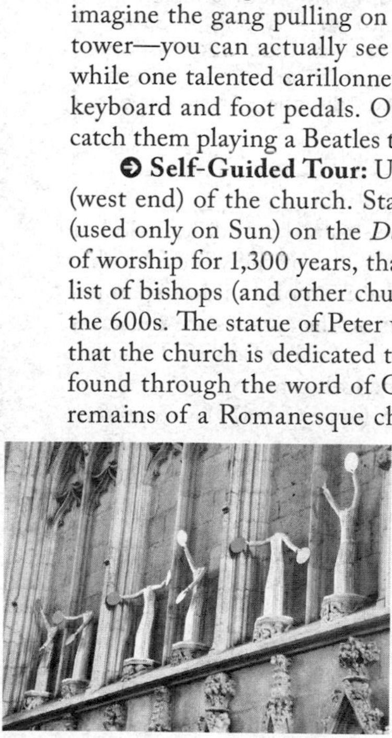

Grab a chair and enjoy the **nave.** Looking down the church, your first impression might be the spaciousness and brightness of

---

England's Anglican Church

The Anglican Church (a.k.a. the Church of England) came into existence in 1534 when Henry VIII declared that he, and not Pope Clement VII, was the head of England's Catholics. The pope had refused to allow Henry to divorce his wife to marry his mistress Anne Boleyn (which Henry did anyway, resulting in the birth of Elizabeth I). Still, Henry regarded himself as a faithful Catholic—just not a *Roman* Catholic—and made relatively few changes in how and what Anglicans worshipped.

Henry's son, Edward VI, later instituted many of the changes that Reformation Protestants were bringing about in continental Europe: an emphasis on preaching, people in the pews actually reading the Bible, clergy being allowed to marry, and a more "Protestant" liturgy in English from the revised Book of Common Prayer (1549). The next monarch, Edward's sister Mary I, returned England to the Roman Catholic Church (1553), earning the nickname of "Bloody Mary" for her brutal suppression of Protestant elements. When Elizabeth I succeeded Mary (1558), she soon broke from Rome again. Today, many regard the Anglican Church as a compromise between the Catholic and Protestant traditions. In the US, Anglicans split off from Britain after the American Revolution, creating the Episcopal Church that still thrives today.

Is the York Minster the leading Anglican church in England? Yes and no (but mostly no). After a long feud, the archbishops of Canterbury and York agreed that York's bishop would have the title "Primate of England" and Canterbury's would be the "Primate of All England," directing Anglicans on the national level.

---

the nave (built 1280-1360). The nave—from the middle period of Gothic, called "Decorated Gothic"—is one of the widest Gothic naves in Europe. Rather than risk a stone roof, builders spanned the space with wood. Colorful shields on the arcades are the coats of arms of nobles who helped tall and formidable Edward I, known as "Longshanks," fight the Scots in the 13th century.

The coats of arms in the clerestory (upper-level) glass represent the nobles who helped his son, Edward II, in the same fight. There's more medieval glass in this building than in the rest of England combined. This precious glass survived World War II—hidden in stately homes throughout Yorkshire.

Walk to the very center

of the church, under the **central tower.** Look up. Look down. Ask a Minster guide about how gifts and skill saved this tower—which weighs the equivalent of 40 jumbo jets—from collapse. (The first tower collapsed in 1407.) While the tower is 197 feet tall, it was intended to be much taller. Use the neck-saving mirror to marvel at it.

From here, you can survey many impressive features of the church:

In the **north transept** (to the left as you face the altar), the grisaille windows—dubbed the "Five Sisters"—are dedicated to British women who died in all wars. Made in 1260 (before colored glass was produced in England), these contain more than 100,000 pieces of glass.

The **south transept** (to the right as you face the altar) features the tourists' entry, where stairs lead down to the undercroft (described later). The new "bosses" (carved medallions decorating the point where the ribs meet on the ceiling) are a reminder that the roof of this wing of the church was destroyed by fire in 1984, caused when lightning hit an electricity box. Some believe the lightning was God's angry response to a new bishop, David Jenkins, who questioned the literal truth of Jesus' miracles. (Jenkins had been interviewed at a nearby TV studio the night before, causing locals to say that the lightning occurred "12 hours too late, and 17 miles off-target.") Regardless, the entire country came to York's aid. *Blue Peter* (England's top kids' show) conducted a competition among their young viewers to design new bosses. Out of 30,000 entries, there were six winners (the blue ones—e.g., man on the moon, feed the children, save the whales).

Look back at the west end to marvel at the **Great West Window,** especially the stone tracery. While its nickname is the "Heart of Yorkshire," it represents the sacred heart of Christ, meant to remind people of his love for the world.

Find the **dragon** on the right of the nave (two-thirds of the way up). While no one is sure of its purpose, it pivots and has a hole through its neck—so it was likely a mechanism designed to raise a lid on a baptismal font.

Turn 180 degrees and face the **choir screen**—the ornate wall of carvings separating the nave from the choir. It's lined with all the English kings from William I (the Conqueror) to Henry VI (during whose reign it was carved, 1461). Numbers indicate the years each reigned. To say "it's slathered in

gold leaf" sounds impressive, but the gold is very thin...a nugget the size of a sugar cube is pounded into a sheet the size of a driveway.

Step into the **choir** (or "quire"), where a service is held daily. All the carving was redone after an 1829 fire, but its tradition of

glorious evensong services (sung by choristers from the Minster School) goes all the way back to the eighth century.

Walk into the north transept. The 18th-century **astronomical clock** is worth a look (the sign helps you make sense of it). It's dedicated to the heroic Allied aircrews from bases here in northern England who died in World War II (as Britain kept the Nazis from invading in its "darkest hour"). The Book of Remembrance below the clock contains 18,000 names.

A corridor that functions as a small church museum leads to the Gothic, octagonal **Chapter House,** the traditional meeting place of the governing body (or chapter) of the Minster. On the pillar in the middle of the doorway, the Virgin holds Baby Jesus while standing on the devilish serpent.

The Chapter House, without an interior support, is remarkable (almost frightening) for its breadth. The fanciful carvings decorating the canopies above the stalls date from 1280 (80 percent are originals) and are some of the Minster's finest. Stroll slowly around the entire room and imagine that the tiny sculpted heads are a 14th-century parade—a fun glimpse of medieval society. Grates still send hot air up robes of attendees on cold winter mornings. A model of the wooden construction illustrates the impressive 1285 engineering.

The Chapter House was the site of an important moment in England's parliamentary history. Fighting the Scots in 1295, Edward I (the "Longshanks" we met earlier) convened the "Model Parliament" here, rather than down south, in London. (The Model Parliament is the name for its early version, back before the legislature was split into the Houses of Commons and Lords.) The government met here through the 20-year reign of Edward II, before moving to London during Edward III's rule in the 14th century.

Go back out into the main part of the church, turn left, and continue all the way down the nave (behind the choir). The church's **east end** is square, lacking a semicircular apse, typical of

England's Perpendicular Gothic style (15th century). Monuments (almost no graves) were once strewn throughout the church, but in the Victorian Age, they were gathered into the east end, where you see them today.

The **Great East Window,** the size of a tennis court, is currently behind scaffolding. In the meantime, interesting displays

explain the ongoing work. Look for the panel of stained glass that is often on display here (it may also in the Chapter House). The panel is exquisitely detailed—its minute features would be invisible from the floor of the church and therefore would be "for God's eyes only." Also, a chart (on the right as you face the window) highlights the core Old Testament scenes in this masterpiece (hard to read from below, even when you can actually see the window). Because of the window's immense size, there's an extra layer of supportive stonework, parts of it wide enough to walk along. In fact, for special occasions, the choir sings from the walkway halfway up the window.

The tower and undercroft are two extra sights to consider, both accessed from the south transept (the tourist entrance). One gets you exercise and a view; the other is a basement full of history. You can scale the 275-step **tower** for the panoramic view. The **undercroft** consists of the crypt, treasury, and foundations. The crypt is an actual bit of the Romanesque church, featuring 12th-century Romanesque art, excavated in modern times. The foundations give you a chance to climb down—archaeologically and physically—through the centuries to see the roots of the much smaller, but still huge, Norman (Romanesque) church from 1100 that stood on this spot and, below that, the excavations of a Roman fort. Peek also at the modern concrete save-the-church foundations. Everything is well-explained. Also in the undercroft is a treasury collection of pewter vessels, silver, and 12th-century statues.

Outside the Minster entrance and across the street, you'll find the **Roman Column.** Erected in 1971, this column commemorates the 1,900th anniversary of the Roman founding of Eboracum (later renamed York). Next to the entrance is a lounging statue of Constantine, who was in York when his father died. The troops declared him the Roman emperor in A.D. 306 at this

site, and six years later, he went to Rome to claim his throne. In A.D. 312, Constantine legalized Christianity, and in A.D. 314, York got its first bishop.

City Wall and Museum Gardens

Get a taste of Roman and medieval York on this easy stroll along a segment of York's wall. The walk begins in the gardens just in front of the Yorkshire Museum (described later).

❍ **Self-Guided Walk:** Start just inside the Museum Gardens Gate, facing into the garden (near the river, where Lendal Street hits Museum Street; gate closes at 20:00).

• *The ruined building about 20 yards to the right of the gate is the...*

Abbey Hospital: The 13th-century facade of the Abbey hospital is interesting mostly because of the ancient Roman tombs stacked just under its vault. These were buried outside the Roman city and discovered in the last century with the building of the train line.

• *Continue into the garden. About 50 yards ahead (on the right) is another remnant of ancient Rome, the...*

Multangular Tower: This 12-sided tower (A.D. 300) was likely a catapult station built to protect the town from enemy river traffic. The red ribbon of bricks was a Roman trademark—both structural and decorative. The lower stones are Roman, while the upper, bigger stones are medieval. After Rome fell, York suffered through two centuries of a dark age. Then the Vikings ruled from 780. They built with wood, so almost nothing from that period remains. The Normans came in 1066 and built in stone, generally atop Roman structures (like this wall). The Roman wall that defined the ancient garrison town worked for the Norman town, too. From the 1600s on, no such fortified walls were needed in England's interior.

• *Continue about 100 yards (past the Neoclassical building holding the fine Yorkshire Museum on the right—worth a visit and described on page 675) to York's ruined...*

St. Mary's Abbey: This abbey dates to the age of William the Conqueror—whose harsh policies of massacres and destruction in this region (called the "Harrowing of the North") made him unpopular. His son Rufus, who tried to improve relations in the 12th century, established a great church here. The church became an abbey that thrived from the 13th century until the Dissolution of the Monasteries in the 16th century. The Dissolution, which came with the Protestant Reformation and break with Rome, was a power play by Henry VIII. He took over the land and riches of the monasteries. Upset with the pope, he wanted his subjects to pay him taxes rather than give the Church tithes. (For more information, see the sidebar on page 668.)

As you gaze at this ruin, imagine magnificent abbeys like this scattered throughout the realm. Henry VIII destroyed most of

them, taking the lead from their roofs and leaving the stones to scavenging townsfolk. Scant as they are today, these ruins still evoke a time of immense monastic power. The one surviving wall was the west half of a very long, skinny nave. The tall arch marked the start of the transept. Stand on the plaque that reads *Crossing beneath central tower,* and look up at the air that now fills the space where a huge tower once stood.

• *Now, backtrack about 50 yards and turn left, walking between the museum and the Roman tower. Continuing between the abbot's palace and the town wall, you're walking along a "snickelway"—a small, characteristic York lane or footpath. The snickelway pops out on...*

Exhibition Square: With the Dissolution, the Abbot's Palace became the **King's Manor** (from the snickelway, make a U-turn to the left and through the gate). Today, it's part of the University of York. Because the northerners were slow to embrace the king's reforms, Henry VIII came here to enforce the Dissolution. He stayed 17 days in this mansion and brought along a thousand troops to make a statement of his determination. You can wander into the grounds and building. The Refectory Café serves cheap cakes, soup, and sandwiches to students, professors, and visitors like you (Mon-Fri 9:30-15:30, closed Sat-Sun).

Exhibition Square is the departure point for various walking and bus tours. You can see the towers of the **Minster** in the distance. (Travelers in the Middle Ages could see the Minster from miles away as they approached the city.) Across the street is a public WC, and **Bootham Bar**—one of the fourth-century Roman gates in York's wall—with access to the best part of the city walls (free, walls open 8:00-dusk).

• *Climb up and...*

Walk the Wall: Hike along the top of the wall behind the Minster to the first corner. York's 12th-century walls are three miles long. Norman kings built the walls to assert control over northern

England. Notice the pivots in the crenellations (square notches at the top of a medieval wall), which once held wooden hatches to provide cover for archers. At the corner with the benches—Robin Hood's Tower—you can lean out and see the moat outside. This was originally the Roman ditch

that surrounded the fortified garrison town. Continue walking for a fine view of the Minster (better when the scaffolding comes down in 2014), with its truncated main tower and the pointy rooftop of its chapter house.

• *Continue on to the next gate, **Monk Bar** (skip the tacky museum in the tower house). Descend the wall at Monk Bar, and step past the portcullis to emerge outside the city's protective wall. Lean against the last bollard and gaze up at the tower, imagining 10 archers behind the arrow slits. Keep an eye on the 12th-century guards, with their stones raised and primed to protect the town. Return through the city wall and go left at the fork in the road to follow Goodramgate a couple of blocks into the old town center. Hiding off Goodramgate on the right is...*

Holy Trinity Church: This church holds rare box pews atop a floor that is sinking as bodies rot and coffins collapse. The church is built in the late Perpendicular Gothic style, with lots of clear and precious stained glass from the 13th to 15th centuries (open Tue-Sun 10:00-16:00, closed Mon). Enjoy the peaceful picnic-friendly gardens.

• *Goodramgate winds up passing...*

King's Square: This lively people-watching zone, with its inviting benches, is prime real estate for buskers and street performers. Just beyond (crossing the square diagonally) is the most characteristic and touristy street in old York: The Shambles (described later). Our walk ends here, at the midpoint between York's main sights.

More Sights Inside York's Walls

I've listed these roughly in geographical order, from near the Minster at the northwest end of town to the York Castle Museum at the southeast end.

Note that several of York's glitzier and most heavily promoted sights (including Jorvik Viking Centre, Dig, Barley Hall, and others) are run by the York Archaeological Trust (YAT). While rooted in real history, YAT attractions are geared primarily for kids and work hard (some say too hard) to make the history entertaining. If you like their approach and plan to visit several, ask about the various combo-ticket options.

▲▲**Yorkshire Museum**—Located in a lush, picnic-perfect park next to the stately ruins of St. Mary's Abbey (described earlier), the Yorkshire Museum is the city's serious "archaeology of York" museum. You can't dig a hole in York without hitting some remnant of the city's long past, and most of what's found ends up here. While the hordes line up at Jorvik Viking Centre, this museum has no crowds and provides a broader historical context. The three main collections—Roman, medieval, and natural history—are well-described, bright, and kid-friendly.

Cost and Hours: £7.50, ticket good for one year, kids under 16 free with paying adult, £13 combo-ticket with York Castle Museum, daily 10:00-17:00, within Museum Gardens, tel. 01904/687-687, www.yorkshiremuseum.org.uk.

Touring the Museum: At the entrance, you're greeted by an original, early fourth-century A.D. Roman statue of the god Mars. From here, the **Roman** collection surrounds a large map on the floor of the Roman Empire. You'll see slice-of-life exhibits about Roman baths, a huge floor mosaic that you can walk on, and skulls accompanied by artists' renderings of how the people originally looked. (One man was apparently killed by a sword blow to the head—making it graphically clear that the struggle between Romans and barbarians was a violent one.) These artifacts are particularly interesting when you consider that you're standing in one of the farthest reaches of the Roman Empire.

The fine seven-minute **"History of York" film** peels back the many fascinating layers of York's story, inspiring an appreciation and curiosity about local history. You'll learn about Margaret Clitherow, who was publicly executed by being crushed to death under her own front door piled with heavy stones, and about the mysterious disappearance of Rome's Ninth Legion—once stationed here.

In the basement are exhibits dedicated to the **medieval** period, when York was England's second city. You can pick up flyers nar-

rating various guided routes through this collection. One large room is dominated by ruins of the St. Mary's Abbey complex (described on page 672; one wall still stands just out front—be sure to see it before leaving). Surrounding the ruins are displays of old weapons, glazed vessels from the 12th and 13th centuries, and a well-preserved 13th-century leather box.

One of the museum's prized pieces is an eighth-century Anglo-Saxon helmet (known as the York Helmet or the Coppergate Helmet), which shows a bit of barbarian refinement. Examine the delicate carving on its brass trim.

The Vikings, who conquered the Anglo-Saxons, also wore some pretty decent shoes and actually combed their hair. The Cawood Sword, nearly a thousand years old, is one of the finest surviving swords from the Viking era. The jewelry collection includes an

exquisitely etched 15th-century pendant called the Middleham Jewel—considered the finest piece of Gothic jewelry in Britain. The noble lady who wore this on a necklace believed that it helped her worship and protected her from illness. The back of the pendant, which rested near her heart, shows the Nativity. The front shows the Holy Trinity crowned by a sapphire (which people believed put their prayers at the top of God's to-do list).

Back upstairs, the small **natural history** exhibit (titled "Extinct") features skeletons of the extinct dodo and ostrich-like moa birds, as well as an ichthyosaurus.

Rounding out the collection are temporary exhibits and a "learning level" for kids. On the top floor, a timeline of the city's history circles all the way around the atrium.

Barley Hall—Uncovered behind a derelict office block in the 1980s, this medieval house has been restored to replicate a 1483 dwelling. It's designed to resurrect the Tudor age for visiting school groups, but feels soulless to adults (who visit with an included audioguide). While it pales in comparison to more authentically "old" sights in town, it could be worth the price for families—especially when bundled with a combo-ticket to other kid-friendly exhibits.

Cost and Hours: £5, kids under 17-£3, combo-tickets with Jorvik Viking Centre or Dig, daily April-Oct 10:00-17:00, until 16:00 in winter, last entry one hour before closing, 2 Coffee Yard off Stonegate, tel. 01904/615-505, www.barleyhall.org.uk.

▲The Shambles—This is the most colorful old street in the half-timbered, traffic-free core of town. Walk to the midway point, at the intersection with Little Shambles. This 100-yard-long street,

next to the old market, was once the "street of the butchers" (the name is derived from *shammell*—a butcher's cutting block). In the 16th century, it was busy with red meat. On the hooks under the eaves once hung rabbit, pheasant, beef, lamb, and pigs' heads. Fresh slabs were displayed on the fat sills. People lived above—as they did even in Roman times. All the garbage

was flushed down the street to a mucky pond at the end—a favorite hangout for the town's cats and dogs. Tourist shops now fill the fine 16th-century, half-timbered Tudor buildings. Look above the modern crowds and storefronts to appreciate the classic old English architecture. The soil here wasn't great for building. Notice how things settled in the absence of a good soil engineer.

Little Shambles leads to the frumpy Newgate Market (popular for cheap produce and clothing), created in the 1960s with the

demolition of a bunch of lanes as colorful as The Shambles. Return to The Shambles a little farther along, through a covered lane (one of York's "snickelways"). Study the 16th-century oak carpentry—mortise-and-tenon joints with wooden plugs rather than nails.

For a cheap lunch, consider the cute, tiny **St. Crux Parish Hall.** This medieval church is now used by a medley of charities that sell tea, homemade cakes, and light meals. They each book the church for a day, often a year in advance. Chat with the volunteers (Mon-Sat 10:00-16:00, closed Sun, on the left at bottom end of The Shambles, at intersection with Pavement).

Dig—This hands-on, kid-oriented archaeological site gives young visitors an idea of what York looked like during Roman, Viking, medieval, and Victorian eras. Sift through "dirt" (actually shredded tires), reconstruct Roman wall plaster, and have a look at what archaeologists have dug up recently. Entry is possible only with a one-hour guided tour (departures every 30 minutes); pass any waiting time by looking at the exhibits near the entry. The exhibits fill the haunted old St. Saviour's Church.

Cost and Hours: £5.50, kids-£5, £13.25 combo-ticket with Jorvik Viking Centre, daily 10:00-17:00, last tour departs one hour before closing, Saviourgate, tel. 01904/615-505, www.digyork.com.

Merchant Adventurers' Hall—Claiming to be the finest surviving medieval guildhall in Britain (from 1357-1361), this vast half-timbered building with marvelous exposed beams contains about 15 minutes' worth of interesting displays about life and commerce in the Middle Ages. You'll see three original, large rooms that are still intact: the great hall itself,

where meetings took place; the undercroft, which housed a hospital and almshouse; and a chapel. Several smaller rooms are filled with exhibits about old York. Sitting by itself in its own little park, this classic old building is worth a stop even just to see it from the outside. Remarkably, the hall is still owned by the same Merchant Adventurers society that built it 650 years ago (now a modern charitable organization).

Cost and Hours: £6, includes audioguide; March-Oct Mon-Thu 9:00-17:00, Fri-Sat 9:00-15:30, Sun 11:00-16:00; Nov-Feb Mon-Sat 9:00-15:30, closed Sun; south of The Shambles between Fossgate and Piccadilly, tel. 01904/654-818, www.theyork company.co.uk.

▲▲**Jorvik Viking Centre**—Take the "Pirates of the Caribbean," sail them northeast and back in time 1,000 years, sprinkle in some real artifacts, and you get Jorvik (YOR-

vik)—as much a ride as a museum. Between 1976 and 1981, more than 40,000 artifacts were dug out of the peat bog right here in downtown York—the UK's largest archaeological dig of Viking-era artifacts. When the archaeologists were finished, the dig site was converted into this attraction. Innovative in 1984, the commercial success of Jorvik inspired copycat ride/museums all over England. Some love Jorvik, while others call it gimmicky and overpriced. If you're thinking Disneyland with a splash of history, Jorvik's fun. To me, Jorvik is a commercial venture designed for kids, with too much emphasis on its gift shop. But it's also undeniably entertaining, and—if you take the time to peruse its exhibits—it can be quite informative.

Cost and Hours: £9.25, £13.25 combo-ticket with Dig, daily April-Oct 10:00-17:00, Nov-March until 16:00, these are last-entry times, tel. 01904/615-505, www.jorvik-viking-centre.co.uk.

Crowd-Beating Tips: This popular attraction can come with long lines. At the busiest times (roughly 11:00-15:00), you may have to wait an hour or more—especially on school holidays. You can book a slot in advance on their website for £1 extra. Or you can avoid the worst lines by coming early or late in the day (when you'll more likely wait just 10-15 minutes).

Touring Jorvik: First you'll walk down stairs (marked with the layers of history you're passing) and explore a small **museum.** Under the glass floor is a re-creation of the archaeological dig that took place right here. Surrounding that are a few actual artifacts (such as a knife, comb, shoe, and cup) and engaging videos detailing the Viking invasions, longships, and explorers, and the history of the excavations. Next to where you board your people-mover is the largest Viking timber found in the UK (from a wooden building on Coppergate). Don't rush through this area: These exhibits offer historical context to your upcoming journey back in time. Viking-costumed docents are happy to explain what you're seeing.

When ready, board a Disney-type **people-mover** for a 12-minute trip through the re-created Viking street of Coppergate. It's the year 975, and you're in the village of Jorvik. You'll glide past reconstructed houses and streets that sit atop the actual excavation site, while the recorded commentary tells you about everyday life in Viking times. Animatronic characters jabber at you in Old Norse, as you experience the sights, sounds, and smells of yore. Everything is true to the original dig—the face of one of the mannequins was computer-modeled from a skull dug up here.

Finally, you'll disembark at the **hands-on area,** where you can actually touch original Viking artifacts. You'll see a big gob of coprolite (fossilized feces that offer archeologists invaluable clues about long-gone lifestyles). Then you'll stroll through a gallery of everyday items (metal, glass, leather, wood, and so on) that provide intimate glimpses of that redheaded culture. Take advantage of the informative touchscreens. The final section is devoted to swords, spears, axes, and shields. You'll also see bashed-in skulls (with injuries possibly sustained in battle) and a replica of the famous Coppergate Helmet (the original is in the Yorkshire Museum).

▲**Fairfax House**—This well-furnished home, supposedly the "first Georgian townhouse in England," is perfectly Neoclassical inside. Each room is staffed by wonderfully pleasant docents eager to talk with you (a comprehensive, free audioguide is planned for the near future). They'll explain how the home was built around 1740 as the dowry for an aristocrat's daughter. The house is compact and bursting with stunning period furniture (the personal collection of a local chocolate magnate), gorgeously restored woodwork, and lavish stucco ceilings that offers clues as to each room's purpose. For example, stuccoed philosophers look down on the library, while the goddess of friendship presides over the drawing room. Taken together, this house provides fine insights into aristocratic life in 18th-century England.

Cost and Hours: £6, £4 souvenir guidebook, Tue-Sat 10:00-16:30, Sun 12:30-16:00, Mon by guided tour only at 11:00 and 14:00—the tours are worthwhile, closed Jan-mid-Feb, near Jorvik Viking Centre at 29 Castlegate, tel. 01904/655-543, www.fairfax house.co.uk.

Clifford's Tower—Perched high on a knoll across from the York Castle Museum, this ruin is all that's left of York's 13th-century castle—the site of the gruesome 1190 mass-suicide of local Jews

(they locked themselves inside and set the castle afire rather than face death at the hands of the bloodthirsty townspeople; read the whole story on the sign at the base of the hill). If you go inside, you'll see a model of the original castle complex as it looked in the Middle Ages, and can climb up to enjoy fine city views from the top of the ramparts—but neither is worth the cost of admission.

Cost and Hours: £3.90; April-Sept daily 10:00-18:00; Oct daily 10:00-17:00; Nov-March Sat-Sun 10:00-16:00, closed Mon-Fri; last entry 15 minutes before closing; tel. 01904/646-940.

▲▲▲**York Castle Museum**—One of Europe's most fascinating museums, this is a Victorian home show, the closest thing

to a time-tunnel experience England has to offer. The one-way plan assures that you'll see everything, including remakes of rooms from the 17th to 20th centuries, the domestic side of World War II, a giant dollhouse from 1715, Victorian toys, and a century of swimsuit fashions.

Cost and Hours: £8.50, ticket good for one year, kids under 16 free with paying adult, £13 combo-ticket with Yorkshire Museum, daily 9:30-17:00, cafeteria at entrance, tel. 01904/650-335, www.yorkcastlemuseum.org.uk. It's at the bottom of the hop-on, hop-off bus route. The museum can call you a taxi (worthwhile if you're hurrying to the National Railway Museum, across town).

Information: The museum's £4 guidebook isn't necessary, but it makes a fine souvenir. The museum proudly offers no audioguides, as its roaming guides are enthusiastic about talking—engage them.

Touring the Museum: The exhibits are divided between two wings: the North Building (to the left as you enter) and the South Building (to the right).

Follow the one-way route through the complex, starting in the **North Building.** You'll first visit the Period Rooms, illuminating Yorkshire lifestyles during different time periods (1600s-1950s) and among various walks of life. The Spotless exhibit examines the mundane but essential task of cleaning throughout history, from the invention of the modern WC to the evolution of the washing machine. The excellent From Cradle to Grave exhibit traces the rites of passage of a typical lifetime during the Victorian Age. For example, most women mourned their husbands for two and a half years, reflected by the color of their clothes. (Queen Victoria herself famously went one better, and swaddled herself in black for four decades after the death of her beloved Prince Albert.) The Hearth and Home exhibit showcases fireplaces and kitchens from the 1600s to the 1980s, and the Barn Gallery explains farming in Yorkshire.

Next you'll stroll down the museum's re-created Kirkgate, a street from the Victorian era—when Britain was at the peak of its power— with old-time storefronts and roaming live guides in period dress. Tucked away down a hallway is the intriguing Reflections of Kirkgate exhibit, with photos and interviews of present-day Yorkers describing their lives.

Circle back to the entry and cross over to the **South Building,** with military-themed exhibits. Look for displays about the Merchant Adventurers (traders and buccaneers on the high seas), Elizabethan soldiers of York, Yorkshire's role in the English Civil War (tracing the events of 1642-1651), and a powerful exhibit called Seeing It Through in York, explaining both the military and civilian experience here during World War II. Downstairs are the Costume Gallery, with 250 years of clothes and textiles, and the Toy Gallery, which takes you from dollhouses to Atari and Transformers.

You'll cross through the castle yard to reach another reconstructed historical street, this one capturing the spirit of the

swinging 1960s—"a time when the cultural changes were massive but the cars and skirts were mini." Slathered with DayGlo colors, this street scene examines fashion, music, and television (including clips of beloved kids' shows and period news reports).

Finally you'll head into the York Castle Prison, which re-creates the experiences of actual people who were thrown into the clink here. Videos, eerily projected onto the walls of individual cells, show actors telling tragic stories about the cells' one-time inhabitants.

Across the River, Behind the Train Station

▲▲**National Railway Museum**—If you like model railways, this is train-car heaven. The thunderous museum shows 200 illustri-

ous years of British railroad his-
tory. Pick up the floor plan to
locate the various exhibits, which
sprawl through several gigantic
buildings on both sides of the
street. Fanning out from a grand
roundhouse (the Great Hall) is an
array of historic cars and engines,
starting with the very first "stage-
coaches on rails," with a crude
steam engine from 1830. You'll trace the evolution of steam-powered transportation, from the Flying Scotsman (the first London-
Edinburgh express rail service), to the era of the aerodynamic
Mallard (famous as the first train to travel at a startling two miles
per minute—a marvel back in 1938) and the striking Art Deco-
style Duchess of Hamilton. The collection spans to the present
day, with a replica of the Eurostar (Chunnel) train and a Japanese
bullet train. The simulator lets you choose between various types
of trains to take for a virtual ride (£3/ride).

The Works is an actual workshop where engineers scurry
about, fixing old trains. A working steam engine is sliced open,
showing cylinders, driving wheels, and smoke box in action. Live
train switchboards show real-time rail traffic on the East Coast
Main Line. Next to the diagrammed screens, you can look out to
see the actual trains moving up and down the line. The Warehouse
is loaded with more than 10,000 items relating to train travel
(including dinnerware, signage, and actual trains). Other exhibits
feature dining cars, post cars, sleeping cars, and train posters.

Crossing back through the entrance area, continue to the
Station Hall, with a collection of older trains, including ones that
the royals have used to ride the rails (including Queen Victoria's
lavish royal car). Behind that are the South Yard and the Depot,
with actual, working trains in storage. Throughout the complex,
red-shirted "explainers" are eager to talk trains. This biggest and
best railroad museum anywhere is interesting even to people who
think "Pullman" means "don't push."

Cost and Hours: Free but donations appreciated, daily 10:00-
18:00, tel. 0844-815-3139, www.nrm.org.uk.

Getting There: It's about a 15-minute walk from the Minster
(southwest of town, up the hill behind the train station). From the
train station itself, the fastest approach is to go all the way to the
back of the station (using the overpass to cross the tracks), exit out
the back door, and turn right up the hill. To skip the walk, a cute

little "road train" shuttles you more quickly between the Minster and the Railway Museum (£2 each way, runs daily Easter-Oct, leaves museum every 30 minutes 11:00-16:00 at the top and bottom of the hour; leaves town—from Duncombe Place, 100 yards in front of the Minster—at :15 and :45 minutes after the hour).

Outside of Town

Riverside Walk or Bike Ride—The New Walk is a mile-long, tree-lined riverside lane created in the 1730s as a promenade for York's dandy class to stroll, see, and be seen—and is a fine place for today's visitors to walk or bike. This hour-long walk along a bike path is a great way to enjoy a dose of countryside away from York. It's clearly described in the TI's *New Walk* flier (£0.60). Start from the riverside under Skeldergate Bridge (near the York Castle Museum), and walk away from town for a mile until you hit the modern Millennium Bridge (check out its thin, modern, stainless-steel design). Cross the river and walk back home, passing through Rowntree Park (a great Edwardian park with lawn bowling for the public, plus family fun including a playground and adventure rides for kids). Energetic bikers can continue past the Millennium Bridge 18 miles to the market town of Selby.

Shopping in York

With its medieval lanes lined with classy as well as tacky little shops, York is a hit with shoppers. I find the **antiques malls** interesting. Three places within a few blocks of each other are filled with stalls and cases owned by antiques dealers from the countryside. The malls sell the dealers' bygones on commission. Serious shoppers do better heading for the country, but York's shops are a fun browse: The **Antiques Centre York** (Mon-Sat 9:00-17:30, Sun 9:00-16:00, 41 Stonegate, tel. 01904/635-888, www.theantiques centreyork.co.uk), the **Red House Antiques Centre** (Mon-Fri 9:30-17:30, Sat 9:30-18:00, Sun 10:30-17:30, a block from Minster at Duncombe Place, tel. 01904/637-000, www.redhouseyork.co.uk), and **Cavendish Antiques and Jewellers** (Mon-Fri 9:30-17:30, Sat 9:30-18:00, Sun 10:00-17:00, 44 Stonegate, tel. 01904/621-666 www.cavendishjewellers.co.uk).

You'll find **thrift shops** run by various charity organizations from the beginning of Goodramgate by the wall to just past Deangate. Good deals abound on clothing, purses, accessories, children's toys, books, CDs, and maybe even a guitar. If you buy something, you're getting a bargain and at the same time helping the poor, elderly, or even a pet in need of a vet (Mon-Sat 9:30-17:00, Sun 11:00-16:00). On Goodramgate alone you'll find shops run by the British Heart Foundation, Save the Children, and

Oxfam (selling donated items as well as free-trade products such as coffee, tea, culinary goods, stationery items, and jewelry and purses made in developing countries and purchased directly from the producers and artisans).

Nightlife in York

Theatre Royal—A full variety of dramas, comedies, and works by Shakespeare entertain the locals in either the main theater or the little 100-seat theater-in-the-round (£10-20, usually Tue-Sat at 19:30, tickets easy to get, on St. Leonard's Place near Bootham Bar and a 5- to 10-minute walk from recommended B&Bs, booking tel. 01904/623-568, www.yorktheatreroyal.co.uk). Those under 25 and students of any age get tickets for only £7.

Ghost Tours—You'll see fliers, signs, and promoters hawking a variety of entertaining but not-so-spooky after-dark tours. I like the one that's genuinely frightening—the "Haunted Walk" (described earlier, under "Tours in York").

Pubs—Atmospheric, half-timbered pubs abound. One of my favorites for old-school York ambience is **The Blue Bell,** a tiny, traditional establishment with a time-warp Edwardian interior. This smallest pub in York serves no food. It has two distinct little rooms—each as cozy as can be. The owners only recently allowed women to enter (daily 11:00-23:00, near the east end of town at 53 Fossgate). **The Maltings,** just over the Lendal Bridge, has a more up-to-date interior (though still classic pub ambience) and—more importantly—seven real ales on tap. Local beer purists swear by this place (£6-7 pub grub served at lunchtime only, open for drinks nightly, cross the bridge and look down and left to Tanners Moat, tel. 01904/655-387). Downtown and great for lunch or dinner, **The House of the Trembling Madness** is another fine watering hole—and is above a "bottle shop" selling a stunning variety of beers by the bottle to go (described later, under "Eating in York").

Movies—The centrally located **City Screen Cinema** is right on the river, playing both art-house and mainstream flicks. They also have an enticing café/bar overlooking the river that serves good food (13 Coney Street, tel. 0871-902-5726).

Sleeping in York

I've listed peak-season, book-direct prices. Don't use the TI. Outside of July and August, some prices go soft. B&Bs will often charge £10 more for weekends and sometimes turn away one-night bookings, particularly for peak-season Saturdays. (York is worth two nights anyway.) Prices spike up for horse races and Bank Holidays (about 20 nights a season). Remember to book ahead dur-

Sleep Code

(£1 = about $1.60, country code: 44, area code: 01904)
S = Single, **D** = Double/Twin, **T** = Triple, **Q** = Quad, **b** = bathroom,
s = shower only. You can assume credit cards are accepted
and breakfast is included unless otherwise noted.

To help you sort easily through these listings, I've divided
the accommodations into three categories based on the price
for a standard double room with bath (during high season):

$$$ **Higher Priced**—Most rooms £90 or more.
$$ **Moderately Priced**—Most rooms between £65-90.
$ **Lower Priced**—Most rooms £65 or less.

Prices can change without notice; verify the hotel's
current rates online or by email. For other updates, see www
.ricksteves.com/update.

ing festival times (mid-Feb, mid-July, mid-Aug, late Sept, and late
Nov—see "Helpful Hints," page 662) and weekends year-round.

B&Bs and Small Hotels

These B&Bs are all small and family-run. They come with plenty
of steep stairs (and no elevators) but no traffic noise. Rooms can be
tight; if maneuverability is important to you, say so when booking.
For a good selection, contact them well in advance. B&B owners
will generally hold a room with an email or phone call and work
hard to help their guests sightsee and eat smartly. Most have per-
mits to lend for street parking.

The handiest B&B neighborhood is the quiet residential area
just outside the old town wall's Bootham gate, along the road called
Bootham. All of these are within a 10-minute walk of the Minster
and TI, and a 10- to 15-minute walk or £5 taxi ride from the station. If driving, head for the cathedral and follow the medieval
wall to the gate called Bootham Bar. The street called Bootham
leads away from Bootham Bar.

Getting There: Here's the most direct way to walk to this
B&B area from the train station: Exit the station to the left on
Station Road. When the road swings right and goes through the
old gate, turn left onto the busy street (Leeman Road). Just before
that street goes under the rail bridge, turn right and follow the
walkway along the tracks, then cross the bridge over the river.
From the far end of the bridge, the Abbey Guest House is a few
yards to your right, facing the river. To reach The Hazelwood and
Ardmore Guest House (closer to the town wall), walk from the
bridge along the river until just before the short ruined tower, then

York Accommodations

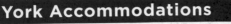

TO A-19 & THIRSK

CLIFTON
BOOTH.CRES.
GROS.TERR.
QUEEN ANNES
BOOTHAM TERR.
SYCAMORE
ST. MARY'S
LONGFIELD
FREDERIC
MARYGATE
EARLS.

P

RAILWAY MUSEUM

RIVER

P

LEEMAN

ROAD

WALKING PATH TO B&B'S

STATION RD.

TRAIN STATION

MICKLE

QUEEN

NUNNERY

BLOSSOM

MICKLEGATE BAR

TO A-64 & LEEDS

1 Abbeyfields Guest House
2 St. Raphael Guesthouse
3 Arnot House
4 Hedley House Hotel
5 Amber House & Number 34
6 Bootham Guest House
7 Queen Annes Guest House
8 Abbey Guest House
9 Number 23 St. Mary's B&B
10 Crook Lodge B&B
11 Airden House
12 The Hazelwood
13 Ardmore Guest House
14 Dean Court Hotel
15 Travelodge York Central
16 Travelodge York Central Mickelgate
17 Premier Inns (2)
18 Ace York Hostel
19 City Screen Cinema
20 Internet Café
21 To Launderette
22 Library (Internet)
23 Bike Rentals (2)

200 YARDS
200 METERS

ACCESS STAIRS TO WALL
PEDESTRIAN ZONE
P PARKING
--- FOOTPATH

YORK

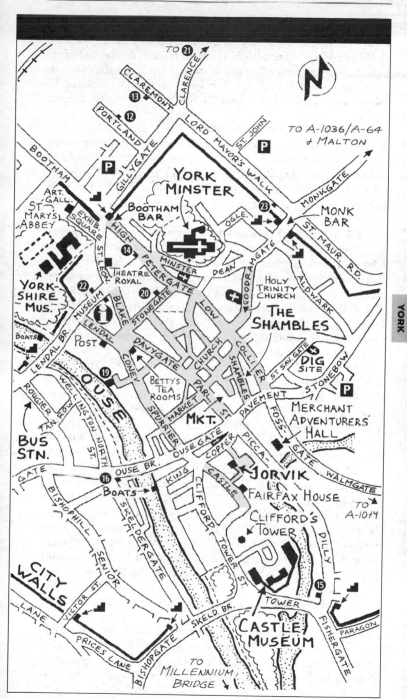

turn inland up onto Marygate. For other B&Bs, follow the path from the bridge, turning left immediately onto a path that skirts the big parking lot (parallel to the train tracks). At the end of the parking lot, you'll turn depending on your B&B: for the places on or near Bootham Terrace, turn left and go under the tracks; or, for B&Bs on St. Mary's Street, take the short stairway on your right.

On or near Bootham Terrace

$$ Abbeyfields Guest House has eight comfortable, bright rooms. This doily-free place, which lacks the usual B&B clutter, has been designed with care (Sb-£49; Db-£78 Sun-Thu, £86 Fri-Sat; less off-season, doesn't price-gouge during races, free Wi-Fi, free parking, 19 Bootham Terrace, tel. 01904/636-471, www.abbeyfields .co.uk, enquire@abbeyfields.co.uk, charming Al and Les).

$$ At St. Raphael Guesthouse, young, creative, and energetic Dom and Zoe understand a traveler's needs. You'll be instant friends. Dom's graphic design training brings a dash of class to their seven comfy rooms, each themed after a different York street, and each lovingly accented with a fresh rose (Sb-£65; Db-£78 Sun-Thu, £90 Fri-Sat; less off-season, free drinks in their guests' fridge, family rooms, free Internet access and Wi-Fi, 44 Queen Annes Road, tel. 01904/645-028, www.straphaelguesthouse.co.uk, info @straphaelguesthouse.co.uk).

$$ Arnot House, run by a hardworking daughter-and-mother team, is old-fashioned, homey, and lushly decorated with Victorian memorabilia. The three well-furnished rooms even have little libraries (Db-£70-80 depending on size of room and demand, 2-night minimum stay unless it's last-minute, no children, free Wi-Fi, huge DVD library, 17 Grosvenor Terrace, tel. 01904/641-966, www.arnothouseyork.co.uk, kim.robbins@virgin.net, Kim).

$$ Hedley House Hotel, well-run by a wonderful family, has 30 clean and spacious rooms. The outdoor hot tub/sauna is a fine way to end your day (Sb-£55-90, Db-£70-110, rates depend on demand, ask for a deal with stay of 3 or more nights, family rooms, good 3-course evening meals for £18, free Wi-Fi, free parking, 3 Bootham Terrace, tel. 01904/637-404, www.hedley house.com, greg@hedleyhouse.com, Greg and Louise Harrand). They also have nine luxury studio apartments—see their website for details.

$ Amber House is a small place with three breezy and well-tended rooms. It's homey, but with elegant touches—a bit more tasteful and upscale-feeling than others in this price range (Db-£64 Sun-Thu, £72 Fri-Sat; Tb-£90; mention Rick Steves when booking direct for these prices in 2012, free Wi-Fi, free parking, 36 Bootham Crescent, tel. 01904/620-275, www.amberhouse-york

.co.uk, amberhouseyork@hotmail.co.uk, John and Linda).

$ Bootham Guest House features gregarious and welcoming Emma. Public spaces are ho-hum, the six en-suite rooms are cheery and stylish, and the two cheaper "standard" rooms—which share one bathroom—are simpler and a bit dull (S-£35; D-£56 Sun-Thu, £60 Fri-Sat; Db-£60 Sun-Thu, £70 Fri-Sat; these prices in 2012 if you mention this book when reserving, free Wi-Fi, 56 Bootham Crescent, tel. 01904/672-123, www.boothamguesthouse.com, boothamguesthouse1@hotmail.com).

$ Number 34, run by hardworking Amy and Jason, has five simple, light, and airy rooms at fair prices. It's a bit masculine-feeling, with modern decor (May-Oct: Sb-£35-45, Db-£60, Tb-£84; Nov-April: Sb-£35, Db-£56, Tb-£75; mention Rick Steves when reserving to get best rates, ground-floor room, free Wi-Fi, 34 Bootham Crescent, tel. 01904/645-818, www.number34york.co.uk, enquiries@number34york.co.uk).

$ Queen Annes Guest House has nine basic rooms in two adjacent houses (#26 is a bit newer) at the best prices in the neighborhood. If you're looking for plush beds and rich decor, look elsewhere. If you'd simply like an affordable and clean place to sleep, this is it (high season: S-£30, D-£48, Db-£55; off-season: S-£26, D-£44, Db-£48; these prices with this book through 2012, family room, ground-floor room, free Wi-Fi, lounge, 24 and 26 Queen Annes Road, tel. 01904/629-389, www.queen-annes-guesthouse.co.uk, info@queen-annes-guesthouse.co.uk, Jason).

On the River
$$ Abbey Guest House is a peaceful refuge overlooking the River Ouse, with five cheerful, beautifully updated, contemporary-style rooms and a cute little garden (Db-£78, four-poster Db with river view-£86, less off-season, ask for Rick Steves discount when you book direct, free Wi-Fi, free parking, £7 laundry service, 13-14 Earlsborough Terrace, tel. 01904/627-782, www.abbeyghyork.co.uk, info@abbeyghyork.co.uk, delightful couple Gill—pronounced "Jill"—and Alec Saville, and a dog aptly named Loofah).

On St. Mary's Street
$$ Number 23 St. Mary's B&B is extravagantly decorated. Chris and Julie Simpson have done everything just right and offer nine spacious and tastefully comfy rooms, a classy lounge, and all the doily touches (Sb-£48-55, Db-£80-95 depending on room size and season, discount for longer stays, family room, DVD library and DVD players, free Wi-Fi, 23 St. Mary's, tel. 01904/622-738, www.23stmarys.co.uk, stmarys23@hotmail.com).

$$ Crook Lodge B&B, with seven tight but elegantly charming rooms, serves breakfast in an old Victorian kitchen. The 21st-century style somehow fits this old house (Db-£74-80, cheaper off-season, check for online specials, one ground-floor room, free Internet access and Wi-Fi, parking, quiet, 26 St. Mary's, tel. 01904/655-614, www.crooklodge.co.uk, crooklodge@hotmail.com, Brian and Louise Aiken).

$$ Airden House rents nine nice rooms (Db-£70-80, this price with 2-night minimum if you mention this book when reserving in 2012, cheaper off-season, lounge, free parking, 1 St. Mary's, tel. 01904/638-915, www.airdenhouse.co.uk, info@airden house.co.uk).

Closer to the Town Wall

$$$ The Hazelwood, my most hotelesque listing, is plush and more formal than a B&B. This spacious house has 14 beautifully decorated rooms with modern furnishings and lots of thoughtful touches. The "standard" rooms have modern, woody decor and small bathrooms, while the bigger "superior" rooms come with newer bathrooms and handcrafted furniture (Sb-£65; four sizes of Db: £80/95, £95/105, £110/115, £110/£125—weekday/weekend rates; two ground-floor rooms, free Internet access and Wi-Fi, £7 laundry service, free parking, light breakfast option, garden patio; fridge, ice, and travel library in pleasant basement lounge; 24 Portland Street, tel. 01904/626-548, www.thehazelwoodyork.com, reservations@thehazelwoodyork.com, Ian and Carolyn). Ask about their bright top-floor two-bedroom apartment, great for families and those with strong legs (continental breakfast only in apartment).

$$ Ardmore Guest House is a fine little four-room place enthusiastically run by Irishwoman Vera, who's given it a green theme. It's about 15 minutes' walk from the station, but only five minutes from Bootham Bar (Sb-£40, Db-£60-75 depending on size, Tb-£75, discount off-season for 3 or more nights, cash only, free Wi-Fi, 31 Claremont Terrace, tel. 01904/622-562, mobile 079-3928-3588, www.ardmoreyork.co.uk, ardmoreguesthouse @crwprojects.co.uk).

Large Hotels

$$$ Dean Court Hotel, a Best Western facing the Minster, is a big, stately hotel with classy lounges and 37 comfortable rooms. A few have views for no extra charge—try requesting one (Sb-£110, small Db-£145, standard Db-£175, superior Db-£205, spacious deluxe Db-£225, 20-25 percent cheaper midweek and off-season, even cheaper Sun, check specific rates at www.bestwestern .com, elevator, free Internet access and Wi-Fi, bistro, restaurant,

Duncombe Place, tel. 01904/625-082, fax 01904/620-305, www .deancourt-york.co.uk, sales@deancourt-york.co.uk).

$$ Travelodge York Central offers 93 identical, affordable, slightly worn rooms near the York Castle Museum. If you book long in advance on their website, this can be amazingly cheap. River views make some rooms slightly less boring—after booking online, call the front desk to try to arrange a view (rates vary wildly depending on demand—as cheap as £9 for a fully prepaid "saver rate" 2 months ahead, cheapest rates are first-come, first-serve; kids' bed free, continental breakfast-£4.50, elevator, pay Internet access and Wi-Fi, parking-£6.50/day, 90 Piccadilly, central reservations tel. 0871-984-6187, front desk tel. 01904/651-852, www .travelodge.co.uk). A newer second location, **Travelodge York Central Mickelgate,** has 104 rooms at the train station end of the Ouse Bridge (similar rates, Mickelgate, tel. 0871-984-6443).

$$ Premier Inn offers 200 rooms in two side-by-side hotels that I hate to recommend, but York has few budget options. They have little character (at one, you enter through a coffee shop), but they offer industrial-strength efficiency and a decent value (Db-£75-100, usually around £84 Sun-Thu, £90 Fri-Sat; check for specials online—occasional deals as low as £29 if you book far enough ahead; up to 2 kids stay free, breakfast-£8, elevator in one building, pay Internet access and Wi-Fi, parking-£8, 5-minute walk to train station, 20 and 28-40 Blossom Street, tel. 0871-527-9194, www.premierinn.com).

Hostel

$ Ace York is a boutique hostel in a large, classy, nicely renovated Georgian house that provides a much-needed option for backpackers. They rent 136 beds in 2- to 14-bed rooms, most with great views and all with private prefab "pod" bathrooms and thoughtful touches such as reading lights for each bed. They also offer fancier, hotel-quality doubles (£16-29/bed depending on size of dorm, Db-£80, family room for up to four-£120, includes continental breakfast, four floors, no elevator, air-con, pay Internet access, free Wi-Fi, self-service laundry-£3, TV lounge, game room, bar, lockers, no curfew, 5-minute walk from train station at 88-90 Mickelgate, tel. 01904/627-720, www.acehotelyork.co.uk, reception@ace-hotelyork.co.uk).

Eating in York

York is bursting with inviting eateries. In the last decade or so, the city has become a hot spot for the new British cuisine—every year seems to bring another bistro serving classy dishes made with fresh, local ingredients. There's also a wide range of ethnic food

York Restaurants

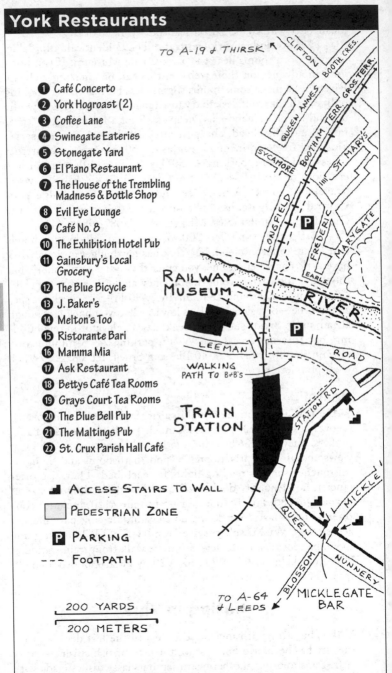

1. Café Concerto
2. York Hogroast (2)
3. Coffee Lane
4. Swinegate Eateries
5. Stonegate Yard
6. El Piano Restaurant
7. The House of the Trembling Madness & Bottle Shop
8. Evil Eye Lounge
9. Café No. 8
10. The Exhibition Hotel Pub
11. Sainsbury's Local Grocery
12. The Blue Bicycle
13. J. Baker's
14. Melton's Too
15. Ristorante Bari
16. Mamma Mia
17. Ask Restaurant
18. Bettys Café Tea Rooms
19. Grays Court Tea Rooms
20. The Blue Bell Pub
21. The Maltings Pub
22. St. Crux Parish Hall Café

ACCESS STAIRS TO WALL

PEDESTRIAN ZONE

P PARKING

--- FOOTPATH

200 YARDS

200 METERS

TO A-19 & THIRSK

CLIFTON

BOOTH. CRES.

GROS. TERR.

QUEEN ANNES

BOOTHAM TERR.

ST. MARY'S

SYCAMORE

LONGFIELD

FREDERIC

MARYGATE

EARLS.

RAILWAY MUSEUM

RIVER

LEEMAN

ROAD

WALKING PATH TO B&B'S

TRAIN STATION

STATION R.D.

MICKLE

QUEEN

BLOSSOM

NUNNERY

TO A-64 & LEEDS

MICKLEGATE BAR

YORK

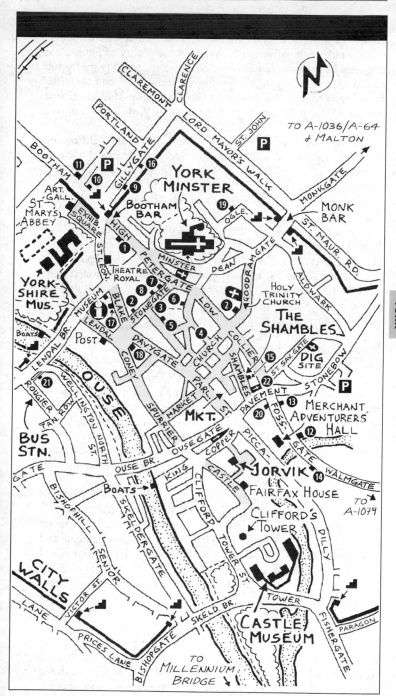

YORK

(including several good choices for Indian, Thai, Italian, Spanish tapas, and so on). The one area where York falters is with good-quality pub grub; while the downtown has plenty of pubs, most serve basic, microwaved food—there's no top-quality gastropub serving food that's a cut above. For something beyond the ordinary, locals head to The House of the Trembling Madness (listed later)...or hop in the car to drive to a countryside gastropub in a nearby village.

If you're in a hurry or on a tight budget, picnic and light-meals-to-go options abound, and it's easy to find a churchyard, bench, or riverside perch upon which to munch cheaply. On a sunny day, perhaps the best picnic spot in town is under the evocative 12th-century ruins of St. Mary's Abbey in the Museum Gardens (near Bootham Bar).

Upscale Bistros: As these trendy, pricey eateries are a York forte, I've listed five of my favorites: Café No. 8, Café Concerto, The Blue Bicycle, J. Baker's, and Melton's Too. These places are each romantic, laid-back, and popular with natives (so reservations are wise for dinner). All have several creative vegetarian options on the menu. Main courses at these places cost about £15-20—not exorbitant by British standards, but not cheap, either.

Near the Minster

Café Concerto, a casual and cozy bistro with wholesome food and a charming musical theme, has an understandably loyal following. The fun menu—which hasn't changed much in years—features updated English favorites with some international options (£9-12 soup, sandwich, and salad meals available before 18:00; otherwise £4-8 starters, £12-17 main dishes; daily 8:30-22:00, smart to reserve for dinner—try for a window seat, also offers take-away, facing the Minster, 21 High Petergate, tel. 01904/610-478).

York Hogroast is a local fixture, serving its delicious and very hearty £3-5 pork sandwiches with a choice of traditional fillings—try the apple (take-away only, Sun-Thu 11:00-23:00, Fri-Sat 11:00-2:00 in the morning, two locations: 82-84 Goodramgate and Stonegate). From the Goodramgate location, grab a sandwich and munch in the yard at the nearby Holy Trinity Church (to your left as you exit, peaceful) or in King's Square (to your right as you exit, lively with buskers).

On Swinegate and Stonegate

The hot new restaurant strip in York is along Swinegate, right in the heart of town. Along here you'll find several stylish restaurants, bars, and lounges serving good food. At the jog in the middle of Swinegate, the snickelway called Coffee Lane leads claustrophobically through the middle of the block to Stonegate, where you'll find more good options.

On Swinegate

Strolling this street, you can just take your pick of the various tempting bars and eateries. Some are trendy, with thumping music, while others are tranquil; some have elaborately decorated dining rooms, while others emphasize heated courtyards. Along here, you'll find two similar, fiercely competitive bar/brasserie/lounges (both open daily and serving £8-12 meals): **Oscar's,** right on Swinegate, has a mod interior and good burgers; **Stonegate Yard,** around the corner on Little Stonegate, has food that's not quite as good in a delightful, ivy-covered courtyard. Others enjoy the courtyard and Mediterranean food at **Lucia** (£4 small plates, £7-12 meals, daily, 12-13 Swinegate). The next three places are also on or near Swinegate:

Indian: Of the multiple decent Indian eateries in town, **The Indian Lounge** is the most appealing—with a modern interior (Bollywood movies on the screen and on the soundtrack) and tasty, fresh food made from good ingredients (£9-13 meals, daily 12:00-14:30 & 17:30-24:00, 26 Swinegate, tel. 01904/639-918).

Vegetarian: **El Piano Restaurant,** just off Swinegate on charming Grape Lane, is a popular veggie option that serves only vegan, gluten-free, and low-sodium dishes in both £4-6 tapas-style portions and full plates. The dishes have Indian/Asian/Middle Eastern flavors, and the inside ambience is bubble gum with blinking lights; they also have a pleasant patio out back. If you're eating family-style, three or four plates serve two. Save money at the take-away window (£3-4 to-go "bamboo boats," £13 three-dish sampler, £30 two-person sampler, Mon-Sat 11:00-23:00, Sun 12:00-17:00, between Low Petergate and Swinegate at 15-17 Grape Lane, tel. 01904/610-676).

Fish-and-Chips: **Mr. Chippy** has cheap and handy carry-out fish-and-chips (£3.50-5) near the top of Swinegate; I'd skip their next-door sit-down restaurant with inflated prices, which defeats the purpose of a chippy (Mon-Sat 11:00-20:15, Sun 12:00-17:00, 37-39 Swinegate).

On Stonegate

The House of the Trembling Madness, the best pub in town, is easy to miss. Enter through The Bottle, a ground-floor shop selling an astonishing number of different take-away beers (called a "bottle shop" in England). Climb the stairs to find a small but cozy pub beneath a high, airy timbered ceiling. While youthful and a bit fashion-forward, it's still accessible to all ages. The food, while not quite achieving "gastropub" status, tries to be locally sourced and is far more creative than standard York pub grub; the chorizo with scrumpy (spicy sausage sautéed in hard apple cider and onions) is delicious (£2-6 snacks, £6-8 meals, daily 10:00-24:00, 48 Stonegate, tel. 01904/640-009).

Evil Eye Lounge serves large portions of delicious, authentic Southeast Asian cuisine. The catch: It's served in a creaky, funky, youthful space that may be a bit too edgy for older customers. You can order downstairs at the bar (with a small terrace out back), or head upstairs for table service (£7 meals, food served Mon-Fri 12:00-21:00, Sat 12:00-19:00, 42 Stonegate, tel. 01904/640-002). On Sundays, the Asian cuisine takes a break, and a full multi-course traditional Sunday roast is served instead (good deal at £7 for adults, £9 for "monsters," Sun 12:00-18:00).

Note that **York Hogroast** also has a location on Stonegate (see earlier).

Near Bootham Bar and Recommended B&Bs

Café No. 8 is your best bistro choice on Gillygate, serving modern European and veggie options. Grab one of eight tables inside or enjoy a shaded little garden and sunroom out back if the weather's good. No. 8 feels like Café Concerto (described earlier) but is more romantic, with jazz, modern art, candles, and hardworking Martin bringing it all together. Chef Chris Pragnell uses what's fresh in the market to shape his menu. The food is simple, elegant, and creative (£6-10 lunches, £6-7 starters, £13-16 dinners, Mon-Fri 12:00-22:00, Sat-Sun 11:00-22:00, 8 Gillygate, tel. 01904/653-074).

The handsome **Exhibition Hotel pub** has a nice bar area inside, as well as a glassed-in conservatory and beer garden out back that's great for kids. While the food is nothing special, it's handy to my recommended B&Bs (£8-11 pub grub, daily 12:00-23:00, until 24:00 on weekends, just outside Bootham Bar at 19 Bootham Street, tel. 01904/641-105).

Supermarket: **Sainsbury's Local** grocery store is handy and open late (daily 6:00-24:00, 50 yards outside Bootham Bar, on Bootham).

At the East End of Town

This neighborhood is across town from my recommended B&Bs, but still central (and a short walk from the York Castle Museum). All three of these places are worth the longer after-dinner stroll.

The Blue Bicycle is no longer a brothel (but if you explore downstairs, you can still imagine when the tiny privacy-snugs needed their curtains). Today, it is passionate about fish. The energy of its happy eaters, its charming canalside setting, and its location just beyond the tourist zone make it worth the splurge. Of my recommended York restaurants, this wins the best ambience award, though the service can be a bit spotty. It's a velvety, hardwood scene, a little sultry but fresh...like its fish. Reservations are a must (£6-12 starters, £16-24 main dishes, vegetarian and meat options, nightly 18:00-21:30, Thu-Sun also 12:00-14:30, 34 Fossgate, tel. 01904/673-990).

J. Baker's is popular for how it turns local produce into high-brow versions of classic dishes. At lunchtime, their "grazing menu" makes it affordable to sample several dishes (available à la carte, or £12 for three courses). At dinnertime, the two earth-tone dining rooms—one downstairs, one upstairs—tend to fill up fast, so reservations are smart. Locals enjoy coming here to celebrate special occasions, but warn that portions can be small (£25 two-course meals, £29 three-course meals, £40 seven-course "grazing" meal, Tue-Sat 12:00-14:30 & 18:00-22:00, closed Sun-Mon, near the end of The Shambles at 7 Fossgate, tel. 01904/622-688). Across the street is the recommended Blue Bell pub (see page 684).

Melton's Too is a fun and casual place to eat. This homey, spacious, youthful restaurant (combining old timbers and plastic chairs) serves up elegantly simple meals and a nice a selection of £5-8 tapas, all with a focus on local ingredients. The seating sprawls on several floors: ground-floor pub, upstairs bistro, and top-floor loft (£7 lunches, £11-14 dinners, Mon-Sat 10:30-22:30, Sun 10:30-21:30, just past Fossgate at 25 Walmgate, tel. 01904/629-222).

Italian

Italian restaurants—many actually run by Italian families—are a dime a dozen in York. Ask your B&B owner for advice on their favorite, or try one of these three.

Ristorante Bari has perhaps the most touristy location in York, right in the middle of The Shambles—but it also has a loyal local following that has kept it in business for more than 50 years. This family-run place has red rustic chairs and an accessible menu of Italian classics (£7-10 pizzas and pastas, £12-18 main dishes, daily 11:30-14:30 & 18:00-22:00, The Shambles, tel. 01904/633-807).

Mamma Mia is the locals' choice for functional, affordable Italian. The casual eating area features a tempting gelato bar, and in nice weather the back patio is *molto bella* (£8-10 pizza

and pasta, daily 11:30-14:00 & 17:30-23:00, 20 Gillygate, tel. 01904/622-020).

Ask Restaurant is a cheap and cheery Italian chain, similar to those found in historic buildings all over England. But York's version lets you dine in the majestic Neoclassical yellow hall of its

Grand Assembly Rooms, lined with Corinthian marble columns. The food may be Italian-chain dull—but the atmosphere is 18th-century deluxe (£9-12 pizza, pastas, and salads; daily 12:00-23:00, Blake Street, tel. 01904/637-254). Even if you're just walking past, peek inside to gape at the interior.

Tea Rooms

York is famous for its elegant teahouses. These two places serve traditional afternoon tea as well as light meals in memorable settings. In both cases, the food is pricey and comes in small portions—I'd come here at 16:00 for tea and cakes, but dine elsewhere.

Ladies love **Bettys Café Tea Rooms,** where you pay £8.25 for a Yorkshire Cream Tea (tea and scones with clotted Yorkshire cream and strawberry jam), or £17 for a full traditional English afternoon tea (tea, delicate sandwiches, scones, and sweets). Your table is so full of doily niceties that the food is served on a little three-tray tower. While you'll pay a little extra here (and the food's nothing special), the ambience and people-watching are hard to beat. If there's a line, it moves quickly (except at dinnertime). Wait for a seat by the windows on the ground level rather than in the much bigger basement (daily 9:00-21:00, "afternoon tea" served all day, piano music nightly 18:00-21:00 and Sun 10:00-13:00, tel. 01904/659-142, St. Helen's Square, fine view of street scene from a window seat on the main floor). Near the WC downstairs is a mirror signed by WWII bomber pilots—read the story.

Grays Court is tucked away behind the Minster, holding court over its own delightful garden just inside the town wall (you'll look down into its inviting oasis if you walk along the top of the wall). For centuries, this was the residence of the Norman Treasurers of York Minster; today it's home to a pleasant tea room. You can either sit outside, at tables scattered in the pleasant garden; or inside, in the Jacobean gallery, a long wood-paneled hall with comfy sofas upstairs in an old mansion. Ask to see the medieval wall of the original Treasurer's House behind the oak paneling. Even if you're not taking tea here, consider dropping by just to poke around the garden (£20 afternoon tea, £5-6 sandwiches, £6-11 light meals, daily 9:00-18:00, Fri-Sat until 21:30 by reservation only, Chapter House Street, tel. 01904/612-613).

York Connections

From York by Train to: Durham (3-4/hour, 45 minutes), **London's** King's Cross Station (2/hour, 2 hours), **Bath** (hourly with change in Bristol, 4.25-4.5 hours, more possible with additional changes), **Cambridge** (roughly hourly, 2.5 hours, change in Peterborough), **Birmingham** (2/hour, 2-2.5 hours), **Keswick/Lake District** (train to Penrith: roughly 2/hour, 3.5-4 hours, 1-2 transfers; then bus, allow about 4.5 hours total), **Manchester Airport** (2/hour, 1.75 hours), **Edinburgh** (1-2/hour, 2.5-2.75 hours). Train info: tel. 0845-748-4950, www.nationalrail.co.uk.

Connections with London's Airports: Heathrow (allow 3 hours minimum; from airport take Heathrow Express train to London's Paddington Station, transfer by Tube to King's Cross, train to York—2/hour, 2 hours; for details on cheaper but slower Tube or bus option from airport to London King's Cross, see page 198), **Gatwick** (allow 3 hours minimum; from Gatwick South, catch First Capital Connect train to London's St. Pancras Station; from there, walk to neighboring King's Cross Station, and catch train to York—2/hour, 2 hours).

NORTH YORKSHIRE

Near York • North York Moors •
The North Yorkshire Coast

The countryside to the north of York—dubbed "North Yorkshire"—is speckled with pleasant attractions: the house and office of the "real" rural vet James Herriot, the desolately beautiful North York Moors, an eclectic mansion often used in movies, an engaging folk museum, a quirky World War II museum at a former POW camp, a kitschy scenic steam train, and several looming skeletons of destroyed abbeys. On the Yorkshire coast, you'll find an appealing pair of salty seaside towns. While none of these is a top-tier sight in itself, they complement each other nicely, so a day driving to several is time well spent.

Getting Around North Yorkshire

By Car: Driving is the best option—distances are short, the towns are small and easy to navigate, and there are plenty of tempting stopovers along the way. Get a good map, and use it thoughtfully to craft an efficient itinerary. As you drive, watch out for "wild" pheasants absentmindedly crossing the road. These birds are bred and fed by locals, and left to range freely through the woods...until autumn, when hunting season begins, and the fat, tame, and naive pheasants become easy prey.

By Public Transportation: You can reach most of these destinations by public transportation, but it requires patience (and, in some cases, a long walk from where the bus or train drops you off). York serves as a fine hub. I've explained particularly handy connections with each listing. As specific bus schedules change frequently with the season—and with funding cuts—always confirm details at the York TI.

York has decent **bus** connections to Thirsk, Castle Howard,

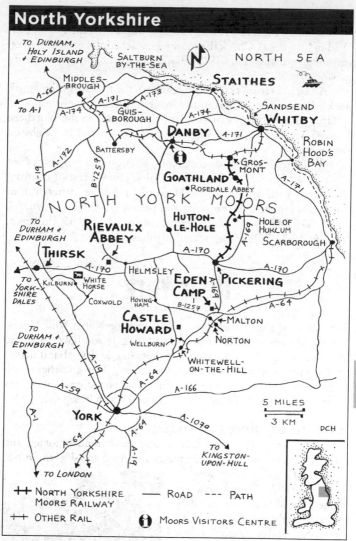

North Yorkshire

TO DURHAM, HOLY ISLAND & EDINBURGH

SALTBURN BY-THE-SEA

NORTH SEA

STAITHES

MIDDLES-BROUGH

SANDSEND

WHITBY

To A-1

GUIS-BOROUGH

DANBY

ROBIN HOOD'S BAY

BATTERSBY

GROS-MONT

GOATHLAND

ROSEDALE ABBEY

NORTH YORK MOORS

RIEVAULX ABBEY

HUTTON-LE-HOLE

HOLE OF HORCUM

THIRSK

HELMSLEY

SCARBOROUGH

KILBURN

WHITE HORSE

EDEN CAMP

PICKERING

COXWOLD

HOVING-HAM

MALTON

CASTLE HOWARD

NORTON

WELLBURN

WHITEWELL-ON-THE-HILL

YORK

5 MILES
3 KM

DCH

TO KINGSTON-UPON-HULL

TO DURHAM & EDINBURGH

TO YORK-SHIRE DALES

TO DURHAM & EDINBURGH

TO LONDON

┿┿ NORTH YORKSHIRE MOORS RAILWAY
┿┿ OTHER RAIL
—— ROAD
--- PATH
🛈 MOORS VISITORS CENTRE

NORTH YORKSHIRE

Eden Camp, Pickering, and Whitby. Buses leave from in front of York's railway station, and some also depart from Exhibition Square near the Minster. Once on the north coast, buses follow the coastal road north and south of Whitby, including Staithes. Various companies operate Yorkshire buses; for most connections, use the route planner at www.yorkshiretravel.net.

The made-for-hikers **Moorsbus** offers various handy routes to middle-of-nowhere hiking destinations in the North York Moors and out-of-the-way sights such as the Ryedale Folk Museum and

Rievaulx Abbey; however, funding cuts have dramatically reduced its frequency (in 2011, it was running Sun only April-Oct, plus Wed in July-Sept). Check the most recent schedules carefully when planning your trip (tel. 01845-597-000, www.northyorkmoors.org.uk/moorsbus).

A fun old **steam train** chugs through the middle of the North York Moors, from Pickering to Grosmont, then sometimes on to Whitby. Other trains can also be helpful (such as the Northern Line #5, which goes from Whitby to Grosmont and to Danby on the moors).

By Tour: Various tour companies offer guided bus excursions from York, focusing on Yorkshire Dales/James Herriot country, the North York Moors, Castle Howard, and more (different tour every day, see websites for tours and prices; try Eddie Brown, tel. 01423/321-248, www.eddiebrowntours.com; or York Pullman, tel. 01904/622-992, www.yorkpullmanbus.co.uk).

Near York

The following sights are between York and the North York Moors. I've listed them in order from west to east. If you have a car and are very speedy, you could see all of these in one day—but it makes more sense to pick a few that appeal to you, then link them with lazy countryside drives. Sparse public-transportation connections mean you'll have to choose just one or two if you lack a car.

▲World of James Herriot

Devotees of the *All Creatures Great and Small* books, movies, and BBC TV series should visit the folksy veterinarian's digs in Thirsk, a pleasant market town west of York. James Herriot was an auto-biographical character created by Alfred Wight, once the Thirsk town vet. Today Wight's home and office have been converted into a museum that painstakingly re-creates the 1940s Skeldale House featured in the novels, and also explores the development of  veterinary science. The worthwhile audioguide, narrated by the vet's son, James Wight, adds even more intimacy to the exhibits. Even non-fans will find the slice-of-1940s-life decor fascinating, and the trivia intriguing. (For example, Alf Wight couldn't use his own name for his autobiographical protagonist without violating an anti-advertising law...so instead he named "himself" for his favorite Scottish soccer goalie, James Herriot.) Fans will be tickled by the museum's reverence for all things Herriot. In the barn, watch the 15-minute documentary about the TV series; even the studio sets from the show have been re-created. The interactive children's section is particularly engaging, even for adults: Try your hand at horse dentistry and find out if you're strong enough to calve a cow.

Cost and Hours: £6.55, recommended £2 audioguide is loud enough to be shared, daily April-Oct 10:00-17:00, Nov-March 11:00-16:00, last entry one hour before closing, 23 Kirkgate, tel. 01845/524-234, www.worldofjamesherriot.org.

Getting There: The museum is just a block up Kirkgate from the main market square in Thirsk. Buses connect York with Thirsk (nearly hourly on Reliance bus #30 or #30X, 1 hour; faster but less frequent on Silverline bus #58—4/day Mon-Sat, 1/day on Sun, 45 minutes; www.yorkshiretravel.net). There are more connections by train, but the train station is about a mile outside of Thirsk, whereas the bus drops you at the main square. Drivers can zip here from York on A19 in about 40 minutes.

Nearby: Die-hard Herriot fans might enjoy exploring the **Yorkshire Dales,** westward from and much tamer than the North York Moors. Get details about the region—and information about guided tours—at the York TI. Approaching Thirsk, keep an eye out on the right side of the road for the **"White Horse"**—a gigantic image in the hillside that overlooks the town of Kilburn. The figure was created by a schoolmaster and his students in 1857, who removed the soil to expose the light-colored bedrock.

NORTH YORKSHIRE

▲Rievaulx Abbey

Rievaulx (ree-VOH) is the sprawling ruins of a 12th-century abbey. Since it's not near any major towns, its pre-cut stones were less susceptible to plunder—so it's been left a bit more intact than

many other ruined abbeys. Its beautiful and secluded setting—tucked away in a gentle, sheep-speckled valley—is appealing, but if you've seen other fine old abbeys, this is a rerun. Start with the little museum, then follow the included audioguide through the ruins. You'll learn how monastic life changed during the four centuries between its founding and its destruction by Henry VIII.

Cost and Hours: £5.60, includes audioguide, £4 parking fee is refunded when you buy abbey ticket; generally

April-Sept daily 10:00-18:00; Oct Thu-Mon 10:00-17:00, closed
Tue-Wed; Nov-March Thu-Mon 10:00-16:00—or maybe even
shorter hours, closed Tue-Wed; café, tel. 01439/798-228, www
.english-heritage.org.uk.

Getting There: Drivers get there in a snap (just a short detour
from A170). Bus transportation is trickier. From York, first catch
a bus to Helmsley (6/day Mon-Sat, none on Sun, 1.25 hours,
Stephensons bus #31 or #31X—confirm bus goes all the way to
Helmsley, www.stephensonsofeasingwold.co.uk). From Helmsley,
you can get to the abbey on foot (2 miles), by taxi (call 01439/770-
981, 01439/770-817, or 01439/770-040), or by infrequent bus
(Moorsbus #M9, runs Sun only April-Oct, plus Wed July-Sept,
but schedules change frequently—confirm before you set out,
www.northyorkmoors.org.uk/moorsbus).

▲▲Castle Howard

Made popular by the filming of the *Brideshead Revisited* TV mini-
series here in 1981, this fine, palatial, 300-year-old home (more a
manor than a "castle") is impres-
sive. It was commissioned on a
whim to John Vanbrugh, a playwright who previously had no
architectural training whatsoever—which explains some of his
unique flourishes (like the grand,
domed entryway that would
seem more at home in a Baroque

church). Vanbrugh went on to build the even grander Blenheim
Palace near Oxford (which is at least twice as interesting, if you're
choosing between them—see page 460). After being damaged in a
1940 fire, Castle Howard lay in ruins for years before being refurbished in the 1950s and opened to the public. The Howard family,
whose precocious daughters are pictured throughout the place, still
lives in one wing—and in winter, when the place is closed to the
public, they actually use the rooms that are normally on the tour
route.

As you follow the one-way route through the house, bor-

row the English descrip-
tions in each room. Chatty
docents posted in key rooms
explain what you're seeing.
Many of the decorations
are "souvenirs" from the
Howards' travels—such as
replicas of Roman busts and
Greek statues, or paintings

that attempt to jam several of a Grand Tour city's landmarks onto a single canvas like today's collage postcards do. (Outside, the mini-pyramid on the horizon—behind the big Atlas Fountain—was inspired by a trip to Egypt.) Also watch for the elaborate, mul-tistory, blue Delft porcelain tulip vase—dating from the "Tulip Fever" era of the late 17th century, when a single flower could cost £1,000. Imagine the extravagance of filling this whole vase. Upstairs are exhibits on the manor's restoration after the 1940 fire, and the filming of *Brideshead Revisited* (both the original TV mini-series and the 2008 big-screen version, starring Emma Thompson and Michael Gambon). The sprawling grounds include several pools, lakes, and fountains, a rose garden, and a quiet wood.

Cost and Hours: £13 for manor and grounds, or £8.50 for grounds only in winter, when the manor is closed. Gardens open daily 10:00-18:30, last entry at 17:30, open until dusk in win-ter; manor open daily late March-Oct 11:00-17:00, last entry at 16:00, closed Nov-late March except late Nov-mid-Dec, when it's decorated for Christmas. Tel. 01653/648-333, www.castlehoward .co.uk.

Getting There: It's in the countryside between Helmsley and Malton. It's ideal by car. You can get here from York on Stephensons bus #180 or #181 (4/day Mon-Sat, none Sun; show bus ticket for a discount on manor admission). On some weekends, York Pullman runs a very convenient direct excursion bus (£17.50, includes manor and grounds entry, some Sat-Sun in summer—check schedule, departs York Memorial Gardens at 10:00 and returns at 16:00, www.yorkpullmanbus.co.uk). Additional connec-tions, through Malton, are more complicated (for details, see the castle's website or www.yorkshiretravel.net).

Eden Camp

Once an internment camp for German and Italian POWs dur-ing World War II, this is now a theme museum on Britain's war experience. Sprawling, cluttered, pleasantly low-tech, and a bit hokey, the exhibit works best for Brits who want to help their kids (or grandkids) understand the war years. But, even though it's overpromoted, its earnestness will win over WWII buffs, as it energetically tries to convey the spirit of a country Hitler couldn't conquer.

The comprehensive exhibits investigate a wide range of World War II and postwar topics. Various barracks detail the rise of Hitler, the fury of the Blitz, and the efforts on the home front—such as rationing and the Local Defense Volunteers, affectionately dubbed "Dads Army." A detailed map and ample posted informa-tion are helpful, if a bit overwhelming. Focus your visit on the top-ics that interest you most. An intense exhibit on the Blitz comes with the sound of bombs, the acrid smell of burning, and wartime mottos such as, "Hitler will send no warning—so always carry your gas mask." Don't miss hut #10, which details the actual purpose of the camp—a prison for captured Nazis and Italians during World War II (think *Hogan's Heroes* in reverse). Enjoy the quirky handmade items—such as a miniature pair of shoes carved out of bread—created by bored POWs who were killing time. Consider the relative delight of being in the care of the gentlemanly English rather than in a Russian camp. It's no wonder the Germans and Italians settled right in.

Cost and Hours: £5.50, daily 10:00-17:00, last entry at 16:00, closed late Dec-mid-Jan, cash only, mess-kitchen cafeteria, tel. 01653/697-777, www.edencamp.co.uk.

Getting There: It's near Malton, 18 miles northeast of York. From York, drivers take A169 toward Scarborough, then follow signs to the camp (notice its proximity to Castle Howard—it's easy to combine these two and more on a day's drive). Or, from York, you can catch Coastliner bus #840 (every 1-2 hours Mon-Sat, fewer on Sun, 50-60 minutes, www.coastliner.co.uk).

North York Moors

In the lonesome North York Moors, sheep seem to outnumber people. Upon this high, desolate-feeling plateau, with spongy and inhospitable soil, bleating flocks jockey for position against scrubby heather for control of the terrain. You can almost imagine the mysterious Heathcliff (from *Wuthering Heights*) plodding across this terrain. As you pass through this haunting landscape, crisscrossed by only a few roads, notice how the gloomy brown  heather—which blooms briefly with purple flowers at summer's end—is actually burned back by wardens to clear the way for new growth. The vast, undulating expanses of nothingness are punctuated by greener, sparsely populated valleys called dales. Park your car and take a hike across the moors on any small road. You'll come upon a few tidy villages and maybe even old Roman roads.

For information on the moors, you can stop at the TI in Pickering (at the south end) and/or the excellent Moors Centre (near Danby, at the north end). Pick up the annual magazine *Out and About in the North York Moors*. Either place can give you hiking tips and sell you essential maps. Popular walks include a 5.5-mile loop near the Hole of Horcum, the 4.5-mile walk between Goathland and Grosmont, or the brief stroll to the waterfall near Goathland. Most villages have at least one general store where you can buy a basic brochure suggesting local hikes.

Getting Around the North York Moors

If you're **driving**, the easiest route across the moors is A169, which roughly parallels the steam-train line north from Grosmont; it passes the Hole of Horcum and comes close to Grosmont, before heading east to Whitby. To the west, smaller roads head north through Hutton-le-Hole (with its folk museum) and the village of Rosedale Abbey. While less straightforward—you'll need a very good map and an even better navigator—this western zone really gets you deep into the moors.

Those relying on **public transportation** will primarily use the North Yorkshire Moors Railway (explained later) and the sporadic Moorsbus system (described on page 701). Study the Moorsbus schedule carefully, and ask around locally, to link up a good day's walking itinerary.

Sights on the Moors

These locations are listed roughly from south to north (as you'd approach them coming from York).

Pickering

This functional town, the southern gateway to the North York Moors, is a major crossroads and a proud hub for this region's meager public transit. Pickering's main parking lot, train station, and TI all cluster on the same block. The helpful **TI** can provide advice for driving and hiking on the moors, and has a room-booking service (tel. 01751/473-791, pickeringtic@btconnect.com).

The main reason to visit Pickering is to catch the **North Yorkshire Moors Railway** steam train into the moors (described next). Pickering is also the jumping-off point for various Moorsbus lines into the moors (lines #M6, #M7, and #M8; for more on this infrequent service, see page 701). Otherwise, you can browse its Monday market (produce, knickknacks) and consider its rural-life museum (Hutton-le-Hole's is better)—but don't bother visiting Pickering unless you're passing through anyway.

With more time, consider stopping by Pickering's ruined 13th-century Norman **castle**, built on the site of a wooden castle from William the Conqueror's 11th-century heyday. Appreciate its textbook motte-and-bailey (stone fort on a grassy hilltop) design, and climb to the top to understand its strategic location (£3.80;

April-Sept Thu-Mon 10:00-17:00, closed Tue-Wed except open daily July-Aug; closed Oct-March, on the ridge above town, tel. 01751/474-989, www.english-heritage.org.uk).Z

Getting There: Drivers find Pickering right on A169 north of York (en route to the coast). Or you can catch Coastliner bus #840 from York (every 1-2 hours Mon-Sat, fewer on Sun, 1.5 hours, www.coastliner.co.uk); you can shave a few minutes off the trip by taking the train to Malton, then catching bus #840 from there.

▲North Yorkshire Moors Railway

This 18-mile, one-hour steam-engine ride between Pickering and Grosmont (GROW-mont) runs almost hourly through some of the best parts of the moors. Sometimes the train continues from Grosmont on to the seaside town of Whitby; otherwise, you might be able to transfer in Grosmont to another, non-steam train to reach Whitby (check schedules as you plan your trip). Once in Whitby, you can use the bus to connect to other towns along the coast (such as to Staithes) or to return to York. (For details on getting to Pickering, see previous paragraph.)

Even with the small and dirty windows (try to wipe off the outside of yours before you roll), and with the track situated mostly in a scenic gully, it's a good ride. You can stop along the way for a walk on the moors (or at the appealing village of Goathland) and catch the next train (£16 round-trip to Grosmont, £21 round-trip to Whitby, includes hop-on, hop-off privileges; runs daily late March-Oct, and some Dec weekends, no trains Nov and Jan-late March, schedule flexes with season but first train generally departs Pickering at 9:00, last train departs Grosmont about 18:30; trip takes about one hour one-way to Grosmont, allow about 2.75 hours round-trip to come back on the same train; tel. 01751/472-508—press 1 for 24-hour timetable info, www.nymr.co.uk). There's nowhere to leave luggage at any stop on the steam-train line (but you can leave your bag for free at the Pickering TI until 17:00)—pack light if you decide to hike.

▲Hutton-le-Hole

This postcard-pretty town, lining up along a river as if posing for its close-up, is an ideal springboard for a trip into the North York Moors. It has some touristy shops and inviting picnic benches, but Hutton-le-Hole's (pronounced "HOO-ton le hole") biggest attraction is its engaging folk museum.

The **Ryedale Folk Museum** illustrates farm life in the moors through reconstructed and furnished 18th-century buildings. At this open-air complex, you'll wander along a line of shops, including a village store—one-stop shopping (the original Costco) to save locals the long trek into the closest market town. Then you'll

come to a humble cluster of traditional, lived-in-feeling thatch-roof cottages. If the beds are unmade, notice the "mattress" is made of rope stretched across a frame, which could be tightened for a firmer night's sleep (giving us the phrase "sleep tight"). The museum is most worthwhile during frequent special weekends, when lively costumed docents explain what you're see-ing along the way—check the online schedule or call ahead (£5.50; mid-March-late Oct daily 10:00-17:30, last entry at 16:30; late Oct-mid-March 10:00-dusk, closes early Dec-mid-Jan; tel. 01751/417-367, www.ryedalefolkmuseum.co.uk).

Getting There: Drivers find it just north of A170. From Hutton-le-Hole, you can plunge northward directly into the North York Moors (which begin suddenly as you leave town). Non-drivers will rely on the sporadic Moorsbus to reach Hutton-le-Hole (#M3 from Helmsley, Sun only April-Oct, plus Wed July-Sept, sched-ules change frequently—confirm before you set out, www.north yorkmoors.org.uk/moorsbus).

In the Heart of the Moors

The Hole of Horcum—This huge sinkhole was supposedly scooped out by a giant. While not too exciting, it offers a good excuse to get out of your car and appreciate the moorland scenery (at the Saltergate car park).

Rosedale Abbey—A tranquil village on the west side of the moors (north of Hutton-le-Hole and far from the Hole of Horcum and Goathland), Rosedale Abbey offers a good dose of small-town moor life. Nestled between hills, it also provides pleasing moor views.

Goathland—This village, huddled along a babbling brook, is worth considering for a sleepy stopover, either on the steam-train trip or for drivers (it's an easy detour from A169). Movie buffs will enjoy Goathland's train station, which was used to film scenes at "Hogsmeade Station" for the early Harry Potter movies (for more on Harry Potter sights, see page 806). But Brits know and love Goathland as the setting for the beloved, long-run-ning TV series *Heartbeat*, about a small Yorkshire

NORTH YORKSHIRE

town in the 1960s. You'll see TV sets intermingled with real buildings, and some shops are even labeled "Aidensfield," for the TV town's fictional name.

▲The Moors Centre

This recently expanded and refurbished visitors center near Danby provides the best orientation for exploring North York Moors National Park. (Unfortunately, it's at the northern end of the park—not as convenient if you're coming from York.) The grand old lodge offers excellent exhibits on various moorland topics, informative films about the landscape, an art gallery showcasing works by local artists inspired by these surroundings, a children's play area, an information desk, plenty of books and maps, guided nature walks, brass rubbing, a cheery cafeteria, and brochures on several good walks that start right outside the front door.

Cost and Hours: Free entry, parking-£2.20/up to 2 hours, £4/day; April-Oct daily 10:00-17:00; March and Nov-Dec daily 11:00-16:00; Jan-Feb Sat-Sun 11:00-16:00, closed Mon-Fri; café, tel. 01439/772-737, www.northyorkmoors.org.uk.

Getting There: The Moors Centre is three-fourths of a mile from Danby in Esk Valley, in the northern part of the park (follow signs from Danby, which is a short drive from A171 running along the northern edge of the park). Danby is where the Moorsbus system (routes #M2, #M3, and #M4) meets the rail network (Danby is on the Northern Line #5, with connections to Grosmont—the terminus for the North Yorkshire Moors Railway described earlier—and Whitby; trains run along here 4/day, less Sun off-season, 20 minutes from Danby to Grosmont, 30 minutes from Danby to Whitby, www.northernrail.org).

The North Yorkshire Coast

Two salty Yorkshire towns—one big (Whitby) and one small (Staithes)—are seaside escapes worth a stop for the seagulls, surf, and Captain Cook lore. If you're not seeing the English coast anywhere else on your trip, and you have an extra day in York, side-tripping here is worthwhile.

Getting to the North Yorkshire Coast

Yorkshire Coastliner buses connect **York** to Whitby (4/day, 1.75-2.75 hours, www.coastliner.co.uk). Alternatively, you can ride the train to Scarborough (hourly, 50 minutes), then catch a bus to Whitby (2/hour in summer, hourly in winter, 1 hour).

To connect Whitby to the **North York Moors,** you can take

the historic steam train from Pickering to Grosmont, which often continues into Whitby (otherwise you may be able to transfer in Grosmont to a Whitby-bound train). Or you can ride the train to Danby, near the Moors Centre.

From **Durham,** you can get to Whitby by train via Darlington and Middlesbrough (Durham-Middlesbrough: at least hourly, 1 hour with transfer in Darlington; then Middlesbrough-Whitby: 4/day, 1.5 hours). The Middlesbrough-Whitby train also stops at two towns on the North York Moors (both described earlier): Grosmont (where you can catch the Moors steam train south to Pickering) and Danby (near The Moors Centre).

Getting Around the North Yorkshire Coast

From Whitby, Arriva buses #5, #5a, and #X5 run up and down the coast north of town, connecting you to Sandsend and Staithes en route to Middlesbrough (2/hour in summer, hourly in winter); south of town, bus #93 run at least hourly to Robin Hood's Bay (www.arrivabus.co.uk).

Whitby

An important port since the 12th century, Whitby is today a fun coastal resort town with about 14,000 people, a gaggle of steep and

salty old streets, and great nautical ambience. Its busy harbor, bristling with ships' masts, is squeezed into a narrow canyon flanked on one side by the stately skeleton of its 11th-century abbey, and on the other by the bluff-topping West Cliff neighborhood. The harborfront zone is a carousel of Coney Island-type amusements and city-dwellers from inland Yorkshire whooping it up. Rounding out Whitby's claim to fame are its connections to Captain Cook and Bram Stoker (whose *Dracula* was partly written here).

Orientation to Whitby

(area code: 01947)

Tourist Information

The TI is on the harbor next to the train and bus stations (daily July-Sept 9:30-19:00, May-June 9:30-18:00, Oct-April 10:00-16:30, tel. 01723/383-636, www.discoveryorkshirecoast.com).

Arrival in Whitby

If driving, consider first stopping by the hilltop sights (the abbey on one side of town, and West Cliff on the other). Then drive down into the old town center and drop your car across the street from the TI in the pay-and-display parking lot near the train and bus stations. Walk about 200 yards toward the harbor—and the lone bridge spanning it—to get oriented.

From the bridge, face the sea to consider your options (described in more detail below): On the left is the waterfront promenade called Pier Road/Fish Quay, lined with tacky carnival distractions, as well as the recommended Magpie Café (popular fish-and-chips) and a tacky Dracula exhibit (skip it); above this scene is the West Cliff area, with fine views over town. On the right (across the bridge) is a warren of touristy lanes filled with hard-candy stores, knickknack shops, and the Captain Cook Memorial Museum; overhead (but not quite visible from here) is the ruined abbey.

Sights in Whitby

Whitby's main landmark is its ruined **abbey,** set on a bluff overlooking the harbor. Built on the site of a seventh-century monas-

tic settlement, the remains of this 11th-century version echo with the chants of ages past... enough to raise goose bumps even on a vampire (*Dracula* was partly set here). Many of the stones from this formerly grand abbey were used to build houses in the town below (£6, includes audio-guide; April-Sept daily 10:00-18:00; Oct-March Thu-Mon 10:00-16:00, closed Tue-Wed—and possibly other weekdays as well; tel. 01947/603-568, www.english-heritage.org.uk).

The abbey is connected to the streets below by a **staircase** of 199 steps called Caedmon's Trod. In the olden days, poor people would carry the coffins of the departed up these steps, resting occasionally on broader steps called "coffin rests"...which, for practical reasons, are more frequent near the top.

Down below, the small **Captain Cook Memorial Museum,** in an old shipowner's house where Cook lodged for a few years, offers a dull look at the famous hometown sailor and his exotic voyages. The most interesting bit is the Voyages Room, with a cutaway model of one of Cook's ships, and miniature replicas of everything that went on board (£4.50, pick up free pamphlet as you enter, daily March 11:00-15:00, April-Oct 9:45-17:00, last entry one hour before closing, closed Nov-Feb; tucked down little Grape Lane behind the Dolphin Hotel, near the bridge on the abbey side of town; tel. 01947/601-900, www.cookmuseumwhitby.co.uk). Two of Captain Cook's boats (*Resolution* and *Endeavour*) were built in the Whitby shipyards; a full-size replica of the *Endeavour*, which has been used in many swashbuckling films, is often moored in Whitby.

Across the harbor from the abbey is a fun little hilltop park called **West Cliff,** with inviting benches and a lively kids' area. Supposedly it was from this vantage point that Bram Stoker contemplated Whitby's abbey...and inspiration bit him in the neck. In *Dracula,* a boat docks at the long pier, and a black dog—the Count in disguise—jumps off the boat and runs up the 199 steps to the abbey...where he hides out for the next three chapters, until he takes to the sea again. Nearby, the whale bones forming an archway over the path recall Whitby's former status as a major whaling city. When whalers returned to port, they'd prop up bones like these on their ships, as a sign to their wives and mothers (who were anxiously waiting ashore) that the trip had gone safely.

To go for a **walk along the beach,** consider strolling to nearby villages, then walking or catching an Arriva bus back: Sandsend to the north (buses #5, #5a, and #X5) is closer than Robin Hood's Bay to the south (bus #93, www.arrivabus.co.uk). Before heading out, check the tide tables carefully (posted in the TI window).

Sleeping in Whitby

A collection of inviting B&Bs perches atop the plateau behind West Cliff. Among these, **$$ Crescent Lodge B&B** is a good choice (8 rooms, Sb-£38, Db-£64, just off the main drag as you enter the upper part of town at 27 Crescent Avenue, tel. 01947/820-073, http://crescentlodgewhitby.co.uk, carol@carolyates.wanadoo.co.uk, Carol).

$ Whitby's **Abbey House youth hostel** is one of England's most impressive. Right on the abbey grounds above town—and literally built with bits and pieces of that abbey—this 17th-century building has undergone an extensive restoration. Now it houses 100 beds in 22 rooms, most of them 4- to 6-bed dormitories with bathrooms. Many rooms have information plaques on the walls explaining the architecture and renovation (£16-22/bed, Db twin-£40-55, price depends on day and season, breakfast-£5, reception open 7:30-10:00 & 14:00-22:30, no curfew, family rooms, fully wheelchair-accessible rooms, pay Internet access and Wi-Fi, laundry, kitchen, cafeteria-style restaurant, tel. 01947/602-878, www.yha.org.uk, whitby@yha.org.uk).

NORTH YORKSHIRE

Sleep Code

(£1 = about $1.60, country code: 44, area code: 01947)
S = Single, **D** = Double/Twin, **T** = Triple, **Q** = Quad, **b** = bathroom, **s** = shower only. Unless otherwise noted, you can assume breakfast is included and credit cards are accepted.

To help you sort easily through these listings, I've divided the accommodations into three categories based on the price for a standard double room with bath (during high season):

$$ Moderately Priced—Most rooms £50 or more.
$ Lower Priced—Most rooms less than £50.

Prices can change without notice; verify the hotel's current rates online or by email. For other updates, see www .ricksteves.com/update.

Eating in Whitby

Fish-and-Chips: In this nautical town, fish-and-chips are on everybody's mind. The **Magpie Café** is a local institution, generally marked by a line of loyal eaters waiting to get in; the carry-out window is to the right (£5 for take-away; in the restaurant: £10-12 fish-and-chips, £12-20 fish dinners; daily 11:30-21:00 except until 20:00 Mon-Thu in winter, closed much of Jan, 14 Pier Road, tel. 01947/602-058). If the Magpie is too crowded—which is quite likely—try these local-approved alternatives: **Quayside,** nearly next door to the Magpie (take-away counter with £5 fish-and-chips, sit-down restaurant with £8-14 meals, daily 11:00-19:00 or 20:00, tel. 01947/602-059); and, across the harbor, the simpler **Mister Chips,** just down the street from the Captain Cook Museum (£3-7 fish-and-chips, take-away only, daily 11:30-22:00, 68-69 Church Street, tel. 01947/604-683).

Pub: The **Dolphin Hotel** offers a scenic location with outdoor seating and serviceable food dead-center in the old town, right at the bridge. They serve £5-9 fish-and-chips and pub grub (food served daily 12:00-14:30 & 18:00-21:00, from Oct-May Sat-Sun only, Bridge Street, tel. 01947/602-197).

Staithes

A ragamuffin village where the boy who became Captain James Cook got his first taste of the sea, Staithes (pronounced "stay-thz," about 10 miles north of Whitby) is a salty jumble of cottages bunny-hopping down a ravine into a tiny harbor. About a tenth the size of its big sister down the coast, Staithes is the yang to

Whitby's yin. This refreshingly unpretentious town is gloriously stubborn about not wooing tourists (www.staithes-town.info).

While dead as a doornail today, in 1816 Staithes was home to 70 boats and the busiest fishing station on the northeast coast of England. Ten years ago, the town supported 20 fishing boats—today, only three. But fishermen (who pronounce their town's name "steers" in the local dialect) still outnumber tourists in undiscovered Staithes. The out-of-towners who do come here rent cottages in the old center and settle in for a long stay as temporary locals. The town has changed little since Captain Cook's days. Lots of flies and seagulls seem to have picked the barren cliffs raw. There's nothing to do but stroll the beach and nurse a harborside beer or ice cream. As you gaze out at the scenery and rich light, imagine Staithes in the early 20th century, when a small artists' colony called the "Staithes Group" enjoyed painting this same scene.

For a bit more activity, drop by the **lifeboat station,** operated by the Royal National Lifeboat Institution (RNLI)—Britain's entirely volunteer answer to the Coast Guard. Entering the big barn, notice the boards up on the eaves with not-quite-stirring accounts of the boats being called to duty. As this organization—England's sole method for responding to maritime emergencies—is entirely funded by donations, consider supporting the cause with a coin or two (flexible hours—typically open daily 10:00-16:00 in summer, most days in winter; shop tel. 01947/840-373, www.rnli.org.uk or www.staithes-lifeboat.co.uk).

Getting to Staithes

Staithes is an easy **drive** north of Whitby. Parking is tough—generally, you can drive in only to unload. Service trucks clog the windy main (and only) lane much of the day. There's a pay-and-display Bank Top lot at the top of the town—an easy downhill walk to the action (but a more strenuous hike back up). While the **bus** #5/#5a/#X5 connection from Whitby to Staithes is fairly straightforward, there's not much in low-key Staithes to justify the

NORTH YORKSHIRE

trip (2/hour in summer, hourly in winter, 30 minutes; 10-minute walk from bus stop into town, www.arrivabus.co.uk).

Eating in Staithes

A pair of lowbrow pubs serves lunch and dinner daily (both open 12:30-14:00 & 18:00-20:00): **The Royal George,** along the main drag, has well-worn, basic decor (tel. 01947/841-432). **The Cod and Lobster,** overlooking the harbor, has scenic outdoor benches and a cozy living room warmed by a coal fire. Drop in to see its old-time Staithes photos (tel. 01947/840-490).

In nice weather, the best option is to enjoy a drink, snack, or light meal (i.e., fish-and-chips) sitting at an outdoor table fronting the harbor. Try the friendly **Seadrift Café,** which specializes in sweets, but also does basic grub (Sun-Thu 10:00-16:00, closed Fri, tel. 01947/841-345).

DURHAM AND NORTHEAST ENGLAND

*Durham • Beamish Museum • Hadrian's Wall •
Holy Island • Bamburgh Castle*

Northeast England harbors some of the country's best historical sights. Go for a Roman ramble at Hadrian's Wall, a reminder that Britain was an important Roman colony 2,000 years ago. Make a pilgrimage to Holy Island, where Christianity gained its first toehold in Britain. Marvel at England's greatest Norman church—Durham's cathedral—and enjoy an evensong service there. At the excellent Beamish Museum, travel back in time to the 18th and 19th centuries.

Planning Your Time

For **train** travelers, Durham is the most convenient overnight stop in this region. But it's problematic to see en route to another destination, since there's no baggage storage in Durham: Either stay overnight, or do Durham as a day trip from York. If you like Roman ruins, visit Hadrian's Wall (tricky but doable by public transportation with transfers, easiest Easter-Oct). The Beamish Museum is an easy day trip from Durham (1 hour by bus, 25 minutes by car).

By **car,** you can easily visit everything in this chapter. Spend a night in Durham and a night near Hadrian's Wall. With a car, you can easily visit Beamish Museum on the way to Hadrian's Wall.

For the best quick visit to Durham, arrive by mid-afternoon, in time to tour the cathedral and enjoy the evensong service (Tue-Sat at 17:15, Sun at 15:30; limited access and no tours during June graduation ceremonies). Sleep in Durham. Visit Beamish the next morning before continuing on to your next destination.

Durham

Without its cathedral, Durham would hardly be noticed. But this magnificently situated structure is hard to miss (even if you're zooming by on the train).

Seemingly happy to go nowhere, Durham sits along the tight curve of its river, snug below its castle and famous church. It has a medieval, cobbled atmosphere and a scraggly peasant's indoor market just off the main square. Durham is the home to England's third-oldest university, with a student vibe jostling against its lingering working-class mining-town feel. You'll see tattooed and pierced people in search of job security and a good karaoke bar. Yet Durham has a youthful liveliness and a small-town warmth that shines—especially on sunny days, when most everyone is out licking ice-cream cones.

Orientation to Durham

(area code: 0191)

As it has for a thousand years, tidy little Durham (pop. 30,000) clusters everything safely under its castle, within the protective hairpin bend of the River Wear. Because of the town's hilly topography, going just about anywhere involves a lot of up and down... and back up again. The main spine through the middle of town (Framwellgate Bridge, Silver Street, and Market Place) is level to moderately steep, but walking in any direction from that area involves some serious uphill climbing. Take advantage of the handy Cathedral Bus to avoid the tiring elevation changes—especially up to the cathedral and castle area, or to the train station (perched high on a separate hill).

Tourist Information

Due to funding cuts, Durham's TI closed in late 2011, but maintains a call center and website (tel. 03000-262-626, www.thisis durham.com, visitor@thisisdurham.com). Look for information racks around town, or ask for help at your B&B or hotel.

Arrival in Durham

By Train: From the train station, the fastest and easiest way to reach the cathedral is to hop on the convenient **Cathedral Bus** (described later, under "Getting Around Durham"). But the town's

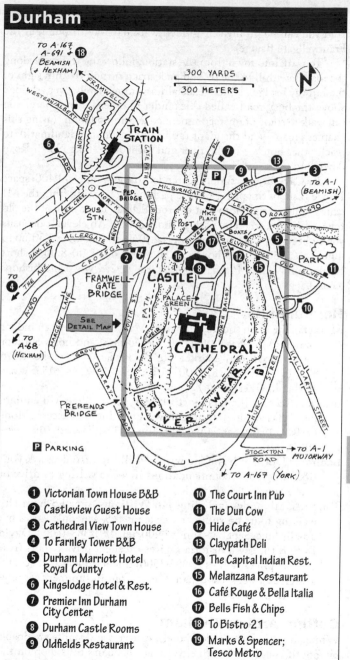

Durham

300 YARDS
300 METERS

TO A-167
A-691 &
(BEAMISH
& HEXHAM)

WESTERN/ALBERT

FRAMWELL

NORTH ROAD

TRAIN STATION

WADD

GATE BETH

FREEMANS PL.

P

MILBURNGATE

PED. BRIDGE

HILBURNGATE

CLAYPATH

TO A-1
(BEAMISH)

ALEX CRES.

BUS STN.

NORTH ROAD

NEVILLE

POST

MKT. PLACE

LEATES ROAD   A-690

P

BOATS

HAW. TER.

ALLERGATE

CROSSGATE

SILVER

SADDLER

ELVET BRIDGE

ELVET

OLD ELVET

PARK

THE AVE.

TO A-690

FRAMWELLGATE BRIDGE

SOUTH ST.

CASTLE

NEW ELVET

MARGERY LANE

PATH

WEIR

PALACE GREEN

NORTH BAILEY

TO A-68
(HEXHAM)

SEE DETAIL MAP

GROVE

QUARRY HEADS

CATHEDRAL

PREBENDS BRIDGE

SOUTH BAILEY

RIVER   WEAR

CHURCH STREET

HALLGARTH STREET

P PARKING

LANE

STOCKTON ROAD

→ TO A-1 MOTORWAY

↓ TO A-167 (YORK)

DURHAM & NE ENGLAND

1 Victorian Town House B&B
2 Castleview Guest House
3 Cathedral View Town House
4 To Farnley Tower B&B
5 Durham Marriott Hotel Royal County
6 Kingslodge Hotel & Rest.
7 Premier Inn Durham City Center
8 Durham Castle Rooms
9 Oldfields Restaurant

10 The Court Inn Pub
11 The Dun Cow
12 Hide Café
13 Claypath Deli
14 The Capital Indian Rest.
15 Melanzana Restaurant
16 Café Rouge & Bella Italia
17 Bells Fish & Chips
18 To Bistro 21
19 Marks & Spencer; Tesco Metro

setting—while steep in places—is enjoyable to stroll through (and you can begin my self-guided walk halfway through, at the Framwellgate Bridge).

To **walk** into town from the station, follow the walkway along the road downhill to the second pedestrian turnoff (within sight of the railway bridge), which leads almost immediately over a bridge above the busy road called Alexander Crescent. From here, you can walk to some of my recommended accommodations (using this chapter's map—and the giant rail bridge as a handy landmark); to reach other hotels—or the river and cathedral—take North Road down into town.

By Car: Drivers simply surrender to the wonderful 400-space Prince Bishops Shopping Centre parking lot (coming from the M1 exit, you'll run right into it at the roundabout at the base of the old town). It's perfectly safe, with 24-hour access. An elevator deposits you right in the heart of Durham (£2.10/up to 2 hours, £3.30/up to 4 hours, £11.50/up to 6 hours, £1.50/overnight 18:00-8:00; a short block from Market Place, tel. 0191/383-9592, www.princebishops .co.uk).

Helpful Hints

Markets: The main square, known as Market Place, has an indoor market (Mon-Sat 9:00-17:00, closed Sun) and hosts outdoor markets (Sat retail market 9:00-16:30, farmers' market third Thu of each month, 9:00-15:30, tel. 0191/384-6153, www .durhammarkets.co.uk).

Internet Access: The **Clayport Library,** set on huge Millennium Place, has about 40 terminals with free Internet access (Mon-Fri 9:30-19:00, Sat 9:00-17:00, Sun 10:30-16:30, tel. 0191/386-4003).

Laundry: Durham has none within walking distance; ask your B&B host for recommendations if you're willing to drive or take a taxi.

Tours: Local guides including **Jan Williams** offer 1.5-hour city walking tours on summer weekends (£5, schedule varies but usually June-Sept Sat-Sun at 14:00, tel. 0191/383-0988). **David Butler,** the town historian, gives excellent private tours (reasonable prices, tel. 0191/386-1500, dhent@dhent.fsnet.co.uk) as well as a weekly Durham Ghost Tour in summer (£5, July-Sept Mon at 19:30).

Getting Around Durham

While all my recommended hotels, eateries, and sights are doable by foot, if you don't feel like walking Durham's hills, hop on the convenient **Cathedral Bus** (#40). This shuttle bus runs between the train station and the cathedral, with stops near the North

Road bus station, Millburngate, Market Place, and some car parks (£0.50 all-day ticket, daily 3/hour; leaves train station Mon-Fri 8:00-17:10, Sat 9:10-17:10; last bus leaves cathedral Mon-Sat at 17:19; none on Sun; tel. 0191/372-5386, www.thisisdurham.com).

Taxis zip tired tourists to their B&Bs or back up to the train station (about £4 from city center, wait on west side of Framwellgate Bridge at the bottom of North Road).

Self-Guided Walk

Welcome to Durham

• *Begin at Framwellgate Bridge (down in the center of town, halfway between the train station and the cathedral).*

Framwellgate Bridge was a wonder when it was built in the 12th century—much longer than the river is wide and higher than

seemingly necessary. It was well-designed to connect stretches of solid high ground, and to avoid steep descents toward the marshy river. Note how elegantly today's Silver Street (which leads toward town) slopes into the Framwellgate Bridge. (Imagine that as recently as the 1970s, this people-friendly lane was congested with traffic and buses.)

• *Follow Silver Street up the hill to the town's main square.*

Durham's **Market Place** retains the same plotting the prince bishop gave it when he moved villagers here in about 1100. Each long and skinny plot of land was the same width (about eight yards), maximizing the number of shops that could have a piece of the Market Place action. Find today's distinctly narrow buildings (Thomas Cook, Whittard, and Thomson)—they still fit the 900-year-old plan. The widths of the other buildings fronting the square are multiples of that original shop width.

Examine the square's **statues.** Coal has long been the basis of this region's economy. The statue of Neptune was part of an ill-fated attempt by a coal baron to bribe the townsfolk into embracing a canal project that would make the shipment of his coal more efficient. The statue of the fancy guy on the horse is Charles Stewart Vane, the Third Marquess of Londonderry. He was an Irish aristocrat, and a general in

Wellington's army, who married a local coal heiress. A clever and aggressive businessman, he managed to create a vast business empire by controlling every link in the coal business chain—mines, railroads, boats, harbors, and so on.

In the 1850s throughout England, towns were moving their markets off squares and into Industrial Age iron-and-glass market halls. Durham was no exception, and today its funky 19th-century **indoor market** (which faces Market Place) is a delight to explore (closed Sun). There are also outdoor markets here on Saturdays and the third Thursday of each month.

Do you enjoy the sparse traffic in Durham's old town? It was the first city in England to institute a "congestion fee." When drivers enter, a camera snaps a photo of each car's license plate, and mails them a bill for £5. This has cut downtown traffic by more than 50 percent. Locals brag that London (which now has a similar congestion fee) was inspired by their success.

• *Head up the hill on Saddler Street towards the cathedral, stopping where you reach the chunk of wall at the top of a stairway. On the left, you'll see a bridge.*

A 12th-century construction, **Elvet Bridge** led to a town market over the river. Like Framwellgate, it's very long (17 arches) and designed to avoid riverside muck and steep inclines. Even today, Elvet Bridge leads to an unusually wide road—once swollen to accommodate the market action. Shops lined the right-hand side of Elvet Bridge in the 12th century, as they do today. An alley separated the bridge from the buildings on the left. When the bridge was widened, it met the upper stories of the buildings on the left, which became "street level."

Turn back to look at the chunk of **wall** by the top of the stairs—a reminder of a once-formidable fortification. The Scots, living just 50 miles from here, were on the rampage in the 14th century. After their victory at Bannockburn in 1314, they pushed farther south and actually burned part of Durham. Wary of this new threat, Durham built thick city walls. As people settled within the walls, the population density soared. Soon, open lanes were covered by residences and became tunnels (called "vennels"). A classic vennel leads to Saddlers Yard, a fine little 16th-century courtyard (immediately opposite Elvet Bridge). While the vennels are cute today, centuries ago they were Dickensian nightmares—the filthiest of hovels.

• *Continue up Saddler Street. Just before the fork at the top of the street, duck through the purple door below the* Georgian Window *sign. You'll*

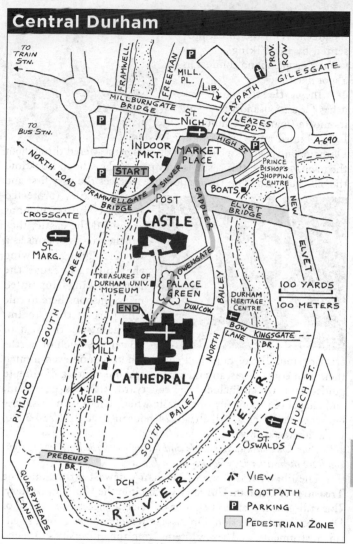

Central Durham

see a bit of the medieval wall incorporated into the brickwork of a newer building, and a turret from an earlier wall. Back on Saddler Street, you can see the ghost of the old wall. (It's exactly the width of the building now housing the Salvation Army.) Veer right at Owengate as you continue uphill, until you reach the Palace Green.

The **Palace Green** was the site of the original 11th-century Saxon town, filling this green between the castle and an earlier church. Later, the town made way for 12th-century Durham's defenses, which now enclose the green. With the threat presented by the Vikings, it's no wonder people found comfort in a spot like this.

The **castle** still stands—as it has for a thousand years—on its motte (man-made mound). Like Oxford and Cambridge, Durham University is a collection of colleges scattered throughout the town, and even this castle is now part of the school. Look into the old courtyard from the castle gate. It traces the very first and smallest bailey (protected

area). As future bishops expanded the castle, they left their coats of arms as a way of "signing" the wing they built. Because the Norman kings appointed prince bishops here to rule this part of their realm, Durham was the seat of power for much of northern England. The bishops had their own army and even minted their own coins. You can enter the castle only with a 45-minute guided tour, which includes the courtyard, kitchens, great hall, and chapel (£5, typically open daily when school is in session—but schedule varies so call ahead, 24-hour info tel. 0191/334-3800, www.dur.ac.uk/university.college/tours).

• *Turning your back to the castle and facing the cathedral, on the right you'll see the university's Palace Green Library.*

The library hosts one of Durham's newest attractions, the **Treasures of Durham University** exhibit in the **Wolfson Gallery.** This still-evolving exhibit showcases eclectic pieces from the U of D's substantial collection. On display are lots of rare books, scientific instruments, and several items from the university's Oriental Museum. One of the best-known pieces is a valuable 1623 copy of Shakespeare's First Folio. Stolen in 1998, it resurfaced in 2008, when Englishman Raymond Scott brought the folio to the Folger Shakespeare Library in Washington, DC, for authentication. Experts immediately recognized it, and the book was returned to Durham. (Scott, an eccentric who lived near Durham, was acquitted of the actual theft but served an eight-year sentence for handling stolen property.) The Durham First Folio had been especially prized by scholars for its good condition and its traceable ownership back to the early 17th century. Unfortunately, it was damaged

Durham's Early Years

Durham's location, tucked inside a tight bend in the River Wear, was practically custom-made for easy fortifications. But it wasn't settled until A.D. 995, with the arrival of St. Cuthbert's body (buried in Durham Cathedral). Shortly after that, a small church and fortification were built upon the site of today's castle and church to house the relic. The castle was a classic "motte-and-bailey" design (with the "motte," or mound, providing a lookout tower for the stockade encircling the protected area, or "bailey"). By 1100, the prince bishop's bailey was filled with villagers—and he wanted everyone out. This was *his* place! He provided a wider protective wall, and had the town resettle below (around today's Market Place). But this displaced the townsfolk's cows, so the prince bishop constructed a fine stone bridge (today's Framwellgate) to connect the new town to grazing land he established across the river. The bridge had a defensive gate, with a wall circling the peninsula and the river serving as a moat.

during the theft, so the book may be out of view while it's being restored (£3, Tue-Fri 10:00-16:45, Sat-Sun 12:00-16:45, Palace Green, tel. 0191/334-3019, www.dur.ac.uk/library/asc).

• *This walk ends at Durham's stunning **cathedral**, described next.*

Sights in Durham

▲▲▲Durham's Cathedral

Built to house the much-venerated bones of St. Cuthbert from Lindisfarne (known today as Holy Island), Durham's cathedral offers the best look at Norman architecture in England. ("Norman"

is British for "Romanesque.") In addition to touring the cathedral and its attached sights, try to fit in an evensong service.

Cost and Hours: Entry to the cathedral itself is free, though a £4 donation is requested and you must pay to enter its several interior sights (described later, under "Other Cathedral Sights"). The cathedral is open to visitors mid-July-Aug daily 9:30-20:00; Sept-mid-July Mon-Sat 9:30-18:00, Sun 12:30-17:30; sometimes closes for special services, opens daily at 7:15 for worship and prayer. Access is limited for two weeks in June, when the cathedral is used for graduation ceremonies.

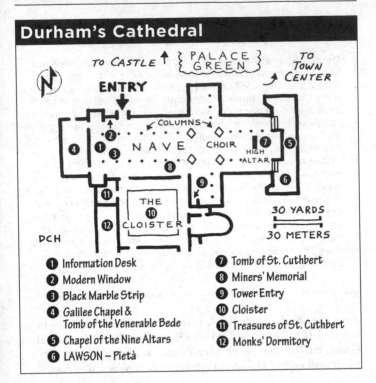

Durham's Cathedral

TO CASTLE ↑ { PALACE GREEN } TO TOWN CENTER

ENTRY

COLUMNS

NAVE   CHOIR   HIGH ALTAR

THE CLOISTER

DCH

30 YARDS
30 METERS

1 Information Desk
2 Modern Window
3 Black Marble Strip
4 Galilee Chapel & Tomb of the Venerable Bede
5 Chapel of the Nine Altars
6 LAWSON – Pietà
7 Tomb of St. Cuthbert
8 Miners' Memorial
9 Tower Entry
10 Cloister
11 Treasures of St. Cuthbert
12 Monks' Dormitory

Information: The £1 pamphlet, *A Short Guide to Durham Cathedral,* is informative but dull. A bookshop, cafeteria, and WC are tucked away in the cloister. No photos, videos, or mobile phones are allowed inside the cathedral. Tel. 0191/386-4266, www.durhamcathedral.co.uk.

Tours: Regular tours run in summer. If one is already in session, you're welcome to join (£4; late July-late Sept Mon-Sat at 10:30, 11:00, and 14:30; tours also possible near Easter and during school vacations in May and Oct; call or check website to confirm schedule).

Evensong: For a thousand years, this cradle of English Christianity has been praising God. To really experience the cathedral, attend an evensong service. Arrive early and ask to be seated in the choir. It's a spiritual Oz, as the choristers (12 men and 20 youngsters—now girls as well as boys) sing psalms—a red-and-white-robed pillow of praise, raised up by the powerful pipe organ. If you're lucky and the service goes well, the organist will run a spiritual musical victory lap as the congregation breaks up (Tue-Sat at 17:15, Sun at 15:30, 1 hour, sometimes sung on Mon; visiting choirs nearly always fill in when choir is off on school break mid-July-Aug; tel. 0191/386-4266). For more on evensong, see page 157.

Organ Recitals: The organ plays most Wednesday evenings in July and August (£8, 19:30).

❍ Self-Guided Tour: Begin your visit outside the cathedral. From the Palace Green, notice how this fortress of God stands boldly opposite the Norman keep of Durham's fortress of man.

Look closely: The **exterior** of this awe-inspiring cathedral has a serious skin problem. In the 1770s, as the stone was crumbling, they crudely peeled it back a few inches. The scrape marks give the cathedral a bad complexion to this day. For proof of this odd "restoration," study the masonry 10 yards to the right of the door. The L-shaped stones in the corner would normally never be found in a church like this—they only became L-shaped when the surface was cut back.

At the cathedral **door,** the big, bronze, lion-faced knocker (a replica of the 12th-century original—now in the treasury) was used by criminals seeking sanctuary (read the explanation).

Inside, purple-robed church attendants are standing by to happily answer questions. Ideally, follow a church tour. A handy information desk is at the back (right) end of the nave.

Notice the **modern window** with the novel depiction of the Last Supper (above and to the left of the entry door). It was given to the church by the local Marks & Spencer department store in 1984. The shapes of the apostles represent worlds and persons of every kind, from the shadowy Judas to the brightness of Jesus. This window is a good reminder that the cathedral remains a living part of the community.

Spanning the nave (toward the altar from the info desk), the **black marble strip** on the floor was as close to the altar as women were allowed in the days when this was a Benedictine church

(until 1540). Sit down (ignoring the black line) and let the fine proportions of England's best Norman nave—and arguably Europe's best Romanesque nave—stir you. All the frilly woodwork and stonework were added in later centuries.

The architecture of the **nave** is particularly harmonious because it was built in a mere 40 years (1093-1133). The round arches and zigzag carved decorations are textbook Norman. The church was also proto-Gothic, built by well-traveled French masons and architects who knew the latest innovations from Europe. Its stone and ribbed roof, pointed arches, and flying buttresses were revolutionary in England. Notice the clean lines and simplicity. It's not as cluttered as other churches for several reasons: Out of respect for St. Cuthbert, for centuries no one else was buried here (so it's not filled with tombs). During Reformation times, sumptuous Catholic decor was removed. Subsequent fires and wars destroyed what Protestants didn't.

Head to the back of the nave and enter the **Galilee Chapel** (late Norman, from 1175). Find the smaller altar just to the left of the main altar. The paintings of St. Cuthbert and St. Oswald (seventh-century king of Northumbria) on the side walls of the niche are rare examples of Romanesque (Norman) paintings. Facing this altar, look above to your right to see more faint paintings on the upper walls above the columns. On the right side of the chapel, the upraised tomb topped with a black slab contains the remains of the **Venerable Bede,** an eighth-century Christian scholar who wrote the first history of England. The Latin reads, "In this tomb are the bones of the Venerable Bede."

Back in the main church, stroll down the nave to the center, under the highest **bell tower** in Europe (218 feet). Gaze up. The ropes turn wheels upon which bells are mounted. If you're stirred by the cheery ringing of church bells, tune in to the cathedral on Sunday (9:15-10:00 & 14:30-15:30) or Thursday (19:30-21:00 practice, trained bell ringers welcome, www.durhambellringers.org .uk) when the resounding notes tumble merrily through the entire town.

Continuing east (all medieval churches faced east), you enter the **choir.** Monks worshipped many times a day, and the choir in the center of the church provided a cozy place to gather in this vast, dark, and chilly building. Mass has been said daily here in the heart of the cathedral for 900 years. The fancy wooden benches are from the 17th century. Behind the altar is the delicately carved Neville Screen from 1380 (made of Normandy stone in London, shipped to Newcastle by sea, then brought here by wagon). Until the Reformation, the niches contained statues of 107 saints. Exit the choir from the far right side (south). Look for the stained-glass window (to your right) that commemorates the church's 1,000th anniversary in 1995. The colorful scenes depict England's history, from coal miners to cows to computers.

Step down behind the high altar into the east end of the church, which contains the 13th-century **Chapel of the Nine Altars.** Built later than the rest of the church, this is Gothic— taller, lighter, and relatively more extravagant than the Norman nave. On the right, see the powerful modern *pietà* made of driftwood, with brass accents by local sculptor Fenwick Lawson.

Climb a few steps to the **tomb of St. Cuthbert.** An inspirational leader of the early Christian Church in north England, St. Cuthbert lived in the Lindisfarne monastery (100 miles north of Durham, today called Holy Island—see page 752). He died in 687. Eleven years later, his body was exhumed and found to be miraculously preserved. This stoked the popularity of his shrine, and pilgrims came in growing numbers. When Vikings raided Lindisfarne in 875, the monks fled with his body (and the famous illuminated Lindisfarne Gospels, now in the British Library in London). In 995, after 120 years of roaming, the monks settled in Durham on an easy-to-defend tight bend in the River Wear. This cathedral was built over Cuthbert's tomb.

Throughout the Middle Ages, a shrine stood here and was visited by countless pilgrims. In 1539, during the Reformation—whose proponents advocated focusing on God rather than saints—the shrine was destroyed. But pilgrims still come, especially on St. Cuthbert's feast day (March 20).

Turn around and walk back the way you came. In the **south transept** (to your left) is the entrance to the tower (described below), as well as an astronomical clock and the Chapel of the Durham Light Infantry, a regiment of the British Army (1881-1968). The old flags and banners hanging above were actually carried into battle.

Beyond the transept, also on the left side of the nave, is the door to the cloister, with more sights—including the treasury collection, the monks' dormitory, and an AV show (all described later). Along the wall by the door to the cloister, notice the **memorial honoring coal miners** who died, and those who "work in darkness and danger in those pits today." (This message is a bit dated—Durham's coal mines closed down in the 1980s.) The nearby book of remembrance lists specific mine victims. As an ecclesiastical center and a major university town as well as a gritty, blue-collar coal-mining town, Durham's population has long been a complicated mix: priests, academics, and the working class.

Tower: The view from the tower will cost you 325 steps and £5 (Mon-Sat 10:00-16:00, closes at 15:00 in winter, closed Sun, last entry 20 minutes before closing; closed during events and in bad weather; must be at least 4'3" tall, no backless shoes; enter through south transept).

Sights in the Cloister: The following sights are within the cloister (which provides a fine view back up to the church towers—made briefly famous in the Harry Potter films, described on page 806). Each sight has a separate ticket, or you can buy a single £5 "Explorer Ticket" that covers all three (ticket available Mon-Sat only, buy at info desk in back of nave).

The well-presented **Treasures of St. Cuthbert** collection is filled with medieval bits and holy pieces. Borrow the descriptions and begin at the far end, where you'll find the actual relics from St. Cuthbert's tomb—his coffin, vestments, and cross. Then work your way chronologically back toward the entrance, passing items from the Norman/medieval period (when the monks of Durham busily copied manuscripts), the Reformation, and the 17th century (£4, Mon-Sat 10:00-16:30, Sun 14:30-16:30).

The **monks' dormitory,** now a library under an original 14th-century timber roof, is filled with Anglo-Saxon stones such as old Celtic crosses (£1, Mon-Sat 10:00-16:00, Sun 13:00-16:00).

In the undercroft, you'll find a dry but informative 17-minute **AV show** telling the history of St. Cuthbert and his ties to this church (£1, Mon-Sat 10:00-16:00, no showings Sun, winter hours vary).

Near the treasury, you'll find the **WCs, bookshop** (in the old kitchen), and fine **Undercroft** cafeteria (daily 10:00-16:30, tel. 0191/386-3721).

More Sights in Durham

There's little to see in Durham beyond its cathedral, but it's a pleasant place to go for a stroll and enjoy its riverside setting.

Durham Heritage Centre—Situated in the old Church of St. Mary-le-Bow near the cathedral, this modest, somewhat hokey, but charming little museum does its best to illuminate the city's history, and is worthwhile on a rainy day. The exhibits, which are scattered willy-nilly throughout the old nave, include a reconstructed Victorian-era prison cell; a look at Durham industries past and present, especially coal mining (in Victorian times, the river was literally black from coal); and a 10-minute movie about 20th-century Durham. In the garden on the side of the church are two modern sculptures by local artist Fenwick Lawson, whose work you'll also see in the cathedral.

Cost and Hours: £2; July-Sept daily 11:00-16:30; June daily 14:00-16:30; April-May and Oct Sat-Sun 14:00-16:30, closed Mon-Fri; closed Nov-March; corner of North Bailey and Bow Lane, tel. 0191/384-5589, www.durhamheritagecentre.org.uk.

Riverside Path—For a 20-minute woodsy escape, walk Durham's riverside path from busy Framwellgate Bridge to sleepy Prebends Bridge.

Boat Cruise and Rental—Hop on the *Prince Bishop* for a relaxing one-hour narrated cruise of the river that nearly surrounds Durham (£7, Easter-Oct; for schedule call 24-hour info line at 0191/386-9525, check their website, or go down to dock at Brown's Boat House at Elvet Bridge, just east of old town; www.prince bishoprc.co.uk). Sailings vary based on weather and tides. For some exercise with identical scenery, you can rent a rowboat at the same pier (£5/hour per person, £10 deposit, Easter-Sept daily 10:00-

18:00, last boat rental one hour before closing or before dusk, tel. 0191/386-3779).

Sleeping in Durham

(area code: 0191)
Close-in pickings are slim in Durham; there are only a handful of B&Bs and a few hotels within easy walking distance of the town center. During graduation (typically the last two weeks of June), everything books up well in advance and prices increase dramatically. Rooms can be tight on weekends anytime of year. If the B&Bs are full, Durham could be a good place to resort to a bigger chain hotel (Premier Inn or Marriott).

B&Bs

$$ Victorian Town House B&B offers three spacious, boutique-like rooms in an 1853 townhouse. It's in a nice residential area just down the hill from the train station, and is handy to the town center (Sb-£50-60, Db-£80-90, family room for up to 4 people-£85-120, cash only, some view rooms, free Wi-Fi, DVD library, 2 Victoria Terrace, 10-minute walk from train or bus station, tel. 0191/370-9963, www.durhambedandbreakfast.com, stay@durhambedandbreakfast.com, friendly Jill and Andy).

$$ Castleview Guest House rents six airy, restful rooms in a well-located, 250-year-old guesthouse next door to a little church. Located on a charming cobbled street, it's just above Silver Street and the Framwellgate Bridge (Sb-£55-60, Db-£80-85, cash preferred, free Internet access and Wi-Fi, free street-parking permit,

---

Sleep Code

(£1 = about $1.60, country code: 44)
S = Single, **D** = Double/Twin, **T** = Triple, **Q** = Quad, **b** = bathroom, **s** = shower only. You can assume credit cards are accepted and breakfast is included unless otherwise noted.

To help you sort easily through these listings, I've divided the accommodations into three categories based on the price for a standard double room with bath (during high season):

$$$ Higher Priced—Most rooms £90 or more.
  $$ Moderately Priced—Most rooms between £50-90.
   $ Lower Priced—Most rooms £50 or less.

Prices can change without notice; verify the hotel's current rates online or by email. For other updates, see www.ricksteves.com/update.

---

4 Crossgate, tel. 0191/386-8852, www.castle-view.co.uk, info @guesthousesdurham.co.uk, Anne and Mike Williams).

$$ Cathedral View Town House rents five rooms a steep 10-minute uphill walk from the library plaza. They have a fine backyard terrace, where you can enjoy the striking namesake panorama and eat your breakfast in good weather (Sb-£70, Db-£85, cathedral-view Db-£90, variety of breakfast options, free Wi-Fi; from Market Place, cross the

bridge, and walk up Claypath—which becomes Gilesgate—to 212 Gilesgate; tel. 0191/386-9566, www.cathedralview.co.uk, cathedral view@hotmail.com, Karen and Jim).

$$ Farnley Tower, a luxurious but impersonal B&B, has 13 large rooms and a quirky staff. On a quiet street at the top of a hill, it's a 15-minute hike up from the town center (Sb-£65, Db-£85, superior Db with cathedral view-£95, family room-£120, 2 percent fee for credit cards, free Wi-Fi, phones in rooms, easy free parking, inviting yard, The Avenue—hike up this steep street and look for the sign on the right, tel. 0191/375-0011, fax 0191/383-9694, www.farnley-tower.co.uk, enquiries@farnley-tower.co.uk, Raj and Roopal Naik). The Naiks also run the inventive Gourmet Spot fine-dining restaurant, in the same building.

Hotels

$$$ Durham Marriott Hotel Royal County scatters its 150 posh, four-star, but slightly scruffy rooms among several buildings sprawling across the river from the city center. The Leisure Club has a pool, sauna, Jacuzzi, and fitness equipment (official rate: Db-£150, but standard rooms usually closer to £100-120, pricier "supreme" rooms—check website for exact prices and deals; breakfast included in some rates but otherwise £15.50 extra, elevator, pay Wi-Fi in lobby, pay cable Internet in rooms, 2 restaurants, bar, free parking, Old Elvet, tel. 0191/386-6821 or tel. 0870-400-7286, fax 0191/386-0704, www.marriott.co.uk).

$$ Kingslodge Hotel & Restaurant is a slightly worn but comfortable 21-room place with charming terraces, an attached restaurant, and a pub. Located in a pleasantly wooded setting, it's convenient for train travelers (Sb-£65, Db-£85, family room-£109-115, free Wi-Fi, free parking, Waddington Street, Flass Vale, tel. 0191/370-9977, www.kingslodge.info, kingslodgehotel@yahoo .co.uk).

$$ Premier Inn Durham City Center, squeezed between Clayport Library and the river, has 103 cookie-cutter purple rooms in a very convenient central location (Sb/Db–usually around £68-78, check online for deals as low as £29 with advance booking, continental breakfast–£5.25, full English breakfast–£8, air-con, elevator, expensive Wi-Fi, Freemans Place, tel. 0871-527-8338 or 0191/374-4400).

$$ Student Housing Open to Anyone: Durham Castle, a student residence actually on the castle grounds facing the cathedral,

rents rooms during the summer break (generally late June-Sept only). Request a room in the stylish main building, which is more appealing than the modern dorm rooms (S–£30-35, Sb–£40-60, D–£52-70, Db–£73-90, fancier Db–£185-200, price depends on room size and amenities, elegant breakfast hall, Palace Green, tel. 0191/334-4106, fax 0191/334-3801, www.dur.ac.uk/university .college, durham.castle@durham.ac.uk). Note that the same office also rents rooms in other university buildings, but most are far less convenient to the city center—make sure to request the Durham Castle location when booking.

Eating in Durham

Durham is a university town with plenty of lively, inexpensive eateries, but there's not much to get excited about. Especially on weekends, the places downtown are crowded with noisy college kids and rowdy townies. Stroll down North Road, across Framwellgate Bridge, up through Market Place, and up Saddler Street, and consider the options suggested below. The better choices are each a five-minute uphill walk from this main artery, and worth the short trek.

Updated British Food: **Oldfields** serves pricey, updated British classics made from locally sourced ingredients. The inviting dining room feels upscale but not snooty, and there's another, more-traditional dining room upstairs. While the service can be spotty and some locals wonder if this place is resting on its laurels, it remains one of the best options in town (£5-7 starters, £13-18 main dishes; lunch specials—£11/two courses, £14/three courses; daily 12:00-22:00, 18 Claypath, tel. 0191/370-9595).

Pubs Across the Elvet Bridge: Two good options are within a five-minute walk of the Elvet Bridge (just east of the old town). **The Court Inn** offers an eclectic menu of pub grub and an open, lively atmosphere (£4-6 sandwiches, £9-10 meals, long list of £3-6 Spanish-style tapas, daily 11:00-22:20; cross the Elvet Bridge, turn right, walk several blocks, and then look left; Court Lane,

tel. 0191/384-7350). For beer and ales, locals favor **The Dun Cow.**
There's a cozy "snug bar" up front, and a more spacious lounge in
the back. Read the legend behind the pub's name on the wall along
the outside corridor. More sedate than the student-oriented places
in the town center, this pub serves only snacks and light meals (£2-
4)—come here to drink and nibble, not to feast (daily 11:00-23:00,
from the Elvet Bridge, walk five minutes straight ahead to Old
Elvet 37, tel. 0191/386-9219).

On Saddler Street: The street leading from Market Place up
to the cathedral is lined with eateries. Among these, the best is the
youthful **Hide Café**—with a popular bar in front, and a sophisticated downstairs dining room in back. Locals appreciate its hip
cachet and modern continental cuisine, and reservations are smart
(£5-10 lunches; dinner—£5-7 starters, £9-14 main dishes; food
served Mon-Sat 12:00-15:00 & 18:00-21:30, Sun 12:00-15:00; 39
Saddler Street, tel. 0191/384-1999).

Deli Lunch: **Claypath Delicatessen** is worth the five-minute
uphill walk above Market Place. Not just any old sandwich shop,
this creative place assembles fresh ingredients into tasty sandwiches, salads, sampler platters, and more. While carry-out is possible, most people eat in the casual, comfortable café setting (£3-5
light meals, Mon-Sat 10:00-17:00, closed Sun; from Market Place,
cross the bridge and walk up Claypath to #57; tel. 0191/340-7209).

Indian: **The Capital,** a five-minute uphill walk above Market
Place (and across the street from Claypath Deli), has well-executed
Indian food in a contemporary setting (£8-12 meals, daily 18:00-
23:30, 69 Claypath, tel. 0191/386-8803).

Italian: **Melanzana** has £9-10 pizzas and pastas, £12 chicken
dishes, and £14-18 steaks in a trendy, romantic setting on the far
end of the Elvet Bridge (daily 9:00-21:00, Fri-Sat until 22:00, 96
Elvet Bridge, tel. 0191/384-0096).

Chain Restaurants with a Bridge View: Two chain places
(that you'll find in every British city) are worth considering in
Durham only because of their delightful setting right at the Old
Town end of the picturesque Framwellgate Bridge: **Café Rouge,**
with French-bistro food and decor (£5-9 starters and light meals,
£11-14 main dishes, Mon-Sat 9:00-23:00, Sun 10:00-22:00, 21
Silver Street, tel. 0191/384-3429); and **Bella Italia,** next door and
down the stairs, with a terrace overlooking the river and surprisingly good food (£5-6 starters, £7-10 pizzas and pastas, Tue-Sat
10:00-23:00, Sun-Mon 10:00-22:30, reservations recommended,
20 Silver Street, tel. 0191/386-1060).

Fish-and-Chips: **Bells,** just off Market Place toward the
cathedral, is a standby for carry-out fish-and-chips. I'd skip their
fancier dining room (£5-7, hours vary but likely Mon-Thu 11:00-
15:00, Fri-Sat 11:00-24:00, Sun 11:30-15:00).

Splurge Outside Town: **Bistro 21,** an untouristy splurge serving modern French/Mediterranean fare and good seafood, is one of Durham's top restaurants. Unfortunately, it's about 1.5 miles out of Durham—practical only for drivers (£7-10 starters, £15-22 main dishes; dinner special available Mon-Fri anytime and Sat before 19:00—£16/two courses, £18/three courses; open Mon-Sat 12:00-14:00 & 18:00-22:00, closed Sun, northwest of town, Aykley Heads, tel. 0191/384-4354).

Supermarket: **Marks & Spencer** is in the old town, just off Market Place (Mon-Sat 8:30-18:00, Sun 11:00-17:00, 4 Silver Street, across from post office). Next door is a **Tesco Metro** (Mon-Sat 7:00-22:00, Sun 11:00-17:00). You can **picnic** on Market Place, or on the benches and grass outside the cathedral entrance (but not on the Palace Green, unless the park police have gone home).

Durham Connections

From Durham by Train to: York (3-4/hour, 45 minutes), **Keswick/Lake District** (train to Penrith—hourly, 3 hours, change in Newcastle and Carlisle; then bus to Keswick—hourly Mon-Sat, Sun 8/day, 40 minutes), **London** (2/hour, 3 hours), **Hadrian's Wall** (take train to Newcastle—4/hour, 15 minutes, then a bus or a train/bus combination to near Hadrian's Wall—see "Getting Around Hadrian's Wall" on page 743), **Edinburgh** (1-2/hour, 1.75-2 hours, less frequent in winter). Train info: tel. 0845-748-4950, www.nationalrail.co.uk.

Route Tips for Drivers

As you head north from Durham on the M1 motorway, you'll pass a famous bit of public art: **The Angel of the North,** a modern, rusted-metal angel standing 65 feet tall with a wingspan of 175 feet (wider than a Boeing 757). While initially controversial when it was erected in 1998, it has since become synonymous with Northeast England, and is a beloved local fixture.

DURHAM & NE ENGLAND

Near Durham: Beamish Museum

This huge, 300-acre open-air museum, which re-creates the years 1825 and 1913 in northeast England, is England's best museum of its type. It takes at least three hours to explore its four sections: Pit Village (a coal-mining settlement with an actual mine), The Town (a 1913 street lined with actual shops), Pockerley Old Hall (a "gentleman farmer's" manor house), and Home Farm (a preserved farm and farmhouse). This isn't a wax museum. If you touch the exhibits, they may smack you. Attendants at each stop happily explain everything. In fact, the place is only really interesting if you talk to

Near Durham

To EDINBURGH

HOLY ISLAND (LINDISFARNE)

BERWICK

BEAL

SCOTLAND

BAMBURGH CASTLE

JEDBURGH

BORDERS

A-68

NORTH SEA

HOUSESTEADS ROMAN FORT

HADRIAN'S WALL

ANGEL OF THE NORTH

B-6318

GREEN HEAD

A-69

NEWCASTLE

TO AMSTERDAM

A-69

HEXHAM

TO CARLISLE & LAKE DISTRICT

HALT-WHISTLE

ONCE BREWED/ TWICE BREWED

VINDO-LANDA ROMAN FORT

BEAMISH MUSEUM

A-693

DURHAM

A-691

SEE DETAIL MAP

ENGLAND

TO YORK & LONDON

DCH

20 MILES

20 KM

DURHAM & NE ENGLAND

the attendants—who make it worth ▲▲▲.

Cost and Hours: £16, 25 percent discount with bus ticket—see below; to visit over several days, choose the "Beamish Unlimited Pass" at no extra charge to make your ticket valid for a year; Easter-Oct open daily 10:00-17:00; Nov-Easter only The Town and Pit Village are open but vintage trams still run, Tue-Thu and Sat-Sun 10:00-16:00, closed Mon and Fri, half-price on weekdays; closed mid-Nov-early

Jan—except open around Christmastime; check events schedule on chalkboard as you enter, last tickets sold at 15:00 year-round, tel. 0191/370-4000, www.beamish.org.uk.

Getting There: By **car,** the museum is five minutes off the A1/M1 motorway (one exit north of Durham at Chester-le-Street/

Junction 63, well signposted, 12 miles and a 25-minute drive north-west of Durham).

Getting to Beamish from Durham by **bus** is a snap on peak-season Saturdays via direct bus #128 (£3.70 day pass, 5/day, 30 minutes, runs April-Oct only, stops at Durham train and bus stations, tel. 0845-606-0260, www.simplygo.com). Otherwise, catch bus #21 or #50/#50A from the Durham bus station (£3.70 day pass, 3-4/hour, 25 minutes) and transfer at Chester-le-Street to bus #28 or #28A, which take you right to the museum entrance (2/hour Mon-Sat, hourly Sun, 15 minutes, leaves from central bus kiosk a half-block away; tel. 0871-200-2233, www.traveline.org.uk). Show your bus ticket for a 25 percent museum discount.

Getting Around the Museum: Pick up a free map at the entry to help navigate the four different zones; while some are side-by-

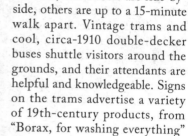

side, others are up to a 15-minute walk apart. Vintage trams and cool, circa-1910 double-decker buses shuttle visitors around the grounds, and their attendants are helpful and knowledgeable. Signs on the trams advertise a variety of 19th-century products, from "Borax, for washing everything" to "Murton's Reliable Travelling Trunks."

Eating at Beamish: There are several eateries scattered around Beamish, including a pub and tea rooms (in The Town), a fish-and-chips stand (in the Pit Village), and various cafeterias and snack stands. Or bring a picnic.

➲ Self-Guided Tour: I've described the four areas in counterclockwise order from the entrance.

From the entrance building, bear left along the road, then watch for the turnoff on the right to the **Pit Village.** This is a company town built around a coal mine, with a schoolhouse, a Methodist chapel, and a row of miners' homes with long, skinny pea-patch gardens out front.

Poke into some of the homes to see their modest interiors. In the Board School, explore the different classrooms, and look for the interesting poster with instructions for avoiding consumption (a.k.a. tuberculosis, a huge public-health crisis back then).

Next, cross to the adjacent **Colliery** (coal mine) where you can take a fascinating—if claustrophobic—20-minute tour into the drift mine (check in at the "lamp camp"—tours depart when enough people gather, generally every 5-10 minutes). Your guide will tell you stories about beams collapsing, gas exploding, and flooding; after that cheerful speech, you'll don a hard hat as you're led into the mine. Nearby (across the tram tracks) is the fascinating **engine works,** where you can see the actual steam-powered winding engine used to operate the mine elevator. The "winderman" demonstrates how he skillfully eases both coal and miners up and down the tight shaft of the mine. This delicate, high-stakes job was one of the most sought-after at the entire Colliery—passed down from father to son—and the winderman had to stay in this building for his entire shift (the seat of his chair flips up to reveal a built-in WC).

A path leads through the woods to Georgian-era **Pockerley,** which has two parts. First you'll see the **Waggonway,** a big

barn filled with steam engines, including the re-created, first-ever passenger train from 1825. (Occasionally this train takes modern-day visitors for a spin on 1825 tracks—a hit with railway buffs.)

Then, climb the hill to **Pockerley Old Hall,** the manor house of a gentleman farmer and his family. The house dates from the 1820s, and—along with the farmhouse described later—is Beamish's only vintage building still on its original site (other buildings at Beamish were relocated from elsewhere and reconstructed here). While not extremely wealthy, the farmer who lived here owned large tracts of land and could afford to hire help to farm it for him. This rustic home is no palace, but it was comfortable for the period. Costumed docents in the kitchen often bake delicious cookies from old recipes...and hand out samples.

The small garden terrace out front provides beautiful views across the pastures. From the garden, turn left and locate the narrow stairs up to the "old house." Actually under the same roof as the gentleman farmer's family, this space consists of a few small rooms that were rented by some of the higher-up workers to shelter their entire families of up to 15 children (young boys worked on the farm, while girls were married off early). While the parents had their own bedroom, the children all slept in the loft up above (notice the ladder in the hall).

From the manor house, hop on a vintage tram or bus, or walk 10 minutes, to the Edwardian-era **The Town** (c. 1913). This bustling street features several working shops and other buildings that are a delight to explore. In the Masonic Hall, ogle the

grand, high-ceilinged meeting room, and check out the fun old metal signs inside the garage. Across the street, poke into the courtyard to find the stables, which are full of carriages. The heavenly smelling candy store sells old-timey sweets, and has an actual workshop in back with trays of free samples. The newsagents sells stationery, cards, and old toys, while in the grocery, you can see old packaging and the scales used for weighing out products. Other buildings include a clothing store, a working pub (The Sun Inn, Mon-Sat 11:00-16:30, Sun 12:00-16:30), Barclays Bank, and a hardware store featuring a variety of "toilet sets" (not what you think).

For lunch, try the Tea Rooms cafeteria (upstairs, daily 10:00-16:30). Or, if the weather is good, picnic in the grassy park with the gazebo next to the tram stop. The row of townhouses includes both homes and offices (if the dentist is in, chat with him to hear some harrowing stories about pre-Novocain tooth extraction). At the circa-1913 railway station at the far end of The Town, you can stand on the bridge over the tracks to watch old steam engines go back and forth—along with a carousel of "steam gallopers." Nearby, look for the "Westoe netty," a circa 1890 men's public urinal. This loo became famous in 1972 as the subject in a nostalgic Norman Rockwell-style painting of six miners and a young boy doing their business while they read the graffiti.

Finally, walk or ride a tram or bus to the **Home Farm**. (This is the least interesting section—if you're running short on time, it's skippable.) Here you'll get to experience a petting zoo and see a "horse gin" (a.k.a. "gin gan")—where a horse walking in a circle turned a crank on a gear to amplify its "horsepower," helping to replace human hand labor. Near the cafeteria, you can

cross a busy road (carefully) to the old farmhouse, still on its original site, where attendants sometimes bake goodies on a coal fire.

Hadrian's Wall

Cutting across the width of the isle of Britain, this ruined Roman wall is one of England's most thought-provoking sights. Once a

towering 20-foot-tall fortification, these days "Hadrian's Shelf," as some cynics call it, is only about three feet wide and three to six feet high. (The conveniently pre-cut stones of the wall were carried away by peasants during the post-Rome Dark Ages, and now form the foundations of many local churches, farmhouses, and other structures.) In most places, what's left of the wall has been covered over by centuries of sod...making it effectively disappear into the landscape. But for those intrigued by Roman history, Hadrian's Wall provides a fine excuse to take your imagination for a stroll. Pretend you're a legionnaire on patrol in dangerous and distant Britannia, at the empire's northernmost frontier... with nothing but this wall protecting you from the terrifying, bloodthirsty Picts just to the north.

Today, several chunks of the wall, ruined forts, and museums thrill history buffs. While a dozen Roman sights cling along the wall's route, I've focused my coverage on an easily digestible six-mile stretch right in the middle, where you'll find the best museums and some of the most enjoyable-to-hike stretches of the wall. Three top sights are worth visiting: Housesteads Roman Fort shows you where the Romans lived; Vindolanda's museum shows you how they lived; and the Roman Army Museum explains the empire-wide military organization that brought them here.

A breeze for drivers, this area can also be seen fairly easily in summer by bus for those good at studying timetables (see "Getting Around Hadrian's Wall," later).

Hadrian's Wall is in vogue as a destination for multi-day hikes through the pastoral English countryside. The Hadrian's Wall National Trail runs 84 miles, following the wall's route from coast to coast (for details, see www.nationaltrail.co.uk/HadriansWall). Through-hikers (mostly British) can walk the wall's entire length in four to ten days. You'll see them bobbing along the ridgeline, drying out their socks in your B&B's mudroom, and recharging at local pubs in the evening. For those with less time, the brief ridge walk next to the wall from Steel Rigg to Sycamore Gap to Housesteads Roman Fort gives you a perfect taste of the scenery and history.

The History of Hadrian's Wall

In about A.D. 122, during the reign of Emperor Hadrian, the Romans constructed this great stone wall. Stretching 73 miles coast to coast across the narrowest stretch of northern England, it was built and defended by some 20,000 troops. Not just a wall, it was a military complex that included forts, ditches, settlements, and roads. At every mile of the wall, a castle guarded a gate, and two turrets stood between each castle. The mile-castles are numbered. (Eighty of them cover the 73 miles, because a Roman mile was slightly shorter than our mile.)

In cross-section, Hadrian's Wall consisted of a stone wall—around 15 to 20 feet tall—with a ditch on either side. The flat-bottomed ditch on the south side of the wall, called the vallum, was flanked by earthen ramparts and likely demarcated the "no-man's land" beyond which civilians were not allowed to pass. Between the vallum and the wall ran a service road called the Military Way. Another less-elaborate ditch ran along the north side of the wall. In some areas—including the region that I describe—the wall was built upon a volcanic ridgeline that provided a natural fortification.

The wall's actual purpose is still debated. While Rome ruled Britain for 400 years, it never quite ruled its people. The wall may have been used for any number of reasons: to protect Roman Britain from invading Pict tribes from the north (or at least cut down on pesky border raids); to monitor the movement of people, as a show of Roman strength and superiority; or to simply give an otherwise bored army something to do. (Emperors understood that nothing was more dangerous than a bored army.) Or perhaps the wall represented Hadrian's tacit admission that the empire had reached its maximum extent; Hadrian was known for consolidating his territory, in some cases giving up chunks of land that had been conquered by his predecessor, Trajan, to create an easier-to-defend (if slightly smaller) empire. His philosophy of "defense before expansion" is embodied by the impressive wall that still bears his name.

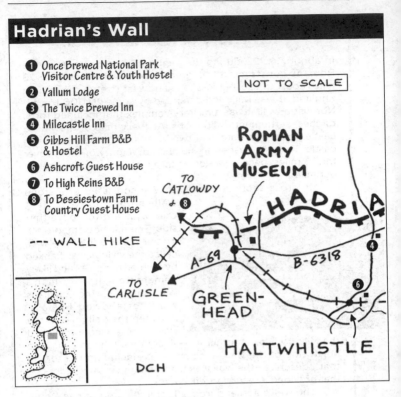

Hadrian's Wall

1 Once Brewed National Park Visitor Centre & Youth Hostel
2 Vallum Lodge
3 The Twice Brewed Inn
4 Milecastle Inn
5 Gibbs Hill Farm B&B & Hostel
6 Ashcroft Guest House
7 To High Reins B&B
8 To Bessiestown Farm Country Guest House

--- WALL HIKE

NOT TO SCALE

ROMAN ARMY MUSEUM

TO CATLOWDY

HADRIA

A-69

B-6318

TO CARLISLE

GREEN-HEAD

HALTWHISTLE

DCH

Orientation to Hadrian's Wall

The area described in this section is roughly between the mid-size towns of Bardon Mill and Haltwhistle, which are located along the busy A69 highway. Each town has a train station and some handy B&Bs, restaurants, and services. However, to get right up close to the wall, you'll need to head a couple of miles north to the adjacent villages of Once Brewed and Twice Brewed (along road B6318).

Tourist Information

Portions of the wall are in Northumberland National Park. The **Once Brewed National Park Visitor Centre** lies along the Hadrian's Wall bus #AD122 route, and has information on the area, including walking guides to the wall. The TV, set in front of a cozy couch, plays a variety of interesting movies about the wall and the surrounding landscape—ideal for a rainy day (Easter-Oct daily 9:30-17:00; Nov-Easter 10:00-15:00 Sat-Sun only, closed Mon-Fri; parking-£3, Military Road/B6318, tel. 01434/344-396,

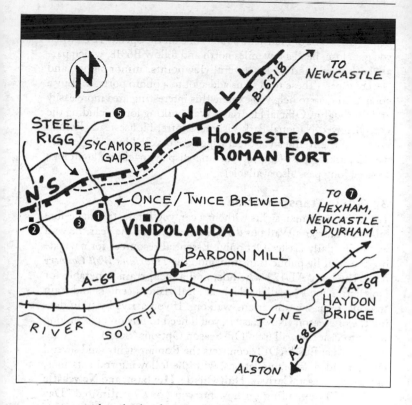

www.northumberlandnationalpark.org.uk, tic.oncebrewed@nnpa
.org.uk).

The helpful **TI** in Haltwhistle, a block from the train station inside the library, has a good selection of maps and guidebooks, and schedule information for Hadrian's Wall bus #AD122
(Easter-Oct Mon-Sat 10:00-13:00 & 13:30-16:30, closed Sun and
Nov-Easter, The Library, Westgate, tel. 01434/322-002, www
.hadrians-wall.org).

Getting Around Hadrian's Wall

Hadrian's Wall is anchored by the big cities of Newcastle to the
east and Carlisle to the west. Driving is the most convenient way
to see Hadrian's Wall. If you're coming by train, consider renting
a car for the day at either Newcastle or Carlisle; otherwise, you'll
need to rely on the bus to connect the sights. If you're just passing
through for the day using public transportation, it's challenging
to stop and see more than just one or two of the sights—study the
bus schedule carefully and prioritize. Non-drivers who want to see
everything—or even hike part of the wall—will need to stay at
least one night along the bus route.

By Car

Zip to this "best of Hadrian's Wall" zone on the speedy A69; when you get close, head a few miles north and follow B6318, which parallels the wall and passes several viewpoints, minor sights, and "severe dips." (These road signs add a lot to a photo portrait.) Buy a good local map to help you explore this interesting area more easily and thoroughly. Official Hadrian's Wall parking lots (including the Once Brewed National Park Visitors Centre, Housesteads Roman Fort, and the trailhead at Steel Rigg) are covered by a single one-day £3 parking pass (coin-op pay-and-display machines at all lots; £8 weeklong pass also available).

By Public Transportation

To reach the Roman sights without a car, you'll take the made-for-tourists Hadrian's Wall **bus #AD122** (named for the year the wall was built; daily Easter-Oct only). Essential resources for navigating the wall by public transit include the *Hadrian's Wall Country Map*, the bus #AD122 schedule, and a local train timetable for Northern Line #4—all available at local visitors centers and train stations, or at www.hadrians-wall.org. If you arrive by train during the off-season (Nov-Easter), you'll need to rely on taxis or long walks to visit the wall (see "Off-Season Options," later).

By Bus: Bus #AD122 connects the Roman sights (and several recommended accommodations) with the following train stations, listed west to east: **Carlisle, Haltwhistle, Hexham,** and **Newcastle** (£1.15-6.70 depending on how far you go, £9 unlimited "Day Rover" ticket, buy tickets on board or at any TI, tel. 01434/322-002, www.hadrians-wall.org). Buses run most frequently between Haltwhistle and Hexham (6/day each way). However, the bus runs less frequently from the end points: from Carlisle, four times a day; and from Newcastle, just once a day (at 9:30—if you miss this bus, take the train to Haltwhistle and pick up the bus there).

By Train: Northern Line's train route #4 runs parallel to and a few miles south of the wall much more frequently than the bus. While the train stops at stations in larger towns—including (west to east) **Carlisle, Haltwhistle, Hexham,** and **Newcastle**—it doesn't take you near the actual Roman sights. But you can catch bus #AD122 at all four of these train stations (train runs daily 1-2/hour; Carlisle to Haltwhistle—30 minutes; Haltwhistle to Hexham—20 minutes; Hexham to Newcastle—40 minutes; www.northernrail.org). Note: To get to or from Newcastle on this line, you must transfer in Hexham.

By Taxi: Four Haltwhistle-based taxi companies can help you connect the dots: Melvin's Taxi (tel. 01434/320-632, mobile 07903-760-230), Turnbull Taxi (tel. 01434/320-105, mobile 07825-004-901), Sprouls (tel. 01434/321-064, mobile 07712-321-064), or

The Doors (tel. 01434/322-556, mobile 07867-668-574). It costs about £11 one-way from Haltwhistle to Housesteads Roman Fort (arrange for return pickup or have museum staff call a taxi). Note that on school days, all of these taxis are busy shuttling rural kids to class in the morning (about 8:00-10:00) and afternoon (about 15:00-16:30), so you may have to wait.

Off-Season Options: Bus #AD122 doesn't run off-season (Nov-Easter), so you can only get as far as the train will take you (i.e., Haltwhistle)—from there, you'll have to take a taxi (described above) to the sights. Or, if you're a hardy hiker, take the Northern Line train to Bardon Mill, then walk about two miles to Vindolanda, and another 2.5 miles to Housesteads Roman Fort.

Luggage: It's difficult to bring your luggage along with you. If you're day-tripping, store your luggage in **Newcastle** (at the left-luggage office at the Newcastle train station, £5/bag per day, Mon-Sat 8:00-20:00, Sun 9:00-20:00, platform 12) or **Carlisle** (across the street from the train station at Bar Solo, £2/bag per day, Mon-Wed 9:00-23:00, Thu-Sat 9:00-24:00, Sun 11:00-22:30, tel. 01228/631-600). If you must travel with luggage, Housesteads Roman Fort and Vindolanda will both let you leave your bags at the sight entrance while you're inside, if you ask nicely. If you want to walk the wall, various baggage-courier services will send your luggage ahead to your next B&B in the region for about £5 per bag (contact Hadrian's Haul, mobile 07967-564-823, www.hadrianshaul.com; or Walkers', tel. 016977/42341, www.walkersbags.co.uk).

Sights at Hadrian's Wall

▲▲**Hiking the Wall**—It's enjoyable to hike along the wall speaking Latin, even if only for a short stretch. Note that park rang

ers forbid anyone from actually walking on top of the wall, except along a very short stretch at Housesteads. On the following hikes, you'll walk alongside the wall.

For a good, craggy, three-mile, up-and-down walk along the wall, hike between Steel Rigg and Housesteads Roman Fort. For a shorter stretch, begin at Steel Rigg (where there's a handy parking lot) and walk a mile to Sycamore Gap, then back again (described next; the Once Brewed National Park Visitor Centre hands out a free sheet outlining this walk). These hikes are moderately strenuous, and are best for those

DURHAM & NE ENGLAND

in good shape and with sturdy shoes.

To reach the trailhead for the short hike from **Steel Rigg to**
Sycamore Gap, take the little road
up from near the Once Brewed
National Park Visitor Centre and
park in the pay-and-display parking lot on the right at the crest of
the hill. Walk through the gate to
the shoulder-high stretch of wall,
go to the left, and follow the wall
running steeply down the valley

below you. Ahead of you are dramatic cliffs, creating a natural
boundary made-to-order for this Roman fortification. Walk down
the steep slope into the valley, then back up the other side (watch
your footing on the stone stairs). Following the wall, you'll do a
similar up-and-down routine three more times, like a slow-motion
human roller coaster. In the second gap is one of the best-preserved
milecastles, #39 (called Castle Nick because it sits in a nick in a
crag).

After walking about a mile, you'll reach the third gap, called

Sycamore Gap for the large
symmetrical tree in the
middle. (Do you remem-
ber the 1991 Kevin Costner
movie *Robin Hood: Prince
of Thieves*? Locals certainly
do—this tree was featured
in it, and tourists fre-
quently ask for directions to
the "Robin Hood Tree.") You can either hike back the way you
came, or cut down toward the main road to find the less strenuous
Roman Military Way path, which skirts the bottom of the ridge
(rather than following the wall); this leads back to the base of the
Steel Rigg hill, where you can huff back up to your car.

▲▲**Housesteads Roman Fort**—With its tiny museum, powerful scenery, and the best-preserved segment of the wall, this is your
best single stop at Hadrian's Wall. It requires a steep hike up from

the parking lot, but once there it's
just you, the bleating sheep, and
memories of ancient Rome.

Cost and Hours: £5 for site
and museum—pay at fort up top,
not at gift shop; daily April-Sept
10:00-18:00; Oct-March closes at
15:50 or dusk, may be open Sat-
Sun only; parking-£3, same park-

ing ticket also good for the Once Brewed National Park Visitor Centre and Steel Rigg parking lots—see page 744, bus #AD122 stops here, museum tel. 01434/344-363, gift shop tel. 01434/344-525, www.english-heritage.org.uk/housesteads.

Services: At the car park are WCs, a snack bar, and a gift shop with a small exhibit of scattered artifacts. They sell a £2 guidebook about the fort or a £5 guidebook covering the entire wall. Ask nicely if you're traveling by bus and want to leave your luggage at the gift shop (same hours as fort).

Touring the Fort: From the gift shop, head outside and hike about a half-mile uphill to the fort. At the top of the hill, duck into the small **museum** (on the left) to buy your ticket before touring the site. This newly expanded but modest museum, with a model of the original fort and a few artifacts, pales in comparison to the one at Vindolanda (explained next).

Then head out to explore the sprawling ruins of the **fort.** Interpretive signs and illustrations explain what you're seeing. All Roman forts were the same rectangular shape and design, containing a commander's headquarters, barracks, and latrines (Housesteads has the best-preserved Roman toilets found any-where—look for them at the lower-right corner). This fort even had a hospital. The fort was built right up to the wall, which runs along its upper end. (This is the one place along the wall where you're actually allowed to get up and walk on top of it for a photo op.) Visually trace the wall to the left to see how it disappears into a bank of overgrown turf.

▲▲Vindolanda—This larger Roman fort (which actually pre-dates the wall by 40 years) and museum are just south of the wall.

Although Housesteads has better ruins and the wall, Vindolanda has the better museum, packed with actual artifacts that reveal intimate details of Roman life.

Cost and Hours: £6.25, £9.50 combo-ticket includes Roman Army Museum, guide-book-£4, daily April-Sept 10:00-18:00, mid-Feb-March and Oct 10:00-17:00, closed Nov-mid Feb, last entry 45 minutes before closing, free parking with entry, bus #AD122 stops here, café, tel. 01434/344-277, www.vindolanda.com.

Tours: Guided tours run twice daily on weekends only (typically at 10:45 and 14:00); in high season, archaeological talks are also offered on weekdays (June-Aug Mon-Fri at 14:00). Both are included in your ticket.

Archaeological Dig: The Vindolanda site is an active dig—

from Easter through September, you'll see the excavation work in progress (usually Mon-Fri, weather permitting). Much of the work is done by volunteers, including armchair archaeologists from the US.

Touring the Site and Museum: From the free parking lot, you'll pay at the entrance, where there's a model of the entire site as it was in Roman times (c. 213-276). Notice that the site had two parts: the fort itself, and the town just outside that helped to supply it.

Then you'll head out to the **site,** walking through 500 yards of grassy parkland decorated by the foundation stones of the Roman fort and a full-size replica chunk of the wall. Over the course of 400 years, at least nine forts were built on this spot. The Romans, by lazily sealing the foundations from each successive fort, left modern-day archaeologists with a 20-foot-deep treasure trove of remarkably well-preserved artifacts: keys, coins, brooches, scales, pottery, glass, tools, leather shoes, bits of cloth, and even a wig. Many of these are now displayed in the museum, well-described in English, German, French, and...Latin.

At the far side of the site, pass through the pleasant riverside garden area on the way to the museum. The well-presented **museum** pairs actual artifacts with insightful explanations—such as a collection of Roman shoes with a description about what each one tells us about its wearer. The weapons (including arrowheads and spearheads) and fragments of armor are a reminder that Vindolanda was an important outpost on Rome's northern boundary—look for the Scottish skull stuck on a pike to discourage rebellion. You'll also see lots of leather; tools that were used for building and expanding the fort; locks and keys (the fort had a password that changed daily—jotting it on a Post-It note wasn't allowed); a large coin collection; items imported here from the far corners of the vast empire (such as fragments of French pottery and amphora jugs from the Mediterranean); beauty aids such as combs, tools for applying makeup, and hairpins; and religious pillars and steles.

But the museum's main attraction is its collection of writing tablets. A good video explains how these impressively well-preserved examples of early Roman cursive were discovered here in 1973. You'll see some of the actual letters—written on thin pieces of wood—and can read the translations. These varied letters, about parties held, money owed, and sympathy shared, bring Romans to life in a way that ruins alone can't. The most famous piece (described but not displayed here) is the first known example of a woman writing to a woman (an invitation to a birthday party).

Finally, you'll pass through an exhibit about the history of the excavations on your way to the shop and cafeteria. Look for the remarkably intact quern stone (similar to a millstone) inscribed with the name *Africanus*.

▲▲**Roman Army Museum**—This museum, a few miles farther west at Greenhead (near the site of the Carvoran Roman fort), was fully renovated in 2011. Its cutting-edge, interactive exhibit illustrates the structure of the Roman Army that built and monitored this wall, with a focus on the everyday lifestyles of the Roman soldiers stationed here. Bombastic displays, life-size figures, and several different films—but few actual artifacts—make this entertaining museum a good complement to the archaeological emphasis of Vindolanda.

Cost and Hours: £5, or buy £9.50 combo-ticket that includes Vindolanda, same hours as Vindolanda, free parking with entry, bus #AD122 stops here, tel. 016977/47485, www.vindolanda.com.

Visiting the Museum: In the first room, a video explains the complicated structure of the Roman Army—legions, cohorts, centuries, and so on. While a "legionnaire" was a Roman citizen, an "auxiliary" was a non-citizen specialist recruited for their unique skills (such as horsemen and archers). A video of an army recruiting officer delivers an "Uncle Caesar wants YOU!" speech to prospective soldiers. A timeline traces the history of the Roman Empire, especially as it related to the British Isles. The good 20-minute *Edge of Empire* 3-D movie offers an evocative look at what life was like for a Roman soldier marking time on the wall, and digital models show reconstructions of the wall and forts. In the exhibit on weapons, shields, and armor (mostly replicas), you'll learn how Roman soldiers trained with lead-filled wooden swords, so when they went into battle, their steel swords felt light by comparison. Another exhibit explains the story of Hadrian, the man behind the wall.

Sleeping and Eating near Hadrian's Wall

(£1 = about $1.60, country code: 44)

If you want to spend the night in this area, set your sights on the adjacent villages of Once Brewed and Twice Brewed, with a few accommodations options, a good pub, and easy access to the most important sights. I've also listed some other accommodations scattered around the region.

In and near Once Brewed and Twice Brewed
(area code: 01434)

These two side-by-side villages, each with a handful of houses, sit at the base of the volcanic ridge along road B6318. (While the mailing address for these hamlets is "Bardon Mill," that town is actually about 2.5 miles away, across the busy A69 highway.) The Twice Brewed Inn, Once Brewed Youth Hostel, Vallum Lodge, and Milecastle Inn are reachable with Hadrian's Wall bus #AD122, which stops nearby several times a day from Easter through October.

$$ Vallum Lodge is a cushy, comfortable, nicely renovated base situated near the vallum (the ditch that forms part of the fortification a half-mile from the wall itself). Its six cheery rooms are all on the ground floor, and it's just up the road from The Twice Brewed Inn—a handy dinner option (Sb-£69, Db-£85, closed late Oct-Easter, free Wi-Fi, lounge, Military Road, tel. 01434/344-248, www.vallum-lodge.co.uk, stay@vallum-lodge.co.uk, cheerful Ann).

$$ The Twice Brewed Inn, two miles west of Housesteads and a half-mile from the wall, rents 14 workable rooms (S-£34, D-£56, Db-£72-84, ask for a room away from the road, free Wi-Fi, free Internet access for hotel guests—otherwise £1/30 minutes, Military Road, tel. 01434/344-534, www.twicebrewedinn.co.uk, info@twicebrewedinn.co.uk). The inn's friendly **pub** serves as the community gathering place (free Wi-Fi), and is a hangout for hikers and the archaeologists digging at the nearby sites. It serves real ales and large portions of good pub grub (£9-12 meals, vegetarian options, fancier restaurant in back with same menu, open daily 11:00-23:00, food served daily 12:00-20:30, Fri-Sat until 21:00).

$ Once Brewed Youth Hostel is a comfortable, institutional place near the Twice Brewed Inn and next door to the Once Brewed National Park Visitor Centre (£16-19/bed with sheets in 2- to 6-bed rooms, private rooms available, non-members-£3 extra, breakfast-£5, packed lunch-£5.50, dinner-£10-12, reception open daily 8:00-10:00 & 16:00-22:00, advanced booking required Dec-Jan, guest kitchen, laundry, Military Road, tel. 01434/344-360 or 0845-371-9753, fax 01434/344-045, www.yha.org.uk, oncebrewed @yha.org.uk).

West of Once/Twice Brewed: **Milecastle Inn,** two miles to the west, cooks up all sorts of exotic game and offers the best dinner around, according to hungry national park rangers. You can order food at the counter and sit in the pub, or take a seat in the table-service area (£9-13 meals, food served daily 12:00-20:30, smart to reserve in summer, North Road, tel. 01434/321-372).

Rural and Remote, North of the Wall: **$$ Gibbs Hill Farm B&B and Hostel** is a friendly working sheep-and-cattle farm set on 700 acres in the stunning valley on the far side of the wall (only practical for drivers). It offers four big, airy rooms in the main house, and three six-bed dorm rooms in a restored hay barn (hostel bed/bedding-£15, Sb-£50, Db-£70, packed lunch-£5, laundry facilities, bikes available for rent, 5-minute drive from

Once Brewed National Park Visitor Centre, tel. 01434/344-030, www.gibbshillfarm.co.uk, val@gibbshillfarm.co.uk, warm Val). They also rent several cottages for two to six people by the week (£280-600).

In Haltwhistle
(area code: 01434)

The larger town of Haltwhistle has a train station, along with stops for Hadrian's Wall bus #AD122 (at the train station and a few blocks east, at Market Place). It also has a helpful TI (see "Tourist Information," on page 742), a launderette, several eateries, and a handful of B&Bs, including this one.

$$ Ashcroft Guest House, a large Victorian former vicarage, is 400 yards from the Haltwhistle train station and 200 yards from the Market Place bus stop. The family-run B&B has eight big, luxurious rooms, huge terraced gardens, and views from the comfy lounge (Sb-£52, Db-£80, four-poster Db-£90, ask about family deals and two-bedroom suite, free Internet access and Wi-Fi, 1.5 miles from the wall, Lanty's Lonnen, tel. 01434/320-213, www.ashcroftguesthouse.co.uk, ashcroft.1@btconnect.com, helpful Geoff and Christine James).

Near Hexham
(area code: 01434)

$$ High Reins offers four rooms in a stone house built by a shipping tycoon in the 1920s (Sb-£46, Db-£69, cash only, lounge, 1 mile south of train station on the western outskirts of Hexham, Leazes Lane, tel. 01434/603-590, www.highreins.co.uk, pwalton@highreins.co.uk, Jan and Peter Walton).

Near Carlisle
(area code: 01228)

$$$ Bessiestown Farm Country Guest House, located far northwest of the Hadrian sights, is convenient for drivers connecting the Lake District and Scotland. It's a quiet and soothing stop in the middle of sheep pastures, with five bedrooms in the main house and two 2-bedroom apartments in the former stables (Sb-£57, Db-£90, Tb-£110, family room for 3 people-£110, fancier suite-£130, discounts for 3-night stays, indoor pool; in Catlowdy, midway between Gretna Green and Hadrian's Wall, a 20-minute drive north of Carlisle; tel. 01228/577-219, fax 01228/577-019, www.bessiestown.co.uk, info@bessiestown.co.uk, gracious Margaret and John Sisson).

Holy Island and Bamburgh Castle

This remote area is worthwhile only for those with a car. It's out of the way for most itineraries—unless you're driving between Durham and Edinburgh on the A1 highway, in which case Holy Island and Bamburgh Castle (and Beamish Museum, described earlier) are easy stop-offs. If you're determined to reach these sights by public transportation, you can go to Newcastle, then take bus #501 to Bamburgh Castle (2-3/day, 2.5 hours); or bus #505 to Beal (5/day Mon-Sat, none direct on Sun, 2 hours), where you can walk a level six miles or catch bus #477 to Holy Island (Wed and Sat only, described under "Getting There," below).

Holy Island (Lindisfarne)

Twelve hundred years ago, this "Holy Island"—then known as Lindisfarne—was Christianity's tenuous toehold on England. In

the A.D. 680s, Holy Island was the home and original burial ground of St. Cuthbert (he's now in Durham). We know it as the source of the magnificent Lindisfarne Gospels (A.D. 698; now in London's British Library), decorated by monks with some of the finest art from Europe's "Dark Ages." By the ninth century, Viking raids forced the monks to take shelter in Durham, but they returned centuries later to re-establish a church on this holy site.

Today Holy Island—worth ▲▲—makes a pleasant stop for modern-day pilgrims: You'll cross a causeway to a quiet town with a striking castle and the ruins of an evocative priory that was originally founded in 635.

Getting There: Holy Island is reached by a two-mile causeway that's cut off twice a day by high tides. Safe crossing times are posted at each end of the causeway (and at www.lindisfarne.org .uk), warning **drivers** when this holy place becomes Holy Island— and you become stranded. Once on the island, signs direct you to a well-marked, mandatory parking lot at the entrance to town (£2.40).

It's also possible to reach Holy Island by **bus** from the nearby town of Beal, but it's not worth the effort unless you're a determined pilgrim (bus #477, 2/day Wed and Sat only; if coming on the bus from Newcastle, get off at Beal to transfer to this bus—but carefully confirm schedule for the complete connection before you head out).

Getting Around Holy Island: From the parking lot, it's an easy 10-minute **walk** into town and to the priory; the castle is about a 20-minute walk away. To save time, ride the convenient **shuttle bus,** which makes a circuit from the parking lot to the village green (next to the priory entrance), then out to the castle, and back again (£1, 3/hour).

Sights on Holy Island

The two main attractions on Holy Island are the ruins of the old priory and the castle outside of town. The town itself is a charming little community of about 150 residents.

Holy Island Town—The town has B&Bs and cafés catering to tourists, a tiny post office, a fire station (with no firefighters— they're helicoptered in when the need arises), a six-student school-house, and a tiny winery offering free tastes of their Lindisfarne mead. There's no official TI, but the **Lindisfarne Centre**—with a well-presented, kid-friendly history exhibit—acts as an unofficial information point and is proudly staffed by native Holy Islanders (£3 to tour the exhibit, daily April-Sept 10:00-17:00, Oct 10:00-16:00, open sporadically Nov-March, Marygate, tel. 01289/389-004, www.lindisfarne.org.uk).

Lindisfarne Priory—The priory has an evocative field of ruined church walls and a tiny but instructive museum. (A priory—run by a prior rather than an abbot—is similar to an abbey, but smaller.)

Cost and Hours: £4.80 ticket includes both museum and priory ruins, guidebook-£4; April-Sept daily 9:30-17:00; Oct daily 9:30-16:00; Nov-Feb Sat-Sun 10:00-14:00, closed Mon-Fri, shorter winter hours possible; March daily 10:00-16:00; tel. 01289/389-200, www.english-heritage.org.uk/lindisfarne.

Touring the Priory: In the **museum,** you'll see exhibits about Holy Island's Anglo-Saxon culture, from stonework to manuscripts—including the famous Lindisfarne Gospels. The Gospels' text was in Latin, the language of scholars ever since the Roman Empire, but the illustrations—with elaborate tracery and interwoven decoration—are a mix of Irish, classical, and even Byzantine forms. These Gospels are a reminder that Christianity almost didn't make it in Europe. After the fall of Rome (which had established Christianity as the Empire's official religion), much of Europe reverted to its pagan ways. In that chaotic era, Lindisfarne—an obscure monastery of Irish monks on a remote island—was one of the few beacons of light, tending the embers of civilization through the long night of the Dark Ages.

You can visit the adjacent church and churchyard without paying, but you need a ticket to get into the actual **priory ruins.** The Lindisfarne monks fled the island in A.D. 875 to escape Viking raids. They made their way to Durham, and built a cathedral to hold the tomb of St. Cuthbert (see page 725). Centuries later, in 1082, the monks returned to Holy Island to re-found the priory and build a fine church in a Norman (Romanesque) style similar to the one in Durham. They fended off invasions by Picts and Scots throughout the 14th century, and fortified the great church. But when Henry VIII "dissolved" (destroyed) the monasteries in the 1530s, the priory was one of his victims. The forgotten ruins were

later excavated in the 1850s as an important example of early English (Anglo-Saxon) history.

As you walk through this site, you're stepping on several layers of history: A ruined Norman church sitting on the ruins of an earlier Anglo-Saxon one (where Cuthbert served as bishop), next to the still-standing Parish Church of St. Mary's, where Holy Islanders worship today. The priory ruins are well-explained by posted plaques and floor plans that help resurrect the rubble.

Lindisfarne Castle—Faintly visible from the priory ruins, the dramatically situated Lindisfarne Castle is enticing from afar,

and makes for a fine photo op. But inside, there's little of interest. Built in 1549—many centuries after the heyday of Cuthbert and the monks—the castle never really saw much action, and it was converted into a holiday home for an aristocratic publisher in the early 1900s. If you do visit, you'll wander through sparsely furnished rooms and stroll out onto the upper battery—an outdoor terrace with views of the priory ruins.

Cost and Hours: £6.95, Tue-Sun 10:00-15:00 or 12:00-17:00 depending on tides—confirm times at the National Trust shop on Marygate in town before heading out, closed Mon except in Aug, tel. 01289/389-244, www.nationaltrust.org.uk/lindisfarne.

Bamburgh Castle

About 10 miles south of Holy Island, this grand castle—worth ▲—dominates the Northumbrian countryside and over-

looks Britain's loveliest beach. Bamburgh (BOMB-ruh) was bought and passionately refurbished by Lord William George Armstrong, a wealthy industrialist, in the 1890s. While it's one of England's most dramatic castles from the outside, the interior (a 19th-century rebuild) lacks soul, barely cracking the country's top ten. But if you're passing by or visiting nearby Holy Island, Bamburgh may be worth a stop.

Cost and Hours: £8.50 includes staterooms and grounds, daily mid-Feb-Oct 11:00-17:00, winter Sat-Sun only 11:00-16:30, last entry one hour before closing, parking-£2, tel. 01668/214-515, www.bamburghcastle.com.

Touring the Castle: Bamburgh's main attraction is its staterooms; as you explore the rest of the grounds, you'll also have the chance to see several smaller exhibits. If arriving late in the day, go directly to the staterooms, which close early (last entry at 16:15). There's virtually no information inside the castle, aside from a few docents; to give meaning to your visit, either rent the £1 audioguide (with two hours of commentary) or buy the £1 guidebook.

The **staterooms** feel lived-in because they still are—with Armstrong family portraits and aristocratic-yet-homey knickknacks hanging everywhere. You'll enter through the medieval kitchen, with its three giant fireplaces, and work your way through smaller storage rooms to the King's Hall, with a fantastic teak ceiling and a J. M. W. Turner painting. At the far end of the great hall is a smaller (but still-grand) alcove separated by an archway, which could be sealed off by gigantic folding doors. Continuing through the stairwell, notice the *private apartment* signs.

The armory once had a very different purpose—you can still see the apse of what was once a chapel. In the keep is a 145-foot-deep Anglo-Saxon well. The scullery (a medieval utility room) includes a long row of sinks and an alcove where they make fresh fudge. You'll wind up in the gift shop; before leaving, check out the archaeology room, with exhibits about the castle's history; and the dungeon, with cheesy mannequins being tortured.

Exploring the **grounds,** you enjoy fine views over the sea and beach, and get a good look at the stout 12th-century keep that's the castle's centerpiece. In the former stables is an art gallery displaying works by local artists. The Armstrong and Aviation Artefacts Museum features the inventions of the family that has owned the castle through modern times. Lord William George Armstrong (1810-1900) was a  pioneer in aviation and a clever innovator, creating (among other things) the first all-steel aircraft structure, a method for in-flight refueling, and the ejector seat. You'll see several of his inventions, along with exhibits on cars, shipbuilding, and more. While the museum is fun for aviation-history buffs, it may be dull to others.

Nearby: The village of Bamburgh is pleasant enough, with tourist-oriented cafés and fine views over a manicured cricket pitch of the looming castle. Better yet, go for a walk on the beach: Crisscrossed by walking paths, rolling dunes lead to a vast sandy beach and lots of families on holiday.

GREAT BRITAIN: PAST & PRESENT

Britain was created by force and held together by force. It's really a nation of the 19th century, when this rich Victorian-era empire reached its financial peak. Its traditional industry, buildings, and the popularity of the notion of "Great" Britain are a product of its past wealth.

To best understand the many fascinating tour guides you'll encounter in your travels, it's helpful to have a basic handle on the sweeping story of this land. (Generally speaking, the nice and bad stories guides tell are not true...and the boring ones are.)

Basic British History for the Traveler

When Julius Caesar landed on the misty and mysterious isle of Britain in 55 B.C., England entered the history books. The primitive Celtic tribes he fought were themselves invaders (who had earlier conquered the even more mysterious people who built Stonehenge). About 90 years later, the Romans came back, building towns and roads and establishing their capital at Londinium. The Celtic natives in Scotland and Wales—consisting of Gaels, Picts, and Scots—were not easily subdued. The Romans built Hadrian's Wall near the Scottish border as protection against their troublesome northern neighbors. Even today, the Celtic language and influence are strongest in these far reaches of Britain.

As Rome fell, so fell Roman Britain—a victim of invaders and internal troubles. Barbarian tribes from Germany and Denmark, called Angles and Saxons, swept through the southern part of the island, establishing Angle-land. These were the days of the real King Arthur, possibly a Christianized Roman general who fought valiantly—but in vain—against invading barbarians. In 793, England was hit with the first of two centuries of savage invasions

Get It Right

Americans tend to use "England," "Britain," and the "United Kingdom" (or "UK") interchangeably, but they're not quite the same:

- **England** is the country occupying the southeast part of the island.
- **Britain** is the name of the island.
- **Great Britain** is the political union of the island's three countries: England, Scotland, and Wales.
- The **United Kingdom (UK)** adds a fourth country, Northern Ireland.
- The **British Isles** (not a political entity) also includes the independent Republic of Ireland.
- The **British Commonwealth** is a loose association of possessions and former colonies (including Canada, Australia, and India) that profess at least symbolic loyalty to the Crown.

You can call the modern nation either the United Kingdom ("the UK"), "Great Britain," or simply "Britain."

by barbarians from Norway, called the Vikings or Norsemen. The island was plunged into 500 years of Dark Ages—wars, plagues, and poverty—lit only by the dim candle of a few learned Christian monks and missionaries trying to convert the barbarians. The sightseer sees little from this Anglo-Saxon period.

Modern England began with yet another invasion. William the Conqueror and his Norman troops crossed the English Channel from France in 1066. William crowned himself king in Westminster Abbey (where all subsequent coronations would take place) and began building the Tower of London. French-speaking Norman kings ruled the country for two centuries. Then followed two centuries of civil wars, with various noble families vying for the crown. In the bitterest feud, the York and Lancaster families fought the Wars of the Roses, so-called because of the white and red flowers the combatants chose as their symbols. Rife with battles, intrigues, and kings, nobles, and ladies imprisoned and executed in the Tower, it's a wonder the country survived its rulers.

England was finally united by the "third-party" Tudor family. Henry VIII, a Tudor, was England's Renaissance king. He was handsome, athletic, highly sexed, a poet, a scholar, and a musician. He was also arrogant, cruel, gluttonous, and paranoid. He went through six wives in 40 years, divorcing, imprisoning, or executing them when they no longer suited his needs. (To keep track of each one's fate, British kids learn this rhyme: "Beheaded, divorced, died; beheaded, divorced, survived.")

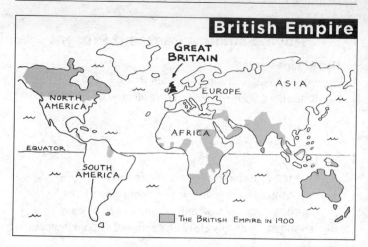

The British Empire in 1900

Henry "divorced" England from the Catholic Church, establishing the Protestant Church of England (the Anglican Church) and setting in motion years of religious squabbles. He also "dissolved" the monasteries (circa 1540), leaving just the shells of many formerly glorious abbeys dotting the countryside while pocketing their land and wealth for the crown.

Henry's daughter, Queen Elizabeth I, who reigned for 45 years, made England a great trading and naval power (defeating the Spanish Armada) and presided over the Elizabethan era of great writers (such as William Shakespeare) and scientists (such as Sir Francis Bacon). But Elizabeth never married, so the English Parliament asked the Protestant ruler to the north, Scotland's King James (Elizabeth's first cousin twice removed), if he'd like to inherit the English throne. The two nations have been tied together ever since.

The longstanding quarrel between England's divine-right kings and Parliament's nobles finally erupted into a civil war in 1643. Parliament forces under the Protestant Puritan farmer Oliver Cromwell defeated—and beheaded—King Charles I. This civil war left its mark on much of what you'll see in Britain. Eventually, Parliament invited Charles' son to take the throne. This "restoration of the monarchy" was accompanied by a great colonial expansion and the rebuilding of London (including Christopher Wren's St. Paul's Cathedral), which had been devastated by the Great Fire of 1666. Parliament gained ultimate authority over the throne when it deposed Catholic James II in 1688, guaranteeing a Protestant succession.

Britain grew as a naval superpower, colonizing and trading with all parts of the globe (although it lost its most important colony to ungrateful Americans in 1776). Admiral Horatio

Royal Families: Past and Present

Royal Lineage

802-1066	Saxon and Danish kings
1066-1154	Norman invasion (William the Conqueror), Norman kings
1154-1399	Plantagenet (kings with French roots)
1399-1461	Lancaster
1462-1485	York
1485-1603	Tudor (Henry VIII, Elizabeth I)
1603-1649	Stuart (civil war and beheading of Charles I)
1649-1653	Commonwealth, no royal head of state
1653-1659	Protectorate, with Cromwell as Lord Protector
1660-1714	Restoration of Stuart dynasty
1714-1901	Hanover (four Georges, Victoria)
1901-1910	Saxe-Coburg (Edward VII)
1910-present	Windsor (George V, Edward VIII, George VI, Elizabeth II)

The Royal Family Today

It seems you can't pick up a British newspaper without some mention of the latest scandal, event, or oddity involving the royal family. Here is the cast of characters:

Queen Elizabeth II wears the traditional crown of her great-great grandmother Victoria. (Elizabeth's late father, George VI, was the subject of the Oscar-winning film *The King's Speech*.) Elizabeth's husband is Prince Philip, who's not considered king.

Their son, Prince Charles (the Prince of Wales), is next in line to become king. But it's Prince Charles' sons who generate the tabloid buzz these days—especially Prince William (b. 1982). A graduate of Scotland's St. Andrews University and an officer in both the Royal Air Force and Royal Navy, William married Catherine "Kate" Middleton, his longtime girlfriend, on April 29, 2011. The TV audience was estimated at one-quarter of the world's population—more than two billion people. Kate—a commoner he met at university—is now the Duchess of Cambridge and will eventually become Britain's queen.

Nelson's victory over Napoleon's fleet at the Battle of Trafalgar secured her naval superiority ("Britannia rules the waves"), and 10 years later, the Duke of Wellington stomped Napoleon on land at Waterloo. Nelson and Wellington—both buried in London's St. Paul's Cathedral—are memorialized by many arches, columns, and squares throughout England.

Economically, Britain led the world into the Industrial Age

William's brother, redheaded Prince Harry (b. 1984), made a media splash as a bad boy when he wore a Nazi armband (as an ill-advised joke) to a costume party. Since then, he's proved his mettle as a career soldier, serving two months in Afghanistan. In 2008, he and his regiment did charity work in Africa, and since then he's been training to become a pilot with the Army Air Corps. Harry's love life—especially his relationship with on-again, off-again girlfriend, Chelsy Davy—is a popular topic for the tabloids.

For years their father's love life was also fodder for the British press. In 1981, Charles married Lady Diana Spencer (Princess Di) who, after their bitter divorce, died in a car crash in 1997. In 2005, Charles married his longtime girlfriend, Camilla Parker Bowles, who is trying to gain respectability with the Queen and the public. But she doesn't call herself a princess—she uses the title "Duchess of Cornwall." Even when Charles becomes king, she will not use "Queen" as her title—instead she plans to call herself the "Princess Consort."

Charles' siblings are occasionally in the news: Princess Anne, Prince Andrew (who married and divorced Sarah "Fergie" Ferguson), and Prince Edward (who married Di look-alike Sophie Rhys-Jones).

For more on the monarchy, see www.royal.gov.uk.

Royal Sightseeing

You can see the trappings of royalty at Buckingham Palace (the Queen's residence) with its Changing of the Guard; Kensington Palace, where members of the extended royal family keep apartments; Clarence House, the London home of Prince Charles and sons; Althorp Estate (80 miles from London), the childhood home and burial place of Princess Diana; Windsor Castle, a royal country home near London; and the crown jewels in the Tower of London.

Your best chances to actually see the Queen are on three public occasions: Opening of Parliament (late October), Remembrance Sunday (early November, at the Cenotaph), or Trooping the Colour (one Saturday in mid-June, parading down Whitehall and at Buckingham Palace).

Otherwise, check the "Latest news and diary" section of www.royal.gov.uk, where you can search for future royal events.

with her mills, factories, coal mines, and trains. By the time of Queen Victoria's reign (1837-1901), Britain was at its zenith of power, with a colonial empire that covered one-fifth of the world.

The 20th century was not kind to Britain. After decades of rebellion, Ireland finally gained its independence—except for the more Protestant north. Two world wars devastated the population. The Nazi Blitz reduced much of London to rubble, although the freedom-loving world was inspired by Britain's determination to stand up to Hitler. Britain was rallied through difficult times by two leaders: Prime Minister Winston Churchill, a remarkable orator, and King George VI, who overcame a persistent stutter. After the war, the colonial empire dwindled to almost nothing, and Britain lost its superpower economic status.

One post-Empire hot spot—Northern Ireland, plagued by the "Troubles" between Catholics and Protestants—heated up, and then finally started cooling off. In the spring of 2007, the unthinkable happened when leaders of the ultra-nationalist party sat down with those of the ultra-unionist party. London returned control of Northern Ireland to the popularly elected Northern Ireland Assembly. Perhaps most important of all, after almost 40 years, the British Army withdrew from Northern Ireland that summer. Three years later, the British government formally apologized for the 1972 shooting of 26 civilians in Derry by British soldiers—a day of infamy known as "Bloody Sunday."

The tradition (if not the substance) of greatness continues, presided over by Queen Elizabeth II, her husband, Prince Philip, and their son Prince Charles. With economic problems, the marital turmoil of Charles and Diana, Princess Di's untimely death in 1997, and a relentless popular press, the royal family has had a tough time over the past few decades. But the Queen has stayed above it all, and most British people still jump at an opportunity to see royalty. With the worldwide hubbub surrounding the 2011 wedding of the Queen's grandson, Prince William, to commoner Kate Middleton, it's clear that the concept of royalty is still alive and well in the third millennium.

Queen Elizabeth, who turns 86 in 2012, will also mark her 60th year on the throne—her Diamond Jubilee. Only her great-great-grandmother, Queen Victoria, had a longer reign. While many wonder who will succeed her—and when—the situation is fairly straightforward: The Queen sees her job as a lifelong position, and legally, Charles (who wants to be king) cannot be skipped over for his son William. Given the longevity in the family (the Queen's mum, born in August of 1900, made it to a ripe old age of 101), Charles might be in for a long wait.

Architecture in Britain

From Stonehenge to Big Ben, travelers are storming castle walls, climbing spiral staircases, and snapping photographs of 5,000 years of architecture. Let's sort it out.

The oldest ruins—mysterious and prehistoric—date from before Roman times back to 3000 B.C. The earliest sites, such as Stonehenge and Avebury, were built during the Stone and Bronze

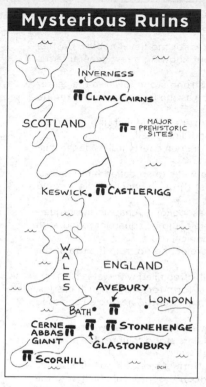

Mysterious Ruins

INVERNESS

𝐓 CLAVA CAIRNS

SCOTLAND

𝐓 = MAJOR PREHISTORIC SITES

KESWICK. 𝐓 CASTLERIGG

W A L E S

ENGLAND

AVEBURY

BATH 𝐓 LONDON

CERNE ABBAS GIANT 𝐓 𝐓 𝐓 STONEHENGE

GLASTONBURY

𝐓 SCORHILL

ages. The remains from these periods are made of huge stones or mounds of earth—some of the hills are even man-made—and were used as celestial calendars, and for worship or burial. Britain is crisscrossed with lines of these mysterious sights (ley lines). Iron Age people (600 B.C.-A.D. 50) left desolate stone forts. The Romans thrived in Britain from A.D. 50 to 400, building cities, walls, and roads. Evidence of Roman greatness can be seen in lavish villas with ornate mosaic floors, temples uncovered beneath great English churches, and Roman stones in medieval city walls. Roman roads sliced across the island in straight lines. Today, unusually straight rural roads are very likely laid directly on these ancient roads.

As Rome crumbled in the fifth century, so did Roman Britain. Little architecture survives from Dark Ages England, the Saxon period from 500 to 1000. Architecturally, the light was switched on with the Norman Conquest in 1066. As William earned his title "the Conqueror," his French architects built churches and castles in the European Romanesque style.

English Romanesque is called Norman (1066-1200). Norman churches had round arches, thick walls, and small windows; Durham Cathedral and the Chapel of St. John in the Tower of London are prime examples. The Tower of London, with its square keep, small windows, and spiral stone stairways, is a typical Norman castle. You'll see plenty of Norman castles—all built to secure the conquest of these invaders from Normandy.

Gothic architecture (1200-1600) replaced the heavy Norman style with light, vertical buildings, pointed arches, soaring spires, and bigger windows. English Gothic is divided into three stages. Early English Gothic (1200-1300) features tall, simple spires; beautifully carved capitals; and elaborate chapter houses (such as the Wells Cathedral). Decorated Gothic (1300-1400) gets fancier, with more elaborate tracery, bigger windows, and ornately carved pinnacles, as you see at Westminster Abbey. Finally, the

Typical Castle Architecture

Castles were fortified residences for medieval nobles. Castles come in all shapes and sizes, but knowing a few general terms will help you understand them.

The Keep (or Donjon): A high, strong stone tower in the center of the castle complex that was the lord's home and refuge of last resort.

Great Hall: The largest room in the castle, serving as throne room, conference center, and dining hall.

The Yard (or Bailey or Ward): An open courtyard inside the castle walls.

Loopholes: Narrow slits in the walls (also called embrasures, arrow slits, or arrow loops) through which soldiers could shoot arrows at the enemy.

Towers: Tall structures serving as lookouts, chapels, living quarters, or the dungeon. Towers could be square or round, with either crenellated tops or conical roofs.

Turret: A small lookout tower projecting up from the top of the wall.

Moat: A ditch encircling the wall, often filled with water.

Motte-and-Bailey: A traditional form for early English castles, with a small fort on top of a hill (motte) next to an enclosed and fortified yard (bailey).

Wall Walk (or Allure): A pathway atop the wall where guards could patrol and where soldiers stood to fire at the enemy.

Parapet: Outer railing of the wall walk.

Crenellation: A gap-toothed pattern of stones atop the parapet.

Hoardings (or Gallery or Brattice): Wooden huts built onto the upper parts of the stone walls. They served as watch towers,

Perpendicular Gothic style (1400-1600, also called "rectilinear") returns to square towers and emphasizes straight, uninterrupted vertical lines from ceiling to floor, with vast windows and exuberant decoration, including fan-vaulted ceilings (King's College Chapel at Cambridge). Through this evolution, the structural ribs (arches meeting at the top of the ceilings) became more and more decorative and fanciful (the most fancy being the star vaulting and fan vaulting of the Perpendicular style).

As you tour the great medieval churches of Britain, remember that almost everything is symbolic. For instance, on the tombs of knights, if the figure has crossed legs, he was a Crusader. If his feet rest on a dog, he died at home; but if the legs rest on a lion, he died in battle. Local guides and books help us modern pilgrims understand at least a little of what we see.

Wales is particularly rich in English castles, which were needed to subdue the stubborn Welsh. Edward I built a ring of powerful castles in Wales, including Conwy and Caernarfon.

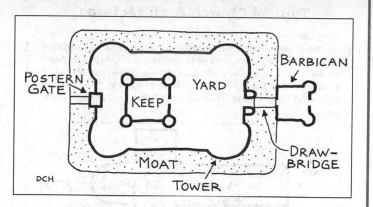

living quarters, and fighting platforms.

Machicolation: A stone ledge jutting out from the wall, fitted with holes in the bottom. If the enemy was scaling the walls, soldiers could drop rocks or boiling oil down through the holes and onto the enemy below.

Barbican: A fortified gatehouse, sometimes a stand-alone building located outside the main walls.

Drawbridge: A bridge that could be raised or lowered, using counterweights or a chain-and-winch.

Portcullis: A heavy iron grille that could be lowered across the entrance.

Postern Gate: A small, unfortified side or rear entrance used during peacetime. In wartime, it could become a "sally-port" used to launch surprise attacks, or as an escape route.

Gothic houses were a simple mix of woven strips of thin wood, rubble, and plaster called wattle and daub. The famous black-and-white Tudor (or "half-timbered") look came simply from filling in heavy oak frames with wattle and daub.

The Tudor period (1485-1560) was a time of relative peace (the Wars of the Roses were finally over), prosperity, and renaissance. Henry VIII broke with the Catholic Church and "dissolved" (destroyed) the monasteries, leaving scores of Britain's greatest churches as gutted shells. These hauntingly beautiful abbey ruins (Glastonbury, Tintern, Whitby, Rievaulx, Battle, St. Augustine's in Canterbury, St. Mary's in York, and lots more) surrounded by lush lawns are now pleasant city parks.

Although few churches were built during the Tudor period, this was a time of house and mansion construction. Heating a home was becoming popular and affordable, and Tudor buildings featured small square windows and many chimneys. In towns, where land was scarce, many Tudor houses grew up and out,

Typical Church Architecture

History comes to life when you visit a centuries-old church. Even if you wouldn't know your apse from a hole in the ground, learning a few simple terms will enrich your experience. Note that not every church has every feature, and that a "cathedral" isn't a type of church architecture, but rather a designation for a church that's a governing center for a local bishop.

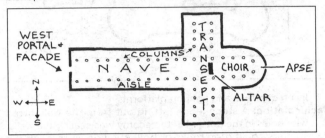

Aisles: The long, generally low-ceilinged arcades that flank the nave.

Altar: The raised area with a ceremonial table (often adorned with candles or a crucifix), where the priest prepares and serves the bread and wine for Communion.

Apse: The space beyond the altar, often bordered with small chapels.

Barrel Vault: A continuous round-arched ceiling that resembles an extended upside-down U.

Choir: A cozy area, often screened off, located within the church nave and near the high altar where services are sung in a more intimate setting.

Cloister: A square-shaped series of hallways surrounding an open-air courtyard, traditionally where monks and nuns got fresh air.

Facade: The outer wall of the church's main (west) entrance, viewable from outside and usually highly decorated.

Groin Vault: An arched ceiling formed where two equal barrel vaults meet at right angles. Less common usage: term for a medieval jock strap.

Narthex: The area (portico or foyer) between the main entry and the nave.

Nave: The long, central section of the church (running west to east, from the entrance to the altar) where the congregation stood through the service.

Transept: The north-south part of the church, which crosses (perpendicularly) the east-west nave. In a traditional Latin cross-shaped floor plan, the transept forms the "arms" of the cross.

West Portal: The main entry to the church (on the west end, opposite the main altar).

getting wider with each overhanging floor.

The Elizabethan and Jacobean periods (1560-1620) were followed by the English Renaissance style (1620-1720). English architects mixed Gothic and classical styles, then Baroque and classical styles. Although the ornate Baroque style never really grabbed Britain, the classical style of the Italian architect Andrea Palladio did. Inigo Jones (1573-1652), Christopher Wren (1632-1723), and those they inspired plastered Britain with enough columns, domes, and symmetry to please a Caesar. The Great Fire of London (1666) cleared the way for an ambitious young Wren to put his mark on London forever with a grand rebuilding scheme, including the great St. Paul's Cathedral and more than 50 other churches.

The celebrants of the Boston Tea Party remember Britain's Georgian period (1720-1840) for its lousy German kings. "Georgian" is English for "Neoclassical." Its architecture was rich and showed off by being very classical. Grand ornamental doorways, fine cast-ironwork on balconies and railings, Chippendale furniture, and white-on-blue Wedgwood ceramics graced rich homes everywhere. John Wood Sr. and Jr. led the way, giving the trendsetting city of Bath its crescents and circles of aristocratic Georgian row houses.

The Industrial Revolution shaped the Victorian period (1840-1890) with glass, steel, and iron. Britain had a huge new erector set (so did France's Mr. Eiffel). This was also a Romantic period, reviving the "more Christian" Gothic style. London's Houses of Parliament are Neo-Gothic—they're just 140 years old but look 700, except for the telltale modern precision and craftsmanship. Whereas Gothic was stone or concrete, Neo-Gothic was often red brick. These were Britain's glory days, and there was more building in this period than in all previous ages combined.

The architecture of the mid-20th century obeyed the formula "form follows function"—it worried more about your needs than your eyes. Modern Britain treasures its heritage and takes great pains to build tastefully in historic districts and to preserve its many "listed" (government-protected) buildings. With a booming tourist trade, these quaint reminders of its past—and ours—are becoming a valuable part of the British economy.

Britain Today

Regardless of the revolution we had 230-some years ago, many American travelers feel that they "go home" to Britain. This most popular tourist destination has a strange influence and power over us. The more you know of Britain's roots, the better you'll get in touch with your own.

What's So Great About Britain?

Geographically, the Isle of Britain is small (about the size of Uganda or Idaho)—600 miles long and 300 miles at its widest point. England occupies the southeastern part of Britain (with about 60 percent of its land—similar in size to Louisiana—and 80 percent of its population). England's highest mountain (Scafell Pike in the Lake District) is 3,206 feet, a foothill by our standards. The population is a fifth that of the United States. At its peak in the mid-1800s, Britain owned one-fifth of the world and accounted for more than half the planet's industrial output. Today, the Empire is down to the Isle of Britain itself and a few token, troublesome scraps, such as the Falklands, Gibraltar, and Northern Ireland.

Economically, Great Britain's industrial production is about 5 percent of the world's total. After emerging from a recession in 1992, Britain's economy enjoyed its longest period of expansion on record. But in 2008, the global economic slowdown, tight credit, and falling home prices pushed Britain back into a recession.

Culturally, Britain is still a world leader. Her heritage, culture, and people cannot be measured in traditional units of power. London is a major exporter of actors, movies, and theater; of rock and classical music; and of writers, painters, and sculptors.

Ethnically, the British Isles are a mix of the descendants of the early Celtic natives (in Scotland, Ireland, Wales, and Cornwall), the invading Anglo-Saxon "barbarians" who took southeast England in the Dark Ages, and the conquering Normans of the 11th century...not to mention more recent immigrants from around the world. Cynics call the United Kingdom an English Empire ruled by London, whose dominant Anglo-Saxon English (50 million) far outnumber their Celtic brothers and sisters (10 million).

Politically, Britain is ruled by the House of Commons, with some guidance from the mostly figurehead Queen Elizabeth and from the House of Lords. Just as the United States Congress is dominated by Democrats and Republicans, Britain's Parliament is dominated by two parties: left-leaning Labour and right-leaning Conservative ("Tories"). Recently the center-left Liberal Democrats ("Lib Dems") have made some inroads, but still remain a distant third.

Strangely, Britain's "constitution" is not one single document; the government's structures and policies are based on centuries of tradition, statues, and doctrine, and much of it is not actually in writing. While this might seem potentially troublesome—if not dangerous—the British body politic takes pride in its ethos of civility and mutual respect, which has long made this arrangement work.

The prime minister is the chief executive. He or she is not elected directly by voters; rather, he or she assumes power as the head of the party that wins a majority in Parliamentary elections. (If no party wins a clear majority—as none did in the 2010 election—it's a "hung parliament," and is usually resolved by at least two parties forming a coalition that adds up to a majority.) In the interest of protocol, the Queen symbolically invites the winner to form a "government" (administration). Instead of imposing term limits, the Brits allow their prime ministers to choose when to leave office. The ruling party also gets to choose when to hold elections, as long as it's within five years of the previous one—so prime ministers carefully schedule elections for times that (they hope) their party will win. (Breaking with tradition, the current coalition government has already announced an election for May 7, 2015.) When an election is announced, the Queen dissolves the Parliament so the parties can focus on a short-and-sweet, one-month campaign.

In the 1980s, Conservatives were in charge under Prime Minister Margaret Thatcher and Prime Minister John Major. As proponents of traditional, Victorian values—community, family, hard work, thrift, and trickle-down economics—they took a Reaganesque approach to Britain's serious social and economic problems.

In 1997, a huge Labour victory brought Tony Blair to the prime ministership. Labour began shoring up a social-service system (health care, education, minimum wage) undercut by years of Conservative rule. Blair started out as a respected and well-liked PM. But after he followed US President George W. Bush into war with Iraq, his popularity took a nosedive. In May of 2007, Blair announced that he would resign; a few weeks later, his Chancellor of the Exchequer and longtime colleague, Gordon Brown, was sworn in as Britain's new prime minister. Burdened with an economic crisis and lacking his predecessor's charisma, Brown never achieved a level of popularity anywhere near Blair's.

Elections in May of 2010 pitted Brown against a Conservative opponent, David Cameron, and a third-party Liberal Democrat challenger, Nick Clegg. Brown, Cameron, and Clegg participated in a series of three television debates—the first in UK history. Thanks to the economic crisis—and his own characteristic stumbles—Brown failed to win a clear majority for his Labour Party. No party won the number of seats needed for a majority—resulting in the first "hung parliament" since 1974. After a few days of wrangling, the Conservatives and the Lib Dems formed a coalition government (the first since World War II), Gordon Brown stepped down, and David Cameron became prime minister.

Brits are turning their attention to the summer of 2012, when the world's eyes will be on their capital city as London hosts the 30th Olympiad. As the city and country spiff up even more than

PAST & PRESENT

Prime Minister David Cameron

David Cameron succeeded Gordon Brown as prime minister in May of 2010, and lives at #10 Downing Street with his wife, Samantha, and their young children. Elected at age 43, Cameron was the youngest PM in two centuries. He heads the Conservative Party (the "Tories"), but has never quite fit the stodgy Conservative image. Rumors still swirl of wild parties and illicit drugs in his student days at Oxford. He's known as "Dave" to his friends, and he developed a habit of riding his bike to work. Cameron rose quickly through the political ranks: He worked to re-elect Conservative PM John Major (1992), assisted the finance minister at #11 Downing Street (1992-1994), and was himself elected to Parliament in 2001, becoming head of the Conservative Party in 2005. By 2008, he was on the cover of *Time* magazine, which hailed him as the future of conservatism.

In 2010, Cameron's Conservative Party came to power, but it was hardly a sweeping Conservative mandate: Three parties split the vote, forcing Cameron's Conservatives to form a coalition with the (more left-leaning) Liberal Democrat Party. The Labour Party, which had held power in Britain for 13 years under Tony Blair and Gordon Brown, is the coalition's chief opposition.

Politically, Cameron is a moderate Conservative who is more pragmatic than ideological. Socially, he's "liberal" in the classical sense, advocating for personal freedoms—gay rights, decriminalization of drugs, allowing hunting and smoking, and ensuring citizens' privacy against government intrusion. Fiscally, he rails against big-government waste. In his early days as PM, he delivered a sober speech about a time of austerity looming on Britain's horizon, when belts would need to be tightened to get the budget under control. His most right-of-center stance is his support for distancing Britain from the euro and the European Union.

Despite his personal appeal, Cameron can't quite shake the Conservatives' image as the party of the upper class. Cameron was born rich, married rich, and has worked within the corporate culture. His colleagues form an old boys' network from his days at Eton, England's most exclusive prep school. The mayor of London, Boris Johnson, is not only an old Oxford frat buddy but also a distant cousin. Cameron's reputation has been tarnished by his links to discredited media mogul Rupert Murdoch, and some have questioned his handling of the riots in London and other urban centers in the summer of 2011.

As the Conservatives try to unite the country to solve Britain's severe economic and cultural problems, it remains to be seen whether David Cameron has brought a fresh enough approach to #10.

PAST & PRESENT

usual for the Olympics, the Brits are hoping their country will come together to celebrate this legendary sporting event.

Current Challenges

From early 2008 to late 2009, the British economy shrank more than 6 percent—the largest decline since the Great Depression. Facing a huge—and growing—budget deficit, soon after his election Prime Minister Cameron announced an austerity program that dramatically cut back spending and increased the VAT (Value-Added Tax—the national sales tax) to 20 percent. The prime minister's budget eliminated more than 500,000 public sector jobs, shortened long-term unemployment benefits to 12 months, imposed higher rents on public housing, slashed funding for the arts and the BBC, cut police services, and raised the retirement age to 66 by 2020. (Visitors might notice reduced bus schedules, unexpected closures of TIs or minor sights, and locals grumbling about tax hikes.)

In this era of uncertainty, British consumers don't seem to be spending much, as they try to gauge the effects of Cameron's austerity measures. It's still unclear whether these bold steps will return Britain to its previous prosperity, or douse the spark of economic recovery. Cutting corners in programs for the working class may have actually cost British society far more money than it saved.

Other hot-button topics in Britain include the ongoing war in Afghanistan, terrorism, immigration, and binge-drinking. While British forces ended combat operations in Iraq in April of 2009, its troops remain in Afghanistan, and every new casualty reinvigorates public debate about the merits and possible outcomes of this war.

Like the US, Britain has been coping with its own string of terrorist threats and attacks. On the morning of July 7, 2005, London's commuters were rocked by four different bombs that killed dozens across the city. In the summer of 2006, authorities foiled a plot to carry liquid bombs onto a plane (resulting in the liquid ban that air travelers are still experiencing today). On June 29, 2007, two car bombs were discovered (and defused) near London's Piccadilly Circus, and the next day, a flaming car drove into the baggage-claim level at Glasgow Airport. Most Brits have accepted that they now live with the possibility of terrorism at home—and that life must go on.

Britain has taken aggressive measures to prevent future attacks, such as installing "CCTV" (closed-circuit) surveillance cameras everywhere, in both public and private places. (You'll frequently see signs warning you that you're being filmed.) As Brits trade their privacy for security, many wonder if they've given up too much.

The terrorist threats have also highlighted issues relating to Britain's large immigrant population (nearly 4 million). Second-generation Muslims—born in Britain, but who strongly identify with other Muslims rather than their British neighbors—were responsible for the July 2005 bombs. Some Brits reacted to the event known as "7/7" as if all the country's Muslims were to blame. At the same time, a handful of radical Islamic clerics justified the bombers' violent actions.

The large Muslim population is just one thread in the tapestry of today's Britain. While nine out of ten Brits are white, the country has large minority groups, mainly from Britain's former overseas colonies: India, Pakistan, Bangladesh, Africa, the Caribbean, and many other places. Despite the tensions between some groups, for the most part Britain is relatively integrated, with minorities represented in most (if not all) walks of life.

But unemployment and the economic downturn have stretched the already-strained relations between communities within Britain. In August of 2011, London police shot and killed a young black man named Mark Duggan, inflaming tensions between the police and the black community. A peaceful protest against the police was followed by violent riots. Opportunistic young people joined in the riots—not necessarily to protest anything in particular (though many were hurting because of the austerity measures), but as an excuse to loot expensive goods from shops. Looting and riots spread to other parts of London and major cities in England. While police contained the violence within a few days, British society as a whole was left to grapple with its causes and social implications: Were the riots about racial and ethnic tensions, the haves versus the have-nots, or simply poor young people eager to grab shiny new smartphones?

Throughout the British Isles, you'll also see many Eastern Europeans (mostly Poles, Slovaks, and Lithuanians) working in restaurants, cafés, and B&Bs. These transplants—who started arriving after their home countries joined the EU in 2004—can make a lot more money working here than back home. British small-business owners have found these new arrivals to be polite, responsible, and affordable. While a few Brits complain that the new arrivals are taking jobs away from the natives, and others are frustrated that their English can be far from perfect, for the most part Britain has absorbed this new set of immigrants gracefully.

Over the last several years, Britain has seen an epidemic of binge-drinking among young people. A 2007 study revealed that one out of every three British men, and one out of every five British women, routinely drink to excess. It's become commonplace for young adults (typically from their mid-teens to mid-20s) to spend weekend nights drinking at pubs and carousing in the streets. (And they ratchet up the debauchery even more when celebrating a "stag night" or "hen night"—bachelor and bachelorette parties.) While sociologists and politicians scratch their heads about this phenomenon, tourists are complaining about weekend noise and obnoxious (though generally harmless) young drunks on the streets.

British TV

Although it has its share of lowbrow reality programming, much British television is still so good—and so British—that it deserves a mention as a sightseeing treat. After a hard day of castle climbing, watch the telly over tea in the living room of your village B&B.

There are currently five free channels that any television can receive. BBC-1 and BBC-2 are government-regulated and commercial-free. Broadcasting of these two channels (and of the five BBC radio stations) is funded by a mandatory £145.50-per-year-per-household television and radio license (hmmm, 65 cents per day to escape commercials and public-broadcasting pledge drives). Channels 3, 4, and 5 are privately owned, a little more lowbrow, and have commercials—but those "adverts" are often clever and sophisticated, providing a fun look at British life. In addition, about 85 percent of households now receive digital cable or satellite television, which offer dozens of specialty channels, similar to those available in North America.

Whereas California "accents" fill our airwaves 24 hours a day, homogenizing the way our country speaks, Britain protects and promotes its regional accents by its choice of TV and radio announcers. See if you can tell where each is from (or ask a local for help).

Commercial-free British TV, while looser than it used to be, is still careful about what it airs and when. But after the 21:00 "watershed" hour, when children are expected to be in bed, some nudity and profanity are allowed, and may cause you to spill your tea.

American programs (such as *Mad Men, CSI, Friends, How I Met Your Mother,* and trash-talk shows) are very popular. But the visiting viewer should be sure to tune the TV to more typically British shows, including a dose of British situation- and political-comedy fun, and the top-notch BBC evening news. British comedies have tickled the American funny bone for years, from sketch comedy *(Monty Python's Flying Circus)* to sitcoms *(Are You Being Served?, Fawlty Towers, Absolutely Fabulous,* and *The Office).* Quiz shows and reality shows are taken very seriously here *(Who Wants to Be a Millionaire?, American Idol, Dancing with the Stars,* and *The X*

Factor are all based on British shows). Jonathan Ross is the David Letterman of Britain for sometimes edgy late-night talk. Other popular late-night "chat show" hosts include Graham Norton and Alan Carr. For a tear-filled, slice-of-life taste of British soaps dealing in all the controversial issues, see the popular and remarkably long-running *Emmerdale, Coronation Street,* or *EastEnders.*

APPENDIX

Contents

Tourist Information

Tourist Information Offices

The Visit Britain office **in the US** is a wealth of knowledge. Request free maps of London and Britain and any specific information you may want (such as regional information, a garden-tour map, urban cultural activities brochures, and so on). The phone line is mainly intended as a customer service number for their online shop and isn't staffed (but they do check their messages). For most questions, it's best to inquire by email (tel. 800-462-2748, www.visitbritain .com, travelinfo@visitbritain.org).

In England, your best first stop in every town is generally the tourist information office—abbreviated **TI** in this book (and abbreviated locally as "TIC," for "tourist information centre"). (The **Britain and London Visitors Centre** in London is particularly good—see page 50.) TIs are good places to get a city map, information on public transit (including bus and train schedules), walking tours, special events, and nightlife. Many TIs have information on the entire country or at least the region, so try to pick up maps for destinations you'll be visiting later in your trip. If you're arriving in town after the TI closes, call ahead to get your questions answered and try to pick up a map in a neighboring town.

For all the help TIs offer, steer clear of their room-finding services (bloated prices, booking fee up to £4, no opinions, and they take a 10 percent cut from your B&B host).

Communicating

Telephones

Smart travelers use the telephone to book or reconfirm rooms, get tourist information, reserve restaurants, confirm tour times, or phone home. Generally, the cheapest way to go is to buy an international phone card in Britain. This section covers dialing instructions, phone cards, and types of phones (for more in-depth information, see www.ricksteves.com/phoning).

How to Dial

Calling from the US to Britain, or vice versa, is simple—once you break the code. The European calling chart in this chapter will walk you through it.

Dialing Domestically Within Britain

Britain, like much of the US, uses an area-code dialing system. To make domestic calls within Britain, punch in just the local number if you're dialing within an area code. If you're calling outside your area code, dial both the area code (which starts with a 0) and the local number.

Area codes are listed in this book, displayed by city on phone-booth walls, and available from directory assistance (dial 118-500, £0.64/minute). It's most expensive to call within Britain between 8:00 and 13:00, and cheapest between 17:00 and 8:00. Still, a short call across the country is inexpensive, so don't hesitate to call long distance.

Certain phone numbers don't have area codes. For example, numbers beginning with 074, 075, 076, 077, 078, and 079 are mobile numbers, which are more expensive to call than a land line. Numbers starting with 080 are toll-free, but those beginning with 084, 087, or 03 are inexpensive toll numbers (£0.10/minute maximum from a land line, £0.20-40/minute from a mobile). Numbers beginning with 09 are pricey toll lines. If you have questions about a prefix, call 100 for free help.

Dialing Internationally to or from Britain

If you want to make an international call, follow these steps:

The English Accent

In the olden days, an English person's accent indicated his or her social standing. Eliza Doolittle had the right idea—elocution could make or break you. Wealthier families would send their kids to fancy private schools to learn proper pronunciation. But these days, in a sort of reverse snobbery that has gripped the nation, accents are back. Politicians, newscasters, and movie stars have been favoring deep accents over the Queen's English. While it's hard for American ears to pick out all of the variations, most English can determine where a person is from based on his or her accent...not just the region, but often the village, and even the part of town.

• Dial the international access code (00 if you're calling from Britain, 011 from the US or Canada).

• Dial the country code of the country you're calling (44 for Britain, or 1 for the US or Canada).

• Dial the area code (without the initial zero) and the local number. (The European calling chart on page 778 lists specifics per country.)

Calling from the US to Britain: To call a London hotel from the US, dial 011 (the US international access code), 44 (Britain's country code), 20 (London's area code without its initial 0), then 7730-8191 (the hotel's number).

Calling from any European Country to the US: To call my office in Edmonds, Washington, from anywhere in Europe, I dial 00 (Europe's international access code), 1 (the US country code), 425 (Edmonds' area code), and 771-8303.

Note: You might see a plus sign (+) in front of a European number. When dialing the number, replace the + with the international access code of the country you're calling from (00 from Europe, 011 from the US or Canada). Or, if calling from a mobile phone, you can insert a + when you dial the number.

Prepaid Phone Cards

International Phone Cards: These are the cheapest way to make international calls from Britain—with the best cards, it costs less than 10 cents a minute to the US, as long as you don't call from a phone booth. British Telecom levies a hefty surcharge for using international phone cards from a pay phone (so instead of 100 minutes for a £5 card, you'll get less than 10 minutes—a miserable deal). But a card is still a good value when calling from a mobile phone or a land line such as a hotel-room phone.

These cards are sold in various denominations at newsstands,

European Calling Chart

Just smile and dial, using this key:
AC = Area Code, LN = Local Number.

European Country	Calling long distance within ...	Calling from the US or Canada to ...	Calling from a European country to ...
Austria	AC + LN	011 + 43 + AC (without the initial zero) + LN	00 + 43 + AC (without the initial zero) + LN
Belgium	LN	011 + 32 + LN (without initial zero)	00 + 32 + LN (without initial zero)
Bosnia-Herzegovina	AC + LN	011 + 387 + AC (without initial zero) + LN	00 + 387 + AC (without initial zero) + LN
Britain	AC + LN	011 + 44 + AC (without initial zero) + LN	00 + 44 + AC (without initial zero) + LN
Croatia	AC + LN	011 + 385 + AC (without initial zero) + LN	00 + 385 + AC (without initial zero) + LN
Czech Republic	LN	011 + 420 + LN	00 + 420 + LN
Denmark	LN	011 + 45 + LN	00 + 45 + LN
Estonia	LN	011 + 372 + LN	00 + 372 + LN
Finland	AC + LN	011 + 358 + AC (without initial zero) + LN	999 (or other 900 number) + 358 + AC (without initial zero) + LN
France	LN	011 + 33 + LN (without initial zero)	00 + 33 + LN (without initial zero)
Germany	AC + LN	011 + 49 + AC (without initial zero) + LN	00 + 49 + AC (without initial zero) + LN
Gibraltar	LN	011 + 350 + LN	00 + 350 + LN
Greece	LN	011 + 30 + LN	00 + 30 + LN
Hungary	06 + AC + LN	011 + 36 + AC + LN	00 + 36 + AC + LN
Ireland	AC + LN	011 + 353 + AC (without initial zero) + LN	00 + 353 + AC (without initial zero) + LN

European Country	Calling long distance within ...	Calling from the US or Canada to ...	Calling from a European country to ...
Italy	LN	011 + 39 + LN	00 + 39 + LN
Montenegro	AC + LN	011 + 382 + AC (without initial zero) + LN	00 + 382 + AC (without initial zero) + LN
Morocco	LN	011 + 212 + LN (without initial zero)	00 + 212 + LN (without initial zero)
Netherlands	AC + LN	011 + 31 + AC (without initial zero) + LN	00 + 31 + AC (without initial zero) + LN
Norway	LN	011 + 47 + LN	00 + 47 + LN
Poland	LN	011 + 48 + LN (without initial zero)	00 + 48 + LN (without initial zero)
Portugal	LN	011 + 351 + LN	00 + 351 + LN
Slovakia	AC + LN	011 + 421 + AC (without initial zero) + LN	00 + 421 + AC (without initial zero) + LN
Slovenia	AC + LN	011 + 386 + AC (without initial zero) + LN	00 + 386 + AC (without initial zero) + LN
Spain	LN	011 + 34 + LN	00 + 34 + LN
Sweden	AC + LN	011 + 46 + AC (without initial zero) + LN	00 + 46 + AC (without initial zero) + LN
Switzerland	LN	011 + 41 + LN (without initial zero)	00 + 41 + LN (without initial zero)
Turkey	AC (if there's no initial zero, add one) + LN	011 + 90 + AC (without initial zero) + LN	00 + 90 + AC (without initial zero) + LN

- The instructions above apply whether you're calling a land line or mobile phone.
- The international access codes (the first numbers you dial when making an international call) are 011 if you're calling from the US or Canada, or 00 if you're calling from virtually anywhere in Europe (except Finland, where it's 999 or another 900 number, depending on the phone service you're using).
- To call the US or Canada from Europe, dial 00, then 1 (the country code for the US and Canada), then the area code and number. In short, 00 + 1 + AC + LN = Hi, Mom!

hole-in-the-wall long-distance shops, and post offices. They generally work only within the country of purchase (e.g., one bought in Britain won't work in France). Buy a lower denomination in case the card is a dud.

To use the card, dial a toll-free access number, then enter your scratch-to-reveal PIN code. (If you have several access numbers listed on your card, you'll save money if you choose the toll-free one starting with 0800, rather than 0845, 0870, or 0871, which cost around £0.10/minute from a fixed line.) To call the US or Britain, see "How to Dial," earlier.

You can also make calls within Britain with an international calling card—but you must dial the area code even if you're just calling across the street.

US Calling Cards: These cards, such as the ones offered by AT&T, Verizon, and Sprint, are the worst option. You'll save money by using an international phone card you've purchased in Britain.

Types of Phones
Public Pay Phones
Coin-op pay phones are almost extinct in Britain, but if you manage to find one, you'll need plenty of coins to make a call (Britain doesn't use insertable phone cards, and calls are pricey). Even prepaid international phone cards are prohibitively expensive on public phones.

Hotel-Room Phones
Calling from your hotel room can be cheap for local calls (ask for the rates at the front desk first), but is often a rip-off for long-distance calls, unless you use an international phone card (explained above). Some hotels charge a fee for dialing supposedly "toll-free" numbers, such as the one for your international phone card—ask before you dial. Incoming calls are free, making this an inexpensive way for friends and family to stay in touch (provided they have a good long-distance plan for calls to Europe—and a list of your hotels' phone numbers).

Phones are rare in B&Bs, but if your room has one, the advice above applies. If there's no phone in your B&B room, and you have an important, brief call to make, you can try very politely asking your host if you may use their personal phone. Ideally use a cheap international phone card with a toll-free access number, or offer to pay your host for the call.

Mobile Phones
Many travelers enjoy the convenience of traveling with a mobile phone.

Using Your Mobile Phone: Your US mobile phone works in Britain if it's GSM-enabled, tri-band or quad-band, and on a calling plan that includes international calls. Phones from AT&T and T-Mobile, which use the same GSM technology that Europe does, are more likely to work overseas than Verizon or Sprint phones (if you're not sure, ask your service provider). Most US providers charge $1.29-1.99 per minute while roaming internationally to make or receive calls, and 20-50 cents to send or receive text messages.

You'll pay cheaper rates if your phone is electronically "unlocked" (ask your provider about this); then, in Britain, you can simply buy a tiny **SIM card,** which gives you a British phone number. SIM cards are sold at mobile-phone stores (such as Carphone Warehouse) and department stores (such as Tesco) for $5-15, and generally include at least that much calling credit—making the SIM card itself effectively free. When you buy a SIM card, you may need to show ID, such as your passport. Insert the SIM card in your phone (usually in a slot on the side or behind the battery), and it'll work like a British mobile phone. When buying a SIM card, always ask about fees for domestic and international calls, roaming charges, and how to check your credit balance and buy more time. When you're in the SIM card's home country, domestic calls are reasonable, and incoming calls are free. You'll pay more if you're roaming in another country.

To call home, save money by using an international calling card (described earlier). Or buy a SIM card that offers cheap direct-dial rates to the US. I've had good luck with Lebara, which charges inexpensive rates for both domestic and international calls (www.lebara-mobile.co.uk).

For tips on traveling with a US smartphone, see "Data Downloading on a Smartphone," later.

Buying a European Mobile Phone: Mobile-phone shops all over Europe sell basic phones—and you can find especially good deals in England. For example, Britain's Carphone Warehouse sells pay-as-you-go mobile phones (locked to work with only one service provider) for as little as £10 plus £10 for calling time. Big department stores (such as Tesco) are another good place to check. Wherever you buy a phone, be sure your package includes a SIM card and prepaid credit for making calls. If you remain in Britain, incoming calls are generally free, and outgoing domestic calls to a fixed line generally run about £0.15-0.20 per minute—less than from a pay phone. (It's more expensive to call a mobile phone or a toll number.) You'll pay more if roaming in another country.

Renting a European Mobile Phone: Car-rental companies and mobile-phone companies offer the option to rent a mobile phone with a European number. While this seems convenient, hidden fees (such as high per-minute charges or expensive shipping costs) can really add up—which usually makes it a bad value. One exception is Verizon's Global Travel Program, available only to Verizon customers.

Data Downloading on a Smartphone: Many smartphones, such as the iPhone, Android, and BlackBerry, work in Europe (note that you can use the AT&T iPhone in Europe, but not the Verizon model). For voice calls and text messaging, smartphones work the same as other US mobile phones (explained earlier). But beware of sky-high fees for data downloading (checking email, browsing the Internet, streaming videos, and so on).

The best solution: Disable data roaming entirely, and only use your device when you find free Wi-Fi. You can ask your mobile-phone service provider to cut off your account's data-roaming capability, or you can manually turn it off on your phone (look under the "Network" menu).

If you want Internet access without being limited to Wi-Fi, you'll need to keep data roaming on—but you can take steps to reduce your charges. Consider paying extra for a limited international data-roaming plan through your carrier, then use data roaming selectively (if a particular task gobbles bandwidth, wait until you're on Wi-Fi). In general, ask your provider in advance how to avoid unwittingly roaming your way to a huge bill. If your smartphone is on Wi-Fi, you can use certain apps to make cheap or free voice calls (see "Calling over the Internet," next).

Calling over the Internet

Some things that seem too good to be true...actually are true. If you're traveling with a wireless device (such as a laptop or smartphone), you can use VoIP (Voice over Internet Protocol) to make free calls over the Internet to another wireless device (or you can pay a few cents to call from your computer to a telephone). If both devices have cameras, you can even see each other while you chat. The major providers are Skype (www.skype.com, also available as a smartphone app), Google Talk (www.google.com/talk), and FaceTime (this app comes standard on newer Apple devices). If you have a smartphone, you can get online at a hotspot and use these apps to make calls without ringing up expensive roaming charges (though call quality can be spotty on slow connections).

Useful Phone Numbers
Emergencies
Police and Ambulance: tel. 999

Embassies and Consulates in London
US Consulate and Embassy: tel. 020/7499-9000, passport info

tel. 020/7894-0563, passport services available Mon-Fri 8:30-11:30, Mon, Wed, Fri also 14:00-16:00 (24 Grosvenor Square, Tube: Bond Street, www.usembassy.org.uk)

Canadian High Commission: tel. 020/7258-6600, passport services available Mon-Fri 9:30-13:30 (Trafalgar Square, Tube: Charing Cross, www.unitedkingdom.gc.ca)

Travel Advisories
US Department of State: tel. 202/647-5225 www.travel.state.gov
Canadian Department of Foreign Affairs: Canadian tel. 800-267-6788, www.dfait-maeci.gc.ca
US Centers for Disease Control and Prevention: US tel. 800-CDC-INFO (800-232-4636), www.cdc.gov/travel

Directory Assistance
Operator Assistance: tel. 100 (free)
Directory Assistance: tel. 118-500 (£0.64/minute, plus £0.23/minute connection charge from fixed lines)
International Directory Assistance: tel. 118-505 (£1.99/minute, plus £0.69 connection charge)

Trains and Buses
Train information for trips within England: tel. 0845-748-4950, overseas tel. 011-44-20-7278-5240 (www.nationalrail.co.uk)
Eurostar (Chunnel Info): tel. 0870-518-6186 (www.eurostar.com)
Trains to all points in Europe: tel. 0870-584-8848 (www.raileurope.com)
National Express Buses: tel. 0871-781-8181 (www.nationalexpress.com)

Airports
For online information on the first three airports, check www.baa.co.uk.
Heathrow (flight info): tel. 0870-000-0123
Gatwick (general info): tel. 0870-000-2468 for all airlines, except British Airways— tel. 0870-551-1155 (flights) or 0870-850-9850 (booking)
Stansted (general info): tel. 0870-000-0303
Luton (general info): tel. 01582/405-100 (www.london-luton.com)
London City Airport (general info): tel. 020/7646-0088 (www.londoncityairport.com)

Airlines
Aer Lingus: tel. 0870-876-5000, US tel. 800-474-7424 (www.aerlingus.com)
Air Canada: tel. 0871-220-1111 (www.aircanada.com)

Alitalia: tel. 0871-424-1424 (www.alitalia.com)
American: tel. 0845-778-9789 (www.aa.com)
bmi: reservations tel. 0870-607-0555, flight info tel. 020/8745-7321 (www.flybmi.com)
British Airways: reservations tel. 0844-493-0787, flight info tel. 0844-493-0777 (www.ba.com)
Brussels Airlines: toll tel. 0905-609-5609—40p/minute, US tel. 516/740-5200 (www.brusselsairlines.com)
Continental Airlines: tel. 0845-607-6760 (www.continental.com)
easyJet: tel. 0843-104-5000 (www.easyjet.com)
KLM Royal Dutch/Northwest Airlines: tel. 0870-507-4074 (www.klm.com)
Lufthansa: tel. 0871-945-9747 (www.lufthansa.com)
Ryanair: tel. 0871-246-0000 (www.ryanair.com)
Scandinavian Airlines (SAS): tel. 0871-521-2772 (www.flysas.com)
United Airlines: tel. 0845-844-4777 (www.unitedairlines.co.uk)
US Airways: tel. 0845-600-3300 (www.usair.com)

Heathrow Airport Car-Rental Agencies
Avis: tel. 0844-544-6000 (www.avis.co.uk)
Budget: tel. 0844-544-4600 (www.budget.co.uk)
Enterprise: tel. 020/8897-2100 (www.enterprise.co.uk)
Europcar: tel. 020/8564-3500 (www.europcar.co.uk)
Hertz: tel. 0870-846-0006 (www.hertz.co.uk)

Internet Access
It's useful to get online periodically as you travel—to confirm trip plans, check train or bus schedules, get weather forecasts, catch up on email, blog or post photos from your trip, or call folks back home (explained earlier, in "Calling over the Internet").

Some hotels and B&Bs offer a computer in the lobby with Internet access for guests. If you ask politely, smaller places may sometimes let you sit at their desk for a few minutes just to check your email. If your hotel doesn't have access, ask your hotelier to direct you to the nearest place to get online. Internet cafés are easy to find in England; for specific listings, see the "Helpful Hints" section for individual destinations.

Traveling with a Laptop or Other Wireless Device: You can get online if your hotel or B&B has Wi-Fi or a port in your room for plugging in a cable. Most accommodations offer Wi-Fi for free;

others charge by the minute or hour. A cellular modem—which lets your laptop access the Internet over a mobile phone network—provides more extensive coverage, but is much more expensive than Wi-Fi.

Warning: While using a public Internet terminal or free Wi-Fi is convenient, it can come with security risks. Some computers are loaded with damaging "malware," such as "key logger" programs that keep track of what you're typing—including passwords. You can ask the Internet café or hotel what sort of security software their machines and Wi-Fi routers are running. If you're not convinced it's secure, don't access any sites (such as online banking) that could be sensitive to fraud. Be careful about storing personal information (such as passport and credit-card numbers) online.

Mail

While you can arrange for mail delivery to your hotel (allow 10 days for a letter to arrive), phoning and emailing are so easy that I've dispensed with mail stops altogether.

You can mail one package per day to yourself worth up to $200 duty-free from Europe to the US (mark it "personal purchases"). If you're sending a gift to someone, mark it "unsolicited gift." For details, visit www.cbp.gov and search for "Know Before You Go."

Transportation

By Car or Public Transportation?

Cars are best for three or more traveling together (especially families with small kids), those packing heavy, and those scouring the countryside. Trains and buses are best for solo travelers, blitz tourists, and city-to-city travelers. While a car gives you the ultimate in mobility and freedom, enables you to search for accommodations more easily, and carries your bags for you, the train zips you effortlessly from city to city, usually dropping you in the center and near the tourist office.

England's 100-mph train system is one of Europe's best. Buses pick you up when the trains let you down. Travelers who don't want (or can't afford) to drive a rental car can enjoy an excellent tour using public transportation.

In England, my choice is to connect big cities by train and to explore rural areas (Cornwall, Dartmoor, the Cotswolds, and the Lake District) footloose and fancy-free by rental car. The mix works quite efficiently (e.g., London, Bath, and York by train, with a rental car for the rest). You might consider a BritRail & Drive Pass, which gives you various combinations of rail days and car days to use within two months' time.

Public Transportation Routes in Britain

Rail
Eurostar
Bus
(8H) Ferry with crossing time

Ferry Note:
Dover - Calais~1.5H
Dover - Boul~1.5 H

50 Kilometers
50 Miles

Orkney Islands
Burwick
Thurso
John o' Groats
Lewis
Skye
Portree
Inverness
Elgin
Kyle
Loch Ness
Culloden
Aviemore
Aberdeen
Mallaig
Fort William
SCOTLAND
Pitlochry
Mull
Iona
Oban
Perth
Dundee
Leuchars
St. Andrews
Stirling
Edinburgh
Glasgow
Berwick
Larne (2H)
Cairnryan
Hexham
Newcastle
To Amsterdam (15H)
Belfast (2-3H)
Stranraer
Carlisle
Durham
NORTHERN IRELAND
Keswick
Penrith
(8H)
Windermere
ENGLAND
North Sea
Isle of Man
Irish Sea
Blackpool
Preston
Leeds
York
Hull
Dublin (7H)
Liverpool
Manchester
Grimsby
Dun Laoghaire (2-3H)
Holyhead
Conwy
Chester
Lincoln
Bangor
Betws-y-Coed
Stoke
Caernarfon
Blaenau
Derby
Peter-borough
King's Lynn
Norwich
REPUBLIC OF IRELAND
Pwllheli
Ffest.
Telf.
Wolv.
Birmingham
Ely
Cambridge
To Esbjerg (18 H)
Harlech
Coventry
Harwich
Aberystwyth
Iron Bridge Gorge
Warwick
Rosslare (3.5H)
WALES
Stratford
Moreton
To Hoek van Holland (6H)
Fishguard
Cheltenham
Stow
Oxford
Ebbs-fleet
Newport
London
Canterbury
Swansea
Cardiff
Bath
Reading
Woking
Ashford
Dover
To Cork (12H)
Bristol
Stonehenge
Calais
Wells
EUROSTAR
Atlantic Ocean
Exeter
Salisbury
Brighton
Dartmoor
Southampton
Portsmouth
Newhaven
To Dieppe (4H)
St. Ives
Truro
Plymouth
English Channel
To Paris & Brussels
Penzance
Falmouth
To Ouistreham (6H)
FRANCE
To Roscoff (6H)
To Cherbourg (3H)

Sample Train Journey

Here is a typical example of a personalized train schedule printed out at England's train stations. At the Salisbury station, I told the clerk that I wanted to leave after 16:30 for Moreton-in-Marsh in the Cotswolds.

Stations	Arrive	Depart	Class
Salisbury	—	16:41	Standard
Bristol	17:48	18:28	1st/Standard
Cheltenham Spa	19:10	19:29	1st/Standard
Worcester	19:52	20:05	1st/Standard
Moreton-in-Marsh	20:42	—	

Even though the trip involved three transfers, this schedule allowed me to easily navigate the rails.

Train departures are listed on overhead boards at the station by their final destination (note that your destination could be an intermediate stop on this route, and therefore not listed on the overhead). It's helpful to ask at the info desk—or any conductor—for the final destination of your next train (such as Oxford), so you'll be able to figure out quickly which platform it's departing from. Upon arrival at Worcester, I looked for *Oxford* on the station's overhead train schedule to determine where to catch my train to Moreton-in-Marsh.

Often the conductor on your previous train can even tell you which platform your next train will depart from, but it's wise to confirm.

England's train system can experience delays, so don't schedule your connections too tight if you need to be at your destination at a specific time.

Trains

Regular tickets on England's great train system (15,000 departures from 2,400 stations daily) are the most expensive per mile in all of Europe. Those who save the biggest book in advance, leave after rush hour (after 9:30), or ride the bus. Now that Britain has privatized its railways, it can be tricky to track down all your options; a single bus or train route can be operated by several companies. However, one British website covers all train lines (www.national rail.co.uk), and another covers all bus and train routes in Britain (www.traveline.org.uk—for information, not ticket sales). Another good resource, which also has schedules for trains throughout Europe, is German Rail's timetable (http://bahn.hafas.de/bin/query.exe/en).

As with airline tickets, British train tickets can come at many different prices for the same journey. A clerk at any station

Railpasses

Prices listed are for 2011 and are subject to change. For the latest prices, details, and train schedules (and easy online ordering), see my comprehensive *Guide to Eurail Passes* at www.ricksteves.com/rail.

"Standard" is the polite British term for "second" class. "Senior" refers to those age 60 and up. No senior discounts for standard class. "Youth" means under age 26. For each adult or senior BritRail or BritRail England pass you buy, one child (5–15) can travel free with you (ask for the **Family Pass,** not available with all passes). Additional kids pay the normal half-adult rate. Kids under 5 travel free.

Note: Overnight journeys begun on the final night of your pass can be completed the day after your pass expires—only BritRail allows this trick. A bunk in a twin sleeper costs $75.

BRITRAIL CONSECUTIVE PASS

	Adult 1st Class	Adult Standard	Senior 1st Class	Youth 1st Class	Youth Standard
3 consec. days	$269	$179	$229	$219	$145
4 consec. days	339	225	289	269	179
8 consec. days	485	319	409	389	259
15 consec. days	725	485	615	579	389
22 consec. days	919	609	779	735	489
1 month	1085	725	925	869	579

BRITRAIL FLEXIPASS

	Adult 1st Class	Adult Standard	Senior 1st Class	Youth 1st Class	Youth Standard
3 days in 2 months	$339	$229	$289	$269	$185
4 days in 2 months	425	285	359	339	229
8 days in 2 months	619	415	525	495	329
15 days in 2 months	929	625	789	745	499

BRITRAIL & DRIVE PASS

Any 4 rail days and 2 car days in 2 months.

	1st Class	2nd Class	Extra Car Day
Mini	$509	$336	$47
Economy	516	339	54
Compact	525	344	63
Compact Auto	556	359	94
Intermed. Auto	569	366	107
Minivan Auto	649	406	187

Prices are per person, two traveling together. Third and fourth persons sharing car buy a regular BritRail pass. To order a Rail & Drive pass, call Rail Europe at 800-438-7245. *Not sold by Europe Through the Back Door.*

Map key:

Approximate point-to-point one-way standard-class fares in US dollars by rail (solid line) and bus (dashed line). First class costs 50 percent more. Add up fares for your itinerary to see whether a railpass will save you money.

BRITRAIL ENGLAND CONSECUTIVE PASS

	Adult 1st Class	Adult Standard	Senior 1st Class	Youth 1st Class	Youth Standard
3 consec. days	$219	$145	$185	$175	$115
4 consec. days	$269	$179	$229	$219	$145
8 consec. days	$385	$259	$329	$309	$205
15 consec. days	$579	$385	$495	$465	$309
22 consec. days	$735	$489	$625	$589	$389
1 month	$869	$579	$739	$695	$465

Covers travel only in England, not Scotland, Wales, or Ireland.

BRITRAIL ENGLAND FLEXIPASS

Type of Pass	Adult 1st Class	Adult Standard	Senior 1st Class	Youth 1st Class	Youth Standard
3 days in 2 months	$269	$185	$229	$219	$145
4 days in 2 months	$339	$229	$289	$269	$185
8 days in 2 months	$495	$329	$419	$395	$265
15 days in 2 months	$745	$499	$635	$595	$399

Covers travel only in England, not Scotland, Wales, or Ireland.

BRITRAIL LONDON PLUS PASS

	Adult 1st Class	Adult Standard
2 out of 8 days	$189	$125
4 out of 8 days	265	199
7 out of 15 days	329	239

Covers much of SE England (see London Plus Coverage Map, above). Includes vouchers to cover two trips on the Heathrow, Stansted, or Gatwick Express, separate from your counted travel days, which can be used up to 6 months from the date you validate the pass in Britain (but not before pass is validated for the 8- or 15-day travel window). Many trains are standard class only. The 7 p.m. rule for night trains does not apply. Kids 5–15 half price; under 5 free.

BRITRAIL FREEDOM OF SCOTLAND PASS

4 out of 8 days	$215
8 out of 15 days	285

For Scotland only, standard class only. Not valid on trains that depart before 9:15 a.m., Monday - Friday. Covers Caledonian MacBrayne and Strathclyde ferry service to popular islands. Discounts on some P&O ferries, some Citylink buses & more. Kids 5–15 half fare; under 5 free.

BRITRAIL CENTRAL SCOTLAND PASS

3 out of 7 days	$75

asses are prevalidated at the time of purchase for a specific, 7-day travel window and cannot be refunded after that planned travel date! Covers frequent service between Edinburgh and Glasgow's Queen St Station (not Glasgow Central), some nearby side-trips (see Central Scotland Coverage Map, below), and the Glasgow Underground (on your three travel days). Standard class only. No highlands or islands. Not valid on trains that depart before 9:15 a.m. Monday - Friday, Glasgow Airport Coach Links, excursion trains, nor private railways. The 7 p.m. rule for night trains does not apply. No child discount; under 5 free.

BRITRAIL PASS PLUS IRELAND

	First Class	Standard Class
5 days in 1 month	$659	$445
10 days in 1 month	1175	795

Covers the entire British Isles (England, Wales, Scotland, Northern Ireland, and the Republic of Ireland). Does not cover ferries. Kids 5-15 pay half fare; under 5 free. No Family Pass, Party Pass, Eurail Discount, nor Off-Peak Special. Before buying the 10-day pass, consider the cost of separate BritRail and Ireland passes.

can figure out the cheapest fare for your trip (or call the helpful National Rail folks at tel. 0845-748-4950, 24 hours daily). Savings can be significant. For a London-York round-trip (standard class), the full fare is more than £100; if you book the day of departure for travel after 9:30, it's around £84; and the cheapest fare, booked a couple of months in advance as two one-way tickets, can cost as little as £27.

While not required on English trains, reservations are free and a good idea for long journeys or any train travel on Sunday. Make them at any train station before 18:00 on the day before you travel.

Buying Train Tickets in Advance: The best fares go to those who book their trips well in advance of their journey. (While only a 7-day minimum advance booking is officially required for the cheapest fares, these sell out fast—especially in summer—so booking 6-8 weeks in advance is often necessary.) Keep in mind that when booking in advance, "return" (round-trip) fares are not always cheaper than buying two "single" (one-way) tickets. Also note that cheap advance tickets often come with the toughest refund restrictions, so be sure to nail down your travel plans before you reserve. To book ahead, you can go in person to any station, book online at www.nationalrail.co.uk, or call 0845-748-4950 (from the US, call 011-44-20-7278-5240, phone answered 24 hours) to find out the schedule and best fare for your journey; then you'll be referred to the appropriate number to call—depending on the particular rail company—to book your ticket. If you order online, be sure you know what you want; it's tough to reach a person who can change your online reservation. You'll pick up your ticket at the station, or you may be able to print it out at home. (BritRail passholders, however, cannot use the Web to make reservations.)

A company called **Megabus** (through their subsidiary Megatrain) sells some discounted train tickets well in advance on a few specific routes, though their focus is mainly on selling bus tickets (tel. 0871-266-3333, www.megatrain.com).

Buying Train Tickets as You Travel: If you'd rather have the flexibility of booking tickets as you go, you can save a few pounds by buying a round-trip ticket, called a "return ticket" (a same-day round-trip, called a "day return," is particularly cheap); buying before 18:00 the day before you depart; traveling after the morning rush hour (this usually means after 9:30 Mon-Fri); and going standard class instead of first class. Preview your options at www.nationalrail.co.uk or www.thetrainline.com.

Senior, Youth, and Family Deals: To get a third off the price of most point-to-point rail tickets, seniors can buy a Senior Railcard (for ages 60 and above), and younger travelers can buy a 16-25 Railcard (for ages 16-25, or for full-time students 26 and above with a valid ISIC card). A Family Railcard allows adults to travel about 33 percent cheaper while their kids ages 5 to 15 receive a 60 percent discount for most trips (maximum of 4 adults and 4 kids). Each Railcard costs £26; see www.railcard.co.uk. Any of these cards are valid for a year on almost all trains except special runs, such as the Heathrow Express or the Eurostar to Paris or Brussels (fill out application at station, brochures on racks in info center, need to show passport; passport-type photo needed for 16-25 Railcard).

Railpasses: Consider getting a railpass, which offers hop-on flexibility and no need to lock in reservations, except for overnight sleeper cars. The BritRail pass comes in "consecutive day" and "flexi" versions, with price breaks for youths, seniors, off-season travelers, and groups of three of more. Most allow one child under 16 to travel free with a paying adult. If you're exploring England's backcountry with a BritRail pass, standard class is a good choice since many of the smaller train lines don't even offer first-class cars. Choose between England-only BritRail passes and ones that cover Scotland and Wales as well.

More BritRail options include England/Ireland passes, "London Plus" passes (good for travel in most of southeast England but not in London itself), and BritRail & Drive passes (which offer you some rail days and some car-rental days). These BritRail passes, as well as Eurailpasses, get you a discount on the Eurostar train that zips you to continental Europe under the English Channel. These passes are sold outside of Europe only. For specifics, contact your travel agent or see www.ricksteves.com/rail.

Buses

Although buses are about a third slower than trains, they're also a lot cheaper. Most buses are operated by **National Express** (tel. 0871-781-8181, www.nationalexpress.com). Note that Brits distinguish between "buses" (for in-city travel with lots of stops) and "coaches" (long-distance cross-country runs)—though for simplicity in this book, I call both "buses."

Round-trip bus tickets usually cost less than two one-way fares (e.g., London-York one-way costs about £26; round-trip cost about £40). And buses go many places that trains don't. Budget travelers can save a wad with a bus pass. National Express sells **Brit Xplorer bus passes** for unlimited travel on consecutive days (£79/7 days, £139/14 days, £219/28 days, sold over the counter, non-UK passport required, tel. 0871-781-8181, www.nationalexpress.com). Check their website to learn about online Funfare deals; senior/youth/family cards and fares; and discounts for advance booking.

If you want to take a bus from your last destination to the nearest airport, you'll find that National Express often offers

airport buses. Bus stations are normally at or near train stations (in London, the main bus station is a block southwest of Victoria Station).

Megabus sells very cheap promotional fares on certain routes, often beating National Express in price. While this can save you some money, you have to book far ahead for the best rates, and journey times tend to be longer than those on National Express (toll tel. 0900-160-0900, www.megabus.com). They also sell discounted train tickets on selected routes.

A couple of companies offer **backpackers' bus circuits.** These easy hop-on, hop-off bus circuits take mostly youth hostelers around the country for super-cheap fares, with the assumption that they'll be sleeping in the hostels along the way. For instance, **Backpacker Tours** offers 1-19-day excursions through England and other destinations in Great Britain (from about £65/1 day, £90/3 days, £266/5 days, tel. 0870-745-1046, www.backpacker tours.co.uk, sales@backpackertours.co.uk).

Renting a Car

If you're renting a car in England, bring your driver's license. It's recommended, but not required, that you also have an International Driving Permit (sold at your local AAA office for $15 plus the cost of two passport-type photos; see www.aaa.com); however, I've frequently rented cars in Britain and traveled problem-free with just my US license.

Rental companies in England require you to be at least 23 years old. Drivers under the age of 25 or over the age of 70 may incur a young- or older-driver surcharge (some rental companies do not rent to anyone 75 and over). If you're considered too young or old, look into leasing (covered later), which has less-stringent age restrictions.

Research car rentals before you go. It's cheaper to arrange most car rentals from the US. Call several companies and look online to compare rates, or arrange a rental through your home-town travel agent.

Most of the major US rental agencies (such as Enterprise, Alamo, National, Avis, Budget, Dollar, Hertz, and Thrifty) have offices throughout Europe. It can be cheaper to use a consolidator, such as Auto Europe (www.autoeurope.com) or Europe by Car (www.ebctravel.com), which compares rates at several companies to get you the best deal. However, my readers have reported problems with consolidators, ranging from misinformation to unexpected fees; because you're going through a middleman, it can be more challenging to resolve disputes that arise with the rental agency.

Regardless of the car-rental company you choose, always read the contract carefully. The fine print can conceal a host of common add-on charges—such as one-way drop-off fees, airport surcharges, or mandatory insurance policies—that aren't included in the "total price," but can be tacked on when you pick up your car. You may need to query rental agents pointedly to find out your actual cost.

For the best deal, rent by the week with unlimited mileage. To save money on gas, ask for a diesel car. I normally rent the smallest, least-expensive model with a stick-shift (cheaper than automatic). An automatic transmission adds about 50 percent to the car-rental cost over a manual transmission. Almost all rentals are manual by default, so if you need an automatic, you must request one in advance; beware that these cars are usually larger models (not as maneuverable on narrow, winding roads). But weigh this against the fact that in England you'll be sitting on the right side of the car, and shifting with your left hand...while driving on the left side of the road. The floor pedals are in the same locations as in the US, and the gears are found in the same basic "H" pattern as at home.

For a three-week rental, allow $900 per person (based on two people sharing) for a small economy car with unlimited mileage, including gas, parking, and insurance. For trips of this length, look into leasing; you'll save money on insurance and taxes.

You can sometimes get a GPS unit with your rental car or leased vehicle for an additional fee (around $15/day; be sure it has all the maps you need before you drive off). Or, if you have a portable GPS device at home, consider taking it with you to Europe (buy and upload European maps before your trip). GPS apps are also available for smartphones, but downloading maps on one of these apps in Europe could lead to an exorbitant data-roaming bill.

Big companies have offices in most cities; ask whether they can pick you up at your hotel. Small local rental companies can be cheaper but aren't as flexible. Compare pickup costs (downtown can be cheaper than the airport) and explore drop-off options. If you pick up the car in a smaller city, such as Bath, you'll more likely survive your first day on the English roads. Returning a car at a big-city train station can be tricky; get precise details on the car drop-off location and hours. Note that rental offices usually close from midday Saturday until Monday.

When you pick up the rental car, check it thoroughly and make sure any damage is noted on your rental agreement. Find out how your car's lights, turn signals, wipers, and gas cap function. Ask what type of fuel your car takes before you fill up. When you return the car, make sure the agent verifies its condition with you.

Car Insurance Options

When you rent a car, you are liable for a very high deductible,

British Radio

Local radio broadcasts can be a treat for drivers sightseeing in Britain. While most rental cars have CD players, very few have adapter ports for MP3 players—so you may wind up listening to a lot of British radio, whether you want to or not.

Many British radio stations broadcast nationwide; your car radio automatically detects the local frequency a station plays on and displays its name (not its frequency) on your radio's digital readout.

The BBC has five nationwide stations, which you can pick up in most of the country. These government-subsidized stations have no ads.

BBC **Radio 1** plays today's pop music, with youthful DJs spinning top 40 hits and interviewing big-name bands. Many of the same songs and artists air stateside, but Radio 1 will acquaint you with British acts that aren't yet known "across the pond." And many hit singles (even those by American groups) get a lot of play here months before they turn up on US radios. You'll be ahead of the curve when you get home, hear a hot "new" song on the radio, and wink knowingly to your friends, "This was a huge hit in the UK last summer."

BBC **Radio 2**—the highest-rated station nationwide—aims at a slightly more mature audience, with adult contemporary, retro pop, and other "middle of the road" music with broad popular appeal.

sometimes equal to the entire value of the car. Limit your financial risk by choosing one of these three options: Buy Collision Damage Waiver (CDW) coverage from the car-rental company, get coverage through your credit card (free, if your card automatically includes zero-deductible coverage), or buy coverage through Travel Guard.

CDW includes a very high deductible (typically $1,000-1,500). Though each rental company has its own variation, basic CDW costs $15-25 a day (figure roughly 25 percent extra) and reduces your liability, but does not eliminate it. When you pick up the car, you'll be offered the chance to "buy down" the basic deductible to zero (for an additional $15-30/day; this is sometimes called "super CDW").

If you opt for **credit-card coverage**, there's a catch. You'll technically have to decline all coverage offered by the car-rental company, which means they can place a hold on your card (which can be up to the full value of the car). In case of damage, it can be time-consuming to resolve the charges with your credit-card company. Before you decide on this option, quiz your credit-card company about how it works.

BBC **Radio 3** features mostly classical music (including live broadcasts of all the concerts in the annual BBC-sponsored Proms music festival), with some jazz and world music.

BBC **Radio 4** is all talk. It's reminiscent of public radio back home—current events, entertaining chat shows, special-interest topics such as cooking and gardening, and lots of radio plays.

BBC **Radio 5 Live**—less widely broadcast than the "big four"—features sporting events, as well as news and sports talk programs.

You'll encounter regional variations of BBC stations, such as BBC London, Radio York, or BBC Scotland. At the top of the hour, many BBC stations broadcast the famous "pips" (indicating Greenwich Mean Time) and a short roundup of the day's news.

Beyond the BBC offerings, several private stations broadcast music and other content with "adverts" (commercials). While many of these are unique to a specific city or region, others are nationwide, including **XFM** (alternative rock), **Classic FM** (classical), **Absolute Radio** (pop), and **Capital FM** (pop).

Traffic Alerts: If you want to stay up-to-date on traffic conditions, ask your rental-car company about turning on automatic traffic alerts that play on the car radio. Once these are enabled (look for the letters *TA* or *TP* on the radio readout), traffic reports for the area you are driving in will periodically interrupt programming.

Finally, you can buy collision insurance from **Travel Guard** ($9/day plus a one-time $3 service fee covers you for up to $35,000, $250 deductible, tel. 800-826-4919, www.travelguard.com). It's valid everywhere in Europe except the Republic of Ireland, and some Italian car-rental companies refuse to honor it. Note that various US states differ on which products and policies are available to their residents.

For more on car-rental insurance, see www.ricksteves.com/cdw.

Leasing

For trips of two and a half weeks or more, consider leasing (which automatically includes zero-deductible collision and theft insurance). By technically buying and then selling back the car, you save lots of money on tax and insurance. Leasing provides you a brand-new car with unlimited mileage and a 24-hour emergency assistance program. You can lease for as little as 17 days to as long as six months. Car leases must be arranged from the US. One of many reliable companies offering affordable lease packages is Europe by Car (US tel. 800-223-1516, www.ebctravel.com).

Driving in England

Driving in England is basically wonderful—once you remember to stay on the left and after you've mastered the roundabouts. Every year, however, I get a few notes from traveling readers advising me that, for them, trying to drive in England was a nerve-racking and regrettable mistake. If you want to get a little slack on the roads, drop by a gas station or auto shop and buy a green *P* (probationary driver with license) sign to put in your car window (don't get the red *L* sign, which means you're a learner driver without a license and thus prohibited from driving on motorways).

Many Yankee drivers find the hardest part isn't driving on the left, but steering from the right. Your instinct is to put yourself on the left side of your lane, which means you may spend your first day or two constantly drifting into the left shoulder. It can help to remember that the driver always stays close to the center line.

Road Rules: Be aware of Britain's rules of the road. Seat belts are mandatory for all, and kids under age 12 (or less than about 4.5 feet tall) must ride in an appropriate child-safety seat. It's illegal to use a mobile phone while driving—pull over or use a hands-free device. For more information about driving in Britain, ask your car-rental company, read the Department for Transport's *Highway Code* (www.direct. gov.uk—click on "Motoring" and look for "The Highway Code" link), or check the US State Department website (www.travel.state.gov, click on "International Travel," then specify "United Kingdom" and click "Traffic Safety and Road Conditions").

STOP AND LEARN THESE ROAD SIGNS

Speed Limit (mph) — Yield — No Passing — End of No Passing Zone — One Way — Intersection — Main Road — Freeway — Danger — No Entry — No Entry for cars — All Vehicles Prohibited — Parking — No Parking — Customs — Peace

Speed Limits: Speed limits are 30 mph in town, 70 mph on the motorways, and 50 or 60 mph elsewhere (though, as back home, many British drivers consider these limits advisory). The national sign for 60 mph is a white circle with a black slash. Motorways have electronic speed limit signs; posted speeds can change depending on traffic or the weather. Follow them accordingly.

Note that road-surveillance cameras strictly enforce speed limits. Any driver (including foreigners renting cars) photographed

speeding will get a nasty bill in the mail. (Cameras—in foreboding gray boxes—flash on rear license plates to respect the privacy of anyone sharing the front seat with someone he or she shouldn't.) Signs (an image of an old-fashioned camera) alert you when you're entering a zone that may be monitored by these "camera cops." Heed them.

Roundabouts: Don't let a roundabout spook you. After all, you routinely merge into much faster traffic on American highways back home. Traffic flows clockwise, and cars already in the roundabout have the right-of-way; entering traffic yields (look to your right as you merge). You'll probably encounter "double-roundabouts"—figure-eights where you'll slingshot from one roundabout directly into another. Just go with the flow and track signs carefully. When approaching an especially complex roundabout, you'll first pass a diagram showing the layout and the various exits. And in many cases, the pavement is painted to indicate the lane you should be in for a particular road or town.

Freeways (Motorways): The shortest distance between any two points is usually the motorway (what we'd call a "freeway"). In Britain, the smaller the number, the bigger the road. For example, M4 is a freeway, while B4494 is a country road.

Motorway road signs can be confusing, too few, and too late. Miss a motorway exit and you can lose 30 minutes. Study your map before taking off. Know the cities you'll be lacing together, since road numbers are inconsistent. British road signs are never marked with compass directions (e.g., *A30 West*); instead, you need to know what major town or city you're heading for *(A30 Penzance)*. The driving directions in this book are intended to be used with a good local map. An England road atlas, easily purchased at gas stations in England, is money well-spent (see "Maps," page 802).

Unless you're passing, always drive in the "slow" lane on motorways (this is the lane farthest to the left). The British are very disciplined about this; ignoring this rule could get you a ticket (or into a road-rage incident). Remember to pass on the right, not the left.

Rest areas are called "services" and often have a number of useful amenities, such as restaurants, cafeterias, gas stations, shops, and motels.

Fuel: Gas (petrol) costs about $9 per gallon and is self-serve. Diesel rental cars are common; make sure you know what kind of fuel your car takes before you fill up. Unleaded pumps are usually green. Note that your US credit and debit cards are unlikely to

How to Navigate a Roundabout

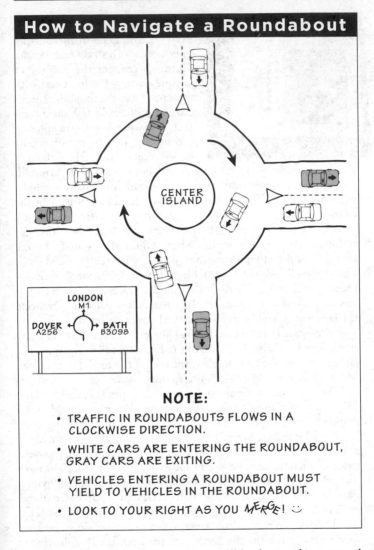

NOTE:

- TRAFFIC IN ROUNDABOUTS FLOWS IN A CLOCKWISE DIRECTION.
- WHITE CARS ARE ENTERING THE ROUNDABOUT, GRAY CARS ARE EXITING.
- VEHICLES ENTERING A ROUNDABOUT MUST YIELD TO VEHICLES IN THE ROUNDABOUT.
- LOOK TO YOUR RIGHT AS YOU MERGE! ☺

work at self-service gas pumps, or at toll bridges and automated parking garages. It might help if you know your card's PIN, but just in case, be sure to carry sufficient cash.

Driving in Cities: Whenever possible, avoid driving in cities. Be warned that London assesses a congestion charge (see page 65). Most cities have modern ring roads to skirt the congestion. Follow signs to the parking lots outside the city core—most are a 5- to 10-minute walk to the center—and avoid what can be an unpleasant grid of one-way streets (as in Bath) or roads that are only available to public transportation during the day (as in Oxford).

England by Car: Mileage & Time

Driving in Rural Areas: Outside of the big cities and the motorways, British roads tend to be narrow. In towns, you may have to cross over the center line just to get past parked cars. Adjust your perceptions of personal space: It's not "my side of the road" or "your side of the road," it's just "the road"—and it's shared as a cooperative adventure. If the road's wide enough, both directions of traffic can pass parked cars simultaneously, but frequently you'll have to take turns—follow the locals' lead and drive defensively. Some narrow country lanes are barely wide enough for one car. Go slowly, and if you encounter an oncoming car, look for the nearest pullout (or "passing place")—the driver who's closest to one is expected to use it, even if they have to back up to reach it. If another car pulls over and blinks its headlights, that means, "Go ahead; I'll wait to let you pass." British drivers—arguably the most courteous on the planet—are quick to offer a friendly wave to thank you for letting them pass (and they appreciate it if you reciprocate). Pull over frequently—to let faster locals pass and to check the map.

Parking: Parking can be confusing. One yellow line marked on the pavement means no parking Monday through Saturday during work hours. Double yellow lines mean no parking at any time. Broken yellow lines mean short stops are OK, but you should always look for explicit signs or ask a passerby. White lines mean you're free to park.

In towns, rather than look for street parking, I generally just pull into the most central and handy "pay and display" parking lot I can find. To "pay and display," feed change into a machine, receive a timed ticket, and display it on the dashboard or stick it to the driver's-side window. Rates are reasonable by US standards, and locals love to share stickers that have time remaining. If you stand by the machine, someone on their way out with time left on their sticker will probably give it to you. Keep a bag of coins in the ashtray or glove box for these machines and for parking meters.

The AA: An Automobile Association membership for Britain comes with most rentals (www.theaa.com). Understand its towing and emergency road-service benefits.

Stock Up: Set your car up for a fun road trip. Establish a cardboard-box munchies pantry. Buy a rack of liter boxes of juice for the trunk, and some Windex and a roll of paper towels (called a "kitchen roll" in Britain) for cleaner sightseeing.

Cheap Flights

London is the hub for many cheap, no-frills airlines, which affordably connect the city with other destinations in the British Isles and throughout Europe. If you're considering a train ride that's more than five hours long, a flight may save you both time and money. When comparing your options, factor in the time it takes to get to the airport and how early you'll need to arrive to check in.

Be aware of the potential drawbacks of flying on the cheap: nonrefundable and nonchangeable tickets, minimal or nonexistent customer service, treks to airports far outside town, and stingy baggage allowances with steep overage fees. If you're traveling with lots of luggage, a cheap flight can quickly become a bad deal. To avoid unpleasant surprises, read the small print before you book.

One of the best websites for comparing inexpensive flights is www.skyscanner.net. Other comparison search engines include www.kayak.com, www.wegolo.com, and www.whichbudget.com. If you're not sure who flies to your destination, check its airport's website for a list of carriers.

With **bmi,** you can fly inexpensively from London to destinations in the UK and beyond. Fares start at about £45 one-way to Edinburgh, Dublin, or Belfast (tel. 0870-607-0555, US tel. 800-788-0555, www.flybmi.com).

Another low-cost airline, **easyJet,** flies from Gatwick, Luton, and Stansted, as well as Liverpool. Prices are based on demand, so the least popular routes make for the cheapest fares, especially if you book early (tel. 0843-104-5000, www.easyjet.com).

Irish-owned **Ryanair** flies from London (mostly Stansted Airport, though also Gatwick and Luton), Liverpool, and Glasgow to often obscure airports near Dublin, Frankfurt, Stockholm, Oslo, Venice, Turin, and many others. Sample fares: London-Dublin—£50 round-trip (sometimes as low as £30), London-Frankfurt—£55 round-trip (Irish toll tel. 0818-303-030, British tel. 0871-246-0000, www.ryanair.com). However, be warned that Ryanair charges additional fees for nearly everything. The company requires a mandatory online-only check-in (£5 charge), from 15 days to four hours before your flight (no airport check-in). When checking in, you must also print out your boarding pass; if you show up without it, there's an additional £40 charge. You can carry on only a small day bag; you'll pay a fee for each checked bag (price depends on number of bags; up to two bags allowed per passenger).

Brussels Airlines (formerly Virgin Express) is a Brussels-based company with good rates and hubs in Bristol, Birmingham, Heathrow, Manchester, and Newcastle (US tel. 516/740-5200, British toll tel. 0905-609-5609—£0.40/minute, www.brusselsair lines.com).

Resources

Resources from Rick Steves

Rick Steves' England 2012 is one of many books in my series on

European travel, which includes country guidebooks, city guidebooks (London, Paris, Rome, Florence, and more), Snapshot Guides (excerpted chapters from my country guides), Pocket Guides (full-color little books on big cities, including London), and my budget-travel skills handbook, *Rick Steves' Europe Through the Back Door.* Most of my titles are available as ebooks. My phrase books—for Italian, French, German, Spanish, and Portuguese—are practical and budget-oriented. My other books include *Europe 101* (a crash course on art and history), *Mediterranean Cruise Ports* (how to make the most of your time in port), and *Travel as a Political Act* (a travelogue sprinkled with tips for bringing home a global perspective). A more complete list of my titles appears near the end of this book.

Video: My public television series, *Rick Steves' Europe*, covers European destinations in 100 shows, including 10 episodes on Great Britain. To watch episodes, visit www.hulu.com/rick-steves-europe; for scripts and other details, see www.ricksteves.com/tv.

Audio: My weekly public radio show, *Travel with Rick Steves*, features interviews with travel experts from around the world. I've also produced free self-guided audio tours of the top sights and neighborhoods in London (and other great cities). All of this audio content is available for free at Rick Steves Audio Europe, an extensive online library organized by destination. Choose whatever interests you, and download it for free to your computer or mobile device

via www.ricksteves.com/audioeurope, iTunes, or the Rick Steves Audio Europe smartphone app.

Maps

The black-and-white maps in this book, drawn by Dave Hoerlein, are concise and simple. Dave, who is well-traveled in Britain, designed the maps to help you locate recommended places and get to local TIs, where you can pick up more in-depth maps of towns or regions (usually free). Better maps are sold at newsstands and bookstores. Before you buy a map, look at it to be sure it has the level of detail you want.

If you'll be lingering in London, buy a city map at a London newsstand; the red *Benson's Handy London Map & Guide* (£2.95) is excellent. Even the vending-machine maps sold in Tube stations are good. The *Rough Guide* map to London is well designed (£5, sold at London and US bookstores). The *Rick Steves' Britain, Ireland & London City Map* has a good map of London ($6, www.ricksteves.com). Many Londoners, along with obsessive-compulsive tourists, rely on the highly detailed *London A-Z* map book (generally £5-7, called "A to Zed" by locals, available at newsstands and www.a-zmaps.co.uk).

If you're driving, get a road atlas (1 inch equals 3 miles) covering all of England. Ordnance Survey, AA, and Bartholomew editions are all available for about £7 at tourist information offices, gas stations, and bookstores. Drivers, hikers, and cyclists may want more in-depth maps for the Cotswolds and the Lake District.

Begin Your Trip at www.ricksteves.com

At ricksteves.com, you'll discover a wealth of free information on European destinations, including fresh monthly news and helpful tips from thousands of fellow travelers. You'll find my latest guidebook updates (www.ricksteves.com/update), a monthly travel e-newsletter (easy and free to sign up), my personal travel blog, and my free Rick Steves Audio Europe smartphone app (if you don't have a smartphone, you can access the same content via podcasts). You can even follow me on Facebook and Twitter.

Our **online Travel Store** offers travel bags and accessories specially designed by me to help you travel smarter and lighter. These include my popular carry-on bags (roll-aboard and backpack versions), money belts, totes, toiletries kits, adapters, other accessories, and a wide selection of guidebooks, planning maps, and DVDs.

Choosing the right **railpass** for your trip—amid hundreds of options—can drive you nutty. We'll help you choose the best pass for your needs and ship it to you for free, plus give you a bunch of free extras.

Rick Steves' Europe Through the Back Door travel company offers **tours** with more than three dozen itineraries and 450 departures reaching the best destinations in this book...and beyond. We offer a 14-day England tour, an 11-day Scotland tour, and a 7-day in-depth London city tour. You'll enjoy great guides, a fun bunch of travel partners (with small groups of generally around 24-28), and plenty of room to spread out in a big, comfy bus. You'll find European adventures to fit every vacation length. For all the details, and to get our Tour Catalog and a free Rick Steves Tour Experience DVD (filmed on location during an actual tour), visit www.ricksteves.com or call us at 425/608-4217.

Other Guidebooks

If you're like most travelers, this book is all you need. But if you're heading beyond my recommended destinations, $40 for extra maps and books is money well-spent. If you'll be focusing on London or traveling elsewhere in Britain, consider *Rick Steves' London 2012* or *Rick Steves' Great Britain 2012*.

The following books are worthwhile, though not updated annually; check the publication date before you buy: The *Lonely Planet* and *Let's Go* guidebooks on London and on Britain are fine budget-travel guides. *Lonely Planet's* guidebooks are more thorough and informative; *Let's Go* books are youth-oriented, with good coverage of nightlife, hostels, and cheap transportation deals. For cultural and sightseeing background, look into Michelin and Cadogan guides to London, England, and Britain. The readable Access guide for London is similarly well-researched. *Secret London* by Andrew Duncan leads the reader on unique walks through a less-touristy London.

Recommended Books and Movies

To learn more about England past and present, check out a few of these books or films.

Nonfiction

For a serious historical overview, wade into *A History of Britain,* a three-volume collection by Simon Schama. *Literary Trails* (Hardyment) reunites famous authors with the environments that inspired them.

In *Notes from a Small Island,* American expat Bill Bryson records his witty notes about every British foible. For more good memoirs, pick up any of the books by Susan Allen Toth on her British travels. If you'll be spending time in the Cotswolds, try *Cider with Rosie,* Laurie Lee's boyhood memoir set just after World War I. Animal-lovers enjoy James Herriot's adventures as a Yorkshire vet, told in *All Creatures Great and Small* and its sequels. And the obsessive world of English soccer is illuminated in Nick Hornby's memoir, *Fever Pitch.*

Fiction

For the classics of British fiction, read anything—and everything— by Charles Dickens, Jane Austen, and the Brontës. Mystery fans can't miss with any of the books by Agatha Christie.

Pillars of the Earth (Follett) traces the building of a fictional 12th-century cathedral in southern England. For a big book on the era of King Richard III, try *The Sunne in Splendour,* one in a series by Sharon Kay Penman. *Wolf Hall* (Mantel) sets its intrigues in the court of Henry VIII, while *Restoration* (Tremain) returns readers to the time of King Charles II.

Set in the 19th-century Anglican church, *The Warden* (Trollope) dwells on moral dilemmas. *Brideshead Revisited* (Waugh) satirizes the British obsession with class and takes place between the World Wars. A rural village in the 1930s is the social battlefield for E. F. Benson's *Mapp and Lucia*. A family saga spanning the interwar years and beyond, *Atonement* (McEwan) takes an intense look at England's upper-middle class. For evocative Cornish settings, try Daphne du Maurier's *Rebecca* or *The House on the Strand*.

For a more contemporary read, check out *Bridget Jones's Diary* (Fielding), *Behind the Scenes at the Museum* (Atkinson), *White Teeth* (Smith), *Saturday* (McEwan), or anything by Nick Hornby *(High Fidelity, About a Boy)*.

Film and Television

In terms of world influence, Britain's filmmaking output rivals its substantial literary contributions. Britain gave birth to the two top-grossing film series of all time: Harry Potter and James Bond. Add to that the fact that much of the Star Wars series (ranked third) was filmed in England, and that the casts of the Pirates of the Caribbean (fourth) and Lord of the Rings (sixth) series were both dominated by British actors—and it's impossible to deny Britain's cinematic clout. But it's not all super-blockbusters. Here are some films that will flesh out your understanding of this small island, past and present.

For a taste of Tudor-era London, try *Shakespeare in Love* (1999), which is set in the original Globe Theatre. In *A Man for All Seasons* (1966), Sir Thomas More faces down Henry VIII. Showtime's racy, lavish series *The Tudors* (2007-2010) is an entertaining, loosely accurate chronicle of the marriages of Henry VIII.

For equally good portraits of Elizabeth I, try *Elizabeth* (1998) and its sequel *Elizabeth: The Golden Age* (2007), or the BBC/HBO miniseries *Elizabeth I* (2005). In *The Duchess* (2008), the 18th-century Duchess of Devonshire glides languidly through life in big skirts and even bigger wigs.

Written and set in the early 19th century, the works of Jane Austen have fared well in film. Among the many versions of *Pride and Prejudice,* the 1995 BBC miniseries starring Colin Firth is the winner. *Persuasion* (1995) was partially filmed in Bath. Other Austen adaptations include *Sense and Sensibility* (1995, with Emma Thompson, Hugh Grant, and Kate Winslet) and *Emma* (1996, with Gwyneth Paltrow). The 1995 SoCal teen comedy *Clueless* also (freely) reinterprets *Emma*. Charlotte Brontë's *Jane Eyre* was filmed in 2011 with Mia Wasikowska and Michael Fassbinder.

In *The Elephant Man* (1980), the cruelty of Victorian London is starkly portrayed in a black-and-white film. *Sweeney Todd* (2007)

Harry Potter Sights

Harry Potter's story is set in a magical Britain. Except for those in London, all of the places mentioned in the books are fictional—though you can still visit many real film locations.

Spoiler Alert: The following will ruin surprises for the three of you who haven't read or seen the Harry Potter books or movies.

London

In the first film, *Harry Potter and the Sorcerer's Stone* (2001), Harry first realizes his wizard powers when talking with a boa constrictor, filmed at the **London Zoo's Reptile House** in Regent's Park (Tube: Great Portland Street).

London bustles along oblivious to the parallel universe of wizards, hidden in the magical Diagon Alley (filmed, like many of the other fictional settings, on a set at Leavesden Studios, north of London). The goblin-run Gringotts Wizarding Bank, though, was filmed in the real-life marble-floored Exhibition Hall of **Australia House** (Tube: Temple), the Australian Embassy.

Harry catches the train to Hogwarts at **King's Cross Station.** Inside, on a **pedestrian bridge** over the tracks, Hagrid gives Harry a train ticket. Harry heads to platform 9¾. You'll find a re-creation—complete with a *Platform 9¾* sign and a luggage cart disappearing into the wall—outside the station, near platform 1.

In *Harry Potter and the Prisoner of Azkaban* (2004), Harry careens through London on a three-decker bus that dumps him at the Leaky Cauldron pub. The exterior was shot on rough-looking Stoney Street at the southeast edge of **Borough Street Market,** by The Market Porter pub (Tube: London Bridge).

In *Harry Potter and the Order of the Phoenix* (2007), the Order takes to the night sky on broomsticks over London, passing over plenty of identifiable landmarks, including the **London Eye, Big Ben,** and **Buckingham Palace.**

The **Millennium Bridge** is attacked and collapses into the Thames in *Harry Potter and the Half-Blood Prince* (2009). In *Order of the Phoenix* and *Harry Potter and the Deathly Hallows: Part I* (2010), the real government offices of **Whitehall** serve as exteriors for the Ministry of Magic. Harry, Ron, and Hermione fight off disguised Death Eaters in a Muggle café, filmed in the West End's bustling **Piccadilly Circus** for *Deathly Hallows: Part I.*

Near Bath

The mysterious side of Hogwarts is often set in the elaborate, fan-vaulted corridors of the **Gloucester Cathedral** cloisters, 50 miles north of Bath. In *Sorcerer's Stone*, when Harry and Ron set out to save Hermione, they look down a long, dark Gloucester hallway and spot a 20-foot troll at the far end.

In *Sorcerer's Stone*, the scene showing Harry being chosen for Gryffindor's Quidditch team was shot in the halls of the 13th-century **Lacock Abbey,** 13 miles east of Bath. Harry attends Professor Snape's class in one of the Abbey's peeling-plaster rooms—appropriate to Snape's temperament. (Mad Max tours include Lacock; see page 365.)

Outdoor scenes from *Deathly Hallows: Part I*, in which Harry, Ron, and Hermione take refuge in the woods, were filmed in the Swinley Forest area of Windsor's **Great Park.**

Oxford

Hogwarts, Harry's prestigious wizarding prep school, is a composite of several locations, many of them real places in Oxford. (For information on Harry Potter tours in Oxford, see page 443.)

Christ Church College inspired two film sets familiar to Potter fans. In *Sorcerer's Stone*, the kids are ferried to Hogwarts and then ascend a **stone staircase** that leads into the Great Hall. Christ Church's high-ceilinged **dining hall** was a model for the one seen throughout the films (with the weightless candles and flaming braziers).

Later in *Sorcerer's Stone*, Harry sneaks into the restricted book section of Hogwarts Library under a cloak of invisibility. This scene was filmed inside Oxford's **Duke Humfrey's Library.** Hermione reads about the Sorcerer's Stone here, too.

At the end of *Sorcerer's Stone*, Harry awakens in the Hogwarts infirmary, filmed in the big-windowed **Divinity School,** on the ground floor of the Bodleian Library; Ron also recuperates here after being poisoned in *Half-Blood Prince*. In *Harry Potter and the Goblet of Fire* (2005), Mad-Eye Moody turns Draco into a ferret in the **New College cloister.**

Durham and Northeast England

In *Sorcerer's Stone*, Harry walks with his white owl, Hedwig, through a snowy cloister courtyard located in **Durham's Cathedral** (see listing on page 725).

Harry first learns to fly a broomstick on the green grass of Hogwarts' school grounds, filmed inside the walls of **Alnwick Castle,** located 30 miles from Newcastle. In *Harry Potter and the Chamber of Secrets* (2002), this is where the Weasleys' flying car crashes into the Whomping Willow.

Southeast England

In *Deathly Hallows: Part II*, the pivotal scene at Lily and James Potter's home in Godric's Hollow—when Harry becomes the "Boy Who Lived"—was shot in the medieval town of **Lavenham,** Suffolk, about 75 miles northeast of London.

Northwest England

Harry and Hagrid speed through **Queensway Tunnel** in Liverpool on Sirius Black's flying motorcycle in *Deathly Hallows: Part I*, as they flee a pack of eager Death Eaters.

captures the gritty Victorian milieu, as does the highly stylized *Sherlock Holmes* (2009). (Sherlock shows up again in an excellent 2010 BBC updating of the detective's story, set in present-day London.) On a lighter note, *Goodbye, Mr. Chips* (1939) is set in a boys' boarding school during Victorian England.

The Edwardian era of the early 20th century has provided a setting for many films. Producer Ismail Merchant and director James Ivory teamed up to create many well-regarded films about this era, including *Howard's End* (1992, which captures the stifling societal pressure underneath the gracious manners), *A Room with a View* (1985), and *The Remains of the Day* (1993).

The all-star *Gosford Park* (2001) is part comedy, part murder mystery, and part critique of England's class stratification in the 1930s. *Chariots of Fire* (1981) ran away with the Academy Award for Best Picture. *Shadowlands* (1993) tells a fictionalized account of author C. S. Lewis' relationship with his future wife.

Wartime London has been captured in many fine movies. *The King's Speech* (2010) won the Best Picture Oscar, with Colin Firth named Best Actor for his portrayal of King George VI on the cusp of World War II. *Hope and Glory* (1987) is a semi-autobiographical story of a boy growing up during WWII's Blitz. *Waterloo Bridge* (1940) is a story of lost love between a woman and a WWI officer. In *Passport to Pimlico* (1949), an explosion in a Tube station is the source of riches and comedy in a time of post-WWII rationing.

British acts were all the rage in the States, thanks to a little band called the Beatles, whose *A Hard Day's Night* (1964) is filled with wit and charm. During this time, "swinging London" also exploded on the international scene, with films such as *Alfie* (1966), *Blowup* (1966), and *Georgy Girl* (1966). (For a swinging spoof of this time, try the Austin Powers comedies.) In *To Sir, with Love* (1967), Sidney Poitier brings order to his undisciplined students.

You can watch Hugh Grant charming the ladies in *Four Weddings and a Funeral* (1994) and *Notting Hill* (1999); Gwyneth Paltrow living two lives in *Sliding Doors* (1998); and John Cleese, Jamie Lee Curtis, and Kevin Kline hilariously double-crossing one other in *A Fish Called Wanda* (1988).

For a departure from the typical Hollywood fare, see *My Beautiful Laundrette* (1986), a gritty story of two gay men (with Daniel Day-Lewis). For another portrayal of urban London—and the racial tensions found in its multiethnic center—look for *Sammy and Rosie Get Laid* (1987). *Lock, Stock and Two Smoking Barrels* (1998) is a violent crime caper set in the city.

Billy Elliot (2000), about a young boy ballet dancer, and *Bend It Like Beckham* (2003), about a young girl of Punjabi descent who plays soccer, were both huge crowd-pleasers. *An Education* (2009), about a bright schoolgirl who falls for an older man, takes place in 1960s London. *V for Vendetta* (2006), based on a British graphic novel, shows a sci-fi future of a London ruled with an iron fist.

In *The Queen* (2006), Helen Mirren expertly channels Elizabeth II during the days after Princess Diana's death. If you enjoy *The Queen*, don't miss two other reality-based films by the same screenwriter and many of the same cast members (most notably Michael Sheen as Tony Blair): *The Special Relationship* (2010, about the friendship between Tony Blair and Bill Clinton) and *The Deal* (2003, about Tony Blair's early relationship with Gordon Brown).

Britain has offered up plenty of comedy choices over the years. If you're in the mood for something completely different, try *Monty Python and the Holy Grail* (1975), a surreal take on the Arthurian legend. The BBC's deeply irreverent "mockumentary" series *The Office* (by Ricky Gervais and Stephen Merchant) inspired the gentler US television show. In *The Full Monty* (1997), some working-class Yorkshire lads take it all off to pay the bills. *Calendar Girls* (2003) has a similar setting and premise, if a slightly more noble cause. *Shaun of the Dead* (2004) combines comedy and horror, when the city's residents turn into zombies; the same filmmakers later merged cop/action films and comedy in *Hot Fuzz* (2007) and sci-fi tropes in *Paul* (2011).

If you're traveling to London or Great Britain with children, consider watching *Mary Poppins* (1964), *My Fair Lady* (1964), *A Little Princess* (1995), the *Wallace & Gromit* movies, Rowan Atkinson's *Mr. Bean* television series and movies, and the *Harry Potter* films.

Holidays and Festivals

This list includes the national holidays observed throughout Great Britain and many—but not all—big festivals in major cities. Many sights and banks close on national holidays—keep this in mind when planning your itinerary. Throughout Britain, hotels get booked up during Easter week; over the Early May, Spring, and Late Summer Bank Holidays; and during Christmas, Boxing Day, and New Year's Day. On Christmas, virtually everything shuts down, even the Tube in London. Museums also generally close December 24 and 26.

Before planning a trip around a festival, make sure you verify its dates by checking the festival's website or contacting the Visit Britain office (tel. 800-462-2748, www.visitbritain.com).

Many British towns have holiday festivals in late November and early December, with markets, music, and entertainment in the Christmas spirit (for instance, Keswick's Victorian Fayre).

2012

	JANUARY					
S	M	T	W	T	F	S
	1	2	3	4	5	6	7
8	9	10	11	12	13	14
15	16	17	18	19	20	21
22	23	24	25	26	27	28
29	30	31				

	FEBRUARY					
S	M	T	W	T	F	S
			1	2	3	4
5	6	7	8	9	10	11
12	13	14	15	16	17	18
19	20	21	22	23	24	25
26	27	28	29			

	MARCH					
S	M	T	W	T	F	S
				1	2	3
4	5	6	7	8	9	10
11	12	13	14	15	16	17
18	19	20	21	22	23	24
25	26	27	28	29	30	31

	APRIL					
S	M	T	W	T	F	S
1	2	3	4	5	6	7
8	9	10	11	12	13	14
15	16	17	18	19	20	21
22	23	24	25	26	27	28
29	30					

	MAY					
S	M	T	W	T	F	S
		1	2	3	4	5
6	7	8	9	10	11	12
13	14	15	16	17	18	19
20	21	22	23	24	25	26
27	28	29	30	31		

	JUNE					
S	M	T	W	T	F	S
					1	2
3	4	5	6	7	8	9
10	11	12	13	14	15	16
17	18	19	20	21	22	23
24	25	26	27	28	29	30

	JULY					
S	M	T	W	T	F	S
1	2	3	4	5	6	7
8	9	10	11	12	13	14
15	16	17	18	19	20	21
22	23	24	25	26	27	28
29	30	31				

	AUGUST					
S	M	T	W	T	F	S
			1	2	3	4
5	6	7	8	9	10	11
12	13	14	15	16	17	18
19	20	21	22	23	24	25
26	27	28	29	30	31	

	SEPTEMBER					
S	M	T	W	T	F	S
						1
2	3	4	5	6	7	8
9	10	11	12	13	14	15
16	17	18	19	20	21	22
23/30	24	25	26	27	28	29

	OCTOBER					
S	M	T	W	T	F	S
	1	2	3	4	5	6
7	8	9	10	11	12	13
14	15	16	17	18	19	20
21	22	23	24	25	26	27
28	29	30	31			

	NOVEMBER					
S	M	T	W	T	F	S
				1	2	3
4	5	6	7	8	9	10
11	12	13	14	15	16	17
18	19	20	21	22	23	24
25	26	27	28	29	30	

	DECEMBER					
S	M	T	W	T	F	S
						1
2	3	4	5	6	7	8
9	10	11	12	13	14	15
16	17	18	19	20	21	22
23/30	24/31	25	26	27	28	29

Here are some major holidays in 2012:

Jan 1	New Year's Day
Feb (one week)	London Fashion Week (www.london fashionweek.co.uk)
Mid-Feb	Jorvik Viking Festival, York (costumed warriors, battles; www.jorvik-viking -centre.co.uk)
March 2-March 11	Literature Festival, Bath (www.bathlit fest.org.uk)
April 6	Good Friday
April 8-9	Easter Sunday and Monday
May 7	Early May Bank Holiday
May 3-6	Jazz Festival, Keswick (www.keswick jazzfestival.co.uk)
Late May	Chelsea Flower Show, London (book tickets in advance for this popular event at www.rhs.org.uk/chelsea)

APPENDIX

May 30–June 10	International Music Festival, Bath (www.bathmusicfest.org.uk)
Late May–early June	Fringe Festival, Bath (alternative music, dance, and theater; www.bathfringe.co.uk)
June 1-2	Beer Festival, Keswick (music, shows; www.keswickbeerfestival.co.uk)
June 2-5	Queen's Diamond Jubilee (www.direct.gov.uk/diamondjubilee)
June 4	Spring Bank Holiday
Early-mid-June	Trooping the Colour, London (military bands and pageantry, Queen's birthday parade; www.trooping-the-colour.co.uk)
June 19-23	Royal Ascot Horse Race, Ascot (near Windsor; www.ascot.co.uk)
Mid-late June	Golowan (Midsummer) Festival, Penzance (www.golowan.org)
Late June–early July	Wimbledon Tennis Championship, London (www.wimbledon.org)
July 6-14	Early Music Festival, York (www.ncem.co.uk)
Late July–early Aug	Cambridge Folk Festival (buy tickets early at www.cambridgefolkfestival.co.uk)
Late Aug	Notting Hill Carnival, London (costumes, Caribbean music, www.thenottinghillcarnival.com)
Aug 27	Late Summer Bank Holiday (England and Wales only, not Scotland)
Sept-Nov	Illuminations, Blackpool (waterfront light festival, www.visitblackpool.com/illuminations)
Sept (one week)	London Fashion Week (www.londonfashionweek.co.uk)
Mid-Sept	Jane Austen Festival, Bath (www.janeausten.co.uk)
Late Sept	York Festival of Food and Drink (www.yorkfoodfestival.com)
Nov 5	Bonfire Night, or Guy Fawkes Night, Britain (fireworks, bonfires, effigy-burning of 1605 traitor Guy Fawkes)
Dec 24-26	Christmas holidays

Conversions and Climate

Numbers and Stumblers

- In Europe, dates appear as day/month/year, so Christmas is 25/12/12.
- What Americans call the second floor of a building is the first floor in Britain.
- On escalators and moving sidewalks, Brits keep the left "lane" open for passing. Keep to the right.
- To avoid the British version of giving someone "the finger," don't hold up the first two fingers of your hand with your palm facing you. (It looks like a reversed victory sign.)
- And please...don't call your waist pack a "fanny pack."

Metric Conversions (approximate)

Britain uses the metric system for everything but driving distances and speed limits, which are expressed in miles. Weight and volume are typically calculated in metric: A kilogram is 2.2 pounds, and one liter is about a quart, or almost four to a gallon. The weight of a person is measured by "stone" (one stone equals 14 pounds). Temperatures are generally given in both Celsius and Fahrenheit.

1 foot = 0.3 meter	1 square yard = 0.8 square meter
1 yard = 0.9 meter	1 square mile = 2.6 square kilometers
1 mile = 1.6 kilometers	1 ounce = 28 grams
1 centimeter = 0.4 inch	1 quart = 0.95 liter
1 meter = 39.4 inches	1 kilogram = 2.2 pounds
1 kilometer = 0.62 mile	32°F = 0°C

Weights and Measures

1 British pint = 1.2 US pints
1 imperial gallon = 1.2 US gallons or about 4.5 liters
1 stone = 14 pounds (a 168-pound person weighs 12 stone)

Clothing Sizes

When shopping for clothing, use these US-to-Britain comparisons as general guidelines (but note that no conversion is perfect).

- Women's dresses and blouses: Add 4
  (US women's size 10 = UK size 14)
- Men's suits and jackets: US and UK use the same sizing
- Men's shirts: US and UK use the same sizing
- Women's shoes: Subtract 2½ (US size 8 = UK size 5½)
- Men's shoes: Subtract about ½ (US size 9 = UK size 8½)

England's Climate

The first line is the average daily high; second line, average daily low; third line, average days without rain. For more detailed weather statistics for destinations in this book (as well as the rest of the world), check www.worldclimate.com.

	J	F	M	A	M	J	J	A	S	O	N	D
LONDON												
	43°	44°	50°	56°	62°	69°	71°	71°	65°	58°	50°	45°
	36°	36°	38°	42°	47°	53°	56°	56°	52°	46°	42°	38°
	16	15	20	18	19	19	19	20	17	18	15	16
YORK												
	43°	44°	49°	55°	61°	67°	70°	69°	64°	57°	49°	45°
	33°	34°	36°	40°	44°	50°	54°	53°	50°	44°	39°	36°
	14	13	18	17	18	16	16	17	16	16	13	14

Temperature Conversion: Fahrenheit and Celsius

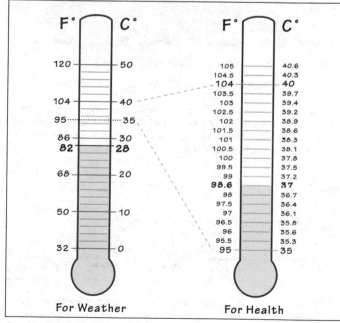

Britain uses both Celsius and Fahrenheit to take its temperature. For a rough conversion from Celsius to Fahrenheit, double the number and add 30. For weather, remember that 28°C is 82°F—perfect. For health, 37°C is just right.

Hotel Reservation

To: _____ _____
        hotel   *email or fax*

From: _____ _____
        name   *email or fax*

Today's date: _____ /_____ /_____
                      day   *month*   *year*

Dear Hotel _____ ,
Please make this reservation for me:

Name: _____

Total # of people: _____ # of rooms: _____ # of nights: _____

Arriving: _____ /_____ /_____ My time of arrival (24-hr clock): _____
              day   month   year   (I will telephone if I will be late)

Departing: _____ /_____ /_____
                day   month   year

Room(s): Single____ Double ____ Twin ____ Triple ____ Quad____

With: Toilet ____ Shower____ Bath ____ Sink only____

Special needs: View____ Quiet____ Cheapest ____ Ground Floor____

Please email or fax confirmation of my reservation, along with the type of
room reserved and the price. Please also inform me of your cancellation
policy. After I hear from you, I will quickly send my credit-card information
as a deposit to hold the room. Thank you.

_____
Name

_____
Address

_____
City   *State*   *Zip Code*   *Country*

Before hoteliers can make your reservation, they want to know the informa-
tion listed above. You can use this form as the basis for your email, or you can
photocopy this page, fill in the information, and send it as a fax (also available
online at www.ricksteves.com/reservation).

Packing Checklist

Whether you're traveling for five days or five weeks, here's what you'll need to bring. Pack light to enjoy the sweet freedom of true mobility. Happy travels!

- ❏ 5 shirts: long- and short-sleeve
- ❏ 1 sweater or lightweight fleece
- ❏ 2 pairs pants
- ❏ 1 pair shorts
- ❏ 1 swimsuit
- ❏ 5 pairs underwear and socks
- ❏ 1 pair shoes
- ❏ 1 rainproof jacket with hood
- ❏ Tie or scarf
- ❏ Money belt
- ❏ Money—your mix of:
  - ❏ Debit card (for ATM withdrawals)
  - ❏ Credit card
  - ❏ Hard cash (in easy-to-exchange $20 bills)
- ❏ Documents plus photo-copies:
  - ❏ Passport
  - ❏ Printout of airline eticket
  - ❏ Driver's license
  - ❏ Student ID and hostel card
  - ❏ Railpass/car rental voucher
  - ❏ Insurance details
- ❏ Daypack
- ❏ Electronics—your choice of:
  - ❏ Camera (and related gear)
  - ❏ Computer/mobile devices (phone, MP3 player, ereader, etc.)
  - ❏ Chargers for each of the above
  - ❏ Plug adapter
- ❏ Empty water bottle

- ❏ Wristwatch and alarm clock
- ❏ Earplugs
- ❏ Toiletries kit
  - ❏ Toiletries
  - ❏ Medicines and vitamins
  - ❏ First-aid kit
  - ❏ Glasses/contacts/sunglasses (with prescriptions)
- ❏ Sealable plastic baggies
- ❏ Laundry soap
- ❏ Clothesline
- ❏ Small towel
- ❏ Sewing kit
- ❏ Travel information (guide-books and maps)
- ❏ Address list (for sending postcards)
- ❏ Postcards and photos from home
- ❏ Notepad and pen
- ❏ Journal

If you plan to carry on your luggage, note that all liquids must be in 3.4-ounce or smaller containers and fit within a single quart-size sealable baggie. For details, see www.tsa.gov/travelers.

British-Yankee Vocabulary

For a longer list, plus a dry-witted primer on British culture, see *The Septic's Companion* (Chris Rae). Note that instead of asking, "Can I help you?" many Brits offer a more casual, "You alright?" or "You OK there?"

advert-advertisement

afters-dessert

anticlockwise-counterclockwise

Antipodean-an Australian or New Zealander

aubergine-eggplant

banger-sausage

bangers and mash-sausage and mashed potatoes

Bank Holiday-legal holiday

bap-small roll

bespoke-custom-made

billion-a thousand of our billions (a million million)

biro-ballpoint pen

biscuit-cookie

black pudding-sausage made from dried blood

bloody-damn

blow off-fart

bobby-policeman ("the Bill" is more common)

Bob's your uncle-there you go (with a shrug), naturally

boffin-nerd, geek

bollocks-all-purpose expletive (a figurative use of testicles)

bolshy-argumentative

bomb-success or failure

bonnet-car hood

boot-car trunk

braces-suspenders

bridle way-path for walkers, bikers, and horse riders

brilliant-cool

brolly-umbrella

bubble and squeak-cabbage and potatoes fried together

bum-butt

candy floss-cotton candy

caravan-trailer

car-boot sale-temporary flea market, often for charity

car park-parking lot

cashpoint-ATM

casualty-emergency room

cat's eyes-road reflectors

ceilidh (KAY-lee)-informal evening of song and folk fun (Scottish and Irish)

cheap and cheerful-budget but adequate

cheap and nasty-cheap and bad quality

cheers-good-bye or thanks; also a toast

chemist-pharmacist

chicory-endive

chippie-fish-and-chips shop; carpenter

chips-French fries

chock-a-block-jam-packed

chuffed-pleased

chunter-mutter

cider-alcoholic apple cider

clearway-road where you can't stop

coach-long-distance bus

concession-discounted admission

concs (pronounced "conks")-short for "concession"

cos-romaine lettuce

cot-baby crib

cotton buds-Q-tips

courgette-zucchini

craic (pronounced "crack")-fun, good conversation (Irish/Scottish and spreading to England)

crisps-potato chips
cuppa-cup of tea
dear-expensive
dicey-iffy, risky
digestives-round graham cookies
dinner-lunch or dinner
diversion-detour
dogsbody-menial worker
donkey's years-ages, long time
draughts-checkers
draw-marijuana
dual carriageway-divided highway (four lanes)
dummy-pacifier
elevenses-coffee-and-biscuits break before lunch
elvers-baby eels
face flannel-washcloth
fag-cigarette
fagged-exhausted
faggot-sausage
fancy-to like, to be attracted to (a person)
fanny-vagina
fell-hill or high plain (Lake District)
first floor-second floor
fiver-£5 bill
fizzy drink-pop or soda
flutter-a bet
football-soccer
force-waterfall (Lake District)
fortnight-two weeks (shortened from "fourteen nights")
fringe-hair bangs
Frogs-French people
fruit machine-slot machine
full Monty-whole shebang, everything
gallery-balcony
gammon-ham
gangway-aisle
gaol-jail (same pronunciation)
gateau (or gateaux)-cake

gear lever-stick shift
geezer-"dude"
give way-yield
glen-narrow valley (Scotland)
goods wagon-freight truck
gormless-stupid
green fingers-green thumbs
half eight-8:30 (not 7:30)
hard cheese-bad luck
heath-open treeless land
hen night-bachelorette party
holiday-vacation
homely-homey or cozy
hoover-vacuum cleaner
ice lolly-Popsicle
interval-intermission
ironmonger-hardware store
ish-more or less
jacket potato-baked potato
jelly-Jell-O
jiggery-pokery-nonsense
Joe Bloggs-John Q. Public
jumble sale-rummage sale
jumper-sweater
just a tick-just a second
kipper-smoked herring
knackered-exhausted (Cockney: cream crackered)
knickers-ladies' panties
knocking shop-brothel
knock up-wake up or visit (old-fashioned)
ladybird-ladybug
lady fingers-flat, spongy cookie
lady's finger-okra
lager-light, fizzy beer
left luggage-baggage check
lemonade-lemon-lime pop like 7-Up, fizzy
lemon squash-lemonade, not fizzy
let-rent
licenced-restaurant authorized to sell alcohol

lift-elevator
listed-protected historic building
loo-toilet or bathroom
lorry-truck
mack-mackintosh raincoat
mangetout-snow peas
marrow-summer squash
mate-buddy (boy or girl)
mean-stingy
mental-wild, memorable
mews-former stables converted to two-story rowhouses
mobile (MOH-bile)-cell phone
moggie-cat
motorway-freeway
naff-tacky or trashy
nappy-diaper
natter-talk on and on
neep-Scottish for turnip
newsagent-corner store
nought-zero
noughts & crosses-tic-tac-toe
off-licence-liquor store
on offer-for sale
OTT-over the top, excessive
panto, pantomime-fairy-tale play performed at Christmas (silly but fun)
pants-underwear, briefs
pasty (PASS-tee)-crusted savory (usually meat) pie from Cornwall
pavement-sidewalk
pear-shaped-messed up, gone wrong
petrol-gas
pillar box-mailbox
pissed (rude), **paralytic, bevvied, wellied, popped up, merry, trollied, ratted, rat-arsed, pissed as a newt**-drunk
pitch-playing field
plaster-Band-Aid
plonk-cheap, bad wine

plonker-one who drinks bad wine (a mild insult)
prat-idiot
publican-pub owner
public school-private "prep" school (e.g., Eton)
pudding-dessert in general
pukka-first-class
pull, to be on the-on the prowl
punter-customer, especially in gambling
put a sock in it-shut up
queue-line
queue up-line up
quid-pound (£1)
randy-horny
rasher-slice of bacon
redundant, made-laid off
Remembrance Day-Veterans' Day
return ticket-round trip
revising; doing revisions-studying for exams
ring up-call (telephone)
roundabout-traffic circle
rubber-eraser
rubbish-bad
sausage roll-sausage wrapped in a flaky pastry
Scotch egg-hard-boiled egg wrapped in sausage meat
Scouser-a person from Liverpool
self-catering-accommodation with kitchen
Sellotape-Scotch tape
services-freeway rest area
serviette-napkin
setee-couch
shag-intercourse (cruder than in the US)
shambolic-chaotic
shandy-lager and 7-Up
silencer-car muffler
single ticket-one-way ticket
skip-Dumpster

sleeping policeman-speed bumps

smalls-underwear

snap-photo (snapshot)

snogging-kissing, making out

sod-mildly offensive insult

sod it, sod off-screw it, screw off

soda-soda water (not pop)

solicitor-lawyer

spanner-wrench

spend a penny-urinate

stag night-bachelor party

starkers-buck naked

starters-appetizers

state school-public school

sticking plaster-Band-Aid

sticky tape-Scotch tape

stone-14 pounds (weight)

stroppy-bad-tempered

subway-underground walkway

suet-fat from animal rendering (sometimes used in cooking)

sultanas-golden raisins

surgical spirit-rubbing alcohol

suspenders-garters

suss out-figure out

swede-rutabaga

ta-thank you

take the mickey/take the piss-tease

tatty-worn out or tacky

taxi rank-taxi stand

telly-TV

tenement-stone apartment house (not necessarily a slum)

tenner-£10 bill

theatre-live stage

tick-a check mark

tight as a fish's bum-cheapskate (watertight)

tights-panty hose

tin-can

tip-public dump

tipper lorry-dump truck

top hole-first rate

top up-refill (a drink, mobilephone credit, petrol tank, etc.)

torch-flashlight

towel, press-on-panty liner

towpath-path along a river

trainers-sneakers

Tube-subway

twee-quaint, cutesy

twitcher-bird-watcher

Underground-subway

verge-grassy edge of road

verger-church official

way out-exit

wee (adj)-small (Scottish)

wee (verb)-urinate

Wellingtons, wellies-rubber boots

whacked-exhausted

whinge (rhymes with hinge)-whine

wind up-tease, irritate

witter on-gab and gab

wonky-weird, askew

yob-hooligan

zebra crossing-crosswalk

zed-the letter Z

INDEX

MAP INDEX

Audio Europe

Join a Rick Steves tour

Enjoy Europe's warmest welcome... with the flexibility and friendship of a small group getting to know Rick's favorite places and people. It all starts with our free tour catalog and DVD.

Great guides, small groups, no grumps.

ricksteves.com

turn your travel dreams into affordable reality

▶ Free Audio Tours & Travel Newsletter

Get your nose out of this guide book and focus on what you'll be seeing with Rick's free audio tours of the greatest sights in Paris, London, Rome, Florence, Venice, and Athens.

Subscribe to our free Travel News e-newsletter, and get monthly articles from Rick on what's happening in Europe.

▶ Great Gear from Rick's Travel Store

Pack light and right—on a budget—with Rick's custom-designed carry-on bags, roll-aboards, day packs, travel accessories, guidebooks, journals, maps and DVDs of his TV shows.

NOW AVAILABLE:
eBOOKS, APPS & BLU-RAY

eBOOKS

Most guides are available as eBooks from Amazon, Barnes & Noble, Borders, Apple, and Sony. Free apps for eBook reading are available in the Apple App Store and Android Market, and eBook readers such as Kindle, Nook, and Kobo all have free apps that work on smartphones.

RICK STEVES' EUROPE DVDs

10 New Shows 2011–2012
Austria & the Alps
Eastern Europe
England & Wales
European Christmas
European Travel Skills & Specials
France
Germany, BeNeLux & More
Greece & Turkey
Iran
Ireland & Scotland
Italy's Cities
Italy's Countryside
Scandinavia
Spain
Travel Extras

BLU-RAY

Celtic Charms
Eastern Europe Favorites
European Christmas
Italy Through the Back Door
Mediterranean Mosaic
Surprising Cities of Europe

PHRASE BOOKS & DICTIONARIES

French
French, Italian & German
German
Italian
Portuguese
Spanish

JOURNALS

Rick Steves' Pocket Travel Journal
Rick Steves' Travel Journal

APPS

Select Rick Steves guides are available as apps in the Apple App Store.

PLANNING MAPS

Britain, Ireland & London
Europe
France & Paris
Germany, Austria & Switzerland
Ireland
Italy
Spain & Portugal

Rick Steves books and DVDs are available at bookstores and through online booksellers.

Credits

Researchers
To help update this book, Rick relied on...

Sarah Murdoch

Sarah Murdoch developed a fascination for Britain over tea and games of whist with her English grandmother. London—full of bookshops, museums, markets, and delicious British accents—is Sarah's idea of heaven. When not tracking down the perfect scone or leading tours for Rick Steves, she lives in Seattle with her understanding husband Patrick and their sons Lucca and Nicola.

Cameron Hewitt

Cameron writes and edits guidebooks for Rick Steves, specializing in Eastern Europe. For this book, he gave old York a fresh look, patrolled Hadrian's Wall, binged on Beatles in Liverpool, and met a ghost in Coventry. When he's not traveling, Cameron lives in Seattle with his wife Shawna.

Lauren Mills

Lauren, a map editor and in-house search engine at Rick Steves, was an ardent Anglophile even before bringing home her British husband as a souvenir. They live in Seattle with their cat Annabel.

Cathy McDonald

Cathy, an editor and researcher for Rick Steves, enjoys England's natural history and how it affects its people. She lives in Seattle, where she has written about the Pacific Northwest for more than 15 years as a freelancer for *The Seattle Times*.

Contributor
Gene Openshaw

Gene is the co-author of ten Rick Steves books. For this book, he wrote material on Europe's art, history, and contemporary culture. When not traveling, Gene enjoys composing music, recovering from his 1973 trip to Europe with Rick, and living everyday life with his daughter.

Chapter Images

The following list identifies the chapter-opening images and credits their photographers.

Introduction: Whitby	Cameron Hewitt
England: Salisbury Cathedral	Cameron Hewitt
London: Houses of Parliament	Rick Steves
Greenwich, Windsor, and Cambridge:	
Windsor's Changing of the Guard	Lauren Mills
Canterbury: Canterbury	Sarah Murdoch
Dover: White Cliffs of Dover	David C. Hoerlein
Brighton: Brighton Pier	Sarah Murdoch
Portsmouth: View from	
the Spinnaker Tower	Cameron Hewitt
Dartmoor: Dartmoor Ponies	Cameron Hewitt
Cornwall: Mousehole	Sarah Murdoch
Bath: Pulteney Bridge	Lauren Mills
Near Bath: Avebury Stone Circle	David C. Hoerlein
Oxford: Spires of Old Souls	Melanie Jeschke
The Cotswolds: Typical Cotswold Scene	Dominic Bonuccelli
Stratford-Upon-Avon:	
Anne Hathaway's Cottage	Rick Steves
Ironbridge Gorge: The Iron Bridge	Lauren Mills
Liverpool: Albert Dock	Cameron Hewitt
Blackpool: Blackpool	Rick Steves
Lake District: Derwentwater	Rick Steves
York: York Minster	Rick Steves
North Yorkshire: Whitby Abbey	Cameron Hewitt
Durham and Northeast England:	
Durham Cathedral	David C. Hoerlein

Acknowledgments

Thanks to Roy and Jodi Nicholls for their research help, to Sarah Murdoch for writing the original version of the southern England chapters, to Melanie Jeschke for the original version of the Oxford chapter, and to friends listed in this book, who put the "Great" in Great Britain.

Rick Steves' Guidebook Series

City, Regional, and Country Guides

Rick Steves' Amsterdam,
    Bruges & Brussels
Rick Steves' Best of Europe
Rick Steves' Budapest
Rick Steves' Croatia
    & Slovenia
Rick Steves' Eastern Europe
Rick Steves' England
Rick Steves' Florence
    & Tuscany
Rick Steves' France
Rick Steves' Germany
Rick Steves' Great Britain
Rick Steves' Greece: Athens
    & the Peloponnese
Rick Steves' Ireland

Rick Steves' Istanbul
Rick Steves' Italy
Rick Steves' London
Rick Steves' Paris
Rick Steves' Portugal
Rick Steves' Prague
    & the Czech Republic
Rick Steves' Provence
    & the French Riviera
Rick Steves' Rome
Rick Steves' Scandinavia
Rick Steves' Spain
Rick Steves' Switzerland
Rick Steves' Venice
Rick Steves' Vienna,
    Salzburg & Tirol

Snapshot Guides

Excerpted from country guidebooks, the Snapshots Guides
cover many of my favorite destinations, such as *Rick Steves'
Snapshot Barcelona, Rick Steves' Snapshot Scotland,* and
Rick Steves' Snapshot Hill Towns of Central Italy.

Pocket Guides

My new Pocket Guides are condensed, colorful guides to
Europe's top cities, including Paris, London, Rome, and more.
These combine the top self-guided walks and tours from my
city guides with vibrant full-color photos, and are sized to slip
easily into your pocket.

Rick Steves' Phrase Books

French
French/Italian/German
German
Italian
Portuguese
Spanish

More Books

Rick Steves' Europe 101: History and Art for the Traveler
Rick Steves' Europe Through the Back Door
Rick Steves' European Christmas
Rick Steves' Mediterranean Cruise Ports
Rick Steves' Postcards from Europe
Rick Steves' Travel as a Political Act

Avalon Travel
a member of the Perseus Books Group
1700 Fourth Street
Berkeley, CA 94710

Text © 2012 by Rick Steves
Portions of this book appeared in *Rick Steves' Great Britain* © 2012, 2011, 2010, 2009,
2008, 2007, 2006, 2005, 2004, 2003, 2002, 2001; and in *Rick Steves' London* © 2012, 2011,
2010, 2009, 2008, 2007, 2006, 2005, 2004, 2003, 2002, 2001
Maps © 2012 by Europe Through the Back Door. All rights reserved.

Printed in the United States by Worzalla
First printing December 2011

ISBN 978-1-59880-981-7
ISSN 1930-4617

For the latest on Rick's lectures, guidebooks, tours, public radio show, and public television
series, contact Europe Through the Back Door, Box 2009, Edmonds, WA 98020, 425/771-
8303, fax 425/771-0833, www.ricksteves.com, rick@ricksteves.com.

Europe Through the Back Door Reviewing Editors: Cameron Hewitt, Jennifer Madison
Davis
ETBD Editors: Suzanne Kotz, Gretchen Strauch, Tom Griffin, Cathy Lu, Cathy
McDonald, Samantha Oberholzer, Candace Winegrad
ETBD Managing Editor: Risa Laib
Research Assistance: Sarah Murdoch, Cameron Hewitt, Lauren Mills, Cathy McDonald,
Samantha Oberholzer, Candace Winegrad
Avalon Travel Senior Editor and Series Manager: Madhu Prasher
Avalon Travel Project Editor: Kelly Lydick
Copy Editor: Patrick Collins
Proofreader: Beatrice Wikander
Indexer: Julie Kawabata
Production and Layout: McGuire Barber Design
Cover Design: Kimberly Glyder Design
Graphic Content Director: Laura VanDeventer
Maps and Graphics: David C. Hoerlein, Laura VanDeventer, Lauren Mills, Twozdai
Hulse, Barb Geisler, Pat O'Connor, Kat Bennett, Mike Morgenfeld, Brice Ticen
Front Matter Color Photos: British Museum, London © Rick Steves; York Minster, York
© Rick Steves
Front Cover Photo: Snowshill, Cotswolds © Cameron Hewitt
Additional Photography: Rick Steves, Cameron Hewitt, Sarah Murdoch, Gene
Openshaw, Lauren Mills, Rich Earl, Bruce VanDeventer, Melanie Jeschke, David C.
Hoerlein, Jennifer Hauseman, Darbi Macy, Pat O'Connor, Sarah Slauson

ABOUT THE AUTHOR

RICK STEVES

Since 1973, Rick Steves has spent 100 days every year exploring Europe. Rick produces a public television series (*Rick Steves' Europe*), a public radio show (*Travel with Rick Steves*), and an app and podcast (*Rick Steves Audio Europe*); writes a bestselling series of guidebooks and a nationally syndicated newspaper column; organizes guided tours that take over ten thousand travelers to Europe annually; and offers an information-packed website (www.ricksteves.com). With the help of his hardworking staff of 80 at Europe Through the Back Door—in Edmonds, Washington, just north of Seattle—Rick's mission is to make European travel fun, affordable, and culturally enlightening for Am